EQUITY

and the

LAW OF TRUSTS

EQUITY

and the

LAW OF TRUSTS

by

PHILIP H. PETTIT, M.A.

of the Middle Temple, Barrister
Professor of Equity at the University of Bristol

THIRD EDITION

LONDON
BUTTERWORTHS
1974

ENGLAND: BUTTERWORTH & CO. (PUBLISHERS) LTD.
LONDON: 88 KINGSWAY, WC2B 6AB

AUSTRALIA: BUTTERWORTHS PTY. LTD.
SYDNEY: 586 PACIFIC HIGHWAY, CHATSWOOD, NSW 2067
MELBOURNE: 343 LITTLE COLLINS STREET, 3000
BRISBANE: 240 QUEEN STREET, 4000

CANADA: BUTTERWORTH & CO. (CANADA) LTD.
TORONTO: 2265 MIDLAND AVENUE, SCARBOROUGH M1P 4S1

NEW ZEALAND: BUTTERWORTHS OF NEW ZEALAND LTD.
WELLINGTON: 26/28 WARING TAYLOR STREET, 1

SOUTH AFRICA: BUTTERWORTH & CO. (SOUTH AFRICA) (PTY.) LTD.
DURBAN: 152/154 GALE STREET

ISBN—Casebound: 0 406 64163 3
Limp: 0 406 64164 1

Printed by Thomson Litho Ltd., East Kilbride, Scotland.

Preface to Third Edition

In preparing the present edition, the main task has been to assimilate the steady flow of decisions, particularly in relation to trusts and the equitable remedies of injunction and specific performance. In many cases it has been possible to do this by means of insertions, or by making amendments to short passages of the text. In other cases advantage has been taken of the opportunity to re-write more extensively, in particular in the following areas:

(i) *Trusts and powers* (pp. 19–29). There has been a good deal of re-writing here, which has resulted in what some may think a disproportionately lengthy treatment of the topic. I would defend this on the grounds of the fundamental importance of the distinction and the insight it gives into the nature of a trust, the number of cases in recent years and their value as an illustration of legal reasoning in courts of equity, and contemporary academic interest in the topic.

(ii) *Gifts to non-charitable unincorporate bodies* (pp. 40–42). This has been re-written following *Re Recher's Will Trusts*, which affirmed the convenient possibility of construing such a gift as one to the present members, subject to their contractual rights *inter se*.

(iii) *The presumptions of a resulting trust and advancement in relation to the matrimonial home* (pp. 106–115). It seems likely that there will be less activity in this field in future in view of the wide statutory powers given to the courts in divorce proceedings.

(iv) *Public benefit in charities* (pp. 187–193). This has been reconsidered following the House of Lords decision in *Dingle* v. *Turner*.

(v) *Gifts to specified charitable institutions whcih have ceased to exist* (pp. 220–223). This is a difficult area which clearly had to be redrafted in the light of *Re Vernon's Will Trust* and *Re Finger's Will Trusts*.

(vi) There is a new section on control of trustees' powers (pp. 360–362), which is partly new, and partly transferred from other parts of the book.

The section on "Completely and Incompletely Constituted Trusts" has been re-arranged into what is thought to be a more logical order, and in connection with the duty of a trustee not to profit from his trust, a clearer distinction has been drawn between trustee cases and those dealing with the analogous duty of other fiduciaries.

In view of the increasing availability of Commonwealth reports in English law libraries—and the sales of previous editions in Commonwealth countries—I have introduced a modest citation of Commonwealth decisions, particularly recent cases illustrating points not dealt with in modern English cases, though

v

I have been conscious of the need to add to the weight of authority as little as possible. By making appropriate deletions there is only a marginal increase in the number of cases referred to. I am disappointed, however, that there is a small increase in the length of the text but at least the rate of increase has been halved in this edition compared with the last.

The present edition was prepared taking account of developments in the law up to the end of 1973, and I have been able to introduce amendments in proof so that (subject to the availability of material to me) it should be substantially up to date to Easter 1974.

As always, I would like to thank my publishers for their co-operation and in particular for revising the index and the table of cases and statutes.

PHILIP H. PETTIT

Faculty of Law
University of Bristol
May 1974

Preface to First Edition

Accepting Maitland's observation that equity is an appendix or gloss on the common law, one might ask why equity is commonly a separate "subject" in a law school, with a consequential need for a corresponding textbook, and why its contents cannot be spread over contract, land law, and other branches of the substantive law. The short practical answer to this question is that there is too much of it—the law of trusts, for instance, could provide enough material to constitute a course, or textbook, by itself. It is, however, possible, while treating the law of trusts to modern university standards, to add other equitable topics to such a course or book without over-weighting the course in comparison with other courses, or making the book excessively long. This seems, in fact, a desirable thing to do, though it naturally leads to the question what other matters of equity should be included and what omitted. On this different minds may well come to different conclusions, and my approach has been entirely pragmatic. Thus I have, for instance, omitted the law relating to mortgages, restrictive covenants and administration of assets on the grounds that the two former are more appropriately treated in textbooks on land law whilst the latter is generally to be found in textbooks on succession. Similarly priorities are commonly considered in connection with mortgages, and equitable assignment in connection with contract, and these matters are likewise omitted. It would be tedious to rehearse the considerations—sometimes nicely balanced—for and against the inclusion of the possible topics. Suffice to say that, apart from a short introduction, with a minimum of the history required for an understanding of the present law, this book deals with the law of trusts as well as with the equitable remedies, which may be available in many contexts but are not dealt with comprehensively in any detail in textbooks on the various branches of the substantive law, and the equitable doctrines of conversion, satisfaction and election which, on balance, seem to be more appropriately included in an equity syllabus than anywhere else.

One other omission perhaps merits special mention, namely any separate treatment of the maxims of equity. It is submitted that there is little value in the long-established practice of attaching the doctrines and rules of equity to a collection of equitable aphorisms, which in fact are commonly later in date than the rules of which they are allegedly the basis. Nevertheless the maxims are referred to whenever it seems appropriate, for they are traditionally a part of equity, and are sometimes a convenient way of referring to some equitable principle. In practice, however, what is really of importance is to know how the wide general principle contained in the maxim is to be applied in the particular context, and what qualifications and limitations are to be attached to it.

Though it is hoped that the book may be found useful by practitioners, it is primarily intended for law students. An attempt has been made, on the one hand, to treat the subjects dealt with at sufficient depth to provide a proper understanding, and, on the other hand, to expound and stress the basic principles without descending into the detail that one expects to find in the larger-scale works for practitioners, where the student first meeting the subject may find it difficult to see the wood for the trees, and where it is naturally less necessary to spend time in explaining the fundamental doctrines.

P. H. P.

March, 1966

Table of Contents

ix

CHAPTER 11—POWERS OF TRUSTEES

CHAPTER 12—BREACH OF TRUST

CHAPTER 13—INJUNCTIONS

CHAPTER 14—SPECIFIC PERFORMANCE

CHAPTER 15—OTHER EQUITABLE REMEDIES

CHAPTER 16—CONVERSION AND RECONVERSION

Table of Statutes

References to "*Statutes*" are to Halsbury's Statutes of England (Third Edition) showing the volume and page at which the annotated text of the Act will be found.

Table of Cases

In the following Table references are given to the English and Empire
Digest where a Digest of each case will be found.

xxiii

PAGE

J

M   PAGE

PAGE

PAGE

PAGE

PAGE

Abbreviations

The following abbreviations have been used in relation to legal periodicals:

A.A.L.R.	*Anglo American Law Review*
A.L.J.	*Australian Law Journal*
A.S.C.L.	*Annual Survey of Commonwealth Law*
B.T.R.	*British Tax Review*
C.B.R.	*Canadian Bar Review*
C.L.C.	*Current Law Consolidation*
C.L.J.	*Cambridge Law Journal*
C.L.P.	*Current Legal Problems*
Col.L.R.	*Colombia Law Review*
Con.	*Conveyancer and Property Lawyer (New Series)*
L.Q.R.	*Law Quarterly Review*
M.L.R.	*Modern Law Review*
M.U.L.R.	*Melbourne University Law Review*
N.I.L.Q.	*Northern Ireland Law Quarterly*
N.L.J.	*New Law Journal*
N.Z.U.L.R.	*New Zealand Universities Law Review*
Sol.Jo.	*Solicitor's Journal*
U.T.L.J.	*University of Toronto Law Journal*
Yale L.J.	*Yale Law Journal*

Case references: Where footnote references to English cases decided since the Judicature Acts are not followed by an indication of the court in which they were decided, it can be assumed that the decision was at first instance in the High Court.

CHAPTER 1

History of the Court of Chancery and Introduction to Equity

1 HISTORY OF THE COURT OF CHANCERY[1]

If law be regarded in general terms as the rules enforced in the courts for the promotion of justice,[2] equity may be described as that part of the law which immediately[3] prior to the coming into force of the Supreme Court of Judicature Acts 1873 and 1875[4] was enforced exclusively in the Court of Chancery, and not at all in the Courts of Common Law—Common Pleas, Exchequer and King's Bench. Although in origin the jurisdiction of the Court of Chancery was undoubtedly based on moral principles designed to remove injustices incapable of being dealt with in the common law courts, equity was always, as Maitland has pointed out,[5] essentially a supplementary jurisdiction, an appendix or gloss on the common law, and it is accordingly not really possible to define it successfully; it can only be described by giving an inventory of its contents or in the historical terms set out above.

The position at the end of the thirteenth century, even after the last of the three common law courts to evolve out of the Curia Regis had become separate, was that a residuum of justice was still thought to reside in the King. If, therefore, the common law courts for any reason failed to do justice, an aggrieved person might petition the King or the King's Council. From early times these petitions seeking the King's extraordinary justice seem to

---

[1] For a fuller account see Holdsworth, *History of English Law*, Vol. I, pp. 395 *et seq.*; Potter's *Historical Introduction to English Law*, 4th Ed., pp. 152 *et seq.*; Kerly, *History of Equity*, and also Milsom, *Historical Foundations of the Common Law*, pp. 74 *et seq.*

[2] This begs the real question, what is justice? which is, however, outside the scope of this book, being a question for jurisprudence and philosophy. Of course, in practice, many matters that justice would demand are not enforced in the courts for various reasons, many being unsuitable for judicial enforcement, and some of the rules enforced fail to achieve justice either generally or in a particular case.

[3] Before 1842 the Court of Exchequer had an equity jurisdiction. The statement following in the text relates to the central courts and disregards the Palatine Courts (abolished by the Courts Act 1971) and the County Courts.

[4] Now repealed and replaced by the Supreme Court of Judicature (Consolidation) Act 1925. It will be convenient to refer to these Acts as the Judicature Acts 1873, 1875 and 1925 respectively. The 1873 and 1875 Acts came into force on 1 November, 1875.

[5] *Equity*, 2nd (Brunyate) Ed., p. 18.

have been referred to the Chancellor, and as early as the reign of Edward I petitions are to be found addressed to the "Chancellor and the Council". This procedure steadily became more frequent, and by the end of the fourteenth century petitions began to be addressed to the Chancellor alone. However they were addressed, the petitions were in fact dealt with by the Chancellor, though at first purely as a delegate of the Council. As the practice became habitual and references frequent, the Chancellor and his office the Chancery inevitably acquired the characteristics of a court, though so far as is known it was not until 1474 that the Chancellor made a decree upon his own authority.[6]

The cases referred to the Chancellor and the Chancery fall into two main groups, first cases where the law was defective, and secondly those where there was theoretically a remedy at common law, but the petitioner was unable to obtain it because of the disturbed state of the country, or the power and wealth of the other party, who might be able to put improper pressure on the jury or even the court. For a long time[7] the latter was the most important and frequent type of case to be dealt with. In exercising jurisdiction in cases of this kind it is unlikely that the Chancellor regarded himself as administering a separate system of law—indeed he was not. It was a jurisdiction which was a cause of considerable complaint and it may be that the Chancellor's powers would have disappeared about the end of the fourteenth century if it had not been for the other head of jurisdiction, which must now be considered.

During the early period of growth of the common law, there was rapid development as new writs were created to meet new cases, and, moreover, the common law judges had a wide discretion to do justice, particularly in the informal procedure by plaint or bill (as opposed to actions begun by writ), and in proceedings in the General Eyre. At first, therefore, there was little scope for a jurisdiction to remedy the defects of the common law. However, this early rapid development ceased with the Provisions of Oxford in 1258, and only proceeded slowly after the controversial[8] *in consimili casu* clause of the Statute of Westminster II in 1285, so that it is fair to say that by the end of the thirteenth century the common law formed a rigid system which was unadaptable, or at least could only be slowly adapted, to meet new types of case. Moreover plaints without writ, for reasons which are not fully explained, apparently ceased to be available in the fourteenth century, and at about the same time General Eyres virtually ceased to be held. Consequently hardship increasingly often arose because of defects in the law, and petitions began to be brought on this ground. In giving relief in these cases new law was being created, and it was this new law which became known as "equity" in contrast to the "common law" dispensed in the common law courts. For a long time there was close con-

---

[6] Though he seems to have dismissed a petition without consulting the Council nearly a century before.

[7] The change seems to have taken place during the reign of Henry VI. The business of the Court of Chancery multiplied three times between 1420 and 1450, by which latter date nine-tenths of its work was concerned with uses—see (1970), 86 L.Q.R. 84 (Margaret E. Avery).

[8] See (1931), 31 Col.L.R. 778 (T. F. T. Plucknett); (1931), 47 L.Q.R. 334 (W. S. Holdsworth); (1936), 52 L.Q.R. 68 (P. A. Landon); (1936), 52 L.Q.R. 220 (T. F. T. Plucknett); (1937), 46 Yale L.J. 1142 (Elizabeth Dix); Fifoot, *History and Sources of the Common Law*, pp. 66 et seq.; Kiralfy, *The Action on the Case*, pp. 19 et seq.

sultation between the Chancellor and the common law judges as to the types of case in which relief should be granted. This reduced the risk of conflict from the point of view of personalities; and from the point of view of principle, conflict between the jurisdictions was reduced by the fact that it was a cardinal rule of the Court of Chancery that equity acts *in personam*. Thus in the central institution of equity jurisdiction, the trust, the Chancellor never denied that the trustee was the legal owner of the trust property, but merely insisted that the trustee should deal with it in accordance with the trust for the benefit of the beneficiaries. Failure to comply with the Chancellor's order would be a contempt of court, which was punishable by imprisonment until the trustee was prepared to comply with the order. Originally this procedure *in personam*, against the person of the defendant, was the only process of the Court of Chancery for enforcing its decrees.[9]

None the less conflict did arise in the sixteenth century as the Chancellor extended and consolidated his jurisdiction, and the dispute centred on injunctions issued by the Chancellor restraining parties to an action at common law either from proceeding with their action at law, or, having obtained judgment, from enforcing it. The dispute finally came to a head under James I, when Coke was Chief Justice and Ellesmere Lord Chancellor. The validity or invalidity of these injunctions would, it was recognised, determine the question whether legal supremacy was vested in the common law courts or the Chancery. The matter was referred by the King to Bacon, the Attorney-General, and other counsel, and in due course he accepted their advice that the injunctions were valid and in 1616 accordingly issued an order in favour of the Chancery. This proved to be a final settlement of the dispute, although it was not fully accepted by the common lawyers until the end of the century.

From a broad point of view the settlement did not prove altogether satisfactory by reason of the defects which grew up in the Court of Chancery during the latter part of the seventeenth and the eighteenth century. There was corruption and abuse of the process of the court,[10] an inadequate number of judicial staff, too many and incompetent officials, an over-elaborate system of rehearing and appeals and a generally unsatisfactory organisation which led to such expense, delays and injustice that the business of the court declined. After piecemeal reforms beginning with the appointment of a Vice-Chancellor in 1813, and becoming much more numerous after the Whig victory in 1830, the Court of Chancery finally ceased to exist as a separate court as a result of the major reorganisation of the whole judicial system by the Judicature Acts 1873 and 1875. Its jurisdiction was transferred to the Supreme Court of Judicature, most of the jurisdiction at first instance being assigned to the Chancery Division of the High Court, though the separation of the High Court into divisions being simply for convenience, all three divisions have the jurisdiction and a duty to recognise and give effect to all equitable rights, obligations and defences.[11]

It should be added in conclusion that limited jurisdiction in equity matters is

---

[9] Sequestration was introduced towards the end of the sixteenth century and now there are various powers for the court to make vesting orders, etc., see e.g. Trustee Act 1925, ss. 44 *et seq.*; Judicature Act 1925, s. 47.

[10] The Chancery became very ready to issue injunctions by reason of the profits which thereby accrued, and litigants were able to use them purely as delaying tactics.

[11] See *Practice Direction*, [1973] 2 All E.R. 233; [1973] 1 W.L.R. 627.

given to the county courts, the relevant statute now being the County Courts Act 1959.[12]

2 JURISDICTION OF THE COURT OF CHANCERY

Originally, as we have seen, the Chancellor did not have any clearly defined jurisdiction, but dispensed an extraordinary justice remedying the defects of the common law courts on grounds of conscience and natural justice, a function for which he was well qualified as he was commonly an ecclesiastic, well versed in both the civil and canon law. He was indeed sometimes called the "Keeper of the King's Conscience". In the absence of fixed principles the decision at first depended to a large degree upon the Chancellor's personal ideas of right and wrong, and there was some truth in Selden's[13] well-worn comment that equity varied according to the conscience of the individual Chancellor in the same way as if the standard measure were a Chancellor's foot. This state of affairs began to be less true in the later seventeenth century as the principles of equity began to become more fixed. Cases in the Chancery began to be reported around the middle of the century and were increasingly cited, relied on and followed in subsequent cases. The Chancellors began to say that although they had a discretion it should be exercised not according to conscience but in accordance with precedent.[14] Lawyers rather than ecclesiastics became appointed Chancellors, the last of the non-legal Chancellors being Lord Shaftesbury, who held office during 1672-73. With his successor, Lord Nottingham, often called the father of modern equity, the development of a settled system of equity really began, to be continued under succeeding Chancellors, notably Lord Hardwicke, and completed in the early nineteenth century by Lord Eldon. The result of their work was to transform equity into a system of law almost as fixed and rigid as the rules of the common law. Accordingly Lord Eldon could observe[15] "Nothing would inflict on me greater pain, in quitting this place,[16] than the recollection that I had done anything to justify the reproach that the equity of this court varies like the Chancellor's foot", and more recently[17] it has been bluntly stated that "This Court is not a Court of conscience". By the early nineteenth century equity, as stated in the opening sentence of this book, had become simply that part of the law enforced in the Court of Chancery.

A related matter is whether it is any longer open to equity to invent new equitable interests. Though there is no fiction in equity as there is said to be at common law that the rules have been established from time immemorial

---

[12] Section 52, as amended by the Administration of Justice Act 1969, s. 5. So far as the estates of deceased persons and trusts are concerned, there is jurisdiction where the estate or fund subject to the trust does not exceed in amount or value the sum of £5,000. There is unlimited jurisdiction by written consent of the parties under s. 53. This section excludes, however, proceedings under the Variation of Trusts Act 1958, to which the normal £5,000 limit applies.

[13] *Table Talk of John Selden* (ed. Pollock 1927), p. 43.

[14] See an article entitled "Precedent in Equity" in (1941), 57 L.Q.R. 245 (W. H. D. Winder).

[15] In *Gee* v. *Pritchard* (1818), 2 Swan. 402, at p. 414.

[16] I.e. the Court of Chancery.

[17] *Per* Buckley J. in *Re Telescriptor Syndicate Ltd.*, [1903] 2 Ch. 174, at pp. 195, 196, echoing Jessel M.R. in *Re National Funds Assurance Co.* (1878), 10 Ch.D. 118, at p. 128.

and though "it is perfectly well known that they have been established from time to time—altered, improved and refined from time to time. In many cases we know the names of the Chancellors who invented them",[18] yet it is doubtful whether a new right can now be created. A few years ago it was suggested[19] that recent cases[20] on licences showed that equity is not yet "of an age past child-bearing",[21] but this suggestion has lost a good deal of its virility in the light of the House of Lords decision in *National Provincial Bank Ltd.* v. *Ainsworth*,[22] overruling a series of authorities beginning with *Bendall* v. *McWhirter*[23] in 1952, which appeared to have created a "deserted wife's equity", entitling a deserted wife to a limited right to remain in occupation of the matrimonial home even as against third parties. Their Lordships held that a wife's rights in relation to occupation of the matrimonial home, where that was the property of her husband, were personal rights against her husband, flowing from her status as wife, and did not confer on her any equitable interest or right of property in the land.[24] Extra-judicially Lord Evershed has observed[25] that s. 25 (11)[26] of the Judicature Act 1873 put a stop to, or at least a very severe limitation on, the inventive faculties of future Chancery judges, while even Lord Denning has said, again extra-judicially,[27] that "the Courts of Chancery are no longer courts of equity. . . . They are as fixed and immutable as the courts of law ever were." The Court of Appeal, moreover, has observed[28] that if a "claim in equity exists, it must be shown to have an ancestry founded in history and in the practice and precedents of the courts administering equity

---

[18] *Per* Jessel M.R. in *Re Hallett's Estate* (1880), 13 Ch.D. 696, at p. 710, C.A.—said, however, to be "rather an overstatement" by Lord Evershed in the 1954 Lionel Cohen Lectures entitled " Aspects of English Equity," p. 13.

[19] (1953), 16 M.L.R. 1 (G. C. Cheshire) and see (1953), 17 Con. 440 (L. A. Sheridan).

[20] *Errington* v. *Errington*, [1952] 1 All E.R. 149; [1952] 1 K.B. 290, C.A., and the cases on the deserted wife's equity starting with *Bendall* v. *McWhirter*, [1952] 1 All E.R. 1307; [1952] 2 Q.B. 466, C.A. But see early doubts in (1952), 68 L.Q.R. 337 (H. W. R. Wade); (1953), 69 L.Q.R. 466 (A. D. Hargreaves).

[21] Allegedly *per* Harman J.—see (1951), 67 L.Q.R. 506 (R. E. Megarry); (1952), 5 C.L.P. 2 (Lord Denning).

[22] [1965] 2 All E.R. 472; [1965] A.C. 1175, H.L., where all the relevant cases are cited. Previous periodical literature includes (1952), 68 L.Q.R. 379 and (1955), 71 L.Q.R. 175 (R. E. Megarry); (1964), 28 Con. 253 (M. A. Peel); (1964), 27 M.L.R. 593 (W. R. Cornish). See now the Matrimonial Homes Act 1967.

[23] *Supra.*

[24] Even before *National Provincial Bank Ltd.* v. *Ainsworth*, *supra*, it had become clear that the alleged right of a deserted wife was at most a mere equity—*Westminster Bank Ltd.* v. *Lee*, [1955] 2 All E.R. 883; [1956] Ch. 7. In the later case in the House of Lords, Lord Upjohn, at pp. 488; 1238, observed that a mere equity, such as the right to have the terms of a deed rectified or set aside on some equitable ground, would not bind a purchaser even with notice unless it was ancillary to, or dependent on, an equitable estate or interest in the land. See also Megarry and Wade, *Law of Real Property*, 3rd ed., pp. 124–126; (1955), 71 L.Q.R. 480 (R. E. Megarry); (1955), 19 Con. 343 (F. R. Crane); (1957), 21 Con. 195 (V. T. H. Delaney).

[25] (1953), 6 C.L.P. 11, 12.

[26] This sub-section is discussed at p. 7, *post*. Lord Evershed's point is that the sub-section necessarily proceeded upon the view that the rules of equity were then a known body of established doctrine.

[27] (1952), 5 C.L.P. 8.

[28] *Re Diplock's Estate*, [1948] 2 All E.R. 318, at p. 326; [1948] Ch. 465, at pp. 481, 482, C.A., affd. *sub nom. Ministry of Health* v. *Simpson*, [1950] 2 All E.R. 1137; [1951] A.C. 251, H.L.; *Thompson* v. *Earthy*, [1951] 2 All E.R. 235; [1951] 2 K.B. 596.

jurisdiction. It is not sufficient that because we may think that the 'justice' of the present case requires it, we should invent such a jurisdiction for the first time." Further, so far as an equitable interest in land is concerned, s. 4 (1) of the Law of Property Act 1925 provides that after 1925 such an interest is only capable of being validly created in any case in which an equivalent equitable interest in property real or personal could have been created before 1926.[29] It seems very doubtful, therefore, whether new equitable interests can any longer be created, except by the extension and development of existing equitable interests by exactly the same process as extension and development may take place at law.

One area in which there has been extension in recent years is that of proprietary estoppel.[30] This however is no new invention, but the development of a doctrine that goes back at least to the early eighteenth century.[1] Another area that has been put forward as an example of the creative activity of equity is that of the contractual licence, but, despite some authority to the contrary,[2] it is submitted that the contractual licence has not become a new equitable interest in land.[3]

The proper approach is, it is submitted, that stated by Bagnall J. in *Cowcher* v. *Cowcher*.[4] "I am convinced", he said, "that in determining rights, particularly property rights, the only justice that can be attained by mortals, who are fallible and are not omniscient, is justice according to law; the justice which flows from the application of sure and settled principles to proved or admitted facts. So in the field of equity the length of the Chancellor's foot has been measured or is capable of measurement. This does not mean that equity is past child-bearing; simply that its progeny must be legitimate—by precedent out of principle. It is well that this should be so; otherwise no lawyer could safely advise on his client's title and every quarrel would lead to a law suit." Of recent years some common law lawyers have sought to give equity a much wider and less precise jurisdiction. Such a development is, it is submitted, not only contrary to precedent and the historical development of equity, but is undesirable for the reasons given by Bagnall J., and unnecessary by reason of the improvements in the machinery for law reform[5] which enable defects in the law to be corrected by legislation more rapidly than in the past.

It is convenient to mention briefly at this point that one distinction between the common law and equity lay in the remedies available. In general the only

---

[29] The answer to this difficulty in the case of a licence suggested in (1952), 16 Con. 323 (F. R. Crane) seems no longer adequate since the decision in *Port Line Ltd.* v. *Ben Line Steamers Ltd.*, [1958] 1 All E.R. 787; [1958] 2 Q.B. 146, where *Strathcona S.S. Co.* v. *Dominion Coal Co.*, [1926] A.C. 108, P.C., was said to be wrongly decided.

[30] I.e. the *Dillwyn* v. *Llewellyn* principle discussed pp. 81–83, *post*.

[1] *Huning* v. *Ferrers* (1711), Gilb. Ch. 85.

[2] *Errington* v. *Errington*, [1952] 1 All E.R. 149; [1952] 1 K.B. 290, C.A.; *Binions* v. *Evans*, [1972] 2 All E.R. 1; [1972] Ch. 359, C.A.

[3] *National Provincial Bank, Ltd.* v. *Ainsworth*, [1965] 2 All E.R. 472; [1965] A.C. 1175, H.L.; *Re A Debtor, Trustee* v. *Solomon*, [1966] 3 All E.R. 255; *sub. nom. Re Solomon, A Bankrupt*, [1967] Ch. 573; Megarry and Wade, *Law of Real Property*, 3rd ed. pp. 780, 781; (1972), 88 L.Q.R. 336 (P.V.B.); (1972), 36 Con. 266 (Jill Martin); (1972), 36 Con. 277 (D. J. Hayton).

[4] [1972] 1 All E.R. 943, at p. 948.

[5] In particular the establishment of the Law Commission.

remedy available at common law was damages, and a plaintiff who established his right and the breach of it by the defendant was entitled to this remedy as a matter of right, no matter how little merit there might seem to be in his claim. Equity, on the other hand, had no power, until Statute intervened,[6] to award damages at all, but invented a variety of remedies, of which the most important are specific performance and injunction. As we shall see,[7] these are orders *in personam* directing a person to do or not to do some specified thing, and disobedience of such an order is a contempt of court. An equitable remedy may be awarded both to enforce a right recognised only in equity, and also to enforce a legal right, though this will only be done where the common law remedy of damages is regarded as inadequate. In any case equitable remedies are always awarded in the discretion of the court.

3 FUSION OF THE ADMINISTRATION OF LAW AND EQUITY

The reorganisation of the courts carried out by the Judicature Acts 1873 and 1875 produced one Supreme Court administering both law and equity. Though for the sake of convenience the High Court, dealing with cases at first instance, was divided into divisions,[8] every judge of each division was given the power and duty to recognise and give effect to both legal and equitable rights, claims, defences and remedies. The administration of law and equity thus being brought into the same courts, provision was made for cases where the rules of law and equity were in conflict. After dealing specifically with a number of particular cases, it was provided[9] in general terms that in all other cases in which there was a conflict or variance between the rules of equity and the rules of common law with reference to the same matter, the rules of equity should prevail. This provision was applied in *Berry* v. *Berry*[10] to prevent a wife succeeding in an action on a separation deed. The deed had been varied by an agreement not under seal, which was no defence to an action at law, but the equitable rule was that a deed may be varied by a simple contract and the equitable rule now prevails. Again in *Walsh* v. *Lonsdale*[11] there was an agreement for a lease of a mill for seven years at a rent payable quarterly in arrears, with a provision entitling the landlord to demand a year's rent in advance. No lease under seal was ever executed and the lease as such was accordingly void at law.[12] The tenant entered into possession and paid rent quarterly in arrears for some eighteen months when a year's rent was demanded in advance. On failure to pay the landlord distrained and the action was for damages for illegal distress. The tenant contended that having gone into possession and paid rent by

---

[6] Lord Cairns' Act (Chancery Amendment Act 1858).

[7] See Chapters 13 and 14, *post*.

[8] Originally five, now three, namely, Chancery, Queen's Bench, and Family Divisions. The Family Division was known as the Probate, Divorce and Admiralty Division prior to the Administration of Justice Act 1970. This Act also makes some changes in the allocation of business between the three divisions.

[9] Judicature Act 1873, s. 25 (11), now replaced by Judicature Act 1925, s. 44.

[10] [1929] 2 K.B. 316, D.C. For other examples see *Job* v. *Job* (1877), 6 Ch.D. 562; *Lowe* v. *Dixon* (1885), 16 Q.B.D. 455.

[11] (1882), 21 Ch.D. 9, C.A.

[12] Section 3 of the Real Property Act 1845, now replaced by s. 52 (1) of the Law of Property Act 1925.

reference to a year he was a yearly tenant upon such of the terms of the agreement as were not inconsistent with the yearly tenancy, that the provision for payment of a year's rent was inconsistent, that the landlord accordingly was not entitled to make the demand and the distress was unlawful. This argument represented the common law view before 1875. The court, however, held that the equitable view must prevail, namely that this being an agreement of which specific performance would be granted, the rights and liabilities of the parties must be ascertained as if the lease had actually been executed containing all the agreed terms. Equity looks upon that as done which ought to be done and, as Jessel M.R. observed,[13]

> "there are not two estates as there were formerly—one estate at common law by reason of the payment of the rent from year to year, and an estate in equity under the agreement. There is only one Court and the equity rules prevail in it. The tenant holds under an agreement for a lease. He holds, therefore, under the same terms in equity as if a lease had been granted, it being a case in which both parties admit that relief is capable of being given by specific performance. That being so he cannot complain of the exercise by the landlord of the same rights as the landlord would have had if a lease had been granted. On the other hand, he is protected in the same way as if a lease had been granted."[14]

In this connection there has been great controversy as to whether there has been a fusion of law and equity or merely a fusion of their administration. The orthodox view is that there has merely been a fusion of administration, "the two streams of jurisdiction, though they run in the same channel, run side by side and do not mingle their waters".[15] More recently the view has been expressed that law and equity themselves are fused.[16] Though it is clear that the decision in a case may well depend upon an amalgam of rules from both common law and equity, as in *Walsh* v. *Lonsdale*,[17] and though on a broader canvas one may regard the law of real property, for instance, as an amalgam of statute, common law and equity, it is submitted that to talk of the fusion of law and equity is misleading. The facts, *inter alia*, that the trust has been unaffected and there is still duality of legal and equitable ownership, that in the law of property legal rights and equitable rights, even though for some purposes equivalent as in *Walsh* v. *Lonsdale*,[18] may have different effects, for instance as regards third parties, and that purely equitable rights can still only be enforced by equitable remedies,[19] are inconsistent with the idea con-

---

[13] *Walsh* v. *Lonsdale* (1882), 21 Ch.D. 9, C.A., at p. 14. Note, however, the qualifications referred to in Megarry and Wade, *Law of Real Property*, 3rd Ed., pp. 632 *et seq.*, and see (1960), 24 Con. 125.

[14] Contrast Maitland, *Equity*, 2nd (Brunyate) Ed., pp. 16–18, and Hohfeld, *Fundamental Legal Conceptions*, pp. 121 *et seq.*

[15] Ashburner's *Principles of Equity*, 2nd Ed., p. 18; (1954), 70 L.Q.R. 326 (Lord Evershed); (1961), 24 M.L.R. 116 (V. T. H. Delaney); Snell's *Principles of Equity*, 27th Ed., p. 17; Megarry and Wade, *Law of Real Property*, 3rd Ed., pp. 133, 134; *Joseph* v. *Lyons* (1884), 15 Q.B.D. 280, C.A.

[16] *Per* Lord Denning in *Errington* v. *Errington*, [1952] 1 All E.R. 149, at p. 155; [1952] 1 K.B. 290, at p. 298, C.A.; Hanbury, *Modern Equity*, 8th Ed., pp. 19 *et seq.*, but Maudsley, editing the 9th Ed., takes a more orthodox view at pp. 17 *et seq.*

[17] (1882), 21 Ch.D. 9, C.A.   [18] *Supra*.

[19] Subject to the power of the court to award damages in lieu of or in addition to an injunction or specific performance—Lord Cairns' Act (Chancery Amendment Act 1858).

veyed by the phrase "fusion of law and equity" which must, if it is to be accurate, be given a limited and special meaning.

4 USES AND TRUSTS

It is convenient to relate briefly at this point the history of the trust, the outstanding creation of equity, under which, in the most general terms,[1] trustees, who get no benefit therefrom, are required to hold property of which they are the legal owners for the benefit of other persons, the *cestuis que trust* or beneficiaries.

Even before the Conquest cases have been found of land being conveyed to one man to be held by him on behalf or "to the use of"[2] another, but for a considerable time this only seems to have been done for a limited time and a limited purpose, such as for the grantor's family while he went on a crusade. From the early thirteenth century the practice grew up of conveying land in a general way for more permanent purposes. For various reasons a landowner might convey land by an ordinary common law conveyance to persons called "feoffees[3] to uses" directing them to hold the land for the benefit of other persons, the *cestuis que use*, who might indeed be or include the feoffor himself. After early doubts the common law refused to take any account of the uses, i.e. the directions given to the feoffees to uses, who, though they were bound in honour, could not be sued either by the feoffor or the *cestuis que use*. The common law in fact treated the feoffees to uses as the unfettered owners of the property, and completely disregarded the claims of the *cestuis que use*.

It was clearly highly unsatisfactory that feoffees to uses should be able to disregard the dictates of good faith, honour and justice with impunity, and from the early fifteenth century the Chancellor began to intervene and compel the feoffees to uses to carry out the directions given to them as to how they should deal with the land. The Chancellor never, however, denied that the feoffees to uses were the legal owners of the land. He merely ordered the feoffees to uses to carry out the directions given to them, and failure to carry out the order would be a contempt of court which would render the feoffees liable to imprisonment until they were prepared to comply.

The device of the use was adopted for various purposes. It enabled a landowner, for example, to evade some of the feudal dues which fell on the person seised of land; to dispose of his land by his will; to evade mortmain statutes; and more effectively to settle his land. The use developed considerably during the fifteenth and early sixteenth centuries, and the rights of the *cestui que use* were so extensive that it became recognised that there was duality of ownership. One person, the feoffee to uses, was the legal owner according to the common law—a title not disputed by the Chancellor. But the feoffee to uses had only the bare legal title; the real beneficial ownership was in the equitable owner, the *cestui que use*. A stop was put to the development of the use in 1535, however, when, largely because the King was losing so many feudal dues by the device of the use, the Statute of Uses was passed to put an end to uses, or at least severely to limit them. In cases where the Act applied the use was

---

[1] The meaning and definition of a trust is discussed in Chapter 2, Section 1.
[2] From the Latin *ad opus*—Pollock and Maitland, *History of English Law*, Vol. 2, p. 228.
[3] The mode of conveyance was normally feoffment with livery of seisin, and the person conveying the land was accordingly the feoffor, the person receiving it the feoffee.

"executed", that is to say, on the one hand the feoffees to uses were deprived of their seisin of the land—indeed they commonly dropped out of the picture altogether—and on the other hand the equitable estates of the *cestuis que use* were turned into equivalent legal estates carrying seisin. Though the Act executed the vast majority of uses there were cases to which it did not apply—where, for instance, the feoffees to uses had active duties to perform—and thus the use never became completely obsolete.

One special case which should be mentioned was the use upon a use, as where land is limited to A and his heirs to the use of B and his heirs to the use of C and his heirs. It was decided before 1535 that C took nothing in such case: A had the legal fee simple, B the equitable fee simple, but the limitation to C was repugnant to B's interest and accordingly void. After the Statute of Uses the second use was still held to be void,[4] though the first use was executed so as to give B the legal fee simple and leave A, like C, with nothing at all. Eventually, however, by steps which are not very clear[5] the Chancellor, about the middle of the seventeenth century,[6] began to enforce this second use and it had become a well-established practice by the end of the century. As a matter of terminology the second use thus enforced became called a trust, and as a matter of drafting the basic formula was "unto and to the use of B and his heirs in trust for C and his heirs". B took the legal fee simple at common law, but the use in his favour prevented the second use being executed by the Statute of Uses, leaving it to be enforced in equity as a trust. The result was to restore duality of ownership, B being the legal and C the equitable owner. The use was in effect resuscitated under the name of trust. The trust, however, became a much more highly developed institution than the use had ever been, and has since been, and now is, used for a wide variety of purposes. In developing the trust equity in general followed the law, and permitted equitable estates to be created corresponding to the legal estates recognised in the common law courts, and these equitable estates were commonly made subject to incidents and rules corresponding to those applying to the equivalent legal estates. Exceptionally, however, the Chancellor regarded himself as entitled to depart from the legal rule where he considered it to be unduly technical or inequitable.

As to the purpose for which a trust is set up, although cases do arise where the whole legal estate is vested in a trustee and the whole equitable interest in a sole beneficiary, it is seldom that such a simple trust is deliberately created. Much more common is some species of settlement constituted by a will, or *inter vivos* upon marriage or on some other occasion, whereby provision is made for a family. The traditional form of strict settlement of land has been largely abandoned for revenue considerations, and the avoidance of income tax and estate duty now commonly dictates the form which a family settlement shall take and, indeed, may be the primary reason why any settlement is made, just as landowners took advantage of the use before 1535 in order to

---

[4] *Tyrrel's Case* (1557), 2 Dyer 155a. But see (1966), 82 L.Q.R. 215 (J. L. Barton).
[5] The political background was that after the abolition of military tenure in 1660 the King ceased to have any substantial interest in the maintenance of feudal dues.
[6] But later than *Sambach* v. *Dalston* (or *Daston*) (1635), Tot. 188 *sub nom. Morris* v. *Darston* Nels. 30. See (1958), 74 L.Q.R. 550 (J. E. Strathdene); (1957), 15 C.L.J. 72 (D. E. C. Yale).

evade the payment of feudal dues. Clubs and societies, unincorporated bodies of all kinds, pension schemes and most charities commonly have their funds and property vested in trustees, while small investors in particular find it simpler to have in effect a varied portfolio by investing in a unit trust.[7]

A unit trust is set up under a trust deed made between parties known as the trustee and the manager. It is in essence the same institution as a particular kind of deed of settlement company known as a management trust which became familiar about the middle of the nineteenth century. Following the Companies Act 1862 the management trust was held to be illegal in Sykes v. Beadon[8] and all but one were wound up or registered as companies under the Companies Act. That one, however, the Submarine Cables' Trust, continued in existence and successfully contended[9] before the Court of Appeal in the following year that Sykes v. Beadon[10] had been wrongly decided. Nevertheless no more management trusts appear to have been created until the early nineteen thirties, when the institution was reintroduced and became known as the unit trust. Unit trust deeds vary widely in their terms, but the general principle is that securities are vested in the trustee under the trust deed, initially on trust for the manager. The beneficial interest thus held by the manager is divided up into a large number of units, sub-units or shares which are offered to the public at a price based on the market value of the securities plus an initial service charge. The investor who purchases units accordingly becomes the beneficial owner of an undivided share of the securities in proportion to the number of units he holds. Many matters are dealt with in the trust deed: provision is made, *inter alia*, for the remuneration of the trustee and the manager out of income; for the manager to repurchase shares from unit holders who wish to dispose of their investment, and for resale by the manager to new investors, though units may be dealt with on the market in the usual way; and for the duration of the trust which has usually been fixed, with perhaps unnecessary caution,[11] at less than twenty-one years to avoid the possible infringement of the rule against perpetuities. Even so, however, the trust deed commonly provides for an extension of the trust if the unit holders so desire. Unit trusts may be either fixed or flexible. The fixed trust under which the portfolio of investments is normally bound to remain unaltered has become unpopular,[12] and the flexible trust which gives the manager power to switch securities is much more common. It gives the unit holder the benefit

---

[7] See the *Report of the Company Law Committee* (the Jenkins Report), 1962 Cmnd. 1749, paras. 307-329; (1960), 23 M.L.R. 129 (H. A. J. Ford). Note that the so-called investment trust is not a trust at all, but a company formed to acquire and hold property by way of investment. In accordance with the principles of company law the shareholders have no direct beneficial interest in the property so acquired.

[8] (1879), 11 Ch.D. 170.

[9] In *Smith* v. *Anderson* (1880), 15 Ch.D. 247, C.A

[10] *Supra.*

[11] Cf. *Re A.E.G. Unit Trust (Managers) Ltd.'s Deed*, [1957] 2 All E.R. 506; [1957] Ch. 415. The practice may alter following the passing of the Perpetuities and Accumulations Act 1964.

[12] The court had to consider a fixed unit trust in *Re Municipal and General Securities Co. Ltd.'s Trust, Municipal and General Securities Co. Ltd.* v. *Lloyds Bank Ltd.*, [1949] 2 All E.R. 937; [1950] Ch. 212.

of the manager's financial skill and acumen, but correspondingly makes him dependent upon the manager's ability, or lack of it, and integrity.[13]

Particularly since the unit trust has an appeal for the relatively small and financially unsophisticated investor, statutory protection has been given.[14] Unit trusts must, in practice,[15] comply with certain conditions so as to become "authorised unit trust schemes", authorised by the Board of Trade[16]. The conditions are designed to ensure that the trustee is financially responsible and independent of the manager, and the trust deed is required to provide for various specified matters to the satisfaction of the Board of Trade. The Board of Trade is entitled to be satisfied not merely that the various matters are dealt with in the deed, but also as to the terms of the relevant provisions. Thus in *Re Electrical and Industrial Development Trust, Allied Investors' Trusts Ltd.* v. *Board of Trade*[17] the Board was held to be entitled to be dissatisfied on the ground that the initial service charge was considered to be excessive. Indeed the Board has taken the view, which has not been challenged in the courts, that it can regulate any matter relating to unit trusts, the sanction being that it can refuse a certificate of authorisation if its views are not met. Thus it has turned down unit trust schemes that would have benefited the funds of the Liberal and Conservative parties respectively. The Board thought that the unit trust concept should be restricted solely to investment, and that it could not authorise a trust in which the unit holder was invited to contribute to any cause, political or otherwise.[18] Once the unit trust is in existence the trustee has considerable control over the manager by reason of the fact that the trust deed must provide for requiring the manager to retire from the trust if the trustee certifies that it is in the interest of the beneficiaries under the trust that he should do so. The Board of Trade is also given a general control over unit trusts by a provision[19] empowering the Board to appoint inspectors to investigate and report on the administration of any unit trust scheme, if it appears to the Board that it is in the interests of unit holders to do so and the matter is one of public concern.

One might sum up the present position by saying that in the complexity of modern society there are few aspects of human activity which do not run more smoothly through the assistance of the trust concept—Roxburgh J. has observed[20] that, "as the principles of equity permeate the complications of modern life, the nature and variety of trusts ever grow". It should perhaps be added from a technical point of view that, although a trust of pure personalty is properly constituted simply by transferring the trust funds to trustees who are directed to hold them on trust for the persons or purposes intended to

---

[13] There has in fact been no case involving a unit trust in which investors have suffered a loss through the dishonesty of the managers of the trust.

[14] The Prevention of Fraud (Investments) Act 1958.

[15] Otherwise they cannot distribute circulars (including newspaper advertisements) inviting the purchase of units—Prevention of Fraud (Investments) Act 1958, s. 14.

[16] In practice the authorisation has been carried out by the Secretary of State for Trade and Industry under powers in S.I. 1970 No. 1537. It is expected that in future the Secretary of State for Trade will act.

[17] [1956] 1 All E.R. 162; [1956] Ch. 232.

[18] *The Times Business News*, 13 June 1968.

[19] Prevention of Fraud (Investments) Act 1958, s. 12.

[20] *Re a Solicitor*, [1952] 1 All E.R. 133; [1952] Ch. 328, at pp. 136; 332.

benefit, it is somewhat more complex with regard to land. Generally it is impossible to set up a trust of land in this way, though occasionally it can be done, where for instance there is a sole beneficiary entitled to the whole equitable interest. This is naturally an unusual case. Much more commonly land is conveyed to trustees on trust to sell it, and the trustees are further directed to hold the proceeds of sale and the net rents and profits until sale in trust for the persons or purposes intended to benefit. In such case the beneficiaries get equitable interests in the proceeds of sale and not in the land itself. It is also possible, however, to create a settlement of land, giving the beneficiaries equitable interests in the land by following the somewhat complex procedure set out in the Settled Land Act 1925, under which, as a general rule, the legal estate is vested, not in the trustees of the settlement, but in the tenant for life under the settlement, who holds the legal estate upon trust for all the beneficiaries under the settlement including himself. Most of the law in relation to settled land is more appropriately dealt with in books on the law of real property.[21]

5 TRUSTS AND TAXATION

With taxation at its present level it is obvious that revenue considerations are in practice commonly of vital importance in trust matters, particularly perhaps when the creation of a trust is under consideration. Most important perhaps are income tax, which in the case of investment income may be as high as 98 per cent, estate duty which may reach 75 per cent in the case of a very large estate, and which is payable not only in respect of property passing or deemed to pass on death, but also on *inter vivos* dispositions made within the seven years preceding death, and *ad valorem* stamp duty, which may be at the rate of 1 per cent on the relevant document. One may also need to consider other taxes such as capital gains tax and corporation tax as well. Accordingly where a man, wishing to make provision for his family, asks his legal advisers to draft the necessary documents, it is not enough for them merely to enquire what beneficial interests the various members of the family should have, to give advice thereon, and draft a settlement to carry out the settlor's expressed wishes. The settlor should also be advised of the tax implications of the proposed provisions, and it will commonly be thought desirable to draft the settlement in a different form and even alter the beneficial provisions so as to reduce the claims of the Inland Revenue. One very simple example to illustrate the point would be a man who proposed to make a will leaving all his property to his wife absolutely relying on her (but not by way of trust) to provide for their children by her will. On his death estate duty would be payable, and on the subsequent death of the wife any property which came to her would be liable

---

[21] E.g. Megarry and Wade, *The Law of Real Property*, 3rd Ed., pp. 287 *et seq.*; Cheshire's *Modern Law of Real Property*, 11th Ed., pp. 139 *et seq.* These books explain, *inter alia*, how, if the proper form is not used to set up an express trust for sale of land, or a settlement under the Settled Land Act 1925, according to the circumstances a trust for sale may be implied (e.g. s. 34 (2) of the Law of Property Act 1925; *Re House, Westminster Bank* v. *Everett*, [1929] 2 Ch. 166), or the imperfect settlement may be perfected so as to comply with the statutory provisions (s. 9 of the Settled Land Act 1925).

to pay estate duty again.[22] If the wife is not expected to need capital,[1] she could be given a life interest only with a power to appoint the capital among the children by her will, and in such case the "surviving spouse" exemption would apply and no further estate duty would be payable on this property on the death of the widow.[2]

In many cases, as already mentioned, the stimulus to create a settlement may not be so much a wish to provide for the family as a desire to reduce the incidence of taxation. It is clear, however, that there are very real limits as to what can be done. Basically, a settlor cannot both eat his cake and have it, and if he wishes to reduce the incidence of tax it can only be by, in effect, giving his property to other persons, though the gift may be by way of trust or settlement under which the interests of individual beneficiaries are restricted. Where large sums of money are involved, however, considerable savings can be made if a man is willing to make his family, rather than himself, the unit and is willing to distribute his wealth among them. Tax considerations may not only be the reason why a trust or settlement is made or why it is made in a particular way, but may also be the reason why the provisions of a trust may be sought to be varied, perhaps with the assistance of the court under the Variation of Trusts Act 1958.[3] Again it may be possible in some circumstances for beneficiaries to join together to break a trust i.e. to bring it to a premature end, and again tax considerations may impel them to do it. Thus if property is settled on X for life, with remainder to Y absolutely, it may be desirable in relation to estate duty for the property to be divided between X and Y. This can be done so that no estate duty will be payable on X's death, in respect of the property acquired by Y on the division, provided he survives the division by seven years or more,[4] while otherwise estate duty would be payable on the capital value of the whole estate. Until recently a very popular device was the discretionary trust,[5] in which, for instance, trustees might have been given an absolute discretion as to the payment of both income and capital of the trust fund to a class of persons such as the settlor's children, grandchildren and their respective spouses. If such a trust was carefully drafted the income was not treated as the income of the settlor, and provided the settlor survived for the appropriate period no estate duty was payable until the death of the last but one of the discretionary beneficiaries. In practice steps were usually taken to wind up the trust before this happened and thus avoid liability to estate duty. The efficacy of this device so far as estate duty is concerned has, however, been eroded by the Finance Act 1969.

---

[22] Though what is known as quick succession relief may be available if the second death occurs within five years of the first—Finance Act 1958, s. 30. It is assumed that she had not disposed of the property during her lifetime: even if she had estate duty may still be payable if the disposition was within seven years of her death.

[1] It would be possible to achieve a partial reduction of duty by giving her a limited amount of capital, or one might give trustees a discretionary power to advance capital, or to make a loan without interest repayable at her death.

[2] Finance Act 1894, s. 5 (2); Finance Act 1898, s. 13; Finance Act 1914, s. 14 (a); Finance Act 1954, s. 32; Finance Act 1956, s. 36; Finance Act 1972, s. 121 and Sched. 26, para. 26.

[3] Discussed pp. 301 et seq., post.

[4] There may be a partial saving after four, five or six years under the Finance Act 1968, s. 35 (2), as amended by Finance Act 1969, s. 40 (1), Sched. 17, Part III, para. 29.

[5] Discussed pp. 84 et seq., post.

It will be realised that each of the taxes mentioned above has its own textbooks—some of them very lengthy—and there are also specialised books dealing with the taxation of trusts and settlements, and even with what is called tax planning.[6] A vital distinction exists between what is usually called "tax evasion" i.e. non-payment of taxes which one is under a legal duty to pay, which is clearly illegal and may result in criminal proceedings, and "tax avoidance" which is the arrangement of one's financial affairs so that no liability or a reduced liability to tax accrues, which is perfectly legal. Though there are judicial dicta which disapprove of schemes which have been entered into to avoid tax, there are many more judgments recognising the right of individuals to dispose of their capital and income so as to attract the least amount of tax. One typical statement is that of Viscount Sumner in *Levene* v. *I. R. Comrs:*[7]

> "It is trite law that His Majesty's subjects are free, if they can, to make their own arrangements, so that their cases may fall outside the scope of the taxing acts. They incur no legal penalties and, strictly speaking, no moral censure if, having considered the lines drawn by the legislature for the imposition of taxes, they make it their business to walk outside them."

The courts themselves have, indeed, been prepared to give their assistance in the creation of tax avoidance schemes, in particular under the Variation of Trusts Act 1958, though in a recent case under the Act Lord Denning M.R. observed:[8] "The avoidance of tax may be lawful, but it is not yet a virtue".

It is not proposed to attempt to deal with any of the above-mentioned taxes even in outline, but it seems desirable at this early stage to stress the practical importance of tax considerations. Fortunately, however, an understanding of equity and trusts does not demand a knowledge of tax law, though it will be found that numerous points of trust law have been decided in litigation with the Inland Revenue. A simple illustration is the meaning of a charitable trust, which has often come before the courts by reason of the fact that charitable trusts enjoy considerable exemptions from taxation. It should be noted, however, that it not uncommonly happens that in a tax statute a word is given a different meaning from the one it has in the ordinary law.

---

[6] An introductory book to all the relevant taxes is Pinson's *Revenue Law*. For Tax Planning see, e.g., the book with that title by Potter and Monroe.

[7] [1928] A.C. 217; [1928] All E.R. Rep. 746 at pp. 227; 751.

[8] *Re Weston's Settlements*, [1968] 3 All E.R. 338, C.A. at p. 342; [1969] 1 Ch. 223, at p. 245.

CHAPTER 2

The Definition and Classification of Trusts

1 DEFINITION OF A TRUST

a Definition

It is commonly observed that no one has succeeded in producing a wholly satisfactory definition of a trust, although the general idea is not difficult to grasp. The general idea is expressed by saying that the trustee is the nominal owner of the trust property, but that the real or beneficial owner is the *cestui que trust*, or, alternatively, that the trustee is the legal owner, the *cestui que trust* the equitable owner. Though adequate to give the general idea, neither statement is altogether satisfactory as a definition, for neither covers, for instance, cases where a sub-trust has been created, such as where trustees hold a fund on trust for X and Y in equal shares, and X and Y both declare themselves trustees of their respective shares for their children. In such case under the head trust, the trustees are nominal owners, but X and Y can hardly be regarded as the real or beneficial owners; and under the sub-trust it is clear that X and Y are not the legal owners at all, but are trustees of the respective equitable half shares. It is difficult indeed to improve fundamentally on the definition put forward by Underhill.[1] This, subject to certain additions printed in italics, is as follows:

> "A trust is an equitable obligation, binding a person (who is called a trustee) to deal with property over which he has control (which is called the trust property) *either* for the benefit of persons (who are called the beneficiaries or *cestuis que trust*[2]) of whom he may himself be one, and any one of whom may enforce the obligation, *or for a charitable purpose, which may be enforced at the instance of the Attorney-General, or for some other purpose permitted by law though unenforceable.*"

The additions have been made to cover cases which critics[3] have said are not included in Underhill's definition, namely charitable trusts and what are

---

[1] *Law of Trusts and Trustees*, 12th Ed., p. 3. See (1899), 15 L.Q.R. 294 (W. G. Hart).
[2] This (which is a part of Underhill's definition) seems the correct plural of *cestui que trust*, not *cestui que trusts* or *cestuis que trustent*—(1910), 26 L.Q.R. 196 (C. Sweet).
[3] E.g. Keeton, *Law of Trusts*, 9th Ed., p. 5; see Keeton's own definition, *ibid.*, p. 5.

known as unenforceable trusts. It is only fair to observe, however, that Underhill's definition was for the purpose of a book dealing only with private trusts,[4] and that unenforceable trusts are recognised as being anomalous and exceptional.[5] The definition by reference to an *equitable* obligation brings out the origins of trusts in the Court of Chancery, though a trust is now, of course, enforceable in any division of the High Court. The trustee must have some control over the trust property in order to be able to deal with it for the benefit of the *cestuis que trust*, though the control may be nominal; in a case[6] in which Underhill's definition was approved, it was held that trustees of a settlement for the purposes of the Settled Land Act 1925 were within that definition. An understanding of the definition may be assisted by a consideration of the differences between trusts and other legal concepts.

b Trust and bailment

Blackstone[7] has caused some confusion by defining bailment as "a delivery of goods in trust, upon a contract expressed or implied, that the trust shall be faithfully executed on the part of the bailee". It may well be that the bailee is, in a popular sense, entrusted with the goods lent, hired out, deposited for safe custody, or whatever it may be; there is, however, no trust in the technical sense and the concepts are distinct. It is indeed better to define bailment as a delivery of personal chattels upon a condition, express or implied, that they shall be redelivered to the bailor, or according to his directions, when the purpose of the bailment has been carried out. Bailment was a recognised common law institution, while trusts, of course, were only recognised by courts of equity. Apart from historical and procedural differences, bailment only applies to personal property, while the trust concept applies to all kinds of property. The essential difference is, perhaps, that the bailee has, as it is said, only a special property in or special ownership of the goods bailed, the general property or general ownership remaining in the bailor, while the trustee is the full owner. Consequently the bailee cannot, as a rule,[8] pass a title to the goods which will be valid as against the bailor, but a trustee can pass a good title to someone who acquires legal ownership *bona fide* for value without notice of the trust.

N.B.

c Trust and contract

Again there is the historical distinction that contract was developed by the common law courts while the trust was a creature of equity. In general the purposes are different: a contract usually represents a bargain between the contracting parties giving each some advantage, while the beneficiary under a trust is commonly a volunteer, and the trustee himself usually obtains no benefit from the trust at all. It is of the essence of a contract that the agreement is

---

[4] Moreover, it is arguable that it does include charitable trusts, though it seems better to put the matter beyond doubt.
[5] *Re Astor's Settlement Trusts*, [1952] 1 All E.R. 1067; [1952] Ch. 534. See *infra*, pp. 39 et seq.
[6] *Re Marshall's Will Trusts*, [1945] 1 All E.R. 550; [1945] Ch. 217.
[7] *Commentaries*, Book II, p. 451; see, generally, Maitland's *Equity*, Lecture IV.
[8] There are important exceptions, e.g. under the Factors' Act 1889; sale in market overt; estoppel.

supported by consideration, but in the case of a trust[9] there is no need for consideration to have been given in order for it to be enforceable. This distinction is blurred by the fact that a contract under seal is enforceable at law without value having been given, the traditional explanation being that a seal imports consideration.

It is a fundamental rule of contract that it can only be enforced by the parties to it, but a completely constituted trust may be enforced by the beneficiaries, even though they may only learn of the existence of the trust long after it has been created. Some confusion may occur because a single transaction may involve both trust and contract. On the one hand there may be a contract to create a trust which can only be enforced where there is consideration[10]; and, on the other hand, although if a contract is entered into with X for the benefit of Y, Y *prima facie* cannot enforce it, if it can be established that X contracted as trustee for Y, and is accordingly a trustee of the benefit of the contract, Y can compel X to enforce the contract in his favour.[11]

d Trust and agency

It is sometimes said that an agent is a trustee for his principal of property belonging to the principal committed to his charge, either generally,[12] or, according to Professor Keeton,[13] only where there is some special, confidential relationship. There is no doubt that a principal can commonly exercise the same remedies against his agent as a *cestui que trust* can against his trustee, but Professor Powell has pointed out[14] that this "does not necessarily mean that an agent is a trustee or that a trustee is an agent. It means simply that agents and trustees have something in common—and that 'something in common' is that they both hold a fiduciary position which imposes on them certain obligations." Thus both agents and trustees are under a duty not to delegate responsibilities, not to let their interests conflict with their duties, not to make any unauthorised profits and to keep proper accounts.

There are, however, considerable differences. Thus the relationship of principal and agent is created by their agreement, but this is not so in the case of trustee and *cestui que trust*. The trustee does not represent the *cestuis que trust*, though he performs his duties for their benefit, as the agent represents his principal. Further the trustee does not bring his *cestuis que trust* into any contractual relationship with third parties, while it is the normal function of an agent to do so. Again the concept of a trust necessarily involves the concept of trust property over which the trustee has at least nominal control, but an agent need never have any control over any property belonging to his principal. Further it may be observed that the statutory provisions relating to trustees do not in general apply to agents. It may, of course, be a matter of some difficulty to decide on the facts whether a particular transaction sets up a trust or agency.[15]

---

[9] Provided it is completely constituted—see Chapter 3, Section 2, pp. 60 *et seq.*, *post*.

[10] As to the possibility of damages where there is a voluntary covenant, see Chapter 3, Section 2, pp. 66, 67, *post*.

[11] See the discussion in Chapter 3, Section 2, pp. 67 *et seq.*, *post*.

[12] See (1898), 14 L.Q.R. 272 (Spencer Brodhurst); (1933), 49 L.Q.R. 578 (W. S. Holdsworth); (1954), 17 M.L.R. 24 (F. E. Dowrick).

[13] *Law of Trusts*, 9th Ed., pp. 214, 215.

[14] *Law of Agency*, 2nd Ed., p. 25; F. E. Dowrick, *loc. cit.*

[15] See (1892), 8 L.Q.R. 220 (C. Sweet).

e Trusts and powers[16]

(i) Basic Distinction

A power can be sufficiently defined for present purposes as an authority vested in a person to deal with or dispose of property not his own.[17] It can be distinguished from a trust succinctly—a trust is imperative, a power discretionary. This distinction may have important consequences, which, as a result of statute, may in some cases seem rather bizarre. For instance, if land is conveyed to trustees in fee simple upon trust to sell it and hold the proceeds on trust for X for life with remainder to Y absolutely, a trust for sale under the provisions of the Law of Property Act 1925 is created under which the trustees have a duty to sell[18] and powers of management,[19] and so far as the beneficiaries are concerned the doctrine of conversion[20] applies so that they are treated from the moment the trust is created as having interests in personalty, not realty. However, if the land is conveyed to trustees in fee simple with power to sell the same on trust for X for life with remainder to Y absolutely, the land is settled land under the Settled Land Act 1925. The trustees, surprisingly, have no power to sell the land, which can be sold only by X, the tenant for life,[21] and the beneficiaries are treated as having interests in land, even if the land is in fact sold and represented by capital money in the hands of the trustees.[22]

One type of power which is liable to be confused with a trust is a special[23] power of appointment. This is a power given to someone (called the donee of the power) under a trust or settlement authorising him to appoint some or all of the trust property among a limited class of persons (called the objects of the power). The donee of the power can choose whether to make an appointment or not, and if by the end of the period during which the power can be exercised he has failed to make a valid appointment whether intentionally or unintentionally, the objects of the power can do nothing about it and the court has no jurisdiction to intervene.[1] If there is a gift over in default of appointment

---

[16] See generally, (1957), 35 C.B.R. 1060 (O. R. Marshall); [1970] A.S.C.L. 187 (J. D. Davies); (1971), 29 C.L.J. 68 (J. Hopkins); (1971), 87 L.Q.R. 31 (J. W. Harris).

[17] *Freme* v. *Clement* (1881), 18 Ch.D., 499; *Re Armstrong* (1886), 17 Q.B.D. 521.

[18] But with a power to postpone the sale indefinitely: Law of Property Act 1925, s. 25.

[19] Though these may often be delegated under s. 29 of the Law of Property Act 1925.

[20] See Chapter 16, *post.*

[21] Settled Land Act 1925, s. 108 (2).

[22] *Ibid.*, s. 75 (5). For another contrast see *Re Mayo, Mayo* v. *Mayo*, [1943] 2 All E.R. 440; [1943] Ch. 302, and *Barker* v. *Addiscott*, [1969] 3 All E.R. 685; *sub nom. Re 90 Thornhill Road, Tolworth, Surrey*, [1970] Ch. 261.

[23] Contrast a general power of appointment, where the person to whom it is given may appoint to himself and make himself owner. In addition to general and special powers there are powers in a hybrid category. See (1949), 13 Con. 20 (J. G. Fleming); (1954), 18 Con. 565 (F. R. Crane). Of increasing importance are what are becoming known as "intermediate powers", i.e. powers exercisable in favour of anyone, with certain exceptions. They enable trustees to deal with virtually all eventualities, and at the same time make the maximum tax savings. See *Re Lawrence's Will Trusts, Public Trustee* v. *Lawrence*, [1971] 3 All E.R. 433; *Re Manisty's Settlement, Manisty* v. *Manisty*, [1973] 2 All E.R. 1203. In the following discussion "power" means a special or intermediate power of appointment.

[1] The court does, of course, have jurisdiction to see that a person does not exceed the power given to him. Thus in relation to a special power of appointment an appointment which goes beyond the limits set to the power by the terms of the power itself or by law, is known as an excessive execution of the power and is void, e.g. appointment to grandchildren under a power to appoint to children. Again an appointment is void if it is "a fraud on a power" i.e. not made *bona fide* for the end designed.

it will take effect: if not, there will be a resulting trust for the testator's[2] estate. Suppose, however, that instead of a person being given a mere power of appointment, a fund is given to trustees on trust to divide it among an ascertainable class of persons: in such case even though the trustees had been directed to divide it in such shares as they in their absolute discretion should think fit,[3] they would be under a duty to make the division, and in case of a failure to distribute any potential beneficiary could apply to the court which would see to it that the division took place.

It will have been observed that in the illustration of a power just given reference was made to a power of appointment arising under a trust. Since 1925 most powers, including all powers of appointment, are equitable only and can therefore only subsist behind a trust or settlement. Accordingly the real question is whether a particular provision in a trust instrument confers a power or imposes a trust. The fact that the provision is contained in a trust instrument does not however mean, on the one hand, that an individual who, under a trust, is given a power of appointment is thereby necessarily constituted a trustee; nor, on the other hand, does it prevent a trustee being given a mere power of appointment, though where a power is given to trustees *ex officio*, the trend of modern decisions suggests that, unlike a power given to individuals, the trustees taking in their fiduciary capacity "cannot simply push aside the power and refuse to consider whether it ought in their judgment to be exercised".[4] Though it is no more than a duty to consider, the existence of such duty must be borne in mind as qualifying statements such as that of Lord Upjohn in *Re Gulbenkian's Settlement Trusts*[5] to the effect that the basic difference between a power and a trust "is that in the first case trustees owe no duty to exercise it and the relevant fund or income falls to be dealt with in accordance with the trusts in default of its exercise, whereas in the second case the trustees *must* exercise [it] and in default the court will".

It is not always easy in practice to decide whether on its true construction a particular provision constitutes a power or a trust, as appears from a series of cases culminating in *McPhail* v. *Doulton*.[6] In that case the judge at first instance and a majority in the Court of Appeal held that the trustees had a mere power, while the House of Lords unanimously agreed that the relevant provision constituted a trust. In the House of Lords, Lord Wilberforce observed[7] how narrow and artificial the distinction could be—"what to one mind may appear as a power of distribution coupled with a trust to dispose of the undistributed surplus, by accumulation or otherwise, may to another appear as a trust for distribution coupled with a power to withhold a portion and accumulate or otherwise dispose of it".

---

[2] Or for the settlor (or his estate) if the trust is created *inter vivos*.
[3] I.e. a discretionary trust, see p. 84, *infra*.
[4] *Per* Lord Reid in *Re Gulbenkian's Settlement Trusts*, [1968] 3 All E.R. 785; [1970] A.C. 508, H.L., at pp. 787; 518; *McPhail* v. *Doulton*, [1970] 2 All E.R. 228; [1971] A.C. 424, H.L. *per* Lord Wilberforce at pp. 240; 449.
[5] *Supra*, at pp. 793; 525.
[6] *Supra*, H.L.
[7] *Supra*, H.L., at pp. 240; 448.

(ii) *Special Power of Appointment—Mere Power or Trust Power*

The inherent difficulty in understanding the relationship between trust and power is not helped by complications in the terminology used. In this context a power is commonly referred to as a mere power, bare power or power collateral—these terms appear to be synonymous—in order to distinguish it from what is variously called a trust power, a power in the nature of a trust, or a power coupled with a duty. A power will be a trust power where, although at first sight it may appear to be a mere power, it is held that on the true construction of the instrument there is an element of trust. It will later be submitted that the term "trust power" is used in two quite different senses.

The question whether a power is a mere power or a trust power has often arisen in family trusts where the person to whom a power of appointment has been given has died without exercising it, and where there is no gift over in default of appointment. In such case, if the court holds that the power is a mere power then, as we have seen, the objects have no claim, and there will be a resulting trust: if, however, the court holds that the power is a trust power, in default of appointment there will be held to be a trust in favour of the objects of the power. A leading case is *Burrough* v. *Philcox*,[8] where a testator gave his surviving child, in the events which happened, power "to dispose of all my real and personal estates amongst my nephews and nieces or their children, either all to one of them, or to as many of them as my surviving child shall think proper". No appointment was made and the court held that the effect of this provision was to create a trust in favour of the nephews and nieces, and their children, subject to a power of selection in the surviving child, and that since the power had not been exercised the nephews and nieces and their children took equally. As Lord Cottenham explained,[9] "when there appears a general intention in favour of a class, and a particular intention in favour of individuals of a class to be selected by another person, and the particular intention fails, from that selection not being made, the court will carry into effect the general intention in favour of the class". In such case it is the duty of the donee of the power to execute it and "the court will not permit the objects of the power to suffer by the negligence or conduct of the donee, but fastens upon the property a trust for their benefit".

Whether a power is a mere power or a trust power is a question of "intention or presumed intention to be derived from the language of the instrument".[10] It is clear, however, that a gift over in default of appointment, though not upon some other event,[11] is conclusive against the power being a trust power for it is inconsistent with an intention to benefit the objects of the power if the donee fails to exercise it.[12] This is so even though the gift over is itself void for some reason.[13] An ordinary residuary gift is not, however, a gift over for this purpose.[14]

---

[8] (1840), 5 My. & Cr. 72; *Brown* v. *Higgs* (1803), 8 Ves. 561; affd. (1813), 18 Ves. 192, H.L.

[9] *Burrough* v. *Philcox* (1840), 5 My. & Cr. 72, at p. 92.

[10] *Per* Evershed M.R. in *Re Scarisbrick's Will Trusts*, [1951] 1 All E.R. 822, at p. 828; [1951] Ch. 622, at p. 635, C.A.

[11] *Re Llewellyn's Settlement*, [1921] 2 Ch. 281.

[12] *Re Mills*, [1930] 1 Ch. 654; [1930] All E.R. Rep. 355, C.A.

[13] *Re Sprague* (1880), 43 L.T. 236.

[14] *Re Brierly* (1894), 43 W.R. 36, C.A.

Where there is no gift over, there is no "inflexible and artificial rule of construction"[15] to the effect that a trust must be implied. As Romer J. explained in *Re Weekes' Settlement*,[16] there is no

> "hard and fast rule that a gift to A for life with a power to appoint to A among a class and nothing more must, if there is no gift over in the will, be held a gift by implication to the class in default of the power being exercised. In my opinion the cases show . . . that you must find in the will an indication that the testatrix did intend the class or some of the class to take—intended in fact that the power should be regarded in the nature of a trust—only a power of selection being given, as, for example, a gift to A for life, with a gift over to such of a class as A shall appoint."

Although Evershed M.R. thought it "clear that, where there is a power to appoint among a class, there will *prima facie* be implied a gift over in default of appointment to all the members of the class in equal shares",[17] it is submitted that the better view is that the court will be unwilling to infer a trust from a power in the absence of other indications of an intention to benefit the class. Thus it was held that there was a mere power and no trust in *Re Weekes' Settlement*,[18] where a testatrix, having given her husband a life interest in certain property, gave him "power to dispose of all such property by will amongst our children"; in *Re Combe*,[19] where, following life interests to his wife and son, a testator directed his trustees to hold the property "in trust for such person or persons as my said son . . . shall by will appoint, but I direct that such appointment must be confined to any relation or relations of mine of the whole blood"; and in *Re Perowne*,[20] where a testatrix gave her husband a life interest in her estate and continued, "knowing that he will make arrangements for the disposal of my estate, according to my wishes, for the benefit of my family".

In most of the family trust cases where the court has decided that the power is a trust power, the court has held that the power remains a power, but, finding an intention on the part of the testator to benefit the objects of the power in any event, has implied a trust in their favour in default of appointment. Thus in *Re Wills's Trust Deeds*[21] Buckley J. said that it really turns on "the question whether on the particular facts of each case it was proper to infer a trust in default of appointment for the objects of the power. The court did not, and, I think, could not compel the donee personally to exercise the power but carried what it conceived to be the settlor's intention into effect by executing an implied trust in default of appointment". Where the court holds that a trust is to be implied in default of appointment, it determines logically who the beneficiaries under the trust should be. A typical case is *Walsh* v. *Wallinger*[22] where a husband

---

15 *Per* Tomlin J. in *Re Combe*, [1925] Ch. 210, at p. 216; [1925] All E.R. Rep. 159, at p. 162.
16 [1897] 1 Ch. 289, at p. 292.
17 *Re Scarisbrick's Will Trusts*, [1951] 1 All E.R. 822, at p. 828; [1951] Ch. 622, at p. 635, C.A.
18 [1897] 1 Ch. 289.
19 [1925] Ch. 210; [1925] All E.R. Rep. 159.
20 [1951] 2 All E.R. 201; [1951] Ch. 785.
21 [1963] 1 All E.R. 390; [1964] Ch. 219.
22 (1830), 2 Russ. and My. 78; *Kennedy* v. *Kingston* (1821), 2 Jac. and W. 431; *Re Arnold's Trusts*, [1946] 2 All E.R. 579; [1947] Ch. 131. For the special position where there is a trust power in favour of relations or members of the donee's family see *I.R.Comrs.* v. *Broadway Cottages Trust*, [1954] 3 All E.R. 120; [1955] Ch. 20, C.A. and cases there cited; *Re Bridgen*, [1937] 4 All E.R. 342; [1938] Ch. 205; *Re Baden's Deed Trusts (No. 2)*, [1972] 2 All E.R. 1304; [1973] Ch. 9, C.A.

left property to his wife "trusting that she will, at her decease, give and bequeath the same to our children in such a manner as she shall appoint". Since the wife's power of appointment could only be exercised by will, an appointment by the wife could only be made to children living at her death. No appointment having been made the court held that there was an implied trust in default of appointment for those children only who survived the wife, [23] as being those whom the testator presumably intended to benefit. Some cases cited in this context are, it is submitted, decisions on the construction of the particular instrument and do not really involve an implied trust at all. An example is Lambert v. Thwaites [24] where the trust was, in effect, to sell real estate and divide the proceeds "amongst all and every the children [of R.W.] in such shares and proportions, manner and form" as R.W. should by will appoint. It was held that on its true construction this was a trust for all the children of R.W., subject, however, to the power of appointment. The children accordingly obtained vested interests liable to be divested if the power of appointment was exercised. R.W. having died without exercising the power, all his children, including the estate of his deceased son Alfred, took equal shares.

It may be added that where the court holds there is an implied trust in default of appointment, it applies the maxim "equality is equity" and divides the property among the beneficiaries equally. [25]

(iii) *Trust in Default of Appointment or Discretionary Trust*

As has just been seen, in most of the family trust cases where a power has been held to be a trust power, the court has implied a trust in default of appointment. In other cases, [1] however, it has also been called a trust power where the court has held that the power was of a fiduciary character which the donee of the power was under a duty to exercise. In such case if he should fail to exercise the power, the court would in some way see to it that the duty was carried out. As Lord Eldon said in *Brown* v. *Higgs* [2]: "the court adopts the principle as to trusts and will not permit his [i.e. the donee of the power] negligence, accident or other circumstances to disappoint the interests of those for whose benefit he is called upon to execute it" but will "discharge the duty in his room and place".

This second construction has been adopted in a number of recent cases concerning large benevolent funds, such as *McPhail* v. *Doulton* [3] where the

---

[23] I.e. the estates of children who had predeceased their mother got nothing.
[24] (1866) L.R. 2 Eq. 151; Kindersley V.C. observed at p. 157: "In the case now before the Court there is in express terms a direct gift to the children".
[25] *Wilson* v. *Duguid* (1883), 24 Ch.D. 244, *Re Llewellyn's Settlement*, [1921] 2 Ch. 281; *Re Arnold's Trusts, supra.*
[1] E.g. *Brown* v. *Higgs* (1803), 8 Ves. 561, affd. (1813), 18 Ves. 192, H.L., though it has not by any means always been so regarded, and was one of the few cases cited in *Re Will's Trust Deeds, supra; Burrough* v. *Philcox* (1840), 5 My. and Cr. 72, where dicta can be found to support both views; *Re Leek*, [1967] 2 All E.R. 1160; [1967] Ch. 1061, affd. [1968] 1 All E.R. 793, [1969] 1 Ch. 563, C.A. See (1971), 29 C.L.J. 68 (J. Hopkins).
[2] *Supra.*
[3] [1970] 2 All E.R. 228, [1971] A.C. 424, H L.

trustees were directed to make grants out of income "at their absolute discretion ... to ... any of the officers and employees or ex-officers or ex-employees of the Company or to any relatives or dependants of any such persons". As already mentioned, in that case all the Law Lords agreed that it was a case of a trust, not a mere power. Though they differed on other points going to the very validity of the trust, they also agreed that, if the trust was valid, the trustees would be under a fiduciary duty to exercise the power, and that if the trustees failed to exercise it, then the court would do so.[4]

It is unfortunate that the term "trust power" has been used in these two different senses, viz. (i) where the court implies a trust in default of appointment, and (ii) where it holds the power to be of a fiduciary nature, which it will itself exercise if necessary. It is, indeed, somewhat curious as well as unfortunate, for a trust power in the second sense is indistinguishable from what is usually referred to as a "discretionary trust" i.e. a trust under which the trustees are given a discretionary and fiduciary power to decide which of the class of potential beneficiaries shall take.[5] Indeed in further proceedings in *McPhail* v. *Doulton*,[6] the term used is discretionary trust and not trust power. It is to be hoped this will become the accepted terminology, and that the term "trust power" will be restricted to the case where a trust is implied in default of appointment.

A trust power in the sense of a discretionary trust has been described as intermediate between trusts and powers: it is, it is submitted, essentially a trust and is in most respects treated as such, but in one important respect, as will be seen shortly, has been virtually assimilated to a mere power.

It should be added that the courts have in fact seldom discussed,[7] and often do not seem to have recognised the existence of, the distinction between (i) implying a trust in default of appointment and (ii) treating the power as a power coupled with a duty to exercise it which the court will exercise if the donee of the power fails to do so, i.e. as a discretionary trust. What has usually happened in practice is that the court has in substance discussed either the question "is it a mere power or is there an implied trust in default of appointment?" or, alternatively, the question "is it a mere power or a discretionary trust?" Assuming that the courts in future distinguish between the two senses of trust power, it seems a clear inference from *McPhail* v. *Doulton*[8] that in the case of a trust power for a large class or classes of beneficiaries, the second sense, that of discretionary trust, is likely to be thought more appropriate, though it may well be that where the trust power is in favour of a small defined class of persons the court will prefer to imply a trust in default of appointment.

---

[4] As to how the court would exercise the power, see p. 87, *infra*.
[5] See p. 84, *infra*.
[6] *Re Baden's Deed Trusts (No. 2)*, [1971] 3 All E.R. 985, affd., [1972] 2 All E.R. 1304, C.A.
[7] Chitty J. noted the distinction in *Wilson* v. *Duguid* (1883), 24 Ch.D. 244, 249, but said that in that case there was a plain implication of a trust in default of appointment, and no need to refer to the concept of a duty to be exercised by the trustees. See (1962), 26 Con. 92 (M. G. Unwin); (1967), 31 Con. 364 (F. R. Crane).
[8] *Supra*, H.L.

(iv)   *Certainty*[9]

In considering what test for certainty of objects has to be applied in order that a disposition shall be valid, it will be convenient to discuss first a mere power, then a fixed trust, i.e. where the interest of the beneficiaries is determined by the settlor and is not dependent upon the discretion of the trustees, and finally a discretionary trust. There is no need to consider separately a trust power in the first sense, where the court implies a trust in default of appointment, for this simply comprises a mere power followed by a fixed trust, to each of which the appropriate test must be applied separately. In this last case it could happen that the power would be valid, but the trust in default void for uncertainty.[10]

So far as a mere power is concerned the law is "that the power is valid if it can be said with certainty whether any given individual is or is not a member of the class and does not fail simply because it is impossible to ascertain every member of the class".[11] Thus in *Re Park*[12] a testator gave his residuary estate to his trustee in trust to pay the income to such person, persons or charitable institutions and in such shares and proportions as his sister should from time to time direct in writing, other than herself, and from and after her decease in trust as to both capital and income for a named charity. It was held that the will conferred on the sister a valid power exercisable by her. In this sort of case, as Harman J. (as he then was) said in *Re Gestetner*[13] "there is no duty to distribute, but only a duty to consider", and it is not necessary that all the possible members of the class should be considered, provided it can be ascertained whether any given postulant is a member of the class or not. Again in *Re Coates*[14] it was held that the following provisions in a will conferred a valid power on the wife: "If my wife feels that I have forgotten any friend I direct my executors to pay to such friend or friends as are nominated by my wife a sum not exceeding £25 per friend with a maximum aggregate payment of £250 so that such friends may buy a small memento of our friendship." In this case Roxburgh J. further attempted to give some guidance as to what is sufficient certainty in this type of case. "This question of uncertainty," he observed,[15] "is a vexed question. Language draws a series of mental pictures in the mind of the person hearing the words spoken. Those pictures are sometimes fairly well defined, and sometimes blurred in outline, but they are never very precise. Language is a medium which disdains mathematical rules." He went on to cite Lord Tomlin,[16] "The question is one of degree in each case, whether, having regard to the language of the will, and the circumstances of the case, there is such uncertainty as to justify the court in coming to the conclusion that the gift is bad".

---

[9] See, generally, 1971 C.L.P. 133 (Harvey Cohen); (1971), 87 L.Q.R. 31 (J. W. Harris); (1971), 29 C.L.J. 68 (J. Hopkins); [1973] 5 N.Z.U.L.R. 348 (Y. F. R. Gubich).
[10] Cf. *Re Sayer Trust*, [1956] 3 All E.R. 600; [1957] Ch. 423.
[11] *Per* Lord Wilberforce in *McPhail* v. *Doulton*, [1970] 2 All E.R. 228; [1971] A.C. 424, H.L.—stating the effect of *Re Gulbenkian's Settlement Trusts*, [1968] 3 All E.R. 785; [1970] A.C. 508, H.L.
[12] [1932] 1 Ch. 580; [1931] All E.R. Rep. 633; *Re Jones*, [1945] Ch. 105.
[13] [1953] 1 All E.R. at p. 1155; [1953] Ch. at p. 688, and see *Fawcett Properties* v. *Buckingham C.C.*, [1960] 3 All E.R. 503, at p. 527; [1961] A.C. 636, at p. 692, H.L.
[14] [1955] 1 All E.R. 26; [1955] Ch. 495.
[15] [1955] 1 All E.R. at p. 28; [1955] Ch. at p. 498; *Re Sayer Trust*, *supra*.
[16] In *Re Ogden*, [1933] Ch. 678, at p. 682; [1933] All E.R. Rep. 720, at p. 722.

Prior to the House of Lords decision in *Re Gulbenkian's Settlement Trusts*,[18] there had been cases[17] proposing a less stringent test, namely that if you could find a person clearly within the description of the class intended to be benefited, the power would be good even though you might be able to envisage cases where it would be difficult or impossible to say whether a person was within the description or not. This test was decisively rejected in *Re Gulbenkian's Settlement Trusts*[18] which was followed in *McPhail* v. *Doulton*,[19] but the judgements in the subsequent proceedings in the latter case, reported as *Re Baden's Deed Trusts (No. 2)*[20], have somewhat confused the position. The test laid down in the two House of Lords decisions was, it will be recalled, whether "it can be said with certainty that *any* given individual is *or is not* a member of the class".[21] The majority of the Court of Appeal in *Re Baden's Deed Trusts (No. 2)*[22] held in effect that a power[23] may be valid even though there may be a substantial number of persons as to whom it is impossible to say whether they are within the class or not, provided, according to Megaw L.J., that as regards at least a substantial number of objects, it can be said with certainty that they fall within it. Sachs L.J. said that so long as the class of persons to be benefited is conceptually certain,[24] evidential uncertainty as to whether or not a given individual is within the class does not matter. The power can only be exercised in favour of persons who are proved to be within it. Stamp L.J., however, gave a forceful dissenting opinion, arguing in substance that this would be to bring in by the back door the test decisively rejected by the House of Lords in *Re Gulbenkian's Settlement Trusts*,[25] namely that the trust is good if there are individuals—or even one—of whom you can say with certainty that he is a member of the class, notwithstanding there may be others whose status is uncertain. The House of Lords test in his view requires it to be possible to say positively of any individual that he either is, or alternatively is not, within the class.

Lastly, reference should be made to a point made by Templeman J. in *Re Manisty's Settlement*.[26] After holding that a power cannot be uncertain merely because it is wide in ambit, and that it does not matter that the power does not attempt to classify the beneficiaries, but only to specify or classify excepted persons, he went on to say that in his view a capricious power could not be validly created. "A power to benefit 'residents of Greater London'," he said, "is capricious because the terms of the power negative any sensible intention on the part of the settlor. If the settlor intended and expected the trustees would have regard to persons with some claim on his bounty or some interest in an institution favoured by the settlor, or if the settlor had any other sensible intention or expectation, he would not have required the trustees to consider only an accidental conglomeration of persons who have no discernible link with the settlor or with any institution. A capricous power negatives a sensible consideration by the trustees of the exercise of the power."

---

[17] *Re Gibbard*, [1966] 1 All E.R. 273; *Re Leek*, at first instance, [1967] 2 All E.R. 1160; [1967] Ch. 1061; *Re Gulbenkian's Settlement Trusts*, in the Court of Appeal [1967] 3 All E.R. 15; [1968] Ch. 126.

[18] *Supra*, H.L.   [19] *Supra*, H.L.

[20] [1972] 2 All E.R. 1304; [1973] Ch. 9, C.A.   [21] Italics supplied.   [22] *Supra*.

[23] Technically the case concerned a discretionary trust to which, as we shall see, the same principles now apply.

[24] E.g. "first cousins" as contrasted with "someone under a moral obligation".

[25] *Supra*, H.L.   [26] [1973] 2 All E.R. 1203.

As regards fixed trusts, Lord Evershed M.R. observed, in *Re Endacott*,[27] that "No principle perhaps has greater sanction or authority behind it than the general proposition that a trust by English law, not being a charitable trust, in order to be effective, must have ascertained or ascertainable beneficiaries". In the present context there is some danger of confusion by reason of the fact that the most elaborate consideration of what is meant by certainty of beneficiaries has been in relation to discretionary trusts at a time when it was thought that they were to be treated for this purpose in the same way as fixed trusts. Until the House of Lords decision in *McPhail* v. *Doulton*[28] the law in relation to discretionary trusts was that where there was a trust for such of a given class of objects as the trustees should select, it was essential that the trustees should know, or be able to ascertain, all the objects from which they were enjoined to select by the terms of the trust. The duty of selection being a fiduciary one, it was considered that trustees could not properly exercise their discretion unless and until they knew of what persons exactly the class consisted among whom they were called on to make their selection. Likewise, if the trustees failed to act, and the court was called upon to do so, it was thought, prior to *McPhail* v. *Doulton*,[1] that the court could only act by way of equal division, which would be impossible unless there was a complete list of potential beneficiaries. Thus in *I.R.Comrs.* v. *Broadway Cottages Trust*,[2] Jenkins L.J., giving the judgement of the Court of Appeal, observed: "Lord Tomlin's view,[3] which we take to be that a trust for such members of a given class of objects as the trustees shall select is void for uncertainty unless the whole range of objects eligible for selection is ascertained or capable of ascertainment, seems to us to be based on sound reasoning and we accept it accordingly". The relevant date for deciding whether the membership of the class was ascertainable or not was the date when the trust came into existence.[4] The fact that it might be difficult or expensive to ascertain the membership of the class did not matter. Thus in *Re Eden*,[5] Wynn-Parry J. stated: "it may well be that a large part, even the whole of the funds available, would be consumed in the inquiry. To say the least of it, that would be very unfortunate, but that cannot of itself constitute any reason why such an inquiry, whether by the trustees or by the court, should not be undertaken." In order to hold the trust valid the court had to be satisfied affirmatively that there was at least a probability of the objects being completely ascertained.[6] So far as concerns the ascertainment of the objects of a fixed trust, these propositions still

---

[27] [1959] 3 All E.R. 562, at p. 568; [1960] Ch. 232, at p. 246.

[28] [1970] 2 All E.R. 228; [1971] A.C. 424, H.L.

[1] *Supra*, H.L. For the present position see p. 87, *infra*.

[2] [1954] 3 All E.R. 120; [1955] Ch. 20, C.A.; *Re Gulbenkian's Settlement Trusts*, [1968] 3 All E.R. 785; [1970] A.C. 508, H.L.

[3] In *Re Ogden*, [1933] Ch. 678; [1933] All E.R.Rep. 720, where a gift of residue, to be distributed among such political bodies having as their object the promotion of Liberal principles as the residuary legatee should select, was held to be a valid trust on evidence that the class benefited was capable of ascertainment.

[4] *Re Hain's Settlement*, [1961] 1 All E.R. 848, C.A.; *Re Gulbenkian's Settlement Trusts*, *supra*, H.L.

[5] [1957] 2 All E.R. 430, at p. 435.

[6] *Re Saxone Shoe Co. Ltd.'s Trust Deed*, [1962] 2 All E.R. 904, *per* Cross J., who also referred to a qualification applying to discretionary trusts which cannot apply to fixed trusts, namely that there is no need to trace persons in whose favour the trustees can say in advance that they will not exercise their discretion. In a fixed trust *ex hypothesi* all the members of the class must take.

seem to represent the law.[7] Suppose, for instance, that a whimsical testator were to direct trustees to divide a fund equally between a class of persons such as the objects of the trust in *McPhail* v. *Doulton*,[8] the trust would seem to be void for uncertainty unless the test of certainty set out above could be satisfied.

Turning to discretionary trusts, as already mentioned, prior to the House of Lords decision in *McPhail* v. *Doulton*[8] a discretionary trust was treated in the same way as a fixed trust and the consequence was that the validity of a disposition might have depended upon the technical question whether it fell on one side or other of the narrow dividing line between trust and power. The result met with judicial criticism. For instance Harman L.J. referring to what he called this "most unfortunate doctrine", said[9]: "it ought to make no difference to the validity of the provisions of the deed whether, on a minute analysis of the language used in this clause, it should be construed as creating a trust or a power . . . the fact that it does is an absurd and embarrassing result". The House of Lords has now decided by a bare majority, that "the test for the validity of [a discretionary trust][10] ought to be similar to that accepted by this House in *Re Gulbenkian's Settlement*[11] for powers, namely that the trust is valid if it can be said with certainty that any given individual is or is not a member of the class".[12] The doubts as to whether the word "similar" meant resemblance rather than identity have been silenced by *Re Baden's Deed Trusts* (No. 2)[13], which makes it clear that the test to be applied to mere powers and discretionary trusts is precisely the same. In relation to trusts Lord Wilberforce in *McPhail* v. *Doulton*[14] further observed that even where the meaning of the words used is clear, the definition of beneficiaries may be so hopelessly wide as not to form "anything like a class", so that the trust is administratively unworkable. It is doubtful whether this proposition applies to powers, which the courts cannot be called upon to administer having in respect of powers a much more limited function.[15]

(v)   *Mere Powers and Discretionary Trusts*

The assimilation of the rules as to certainty for powers and discretionary trusts has removed the main practical reason for having to distinguish between them. Certain differences remain however, and in appropriate circumstances may be of considerable importance. There is still a vital distinction where the

---

[7] Maudsley shares this view (Supplement to Hanbury's Modern Equity, 9th Edn., p. 125). *Contra*, Parker and Mellows, The Modern Law of Trusts, 2nd Edn., pp. 19, 76.

[8] [1970] 2 All E.R. 228; [1971] A.C. 424, H.L. The objects are set out above at p. 24.

[9] *Re Baden's Deed Trusts*, [1969] 1 All E.R. 1016; [1969] 2 Ch. 388, C.A. at pp. 1019; 397, reversed H.L. *sub. nom. McPhail* v. *Doulton, supra.*

[10] Lord Wilberforce actually used the phrase "trust powers".

[11] *Supra*, H.L.

[12] *Per* Lord Wilberforce, in *McPhail* v. *Doulton*, [1970] 2 All E.R. 228; [1971] A.C. 424, H.L. Hopkins in (1971), 29 C.L.J. at p. 101 raises the question as to the application of the new rule to discretionary trusts of capital as opposed to income. It is submitted that it should apply equally to both.

[13] *Supra*, C.A., and *per* Brightman J. at first instance, [1971] 3 All E.R. 985.

[14] [1970] 2 All E.R. 228; [1971] A.C. 424, H.L. at pp. 247; 457, discussed in *Re Manisty's Settlement*, [1973] 2 All E.R. 1203.

[15] *Re Manisty's Settlement, supra.* Such a power may be attacked on other grounds—see p. 26, *supra.*

power or trust is not exercised. In the case of a mere power the property goes to the persons entitled in default of appointment, either by express or implied gift over or by way of resulting trust, while in the case of a discretionary trust the beneficiaries will not be allowed to suffer by reason of the default of the trustees and the court will in some way ensure that the trust is executed. Another difference was referred to by Lord Wilberforce in *McPhail* v. *Doulton*.[16] "As to the trustees' duty of enquiry or ascertainment," he said, "in each case the trustees ought to make such a survey of the range of objects or possible beneficiaries as will enable them to carry out their fiduciary duty. A wider and more comprehensive range of enquiry is called for in the case of [discretionary trusts][17] than in the case of powers." In so far as it relates to powers, this rather vague dictum must, it is submitted, be restricted to powers given to trustees. An individual to whom a mere power is given is normally under no fiduciary duty to survey the range of objects.

A blurring of the line between powers and trusts occurs where a power is given to a trustee. At one extreme, if a mere power is given to an individual he is under no duty to exercise it or even to consider whether he should exercise it. He owes no duty at all to the objects of the power, which he is free to release even if he does so because as a consequence he will receive some benefit from one or other of the persons who take in default of appointment.[18] The objects can only complain if there is an excessive execution of the power, or if the appointment made constitutes a fraud on the power. At the other extreme if property is given to trustees on discretionary trusts, as we have seen the Court will see to it that the trust is carried out. In between these two extremes is the case where a power is given to a trustee. In this case by reason of his fiduciary position the trustee, unlike an individual, is under a duty to consider whether and in what way he should exercise the power and cannot refuse to consider whether it ought to be exercised. As we shall see,[19] in relation to any of a trustee's discretionary powers, the court has jurisdiction to interfere not only where it is improperly exercised, but also where a trustee refuses to consider whether or not to exercise it. But the decision of the trustees in the exercise of their discretion will not normally be interfered with by the court. It should be added that a power given to trustees *ex officio* is not capable of being released,[20] in the absence of words in the trust deed authorising them to do so.[21]

(vi) *Unenforceable Trusts or Trusts of Imperfect Obligation*

These trusts, as the alternative names imply, constitute an exception to the principle that trusts are imperative, powers discretionary. In these trusts the trustees cannot be compelled to carry out their duties; they are, in substance, powers rather than trusts and, as previously mentioned, admittedly anomalous and exceptional. They are discussed later.[22]

---

[16] [1970] 2 All E.R. 228, at p. 247; [1971] A.C. 424 at p. 457, H.L.
[17] Lord Wilberforce actually used the term "trust powers".
[18] *Re Greaves' Will Trusts*, [1954] 1 All E.R. 771; [1954] Ch. 434, C.A.; *Re Gulbenkian's Settlement Trusts*, [1968] 3 All E.R. 785; [1970] A.C. 508, H.L. *per* Lord Reid at pp. 787; 518.
[19] *Infra*, p. 361.
[20] *Re Wills's Trust Deeds* [1963] 1 All E.R. 390; [1964] Ch. 219; *Re Manisty's Settlement*, [1973] 2 All E.R. 1203.
[21] *Muir* v. *I.R. Comrs.*, [1966] 3 All E.R. 38, C.A.
[22] See pp. 39 *et seq.*, *infra*.

f   Trusts and the administration of estates of deceased persons[1]

Though different in origin, trusts having been developed by the Lord Chancellor and the jurisdiction over personal representatives having been at first exercised only in the ecclesiastical courts, it is not now possible to draw a clear line between trustees and personal representatives. In fact a person may well be at the same time both trustee and personal representative, though for particular purposes one office may be predominant. The main principles which produce this somewhat confusing situation are as follows.

First a personal representative retains his office for the whole of his life,[2] unless that grant was originally of a limited duration, or is subsequently revoked by the court. An example of a limited grant arises where a minor is appointed sole executor. In this case a grant of administration is made to his parents or guardians for his use and benefit until he attains the age of eighteen years. Such a grant automatically determines on his attaining that age or earlier death. As to revocation, this may occur for various reasons, for example if it appears that the presumed deceased is still alive.

Secondly, in a number of cases of which *Re Ponder*[3] is perhaps the best known, it has been held that a personal representative who has paid all expenses and debts, cleared the estate and completed his duties in a proper way, becomes *functus officio* as such, and holds the residue not as a personal representative, but as a trustee, and can accordingly exercise the statutory power to appoint new trustees.[4] Some doubt was cast upon this view by a reserved judgment of a strong Court of Appeal in *Harvell* v. *Foster*,[5] where an administrator was held liable as such[6] when all the duties of his office had been performed save the distribution of the net residue, which was impossible by reason of the infancy of the residuary legatee. Danckwerts J. criticised dicta in this case in *Re Cockburn*[7] and had no doubt that a personal representative who has completed his duties in a proper way can appoint new trustees. There seems in fact to be no necessary conflict between *Re Cockburn*[7] and *Re Ponder*[8] on the one hand, and *Harvell* v. *Foster*[9] on the other, if it is accepted, as it was by the Court of Appeal in the last-mentioned case, disapproving on this point Sargant J.'s view in *Re Ponder*,[8] that the offices of personal representative and trustee are not mutually exclusive. On this basis he can, *qua* trustee, exercise the statutory power to appoint new trustees[10], while, *qua* personal representative, he remains liable for any failure to carry out his duties as such. It should be observed that until the estate, whether of a testator[11] or an intestate,[12] is fully administered,

---

1 See, generally, (1955), 19 Con. 199 (B. S. Ker).
2 *Re Timmis*, [1902] 1 Ch. 176, *per* Kekewich J. at p. 183; *Attenborough* v. *Solomon*, [1913] A.C. 76, H.L., *per* Haldane L.C. at p. 83; *Harvell* v. *Foster*, [1954] 2 All E.R. 736; [1954] 2 Q.B. 367, C.A., *per* Evershed M.R. at pp. 745, 383; *Re Aldhous*, [1955] 2 All E.R. 80.
3 [1921] 2 Ch. 59; *Eaton* v. *Daines*, [1894] W.N. 32; *Re Pitt* (1928), 44 T.L.R. 371; *Re Yerburgh*, [1928] W.N. 208; *Re Cockburn*, [1957] 2 All E.R. 522; [1957] Ch. 438.
4 See Chapter 8, at p. 228, *post*.
5 *Supra*.
6 The action was actually against the sureties in the administration bond. As to sureties, see now the Administration of Estates Act 1971, s. 8.
7 *Supra*.   8 *Supra*.   9 *Supra*.
10 But where land is concerned see *Re King's Will Trusts*, [1964] 1 All E.R. 833; [1964] Ch. 542 and p. 31 n. 16, *infra*.
11 *Commissioner of Stamp Duties* v. *Livingston*, [1964] 3 All E.R. 692; [1965] A.C. 694, P.C.
12 *Eastbourne Mutual Building Society* v. *Hastings Corporation*, [1965] 1 All E.R. 779.

the residuary legatees, or the next of kin of an intestate, are not to be regarded as the beneficial owners of the unadministered assets. The personal representatives hold the assets in full ownership without distinction between legal and equitable interests. It is also true, however, that they hold them for the purpose of carrying out the functions and duties of administration, not for their own benefit, and that these functions and duties may be enforced by creditors and beneficiaries. The result therefore is that a personal representative is in a fiduciary position with regard to the assets that come to him in the right of his office and for certain purposes and in some aspects he is treated by the court as a trustee. But equity has never recognised or created for residuary legatees, or the next of kin of an intestate, a beneficial interest in the assets in the hands of the personal representatives during the course of administration.[13] One consequence of this is that personal representatives are not under the same duty as trustees to hold the balance evenly between the beneficiaries.[14]

Thirdly, the same persons are commonly appointed as executors and trustees by a testator. In the absence of an express assent, an implied assent to themselves as trustees will readily be inferred from their conduct where executors have completed their duties as such. This was of vital importance in *Attenborough* v. *Solomon*[15] by reason of the fact that trustees can only act jointly, whereas one of several executors has full power to deal with and dispose effectively of the pure personalty. What happened here was that long after the debts and pecuniary legacies had been paid and the residuary account passed, one of two persons appointed as executors and trustees pledged certain plate forming part of the residuary estate with pawnbrokers and misapplied the money so raised. After the death of the pledgor, the transaction was discovered and an action was brought by the surviving co-executor and a new trustee against the pawnbroker to recover the plate. They were held entitled to succeed on the ground that the proper inference to be drawn was that before the date of the pledge the executors had assented to the trust disposition taking effect and held the plate not as executors but as trustees. Since 1925, however, an assent in relation to land must be in writing, even in the case of a personal representative assenting to himself as a trustee.[16]

Fourthly, the amount of overlapping has been increased by the definition in the Trustee Act 1925[17] of a trustee as including a personal representative, where the context admits, and by the provisions of the Administration of Estates Act

---

[13] *Commissioner of Stamp Duties* v. *Livingston, supra*; *Lall* v. *Lall*, [1965] 3 All E.R. 330; *Re Leigh's Will Trusts*, [1969] 3 All E.R. 432; [1970] Ch. 277. See (1965), 23 C.L.J. 44 (S. J. Bailey).

[14] *Re Hayes's Will Trusts*, [1971] 2 All E.R. 341 (power to sell to a beneficiary at estate duty valuation. Executors bound to consider interest of estate as a whole, but under no duty to consider effect between trust beneficiaries). See pp. 281 *et seq.* as to duty of trustees.

[15] [1913] A.C. 76, H.L.; *Phillipo* v. *Munnings* (1837), 2 My. & Cr. 309; *Re Claremont*, [1923] 2 K.B. 718.

[16] Administration of Estates Act 1925, s. 36; *Re King's Will Trusts*, [1964] 1 All E.R. 833, criticised in (1964), 28 Con. 298 (J. F. Garner). According to this not altogether convincing decision, without a written assent a personal representative who has become a trustee cannot, as regards land, take advantage of s. 40 of the Trustee Act 1925 (discussed in Chapter 8, Section 2) on the appointment of new trustees, cf. *Re Cockburn*, [1957] 2 All E.R. 522; [1957] Ch. 438, apparently not cited in *Re King's Will Trusts, supra*.

[17] Section 68 (17).

1925[18] which constitute an administrator an express trustee both on a total and a partial[19] intestacy.

In addition to the matters mentioned incidentally above, the distinction between personal representative and trustee may be relevant with regard to the Statutes of Limitation,[20] and by reason of the rule that a sole personal representative, whether or not a trust corporation, can give a valid receipt for capital money arising on a sale of the deceased's land, while there must be at least two trustees of a trust for sale of land for this purpose, unless the sole trustee happens to be a trust corporation.[21] For most purposes, however, Jessel M.R. correctly summarised the position when he observed in Re Speight,[1] "In modern times the Courts have not distinguished between . . . executors and trustees but they have put them all together and considered that they are all liable under the same principles."

2 CAPACITY OF SETTLOR AND BENEFICIARIES

a Capacity of settlor

Capacity to create a trust is, in general, the same as capacity to hold and dispose of any legal or equitable estate or interest in property.

An infant or minor[2] cannot, since 1925, hold a legal estate in land[3] and accordingly cannot settle it.[4] As regards other property, the position is similar to the general rule in relation to contracts; accordingly an *inter vivos* settlement by a minor is voidable in the sense that it will be binding upon the minor after he comes of age unless he repudiates it on, or shortly after, attaining his majority.[5] So far as a settlement by will is concerned, a minor cannot make a valid will,[6] unless he is a soldier[7] being in actual military service or a mariner or seaman being at sea.[8] The provisions of the Infant Settlements Act 1855[9] were repealed

---

[18] Section 33. Cf. Land Transfer Act 1897, s. 2, and *Toates* v. *Toates*, [1926] 2 K.B. 30, D.C.

[19] Administration of Estates Act 1925, s. 49, as amended by the Intestates' Estates Act 1952.

[20] See Chapter 12, Section 3C, p. 375, *post.*

[21] Law of Property Act 1925, s. 27 (2), as substituted by the Law of Property (Amendment) Act 1926, s. 7, and Schedule.

[1] (1883), 22 Ch.D. 727, C.A., at 742, affirmed *sub nom. Speight* v. *Gaunt* (1884), 9 App. Cas. 1, H.L.

[2] I.e., since 31st December 1969, someone under the age of 18—Family Law Reform Act 1969 ss. 1 and 2. Previously the age of majority was 21.

[3] Law of Property Act 1925, s. 1 (6).

[4] From a practical point of view this is unimportant, as a minor can have an equitable interest and dispose of this as effectively as he could a legal estate before 1926.

[5] *Edwards* v. *Carter*, [1893] A.C. 360, H.L.

[6] Wills Act 1837, s. 7, as amended by s. 3 Family Law Reform Act 1969.

[7] Including a member of the Royal Air Force: Wills (Soldiers and Sailors) Act 1918, s. 5 (2).

[8] Wills Act 1837, s. 11, as amended by the Wills (Soldiers and Sailors) Act 1918. The privilege extends to a member of the Royal Naval and Marine Forces not only when at sea, but also when so circumstanced that if he were a soldier he would be in actual military service.

[9] This provided that a male infant of the age of 20 and upwards, or a female infant of the age of 17 and upwards, could make an immediately binding settlement. The Act applied only to marriage settlements, including post-nuptial settlements if made within a short time

by s. 11 of the Family Law Reform Act 1969, except in relation to anything done before the latter Act came into force.

Where a person, referred to in the Mental Health Act 1959 as a patient, is incapable, by reason of mental disorder, of managing and administering his property and affairs, and a receiver has been appointed,[10] any purported disposition including a settlement executed by him will, it is thought, be void since the 1959 Act for the same reasons as it was held void under the old law, namely that by the appointment the right of the patient to manage his affairs is suspended, and the sole management thereof in the meantime is committed to the receiver.[11] The result is probably the same even where a receiver has not been appointed, unless the disposition takes place during a lucid interval,[12] though the person who wishes to set the disposition aside will, in this case, have to establish the mental disorder. It seems that a disposition will not be set aside as against one who gave consideration and at the time of the disposition was unaware of the incapacity.[13] By the Mental Health Act 1959[14] jurisdiction is given to the judges of the Supreme Court nominated for this purpose by the Lord Chancellor to make orders or give directions for the settlement of any property of a patient as defined above, provided the patient is of full age.[15] This involves power to make such consequential vesting or other orders as may be required[16]; and to vary the settlement, at any time before the death of the patient, if it appears that some material fact was not disclosed when the settlement was made, or that there has been some substantial change in circumstances.[17] It seems that in exercising the jurisdiction the judge will be guided by what it is thought likely the patient would himself do if he were not under disability, but on the assumption that his circumstances in other respects are what they are in fact.[18] Thus in Re T.B.[19] the court approved a revocable settlement of the whole of a patient's property in favour of the patient's illegitimate son and his family. The effect of this was to benefit the son and his family, who otherwise[20] would get nothing at all, to the exclusion of the patient's collateral next-of-kin,

---

of marriage, but it is not clear whether it applied where the marriage took place before the specified age, though the settlement took place after it. The Act applied to all kinds of property, whether real or personal, and whether in possession, reversion, remainder, or expectancy, including property over which the infant had a power of appointment. The Act, however, only made the settlement valid and binding where the sanction of the court had been obtained.

[10] Mental Health Act 1959, ss. 101, 105.

[11] Re Walker, [1905] 1 Ch. 160, C.A. (lunatic so found by inquisition); Re Marshall, [1920] 1 Ch. 284; [1920] All E.R. Rep. 190 (receiver appointed under Lunacy Act 1890).

[12] Clerk v. Clerk (1700), 2 Vern. 412; Towart v. Sellars (1817), 5 Dow. 231; Daily Telegraph Newspaper Co. Ltd. v. McLaughlin, [1904] A.C. 776, P.C.

[13] Niell v. Morley (1804), 9 Ves. 478; Molton v. Camroux (1848), 2 Exch. 487, affd. (1849), 4 Exch. 17; Price v. Berrington (1851), 3 Mac. & G. 486.

[14] Sections 102 and 103 (1).   [15] Ibid., s. 103 (3).

[16] Ibid., s. 103 (2).   [17] Ibid., s. 103 (4).

[18] Re D.M.L., [1965] 2 All E.R. 129; [1965] Ch. 1133 (Ct. of Protection); Re W.J.G.L., [1965] 3 All E.R. 865; [1966] Ch. 135 (Ct. of Protection). Reference may also usefully be made to decisions on earlier legislation; e.g. Re C., [1960] 1 All E.R. 393 (Ct. of Protection). Cf. Re Evans (1882), 21 Ch.D. 297, C.A.; Re C.L., [1968] 1 All E.R. 1104; [1969] 1 Ch. 587 (Ct. of Protection).

[19] [1966] 3 All E.R. 509; [1967] Ch. 247 (Ct. of Protection).

[20] But see now s. 14, Family Law Reform Act 1969.

if, as was anticipated, the patient were to die without recovering his testamentary capacity. Until recently the jurisdiction did not include power to make a will for a patient, though it was, and is still, possible to order an immediate settlement which will also determine what will happen after the patient's death. The Administration of Justice Act 1969,[21] by way of amendment of the 1959 Act, has now expressly conferred such a power on the court. It may be added that the inherent jurisdiction under royal prerogative is now in practice obsolete, for there is now no one entrusted under sign manual with its exercise; moreover, this jurisdiction only applied to persons found of unsound mind by inquisition, and there is now no one qualified to hold an inquisition.

b Capacity of beneficiary

In general, anyone who can hold an interest in property can be a beneficiary under a trust. A minor can have an equitable interest in land, although he cannot hold a legal estate.[1] Married women are no longer in a special position, and, the mortmain acts having been repealed,[2] there is no special restriction on trusts for corporations. Aliens can be beneficiaries under a trust of any property, except a British ship.[3] It should be added that a beneficiary may be a trustee, even a sole trustee, though a sole trustee cannot hold on trust for himself as sole beneficiary. No trust can exist where the entire estate, both legal and equitable, is vested in one person.[4]

3   THE ESSENTIALS OF A TRUST

Lord Langdale's judgment in *Knight* v. *Knight*[5] is frequently referred to as setting out the proposition that in order for a trust to be valid the "three certainties" must be present—certainty of words, certainty of subject, and certainty of object. There was, however, nothing novel in this statement. Lord Eldon, for instance,[6] said that in order for a trust to be valid, "first, that the words must be imperative . . .; secondly, that the subject must be certain . . .; and, thirdly, that the object must be as certain as the subject". Before discussing these three certainties, reference may be made to a decision in which the question of uncertainty arose in an unusual form. In *Muir* v. *I.R.Comrs.*[7] income was payable among a class of defined beneficiaries for a period which was certain up to a given point of time and only after that point of time could, on what was actually held to be the wrong construction, become uncertain. The court took the view that, even if it were possible that uncertainty might

---

21 Sections 17 and 18. See (1970), 34 Con. 150 (D. E. Hunt and M. E. Reed).
1 Law of Property Act 1925, s. 1 (6).
2 Charities Act 1960, s. 38.
3 Status of Aliens Act 1914, s. 17; Merchant Shipping Act 1894, ss. 1 and 9 (v). Note, however, that there are restrictions under s. 29 of the Exchange Control Act 1947 on making an *inter vivos* settlement where a proposed beneficiary, whether an alien or not, is resident outside the sterling area.
4 *Re Cook*, [1948] 1 All E.R. 231; [1948] Ch. 212.
5 (1840), 3 Beav. 148.
6 In *Wright* v. *Atkyns* (1823), Turn. & R. 143, 157.
7 [1966] 3 All E.R. 38, C.A.

later supervene, the trust was presently certain and valid, and the prospect that at some future stage it might become uncertain did not render it invalid during the certain period.

a Certainty of words

Since "equity looks to the intent rather than the form" there is no need for any technical expression to be used in order to constitute a trust. It is a question in every case of construction of the words used to ascertain whether they (together with any admissible extrinsic evidence) establish an intention to set up a trust. The question has often arisen under wills whether a trust is created where the testator has in terms expressed his confidence, wish, belief, desire, hope or recommendation that the legatee or devisee will use the gift in a certain way, or whether in such a case the legatee or devisee takes beneficially with at most a moral obligation to use the gift in the way indicated. In the earlier cases[8] the courts were very ready to hold that such precatory words set up what is commonly called a "precatory trust". Rigby L.J.[9] has, however, castigated this phrase as "a misleading nickname", pointing out that if, as a matter of construction, precatory words are held to set up a trust, the trust so constituted is a perfectly ordinary trust with no special or unusual characteristics.

It is generally agreed that there was a change of approach by the courts during the nineteenth century. Lambe v. Eames,[10] in 1871, is sometimes said to be the turning point,[11] but Lord St. Leonards had pointed out the change of attitude more than twenty years before.[12] There is, in fact, no clear dividing line and even after Lambe v. Eames[13] there are cases[14] where the older approach is still adopted. As to the older cases James L.J. observed,[15] "in hearing case after case cited, I could not help feeling that the officious kindness of the Court of Chancery in interposing trusts where in many cases the father of the family never meant to create trusts, must have been a very cruel kindness indeed".

The proper attitude to precatory words is stated in the judgment of Cotton L.J. in Re Adams and the Kensington Vestry,[16] where it was held that there was no trust created by a testator who gave all his property to his wife "in full confidence that she will do what is right as to the disposal thereof between my children, either in her lifetime or by will after her decease". He said,

---

[8] E.g. Palmer v. Simmonds (1854), 2 Drew. 221; Hart v. Tribe (1854), 18 Beav. 215; Gully v. Cregoe (1857), 24 Beav. 185.

[9] In Re Williams, [1897] 2 Ch. 12, at p. 27, C.A.

[10] (1871), 6 Ch. App. 597.

[11] E.g. Cozens-Hardy M.R. in Re Atkinson (1911), 103 L.T. 860, at p. 862, C.A.

[12] A Treatise of the Law of Property, pp. 375 et seq., published in 1849. See also the argument of Mr. Richards in Knight v. Knight (1840), 3 Beav. 148, at p. 165 et seq.

[13] Supra.

[14] E.g. Curnick v. Tucker (1874), L.R. 17 Eq. 320; Le Marchant v. Le Marchant (1874), L.R. 18 Eq. 414.

[15] In Lambe v. Eames, supra, at p. 599.

[16] (1884), 27 Ch.D. 394, at p. 410, C.A. A similar case is Re Hutchinson & Tenant (1878). 8 Ch.D. 540.

"I have no hesitation in saying myself, that I think some of the older authorities went a great deal too far in holding that some particular words appearing in a will were sufficient to create a trust. Undoubtedly confidence, if the rest of the context shows that a trust is intended, may make a trust,[17] but what we have to look at is the whole of the will which we have to construe, and if the confidence is that she will do what is right as regards the disposal of the property, I cannot say that that is, on the true construction of the will, a trust imposed upon her. Having regard to the later decisions, we must not extend the old cases in any way, or rely upon the mere use of any particular words, but, considering all the words which are used, we have to see what is their true effect, and what was the intention of the testator as expressed in his will."

Again, there was held to be no trust created in *Re Hamilton*,[18] and the legatees took beneficially where, after giving legacies to two nieces, a testator continued "I wish them to bequeath them equally between the families of O and P in such mode as they shall consider right". Lindley L.J. in his judgment in that case stated[19]

"You must take the will which you have to construe and see what it means, and if you come to the conclusion that no trust was intended, you say so, although previous judges have said the contrary on some wills more or less similar to the one which you have to construe,"

and, in the same case, Lopes L.J. observed[20]

"it seems to me perfectly clear that the current of decisions with regard to precatory trusts is now changed, and that the result of the change is this, that the Court will not allow a precatory trust to be raised unless on the consideration of all the words employed it comes to the conclusion that it was the intention of the testator to create a trust".

Other cases illustrating the modern approach, and in which it was held that no trust was constituted, include *Mussoorie Bank Ltd.* v. *Raynor*,[1] where a testator gave all his estate to his wife "feeling confident that she will act justly to our children in dividing the same when no longer required by her", *Re Diggles*,[2] where the relevant words were "it is my desire that she allows X an annuity of £25", and *Re Johnson*,[3] where, after leaving half of his estate to his mother, the testator provided "I request that my mother will on her death leave the property or what remains of it . . . to my four sisters".

The modern attitude does not, of course, prevent the court from holding that a trust is created by precatory words where, as a matter of construction, this appears to be the intention of the testator[4]; and, at any rate according to Wynn-Parry J. in *Re Steele's Will Trusts*,[5] if a testator uses language which is the same, *mutatis mutandis*, as that used in an earlier case in which it was held

---

[17] Cf. *Comiskey* v. *Bowring-Hanbury*, [1905] A.C. 84, H.L.
[18] [1895] 2 Ch. 370, C.A.
[19] *Re Hamilton*, *supra*, at p. 373.
[20] *Re Hamilton*, *supra*, at p. 374.
[1] (1882), 7 App. Cas. 321, P.C.
[2] (1888), 39 Ch.D. 253, C.A. Cf. *Re Oldfield*, [1904] 1 Ch. 549, C.A., where at first instance, Kekewich J. said, "a desire carries no obligation except a moral one".
[3] [1939] 2 All E.R. 458; *Re Atkinson* (1911), 103 L.T. 860, C.A.
[4] *Comiskey* v. *Bowring-Hanbury*, [1905] A.C. 84, H.L.; *Re Burley*, [1910] 1 Ch. 215.
[5] [1948] 2 All E.R. 193; [1948] Ch. 603. The earlier case here was *Shelley* v. *Shelley* (1868), L.R. 6 Eq. 540.

that a trust was constituted, he thereby shows an intention in like manner to set up a trust. If rightly decided, it is submitted that the principle of *Re Steele's Will Trusts*[6] should be restricted to cases where the older authority comprises a more or less complex limitation which might reasonably be regarded as having been used as a precedent for the later will.

b Certainty of subject

It has been pointed out[7] that there is some ambiguity here, for the phrase may mean that the property subject to the trust must be certain, or that the beneficial interests of the *cestuis que trust* must be certain.

Where the trust property cannot be clearly identified, the purported trust is altogether void as, for instance, in *Palmer* v. *Simmonds*,[8] where the subject of the alleged trust was "the bulk of my said residuary estate". *Sprange* v. *Barnard*[9] illustrates the way in which the question has arisen in a number of cases. There a testatrix gave property to her husband "for his sole use" and continued "at his death, the remaining part of what is left, that he does not want for his own wants and use, to be divided between" a brother and sisters. It was held that there was no trust since it was uncertain what would be left at the death of the husband. The husband accordingly took absolutely. In practice, the question of certainty of subject is often associated with that of certainty of words. In giving the advice of the Privy Council in *Mussoorie Bank Ltd.* v. *Raynor*,[10] Sir Arthur Hobhouse observed, "uncertainty in the subject of the gift has a reflex action upon the previous words, and throws doubt upon the intention of the testator, and seems to shew that he could not possibly have intended his words of confidence, hope, or whatever they may be,—his appeal to the conscience of the first taker,—to be imperative words".

If there is certainty of words, and the property subject to the trust is clearly identified, the trust will be valid. If, however, the beneficial interests to be taken are not certain, those interests will fail for uncertainty, and the trustees will hold on a resulting trust for the settlor, as in *Boyce* v. *Boyce*,[11] where a testator devised two houses to trustees on trust to convey one to Maria "whichever she may think proper to choose or select" and the other to Charlotte. Maria predeceased the testator and it was accordingly held that Charlotte had no claim. There is no uncertainty, however, where there is a discretion given to the trustees to determine the exact quantum of the beneficial interests,[12] or where the words used by the testator are a sufficient indication of his intention to provide an effective determinant of what he intends. Thus in *Re Golay*[13] the testator directed his executors to let T. "enjoy one of my flats during her lifetime and to receive a

---

[6] *Supra.*
[7] (1940), 4 M.L.R. 20 (Glanville Williams).
[8] (1854), 2 Drew. 221; cp. *Bromley* v. *Tryon*, [1952] A.C. 265, H.L., and on another point, *Richardson* v. *Watson* (1833), 4 B. & Ad. 787.
[9] (1789), 2 Bro.C.C. 585. Principle of case valid though decision perhaps doubtful— contrast *Re Stringer's Estate* (1877), 6 Ch.D. 1, C.A.; *Re Last*, [1958] P. 137. Cf. *Re Jones*, [1898] 1 Ch. 438 (absolute gift—gift over of what remains void for repugnancy).
[10] (1882), 7 App. Cas. 321, at p. 331, P.C.   [11] (1849), 16 Sim. 476.
[12] As to discretionary trusts see Chapter 3, Section 4b, p. 84, *post.*
[13] [1965] 2 All E.R. 660. See (1965), 81 L.Q.R. 481 (R. E. Megarry).

reasonable income from my other properties". It was held that the words "reasonable income" directed an objective determinant of amount which the court could if necessary apply, and accordingly the gift did not fail for uncertainty. Again, in other circumstances the court may cure an apparent uncertainty by applying the maxim that equality is equity. Further, if there is an absolute gift in the first instance, and trusts are engrafted or imposed on that absolute interest which fail for uncertainty, or indeed any other reason, then the absolute gift takes effect so far as the trusts have failed.[14]

c   Certainty of objects

With the exception or quasi-exception of gifts to charity, it is a fundamental rule that the object of a trust must be certain. One aspect of this rule has already been discussed in connection with the distinction between trust and power.[15] On the same principle trusts for philanthropic,[16] or patriotic,[17] or public,[18] or benevolent[19] purposes are all void, for these words have no technical legal meaning and the court would accordingly be unable to determine whether the trustees had or had not carried out their trust by applying the trust funds in any particular way. Similarly if there is a gift on trust to apply the subject-matter in such manner or for such purposes, or whatever the words may be, as the donee may think fit, then that represents a trust for undefined objects such as the court cannot execute, and the trust is accordingly void.[20] Charity, however, is a term of art and, even though there may be uncertainty in the sense that no particular charitable purpose is specified, or only referred to in vague terms, this does not matter, provided the gift is exclusively for charitable purposes. In another sense charity is one and indivisible, and if necessary a scheme will be made to specify the particular charity which is to benefit.[1] In any case where there is uncertainty of objects, assuming the other two certainties are present, the trustee cannot take beneficially, but will hold the trust property on a resulting trust for the settlor, or, where the trust arises under a will, for the persons entitled to the residue, or on intestacy, as the case may be.

Difficult problems have arisen where the object of a trust is a non-human beneficiary, such as a dog, an unincorporated association, or a non-charitable purpose.[2] The basic principle, subject perhaps to the possibility of review of the decisions by the House of Lords, and with the exception of charitable trusts, is that "a trust to be valid must be for the benefit of individuals".[3] This is the principle stated by Grant M.R. in _Morice_ v. _Bishop of Durham,_[4] that "there must be somebody in whose favour the court can decree performance", restated by

---

[14] _Lassence_ v. _Tierney_ (1849), 1 Mac. & G. 551; _Hancock_ v. _Watson,_ [1902] A.C., 14, H.L.
[15] See pp. 25 _et seq., supra._
[16] _Re Macduff,_ [1896] 2 Ch. 451, C.A.
[17] _A.G._ v. _National Provincial Bank,_ [1924] A.C., 262, H.L.
[18] _Houston_ v. _Burns,_ [1918] A.C. 337, H.L.
[19] _Chichester Diocesan Fund_ v. _Simpson,_ [1944] A.C. 341, H.L.
[20] _Re Pugh's Will Trusts,_ [1967] 3 All E.R. 337.
[1] See Chapter 7, Section 3, pp. 211 _et seq., post._
[2] For a full and penetrating discussion see Morris and Leach, _The Rule Against Perpetuities,_ 2nd Edn., pp. 307 _et seq.,_ where reference is made to much periodical literature including (1953), 6 C.L.P. 151 (O. R. Marshall); (1953), 17 Con. 46 (L. A. Sheridan); (1955), 18 M.L.R. 120 (L. H. Leigh).
[3] _Per_ Lord Parker in _Bowman_ v. _Secular Society,_ [1917] A.C. 406, at p. 441, H.L.
[4] (1805), 10 Ves. 522, affirming (1804), 9 Ves. 399, at p. 405.

Harman J. in *Re Wood*,[5] who observed "that a gift on trust must have a *cestui que trust*", and since affirmed by Roxburgh J. in *Re Astor's Settlement Trusts*[6] and the Court of Appeal in *Re Endacott*.[7] Accordingly it has been said[8]: "A gift can be made to persons (including a corporation) but it cannot be made to a purpose or to an object; so, also, a trust may be created for the benefit of persons as *cestuis que trust*, but not for a purpose or object unless the purpose or object be charitable". The idea behind this seems to be that otherwise the validity of the trust would depend upon the whim of the trustee, and "a court of equity does not recognise as valid a trust which it cannot both enforce and control".[9]

To this general principle there are exceptions "properly to be regarded as anomalous and exceptional",[10] perhaps "concessions to human weakness or sentiment",[11] or "merely occasions when Homer has nodded".[12] These exceptions, which are known as "unenforceable trusts" or "trusts of imperfect obligation", seem to be restricted to trusts arising under wills where the legacy will fall into a residuary gift if the unenforceable trust is not carried out.[13] The court can indirectly enforce the trust in such a case by obtaining an undertaking from the trustee to apply the legacy towards the unenforceable purpose, and giving the residuary legatees liberty to apply if the undertaking is not carried out. Evershed M.R. in *Re Endacott*[14] referred with apparent approval to the classification of these exceptions put forward by Morris and Leach[15] into five groups, namely:

i Trusts for the erection or maintenance of monuments or graves. If the tomb can be regarded as a part of the fabric of a church,[16] or the trust is for the maintenance of a churchyard in general,[17] the trust is charitable and clearly valid. Equally clearly a trust for the maintenance of a tomb or a monument

---

[5] [1949] 1 All E.R. 1100, at p. 1101; [1949] Ch. 498, at p. 501.
[6] [1952] 1 All E.R. 1067; [1952] Ch. 534; *Re Shaw*, [1957] 1 All E.R. 745, compromised, [1958] 1 All E.R. 245, C.A.
[7] [1959] 3 All E.R. 562; [1960] Ch. 232, C.A. Yet two years later in *Re Harpur's Will Trusts*, [1961] 3 All E.R. 588; [1962] Ch. 78, C.A., Evershed M.R., who was a member of the court in *Re Endacott*, observed, at pp. 592; 91, that a trust to apply income, restricted to the perpetuity period, "for certain named purposes such as the trustees think fit, some of the purposes being charitable and some not charitable" would be valid. But see *Re Denley's Trust Deed*, [1968] 3 All E.R. 65; [1969] 1 Ch. 373.
[8] *Leahy v. A.-G. of New South Wales*, [1959] 2 All E.R. 300, at p. 307; [1959] A.C. 457, at p. 478, P.C. *per* Viscount Simonds; *Re Recher's Will Trusts*, [1971] 3 All E.R. 401; [1972] Ch. 526.
[9] *Per* Roxburgh J. in *Re Astor's Settlement Trusts*, supra, at pp. 1075; 549.
[10] *Ibid.* at pp. 1074, 547, and *per* Evershed M.R. in *Re Endacott*, supra, C.A.
[11] *Ibid.*
[12] *Per* Harman L.J. in *Re Endacott*, [1959] 3 All E.R. 562, at p. 571; [1960] Ch. 232, at p. 250, C.A.
[13] *Re Astor's Settlement Trusts*, supra. *Sed quaere*—there will always be someone entitled to the fund if the unenforceable trust is not carried out, either under the intestacy rules, or by way of resulting trust or otherwise, who could be given liberty to apply.
[14] *Supra.*   [15] *Op. cit.*, p. 310.
[16] *Hoare* v. *Osborne* (1866), L.R. 1 Eq. 585; *Re King*, [1923] 1 Ch. 243.
[17] *Re Vaughan* (1886), 33 Ch.D. 187 (*per* North J. at p. 192, "I do not see any difference between a gift to keep in repair what is called 'God's House' and a gift to keep in repair the churchyard round it which is often called 'God's Acre')"; *Re Manser*, [1905] 1 Ch. 68; *Re Eighmie*, [1935] Ch. 524.

not in a church for ever or for an indefinite period is void as offending against the rule against perpetual trusts.[18] A trust for the erection of a monument to the testator or some member of his family, or for the maintenance of a tomb has, however, been held valid, where it would not continue beyond the perpetuity period.[19] Though valid, such a trust is unenforceable in that no one can compel the trustee to carry it out; but if he wishes to perform it, no one can prevent him from doing so, and only if and in so far as he chooses not to do so will there be a resulting trust for the residuary legatees.

ii   Trusts for the saying of masses, if these are not charitable. Trusts for the saying of masses have been held charitable at first instance.[20] In view of the stress which the House of Lords has put[1] on the requirement of an element of public benefit there must be some doubt about the validity of this decision, particularly where the masses are to be said privately. If such trusts are eventually held not to be charitable, it seems they would be valid unenforceable trusts[2] provided they are restricted to the perpetuity period, with like effects to those referred to under i above.

iii Trusts for the maintenance or benefit of animals in general, or of a class of animals are charitable.[3] A trust for the benefit of specific animals is, however, not charitable, but in several cases[4] such a trust has been held to be a valid unenforceable trust, if restricted to the perpetuity period, again with like effects to those referred to under i above. It may be observed that in the only case in which this point was discussed,[5] the judge, North J., did not treat animal cases as exceptions to a rule, but dissented from the view that the court will not recognise a trust unless it is capable of being enforced by someone.

iv   Trusts for the benefit of unincorporated associations. There is no difficulty where the purposes of the association are charitable—the trust will not then be void either for uncertainty or perpetuity. Cases of non-charitable associations were said to form a more doubtful group by Morris and Leach,[6] and the trend of recent decisions suggests that this group should be deleted as an exception. The difficulty largely arises out of "the artificial and anomalous conception of an unincorporated society which, though it is not a separate entity in law, is yet for many purposes regarded as a continuing entity and, however inaccurately, as

---

[18] *Hoare* v. *Osborne, supra*; *Re Vaughan, supra*; *Re Elliott*, [1952] Ch. 217. See Chapter 5, Section 1b, p. 127, *post*.

[19] *Trimmer* v. *Danby* (1856), 25 L.J.Ch. 424; *Pirbright* v. *Salwey*, [1896] W.N. 86; *Re Hooper*, [1932] 1 Ch. 38.

[20] *Re Caus*, [1934] Ch. 162; [1933] All E.R. Rep. 818; and see *Carrigan* v. *Redwood* (1910), 30 N.Z.L.R. 244.

[1] *Gilmour* v. *Coats*, [1949] 1 All E.R. 848; [1949] A.C. 426, H.L. Their Lordships were careful, however, to reserve their opinion on this point.

[2] *Bourne* v. *Keane*, [1919] A.C. 815, H.L.

[3] *Re Wedgwood*, [1915] 1 Ch. 113, C.A.; *National Anti-Vivisection Society* v. *I.R.Comrs.*, [1947] 2 All E.R. 217; [1948] A.C. 31, H.L.; *Re Moss*, [1949] 1 All E.R. 495.

[4] *Pettingall* v. *Pettingall* (1842), 11 L.J.Ch. 176; *Mitford* v. *Reynolds* (1848), 16 Sim. 105; *Re Dean* (1889), 41 Ch.D. 552; *Re Haines* (1952), *The Times*, Nov. 7th, p. 11.

[5] *Re Dean, supra*. So far as the perpetuity period is concerned this case is generally thought to be wrong in so far as it suggests the lives can be other than human lives—Morris and Leach, *op. cit.*, p. 63.

[6] *Op. cit.*, p. 310.

something other than an aggregate of its members"[7] In the case of a gift to an unincorporated non-charitable association one must first construe the gift, and then decide what results flow from that construction. It appears from *Re Recher's Will Trusts*[8] that there are four possible interpretations of such a gift.

First, and this seems to be the *prima facie* construction, it may be construed as a gift to the individual members of the association at the date of the gift for their own benefit as joint tenants or tenants in common, so that they could at once, if they pleased, agree to divide it amongst themselves, each putting his share into his own pocket. On the basis that the gift is to the individual members it follows that any member, after severance if he took as a joint tenant, can claim an *aliquot* share whether or not he continues to be a member of the association and irrespective of the wishes of the other members. In *Leahy v. A.-G. of New South Wales,*[9] it was observed that it is by reason of this construction

> "that the prudent conveyancer provides that a receipt by the treasurer or other proper officer of the recipient society for a legacy to the society shall be a sufficient discharge to executors.[10] If it were not so, the executors could only get a valid discharge by obtaining a receipt from every member. This must be qualified by saying that, by their rules, the members might have authorised one of themselves to receive a gift on behalf of them all."

This first construction may even be given to a gift for the general purposes of the association,[11] although it may clearly not be contemplated that the individual members shall divide it amongst themselves, provided there is nothing in the constitution of the society to prohibit it.[12]

Secondly, it may be construed as a gift not only to present members, but also to future members for ever or for an indefinite period. On this construction, unless the duration is limited to the perpetuity period, it will fail for perpetuity.

Thirdly, it may be construed as a gift to the trustees or other proper officers of the association on trust to carry into effect the purposes of the association. On this construction the rule in *Morice v. Bishop of Durham*[13] applies and the gift will fail for want of a beneficiary. It is only if on this construction the gift were to be held valid—which, it is submitted, is not the case—that unincorporated associations would constitute an exception to the general principle, for each other construction is based on a gift to individuals.

---

[7] *Leahy v. A.-G. of New South Wales,* [1959] 2 All E.R. 300, at p. 306; [1959] A.C. 457, at p. 477, P.C., *per* Viscount Simonds.

[8] [1971] 3 All E.R. 401; [1972] Ch. 526 following *Leahy v. A.-G. of New South Wales, supra,* P.C. and *Neville Estates Ltd. v. Madden,* [1961] 3 All E.R. 769; [1962] Ch. 832. See (1960), 24 Con. 278 (E. O. Walford); (1965), 29 Con. 165 (J. A. Andrews); (1971), 8 M.U.L.R. 1 (P. W. Hogg); (1973), 47 A.L.J. 305 (R. Baxt).

[9] [1959] 2 All E.R. 300, at p. 306; [1959] A.C. 457, at p. 477 P.C.

[10] But even this will not save the gift where there is in fact no association. Thus the gift to the Oxford Group failed in *Re Thackrah,* [1939] 2 All E.R. 4. See E. O. Walford, *loc. cit.*

[11] *Bowman v. Secular Society Ltd.,* [1917] A.C. 406, H.L.; *Re Ogden,* [1933] Ch. 678; [1933] All E.R. Rep. 720.

[12] *Re Clarke,* [1901] 2 Ch. 110. Cf. *Re Drummond,* [1914] 2 Ch. 90; [1914–15] All E.R. Rep. 223; disapproved *Leahy v. A.-G. of New South Wales, supra.*

[13] (1805), 10 Ves. 522 affirming (1804), 9 Ves. 399.

Fourthly and lastly it may be construed as a gift to the existing members of the association beneficially, but on the basis that the subject matter of the gift falls to be dealt with in accordance with the rules of the association by which the members are contractually bound *inter se*. On this construction the gift will be valid. Though beneficially entitled an individual member cannot claim to be paid out his share. His share will accrue to the other members on his death or resignation, even though such members include persons who become members after the gift took effect.[14] This fourth construction was held to be the proper way to construe the gift to the Anti-Vivisection society in *Re Recher's Will Trusts*[15] itself. The gift would accordingly have been held good had the society still been in existence, but on the facts it was held to fail because it had been dissolved before the testatrix died.

v Miscellaneous cases. The most important case is *Re Thompson*,[16] where a testator gave a legacy of £1,000 to his friend G. W. L. to be applied by him in such manner as in his discretion he might think fit towards the promotion and furtherance of fox-hunting. Clauson J. refused to accept the argument based on *Morice v. Bishop of Durham*[17] that the trust was invalid, and indirectly enforced the trust in the usual way by requiring an undertaking from the trustee to apply the legacy towards the object expressed in the will, and giving the residuary legatees liberty to apply to the court in case the trustee failed to carry out his undertaking.

In addition to these five exceptions, an important qualification appears from the recent case of *Re Denley's Trust Deed*,[18] where the judge drew a distinction between "purpose or object trusts which are abstract or impersonal" and which are void on the principle set out above, and a trust which "though expressed as a purpose, is directly or indirectly for the benefit of an individual or individuals" Such a trust, he said, is in general outside the mischief of the principle that every trust must have a certain *cestui que trust*. He accordingly held valid a trust for the provision of a recreation or sports ground, during a period limited within the perpetuity period, for the benefit of what he held to be an ascertainable class. There are, however, difficulties in reconciling this decision with *dicta* in *Leahy v. A.-G. of New South Wales*.[1]

Finally, it should be mentioned that in the present state of the authorities it seems impossible to accept the attractive proposition that an unenforceable trust should be allowed to take effect as a power.[2] In two cases[3] the Court of Appeal has made clear statements to the contrary observing, for instance, in

---

[14] It is not easy to see how this proposition is to be reconciled with the Law of Property Act 1925, s. 53 (1) (c), which requires the disposition of an equitable interest to be in writing, and there are also difficulties in regard to infant members. See [1971] A.S.C.L., p. 379 (J. Hackney).

[15] [1971] 3 All E.R. 401; [1972] Ch. 526.

[16] [1934] Ch. 342; [1933] All E.R. Rep. 805.   [17] *Supra*.

[18] [1968] 3 All E.R. 65; [1969] 1 Ch. 373.

[1] *Supra*. See [1968] A.S.C.L., pp. 437 *et seq*. (J. D. Davies) (1969), 32 M.L.R. 96 (J. M. Evans); (1970) 34 Con. 77 (P. A. Lovell); (1973), 37 Con. 420 (L. McKay).

[2] Morris and Leach, *op. cit.*, pp. 319 *et seq*. See the American Law Institute's Restatement of Trusts, 2d (1959), para. 124.

[3] I.R.Comrs. v. *Broadway Cottages Trust*, [1954] 3 All E.R. 120; [1955] Ch. 20, C.A ; *Re Endacott*, [1959] 3 All E.R. 562; [1960] Ch. 232, C.A.; *Re Shaw*, [1957] 1 All E.R. 745, compromised, [1958] 1 All E.R. 245, C.A.

I.R.Comrs. v. *Broadway Cottages Trust*[4] "We do not think a valid power is to be spelt out of an invalid trust". If, however, a provision is drafted as a mere power to appoint for a specific non-charitable purpose, limited in its exercise to the perpetuity period, it seems it may well be valid.[5] The donee of the power may exercise it if he wishes to do so, and if he does not the property will pass to the persons entitled in default of appointment, or be held on a resulting trust for the settlor or his estate.

4   CLASSIFICATION OF TRUSTS

a   Express, resulting, implied and constructive trusts

There is no generally agreed classification, and it has even been judicially suggested[6] that the boundaries of constructive trust may have been left deliberately vague, so as not to restrict the court by technicalities in deciding what the justice of a particular case may demand. Nevertheless it may be important in particular contexts to be able to put a trust in one category or another. Thus as a general rule a declaration of trust of land must be evidenced by writing, but this rule does not apply to resulting, implied and constructive trusts[7]; and although the appointment of an infant as an express trustee is void,[8] he can hold property as a trustee upon a resulting trust.[9] At one time express trustees were treated differently from constructive trustees for the purposes of limitation, and to increase the difficulties of classification, in this context express trustees included many persons who were generally regarded as constructive trustees.[10] This distinction, however, does not exist under the modern law.

An express trust is *prima facie* one where the settlor has expressed his intention to set up a trust.

The term implied trust is used in more than one sense. In one sense an implied trust arises where the intention of the settlor to set up a trust is inferred from his words or actions, i.e. where his intention is not directly expressed but presumed. Precatory trusts[11] are implied trusts in this sense, though some writers,[12] probably rightly, consider they are essentially express trusts, in that the trust is expressed, albeit in ambiguous and uncertain language. Again, as mentioned below, many resulting trusts depend upon the implied intention of the grantor, and sometimes the term implied trust is used as synonymous with constructive trust.

The term resulting trust seems to be limited to three fairly well defined types of case,[13] first, where a man purchases property and has it conveyed or

---

[4] [1954] 3 All E.R. 120; [1955] Ch. 20, C.A., at 128; 36.
[5] *Re Douglas* (1887), 35 Ch.D. 472, C.A
[6] Per Edmund Davies L.J. in *Carl-Zeiss-Stiftung* v. *Herbert Smith & Co.* (No. 2), [1969] 2 All E.R. 367, 381, C.A.
[7] Law of Property Act 1925, s. 53 (2).
[8] Law of Property Act 1925, s. 20.
[9] *Re Vinogradoff*, [1935] W.N. 68.
[10] See *Soar* v. *Ashwell*, [1893] 2 Q.B. 390, C.A.
[11] See pp. 35, 36, *ante*.
[12] E.g. Underhill, *Law of Trusts and Trustees*, 12th Ed., p. 11
[13] Discussed fully in Chapter 4, on pp. 100–120, *post*.

transferred into the name of another or the joint names of himself and another when the beneficial interest will normally, as it is said, result to the man who put up the purchase money; secondly, where there is a voluntary conveyance or transfer into the name of another or into the joint names of the grantor and another where likewise there is *prima facie* a resulting trust for the grantor; and thirdly, where there is a transfer of property to another on trusts which leave some or all of the equitable interest undisposed of. Again there is a resulting trust, whether the reason is that there is no attempt to dispose of part of the equitable interest, as where property is given to trustees on trust for X for life, and nothing is said as to what is to happen after X's death, or that a purported disposition fails, as where a declared trust is void for uncertainty.

According to Underhill[14] resulting trusts may be classified into two groups: (a) those where the resulting trust depends upon the presumed or implied intention of the grantor—when in Underhill's view they are to be treated as express trusts. This will be the position in the first two types of case referred to above, and in the third type where there has been no attempt to dispose of a part of the beneficial interest which is consequently held upon a resulting trust, and (b) those where there can be no such implied intention, for instance, where the declared trust is void for uncertainty or illegality, when they are to be treated as constructive trusts. In *Re Vandervell's Trusts*[15] Megarry J. classified resulting trusts a little differently. In his view the first two types of cases are "presumed resulting trusts", for the reason stated by Underhill. Megarry J., however, appears to be of the opinion that the third type of case is always what he calls an "automatic resulting trust", i.e. it does not depend on any intentions or presumptions, but is the automatic consequence of the transferor's failure to dispose of what is vested in him. It should be added that Megarry J. did not discuss the question whether resulting trusts are express or constructive trusts.

Lastly a constructive trust is one imposed by a court of equity regardless of the intention of the owner of the property. The term is commonly used as including resulting trusts, and by Underhill as comprehending all trusts which are not express in his wide definition of that word. The most important cases of what we may perhaps call pure constructive trust are where a stranger to the trust, not being a *bona fide* purchaser for value without notice, is found in possession of trust property, which he will be compelled to hold on trust for the beneficiaries as a constructive trustee,[16] and where a trustee makes some profit out of his trust which he will be compelled to hold as a part of the trust property.[17] Apart from these cases, wherever the legal and equitable ownership of property is separated, and there is no trust express, implied or resulting, equity will treat the person in whom the property is vested as a constructive

---

[14] *Op. cit.*, pp. 10, 11.
[15] [1974] 1 All E.R. 47.
[16] See Chapter 4, Section 5, p. 122, *post*.
[17] See Chapter 10, Section 2b, p. 310, *post*. Hanbury's unorthodox view (*Modern Equity*, 8th Ed., p. 111) that this case is no part of constructive trusts, because the trustee holds the profits on the same express trust as that on which he holds the property out of which it is made, is not followed by Maudsley editing the 9th Ed., at p. 101.

trustee for the beneficial owner. Thus, for instance, under a contract for the sale of land a vendor is a constructive trustee for the purchaser until completion, though it may well be, as in this case, that the constructive trust has special characteristics.[18]

The generally accepted view in English law is that the constructive trust is a substantive institution. It is in principle like any other trust, the difference lying in the mode of creation. Express trusts and constructive trusts are two species of the same genus. In America, however, a constructive trust is usually treated rather as a remedy, i.e. a person who would be unjustly enriched if he was permitted to retain property is held to be under an obligation to transfer that property to the person entitled in equity and accordingly to be a constructive trustee.[19] Lord Denning M.R. is, perhaps, the first English judge who can be cited in support of the American approach. He said, in *Hussey* v. *Palmer*[20] that the constructive trust "is an equitable remedy by which the court can enable an aggrieved party to obtain restitution". It is submitted it would be premature to treat this *dictum* as establishing the acceptance of the American view as part of English law.

b Statutory trusts

In contrast to the trusts considered in sub-section **a** above, which were either set up by act of parties or imposed by a court of equity, a trust may be created by statute in specified circumstances. Among the most important are the trust for sale on intestacy under s. 33 of the Administration of Estates Act 1925, and the trust for sale imposed by ss. 34–36 of the Law of Property Act 1925 in cases of undivided shares and joint tenancy of land where no express trust for sale was set up by the relevant instrument.

c Executory and executed trusts

This is a division of express trusts. Although as Lord St. Leonards pointed out in *Egerton* v. *Brownlow*,[21] in one sense all trusts are executory in that there is always something to be done, the terms "executory" and "executed" are used, he continued, with a technical meaning. An executed trust is where the settlor has been his own conveyancer, i.e. where he has defined exactly the interests to be taken by the beneficiaries or, in other words, has set out the

---

[18] See Chapter 4, Section 4, p. 120, *post*.

[19] See *Scott on Trusts*, 3rd Ed. Vol. V. Sections 461 and 462, who stated in section 462.1 that express and constructive trusts "are distinct concepts. They are not two species of a single genus"; American restatement of the Law of Restitution, Section 160. By contrast, in English Law, in appropriate circumstances a person may be held to be a constructive trustee, from which it may follow, on ordinary trust principles discussed *infra*, pp. 333 *et seq.*, that the beneficiary may be able to call for a transfer of the trust property.

[20] [1972] 3 All E.R. 744, 747, C.A. discussed *infra*, pp. 82, 83. The case for treating the constructive trust as a remedy rather than a substantive institution has recently been fully argued by D. W. M. Waters in *The Constructive Trust*. See also (1955), 71 L.Q.R. 39 (A. W. Scott); (1959), 75 L.Q.R. 234 (R. H. Maudsley); (1963), 21 C.L.J. 119 (L. J. Sealy); Goff & Jones, *The Law of Restitution*, pp. 36 *et seq.*; (1973), 26 C.L.P. 17 (A. J. Oakley).

[21] (1853), 4 H.L.Cas. 1, 210.

limitations of the equitable interests in complete and final form. An executory trust is where he has merely expressed his general intention as to the way in which the property shall go, the limitations really only being intended as instructions as to the mode in which a formal settlement should ultimately be made.[22]

> "The instrument does not profess to carry into execution the purpose of the testator. It professes only to express the purpose or intention of the testator, and to give to other persons power and instructions for carrying that intention into execution. The intention may be more or less clearly expressed, the direction or instruction may be more or less explicit. The language of the trust is not to be assumed to be the language in which the ultimate deed is to be expressed."[1]

The doctrine of executory trusts, however, has its limits. Before it can be applied, it must be possible to ascertain from the language of the document directing the setting-up of the trust, at least in general terms, the trusts which one is to impose on the property to be settled. It was held that this could not be done, and the trust accordingly failed, in *Re Flavel's Will Trusts*,[2] where a testator left a share of residue to trustees "for formation of a superannuation bonus fund for the employees" of a named company.

The importance of the distinction between executory and executed trusts lies in their construction. In the case of an executed trust equity will follow the law and give a strict construction to technical words; if strict conveyancing language with a definite legal meaning is used in the creation of a trust of an equitable estate, it is not competent to a court to disregard that legal meaning even though a contrary intention may appear from the rest of the deed.[3] However, even in an executed trust the use of untechnical expressions may enable the court to give effect to the settlor's intentions.[4] By contrast in the case of an executory trust the court is not bound to construe technical expressions in a technical way, but can look at the whole instrument in order to discover what is the real intention of the settlor, or testator, and order the formal settlement to be drafted so as to fulfil, so far as possible, these real intentions. It has been said[5] "In construing the words creating an executory trust a court of Equity exercises a large authority in subordinating the language to the intent".

Most cases on executory trusts have been cases on marriage articles, where the articles direct a more formal conveyance to be made, and themselves express the limitations in an informal manner, but executory trusts may arise under wills,[6] or indeed under *inter vivos* dispositions other than marriage articles.[7] Although in strict theory there is no difference in the construction to be put upon executory trusts in marriage articles as opposed to those found elsewhere, in practice in the case of marriage articles there is a strong presump-

---

[22] For cases establishing this classification see *Stanley* v. *Lennard* (1758), 1 Eden, 87; *Austen* v. *Taylor* (1759), 1 Eden. 361; *Jervoise* v. *Northumberland* (1820), 1 Jac. & W. 559.
[1] Per Lord Colonsay in *Sackville-West* v. *Holmesdale* (1870), L.R. 4 H.L. 543, at p. 570.
[2] [1969] 2 All E.R. 232.
[3] *Re Bostock's Settlement*, [1921] 2 Ch. 469, C.A.
[4] *Re Arden*, [1935] Ch. 326.
[5] Per Lord Westbury in *Sackville-West* v. *Holmesdale* (1870), L.R. 4 H.L. 543, at p. 565; *Re Bostock's Settlement*, [1921] 2 Ch. 469, C.A.
[6] *Re Spicer* (1901), 84 L.T. 195.
[7] *Mayn* v. *Mayn* (1867), L.R. 5 Eq. 150.

tion that there was an intention to provide for the issue of the marriage. "Words may be used which, technically construed, would imply that the issue of the marriage should be left to the chance of taking by descent an estate of inheritance vested in the parent; yet so strong is the evidence, arising out of the occasion of the contract, of an intention to give to the issue a provision independent of their parents, that, as a general rule, limitations will be introduced into the completed settlement giving a life estate to the parent, and estates by purchase to the issue. This is not because there is any rule of law peculiarly applicable to marriage articles, but because in such documents, *res ipsa loquitur*, the occasion itself testifies what the paramount object of the parties must have been."[8] It may be added that the practical importance of the distinction between executed and executory trusts has been considerably reduced as a result of the abolition[9] of the rule in *Shelley's Case*,[10] and the provisions of ss. 60 and 130 of the Law of Property Act 1925.

d Private and charitable trusts

A private trust is for the benefit of an individual, or a number or class of specified persons, all of whom must be definitely ascertained within the perpetuity period; a public or charitable trust has as its object charity in a technical sense and usually requires an element of public benefit. The definition of charity, and the advantages and disadvantages of charitable trusts, are discussed in Chapter 6.

e Completely and incompletely constituted trusts

This distinction is discussed in Chapter 3, Section 2, p. 60, *post.*

f Simple and special trusts

The distinction has not been fully worked out by the courts. The term "bare trust", which seems to be synonymous with "simple trust" or "naked trust" has been the subject of conflicting views in several cases where the point has arisen on the construction of that term in a statute. Hall V.C. in *Christie* v. *Ovington*[11] took the view, in connection with s. 5 of the Vendor and Purchaser Act 1874, repealed and replaced by s. 48 of the Land Transfer Act 1875,[12] that a bare trustee was "a trustee to whose office no duties were originally attached, or who, although such duties were originally attached to his office, would, on the requisition of his *cestuis que trust*, be compellable in equity to convey the estate to them, or by their direction". Jessel M.R. in *Morgan* v. *Swansea Urban Sanitary Authority*[13] criticised this definition on two grounds: first, he said the concept of a trustee necessarily connotes duties, and the definition would be meaningless unless "duties" means active duties in the sense of trusts

---

[8] *Sackville-West* v. *Holmesdale, supra, per* Lord Cairns at p. 572; *Blackburn* v. *Stables* (1814), 2 Ves. & B. 367.
[9] By the Law of Property Act 1925, s. 131.
[10] (1581), 1 Co. Rep. 93b.
[11] (1875), 1 Ch.D. 279.
[12] Repealed by the Land Registration Act 1925, s. 147, and Schedule.
[13] (1878), 9 Ch.D. 582.

to sell or lease or something of that sort. Secondly, he said that as it stands the second part of the definition is totally unhelpful, since in any trust all the *cestuis que trust*, if *sui iuris*, can together compel the trustees to convey the estate. It would, he said, have a meaning, if it continued "and has been requested by them so to convey it" for after such request it would be wrong of the trustee to continue to hold the estate. However, Jessel M.R.'s own view was that a bare trustee meant a trustee without any beneficial interest.

Jessel M.R.'s view is supported by *Re Blandy Jenkins' Estate*,[14] where the point arose under the Fines and Recoveries Act 1833,[15] and by the opinion of Kenyon C.J. in the older case of *Roe d. Reade* v. *Reade*.[16] On the other side the view that the test is whether the trustee has active duties[17] to perform was applied in *Re Docwra*,[18] *Re Cunningham and Frayling*[19] and *Schalit* v. *Joseph Nadler Ltd.*,[20] though in the last case the earlier cases were not referred to. This view or a variant of it also seems to be the one preferred by textbook writers.[1] In practice a bare trustee may well be such whichever test is applied, as where T holds a fund on trust for X absolutely, and whether he is a bare trustee or not will seldom affect his legal position.

If a trust is not a simple one, it is a special one. On the basis that under a special trust the trustee has active duties to perform, a further subdivision can be made into ministerial and discretionary, according to the degree of judgment and discretion that the trustee is required to exercise.

5 NATURE OF A TRUST[2]

It may seem strange, though it is perhaps not untypical of English law, that although the trust is so highly developed an institution, it is impossible to say with assurance what is the juristic nature of the interest of a *cestui que trust*.[3] If one considers the traditional classification of rights into rights *in rem* which are good against persons generally and rights *in personam* which are rights against a specified person or persons, the right of a *cestui que trust* seems to be rather less than one and rather more than the other. The traditional view which was insisted upon by Maitland[4] is that the interest of the *cestui que trust* is necessarily a right *in personam*. The main reason why Maitland thought the contrary view untenable was the undoubted rule[5] that an equitable interest

---

[14] [1917] 1 Ch. 46.
[15] Sections 27 and 22.
[16] (1799), 8 Term.Rep. 118.
[17] Or, according to Snell's *Principles of Equity*, 27th Ed., p. 100, duties imposed by the settlor as opposed to the duties imposed by law.
[18] (1885), 29 Ch.D. 693.
[19] [1891] 2 Ch. 567.
[20] [1933] 2 K.B. 79; [1933] All E.R. Rep. 708, D.C.
[1] Underhill, *Law of Trusts and Trustees*, 12th Ed., p. 12; Lewin on *Trusts*, 16th Ed., p. 6; Keeton, *Law of Trusts*, 9th Ed., p. 35.
[2] See, generally, (1967), 45 C.B.R. 219 (D. W. M. Waters).
[3] As to the interest of persons entitled to the estate of a deceased person, see p. 31, *ante*.
[4] *Equity*, 2nd (Brunyate) Ed., pp. 106 *et seq.*; (1917), 17 Col.L.R. 467 (H. F. Stone). See generally Winfield, *Province of the Law of Tort*, pp. 108 *et seq.*; (1954), 32 C.B.R. 520 (V. Latham).
[5] Now considerably affected by the provisions as to registration under the Land Charges Act 1972, which do not, however, apply to the ordinary trust interest.

will not avail against a subsequent *bona fide* purchaser for value of a legal estate without notice of the trust—"such a purchaser's plea of a purchase for valuable consideration without notice is an absolute, unqualified, unanswerable defence, and an unanswerable plea to the jurisdiction of this court".[6] This view is also consistent with the historical development of the trust under which the beneficiary could originally only sue the original feoffee to uses, then a rapidly increasing number of classes of persons until ultimately it became convenient and possible, instead of listing the persons against whom the right could be enforced, to say it was enforceable against all except the *bona fide* purchasers for value of a legal estate without notice.

This traditional view has met with some criticism. Scott[7] has argued that the right of the *cestui que trust* is a right *in rem* because it is available against persons generally, although there are some exceptions, in the same way as the owner of a cheque is regarded as having a right *in rem* to it, although he may be defeated by a holder in due course. Further it has been suggested that the traditional view is not adequate to explain the rules as to following the trust property.[8] In so far as a *cestui que trust* can do this he is, it is said, exercising a right *in rem*, a proprietary right which is clearly greater than a right *in personam*. Moreover the House of Lords, in *Baker* v. *Archer-Shee*,[9] which depended upon the nature of a life interest in a settled fund, seems to have committed English law[10] to what is sometimes called the "realist" view, which can hardly be reconciled with traditional theory. In the court of first instance Rowlatt J. observed,[11]

> "[Counsel] says that she has no interest specifically in the stocks, shares and rents constituting the trust fund, and that they are not her possessions. . . . What this lady enjoys is not the stocks, shares and rents or other property constituting the trust fund under the will; what she has is the right to call upon the trustees, and, if necessary, to compel the trustees to administer this property during her life so as to give her the income arising therefrom according to the provisions of the trust. Her interest is merely an equitable one, and it is not an interest in the specific stocks and shares constituting the trust fund at all."

This opinion was accepted by the Court of Appeal and by the minority in the House of Lords, being cited with approval by Lord Blanesburgh,[12] while Viscount Sumner, also in the minority,[10] said, "All that the [beneficiary] can do is to claim the assistance of a court of equity to enforce the trust and to compel the trustee to discharge it." The majority of the House of Lords,[14] however, took the view that a beneficiary "was sole beneficial owner of the interest and dividends of all the securities, stocks and shares forming part of

---

[6] *Pilcher* v. *Rawlins* (1872), 7 Ch. App. 259, *per* James L.J. at pp. 268, 269.
[7] (1917), 17 Col.L.R. 269.
[8] See Chapter 15, Section 2, p. 460, *post*.
[9] [1927] A.C. 844, H.L.; (1928), 44 L.Q.R. 468 (H. G. Hanbury).
[10] Contrast the law of New York—*Archer-Shee* v. *Garland*, [1931] A.C. 212, H.L.
[11] [1927] 1 K.B. 109, at p. 116.
[12] [1927] A.C. 844, 877, H.L.   [13] *Ibid.*, at p. 850.
[14] Lords Atkinson, Carson and Wrenbury.

the trust fund",[15] and in a subsequent case[16] the House unanimously agreed that this constituted the binding *ratio decidendi* of the former case. Thus Viscount Dunedin observed[17] that Viscount Sumner's opinion had been "rejected by the majority on the view that there was in the beneficiary a specific equitable interest in each and every one of the stocks, shares, etc., which formed the trust fund", and Lord Tomlin said,[18] "I do not think that it can be doubted that the majority of your Lordships' House in the former case founded themselves upon the view that according to English law . . . [the beneficiary] had a property interest in the income arising from the securities, stocks and shares constituting the American trust, and that but for the existence of that supposed property interest the decision would have been different." It may be added that the traditional view was repeated by the Divisional Court in *Schalit* v. *Joseph Nadler Ltd.*,[19] but it can carry little weight as *Baker* v. *Archer-Shee*[20] does not even appear to have been cited.[1]

In the light of the considerations discussed, some modern writers have attempted to find a compromise solution. Thus Hanbury[2] regards equitable interests as hybrids, not quite rights *in rem* because of the doctrine of the *bona fide* purchaser, and not quite rights *in personam* because of the doctrine of following trust funds, while Marshall[3] says that a *cestui que trust* always has a personal right, and in some cases he has a real right also. There seems much to be said for treating the interest of a *cestui que trust* as *sui generis*, instead of trying to force it into a classification which is really inadequate. It may be added that the position is further complicated by the possibility of the registration of certain equitable interests under the Land Charges Act 1972. Whatever the nature of an equitable interest may be before registration, it would seem to become a right *in rem* by virtue thereof, since registration is deemed to constitute actual notice to all persons and for all purposes connected with the land affected.[4] An equitable interest under a trust, however, is not in general capable of registration but one exception is under a contract for the sale of land where, on the one hand, the vendor is regarded as a constructive trustee for the purchaser,[5] and, on the other hand, the equitable interest of the purchaser is registrable as a land charge class C (iv) under s. 2(4) of the Land Charges Act 1972. In such case, after registration, the purchaser would clearly seem to be properly referred to as the equitable owner of the subject matter of the contract.

---

[15] *Supra*, at p. 870, *per* Lord Carson. Cf. *O'Rourke* v. *Darbishire*, [1920] A.C. 581; [1920] All E.R. Rep. 1, H.L.
[16] *Archer-Shee* v. *Garland*, [1931] A.C. 212, H.L., and see *Pritchard* v. *M.H. Builders (Wilmslow), Ltd.*, [1969] 2 All E.R. 670.
[17] *Archer-Shee* v. *Garland, supra*, at p. 221.
[18] *Ibid*, at p. 222.
[19] [1933] 2 K.B. 79; [1933] All E.R.Rep. 708, D.C.
[20] *Supra*.
[1] But see (1954), 32 C.B.R. 520, at p. 537 (V. Latham) for a contrary view.
[2] *Modern Equity*, 8th Ed., p. 446. But Maudsley, editing the 9th Ed. at p. 17, considers that the whole argument contains less substance than has been thought to attach to it in the past. See also Holdsworth, *History of English Law*, Vol. IV, pp. 432 *et seq.*
[3] Nathan & Marshall, *A Casebook on Trusts*, 5th Ed., p. 9.
[4] Law of Property Act 1925, s. 198.
[5] See Chapter 4, at p. 120, *post*.

CHAPTER 3

Express Trusts

1 REQUIREMENTS OF WRITING

Apart from statute, there are no requirements as to writing or other formalities in connection with the creation of trusts or dealings with equitable interests, whether *inter vivos* or testamentary, and whether relating to real or personal property. The statutory provisions, however, are of wide ambit and must now be considered. The first four subsections below deal with *inter vivos* transactions and the fifth deals with wills.

a A contract to create a trust and a contract to dispose of a subsisting equitable interest

i *Land*—Such contracts if relating to land or any interest therein come within the scope of s. 40 (1) of the Law of Property Act 1925[1]—

"No action may be brought upon any contract for the sale or other disposition of land or any interest in land, unless the agreement upon which such action is brought, or some memorandum or note thereof, is in writing, and signed by the party to be charged or by some other person thereunto by him lawfully authorised."[2]

"Land" is widely defined in the Law of Property Act 1925[3] as including, *inter alia*, land of any tenure,[4] mines and minerals, buildings or parts of buildings, and other corporeal hereditaments, and also incorporeal hereditaments. The

---

[1] Replacing in part s. 4 of the Statute of Frauds 1677. The authorities on the old Act are still applicable: some of the cases cited below are actually decisions on s. 17 of the Statute of Frauds (later replaced by s. 4 of the Sale of Goods Act 1893 and finally repealed by the Law Reform (Enforcement of Contracts) Act 1954) to which the same principles apply.
[2] For a fuller discussion of this section reference should be made to textbooks on real property, e.g. Cheshire, *Modern Real Property*, 11th Ed., pp. 374 *et seq.*; Megarry and Wade, *The Law of Real Property*, 3rd Ed., pp. 554 *et seq.* The section is exhaustively considered in Williams's *The Statute of Frauds: Section Four*.
[3] Section 205 (1) (ix).
[4] This includes leaseholds: *Re Brooker*, [1926] W.N. 93; *Re Berton*, [1939] Ch. 200.

definition specifically excludes an undivided share in land, but an interest in the proceeds to arise from a sale of land is an "interest in land" and accordingly within the section.[5]

Section 40 (1) does not require that the actual contract shall be in writing; it merely requires that appropriate writing must be[6] in existence, as evidence of the contract, at the time when the action is commenced.[7] There is no need for the writing to be in any particular form,[8] but it must contain all the material terms of the contract,[9] and also an express or implied recognition that a contract has in fact been entered into.[10] The writing must be signed[11] by the party to be charged, i.e. the defendant against whom the action is brought, and signature by a duly authorised agent is expressly permitted. The requirement of signing has been so construed as to permit an unsigned document to be read together with a signed document where there is sufficient reference in the latter to the former, the two (or more) documents being regarded as one for the purpose of the statute.[12] It has been settled that the absence of writing does not make the contract void, still less illegal, but merely unenforceable by action.[13]

ii *Pure personalty*—There are no requirements of writing in connection with contracts to create a trust or to dispose of equitable interests in pure personalty.

iii *Equitable interests in pure personalty and, semble, land*—By way of qualification to what has been said in (i) and (ii) above, it should be mentioned that a contract to assign an equitable interest may come within the scope of s. 53 (1) (c)[14] of the Law of Property Act 1925 as being a "disposition" of a subsisting equitable interest. The point is far from clear, and the House of Lords was able to avoid deciding the question in *Oughtred* v. *I.R.Comrs*.[15] by treating the transaction in question as an agreement for sale followed by a transfer in the usual way.

b Declarations of trust inter vivos

The more obvious use of the phrase "declaration of trust" is to describe the case where the owner of property declares that henceforth he will hold it on

---

[5] *Cooper* v. *Critchley*, [1955] 1 All E.R. 520; [1955] Ch. 431, C.A.; *Steadman* v. *Steadman*, [1973] 3 All E.R. 977, C.A. *Contra*, Lewin, *Trusts*, 16th Ed., p. 23, on similar words in s. 53 (1) (b). Cf. *Irani Finance, Ltd.* v. *Singh*, [1970] 3 All E.R. 199; [1971] Ch. 59, C.A.

[6] Or must have been. If it was in existence and has been destroyed secondary evidence may be admissible: *Barber* v. *Rowe*, [1948] 2 All E.R. 1050, C.A.

[7] *Re Holland*, [1902] 2 Ch. 360, C.A.

[8] See, e.g., *Gibson* v. *Holland* (1865), L.R. 1 C.P. 1; *Cohen* v. *Roche*, [1927] 1 K.B. 169; *Hill* v. *Hill*, [1947] 1 All E.R. 54; [1947] Ch. 231, C.A.

[9] *Hawkins* v. *Price*, [1947] 1 All E.R. 689; [1947] Ch. 645; *Beckett* v. *Nurse*, [1948] 1 All E.R. 81; [1948] 1 K.B. 535, C.A.

[10] *Tiverton Estates, Ltd.* v. *Wearwell Ltd.*, [1974] 1 All E.R. 209, C.A.

[11] *Schneider* v. *Norris* (1814), 2 M. & S. 286; *Evans* v. *Hoare*, [1892] 1 Q.B. 593, D.C.; *Leeman* v. *Stocks*, [1951] 1 All E.R. 1043; [1951] Ch. 941.

[12] *Timmins* v. *Moreland Street Property Co. Ltd.*, [1957] 3 All E.R. 265; [1958] Ch. 110, C.A., and cases therein cited; and see (1958), 22 Con. 275 (G. H. L. Fridman).

[13] *Leroux* v. *Brown* (1852), 12 C.B. 801; *Britain* v. *Rossiter* (1879), 11 Q.B.D. 123, C.A.; *Maddison* v. *Alderson* (1883), 8 App. Cas. 467, H.L.

[14] The requirements of this provision are discussed in sub-s. c, *infra*, p. 56.

[15] [1959] 3 All E.R. 623; [1960] A.C. 206, H.L., discussed *infra*, p. 56; and see (1960), 24 Con. 70 (F. R. Crane).

certain trusts. There are two cases. First, where the settlor was owner of the property both at law and in equity, when the result is that he remains the legal owner while the equitable title is vested in the beneficiaries under the trust. Secondly, where the settlor was merely the equitable owner before the declaration of trust, when the effect seems to depend upon whether the trust declared is a bare or simple trust, or whether it is a special trust under which the trustee has some active duties to perform.[16a] If the trust is or becomes a bare trust, imposing no active duties on the settlor-trustee, it seems that the settlor-trustee "disappears from the picture"[17] and the legal owner becomes a trustee for the ultimate beneficiary. Thus in *Grainge* v. *Wilberforce*,[18] Chitty J. is reported as holding that the case before him "fell within the principle that where A was trustee for B, who was trustee for C, A held in trust for C, and must convey as C directed". If, however, the trust declared imposes any duties on the trustee it would, it is submitted, be impossible for the settlor-trustee to drop out of the picture, and the effect would be to create a sub-trust[19] under which the settlor would henceforth hold the equitable property as a trustee for the beneficiaries who would have subsidiary equitable interests.

The perhaps less obvious use of the phrase "declaration of trust" is to describe an alternative mode in which a trust may be created, namely, by a transfer of the property to trustees and a direction to the trustees to hold the property on specified trusts, the direction to the trustees by the equitable owner really constituting the declaration of trust.

(i) *Land*—As regards land or any interest therein,[20] s. 53 (1) (b)[21] of the Law of Property Act 1925 provides—

> "A declaration of trust respecting any land or any interest therein must be manifested and proved by some writing signed by some person who is able to declare such trust or by his will."

Although the wording is somewhat different, the requirement of writing in s. 53 (1) (b) is generally thought to be the same as under s. 40 (1).[1] Thus the

---

[16] As to the distinction between a simple and a special trust see Chapter 2, Section 4f, p. 47, *ante*.

[17] *Per* Upjohn J. in *Grey* v. *I.R.Comrs.*, [1958] 1 All E.R. 246, at p. 251; [1958] Ch. 375, at p. 382; reversed on appeal [1958] 2 All E.R. 428; [1958] Ch. 690. The C.A. decision was affirmed by H.L. on different grounds, [1959] 3 All E.R. 603; [1960] A.C. 1.

[18] (1889), 5 T.L.R. 436, citing *Head* v. *Lord Teynham* (1783), 1 Cox. Eq. Cas. 57. Cf. *B. S. Lyle, Ltd.* v. *Rosher*, [1958] 3 All E.R. 597, H.L.

[19] In *Re Lashmar*, [1891] 1 Ch. 258, C.A., where it was held that the trustee disappeared from the picture, Lindley L.J. expressly pointed out that *Onslow* v. *Wallis* (1849), 1 Mac. & G. 506, was to be distinguished on the ground that there the trustee had duties to perform, and said that had there been any duties to perform in the case before them, the decision of the court would have been the other way.

[20] "Land" has the same meaning as in s. 40 (1) discussed at p. 51, *ante*.

[21] Replacing s. 7 of the Statute of Frauds 1677. Care must be taken in applying decisions on the old Act where there have been changes in the wording—see *Grey* v. *I.R.Comrs.*, [1959] 3 All E.R. 603; [1960] A.C. 1, H.L.

[1] See pp. 51 and 52, *ante*.

writing is only required as evidence of the declaration of trust,[2] and need not
therefore be contemporaneous with it.[3] The writing need not be in any
particular form,[4] but must contain all the material terms of the trust,[5] and
joinder of documents is permitted as under s. 40 (1).

Section 53 (1) (b) differs from s. 40 (1) in that signature by an agent is not
permitted; the signature under s. 53 (1) (b) must be by "some person who is
able to declare such trust". In the first type of declaration of trust, where the
owner of property declares himself to be a trustee thereof, he is clearly the
person who must sign the writing. In the second type of declaration of trust,
where there is separation of the legal and equitable interests and the declaration
of trust takes the form of a direction to the trustees by the equitable owner, it
has been settled that it is the equitable owner who must sign the writing if it is
to be effective.[6]

It seems generally to have been assumed, consistently with the view that
writing was merely required as evidence,[7] that the effect of absence of writing
was the same under s. 7 of the Statute of Frauds as under s. 4.[8] No point seems
to have been taken in any reported case on the difference in wording—"no
action shall be brought" in s. 4, "or else they shall be utterly void and of none
effect" under s. 7. There is no substantial change of wording from the Statute
of Frauds in s. 40 (1), but s. 53 (1) (b) does not contain any express sanction
for failure to comply with its provisions. The assumption of most textbook writers[9] is probably right, that since s. 53 (1) (b) merely requires
writing as evidence, absence of writing does not make the declaration of trust
void.[10]

(ii) *Pure personalty*—There is no requirement of writing and a trust may
accordingly be declared by unsigned writing, by word of mouth, and even by
conduct.[11]

(iii) *Equitable interests in real or personal property*—By way of qualification to
what has been said above, writing may be required in some cases under
s. 53 (1) (c)[12] as a declaration of trust may also be a disposition within that
section. The distinction between the two types of declaration of trust must be
borne in mind.

---

[2] *Forster* v. *Hale* (1798), 3 Ves. 696; affd. (1800), 5 Ves. 308.
[3] *Rochefoucauld* v. *Boustead*, [1897] 1 Ch. 196, C.A.
[4] See, e.g., *Deg* v. *Deg* (1727), 2 P.Wms. 412—recital in deed; *Forster* v. *Hale* (1798), 3 Ves.
696; affd. (1800), 5 Ves. 308—correspondence.
[5] *Smith* v. *Matthews* (1861), 3 De G.F. & J. 139.
[6] *Tierney* v. *Wood* (1854), 19 Beav. 330; *Kronheim* v. *Johnson* (1877), 7 Ch.D. 60; *Grey* v.
I.R.Comrs., [1958] 2 All E.R. 428, at p. 433; [1958] Ch. 690, at p. 709, C.A.; affd. [1959]
3 All E.R. 603; [1960] A.C. 1, H.L.
[7] Cf. *Leroux* v. *Brown* (1852), 12 C.B. 801, *per* Jervis C.J. at pp. 824–825.
[8] *Gardner* v. *Rowe* (1825), 2 Sim. & St. 346; affd. (1828). 5 Russ, 258; *Rochefoucauld* v.
Boustead, [1897] 1 Ch. 196, C.A.
[9] See, e.g., Underhill's *Law of Trusts and Trustees*, 12th Ed., p. 123.
[10] Contrast the effect of s. 53 (1) (c) replacing s. 9 of the Statute of Frauds. p. 56, *post*.
[11] *Kilpin* v. *Kilpin* (1834), 1 My. & K. 520; *M'Fadden* v. *Jenkyns* (1842), 1 Ph. 153; *Jones* v.
Lock (1865), 1 Ch. App. 25; *Grey* v. *I.R.Comrs.*, *supra*, in C.A. *per* Evershed M.R. at
pp. 432; 708, *per* Morris L.J. at pp. 440; 719. Both judges refer to "personal property",
but it is thought that they cannot have meant to include leaseholds.
[12] The nature of the requirement of writing under s. 53 (1) (c) and the effect of failure to
observe it are dealt with in sub-s. (c), p. 56, *post*.

Where the declaration of trust consists of a direction to the trustees by the equitable owner, it is now settled beyond dispute that, at any rate where an equitable interest in pure personalty is concerned, such a declaration is a disposition within s. 53 (1) (c),[13] though it does not, of course, fall within s. 53 (1) (b). The point arose in *Grey v. I.R.Comrs.*[14] where on February 1, 1955 a settlor transferred 18,000 shares to trustees. On February 18, 1955 he orally directed the trustees to hold the shares on specified trusts and on March 25, 1955 the trustees executed a deed of declaration of trust reciting the directions given to them on February 18 and declaring that they had been holding the shares on the specified trusts since that date. The object of dealing with the matter in this way was to avoid liability to stamp duty. If the directions of February 18 were valid they would, being oral, attract no duty themselves, and the deed of March 25 would likewise attract no duty as it would not be a "disposition". The House of Lords, however, held that the oral direction given by the settlor on February 18 was a purported disposition of an equitable interest within s. 53 (1) (c) and was thereby rendered invalid as it was not in writing. Therefore the deed of March 25 was an effective disposition attracting *ad valorem* stamp duty. Where the declaration of trust is in respect of an equitable interest in land, writing is already required by s. 53 (1) (b).[15] It may, however, be important to know whether s. 53 (1) (c) also applies, as the requirement of writing, and probably the effects of absence of writing, differ[16] under the two provisions. Though the point is not referred to, the reasoning in *Grey v. I.R.Comrs.*[17] would seem to apply equally to interests in land and interests in pure personalty.

It has been suggested[18] that *Grey v. I.R.Comrs.*[19] is authority for the proposition that s. 53 (1) (c) also applies where the equitable owner of pure personalty[20] declares a trust not by giving a direction to the trustees but by declaring himself a trustee thereof. It is submitted, however, that this will be the case only where the trust declared is a bare or simple trust under which the trustee has no active duties to perform, when the settlor disappears from the picture and the equitable interest is in effect transferred to the ultimate beneficiary.[21] Otherwise, where the settlor-trustee has some active duties to perform, it is submitted that he does not disappear from the picture, but remains the owner of the original equitable interest, while under the sub-trust thus created a new subsidiary equitable interest becomes vested in the ultimate beneficiary. In this case there would seem to be no disposition of the original equitable interest and accordingly s. 53 (1) (c) would appear not to apply.

iv Resulting, implied and constructive trusts are not within the scope of this chapter, but for the avoidance of doubt it may be mentioned that the Law

---

[13] Whether it came within its predecessor s. 9 of the Statute of Frauds is a question which is now never likely to be answered. *Per* Lord Radcliffe in *Grey v. I.R.Comrs.*, [1960] A.C. 1, at p. 16; [1959] 3 All E.R. 603, at p. 608, H.L.

[14] [1959] 3 All E.R. 603; [1960] A.C. 1, H.L.

[15] *Tierney v. Wood* (1854), 19 Beav. 330.

[16] For the requirements and effect of s. 53 (1) (c) see sub-s. (c), *infra*.

[17] *Supra*.

[18] Underhill's *Law of Trusts and Trustees*, 12th Ed., p. 124.

[19] *Supra*.

[20] The reasoning would seem equally to apply to land.

[21] See the discussion at p. 53, *ante*.

of Property Act 1925, s. 53 (2), expressly provides that s. 53 does not affect the creation or operation of resulting, implied or constructive trusts.

c Dispositions of equitable interests inter vivos

Section 53 (1) (c)[1] of the Law of Property Act 1925 provides—

> "A disposition of an equitable interest or trust subsisting at the time of the disposition, must be in writing signed by the person disposing of the same, or by his agent thereunto lawfully authorised in writing or by will."

There are considerable differences between this provision and the provisions of s. 53 (1) (b) and s. 40. Unlike those provisions, s. 53 (1) (c) requires that the disposition shall actually be in writing, and not merely evidenced in writing; signature must be by the person making the disposition, or, like s. 40 (1) but unlike s. 53 (1) (b), by his duly authorised agent. The requirement that the disposition must actually be in writing, if not complied with at the time, clearly cannot be rectified subsequently,[2] and accordingly it always seems to have been assumed that absence of writing makes the purported disposition void. This view seems to be implicit in two important decisions of the House of Lords, *Grey* v. *I.R.Comrs.*[3] and *Oughtred* v. *I.R.Comrs.*[4] It was held in *Re Tyler's Fund Trusts*,[5] however, that there is no need, where the assignee is to take in a fiduciary capacity, for the writing to contain particulars of the trust.

Grey v. *I.R.Comrs.*[3] and *Oughtred* v. *I.R.Comrs.*[4] are also important authorities on the meaning of the phrase "disposition of an equitable interest or trust". It clearly includes an assignment of the interest directly. As has been explained in the preceding sub-sections, it also includes the case where the equitable owner directs the trustee to hold the property in trust for a third party,[6] and may include the case where the equitable owner declares himself to be a trustee of the equitable interest for the third party.[7] It may also include the case where the equitable owner contracts with a third party for valuable consideration to assign the equitable interest to him. This last point arose in *Oughtred* v. *I.R. Comrs.*[8] The facts were that there was a settlement under which shares were limited to O. for life with remainder to her son P. absolutely. By an oral agreement on June 18, 1956 made between O. and P. it was agreed that on June 26, 1956 they would effect an exchange: P. would make over to his mother his reversionary interest in the settled shares, and she, in exchange, would make over to him absolutely a separate block of shares in the same company which were her absolute property. In an attempt to save liability to stamp duty, the agreement was carried into effect on June 26 by the execution of three documents (i) a transfer of her own shares by O. to P.; (ii) a deed of release whereby O. and P. gave a release to the trustees in respect of anything done by the trustees in the execution of the trusts of the settlement and (iii) a transfer (referred to as "the disputed transfer") of the previously settled shares by the

---

[1] Replacing, with considerable amendments, s. 9 of the Statute of Frauds 1677.
[2] Except, of course, by a fresh independent disposition in writing.
[3] [1959] 3 All E.R. 603; [1960] A.C. 1. Cf. (1959), 17 C.L.J. 99 (J. C. Hall).
[4] [1959] 3 All E.R. 623; [1960] A.C. 206.   [5] [1967] 3 All E.R. 389.
[6] See p. 55, *ante*.   [7] See p. 53, *ante*.
[8] *Supra*. See also the judgment of Upjohn J. at first instance [1958] 1 All E.R. 252; [1958] Ch. 383 and of the C.A., [1958] 2 All E.R. 443; [1958] Ch. 678.

trustees to O . Stamp duty was claimed on the disputed transfer, and one contention by the Inland Revenue was that the oral agreement of June 18 could not, because of s. 53 (1) (c), effect a disposition of P.'s reversionary interest, which remained vested in him until the execution of the disputed transfer. Against this it was argued that the effect of the oral contract was to make P. a constructive trustee of the reversionary interest in favour of O., under a well-settled principle discussed later,[9] so that the entire beneficial interest had already passed to her before the disputed transfer was executed. The transfer on this basis, it was said, would only operate on the bare legal estate and would not attract stamp duty. As we have seen a constructive trust is exempted from the requirement of writing by s. 53 (2). Unfortunately for legal theory only one of the Law Lords decided in terms that s. 53 (2) did not do away with the necessity of writing. The other two Law Lords in the majority held that stamp duty was payable, without finding it necessary to decide whether s. 53 (1) (c) applied or was excluded by s. 53 (2).

It has further been held that s. 53 (1) (c) does not apply to the case where the equitable owner directs the trustee to transfer the legal estate to a third party and the transfer duly takes place. The point arose in *Vandervell* v. *I.R. Comrs.*[10] where a bank holding shares as a bare trustee transferred them on the directions of the equitable owner to a charity. In dismissing the argument that no beneficial interest passed to the charity in the absence of a writing signed by the equitable owner, Lord Upjohn pointed out[11] that the object of the section is "to prevent hidden oral transactions in equitable interests in fraud of those truly entitled, and making it difficult, if not impossible, for the trustees to ascertain who are in truth his (sic) beneficiaries". However, he continued, when the beneficial owner "owns the whole beneficial estate and is in a position to give directions to his bare trustee with regard to the legal as well as the equitable estate there can be no possible ground for invoking the section where the beneficial owner wants to deal with the legal estate as well as the equitable estate". Accordingly if a bare trustee, on the directions of the beneficial owner who intends the beneficial interest to pass, transfers the legal estate to a third party, that third party will also acquire the beneficial interest without any need for any further document.

Finally, Megarry J. thought[12] it very doubtful whether the section would apply to a nomination made under a staff pension fund, where a member had power to appoint a nominee to receive the moneys otherwise due to his personal representatives in the event of his death.

d   Equity will not permit a statute to be used as an instrument of fraud

All the statutory provisions that have been discussed have their origin in the Statute of Frauds 1677 the purpose of which appears from its title, namely, to

---

[9] See p. 120, *infra*, and cf. *Re Holt's Settlement*, [1968] 1 All E.R. 470, at p. 476; [1969] 1 Ch. 100, at p. 116.

[10] [1967] 1 All E.R. 1; [1967] 2 A.C. 291, H.L.; (1966), 24 C.L.J. 19 (G. Jones); (1967), 31 Con. 175 (S. M. Spencer); (1967) 30 M.L.R. 461 (N. Strauss).

[11] At p. 311. There seems to be much to be said for Harman L.J.'s succinct statement in C.A. that "s. 53 (1) (c) in dealing with dispositions of an equitable interest, only applies where the disponer is not also the controller of the legal interest": [1965] 2 All E.R. 37, 49.

[12] In *Re Danish Bacon Co., Ltd. Staff Pension Fund Trusts*, [1971] 1 All E.R. 486.

prevent the injustice that was thought likely to occur from perjury or fraud when oral evidence was admitted. Although the Court of Chancery was bound by statute, it nevertheless regarded itself as having power to intervene where the strict application of the statute would actually promote the fraud it was intended to prevent.

i A most important illustration of the maxim heading this section is the equitable doctrine of part performance which has been elaborated in many cases. This is adequately discussed in textbooks on real property and contract[13]: for present purposes it will suffice to state the fundamental proposition, that where there is a contract which falls within s. 40 (1),[14] but the plaintiff is unable to produce the required evidence in writing, he may nevertheless succeed in obtaining the equitable remedy of specific performance[15] where he has partly fulfilled his own obligations under the contract in reliance on the defendant's promise, provided that his acts of part performance are such as must be referred to some contract and may be referred to the alleged one.[16] It is expressly provided that the provisions[17] of ss. 40 (1) and 53 of the Law of Property Act 1925, do not affect the law relating to part performance.

ii In the leading case of *Rochefoucauld* v. *Boustead*[18] it was said, "It is further established by a series of cases, the propriety of which cannot now be questioned, that the Statute of Frauds does not prevent the proof of a fraud; and that it is a fraud on the part of a person to whom land is conveyed as a trustee, and who knows it was so conveyed, to deny the trust and claim the land himself. Consequently, notwithstanding the statute, it is competent for a person claiming land conveyed to another to prove by parol evidence that it was so conveyed upon trust for the claimant, and that the grantee, knowing the facts, is denying the trust and relying upon the form of conveyance and the statute, in order to keep the land himself." It is not necessary that the actual conveyance shall have been fraudulently obtained, nor is there any need for the conveyance to include any express stipulation that the grantee is in so many words to hold as trustee.[19] "The fraud which brings the principle into play arises as soon as the absolute character of the conveyance is set up for the purpose of defeating the beneficial interest."[20] Three illustrations of this principle may be given.[21]

First, in *Davies* v. *Otty* (*No.* 2)[22] the plaintiff, being apprehensive that he would be indicted for bigamy, for which it eventually turned out he was not liable, conveyed certain real property to the defendant under a parol agreement that

---

[13] E.g. Megarry and Wade, *The Law of Real Property*, 3rd Ed., pp. 569 *et seq.*; Cheshire, *Modern Real Property*, 11th Ed., pp. 379 *et seq.*; Cheshire and Fifoot, *Law of Contract*, 8th Ed., pp. 191 *et seq.*

[14] Of the Law of Property Act 1925.

[15] As to the possibility of an injunction see *J. C. Williamson Ltd.* v. *Lukey and Mulholland*, (1931), 45 C.L.R. 282 (High Ct. of Australia).

[16] *Steadman* v. *Steadman*, [1973] 3 All E.R. 977; [1974] Q.B. 161, C.A.

[17] Law of Property Act 1925, ss. 40 (2) and 55 (d).

[18] [1897] 1 Ch. 196, C.A., at p. 206.

[19] *Bannister* v. *Bannister*, [1948] 2 All E.R. 133, C.A.

[20] *Bannister* v. *Bannister*, *supra*, at p. 136.

[21] See also in connection with secret trusts, p. 91, *post*.

[22] (1865), 35 Beav. 208.

he would retransfer the property when the plaintiff's difficulties had passed.[1] The defendant refused to retransfer the property when called upon to do so by the plaintiff, and, in this action brought to compel him to reconvey, the defendant argued that the alleged trust was unenforceable by reason of the absence of writing. The court held, however, that this was a case of fraud and that the Statute of Frauds did not apply. In the words of Romilly M.R.[2] "I am of opinion that it is not honest to keep the land. If so, this is a case in which, in my opinion, the Statute of Frauds does not apply".

Secondly, in *Bannister* v. *Bannister*,[3] on the plaintiff's oral undertaking that the defendant would be allowed to live in a cottage rent free for as long as she desired, the defendant agreed to sell to him[4] that and an adjacent cottage. The conveyance executed in due course contained no reference to the plaintiff's undertaking. Subsequently the plaintiff claimed possession of the premises occupied by the defendant, and claimed that the alleged trust[5] contained in the oral understanding was, under the provisions of ss. 53 and 54 of the Law of Property Act 1925 defeated by the absence of writing. It was held, however, that this was a case of fraud on the part of the plaintiff and that accordingly the argument based on the absence of writing must fail.

Lastly, in *Hodgson* v. *Marks*[6] the plaintiff had transferred a house to one Evans, it being orally agreed between her and Evans that the house was to remain her house though in Evans's name. The Court of Appeal said that quite plainly Evans could not have placed any reliance on s. 53 (1) for that would have been to use the section as an instrument of fraud. At first instance Ungoed-Thomas J. had held that the defendant, a purchaser for value without notice from Evans, would likewise be unable to rely upon s. 53 (1), but this point was left open in the Court of Appeal.

e The creation of trusts and the disposition of equitable interests by will

The provisions of the Law of Property Act 1925 do not affect wills,[7] but the requirements of the Wills Act 1837, which apply equally to both legal estates and equitable interests in all forms of property, both land and pure personalty, are even more stringent. Section 9 of the Act provides as follows:

---

[1] The effect of the parol agreement, unless invalidated by absence of writing under the Statute of Frauds, was to make the defendant a trustee of the property for the plaintiff. The reason for the transaction was that before the Forfeiture Act 1870 property was liable to forfeiture on conviction of felony.

[2] *Davies* v. *Otty* (*No. 2*), *supra*, at p. 215.

[3] [1948] 2 All E.R. 133, C.A.; *Neale* v. *Willis* (1968), 19 P. & C.R. 836, C.A. Cf. *Binions* v. *Evans*, [1972] 2 All E.R. 70; [1972] Ch. 359, C.A., and see (1973), 32 C.L.J. 123 (R. J. Smith); (1973), 26 C.L.P. 17 (A. J. Oakley).

[4] At a price well below the contemporary value of the two cottages.

[5] It was ultimately held that the effect of the undertaking was that the plaintiff held the cottage in trust during the life of the defendant to permit the defendant to occupy the same for as long as she might desire to do so.

[6] [1971] 2 All E.R. 684; [1971] Ch. 892, C.A. The main point of the decision was whether the plaintiff had an overriding interest under s. 70 (1) (g) of the Land Registration Act 1925. See (1971), 35 Con. 255 (I. Leeming); (1973), 36 M.L.R. 25 (R. H. Maudsley).

[7] Law of Property Act 1925, s. 55 (a).

"No will shall be valid unless it shall be in writing . . . signed at the foot or end thereof[8] by the testator, or by some other person in his presence and by his direction; and such signature shall be made or acknowledged by the testator in the presence of two or more witnesses present at the same time and such witnesses shall attest and shall subscribe the will in the presence of the testator, but no form of attestation shall be necessary."[9]

Failure to comply with the statutory requirements makes the purported will absolutely void.

It was at one time thought that the cases on fully-secret and half-secret trusts[10] represented an exception to the operation of s. 9, being a further application of the maxim that equity will not permit a statute to be used as an instrument of fraud.[11] As will be explained later,[12] it can now be regarded as settled that there is no conflict between the rules relating to fully-secret and half-secret trusts and the provisions of the Wills Act 1837 and accordingly it would be inappropriate and indeed misleading to discuss the former in this section.

2 COMPLETELY AND INCOMPLETELY CONSTITUTED TRUSTS

a The perfect creation of a trust

The classic statement of the law as to what is meant by the perfect creation, or complete constitution, of a trust is to be found in the judgment of Turner L.J. in the leading case of *Milroy* v. *Lord*[13]:

"I take the law of this court to be well settled, that, in order to render a voluntary settlement valid and effectual, the settlor must have done everything which, according to the nature of the property comprised in the settlement, was necessary to be done in order to transfer the property and render the settlement binding upon him. He may, of course, do this by actually transferring the property to the persons for whom he intends to provide, and the provision will then be effectual, and it will be equally effectual if he transfers the property to a trustee for the purposes of the settlement, or declares that he himself holds it in trust for those purposes; . . . but, in order to render the settlement binding, one or other of these modes must, as I understand the law of this court, be resorted to, for there is no equity in this court to perfect an imperfect gift. The cases I think go further to this extent, that if the settlement is intended to be effectuated by one of the modes to which I have referred, the court will not give effect to it by applying another of those modes. If it is intended to take effect by transfer, the court will not hold the intended transfer to operate as a declaration of trust, for then every imperfect instrument would be made effectual by being converted into a perfect trust."

Each of the two alternative modes of constituting a trust—the effective transfer of the trust property to trustees, or the declaration by the settlor that he is a trustee thereof—requires further consideration.

---

[8] As to the position of the signature, see the Wills Act Amendment Act 1852.

[9] For details of the meaning given to these provisions, and as to privileged testators who may make valid informal wills, see e.g. *Williams on Wills*, 3rd Ed., pp. 54 *et seq.*; *Jarman on Wills*, 8th Ed., Vol. 1, pp. 117 *et seq.*; Bailey, *The Law of Wills*, 7th Ed., Chapter IV.

[10] Discussed in Section 5 of this chapter, p. 89, *post*.

[11] This was undoubtedly the principle upon which the doctrine of secret trusts was originally based, but in course of time the basis of the doctrine has changed.

[12] See p. 90, *post*.

[13] (1862), 4 De G.F. & J. 264 at pp. 274–275.

i *The effective transfer of the trust property to trustees*—Where the settlor is
the owner of the property both at law and in equity he must normally, if he
intends to constitute the trust by transfer, vest the legal interest in the property
in the trustee: exceptionally, if he cannot do this, the trust may nevertheless
be effective if it can be established that the settlor has done everything in his
power, according to the nature of the property given, to give the trustee a
complete legal title. What is necessary to pass the legal title depends on the
nature of the property: for instance, in the case of land, whether freehold or
leasehold, there must be a deed,[14] in the case of personal chattels capable of
passing by delivery, there must be either delivery or a deed of gift,[15] and in
the case of registered shares there must be an appropriate entry in the company's
register made in pursuance of a proper instrument of transfer.[16] Thus in *Milroy*
v. *Lord*[17] itself the attempt to create a trust failed, the legal title not having
been vested in the trustee due to the fact that the wrong form of transfer was
used for the purpose of transferring the bank shares which were intended to
constitute the trust property.

Milroy v. *Lord*[18] is also a leading authority for the rule that if a prospective
settlor attempts to set up a trust by transferring property to a trustee, and the
attempted transfer is for any reason ineffective, it is impossible to construe it
as a declaration of trust. Exactly the same principle applies where a prospective
donor attempts to transfer property to a person beneficially, when the transfer
is ineffective. In either case there is no equity to complete the imperfect gift
by construing it as a declaration of trust, whether the imperfect gift was direct
or through the intervention of trustees. There is a vital distinction between an
intention to transfer property and an intention to retain it albeit in an altered
capacity as trustee. An intention to do the former, even though the execution
is ineffective, cannot be construed as the latter quite different intention. An
illustration is to be found in *Richards* v. *Delbridge*[19] where J. D., who was
possessed of certain leasehold business premises, indorsed and signed on the
lease a memorandum in these terms: "This deed and all thereto belonging I
give to E. B. R. from this time forth, with all the stock-in-trade." E. B. R. was
J. D.'s infant grandson. J. D. shortly afterwards delivered the lease to E. B. R.'s
mother on his behalf. Subsequently, after J. D.'s death, it was claimed that
there was a trust in favour of E. B. R. It was held, however, that there was no
effective transfer of the lease,[20] and, further, that the ineffective attempt to do
so could not be construed as a declaration of trust.

---

[14] Law of Property Act, 1925, s. 52 (1).
[15] *Cochrane* v. *Moore* (1890), 25 Q.B.D. 57, C.A.; *Re Cole*, [1963] 3 All E.R. 433; [1963]
Ch. 175, C.A.; *Thomas* v. *Times Book Co., Ltd.*, [1966] 2 All E.R. 241 (this concerned
the original manuscript of "Under Milk Wood"); and see [1953] C.L.J. 355 (J. W. A.
Thornely); (1964), 27 M.L.R. 357 (A. C. Diamond).
[16] Note, however, that neglect of unessential matters on a transfer is not necessarily fatal
to a transfer's validity, but may be treated as a mere irregularity and disregarded—*Re
Paradise Motor Co., Ltd.*, [1968] 2 All E.R. 625, C.A.
[17] (1862), 4 De G.F. & J. 264. See also *Re Fry*, [1946] 2 All E.R. 106; [1946] Ch. 312; *Re
Wale*, [1956] 3 All E.R. 280; *Spellman* v. *Spellman*, [1961] 2 All E.R. 498, C.A.
[18] *Supra*.
[19] (1874), L.R. 18 Eq. 11. See also the cases cited in note 17, *supra*.
[20] This would have required an assignment under seal, Law of Property Act 1925, s. 52 (1),
replacing Real Property Act 1845, s. 3.

"The true distinction appears to me to be plain and beyond dispute: for a man to make himself a trustee there must be an expression of intention to become a trustee, whereas words of present gift show an intention to give over property to another,[1] and not retain it in the donor's own hands for any purpose, fiduciary or otherwise."[2]

More recent cases have added the qualification that although the legal title may remain vested in the settlor, an attempted transfer by him to a trustee may nevertheless be effective in equity and may enable an enforceable trust to be established where the settlor has done everything in his power to divest himself of the property in favour of the trustee.[3] It is essential that no further step remains to be taken by the settlor. Where this is the position, the property is regarded as effectively transferred in equity, the settlor[4] retaining the bare legal title on trust for the transferee.[5] Thus in *Re Rose*[6] the deceased executed two transfers in proper form dated 30th March, 1943, each in respect of 10,000 shares in an unlimited company, one transfer being in favour of his wife beneficially and the other in favour of his wife and X as trustees. At the date of their execution the transfers and the relative share certificates were handed to the transferees. The legal title to the shares could, of course, only pass by an appropriate entry in the register of the company, whose articles of association authorised the directors to refuse to register any transfer. The transfers were in fact registered on 30th June, 1943. The deceased died on 16th February, 1947, and whether or not estate duty was payable on the shares transferred by the two transfers of 30th March, 1943, depended upon whether the transfers were effective before 10th April, 1943. Although the legal title clearly did not vest in the respective transferees until 30th June, 1943, the principle set out above was laid down. It was accordingly held that, the deceased having "done all in his power to divest himself of and to transfer to the transferees the whole of his right, title and interest, legal and equitable, in the shares in question",[7] the gift of the beneficial interest in the shares had been made and completed on 30th March, 1943. Between that date and 30th June, 1943, the deceased was a trustee of the bare legal title for the transferees.[8]

So far we have been considering the case where the settlor is the owner of the property both at law and in equity; if the settlor merely possesses an equitable interest in the property, a trust[9] of that equitable interest can be completely constituted by an assignment[10] of that interest to trustees: there is no need for

---

[1] Either beneficially or as a trustee.
[2] *Per* Jessel M.R. (1874), L.R. 18 Eq. 11, 15.
[3] The same principle applies to the case of a gift to a donee beneficially.
[4] Or donor.
[5] The transferee may himself be a trustee, or may take beneficially.
[6] [1952] 1 All E.R. 1217; [1952] Ch. 499, C.A. See also *Re Fry*, [1946] 2 All E.R. 106; [1946] Ch. 312; *Re Rose*, [1948] 2 All E.R. 971; [1949] Ch. 78; *Vandervell* v. *I.R. Comrs*, [1967] 1 All E.R. 1; [1967] 2 A.C. 291, at pp. 18, 330, H.L.
[7] *Re Rose*, [1952] 1 All E.R. at p. 1225; [1952] Ch. at p. 515, *per* Jenkins L.J.
[8] The Court of Appeal actually considered the case of the transfer to the wife beneficially, saying that the same principle would apply in the case of the transfer to trustees, where there would be a sub-trust in favour of the ultimate beneficiaries.
[9] Strictly a sub-trust.
[10] In *Re McArdle*, [1951] 1 All E.R. 905; [1951] Ch. 669, C.A. Evershed M.R. adopted the statement in White and Tudor's *Leading Cases in Equity* that "the mode or form of

him to compel a transfer of the legal title, even if he can do so. As we have already seen, a disposition of an equitable interest must be in writing.[11] Thus in *Kekewich* v. *Manning*[12] trustees held certain shares on trust for A for life with remainder to B absolutely. B in effect executed a voluntary assignment of his equitable reversionary interest to C upon trust for D. It was held, even on the assumption that the assignment was purely voluntary, that a valid trust was effectively created of the equitable interest, though the legal title, of course, remained vested in the original trustees. Note, however, that if C were a bare trustee no new trust would seem to be created, for C would presumably drop out of the picture leaving D as a direct beneficiary under the head trust.[13] In such case B could deal with his equitable interest so as to achieve substantially the same result either by assigning his equitable interest directly to D beneficially, or by directing the original trustees henceforth to hold that interest for the benefit of D. Such methods are commonly included within the meaning of the phrase "declaration of trust", in addition to the meaning of the phrase now to be discussed.

ii *A declaration of trust*—Whether the settlor has a legal or merely an equitable interest in property, he can completely constitute a trust by declaring himself[14] a trustee thereof for the intended *cestui que trust*. "Where a declaration of trust is relied on the Court", it has been said,[15] "must be satisfied that a present irrevocable declaration of trust has been made." A settlor, however, "need not use the words, 'I declare myself a trustee', but he must do something which is equivalent to it and use expressions which have that meaning; for, however anxious the Court may be to carry out a man's intention, it is not at liberty to construe words otherwise than according to their proper meaning".[16] It is even possible for a declaration of trust to be implied from conduct.[17] Most of the cases have been concerned with the rule already dealt with, that an attempted transfer of property will not be construed as a declaration of trust,[18] and need not be further discussed. It should, however, be observed that there

---

assignment is absolutely immaterial provided the intention of the parties is clear". In the same case, however, Jenkins L.J. observed that "A voluntary equitable assignment, to be valid, must be in all respects complete and perfect so that the assignee is entitled to demand payment from the trustee or holder of the fund, and the trustee is bound to make payment to the assignee, with no further act on the part of the assignor remaining to be done to perfect the assignee's title". Cf. *Re Wale*, [1956] 3 All E.R. 280; *Letts* v. *I.R.Comrs.*, [1956] 3 All E.R. 588.

[11] Law of Property Act 1925, s. 53 (1) (c).
[12] (1851), 1 De G.M. & G. 176, and see *Gilbert* v. *Overton* (1864), 2 Hem. & M. 110; *Ellison* v. *Ellison* (1802), 6 Ves. 656. [13] See p. 53, *ante*.
[14] The formal requirements were discussed in Section 1 of this chapter.
[15] *Re Cozens*, [1913] 2 Ch. 478, *per* Neville J., at p. 486.
[16] *Richards* v. *Delbridge* (1874), L.R. 18 Eq. 11, *per* Jessel M.R., at p. 14.
[17] See, e.g., *Gray* v. *Gray* (1852), 2 Sim.N.S. 273; *Gee* v. *Liddell* (1866), 35 Beav. 621; *New, Prance and Garrard's Trustee* v. *Hunting*, [1897] 2 Q.B. 19, C.A.; and contrast *Re Cozens*, [1913] 2 Ch. 478.
[18] Cf. Maitland's *Equity*, 2nd (Brunyate) Ed., p. 72. "The two intentions are very different— the giver means to get rid of his rights, the man who is intending to make himself a trustee intends to retain his rights but to come under an onerous obligation. The latter intention is far rarer than the former. Men often mean to give things to their kinsfolk, they do not often mean to constitute themselves trustees. An imperfect gift is no declaration of trust."

is no need for the declaration of trust to be communicated to the *cestui que trust*.[19]

b Meaning of the term volunteer

A beneficiary under a trust is a volunteer unless either he has provided valuable consideration in a common law sense, or he is, as it is said, within the scope of the marriage consideration. So far as value in the common law sense is concerned, reference may be made to the discussion of consideration in works on the law of contract,[20] but some explanation must be given of what is meant by marriage consideration.

Marriage has been said to be "the most valuable consideration imaginable"[1] and a settlement or trust made or agreed to be made before[2] and in consideration of marriage is accordingly regarded as made for value. The question is who can take advantage of this, or, in other words, who is within the scope of the marriage consideration. It is now clear that only the husband, wife and issue[3] of the marriage are within the scope of the marriage consideration.[4] Some other cases[5] which held, or suggested, that other persons such as illegitimate children or children by a former or possible second marriage were within the marriage consideration, can now, it seems, in the light of the cases cited,[4] only be supported on the ground that the interests of such persons, on the special facts of the case, were so intermingled with the interests of issue of the marriage, that they could not be separated, and the latter could only be enforced if the former were also admitted.

c Equity will not assist a volunteer[6]

The main importance of knowing whether or not a trust has been completely constituted arises in connection with the enforcement of the trust by a *cestui que trust* thereunder who is a volunteer. If a *cestui que trust* has provided valuable consideration, then he can have the trust enforced even though it has not been com-

---

[19] *Tate* v. *Leithead* (1854), Kay 658; *Middleton* v. *Pollock* (1876), 2 Ch.D. 104; *Standing* v. *Bowring* (1885), 31 Ch.D. 282, C.A.

[20] See, e.g., Cheshire and Fifoot, *The Law of Contract*, 8th Ed., pp. 57 *et seq.*

[1] *A.-G.* v. *Jacobs Smith*, [1895] 2 Q.B. 341, C.A., *per* Kay L.J. at p. 354. Note, however, the provisions of s. 4 (6) of the Land Charges Act 1972, which put a purchaser for money or money's worth in a better position than one who can only rely on the consideration of marriage. See also *A.-G. for Ontario* v. *Perry*, [1934] A.C. 477; [1934] All E.R. Rep. 422, P.C.

[2] A post-nuptial settlement executed in pursuance of an ante-nuptial agreement would be regarded as made for value (*Re Holland*, [1902] 2 Ch. 360, C.A.); but neither a post-nuptial settlement made otherwise than in pursuance of an ante-nuptial agreement nor a mere post-nuptial agreement.

[3] Whether children or more remote issue—*MacDonald* v. *Scott*, [1893] A.C. 642, H.L., *per* Lord Herschell at p. 650.

[4] *De Mestre* v. *West*, [1891] A.C. 264, P.C.; *A.-G.* v. *Jacobs Smith*, [1895] 2 Q.B. 341, C.A.; *Rennell* v. *I.R.Comrs.*, [1961] 3 All E.R. 1028; [1962] Ch. 329, C.A., affd. *sub nom.* *I.R.Comrs.* v. *Rennell*, [1963] 1 All E.R. 803; [1964] A.C. 173, H.L.; *Re Cook's Settlement Trusts*, [1964] 3 All E.R. 898; [1965] Ch. 902. It is submitted that the position is unaffected by the Family Law Reform Act 1969.

[5] *Newstead* v. *Searles* (1737), 1 Atk. 265; *Clarke* v. *Wright* (1861), 6 H. & N. 849.

[6] The maxim is sometimes expressed as, Equity will not perfect an imperfect gift.

pletely constituted; that is to say, he can enforce a contract or covenant to create a trust; but if he is a volunteer, even though he may be specially an object of the intended trust,[7] he will only succeed if the trust has been completely constituted.[8]

(i) *Cestui que trust not a volunteer.* In this case the *cestui que trust* can enforce not only a completely but also an incompletely constituted trust. He can, if need be, compel his trustee to bring an action at law for damages for breach of the contract or covenant to create a trust; to such an action the settlor, in appropriate circumstances, might plead the Limitation Act 1939. In most cases, however, the *cestui que trust* would choose to assert his equitable rights based on the availability of the equitable remedy of specific performance,[9] as a result of which the property contracted or covenanted to be settled would be regarded as subject to a trust. Thus in *Pullan* v. *Koe*[10] there was a marriage settlement in 1859 which contained a covenant by the husband and wife with the trustees to settle the wife's after acquired property of the value of £100 or upwards. In 1879 the wife had received £285 which she had paid into her husband's banking account, on which she had power to draw. Shortly afterwards, part of this sum was invested in two bearer bonds which remained at the bank until the death of the husband in 1909 and at the time of the action were in the possession of the executors. The trustees of the marriage settlement, with the object of benefiting the widow and nine surviving children of the marriage, brought an action against the husband's executors. Any claim by the trustees at law for damages for breach of the covenant would long since have been barred by the Statutes of Limitation since the cause of action had arisen when the covenant was broken in 1879; the court, however, held that the moment the wife received the £285 it was specifically bound by the covenant and was consequently subject to a trust enforceable[11] in favour of the wife and children being persons within the marriage consideration. It seems clear that the *cestuis que trust*, not being volunteers, would have had their interests equally protected, even if the trustees had been unwilling to bring proceedings to enforce the covenant.

It should be noted, however, that even a *cestui que trust* who has provided consideration, will be unable to do more than compel his trustee to exercise his remedy at law, where the contract or covenant is one to which the remedy of specific performance is not appropriate so that there is never any property subject to a trust. This would be the position where there was a covenant merely to pay money, as in *Stone* v. *Stone*,[12] in which case it was held that an action at law on the covenant to settle £1,000 being barred by the Statute of Limitations, the *cestuis que trust*, though purchasers, were without remedy.

---

[7] *Re Cook's Settlement Trusts*, [1964] 3 All E.R. 898; [1965] Ch. 902.

[8] For a pseudo-exception see sub-s. (*e*), p. 72, *post.* Note also that if an incompletely constituted trust is enforced by a beneficiary who has given valuable consideration it enures for the benefit of a volunteer—*Davenport* v. *Bishopp* (1843), 2 Y. & C.Ch. 451; affirmed (1846), 1 Ph. 698.

[9] This remedy is discussed in Chap. 14, *infra.* For present purposes it can be regarded as an order directing the settlor (or his personal representatives) to transfer to the trustees the property which the settlor under the contract or covenant agreed to transfer to them.

[10] [1913] 1 Ch. 9.

[11] The claim could, of course, have been defeated by a *bona fide* purchaser for value without notice who acquired the legal title, but neither the husband, nor his executors claiming through him, were in this position.

[12] (1869), 5 Ch.App. 74. In *Pullan* v. *Koe, supra,* a specific fund of money was impressed with a trust.

(ii) *Cestui que trust a volunteer.*—If the trust is completely constituted the fact that a *cestui que trust* is a volunteer is irrelevant: he is just as much entitled to enforce the trust as a *cestui que trust* who has provided consideration. If, however, the trust is not completely constituted, a volunteer *cestui que trust* will get no assistance from a court of equity. This can be illustrated by *Re Plumptre's Marriage Settlement.*[13] There, under a marriage settlement made in 1878, certain funds coming from the wife's father were settled upon the usual trusts of a wife's fund, with an ultimate remainder, in the events which happened, for the wife's statutory next-of-kin. The settlement contained an after-acquired property clause, which was held to cover a sum of stock given by the husband to the wife, which she subsequently sold and reinvested and which remained registered in her name on her death in 1909. The facts of this case, it will have been observed, are very similar to those in *Pullan* v. *Koe*[14] and it was likewise held that any action at law would be barred by the Statutes of Limitation. By contrast with *Pullan* v. *Koe*,[14] however, the beneficiaries under the settlement who were seeking to enforce the covenant, i.e. the next-of-kin, were not within the marriage consideration but were mere volunteers. It was accordingly held that they could not enforce the covenant against the husband, as administrator of his wife's estate.

Another illustration is *Jefferys* v. *Jefferys*,[15] where the contrast between a completely and an incompletely constituted trust as regards volunteers was brought out neatly. There by a voluntary settlement a father conveyed certain freehold and covenanted to surrender[16] certain copyhold estates to trustees in trust for the benefit of his daughters. Subsequently he devised part of the same estates to his widow who, after his death, was admitted[16] to some of the copyholds. It was held that as to the freeholds the trust in favour of the daughters was enforceable by them, since the trust was completely constituted by the conveyance thereof to the trustees: but as to the copyholds, the trust was not complete and the court refused to compel the performance of a voluntary contract.

As appears from the above cases, the fact that the obligation is contained in a deed makes no difference in equity which has no special regard to the form of a seal.[17] It may well be asked, however, whether the trustees with whom the covenant is made can, or should, bring an action at law for damages since the common law regards consideration and a seal as alternative requirements. On this question it has been held that volunteers cannot compel trustees to take proceedings for damages, and further, that if the trustees ask the court for directions as to what they should do, they will be directed not to take any steps either to compel performance of the covenant or to recover damages through the failure to implement it. Thus in the leading case of *Re Pryce*[18] there was a marriage settlement under which the wife covenanted to settle after-acquired

---

[13] [1910] 1 Ch. 609; *Re D'Angibau* (1880), 15 Ch. D. 228, C.A.
[14] [1913] 1 Ch. 9, discussed *supra*, p. 65.
[15] (1841), Cr. & Ph. 138.
[16] The mode of conveyance of copyhold was by surrender and admittance.
[17] See, e.g., *Jefferys* v. *Jefferys* (1841), Cr. & Ph. 138; *Kekewich* v. *Manning* (1851), 1 De G.M. & G. 176.
[18] [1917] 1 Ch. 234; *Re Kay's Settlement*, [1939] Ch. 329. See generally, "Incompletely Constituted Trusts" by R. H. Maudsley in "Perspectives of Law" (ed. R. Pound), p. 240.

property. The beneficial limitations of funds brought into the settlement by the wife (including any after-acquired property) were successive life interests to the wife and the husband, remainder to the children of the marriage (of whom there were never in fact any), and an ultimate remainder to the wife's next-of-kin, who were of course volunteers. The husband was dead and the wife did not wish the covenant to be enforced. The court held that the trustees ought not to take any steps to compel the transfer or payment to them of the after-acquired property. The principle of Re Pryce[19] has been strongly criticised,[20] and it has been further contended[21] that the court should not in such cases have left it open whether the trustees could sue for damages for breach of covenant if they wished, but should have directed them to sue, on the ground that there was a completely constituted trust of the benefit of the covenant.[22] Since these critical articles, however, Re Pryce[1] and Re Kay's Settlement[2] have been followed in Re Cook's Settlement Trusts[3] and have found academic support.[4] On the cases as they stand there is no clear authority as to the position if the trustees do not ask the court for directions, but choose to bring an action. Professor Elliott[5] takes the view that if an action would lie any damages recovered would become trust property, and that such damages would be substantial.[6] The authorities for this view are not very weighty, and even if valid as regards a covenant to pay money or transfer specific property, do not establish the point in the case of a covenant to settle after-acquired property.[7] Lee[8] considers that any damages recovered would be held on a resulting trust for the settlor.

(iii) *Cestui que trust a covenantee*—Even where the *cestui que trust* is a volunteer, there is a clear decision at first instance,[9] that if the covenant is made with him, there is no answer to an action by him at common law on the covenant, and substantial damages for breach thereof will be awarded.

(iv) *Performance of unenforceable covenant*—It is clear that if the settlor has in fact transferred property to trustees in compliance with an unenforceable covenant to settle the same in favour of volunteers, he thereby completely constitutes the trust, and cannot thereafter claim to recover the property, which must be held by the trustees on the declared trusts.[10]

d Trusts of a chose in action

There is no difficulty over the concept of a chose in action constituting the trust property: to give a simple illustration, if A owes B £250, B may assign

---

[19] [1917] 1 Ch. 234.
[20] In (1960), 76 L.Q.R. 100 (D. W. Elliott).   [21] (1962), 78 L.Q.R. 228 (J. A. Hornby).
[22] See sub-s. (e), p. 72, post.   [1] Supra.   [2] Supra.
[3] [1965] Ch. 902; [1964] 3 All E.R. 898; and see (1965), 23 C.L.J. 46 (Gareth Jones). Cf. Re Ralli's Will Trusts, [1963] 3 All E.R. 940; [1964] Ch. 288.
[4] [1967] A.S.C.L., pp. 387 et seq. (J. D. Davies); (1969) 85 L.Q.R. 213 (W. A. Lee).
[5] Loc. cit.
[6] See (1960), 76 L.Q.R. 100 (D. W. Elliott), citing, inter alia, Re Cavendish Browne's Settlement Trusts, [1916] W.N. 341.
[7] See R. H. Maudsley, op. cit., p. 244, and J. D. Davies, op. cit., p. 392. Cf. pp. 68 and 73, infra.
[8] Loc. cit.
[9] Cannon v. Hartley, [1949] 1 All E.R. 50; [1949] Ch. 213.
[10] Paul v. Paul (1882), 20 Ch.D. 742, C.A.; Re Adlard, [1953] 2 All E.R. 1437; [1954] Ch. 29; Re Ralli's Will Trusts, [1963] 3 All E.R. 940; [1964] Ch. 288.

the debt to trustees on trust for X and Y equally so as to create an effective trust. Suppose, however, A enters into a contract with B under which A is to confer some benefit upon C. At common law the rule is that only a person who is a party to a contract can sue on it[11]: in this case this means that C will be unable to sue either directly or indirectly for the benefit which A had agreed with B to give him. "A by entering into the contract with B has assumed liabilities towards B, but not towards anyone else, and business is conducted on the basis of contractual liability being limited in that way and not extending to include liability to third parties. Otherwise it would be too perilous to make a contract."[12] However, if A fails to confer the benefit on C, B, the promisee, will always be able to sue A, the promisor, although the nature of the remedy which the court will grant will depend on the circumstances of each case.[13]

B can, in fact, always bring an action for damages for breach of contract though it is not clear whether he can obtain substantial damages measured by the loss to C, or whether he can only obtain damages to compensate him for his own loss which will normally be nominal, though they could be substantial if substantial damage were proved.[14] The latter is, it is submitted, the better opinion though both views found supporters in *Beswick* v. *Beswick*.[15] Those judges in *Beswick* v. *Beswick*[16] who supported the view that substantial damages should be recoverable also took the view that the moneys recovered would become subject to a trust for C.[17] On the other view, there will be no need to account to C for any damages that B recovers, which represent B's own loss.

As an alternative to damages, according to the circumstances, some equitable remedy may be available. Thus all the Law Lords agreed in *Beswick* v. *Beswick*,[18] as indeed had the judges in the Court of Appeal, that in an appropriate case B could obtain a decree of specific performance against A, compelling him to confer the agreed benefit on C, even though the obligation of A may merely be to make a money payment. If damages would be nominal, this has been said to be an argument in favour of, rather than against, the availability of specific performance.[19] In other circumstances some other remedy such as an injunction may be appropriate.[20]

It will be useful to consider the application of these principles to the facts

---

11 *Tweddle* v. *Atkinson* (1861), 1 B. & S. 393; *Dunlop Pneumatic Tyre Co. Ltd.* v. *Selfridge & Co. Ltd.*, [1915] A.C. 847, H.L.; *Scruttons Ltd.* v. *Midland Silicones Ltd.*, [1962] 1 All E.R. 1; [1962] A.C. 446, H.L.; *Beswick* v. *Beswick*, [1967] 2 All E.R. 1197; [1968] A.C. 58, H.L. See also (1960), 23 M.L.R. (M. P. Furmston); (1956), 19 M.L.R. 374 (F. E. Dowrick).

12 *Per* Pearson L.J. in *Rookes* v. *Barnard*, [1962] 2 All E.R. 579, 608; [1963] 1 Q.B. 623, 695, C.A., reversed in part [1964] 1 All E.R. 367; [1964] A.C. 1129, H.L., but this dictum unaffected.

13 *Snelling* v. *John G. Snelling, Ltd.*, [1972] 1 All E.R. 79; [1973] Q.B. 87.

14 See, generally, [1967] A.S.C.L., pp. 397 *et seq.* (J. D. Davies); (1969), 85 L.Q.R. 213 (W. A. Lee).

15 [1967] 2 All E.R. 1197; [1968] A.C. 58, H.L. See also the judgments in C.A.—[1966] 3 All E.R. 1; [1966] Ch. 538. Cf. *West* v. *Houghton* (1879), 4 C.P.D. 197, D.C.

16 *Supra.*

17 *Sed quaere.* *Ex hypothesi*, B has not contracted as trustee for C as in the cases shortly to be discussed.

18 *Supra.* See also *Gurtner* v. *Circuit*, [1968] 1 All E.R. 328; [1968] 2 Q.B. 587, C.A.

19 But see p. 426, *infra.*

20 See *Snelling* v. *John G. Snelling, Ltd.*, *supra*, and (1973), 36 M.L.R. 214 (Alan Wilkie).

of *Beswick* v. *Beswick*.[21] In this case one Peter Beswick agreed with his nephew, the defendant, to assign to him the goodwill and assets of the business of a coal merchant carried on by him in consideration of the defendant employing him as consultant to the business for the remainder of his life at a weekly rate of £6 10s. od.; and for the like consideration the defendant agreed to pay, after Peter Beswick's death, an annuity of £5 per week to his widow. Peter Beswick died intestate, having been duly paid £6 10s. od. per week during his lifetime. Having made one payment of £5 to his widow, the defendant repudiated his liability. The widow took out letters of administration to Peter Beswick's estate and brought an action suing both personally and as administratrix. The claim in the personal capacity failed, but as administratrix it was held that she was entitled to a decree of specific performance.[22] It should be added that Lord Denning M.R. recently appears to have taken the view that in the sort of third party contract under discussion, if the contracting party B can obtain specific perform-ance, the same remedy is directly available to the third party, C. In *Neale* v. *Willis*[23] a husband borrowed £50 from his mother-in-law to assist in buying a house, on the express undertaking that the house would be in the joint names of his wife and himself. He broke the undertaking and had the house conveyed into his name alone. Lord Denning observed correctly that, following *Beswick* v. *Beswick*,[24] the mother-in-law could have obtained specific performance. Counsel had, however, pointed out that this was an action by the wife—the third party—and that the mother-in-law was not even a party to the action. Lord Denning expressed himself unimpressed by this distinction and was pre-pared to enforce the agreement at the instance of the wife. It is respectfully submitted that *Beswick* v. *Beswick*[24] cannot be called in aid in this way to support an action by a third party. Their Lordships in that case, as we have seen, drew a clear distinction between the widow *qua* third party suing person-ally and the widow *qua* administratrix suing in her representative capacity. It was only in the latter capacity that her claim succeeded. Lord Hodson[25] made explicit what is implicit in the speeches of the other Law Lords when he said: "Although the widow cannot claim specific performance in her personal capacity . . .". It is accordingly respectfully submitted that the opinion of Lord Denning in *Neale* v. *Willis*[1] is wrong on this point, though it may well be that the case itself is rightly decided on the other ground[2] supported by the other members of the court.

A further rule at common law is that B cannot require A to confer the benefit on him instead of C: A is fully entitled to insist on carrying out the contract according to its terms by conferring the benefit on C.[3] If he does so, B cannot sue C at common law in an action for money had and received.[4]

---

[21] [1967] 2 All E.R. 1197; [1968] A.C. 58, H.L.
[22] See Chap. 14 *infra*, p. 426.   [23] (1968), 19 P. & C.R. 836, C.A.   [24] *Supra*, H.L.
[25] *Supra*, at pp. 1207; 81. The distinction is also clearly drawn by Ormrod J. in *Snelling* v. *John G. Snelling Ltd.*, [1972] 1 All E.R. 79; [1973] Q.B. 87.
[1] *Supra*.
[2] The principle applied in *Bannister* v. *Bannister*, [1948] 2 All E.R. 133, C.A. discussed *supra*, p. 59.
[3] *Re Stapleton-Bretherton*, [1941] 3 All E.R. 5; [1941] Ch. 482; *Re Schebsman*, [1943] 2 All E.R. 768; [1944] Ch. 83, C.A.; *Re Miller's Agreement*, [1947] 2 All E.R. 78; [1947] Ch. 615.
[4] *Re Schebsman, supra*.

It may be, however, that *prima facie* C could be called on to account to B in equity, on the basis that he holds on a resulting trust for B who has furnished the consideration.[5] The presumption of a resulting trust, if it exists, will often in practice be rebutted by the presumption of advancement,[6] or proof of an intent that C should take the property for his own use and benefit. Apart from presumptions, whether the parties intended C to be a mere nominee, or to take for his own use and benefit, is a question of construction of the agreement read in the light of all the circumstances which were known to the parties.[7] Further, A and B may come to a fresh agreement, releasing the old one, or varying it as they wish,[8] or B may simply release A from his obligation.

In some circumstances the above rules may be qualified by the intervention of equity:[9] this will be so if it can be established that B has constituted himself a trustee for C of the benefit of the contract. If this can be shown, ˋB, as trustee for C, can sue A and recover substantial damages, the measure of damages being the loss suffered by C.[10] If B refuses to sue, C, the *cestui que trust*, can himself bring proceedings, but he must join B in the action as co-plaintiff, if he consents, or as defendant, if he refuses.[11] It is important to observe that if a trust is established, it is not open to A and B to release A from his obligation to benefit C or in any way to vary it.[12]

The problem is to know in what circumstances B will be regarded as a trustee: no satisfactory test can be suggested, and it has been said that "the way in which the court will decide a novel case is almost completely unpredictable".[13] What can be said with a fair degree of confidence is that the onus of establishing a trust is a heavy one—"the intention to constitute the trust must be affirmatively proved",[14] or, as was said in another case,[15] "It is not legitimate to import into the contract the idea of a trust when the parties have given no indication that such was their intention".

---

[5] *Re Policy No. 6402 of the Scottish Equitable Life Assurance Society*, [1902] 1 Ch. 282; and see the cases cited in n. 3, *supra*. See also (1944), 7 M.L.R. 123 (Glanville Williams).
[6] See Chapter 4, Section 2d, p. 104, *post*.
[7] *Beswick* v. *Beswick*, [1967] 2 All E.R. 1197; [1968] A.C. 58, H.L.
[8] *Re Schebsman*, [1943] 2 All E.R. 768; [1944] Ch. 83, C.A.; *Green* v. *Russell*, [1959] 2 All E.R. 525; [1959] 2 Q.B. 226, C.A.
[9] In other cases by the intervention of the legislature, e.g. Road Traffic Act 1972, s. 148 (4); Married Women's Property Act 1882, s. 11, as amended by the Statute Law (Repeals) Act 1969, discussed in (1961), 25 Con 454 (P. Elman); Third Parties (Rights against Insurers) Act 1930. As to Law of Property Act 1925, s. 56, see *Beswick* v. *Beswick*, *supra*, H.L.
[10] *Lamb* v. *Vice* (1840), 6 M. & W. 467; *Robertson* v. *Wait* (1853), 8 Exch. 299; *Lloyds* v. *Harper* (1880), 16 Ch.D. 290, C.A.
[11] *Gandy* v. *Gandy* (1885), 30 Ch.D. 57, C.A.; *Vandepitte* v. *Preferred Accident Insurance Corporation of New York*, [1933] A.C. 70, P.C.; *Harmer* v. *Armstrong*, [1934] Ch. 65; [1933] All E.R. Rep. 778, C.A.
[12] *Re Schebsman*, [1943] 2 All E.R. 768; [1944] Ch. 83, C.A.; but see *Hill* v. *Gomme* (1839), 5 My. & Cr. 250, where the contrary is suggested. *Re Empress Engineering Co.* (1880), 16 Ch.D. 125, at p. 129, C.A.; *Re Flavell* (1883), 25 Ch.D. 89, at p. 102, C.A.
[13] (1944), 7 M.L.R. 123 (G. L. Williams).
[14] *Vandepitte* v. *Preferred Accident Insurance Corporation of New York*, [1933] A.C. 70, 79–80, P.C.
[15] *Re Schebsman*, [1943] 2 All E.R. 768, at p. 770; [1944] Ch. 83, at p. 89, C.A., *per* Lord Greene, M.R.

The earliest case seems to be *Tomlinson* v. *Gill*,[16] decided by Lord Hardwicke. There Gill promised the widow of an intestate that if she would permit him to be joined with her in the letters of administration, he would make good any deficiency of assets to pay debts. Joint administration was accordingly taken out, and proceedings were brought by the creditors of the intestate against Gill, for satisfaction of their debts and the enforcement of the promise made by Gill to the intestate's widow. It was held that, though no action would lie at law, "the plaintiff is proper here,[17] for the promise was for the benefit of the creditors and the widow is a trustee for them".

In *Fletcher* v. *Fletcher*[18] the settlor, by a voluntary deed, covenanted with trustees that in case A and B (his natural sons, at that time infants) or either of them should survive him and attain full age, his personal representatives should within twelve months of his death pay £60,000 to the trustees on trust for A and B or such one of them as should attain the age of 21. A and B both survived the settlor, but B died without attaining full age. The trustees refused to sue, but the court held that this fact did not prejudice the right of A to recover payment of the debt out of the assets of the covenantor. In the course of the judgment Wigram V.C. said[19] "One question made in argument has been, whether there can be a trust of a covenant the benefit of which shall belong to a third party; but I cannot think there is any difficulty in that. . . ." There was a completely constituted trust of the chose in action, the benefit of the covenant, which the *cestui que trust* could enforce if the trustee failed or refused to act.

Numerous cases have arisen in connection with policies of insurance; two points emerge from the cases[20]: first that the mere fact that A takes out a policy which is expressed to be for the benefit of B or on behalf of B does not constitute a trust for B; second, that the mere fact that the policy provides that the policy moneys are to be payable to B does not create a trust in favour of B.

> "The whole question in these cases depends upon the true construction of the particular policy. I think that one must assume that, unless there is in the policy something establishing reasonably clearly that the assured was in fact constituting and intending to constitute himself a trustee for the [third party] of the assurance moneys, the [third party] is not, and the personal representatives of the [assured] are, entitled to the moneys payable."[1]

The more recent decisions in the higher courts suggest that the burden of establishing a trust is not easy to discharge.[2] It should be observed, however,

---

[16] (1756), Amb. 330. Another early case was *Gregory* v. *Williams* (1817), 3 Mer. 582. For a full discussion of the cases up to 1930 see (1930), 46 L.Q.R 12 (Corbin).

[17] I.e. in the Court of Chancery.

[18] (1844), 4 Hare. 67. *Re Cavendish Browne's Settlement Trusts*, [1916] W.N. 341, may also be explained on the same basis. Contrast *Colyear* v. *Lady Mulgrave*. (1836), 2 Keen. 81, where the covenantee was not intended to be a trustee.

[19] (1844), 4 Hare. 67, 74. See note 3 on p. 74.

[20] *Re Webb*, [1941] 1 All E.R. 321; [1941] Ch. 225 where the earlier cases are reviewed; *Re Foster's Policy*, [1966] 1 All E.R. 432. Cf. *Re Leek*, [1967] 2 All E.R. 1160; [196 Ch. 1061 affd. on different grounds [1968] 1 All E.R. 793; [1969] 1 Ch. 563, C.A. 71

[1] *Re Webb*, [1941] 1 All E.R. 321; [1941] Ch. 225, per Farwell J. at pp. 325, 234.

[2] *Vandepitte* v. *Preferred Accident Insurance Corporation of New York*, [1933] A.C. 70, P.C.; *Re Schebsman*, [1943] 2 All E.R. 768; [1944] Ch. 83, C.A.; *Green* v. *Russell*, [1959] 2 All E.R. 525; [1959] 2 Q.B. 226, C.A. A trust was established in *Royal Exchange*

that if the policy moneys are actually paid over to the third party, the third party will, even in the absence of a trust, be entitled to retain them as against the assured's estate, provided that under the contract on its true construction the policy moneys were to be paid to him <u>for his own use and benefit</u>.[3]

The same problem has arisen in cases where a partnership deed, or a deed of dissolution of partnership, contains a covenant by the surviving partners to pay an annuity to the wife or children of a deceased or retiring partner. Again, the latest cases suggest that it is far from easy to establish a trust,[4] though in an earlier case[5] a covenant in a partnership deed was held, in the events which happened, to constitute the personal representative of the deceased partner a trustee, notwithstanding the fact that the existence of the trust would have disabled the partners from cancelling or varying the partnership deed in so far as doing so might affect the trust.

e Trusts of the benefit of a contract and volunteers

Some of the cases just considered seem to offend against the maxim previously discussed[6] that equity will not assist a volunteer. Assuming that the intention to create a trust has been established, the difficulty is to establish that the trust has been completely constituted by the vesting of the trust property in the trustee, and, indeed, of what the trust property consists.

One answer to the difficulty is said to be that the maxim does not apply to a completely constituted trust, and that in such cases the trust property, i.e. a chose in action, the benefit of the contract, is fully vested in the trustee. This view explains cases such as *Fletcher* v. *Fletcher*,[7] but should it seems have produced a different result in *Re Pryce*[8] and *Re Kay's Settlement*[9] and at first sight seems inconsistent with the principle frequently laid down by Lord Eldon, which has been repeated in and formed the basis of subsequent decisions, that there is a vital distinction between the case where the trust has been completely constituted by the transfer of the property, and the case where the matter "rests in covenant, and is purely voluntary",[10] when equity will refuse to give any assistance towards the constitution of the trust. As to *Re Pryce*[11] and *Re Kay's Settlement*,[11] the answer, it has been contended,[12] is that these cases were wrongly

---

Assurance v. Hope, [1928] Ch. 179, C.A.; In re Gordon, [1940] Ch. 851; Re Webb, [1941] 1 All E.R. 321; [1941] Ch. 225; Prudential Staff Union v. Hall, [1947] K.B. 685; Re Foster's Policy, [1966] 1 All E.R. 432.

[3] Beswick v. Beswick, [1967] 2 All E.R. 1197; [1968] A.C. 58, H.L.

[4] Re Miller's Agreement, [1947] 2 All E.R. 78; [1947] Ch. 615. This may have advantages from the estate duty angle: Beswick v. Beswick, supra.

[5] Re Flavell (1883), 25 Ch.D. 89, C.A., not cited in either of the cases in the previous note.

[6] See pp. 64 et seq., ante.

[7] (1844), 4 Hare 67, discussed at p. 71, ante; Williamson v. Codrington (1750), 1 Ves.Sen. 511; Cox v. Barnard (1850), 8 Hare 310; Clough v. Lambert (1839), 10 Sim. 174; Gandy v. Gandy (1885), 30 Ch.D. 57, C.A.

[8] [1917] 1 Ch. 234, and see pp. 66, 67, ante.   [9] [1939] Ch. 329, and see p. 67, ante.

[10] Ellison v. Ellison (1802), 6 Ves. 656, at p. 662, per Lord Eldon. See also Colman v. Sarrel (1789), 1 Ves. 50; Pulvertoft v. Pulvertoft (1811), 18 Ves. 84; Ex parte Pye (1811), 18 Ves. 140; Jefferys v. Jefferys (1841), Cr. & Ph. 138; Re D'Angibau (1880), 15 Ch.D. 228, C.A.; Re Plumptre's Marriage Settlement, [1910] 1 Ch. 609; Re Kay's Settlement, [1939] 1 All E.R. 245; [1939] Ch. 329.   [11] Supra.

[12] See (1960), 76 L.Q.R. 100 (D. W. Elliott); (1962), 78 L.Q.R. 228 (J. A. Hornby); (1965), 23 C.L.J. 46 (Gareth Jones); (1966), 29 M.L.R. 397 (Duncan Matheson); and p. 67, ante.

decided, while as to Lord Eldon's rule the point is said to be that the trust of the benefit of the contract or covenant is completely constituted. Lord Eldon's rule prevents the volunteer from claiming specific performance of a covenant to settle specified property, and disables him from claiming that such specified property is subject to the trusts of the settlement unless and until it is conveyed to the trustees, but, according to this argument, even a volunteer should be able to compel the trustees to sue for damages for breach of the covenant, for the right to sue, i.e. the benefit of the contract, is held by the trustees on a completely constituted trust.

Another view has recently been put forward by a writer[13] in the Law Quarterly Review. He supports *Re Pryce*[14] and *Re Kay's Settlement*[15], and suggests the criticisms of these decisions depend upon two assumptions whose validity he doubts. The first is that a covenant to settle after-acquired property generates *per se* a legal chose in action quite divorced from considerations of equity. The second is that any such chose is of a kind capable of forming the subject matter of a trust. An expectancy, he says, is not property and cannot be settled upon trust.[16] The writer concludes by observing that in all the cases cited by the critics of *Re Pryce*[17] and *Re Kay's Settlement*[18] where the covenant had been held enforceable by volunteers, there had been existing property for the subject matter of the trust. He cites *Re Cook's Settlement Trusts*[19] where the judge had pointed out that the covenant with which he was concerned did not create a property right. It was, the judge said, "an executory contract to settle a particular fund or particular funds of money which at the date of the covenant did not exist and which might never come into existence. . . . The case . . . involves the law of contract, not the law of trusts."

It is suggested, that notwithstanding the closely reasoned argument of the critics, *Re Pryce*[17] and *Re Kay's Settlement*,[18] which have stood for many years, and were recently followed without disapproval in *Re Cook's Settlement Trusts*,[19] are not likely to be overruled. There is after all somewhat of a paradox in the proposition that a contract to create a trust which equity would not permit trustees to enforce in the Court of Chancery should, in effect,[20] be enforceable at common law. Even on the basis that there is a trust of the benefit of the contract or covenant, an argument could be put forward not only to deprive the volunteers of any right to compel the trustees to sue, but also to deprive the trustees of power to choose whether to sue or not, namely that the trusts

---

[13] (1969), 85 L.Q.R. 213 (W. A. Lee).
[14] [1917] 1 Ch. 234.   [15] [1939] Ch. 329.
[16] This point had previously been made by J. D. Davies in A.S.C.L. [1967], pp. 387 *et seq.*, where he observed that where someone claiming to be a trustee proceeds against an alleged settlor or covenantor, there is nothing to stop the latter alleging the invalidity of the trust he purported to create. This may be on the ground that a trust must have a subject matter which is property in a technical sense. This does not include a mere *spes* (e.g. a covenant to settle after-acquired property) as opposed to a future interest. See *Williams* v. *Commissioners of Inland Revenue*, [1965] N.Z.L.R. 395, C.A.; *Re Ellenborough*, [1903] 1 Ch. 697.
[17] *Supra*.   [18] *Supra*.
[19] [1964] 3 All E.R. 898; [1965] Ch. 902; (1966), 30 Con. 286 (M. C. Cullity and H. A. J. Ford).
[20] It is of course, recognised that there is a vast difference between an action in equity for specific performance and an action at law for damages, but in most cases the beneficiary will be unconcerned whether the trust property comprises the property covenanted to be settled or its monetary equivalent.

attaching to the benefit of the contract or covenant are not necessarily the same as those which will attach to any property actually transferred thereunder. The leaning of equity against volunteers might lead the court to hold that the volunteer has no equitable interest in the benefit of the contract, and on this basis if all the beneficiaries under the settlement are volunteers the whole equitable interest in the benefit of the contract would result to the settlor, on which basis the court would surely, and rightly, direct the trustees not to sue, even if an application of the *Saunders* v. *Vautier*[1] principle does not enable the settlor himself to do so. But if, as in *Davenport* v. *Bishopp*,[2] someone who has or is deemed to have furnished consideration, enforces the covenant as he may the trusts of the settlement, including the interest of volunteers, will naturally attach to the property which actually comes into the hands of the trustees.

On this last view the main difficulty is to discover the intention of the settlor. If as in *Fletcher* v. *Fletcher*,[3] the intention is to create an immediate trust of the benefit of the covenant at law in favour of volunteers, the trust is completely constituted as from the moment the covenant is executed and the volunteer beneficiaries have immediate equitable rights which they can enforce by compelling the trustees to sue on the covenant. If, however, the intention is not to give volunteers any equitable rights in the benefit of the covenant, they have no rights which they can enforce either directly or indirectly, unless and until property is actually transferred to the trustees under the covenant. And in construing the settlement to ascertain the intention one would have to bear in mind that, as we have seen,[4] the intention to create a trust must be affirmatively proved.

3   EXCEPTIONS TO THE MAXIM THAT EQUITY WILL NOT ASSIST A VOLUNTEER

a. The rule in Strong v. Bird[5]

Where a donor has attempted to make an immediate gift *inter vivos* of either real[6] or personal[7] property to a donee, which gift has failed by reason of the fact that the legal formalities necessary for the proper transfer of title to the particular property in question have not been complied with, then if the donee has subsequently become the executor or administrator[8] of the donor, the gift is considered to have been perfected by the vesting of the legal title in the

---

[1] See Chapter 10, Section 7, p. 333, *post*.   [2] (1843), 2 Y. & C.Ch.Cas. 451.

[3] (1844), 4 Hare 67. Maudsley, editing the 9th Ed. of Hanbury's *Modern Equity* at p. 146, points out two difficulties of this decision. First, that positive evidence of the intention to create a trust of the benefit of the covenant is lacking. Secondly, that a trust of such a chose in action should be created by the covenantee and not the covenantor, and on the facts the covenantee did not originally know of the arrangement, and, as soon as he did, wished to decline the trust.

[4] See p. 70, *ante*.

[5] (1874), L.R. 18 Eq. 315.

[6] *Re James*, [1935] Ch. 449; [1935] All E.R.Rep. 235. The rule was limited to personal property prior to the Land Transfer Act 1897.

[7] The rule applies to the release of a debt, as in *Strong* v. *Bird*, *supra*, itself.

[8] It makes no difference that the donee is merely one of several executors or administrators, for in the eye of the law the whole of the property vests in each personal representative. *Re Stewart*, [1908] 2 Ch. 251; *Re James*, [1935] Ch. 449; [1935] All E.R.Rep. 235.

donee. For the rule to apply it is necessary to show that the testator had up to the moment of his death a continuing intention that the gift should have been given at the time when it was given,[9] and, where the donor has appointed the donee his executor, that the testator had not any intention inconsistent with an intention to bring about the result flowing from the appointment.[10] The rule does not apply where there is a mere promise to make a gift in the future,[11] or where there is an intention to give, and the gift is not completed because the intending donor desires first to apply the subject matter of the contemplated gift to some other purpose.[12] The rule in *Strong* v. *Bird*[13] has been said[14] to rest on two grounds, first that the vesting of the property in the personal representative at the donor's death completes the imperfect gift made in the lifetime, and, secondly, that the intention of the donor to give the benefit to the donee is sufficient to countervail the equity of the beneficiaries under the will.

An interesting extension of the *Strong* v. *Bird*[13] principle is to be seen in *Re Ralli's Will Trusts*.[15] In this case the testator, who died in 1899, left a half share of his residue to his widow for life with remainder to his daughter Helen absolutely. By her marriage settlement in 1924 Helen covenanted to assign, *inter alia*, her reversionary interest in the testator's estate to the trustees on trust, in the events which happened, after her death for persons who were mere (her sister's children) volunteers. The widow died in 1961, Helen having predeceased her without having executed an assignment of the reversionary interest to the trustees. The plaintiff became the sole surviving trustee of both the will of the testator and Helen's marriage settlement. Helen's personal representatives claimed that her share of residue should be paid over to them, and that they would not then be compelled to pay it over to the plaintiff as trustee of the marriage settlement, as equity would not assist the beneficiaries thereunder being mere volunteers. The court held, however, that it was irrelevant that the plaintiff, the settlement trustee, had acquired the legal title as trustee of the will. The question was, who was entitled in equity? Helen, having covenanted to assign her share to the plaintiff would not be allowed to assert a claim in equity against him, and her personal representatives could be in no better position. The inability[16] of the volunteers under the settlement to enforce their rights against Helen was irrelevant: it was sufficient for them to rely on their claim against the plaintiff as settlement trustee. The imperfect gift of the reversionary interest by Helen to the settlement trustee was thus completed by the chance acquisition by the sole surviving trustee of the legal estate in a different capacity. If, as might easily have happened, the will trustee and the settlement trustee had been different persons, the result would have been quite different. Helen's personal representatives would then have been able to claim her share from the will trustee, and the volunteers under the marriage settlement would have been unable to compel the enforcement of the covenant.

---

[9] *Re Pink*, [1912] 2 Ch. 528, C.A.; *Re Freeland*, [1952] Ch. 110, *sub nom. Jackson* v. *Rodgers*, [1952] 1 All E.R, 16, C.A.
[10] *Re Pink, supra.*   [11] *Re Innes*, [1910] 1 Ch. 188.
[12] *Re Freeland, supra.*
[13] *Supra.*
[14] See, e.g., *Re Stewart*, [1908] 2 Ch. 251, *per* Neville J. at pp. 254–255.
[15] [1963] 3 All E.R. 940; [1964] Ch. 288.
[16] See p. 66, *supra.*

b Donatio mortis causa

"The principle of not assisting a volunteer to perfect an incomplete gift does not apply to a *donatio mortis causa*",[17] though it is not in every case that the assistance of equity is required. A *donatio mortis causa* has been described as

"a singular form of gift. It may be said to be of an amphibious nature, being a gift which is neither entirely *inter vivos* nor testamentary. It is an act *inter vivos* by which the donee is to have the absolute title to the subject of the gift not at once but if the donor dies. If the donor dies the title becomes absolute not under but as against his executor. In order to make the gift valid it must be made so as to take complete effect on the donor's death."[18]

The title of the donee can never be complete until the donor is dead,[19] and, accordingly, the *donatio* will fail if the donee predeceases the donor.[20]

In order for a *donatio mortis causa* to be effective, there are three conditions which must be complied with. "Firstly, a clear intention to give, but to give only if the donor dies, whereas if the donor does not die then the gift is not to take effect and the donor is to have back the subject-matter of the gift. Secondly, the gift must be made in contemplation of death, by which is meant not the possibility of death at some time or other, but death within the near future, what may be called death for some reason believed to be impending. Thirdly, the donor must part with dominion over the subject matter of the *donatio*."[1] Before discussing each of these conditions, it should be mentioned that if there has been a complete transfer of the subject-matter of the *donatio* such as would suffice in an *inter vivos* gift, the *donatio* will be effective and complete on the death without any further act being necessary; but even where the transfer has been inchoate or incomplete, so that it would be ineffective in an *inter vivos* gift, it may suffice to constitute a valid *donatio*.[2] In such case the legal title will be held by the personal representatives on trust for the donee, and the donee will, if need be, be able to compel the personal representatives to lend their names to any necessary action, on receiving an appropriate indemnity.[3] It is where the transfer has been inchoate or incomplete that equity allows an exception to the rule that it will not complete an imperfect gift.

Each of the conditions referred to above must now be considered.

i First, as to the intention required, this must be distinguished on the one hand from an intention to make an immediate or irrevocable gift,[4] and on

---

17 *Per* Lindley L.J. in *Re Dillon* (1890), 44 Ch.D. 76, at p. 83, C.A., citing *Duffield* v. *Elwes* (1827), 1 Bli. N.S. 497.
18 *Re Beaumont*, [1902] 1 Ch. 889, *per* Buckley J., at p. 892.
19 *Duffield* v. *Elwes*, *supra*; *Delgoffe* v. *Fader*, [1939] 3 All E.R. 682; [1939] Ch. 922.
20 *Tate* v. *Hilbert* (1793), 2 Ves. 111, at p. 120; *Walter* v. *Hodge* (1818), 2 Swans 92, 99.
 1 *Re Craven's Estate*, [1937] 3 All E.R. 33, at p. 37; [1937] Ch. 423, at p. 426, *per* Farwell J. See to the same effect *Cain* v. *Moon*, [1896] 2 Q.B. 283, 288, D.C., *per* Lord Russell of Killowen; *Delgoffe* v. *Fader*, [1939] 3 All E.R. 682, at p. 685; [1939] Ch. 922, at p. 927, *per* Luxmoore L.J.
 2 *Ward* v. *Turner* (1752), 2 Ves.Sen. 431; *Re Wasserberg*, [1915] 1 Ch. 195; [1914-15] All E.R.Rep. 217.
 3 *Duffield* v. *Elwes*, *supra*; *Delgoffe* v. *Fader*, *supra*; *Re Lillingston*, [1952] 2 All E.R. 184.
 4 If the intention is to make an *inter vivos* gift, which is incomplete and accordingly fails, it cannot be treated as a *donatio mortis causa* even though this might validate it. *Edwards* v. *Jones* (1836), 1 My. & Cr. 226.

the other hand from an attempted nuncupative will.[5] The intention must be that the gift shall automatically become complete on death, but subject to the condition that it may be revoked by the donor expressly, and will automatically be revoked if he should recover. If it is revoked, the donee will thereafter hold any property that has been transferred as trustee for the donor.[6] The condition need not be express, and will readily be implied where the gift is made in expectation of death.[7] Probably, somewhat illogically, the better view is that the necessary condition may be implied notwithstanding the fact that the donor knows that there cannot be any recovery.[8] In his lifetime the *donatio* will be revoked by the donor recovering dominion over the subject-matter of the gift,[9] but not by the mere fact of the donor taking the property back for safe custody.[10] It is said to be impossible, however, to revoke a *donatio mortis causa* by will, for death makes the gift complete,[11] though a *donatio* may be satisfied by a legacy contained in a subsequent testamentary instrument.[12]

ii The requirement that the gift must be made in contemplation of death will readily be treated as satisfied where it was made during the donor's last illness. The reported cases all contemplate death through illness, but on principle there seems no reason why the contemplation of death from some other source should not be equally effective.[13] But, of course, a merely general contemplation of death, on the ground that everyone must die at some time or other, is inadequate. Prior to the Suicide Act 1961, which provided that suicide should no longer be a crime, it had been held[14] that a purported *donatio mortis causa* in contemplation of suicide was not valid, as it would otherwise allow the donor to give effect to his gift by means of committing a crime. By virtue of the Act this reason is no longer applicable, though it is arguable that such a *donatio mortis causa* should not be recognised on grounds of public policy. It does not matter that death actually occurs from a disease[15] other than that contemplated.[16]

iii Parting with the dominion means, primarily, physical delivery of the subject matter of the *donatio* with intent to part with the dominion and not merely, for instance, with intent to ensure its safe custody.[17] Failure to part with the dominion inevitably means failure of the *donatio mortis causa*, as, for instance, in *Bunn* v. *Markham*,[18] where the property was, by the deceased's

---

[5] *Solicitor to the Treasury* v. *Lewis*, [1900] 2 Ch. 812.

[6] *Stanilund* v. *Willott* (1852), 3 Mac. & G. 664; *Re Wasserberg*, [1915] 1 Ch. 195; [1914–15] All E.R.Rep. 217.

[7] *Gardner* v. *Parker* (1818), 3 Madd. 184; *Re Lillingston*, [1952] 2 All E.R. 184.

[8] *Wilkes* v. *Allington*, [1931] 2 Ch. 104, at p. 111, per Lord Tomlin; *Re Lillingston, supra*; *Re Mustapha* (1891), 8 T.L.R. 160.

[9] *Bunn* v. *Markham* (1816), 7 Taunt. 224.

[10] *Re Hawkins*, [1924] 2 Ch. 47; [1924] All E.R.Rep. 430.

[11] See, e.g., White and Tudor's *Leading Cases in Equity*, 9th Ed., Vol. 1, p. 355.

[12] *Jones* v. *Selby* (1710), Prec.Ch. 300, where satisfaction was said to be equivalent to a revocation; *Hudson* v. *Spencer*, [1910] 2 Ch. 285.

[13] See the discussion in *Agnew* v. *Belfast Banking Co.*, [1896] 2 I.R. 204.

[14] *Re Dudman*, [1925] Ch. 553.

[15] Or, probably, from any other source, including suicide not contemplated at the date of the gift: *Mills* v. *Shields*, [1948] Ir.R. 367.

[16] *Wilkes* v. *Allington*, [1931] 2 Ch. 104.

[17] *Hawkins* v. *Blewitt* (1798), 2 Esp. 663.

[18] (1816), 7 Taunt. 224.

directions, sealed in three parcels and the names of the intended donees written thereon. The deceased declared that they were intended for the named donees and directed that they should be given to them after his death. The parcels were then replaced in a chest to which the deceased retained the key, and it was held that there was no sufficient delivery and accordingly no effective *donatio mortis causa*.

Delivery, however, need not be by the donor personally into the hands of the donee. It may be made by a duly authorised agent of the donor,[19] or like-wise to an agent for the donee,[20] but mere delivery to an agent of the donor is ineffective.[1] Again, an antecedent delivery of the chattel, i.e. anterior to the date of the actual gift, is adequate, even though made *alio intuito*,[2] e.g. for safe custody only, and it seems that words of gift subsequently followed by delivery may suffice.[3] Further, a *donatio mortis causa* is not invalidated by the fact that it is expressed to be subject to an express charge or trust, even to an indefinite extent, e.g. to pay funeral expenses.[4]

It is settled, however, that delivery of the key to the box or other receptacle or place in which the subject matter of the alleged *donatio* is contained may be a sufficient delivery of such subject matter if the requisite intent appears.[5] The better view, it is submitted, is that this is not to be regarded as a symbolic delivery, but as giving to the donee the means of getting at the subject matter, and correspondingly depriving the donor of his power of dealing with it[6]; and, further, that it applies not only to bulky articles, but also to things which are capable of actual manual delivery.[7] Even where delivery of the key only transfers a partial dominion over the subject of the *donatio*, as where the key of a safe deposit at Harrod's Ltd., was handed over, but under the terms of the contract of deposit the contents would only be handed over to anyone other than the actual depositor on production, in addition to the key, of a signed authority and the giving of a password, this may be a sufficient delivery and equity will complete the imperfect gift.[8] Delivery of a key will be equally effective if it merely gives the donee the means of getting at another key which in its turn gives access to the place in which the subject matter of the *donatio* is contained.[9] But if the donor retains a duplicate key, it seems there is no effective delivery, for the donor is still able to deal with the subject matter

---

[19] *Re Craven's Estate*, [1937] 3 All E.R. 33; [1937] Ch. 423.
[20] *Moore* v. *Darton* (1851), 4 De G. & Sm. 517. Perhaps a doubtful decision on the facts.
[1] *Powell* v. *Hellicar* (1858), 26 Beav. 261; *Farquharson* v. *Cave* (1846), 2 Coll. 356.
[2] *Cain* v. *Moon*, [1896] 2 Q.B. 283, D.C.; *Birch* v. *Treasury Solicitor*, [1950] 2 All E.R. 1198; [1951] Ch. 298, C.A.
[3] *Re Weston*, [1902] 1 Ch. 680.
[4] *Hills* v. *Hills* (1841), 8 M. & W. 401; *Re Ward*, [1946] 2 All E.R 206; *Birch* v. *Treasury Solicitor, supra*.
[5] *Jones* v. *Selby* (1710), Prec.Ch. 300; *Re Mustapha* (1891), 8 T.L.R. 160. Cf. (1956), 19 M.L.R. 394 (A. C. H. Barlow).
[6] *Birch* v. *Treasury Solicitor, supra*; *contra, Jarman on Wills*, 8th Ed., Vol. 1, p. 47.
[7] It is submitted that decisions such as *Jones* v. *Selby, supra*, and *Re Mustapha, supra*, are to be preferred on this point to dicta in other cases, e.g. *Re Wasserberg*, [1915] 1 Ch. 195; [1914–15] All E.R. Rep. 217.
[8] *Re Lillingston*, [1952] 2 All E.R. 184; *Re Wasserberg, supra*.
[9] *Re Lillingston, supra*, "it does not matter in how many boxes the subject of a gift may be contained or that each, except the last, contains a key which opens the next, so long as the scope of the gift is made clear". *Per* Wynn-Parry J., [1952] 2 All E.R. 184, 191.

and cannot be said to have parted with dominion.[10] For the same reason there can be no *donatio mortis causa* if the alleged donor parts with possession of a locked box or other receptacle, but retains possession of the key.[11]

There may be more difficulty where the subject matter of the alleged *donatio mortis causa* is not a chattel capable of actual delivery as explained in the preceding paragraphs, but is a chose in action. There will be no problem where there has been such delivery of a banknote,[12] or a negotiable instrument, other than one drawn by the donor,[13] in such a condition that mere delivery of the document will effect a transfer of the chose in action which it represents; nor in any other case where the formalities of transfer have been carried out so as to pass the legal title.[14] Where, however, the title to the chose in action does not pass by mere delivery of any document, and where there has been no formal transfer of the legal title, it is the law that for the purposes of a *donatio mortis causa* delivery of the appropriate documents may be regarded as equivalent to a transfer and equity will complete the imperfect gift. The question what are the appropriate documents which must be delivered is to be answered by applying the test propounded by the Court of Appeal in *Birch* v. *Treasury Solicitor*,[15] namely, "that the real test is whether the instrument 'amounts to a transfer'[16] as being the essential *indicia* or evidence of title, possession or production of which entitles the possessor to the money or property purported to be given".[17] In that case it was held that the choses in action respectively represented by a Post Office Savings Bankbook, a London Trustee Savings Bankbook, a Barclay's Bank deposit pass book and a Westminster Bank deposit account book were each the subject of a valid *donatio mortis causa* by delivery of the appropriate book. Other cases have held valid the *donatio mortis causa* of a bond,[18] bills of exchange, cheques and promissory notes payable to the donor, even though unendorsed and therefore not transferable by delivery,[19] a banker's deposit note,[20] national savings certificates,[1] an insurance policy[2] and even a mortgage.[3]

iv It is commonly stated that some things cannot form the subject matter of a *donatio mortis causa*. These seem to fall into three categories:

First, no attempt appears ever to have been made to establish a *donatio mortis causa* of land, and *dicta* of Lord Eldon in *Duffield* v. *Elwes*[4] deny the possibility.

---

[10] *Re Craven's Estate*, [1937] 3 All E.R. 33, at p. 38; [1937] Ch. 423, at p. 428, *per* Farwell J.

[11] *Re Johnson* (1905), 92 L.T. 357; *Reddel* v. *Dobree* (1839), 10 Sim. 244.

[12] *Miller* v. *Miller* (1735), 3 P.Wms. 356; *Re Hawkins*, [1924] 2 Ch. 47; [1924] All E.R.Rep. 430.

[13] See p. 80, *post*.

[14] *Staniland* v. *Willott* (1850), 3 Mac. & G. 664.

[15] [1950] 2 All E.R. 1198; [1951] Ch. 298, C.A., at pp. 1207, 311.

[16] Adopting the phrase uttered by Lord Hardwicke L.C. in *Ward* v. *Turner* (1752), 2 Ves.Sen. 431 at p. 444.

[17] It is no longer regarded as necessary that the document handed over should contain a record of all the essential terms of the contract. Cf. *Re Weston*, [1902] 1 Ch. 680; *Delgoffe* v. *Fader*, [1939] 3 All E.R. 682; [1939] Ch. 922.

[18] *Gardner* v. *Parker*, *supra*; *Re Wasserberg*, [1915] 1 Ch. 195; [1914–15] All E.R.Rep. 217.

[19] *Re Mead* (1880), 15 Ch.D. 651; *Clement* v. *Cheesman* (1885), 27 Ch.D. 631.

[20] *Re Dillon* (1890), 44 Ch.D. 76, C.A.

[1] *Darlow* v. *Sparks*, [1938] 2 All E.R. 235.

[2] *Witt* v. *Amis* (1861), 1 Best. & Sm. 109; *Amis* v. *Witt* (1863), 33 Beav. 619.

[3] *Duffield* v. *Elwes* (1827), 1 Bli.N.S. 497; *Wilkes* v. *Allington*, [1931] 2 Ch. 104.

[4] *Supra*, at pp. 530, 539, 543. *Sed quaere*. Particularly in the event of an actual conveyance of land to an intended donee complying with the necessary conditions.

Secondly,[5] it was stated in *Moore* v. *Moore*[6] that railway stock, and in *Re Weston*[7] that building society shares, are not a proper subject of a *donatio mortis causa*. In *Re Weston*[7] the court held that the building society shares were not distinguishable from the railway stock in *Moore* v. *Moore*,[6] which in its turn merely followed *Ward* v. *Turner*,[8] which was treated as deciding that the South Sea annuities the subject of the case could not be the subject of a *donatio mortis causa*. It is submitted that *Ward* v. *Turner*[9] should be regarded as deciding not that South Sea annuities could never be the subject of a *donatio mortis causa*, but that the delivery of the receipts in that case did not "amount to a transfer". It is noteworthy that Lord Hardwicke in his judgment said that, after acceptance of the stock, the receipts "are nothing but waste paper, and are seldom taken care of afterwards".[10] If *Ward* v. *Turner*[9] is properly to be explained on this ground, it would undermine the authority of *Moore* v. *Moore*[11] and *Re Weston*[12] on this point. These latter cases, moreover, are not easy to reconcile with *Staniland* v. *Willott*,[13] where it was held that a valid *donatio mortis causa* was constituted by a complete transfer of shares in a public company. On the view now being suggested this second category altogether disappears.

Thirdly, it is clear that there cannot be a valid *donatio mortis causa* of the donor's own cheque or promissory note.[14] The point here is that a man's own cheque or promissory note is not property when given by the donor to the donee; a cheque is merely a revocable order to the banker to make the payment to the person in whose favour the cheque is drawn and the gift of a promissory note is merely a gratuitous promise. It may be otherwise if a cheque has actually been paid during the donor's lifetime,[15] or immediately after the death before the banker has been apprised of it,[16] or negotiated for value.[17]

c **Statutory provisions**

It is convenient to mention briefly that there are two cases under the Settled Land Act 1925 where statute will complete an imperfect gift.

i An instrument *inter vivos* which is intended to create a settlement of a legal estate in land, but which does not comply with the provisions of the Settled Land Act 1925 will not operate to transfer or create a legal estate,[18] and

---

[5] See, generally, (1966), 30 Con. 189 (Alec Samuels).
[6] (1874), L.R. 18 Eq. 474.
[7] [1902] 1 Ch. 680, but see (1947), 204 L.T.Jo. 142.
[8] (1752), 2 Ves.Sen. 431.
[9] (1752) 2 Ves.Sen, 431. See *per* Lord Hardwicke L.C. at p. 444.
[10] At p. 443. He also added "what I very seldom do . . . I should be very glad to have this point settled by the supreme authority".
[11] *Supra.*
[12] *Supra.*
[13] (1850), 3 Mac. & G. 664. See also *Re Craven's Estate,* [1937] 3 All E.R. 33; [1937] Ch. 423.
[14] *Re Beaumont,* [1902] 1 Ch. 889; *Re Leaper,* [1916] 1 Ch. 579; *Re Swinburne,* [1926] Ch. 38; [1925] All E.R.Rep. 313, C.A. (actually a decision on an *inter vivos* gift).
[15] *Bouts* v. *Ellis* (1853), 17 Beav. 121, *affd.* 4 De G.M. & G. 249. It is enough if it has been accepted by the banker during the donor's lifetime; *Re While,* [1928] W.N. 182; *Re Beaumont,* [1902] 1 Ch. 889.
[16] *Tate* v. *Hilbert* (1793), 2 Ves. 111.
[17] *Tate* v. *Hilbert, supra; Rolls* v. *Pearce* (1877), 5 Ch.D. 730.
[18] Settled Land Act 1925, s. 4.

is thus imperfect. Even though the imperfect settlement may be voluntary, it may be perfected under the provisions contained in s. 9 of the Act.

ii A legal estate in land is not capable of being held by an infant.[19] A purported conveyance of a legal estate in land to an infant accordingly cannot vest any legal estate in him; it is, however, provided by s. 27 of the Settled Land Act 1925 that such a conveyance shall operate as an agreement for valuable consideration[20] to execute a settlement in proper form in favour of the infant and in the meantime to hold the land in trust for him.

d The Dillwyn v. Llewellyn[21] principle—Proprietary estoppel

In this case a father placed one of his sons in possession of land belonging to the father, and at the same time signed a memorandum that he had presented the land to the son for the purpose of furnishing him with a dwelling-house, but no formal conveyance was ever executed. The son, with the assent and approbation of the father, built at his own expense a house upon the land and resided there. After the father's death the question arose what estate, if any, the son had in the land. The judgment of Lord Westbury L.C. does not make it clear whether he considered the case to be one of gift or of contract, but he did say, after repeating the rule that equity will not complete an imperfect gift, that the subsequent acts of the donor might give the donee a right or ground of claim which he did not have under the original gift. The ratio of his actual decision in this case seems to be that putting the son into possession and the subsequent expenditure incurred with the approbation of the father were grounds for equity intervening to complete the imperfect gift by compelling a conveyance of the fee simple to the son,[1] though it has been thought that the case is to be explained on a contractual basis.[2] The Privy Council has since asserted[3] that there can be no doubt "that where an owner of land has invited or expressly encouraged[4] another to expend money on part of his land on the faith of an assurance or promise that that part of the land will be made over to the person so expending his money a court of equity will *prima facie* require the owner by appropriate conveyance to fulfil his obligation: and when, for example, for reasons of title, no such conveyance can effectively be made, a court of equity may declare that the person who has expended the money is entitled to an equitable charge or lien for the amount so expended". Such a lien had been the remedy granted in *Unity Joint State Mutual Banking Association* v *King*,[5] where a father had allowed his sons to occupy and expend money on his land.

---

[19] Law of Property 1925, 1 (6).
[20] And therefore enforceable, even though the purported conveyance was in fact voluntary.
[21] (1862), 4 De G.F. & J. 517. Cf. *Ramsden* v. *Dyson* (1866), L.R. 1 H.L. 129; *Plimmer* v. *Wellington Corpn.* (1884), 9 App. Cas. 699, P.C.; *Chalmers* v. *Pardoe*, [1963] 3 All E.R. 552, P.C.
[1] See (1963), 79 L.Q.R. 238 (D. E. Allan).
[2] E.g. Wynn-Parry J. at first instance in *Re Diplock*, [1947] 1 All E.R. 522, at p. 549; [1947] Ch. 716, at pp. 781–784.
[3] *Chalmers* v. *Pardoe*, [1963] 3 All E.R. 552, 555, P.C.
[4] Or, it seems, merely allowed—*Inwards* v. *Baker*, [1965] 1 All E.R. 446, at p. 448; [1965] 2 Q.B. 29, at p. 37, C.A.; *Ward* v. *Kirkland*, [1966] 1 All E.R. 609; [1967] Ch. 194.
[5] (1858), 25 Beav. 72.

The basic equitable principle involved is, however, even wider, and its application to particular facts is very much in the discretion of the court. Wherever the person who has made the expenditure on the land was induced to do so by the expectation of obtaining protection, equity will in a proper case protect him so that no injustice will be perpetrated. It is for the court to say in which way the equity can be satisfied. Recent cases illustrate the different ways in which the same basic equity has been applied.

In *Inwards* v. *Baker*,[6] the defendant was, in 1931, considering building a bungalow on land which he would have to purchase. His father, who owned some land, suggested that the defendant should build the bungalow on his land and make it a little bigger. The defendant accepted that suggestion and built the bungalow himself, with some financial assistance from his father, part of which he had repaid. He had lived in the bungalow ever since. In 1951 the father died and in 1963 the trustees of his will claimed possession from the defendant. The court held that the defendant was entitled to remain in possession of the bungalow as a licensee so long as he desired to use it as his home. In *Ward* v. *Kirkland*[7] a landowner gave his neighbour permission to lay drainpipes in his land. The neighbour incurred expense in putting the drains in, on the footing and in the belief and conviction that he had permission for putting the drains there for an indefinite time. It was held that he thereby acquired an equity of a permanent nature to have the drains in the land. In *E.R. Ives Investments, Ltd.* v. *High*[8], the facts were very different and the application of the principle was varied accordingly. The defendant and the predecessors in title of the plaintiff had, in 1949, entered into an agreement whereby the defendant agreed that the foundations of the plaintiff's building should remain on the defendant's land, and it was further agreed that the defendant should have a right of access across the plaintiff's land. The agreement was never put into a formal document. Subsequently the defendant, with the encouragement of the plaintiff's predecessors in title built a garage, the only access to which was across the plaintiff's land. The plaintiff, who took with full knowledge of the facts, nevertheless brought an action for damages for trespass and an injunction to restrain the defendant from further trespass. On the basis of the above principle the Court of Appeal affirmed the dismissal of the action by the county court judge.[9] It was also held that the equity does not require to be protected by registration under the Land Charges Act, 1925.[10]

Lastly there is the unsatisfactory decision in *Hussey* v. *Palmer*.[11] In that case the

---

[6] *Supra.* See also *Siew Soon Wah* v. *Yong Tong Hong*, [1973] A.C. 836, P.C.

[7] [1966] 1 All E.R. 609; [1967] Ch. 194.

[8] [1967] 1 All E.R. 504; [1967] 2 Q.B. 379, C:A. See (1967), 31 Con. 332 (F. R. Crane); (1967) 30 M.L.R. 580 (H. W. Wilkinson); (1968) 32 Con. 96 (R. E. Poole).

[9] The Court also relied on the principle of *Halsall* v. *Brizell*, [1957] 1 All E.R. 371; [1957] Ch. 169, viz. that he who takes the benefit (i.e., on the facts here, of keeping his foundations in the defendant's land) must accept the burden (i.e., of allowing the defendant the agreed access), though that case concerned the benefit and burden under a deed.

[10] Now largely repealed and replaced by the Land Charges Act 1972. See F. R. Crane, *loc. cit.*; (1967), 31 Con. 394 (J. F. Garner); (1969), 33 Con. 135 (P. Jackson); *Shiloh Spinners, Ltd.* v. *Harding*, [1971] 2 All E.R. 307; [1972] Ch. 326, C.A. (esp. *per* Russell L.J. at pp. 315; 343), reversed H.L., [1973] 1 All E.R. 90; [1973] A.C. 691.

[11] [1972] 3 All E.R. 744, C.A. discussed (1973), 37 Con. 65 (D. J. Hayton); (1973), 89 L.Q.R. 2; (1973), 32 C.L.J. 41 (P. B. Fairest); (1973), 36 M.L.R. 426 (T. C. Ridley).

plaintiff paid £607 for an additional bedroom to be built on to a house belonging to her son-in-law, the defendant, in order to enable her to go and live with him and her daughter. After a short time differences arose between the plaintiff and her daughter and the plaintiff left to live elsewhere. She soon became hard up and asked for her money back. On being refused, she brought her action for repayment, which succeeded in the Court of Appeal. *Unity Joint State Mutual Banking Association* v. *King*,[12] *Chalmers* v. *Pardoe*[13] and *Inwards* v. *Baker*[14] were all referred to, and the principle of these cases formed one ground of the decision. It seems doubtful, however, whether this principle applied on the facts, in the absence of evidence of the required expectation on the part of the plaintiff induced by the acts or conduct of the defendant.[15] The second, and, it seems, the main ground for the decision, though the two grounds were not kept distinct, involved the undoubted principle that where two persons contribute to the purchase price of property which is put into the name of one only, that one holds on a resulting trust for the other to an extent proportionate to his contribution.[16] In *Hussey* v. *Palmer*[17] Lord Denning said that this principle applied equally where a person pays for an improvement to property. No reference was made, however, to *Pettitt* v. *Pettitt*[18] where Lord Upjohn said,[19] "It has been well settled in your Lordships' House that if A expends money on the property of B *prima facie* he has no claim on such property", or to *Davis* v. *Vale*[20] where Lord Denning himself seems to have assumed that this was the law. In any case it is submitted that the dissenting judgment of Cairns L.J. regarding the matter purely one of loan, is to be preferred.[1]

4 DISCRETIONARY AND PROTECTIVE TRUSTS

a Limitations upon condition and determinable interests

One might think that a gift to X for life or until he becomes bankrupt would have the same effect as a gift to X for life on condition that if he becomes bankrupt his interest shall determine. In fact, however, a distinction must be drawn between a determinable interest, where the determining event is incorporated in the limitation so that the interest automatically and naturally determines if and when the event happens, and a grant upon a condition subsequent, where an interest is granted subject to an independent proviso that the interest may be brought to a premature end if the condition is fulfilled.[2] In the latter case, if for any reason the condition is void, the grant becomes absolute and the interest will not be liable to premature determination.[3]

---

[12] *Supra.*   [13] *Supra.*   [14] *Supra.*
[15] The only expectation on the evidence seems to have been of a licence to live there so long as she wanted.
[16] See *infra*, pp. 100, 101.   [17] *Supra*, C.A.
[18] [1969] 2 All E.R. 385; [1970] A.C. 777, H.L.; Cf. *Re Vandervell's Trusts*, [1974] 1 All E.R. 47.
[19] At pp. 449; 818.   [20] [1971] 2 All E.R. 1021, C.A.
[1] It is not altogether clear whether the majority held the plaintiff entitled to £607, or to a share of the house proportionate to the £607 paid.
[2] For a discussion of the distinction see Cheshire, *Modern Real Property*, 11th Ed., pp. 310 *et seq.*; Megarry and Wade, *The Law of Real Property*, 3rd Ed., pp. 75 *et seq.*
[3] *Sifton* v. *Sifton*, [1938] A.C. 656, at p. 677, P.C.

These principles apply in general to all estates and interests in property, but for present purposes we are concerned with their effect upon life interests.

Conditions which have been held void include conditions intended to secure the premature determination of the interest granted on alienation[4] or bankruptcy.[5] There is no doubt, however, that the corresponding determinable limitation, i.e. a grant of a life interest to X until he attempts to alienate the same or becomes bankrupt, is perfectly valid,[6] and in dealing with life interests the courts, it seems, will not be astute to construe a provision as a condition if it can be construed as a determinable limitation.

An important restriction on the validity of such a determinable limitation is that a man cannot settle his own property on himself until his bankruptcy, so as to defeat the claim of his trustee in bankruptcy,[7] though there is no objection to a limitation which takes effect so as to defeat a particular alienee.[8] Where a man does settle property on himself, and, as is usually the case, the life interest is determinable not only on bankruptcy but also upon other events such as an attempted alienation or charge, then, on the one hand, if bankruptcy is the first determining event to happen, the life interest will vest indefeasibly in the trustee in bankruptcy and will no longer be capable of being determined by the happening of any subsequent specified determining event[9]; on the other hand, if one of the other determining events is the first to happen, the life estate will automatically come to an end and if the life tenant subsequently becomes bankrupt the bankrupt will have no interest in the property which can pass to his trustee in bankruptcy.[10]

b   Discretionary trusts[11]

Trustees are often given discretions of varying kinds, but the phrase discretionary trust usually[12] means a trust under which the trustees are given a discretion to pay or apply income to or for the benefit of all, or any one or more exclusively of the others, of a specified class or group of persons, no beneficiary being able to claim as of right that all or any part of the income is to be paid to him or applied for his benefit. A discretionary trust may be exhaustive, that is where the trustees are bound to distribute the whole income, but have a discretion as to how the distribution is to be made between the objects. Alternatively according to the cases cited below a discretionary trust may be non-

---

[4] *Brandon* v. *Robinson* (1811), 18 Ves. 429; *Graves* v. *Dolphin* (1826), 1 Sim. 66; *Rochford* v. *Hackman* (1852), 9 Hare 475; *Re Smith*, [1916] 1 Ch. 369. See, generally, *Re Brown*, [1953] 2 All E.R. 1342; [1954] Ch. 39; (1943), 59 L.Q.R. 343 (Glanville Williams).
[5] *Re Dugdale* (1888), 38 Ch.D. 176.
[6] See, e.g., *Brandon* v. *Robinson*, *supra*.
[7] *Wilson* v. *Greenwood* (1818), 1 Swan. 471, 481, footnote; *Mackintosh* v. *Pogose*, [1895] 1 Ch. 505; *Re Wombwell* (1921), 125 L.T. 437.
[8] *Re Johnson, Ex parte Matthews*, [1904] 1 K.B. 134, D.C.
[9] *Re Burroughs-Fowler*, [1916] 2 Ch. 251.
[10] *Re Richardson's Will Trusts*, [1958] 1 All E.R. 538; [1958] Ch. 504; *Re Detmold* (1889), 40 Ch.D. 585; *Re Brewer's Settlement*, [1896] 2 Ch. 503.
[11] See generally (1957), 21 Con. 55 (L. A. Sheridan); (1967), 31 Con. 117 (A. J. Hawkins).
[12] One may have a discretionary trust as to capital, where the trustees are bound to distribute the fund among a class but are given a discretionary power to decide in what shares and proportions the potential beneficiaries are to take, or trustees could be given a discretion as to both income and capital.

exhaustive, in which case the trustees have a discretion not only as to how the distribution is to be made, but also as to whether and to what extent it is to be made at all. It is submitted that the term "non-exhaustive discretionary trust" in fact conceals the two alternatives referred to by Lord Wilberforce in *McPhail* v. *Doulton*[13] viz. a power of distribution coupled with a trust to dispose of the undistributed surplus, by accumulation or otherwise, and a trust for distribution coupled with a power to withhold a portion and accumulate or otherwise dispose of it. The distinction between these alternatives does not appear to have been raised in *Gartside* v. *I.R. Comrs.*[14] and it is submitted that it is only if the provision there in question was construed in the latter sense that it should properly have been called a discretionary trust. It was in fact consistently so called by their Lordships, though the language of the will is similar to that given as a typical example of a mere power by Russell L.J. in *Re Baden's Deed Trusts.*[15]

The nature of the interest of a discretionary beneficiary has been discussed in relation to statutory provisions relating to estate duty.[16] In *Gartside* v. *I.R. Comrs.,*[17] which involved a non-exhaustive trust, Lord Reid made it clear that the objects of a discretionary trust do not have concurrent interests in the income, nor do they have a group interest. They all have individual rights: they are in competition with each other and what the trustees give to one is his alone. The reference to a class or group of objects under a discretionary trust is merely a convenient form of reference to indicate individuals who satisfy requirements to qualify as objects who may separately receive benefits under the exercise of the discretion. Subsequently Cross J. in *Re Weir's Settlement*[18] and Ungoed-Thomas J. in *Sainsbury* v. *I.R. Comrs.*[19] have taken the same view in the case of an exhaustive trust. The cases cited also lay down that the separate "interest" of each separate object is unquantifiable, and of a limited kind. What he has is a right to be considered as a potential beneficiary, a right to have his interest protected by a court of equity and a right to take and enjoy whatever part of the income the trustees choose to give him. He could accordingly go to the court if the trustees refused to exercise their discretion at all, or exercised it improperly.[20] It follows from what has been said that it is very difficult to explain where the equitable interest lies in the case of discretionary trusts. Further it may be observed that the description of the rights of a potential

---

[13] [1970 2 All E.R. 228, at p. 240; [1971] A.C. 424, at p. 448, H.L.
[14] [1968] 1 All E.R. 121; [1968] A.C. 553, H.L.
[15] [1969] 1 All E.R. 1016, at p. 1022, C.A. In *Re Weir's Settlement*, [1970] 1 All E.R. 297, 300; [1971] Ch. 145 at p. 164, C.A., Russell L.J. referred to *Gartside* v. *I.R.Comrs.*, supra, H.L. as "a case of a non-exhaustive discretionary power or trust".
[16] So far as estate duty is concerned the Finance Act 1968, s. 39 provided that the object of a discretionary trust had an interest in the trust property, even an interest in possession. This section has been repealed and the code of liability recast by the Finance Act 1969, see especially s. 36.
[17] [1968] 1 All E.R. 121; [1968] A.C. 553, H.L.
[18] [1968] 2 All E.R. 1241; [1969] 1 Ch. 657, reversed C.A., [1970] 1 All E.R. 297; [1917] Ch. 145, without casting doubt on relevant dicta in court below.
[19] [1969] 3 All E.R. 919; [1970] Ch. 712.
[20] *Tempest* v. *Lord Camoys* (1882), 21 Ch.D., 571; [1881–5] All E.R. Rep. 836, C.A.; *Martin* v. *Martin*, [1919] P. 283; [1918–19] All E.R. Rep. 1116, C.A.; *Gartside* v. *I.R.Comrs.*, supra, H.L. see p. 361, *infra*.

beneficiary under a discretionary trust is in fact similar to that of the objects of a mere power given to trustees in their fiduciary capacity. The main difference lies in the fact that the object of a mere power has no ground of complaint if, after due consideration, the trustees decide not to exercise the power at all. It should be added that an object of a discretionary trust may renounce his right to be considered as a potential beneficiary and, at any rate if he does so for valuable consideration, he thereupon ceases to be an object of the trust.[1]

If an object of a discretionary trust assigns his interest or becomes bankrupt, it is clear that the assignee or trustee in bankruptcy cannot, any more than the discretionary beneficiary could have done, demand payment of any part of the fund. If the trustees exercise their discretion in favour of a discretionary beneficiary by paying or delivering money or goods to him, or even, it seems, by appropriating money or goods to be paid or delivered to him, the title to the money or goods passes to the assignee or trustee in bankruptcy.[2] And, where the trustees have actually paid the discretionary beneficiary after notice of an assignment or bankruptcy, they have been held liable to the assignee or trustee in bankruptcy for all the money paid.[3] It seems, however, that the trustees can validly expend the whole or any part of the fund for his maintenance, for instance, in paying an hotel keeper to give him a dinner, or in paying the rent of the house in which he is living,[4] and in respect of any such payment an assignee or trustee in bankruptcy will have no claim.[5]

The position is quite different where the trustees are bound to apply the whole fund for the benefit of a particular person, even though they may be given a discretion as to the method in which the fund is to be applied for his benefit. In this case the beneficiary, if *sui iuris*, is entitled to demand payment of the whole fund, which will pass to an assignee or trustee in bankruptcy.[6] Similarly where two or more persons together (constituting a closed class) are the sole objects of an exhaustive discretionary trust and between them entitled to have the whole fund applied to them or for their benefit, though no one by himself may be able to demand any payment, they can, if *sui iuris*, all join together and require the trustees to pay over the fund to them.[7] Similarly they may agree and assign to a third party all the capital or income as the case may be of the trust fund, when the trustees will become obliged to pay it to the third party.[8] Discretionary beneficiaries for the time being constituting the sole objects of an exhaustive discretionary trust of income have a corresponding

---

[1] *Re Gulbenkian's Settlement Trusts (No. 2)*, [1969] 2 All E.R. 1173, [1970] Ch. 408.
[2] *Re Coleman* (1888), 39 Ch.D. 443, C.A.
[3] *Re Neil* (1890), 62 L.T. 649; *Re Bullock* (1891), 60 L.J.Ch. 341. According to *Re Ashby*, [1892] 1 Q.B. 872, however, the trustee in bankruptcy or assignee can only claim to the extent to which sums are paid in excess of the amount necessary for the mere support of the object of the trust.
[4] *Re Allen-Meyrick's Will Trusts*, [1966] 1 All E.R. 740.
[5] *Re Coleman, supra; Re Bullock, supra*.
[6] *Green* v. *Spicer* (1830), 1 Russ. & My. 395; *Younghusband* v. *Gisborne* (1844), 1 Coll. 400; *Re Smith*, [1928] Ch. 915. Cf. *Saunders* v. *Vautier* (1841), Cr. & Ph. 240; *Wharton* v. *Masterman*, [1895] A.C. 186, H.L. and *infra*, Chapter 10, Section 7, p. 333, *post*.
[7] *Re Smith, supra; Re Nelson*, [1928] Ch. 920, n., C.A.
[8] See *Re Weir's Settlement, supra*, at first instance at pp. 1248; 683; *Sainsbury* v. *I.R.Comrs., supra*, at p. 927; 725.

power even if the class is not a closed class, but the direction or assignment will in such case cease to be effective if a new member of the class comes into being.

A quite separate problem is as to what should happen if trustees fail to execute a discretionary trust. Being a trust, the court will see to it that it does not fail, and before *McPhail* v. *Doulton*[9] it was thought that all that the court could do was to order equal division. This, it will be recalled, is the reason why before that decision it was thought that a discretionary trust would only be valid if you could get a complete list of potential beneficiaries. In that case, however, it was held that the court was not so restricted. As Lord Wilberforce explained[10]: "The Court, if called upon to execute the trust power, will do so in the manner best calculated to give effect to the settlor's or testator's intentions. It may do so by appointing new trustees, or by authorising or directing representative persons of the classes of beneficiaries to prepare a scheme of distribution, or even, should the proper basis for distribution appear by itself directing the trustees so to distribute."[11]

c Protective trusts[12]

This expression is used to describe a life interest determinable on an event such as bankruptcy, and followed by discretionary trusts in favour of the person whose interest has determined and his near relatives. The trusts may be set out expressly,[13] or the instrument may incorporate the statutory provisions appearing in s. 33 of the Trustee Act 1925, which section does not, however, apply to trusts coming into operation before 1926, and takes effect subject to any modifications contained in the instrument creating the trust. Section 33 (1) provides as follows:

"Where any income, including an annuity or other periodical income payment, is directed to be held on protective trusts for the benefit of any person (in this section called 'the principal beneficiary') for the period of his life or for any less period, then, during that period (in this section called the 'trust period') the said income shall, without prejudice to any prior interest, be held on the following trusts, namely:

(i) Upon trust for the principal beneficiary during the trust period or until he, whether before or after the termination of any prior interest, does or attempts to do or suffers any act or thing, or until any event happens, other than an advance under any statutory or express power, whereby if the said income were payable during the trust period to the principal beneficiary absolutely during that period, he would be deprived of the right to receive the same or any part thereof . . . [and thereafter] . . .

---

[9] [1970] 2 All E.R. 228; [1971] A.C. 424, H.L.
[10] In *McPhail* v. *Doulton*, *supra*, at pp. 247, 457.
[11] See (1967) 31 Con. 117 (A. J. Hawkins); (1971), 29 C.L.J. 68 (J. Hopkins).
[12] See, generally (1957), 21 Con. 110 (L. A. Sheridan).
[13] See, e.g., *Re Munro's Settlement Trusts*, [1963] 1 All E.R. 209, where it is pointed out that a beneficiary under a discretionary trust is in a somewhat different, and perhaps stronger, position than a mere expectant heir.

(ii) upon trust for the application thereof for the maintenance or support,[14] or otherwise for the benefit, of all or any one or more exclusively of the other or others of the following persons (that is to say)—

(a) the principal beneficiary and his or her wife or husband, if any, and his or her children[15] or more remote issue,[16] if any; or

(b) if there is no wife or husband or issue[16] of the principal beneficiary in existence, the principal beneficiary and the persons who would, if he were actually dead, be entitled to the trust property or the income thereof or to the annuity fund, if any, or arrears of the annuity, as the case may be; as the trustees in their absolute discretion, without being liable to account for the exercise of such discretion, think fit."

The section specifically provides that nothing therein contained shall validate any trust which would otherwise be invalid,[17] such as a settlement by a man of his own property on himself until bankruptcy.[18]

It is not necessary in order to invoke the section to use the actual words mentioned therein, provided the reference is sufficiently clear. *In Re Platt*[1] a gift to be held "for a protective life interest" was held to be effective, and in *Re Wittke*[2] a gift of income "upon protective trusts for the benefit of my sister" was also held to be adequate, consequent upon the decision as a question of construction that the sister was intended to take a life interest.

It is, of course, a question of construction of the particular terms of the relevant clause in s. 33 or the express limitation as the case may be, whether a particular event determines the interest of the principal beneficiary. Where the protective trusts under s. 33 have applied, events which have been held to have this effect have included the Trading with the Enemy Act 1939 and Orders[3] made thereunder, whereby money payable to a person resident in enemy territory was directed to be paid to the Custodian of Enemy Property,[4] and an order made in the Probate Divorce and Admiralty Division of the High Court that the principal beneficiary should charge his interest with the payment of £50 per annum,[5] but not an order diverting a part of the income

---

[14] The trustees may apply the income to the maintenance and support of the principal beneficiary without regard to any debt he may owe to the trust estate—*Re Eiser's Will Trusts*, [1937] 1 All E.R. 244.

[15] Including, in relation to any disposition made after 31 December, 1969, illegitimate children—s. 15 (3), Family Law Reform Act 1969.

[16] Including, in relation to any disposition made after 31 December, 1969, anyone who would rank as such issue if he, or some other person through whom he is descended from the principal beneficiary, had been born legitimate—s. 15 (3), Family Law Reform Act 1969.

[17] Trustee Act 1925, s. 33 (3).

[18] See p. 84, *ante*.

[1] [1949], 1 C.L.C. 10917.

[2] [1944] 1 All E.R. 383; [1944] Ch. 166.

[3] Trading with the Enemy (Custodian) Order 1939 (S.R. & O. 1939 No. 1198). Later orders of this kind contained a proviso that vesting in the Custodian of Enemy Property should not take place if it would cause a forfeiture, e.g. The Trading with the Enemy (Custodian) (No. 2) Order 1946 (S.R. & O. 1946 No. 2141).

[4] *Re Gourju's Will Trusts*, [1943] Ch. 24; *Re Wittke*, [1944] 1 All E.R. 383; [1944] Ch. 166; contrast *Re Harris*, [1945] 1 All E.R. 702; [1945] Ch. 316; *Re Pozot's Settlement Trusts*, [1952] 1 All E.R. 1107; [1952] Ch. 427, C.A., where the protective trusts were not in the statutory form.

[5] *Re Richardson's Will Trusts*, [1958] 1 All E.R. 538; [1958] Ch. 504; *Edmonds* v. *Edmonds*, [1965] 1 All E.R. 379.

from a husband to a wife in priority to the protective trust.[6] Decisions on express provisions, differing to a greater or lesser extent from the provisions of s. 33, suggest that the interest of the principal beneficiary under s. 33 would be determined, *inter alia*, by the trustee impounding part of the income of the principal beneficiary in order to repair a breach of trust by the trustee in paying part of the trust fund to the principal beneficiary at his own instigation,[7] or an order of sequestration of the income[8]; but not by an order of the court under s. 57 of the Trustee Act 1925 varying the effect of the trusts,[9] nor by an authority to the trustees to pay dividends from trust shares to creditors, if no dividend is in fact declared.[10]

If an event happens which determines the interest of the principal beneficiary and brings the discretionary trust into play, the trustees are not entitled to retain the income, but must apply it as and when they receive it for the purposes set out in the discretionary trusts, with such necessary limitations on absolute obligation as the practical necessities of the case demand.[11] There is no reason why there should not be a series of two or more protective trusts in favour of the same beneficiary, e.g. the first trust until he attains the age of 30, the second for the remainder of his life thereafter. This would give the principal beneficiary a second chance to enjoy the income as of right, and thus prevent a youthful indiscretion from making him dependent on the discretion of the trustees for the rest of his life.[12]

5 FULLY-SECRET AND HALF-SECRET TRUSTS [13]

a The principle upon which secret trusts are enforced

A typical case of a fully-secret trust would be where a testator had left property by his will to X absolutely, on the face of the will for his own benefit, but where in fact during his lifetime the testator had informed X that the property left to him by will was not for his own benefit but for certain specified persons or purposes, and where X had promised to carry the testator's intention into effect. From early times the Court of Chancery would, in such cases, compel X to carry out the trusts: though difficulty was felt in reconciling the

---

[6] *General Accident Fire and Life Assurance Corporation, Ltd.* v. *I.R.Comrs.*, [1963] 3 All E.R. 259, C.A.

[7] *Re Balfour's Settlement*, [1938] 3 All E.R. 259; [1938] Ch. 928. Contrast *Re Brewer's Settlement*, [1896] 2 Ch. 503. As to impounding of a beneficiary's income see Chapter 12, Section 3b, p. 373, *post*.

[8] *Re Baring's Settlement Trusts*, [1940] 3 All E.R. 20; [1940] Ch. 737.

[9] *Re Mair*, [1935] All E.R.Rep. 736; [1935] Ch. 562. Contrast *Re Salting*, [1932] 2 Ch. 57. As to the effect of s. 57 of the Trustee Act 1925, see Chapter 10, Section 1b, p. 297, *post*.

[10] *Re Longman*, [1955] 1 All E.R. 455.

[11] *Re Gourju's Will Trusts*, [1943] Ch. 24, *per* Simmonds J., at p. 34. But they cannot validly exercise their discretion in advance—*Re Vestey's Settlement*, [1950] 2 All E.R. 891, C.A., *per* Evershed M.R. at p. 895 (not reported on this point in [1951] Ch. 209). See also *Re Allen-Meyrick's Will Trusts*, [1966] 1 All E.R. 740; *Re Gulbenkian's Settlement Trusts (No. 2)*, [1969] 2 All E.R. 1173; [1970] Ch. 408.

[12] See (1958), 74 L.Q.R. 182 (R. E. Megarry), and *Re Richardson's Will Trusts*, [1958] 1 All E.R. 538; [1958] Ch. 504.

[13] See, generally (1947), 12 Con. 28 (J. G. Fleming); (1963), 27 Con. 92 (J. A. Andrews).

result with the provisions of s. 9 of the Wills Act 1837,[14] which require a testamentary disposition to be made in a specified form. At first the accepted explanation was that this was an application of the maxim we have already met, that "equity will not permit a statute to be used as an instrument of fraud"[15]: it would be fraud on the part of the secret trustee to rely on the absence of the statutory formalities in order to deny the trust and keep for himself property which he well knew the testator did not intend him to enjoy beneficially. More recent cases, however, appear to establish that there is no conflict with the Wills Act 1837, since the trust operates outside or, as it is said, dehors the will. Where the will is executed in proper form, X will be able to establish his legal title to the property: but if the intention of the testator has been communicated to X by the testator in his lifetime, and X has acquiesced, his conscience will be bound in equity and he will be compelled to hold the property on trust for the persons or purposes indicated by the testator.[16] This trust is not regarded as a testamentary disposition coming within the Wills Act, but as a trust within the ordinary equity jurisdiction.

A half-secret trust differs from a fully-secret trust in that the will declares that the property is given to X on trust, though the trusts are not expressed in the will, but have likewise been communicated to X by the testator during his lifetime.[17] Though there are authorities going back as far as the seventeenth century, there was greater difficulty in establishing their validity. So long as the basis was thought to be fraud, the difficulty was that even if the intended beneficiaries did not take, it was clear that the secret trustee could not keep the property for himself as he was expressed to be a mere trustee in the will. If the Wills Act applied to invalidate the secret trust there would be a resulting trust to the estate. In *Blackwell* v. *Blackwell*,[18] however, it was finally established that half-secret and fully-secret trusts are enforced on the same principles.

Two cases may be mentioned as clear illustrations of the modern view. In *Re Gardner*[19] there was a secret trust and one of the beneficiaries thereunder had predeceased the testatrix. Although a gift by will lapses if the beneficiary predeceases the testator it was held that the share of the deceased beneficiary did not lapse, but passed to her personal representative, since her title arose not under the will, but by the trust created[20] during her lifetime by communication and acceptance thereof by the secret trustee. In *Re Young*[1] the problem arose

---

[14] Prior to this Act, the Statute of Frauds 1677, and see p. 59, *supra*.

[15] See, e.g., *Jones* v. *Badley* (1868), 3 Ch.App. 362, *per* Lord Cairns; *McCormick* v. *Grogan* (1869), L.R. 4 H.L. 82, *per* Lord Hatherley.

[16] See, e.g., *Cullen* v. *A.G. for Ireland* (1866), L.R. 1 H.L. 190, *per* Lord Westbury; *Blackwell* v. *Blackwell*, [1929] A.C. 318, H.L. See also the discussion in Nathan and Marshall, *A Casebook on Trusts*, 5th Ed., pp. 285-287.

[17] See p. 95, *infra*, for the position as to the time of communication in the case of a half-secret trust.

[18] *Supra*, approving *Re Fleetwood* (1880), 15 Ch.D., 594; *Re Huxtable*, [1902] 2 Ch. 793, C.A.

[19] [1923] 2 Ch. 230.

[20] Though it illustrates the present point well, it is difficult to see how the beneficiary could have obtained a transmissible interest before the trust was completely constituted by the trust property vesting in the secret trustee on the death of the testatrix.

[1] [1950] 2 All E.R. 1245; [1951] Ch. 344.

in an acute form. Section 15 of the Wills Act 1837[2] provides that a legacy to an attesting witness is ineffective; the facts were that one of the attesting witnesses was a beneficiary under a secret trust. It was held that he did not take under the will and that he was therefore unaffected by the statutory provisions. "The whole theory," it was said,[3] "of the formation of a secret trust is that the Wills Act 1837 has nothing to do with the matter." It may be added that where it is the secret trustee, and not the beneficiary thereunder, who predeceases the testator, or renounces or disclaims the devise or legacy, the better view is, perhaps, that the secret trust fails, on the ground that it only affects the property by reason of the personal obligation binding the individual devisee or legatee.[4]

There is no general agreement as to whether secret trusts are express or constructive. Snell[5] and Underhill[6], for example, both deal with secret trusts under the head of express trusts: Marshall[7], while observing that this represents the current of opinion, himself takes the contrary view that both fully secret and half-secret trusts are constructive trusts, on the ground that "the court of equity finds the legatee or devisee in possession of the legal title to property and imposes on him an equitable obligation to hold that legal title on trust for a third party as a result of what has taken place outside the will". Sheridan[8] considers that although half-secret trusts are express, fully-secret trusts are constructive. But, it may be asked, as the trust operates outside the will, why should the fact that the existence of the trust is disclosed in the will alter the character of the trust? It is submitted that secret trusts are express trusts, being based on the expressed intention of the testator communicated to and acquiesced in by the secret trustee. On this basis one runs into the difficulty that s. 53 (1) (b) of the Law of Property Act 1925[9] would seem to require writing where the subject of the secret trust is land. This was in fact held to be the case in Re Baillie[10], which concerned a half-secret trust, but more recently, in Ottaway v. Norman,[11] a fully-secret trust of land was held valid on parol evidence. In this case the trust seems to have been treated as constructive rather than express, but there was no discussion of this point, and no reference was made to any possible requirement of writing. However, even if a secret trust is express, it is arguable that it should be enforced notwithstanding the absence of writing by an application of the maxim that equity will not permit a statute to be used as an instru-

---

[2] Now modified by the Wills Act 1968, which allows the attesting witness-legatee to take if the will is duly executed without his attestation.
[3] Per Danckwerts J., at pp. 1250, 350.
[4] Re Maddock, [1902] 2 Ch. 220, C.A., per Cozens Hardy L.J., at p. 231; contra Blackwell v. Blackwell, [1929] A.C. 318, 328, H.L., per Lord Buckmaster.
[5] Principles of Equity, 27th Ed., pp. 106 et seq.
[6] Law of Trusts and Trustees, 12th Ed., pp. 125 et seq.
[7] Editing Nathan and Marshall, A Casebook on Trusts, 5th Ed., p. 286; (1972), 23 N.I.L.Q. 263 (R. Burgess).
[8] (1951), 67 L.Q.R. (L. A. Sheridan).
[9] See Section 1b, p. 52, ante.
[10] (1886), 2 T.L.R. 660. In Re Young, [1950] 2 All E.R. 1245; [1951] Ch. 344, where the trust was held to have been validly established by parol evidence, no point was taken on s. 53 (1) (b).
[11] [1971] 3 All E.R. 1325; [1972] Ch. 698.

ment of fraud.[12] Maudsley[13] also takes the view that secret trusts are express trusts, but considers that in the case of a fully secret trust, on the ground of fraud the apparent beneficiary under the will would be bound by a constructive trust, which would not require writing even if it involved land.[14]

It should be added that in the recent case of *Nichols* v. *I.R. Comrs.*[15] it was conceded by counsel that the doctrine of secret trusts applies to *inter vivos* gifts, and reference was made to *Bannister* v. *Bannister*,[16] which has already been discussed. It is suggested, however, that the better view is that of Pennycuick J. who observed, in *Re Tyler's Fund Trusts*:[17] "It is probably true to say that the particular principles of law applicable to secret trusts are really concerned only with trusts created by will".

b Fully-secret trusts

As already indicated, the essential factors that must be present in order to raise a trust are the communication of the intention of the testator to the secret trustee, and his express or tacit[18] promise to carry out the testator's intention on the faith of which the testator either makes a disposition in favour of the secret trustee,[19] or leaves an existing disposition unrevoked.[20] A trust is raised in exactly the same way if on the strength of such a promise by an intestate successor, a man fails to make a will,[1] or if he destroys a codicil so as to revive the effect of prior testamentary provisions in favour of the secret trustee.[2] In most of the cases the obligation imposed on the secret trustee is to make some form of *inter vivos* transfer, but in *Ottaway* v. *Norman*[3] the doctrine was held to apply equally where the obligation was to make a will in favour of the beneficiary under the secret trust.

The communication to the secret trustee, which may be through an authorised agent,[4] must take place during the testator's lifetime, though it matters not whether it is before or after the date of the will. If, however, the alleged secret trustee only learns of the alleged trust after the death of the testator, the trust will be ineffective. On the death the property passes under the will to a

---

[12] See s. 1 d, p. 57, *ante.*
[13] Editing Hanbury's *Modern Equity*, 9th Ed., pp. 169-170.
[14] Section 53 (2) of the Law of Property Act 1925.
[15] [1973] 3 All E.R. 632.
[16] [1948] 2 All E.R. 133, C.A. discussed *supra*, p. 59.
[17] [1967] 3 All E.R. 389, at p. 392. The dictum of Pennycuick J. requires slight modification to cover the analogous cases referred to in the next following paragraph *infra*. The phrase "created by will" is not a very happy one—see pp. 90, 91, *supra*—but the meaning seems clear.
[18] If the intention is communicated to the secret trustee, it seems that silence on his part will normally be treated as consent to act—*Moss* v. *Cooper* (1861), 1 J. & H. 352.
[19] *Drakeford* v. *Wilks* (1747), 3 Atk. 539.   [20] *Moss* v. *Cooper* (1861), 1 John & H. 352.
[1] *Stickland* v. *Aldridge* (1804), 9 Ves. 516; *Re Gardner*, [1920] 2 Ch. 523, C.A.
[2] *Tharp* v. *Tharp*, [1916] 1 Ch. 142; compromised on appeal [1916], 2 Ch. 205, C.A.
[3] [1971] 3 All E.R. 1325; [1972] Ch. 698—the secret trustee was beneficially entitled for life. It was observed in this case that if a will contains a gift which is in terms absolute, clear evidence is needed before the court will assume that the testator did not mean what he said. The decision is not without its difficulties—see (1973), 36 M.L.R. 210 (S. M. Bandali).
[4] *Moss* v. *Cooper, supra*, where the question of communication through an unauthorised agent was raised but not answered.

beneficiary whose conscience is perfectly clear, and his absolute title will not be affected by anything he may subsequently learn about the testator's intentions, which have not been expressed in compliance with the Wills Act 1837. Thus in *Wallgrave* v. *Tebbs*[5] the testator bequeathed £12,000 and devised certain lands to T. and M. as joint tenants. Neither T. nor M. had ever had any communication with the testator about his will, or about any of his intentions or wishes with respect to the disposition of his property. The evidence showed that the testator wished certain charitable purposes to be carried out and felt confident that T. and M. would carry them out. T. and M. claimed to take the property absolutely, free from the trust, though they admitted that they would, if they succeeded, apply the property substantially as the trustee wished. It was held that in the absence of any communication in the testator's lifetime, T. and M. took absolutely.

It is not sufficient to communicate merely the fact of the trust to the secret trustee: the details of the trust must also be communicated to and accepted by him. If there is merely communication and acceptance of the fact of the trust, the secret trustee will hold on trust for the residuary devisees or legatees, or the persons entitled on intestacy if there is no residuary gift, or if residue is given on a secret trust.[6] He cannot take beneficially, as he has accepted the position of trustee, but communication of the particular trusts after the death by an unattested paper is not permitted, as this would be a means by which a testator could evade the provisions of the Wills Act 1837.[7] It would, however, probably be a sufficient communication if the details of the trust were handed over to the secret trustee by the testator during his lifetime in a sealed envelope, even though this was marked "Not to be opened until after my death".[8]

Difficulties have arisen where there has been communication to one, or some only, of two or more secret trustees[9]. If the gift in the will is to two or more persons as tenants in common, then only the person, or persons, to whom the secret trust was communicated in the testator's lifetime are bound by it; the other person or persons take their respective shares beneficially.[10] Where the gift is to persons as joint tenants a curious distinction is drawn between the

---

[5] (1855), 2 K. & J. 313. See also *Jones* v. *Badley* (1868), 3 Ch. App. 362.

[6] The same result would follow if the trusts were communicated but were void for uncertainty, illegality, or other cause. For this reason in many cases prior to the Mortmain and Charitable Uses Act 1891, where the alleged trust was for charitable purposes, it was the residuary devisees or legatees or intestate successors who alleged that there was a secret trust since, so far as the property comprised realty or impure personalty, such a trust would be void under the Statute of Mortmain 1736, and the secret trustees would therefore hold on trust for them. The alleged secret trustees, who argued that no trust existed, often in fact fully intended to carry out the testator's wishes if they succeeded in their claim, though, of course, they could not be compelled to do so.

[7] *Re Boyes* (1884), 26 Ch.D. 531.

[8] *Re Boyes, supra*; *Re Keen*, [1937] 1 All E.R. 452; [1937] Ch. 236, C.A., where arguing by analogy Lord Wright M.R. said "a ship which sails under sealed orders is sailing under orders though the exact terms are not ascertained by the captain till later".

[9] The propositions below are disputed in (1972), 88 L.Q.R. 225 (B. Perrins) where it is argued that in every case where there has been a communication to X (one of two secret trustees X and Y) only, yet it is alleged that X and Y are both bound by the secret trust, the question is whether the gift to Y in the will was induced by the promise made by X to the testator.

[10] *Tee* v. *Ferris* (1856), 2 K. & J. 357; *Re Stead*, [1900] 1 Ch. 237.

case where one, or more, of the secret trustees have accepted the trust prior to the execution of the will, and the case where the acceptance was subsequent to the will (though, of course, during the testator's lifetime). In the first case all the joint tenants are bound by the trust,[11] on the ground that no one can take a benefit which has been procured by fraud. For no satisfactory reason this principle does not apparently apply in the latter case, where only the person or persons who have accepted the trust are bound by it.[12]

c Half-secret trusts

Here, as we have seen, the will expressly states that the gift is on trust, so there is no possibility of the secret trustee claiming beneficially. The problem accordingly is whether he holds on trust for the residuary devisees or legatees, or the persons entitled on intestacy, if there is no residuary gift or if residue is given, or whether the secret trusts communicated to and accepted by him can be enforced. There are, however, rather more difficulties and uncertainties in the relevant law than in the case of fully-secret trusts.

What may, perhaps, be called the primary rule is the rule that evidence as to the alleged half-secret trust is inadmissible if it contradicts the terms of the will. Thus in *Re Keen*[13] the testator bequeathed £10,000 to X and Y "to be held upon trust and disposed of by them among such person, persons or charities as may be notified by me to them or either of them during my lifetime". As a matter of construction it was held that the will referred to a future notification, and the court held that evidence of a prior notification was inadmissible as it would be inconsistent with the express terms of the will. Another aspect of this rule is that a person named as trustee in the will is not permitted to set up any beneficial interest in himself,[14] though it is a different matter if on its true construction the will gives property to a person conditionally on his discharging the testator's wishes communicated to him.[15]

A further problem in connection with this rule is where the will gives property to persons in some such terms as in *Re Spencer's Will*[16] "relying, but not by way of trust, upon their applying the sum in or towards the objects privately communicated to them" by the testator. In that case itself the Court of Appeal held that evidence would be admissible to show that the legatees had in fact accepted a secret trust,[17] though it is not made clear how this is to be reconciled with the rule, as such evidence would contradict the terms of the will. Indeed, it seems doubtful whether the point was argued. This decision was distinguished in *Re Falkiner*,[18] where it was held that the true inference was that the alleged secret trustee, knowing the contents of the will, had agreed to give effect to the testatrix's wishes in accordance with the scheme of

---

[11] *Russell* v. *Jackson* (1852), 10 Hare 204; *Re Stead, supra.*
[12] *Moss* v. *Cooper* (1861), 1 John & H. 352; *Re Stead, supra.*
[13] [1937] 1 All E.R. 452; [1937] Ch. 236, C.A. See also *Re Spence*, [1949] W.N. 237.
[14] *Re Rees' Will Trusts*, [1949] 2 All E.R. 1003; [1950] Ch. 204, C.A.; *Re Huxtable, supra.*
    Re Pugh's Will Trusts, [1967] 3 All E.R. 337, Cp. *Re Tyler's Fund Trusts*, [1967] 3 All
    E.R. 389.
[15] See, e.g., *Irvine* v. *Sullivan* (1869), L.R. 8 Eq. 673.
[16] (1887), 3 T.L.R. 822, C.A.
[17] This, of course, would be a fully-secret trust, not a half-secret trust.
[18] [1924] 1 Ch. 88, applied in *Re Stirling*, [1954] 2 All E.R. 113.

the will, which included a provision that there should be no trust or legal obligation.

Turning to another matter, the most important distinction between fully-secret and half-secret trusts is that in the latter case the communication to and acceptance of the trusts will not merely be ineffective if it takes place after the testator's death, but even if it takes place during his lifetime but after the execution of his will. "A testator," it has been said,[19] "cannot reserve to himself a power of making future unwitnessed dispositions by merely naming a trustee and leaving the purposes of the trust to be supplied afterwards, nor can a legatee give testamentary validity to an unexecuted codicil by accepting an indefinite trust, never communicated to him in the testator's lifetime", and on this basis it has been stated that in the case of a half-secret trust communication cannot be effective if made after the date of the will. This argument, which, if valid, would apply equally to fully-secret trusts, is, it is submitted, invalid as it fails to take into account the basis of secret trusts, i.e. that they operate entirely outside the will. The secret trustee, whether it is a fully-secret or half-secret trust, should, on principle, take the property bound by an equitable obligation if he has accepted the trust at any time during the testator's lifetime, whether before or after the date of the will being irrelevant. However, although not finally settled, the weight of dicta favours the view that in the case of half-secret trusts the communication and acceptance of the trust must be prior to, or contemporaneously with, the execution of the will,[20] and the contrary view seems to have been considered unarguable in Re Bateman's Will Trusts,[1] the most recent case.

Where a testator makes a gift to two or more persons who on the face of the will are trustees, who always hold as joint tenants, it is clear, assuming that the law as stated in the preceding paragraph is correct, that if there had been no communication of the trusts by the time that the will was executed, the trustees would hold the property on trust for the residuary devisees or residuary legatees, or the persons entitled on intestacy if there is no residuary gift or if it is a gift of residue.[2] Where the trust has been communicated to and accepted before the date of the will by one, or some only, of the trustees the position seems to be the same as in fully-secret trusts, i.e. the gift being to them as joint

---

[19] Per Viscount Sumner in Blackwell v. Blackwell, [1929] A.C. 318, at p. 339, H.L.

[20] Johnson v. Ball (1851), 5 De.G. & Sm. 85; Blackwell v. Blackwell, supra; Re Keen, [1937] 1 All E.R. 452; [1937] Ch. 236, C.A. The apparent rule is criticised by Holdsworth (1937), 53 L.Q.R. 501, but approved (1972), 23 N.I.L.Q. 263 (R. Burgess). The unsatisfactory position is, perhaps, due to confusion with the probate doctrine of incorporation by reference, under which a document not properly executed in accordance with the provisions of the Wills Act 1837 may be incorporated in the will and granted probate. In order for this to happen the document sought to be incorporated must already be in existence when the will is executed and referred to therein as an existing document in terms enabling it to be clearly identified. See In the Goods of Smart, [1902] P. 238; Re Jones, [1942] 1 All E.R. 642; [1942] Ch. 328; Re Schintz's Will Trusts, [1951] 1 All E.R. 1095; [1951] Ch. 870.

[1] [1970] 3 All E.R. 817.

[2] The same result would follow if the trusts were duly communicated in time, but were void for uncertainty, illegality or other cause. See, e.g., Re Hawksley's Settlement, [1934] Ch. 384; [1934] All E.R. Rep. 94.

tenants, acceptance by one binds all.[3] What has been said is subject to the qualification that, as we have already seen, if the evidence as to communication contradicts the terms of the will it is inadmissible; so if the will states that the trusts have been communicated to all the trustees, evidence of communication to one only would seem to be inadmissible.[4]

The last point to be mentioned was decided in *Re Cooper*.[5] There the testator bequeathed £5,000 to two persons as trustees on the face of the will, and the trusts were duly communicated to them by the testator and accepted prior to the execution of the will. Subsequently the testator executed a codicil whereby he, in effect, increased the legacy to £10,000, the trustees "knowing my wishes regarding that sum". The increase of the legacy was never communicated to the trustees by the testator. It was held that the secret trusts were effective as to the first £5,000 but failed as to the additional £5,000 given by the codicil.

---

[3] *Re Young*, [1950] 2 All E.R. 1245; [1951] Ch. 344.
[4] *Re Spence*, [1949] W.N. 237. Contrast *Re Keen*, [1937] 1 All E.R. 452; [1937] Ch. 236, C.A., where the will referred to communication to the trustees "or one of them".
[5] [1939] 3 All E.R. 586; [1939] Ch. 811, C.A.

CHAPTER 4

Implied, Resulting and Constructive Trusts

The somewhat confused classification of trusts has already been discussed.[1] In this chapter five different types of circumstances are considered. Mutual wills, discussed in the first section, are generally regarded as a case of implied trust. The following two sections—transfer into and purchase in the name of another, and failure to dispose of the equitable interest—are cases of resulting trust. The last two sections—vendor under a contract for the sale of land, and strangers to the trust—are both cases of constructive trust.

1 MUTUAL WILLS[2]

Where two persons, usually, but not essentially,[3] husband and wife, have made an agreement as to the disposal of their property, and each has in accordance with the agreement executed a will, the two wills containing, *mutatis mutandis*, similar provisions, such wills are known as mutual wills. The mutual wills may give the survivor only a life interest,[4] or, it seems, after some hesitation, an absolute interest.[5] In either case it may well be a term of the agreement that the wills shall not be revoked,[6] and if one or the other nevertheless purports to revoke his mutual will, various problems may arise.

In the first place, it is quite clear that a will cannot be made irrevocable.[7] In *In the Estate of Heys*[8] a husband and wife made mutual wills in 1907. The husband died in 1911 and his will was duly proved, under which the wife took certain benefits. Subsequently the wife executed a codicil in 1912 and a fresh

---

[1] See Chapter 2, Section 4, p. 43, *ante*.
[2] See, generally (1951), 15 Con. 28 (G. Boughen Graham); (1970), 34 Con. 230 (R. Burgess).
[3] *Walpole* v. *Orford* (1797), 3 Ves. 402.
[4] E.g. *Dufour* v. *Pereira* (1769), Dick. 419—the earliest and leading case on mutual wills.
[5] *Re Green*, [1950] 2 All E.R. 913; [1951] Ch. 148, disregarding doubts suggested by *Re Oldham*, [1925] Ch. 75.
[6] Except, of course, as a result of a subsequent agreement.
[7] *Vynior's Case* (1609), 8 Co.Rep. 81b.
[8] [1914] P. 192.

will in 1913. These later instruments were made in breach of a definite agreement between the husband and wife in 1907 when the mutual wills were executed that they should be irrevocable. It was held that the will of 1907 was none the less revocable, for our testamentary law regards revocability as an essential characteristic of a will, and probate was accordingly ordered of the will of 1913.

It by no means follows, however, that an agreement such as that entered into by the husband and wife above in 1907 is worthless. At law, an action for damages will lie for breach of a covenant or contract not to revoke a will,[9] and, in equity, a mutual will of which probate will not be granted may be enforced under a trust. Equity takes the view, where two persons have agreed to make and have in fact executed mutual wills, and where it was a term of the agreement that such wills should not be revoked, that the first of them to die dies with the implied promise of the survivor that the agreement shall hold good. Accordingly, if the survivor revokes[10] or alters his will, as we have seen he can, his personal representatives will take his property upon trust to perform the agreement, for the will of the one who has died first has, by his death, become irrevocable.[11]

In order to establish the trust it is not sufficient to establish an agreement to make mutual wills followed by their due execution: it is essential that an agreement not to revoke them be proved. This agreement, although it does not restrain the legal right to revoke, is the foundation of the right in equity.[12] Such an agreement will not be implied from the mere making of mutual wills. In *Re Oldham*[13] it was pointed out that "the fact that those two wills were made in identical terms connotes no more than an agreement of so making them"; other evidence, which may consist of recitals in the mutual wills,[14] or of evidence outside them[15] must be brought to establish the agreement not to revoke them.

Even assuming that an agreement not to revoke the mutual wills is established, a trust is not created at once, and, indeed, may never arise at all. Clearly the parties may release each other from their bargain by mutual agreement, and it seems that during their joint lifetimes either may revoke his will separately, provided he gives notice of the revocation to the other party.[16] Such other party thereby acquires an opportunity to alter his own will, and the ground upon which a trust is raised ceases to exist. Further, even though no notice be given during their joint lives, where the one who dies first has departed from the bargain by executing a fresh will revoking the former one, the survivor, who has, on the death of the other party to the agreement, notice of the alteration, cannot claim to have the later will of the deceased set aside or modified, or indirectly enforced by way of declaration of trust or other-

---

[9] *Robinson* v. *Ommanney* (1883), 23 Ch.D. 285, C.A.—but not where the revocation is by the subsequent marriage of the covenantor.
[10] This includes revocation by a subsequent marriage.
[11] *Dufour* v. *Pereira* (1769), Dick. 419; *Stone* v. *Hoskins*, [1905] P. 194.
[12] *Gray* v. *Perpetual Trustee Company Ltd.*, [1928] A.C. 391, P.C.
[13] [1925] Ch. 75.
[14] *Re Green*, [1950] 2 All E.R. 913; [1951] Ch. 148.
[15] *In the Estate of Heys*, [1914] P. 192.
[16] *Dufour* v. *Pereira*, *supra*.

wise.[17] In such case, therefore, no trust will ever come into being. It is the death of the first to die, leaving his will unrevoked by which he carries his part of the bargain into execution and makes his will irrevocable that brings the trust into being. This appears from *Re Hagger*,[18] a case in which a husband and wife made not mutual wills, but a joint will, to which the same principles apply. By the joint will the survivor was to have a life interest in certain joint property with remainders over. The husband and wife agreed not to revoke the joint will. The wife was the first to die, and subsequently, but before the death of the husband, one of the remaindermen died. It was held that from the death of the wife the husband held the property upon the trusts of the joint will, and accordingly there was no lapse of the share of the beneficiary who survived the wife but predeceased the husband, and his share was payable to his personal representatives as part of his estate.

It is submitted that the better view where the above conditions are fulfilled is that the trust arises automatically on the death of the first to die, and does not depend upon the acceptance by the survivor of benefits given to him by the will of the first to die.[19] There are *dicta*,[20] however, in some cases which suggest that it is the acceptance of benefits by the survivor which gives rise to the trust: the point has not arisen directly for decision and the former view seems more consistent with the principles upon which mutual wills are enforced, namely, that the first to die made his will in reliance on the promise of the survivor and that by his death the will of the first to die has become irrevocable.[1]

In practice, the most difficult problem may well be to ascertain exactly what property is subject to the trusts: this is strictly a question of the construction of the mutual wills. In *Re Hagger*,[2] the facts of which have already been mentioned, it was held that the joint will effected a severance of the joint interest of the husband and wife, and the trust operated as from the wife's death, not only on her interest in the property, but also on the interest of the surviving husband. In *Re Green*,[3] the mutual wills of husband and wife were in identical form, *mutatis mutandis*. Apart from certain specific real property, the husband divided his residue into two equal shares, one moiety being considered as his own personal estate and the other moiety as the equivalent to any benefit which he had received from his wife by reason of her predeceasing him, as in fact happened. The husband subsequently revoked his first, mutual, will and after the husband's death the court held that the trust operated only on one-half of the husband's residuary estate, i.e. the moiety which he had notionally received from his wife. The other moiety passed under his fresh will. The questions as to how far in such circumstances the survivor is entitled to dispose of his own property in his lifetime, and as to

---

[17] *Stone* v. *Hoskins*, [1905] P. 194. But there may be a claim for damages where there has been unilateral revocation in breach of contract.

[18] [1930] 2 Ch. 190.

[19] This view seems to have been preferred by Lord Camden in *Dufour* v. *Pereira*, *supra*, and by Clauson J. in *Re Hagger*, *supra*.

[20] Cf. Gorrel Barnes P. in *Stone* v. *Hoskins*, *supra*, and Astbury J. in *Re Oldham*, [1925] Ch. 75.

[1] See (1951), 14 M.L.R. 136 (J. D. B. Mitchell).

[2] *Supra*.

[3] [1950] 2 All E.R. 913; [1951] Ch. 148.

what extent after-acquired property is subject to the trust have not yet been judicially explored.[4]

As has been mentioned in connection with *Re Hagger*,[5] the same principles apply where two persons have executed a joint will.[6] In such case on the death of one of the joint testators probate will be granted of so much of the joint will as becomes operative on his death.[7] The survivor of joint testators will be bound by a trust in the same way and to the same extent as if they had executed mutual wills.

2 TRANSFER INTO AND PURCHASE IN THE NAME OF ANOTHER AND RELATED CASES

a Purchase in the name of another or in the joint names of the purchaser and another

Whenever a man buys either real or personal property and has it conveyed or registered or otherwise put into the name of another, or of himself and another jointly, it is presumed that that other holds the property on trust for the person who has paid the purchase money. The classic statement of the law is to be found in the judgment of Eyre C.B. in *Dyer v. Dyer*[8]:

> "The clear result of all the cases, without a single exception, is that the trust of a legal estate, whether freehold, copyhold, or leasehold; whether taken in the names of the purchasers and others jointly, or in the names of others without that of the purchaser; whether in one name or several; whether jointly or successive—results to the man who advances the purchase-money."

Although *Dyer v. Dyer*[9] refers only to interests in land, the principle has always been treated as equally applicable to pure personalty.[10] The same principle governs analogous cases, as in *Re Howes*,[11] where a testatrix put £500 on deposit at a bank in the name of her niece.[12] She never informed the niece of what she had done, retained the deposit note and purported to dispose of the money by a codicil to her will. It was held that even though this was not strictly a purchase, the equitable principle gave rise to a resulting trust to the testatrix. It also applies in a similar way where there is a joint advance by

---

[4] See the discussion in (1951), 14 M.L.R. 136 (J. D. B. Mitchell).

[5] *Supra.*

[6] It was at one time thought that a joint will was impossible (e.g. *per* Lord Mansfield in *Earl of Darlington v. Pulteney* (1775), 1 Cowp. 260, 268), but there is now no doubt that it can be valid (see, e.g., *Re Duddell*, [1932] 1 Ch. 585; [1932] All E.R. Rep. 714). Joint wills are rare in practice and Underhill's *Law of Trusts and Trustees*, 12th Ed., p. 49, states that they are to be deprecated and that practitioners should refuse to draft them.

[7] *In the Goods of Piazzi-Smyth*, [1898] P. 7.

[8] (1788), 2 Cox. Eq. Cas. 92, 93: cited with approval by Lord Upjohn in *Pettitt v. Pettitt*, [1969] 2 All E.R. 385; [1970] A.C. 777, H.L.

[9] *Supra.*

[10] See, e.g., *The Venture*, [1908] P. 218, C.A.; *Re Policy No. 6402 of the Scottish Equitable Life Assurance Society*, [1902] 1 Ch. 282; *Shephard v. Cartwright*, [1954] 3 All E.R. 649, [1955] A.C. 431, H.L.; *Bateman Television, Ltd. v. Bateman and Thomas*, [1971] N.Z.L.R. 453, C.A.

[11] (1905), 21 T.L.R. 501.

[12] She was not *in loco parentis* to the niece, so the presumption of advancement did not apply—see p. 105, *post.*

two or more persons, but the conveyance or transfer is taken in the name of one only. For instance, if X advances £3,000 and Y advances £1,500 towards the purchase of property which is conveyed into the name of X alone, X will hold the property as to one-third on a resulting trust for Y.[13]

There is no need for the conveyance or other instrument of transfer to contain any reference to the fact that the purchase price has been paid by someone other than the transferee. Parol evidence is always admissible to establish who in fact advanced the money,[14] and this is so, even though the consideration is expressed to be paid by the nominal purchaser. The fact of the advance must, of course, be satisfactorily proved by evidence,[15] which may, however, be circumstantial evidence, such as that the nominal purchaser had not the means to provide the purchase money.[16] Evidence must also show that the money was intended to be advanced by the person alleging the resulting trust in the character of purchaser: if the evidence merely established a loan of some or all the money used for the purchase, there would be no resulting trust and the person lending the money would be a mere creditor.[17] If the fact of the advance is established, absence of writing is immaterial, even in the case of land, since the statutory provisions as to writing expressly exclude the creation and operation of resulting, implied and constructive trusts.[18]

An attempt was recently made[19] to extend the principle of *Dyer* v. *Dyer*[20] to an informal flat-sharing arrangement where the tenancy agreement was in the name of the defendant, but the rent and other expenses were shared equally between the plaintiffs and the defendant. It was held that "purchase money" does not include rent, and accordingly the sharing of the rent[21] did not establish a resulting trust in favour of the plaintiffs. Rent, unlike purchase money, is not paid for the acquisition of a capital asset, but for the use of a property during the term.

The presumption of a resulting trust applies equally where the parties were at the relevant time husband and wife. There has been much litigation, in particular in relation to the matrimonial home. Further discussion of this aspect of resulting trusts will be found at pp. 106 *et seq.* below in conjunction with the presumption of advancement.

As to a claim that there is a resulting trust, which involves setting up a transaction which is fraudulent, illegal, or contrary to public policy, see Chapter 5, Section 1d and h, pp. 129, 134, *post.*

---

[13] *Diwell* v. *Farnes*, [1959] 2 All E.R. 379, C.A.; *Bull* v. *Bull*, [1955] 1 All E.R. 253; [1955] 1 Q.B. 234, C.A. But if X and Y had contributed equally to the purchase price, they would presumably be entitled as joint tenants in equity by analogy to the position where the conveyance or transfer is into joint names. In such case the presumption is that if the contributions are equal they take jointly, but if their contributions are unequal they take as tenants in common in shares proportionate to their contributions—see *Lake* v. *Gibson* (1729), 1 Eq. Cas. Abr. 290; *Aveling* v. *Knipe* (1815), 19 Ves. 441; *Robinson* v. *Preston* (1858), 4 K. & J. 505.

[14] *Heard* v. *Pilley* (1869), 4 Ch. App. 548.

[15] *Willis* v. *Willis* (1740), 2 Atk. 71; *Groves* v. *Groves* (1829), 3 Y. & J. 163.

[16] *Willis* v. *Willis, supra.*

[17] *Aveling* v. *Knipe* (1815), 19 Ves. 441.

[18] Law of Property Act 1925, s. 53 (2), replacing the Statute of Frauds 1677, s. 8.

[19] *Savage* v. *Dunningham*, [1973] 3 All E.R. 429.

[20] *Supra.*

[21] *A fortiori* the sharing of the other expenses.

b Voluntary conveyance or transfer into the name of another or into the joint names of the grantor and another

It is necessary to draw a distinction between land and pure personalty.

i As to land, the position has for long been curiously unsettled. Before the Statute of Uses 1535 on a voluntary conveyance a resulting use was raised in favour of the grantor. After 1535 this use was executed by the statute with the result that nothing passed by the grant. Later land was conveyed unto and to the use of the grantee, and the words "to the use" would then operate to prevent the resulting use being implied. Whether the grantee, who thus obtained the legal estate, held it on a resulting trust for the grantor was much disputed, and has never been definitely settled.[22] Nor has the matter been put beyond dispute by s. 60 (3) of the Law of Property Act 1925, which provides:

> "In a voluntary conveyance a resulting trust for the grantor shall not be implied merely by reason that the property[23] is not expressed to be conveyed for the use or benefit of the grantee."

Though recently referred to[24] by the Court of Appeal as a "debatable question", the better view, since 1925, seems to be that, in the absence of evidence to the contrary, there will be no resulting trust on a voluntary conveyance to another,[1] though some[2] take the contrary view on the ground that there is nothing to show that the equitable estate is to pass.

There seems to be neither decision nor academic discussion of the effect of a conveyance of land into the joint names of the grantor and another: all that can usefully be said is that there is here a stronger argument for a resulting trust than where there is a conveyance into the name of another alone.

ii As to pure personalty, it seems to be settled that on a transfer into the joint names of the transferor and another, there is a presumption of a resulting trust for the transferor. A clear example is *Re Vinogradoff*,[3] where a testatrix, during her lifetime, had transferred £800 War Loan into the joint names of herself and her infant granddaughter aged four years. After the death of the testatrix, it was held that her granddaughter held the War Loan on a resulting trust for the testatrix's estate.

It is less certain whether there is a presumption of a resulting trust where there is a transfer into the name of another alone. The weight of opinion

---

[22] In favour of a resulting trust are Maitland's *Equity*, 2nd (Brunyate) Ed., p. 77; White and Tudor's *Leading Cases in Equity*, 9th Ed., Vol. 2, p. 762; *contra*, dicta in *Young* v. *Peachy* (1741), 2 Atk. 254, 257; *Lloyd & Jobson* v. *Spillet* (1740), 2 Atk. 148, 150; *Fowkes* v. *Pascoe* (1875), 10 Ch. App. 343, 348. See discussion in Hanbury's *Equity*, 3rd Ed., pp. 180–182.

[23] By s. 205 (1) (xx) this means, unless the context otherwise requires, any interest in real or personal property. It is submitted that the context restricts the meaning to land.

[24] *Hodgson* v. *Marks*, [1971] 2 All E.R. 684; [1971] Ch. 892 *per* Russell L.J. giving the judgment of the court. See *Neazor* v. *Hoyle* (1962), 32 D.L.R. (2d) 131.

[1] As stated, e.g., in Snell's *Principles of Equity*, 27th Ed., p. 180; Nathan and Marshall, *A Casebook on Trusts*, 5th Ed., pp. 261, 262.

[2] E.g. Underhill, *Law of Trusts and Trustees*, 12th Ed., p. 219.

[3] [1935] W.N. 68. See also *Batstone* v. *Salter* (1875), 10 Ch. App. 431; *Standing* v. *Bowring* (1885), 31 Ch. D. 282, C.A.; *Young* v. *Sealey*, [1949] 1 All E.R. 92; [1949] Ch. 278.

seems to be in favour of a resulting trust in such case,[4] though there seems
something to be said for the opinion expressed by Richards C.B.[5] that "if I
deliver over money, or transfer stock to another, even though he should be a
stranger, it would be *prima facie* a gift".

c   Rebutting the presumption of a resulting trust

"Trusts," it has been said,[6] "are neither created nor implied by law to defeat
the intentions of donors or settlors; they are created or implied or are held to
result in favour of donors or settlors in order to carry out and give effect to
their true intentions, expressed or implied . . ." In practice, in this context,
this means that the somewhat artificial and formal rule that the circumstances
we have been discussing give rise to a resulting trust, only applies in the absence
of sufficient evidence to the contrary. Accordingly, the presumed intention
of a person who purchases property in the name of another whether alone or
jointly, that that other shall be a bare trustee for him, will not necessarily
prevail if evidence is adduced to show that the true intention is otherwise.
The same is true where there is a voluntary conveyance or transfer which gives
rise to a presumption of a resulting trust. Even parol evidence[7] may suffice to
establish that at the relevant time the true intention of the person who provided
the purchase money or transferred the property was that the person into whose
name the property was conveyed or transferred solely or jointly with his own
should take some beneficial interest. The relevant time is, of course, the date
of the purchase or transfer and if the evidence[8] establishes an intention at that
time to make an absolute gift, the donor cannot subsequently change his mind
and recall the property which he has had put in the then intended donee's
name.[9]

Evidence to rebut a resulting trust may establish that there is no resulting
trust at all, and that the person in whose name the property is purchased was
intended to take absolutely and beneficially,[10] but it may merely rebut the
presumption of a resulting trust in part, leaving it to prevail as to the remainder.
In particular, the courts, it seems, will be very ready to accept evidence, where
there has been a purchase in or transfer into the joint names of the person
providing the purchase money or transferring the property, and another, that
the intention was that the former should receive the income during his life, i.e.
to this extent the resulting trust prevails, but that the property should belong
to the other after his death, i.e. the resulting trust is rebutted as to the

---

[4] See, e.g., *Hepworth* v. *Hepworth* (1870), L.R. 11 Eq. 10; *Fowkes* v. *Pascoe* (1875), 10 Ch.
App. 343, at 348; *Vandervell* v. *I.R.Comrs.*, [1967] 1 All E.R. 1; [1967] 2 A.C. 291, H.L.
See also *Seldon* v. *Davidson*, [1968] 2 All E.R. 755, C.A., where the question was whether
a payment of money was a loan or a gift, and it was held that it was *prima facie* the former
in the absence of circumstances raising the presumption of advancement—as to which see
infra, pp. 104 *et seq.*
[5] In *George* v. *Howard* (1819), 7 Price 646, 651.
[6] *Per* Lindley L.J. in *Standing* v. *Bowring* (1885), 31 Ch. D. 282, 289, C.A., and see generally
Vandervell v. *I.R.Comrs.*, *supra*, H.L.
[7] *Fowkes* v. *Pascoe* (1875), 10 Ch. App. 343.
[8] As to what evidence is admissible see *Shephard* v. *Cartwright*, [1954] 3 All E.R. 649;
[1955] A.C. 431, H.L.
[9] *Groves* v. *Groves* (1829), 3 Y. & J. 163; *Re Gooch* (1890), 62 L.T. 384; *Shephard* v. *Cart-*
wright, *supra*.
[10] *Currant* v. *Jago* (1844), 1 Coll. 261.

remainder.[11] Indeed, in cases where stock has been transferred or money paid into a bank account in joint names, the person providing the stock or money has been held entitled on the evidence not only to the income during his life, but also to sell and transfer the stock or withdraw the money. Nevertheless on that person's death an intention that the other should take beneficially what is left in the joint names has been established and held to be valid.[12]

It may be added that the presumption of a resulting trust naturally weakens with the passage of time, at any rate if there has been acquiescence as where the person in whose name the property has been purchased is allowed to remain in possession.[13]

d The presumption of advancement

In addition to rebutting the presumption of a resulting trust by evidence as to the true intention, the existence of certain special relationships between the person who provides the purchase money or who transfers the property and the person into whose name the property is conveyed or transferred, either alone or jointly, gives rise to a presumption of advancement, which displaces the presumption of a resulting trust. Although the law is commonly expressed in such a way, it is perhaps more accurate to say that the special relationship will be treated as *prima facie* evidence that the person who paid the purchase money or transferred the property intended to make a gift to the person into whose name the property was conveyed or transferred. In any case evidence is admissible to rebut the presumption of advancement in whole or in part and to reinstate wholly or partially the presumption of a resulting trust by showing that the intention of the person who paid the purchase money or transferred the property was that he should retain the whole or some part of the equitable interest. Another way in which the law is sometimes expressed is by saying that the presumption of a resulting trust, referred to in subsections a and b, *supra*, arises only where there is a purchase or transfer into the name of a stranger, i.e. someone who is not in one of the special relationships to the purchaser or transferor, but that where the special relationship exists there is no presumption of a resulting trust but a presumption of advancement.

i *Father and child*—Perhaps the primary relationship which has consistently been held to give rise to a presumption of advancement is that of father and child. There have been many cases where on the purchase or transfer of

---

[11] *Fowkes* v. *Pascoe* (1875), 10 Ch. App. 343; *Benbow* v. *Townsend* (1833), 1 My. & K. 506; *Batstone* v. *Salter* (1875), 10 Ch. App. 431; *Standing* v. *Bowring* (1885), 31 Ch. D. 282, C.A.; *Young* v. *Sealey*, [1949] 1 All E.R. 92; [1949] Ch. 278. See also *Rider* v. *Kidder* (1805), 10 Ves. 360, where the court contemplated the rebuttal of the presumption as to a life interest to the stranger, but its prevailing as to the remainder. It is submitted that there is no difference in principle between realty and personalty—see (1966), 30 Con. 223 (E. L. G. Tyler).

[12] *Beecher* v. *Major* (1865), 2 Drew. & Sm. 431; *Young* v. *Sealey*, *supra*. In the latter case it was held that having regard to previous decisions the gift was not defeated by the Wills Act 1837, although it appeared in fact to be testamentary in nature. The earlier decisions on similar facts were followed notwithstanding that the point on the Wills Act had apparently not been raised. The latter case was considered in *Re Figgis*, [1968] 1 All E.R. 999; [1969] 1 Ch. 123.

[13] *Groves* v. *Groves* (1829), 3 Y. & J. 163; *Clegg* v. *Edmondson* (1857), 8 De G.M. & G. 787.

property by a father into the name of his child[14] the question has been whether the evidence was sufficient to rebut the presumption of advancement arising by virtue of the relationship. The Privy Council, in *Commissioner of Stamp Duties* v. *Byrnes*,[15] citing *Grey* v. *Grey*,[16] said that the fact that the son permits his father to receive the profits during his lifetime is not evidence which rebuts the presumption, as it is merely an act of reverence and good manners, but a later case shows that the retention of the title deeds to the property by the father may have a different result.[17] The presumption of advancement was rebutted in *Re Gooch*,[18] where a father bought shares in a company in the name of his son in order to qualify the son to be a director. The son always handed the dividends received on the shares to his father, and later handed over the actual share certificates. And it seems that the fact that the son is his father's solicitor is by itself a fact which will rebut the presumption.[19] On the other hand, the fact that property is conveyed or transferred into the joint names of a child and a stranger, does not prevent the presumption of advancement from applying.[20]

It is usually said,[1] and was recently assumed by the Court of Appeal,[2] that the presumption of advancement also arises where a man is *in loco parentis* to the person into whose name the property is conveyed or transferred, that is to say, where he has taken upon himself what is regarded in equity as the father's natural office and duty of making provision for the child.[3] This proposition is supported by reference to cases where the child was an illegitimate son,[4] or a grandchild where the father was dead,[5] or the nephew of his wife who had been virtually adopted as a son.[6] It was pointed out in *Tucker* v. *Burrow*,[7] however, that in no reported case where one is *in loco parentis* to another has the court relied solely on such circumstance giving rise to a presumption of advancement: there has always been other evidence to rebut the presumption of a resulting trust. On the authority of *Tucker* v. *Burrow*[8] it is still perhaps arguable that even though a man be *in loco parentis* to the person in whose name the purchase is taken, there will not be any presumption of advancement if that person is not closely related but is a remote relation or stranger, such as the illegitimate child of a legitimate daughter.

The better opinion is perhaps that the relationship of mother[9] and child does not

---

[14] There is no presumption of advancement on a purchase or transfer of property by a child into the name of its father.

[15] [1911] A.C. 386, P.C.

[16] (1677), 2 Swan. 594.

[17] *Warren* v. *Gurney*, [1944] 2 All E.R. 472, C.A.

[18] (1890), 62 L.T. 384. See also *Stock* v. *McAvoy* (1872), L.R. 15 Eq. 55.

[19] *Garrett* v. *Wilkinson* (1848), 2 De G. & Sm. 244.

[20] *Crabb* v. *Crabb* (1834), 1 My. & K. 511.

[1] E.g. by Viscount Simonds in *Shephard* v. *Cartwright*, [1954] 3 All E.R. 649; [1955] A.C. 431, H.L.; Snell's *Equity*, 27th Ed., p. 177; Underhill's *Law of Trust and Trustees*, 12th Ed., p. 218.

[2] *Re Paradise Motor Co., Ltd.*, [1968] 2 All E.R. 625, C.A.

[3] The meaning of the term *in loco parentis* seems to be the same here as in connection with satisfaction, discussed fully in Chapter 17, Section 3c, p. 517, *post*.

[4] *Kilpin* v. *Kilpin* (1834), 1 My. & K. 520, 542; *Soar* v. *Foster* (1858), 4 K. & J. 152.

[5] *Ebrand* v. *Dancer* (1680), 2 Cas. in Ch. 26.   [6] *Currant* v. *Jago* (1844), 1 Coll. 261.

[7] (1865), 2 Hem. & M. 515, at 526–527.

[8] *Supra*. And see Lewin, *Trusts*, 16th Ed., p. 139.

[9] *A fortiori*, stepmother and stepchild—*Todd* v. *Moorhouse* (1874), L.R. 19 Eq. 69, 71.

give rise to any presumption of advancement,[10] the reason given being that equity does not recognise any obligation on the part of a mother to provide for her child. Since the point is the absence of equitable obligation, the fact that there may be a statutory obligation under the National Assistance Act 1948[11] is on this view irrelevant. In practice, however, as Jessel M.R. observed[12] "in the case of a mother . . . it is easier to prove a gift than in the case of a stranger; in the case of a mother very little evidence beyond the relationship is wanted, there being very little additional motive required to induce a mother to make a gift to her child".

ii *Husband and wife*[13]—

Questions often arise between husband and wife as to the ownership of property, more often than not after the break-up of a marriage. In some circumstances a wife may place reliance on the presumption of advancement. Certain important principles should, however, be referred to before investigating the different situations that may arise. First, property rights have to be ascertained as at the time of purchase or transfer, and the rights so ascertained cannot be altered by subsequent events unless there has been an agreement to vary them. In particular, as Lord Morris said in *Pettitt* v. *Pettitt*[14]: "the fact of a break-down of the marriage is irrelevant in the determination of a question as to where ownership lay before the break-down: the break-down will then merely have caused the need for a decision but will not of itself have altered whatever was the pre-existing position as to ownership".[15] In the same case[16] Lord Upjohn stated the position as follows: "In the first place, the beneficial ownership of the property in question must depend on the agreement of the parties determined at the time of its acquisition. If the property in question is land there must be some lease or conveyance which shows how it was acquired. If that document declares not merely in whom the legal title is to vest but in whom the beneficial title is to vest that necessarily concludes the question of title as between the spouses for all time,[17] and in the absence of fraud or mistake at the time of the transaction the parties cannot go behind it at any time thereafter even on death or the break-up of the marriage. . . . But the document may be silent as to

---

[10] *Bennet* v. *Bennet* (1879), 10 Ch.D. 474; *Re De Visme* (1863), 2 De G.J. & Sm. 17. *Contra*, particularly in the case of a widowed mother, *Sayre* v. *Hughes* (1868), L.R. 5 Eq. 376; *Garrett* v. *Wilkinson* (1848), 2 De G. & Sm. 244. Underhill, *Law of Trusts and Trustees*, 12th Ed., p. 216.

[11] Section 42 (1), replacing earlier legislation.

[12] In *Bennet* v. *Bennet*, *supra*, at pp. 479–480. Cf. *Edwards* v. *Bradley* (1957), 9 D.L.R. (2d) 673, where the Supreme Court of Canada held that there was no presumption of advancement (nor, on the facts, evidence) to rebut the presumption of a resulting trust.

[13] Note the wide powers of the court under the Matrimonial Causes Act 1973 (a consolidating act). The rules applied to determine property disputes between husband and wife apply also to property disputes between formerly engaged couples by virtue of s. 2 of the Law Reform (Miscellaneous Provisions) Act 1970. See Law Commission Report No. 52—First Report on Family Property: A New Approach; (1973), 26 C.I.P. 17 (A. J. Oakley); (1973) 23 U.T.L.J. 148 (H. Lesser).

[14] [1969], 2 All E.R. 385, at p. 397; [1970] A.C. 777, at p. 803, H.L.

[15] Lord Morris went on to say that it would be relevant to some questions which could be the subject of a s. 17 application—see p. 115, *infra*.

[16] *Pettitt* v. *Pettitt*, *supra*, at pp. 405; 813; *Re John's Assignment Trusts*, [1970] 2 All E.R. 210n.

[17] Presumably this means concludes for all time the question of title as at the date of acquisition. It may be varied by subsequent agreement. The author shares the opinion of H. K. Bevan and F. W. Taylor in (1966), 30 Con. 354, 438 and E. H. Scamell in (1967), C.L.P. 120, that the view stated in the text is the better one. See also (1970), 34 Con. 156 (Gareth Miller).

the beneficial title. . . . If there is no . . . available evidence then what are called the presumptions come into play."

The presumptions to which Lord Upjohn referred are the presumption of a resulting trust on a purchase in the name of, or voluntary conveyance to, another—which has already been discussed[18]—and the presumption of advancement. As to the latter, with which we are now primarily concerned, it can be taken as settled, in the light of clear statements by three of the Law Lords in *Pettitt* v. *Pettitt*[19] that the strength of this presumption has been much diminished with changing conditions of society.

Lastly, in *Gissing* v. *Gissing*,[20] Viscount Dilhorne referred to *Pettitt* v. *Pettitt*[21] as establishing that there is not one law of property applicable where a dispute as to property is between spouses, and another law of property where the dispute is between other persons. In some cases before *Pettitt* v. *Pettitt*[21]—and indeed in some after it—the phrase "family assets" is used. This may be a useful loose expression to refer to possessions of a family, but it has no legal meaning, and family assets are not a special class of property known to the law. English law knows no doctrine of community of goods or joint family property, and such a doctrine could only be established by legislation.

(a) *Purchase or transfer by a husband into the name of his wife, or into the joint names of his wife and himself.* The classic statement of the presumption of advancement in this situation is that of Malins V.C. in *Re Eykyn's Trusts*,[22] cited with approval by Lord Upjohn in *Pettitt* v. *Pettitt*.[23]

"The law of this court is perfectly settled that when a husband transfers money or other property into the name of his wife only, then the presumption is, that it is intended as a gift or advancement to the wife absolutely at once. . . . And if a husband invests money, stock or otherwise, in the names of himself and his wife, then also it is an advancement for the benefit of the wife absolutely if she survives her husband, but if he survives her, then it reverts to him as joint tenant with his wife. This principle is established by the authority of *Dummer* v. *Pitcher*[24] and cannot now be disputed."

In 1958 it was said[1] that "in this day and age one may feel that the presumption is more easily capable of rebuttal" and, as mentioned above, the House of Lords has stated that the strength of presumption is now greatly diminished. Despite this the Court of Appeal relied on the presumption in *Tinker* v. *Tinker*.[2] The court did not attempt to explain why it applied the presumption without hesitation in this case, which contrasts with all the other husband and wife cases since *Pettitt* v. *Pettitt*[19] where the presumption has been treated as of little or no importance. All the other relevant cases have in fact involved contribu-

---

[18] *Supra*, pp. 100–103.

[19] [1969] 2 All E.R. 385; [1970] A.C. 777, H.L., *per* Lord Reid at pp. 389; 793, Lord Hodson at pp. 404; 811, and Lord Diplock at pp. 414; 824. Lord Upjohn, however, thought the presumptions as useful as ever, though he said that they only come into play in the absence of evidence.

[20] [1970] 2 All E.R. 780; [1971] A.C. 886, H.L.   [21] *Supra*, H.L.

[22] (1877), 6 Ch.D. 115, at p. 118, where it was held that the presumption of advancement was unaffected by the fact that the property was placed in the name also of another person. It makes no difference whether one is dealing with realty or personalty—see (1966), 30 Con. 223 (E. C. G. Tyler), Dymond, *Death Duties*, 15th Ed., Vol. I, p. 447, and Lewin, *Trusts*, 16th Ed., p. 137.

[23] *Supra*.   [24] (1833), 2 My. & K. 262.

[1] *Silver* v. *Silver*, [1958] 1 All E.R. 523, 525, C.A., *per* Evershed M.R.

[2] [1970] 1 All E.R. 540; [1970] P. 136, C.A., where the evidence in fact supported the presumption.

tions to the purchase by both husband and wife—a situation which is discussed in (c) below—and *Tinker* v. *Tinker*[2] may be distinguished on that ground, for there the husband had provided the whole of the purchase price of the house which he had put into his wife's name. It may be that the strength of the presumption of advancement is less impaired in the situation under consideration, i.e. where there has been a purchase or transfer by a husband into the name of his wife, and no contribution is made by the wife.

It has always, of course, been possible to rebut the presumption by evidence that no gift was intended. The older cases, particularly those in which the presumption of advancement was upheld, must, however, be read with care in the light of the possible change in the weight to be attached to the presumption. The presumption of advancement was rebutted in *Re Salisbury-Jones*,[3] where the wife entered into a mortgage of her property under which the husband was a surety. When the husband was called upon to pay the money due under the mortgage it was held that in so doing he was discharging a legal obligation and there was no question of his making a gift to his wife. He was therefore entitled as against her to all the remedies of a surety. On general principles, a husband will not be permitted to set up his own illegality or fraud in order to rebut the presumption of advancement. In *Gascoigne* v. *Gascoigne*,[4] where the husband's fraudulent design was to protect his property from his creditors, it was held that the wife was entitled to retain the property conveyed to her for her own use, notwithstanding that she was a party to the fraud, and in *Re Emery's Investment's Trusts*,[5] where shares were put into the sole name of the wife in order to evade the revenue laws of a friendly foreign country, the wife was able to rely on the presumption of advancement and the husband was not permitted to set up his inequitable intention in order to rebut it. The Court of Appeal agreed in *Tinker* v. *Tinker*[6] that these last two cases were correctly decided. In *Tinker* v. *Tinker*[6] itself the husband, on the purchase of the matrimonial home, had it conveyed into his wife's name, to avoid its being taken by his creditors in case his business failed. It was found as a fact that he had acted honestly, not fraudulently. This evidence of his intention was held to strengthen the presumption of advancement, and accordingly the husband had no claim to the house when the marriage broke up, although the wife had made no contribution to its purchase.[7]

The presumption has been applied not only to a once for all purchase or transfer, but also to analogous transactions, such as a purchase of land with the aid of an instalment mortgage which is paid off by the husband over a period of years, when the payment of each instalment is, as it were, a supplementary gift.[8] Since *Pettitt* v. *Pettitt*[9] however, the court will, it seems, be slow to apply the

---

[2] See footnote 2, p. 107.

[3] [1938] 3 All E.R. 459, applied to a guarantee of an overdraft; *Anson* v. *Anson*, [1953] 1 All E.R. 867; [1953] 1 Q.B. 636.

[4] [1918] 1 K.B. 223, D.C.   [5] [1959] 1 All E.R. 577; [1959] Ch. 410.

[6] [1970] 1 All E.R. 540; [1970] P. 136, C.A., somewhat unconvincingly distinguished in *Heseltine* v. *Heseltine*, [1971] 1 All E.R. 952; C.A. See (1971), 115 Sol. Jo. 614 (S. Cretney).

[7] Note, however, that such a conveyance into the wife's name may constitute a post-nuptial settlement which the court has jurisdiction to vary under s. 24 (1) (c) of the Matrimonial Causes Act 1973.

[8] *Moate* v. *Moate*, [1948] 2 All E.R. 486; *Silver* v. *Silver*, *supra*.

[9] [1969] 2 All E.R. 385; [1970] A.C. 777, H.L.

presumption in such case, at any rate where the wife has made a contribution.[10]

Until the Married Women's Property Act 1964 it was the law that savings by a wife out of payments made to her by her husband by way of housekeeping allowance,[11] and investments,[12] made out of such savings, belonged to the husband. In *Richards* v. *Richards*,[13] however, where the husband was a naval officer far away from home, it was held that the naval allotment was not a payment by way of housekeeping allowance, but was paid in such a way as to be beyond recall by him and as not to require any accounting by her. The husband was accordingly not entitled to any beneficial interest in a house bought by the wife, even though it may have been bought in part out of the money which had come to the wife in this way from her husband. Now, money derived from any allowance made by a husband for the expenses of the matrimonial home or for similar purposes,[14] or any property acquired out of that money, is to be treated as belonging to the husband and wife in equal shares, in the absence of any agreement between them to the contrary.[15]

Special mention should be made of joint bank accounts[16] between husband and wife where both parties have power to draw cheques on the account. *Prima facie* in such a case during their joint lives each spouse has power to draw cheques not only for the joint benefit of both, but also for his or her own separate benefit, and accordingly if either spouse draws on the account to purchase a chattel or an investment in his or her name alone, that spouse will be the sole owner of the chattel or investment both at law and in equity. If the purchase were in joint names[17] they would *prima facie* be joint tenants. And on the death of one spouse the survivor will be entitled to the balance of the account.[18] These *prima facie* rules may be displaced by the evidence. On the one hand, this may rebut the presumption of advancement and show that a banking account placed in joint names is to be held beneficially for the husband[19] alone. Thus in *Marshall* v. *Crutwell*[20] a husband in failing health transferred his banking account from his own name into the names of himself and his wife and

---

[10] *Falconer* v. *Falconer*, [1970] 3 All E.R. 449, C.A.

[11] *Blackwell* v. *Blackwell*, [1943] 2 All E.R. 579, C.A.

[12] *Hoddinott* v. *Hoddinott*, [1949] 2 K.B. 406, C.A., investment (*sic*) in football pools. The dissenting judgment of Denning L.J. should be studied.

[13] [1958]3 All E.R. 513, C.A.

[14] This phrase was held not to include mortgage repayments towards the purchase of the matrimonial home in *Tymoszczuk* v. *Tymoszczuk* (1964), 108 Sol. Jo. 676 where it was held that the Act was retrospective. This decision was doubted on both points by Goff J. in *Re John's Assignment Trusts*, [1970] 2 All E.R. 210n.

[15] Married Women's Property Act 1964.

[16] See (1969), 85 L.Q.R. 530 (M. C. Cullity).

[17] Vaisey J.'s dictum in *Jones* v. *Maynard*, [1951] 1 All E.R. 802, 804; [1951] Ch. 572, 575, to the effect (*semble*) that if the husband draws on the account to purchase investments in his wife's name, the presumption of advancement will apply and the wife will be entitled, seems to be right on principle. It is somewhat less certain whether the general rule of a resulting trust for the wife (see p. 110, *post*) would apply to a similar purchase by the wife in the husband's name.

[18] The authorities for the above propositions are *Re Young* (1885), 28 Ch. D. 705; *Re Bishop*, [1965] 1 All E.R. 249; [1965] Ch. 450.

[19] *Hoddinott* v. *Hoddinott*, [1949] 2 K.B. 406, C.A.

[20] (1875), 2 L.R. 20 Eq. 328. *A fortiori* where the account is fed by the wife alone, she alone is beneficially entitled—*Heseltine* v. *Heseltine*, [1971] 1 All E.R. 952, C.A.

directed his bankers to honour cheques drawn either by himself or his wife. He afterwards paid considerable sums into the account. All cheques were thereafter drawn by the wife at the direction of her husband, and the proceeds were applied in payment of household and other expenses. After his death the wife claimed to be entitled to the balance, but it was held that the transfer of the account was not intended to be a provision for the plaintiff, but merely a mode of conveniently managing her husband's affairs. The presumption was not, however, rebutted in *Re Figgis*,[1] where the joint account had been in existence for nearly fifty years, but had only been operated by the wife during the first world war, and, without the husband's knowledge, during his last illness. This case involved both a current and a deposit account, and as to the latter the judge observed that in the nature of things it was far less appropriate than a current account as a provision made for convenience. He added that even if the current account had been opened merely for convenience, in his view this could change and later become an advancement for the wife. On the other hand, where one spouse has drawn on the account to purchase an investment in his or her name alone, the evidence may show, as in *Jones* v. *Maynard*[2], that the parties intended "a common purse and a pool of their resources".[3] In that case the investment purchased out of the joint[4] account by the husband in his sole name was accordingly directed to be held by him as to one half on trust for his wife.

If at the relevant time, i.e. the time of the purchase or transfer, the relationship of husband and wife was in existence, the presumption of advancement will be applied notwithstanding that the parties were subsequently divorced,[5] or, in the case of a voidable marriage, that a decree of nullity has been pronounced.[6] The presumption may be even stronger where the parties were engaged to be married, provided that the marriage was subsequently duly solemnised.[7] There is, however, no presumption of advancement if the purported marriage is void.[8] The presumption has never been applied where man and woman are living together without having gone through any ceremony of marriage at all. Some support for the contrary view may now, perhaps, be found in recent cases which to some extent assimilate the position of man and mistress to that of husband and wife.[9]

(b) *Purchase or transfer by a wife into the name of her husband or into the joint names of her husband and herself.* Here there is no presumption of advancement, and accordingly the husband will hold on a resulting trust for the wife.[10] Thus

---

[1] [1968] 1 All E.R. 999; [1969] 1 Ch. 123.   [2] *Supra.*
[3] *Jones* v. *Maynard*, *supra*, at p. 803.
[4] Technically, it seems, it was not a joint account, as it remained in the name of the husband alone, but it was said to be a joint account "to all intents and purposes", because both spouses had power to draw on it.
[5] *Thornley* v. *Thornley*, [1893] 2 Ch. 229.   [6] *Dunbar* v. *Dunbar*, [1909] 2 Ch. 639.
[7] *Moate* v. *Moate*, [1948] 2 All E.R. 486. Cf. *Zamet* v. *Hyman*, [1961] 3 All E.R. 933, C.A.
[8] *Soar* v. *Foster* (1858), 4 K. & J. 152—"marriage" with deceased wife's sister, at that time illegal. So held notwithstanding the judicial observation that "any moralist would say that a man was bound to make provision for the woman with whom he had so cohabitated". Whether or not a decree of nullity has been pronounced would seem to be irrelevant.
[9] See *Cooke* v. *Head*, [1972] 2 All E.R. 38, C.A., preferring the dissenting judgment of Willmer J. in *Diwell* v. *Farnes*, [1959] 2 All E.R. 379; *Richards* v. *Dove*, [1974] 1 All E.R. 888, and see p. 112 n. 20, *infra*.
[10] *Re Curtis* (1885), 52 L.T. 244; *Rich* v. *Cockell* (1802), 9 Ves. 369.

in *Mercier* v. *Mercier*[11] husband and wife had a joint banking account almost entirely composed of the wife's income. Land was purchased and paid for out of the joint account, but conveyed into the name of the husband alone. In holding that the husband held the property on a resulting trust for the wife, it was pointed out that there was no distinction in principle between payment out of capital or income. And in *Pearson* v. *Pearson*,[12] where the matrimonial home was conveyed into joint names, but the wife not only provided the initial payment but paid all the mortgage instalments, it was held that the wife alone was entitled. In *Pettitt* v. *Pettitt*,[13] however, Lord Upjohn observed:

> "If a wife puts property into her husband's name it may be that in the absence of all other evidence he is a trustee for her, but in practice there will in almost every case be some explanation (however slight) of this (today) rather unusual course. If a wife puts property into their joint names I would myself think that a joint beneficial tenancy was intended, for I can see no other reason for it."

In *Heseltine* v. *Heseltine*[14] a wealthy wife transferred two sums of £20,000 to her relatively poor husband for the purpose of equalising their property for estate duty purposes, and a further sum of £20,000 to enable the husband, as a candidate for membership of Lloyd's, to sign a certificate that he was worth £90,000. One might expect the court to have held that there was a presumption of a resulting trust, rebutted by the evidence. In fact after the break-up of the marriage it was held that all these sums were held by the husband on trust for the wife. Lord Denning M.R. called it a resulting trust, but in fact the court seems to have imposed a constructive trust, though it is doubtful whether it was justified in doing so on the facts.

An established, though limited, exception to the presumption of a resulting trust arises where a husband and wife are living together and the wife consents to or acquiesces in the husband receiving income from her property, when to that extent only there will be a presumption of gift.[15] But if without the wife's knowledge the husband sold the property and misappropriated the proceeds of sale, he would not only be liable to replace the capital, but also to account for the income that would have been produced after the date of the sale, for whatever the position may have been as to income arising before that date, the wife not having known of the sale could not have assented or acquiesced thereafter.[16] The same principles underlie what is known as the equity of exoneration.[17] This applies where a married woman charges her property with money for the purpose of paying her husband's debts and the money raised by her is so applied. In such case she is *prima facie* regarded in equity and as between herself and him, as lending him and not giving him the money raised on her property and as entitled to have the property exonerated by him from the charge she has created. The presumption of the equity of exoneration, however,

---

[11] [1903] 2 Ch. 98, C.A.
[12] (1965), *Times*, November 30.
[13] *Supra*, at pp. 407; 815.
[14] [1971] 1 All E.R. 952, C.A. Possibly the wife could have had the transfers set aside on the grounds of undue influence. This case also raises difficulties as to what has been called the "floating trust" concept, and the idea of a "trust for the family"—see (1971), 115 Sol. Jo. 614 (S. Cretney).
[15] *Caton* v. *Rideout* (1849), 1 Mac. & G. 599; *Edward* v. *Cheyne* (No. 2) (1888), 13 App. Cas. 385, H.L.; the presumption is, of course, rebuttable, *Re Young* (1913), 29 T.L.R. 391.
[16] *Dixon* v. *Dixon* (1878), 9 Ch.D. 587.
[17] *Clinton* v. *Hooper* (1791), 1 Ves. 173; *Hudson* v. *Carmichael* (1854), Kay. 613.

may be rebutted by evidence showing that the proper inference is that the money was intended to be given, not merely lent, as might be the case, for instance, where the debts have been incurred with the assent of the wife in order to maintain the husband and wife in a standard of living above their income.[18]

(c) *Contributions*[19] *by both spouses*[20] *to purchase price of property*. In this situation the role of the presumption of advancement is now negligible. Even if the property is conveyed into the name of the wife alone the strength of the presumption has diminished virtually to vanishing point.[21] The relevant law was discussed by the House of Lords in the recent cases of *Pettitt* v. *Pettitt*[1] and *Gissing* v. *Gissing*,[2] from which it appears that in this sort of case by virtue of the contributions that a party has made towards the purchase price there will be a resulting trust in his favour to a proportionate extent no matter in whose name the legal title may be put. It was further pointed out in *Gissing* v. *Gissing*[3] that the courts should make a serious attempt to evaluate the contribution made by each party, and should only fall back on the maxim "Equality is equity" where each has clearly made a substantial contribution but it is virtually impossible to quantify the contributions precisely.

A number of cases have come before the courts since *Gissing* v. *Gissing*[1] and a difference of opinion has emerged as to the meaning of the House of Lords' decisions. In a series of cases[4] dealing mainly with the matrimonial home the Court of Appeal has stated the effect of these decisions in very broad terms, namely that if both husband and wife make substantial[5] contributions, whether directly or indirectly, in money or money's worth to the initial deposit or to the mortgage instalments, the court will impute, impose or infer a trust whereby the legal owner holds the house on trust for them both, giving to each a beneficial interest of such an extent as may in all the circumstances seem just. In relation to indirect contributions, in the case of a claim by a wife, for instance, if her efforts or her contributions relieved the husband of other expenses which he would otherwise have had to bear—so that he would not have been able to meet the mortgage instalments without her help—then she is regarded as having made an indirect contribution. Indeed, even if the husband does not strictly need the wife's help—because, for instance, he has enough money of his own, or could find it by cutting down his smoking or drinking, or selling his car—if in fact he accepts it, she becomes entitled to a share. The Court of Appeal has indeed expressly rejected[6] the argument that indirect contributions can only be

---

18 *Paget* v. *Paget*, [1898] 1 Ch. 470, C.A., explained in *Hall* v. *Hall*, [1911] 1 Ch. 487.
19 Including contributions before marriage with a view to setting up the matrimonial home —*Ulrich* v. *Ulrich*, [1968] 1 All E.R. 67, C.A.
20 Similar principles apply to a man and his mistress. *Richards* v. *Dove*, [1974] 1 All E.R. 888—though the result may be different because of the absence of the legal duty owed by a husband to his wife.
21 Even Lord Upjohn in *Pettitt* v. *Pettitt*, *supra*, thought that a wife would not be able to rely on the presumption of advancement unless the husband's contribution was very small. And see *Falconer* v. *Falconer*, [1970] 3 All E.R. 449, C.A.
1 *Supra*, H.L.
2 [1970] 2 All E.R. 780; [1971] A.C. 886, H.L.
3 *Supra*, per Lord Reid at 783; 897 and per Lord Pearson at 788; 903.
4 Including *Falconer* v. *Falconer*, [1970] 3 All E.R. 449, C.A.; *Davis* v. *Vale*, [1971] All E.R. 1021, C.A.; *Hargrave* v. *Newton*, [1971] 3 All E.R. 866, C.A.; *Hazell* v. *Hazell*, [1972] 1 All E.R. 923, C.A.; *Kowalczuk* v. *Kowalczuk*, [1973] 2 All E.R. 1042, C.A.
5 See *Falconer* v. *Falconer*, *supra*, C.A. and *Hargrave* v. *Newton*, *supra*, C.A.
6 *Hargrave* v. *Newton*, *supra*, C.A.; *Hazell* v. *Hazell*, *supra*, C.A.

taken into account if they are referable to the purchase of the property in question, though, as has been pointed out,[7] it is doubtful whether the court is entitled to do this in the light of the speeches in *Gissing* v. *Gissing*.[8] The Court of Appeal has relied mainly on the opinion of Lord Reid which, as pointed out by Bagnall J. in *Cowcher* v. *Cowcher*,[9] in significant respects did not accord with the other four opinions. Viscount Dilhorne, for instance, said[10] in so many words that proof of expenditure for the benefit of the family by one spouse will not of itself show any common intention as to the ownership of the matrimonial home.

Cowcher v. *Cowcher*[11] is difficult to reconcile with the line of Court of Appeal decisions referred to above. Although Bagnall J. made a gallant attempt to do so in respect of the decisions then available to him, the truth of the matter seems to be that his interpretation of the House of Lords decisions in *Pettitt* v. *Pettitt*[12] and *Gissing* v. *Gissing*[13] is inconsistent with that put upon them by the Court of Appeal. Bagnall J.'s view is that one must first determine the actual sources of the purchase money, that is from whose bank account or savings account or other resources it was provided. *Prima facie* the property will be held on a resulting trust for the spouses in corresponding proportions. Secondly, it may in some cases be possible to establish an express agreement ("interest consensus") showing an intention that the property shall be held on different trusts. These would be express trusts. If effective there will be no difficulty. If ineffective for any reason—it may, for instance, be oral but come within statutory provisions requiring writing—it will nevertheless preclude the possibility of any implied agreement and the *prima facie* resulting trust will operate. Thirdly, in the absence of an express agreement, the court must determine whether, from the whole of the evidence including acts of the parties before, at the time of and after the purchase, there can be inferred an agreement as to the proportions in which they were to be treated as providing the purchase money. If so, there will be a resulting trust for the parties in corresponding proportions. It should be observed that the agreement last referred to, called by the judge "money consensus", is to be distinguished from "interest consensus". By "money consensus" he means an agreement that, irrespective of who makes the actual payments, as between themselves the parties are to be treated as contributing to the purchase price in certain agreed shares. Whoever held the legal title would then hold it on a corresponding resulting trust. By "interest consensus" he means an agreement that, irrespective of their contributions to the purchase price, the property is to be held in an *express* trust for the parties in certain agreed shares. In Bagnall J.'s view it would be very difficult to infer interest consensus from conduct, and in any case he considers that the House of Lords contemplated money consensus.

It should be added that where there has been a divorce it is now seldom necessary to decide the exact property rights of husband and wife by reason of

---

[7] (1972), 88 L.Q.R. 333 (J. M. Eekelaar) where the difficulties flowing from the absence of a requirement of referability are pointed out.
[8] [1970] 2 All E.R. 780; [1971] A.C. 886, H.L.   [9] [1972] 1 All E.R. 943.
[10] *Gissing* v. *Gissing*, *supra*, H.L. at pp. 786; 901.
[11] *Supra*, noted (1972), 88 L.Q.R. 333 (J. M. Eekelaar); (1972), 35 M.L.R. 547 (J. Levin).
[12] [1969] 2 All E.R. 385; [1970] A.C. 777, H.L.
[13] *Supra*, H.L.

the wide powers given to the court under the Matrimonial Causes Act, 1973, which enable the court to do what is just having regard to all the circumstances.[14] In other circumstances it may still be essential.[15]

(d) *Improvements.*   So far as improvements to matrimonial property are concerned the disputes in the cases have been silenced by the enactment of s. 37 of the Matrimonial Proceedings and Property Act 1970, which provides:[16]

> "It is hereby declared that where a husband or wife contributes in money or money's worth to the improvement of real or personal property in which or in the proceeds of sale of which either or both of them has or have a beneficial interest, the husband or wife so contributing shall, if the contribution is of a substantial nature and subject to any agreement between them to the contrary express or implied, be treated as having then acquired by virtue of his or her contribution a share or an enlarged share, as the case may be, in that beneficial interest of such an extent as may have been then agreed or, in default of such agreement, as may seem in all the circumstances just to any court before which the question of the existence or extent of the beneficial interest of the husband or wife arises (whether in proceedings between them or in any other proceedings)."

The section has been held[17] to have retrospective effect and according to Lord Denning, M.R.[18] is a declaration not only of what the law is now and is to be in the future, but also as to what it was before the Act. Even Lord Denning, M.R. seems to agree, however, that under s. 37 only contributions referable to the improvement to the property can be taken into account.[19]

The task of the court, according to Arnold, J. in *Griffiths* v. *Griffiths*[20] "is to come to a conclusion as to what share in the beneficial interest of the house will in all the circumstances be a just share for the husband[1] to have in requital for the achievement of those improvements. It does not seem to me," he continued, "that it would be just that he should have the cost of an improvement which has added nothing to the value of the house when it comes to be realised and, conversely, that he should be denied more than the cost of an improvement when in fact it has contributed very largely indeed, and far beyond its intrinsic worth, to the ultimate sale price of the house. It seems to me what is just is to look at the situation in the round, to see what has been achieved by means of the improvements in the realisation, if there be a realisation, or in the current value if there be a current value. Moreover, it seems logical and just to ignore the

---

[14] See *Wachtel* v. *Wachtel*, [1973] 1 All E.R. 829; [1973] Fam. at p. 81, C.A., *per* Lord Denning, M.R. at pp. 837; 92; *Kowalczuk* v. *Kowalczuk*, [1973] 2 All E.R. 1042 *per* Lord Denning, M.R. at p. 1045; *Gordon* v. *Gordon* (1973), 123 N.L.J. 969, C.A.; *Griffiths* v. *Griffiths*, [1974] 1 All E.R. 932, C.A.

[15] See e.g. *Re Cummins, Cummins* v. *Thompson*, [1971] 3 All E.R. 782; [1972] Ch. 62, C.A.

[16] See (1970), 120 N.L.J. 1008 (R. T. Oerton) and the correspondence at p. 1082.

[17] *Davis* v. *Vale*, [1971] 2 All E.R. 1021, C.A.

[18] *Davis* v. *Vale*, supra, C.A., at p. 1025; *Kowalczuk* v. *Kowalczuk*, [1973] 2 All E.R. 1042, C.A., at p. 1045. It is submitted, however, that there is much to be said for the view that before the Act improvements gave rise to no claim in the absence of agreement.

[19] *Kowalczuk* v. *Kowalczuk*, supra, C.A., at p. 1045.

[20] At first instance, [1973] 3 All E.R. 1155; [1973] 1 W.L.R. 1454, at pp. 1159; 1457, not discussed on appeal, supra, where improvements were treated simply as a factor in deciding what financial provisions should be made on divorce. It seems that s. 37 should only be used in proceedings under s. 17 of the Married Women's Property Act 1882, infra, p. 115.

[1] Or wife, as the case may be.

enjoyment value of the improvements which happened in the course of the marriage."

(e) *Section 17 of the Married Women's Property Act 1882.*[2] This section provides as follows: "In any question between husband and wife as to the title to or possession of property, either party . . . may apply [to a judge who] may make such order with respect to the property in dispute . . . as he thinks fit." So far as title to property is concerned, it was finally settled by the House of Lords in *Pettitt* v. *Pettitt,*[3] after a long series of cases demonstrating acute differences of opinion in the Court of Appeal, that s. 17 is a purely procedural section which confers no jurisdiction to transfer any proprietary interest from one spouse to the other or to create new proprietary rights in either spouse.[4] By an extension contained in s. 39 of the Matrimonial Proceedings and Property Act 1970 an application may be made for three years after the marriage has been dissolved or annulled. Usually, however, there is no point in going on with an application under s. 17 once there has been a divorce. The proper course is to take out proceedings under the Matrimonial Causes Act 1973, which gives wide powers to the court to do what is just having regard to all the circumstances.[5]

It should be added that it is equally clear from *Pettitt* v. *Pettitt*[6] that where the question is not one of title to property, but whether an established property right can be enforced, it is agreed that the court has a discretion to restrain or postpone the enforcement of a spouse's legal rights, in relation, for instance, to sale of the property or to possession, having regard to the mutual matrimonial duties of the spouses.

3 FAILURE TO DISPOSE OF THE EQUITABLE INTEREST IN WHOLE OR IN PART

a The principle involved

"Equity," it has been said,[7] "abhors a beneficial vacuum." Accordingly where a settlor conveys or transfers property to trustees, but fails to declare the trusts upon which it is to be held; or where the expressed trusts fail altogether

---

[2] As extended by s. 7 of the Matrimonial Causes (Property and Maintenance) Act 1958 and amended by the Statute Law (Repeals) Act 1969.

[3] [1969] 2 All E.R. 385; [1970] A.C. 777, H.L.

[4] Perhaps the clearest and most extreme statement of the contrary view was that of Lord Denning M.R. in *Hine* v. *Hine,* [1962] 3 All E.R. 345, 347, C.A. when he said: "The jurisdiction of the court over family assets under s. 17 is entirely discretionary. Its discretion transcends all rights, legal or equitable, and enables the court to make such order as it thinks fit. This means . . . that the court is entitled to make such order as appears to be fair and just in all the circumstances of the case."

[5] See the cases cited in n. 15, p. 114, *supra.*

[6] *Supra.* See also *National Provincial Bank, Ltd.* v. *Ainsworth,* [1965] 2 All E.R. 472; [1965] A.C. 1175, H.L.; *Jones* v. *Jones,* [1971] 2 All E.R. 737, C.A.; *Morris* v. *Tarrant,* [1971] 2 All E.R. 920; [1971] 2 Q.B. 143; (1967), 30 M.L.R. 219 (S. Roberts). Note that, by the Matrimonial Homes Act 1967, as amended by s. 38 of the Matrimonial Proceedings and Property Act 1970, where one spouse has a right to occupy a dwelling house which has at some time been the matrimonial home and the other spouse has no such right, such other spouse is given rights of occupation so long as the marriage subsists—see (1968), 32 Con. 85 (F. R. Crane); *Tarr* v. *Tarr,* [1972] 2 All E.R. 295; [1973] A.C. 254, H.L.

[7] *Vandervell* v. *I.R.Comrs.,* [1965] 2 All E.R. 37; [1966] Ch. 261, C.A., *per* Diplock L.J., at pp. 46, 291. Contrast dicta in *Wood Preservation, Ltd* v. *Prior,* [1969] 1 All E.R. 364, C.A., esp. *per* Lord Donovan, at p. 367.

on the ground,[8] for instance, of uncertainty, or non-compliance with statutory requirements as to writing[9]; or where they fail partially on similar grounds, or because the trusts expressed only dispose of a part of the equitable interest; in any such case the entire equitable interest, or such part thereof as has not been effectively disposed of, remains vested in the settlor or, in technical language, is said to result to him, and the property is accordingly said to be held by the trustees upon a resulting trust for him.[10] *Ex hypothesi* in these cases the transfer is on trust, and accordingly the resulting trust does not establish the trust but merely carries back to the transferor the beneficial interest that has not been disposed of. As previously mentioned[11] this is the automatic consequence of the transferor's failure to dispose of what is vested in him, and may therefore be called an automatic resulting trust. The same principle applies to a devise or bequest by a testator to trustees upon trusts which fail similarly either altogether or in part, when the trustees will hold on a resulting trust, wholly or *pro tanto*, for the persons entitled to residue, or, if the gift which fails is a gift of residue, or if there is no residuary gift, then for the persons entitled on intestacy.[12] We have, indeed, already come across an application of the principle in connection with alleged half-secret trusts which have not been established.[13] Another illustration is where there has been a marriage settlement in contemplation of a particular marriage and the contract to marry has been "definitely and absolutely put an end to"[14]; the trustees of the settlement will in such case hold the property on a resulting trust for the person who put the property into the settlement.[15] And the same result has been reached where a decree of nullity has been pronounced.[16] Of a very different character is a series of bankruptcy cases,[17] applying the same basic principle, which establish that a loan of

---

[8] The special considerations which apply where the trusts fail on the ground of illegality, or because they offend against public policy, are discussed in Chapter 5, Section 1, p. 126, *post*.

[9] *Hodgson* v. *Marks*, [1971] 2 All E.R. 684; [1971] Ch. 892, C.A.

[10] Or, if he is dead, for his estate.

[11] *Supra*, p. 44; *Re Vandervell's Trusts (No. 2)*, [1974] 1 All E.R. 47.

[12] See, e.g., *Morice* v. *Bishop of Durham* (1805), 10 Ves. 522; *Chichester Diocesan Fund* v. *Simpson*, [1944] A.C. 341, H.L.

[13] See, e.g., *Johnson* v. *Ball* (1851), 5 De G. & Sm. 85; *Re Keen*, [1937] 1 All E.R. 452; [1937] Ch. 236, C.A. The result is the same in a fully-secret trust if the apparent beneficiary admits that he is or is proved to be a mere trustee—*Re Boyes* (1884), 26 Ch.D. 531.

[14] *Per* Pearson J. in *Essery* v. *Cowlard* (1884), 26 Ch.D. 191, 193. In this case the parties had in fact lived together without marriage and had had three children; *Bond* v. *Walford* (1886), 32 Ch. D. 238. For a case where no trusts were sufficiently declared see *Re Wilcock* (1890), 62 L.T. 317.

[15] Note that a well-drafted settlement will contain express provisions to cover this situation.

[16] *Re Ames' Settlement*, [1946] 1 All E.R. 689; [1946] Ch. 217 and see *Re d'Altroy's Will Trusts*, [1968] 1 All E.R. 181, discussed in (1969), 32 M.L.R. 210 (J. Tiley); *Re Rodwell*, [1969] 3 All E.R. 1363; [1970] Ch. 726. But note the power of the Divorce Court under the Matrimonial Causes Act 1973, s. 24. S. 16 of the Act, replacing the Nullity of Marriage Act 1971, s. 5, now provides that a decree of nullity in respect of a voidable marriage shall end the marriage from the date of the decree absolute and not retrospectively.

[17] Discussed and followed in *Barclays Bank, Ltd.* v. *Quistclose Investments, Ltd.*, [1968] 3 All E.R. 651; [1970] A.C. 567, H.L. Note, however, that, subject to agreement to the contrary, an estate agent is not a trustee in relation to either a contract or pre-contract deposit paid to him as stakeholder—*Potters* v. *Loppert*, [1973] 1 All E.R. 658.

money on a specific condition creates a trust attaching to the money in the hands of the borrower, a trust which subsists in favour of the lender if the condition fails. The existence of a contractual obligation to repay is not invariably inconsistent with the existence of a trust.[1]

Where the expressed trusts are in part valid but do not exhaust the beneficial interest there will be a resulting trust whether the expressed trusts are of a non-charitable, or of a charitable nature, unless in the latter case the *cy-près* doctrine[2] applies. A case involving a non-charitable trust was *Re the Trusts of the Abbott Fund*,[3] in which a fund had been raised by subscription for the maintenance and support of two distressed ladies. On the death of the survivor, a portion of the fund remained unapplied in the hands of the trustees. It was held that there was a resulting trust of the balance of the fund for the subscribers thereto. Again in *Re Gillingham Bus Disaster Fund*,[4] following an accident in which a number of cadets were killed and injured, a fund was raised by subscription for the benefit of the victims and other worthy causes in memory of the boys who were killed. These trusts were not charitable, the trust for worthy causes being void for uncertainty. Consequently it was held that the balance of the fund not applied for the benefit of the victims was held on a resulting trust for the subscribers. It was further held in that case that the position was unaffected by the fact that a large number of the subscribers, such as contributors to street collections, were, as it was assumed, unascertainable, but the better view seems to be that where money is raised by means of entertainments, raffles and sweepstakes, or street collections, the donor parts with his money out and out, and there is no resulting trust.[5]

Another type of case in which there may be a resulting trust is where the provisions of a settlement fail to cover the events which in fact happen. In *Re Cochrane's Settlement Trusts*[6] there was a post-nuptial settlement in an unusual form. Husband and wife each brought property into the settlement, the beneficial limitations of which were that income was payable to the wife for life

---

[1] Normally payment by way of loan is inconsistent with the creation of a resulting trust. In *Hussey* v. *Palmer*, [1972] 3 All E.R. 744, C.A., it is submitted that the view of Cairns L.J. at p. 749 on this point is to be preferred to that of Phillimore L.J. at p. 748. See (1973) 37 Con. 65 (D. J. Hayton).

[2] The *cy-près* doctrine is discussed in Chapter 7, Section 4, pp. 215 et seq., post.

[3] [1900] 2 Ch. 326. See also *Re Customs and Excise Officers' Mutual Guarantee Fund*, [1917] 2 Ch. 18; *Re Hobourn Aero Components, Ltd.'s Air Raid Distress Fund*, [1945] 2 All E.R. 711; *Re St. Andrews Allotment Association's Trusts*, [1969] 1 All E.R. 147; *Re Sick and Funeral Society of St. John's Sunday School, Golcar*, [1972] 2 All E.R. 439; [1973] Ch. 51.

[4] [1958] 1 All E.R. 37; [1958] Ch. 300, affd. C.A., [1958] 2 All E.R. 749; [1959] Ch. 62, though the present point did not arise on appeal.

[5] *Re West Sussex Constabulary's Widows, Children and Benevolent* (1930) *Fund Trusts*, [1970] 1 All E.R. 544; [1971] Ch. 1, criticized on another ground (1971), 87 L.Q.R. 466 (Michael Albery); and see (1958), 74 L.Q.R. 190, 489; (P. S. Atiyah) (1973), 37 Con. 126 (Penelope Pearce and A. Samuels).

[6] [1955] 1 All E.R. 222; [1955] Ch. 309; see also *Re Llanover Settled Estates*, [1926] Ch. 626; [1926] All E.R. Rep. 631; *Re Flower's Settlement Trusts*, [1957] 1 All E.R. 462, C.A. The resulting trust may, however, be ousted by the doctrine of acceleration—*Re Hodge*, [1943] 2 All E.R. 304; [1943] Ch. 300; *Re Flower's Settlement Trusts*, *supra*; *Re Dawson's Settlement*, [1966] 3 All E.R. 68—or the court may even, in a clear case, supply words to fill in a gap in the limitations with the result that there will be no place for a resulting trust—*Re Akeroyd's Settlement*, [1893] 3 Ch. 363, C.A.; *Re Cory*, [1955] 2 All E.R. 630.

"so long as she shall continue to reside with the husband" and after her death "or the prior determination of the trust in her favour" to the husband for life with a gift over of capital, "from and after the decease of the survivor of them". The wife ceased to reside with the husband, who later died, leaving the wife surviving him. It was held that during the remainder of the life of the wife there were resulting trusts in favour of the estate of the husband and in favour of the wife of the income of their respective parts of the trust fund.

Where charitable trusts are declared which fail in whole or in part, there may likewise be a resulting trust though here, as already mentioned, it will often be ousted by the *cy-près* doctrine, which will be discussed later in connection with charitable trusts. In the absence of the requirements for the application of the *cy-près* doctrine, there has been held to be a resulting trust both in cases where the trust has failed altogether, and in cases where the court has had to deal with a surplus after the particular charitable purpose has come to an end. In *Re Ulverston and District New Hospital Building Fund*[7] a fund was opened for the building of a new hospital, but the scheme became impracticable so that there was a total failure *ab initio* of the purpose of the fund. It was held that so far as money had been received from identifiable[8] sources there was a resulting trust for the subscribers. There will likewise be a resulting trust for the subscribers where there is a surplus after the particular charitable trust has been fulfilled,[9] and for the settlor or his representatives where a charitable trust for a limited period or a limited purpose has come to an end.[10]

b   The preliminary question of construction

In various circumstances where at first sight one might think that there was a resulting trust it has been held that on the true construction of the relevant documents a resulting trust does not arise. One type of case where this is so is where a donor parts with his money out and out and has no intention of retaining any interest therein. In such case, since, *ex hypothesi*, neither the beneficiaries named to whom some interest is given, nor the donor, are in a position to put forward any claim to the equitable interest not expressly disposed of, it necessarily falls to the Crown as *bona vacantia*. Thus in *Cunnack v. Edwards*[11] a society was formed to raise a fund by subscriptions from the members to provide for widows of deceased members. On the death of the last widow of a member there was a surplus. It was held that having regard to the constitution of the fund, no interest could possibly be held to remain in the contributors, each of whom had parted with his money once and for all under a contract for the benefit of his widow. When this contract had been

---

7   [1956] 3 All E.R. 164; [1956] Ch. 622, C.A.   See also *Re University of London Medical Sciences Institute Fund*, [1909] 2 Ch. 1, C.A.
8   As to anonymous subscribers see the Charities Act 1960, s. 14 and pp. 218, 219, *post*.
9   *Re British Red Cross Balkan Fund*, [1914] 2 Ch. 419—the subscribers are entitled to the surplus rateably in proportion to their subscriptions.
10   *Gibson v. South American Stores (Gath & Chaves), Ltd.*, [1949] 2 All E.R. 985; [1950] Ch. 177, C.A.; *Re Cooper's Conveyance Trusts*, [1956] 3 All E.R. 28; *Bankes v. Salisbury Diocesan Council*, [1960] 2 All E.R. 372; [1960] Ch. 631. See (1957), 21 Con. 213; and note the effect of the Perpetuities and Accumulations Act 1964, s. 12.
11   [1896] 2 Ch. 679, C.A.; see also *Braithwaite v. A.G.*, [1909] 1 Ch. 510; (1966), 30 Con. 117 (H. A. Hickling).

carried into effect each contributor had received all that he had contracted to get for his money and could not ask for any more. The surplus accordingly passed to the Crown as *bona vacantia*. The result is the same, according to the better view, in relation to money raised by means of entertainments, raffles and sweepstakes, or street collections.[12]

In other circumstances it may be held that on the true construction of the instrument there is in fact no equitable interest undisposed of so that the whole foundation for a resulting trust disappears. In one line of cases the problem has been to decide whether there is a gift to a donee upon trust, when any property not required to carry out the expressed trust will be held on a resulting trust for the testator's estate,[13] or whether there is a beneficial gift to a donee subject to carrying out some particular trust or obligation. What has been called[14] the classic statement of the principles applicable to this problem is contained in the judgment of Lord Eldon in *King* v. *Denison*[15]:

> "If I give to A. and his heirs all my real estate, charged with my debts, that is a devise to him for a particular purpose, but not for that purpose only. If the devise is upon trust to pay my debts, that is a devise for a particular purpose, and nothing more; and the effect of these two modes admits just this difference. The former is a devise of an estate of inheritance for the purpose of giving the devisee the beneficial interest, subject to a particular purpose; the latter is a devise for a particular purpose; with no intention to give him any beneficial interest."[16]

It is, of course, only in the latter case that a resulting trust can arise. Whether the former or the latter view is the true construction of the particular will depends on the whole contents of the will, but extrinsic evidence will not be admitted to show that someone who on the construction of the will by itself is a mere trustee was intended by the testator to take beneficially.[17] Although it has been said that "there is a presumption that a gift in trust is not a beneficial gift"[18] so that any surplus will be held on a resulting trust, "the cases show that slight indications may well suffice to persuade the court that the intention of the testator was not to create a trust estate in the devisee, but to give him a conditional gift",[19] particularly, it seems, if the donee in trust is a wife, fiancée or relative for whom the testator might be supposed to have intended to make provision.[20]

---

[12] See p. 117, *ante*, especially references in n. 5.
[13] The cases all seem to have arisen on wills, though there seems to be no reason why the same problem should not arise on an *inter vivos* disposition.
[14] *Per* Bowen L.J. in *Croome* v. *Croome* (1888), 59 L.T. 582, at p. 585, C.A.; affd. (1889), 61 L.T. 814, H.L.
[15] (1813), 1 Ves. & B. 260, at p. 272, citing *Hill* v. *Bishop of London* (1738), 1 Atk. 618.
[16] Although Lord Eldon refers only to real estate, exactly the same principles apply to personal property.
[17] *Re Rees' Will Trusts*, [1949] 2 All E.R. 1003; [1950] Ch. 804, C.A. Cf. *Re Tyler's Fund Trusts*, [1967] 3 All E.R. 389.
[18] *Re West*, [1900] 1 Ch. 84, *per* Kekewich J. at p. 87.
[19] *Re Rees' Will Trusts*, *supra*, *per* Evershed M.R. at p. 1005. Cf. *Re Pugh's Will Trusts*, [1967] 3 All E.R. 337.
[20] There was held to be a resulting trust in *Re West*, *supra*; *Re Rees' Will Trusts*, *supra*; but the donee was held to take the surplus beneficially in *Irvine* v. *Sullivan* (1869), L.R. 8 Eq. 673; *King* v. *Denison*, *supra*; *Croome* v. *Croome* (1888), 59 L.T. 582, C.A., affd. (1889), 61 L.T. 814, H.L.

Another type of case where at first sight one might expect to find a resulting trust is illustrated by *Re Andrew's Trust*.[21] There a fund was subscribed for the education of the children of a deceased clergyman. When the children were all of age and their education had been completed, there remained a surplus. It was held that it should be divided equally among the children and not on a resulting trust for the subscribers. It is interesting to compare this case with the somewhat similar facts of *Re the Trusts of the Abbott Fund*,[1] where it will be recalled it was held that there was a resulting trust for the subscribers. The point of distinction seems to be that in *Re Andrew's Trust*[2] there was in fact no equitable interest undisposed of; for the fund was treated as having been subscribed for the benefit of the children generally, with particular reference to their education.[3] Accordingly there was nothing to form the subject-matter of a resulting trust.

Finally, mention should be made of the rule in *Lassence* v. *Tierney*,[4] namely, "that if you find an absolute gift to a legatee in the first instance, and trusts are engrafted or imposed on that absolute interest which fail, either from lapse or invalidity or any other reason, then the absolute gift takes effect so far as the trusts have failed to the exclusion of the residuary legatee or next of kin[5] as the case may be".[6]

4 THE VENDOR UNDER A CONTRACT FOR THE SALE OF LAND

Numerous cases[7] from the middle of the seventeenth century onwards establish[8] the general proposition that where there is a contract for the sale of land the purchaser becomes the owner in equity of the land or, as Lord Hardwicke put it,[9] the rule is "that the vendor of the estate is, from the time of his contract, considered as a trustee for the purchaser".[10] There are, however, difficulties, some of which are due to the fact that the nature of the trust and the duties of the vendor as trustee may undergo important changes. When the purchaser has paid the purchase price in full and has no other obligation to perform under the contract, the vendor is a trustee without qualification, a naked, bare, or mere trustee, but until that state has been reached, he " is only

---

[21] [1905] 2 Ch. 48; see also *Smith* v. *Cooke*, [1891] A.C. 297, H.L.

[1] [1900] 2 Ch. 326. See p. 117, *ante*.

[2] *Supra.*

[3] The court was, perhaps, influenced by the fact that in the later case the children were alive, while in the earlier one the ladies were dead.

[4] (1849), 1 Mac. & G. 551, also known as the rule in *Hancock* v. *Watson*, [1902] A.C. 14, H.L. *Re Burton's Settlement Trusts*, [1955] 1 All E.R. 433; [1955] Ch. 348, C.A.

[5] Who could, of course, only claim on a resulting trust.

[6] *Per* Lord Davey in *Hancock* v. *Watson*, [1902] A.C. 14, 22, H.L.

[7] See (1960), 24 Con. 47 (P. H. Pettit); *Musselwhite* v. *C. H. Musselwhite & Son, Ltd.*, [1962] 1 All E.R. 201; [1962] Ch. 964.

[8] The only dissenting voice seems to be that of Brett L.J. in *Rayner* v. *Preston* (1881), 18 Ch.D. 1, C.A.

[9] *Green* v. *Smith* (1738), 1 Atk. 572, at p. 573.

[10] See Chapter 16, Section 1e, p. 496, *post*.

a trustee in a modified sense",[11] a "quasi-trustee",[12] or as Jessel M.R. put it,[13] "He is certainly a trustee for the purchaser, a trustee, no doubt, with peculiar duties and liabilities, for it is a fallacy to suppose that every trustee has the same duties and liabilities; but he is a trustee". The transition was recognised by Plumer M.R. in *Wall* v. *Bright*,[14] as follows:

"The vendor is, therefore, not a mere trustee; he is in progress towards it, and finally becomes such when the money is paid, and when he is bound to convey. In the meantime he is not bound to convey; there are many uncertain events to happen before it will be known whether he will ever have to convey, and he retains, for certain purposes, his old dominion over the estate. There are these essential distinctions between a mere trustee, and one who is made a trustee constructively, by having entered into a contract to sell; and it would, therefore, be going too far to say that they are alike in all respects; the principle that the agreement is to be considered as performed, which is a fiction of equity, must not be pursued to all its practical consequences. It is sufficient to say that it governs the equitable estate, without affecting the legal."

The reason for the special position of the vendor-trustee is given by Lord Cairns in *Shaw* v. *Foster*.[15] The vendor-trustee, he explained, "was not a mere dormant trustee, he was a trustee having a personal and substantial interest in the property, a right to protect that interest, and an active right to assert that interest if anything should be done in derogation of it. The relation, therefore, of trustee and *cestui que trust* subsisted, but subsisted subject to the paramount right of the vendor and trustee to protect his own interest as vendor of the property." For a full discussion of the special position of a vendor-trustee, reference should be made to works on vendor and purchaser[16]; for present purposes it is sufficient to observe by way of illustration that, on the one hand, like any other trustee, he is under a duty to use reasonable care to maintain the property in a reasonable state of preservation,[17] though, by way of qualification, he will be under no liability to the purchaser for neglect or even misfeasance if the contract ultimately goes off.[18] On the other hand, by way of contrast with an ordinary trustee the vendor-trustee is entitled to retain for his own benefit the rents and profits until the date fixed for completion, and is entitled to retain possession of the property until the contract is completed by payment of the purchase price.

---

[11] *Royal Bristol Permanent Building Society* v. *Bomash* (1887), 35 Ch.D. 390, *per* Kekewich J. at p. 397.
[12] *Cumberland Consolidated Holdings Ltd.* v. *Ireland*, [1946] 1 All E.R. 284; [1946] K.B. 264, *per* Lord Greene M.R. giving the judgment of the Court of Appeal, at pp. 286, 269.
[13] In *Earl of Egmont* v. *Smith* (1877), 6 Ch.D. 469, at p. 475.
[14] (1820), 1 Jac. & W. 494, at p. 503.
[15] (1872), L.R. 5 H.L. 321, at p. 338.
[16] E.g. Williams on *Vendor and Purchaser*, 4th Ed., Vol. 1, pp. 545 *et seq.*; Emmet on *Title*, 15th Ed., Vol. 1, pp. 207 *et seq.*; Dart on *Vendor and Purchaser*, 8th Ed., Vol. I, pp. 265 *et seq.*; (1959), 23 Con. 173 (V. G. Wellings).
[17] See, e.g., *Phillips* v. *Silvester* (1872), 8 Ch. App. 173; *Golden Bread Co.* v. *Hemmings* [1922] 1 Ch. 162; *Cumberland Consolidation Holdings Ltd.* v. *Ireland*, *supra*, C.A.; *Phillips* v. *Lamdin*, [1949] 1 All E.R. 770; [1949] 2 K.B. 33.
[18] *Plews* v. *Samuel*, [1904] 1 Ch. 464.

5 STRANGERS TO THE TRUST

a "Knowing receipt or dealing" and "knowing assistance"[19]

The cases in which a stranger to the trust is said to be a constructive trustee fall into two categories. First there are cases where a person knowingly receives trust property in breach of trust,[20] or, even though he may have received it innocently, subsequently deals with it in a manner inconsistent with the performance of trusts of which he has become cognisant.[21] There is no need to show that such person has been "unjustly enriched" or that he obtained any other personal advantage.[22] In this category, i.e. knowing receipt or dealing, an objective test of knowledge has to be applied, i.e. the question is whether the stranger had, at the material time, actual or constructive notice of the trusts.[1]

Secondly, there are cases where a person has knowingly assisted in a dishonest and fraudulent design on the part of the trustees even though no part of the trust property ever comes into his hands.[2] The meaning of knowledge in relation to cases in this category, i.e. knowing assistance, was carefully considered by Ungoed-Thomas J. in *Selangor United Rubber Estates Ltd.* v. *Cradock* (No. 3)[3] who concluded[4] that "the knowledge required to hold a stranger liable as constructive trustee in a dishonest and fraudulent design is knowledge of circumstances which would indicate to an honest, reasonable man that such a design was being committed or would put him on enquiry, which the stranger failed to make, whether it was being committed. Acts in the circumstances normal in the honest conduct of affairs do not indicate such a misapplication, though compatible with it; and answers to enquiries are *prima facie* to be presumed to be honest." Subsequently, in *Karak Rurber Co. Ltd.* v. *Burden* (No. 2),[5] Brightman J. reiterated that the test is an objective one, and made it clear that there is no need to establish any want of probity on the part of the constructive trustee. In the *Selangor*[6] case Ungoed-Thomas J. also discussed the meaning of "a dishonest and fraudulent design". The phrase, he said,[7] is not

---

19 Convenient catch-phrases taken by Brightman J. from Snell's Equity, 26th Ed., pp. 202, 203 and used in *Karak Rubber Co. Ltd.* v. *Burden* (No. 2), [1972] 1 All E.R. 1210, at pp. 1234, 1235.

20 *Gray* v. *Lewis* (1869), L.R. 8 Eq. 526, affd. (1873), 8 Ch. App. 1035; *Nelson* v. *Larholt*, [1947] 2 All E.R. 751; [1948] 1 K.B. 339; *G. L. Baker Ltd.* v. *Medway Building & Supplies Ltd.*, [1958] 3 All E.R. 540, C.A. Cp. *Williams* v. *Williams* (1881), 17 Ch.D. 437.

21 *Lee* v. *Sankey* (1873), L.R. 15 Eq. 204; *Barnes* v. *Addy* (1874), 9 Ch.App. 244; *Re Barney*, [1892] 2 Ch. 265; *Soar* v. *Ashwell*, [1893] 2 Q.B. 390, C.A.; *Re Eyre-Williams*, [1923] 2 Ch. 533.

22 Per Edmund Davies L.J. in *Carl-Zeiss-Stiftung* v. *Herbert Smith & Co.* (No. 2), [1969] 2 All E.R. 367; [1969] 2 Ch. 277, C.A., at pp. 381; 300.

1 *Karak Rubber Co. Ltd.* v. *Burden* (No. 2), supra, at p. 1241.

2 *Eaves* v. *Hickson* (1861), 30 Beav. 136; *Barnes* v. *Addy*, supra; *Soar* v. *Ashwell*, supra, and see *Andrews* v. *Bousfield* (1847), 10 Beav. 511. A contrary inference can be drawn from *Selangor United Rubber Estates Ltd* v. *Cradock* (No. 3), [1968] 2 All E.R. 1073 at pp. 1123–1124—criticised (1969) 32 M.L.R. 328 (M. R. Chesterman and A. S. Grabiner).

3 [1968] 2 All E.R. 1073.   4 At p. 1104.

5 *Supra*. There are *dicta* of Sachs L.J. and Edmund Davies L.J., in *Carl-Zeiss-Stiftung* v. *Herbert Smith & Co.* (No. 2), [1969] 2 All E.R. 367; [1969] 2 Ch. 277, which may be used to support the contrary view as to want of probity, particularly in relation to an innocent, even though negligent, failure to enquire.   6 *Supra*.

7 In the *Selangor* case, supra, at p. 1105.

a term of art, and the words "are to be understood 'according to the plain principles of a court of equity' . . . (which) in this context at any rate, are just plain, ordinary commonsense. I accept that 'dishonest and fraudulent', so understood, is certainly conduct which is morally reprehensible; but what is morally reprehensible is best left open to identification and not to be confined by definition."

Where the stranger has trust property in his possession, but is not fixed with liability as a constructive trustee in accordance with the above principles, there are two possibilities: first, if the stranger can establish he is a *bona fide* purchaser for value of a legal estate, there will on general principles be no remedy against him at all.[8] Secondly, if he cannot establish this and is, as it is said, an innocent volunteer, although he may be under a liability to restore the trust fund in some circumstances,[9] even so he will not be liable as a constructive trustee.[10]

b Possession by an agent of trustees

The question has often arisen as to whether an agent of trustees, such as a solicitor, banker or broker, has himself become a constructive trustee of trust property which has come into his hands. It is clear that in this context such an agent is a stranger to the trust[11], and the same principle[12] has been formulated in terms to cover the special case. In *Lee* v. *Sankey*,[13] Bacon V.C. said,

> "It is well established by many decisions, that a mere agent of trustees is answerable only to his principal and not to *cestuis que trust* in respect of trust moneys coming to his hands merely in his character of agent. But it is also not less clearly established that a person who receives into his hands trust moneys, and who deals with them in a manner inconsistent with the performance of trusts of which he is cognisant, is personally liable for the consequences which may ensue upon his so dealing."

The same proposition was expressed in different words more recently by Bennett J.,[14] "an agent in possession of money which he knows to be trust money, so long as he acts honestly, is not accountable to the beneficiaries interested in the trust money unless he intermeddles in the trust by doing acts characteristic of a trustee and outside the duties of an agent". Three cases may be mentioned to illustrate what has been said. On the one hand, in *Mara* v. *Browne*[15] trustees employed a solicitor who advised improper investments,

---

[8] *Pilcher* v. *Rawlins* (1872), 7 Ch.App. 259.

[9] See Chapter 15, Section 2, p. 460, *post*.

[10] *Re Diplock's Estate*, [1948] 2 All E.R. 318, at 324–325, 347; [1948] Ch. 465, at 478–479, C.A.; affd. *sub nom. Ministry of Health* v. *Simpson*, [1950] 2 All E.R. 1137; [1951] A.C. 251, H.L.

[11] An agent in receipt of trust property has been said to be in the second category above— *Karak Rubber Co. Ltd.* v. *Burden* (*No. 2*), *supra*, at p. 1235.

[12] It is perhaps arguable that an agent in some respects may be in a different position from other strangers—*Carl-Zeiss-Stiftung* v. *Herbert Smith & Co.* (*No. 2*), [1969] 2 All E.R. 367; [1969] 2 Ch. 277, *per* Sachs L.J. at pp. 380; 299.

[13] (1873), L.R. 15 Eq. 204.

[14] In *Williams-Ashman* v. *Price*, [1942] 1 All E.R. 310, at p. 313; [1942] Ch. 219, at p. 228, citing *Mara* v. *Browne*, [1896] 1 Ch. 199, C.A.

[15] *Supra.* See also *Barnes* v. *Addy* (1874), 9 Ch.App. 244; *Re Blundell* (1888), 40 Ch.D. 370. Also contrast *Bridgman* v. *Gill* (1857), 24 Beav. 302, with *Thomson* v. *Clydesdale Bank Ltd.*, [1893] A.C. 282, H.L., and *Coleman* v. *Bucks and Oxon Union Bank*, [1897] 2 Ch. 243, a rather surprising decision on the facts.

which were actually carried through by him on being paid trust moneys for the purpose. It was held that the solicitor had acted only in his character of solicitor to the trustees and that consequently he was not liable as a constructive trustee. It may be added that an action brought in due time against the solicitor for negligence in advising an improper investment would probably have succeeded, but at the time of the action such a claim had become barred by the Statute of Limitations; the Statute, however, would not have affected a claim based on a breach of trust. The solicitors were also absolved from liability in the novel case of *Carl-Zeiss-Stiftung* v. *Herbert Smith & Co. (No 2).*[16] The plaintiff in this case had some years previously brought an action, as yet unheard, against X, the defendant solicitors' clients, claiming in effect that all X's property was held on trust for the plaintiff. X had paid fees in the ordinary way to the defendant solicitors, who had acted throughout with perfect propriety. The plaintiff now claimed that the moneys paid to the solicitors were held by them on a constructive trust for the plaintiff. The principles applied were that whatever might be the nature of the knowledge or notice required, cognisance of a "doubtful equity" is not enough: no stranger can become a constructive trustee merely because he is made aware of a disputed claim the validity of which he cannot properly assess. In particular the law is reluctant to make a mere agent a constructive trustee. Accordingly mere notice of a claim asserted by a third party is insufficient to render the agent guilty of a wrongful act in dealing with property derived from his principal in accordance with the latter's instructions unless the agent *knows* that the third party's claim is well founded and that the principal accordingly had no authority to give such instructions. The only possible exception would be the existence of a duty to enquire which had not been carried out. On the other hand, in *Lee* v. *Sankey*[17] trustees of a will employed solicitors to receive the proceeds of the sale of their testator's real estate. The solicitors improperly paid over the proceeds of sale to one only of the trustees, who subsequently became bankrupt, without the receipt or authority of the other. It was held that the solicitors were liable to make good the loss to the trust estate which accrued.

c Trustee *de son tort*

One point which is really only a matter of terminology should perhaps be mentioned. This is as to the meaning of the phrase "trustee *de son tort*" which is often used in this context. A trustee *de son tort* has been said to be the same thing as a constructive trustee,[18] though in this context "constructive trustee" seems to be limited to the particular circumstances being considered in the present section. It has been suggested[19], however, that a constructive trustee is one who has actually received the trust property or had it under his control, while a trustee *de son tort* is one who, without receiving the trust property, has knowingly assisted the trustee in a fraudulent breach of trust, or has mixed himself up in the affairs of the trust by assuming to act as trustee. It is sub-

---

[16] [1969] 2 Ch. 277; [1969] 2 All E.R. 367 C.A.
[17] (1873), L.R. 15 Eq. 204. See also *Blyth* v. *Fladgate*, [1891] 1 Ch. 337; *Soar* v. *Ashwell*, [1893] 2 Q.B. 390, C.A.
[18] *Mara* v. *Browne*, [1896] 1 Ch. 199, C.A.; *Re Barney*, [1892] 2 Ch. 265.
[19] Nathan and Marshall, *A Casebook on Trusts*, 5th Ed., pp. 310, 311.

mitted that the better view is that the expression trustee *de son tort*, which seems to have been adopted from the expression executor *de son tort* in the law relating to administration of assets, is not to be contrasted with a constructive trustee, but is an expression used to describe one type of constructive trust, namely, where a stranger has positively assumed to act as trustee. This seems in effect to represent the opinion of Ungoed-Thomas J. in *Selangor United Rubber Estates, Ltd.* v. *Cradock (No. 3)*,[20] where he distinguished between what he called "two very different kinds of so-called constructive trustees. (i) Those who, though not appointed trustees, take on themselves to act as such and to possess and administer trust property for the beneficiaries, such as trustees *de son tort*. Distinguishing features [include] (a) they do not claim to act in their own right but for the beneficiaries, and (b) their assumption to act is not of itself a ground of liability (save in the sense of course of liability to account and for any failure in the duty so assumed), and so their status as trustees precedes the occurrence which may be the subject of claim against them. (ii) Those whom a court of equity will treat as trustees by reason of their action, of which complaint is made. Distinguishing features are (a) that such trustees claim to act in their own right and not for beneficiaries, and (b) no trusteeship arises before, but only by reason of, the action complained of." In any case, the meaning of the expression trustee *de son tort*, as already indicated, is not a matter of practical importance for, even if he is to be distinguished from a constructive trustee, his liability is the same.

---

[20] [1968] 2 All E.R. 1073 at p. 1095.

CHAPTER 5

Void and Voidable Trusts

1 UNLAWFUL TRUSTS

It is against the policy of the law to enforce certain trusts, and the following are the more important categories of trust which are liable to be declared void. It is not intended to give an exhaustive list, and in any case there is no reason why a novel kind of trust should not be declared void on the ground of public policy. As Danckwerts L.J. said in *Nagle* v. *Feilden:*[1] "The law relating to public policy cannot remain immutable. It must change with the passage of time. The wind of change blows on it". Some cases are really isolated instances, such as *Brown* v. *Burdett*.[2]

a   Trusts which offend against the rule against perpetuities

Since the Perpetuities and Accumulations Act 1964 it will only be rarely that the rule against perpetuities will make void a limitation contained in an instrument taking effect after the commencement of the Act.[3] Until amended by the Act, however, the rule was one of the commonest causes of the failure of a trust. In its unamended form it laid down that a future interest[4] in any kind of property, real or personal, would be void *ab initio* if it might possibly vest outside the perpetuity period, namely, the compass of a life or any number of lives in being[5] at the time when the instrument creating it came into effect, and twenty-one years thereafter, with the possible addition of the period of gestation in the case of some person entitled being *en ventre sa mère* at the end of the period. The main alteration made by the 1964 Act was to change the rule from one concerned with possibilities to one concerned with actual events—the wait and see principle. The rule is discussed at length in books on the law of real property, to which the reader is referred.[6]

---

[1] [1966] 1 All E.R. 689, at p. 696, C.A., admittedly in a different context.
[2] (1882), 21 Ch.D. 667 (trust to block up a house for twenty years).
[3] 16th July, 1964. With one limited exception (in s. 8 (2)) the Act has no retrospective effect—s. 15 (5).
[4] Since 1925 a future interest, other than a reversionary lease, must be an equitable interest under a trust. For a possible qualification see (1908), 24 L.Q.R. 431 (D. T. Oliver).
[5] Including the life of a person *en ventre sa mère* at the relevant time.
[6] See, e.g., Cheshire's *Modern Real Property*, 11th Ed., pp. 263 *et seq.*; Megarry and Wade, *The Law of Real Property*, 3rd Ed., pp. 214 *et seq.*; Morris and Leach, *The Rule against Perpetuities*, 2nd Ed., and Supp.

b Trusts which offend against the rule against perpetual trusts

Closely related to and sometimes confused with the rule against perpetuities is the rule that a gift which requires capital to be retained beyond the perpetuity period is void. This rule is sometimes known as the rule against inalienability, and it should perhaps be made clear that it cannot be evaded merely by giving a power to change investments sufficiently wide to enable the property given to be disposed of, if the proceeds of sale are required to be re-invested and the capital fund has to be retained in perpetuity. This rule, which does not apply to charities, is, like the rule against perpetuities, discussed in books on the law of real property.[7]

c Trusts for illegitimate children

The law has recently been altered by s.15 of the Family Law Reform Act 1969, but it will for some time be necessary to know the old law, which still applies to dispositions made before the section came into effect on the 1st January, 1970. It should be observed in particular that so far as dispositions by will are concerned, what matters is the date the will was executed, not the date of the testator's death, and for this purpose a disposition in a will executed before 1st January, 1970 is not treated as made on or after that date by reason only that it is confirmed by a codicil executed on or after that date:

(i) *The law relating to dispositions made before 1st January, 1970.* The courts had, in the more recent cases, already recognised that the objection to gifts to illegitimate children on the ground of their being contrary to public policy was less strong than had formerly been thought to be the case. The basis of the objection is that such gifts are *contra bonos mores*, as tending to encourage immorality, but as was observed in *Re Hyde*,[8] "the view of the legislature is that no useful purpose is served by penalising illegitimate children, and that the true interests of public policy do not require innocent persons to be punished in that manner".

Before reaching the objection of public policy, however, an illegitimate child, if he is to take, must establish that he is an intended beneficiary under the disposition in question.[9] This may be a matter of some difficulty where there is a gift to children as a class, for the rule is that children *prima facie* means legitimate children,[10] though the wording of the instrument and admissible extrinsic evidence may establish that in a particular context children means or includes illegitimate children.[11] There is no difficulty on the ground of uncertainty where there is a gift to the illegitimate children of a woman—maternity is, it has been said, "a fact perhaps of all others the most easily capable of

---

[7] See, e.g., Megarry and Wade, *op. cit.*, pp. 272 *et seq.*; Morris and Leach, *op. cit.*, pp. 321 *et seq.*

[8] [1932] 1 Ch. 95, 98.

[9] For a full discussion see Jarman on *Wills*, 8th Ed., Vol. III, pp. 1750 *et seq.*

[10] *Hill* v. *Crook* (1873), L.R. 6 H.L. 265; *Dorin* v. *Dorin* (1875), L.R. 7 H.L. 568; *Re Pearce*, [1914] 1 Ch. 254, C.A.; *Re Wohlgemuth*, [1948] 2 All E.R. 882; [1949] Ch. 12. Cf. *Sydall* v. *Castings, Ltd.*, [1966] 3 All E.R. 770; [1967] 1 Q.B. 302, C.A. (descendant).

[11] See, e.g., *Re Haseldine* (1886), 31 Ch.D. 511, C.A.; *Re Loveland*, [1906] 1 Ch. 542; *Re Herwin*, [1953] 2 All E.R. 782; [1953] Ch. 701, C.A. Cf. *Re Gilpin*, [1953] 2 All E.R. 1218; [1954] Ch. 1; *Re Jebb*, [1965] 3 All E.R. 358; [1966] Ch. 667, C.A. (both concerned with an adopted child) and see the criticism of the latter case in (1966), 582 L.Q.R. 196 (J. H. C. Morris).

conclusive proof".[12] As to the illegitimate children of a man, public policy forbids an inquiry into actual paternity,[13] but reputed illegitimate children may be able to claim on the basis of reputation—"although the fact of paternity cannot be inquired into, the reputation of paternity may".[14] If a gift extends to illegitimate children of a man, reputed illegitimate children in existence when the deed is executed, or in the case of a will, when it is actually made, are clearly capable of taking. The better view, it is submitted, is that reputed illegitimate children who are born after the date of the will but before the date of the death of a testator are also capable of establishing the necessary reputation.[15] It is, however, doubtful whether a child *en ventre sa mère* at the relevant date can subsequently establish that at the material point of time he had the reputation of being the child of a particular man[16]: but, of course, if there is simply a gift to an illegitimate child *en ventre sa mère*, without any reference to paternity, the gift will be good.[17]

Public policy comes into play and declares a disposition void only where the gift is by deed to future illegitimate children, or by will to illegitimate children to be begotten after the death of the testator.[18] The law, and the reason behind it, are explained by Mellish L.J. in *Occleston* v. *Fullalove*[19]:

> "If a man, at the commencement of an illicit intercourse with a particular woman, could make a valid settlement on his expected illegitimate children, this would, I think, manifestly encourage the immoral connection and discourage marriage, which the law favours . . . it is necessary to consider how far the same doctrine applies to wills. Now if a will was so worded as to give a bequest to illegitimate children to be begotten after the death of the testator, I think it would be subject to the same objection as a settlement by deed."

Mellish L.J. went on to explain that there could be no objection to a gift to illegitimate children by the will of the putative father himself,[20] for obviously such a gift could not encourage an immoral intercourse after his death.

A restrictive application of the rule as to public policy appears in *In re Hyde*,[1] where a testator gave his residue on trust for his son for life, with remainder to such of the children or reputed children of his son as the son should by will appoint. It was held that an appointment could validly be made in favour of reputed children born and begotten after the death of the testator, the court taking the view that the power would not encourage immorality. Finally, it should be observed that under a gift to a class which may include future illegitimate children the gift may be valid as to the illegitimate children then

---

[12] *Occleston* v. *Fullalove* (1874), 9 Ch. App. 147, *per* James L.J. at p. 164.

[13] *Occleston* v. *Fullalove*, *supra*; *Re Bolton* (1886), 31 Ch.D. 542, C.A; *Re Homer* (1916), 115 L.T. 703.

[14] *Per* Bowen L.J. in *Re Bolton*, *supra*, at p. 553.

[15] *Occleston* v. *Fullalove* (1874), 9 Ch. App, 147; *Re Hyde*, [1932] 1 Ch. 95.

[16] *Metham* v. *Duke of Devon* (1718), 1 P. Wms. 529; *Earle* v. *Wilson* (1811), 17 Ves. 528.

[17] *Gordon* v. *Gordon* (1816), 1 Mer. 141.

[18] *Occleston* v. *Fullalove*, *supra*; *Re Hastie's Trust* (1887), 35 Ch.D. 728; *Re Hyde*, *supra*.

[19] *Supra*, at p. 171.

[20] *A fortiori* a gift by a mother to her illegitimate child, even though begotten and born after the date of the will; *Re Frogley*, [1905] P. 137.

[1] *Supra*.

existing, or begotten but not yet born, even though it fails as to those neither born nor begotten when the deed or will comes into effect.[2]

(ii) *The law relating to dispositions made after 31st December, 1969.* Both of the old difficulties have disappeared. By s.15(1) of the Family Law Reform Act 1969 the presumption that "children" means "legitimate children" is reversed: *prima facie* it is to be construed as meaning, or including, illegitimate children, and by s.15(7) the rule that a disposition in favour of illegitimate children not in being when the disposition takes effect is void as being contrary to public policy is abolished.

d The effect of declaring a trust void as offending against the policy of the law

In the types of case discussed in the three preceding subsections, the usual result of an expressed trust being declared void will be that the property must be held on a resulting trust for the settlor, or, where the trust arises under a will, the property will fall into the residuary estate[3] of the testator. The particular provisions of the instrument creating the trust must, however, be taken into account. Suppose, for instance, the limitations under a trust were to X for life, with remainder for life to X's first son to become a barrister, remainder in fee simple to Y. Suppose further that when the limitation came into effect X had no children though he subsequently had sons who survived him by more than 21 years. Before the Perpetuities and Accumulations Act 1964, the second limitation would have been void *ab initio* as infringing the rule against perpetuities, and even now will become void for the same reason if no son has become a barrister within 21 years of the death of X. Neither before nor after the Act, however, would there have been a resulting trust, but the vested remainder of Y would have been or would be accelerated.[4] Again, as we have seen,[5] where a gift to existing and future illegitimate children is void as to the future children, the interest which they would have taken may accrue to the benefit of any children in existence.

In the types of case discussed in the following three subsections, the question is not strictly one as to the validity of the trust itself, but as to the validity of a condition to which the trust is made subject. It is a question of construction whether a condition is a condition precedent, i.e. where the gift is not intended to take effect unless and until the condition is fulfilled, or a condition subsequent, i.e. where the gift vests immediately, but is liable to be divested if and when the condition is fulfilled, the court in general, it seems, preferring the latter construction where the intention is not made clear. If a condition subsequent

---

[2] *Ebbern* v. *Fowler*, [1909] 1 Ch. 578, C.A.; *Hill* v. *Crook* (1873), L.R. 6 H.L. 265; *Crook* v. *Hill* (1876), 3 Ch.D. 773. Contrast the position as to class gifts in connection with the rule against perpetuities, Cheshire, *Modern Real Property*, 11th Ed., pp. 274 *et seq.*; Megarry and Wade, *The Law of Real Property*, 3rd Ed., pp. 234 *et seq.*; Morris and Leach, *Rule against Perpetuities*, 2nd Ed., pp. 101 *et seq.*, now altered by the Perpetuities and Accumulations Act 1964, ss. 3 and 4.

[3] If the subject of the gift is residue, or if there is no residuary gift, it will become property undisposed of by will and devolve accordingly.

[4] Cf. *Re Flower's Settlement Trusts*, [1957] 1 All E.R. 462, C.A.; *Re Allan's Will Trusts*, [1958] 1 All E.R. 401, overruled on another point, *Re Gulbenkian's Settlement Trusts* [1967] 3 All E.R. 15; [1968] Ch. 126, C.A. affd. [1968] 3 All E.R. 785; [1970] A.C. 508, H.L. and see Perpetuities and Accumulations Act 1964, s. 6.; (1973), 32 C.L.J. 246 (A. M. Pritchard).

[5] *Supra*, pp. 128, 129.

is void,[6] the gift, whether of realty or personalty, remains good and is not liable to be determined by breach of the condition, the presence of a gift over being irrelevant. In the case of conditions precedent it seems that a distinction has to be drawn between gifts of realty and gifts of personalty. If a gift of real property is made dependent upon a condition precedent which is void, the gift fails. In the case of a gift of personal property where a condition precedent is illegal and void, a further distinction is drawn according to whether the illegality involves *malum in se*, or *malum prohibitum*. In the former case, the gift fails, as in the case of real property, but in the latter case the gift is good, and will pass to the donee unfettered by the condition. Unfortunately "the difference between *malum prohibitum* and *malum in se* has never been very precisely defined or considered"[7]; *malum in se* seems to mean some act which is intrinsically and morally wrong, such as murder, *malum prohibitum* some act which offends against a rule of law but is not wrong in itself, such as smuggling.

e   Trusts tending to prevent the carrying out of parental duties

The cases have usually arisen on the validity of a condition subsequent, and in deciding the matter the courts have referred to the principle set out in Sheppard's *Touchstone*,[8] that "if the matter of the condition tend to provoke or further the doing of some unlawful act, or to restrain or forbid a man the doing of his duty; the condition for the most part is void". Thus in *Re Sandbrook*[9] a testatrix, having given the bulk of her residuary estate to trustees on trust for two grandchildren, declared that if one or both of them should "live with or be or continue under the custody, guardianship or control of their father, . . . or be in any way directly under his control", they should forfeit their interest. It was held that the case fell directly within the principle laid down in Sheppard's *Touchstone*. The condition, Parker J. said,[10] "is inserted in the will with the direct object of deterring the father of these two children from performing his parental duties with regard to them, because it makes their worldly welfare dependent on his abstaining from doing what it is certainly his duty to do, namely, to bring his influence to bear and not give up his right to the custody, the control and education of his children". It was accordingly declared to be void, with the result that the gift remained valid and not liable to be determined by breach of the condition. The same principle was applied to a condition subsequent against embracing the Roman Catholic faith in *Re Borwick*,[11] where it was observed,[12] "The parents' duty[13] is to be discharged solely with a view to the moral and spiritual welfare of their children, and ought not to be influenced by mercenary considerations affecting the infant's worldly welfare."

---

[6] The requirement of certainty is stricter for a condition subsequent than a condition precedent; *Re Allen*, [1953] 2 All E.R. 898; [1953] Ch. 810, C.A.; *Re Lysaght*, [1965] 2 All E.R. 888; [1966] Ch. 191; *Re Lowry's Will Trusts*, [1966] 3 All E.R. 955; [1967] Ch. 638.

[7] Per Romer J. in *Re Piper*, [1946] 2 All E.R. 503, at p. 505. See Sheppard's *Touchstone*, p. 132; *Re Moore* (1888), 39 Ch.D. 116, C.A.; *Re Elliott*, [1952] 1 All E.R. 145; [1952] Ch. 217; (1955), 19 Con. 176 (V. T. H. Delaney).   [8] P. 132.

[9] [1912] 2 Ch. 471. See also *Re Morgan* (1910), 26 T.L.R. 398—bequest to grandchildren on condition of living with mother if she and father live separately.

[10] *Re Sandbrook*, [1912] 2 Ch. 471, at p. 476.

[11] [1933] Ch. 657. See also *Re Boulter*, [1922] 1 Ch. 75.

[12] Per Bennett J. at p. 666.

[13] As to religion. See also *Re Tegg*, [1936] 2 All E.R. 878.

Perhaps the strongest case is *Re Piper*,[14] where a condition[15] against residence with the father was held void as being calculated to bring about the separation of parent and child, notwithstanding the fact that the father had been divorced before the date of the will under which the gift to the children was made. The condition was further held to be *malum prohibitum*, and, accordingly, the gift to the children, being a gift of personalty, took effect free from it.

f Trusts designed or tending to induce a future separation of husband and wife, or to encourage an invasion of the sanctity of the marriage bond

Where a husband and wife have decided upon an immediate separation, trusts contained in a deed of separation entered into at that time are valid and will be enforced[16]; the point is that the separation in such case is not in any way induced by the trusts contained in the deed. By contrast, trusts which are made in contemplation of the future separation of a husband and wife then living together are void, for their existence might tend to bring about a separation which would not otherwise take place.[17]

A condition contained in a bequest to a married woman that she should live apart from her husband has been held[18] *contra bonos mores* and void on this ground. Again in the case of the will of a testatrix giving her residue to her son absolutely with a proviso modifying the gift so long as the son's wife should be alive and married to him, but declaring that the absolute gift should take effect if the wife should die or the marriage be otherwise terminated, it was held that the provision was designed, or tended, to encourage an invasion of the sanctity of the marriage bond, and was, therefore, void as being against public policy.[19] The facts were somewhat similar and the decision the same in *Re Johnson's Will Trusts*,[20] where a testator gave his residue of over £11,000 on protective trusts for his daughter for life, with a proviso cutting down her interest to £50 p.a. so long as she was married and living with her husband, but giving her the whole income in the event of the husband's death, or her divorce or separation from him. The result will be the same where the provision in question operates indirectly as in *Wilkinson* v. *Wilkinson*,[1] where a condition in the will took away a gift to a married woman "should she not cease to reside in Skipton", where her husband lived and where his business was. It was held that the condition was void, as it was designed to induce her not to carry out her duties as a wife.

The effect of each particular provision has to be carefully considered in every case. Thus in *Re Lovell*,[2] a man, by his will, gave an annuity to his mistress,

---

[14] [1946] 2 All E.R. 503.
[15] In this case a condition precedent. See (1947), 11 Con. 218 (J. H. C. Morris).
[16] *Wilson* v. *Wilson* (1848), 1 H.L.C. 538; *Vansittart* v. *Vansittart* (1858), 2 De G. & J. 249.
[17] *Westmeath* v. *Westmeath* (1830), 1 Dow. & Cl. 519; *Re Moore* (1888), 39 Ch.D. 116, C.A.
[18] *Wren* v. *Bradley* (1848), 2 De G. & Sm. 49; *Re Freedman* (unreported, 2nd December, 1942—referred to in *Re Caborne*, [1943] 2 All E.R. 7; [1943] Ch. 224).
[19] *Re Caborne*, [1943] 2 All E.R. 7; [1943] Ch. 224; *Re Hope Johnstone*, [1904] 1 Ch. 470.
[20] [1967] 1 All E.R. 553; [1967] Ch. 387.
[1] (1871), L.R. 12 Eq. 604.
[2] [1920] 1 Ch. 122.

a married woman living apart from her husband "provided and so long as she shall not return to live with her present husband . . . or remarry". It was held that the provision was valid, as its object was not to induce her to continue to live apart from her husband and not to remarry, but to make provision for her until she returned to her husband or remarried. A similar decision was reached in Re Thompson,[3] where a testator gave his daughter an annuity of £300, if still married to her present husband, but the income of the whole estate if she should become a widow, or remarried to another person, or divorced and not remarried to her present husband. It was held that the provision was not contrary to public policy as the purpose was not to induce a divorce, but to prevent the income coming into the hands of the husband, regarded by the testator as a spendthrift. It has been suggested,[4] however, that this decision disregards the rule that the law looks to the general tendency of the disposition, and not to the possibility of public mischief occurring in the particular instance.

g   Trusts in restraint of marriage

The law is difficult,[5] being complicated both by the differences in the rules relating to general and partial restraints and also by the distinctions that have to be drawn between dispositions of realty, where the rules are based on the common law, and dispositions of personalty, where the rules adopted by the Court of Chancery came to it, with considerable modifications, from Roman Law by way of the Ecclesiastical Courts.[6]

So far as realty is concerned there is no clear decision, but the weight of opinion is in favour of the view that a general restraint is prima facie void.[7] It seems, however, that whatever the form of the disposition it will readily be treated as a limitation until marriage, which is valid, if the intention appears to be, not to promote celibacy, but to make provision until marriage takes place.[8]

So far as personalty[9] is concerned, it is settled that a general restraint is prima facie void,[10] whether the restraint is general in so many words, or whether,

---

[3] [1939] 1 All E.R. 681.

[4] By Simonds J. in Re Caborne, [1943] 2 All E.R. 7; [1943] Ch. 224. Cf. Re Fentem, [1950] 2 All E.R. 1073; Re Johnson's Will Trusts, supra.

[5] "Proverbially difficult", at least as to personalty, per Younger J. in Re Hewett, [1918] 1 Ch. 458, 463.

[6] See Re Whiting's Settlement, [1905] 1 Ch. 96, C.A., per Vaughan Williams L.J. at pp. 115–116; Bellairs v. Bellairs (1874), L.R. 18 Eq. 510, per Jessel M.R. at p. 513.

[7] White and Tudor, Leading Cases in Equity, 9th Ed., Vol. I, p. 487; Jarman on Wills, 8th Ed., Vol. II, p. 1528; (1896), 12 L.Q.R. 36 (Cyprian Williams). Contra, Theobald on Wills, 13th Ed., p. 585, citing Bellairs v. Bellairs, supra, criticised in Duddy v. Gresham (1878), 2 L.R. Ir. 442, and Jones v. Jones (1876), 1 Q.B.D. 279, D.C., which however, seems rather to support the contrary view, stressing the qualification immediately following in the text. Theobald, loc. cit., agrees that a general restraint is void in the case of an estate tail, as being repugnant to the interest granted—Earl of Arundel's Case (1575), 3 Dyer. 342b.

[8] Jones v. Jones (1876), 1 Q.B.D. 279, D.C.

[9] Or a mixed fund representing the proceeds of sale of real estate and personalty—Bellairs v. Bellairs (1874), L.R. 18 Eq. 510.

[10] Bellairs v. Bellairs, supra; Re Bellamy (1883), 48 L.T. 212; Re Hewett, [1918] 1 Ch. 458.

although in terms partial, it is from its nature probable that in practice it would amount to a prohibition of marriage.[11] However, where the intention was not to promote celibacy, but, for instance, to make provision for the child of the person restrained,[12] or to ensure that after the death of the person restrained the property given would be dealt with in a particular manner,[13] the restraint has been held good. On principle one might have thought that the court would not be entitled to look behind the general tendency of the provision, and examine its motive and intention in the light of the particular circumstances and the ground of public policy involved. However, in the cases above referred to, the court has regarded itself as entitled to make the necessary inquiry.[14] It is clear, however, that a gift until marriage is perfectly good,[15] the intention in such case being assumed to be to provide for the beneficiary while unmarried, and not to prevent a marriage from taking place.

Partial restraints, whether with regard to realty or to personalty are *prima facie* valid,[16] and accordingly the following conditions have been held good: against marriage with any person born in Scotland or of Scottish parents,[17] against marriage with a person who did not profess the Jewish religion and was not born a Jew,[18] against marriage with a domestic servant, or a person who had been a domestic servant,[19] against marriage with either of two named persons,[20] or against marriage without the consent of named persons.[1] For this purpose a condition in restraint of a second or subsequent marriage, whether of a man or a woman, and whether the gift was by one spouse to the survivor, or by a stranger, is regarded as a partial restraint, and it is accordingly *prima facie* valid.[2]

There is, however, an important difference in the effect of a partial restraint imposed on realty and personalty respectively. Lord Radcliffe[3] has stated the position in these words:

"For, whereas a condition subsequent in partial restraint of marriage was effective to determine the estate in the case of a devise of realty even without any new limitation to take effect on the forfeiture, so that a residuary devisee or heir came

---

[11] *Re Lanyon,* [1927] 2 Ch. 264—marriage with a blood relation.

[12] *Re Hewett,* [1918] 1 Ch. 458, where the woman restrained was the testator's mistress and the child the fruit of their irregular union.

[13] *Re Fentem,* [1950] 2 All E.R. 1073—a gift by a testatrix to her brother for life, with remainder to his personal representatives. The condition was attached only to the gift over after the brother's death.

[14] *Re Hewett,* [1918] 1 Ch. 458; *Re Fentem,* [1950] 2 All E.R. 1073. See also *Jones v. Jones, supra.* Cf. *Re Caborne,* [1943] 2 All E.R. 7; [1943] Ch. 224.

[15] *Morley v. Rennoldson* (1843), 2 Hare 570; *Webb v. Grace* (1848), 2 Ph. 701.

[16] Unless void on some other ground, such as uncertainty. See, e.g., *Clayton v. Ramsden,* [1943] 1 All E.R. 16; [1943] A.C. 320, H.L.; *Re Moss's Trusts,* [1945] 1 All E.R. 207.

[17] *Perrin v. Lyon* (1807), 9 East. 170.

[18] *Hodgson v. Halford* (1879), 11 Ch.D. 959. Cf. *Re Selby's Will Trusts,* [1965] 3 All E.R. 386 (condition precedent).

[19] *Jenner v. Turner* (1880), 16 Ch.D. 188.

[20] *Re Bathe,* [1925] Ch. 377; *Re Hanlon,* [1933] Ch. 254.

[1] *Dashwood v. Lord Bulkeley* (1804), 10 Ves. 230; *Lloyd v. Branton* (1817), 3 Mer. 108.

[2] *Leong v. Chye,* [1955] 2 All E.R. 903; [1955] A.C. 648, P.C.; *Allen v. Jackson* (1875), 1 Ch.D. 399, C.A.

[3] Giving the judgment of the Judicial Committee of the Privy Council in *Leong v. Chye, supra,* at 906; 660.

E.T.   9

in of his own right,[4] it was early determined and consistently maintained that a condition subsequent in partial restraint of marriage, when annexed to a bequest of personalty,[5] was ineffective to destroy the gift unless the will in question contained an explicit gift over of the legacy to another legatee. And for this purpose a mere residuary bequest was not treated as a gift over."

In the latter case, where there is no gift over, the condition is said to be merely *in terrorem*, that is, intended merely in a monitory sense. Lord Radcliffe,[6] after emphasising that it is impossible to give an account of the origin of the rule that is wholly logical, suggested that rather than base the rule on an artificial presumed intention, it is better to say simply that it is the presence in the will of the express gift over that determines the matter in favour of forfeiture.

h   Trusts which are not merely unlawful but also fraudulent

As we have seen,[7] where the object of a trust is unlawful, in general there will be a resulting trust for the settlor, or where the trust is declared by will, the property given will fall into the residuary estate of the testator. This is so not only when the trust offends against a technical rule such as the rule against perpetuities, but also when it is *contra bonos mores*, such as a trust for future illegitimate children, or where the trust is calculated to encourage an offence prohibited by statute.[8] Where, however, the object is not merely against the policy of the law, but is also fraudulent, further considerations have to be taken into account.

In the first place it should be made clear that if the matter is still in the stage of contract or covenant, the fraud or illegality will, of course, make it unenforceable. This is not a matter of trust, but a matter of contract. We are concerned, however, to consider at this point cases where a man, having conveyed or transferred property to another for some fraudulent and illegal purpose, subsequently claims that that other holds the property upon a resulting trust for him. Although it is usually clear in cases of this type that no beneficial interest was intended to pass, it seems that, in general, a claim by way of resulting trust will nevertheless fail, if it is necessary for the plaintiff to disclose his own illegality,[9] the maxim of law that *in pari delicto melior est conditio possidentis*[10] being supported by the equitable maxim that "he who seeks equity must come with clean hands". As Lord Eldon explained[11]: ". . . the plaintiff stating, he had been guilty of a fraud upon the law . . . and coming to equity to be relieved against his own act, and the defence being dishonest, between the two species of dishonesty the Court would not act; but would say 'Let the estate lie, where it falls'." Accordingly, it has been held, or at least an opinion expressed, that a claim should fail on this ground, in cases where a ship was registered in the name of one partner only, to enable profits to be made by government contracts into which the other partner, who alleged a trust, could

---

[4] *Haughton* v. *Haughton* (1824), 1 Moll. 611; *Jenner* v. *Turner, supra.*
[5] And, possibly, where realty and personalty are given together: *Duddy* v. *Gresham* (1878), 2 L.R.Ir. 442.
[6] *Leong* v. *Chye*, [1955] 2 All E.R. 903, at p. 908; [1955] A.C. 648, at p. 662, P.C.
[7] See p. 129, *ante.*
[8] *Thrupp* v. *Collett* (1858), 26 Beav. 125.
[9] *Chettiar* v. *Chettiar*, [1962] 1 All E.R. 494; [1962] A.C. 294, P.C. Cf. *Shaw* v. *Shaw*, [1965] 1 All E.R. 638, C.A.
[10] See (1955), 71 L.Q.R. 254 (J. K. Grodecki).
[11] In *Muckleston* v. *Brown* (1801), 6 Ves. 52, 69.

not enter, being a Member of Parliament[12]; or where property has been transferred in order to give a colourable qualification to kill game,[13] or to sit in
Parliament,[14] or to vote at an election[15]; or where money was placed to the
credit of a company to enable it to have a fictitious credit in case of inquiries
at their bankers.[16]

A claim to relief may, however, succeed if it turns out that no fraud has in
fact been perpetrated, whatever the motive or intention may have been,[17] and
there will, of course, be no fraud and a resulting trust can be set up where
property has been transferred in order to give a qualification for some purpose,
and this qualification is satisfied by possession of the bare legal title.[18] Further,
the better opinion is, perhaps, that a settlor may recover if he repents of his
fraudulent and illegal purpose before its performance has been begun,[19] though
some cases suggest a stricter view.[20] In any case where the plaintiff does not
have to disclose any illegality it seems that a defendant who wishes to rely on
the fraud and illegality of a transaction as a defence to a claim that he is a
trustee holding on a resulting trust for the grantor, must plead it in distinct
terms: as has been said,[1] he "must clearly put forward his own scoundrelism
if he means to reap the benefit of it".

Mention should also be made of the proposition that although a settlor who
has transferred property to another for a fraudulent and illegal purpose may
be unable to recover it, the position may be otherwise if the claim is made by
someone claiming through the settlor who is himself personally not *in delicto*.
It is difficult to see on what satisfactory principle this view can be supported,
although it has been put forward by no less an authority than Lord Eldon.[2]
It was held to be erroneous and contrary to law by Lord Selborne,[3] though
without having been referred to Lord Eldon's dictum.

In another type of case the real question has been whether the settlor can
successfully allege a resulting trust on the ground that the expressed trust has
failed, as being created for an illegal consideration. It is submitted that the
correct principle was applied in *Ayerst* v. *Jenkins*,[4] where the plaintiffs' claim was

[12] *Curtis* v. *Perry* (1802), 6 Ves. 739; *Ex parte Yallop* (1808), 15 Ves. 60, where the allegation
of a resulting trust failed purely on the ground that to admit it would defeat the purpose
of the statute requiring registration.
[13] *Druckenbury* v. *Druckenbury* (1820), 2 Jac. & W. 441.
[14] *Platamore* v. *Staple* (1815), Coop. G. 250.
[15] *Groves* v. *Groves* (1829), 3 Y. & J. 163.
[16] *Re Great Berlin Steamboat Co.* (1884), 26 Ch.D. 616, C.A.
[17] *Davies* v. *Otty* (No. 2) (1865), 35 Beav. 208.
[18] *Childers* v. *Childers* (1857), 1 De G. & J. 482.
[19] *Symes* v. *Hughes* (1870), L.R. 9 Eq. 475; *Chettiar* v. *Chettiar, supra*; or, possibly, even at a
later point of time—*Ayerst* v. *Jenkins* (1873), L.R. 16 Eq. 275, *per* Lord Selborne L.C.
at p. 284.
[20] *Groves* v. *Groves, supra*; *Roberts* v. *Roberts* (1818), Dan. 143.
[1] *Haigh* v. *Kaye* (1872), 7 Ch. App. 469, at p. 473, *per* James L.J.; *Chettiar* v. *Chettiar
supra*.
[2] *Muckleston* v. *Brown* (1801), 6 Ves. 52, 68; *Matthew* v. *Hanbury* (1690), 2 Vern.
187.
[3] *Ayerst* v. *Jenkins* (1873), L.R. 16 Eq. 275, at p. 281.
[4] (1873), L.R. 16 Eq. 275. Cf. cases where there is a prior trust until the solemnisation of a
marriage, which either cannot in law take place because the parties are within the
prohibited degrees, or which is subsequently avoided *ab initio* by the grant of a decree
of nullity—*Pawson* v. *Brown* (1879), 13 Ch.D. 202; *Re Wombwell's Settlement*, [1922]
2 Ch. 298; *Re d'Altroy's Will Trusts*, [1968] 1 All E.R. 181.

dismissed. In that case the settlor, shortly before going through a ceremony of marriage with his deceased wife's sister, which to the knowledge of both parties was invalid under the then existing state of the law, transferred certain property to trustees for the lady. The settlor and the lady cohabited unlawfully as man and wife until the settlor's death. Subsequently his personal representatives claimed the property on the ground that the settlement was founded on an immoral consideration. The court distinguished cases where relief was sought against a bond or covenant or other obligation resting *in fieri*, where the consideration was illegal, and held that in the case of an executed trust, a settlor was not entitled to relief on the ground of the illegality of his own intention and purpose. In discussing the claim it was observed, however, that the position might be otherwise in a case where to refuse "relief to a particular plaintiff might be to effectuate an unlawful object, or to defeat a legal prohibition, or to protect a fraud".[5] The decision in this case is consistent with the *ratio decidendi* of a line of cases in which it has been held that although a deed or bond entered into with a woman in consideration of future illicit cohabitation is illegal and void, a deed in consideration of past cohabitation is valid, and the mere contemplation of future cohabitation is not enough to invalidate it, it making no difference that cohabitation in fact subsequently takes place.[6]

Ayerst v. *Jenkins*[7] was, however, distinguished in the unsatisfactory decision on similar facts of *Phillips* v. *Probyn*[8] on the ground that there was not a claim by the settlor or anyone claiming under him, but an application by the trustees for directions as to whom they ought to pay. On principle the illegality of the consideration would not seem to be any ground for a trustee in whom that property is vested failing to carry out his trust,[9] but in this case North J. held that the trustees must account to the representatives of the settlor.[10]

2 VOIDABLE CONVEYANCES UNDER SECTION 172 OF THE LAW OF PROPERTY ACT 1925

a General

This section replaces, and in effect and in more modern language, re-enacts, certain provisions[11] of the statute 13 Eliz. I c. 5, which itself has been said to be

---

[5] *Per* Lord Selborne in *Ayerst* v. *Jenkins* (1873), L.R. 16 Eq. 275 at p. 283.

[6] *Re Vallance* (1884), 26 Ch.D. 353; *Re Wootton Isaacson* (1904), 21 T.L.R. 89.

[7] *Supra.*

[8] [1899] 1 Ch. 811; *Chapman* v. *Bradley* (1863), 33 Beav. 61, affd. on different grounds (1863), 4 De G.J. & S. 71.

[9] Cf. *Thomson* v. *Thomson* (1802), 7 Ves. 470; *Sharp* v. *Taylor* (1849), 2 Ph. 801, 818.

[10] If the decisions in *Ayerst* v. *Jenkins, supra*, and *Phillips* v. *Probyn, supra*, are both to stand, the trustees would not seem to be liable to be attacked, whether they account to the expressed beneficiary or the settlor. If they choose the first alternative any claim by the settlor can be met by the plea of his illegality, while if they choose the second alternative, a claim by the beneficiary would hardly succeed if the trustees have merely done what they would have been directed to do by the court. In practice, they should seek the directions of the court.

[11] The provisions for penalties were repealed by Sched. 7 to the Law of Property Act 1925, but not replaced.

merely declaratory of the common law.[12] It may well be that in most respects the new section has not altered the previous law, and cases on the old Act are commonly regarded as applicable to it. Harman L.J. took this view in *Re Eichholz*,[13] on the ground that the Law of Property Act 1925 is a consolidating Act and is not therefore to be taken as making an alteration in the law unless the words admit of no other interpretation. This view has, however, been cogently criticised[14] on the ground that it fails to take into account that the section in its 1925 form derived from what is professedly an amending Act i.e. the Law of Property (Amendment) Act 1924. It should also be noted that in the older cases on this subject it is not always made clear whether the judges are dealing with the operative part of the old Act, now represented by s. 172 (1), or with the proviso, now represented by s. 172 (3).[15]

The section provides as follows:

"(1) Save as provided in this section, every conveyance of property, made whether before or after the commencement of this Act, with intent to defraud creditors, shall be voidable, at the instance of any person thereby prejudiced.

(2) This section does not affect the operation of a disentailing assurance, or the law of bankruptcy for the time being in force.

(3) This section does not extend to any estate or interest in property conveyed for valuable consideration and in good faith or upon good consideration and in good faith to any person not having, at the time of the conveyance, notice of the intent to defraud creditors."

The object of this section, like its predecessor the statute 13 Eliz. I c. 5, is to prevent debtors disposing of their property to the prejudice of their creditors. "The principle on which the statute of 13 Eliz. I c. 5 proceeds," said Lord Hatherley,[16] "is this, that persons must be just before they are generous, and that debts must be paid before gifts can be made." Unlike the bankruptcy laws, however, whose aim is to achieve an equal distribution of the available assets between all the creditors, the provisions under consideration do not prohibit the preference of one creditor to another.[17] As Fletcher Moulton L.J. said in *Glegg* v. *Bromley*,[18] "it is well settled law that apart from the rules of bankruptcy a person may pay his debts in any order he pleases, and may charge his property as he will as security for paying those debts". And Jessel M.R. in *Middleton* v. *Pollock*[19] explained, "the meaning of the statute is that the debtor

---

[12] See. e.g. Lord Mansfield in *Cadogan* v. *Kennett* (1776), 2 Cowp. 432, 434; Lord Campbell in *Rickards* v. *A.G.* (1844), 12 Cl. & F. 30, 42.

[13] [1959] 1 All E.R. 166; [1959] Ch. 708. See the treatment in Kerr on *Fraud and Mistake*, 7th Ed., pp. 298 *et seq.*; Smith's *Leading Cases*, 13th Ed., Vol. I, p. 11.

[14] (1959), 75 L.Q.R. 307 (R.E.M.). See Williams on *Bankruptcy*, 18th Ed., p. 371; *Grey* v. *I.R.Comrs.*, [1959] 3 All E.R. 603; [1960] A.C. 1, H.L.; *Beswick* v. *Beswick*, [1967] 2 All E.R. 1197; [1968] A.C. 58, H.L.; *Lloyds Bank Ltd.* v. *Marcan*, [1973] 2 All E.R. 359; affd. [1973] 3 All E.R. 754, C.A.

[15] *Glegg* v. *Bromley*, [1912] 3 K.B. 474, at p. 492; [1911–13] All E.R. Rep. 1138, at p. 1147, C.A. *per* Parker J.

[16] In *Freeman* v. *Pope* (1870), 5 Ch. App. 538, at p. 540.

[17] *Alton* v. *Harrison* (1869), 4 Ch. App. 622; *Re Lloyd's Furniture Palace Ltd.*, [1925] Ch. 853; [1925] All E.R. Rep. 439.

[18] [1912] 3 K.B. 474, at p. 485; [1911–13] All E.R. Rep. 1138, at p. 1144, C.A.

[19] (1876), 2 Ch.D. 104, at pp. 108, 109.

must not retain a benefit for himself. It has no regard whatever to the question of preference or priority amongst the creditors of the debtor". This is subject to the qualification that the conveyance will be void if it is a mere cloak for retaining a benefit to the grantor[20]; if this is the position the transaction will not be saved by the fact that one creditor incidentally gets some benefit.[1]

Despite this important difference in the objects of s. 172 of the Law of Property Act and the Bankruptcy Act 1914, the provisions do overlap to a considerable extent. The position can be summarised by saying that, on the one hand, dispositions of property which are void in bankruptcy are not necessarily void under s. 172, while, on the other hand, a conveyance which is void under s. 172, is an act of bankruptcy within s. 1 (1) (b) of the Bankruptcy Act 1914 upon which a bankruptcy petition may be founded. It only remains an available act of bankruptcy, however, for three months.[2] It may also be noted that a voluntary settlement cannot be avoided in bankruptcy if it was made more than ten years before the settlor became bankrupt,[3] while it may be set aside under s. 172 at any time until the right to receive the debt has become barred by the Limitation Act 1939.[4]

The word "conveyance" is widely defined in the Law of Property Act 1925.[5] The corresponding provision in the statute 13 Eliz. I c. 5 referred to "feoffment, gift, grant, alienation, bargain and conveyance" and was held to include any kind of disposition of property, most of the cases being concerned with settlements and trusts. It is not clear whether the single word "conveyance" used in s. 172 has the same scope as the earlier phrase; in the only reported case on this point since 1925,[6] Harman J. thought that it had and took the view that an oral transaction would be included. This seems doubtful in the light of a subsequent decision[7] by the House of Lords that, as defined by the Law of Property Act 1925, "conveyance" is restricted to instruments in writing, unless the context otherwise requires. Section 172 was not referred to, but it is not easy to find in it the necessary contrary context.

"Property" is defined[8] as including "any thing in action, and any interest in real or personal property", and accordingly the only property which is not within the provision is that which cannot be affected either by legal or equitable execution,[9] for creditors can obviously not be prejudiced by the alienation of

---

[20] See the cases cited in the three preceding footnotes.
[1] *Re Fasey*, [1923] 2 Ch. 1, C.A.
[2] Bankruptcy Act 1914, s. 4 (1) (c)
[3] Bankruptcy Act 1914, s. 42.
[4] *Re Maddever* (1884), 27 Ch.D. 523, C.A.
[5] Section 205 (1) (ii), as including "a mortgage, charge, lease, assent, vesting declaration, vesting instrument, disclaimer, release and every other assurance of property or of an interest therein by any instrument, except a will".
[6] *Re Eichholz*, [1959] 1 All E.R. 166; [1959] Ch. 708. Cf. the opinion of the same judge in the Court of Appeal in *Rye* v. *Rye*, [1960] 3 All E.R. 810, C.A., affd. [1962] 1 All E.R. 146, H.L. See also (1959), 75 L.Q.R. 307 (R. E. M.).
[7] *Rye* v. *Rye, supra.*
[8] Section 205 (1) (xx) of the Law of Property Act 1925.
[9] See *Mathews* v. *Feaver* (1786), 1 Cox Eq. Cas. 278. The qualification is of minimal importance as virtually all property can now be taken in execution; for an exception see, e.g., *Lucas* v. *Harris* (1886), 18 Q.B.D. 127, C.A.; *Crowe* v. *Price* (1889), 22 Q.B.D. 429, C.A.

property against which they could have no remedy. It is not necessary to trace historically the steps whereby different kinds of property have been brought within the reach of creditors, but whenever a new right of proceeding came into existence the courts promptly recognised that the property which could thereby be reached could be disposed of fraudulently as against creditors and was therefore brought within the scope of the statute 13 Eliz. I c. 5.[10] The relevant date was the date of the conveyance, and if the property could not be taken in execution at that date, a subsequent statute making the property liable would not assist creditors, who would remain defeated by the prior conveyance.[11]

b The intent to defraud creditors

The word "defraud" in this sub-section, according to Pennycuick V.C.,[12] is "designed to reproduce the expression 'hinder, delay or defraud' in the Statute of Elizabeth, and is not intended to be confined to cases of fraud in the ordinary modern sense of that word, i.e. as involving actual deceit or dishonesty". He defined it as meaning "depriving creditors of timely recourse to property which would otherwise be applicable for their benefit". Thus in *Lloyd's Bank, Ltd.* v. *Marcan*[13] the defendant had mortgaged property to the plaintiff. After the plaintiff had started proceedings for possession, the defendant granted a 20 year lease to his wife, which, apart from s. 172, would have been valid. The lease was granted, after receiving the advice of counsel that it was legitimate to do so, with the admitted intention of enabling his wife and family, including himself, to retain possession of the property and thereby to exclude the plaintiff bank from possession of the property. It was held the intent to defraud was clearly established.

The intent to defraud referred to is that of the grantor,[14] and is a question of fact to be ascertained by considering all the circumstances of the case. It may be proved by direct evidence, inferred from surrounding circumstances, or imputed on the basis that a man must be presumed to intend the natural consequences of his own acts.[15] An important circumstance is whether the settlement is voluntary or for valuable consideration. Although the mere fact of a settlement being voluntary does not make it fraudulent,[16] want of consideration is material in deciding whether there was a fraudulent intent,[17] and according to some writers[18] affects the burden of proof. On this

---

[10] *Ideal Bedding Company Ltd.* v. *Holland*, [1907] 2 Ch. 157.

[11] *Sims* v. *Thomas* (1840), 12 Ad. & El. 536.

[12] At first instance, in *Lloyd's Bank Ltd.* v. *Marcan*, [1973] 2 All E.R. 359, 367; affd. [1973] 3 All E.R. 754, C.A., where, however, Cairns L.J. thought that a dishonest intention must be shown, at any rate where the conveyance is for consideration.

[13] *Supra.*

[14] Note, however, the exceptional case of *Cornish* v. *Clark* (1872), L.R. 14 Eq. 184, where the grantees, not the grantor, had the requisite intent. They had instigated the grant, which was, indeed, said to be their act assented to by the grantor, who was assumed not to have had the primary intention of defeating his creditors thereby.

[15] *Godfrey* v. *Poole* (1888), 13 App. Cas. 497, at p. 503, P.C.; *Glegg* v. *Bromley*, [1912] 3 K.B. 474, 492; [1911–13] All E.R. Rep. 1138, at p. 1147, C.A., *per* Parker J.; *Denny's Trustee* v. *Denny & Warr*, [1919] 1 K.B. 583.; *Lloyds Bank Ltd.* v. *Marcan, supra.*

[16] *Holmes* v. *Penney* (1856), 3 K. & J. 90.

[17] *Glegg* v. *Bromley, supra.*

[18] 17 *Halsbury's Laws* (3rd Ed.), 657.

view, if the settlement is for valuable consideration, the onus of proof of intent to defraud rests upon those who seek to attack the settlement—"the fact that there is valuable consideration shows at once that there may be purposes in the transaction other than the defeating or delaying of creditors, and renders the case, therefore, of those who contest the deed more difficult"[19]; while if the settlement is voluntary, proof of the fact that the settlor was insolvent at the time of the settlement, or that shortly after the date of the settlement he engaged in trade of a hazardous character,[20] or of any of the so-called badges or indications of fraud discussed below, puts the onus of disproving the intent to defraud on those who seek to maintain the settlement. The better view,[21] is that even in the case of a voluntary settlement the onus of proving the fraudulent intention is on those who seek to impeach the settlement, except perhaps in the case discussed in the following paragraph. The so-called badges of fraud are on this view merely factors which the court takes into account in determining whether the fraudulent intent existed in any particular case, though they might be regarded as stronger evidence in the case of a voluntary conveyance.

In one type of case there are dicta which suggest that proof of certain circumstances raises an irrebuttable inference that the requisite intent was there when the settlement was made. Thus Lord Hatherley L.C. said in *Freeman* v. *Pope*,[22] with reference to a voluntary settlement,

> "if a person owing debts makes a settlement which subtracts from the property which is the proper fund for the payment of those debts, an amount without which the debts cannot be paid, then, since it is the necessary consequence of the settlement (supposing it effectual) that some creditors must remain unpaid, it would be the duty of the judge to direct the jury that they must infer the intent of the settlor to have been to defeat or delay his creditors, and that the case is within the statute."

It is very difficult to reconcile this with the forceful opinion of Lord Esher in *Ex parte Mercer, Re Wise*[23] where he stigmatized as monstrous the argument that, if the necessary consequence of a settlement was to defeat or delay the settlor's creditors, then "as a proposition of law, the tribunal which had to consider whether he did intend to defeat and delay his creditors was bound to find that he did". In that case Wise, the captain of a merchant ship, was engaged to be married to Emily Vyse. He went on a voyage to Hong Kong and there married someone else. Shortly afterwards he received information that he had become entitled to a legacy of £500, and also, by the same post, information that Emily Vyse had brought an action against him for breach of promise of marriage.[24] He immediately settled the legacy on his wife and any children he might have. The court accepted his statement that the breach of promise action, which he

---

[19] *Re Johnson* (1881), 20 Ch.D. 389, *per* Fry J. at 393; affd. *sub. nom Golden* v. *Gillam* (1882), 51 L.J. Ch. 503, C.A.

[20] *Mackay* v. *Douglas* (1872), L.R. 14 Eq. 106; *Re Butterworth, Ex parte Russell* (1882), 19 Ch.D. 588, C.A.

[21] Kerr on *Fraud and Mistake*, 7th Ed., p. 322.

[22] (1870), 5 Ch. App. 538, 541. See also *per* Giffard L.J. at p. 545; *Green* v. *Paterson* (1886) 32 Ch.D. 95, C.A., *per* Cotton L.J. at p. 105; *Re Holland*, [1902] 2 Ch. 360, C.A., *per* Vaughan Williams and Stirling L.JJ. at 373, 381. See ((1973), 47 A.L.J. 365 (W. A. Lee).

[23] (1886), 17 Q.B.D. 290, C.A, at p. 298.

[24] This action was abolished by the Law Reform (Miscellaneous Provisions) Act 1970.

thought was merely a threat he would hear nothing more about, had no influence in inducing him to make the settlement. However, Emily Vyse not only pursued the action, but obtained judgment for £500 damages and costs, and on his failing to pay took steps to have him adjudicated bankrupt. The trustee in bankruptcy sought to have the settlement set aside, but it was held that the intent to defraud was not established.

It is submitted that the better opinion[1] is that even the circumstances referred to in *Freeman* v. *Pope*[2] do no more than raise a presumption that the requisite intent was there, but it remains open to those who seek to uphold the settlement to bring evidence to show that no such intention existed. It seems clear that in such circumstances the burden of disproving the fraudulent intent is a heavy one. These observations apply not only where actual insolvency[3] at the date of the voluntary settlement is established, but also where a man is substantially indebted at the date of the settlement, and shortly afterwards[4] becomes absolutely insolvent. In the last case the burden of proving solvency at the date of the settlement rests upon those who seek to uphold it.[5]

Six badges of fraud were put forward in *Twyne's Case*[6]: none is conclusive by itself, though some are stronger evidence than others. First, the fact that the conveyance comprises all or substantially all the property of the grantor.[7] Since *Twyne's Case*[8] there has been no doubt that this is a most material circumstance, and many of the more recent cases have been directed to settling the point that it is not conclusive.[9] Secondly, perhaps the strongest indication is the fact of the continuance in possession by the grantor of the property he has purported to convey; indeed in some of the early cases it is said that this is conclusive evidence of fraudulent intent.[10] It is now settled, however, that continuance in possession is only evidence, raising a presumption of fraud which may be explained away or rebutted, or, of course, confirmed, by other circumstances.[11] Further, the nature of the grant is of importance; continuance in possession is no evidence of fraudulent intent where it takes place under the terms of the deed or agreement; this was recognised even in *Edwards* v. *Harben*,[12] where Buller J. said,

"unless possession accompanies and follows the deed, it is fraudulent and void; . . . but if the deed or conveyance be conditional, there the vendor's continuing in possession does not avoid it, because by the terms of the conveyance the vendee

---

[1] This was the view of the Manitoba Court of Appeal in *Mandryk* v. *Merko* (1971), 19 D.L.R. (3d) 238, where evidence submitting the inference was accepted. [2] *Supra.*

[3] "The question is, what is meant by insolvency ? If by the act of assignment the party makes himself insolvent, that is, if the property left over after the conveyance is not enough to pay his debts, that is insolvency sufficient for the purposes of the plaintiff in this action", *per* Erskine J. in *Jackson* v. *Bowley* (1841), Car. & M. 97, at p. 103.

[4] As much as three years in *Townsend* v. *Westacott* (1840), 2 Beav. 340.

[5] *Townsend* v. *Westacott, supra; Crossley* v. *Elworthy* (1871), L.R. 12 Eq. 158.

[6] (1601), 3 Co. Rep. 80b.

[7] *Thompson* v. *Webster* (1859), 4 Drew. 628.

[8] *Supra.*

[9] *Alton* v. *Harrison* (1869), 4 Ch. App. 622; *Ex parte Games, Re Bamford* (1879), 12 Ch.D. 314, C.A.; *Re Fasey,* [1923] 2 Ch. 1, C.A.

[10] See, e.g., *Edwards* v. *Harben* (1788), 2 Term. Rep. 587.

[11] *Arundell* v. *Phipps* (1804), 10 Ves. 139; *Martindale* v. *Booth* (1832), 3 B. & Ad. 498.

[12] (1788), 2 Term. Rep. 587, at pp. 595, 596, after consultation with all the judges, whose opinion was unanimous. See also *Alton* v. *Harrison* (1869), 4 Ch. App. 622.

is not to have possession till he has performed the condition . . . [as to deeds or bills of sale to take place at some future time] the possession continuing in the vendor till that future time, or till that condition is performed, is consistent with the deed; and such possession comes within the rule, as accompanying and following the deed."

One most obvious case where continuance in possession is no evidence of fraud, is in the case of a mortgage of land where the mortgagor, as is usual, remains in possession.[13] Thirdly, secrecy of conveyance.[14] Fourthly, the fact that the conveyance was made after a writ has been issued against the grantor, or after execution has been issued. This is an important factor in the case of a voluntary conveyance,[15] though even here not conclusive.[16] But it is less strong evidence in the case of a conveyance for valuable consideration, for it is settled that it is not a ground for invalidating a *bona fide* sale that it is made in order to defeat an intended execution.[17] It may, however, help to establish fraudulent intent when taken together with other circumstances.[18] Fifthly, the existence of a trust or reservation for the benefit of the grantor. The question is always,

> "Is the deed one for the benefit of creditors, or does it seek to benefit the debtor at the expense of the creditors ? . . . not necessarily giving him an actual benefit, but giving him a chance of a benefit at his creditors' expense. . . . Where a deed of this sort is substantially for the benefit of creditors, the court should not draw the inference that it is fraudulent from the fact that it contains a proviso which, though favourable to the debtor, is consistent with the tenor and object of the deed."[19]

Sixthly, the fact that it contains some unusual and unnecessary statement that the conveyance is made without any fraudulent intent.

In addition to these six cases set out in *Twyne's Case*,[20] it has been held that the fact that a settlor reserved to himself a power of revocation is a badge of fraud, since the property remains virtually in the settlor's control,[1] but it has more recently been said[2] that such a power cannot defraud creditors since it may be used by the trustee in bankruptcy for their benefit. And finally the presence of false statements in the conveyance is a badge of fraud,[3] though not

---

[13] *Stone* v. *Grubham* (1615), 2 Bulst. 225.
[14] *Ex parte Chaplin, Re Sinclair* (1884), 26 Ch.D. 319, C.A.; *Corbett* v. *Radcliffe* (1860), 14 Moo. P.C. 121, at p. 139.
[15] *Blenkinsopp* v. *Blenkinsopp* (1852), 1 De G.M. & G. 495; *Barling* v. *Bishopp* (1860), 29 Beav. 417.
[16] *Ex parte Mercer, Re Wise* (1886), 17 Q.B.D. 290, C.A.
[17] *Wood* v. *Dixie* (1845), 7 Q.B. 892; *Hale* v. *Saloon Omnibus Co.* (1859), 4 Drew. 492. It will be remembered that the statute does not affect the preference of one creditor over another, even though it was intended to defeat that other.
[18] *Cadogan* v. *Kennett* (1776), 2 Cowp. 432; *Bott* v. *Smith* (1856), 21 Beav. 511; *Re Maddever* (1884), 27 Ch.D. 523, C.A.
[19] *Maskelyne & Cooke* v. *Smith*, [1903] 1 K.B. 671, C.A., *per* Vaughan Williams L.J. at pp. 676–677; *Alton* v. *Harrison* (1869), 4 Ch. App. 622.
[20] (1601), 3 Co. Rep. 80b.
[1] *Peacock* v. *Monk* (1748), 1 Ves. Sen. 127, at p. 132; *Smith* v. *Hurst* (1852), 10 Hare 30, at p. 44.
[2] *Re H. W. Baker*, [1936] Ch. 61; [1935] All E.R. Rep. 843, *per* Farwell J.
[3] *Ex parte Chaplin, Re Sinclair* (1884), 26 Ch.D. 319, C.A.

as against a party who neither knew nor ought to have known of the falsity of the statement.[4]

c   Who can avoid settlements

Where s. 172 applies, the settlement is not void, but voidable "at the instance of any person thereby prejudiced". It is thought[5] that these words will be interpreted in the same way as the corresponding words in the statute 13 Eliz. I c. 5. In all other respects and as against other persons, including the grantor himself, the settlement remains valid.[6]

It was settled at an early date that subsequent creditors may attack a settle-ment as well as creditors existing at the time the settlement was made,[7] at any rate so long as any debt in existence at the date of the settlement remains unpaid.[8] The better view would seem to be that even if all the prior creditors have been paid, a subsequent creditor can invoke s. 172.[9] He may, however, have some difficulty in establishing the fraudulent intent, the mere fact that the settlor was insolvent at the date of the settlement clearly not being sufficient by itself, if the prior creditors have all been paid.

d   Persons taking bona fide, without notice of intent to defraud creditors

Under the statute 13 Eliz. I c. 5, protection was afforded to such persons who took "upon good consideration". This was held to mean valuable considera-tion,[10] including marriage,[11] but not the consideration of natural love and affection for relatives, sometimes called meritorious consideration. Section 172 (3) of the Law of Property Act 1925, however, refers to both valuable consideration[12] and good consideration, and textbook writers[13] have accordingly taken the view, that under the modern law,[14] good consideration in the sense of natural love and affection will be sufficient to support a settlement, if the other circumstances of the subsection are complied with. If this construction is right, the section will seldom be of assistance to creditors; as was said in *Twyne's Case*,[15] "if consideration of nature or blood should be a good con-sideration within this proviso, the statute would serve for little or nothing, and no creditor would be sure of his debt". In *Re Eichholz*,[16] however, it seems

---

[4] *Kevan* v. *Crawford* (1877), 6 Ch.D. 29, C.A.
[5] See, e.g., 17 *Halsbury's Laws*, 3rd Ed., 659; Kerr on *Fraud and Mistake*, 7th Ed., p. 317.
[6] *Robinson* v. *M'Donnell* (1818), 2 B. & Ald. 134; *Steel* v. *Brown & Perry* (1808), 1 Taunt, 381.
[7] See, e.g., *Mackay* v. *Douglas* (1872), L.R. 14 Eq. 106; *Ex parte Russell, Re Butterworth* (1882), 19 Ch.D. 588, C.A.
[8] *Jenkyn* v. *Vaughan* (1856), 3 Drew. 419.
[9] *Holmes* v. *Penny* (1856), 3 K. & J. 90; *Mackay* v. *Douglas, supra*; *Re Lane-Fox*, [1900] 2 Q.B. 508. See also *Re Kelleher*, [1911] 2 I.R. 1.
[10] *Twyne's Case* (1602), 3 Co. Rep. 80b; *Mathews* v. *Feaver* (1786), 1 Cox Eq. Cas. 278; *Re David & Adlard*, [1914] 2 K.B. 694.
[11] See, e.g., *Campion* v. *Cotton* (1810), 17 Ves. 263; *Hardey* v. *Green* (1849), 12 Beav. 182.
[12] Defined to include marriage, though not a nominal consideration in money—Law of Property Act 1925, s. 205 (1) (xxi).
[13] See, e.g., 17 *Halsbury's Laws*, 3rd Ed., 654; Kerr on *Fraud and Mistake*, 7th Ed., p. 341.
[14] Which applies to conveyances whenever made—Law of Property Act 1925, s. 172 (1).
[15] (1602), 3 Co. Rep. 80b, at 81b.
[16] [1959] 1 All E.R. 166; [1959] Ch. 708.

to have been assumed, without argument, that good consideration still means valuable consideration as under the old law.

The next requirement is that of good faith. Doubts were raised in *Lloyds Bank, Ltd.* v. *Marcan*[17] as to whose good faith is in question, and as to whether the requirement adds anything, and, if so, what, to what is already contained in sub-s. (1) and in the final requirement of sub-s. (3) discussed below. At first instance Pennycuick V.C. did not find it necessary to express a conclusion on the point, and it was not discussed on appeal.

Lastly the person claiming the benefit of sub-s. (3) must not, at the time of the conveyance, have had notice of the intent to defraud creditors. Thus it has been held that a marriage settlement cannot be impeached as against a wife who has been unaware of the intent to defraud,[18] even as regards a covenant to settle all the after-acquired property of the husband,[19] and notwithstanding the fact that the settlement contains false recitals.[20] It would accordingly seem to be impossible to impeach a settlement as against infant children,[21] and if good consideration, *stricto sensu*, is sufficient, this is so even in the case of a post-nuptial settlement not in pursuance of an ante-nuptial agreement, i.e. where the marriage consideration is past. It is not however sufficient for the person claiming the benefit of sub-s. (3) to establish that there was no intent to defraud on his part. He must establish that he had no notice, actual or constructive, of the intent to defraud on the part of the conveying party.[1] Finally, it should be observed that the protection of s. 172 (3) may be claimed not only by the original grantees under the conveyance, but also by persons claiming through them who satisfy the requisite conditions.[2]

3 VOLUNTARY DISPOSITION FOLLOWED BY CONVEYANCE FOR VALUABLE CONSIDERATION

a Law of Property Act 1925, s. 173 (1)

This subsection, which replaces the statute 27 Eliz. I c. 4, is in the following terms:

> "Every voluntary disposition of land made with intent to defraud a subsequent purchaser is voidable at the instance of that purchaser."

Under the old statute it was settled law that the mere fact that a voluntary disposition of land was subsequently followed by a disposition for value was

---

[17] [1973] 2 All E.R. 359 affd. [1973] 3 All E.R. 754, C.A.
[18] *Aliter* where the wife is a party to a scheme to protect property against the rights of creditors—*Re Pennington, Ex parte Pennington* (1888), 5 Morr. 268, C.A.
[19] *Re Reis*, [1904] 2 K.B. 769, C.A., *on appeal sub nom., Clough* v. *Samuel*, [1905] A.C. 442, H.L.
[20] *Campion* v. *Cotton* (1810), 17 Ves. 263; *Kevan* v. *Crawford* (1877), 6 Ch.D. 29, C.A.
[21] Unless of years of discretion when the settlement was made.
[1] *Re Johnson* (1881), 20 Ch.D. 389, affd. C.A. *sub nom. Golden* v. *Gillam* (1882), 51 L.J.Ch. 503; *Re Fasey*, [1923] 2 Ch. 1, C.A.; *Lloyds Bank, Ltd.* v. *Marcan, supra*.
[2] *Halifax Banking Co.* v. *Gledhill*, [1891] 1 Ch. 31; *Harrods Ltd.* v. *Stanton*, [1923] 1 K.B. 516; [1923] All E.R. Rep. 592, D.C.

conclusive proof that an intention to defraud the subsequent purchaser existed when the voluntary disposition was made. This was unaffected by the fact that the grantor had other property at the time of the voluntary disposition and did not appear to be then indebted, or that there was no fraud in fact in the transaction, or even that the subsequent purchaser had notice of the prior voluntary disposition.[3] It did not apply where the voluntary disposition was to a charity,[4] nor where the subsequent purchaser did not take from the grantor under the voluntary disposition, but from a devisee under such grantor's will.[5]

It should be noted that s. 173 applies to land only, not, as s. 172, to property generally.

b Law of Property Act 1925, s. 173 (2)

This subsection, which replaces the Voluntary Conveyances Act 1893, provides:

> "For the purposes of this section, no voluntary disposition, whenever made, shall be deemed to have been made with intent to defraud by reason only that a subsequent conveyance for valuable consideration was made. . . ."[6]

It will be realised from what has been said, that the strained interpretation put upon 27 Eliz. I c. 4 in effect enabled anyone, who had made a voluntary settlement of land, to change his mind by subsequently selling the subject-matter of the settlement. The unsatisfactory state of the law was radically altered by the Voluntary Conveyances Act 1893, since when it has been necessary to establish an actual intent to defraud in order to avoid a voluntary disposition of land. The onus of proving bad faith is cast on the party alleging it.[7] The result is that, taken as a whole, s. 173 of the Law of Property Act 1925 is of little practical significance.

4 SECTION 42 OF THE BANKRUPTCY ACT 1914

a Voluntary settlements under s. 42 (1)[8]

Under sub-s. (1) it is provided that a trustee in bankruptcy may in some cases avoid a settlement of property, even though it is neither in fact, nor deemed to be, fraudulent. In general the operation of the subsection is restricted to voluntary settlements, by reason of the fact that certain settlements, dealt with below,[9] are expressly excluded from its ambit.

Sub-s. (1) begins by referring to "any settlement of property". "Property",

---

[3] *Doe d. Otley* v. *Manning* (1807), 9 East 59; *Re Barker's Estate* (1875), 44 L.J. Ch. 487.
[4] *Ramsay* v. *Gilchrist*, [1892] A.C. 412, P.C.
[5] *Doe d. Newman* v. *Rusham* (1851), 17 Q.B. 723.
[6] The subsection only applies where the subsequent conveyance was made after 28th June, 1893.
[7] *Moore* v. *Kelly*, [1918] 1 I.R. 169.
[8] Replacing earlier legislation. Many of the cases cited below are on corresponding provisions in earlier Acts.
[9] See pp. 149 *et seq., post.*

by the definition section,[10] includes "money, goods, things in action, land, and every description of property, whether real or personal, and whether situate in England or elsewhere; also obligations, easements, and every description of estate, interest and profit, present or future, vested or contingent, arising out of or incident to property as above defined". Though very extensive, this does not include property over which the settlor had even a general power of appointment[11]; nor does it include a statutory tenancy under the Rent Restriction Acts.[12]

"Settlement" is defined[13] to "include any conveyance or transfer of property". Notwithstanding the definition the courts have held that

> "that section applies only to such conveyances or transfers as are in the nature of settlements, in the sense of being dispositions of property by a person to be held and preserved for the enjoyment of some other person. The retention of the property in some sense must . . . be contemplated, and not its immediate alienation or consumption. But it is not necessary . . . that there should be any actual restriction of the power of alienation by the donee".[14]

The cases, it has been said,[15] show that whether a disposition of property constitutes a settlement within what is now s. 42 depends "on the intention of the 'donor', at all events, to this extent, that the section did not apply to cases where the circumstances of the gift made it manifest that the subject-matter of the gift was not intended to be preserved by the 'donee', as would be manifest in the case of a gift of money to a son to advance him in business,[16] or to a son for his maintenance". Accordingly the purchase by a father of shares, which are registered in the son's name, and upon which the son receives the dividends, has been said to constitute a settlement,[17] and this has been held to be so where the actual gift has been of money to be applied in the purchase of shares.[18] Again a gift of jewellery to a wife by a husband who became bankrupt within two years has been held to be a settlement, on the ground that the husband contemplated the retention by his wife of the gift.[19] It was said in the last-mentioned case that the decision would have been the same if the wife had

---

[10] Bankruptcy Act 1914, s. 167.

[11] *Re Mathieson*, [1927] I Ch. 283; [1926] All E.R. Rep. 306, C.A.; *Re Armstrong, Ex parte Gilchrist* (1886), 17 Q.B.D. 521, C.A. See also *Re Schebsman*, [1943] 2 All E.R. 768; [1944] Ch. 83, C.A.

[12] *Sutton* v. *Dorf*, [1932] 2 K.B. 304, D.C.; *Smith* v. *Odder*, [1949] W.N. 249, C.A.

[13] By Bankruptcy Act 1914, s. 42 (4).

[14] *Re Tankard*, [1899] 2 Q.B. 57, *per* Wright J. at p. 59.

[15] *Re Vansittart*, [1893] I Q.B. 181; [1891–4] All E.R. Rep. 1111, *per* Vaughan Williams J. at pp. 183, 1112. The construction adopted in this case and in *Re Player* (1885), 15 Q.B.D. 682, D.C., was approved and followed in *Re Tankard, supra*, and by the Court of Appeal in *Re Plummer*, [1900] 2 Q.B. 790.

[16] As was the case in *Re Player* (1885), 15 Q.B.D. 682, *per* Cave J. at p. 687. The fact that there were two applications in the same bankruptcy separately reported has caused some confusion in the references. For instance, both *Re Vansittart*, [1893] I Q.B. 181, and *Re Tankard*, [1899] 2 Q.B. 57, cite *Re Player* and give the above reference, on points for which the reference should clearly be to the other *Re Player* (1885), 2 Morr. 261, D.C. In both cases both the decisions in *Re Player* seem to be referred to.

[17] See *Re Player* (1885), 15 Q.B.D. 682, at p. 687, D.C.

[18] *Re Player* (1885), 2 Morr. 261.

[19] *Re Vansittart, supra*.

been given money to buy herself a present. In contrast to these cases it was held in *Re Player*[20] that there was no settlement and accordingly s. 42 did not apply where a father advanced £650 to provide stock-in-trade to enable a son to set up in business.

b The time when the settlement was made

Assuming that there is a settlement within the section, the main provisions distinguish between the case where the settlor becomes bankrupt[1] within two years after the date of the settlement and the case where the settlor becomes bankrupt at some subsequent time within ten years after the date of the settlement.

In the first case, the settlement is void against the trustee in bankruptcy, even though the settlor may have been solvent when the settlement was made. In the second case, however, where the settlement was made within ten but not within two years of the bankruptcy, although still *prima facie* void, it will be upheld if the parties claiming under the settlement[2] can establish two things, *viz.*:

i that the settlor was, at the time of making the settlement, able to pay all his debts without the aid of the property comprised in the settlement,[3] and

ii that the interest[4] of the settlor in such property passed to the trustee of such settlement on the execution thereof.

c The effect of s. 42 (1) on settlements which fall within it

According to the words of the section, a settlement, if the requisite conditions are fulfilled, is void against the trustee in bankruptcy. The cases, however, make it clear that "void" is to be construed as meaning "voidable". This has various consequences. It means that the settlement remains valid unless and until the trustee in bankruptcy takes the necessary steps to have the settlement set aside. This, according to Cozens-Hardy M.R.,[5] requires an application to the court by the trustee in bankruptcy for a declaration to that effect and for

---

[20] (1885), 15 Q.B.D. 682, D.C. See also *Re Branson*, [1914] 3 K.B. 1086, C.A.; *Re Harrison and Ingram*, [1900] 2 Q.B. 710, C.A.

[1] The doctrine of relation back applies so that the relevant date is the date on which the bankrupt first committed an available act of bankruptcy—*Re Reis*, [1904] 1 K.B. 451, reversed on different grounds, [1904] 2 K.B. 769, C.A.; *sub nom. Clough* v. *Samuel*, [1905] A.C. 442, H.L.; *Re Hart*, [1912] 3 K.B. 6, C.A.

[2] The burden of proof is upon them—*Ex parte Russell* (1882), 19 Ch.D. 588, C.A.

[3] This means "without the aid of the property which by the settlement passes to other persons", and accordingly a life interest reserved to the settlor (*Re Lowndes* (1887), 18 Q.B.D. 677, D.C.), or an unfettered power to raise a capital sum (*Re H. W. Baker*, [1936] Ch. 61; [1935] All E.R. Rep. 843) must be taken into account. See also *Ex parte Huxtable* (1876), 2 Ch.D. 54, C.A.; *Ex parte Russell* (1882), 19 Ch.D. 588, C.A.

[4] See *Shrager* v. *March*, [1908] A.C. 402, P.C. In this case it was held that this provision had been complied with where a settlor had altered his position from that of beneficial owner to that of a trustee for his wife and children, though ultimately on their default for himself.

[5] *Re Hart*, [1912] 3 K.B. 6, 10, C.A. Cf. r. 8 (1) (e) of the Bankruptcy Rules 1952.

consequential relief. Fletcher-Moulton L.J.,[6] however, has expressed the view that formal avoidance is not required, stating that an action to recover the settled property would be an ample exercise of the election of the trustee in bankruptcy to treat the settlement as void. If it is declared void, it is not avoided *ab initio*, but only from the date of the act of bankruptcy to which the title of the trustee relates back,[7] or, possibly, from the date of the actual avoidance.[8] Accordingly a *bona fide* purchaser for value from a donee under a voluntary settlement who purchased prior to such act of bankruptcy has a title good against the trustee in bankruptcy, even if he purchased with notice that the donee claimed under a voluntary settlement.[9] On general equitable principles such a *bona fide* purchaser for value has even been held to be protected where the purchase was subsequent to the act of bankruptcy, provided of course he had no notice of it.[10] Again trustees of a settlement which is avoided under these provisions have been held to be entitled to a lien on the settled property for their proper expenses previously incurred, such as the costs of defending an action by the settlor to set aside the settlement,[11] on the ground that when the costs were incurred the trustees were acting properly in the administration of a valid trust. Further trustees who have acted in defending, unsuccessfully, an action to set aside the settlement brought by the trustee in bankruptcy himself, may be empowered by the court to retain their costs out of the trust estate before handing it over to the trustee in bankruptcy.[12]

If the settlement is declared void, it is void altogether.[13] Problems have arisen where the settlor has created a charge on the property between the date of the settlement and the bankruptcy. It has been held that the trustee in bankruptcy cannot claim priority over such incumbrances by alleging that he stands in the place of the beneficiaries under the settlement, or that as trustee in bankruptcy he has a paramount title on behalf of the unsecured creditors. The true view is that the settlement being avoided, the property reverts to the settlor, inevitably subject to any subsequent incumbrances he may have created. It is as the settlor's property that it vests in the trustee in bankruptcy, still subject to the incumbrances. The result of avoidance by the trustee in bankruptcy, therefore, is to accelerate subsequent incumbrances generally, and not necessarily to benefit the unsecured creditors directly[14] at all.[15]

The proposition that, if duly avoided, a settlement is void altogether, is subject to one important qualification. The avoidance only operates to the

---

[6] *Lister* v. *Hooson*, [1908] 1 K.B. 174, at p. 178, C.A.
[7] *Re Brall*, [1893] 2 Q.B. 381; *Re Carter & Kenderdine's Contract*, [1897] 1 Ch. 776, C.A.; *Re Hart*, *supra*, *per* Kennedy L.J.; *Re Gunsbourg & Co. Ltd.*, [1920] 2 K.B. 426, C.A., *per* Younger L.J. dissenting.
[8] *Re Gunsbourg & Co. Ltd.*, *supra*, *per* Lord Sterndale and Warrington L.J. *obiter*, explaining *Re Hart*, *supra*.
[9] *Re Brall*, *supra*; *Re Carter & Kenderdine's Contract*, *supra*.
[10] *Re Hart*, [1912] 3 K.B. 6, C.A. But see the explanation of the majority of C.A. in *Re Gunsbourg & Co. Ltd.*, *supra*.
[11] *Re Holden* (1887), 20 Q.B.D. 43, D.C.
[12] *Merry* v. *Pownall*, [1898] 1 Ch. 306; *Ideal Bedding Co. Ltd.* v. *Holland*, [1907] 2 Ch. 157.
[13] Subject to the qualification contained in the next paragraph.
[14] They will get a limited indirect benefit by the reduction or elimination of the secured creditors.
[15] *Sanguinetti* v. *Stuckey's Banking Co.*, [1895] 1 Ch. 176; *Re Farnham*, [1895] 2 Ch. 799, C.A.

extent of the debts[16] and costs of the bankruptcy, and any surplus of the settled property there may be reverts to the trustees of the settled property subject to the trusts thereof.[17]

d Settlements excluded from the operation of s. 42 (1)

The subsection itself excludes three types of settlement from its operation. Each of these exceptions must be considered separately.

i "Any settlement made before and in consideration of marriage." The Irish Court of Appeal has held,[18] on the same words in an Irish statute, that this exception is not restricted to the marriage of the bankrupt; it was further held that the exception was not invalidated by fraudulent intent, even though the beneficiaries under the settlement were parties to it. Where there is an intent to defraud creditors, however, to which all parties are privy, the settlement, even though it may not be void under this section, will be voidable under s. 172 of the Law of Property Act 1925,[19] and it will itself constitute an act of bankruptcy.[20]

ii "Any settlement . . . made in favour of a purchaser or incumbrancer in good faith and for valuable consideration." The word purchaser in this context has been held to mean a buyer in the ordinary commercial sense, not a purchaser in the legal sense of the word. In other words, it is not to be treated as a conveyancing term, but must be considered as applying to cases where there is a *quid pro quo*.[1] In order to constitute a purchaser in good faith, it is sufficient that there is good faith on the part of the purchaser; it is not necessary to establish good faith on the part of any other person.[2] In a settlement for valuable consideration, the fact that the settlor has extravagant habits so that it is probable that future creditors will be delayed or defeated is not in itself sufficient evidence of an intent to defraud creditors, even where the settlor himself proposed the settlement.[3]

To constitute a person a purchaser for valuable consideration, it is not necessary that either money or physical property should be given; the release of a right, or the compromise of a claim may be sufficient. This proposition is taken from the headnote in *Re Pope*,[4] where the bankrupt executed a post-nuptial settlement in favour of his wife and children in consideration of his wife refraining from taking proceedings in the Divorce Court. It was held that the case fell within this exception and the settlement was accordingly valid. In a subsequent case, Harman J. commented,[5] "I can well see that that was a good consideration. It was a detriment to her, because she might have got alimony.

---

[16] Including, of course, the prior claim of incumbrancers considered in the preceding paragraph.
[17] *Re Sims* (1896), 45 W.R. 189; *Re Parry*, [1904] 1 K.B. 129.
[18] *Re Downes*, [1898] 2 I.R. 635.
[19] *Re Pennington* (1888), 5 Morr. 268, C.A.
[20] *Colombine* v. *Penhall* (1853), 1 Sm. & G. 228; *Bulmer* v. *Hunter* (1869), L.R. 8 Eq. 46.
[1] *Hance* v. *Harding* (1888), 20 Q.B.D. 732, C.A.; *Re A Debtor*, [1965] 3 All E.R. 453.
[2] *Mackintosh* v. *Pogose*, [1895] 1 Ch. 505.
[3] *Re Tetley* (1896), 66 L.J.Q.B. 111, affd. 3 Mans. 321, C.A.
[4] [1908] 2 K.B. 169, C.A.
[5] *Re Macadam*, [1950] 1 All E.R. 303, at p. 306, D.C.

It was an advantage to him, because he avoided the publicity and also the costs of divorce proceedings." Again, a wife's agreement to live apart from her husband[6] and a *bona fide* compromise of a *bona fide* action claiming rights against a defendant's property[7] have been held to constitute valuable consideration for the present purpose.

According to *Hance* v. *Harding*,[8] it is not necessary either that the consideration should have been provided by a beneficiary under the settlement, or that the bankrupt should get the benefit of it. Thus a settlement was upheld within this exception where the bankrupt assigned a policy of life insurance to trustees for the benefit of his children, and the bankrupt's father assigned certain leasehold property to the trustees on like trusts.[9] Having held that the transaction was entered into by all parties with perfect *bona fides*, Lord Esher M.R. said[10]: "Then can he be called a purchaser? He has given something to get something for other persons, *viz.*, the family of his son. He has given up his interest in certain leaseholds to induce his son to give up his interest in these policies. That being so, I think he is a purchaser from the bankrupt within the meaning of the section." Some doubts have been raised, however, by a later case[11] where it was held[12] that "the consideration spoken of in s. 42 is a consideration moving to the bankrupt which replaces the property extracted from his creditors". It is submitted that this dictum cannot stand, being inconsistent with the Court of Appeal decision in *Hance* v. *Harding*,[13] which does not appear to have been cited to the court.

There is, however, no valuable consideration where the bankrupt has substituted a voluntary settlement upon his wife, for a voluntary allowance to her for maintenance.[14] It also has been held that where trustees of a settlement, at the request of the bankrupt, exercise some power or discretion which they have under it, there is no valuable consideration for the bankrupt's bringing further property into the settlement, even though the trustees only agreed to exercise the power on condition that this was done.[15]

It has been held by the Privy Council, on similar words, that the onus is upon the trustee in bankruptcy to prove that a conveyance which he is seeking to set aside was not made in good faith or for valuable consideration.[16] The court is not, of course, bound by the outward appearance of the documents involved. On the one hand, a settlement was held to be outside this exception and void, notwithstanding a recital therein of the payment of £5 as the consideration. It was said that, even if it had been paid, it was not a real and substantial consideration having regard to the value of the property settled.[17] On the other hand, where a settlement was on the face of it voluntary, it was held that

---

[6] *Re Weston*, [1900] 2 Ch. 164.
[7] *Re Cole*, [1931] 2 Ch. 174.
[8] (1888), 20 Q.B.D. 732, C.A.
[9] *Hance* v. *Harding* (1888), 20 Q.B.D. 732, C.A.   See also *Re Tetley*, *supra*.
[10] *Hance* v. *Harding*, *supra*, at pp. 737, 738.
[11] *Re A Debtor*, [1965] 3 All E.R. 453.
[12] *Re A Debtor*, *supra*, per Stamp J. at 457.
[13] *Supra*.
[14] *Re Macdonald*, [1920] 1 K.B. 205.
[15] *Re Parry*, [1904] 1 K.B. 129; *Re Macadam*, [1950] 1 All E.R. 303, D.C.
[16] *Cheah Soo Tuan (Official Assignee of the Estate of)* v. *Khoo Saw Cheow*, [1931] A.C. 67, P.C.
[17] *Re Naylor* (1893), 69 L.T. 355.

valuable consideration could be established by extrinsic evidence so as to bring the case within the exception.[18]

iii "Any settlement made on or for the wife or children of the settlor of property which has accrued to the settlor after marriage in right of his wife." Although it was argued in *Re Bower Williams*[19] that this provision was only retained to meet the case where there had been a marriage before the Married Women's Property Act 1882 and the husband acquired his wife's property during the coverture, it was held in that case to cover property which vested in a husband, married in 1913, on the death of his wife intestate in 1925. The reasoning in this case would seem to apply to property taken by a husband on the death of his wife intestate under the provisions of the Administration of Estates Act 1925.[20]

iv In addition to the above three cases referred to in s. 42 (1) itself, it should be noted that the Married Women's Property Act 1882, s. 11,[1] provides that a policy of assurance effected by any man on his own life and expressed to be for the benefit of his wife or children[2] shall create a trust in their favour, and the moneys payable under any such policy shall not be subject to his debts so long as any object of the trusts remains unperformed. It is provided, however, that if it shall be proved that the policy was effected and the premiums paid with intent to defraud the creditors of the insured, they shall be entitled to receive, out of moneys payable under the policy, a sum equal to the premiums so paid.

e Section 42 (2)

This subsection provides that any covenant or contract made by a settlor in consideration of his or her marriage,[3] either

i for the future payment of money[4] for the benefit of the settlor's wife or husband or children, or

ii for the future settlement on or for the settlor's wife or husband or children, of property, wherein[5] the settlor had not at the date of the marriage any estate or interest,[6] whether vested or contingent, in possession or remainder,

---

[18] *Pott v. Todhunter* (1845), 2 Coll. 76; *Re Holland*, [1902] 2 Ch. 360, C.A.

[19] [1927] 1 Ch. 441, C.A.

[20] As amended by the Intestates' Estates Act 1952 and the Family Provision Act 1966.

[1] As amended by the Statutes Law (Repeals) Act 1969.

[2] Including illegitimate children—s. 19 (1), Family Law Reform Act 1969 as to policies coming into force after 31 December, 1969.

[3] Contrast s. 42 (1), where the first excepted case does not appear to be restricted to the marriage of the settlor. See p. 149, *ante*.

[4] This has been held to include a covenant to pay the premiums on a life policy brought into the settlement: *Re Cumming and West*, [1929] 1 Ch. 534.

[5] The clause introduced by the word "wherein" applies only to "property"—*Re Cumming and West*, [1929] 1 Ch. 534. This is clear as set out in the text, but less clear in the actual terms of the sub-section.

[6] See *Re Andrews' Trusts* (1878), 7 Ch.D. 635; *Re Bulteel's Settlements*, [1917] 1 Ch. 251, 258, where it was held that "if a settlor has any estate or interest in property at the date of his marriage, then that property passes to the trustees of the settlement comprising it unaffected by this enactment, even although the property ultimately reaches them under some title other than that derived from the estate or interest actually possessed in the property by the settlor at the relevant moment".

not being money or property in right of the settlor's wife or husband, shall, if the settlor is adjudged bankrupt and the covenant or contract has not been executed[7] at the date of the commencement of his bankruptcy, be void against the trustee in the bankruptcy.

For what it may be worth the subsection gives the persons entitled under the covenant or contract a special right to claim for dividend in the bankruptcy, in respect thereof. This does not technically make them creditors,[8] and the section expressly provides that any such claim is to be postponed until all claims of the other creditors for valuable consideration in money or money's worth have been satisfied, which includes the creditors' claim to statutory interest.[9]

f Section 42 (3)

This subsection provides that any payment of money (not being payment of premiums on a policy of life assurance) or any transfer of property[10] made by the settlor in pursuance of a covenant or contract under sub-s. (2) shall be void against the trustee in bankruptcy unless the persons to whom the payment was made prove one of three things, viz.:

i   that the payment or transfer was made more than two years before the date of the commencement of the bankruptcy, or

ii   that at the date of the payment or transfer the settlor was able to pay all his debts without the aid of the money so paid or the property so transferred, or

iii that the payment or transfer was made in pursuance of a covenant or contract to pay or transfer money or property expected to come to the settlor from or on the death of a particular person named in the covenant or contract and was made within three months after the money or property came into the possession or under the control of the settlor.

In the event of a payment or transfer being declared void it is provided that the persons to whom it was made are entitled to claim for dividend under or in respect of the covenant or contract, and it seems that in this case, unlike the case under sub-s. (2), they are not postponed to other creditors.

5 SECTION 37 OF THE MATRIMONIAL CAUSES ACT 1973

By virtue of this section a wife[11] who has brought proceedings for financial relief under the Act against her husband may apply to the Court for an order

---

[7] Cf. Re Magnus, [1910] 2 K.B. 1049, C.A., which would probably be decided the same way today, although it was a case on different words contained in the Bankruptcy Act 1883.

[8] Re Cumming and West, [1929] 1 Ch. 534; Re A Debtor, Re Baughan, [1947] 1 All E.R. 417; [1947] Ch. 313.

[9] Re a Debtor, Re Baughan, supra.

[10] "Transfer of property . . . means an actual transfer made by the bankrupt in pursuance of the antecedent contract to settle the after acquired property"—per P. O. Lawrence J. in Re Dent, [1923] 1 Ch. 113, 122.

[11] Including a former wife. Though less often needed in practice the section applies equally to an application by a husband, or former husband.

setting aside any "reviewable" disposition[12] made with the intention of defeating the claim for financial relief. If the application is made before financial relief has been granted, the wife must show that if the disposition were set aside the court would grant her financial relief or different financial relief. A disposition is a "reviewable disposition" unless it was "made for valuable consideration (other than marriage) to a person who, at the time of the disposition, acted in relation to it in good faith and without notice of any intention on the part of the other party to defeat the applicant's claim for financial relief."[13] This provision operates to protect intermediate *bona fide* dealings for value between the date of the disposition and the date of its being set aside.[14]

Where the disposition was made three years or more before the application the wife must prove affirmatively the husband's intention to defeat her claim. Where, however, the disposition was made less than three years before the application, this intention is presumed, if the effect of the disposition would be to defeat the claim, or, where an order for relief is already in force, if it has had this effect: the presumption can be rebutted by evidence to the contrary, but the onus of proof in this case rests on the husband.[15]

6 ILLUSORY TRUSTS

a Trusts for the benefit of creditors[16]

If a valid trust is created it cannot be revoked, unless the settlement itself contains a power of revocation. There appears to be an exception to this rule where a debtor conveys or transfers property to trustees for the benefit of his creditors. Such a disposition is *prima facie* revocable by the debtor, but the true view in such case is that the apparent beneficiaries have never acquired any equitable interest in the property at all. The trustees, in the eye of equity, hold the property conveyed or transferred to them on trust for the debtor himself absolutely.[17] The debtor "proposes only a benefit to himself by the payment of his debts—his object is not to benefit his creditors".[18] The trustees are in effect mere mandatories or agents[19] of the debtor, who, it has been said,[20] "is merely directing the mode in which his own property shall be applied for his own benefit, and . . . the general creditors, or the creditors named in the schedule, are merely persons named there for the purpose of shewing how the trust property under the voluntary deed shall be applied for the benefit of the

---

[12] "Disposition" is defined by s. 37 (6) in terms wide enough to include a trust.
[13] Section 37 (4).
[14] *National Provincial Bank, Ltd.,* v. *Hastings Car Mart, Ltd.,* [1964] 1 All E.R. 688; [1964] Ch. 665, C.A. There was no appeal to the H.L. on this point.
[15] Section 37 (5).
[16] See generally (1957), 21 Con. 280 (L. A. Sheridan).
[17] *Bill* v. *Cureton* (1835), 2 My. & K. 503.
[18] *Bill* v. *Cureton, supra,* per Pepys M.R. at 511.
[19] See *Acton* v. *Woodgate* (1833), 2 My. & K. 492, per Leach M.R.
[20] *Garrard* v. *Lord Lauderdale* (1830), 3 Sim. 1, per Shadwell V.C. at 12; affd. (1831), 2 Russ. & My. 451.

volunteers". The deed, in substance, operates merely as a power to the trustees which is revocable by the debtor.

b Where the trust becomes irrevocable

In various circumstances, the court will draw the inference that the *prima facie* rule does not represent the intention of the debtor, and that the deed accordingly creates a true trust for the benefit of the creditors, or at any rate some of them. This will clearly be the case as regards those creditors who have executed the deed,[1] or who have acted on the deed, for instance by forbearing to sue,[2] or have expressly assented, not necessarily formally, to the trust,[3] or where they have been expressly or impliedly told by the debtor that they may look to the trust property for the payment of their debts.[4] Mere communication of the trust to a creditor which is not dissented from by him may well be sufficient by itself to make the trust irrevocable, but the law on this point is confused.[5]

A deed has been held to be irrevocable where the obvious intention of the transaction would be frustrated if the debtor retained a power of revocation. Thus in *New, Prance and Garrard's Trustee* v. *Hunting*[6] the debtor conveyed the property to trustees on trust to raise £4,200 to make good breaches of trust committed by the debtor. The obvious purpose, it was said, was thereby to mitigate the penal consequences of the breaches of trust, which purpose required the creation of an irrevocable binding trust. An alternative ground for the judgment of one of the members of the Court of Appeal, Lord Esher M.R., in this case, was that the mere fact that the deed was expressed to be in favour of particular persons only and not in favour of creditors generally raises an inference that an irrevocable trust was intended.[7] This latter ground is, it is submitted, of doubtful validity in view of the number of cases, including the leading case of *Garrard* v. *Lord Lauderdale*[8] itself, where a debtor has been held entitled to revoke a conveyance to trustees on trust for creditors expressly named in a schedule thereto.

The effect of the death of the debtor is not clear. If the trust is to commence only after the debtor is dead, it seems that it makes it irrevocable.[9] Where the trust is to pay either during the debtor's lifetime or after his death the authorities are contradictory as to whether the death of the debtor makes the trust irrevocable.[10]

---

1 *Montefiore* v. *Browne* (1858), 7 H.L.Cas. 241; *Mackinnon* v. *Stewart* (1850), 1 Sim. N.S. 76; *Johns* v. *James* (1878), 8 Ch.D. 744, C.A.

2 *Nicholson* v. *Tutin* (1855), 2 K. & J. 18; *Re Baber's Trusts* (1870), L.R. 10 Eq. 554.

3 *Harland* v. *Binks* (1850), 15 Q.B. 713.   4 *Synnot* v. *Simpson* (1854), 5 H.L.Cas. 121.

5 In favour of a trust *Adnitt* v. *Hands* (1887), 57 L.T. 370, D.C.; *Re Sanders' Trusts* (1878), 47 L.J.Ch. 667; *contra, Cornthwaite* v. *Frith* (1851), 4 De G. & Sm. 552; *Re Michael* (1891), 8 Morr. 305, D.C. See also *Mackinnon* v. *Stewart* (1850), 1 Sim. N.S. 76; *Montefiore* v. *Browne* (1858), 7 H.L.Cas. 241.

6 [1897] 2 Q.B. 19, C.A., affd. on another ground [1899] A.C. 419, H.L. See also *Radcliffe* v. *Abbey Road & St. John's Wood Permanent Building Society* (1918), 87 L.J.Ch. 557.

7 *New, Prance & Garrard's Trustee* v. *Hunting, supra,* at p. 26, following *Smith* v. *Hurst* (1852), 10 Hare 30.   8 (1830), 3 Sim. 1.

9 *Re Fitzgerald's Settlement* (1887), 37 Ch.D. 18, C.A.; *Priestley* v. *Ellis,* [1897] 1 Ch. 489.

10 In favour of a continued power of revocation—*Garrard* v. *Lord Lauderdale, supra* (assumed without discussion); *Re Sanders' Trusts* (1878), 47 L.J.Ch. 667; *contra, Montefiore* v. *Browne* (1858), 7 H.L.C. 241; *Priestley* v. *Ellis, supra.*

Lastly, it has been held that the mandatory theory does not apply to an assignment made to a creditor as trustee for himself and other creditors; the debtor cannot revoke such a deed after it has been communicated to the assignee.[11]

c Deeds of Arrangement Act 1914

This Act considerably reduces the practical importance of the law as stated above. It provides that a deed of arrangement[12] made by a debtor for the benefit of his creditors generally, or, if he was insolvent at the date of the execution thereof, for the benefit of any three or more of them, shall be void if not registered with the registrar appointed by the Board of Trade within seven days of its execution.[13] Further, if a deed of arrangement is expressed to be or is in fact for the benefit of a debtor's creditors generally, it will be void unless it has received the written assent of a majority in number and value of the creditors within twenty-one days after registration.[14]

It should also be noted that a deed of arrangement affecting unregistered land may be registered under the Land Charges Act 1972,[15] and if not so registered will be void as against a purchaser for valuable consideration.[16] In the case of registered land the procedure to protect a deed of arrangement is to lodge a caution against dealing, and a purchaser will not be concerned with or affected by any deed of arrangement which is not so protected.[17]

d Bankruptcy Act 1914

A deed of arrangement, even though duly registered, will constitute an act of bankruptcy, under s. 1 (1) (a), where a debtor has made a conveyance or assignment of all or substantially all[18] his property to a trustee for the benefit of his creditors generally. As such it may be used to support a bankruptcy petition by any creditor who has not assented to or acquiesced in it,[19] and even by an assenting creditor if the deed has become void under the Deeds of Arrangement Act 1914.[20] It remains an available act of bankruptcy for three months,[1] though this time may be reduced to one month from the service of a specified notice on the creditor by the trustee under the deed of arrangement.[2] The deed of arrangement will be void as against the trustee in bankruptcy if the debtor is actually adjudicated bankrupt on a petition presented within three months of the date of its execution.

A deed of arrangement which is not an act of bankruptcy under the Bankruptcy Act 1914, s. 1 (1) (a), may nevertheless constitute an act of bankruptcy under s. 1 (1) (b) or s. 1 (1) (c) where the transaction is a fraudulent conveyance, gift, delivery or transfer, or where it would amount to a fraudulent preference under s. 44 if the debtor were adjudged bankrupt. If it does, however, there

---

[11] *Siggers* v. *Evans* (1855), 5 E. & B. 367.   [12] Defined in s. 1.
[13] Section 2, subject to the Administration of Justice Act 1925, s. 22 (1).
[14] Deeds of Arrangement Act 1914, s. 3.
[15] Land Charges Act 1972, s. 7 (1).
[16] Land Charges Act 1972, ss. 7 (2) and 17 (2).
[17] Land Registration Act 1925, ss. 59 (1) and (6) and 100 (7).
[18] *Re Spackman* (1890), 24 Q.B.D. 728, C.A.
[19] As to withdrawal of assent see *Re Clarke*, [1966] 3 All E.R. 622; [1967] Ch. 1121, D.C.
[20] Deeds of Arrangement Act 1914, s. 24 (2).
[1] Bankruptcy Act 1914, s. 4 (1) (c).
[2] Deeds of Arrangement Act 1914, s. 24 (1).

is this difference that it is not within the provisions of s. 24 of the Deeds of Arrangement Act 1914. Accordingly it would appear that in this case the trustee under the deed of arrangement cannot under sub-s. (1) abridge the time during which it remains an available act of bankruptcy. As regards sub-s. (2), however, it seems that this merely puts the existing law into statutory form; so that an assenting creditor will be able to rely on a deed which has become void under the Deeds of Arrangement Act 1914 as an act of bankruptcy. The point is that where the deed itself is void, the assent to it is equally void and incapable of binding the creditor.[3]

7 THE RACE RELATIONS ACT 1968

Apart from statute, it does not seem that a provision in a trust instrument discriminating against potential beneficiaries on the ground, for instance, of colour or religion, is regarded as being against public policy or otherwise unlawful, even in the case of a charitable trust. This was impliedly assumed in *Re Dominion Students' Hall Trusts*,[4] a case concerning a colour bar, and expressly stated in *Re Lysaght*,[5] a case concerning a provision excluding students of the Jewish or Roman Catholic faith from benefit, though the judge stigmatized this provision as "unamiable" and "undesirable".

The Race Relations Act 1968, now declares that discrimination, as defined in the Act, on the ground of colour, race, or ethnic or national origins, is unlawful. For the purposes of the Act, a person discriminates against another if on any of these grounds he treats that other in certain specified situations less favourably than he treats or would treat other persons. The specified situations would commonly seem to include the administration of a charitable, though not a private, trust.

The Act contains two special provisions relating to charitable trusts. Section 9 (1) (a) seems intended to distinguish between discriminating in favour of someone for whom one feels sympathy, and discriminating against someone because one thinks he is inferior. It provides that nothing in the Act affects a provision which is contained in a charitable instrument taking effect after 25 November 1968 and confers benefits on persons of a particular race, particular descent, or particular ethnic or national origins. Section 9 (1) (b) provides that nothing in the Act renders unlawful an act done in order to comply with the provisions of any charitable instrument taking effect before 25 November 1968: charitable trusts may continue in perpetuity, and this provision by itself means that any discriminatory provision taking effect before the specified date remains lawful indefinitely.

It should be observed, however, that in the administration of a charitable trust a procedure may be available for the removal[6] of a discriminatory provision saved by s. 9 (1) (b), or one altogether outside the scope of the Act, such as a provision for religious discrimination. This is by means of a cy-près scheme, which is discussed in Chapter 7, Section 4, *post*.

---

[3] *Re A Bankruptcy Notice,* [1924] 2 Ch. 76, C.A.; *Huddersfield Fine Worsteds Ltd.* v. *Todd* (1925), 42 T.L.R. 52.

[4] [1947] Ch. 183, and see *infra*, p. 216.

[5] [1965] 2 All E.R. 888; [1966] Ch. 191.

[6] As was done both in *Re Dominion Students' Hall Trust, supra,* and *Re Lysaght, supra*.

CHAPTER 6

Charitable Trusts

1 DIFFERENCE BETWEEN CHARITABLE AND NON-CHARITABLE TRUSTS

Although in most ways the rules relating to charitable and non-charitable trusts are the same, there are certain very important differences, which may go to the very validity of the trust, for instance, in relation to certainty and perpetuity, or may have important economic results, for instance, in relation to income tax. It seems convenient to begin by discussing the most important of these differences, in order to appreciate the reasons why it may be necessary to contend that a trust is or is not charitable. Other differences will appear incidentally from time to time.

a Certainty

The ordinary rule, as we have seen,[1] is that a private trust will fail if there is no certainty of objects, and thus, for instance, gifts for public or for benevolent purposes are void for uncertainty since the words used have no technical legal meaning. Where, however, there is a clear intention to give property for charitable purposes the gift will not fail on that ground. Charity is a word with a technical legal meaning, and accordingly if trustees are given a discretion to distribute property amongst charitable objects, the court can determine whether any object chosen is charitable or not, and as we shall see,[2] a procedure is available for selecting the objects of a gift to charity where the settlor or testator either makes no provisions for the purpose or the provisions are for any reason ineffective. The certainty required is certainty of intention to devote the property to charitable purposes.[3]

Although a gift for charity may be good notwithstanding that the particular objects are left undefined by the trust instrument, the gift will none the less fail if the trust is drafted in such a way that it is possible, without a breach of trust, for the whole of the gift to be devoted to non-charitable purposes. It

---

[1] Chapter 2, Section 3c, p. 38, *ante.*
[2] Chapter 7, Section 3, pp. 211, *et seq., post.*
[3] It could well be argued that there is certainty of objects by reason of the maxim *id certum est quod certum reddi potest.*

was for this reason that gifts have wholly failed in numerous cases, such as *Blair* v. *Duncan*,[4] where there was a bequest "for such charitable or public purposes as my trustee thinks proper," and *Houston* v. *Burns*,[5] where residue was given "for such public, benevolent or charitable purposes . . . as [my trustees] in their discretion shall think proper". In both cases the trustees, according to the terms of the trust, could quite properly have applied the whole fund for, in the one case public, and in the other case public or benevolent, non-charitable purposes. Similarly if a specified part of the fund must be applied for charitable purposes, but the remainder may be applied for non-charitable purposes, the gift will fail as to the latter part.

This principle still remains in full force in respect of trust instruments coming into operation on or after 16th December 1952,[6] but is qualified by the Charitable Trusts (Validation) Act 1954 in respect of what the Act calls "imperfect trust instruments" coming into operation before that date.[7] Some of the judges[8] have found this Act very difficult to interpret and its objects obscure. Thus Cross J. observed in *Re Harpur's Will Trusts*[9]: "The Act leaves the law untouched for the future but, for some reason which I do not pretend to understand, validates retrospectively a limited number of dispositions which had already failed. I do not know on what principle these particular dispositions were selected for favourable treatment, and so I see no reason for construing this Act liberally." And Harman L.J.[10] thought the Act so difficult to construe that in his view one could only go along step by step giving each word the best meaning one could. Other judges,[11] however, who, as we shall see, have been willing to give the Act a wider construction, have found less difficulty, and even regarded the main provision in s. 1 (1) as "clear and unambiguous".[12]

Turning to the terms of the Act, sub-ss. (1)-(3) of s. 1 provide as follows:

---

[4] [1902] A.C. 37, H.L.
[5] [1918] A.C. 337; [1918–19] All E.R. Rep. 817, H.L.; *Chichester Diocesan Fund* v. *Simpson*, [1944] 2 All E.R. 60; [1944] A.C. 341, H.L.
[6] The date of the publication of the *Nathan Report on Charitable Trusts* (Cmd. 8710).
[7] The Act is based on the recommendation of the Nathan Report, this point having become notorious as a result of the decisions in *Chichester Diocesan Fund* v. *Simpson*, *supra*; *Oxford Group* v. *I.R.Comrs.*, [1949] 2 All E.R. 537, C.A.; *Ellis* v. *I.R.Comrs.* (1949), 31 Tax Cas. 178, C.A. The time limit on the operation of the Act is apparently based on the unsatisfactory theory that after the publication of the report everyone is presumed to know the law. For a discussion of the Act in the light of the cases see (1962), 26 Con. 200 (Spencer G. Maurice). There are provisions in s. 3 saving, to some extent, the rights of persons entitled on the basis of invalidity—see *Re Thomas's Will Trust*, [1969] 3 All E.R. 1492 *sub. nom. Re Chitty's Will Trusts*, [1970] Ch. 254.
[8] See, e.g., *Re Harpur's Will Trusts*, [1961] 3 All E.R. 588; [1962] Ch. 78, C.A., *per* Evershed M.R. at 590; 87, and *per* Harman L.J., who admitted at 595; 95, "It has been my misfortune on a previous occasion in *Re Gillingham Bus Disaster Fund* to have to wrestle with the terms of this statute, and I confess to having been floored by them on that occasion and this".
[9] [1960] 3 All E.R. 237, 243; [1961] Ch. 38, 49, affirmed, [1961] 3 All E.R. 588; [1962] Ch. 78, C.A. In *Re Saxone Shoe Co. Ltd.'s Trust Deed*, [1962] 2 All E.R. 904, the same judge said, at p. 914, "the Act is a very odd one, and it is no answer to an argument founded on it that it produces a result which is surprising or even absurd".
[10] In *Re Harpur's Will Trusts*, *supra*, C.A., at 596; 96.
[11] Ormerod L.J., dissenting, in *Re Gillingham Bus Disaster Fund*, [1958] 2 All E.R. 749; [1959] Ch. 62, C.A.; Buckley J. in *Re Wykes' Will Trusts*, [1961] 1 All E.R. 470; [1961] Ch. 229.
[12] *Per* Buckley J. in *Re Wykes' Will Trusts*, *supra*, at 476; 242.

"(1) In this Act, 'imperfect trust provision' means any provision declaring the objects for which property is to be held or applied, and so describing those objects that, consistently with the terms of the provision, the property could be used exclusively for charitable purposes, but could nevertheless be used for purposes which are not charitable.

(2) Subject to the following provisions of this Act, any imperfect trust provision contained in an instrument taking effect before the sixteenth day of December, nineteen hundred and fifty-two, shall have, and be deemed to have had, effect in relation to any disposition or covenant to which this Act applies—

(a) as respects the period before the commencement of this Act,[13] as if the whole of the declared objects were charitable; and

(b) as respects the period after that commencement as if the provision had required the property to be held or applied for the declared objects in so far only as they authorise use for charitable purposes.

(3) A document inviting gifts of property to be held or applied for objects declared by the document shall be treated for the purposes of this section as an instrument taking effect when it is first issued."

The first case on the Act, *Vernon* v. *I.R.Comrs.*,[14] concerned a scheme sanctioned by the court under which certain property was to be held as a recreation ground and club house for the employees of a particular company and such other persons as might be authorised by the trustees. In order for the Act to apply it had to be shown, under s. 1 (1), that the property could be used "exclusively for charitable purposes". At the time the scheme was sanctioned it had been assumed that the trusts declared would be charitable, but in 1956 it was manifest that this could not be so in respect of the primary trust for the benefit of the employees.[15] It was, therefore, argued that the trustees, under their powers, might, for instance, properly invite the inhabitants of some defined area to enjoy the recreation ground and club house, and it would then be a charitable trust because it would be for the benefit of a defined section of the public. This argument was rejected, however, on the ground that the discretionary power of the trustees to admit other persons did not confer on the scheme the necessary character of being a public trust and accordingly it could not be said that the property could be used "exclusively for charitable purposes". For the same reason, in the next case, *Re Gillingham Bus Disaster Fund*,[16] it was clear, subject to an argument on s. 2 (3) discussed below, that the Act could not apply where the two primary objects of the trust (defraying the funeral expenses and caring for the boys who were disabled) were admittedly non-charitable, and subject thereto the fund was to be held for such worthy cause or causes as the trustees should determine.

In this last case Lord Evershed pointed out[17] that the Act distinguishes between (i) an "imperfect trust provision" which, to the extent and subject to the qualifications stated in the Act, is thereby validated; (ii) the "instrument" in which the imperfect trust provision is contained; and (iii) the "disposition"

---

[13] 30th July, 1954.
[14] [1956] 3 All E.R. 14.
[15] See *infra* Section 2g, pp. 187 *et seq.*, *post*, where it is explained that as a general rule a trust cannot be charitable unless it is for the benefit of the public or a sufficiently important section thereof.
[16] [1958] 2 All E.R. 749; [1959] Ch. 62, C.A.
[17] In *Re Gillingham Bus Disaster Fund*, *supra*, at 751–752; 70.

or "covenant" to which the Act is expressed to apply and in relation to which the validation takes effect. Bearing in mind these distinctions, we can now turn to consider s. 2 (3) which, it was contended, got over the difficulty that the property could not be used "exclusively for charitable purposes", since the two primary objects were non-charitable. The sub-section is in these terms:

> "A disposition in settlement or other disposition creating more than one interest in the same property shall be treated for the purposes of this Act as a separate disposition in relation to each of the interests granted."

The argument, which was accepted only by the dissenting judge in the Court of Appeal, Ormerod L.J., was that each contribution to the fund, made on the understanding that it would be dealt with on the terms of the published appeal, constituted a disposition of property creating separate interests in favour of the three objects respectively. The majority,[18] however, though they accepted with regard to each disposition, consisting of the donor's contribution, that it would not be a fatal objection, if separate interests had been created, that the extent of the separate interests could not have been quantified at the time the disposition was made, held that the argument failed. Neither Evershed M.R. nor Romer L.J. considered that a donor could fairly be said by his disposition to have created separate or distinct interests in favour of the "worthy causes" mentioned in the relevant instrument. Evershed M.R. put it on the rather technical ground that if an interest in favour of worthy causes could be said to have been created at all, it must have been by the joint effect of the disposition and of the instrument or by the exercise by the trustees of their discretionary powers, and not by the disposition alone; while Romer L.J. thought that the effect of a donor giving a contribution to the fund was to vest in the trustees a legal interest in the subject matter of the contribution coupled with an enforceable obligation to apply the gift in accordance with the provisions of the appeal. Subject to this no interests were, in his view, "created" by the various donors in the contributions which they made.

By virtue of their decision on s. 2 (3) the majority of the Court of Appeal in Re Gillingham Bus Disaster Fund[19] did not need to decide whether the Act would apply to a separate disposition to "such worthy cause or causes as the trustees should determine". The point is whether the Act applies only to a gift which is expressed to be for charitable purposes as well as for other non-charitable purposes, or whether it also applies to a gift such as, for example, a gift for public purposes, or a gift for worthy causes, in which charity is not expressly mentioned but where the terms of the gift in fact could include both charitable and non-charitable purposes, and the gift could accordingly in fact be used exclusively for charitable purposes. At first instance, in Re Gillingham Bus Disaster Fund,[1] Harman J. took the former view,[2] with which the majority expressed some sympathy on appeal, but Ormerod L.J., dissenting, thought it was clear that the Act covered both types of gift. This latter view was

---

[18] Affirming Harman J. in the court below: [1958] 1 All E.R. 37; [1958] Ch. 300.
[19] [1958] 2 All E.R. 749; [1959] Ch. 62, C.A.
[1] [1958] 1 All E.R. 37; [1958] Ch. 300.
[2] It seems this was intended as an alternative ground for his decision—Re Harpur's Will Trusts, [1961] 3 All E.R. at 595; [1962] Ch. at 95, C.A., per Harman L.J.; Re Saxone Shoe Co. Ltd.'s Trust Deed, [1962] 2 All E.R. 904, 915; though Buckley J. regarded it as an obiter dictum in Re Wykes' Will Trusts, [1961] 1 All E.R. 470; [1961] Ch. 229.

preferred by Buckley J. in *Re Wykes' Will Trusts*,[3] where a fund was given to the board of directors of a company "to be used at their discretion as a benevolent or welfare fund or for welfare purposes for the sole benefit of the past present and future employees of the company". This disposition in fact raised two distinct questions: first, the one just mentioned, namely, whether the Act applies to a trust to promote purposes which contains no reference to charity either generally or in the shape of some specific purpose but under which the fund could be wholly applied for charitable purposes; and, secondly, whether the Act applies to a case where the invalidity of the trust is not due, or not solely due, to the fact that the declared purposes are not wholly charitable, but is due in whole or in part to the fact that having regard to the nature of the class of potential beneficiaries only one particular sort of charitable trust, namely, a trust for the relief of poverty, could be validly created.[4] Here by reason of the fact that the class of persons to be benefited was restricted to employees, the trust could only be charitable if it was for the relief of poverty; this was clearly within the terms of the trust, though equally clearly according to its terms the fund, or its income, could be applied to other, i.e., necessarily non-charitable, purposes. The judge held that since, consistently with the terms of the trust, the whole fund could be applied by the trustees for the relief of poverty, i.e., exclusively for charitable purposes, the Act applied, notwithstanding the absence of any express reference to charity, and notwithstanding that the validation could be effected only by confining the purposes of the trust to a particular charitable purpose, namely, the relief of poverty. In a subsequent case, *Re Saxone Shoe Co. Ltd.'s Trust Deed*,[5] Cross J. proceeded on the footing that *Re Wykes' Will Trusts*[6] was rightly decided on both points, though at first instance in *Re Harpur's Will Trusts*[7] the same judge had on the first question felt himself bound by Harman J.'s contrary opinion.[8] On the second point Cross J. had already followed *Re Wykes' Will Trusts*[9] in *Re Mead's Trust Deed*,[10] where the objects of the trust were the provision of a sanitorium for consumptive members of a trade union, a convalescent home for members recovering from any kind of illness, and a home for aged members who were no longer able to support themselves by working at their trade and the wives of such members. The last object was admittedly charitable, but the first two were not, lacking the required element of public benefit.[11] It was held that the Act applied and the trust was validated, the court declaring that, as from 30th July 1954, the trust property had been held by the trustees as regards the first two objects for the benefit of those members of the society only who were from time to time poor persons.

It might appear that the principles of *Re Wykes' Will Trusts*[12] would make the Act apply so as to validate many invalid private trusts by turning them

---

[3] [1961] 1 All E.R. 470; [1961] Ch. 229.
[4] See Section 2g & h, pp. 187 *et seq., post.*
[5] [1962] 2 All E.R. 904.
[6] *Supra.*
[7] [1960] 3 All E.R. 237; [1961] Ch. 38, affd. [1961] 3 All E.R. 588; [1962] Ch. 78, C.A., where, however, this point was not discussed.
[8] At first instance in *Re Gillingham Bus Disaster Fund*, [1958] 1 All E.R. 37; [1958] Ch. 300.
[9] *Supra.*
[10] [1961] 2 All E.R. 836.
[11] See Section 2g, pp. 187 *et seq., post.*
[12] *Supra.*

into trusts for the relief of such potential beneficiaries as should from time to time be poor. In *Re Saxone Shoe Co. Ltd.'s Trust Deed*[13] a fund was to be applied in the discretion of the trustees for various specified purposes and any other purposes the trustees should consider to be for the benefit, in every case, of employees and former employees of the company and their dependants. It was contended that the trust had been validated by being turned into a trust for the relief of poverty among such members of the class of beneficiaries as might from time to time be poor persons. This contention was rejected on the ground that the trust in question was simply a trust to pay or apply the fund for the benefit of such members of a class (not being a section of the public) as the trustees should think fit, as opposed to a trust to promote some purposes, for example, welfare purposes which would include the relief of poverty, among such a class. The Act, Cross J. said, does not apply to a private discretionary trust as opposed to a trust for the promotion of quasi-charitable purposes. The distinction, he admitted, is very fine, and, unfortunately, little assistance was given as to what constitutes a quasi-charitable purpose.

Difficulty has also arisen in the interpretation of s. 2 (1)[14] which provides that the Act "applies to any disposition of property to be held or applied for objects declared by an imperfect trust provision . . . where apart from this Act the disposition . . . is invalid . . . but would be valid if the objects were exclusively charitable". It seems reasonably clear, however, that one effect of this provision is that the Act cannot apply where the trusts are contained in a scheme settled or sanctioned by the court. In such case when the imperfect quality of the trusts has been pointed out, the court must amend the scheme and accordingly the disposition cannot be said to be invalid.[15] The last point to be observed on this Act is that its provisions have no application to a trust for institutions as opposed to one for objects or purposes.[16]

Quite apart from the 1954 Act, there are various cases which at first sight might seem to be void for uncertainty on the principle explained above, but in which the trust has been held to be good. One class of case is where there is a trust under which a fund or the income thereof is to be applied primarily to purposes which are not charitable and accordingly void, and as to the balance or residue to purposes which are charitable. In this class of case if, on the one hand, as a matter of construction, the gift to charity is a gift of the entire fund or income subject to the payments thereout required to give effect to the non-charitable purpose, the amount set free by the failure of the non-charitable gift will be caught by and pass under the charitable gift.[17] On the other hand, if the gift of the residue is to be read as a gift of the mere balance of the fund after deducting the amount of the sum previously given out of it, the gift will wholly fail, on the ground that no ascertainable part of the fund or the income is devoted to charity, unless the amount applicable to the non-charitable purpose can be quantified. If this can be done the gift will fail, quoad that amount only, and will take effect in favour of the charitable purpose as regards

---

[13] *Supra.* Cf. *Vernon v. I.R.Comrs.*, [1956] 3 All E.R. 14.
[14] See *Re Harpur's Will Trusts*, [1961] 3 All E.R. 588; [1962] Ch. 78, C.A.
[15] *Vernon v. I.R.Comrs.*, [1956] 3 All E.R. 14.
[16] *Re Harpur's Will Trusts, supra.*
[17] *Re Parnell*, [1944] Ch. 107; *Re Coxen*, [1948] 2 All E.R. 492; [1948] Ch. 747. Cf. *Mitford v. Reynolds* (1848), 16 Sim. 105.

the remainder.[18] Exceptionally and anomalously if the primary non-charitable trust is the maintenance in perpetuity of a tomb not in a church, it is simply ignored, even though it may be capable of being quantified, and the whole fund or income is treated as being devoted to charitable purposes.[19] Further in some cases the true view of the matter may be that the alleged non-charitable trusts are essentially ancillary to the charitable trusts and it is settled that purposes merely ancillary to a main charitable purpose, which if taken by themselves would not be charitable, will not vitiate the claim of an institution to be established for purposes that are exclusively charitable.[20] Thus in *Re Coxen*[21] a fund of some £200,000 was given to the Court of Aldermen for the City of London upon trust

(a) to apply annually a sum not exceeding £100 to a dinner for the Court of Aldermen upon their meeting upon the business of the trust;

(b) to pay one guinea to each alderman who attended during the whole of a committee meeting in connection with the trust, and

(c) to apply the balance for a specified charitable purpose.

It was held that all the trusts were charitable as the provisions in favour of the aldermen were given for the better administration of the principal charitable trust and not for the personal benefit of the recipients.

Another class of case involves what is sometimes called apportionment, though it does not seem that it should make any difference whether trustees are directed to apportion a fund between different objects as opposed to being given a power of selection, division, or appointment. It must be remembered that where there is a power of selection or appointment between two or more persons or objects, the whole may be appointed to one to the total exclusion of the other or others, unless there is some express provision that each object is to have a minimum amount.[22] In the first place, if each object taken by itself is a valid object, whether charitable or non-charitable, the trust will be good even though the share that each object is to take is not declared by the trust instrument, and even though the trustees, having been given a power of selection, apportionment, division or appointment, fail to exercise it. In such case the court will divide the property between the objects equally, unless there is some contrary intention in the trust instrument.[1] Secondly, this principle was applied in *Re Clarke*[2] to a case where residue was given to

(a) indefinite charitable objects;

(b) a definite charitable object;

---

[18] *Re Vaughan* (1886), 33 Ch.D. 187; *Re Taylor* (1888), 58 L.T. 538; *Re Porter*, [1925] Ch. 746.

[19] *Re Birkett* (1878), 9 Ch.D. 576; *Re Vaughan, supra*; *Re Rogerson*, [1901] 1 Ch. 715.

[20] *Incorporated Council of Law Reporting for England and Wales v. A.-G.*, [1971] 3 All E.R. 1029; [1972] Ch. 73, C.A., *per* Russell L.J. at pp. 1033; 84.

[21] *Supra; Royal College of Surgeons of England v. National Provincial Bank Ltd.*, [1952] 1 All E.R. 984; [1952] A.C. 631, H.L. Contrast *Re Barnett* (1908), 24 T.L.R. 788.

[22] Section 158 of the Law of Property Act 1925 replacing the Illusory Appointments Act 1830 and the Powers of Appointment Act 1874.

[1] *Salusbury v. Denton* (1857), 3 K. & J. 529; *Re Douglas* (1887), 35 Ch.D. 472, C.A.; *Hunter v. A.-G.*, [1899] A.C. 309, H.L., *per* Lord Davey at p. 324. It seems doubtful whether the principle was properly applied in *Hoare v. Osborne* (1866), L.R. 1 Eq. 585.

[2] [1923] 2 Ch. 407; *Re King*, [1931] W.N. 232.

(c) another definite charitable object;

(d) such indefinite charitable and non-charitable objects as the executors should think fit,

and the residue was directed to be divided among the four objects or sets of objects in such shares and proportions as the executors should determine. It was held that the power of distribution or appointment given to the executors was void, as they could appoint the whole fund to object (d), which was void for uncertainty, and this was clearly correct. It was further held, however, that the principle of *Lambert* v. *Thwaites*[3] applied. In this case, it will be recalled, it was held that on its true construction the will set up a trust for all the children giving them vested interests, liable to be divested if the power of appointment was exercised. Similarly here the residue was held to have vested in the four objects equally: *prima facie* their interests were liable to be divested by the exercise by the executors of their power of distribution or appointment, but this power being void, their interests were indefeasible. The gifts to objects (a), (b) and (c) were accordingly good, but the gift of the remaining one-fourth share to object (d) failed on the ground of uncertainty, and went to the persons entitled on intestacy. The principle of the trust power cases such as *Walsh* v. *Wallinger*[4] does not, however, enable one, in, for instance, a gift to "such charitable or benevolent objects as my trustees shall select", to imply a gift over in default of appointment to charitable and benevolent objects in equal shares so as to save the gift as to one-half for charity. The courts are unwilling to make any apportionment in this sort of case,[5] and, as we have seen,[6] numerous decisions, including many in the House of Lords, have held such gifts altogether void. In this sort of case there is no gift to objects, but only a power given to the trustees to distribute among an uncertain group of objects, and the court will not imply any gift in default of appointment when, as has been said[7] "charitable purposes are mixed up with other purposes of such a shadowy and indefinite nature that the court cannot execute them".

b Perpetuities

In general the rule against perpetuities, which is shortly stated in Section 1a of the preceding chapter,[8] applies to gifts to charity. As Lord Selborne L.C. said,[9] "if the gift in trust for charity is itself conditional upon a future and uncertain event, it is subject . . . to the same rules and principles as any other estate depending for its coming into existence upon a condition precedent. If the condition is never fulfilled, the estate never arises; if it is so remote and

---

[3] (1866), L.R. 2 Eq. 151, discussed in Chapter 2, Section 1e, p. 23, *ante.*
[4] (1830), 2 Russ. & My. 78; see Chapter 2, Section 1e, pp. 22, 23, *ante.*
[5] See *per* Lord Wright in *Chichester Diocesan Fund* v. *Simpson*, [1944] 2 All E.R. 60, at p. 66; [1944] A.C. 341, 356, H.L.
[6] See p. 158, *ante.*
[7] *Hunter* v. *A.-G.* [1899] A.C. 309, H.L. *per* Lord Davey at p. 323.
[8] See, generally, Cheshire, *Modern Real Property*, 11th Ed., pp. 263 *et seq.*; Megarry and Wade, *The Law of Real Property*, 3rd Ed., pp. 214 *et seq.*; Morris and Leach, *The Rule against Perpetuities*, 2nd Ed. and Supplement. The law has recently been altered by the Perpetuities and Accumulations Act 1964.
[9] *Chamberlayne* v. *Brockett* (1872), 8 Ch. App. 206, at p. 211; *Re Lord Stratheden and Campbell*, [1894] 3 Ch. 265; *Re Mander*, [1950] 2 All E.R. 101; [1950] Ch. 547.

indefinite as to transgress the limits of time prescribed by the rules of law against perpetuities, the gift fails *ab initio*".[10] Thus gifts to charity to take effect on the appointment of the next lieutenant-colonel of a volunteer corps,[11] or when a candidate for the priesthood comes forward from a particular church,[12] have been held void on the ground that the event might not occur until after the expiration of the perpetuity period.[13] The general rule applies equally when the limitation to charity is by way of a gift over following a gift in favour of private individuals.[14]

Exceptionally, however, the rule against perpetuities has no application to a gift to one charity with a gift over to another charity upon some contingency, notwithstanding that the contingency may occur outside the perpetuity period.[15] The exception, however, does not cover the case of a gift over from a charity to an individual. The gift over in such case is subject to the rule.[16]

c The rule against perpetual trusts

As has been seen,[17] gifts for non-charitable purposes are generally void, and, in the exceptional cases where they are valid, must, if they are to be effective at all, be limited so as not to continue beyond the perpetuity period.[18] Trusts for charitable purposes are, however, completely unaffected by the rule against perpetual trusts, and it is no objection to a charitable trust that it may continue for ever and that it may never be possible to expend the capital as opposed to the income of the property subject to the trust.

It is convenient to mention at this point some of the cases that have arisen in connection with the upkeep of tombs. Though the upkeep of a tomb, other than a tomb in a church, is not a charitable purpose, it may nevertheless be possible to some extent to effect the desired purpose. If the provision is limited to the perpetuity period it is apparently valid, though unenforceable,[17] and various devices may be adopted which may, in practice, provide for its upkeep for an even longer period. First, if the gift is for the upkeep of the whole of a churchyard, including the particular tomb in question, the gift is charitable even though the motive for it may be the non-charitable one of maintaining one particular tomb. Secondly, advantage may be taken of the principle of *Christ's Hospital* v. *Grainger*[19] by granting property to one charity with a gift over to another charity if the tomb is not kept in repair. Care must be taken, however, not to impose any trust for the non-charitable purpose of maintaining the tomb on the subject-matter of the gift—failure to observe

---

[10] But see now the Perpetuities and Accumulations Act 1964, s. 3.
[11] *Re Lord Stratheden and Campbell, supra.*
[12] *Re Mander, supra.*
[13] But see now the Perpetuities and Accumulations Act 1964, s. 3.
[14] *Re Bowen*, [1893] 2 Ch. 491; [1891–94] All E.R. Rep. 238; *Re Wightwick's Will Trusts*, [1950] 1 All E.R. 689; [1950] Ch. 260.
[15] *Christ's Hospital* v. *Grainger* (1849), 1 Mac. & G. 460; *Re Tyler*, [1891] 3 Ch. 252, C.A.; *Royal College of Surgeons of England* v. *National Provincial Bank*, [1952] 1 All E.R. 984; [1952] A.C. 631, H.L. Cf. *Re Martin*, [1952] W.N. 339.
[16] *Re Bowen, supra*; *Gibson* v. *South-American Stores (Gath & Chaves), Ltd.* [1949] 2 All E.R. 985; [1950] Ch. 177, C.A.; *Re Cooper's Conveyance Trusts*, [1956] 3 All E.R. 28.
[17] Chapter 2, Section 3c, pp. 38 *et seq.*, *ante*.
[18] This is unaffected by the Perpetuities and Accumulations Act 1964 (s. 15 (4)).
[19] (1849), 1 Mac. & G. 460. See Section 1b of this chapter, *supra*.

this point led to a failure of the scheme in *Re Dalziel*.[20] From a practical point of view the validity of this device depends on the trust income exceeding the sums needed for the upkeep of the tomb and on the availability of other income to carry out the necessary maintenance. Thirdly, until the Perpetuities and Accumulations Act 1964, by creating a trust to pay the income of a fund to a corporation, so long as the tomb was kept in repair.[21] This created a determinable interest in the corporation which automatically came to an end if the tomb ceased to be kept in repair, and the subject-matter of the gift in that event fell into residue even though the determining event might happen outside the perpetuity period.[1] Again this scheme failed if any trust for non-charitable purposes was imposed on the income.[2] This device can, however, no longer be effective to maintain a tomb beyond the perpetuity period, for the 1964 Act provides that if and when it becomes established that the determining event must occur, if at all, outside the perpetuity period, the determinable interest shall become an absolute interest, though the determining event will be operative if it occurs during the perpetuity period.[3] Finally it may be noted that a burial authority or a local authority may undertake the maintenance of a private grave for a period not exceeding 99 years from the date of the agreement.[4]

d   Exemptions from rates and taxes[5]

The income of bodies of persons or trusts established in the United Kingdom[6] for charitable purposes only, so far as it is applied accordingly,[7] is wholly exempt from income tax[8] and there is a similar exemption in relation to capital gains tax.[9] Charities[10] are entitled to a 50 per cent remission of rates on hereditaments occupied by them, and wholly or mainly used for charitable purposes,[11] and may be granted a further remission by the rating authority.[12]

---

[20] [1943] 2 All E.R. 656; [1943] Ch. 277.
[21] *Re Chardon*, [1928] Ch. 464; *Re Chambers Will Trusts*, [1950] Ch. 267.   See (1937), 53 L.Q.R. 24 (W. O. Hart); (1938), 54 L.Q.R. 258 (M. J. Albery).
[1] An express gift over would have been void for perpetuity.
[2] *Re Wightwick's Will Trusts*, [1950] 1 All E.R. 689; [1950] Ch. 260.
[3] Sections 12 (1) and 3. Note also s. 1.
[4] Parish Councils and Burial Authorities (Miscellaneous Provisions) Act 1970, s. 1.
[5] See, [1972] B.T.R. 346.
[6] *Camille & Henry Dreyfus Foundation Inc.* v. *I.R.Comrs.*, [1956] A.C. 39, H.L.
[7] See *I.R.Comrs.* v. *Educational Grants Association, Ltd.*, [1967] 2 All E.R. 893; [1967] Ch. 993, C.A.
[8] Income and Corporation Taxes Act 1970, s. 360, as amended by Finance Act 1971, ss. 56 (3) (4), 69 (7) and Sched. 14, Part IV. An interesting recent decision is *Trustees of G. Drexler Ofrex Foundation* v. *I.R.Comrs.*, [1965] 3 All E.R. 529; [1966] Ch. 675.
[9] Finance Act 1965, s. 35 (1) and (2), as amended by Income and Corporation Taxes Act 1970, s. 538 (1) and Sched. 15. The donor may obtain relief from capital gains tax on gifts to charities—Finance Act 1972, s. 119.
[10] With the exception of certain universities and colleges set out in the Eighth Schedule to the General Rate Act 1967, as amended by Statutory Instruments.
[11] *Aldous* v. *Southwark Corporation*, [1968] 3 All E.R. 498, C.A.; *Valuation Comr.* v. *Redemptorist Order Trustees*, [1971] N.I. 114, C.A.   It is not settled whether a charity shop is entitled to relief, or whether it fails to qualify, as being used for the purposes of fund-raising and not for the purposes of the charity.
[12] General Rate Act 1967, s. 40. See also s. 50 and, generally, (1964), 28 Con. 20 (Spencer G. Maurice).

As regards estate duty the charge on *inter vivos* gifts within the seven years preceding the death of the donor only applies to gifts within one year preceding death where the donee is a charity.[13]

Further in connection with estate duty, for the purpose of calculating the principal value of an estate property given to charities is to be left out of account up to a limit of £50,000, and property given to any of the bodies specified in Schedule 25 of the Finance Act 1972[14] is to be left out of account entirely. It follows that no estate duty is payable on property comprised in such gifts.[15]

Charities are generally liable to Value Added Tax. In the case of charities established for the relief of distress, however, an order[16] has been made which relieves from V.A.T. most sales by such a charity of goods donated to it, whether new or used. It does not matter whether the sale takes place in a charity shop, or on an occasion such as a fête or coffee morning.

2 DEFINITION OF CHARITY

a General[17]

In order for a trust to be legally charitable, its purposes must fall within the spirit and intendment of the preamble to the Statute 43 Eliz. 1, c. 4, sometimes referred to as the Charitable Uses Act 1601.[18] This proposition has recently been reaffirmed by the House of Lords[19] notwithstanding the repeal of the preamble by the Charities Act 1960.[20] The purposes set out in the preamble are, in modernised English, as follows:

"The relief of aged, impotent and poor people; the maintenance of sick and maimed soldiers and mariners, schools of learning, free schools and scholars in universities; the repair of bridges, ports, havens, causeways, churches, sea-banks and highways; the education and preferment of orphans; the relief, stock or maintenance for houses of correction; the marriages of poor maids, the supportation, aid and help of young tradesmen, handicraftsmen and persons decayed; the relief or redemp-

---

[13] Customs and Inland Revenue Act 1881, s. 38 (2) (*a*); Finance Act 1894, s. 2 (1) (*c*); Finance Act 1968, s. 35 (1).

[14] E.g. the National Gallery and the British Museum.

[15] See Finance Act 1972, s. 121.

[16] The V.A.T. (Charities) Order 1973, S.I. No. 385. The order defines "the relief of distress".

[17] Useful articles include (1945), 61 L.Q.R. 268 (J. Brunyate); (1956), 72 L.Q.R. 187 (G. Cross); and on the Charities Act 1960, (1960), 24 Con. 390 (Spencer G. Maurice); (1961), 24 M.L.R. 444 (O. R. Marshall).

[18] Repealed by the Mortmain and Charitable Uses Act 1888, the preamble, however being preserved by s. 13 (2). The 1888 Act was itself repealed by the Charities Act 1960 and with it the preamble, but s. 38 (4) provides that "any reference in any enactment or document to a charity within the meaning, purview and interpretation of the Charitable Uses Act 1601, or of the preamble to it, shall be construed as a reference to a charity within the meaning which the word bears as a legal term according to the law of England and Wales".

[19] *Scottish Burial Reform and Cremation Society, Ltd.* v. *Glasgow City Corporation*, [1967] 3 All E.R. 215; [1968] A.C. 138, H.L.; see also *Re Banfield*, [1968] 2 All E.R. 276.

[20] See n. 18, *supra*. Cf. the articles on the Charities Act 1960 referred to in note 17, *supra*, and Nathan, *Charities Act 1960*, at p. 24. The opinion expressed in the text above is also the opinion of the Charity Commissioners—Report of the Charity Commissioners for 1966, para. 31.

tion of prisoners or captives; and the aid or ease of any poor inhabitants concerning payment of fifteens, setting out of soldiers and other taxes."

While, as Lord Upjohn said in *Scottish Burial Reform and Cremation Society, Ltd.* v. *Glasgow City Corporation*,[21] "it may seem almost incredible to anyone not familiar with this branch of the English law that this should still be taken as the test, it is undoubtedly the accepted test, though only in a very wide and broad sense". In the same case, however, Lord Wilberforce pointed out[22] that the requirement that the purpose in order to be charitable must be within the spirit and intendment of the preamble does not mean quite what it says; "for it is now accepted that what must be regarded is not the wording of the preamble itself, but the effect of decisions given by the courts as to its scope, decisions which have endeavoured to keep the law as to charities moving according as new social needs arise or old ones become obsolete or satisfied". The process was described by Lord Reid[23]: "The courts appear to have proceeded first by seeking some analogy between an object mentioned in the preamble and the object with regard to which they had to reach a decision. Then they appear to have gone further, and to have been satisfied if they could find an analogy between an object already held to be charitable and the new object claimed to be charitable". The result, in Lord Upjohn's words,[24] is that " 'the spirit and intendment' of the preamble to the statute of Elizabeth have been stretched almost to breaking point". He went on to give what is thought to be the first judicial hint of the possibility of a change of approach. "In the nineteenth and early twentieth centuries this was often due to a desire on the part of the courts to save the intentions of the settlor or testator from failure from some technical rule of law. Now that it is used so frequently to avoid the common man's liability to rates or taxes, this generous trend of the law may one day require reconsideration."

Be this as it may, the accepted classification of the multitude of single instances is set out in the speech of Lord Macnaghten in *Commissioners for Special Purposes of Income Tax* v. *Pemsel*[1]: "Charity," he said, "in its legal sense comprises four principal divisions: trusts for the relief of poverty; trusts for the advancement of education; trusts for the advancement of religion; and trusts for other purposes beneficial to the community, not falling under any of the preceding heads". Lord Macnaghten went on to observe that "the trusts last referred to are not the less charitable in the eye of the law, because incidentally they benefit the rich as well as the poor, as indeed, every charity that deserves the name must do either directly or indirectly". But it is very doubtful whether a trust would be declared to be charitable which excluded the poor.[2] Lord

---

[21] [1967] 3 All E.R. 215; [1968] A.C. 138 at pp. 221; 151, H.L.

[22] In *Scottish Burial Reform and Cremation Society, Ltd.* v. *Glasgow City Corporation, supra,* at p. 223; 154.

[23] In *Scottish Burial Reform and Cremation Society, Ltd.* v. *Glasgow City Corporation, supra,* at p. 218; 147.

[24] *Scottish Burial Reform and Cremation Society, Ltd.* v. *Glasgow City Corporation, supra,* at p. 222; 153. Cf. *Dingle* v. *Turner,* [1972] 1 All E.R. 878; [1972] A.C. 601, H.L., and see p. 191, *infra.*

[1] [1891] A.C. 531, 583, H.L., based on the classification put forward by Sir Samuel Romilly as counsel in *Morice* v. *Bishop of Durham* (1805), 10 Ves. 522.

[2] *Re Macduff,* [1896] 2 Ch. 451, C.A., *per* Lindley L.J. at 464; *Le Cras* v. *Perpetual Trustee Co., Ltd.,* [1967] 3 All E.R. 915; *sub. nom. Re Resch's Will Trusts* [1969] A.C. 514, P.C.

Macnaghten's classification has constantly been referred to in later cases. Lord Wilberforce, in *Scottish Burial Reform and Cremation Society, Ltd.* v. *Glasgow City Corporation*[3] reaffirmed its value and its usefulness in solving many problems, but made three observations, which, he said, its author would surely not have denied. These were "first, that, since it is a classification of convenience, there may well be purposes which do not fit neatly into one or other of the headings: secondly, that the words used must not be given the force of a statute to be construed; and, thirdly, that the law of charity is a moving subject which may well have evolved even since 1891".[4]

Whether or not a trust is charitable is a question of law[5] to be decided by the judge in the light of the circumstances in which the institution or trust came into existence and the sphere in which it operates.[6] In reaching his decision the judge[7] is completely unaffected by the settlor's or testator's opinion as to whether the purpose he has indicated is charitable or not.[8] Otherwise, as Russell J. observed,[9] "trusts might be established in perpetuity for the promotion of all kinds of fantastic (though not unlawful) objects, of which the training of poodles to dance might be a mild example". Equally the motive of the settlor or testator will not prevent a gift from being charitable if the purpose is one which is charitable in the eye of the law. Thus a bequest to provide for the erection of a stained glass window in a church was held to be charitable notwithstanding that the motive of the testatrix was to perpetuate her memory and not to beautify the church or to benefit the parishioners.[10] As Farwell J. said in *Re Delany*,[11] "the care of the aged, poor and the like is a charity . . . whether the persons who devote their lives to it are actuated by the love of God, a desire for their own salvation, or mere pique, or disgust with the world".

Generally the trust instrument comes into existence before, or at the same time as, the trust fund. Sometimes, however, the order may be reversed, as may be the case, for instance, where a fund is set up as a result of a public appeal which does not clearly define the trusts. The position in such a case was explained in the following terms by Cozens-Hardy L.J. in *A.-G.* v. *Mathieson*[12]:

"When money is given by charitable persons for somewhat indefinite purposes, a time comes when it is desirable, and indeed necessary, to prescribe accurately the terms of the charitable trust, and to prepare a scheme for that purpose. In the

---

[3] [1967] 3 All E.R. 215, 223; [1968] A.C. 138, 154, H.L.

[4] I.e. when *Commissioners for Special Purposes of Income Tax* v. *Pemsel, supra*, was decided.

[5] *Royal Choral Society* v. *Inland Revenue Commissioners*, [1943] 2 All E.R. 101, C.A.

[6] *Incorporated Council of Law Reporting for England and Wales* v. *A.-G.*, [1971] 3 All E.R. 1029; [1972] Ch. 73, C.A. *per* Sachs L.J. at pp. 1038; 91.

[7] Commonly in practice the Charity Commissioners on an application for registration— see p. 211, *post*.

[8] *Re Hummeltenberg*, [1923] 1 Ch. 237; *National Anti-Vivisection Society* v. *Inland Revenue Commissioners*, [1947] 2 All E.R. 217; [1948] A.C. 31, H.L.; Cf. *Re Cox*, [1955] 2 All E.R. 550; [1955] A.C. 627, P.C. Similarly where the trust instrument purports to leave the matter to the opinion of the trustees—*Re Wootton's Will Trusts*, [1968] 2 All E.R. 618.

[9] In *Re Hummeltenberg*, [1923] 1 Ch. 237, 242, approved by the House of Lords in *National Anti-Vivisection Society* v. *Inland Revenue Commissioners, supra*.

[10] *Re King*, [1923] 1 Ch. 243; *Re Delius' Will Trusts*, [1957] 1 All E.R. 854; [1957] Ch. 299.

[11] [1902] 2 Ch. 642 at pp. 647, 648; *Valuation Comr.* v. *Redemptorist Order Trustees*, [1971] N.I. 114, C.A.

[12] [1907] 2 Ch. 383, at p. 394, C.A.

absence of evidence to the contrary, the individual or the committee entrusted with the money must be deemed to have implied authority for and on behalf of the donors to declare the trusts to which the sums contributed are to be subject. If the individual or the committee depart from the general objects of the original donors, any deed of trust thus transgressing reasonable limits might be set aside by proper proceedings instituted by the A.-G., or possibly by one of the donors. But unless and until set aside or rectified, such a deed must be treated as in all respects decisive of the trusts which, by the authority of the donor, are to regulate the charity."

It should be added that it is quite clear that the mere making of a charge for the services rendered does not prevent an organisation, otherwise charitable, from being charitable, and there is no reason why the position should be altered by the mere fact that a commercial undertaking comes into the field and supplies similar services on a commercial basis.[13]

We must now turn to consider Lord Macnaghten's four heads of charity, which will be discussed in turn. One should add the warning, however, that it is often arguable that the facts of a case bring it under more than one head of charity, or that it does not decisively fit into one rather than another category,[14] and the court may well declare a trust to be charitable without making it clear exactly on what ground it does so.

b Trusts for the relief of poverty

"Poverty, of course, does not mean destitution. It is a word of wide and somewhat indefinite import, and, perhaps, it is not unfairly paraphrased for present purposes as meaning persons who have to 'go short' in the ordinary acceptation of that term, due regard being had to their status in life and so forth."[15] "There may be a good charity for the relief of persons who are not in grinding need or utter destitution . . . [but] relief connotes need of some sort, either need for a home, or for the means to provide for some necessity or quasi-necessity, and not merely an amusement, however healthy."[16]

In accordance with these dicta, gifts for ladies in reduced circumstances,[17] for the aid of distressed gentlefolk,[18] to provide a temporary residence for ladies of limited means,[19] and a nursing home for persons of moderate means,[1] have all been held charitable. The fact that no one in receipt of an income less than a certain amount is eligible to benefit, does not necessarily prevent a trust from being charitable.[2]

The intention that the gift shall be for the relief of poverty may be inferred

---

[13] *Scottish Burial Reform and Cremation Society, Ltd., v. Glasgow City Corporation,* [1967] 3 All E.R. 215; [1968] A.C. 138, H.L.

[14] *Re Hopkins' Will Trusts,* [1964] 3 All E.R. 46, at p. 51; [1965] Ch. 669, at pp. 678, 679; *Scottish Burial Reform and Cremation Society, Ltd. v. Glasgow City Corporation,* [1967] 3 All E.R. 215; [1968] A.C. 138, H.L.

[15] *Per* Evershed M.R. in *Re Coulthurst's Will Trusts,* [1951] 1 All E.R. 774, at p. 776; [1951] Ch. 661, at p. 666, C.A.

[16] *Per* Lord Simonds in *I.R.Comrs. v. Baddeley,* [1955] 1 All E.R. 525, 529; [1955] A.C. 572, at p. 585, H.L.

[17] *Shaw v. Halifax Corporation,* [1915] 2 K.B. 170, C.A.

[18] *Re Young,* [1950] 2 All E.R. 1245; [1951] Ch. 344.

[19] *Re Gardom,* [1914] 1 Ch. 662, C.A.

[1] *Re Clarke,* [1923] 2 Ch. 407.

[2] *Re De Carteret,* [1933] Ch. 103; *Re Lacy,* [1899] 2 Ch. 149.

from the nature of the gift, as in *Re Lucas*,[3] where the income of a fund was given "to the oldest respectable inhabitants in Gunville to the amount of 5s. per week each". It was held that the smallness of the amounts payable showed that the purpose of the gift was to assist the aged poor. It is, of course, sufficient if the gift is to an institution the object of which is the relief of poverty.[4]

By way of contrast a gift to provide a contribution towards the holiday expenses of workpeople was held not to be charitable on the ground that, although employed at a very small wage, the workpeople could not be described as poor people within the meaning of the statute of Elizabeth.[5] And it has been held that the working classes do not constitute a section of the poor for the purpose of the law of charity.[6]

It is convenient to mention here, since the statute of Elizabeth refers in one phrase to "the relief of aged, impotent and poor people", that a series of decisions[7] at first instance has held that these words are to be read disjunctively so that a gift may be charitable if the beneficiaries conform to any one of these descriptions. This was applied in *Re Cottam's Will Trusts*[8] to a gift to a local authority to provide flats for aged persons notwithstanding that the flats were to be let at economic rents. It has been pointed out[9] that the principle of these decisions would seem to lead to the result that trusts for "aged peers" or "impotent millionaires" would be charitable. Megarry's suggestion[9] that such trusts would fail as lacking an element of public benefit is criticised by Atiyah,[10] but it is submitted that his own view, that where direct benefit to a section of the public is relied on there must be an indirect benefit to the public at large, is insufficiently supported. It is submitted that a trust for impotent millionaires would fail on the ground put forward by Lindley L.J. in *Re Macduff*,[11] namely, that no trust would be charitable which excluded the poor. If the disjunctive principle is correct, a trust for aged peers might well be good, unless it could successfully be contended that the number of peers is inadequate to form a section of the public.[12]

c Trusts for the advancement of education

Schools of learning, free schools and scholars in universities are specifically mentioned in the Statute of Elizabeth, and many other educational purposes

[3] [1922] 2 Ch. 52; *Re Dudgeon* (1896), 74 L.T. 613; *Re Wall* (1889), 42 Ch.D. 510.
[4] *Biscoe* v. *Jackson* (1887), 35 Ch.D. 460, C.A. (soup-kitchens).
[5] *Re Drummond*, [1914] 2 Ch. 90; [1914–15] All E.R. Rep. 223.
[6] *Re Sanders' Will Trusts*, [1954] 1 All E.R. 667; [1954] Ch. 265, where it was said that the term "working class" is now an anachronism.
[7] As to aged persons see *Re Robinson*, [1950] 2 All E.R. 1148; [1951] Ch. 198; *Re Glyn's Will Trusts*, [1950] 2 All E.R. 1150 n; *Re Bradbury*, [1950] 2 All E.R. 1150, n. As to impotent persons see *Re Lewis*, [1954] 3 All E.R. 257; [1955] Ch. 104 ("to ten blind girls, Tottenham residents if possible, the sum of £100 each"); *Re Elliott* (1910), 102 L.T. 528; *Re Hillier*, [1944] 1 All E.R. 480.
[8] [1955] 3 All E.R. 704. Cf. *Re Payling's Will Trusts*, [1969] 3 All E.R. 698.
[9] By R. E. Megarry at (1951), 67 L.Q.R. 164; (1955), 71 L.Q.R. 16.
[10] (1958), 21 M.L.R. at pp. 140, 141. As to the requirement of public benefit, see p. 187, *infra*.
[11] [1896] 2 Ch. 451, at p. 464; [1895–99] All E.R. Rep. 154, at p. 157, C.A. The same result is reached by stressing that a trust to be charitable must be for the *relief* of age, impotence or poverty—[1970] A.S.C.L. 199 (J. D. Davies).
[12] *Re Compton*, [1945] 1 All E.R. 198; [1945] Ch. 123, C.A.

have been held to come within its spirit and intendment. Education is not restricted to the narrow sense of a master teaching a class, but includes the education of artistic taste,[13] "the promotion or encouragement of those arts and graces of life which are, perhaps, the finest and best part of the human character",[14] and the improvement of a useful branch of human knowledge and its public dissemination.[15] On the other hand, it has been said[16] that "if the object be merely the increase of knowledge, that is not in itself a charitable object unless it be combined with teaching or education", for otherwise there would be no element of public benefit, though it has since been explained[17] that education was used here in a wide sense "certainly extending beyond teaching, and that the requirement is that, in order to be charitable, research must either be of educational value to the researcher or must be so directed as to lead to something which will pass into the store of educational material, or so as to improve the sum of communicable knowledge in an area which education may cover— education in this last context extending to the formation of literary taste and appreciation". It is not enough, however, that the object should be educational in the sort of loose sense in which all experience may be said to be educative.[18]

In accordance with these principles, gifts to endow and build a Cambridge college,[19] to found lectureships and professorships,[20] and to augment fellows' stipends[21] have all been held to be charitable. Of special interest is *Incorporated Council of Law Reporting for England and Wales* v. *A.-G.*[22] The main object of the Council is the preparation and publication of law reports, not for profit, for the purpose of providing essential material for the study of law—in the sense of acquiring knowledge of what the law is, how it is developing, and how it applies to the enormous range of human activities which it affects. This was held to be for the advancement of education, as would be the institution and maintenance of a library for the study of any other learned subject or science. As regards the subjects of education, a wide variety have been held to be edu-

---

[13] *Royal Choral Society* v. *I.R.Comrs.*, [1943] 2 All E.R. 101, C.A.

[14] *Per* Vaisey J. in *Re Shaw's Will Trusts*, [1952] 1 All E.R. 49, 55; [1952] Ch. 163, 172 (the wife of G. Bernard Shaw). Cf. Farwell J. in *Re Lopes*, [1931] 2 Ch. 130, 136, "a ride on an elephant may be educational. At any rate it brings the reality of the elephant and its uses to the child's mind, in lieu of leaving him to mere book learning. It widens his mind, and in that broad sense is educational".

[15] *Incorporated Council of Law Reporting for England and Wales* v. *A.-G.*, [1971] 3 All E.R. 1029; [1972] Ch. 73, C.A., *per* Buckley L.J. at pp. 1046; 102.

[16] *Per* Harman J. in *Re Shaw*, [1957] 1 All E.R. 745, at p. 752 (G. Bernard Shaw), compromised C.A. [1958] 1 All E.R. 245. Cf. *Re Macduff*, [1896] 2 Ch. 451; [1895–99] All E.R. Rep. 154, C.A., *per* Rigby L.J. at 472; 162. "Education is no doubt a charitable purpose within the statute, learning is not."

[17] *Re Hopkins' Will Trusts*, [1964] 3 All E.R. 46, 52; [1965] Ch. 669, 680, *per* Wilberforce J. See (1965), 29 Con. 368 (M. Newark and A. Samuels).

[18] *I.R.Comrs.* v. *Baddeley*, [1955] 1 All E.R. 525; [1955] A.C. 572, H.L., *per* Lord Simonds at 529; 585.

[19] *A.-G.* v. *Downing* (1766), Amb. 550; (1769), Amb. 571.

[20] *A.-G.* v. *Margaret and Regius Professors in Cambridge* (1682), 1 Vern. 55.

[21] *The Case of Christ's College, Cambridge* (1757), 1 W.Bl. 90.

[22] [1971] 3 All E.R. 1029; [1972] Ch. 73, C.A. Russell L.J. reached the same result, but on the ground that the case fell under Lord Macnaghten's fourth head. The fact that the reports are used by members of the legal profession for earning fees is incidental and does not detract from the exclusively charitable character of the Council's objects. See (1972), 88 L.Q.R. 171.

cational, including the promotion and advancement of the art and science of surgery,[1] of choral singing in London,[2] of organists and organ music,[3] of the music of a particular composer,[4] of Egyptology,[5] of a search for the Bacon-Shakespeare manuscripts,[6] of economic and sanitary science,[7] of industry and commerce,[8] of legal education,[9] of zoology,[10] and of English classical drama and the art of acting.[11] Even a trust[12] for "the teaching, promotion and encouragement in Ireland of self-control, elocution, oratory, deportment, the arts of personal contact, of social intercourse, and the other arts of public, private, professional and business life", described by the judge[13] as "a sort of finishing school for the Irish people" has been held to be charitable, as have trusts for an annual chess tournament for boys and young men in the city of Portsmouth,[14] and to provide an annual treat or field day for schoolchildren, on the ground that this would encourage nature study.[15]

These last cases are very near the border line, and cases which have fallen on the other side include trusts for artistic purposes,[16] and to present artistic dramatic works.[17] Political propaganda masquerading as education is not charitable,[18] and education for some purposes may lack the necessary element of public benefit and therefore not be charitable as in the illustrations of schools or colleges for prostitutes, or pickpockets, given by Harman L.J.,[19] and the college for training spiritualistic mediums in Re Hummeltenberg.[20] Although a

---

[1] Royal College of Surgeons of England v. National Provincial Bank, [1952] 1 All E.R. 984; [1952] A.C. 631, H.L.
[2] Royal Choral Society v. I.R.Comrs., [1943] 2 All E.R. 101, C.A. (It is irrelevant and, according to Lord Greene, curious, that incidentally people may find pleasure either in providing education or in being educated.) [3] Re Levien, [1955] 3 All E.R. 35.
[4] Re Delius' Will Trusts, [1957] 1 All E.R. 854; [1957] Ch. 299—a gift by the widow of the composer Delius for the advancement of his musical works. All the counsel in the case agreed that the works were of a high standard. In Re Pinion, [1964] 1 All E.R. 890; [1965] Ch. 85, C.A., the testator sought to found a small museum with his own paintings and his collection of paintings and antiques. On expert evidence that as a means of education the collection was worthless, it was held the gift was not charitable.
[5] Re British School of Egyptian Archaeology, [1954] 1 All E.R. 887.
[6] Re Hopkins' Will Trusts, [1964] 3 All E.R. 46; [1965] Ch. 669.
[7] Re Berridge (1890), 63 L.T. 470, C.A.
[8] Crystal Palace Trustees v. Minister of Town & Country Planning, [1950] 2 All E.R. 857; [1951] Ch. 132.
[9] Smith v. Kerr, [1902] 1 Ch. 774, C.A.—a gift to Clifford's Inn—one of the Inns of Chancery established to provide legal education.
[10] Re Lopes, [1931] 2 Ch. 130; North of England Zoological Society v. Chester R.D.C., [1959] 3 All E.R. 116, C.A.
[11] Re Shakespeare Memorial Trust, [1923] 2 Ch. 398.
[12] Re Shaw's Will Trusts, [1952] 1 All E.R. 49; [1952] Ch. 163.
[13] Vaisey J., supra, at 52; 167.
[14] Re Dupree's Deed Trusts, [1944] 2 All E.R. 443; [1945] Ch. 16.
[15] Re Mellody, [1918] 1 Ch. 228. Cf. Re Pleasants (1923), 39 T.L.R. 675.
[16] Re Ogden (1909), 25 T.L.R. 382, C.A. Cf. Crystal Palace Trustees v. Minister of Town & Country Planning, [1950] 2 All E.R. 857; [1951] Ch. 132.
[17] Associated Artists, Ltd. v. I.R.Comrs., [1956] 2 All E.R. 583.
[18] Bonar Law Memorial Trust v. I.R.Comrs. (1933), 17 Tax. Cas. 508; Re Hopkinson, [1949] 1 All E.R. 346; Re Strakosch, [1949] 2 All E.R. 6; [1949] Ch. 529, C.A.
[19] In Re Pinion, [1964] 1 All E.R. 890, at p. 893; [1965] Ch. 85, at p. 105, C.A.; Re Shaw, [1957] 1 All E.R. 745, at p. 752, compromised C.A., [1958] 1 All E.R. 245.
[20] [1923] 1 Ch. 237; [1923] All E.R. Rep. 49.

trust for mere sport is not charitable,[21] a gift for sport in a school is charitable as being for the advancement of education, which involves development of the body as well as the mind.[1] And a gift for the Boy Scouts is charitable, on the ground that the purpose of the association is the instruction of "boys of all classes in the principles of discipline, loyalty and good citizenship", one of the most important elements in education.[2]

It may be added that the mere fact that membership of an institution may confer some benefit on the members does not necessarily prevent the institution from being a charitable body. The test is whether the main object of the institution is the promotion and advancement of a science (using this word in a wide sense) or the protection and advantage of those practising a particular profession.[3]

d   Trusts for the advancement of religion

This is a separate head of charity under Lord Macnaghten's classification, although the only matter relating to the purposes of religion referred to in the Statute of Elizabeth is the repair of churches. Many religious purposes, however, have been held to fall within its spirit and intendment. It is generally accepted that "the Court of Chancery makes no distinction between one religion and another, . . . [or] one sect and another . . . [unless] the tenets of a particular sect inculcate doctrines adverse to the very foundations of all religion and . . . subversive of all morality. . . . If the tendency were not immoral and although this Court might consider the opinions sought to be propagated foolish or even devoid of foundation" the trust would nevertheless be charitable.[4] "As between different religions the law stands neutral, but it assumes that any religion is at least likely to be better than none."[5] These propositions are undoubtedly true so far as the various Christian denominations are concerned; there is no doubt as to the charitable character of religious trusts not only for the established church, but also for non-conformist bodies,[6] Unitarians,[7] Roman Catholics,[8] and, it has been held, even for the publication of the works of Joanna Southcott.[9] Similarly with regard to organisations which

---

[21] *Re Nottage*, [1895] 2 Ch. 649, C.A. (yacht racing); *I.R.Comrs.* v. *City of Glasgow Police Athletic Association*, [1953] 1 All E.R. 747; [1953] A.C. 380, H.L. See the Recreational Charities Act 1958, discussed at pp. 186, *et seq. post.*

[1] *Re Mariette*, [1915] 2 Ch. 284; [1914-15] All E.R. Rep. 794.

[2] *Re Webber*, [1954] 3 All E.R. 712, at p. 713.

[3] *Royal College of Surgeons of England* v. *National Provincial Bank*, [1952] 1 All E.R. 984; [1952] A.C. 631, H.L.; *Royal College of Nursing* v. *St. Marylebone Corporation*, [1959] 3 All E.R. 663, C.A.; *Re Mason*, [1971] N.Z.L.R. 714.

[4] Per Romilly M.R. in *Thornton* v. *Howe* (1862), 31 Beav. 14, at p. 19; *Gilmour* v. *Coats*, [1949] 1 All E.R. 848; [1949] A.C. 427, H.L.; *Re Watson, Hobbs* v. *Smith*, [1973] 3 All E.R. 678.

[5] Per Cross J. in *Neville Estates Ltd.* v. *Madden*, [1961] 3 All E.R. 769, at p. 781; [1962] Ch. 832, at p. 853.

[6] Since the Toleration Act 1688. See, e.g. *Re Strickland's Will Trusts*, [1936] 3 All E.R. 1027, appeal dismissed by consent, [1937] 3 All E.R. 676, C.A. (Baptist); *Re Manser*, [1905] 1 Ch. 68 (Quakers).

[7] Since the Unitarian Relief Act 1813. E.g. *Re Nesbitt's Will Trusts*, [1953] 1 All E.R. 936.

[8] Since the Roman Catholic Charities Act 1832. E.g. *Dunne* v. *Byrne*, [1912] A.C. 407; [1911-13] All E.R. Rep. 1105, P.C.; *Re Flinn*, [1948] 1 All E.R. 541; [1948] Ch. 241.

[9] *Thornton* v. *Howe, supra.* Joanna Southcott claimed that she was with child by the Holy Ghost, and would give birth to a second Messiah.

exist for the advancement of religion, such as the Church Army,[10] the Salvation Army,[11] the Church Missionary Society,[12] the Society for the Propagation of the Gospel in Foreign Parts,[13] the Sunday School Association,[14] the Protestant Alliance and kindred institutions,[15] and even, it has been held, a society of clergymen, in connection with a trust to provide dinners, on the ground that the free meals would increase the usefulness of the society by attracting a greater number of clergymen to the meetings.[16] But not, it has been decided, the Oxford Group Movement.[17]

Beyond the Christian religion, trusts for the advancement of the Jewish religion are undoubtedly charitable,[18] but there seems to be no authority on wholly distinct religions such as Mohammedism or Buddhism, though regulations[19] made under the Charities Act 1960 assume that a trust for the advancement of a religion other than Christianity is charitable. The objects of the Theosophical Society are not charitable,[20] as being for the advancement of religion or otherwise, and it has not been thought arguable that gifts for the maintenance of a masonic temple[1] or a college for training spiritualistic mediums[2] are charitable, and the same must surely be true of an atheistic society.[3]

The advancement of religion means the promotion of spiritual teaching in a wide sense, and the maintenance of the doctrine on which it rests, and the observances that serve to promote and manifest it.[4] Gifts for religious purposes or to religious societies have been held to be *prima facie* good as being restricted to such purposes as are charitable,[5] though, as we shall see,[6] religious purposes

---

[10] *Re Smith* (1938), 54 T.L.R. 851.

[11] *Re Fowler* (1914), 31 T.L.R. 102, C.A.; *Re Smith, supra.*

[12] *Re The Clergy Society* (1856), 2 K. & J. 615.   [13] *Re Maguire* (1870), L.R. 9 Eq. 632.

[14] *R. v. Special Commissioners of Income Tax*, [1911] 2 K.B. 434, C.A.

[15] *Re Delmar Charitable Trust*, [1897] 2 Ch. 163 (societies having as their object "to maintain and defend the doctrines of the Reformation, and the principles of civil and religious liberty against the advance of Popery").

[16] *Re Charlesworth* (1910), 26 T.L.R. 214.

[17] *Re Thackrah*, [1939] 2 All E.R. 4; *Oxford Group v. I.R.Comrs.*, [1949] 2 All E.R. 537, C.A. (the movement is probably a social movement founded on Christian ethics rather than a movement for the advancement of religion).

[18] Since the Religious Disabilities Act 1846, according, *inter alia*, to *Neville Estates Ltd. v. Madden*, [1961] 3 All E.R. 769; [1962] Ch. 832. But a Jewish religious trust was held charitable in *Straus v. Goldsmid* (1837), 8 Sim. 614, not following Lord Hardwicke's decision in *Da Costa v. De Paz* (1754), 2 Swan. 487, n.

[19] S.I. 1962 No. 1421; S.I. 1963 No. 2074.

[20] *Re Macaulay's Estate*, [1943] Ch. 435, n, H.L. ("to form a nucleus of Universal Brotherhood of Humanity without distinction of race, creed, caste or colour"). Cf. *Re Price*, [1943] 2 All E.R. 505; [1943] Ch. 422 (Anthroposophical Society).

[1] *Re Porter*, [1925] Ch. 746.

[2] *Re Hummeltenberg*, [1923] 1 Ch. 237; [1923] All E.R. Rep. 49.

[3] The point did not arise in *Bowman v. Secular Society, Ltd.*, [1917] A.C. 406; [1916–17] All E.R. Rep. 1, H.L., where it was held that there is nothing contrary to law in an attack on or a denial of the truth of Christianity unaccompanied by vilification, ridicule or irreverence. Christianity is not a part of the law of England.

[4] *Keren Kayemeth Le Jisroel, Ltd. v. I.R.Comrs.*, [1931] 2 K.B. 465, C.A., affirmed H.L., [1932] A.C. 650; [1932] All E.R. Rep. 971, *per* Hanworth M.R. at 477; *Oxford Group v. I.R.Comrs.*, [1949] 2 All E.R. 537, C.A.; *Berry v. St. Marylebone Corporation*, [1957] 3 All E.R. 677; [1958] Ch. 406, C.A.

[5] *Re White*, [1893] 2 Ch. 41, C.A. *Sed quaere*. See the doubts suggested in *Dunne v. Byrne*, [1912] A.C. 407, 411; [1911–13] All E.R. Rep. 1105, 1108, P.C.; *Re Smith's Will Trusts*, [1962] 2 All E.R. 563, C.A.

[6] See pp. 187 *et seq., post.*

are not necessarily charitable for they may, for instance, lack the vital element of public benefit, and similarly a religious body may engage in a number of subsidiary activities which are not purely religious. A trust in favour of such a body *simpliciter* may nevertheless be a good charitable trust, but the income can only be applied to the activities of the body which are purely religious.[7] A trust, however, which is so worded as to permit the income to be used by a religious body in activities which are not purely religious is not a good charitable trust.[8]

A gift for missionary purposes is ambiguous and may comprise objects which are not charitable,[9] but the court will readily find in the context or surrounding circumstances evidence to show that the gift is restricted to the popular sense of Christian missionary work which is charitable.[10] Gifts in popular language such as to "the service of God"[11] or "for God's work"[12] have also been held to be applicable only to charitable purposes for the advancement of religion, but not a gift for "good works".[13]

More clearly analogous to the repair of churches referred to in the Statute of Elizabeth, the erection, maintenance or repair of any church, chapel or meeting house or any part of the fabric thereof is charitable, and there have been held charitable gifts in connection with, *inter alia*, stained glass windows,[14] the spire,[15] chancel,[16] gallery,[17] seating,[18] organ,[19] and a monument in a church.[20] By a slight extension gifts for the upkeep of a churchyard or burial ground,[1] are charitable, even though restricted to some particular denomination,[2] but not a gift for the erection or repair of a particular tomb in a churchyard,[3] though it was held otherwise in the case of a gift to erect and maintain headstones to the graves of the pensioners of certain almshouses.[4]

Trusts for the support of the clergy are clearly charitable, even though subject to a condition such as promoting some specified doctrine,[5] wearing a

---

[7] *Oxford Group* v. *I.R.Comrs.*, [1949] 2 All E.R. 537, C.A. *per* Tucker L.J. at p. 539; *Re Banfield*, [1968] 2 All E.R. 276.

[8] *Oxford Group* v. *I.R.Comrs.*, *supra.*

[9] *Scott* v. *Brownrigg* (1881), 9 L.R. Ir. 246.

[10] *Re Kenny* (1907), 97 L.T. 130; *Re Moon's Will Trusts*, [1948] 1 All E.R. 300.

[11] *Re Darling*, [1896] 1 Ch. 50.

[12] *Re Barker's Will Trusts* (1948), 64 T.L.R. 273.

[13] *Re How*, [1930] 1 Ch. 66; [1929] All E.R. Rep. 354.

[14] *Re King*, [1923] 1 Ch. 243; *Re Raine*, [1956] 1 All E.R. 355; [1956] Ch. 417.

[15] *Re Palatine Estate Charity* (1888), 39 Ch.D. 54.

[16] *Hoare* v. *Osborne* (1866), L.R. 1 Eq. 585.

[17] *A.-G.* v. *Day*, [1900] 1 Ch. 31.

[18] *Re Raine*, *supra.*

[19] *A.-G.* v. *Ockover* (1736), cited in 1 Ves. Sen. 536.

[20] *Hoare* v. *Osborne*, *supra.*

[1] *Re Douglas*, [1905] 1 Ch. 279; *Re Vaughan* (1886), 33 Ch.D. 187 (*per* North J. at 192, "I do not see any difference between a gift to keep in repair what is called 'God's House' and a gift to keep in repair the churchyard round it, which is often called 'God's Acre'.")

[2] *Re Manser*, [1905] 1 Ch. 68 (Quakers). Cf. *Re Eighmie*, [1935] Ch. 524 and see *Scottish Burial Reform and Cremation Society, Ltd.* v. *Glasgow City Corporation*, [1967] 3 All E.R. 215; [1968] A.C. 138, H.L.

[3] *Hoare* v. *Osborne* (1848), L.R. 1 Eq. 585; *Re Vaughan*, *supra*; *Re Hooper*, [1932] 1 Ch. 38.

[4] *Re Pardoe*, [1906] 2 Ch. 184.

[5] *A.-G.* v. *Molland* (1832), 1 You. 562.

black gown in the pulpit,[6] or even preaching an annual sermon in commemoration of the testator.[7] Also charitable was a gift to a society for the relief of infirm, sick and aged Roman Catholic secular priests in the Clifton diocese, on the ground that this would tend to make the ministry more efficient, by making it easy for the sick and old to retire and give place to the young and healthy,[8] and somewhat similarly in the case of a gift for retired missionaries.[9]

Somewhat less obviously charitable perhaps is a gift for the benefit of a church choir,[10] and a case which seems to be at least on the extreme limit is Re Pardoe,[11] where a trust to endow the ringing of a peal of bells on 29th May in each year to commemorate the restoration of the monarchy to England was held to be for the advancement of religion as calculated to bring back "happy thoughts" which would necessarily connote "a feeling of gratitude to the Giver of all good gifts".[12] This principle was not applied, however, where the bells were directed to be rung half-muffled on the anniversary of the testator's death.[13]

It is convenient to consider at this point the effect of a gift to a person not as an individual but as the holder of a particular office. The relevant principles are not in fact restricted to gifts for the advancement of religion, and would apply equally, for instance, to a gift to the head of a school or college,[14] but they have been worked out mainly in connection with gifts to bishops and vicars.[15] The principles are, in fact, relatively easy to state, but their application has led to very fine distinctions. The basic principle is that in determining whether or not trusts are charitable, the character of the trustees is *prima facie* irrelevant. What matters is the purpose of the trust not the character of the trustee. Where, however, there is a gift to a person who holds an office the duties of which are in their nature wholly charitable, and the gift is made to him in his official name and by virtue of his office, then, if the purposes are not expressed in the gift itself, the gift is assumed to be for the charitable purposes inherent in the office. But where the purposes of the gift are expressed in terms not confining them to purposes which are in the legal sense charitable, they cannot be confined to charitable purposes merely by reference to the character of the trustee.

Thus a gift to the bishop of a diocese, or the vicar or vicar and churchwardens of a particular parish, *simpliciter*, is a valid charitable gift, for the bishop or vicar must use the gift exclusively for the charitable purposes inherent in his office. The gift is equally charitable where the gift is followed by words which merely indicate that the bishop or vicar is to have a full discretion in settling the particular mode of application within the charitable purposes of the gift. Thus gifts were held charitable in Re Garrard,[16] where there was a legacy "to the

---

[6] *Re Robinson*, [1897] 1 Ch. 85, C.A., but the condition was subsequently removed—*Re Robinson*, [1923] 2 Ch. 332.

[7] *Re Parker's Charity* (1863), 32 Beav. 654; cf. *Re Hussey's Charities* (1861), 7 Jur. N.S. 325.

[8] *Re Forster*, [1938] 3 All E.R. 767; [1939] Ch. 22.

[9] *Re Mylne*, [1941] 1 All E.R. 405; [1941] Ch. 204.

[10] *Re Royce*, [1940] 2 All E.R. 291; [1940] Ch. 514.   [11] [1906] 2 Ch. 184.

[12] *Per* Kekewich J., at p. 186.

[13] *Re Arber* (1919), *Times*, 13th December.

[14] Cf. *Re Spensley's Will Trusts*, [1954] 1 All E.R. 178; [1954] Ch. 233, C.A.

[15] See (1960), 24 Con. 306 (V. T. H. Delany).

[16] [1907] 1 Ch. 382; [1904–7] All E.R. Rep. 237; *Re Norman*, [1947] 1 All E.R. 400; [1947] Ch. 349.

vicar and churchwardens—to be applied by them in such manner as they shall in their sole discretion think fit", in *Re Flinn*,[17] where residue was given to "His Eminence the Archbishop of Westminster Cathedral London for the time being . . . to be used by him for such purposes as he shall in his absolute discretion think fit", and in *Re Rumball*,[18] where residue was given to "the Bishop for the time being of the Diocese of the Windward Islands to be used by him as he thinks fit in his diocese".

Where, however, the added words set out the purposes for which the gift is to be held, it must be seen whether or not those declared purposes are charitable. Thus in *Dunne* v. *Byrne*,[19] residue was left to "the Roman Catholic Archbishop of Brisbane and his successors to be used and expended wholly or in part as such archbishop may judge most conducive to the good of religion in this diocese". It was held this was not charitable since a thing could be most conducive to the good of religion without being charitable in the legal sense, or even in itself religious. This principle was applied in *Re Stratton*,[20] where there was a gift to the vicar of a parish "to be by him distributed at his absolute discretion among such parochial institutions or for such parochial purposes as he shall select" and in *Farley* v. *Westminster Bank Ltd.*,[1] where the gift was to the vicars and churchwardens of two named churches "for parochial work". A gift for parochial purposes or for parish work means that the gift is not a gift for ecclesiastical or religious purposes in the strict sense, but that it is a gift for the assistance and furtherance of those various activities connected with the parish church which are to be found in every parish but which include many objects which are not charitable in the legal sense of the word. On the other hand, a gift to the vicar of a church "to be used for his work in the parish" has been held to be charitable,[2] for the added words merely had the effect of imposing a limitation on the scope of the trust which would have been created simply by a gift to the vicar. Again gifts to the vicar of St. Alban's Church "for such objects connected with the Church as he shall think fit",[3] and to the vicar and churchwardens of St. George's Church "for any purposes in connection with the said church which they may select"[4] have been held to be charitable. In both cases the objects or purposes were construed as relating to the church—its fabric and services—in contradistinction to the parish. The court in both cases refused to import into the objects or purposes parochial activities, holding that the funds were to be held in each case on the more limited, and, accordingly, charitable trusts.

---

[17] [1948] 1 All E.R. 541; [1948] Ch. 241.
[18] [1955] 3 All E.R. 71; [1956] Ch. 105, C.A.
[19] [1912] A.C. 407; [1911–13] All E.R. Rep. 1105, P.C.
[20] [1931] 1 Ch. 197; [1930] All E.R. Rep. 255, C.A.
[1] [1939] 3 All E.R. 491; [1939] A.C. 430, H.L.
[2] *Re Simson*, [1946] 2 All E.R. 220; [1946] Ch. 299.
[3] *Re Bain*, [1930] 1 Ch. 224; [1929] All E.R. Rep. 387, C.A.
[4] *Re Eastes*, [1948] 1 All E.R. 536; [1948] Ch. 257. The gift continued "it being my wish that they shall especially bear in mind the requirements of the children in the said parish", but it was held that these (and other) superadded directions were not words of trust, but mere precatory words which in no way enlarged the purposes of the gift.

e Trusts for other purposes beneficial to the community

In putting forward the classification[5] of charitable trusts adopted by Lord Macnaghten in *Income Tax Special Purposes Comrs.* v. *Pemsel*[6] Sir Samuel Romilly called this fourth head the most difficult, and it is indeed impossible to devise any satisfactory test to decide whether or not any particular purpose is within it. It is not sufficient under this head that a gift is for the public benefit: it must be beneficial in a way which the law regards as charitable, which brings one back to the question whether the particular purpose is within the spirit and intendment of the Statute of Elizabeth as revealed in the cases. As Lindley L.J. observed in *Re Macduff*,[7] "this court has taken great liberties with charities, but the liberty is always restricted by falling back, or professing to fall back, upon the Statute of Elizabeth". The position was explained by Viscount Cave L.C. in *A.-G.* v. *National Provincial Bank*[8] as follows:

> "Lord Macnaghten[9] did not mean that all trusts for purposes beneficial to the community are charitable, but that there were certain charitable trusts which fell within that category: and accordingly to argue that because a trust is for a purpose beneficial to the community it is therefore a charitable trust is to turn round his sentence and to give it a different meaning. So here it is not enough to say that the trust in question is for public purposes beneficial to the community or for the public welfare; you must also show it to be a charitable trust."

Recently, however, the Court of Appeal has put forward a more pragmatic approach. In *Incorporated Council of Law Reporting for England and Wales* v. *A.-G.*[10] Russell L.J. stated that the courts in substance accept that if a purpose is shown to be beneficial to the community or, as it is sometimes put, of general public utility it is *prima facie* charitable in law, but have left open a line of retreat based on the spirit and intendment of the statute in case they are faced with a purpose (e.g. a political purpose) which could not have been within the contemplation of the statute even if the then legislators had been endowed with the gift of foresight into the circumstances of later centuries. If *prima facie* charitable, the onus seems to be on those who say it is not to show some sufficient reason to support their contention. In another recent case[11] the Privy Council explained the process that a court must follow:

> "It must first consider the trend of those decisions which have established certain objects as charitable under this heading and ask whether, by reasonable extension or analogy, the instant case may be considered to be in line with these. Secondly it must examine certain accepted anomalies to see whether they fairly cover the objects under consideration. Thirdly—and this is really a cross-check upon the others—it must ask whether, consistently with the objects declared, the income and property in question can be applied for purposes clearly falling outside the scope of charity: if so, the argument for charity must fail."

---

[5] In *Morice* v. *Bishop of Durham* (1805), 10 Ves. 522.
[6] [1891] A.C. 531, at p. 583, H.L.
[7] [1896] 2 Ch. 451, at p. 467; [1895–99] All E.R. Rep. 154, at p. 159, C.A.
[8] [1924] A.C. 262, 265, H.L. See also *Williams' Trusts* v. *I.R.Comrs.*, [1947] 1 All E.R. 513; [1947] A.C. 447, H.L.; *Re Strakosch*, [1949] 2 All E.R. 6; [1949] Ch. 529, C.A.; *Scottish Burial Reform and Cremation Society, Ltd.* v. *Glasgow City Corporation*, [1967] 3 All E.R. 215; [1968] A.C. 138, H.L.
[9] In *Pemsel's Case, supra.*
[10] [1971] 3 All E.R. 1029; [1972] Ch. 73, C.A., esp. *per* Russell L.J. at p. 1036; 88.
[11] *D'Aguiar* v. *I.R.Comrs.* (1970), 15 W.I.R. 198, P.C.

In the light of the above principles, let us now look at some of the most important kinds of purposes that have commonly come before the courts.

As might be expected in English courts, gifts in favour of animals generally, or a class of animals, as opposed to gifts for specific animals[12], may be charitable; not, however, on the ground that they benefit the animals, but on the ground that they produce a benefit to mankind. Thus in *Re Wedgwood*[13] a trust for the protection and benefit of animals was held to be charitable on the ground, according to Cozens-Hardy M.R.,[14] that "it tends to promote public morality by checking the innate tendency to cruelty", and in the same case Swinfen Eady L.J. observed,[15] "a gift for the benefit and protection of animals tends to promote and encourage kindness towards them, to discourage cruelty, and to ameliorate the condition of the brute creation, and thus to stimulate humane and generous sentiments in man towards the lower animals; and by these means promote feelings of humanity and morality generally, repress brutality, and thus elevate the human race". Accordingly a bequest "for the establishment of a hospital in which animals, which are useful to mankind, should be properly treated and cured and the nature of their diseases investigated, with a view to public advantage" was held to be charitable in *University of London* v. *Yarrow*[16] and in *Re Douglas*[17] the Home for Lost Dogs was said to be a charitable institution. Again in *Re Moss*[18] a gift to a lady "for her to use at her discretion for her work for the welfare of cats and kittens needing care and protection" was held to be charitable on evidence that for many years she had carried on the work of receiving, sheltering and caring for unwanted or stray cats, the judge observing[19] that "the care of and consideration for animals which through old age or sickness or otherwise are unable to care for themselves are manifestations of the finer side of human nature, and gifts in furtherance of these objects are calculated to develop that side and are, therefore, calculated to benefit mankind".

Russell L.J., however, has said,[20] "the authorities have, in my opinion, reached the furthest admissible point of benevolence in construing, as charitable, gifts in favour of animals, and, for myself, I am not prepared to go any further". This probably represents the weight of judicial opinion, and Lord Sterndale pin-pointed an anomaly when he said,[1] "I confess I find considerable difficulty in understanding the exact reason why a gift for the benefit of animals, and for the prevention of cruelty to animals generally, should be a good charitable gift, while a gift for philanthropic purposes which, I take it, is for the benefit

---

[12] *Re Dean* (1889), 41 Ch.D. 552.
[13] [1915] 1 Ch. 113; [1914–15] All E.R. Rep. 322, C.A.; *Re Grove-Grady*, [1929] 1 Ch. 557; [1929] All E.R. Rep. 158, C.A., compromised on appeal *sub nom. A.-G.* v. *Plowden*, [1931] W.N. 89, H.L.; *National Anti-Vivisection Society* v. *I.R.Comrs.*, [1947] 2 All E.R. 217; [1948] A.C. 31, H.L.
[14] At pp. 117; 324.
[15] At pp. 122; 327.
[16] (1857), 1 De G. & J. 72, at p. 79.
[17] (1887), 35 Ch.D. 472, C.A. Also the R.S.P.C.A.—see *Re Wedgwood, supra.*
[18] [1949] 1 All E.R. 495.
[19] At pp. 497, 498.
[20] In *Re Grove-Grady*, [1929] 1 Ch. 557, at p. 588; [1929] All E.R. Rep. 158, at p. 171, C.A.
[1] In *Re Tetley*, [1923] 1 Ch. 258, at p. 266, C.A., affirmed *sub nom. A.-G.* v. *National Provincial Bank*, [1924] A.C. 262, H.L.

of mankind generally, should be bad as a charitable gift." Though it is hard to believe that in any 'true sense gifts in favour of animals come within the spirit and intendment of the Statute of Elizabeth, their charitable character is, within limits, firmly settled. To be charitable, however, the gift must be regarded as producing a benefit to mankind, and in this sense be for the public benefit. The limits were passed, and the gift accordingly held not to be charitable, in Re Grove-Grady,[2] where the purpose was to provide "a refuge or refuges for the preservation of all animals, birds or other creatures not human . . . so that [they] shall there be safe from molestation or destruction by man". The purpose was held not to afford any advantage to animals that are useful to mankind in particular, or any protection from cruelty to animals generally, and not to denote any elevating lesson to mankind. And one ground on which the National Anti-Vivisection Society was held by the House of Lords not to be a charitable institution was that it lacked the element of public benefit.[3] It may be added that the validity of cases[4] which decided that vegetarian societies whose object was to stop the killing of animals for food were charitable, seems very doubtful in the light of the National Anti-Vivisection Society's Case,[5] though Lord Simonds expressly refused[6] to express an opinion as to whether they were rightly decided.

The alternative ground upon which the National Anti-Vivisection Society's Case[7] was decided was that a, if not the, main object of the society was to obtain an alteration of the law, that this was a political object, and that, in the words of Lord Parker,[8] "equity has always refused to recognise such objects as charitable". The law, it is said,[9] cannot stultify itself by holding that it is for the public benefit that the law itself should be changed; the court must decide on the principle that the law is right as it stands. This rather narrow legalistic view undoubtedly represents the law, though it is, perhaps, a little surprising, as elsewhere in their speeches both Lord Wright and Lord Simonds frankly recognised that in changing conditions the same purpose may at one time be beneficial, and at another injurious, to the public.[10] As is commonly the case in charity matters, the cases run to fine distinctions; thus a gift to a temperance society whose object was the promotion of temperance mainly by political means was held not to be charitable,[11] while in a subsequent case the Court of Appeal held that a gift for the promotion of temperance generally was.[12]

---

[2] Supra.

[3] National Anti-Vivisection Society v. I.R.Comrs., [1947] 2 All E.R. 217; [1948] A.C. 31, H.L.

[4] Re Cranston, [1898] 1 I.R. 431, C.A.; Re Slatter (1905), 21 T.L.R. 295.

[5] Supra.

[6] National Anti-Vivisection Society v. I.R.Comrs., [1947] 2 All E.R. 217, at p. 238; [1948] A.C. 31, at p. 73, H.L.

[7] [1947] 2 All E.R. 217; [1948] A.C. 31, H.L.

[8] In Bowman v. Secular Society Ltd., [1917] A.C. 406, at p. 442; [1916–17] All E.R. Rep. 1, at p. 18, H.L.

[9] See National Anti-Vivisection Society v. I.R.Comrs., supra, especially per Lord Wright at pp. 224–225; 50, and per Lord Simonds at pp. 232; 62, approving the statement in Tyssen on Charitable Bequests. Lord Parker, dissenting, thought that political objects here should be restricted to those whose only means of attainment is a change of law.

[10] See the discussion at p. 192, post.

[11] I.R.Comrs. v. Temperance Council of Christian Churches of England and Wales (1926), 136 L.T. 27.   [12] Re Hood, [1931] 1 Ch. 240, C.A.

The Charity Commissioners have recently[13] pointed out the dangers to charities arising from the increasing desire of voluntary organisations for "involvement" in the causes with which their work is connected. After referring to the "well-established principle of charity law that a trust for the attainment of a political object is not a valid charitable trust and that any purpose with the object of influencing the legislature is a political purpose" the Commissioners observed, it is submitted correctly, that "it is very unlikely that it will lie within any charity's purposes and powers to sponsor action groups or bring pressure to bear on the government to adopt or alter a particular line of action". Nor, as we have seen,[14] can activities primarily of a propagandist nature be regarded as charitable by being represented as educational.

A gift for the relief of the sick is charitable, falling by close analogy within the phrase "the relief of the impotent" in the Statute of Elizabeth, and it has always been assumed that gifts for the ordinary hospitals which, before the National Health Service Act 1946, were supported by voluntary contributions and were generally referred to as voluntary hospitals, were charitable, as opposed to private nursing homes run for profit. Thus in one case[15] a gift in a will to hospitals was held to be charitable for as a matter of construction it was held that the term referred only to voluntary hospitals which were charitable institutions. There have also been held charitable gifts to a hospital to provide accommodation for the use of relatives of patients who were critically ill,[16] to provide a home of rest for nurses, for this would be calculated to increase the efficiency of the hospital by providing the means of restoring the efficiency of the nurses,[17] and a gift to trustees "in their absolute discretion to apply the same to the medical profession for the furtherance of psychological healing in accordance with the teaching of Jesus Christ", for this was a gift to further the art of healing.[18] The hospital cases have been extended so as to render charitable Homes of Rest, as they were called, for lady teachers,[19] for the sisters of a charitable community and such persons as the Mother Superior should appoint,[20] and generally so as to "afford the means of physical and/or mental recuperation to persons in need of rest by reason of the stress and strain caused or partly caused by the conditions in which they ordinarily live and/or work".[21] It should be observed that where a gift for the purposes of a hospital is *prima facie* charitable, it does not lose this character merely because charges are made to patients and the courts will be very slow to hold that in such case it has ceased to be charitable on the ground that the charges are so high that the poor are excluded from benefit.[22] The test is essentially one of public benefit, and indirect as well as direct benefit enters into the account.

---

[13] Report for 1969 paras. 7–16.
[14] See p. 173, *supra*.
[15] *Re Smith's Will Trusts*, [1962] 2 All E.R. 563, C.A.
[16] *Re Dean's Will Trusts*, [1950] 1 All E.R. 882.
[17] *Re White's Will Trusts*, [1951] 1 All E.R. 528.
[18] *Re Osmund*, [1944] 1 All E.R. 262; [1944] Ch. 206, C.A.
[19] *Re Estlin* (1903), 72 L.J.Ch. 687.
[20] *Re James*, [1932] 2 Ch. 25.
[21] *Re Chaplin*, [1933] Ch. 115; *Re Banfield*, [1968] 2 All E.R. 276.
[22] *Re Macduff*, [1896] 2 Ch. 451, C.A.; *Le Cras v. Perpetual Trustee Co., Ltd.*, [1967] 3 All E.R. 915; *sub. nom. Re Resch's Will Trusts*, [1969] A.C. 514, P.C., and see p. 170, *supra*.

To increase the efficiency of the armed forces or the police forces is a charitable purpose and gifts calculated to have this effect are accordingly charitable, for instance, gifts for the benefit of a volunteer corps,[1] for teaching shooting,[2] and to promote the defence of the United Kingdom from the attack of hostile aircraft.[3] This principle was said to be unassailable in *I.R.Comrs.* v. *City of Glasgow Police Athletic Association*,[4] but doubt was cast on whether it had been correctly applied in earlier cases where there had been held charitable gifts to maintain a library and purchase plate for an officers' mess,[5] and for the promotion of sport in a regiment as calculated to improve the physical efficiency of the army.[6] By way of contrast a gift for the welfare benefit or assistance of members of the Royal Navy whether past, present, or future, has been held not to be charitable as it could be used purely for the benefit of ex-members of the navy not being necessarily poor or aged or in any other way objects of charity.[7]

The relief of distress is clearly within the spirit and intendment of the Statute of Elizabeth, and there have accordingly been held charitable the Royal National Life-boat Institution,[8] a trust for the provision of a fire brigade,[9] and, in the case of the disastrous floods in the Lyn Valley, a trust to relieve hardship and suffering by the local people and others who were in the area at the time of the disaster and suffered by it.[10] There has also been held charitable a trust for the founding of a children's home,[11] but the Court of Appeal has decided by a majority that a gift for the general benefit and general welfare of the children for the time being in a home provided and maintained by a local authority was not charitable as it might be possible to use the fund for non-charitable purposes, such as, it was suggested, the provision of television sets for juvenile delinquents and refractory children, or even the inmates of a Borstal institution.[12]

The National Trust is a charitable body,[13] and likewise a trust to preserve two ancient cottages,[14] and, it seems, a trust to enclose land as a breathing space and air zone for a town, though in the last case the trust was vitiated by a provision for the establishment of a hotel on the land for the use of distinguished visitors.[15] Of a very different character were the purposes of the appellant company in

---

[1] *Re Lord Stratheden and Campbell*, [1894] 3 Ch. 265.
[2] *Re Stephens*, [1892] 8 T.L.R. 792.
[3] *Re Driffill*, [1949] 2 All E.R. 933; [1950] Ch. 92. See also *Re Corbyn*, [1941] 2 All E.R. 160; [1941] Ch. 400.
[4] [1953] 1 All E.R. 747; [1953] A.C. 380, H.L.
[5] *Re Good*, [1905] 2 Ch. 60.
[6] *Re Gray*, [1925] Ch. 362. There would seem to be less doubt about this case than about *Re Good*, *supra*.
[7] *Re Meyers*, [1951] 1 All E.R. 538; [1951] Ch. 534. Nor a gift of a house for the use of ex-officers at a small rent during their lives—*Re Good*, *supra*.
[8] *Thomas* v. *Howell* (1874), L.R. 18 Eq. 198.
[9] *Re Wokingham Fire Brigade Trusts*, [1951] 1 All E.R. 454; [1951] Ch. 373.
[10] *Re North Devon & West Somerset Relief Fund Trusts*, [1953] 2 All E.R. 1032.
[11] *Re Sahal's Will Trusts*, [1958] 3 All E.R. 428.
[12] *Re Cole*, [1958] 3 All E.R. 102; [1958] Ch. 877, C.A. There seems much to be said for the dissenting judgment of Lord Evershed M.R.
[13] *Re Verrall*, [1916] 1 Ch. 100.
[14] *Re Cranstoun*, [1932] 1 Ch. 537.
[15] *Re Corelli*, [1943] 2 All E.R. 519; [1943] Ch. 332 (Stratford-upon-Avon).

Scottish Burial Reform and Cremation Society, Ltd. v. *Glasgow City Corporation*,[16] namely, primarily, to promote and afford facilities for cremation. These were held to be charitable under the fourth head, through an extension of the burial ground cases which, though apparently at first held charitable as being for the advancement of religion, are probably best regarded as falling on the border-line between that head and the fourth head of trusts otherwise beneficial to the community.[17] Different again, and also charitable, are the purposes of the Incorporated Council of Law Reporting for England and Wales, which publishes law reports, not for profit, in order to further the sound development and administration of the law in this country.[18]

Trusts which have been held not to be charitable include a trust to provide knickers for boys living in a certain area,[19] a trust to encourage emigration,[20] a trust to strengthen the bonds between South Africa and the United Kingdom,[21] and the trust under George Bernard Shaw's will to provide for research into and propaganda on the advantages of a reform of the alphabet.[22] The Charity Commissioners have taken the view that the provision of a service for charities is not necessarily a charitable purpose of itself, and accordingly refused to register as a charity a company formed to provide catering staff at cost exclusively for charities such as voluntary hospitals and old people's homes.[23] Again it has been held that it is not open to one charity to subscribe to the funds of another charity unless the recipient charity is expressly or by implication a purpose or object of the donor charity.[1] Further the National House-Builders Registration Council was held not to be charitable on the ground that on balance it conferred more benefit on those engaged in the industry than it did on the public, and could not therefore be regarded as an altruistic organisation.[2]

In *Re Smith*[3] a gift of residue "unto my country England to and for ... own use and benefit absolutely" was held to be charitable, and this may be justified on the ground that, where no purpose is defined, a charitable purpose may be implicit in the context.[4] There is considerable difficulty as regards gifts limited to a particular locality. One line of cases[5] establishes the principle that if the purposes are not charitable *per se*, the localisation of them will not make them charitable. The diffi-

---

[16] [1967] 3 All E.R. 215; [1968] A.C. 138, H.L.
[17] See the cases cited *supra*, p. 176 in nn. 1 and 2.
[18] *Incorporated Council of Law Reporting for England and Wales* v. *A.-G.*, [1971] 3 All E.R. 1029; [1972] Ch. 73, C.A. (Also for the advancement of education—see p. 172, *supra*.)
[19] *Re Gwyon*, [1930] 1 Ch. 255 (not for the relief of poverty and not saved by restriction to a particular area).
[20] *Re Sidney*, [1908] 1 Ch. 488, C.A. Contrast *Re Tree*, [1945] Ch. 325 (a trust to help poor emigrants, charitable as being for the relief of poverty).
[21] *Re Strakosch*, [1949] 2 All E.R. 6; [1949] Ch. 529, C.A.
[22] *Re Shaw*, [1957] 1 All E.R. 745, compromised on appeal, [1958] 1 All E.R. 245, C.A.
[23] Report of the Charity Commissioners for 1969, para. 20.
[1] *Baldry* v. *Feintuck*, [1972] 2 All E.R. 81.
[2] Report of the Charity Commissioners for 1969, para. 22.
[3] [1932] 1 Ch. 153, C.A. See (1940), 56 L.Q.R. 49 (M. Albery).
[4] *Williams' Trusts* v. *I.R.Comrs.*, [1947] 1 All E.R. 513, 521; [1947] A.C. 447, 459, H.L.; *Re Strakosch*, [1949] 2 All E.R. 6; [1949] Ch. 529, C.A.
[5] *Houston* v. *Burns*, [1918] A.C. 337; [1918–19] All E.R. Rep. 817, H.L.; *Re Gwyon*, [1930] 1 Ch. 255; *Williams' Trusts* v. *I.R.Comrs.*, *supra*; *Re Sanders' Will Trusts*, [1954] 1 All E.R. 667; [1954] Ch. 265.

culty is really caused by *Goodman* v. *Saltash Corporation*,[6] unfortunately a decision of the House of Lords. Always cited in this context are the words of Lord Selbourne L.C.[7] " A gift subject to a condition or trust for the benefit of the inhabitants of a parish or town or of any particular class of such inhabitants is (as I understand the law) a charitable trust." Accordingly it would seem that under such a charitable trust the trust funds may properly be used for public or benevolent purposes in a parish, though a gift for public or benevolent purposes in a parish would not be charitable. This anomalous[8] situation will not be extended. Being a House of Lords decision, it must be followed by lower courts in an appropriate case, as was done in *Re Norton's Will Trusts*,[9] where the gift was "for the benefit of the church and parish", but the Court of Appeal felt able to distinguish it in *Re Endacott*,[10] where the testator gave his residuary estate "to North Tawton Devon Parish Council for the purpose of providing some useful memorial to myself ", and Jenkins L.J. has even observed[11] that the line of cases based on *Goodman* v. *Saltash Corporation*[12] "should not now be regarded as authoritative save in so far as they can be explained on the ground that the particular purpose was regarded as falling within the spirit and intendment of the preamble to the Statute of Elizabeth I".

f Recreational charities

On general principles, a purely recreational trust will not be charitable because it is not within the spirit and intendment of the preamble to the Statute of Elizabeth, and accordingly it has never been doubted since *Re Nottage*[13] that a gift to promote mere sport, whether a particular sport or sport in general,[14] is not charitable: the fact that it is beneficial to the public is not enough. Despite this, however, it seems that the provision of land for use as a recreation ground by the community at large or by the inhabitants of a particular area is charitable.[15] The Court of Appeal in Northern Ireland had to consider, in *Valuation Comr. for Northern Ireland* v. *Lurgan Borough Council*,[16] whether the recreation ground cases would cover an indoor swimming pool. In holding that they would not

---

[6] (1882), 7 App. Cas. 633, H.L.

[7] At p. 642.

[8] See the discussion by Lord Simonds in *Williams' Trusts* v. *I.R.Comrs.*, *supra*, at pp. 521; 459; *I.R.Comrs.* v. *Baddeley*, [1955] 1 All E.R. 525; [1955] A.C. 572, H.L.

[9] [1948] 2 All E.R. 842. Cf. *Verge* v. *Somerville*, [1924] A.C. 496; [1924] All E.R. Rep. 121, P.C.

[10] [1959] 3 All E.R. 562; [1960] Ch. 232, C.A.

[11] In the Court of Appeal in *Baddeley* v. *I.R.Comrs.*, [1953] 2 All E.R. 233, at p. 246; [1953] Ch. 504, at p. 527.

[12] (1882), 7 App. Cas. 633, H.L.

[13] [1895] 2 Ch. 649; [1895–99] All E.R. Rep. 1203, C.A. (annual cup in perpetuity for the most successful yacht of the season). As to sport in a school, see *Re Mariette*, referred to at p. 174, *ante*, and, as to sport in the army, *Re Gray*, at p. 183, *ante*.

[14] *I.R.Comrs.* v. *City of Glasgow Police Athletic Association*, [1953] 1 All E.R. 747; [1953] A.C. 380, H.L.

[15] *Re Hadden*, [1931] All E.R. Rep. 539; [1932] 1 Ch. 133; *I.R.Comrs.* v. *Baddeley*, [1955] 1 All E.R. 525; [1955] A.C. 572, H.L.; *Re Morgan*, [1955] 2 All E.R. 632.

[16] [1968] N.I. 104, C.A. The provision and maintenance of the swimming pool was, however, held to constitute a recreational charity within the meaning of the Recreational Charities Act (Northern Ireland), 1958. This Act is in similar terms to the English Act discussed in the following paragraphs.

Lord MacDermott L.C.J. took the view that the law does not regard the mere provision of recreational facilities charitable unless they are provided in the open air on land dedicated to the use and enjoyment of the public. This, he admitted, was an arbitrary as well as a fine distinction, but the line had to be drawn somewhere. The decision of the House of Lords in *I.R.Comrs.* v. *Baddeley*[17] that a trust "for the promotion of the moral social and physical well-being of persons resident [in a certain area] by the provision of facilities for moral social and physical training and recreation and by promoting and encouraging all forms of such activities as are calculated to contribute to the health and well-being of such persons" was not charitable raised doubts as to the charitable status of many institutions, and in particular many village halls, and for the removal of these doubts there was passed the Recreational Charities Act 1958.[18] It has been pointed out[19] that the Act itself is by no means free from difficulties of interpretation, and it is doubtful whether *I.R.Comrs.* v. *Baddeley*[20] would be decided differently today by reason of its provisions.

The main provisions are contained in s. 1 (1) of the Act, which provides that:

> ". . . it shall be and be deemed always to have been charitable to provide, or assist in the provision of, facilities for recreation or other leisure-time occupation, if the facilities are provided in the interests of social welfare."

The meaning of the requirement of social welfare[21] is to some extent explained in sub-s. (2), which provides that the requirements shall not be treated as satisfied unless:

> "(a) the facilities are provided with the object of improving the conditions of life for the persons for whom the facilities are primarily intended; and
> (b) either—
> (i) those persons have need of such facilities as aforesaid by reason of their youth, age, infirmity or disablement, poverty or social and economic circumstances;
> or—
> (ii) the facilities are to be available to the members or female members of the public at large."

Subject to the requirement of social welfare, sub-s. (3) provides that the Act

> ". . . . applies in particular to the provision of facilities at village halls, community centres and women's institutes, and to the provision and maintenance of grounds and buildings to be used for purposes of recreation or leisure-time occupation, and extends to the provision of facilities for those purposes by the organising of any activity."

---

[17] *Supra.*
[18] See, generally (1959), 23 Con. 15 (Spencer G. Maurice).
[19] E.g. Nathan and Marshall, *A Casebook on Trusts*, 5th Ed., p. 200.
[20] *Supra.*
[21] See, generally (1959), 23 Con. 365 (D. W. M. Waters); *Valuation Comr. for Northern Ireland* v. *Lurgan Borough Council*, [1968] N.I. 104, C.A.

It is specifically provided that nothing in s. 1 is to derogate from the principle that a trust or institution to be charitable must be for the public benefit.[1]

The meaning of the word "need" in s. 1 (2) (b) (i) is not altogether clear. It has been contended[2] that the Act accepts as a fact that suitable recreation or other leisure-time occupation improves the conditions of life and in that sense everyone has "need" of facilities for it. On this view "need" in s. 1 (2) (b) (i) must be used in some other sense. Another point is that it seems that, under s. 1 (2) (b) (ii), a trust cannot be charitable by virtue of the Act if it is available only to male members of the public at large, or, apparently, if it is available only to members or female members of the public in a particular geographical area. It has, however, been held that s. 1 (2) (b) (ii) does not require that the facilities should be available to members of the public at large primarily or without being subject to the primary intention of benefit to others.[3]

The provisions of the 1958 Act do not appear directly to affect the principle that a gift for mere sport is not charitable, though in practice the result would now seem to be otherwise where sporting facilities are provided in the interests of social welfare, for instance, organised games in a youth club. However it is by no means clear that the Act would affect a case such as *I.R.Comrs.* v. *Glasgow City Police Athletic Association*,[4] where it was held that although the association had official importance and a public aspect, its provision of recreation for members was an essential non-charitable purpose which was not subsidiary or incidental to the furtherance of a public purpose, and, therefore, the association was not a body established for charitable purposes only. Members of the police would hardly seem to fall within s. 1 (2) (b) (i).

g   The requirement of public benefit[5]

Even if it has been established that the purposes of a trust fall within one of the four heads of charity under Lord Macnaghten's classification, the trust will still not be legally charitable unless it can also be shown that it is for the benefit of the community (or public) or an appreciably important section of the community (or public). As will be seen trusts for the relief of poverty constitute an exception to the general rule, but in relation to the other heads of charity the requirement of public benefit has frequently proved a trap for the unwary. Thus in *Gilmour* v. *Coats*[6] a trust for an association of strictly cloistered and purely contemplative nuns, though undoubtedly for the advancement of religion, was held not to be charitable as lacking the element of public benefit. So far as the intercessory prayers of the nuns were alleged to be productive of public benefit, the court could not consider it; the court could only act on

---

[1] See *Wynn* v. *Skegness Urban District Council*, [1966] 3 All E.R. 336.
[2] See *Trustees of the City of Belfast Y.M.C.A.* v. *Valuation Comr. for Northern Ireland*, [1969] N.I. 3, C.A., esp. *per* Curran L.J. at p. 23.
[3] *Wynn* v. *Skegness Urban District Council*, *supra*.
[4] [1953] 1 All E.R. 747; [1953] A.C. 380, H.L.
[5] See, generally (1956), 72 L.Q.R. 187 (G. Cross); (1958), 21 M.L.R. 138 (P. S. Ariyah).
[6] [1949] 1 All E.R. 848; [1949] A.C. 426, H.L.; *Cocks* v. *Manners* (1871), L.R. 12 Eq. 574. (*Per* Wickens V.C. at 585, "A voluntary association of women for the purpose of working out their own salvation by religious exercises and self-denial seems to me to have none of the requisites of a charitable institution.") These cases were rightly distinguished in *Re Banfield*, [1968] 2 All E.R. 276.

evidence before it and no temporal court could determine the truth of any religious belief. And the benefit alleged to be derived by others from the example of pious lives was held to be too vague and intangible to satisfy the test of public benefit.[7] Elsewhere Farwell J. has observed[8] that "there is, in truth, no charity in attempting to improve one's own mind or save one's own soul. Charity is necessarily altruistic and involves the idea of aid or benefit to others."

Whether or not the required element of public benefit is present is a question of law for the judge to decide on the evidence before him. However, as Lord Simonds has pointed out[9] "when a purpose appears broadly to fall within one of the familiar categories of charity, the court will assume it to be for the benefit of the community, and, therefore, charitable unless the contrary is shown, and further the court will not be astute in such a case to defeat upon doubtful evidence the avowed benevolent intention of a donor".

The most baffling problem[10] in this context is to determine whether or not the common characteristic which is shared by a number of persons is or is not such as to make them a section of the public. The test which has been most consistently applied during the last thirty or so years, often referred to as the "Compton test",[11] was approved by the majority of the House of Lords in Oppenheim v. Tobacco Securities Trust Co., Ltd.[12] According to this test in order to constitute a section of the public the possible beneficiaries must not be numerically negligible, and the quality which distinguishes them from other members of the public, so that they form by themselves a section of it, must be a quality which does not depend on their relationship to a particular individual. It must be essentially impersonal and not personal. A section of the public in this sense has been contrasted with a fluctuating body of private individuals. Applying this test the inhabitants of a named place normally constitute a section of the public. On the other hand in Re Compton[13] itself a trust for the education of the lawful descendants of three named persons was held not to be for a section of the public and thus not charitable, and the same result was reached in the Oppenheim[14] case, where the trust was again for the advancement of education and the potential beneficiaries were the children of employees and former employees of one or other of a group of companies. They were held not to constitute a section of the public, notwithstanding that the number of employees was over 110,000. In the Oppenheim[15] case, counsel had pointed out some of the

---

[7] As Greene M.R. said in the Court of Appeal, sub nom. Re Coats' Trusts, [1948] 1 All E.R. 521, at p. 528; [1948] Ch. 340, at p. 353, "they are to be paid, not to do good, but to be good".

[8] In Re Delany, [1902] 2 Ch. 642, at pp. 648, 649.

[9] In National Anti-Vivisection Society v. I.R.Comrs., [1947] 2 All E.R. 217; [1948] A.C. 31, H.L., at p. 233; 65; Re Watson, [1973] 3 All E.R. 678.

[10] See e.g. Re Mead's Will Trust Deed, [1961] 2 All E.R. 836, at p. 840 (members of a trade union not a section of the public for a trust under Lord Macnaghten's fourth head) where Cross J., as he then was, said despairingly not only that this is a very difficult question, but that "there appears to be no principle by reference to which it can be answered".

[11] Re Compton, [1945] 1 All E.R. 198; [1945] Ch. 123, C.A.; Re Hobourn Aero Components Ltd.'s Air Raid Disaster Fund, [1946] 1 All E.R. 501; [1946] Ch. 194, C.A.

[12] [1951] 1 All E.R. 31; [1951] A.C. 297, H.L.

[13] Supra, C.A.

[14] Supra, H.L.

[15] Supra, H.L.

anomalies that may flow from an application of the *Compton* test. In his speech in the House of Lords, Lord Simonds first set out counsel's argument: "Admittedly, those who follow a profession or calling—clergymen, lawyers, colliers, tobacco-workers and so on—are a section of the public, and how strange then it would be if, as in the case of railwaymen, those who follow a particular calling are all employed by one employer. Would a trust for the education of men employed on the railways by the Transport Board not be charitable? And what of service of the Crown, whether in the civil service or the armed forces? Is there a difference between soldiers and soldiers of the King?" His comment was short but clear: "My Lords, I am not impressed by this sort of argument . . ."[16] This, indeed, represented the view of the majority of the Law Lords, though it was not necessary for a definitive ruling to be given on this point.

The *Compton* test was, however, regarded as inadequate by Lord MacDermott, giving the only dissenting speech in the *Oppenheim*[17] case, and his views have since received strong support from *obiter dicta* of Lord Cross in *Dingle* v. *Turner*,[18] dicta in which all the other Law Lords concurred. In the opinion of Lord Cross the distinction between personal and impersonal relationships is unsatisfactory—as Lord MacDermott had pointed out in the *Oppenheim*[19] case it is accepted that the poor and the blind are sections of the public, but what is more personal than poverty or blindness? Further the attempt to elucidate the phrase "a section of the public" by contrasting it with "a fluctuating body of private individuals" is unhelpful, since a particular group of persons might equally well answer both descriptions. At the end of the day, Lord Cross said, one is left where one started with the bare contrast between "public" and "private" and in his view the question whether or not the potential beneficiaries of a trust can fairly be said to constitute a section of the public is (as it was generally thought to be before *Re Compton*[20]) a question of degree. In the light of these dicta the precise standing of the *Compton* test is uncertain. It may still be considered binding at first instance, but the House of Lords might well take a different view, particularly if the trust in question should be other than for the advancement of education.

In *Dingle* v. *Turner*[1] Lord Cross went on to say that in his view much must depend on the purpose of the trust. "It may well be," he said, "that, on the one hand, a trust to promote some purpose, *prima facie* charitable, will constitute a charity even though the class of potential beneficiaries might fairly be called a private class and that, on the other hand, a trust to promote another purpose, also *prima facie* charitable, will not constitute a charity even though the class of potential beneficiaries might seem to some people fairly describable as a section of the public." This, it is submitted, is eminently reasonable and entirely consistent with the view that whether or not a class constitutes a section of the

---

[16] *Per* Lord Simonds in *Oppenheim* v. *Tobacco Securities Trust Co. Ltd., supra*, at pp. 34, 35; 307.
[17] *Supra*, H.L. Contrast *I.R.Comrs.* v. *Baddeley*, [1955] 1 All E.R. 525; [1955] A.C. 572, H.L. *per* Lord Reid at p. 543; 606.
[18] [1972] 1 All E.R. 878; [1972] A.C. 601; H.L. noted (1972), 36 Con. 210.
[19] [1951] 1 All E.R. 31; [1951] A.C. 297, H.L.
[20] *Supra*, C.A.
[1] *Supra*, H.L. at pp. 889; 624.

public is a question of degree, taking into account all the facts of the case. It is difficult however to see that an application of the *Compton* test can permit any variation in the meaning of the phrase "a section of the public" according to the kind of charitable purpose involved. Yet there are clear statements and decisions recognising that such variation exists, though unfortunately they do not advert to the difficulties of reconciling this with the *Compton* test. For instance, Lord Somerwell, in *I.R.Comrs.* v. *Baddeley*[2] declared himself unable to accept the principle "that a section of the public sufficient to support a valid trust in one category must, as a matter of law, be sufficient to support a trust in any other category . . . There might well be a valid trust for the promotion of religion benefiting a very small class. It would not follow at all that a recreation ground for the exclusive use of the same class would be a valid charity, though it is clear . . . that a recreation ground for the public is a charitable purpose." In that case the majority of the Law Lords took the view that the social purposes were too wide to fall within Lord Macnaghten's fourth class and the trusts were for that reason not charitable. Lord Simonds[3] however went on to express the view that had the purpose fallen within the fourth head, the trusts would still not have been charitable as the prospective beneficiaries—members and potential members of the Methodist church in West Ham and Leyton—were "a class within a class" and did not constitute a section of the public.[4] By contrast in the case of religious trusts a similar group has been held to constitute a section of the public, as in *Neville Estates, Ltd.* v. *Madden*[5] where the group—members for the time being of the Catford Synagogue—was even narrower than persons of the Jewish faith living in Catford. In this case the judge accepted that the members of the Catford Synagogue were no more a section of the public than the members of the Carmelite priory in *Gilmour* v. *Coats*,[6] and justified the contrasting result on the ground that the nuns of the priory lived secluded from the world, while the members of the synagogue spent their lives in the world. The court, he said,[7] is "entitled to assume that some benefit accrues to the public from the attendance at places of worship of persons who live in this world and mix with their fellow citizens".

Several further separate points should be noted. First, the validity of a trust

---

[2] [1955] 1 All E.R. 525, at p. 549; [1955] A.C. 572, at p. 615, H.L. See also *per* Lord Simonds in *National Anti-Vivisection Society* v. *I.R.Comrs.*, [1947] 2 All E.R. 217, at p. 233; [1948] A.C. 31, at p. 65. H.L. where he said that it would not be "surprising to find that, while in every category of legal charity some element of public benefit must be present, the court had not adopted the same measure in regard to different categories, but had accepted one standard in regard to those gifts which are alleged to be for the advancement of education, and another for those which are alleged to be for the advancement of religion, and it may be yet another in regard to the relief of poverty". This case was not concerned however with the meaning of "a section of the public".

[3] Lord Reid took a contrary view and Lords Porter and Tucker expressly refused to express an opinion on the point.

[4] See also *Williams' Trusts* v. *I.R.Comrs.*, [1947] 1 All E.R. 513; [1947] A.C. 447, H.L. *per* Lord Simonds at p. 520, 457 who, in relation to similar trusts, expressed the opinion that Welsh people, defined as persons of Welsh nationality by birth or descent or born or educated or at any time domiciled in the Principality of Wales or the county of Monmouth, did not constitute a section of the community for this purpose.

[5] [1961] 3 All E.R. 769; [1962] Ch. 832.

[6] [1949] 1 All E.R. 848; [1949] A.C. 426, H.L. See p. 187, *supra.*

[7] *Neville Estates, Ltd.* v. *Madden, supra,* at p. 751; 853.

is not affected by the fact that, by its very nature, only a limited number of persons are likely to avail themselves or are, perhaps, even capable of availing themselves, of its benefits. It is otherwise if a form of relief is offered to a selected few out of a larger number equally willing and able to take advantage of it. Thus trusts for the maintenance of sea-walls[8] generally, or along a particular stretch of coast, or for some form of child welfare, or for repatriated New South Wales soldiers,[9] may all be charitable. "A bridge which is available for all the public may undoubtedly be a charity, and it is indifferent how many people use it. But confine its use to a selected number of persons, however numerous and important, it is then clearly not a charity. It is not of general public utility, for it does not serve the public purpose which its nature qualifies it to serve".[10]

Secondly, anything in the nature of a mutual benefit society[11] does not have the necessary quality of public benefit, as in *Re Hobourn Aero Components, Ltd.'s Air Raid Distress Fund*,[12] where voluntary collections from employees of the munition factories belonging to a certain company were to be used to relieve, without a means test, the distress suffered by the employees from air raids. This was held not to be charitable, Greene M.R. observing,[13] "the point, to my mind, which really puts this case beyond reasonable doubt is the fact that a number of employees of this company, actuated by motives of self-help, agreed to a deduction from their wages to constitute a fund to be applied for their own benefit without any question of poverty coming into it. Such an arrangement seems to me to stamp the whole transaction as one having a personal character, money put up by a number of people, not for the general benefit, but for their own individual benefit." This principle does not, however, apply with full force in the case of trusts for religious purposes, which may be valid even though in favour of the members of a religious organisation.[14]

Thirdly, in deciding the question of law whether or not an element of public benefit is present, it is unsettled whether regard should be had to the fiscal privileges accorded to charities. In *Dingle* v. *Turner*[15] Lord Cross, with whose speech Lord Simon concurred, thought that it should, but the other three Law Lords expressed their doubts, and there is no case in which fiscal privileges have been expressly taken into account. Lord Cross however said that in his opinion the *Compton*[16] and *Oppenheim*[17] cases had been influenced by fiscal considerations—a trust for the education of the children of employees of a company represents a fringe benefit for the employees and does not deserve fiscal privileges. There is not the same risk of abuse in the case of trusts for the relief of poverty, whose privileged position Lord Cross thought might be thus justified

---

[8] See 43 Eliz. I, c. 4, p. 167, *ante*.
[9] *Verge* v. *Somerville*, [1924] A.C. 496, P.C.
[10] *Per* Lord Simonds in *I.R.Comrs.* v. *Baddeley*, [1955] 1 All E.R. 525, at p. 533; [1955] A.C. 572, at p. 592, H.L.
[11] Unless it comes within the "poverty" exception discussed in the following subsection by reason of a means test for benefits.
[12] [1946] 1 All E.R. 501; [1946] Ch. 194, C.A.; *I.R.Comrs.* v. *City of Glasgow Police Athletic Association*, [1953] 1 All E.R. 747; [1953] A.C. 380, H.L.
[13] *Supra*, at pp. 506; 200.
[14] *Neville Estates, Ltd.* v. *Madden*, [1961] 3 All E.R. 769; [1962] Ch. 832.
[15] [1972] 1 All E.R. 878; [1972] A.C. 601, H.L.
[16] [1945] 1 All E.R. 198; [1945] Ch. 123, C.A.
[17] [1951] 1 All E.R. 31; [1951] A.C. 297, H.L.

on practical grounds. Lord Cross even suggested that for the same sort of reason a trust to promote religion among the employees of a company might be charitable, provided the benefits were purely spiritual, though purposes under Lord Macnaghten's fourth head would normally be on a par with educational trusts.

Fourthly, it must be borne in mind that the courts' understanding of public benefit may vary with the passing of time. Thus in *National Anti-Vivisection Society* v. *I.R.Comrs.*[18] Lord Wright observed[19] "where a society has a religious object it may fail to satisfy the test (of public benefit) if it is unlawful, and the test may vary from generation to generation as the law successively grows more tolerant . . . It cannot be for the public benefit to favour trusts for objects contrary to the law. Again eleemosynary trusts may, as economic ideas and conditions and ideas of social service change, cease to be regarded as being for the benefit of the community, and trusts for the advancement of learning or education may fail to secure a place as charities, if it is seen that the learning or education is not of public value." Lord Simonds made the same point when he said,[20] "if, today, a testator made a bequest for the relief of the poor, and required, that it should be carried out in one way only, and the court was satisfied by evidence that that way was injurious to the community, I should say that it was not a charitable gift, though three hundred years ago the court might, upon different evidence, or in the absence of any evidence, have come to a different conclusion". As will be seen, however,[21] it might well be different if there were no condition that the gift should be carried out in one way only, or if a purpose originally charitable ceases to be so owing to changing circumstances.

Lastly, it may be added that it appears that a trust may be charitable, and the test of public benefit presumably passed, where the persons to benefit are all outside the jurisdiction.[22] This last matter has not been much considered in the cases, and one view[1] is that although the advancement of religion, the advancement of education and the relief of poverty are charitable purposes in whatever part of the world they are carried out, purposes within the fourth head of the classification in *Pemsel's Case*,[2] i.e. other purposes beneficial to the community, will be charitable only if of benefit to the community of the United Kingdom. In a recent case,[3] however, it was held that the planting of a grove of trees in Israel was a valid charitable gift, though this point does not appear to have been discussed in the judgment.

---

[18] [1947] 2 All E.R. 217; [1948] A.C. 31, H.L.
[19] *Supra*, at pp. 220; 42.
[20] At pp. 236; 69.
[21] Chapter 7, Section 3, pp. 211, *et seq.*, *post*.
[22] *Pemsel's Case*, [1891] A.C. 531, H.L. ("for the general purposes of maintaining, supporting and advancing the missionary establishments among heathen nations of the Protestant Episcopal Church"); *Re Robinson*, [1931] 2 Ch. 122 ("to the German Government for the time being for the benefit of its soldiers disabled in the late war"); and other cases on foreign missions such as *Re Kenny* (1907), 97 L.T. 130; *Re Redish* (1909), 26 T.L.R. 42. *Sed quaere*. See (1965), 29 Con. 123 (D. M. Emrys Evans).
[1] That of the Charity Commissioners as appears from their report for 1963, para. 72. This view is criticised by Emrys Evans, *loc. cit.*
[2] *Supra*.
[3] *Re Jacobs* (1970), 114 Sol. Jo. 515.

h Exceptions to the requirement of public benefit

The major anomalous head of charity for which the requirement of public benefit is not essential or is at least greatly modified is trusts for the relief of poverty. The law of charity in relation to poverty has followed its own line, and a series of cases, beginning with *Isaac* v. *Defriez*,[4] has established the validity of trusts for "poor relations", or other groups of persons who are not normally regarded as forming for this purpose a section of the community. Thus a trust for the relief of poverty was held to be charitable in *Gibson* v. *South American Stores*, (*Gath and Chaves, Ltd.*)[5] where the beneficiaries were selected by the tie of common employment, and in *Re Young's Will Trusts*,[6] where there was a gift to the trustees of the Savage Club "upon trust to be used by them as they shall in their absolute discretion think fit for the assistance of my fellow members by way of pensions or grants who may fall on evil days". The existing cases on this matter were considered by the Court of Appeal in *Re Scarisbrick*,[7] where, following life interests to her children, a testatrix gave half her residue to such relations, i.e. relations in any degree, of her children as should be in needy circumstances. It was held that the exceptional rule in relation to trusts for the relief of poverty applied just as much to a trust for immediate distribution as to a perpetual trust. It was pointed out, however, that it would be different where the trust was not for the relief of poverty, albeit among a class not normally regarded as forming a section of the public, but an ordinary gift to some particular individual or individuals, even though limited to the amount required to relieve his or their necessities if in necessitous circumstances—such as gifts to named persons in needy circumstances, or to a narrow class of near relatives, for example, such of a testator's statutory next of kin as at his death should be in needy circumstances. Most of the cases were reviewed by the House of Lords in *Dingle* v. *Turner*,[8] where the validity of the poverty exception was confirmed. Their Lordships agreed that it was a natural development of the "poor relations" decisions to hold as charitable trusts for "poor employees" of an individual or company (the case before the House), or poor members of a club or society, and they held that it would be illogical to draw a distinction between different kinds of poverty trusts.

There seems to be a second minor and equally anomalous exception to the requirement of public benefit in what the Privy Council has called[9] "the ancient English institution of educational provision for 'Founder's Kin' in certain schools and colleges". Such foundations giving preference to descendants of the donor are valid, "though there seems to be virtually no direct authority as to the principle on which they rested and they should probably be

---

[4] (1754), 2 Amb. 595; *A.-G.* v. *Price* (1810), 17 Ves. 571.
[5] [1949] 2 All E.R. 985; [1950] Ch. 177, C.A.; *Re Coulthurst's Will Trusts*, [1951] 1 All E.R. 774; [1951] Ch. 661, C.A.
[6] [1955] 3 All E.R. 689.
[7] [1951] 1 All E.R. 822; [1951] Ch. 622, C.A.; *Re Cohen*, [1973] 1 All E.R. 889.
[8] [1972] 1 All E.R. 878; [1972] A.C. 601, H.L.
[9] In *Mohamed Falil Abdul Caffoor* v. *Income Tax Commissioners*, [1961] 2 All E.R. 436, at p. 444; [1961] A.C. 584, at p. 602 P.C. See, generally, Squibb, *Founders' kin*.

regarded as belonging more to history than to doctrine".[10] Most founder's fellowships at Oxford and Cambridge were abolished by the Oxford University Act 1854 and the Cambridge University Act 1856, respectively, but some still exist, and there have been two new foundations during the present century.

Though hardly an exception to the rule as to public benefit, it is convenient to refer at this point to a way in which it may be possible, from a practical point of view, to evade it. It was held in *Re Koettgen*[11] that the charitable character of the primary trust for the advancement of education being of a sufficiently public nature, its validity was unaffected by the expression of the testator's imperative wish that in selecting beneficiaries the trustees should give preference to the employees of a particular company and members of their families. It was held that it was at the stage when the primary class of eligible persons was ascertained that the question of the public nature of the trust arose to be decided. Doubts have been raised,[12] however, as to whether this decision is consistent with the principle of *Oppenheim* v. *Tobacco Securities Trust Ltd.*[13]

Finally it should be mentioned that it does not follow from the general rule that in order to be charitable a trust must be for the public benefit, that a trust for the public benefit is necessarily charitable.[14]

i "Charity" for the purposes of the Charities Act 1960

In this Act, which provides a code for the administration of charities, "charity" is defined[15] as meaning "any institution, corporate[16] or not, which is established[17] for charitable purposes[18] and is subject to the control[19] of the High Court in the exercise of the court's jurisdiction[20] with respect to charities". "Institution" is itself defined[1] as including any trust or undertaking, so the definition clearly includes the ordinary case of trustees holding property upon charitable trusts. If a trustee[2]—which may be a corporate charity with its own corporate property—holds separate funds on special trusts, each fund will

---

[10] *Mohamed Falil Abdul Caffoor* v. *Income Tax Commissioners, supra; Spencer* v. *All Souls College* (1762), Wilm. 163; *A.-G.* v. *Sidney Sussex College* (1869), 4 Ch. App. 722; *Re Compton*, [1945] 1 All E.R. 198; [1945] Ch. 123, C.A.

[11] [1954] 1 All E.R. 581. Contrast *Vernon* v. *I.R.Comrs.*, [1956] 3 All E.R. 14; *Trustees of G. Drexler Ofrex Foundation* v. *I.R.Comrs.*, [1965] 3 All E.R. 529; [1966] Ch. 675.

[12] *Mohamed Falil Abdul Caffoor* v. *Income Tax Commissioners, supra; I.R.Comrs.* v. *Educational Grants Association, Ltd.*, [1967] 2 All E.R. 893; [1967] Ch. 993, C.A.

[13] *Supra.*   [14] See *supra*, p. 179.
[15] In s. 45 (1).   [16] See also s. 30.

[17] The relevant date is the foundation date. *Incorporated Council of Law Reporting for England and Wales* v. *A.-G.*, [1971] 3 All E.R. 1029; [1972] Ch. 73, C.A. *per* Sachs L.J., at pp. 1038; 91.

[18] I.e. exclusively charitable—s. 46. The definition thus does not include a valid discretionary trust for "charities" and non-charities.

[19] It seems from *Construction Industry Training Board* v. *A.-G.*, [1972] 2 All E.R. 1339; [1973] Ch. 173, C.A., that it is sufficient that the institution should be subject to the control of the court in some significant respect, even though in other respects the jurisdiction of the courts is ousted.

[20] The court has jurisdiction in any case where the revenues are to be applied in England and Wales, and if the charity is founded here though the revenues are to be applied abroad—*Re Duncan* (1867), 2 Ch. App. 356; *Keren Kayemeth Le Jisroel, Ltd.* v. *I.R.Comrs.*, [1931] 2 K.B. 465, C.A.

[1] Charities Act 1960, s. 46.

[2] *E.g. Re Royal Society's Charitable Trusts*, [1955] 3 All E.R. 14; [1956] Ch. 87.

constitute a separate institution and accordingly a separate charity for the purposes of the Act, though the Charity Commissioners may direct that for all or any of the purposes of the Act an institution established for any special purposes of or in connection with a charity (being charitable purposes) shall be treated as forming part of that charity or as forming a distinct charity.[3]

The Act specifically excludes from the definition[4] of charity any ecclesiastical corporation (i.e. any corporation in the Church of England, whether sole or aggregate, which is established for spiritual purposes) in respect of the corporate property of the corporation, except a corporation aggregate having some purposes which are not ecclesiastical in respect of its corporate property held for those purposes[5]; or any trust of property for purposes for which the property has been consecrated. Further certain charities listed in the Second Schedule to the Act[6] and known as "exempt charities" are not subject to the mandatory provisions of the Act. These exempt charities, which are subject to their own special provisions as to supervision, include most universities and colleges and the British Museum,[7] and other institutions administered by them or on behalf of any of them, the Church Commissioners and any institution administered by them, and Industrial and Provident Societies and Friendly Societies. Though free from the supervisory provisions of the Act, exempt charities may take advantage of its enabling provisions. In addition to and quite distinct from exempt charities are excepted charities, who may be excepted from some of the obligations of the Act though in general subject to it.[8]

j The expression "common good"

The Nathan Report[9] was strongly in favour of establishing Common Good Funds,[10] both national and local, for the general benefit of the community. The idea of national common good funds was not accepted by the government, which agreed, however, that it would be advantageous if local common good funds were established more widely.

With a view to encouraging the formation of such funds and at the same time ensuring that only suitable funds were given this title, Section 31 of the Charities Act 1960 makes it an offence,[11] without the consent of the Commissioners,[12] to invite gifts in money or in kind to the funds of, or to any fund managed by, an

---

[3] Charities Act 1960, s. 45 (5).
[4] *Ibid.*, s. 45 (2).   [5] E.g. Christ Church, Oxford.
[6] Also certain institutions added by Order in Council under para. (*c*) of the Schedule: S.I. 1962, No. 1343; S.I. 1965, No. 1715; S.I. 1966, No. 1460; S.I. 1967, No. 821; S.I. 1969, No. 1496.
[7] This includes the British Museum (Natural History)—British Museum Act 1963, s. 8 (4.) and Sched. 2, para. 3. Also the Museum of London: Museum of London Act 1965, s. 11, and the British Library Board—British Library Act 1972, s. 4 (2).
[8] The three obligations from which they may be excepted are the obligation to transmit annual accounts, to register, and in relation to dealings with land. See Chapter 7, Sections 1b, 2 and 5, pp. 201, 208, 225, *post.*
[9] Cmd. 8710, paras. 603–621.
[10] The term comes from Scotland, where most of the Royal Burghs possess funds held by the Town Council "in trust for behoof of the community".
[11] Punishable by a fine not exceeding £50—s. 31 (3).
[12] See Chapter 7, Section 1b, pp. 199 *et seq.*, *post.*

institution which has the words "common good" in its name, other than a body corporate established by royal charter, or to any fund described in or in connection with the invitation by a name which includes the words "common good" otherwise than as part of the name of such a body corporate. It is likewise an offence, without the same consent, to use the words "common good" in the name of any institution established in England or Wales, other than a body corporate established by royal charter. The consent of the Commissioners is only given rarely, and only where a charity's features comprise a sizeable permanent endowment, a wide range of charitable benefits over a considerable sector of the population, and some authoritative and representative board of trustees for its direction.

The idea of common good funds has not, however, found much favour. There are only four such funds in existence.

CHAPTER 7

The Administration of Charities

The law relating to the administration of charities was brought up to date by the Charities Act 1960 following the comprehensive report[1] (usually known as the Nathan Report) of the Committee on the Law and Practice relating to Charitable Trusts which was appointed in 1950. Viscount Kilmuir L.C., in moving the second reading, said that the Act had four main aims:

(i) to modernise the machinery of administration of charity law;

(ii) to establish a statutory foundation for voluntary co-operation between charity and the statutory welfare services on a basis of equality and partnership;

(iii) to establish a central register of charities; and

(iv) to extend and specify the conditions which must be satisfied before the purposes of a charitable trust can be altered, by what is known as a *cy-près* scheme.

Much of this chapter will be concerned with the provisions of the Act.

1 CHARITY TRUSTEES AND PERSONS AND BODIES HAVING POWERS AND DUTIES IN CONNECTION WITH CHARITIES

a Trustees[2]

In general the trustees of a charity have exactly the same powers, duties and liabilities as trustees of a private trust. Unlike the trustees of a private trust, however, they need not act unanimously, but the decision and act of a majority will be treated as the decision and act of the whole body of trustees and thus bind a dissenting minority;[3] moreover s. 34 of the Trustee Act 1925, which restricts the number of trustees of land to four, does not apply to land vested

---

[1] Cmd. 8710 published in December 1952.

[2] "Charity trustees" for the purposes of the Charities Act 1960 "means the persons having the general control and management of the administration of a charity"—s. 46—which would mean the directors in the case of a charity incorporated under the Companies Acts.

[3] *Wilkinson* v. *Malin* (1832), 2 Cr. & J. 636; *Perry* v. *Shipway* (1859), 1 Giff. 1; *Re Whiteley*, [1910] 1 Ch. 600.

in trustees for charitable purposes.[4] Further the Charity Commissioners have stated[5] clearly that in their view s. 19 of the Trustee Act 1925, which gives private trustees a limited power to insure the trust property[6] does not apply to charity trustees, who are under a larger duty to keep the charity property insured for its full value. Otherwise the provisions of the Trustee Act 1925[7] and the Trustee Investments Act 1961 apply to charity trustees, who, by s. 29 of the Settled Land Act 1925,[8] are also given in relation to land all the powers which are conferred on a tenant for life and the trustees of a settlement. Technically, indeed, trustees appear to have inherent powers of management, including powers of sale, leasing and mortgaging, in the provident administration of charity property,[9] but in practice should only act if they can point to some express power such as a provision in the trust instrument or a statutory power. Otherwise if the transaction is attacked, it will be very difficult to satisfy the court that the trustees have not been guilty of a breach of trust, for it will have to be shown that the transaction was beneficial to the charity and justified by the circumstances.

All trustees are required to keep accounts,[10] and charity trustees are statutorily[11] required to do so, and to preserve the accounts for seven years at least, unless the charity ceases to exist and the Commissioners permit them to be destroyed or otherwise disposed of. They are under a duty to apply for registration,[12] and to notify the Commissioners if the charity ceases to exist or of any change in its trusts. They must also take steps to enable the trust property to be applied cy-près where the case permits and requires.[13] Any charity trustee may make a written application to the Commissioners for their opinion or advice[14] on any matter affecting the performance of his duties as such. A trustee who acts in accordance with such opinion or advice is deemed to have acted in accordance with his trust unless he knows or has reasonable cause to suspect that the opinion or advice was given in ignorance of material facts, or that the decision of the court has been obtained on the matter or proceedings are pending to obtain one.[15]

Under the Trustee Appointment Acts 1850, 1869 and 1890, which applied only to certain religious and educational trusts, mainly in relation to chapel premises and the like, it was often[16] possible to appoint new trustees at a meeting

---

[4] Trustee Act 1925, s. 34 (3) (a). A power to execute instruments may be delegated to two or more trustees—Charities Act 1960, s. 34.

[5] Report for 1972, paras. 82–84.   [6] Discussed infra, pp. 340, 341.

[7] With the exception of s. 16, which ground however is largely covered by the provisions of s. 29 of the Settled Land Act 1925.

[8] As amended by the Charities Act 1960. It is a somewhat difficult section—see Re Booth & Southend-on-Sea Estates Company's Contract, [1927] 1 Ch. 579.

[9] A.-G. v. Warren (1818), 2 Swans. 291.

[10] See Chapter 10, Section 6, p. 330, post.

[11] Charities Act 1960, s. 32. This section applies to exempt charities. But see s. 8 as to the duty to transmit accounts discussed at p. 201, post.

[12] Section 4 (6), discussed at p. 210, post.

[13] Section 13 (5), discussed in Section 4, p. 215, post.

[14] Which, semble, need not be in writing.

[15] Charities Act 1960, s. 24. A trustee of an exempt charity may take advantage of this section.

[16] Reference must be made to the Acts themselves for details as to what trusts they applied to, the circumstances in which the power was available and other matters.

of the congregation or society, and if a memorandum was properly executed in the statutory form, land held on these trusts would, without any conveyance, be vested in the new trustees jointly with the continuing trustees, if any. It has, however, never been settled whether such trustees merely took the legal estate, or whether they were enabled to exercise the powers vested in the former trustees.[17] By the Charities Act 1960,[18] these Acts cease to have effect, except that in relation to land to which they applied on the 1st January, 1961, they continue to have effect "as if contained in the conveyance or other instrument declaring the trusts on which the land is then held".[19] These Acts are replaced by s. 35 of the Charities Act 1960, which applies to all charities, but only where, under the trusts of the charity, trustees of property held for the purpose of the charity may be appointed by resolution of a meeting of the charity trustees, members or other persons. A memorandum in accordance with the Act, if executed as a deed, brings into play s. 40[20] of the Trustee Act 1925.[21]

It may be added that by the Charitable Trustees Incorporation Act 1872, the Charity Commissioners[22] are empowered, upon the application of the trustees, to grant to the trustees of a charity a certificate of registration as a corporate body. Except as regards property vested in the Official Custodian for Charities,[1] the certificate of incorporation vests in the body corporate all the property belonging to or held in trust for the charity, but the liability of the trustees is unaffected. The Act has never found much favour with practitioners, and the advantages sought by incorporation can be equally well obtained by the appointment of the Official Custodian for Charities, which is now the procedure generally preferred.

b The Charity Commissioners

These were first appointed under the Charitable Trusts Act 1853, and the 1960 Act[2] has provided for their continuance. There is a Chief Charity Commissioner and two other commissioners, who are appointed by the Home Secretary, and at least two of the three must be barristers or solicitors. In the past charity trustees have often tended to look upon the Charity Commissioners with suspicion, and the Act now makes it clear that their duty is to help trustees and not to interfere with their work. The general function[3] of the Commissioners is stated to be to promote "the effective use of charitable resources by encouraging the development of better methods of administration, by giving charity trustees information or advice on any matter affecting the charity, and by investigating and checking abuses", and their general object,[4] "so to act in the case of any charity (unless it is a matter of altering its purposes) as best to

---

[17] See *Bunting* v. *Sargent* (1879), 13 Ch.D. 330.
[18] Section 35.
[19] Since the Acts now operate not with the force of statute, but only with the force of a deed, it seems doubtful whether they can be relied on to divest any old trustees of a legal estate vested in them.
[20] See Chapter 8, Section 2, p. 244, *post*.
[21] See also s. 18 of the Charities Act 1960, discussed at p. 200, *post*.
[22] See sub-sect. b, *infra*.
[1] See sub-sect. e, p. 202, *infra*.
[2] Section 1 and the First Schedule.   [3] Section 1 (3).
[4] Section 1 (4).

promote and make effective the work of the charity in meeting the needs designated by its trusts". To reassure charity trustees that in seeking the assistance of the Commissioners they would not run any danger of losing their independence in the administration of their charity, it was expressly provided that the Commissioners should themselves have no power to act in the administration of a charity.[5]

The Commissioners have the same powers[6] as are exercisable by the High Court in charity proceedings for establishing schemes,[7] and for appointing, discharging or removing charity trustees and for vesting or transferring property, though generally only on the application of the charity.[8] The Commissioners, however, are not to exercise their jurisdiction in any case which, by reason of its contentious character, or of any special question of law or of fact which it may involve, or for other reasons, the Commissioners may consider more fit to be adjudicated on by the court.[9] There are provisions for appeal to the High Court with a certificate from the Commissioners or leave of a Chancery Judge.[10]

The Commissioners may from time to time institute inquiries with regard to charities or a particular charity or class of charities, either generally or for particular purposes. The inquiry may be conducted by the Commissioners themselves, or they may appoint someone else to conduct it and report to them, and in either case there is power to compel the attendance of witnesses and take evidence on oath.[11] They may also inspect and call for copies of documents relating to a charity from any person having them in his possession or control.[12] If the Commissioners are satisfied as a result of an inquiry that there has been any misconduct or mismanagement in the administration of the charity and that it is necessary or desirable to act for the purpose of protecting the property of the charity or securing a proper application for the purposes of the charity of that property or of property coming to the charity, they may take various steps, including the removal of any trustee or other person connected with the charity who has been responsible for or privy to the misconduct or mismanagement or has by his conduct contributed to it or facilitated it, and the vesting in or transfer to the official custodian for charities of property held by or in trust for the charity[13].

---

[5] Section 1 (4).

[6] It will be recalled that the supervisory powers of the Act as opposed to the enabling powers do not extend to exempt charities.   [7] Discussed in Section 3, post.

[8] Charities Act 1960, s. 18. But by s. 18 (5), in the case of non-exempt charities with an income from property not exceeding £50 p.a., on the application of the Attorney-General, a charity trustee or any other person interested in the charity, or, in the case of any local charity, any two or more inhabitants of the area.

[9] Ibid., s. 18 (9).

[10] Section 18 (11) (12); Child v. A.-G., [1973] 2 All E.R. 108. By sub. s. 10 the A.-G. has an unqualified right of appeal.

[11] Charities Act 1960, s. 6. The section does not apply to exempt charities.

[12] Ibid., s. 7. The section does not apply to documents of an exempt charity.

[13] Section 20 (1). The power was first exercised in 1964 following the report of an accountant appointed under ss. 6 and 8 (Report of the Charity Commissioners for 1964, paras. 12, 57, 58). For other cases see Report for 1971, paras. 90–96; Report for 1972, paras. 78–81. A right of appeal is given by s. 20 (7), and on appeal it is for the appellant to show that the order was wrongly made—Jones v. A.-G., [1973] 3 All E.R. 518, C.A. Section 20 does not apply to an exempt charity.

As to trustees it is further provided that the Commissioners may discharge a charity trustee on his application,[14] or remove a charity trustee by order made of their own motion[15]—

"(a) where the trustee is a bankrupt or a corporation in liquidation, or is incapable of acting by reason of mental disorder within the meaning of the Mental Health Act 1959;

(b) where the trustee has not acted, and will not declare his willingness or unwillingness to act;

(c) where the trustee is outside England and Wales or cannot be found or does not act, and his absence or failure to act impedes the proper administration of the charity."

Similarly they may appoint a person to be a charity trustee, and make orders with regard to the vesting and transfer of property[16]—

"(a) in place of a charity trustee removed by them under this section or otherwise;

(b) where there are no charity trustees, or where by reason of vacancies in their number or the absence or incapacity of any of their number the charity cannot apply for the appointment;

(c) where there is a single charity trustee, not being a corporation aggregate, and the Commissioners are of opinion that it is necessary to increase the number for the proper administration of the charity;

(d) where the Commissioners are of opinion that it is necessary for the proper administration of the charity to have an additional charity trustee, because one of the existing charity trustees who ought nevertheless to remain a charity trustee either cannot be found or does not act or is outside England and Wales."

On request, charity trustees must supply the Commissioners with accounts, and a charity having a permanent endowment[17] must supply its accounts[18] yearly without request, unless it is a charity excepted by order or regulation.[19] There is, however, no legal requirement that the accounts must be audited, though it is prudent and proper for the trustees to arrange for this to be done by an independent person. Moreover, the Commissioners may direct an investigation and audit, at the Commissioners' expense.[20] It may be added that the Commissioners may provide books in which any deed, will or other document relating to a charity may be enrolled, and may accept for safe keeping any document of or relating to a charity.[1]

---

[14] Section 18 (7). In many cases a trustee will be able to retire under s. 39 of the Trustee Act 1925, or, as a last resort, pay into court under s. 63 of the Trustee Act 1925—see Chapter 8, Section 3c, p. 250, *post*.

[15] Section 20 (3) as amended by the Criminal Law Act 1967, s. 10 and Sched. 3, Part III.

[16] Section 20 (4) and (5).   [17] For the definition of this term see *ibid.*, s. 46.

[18] The prescribed information required is set out in S.I. 1960 No. 2425.

[19] *Ibid.*, s. 8 (1), (2) and (6). This section does not apply to an exempt charity. Excepted charities comprise certain religious charities excepted by S.I. 1963 No. 2074 and S.I. 1964 No. 1825 and, with some exceptions, charities for the promotion of the efficiency of the armed forces excepted by S.I. 1965 No. 1056. S.I. 1963 No. 210 excepted various Health Authorities, most of which were extinguished by the National Health Service Reorganisation Act 1973, though it still applies to Boards of Governors preserved by s. 15 of the Act. No provision has yet been made in respect of charities administered by the new Health Authorities set up by the Act, but it is expected that an appropriate order or regulation will be made in due course.

[20] *Ibid.*, s. 8 (3)–(6).   [1] Section 25. Exempt charities may take advantage of this provision.

Finally, s. 23 of the Charities Act 1960 gives the Commissioners wide power to authorise dealings with charity property which may be compared with s. 57 of the Trustee Act 1925[2] and s. 64 of the Settled Land Act 1925.[3] Where it appears to the Commissioners that any action proposed or contemplated in the administration of a charity is expedient in the interests of the charity, they may by order sanction that action, whether or not it would otherwise be within the powers exercisable by the charity trustees in the administration of the charity,[4] and the order may be made so as to authorise a particular transaction, compromise or the like, or a particular application of property, or so as to give a more general authority.[5] In practice the procedure of establishing a scheme[6] is preferred for this last purpose. In particular the order may authorise a charity to use common premises, or employ a common staff, or otherwise combine for any purpose of administration, with any other charity,[7] and it may give directions as to the manner in which any expenditure is to be borne and as to other matters connected with or arising out of the action thereby authorised.[8]

It should be added that prior to 1 February 1974 the functions of the Charity Commissioners in relation to educational trusts were carried out by the Secretary of State for Education and Science.[9] By the Education Act 1973 the powers of the Secretary of State to carry out these functions were terminated, and the Charity Commissioners, who previously had concurrent jurisdiction over educational trusts, now have exclusive jurisdiction over them in exactly the same way as they have jurisdiction over other charitable trusts.

c The Official Custodian for Charities

The Official Custodian for Charities, a corporation sole having perpetual succession and using an official seal, was created by s. 3 of the 1960 Act. He is the successor for all purposes both of the official trustee of charity lands and of the official trustees of charitable funds.[10] Charity property may become vested in the Official Custodian by an order of the court,[11] either directly vesting the property in the Official Custodian, or authorising or requiring the persons in whom the property is vested to transfer it to him, or appointing any person to transfer it to him.[12] So far as personal property, including real securities, is concerned, it may be transferred to the Official Custodian with his consent without any such order.[13]

Where property is vested in the Official Custodian in trust for a charity, he must not exercise any powers of management, but has the same powers,

---

[2] Discussed in Chapter 10, Section 1b, p. 298, *post.*
[3] Discussed *ibid.*, p. 300, *post.*
[4] Charities Act 1960, s. 23 (1). This section was used by the Commissioners in August 1962 to authorise the sale of the Leonardo cartoon by the Royal Academy of Arts at a price lower than that obtainable on the open market, subject however to the condition that upon sale the cartoon should be held on trust for exhibition to the public.
[5] *Ibid.*, s. 23 (2).   [6] See Section 3, *post.*
[7] *Ibid.*, s. 23 (2)   [8] *Ibid.*, s. 23 (3).
[9] He replaced the Minister of Education on 1 April 1964—S.I. 1964 No. 490.
[10] *Ibid.*, s. 48 (6).
[11] Or, under s. 18, of the Commissioners, but in their case generally only on the application of the charity. See also s. 20, discussed at p. 200, *ante.*
[12] *Ibid.*, s. 16 (1).
[13] *Ibid.*, s. 16 (2).

duties and liabilities, and is entitled to the same rights and immunities, and is subject in the same way to the control and orders of the court as a corporation appointed custodian trustee under s. 4 of the Public Trustee Act 1906,[14] except that he has no power to charge fees.[15] The absence of any power of management means, for instance, that any trust property uninvested in his hands will remain uninvested unless and until he receives precise instructions from the trustees.

d The Attorney-General

The Attorney-General acts in charity cases on behalf of the Crown as *parens patriae*, and represents all the objects of the charity. It has always been recognised that it is his duty to intervene for the purpose of protecting charities and affording advice and assistance to the court in the administration of charitable trusts.[16] No-one other than the Attorney-General is entitled to maintain an action against supposed trustees to establish the existence of a charitable trust, and only the Attorney-General or the trustees of a charity can bring proceedings to recover charity property from a third person.[17] No authorisation or leave has to be obtained for the Attorney-General to take proceedings, whether *ex officio* or *ex relatione*.[18] The Commissioners are under a duty to inform the Attorney-General if it appears to them that it is desirable that he should bring proceedings with reference to a charity.[19]

One particular power apparently possessed by the Attorney-General, and the court, is to authorise charity trustees to make *ex gratia* payments out of funds held on charitable trusts. This power is not to be exercised lightly on slender grounds, but only in cases where it can fairly be said that, if the charity were an individual, it would be morally wrong of him to refuse to make the payment.[20]

e Local authorities

Whatever validity there may at one time have been in the theory that charitable and public funds should not be applied to the same objects, it is clear that the theory is now untenable. As the Nathan Committee pointed out,[21] with the wide and continual extension of public services it is becoming increasingly true that the charitable purposes to which rates and taxes may not be applied are almost non-existent. The Committee thought that co-operation and partnership between charity trustees and local authorities should be

---

[14] See Chapter 8, Section 6, p. 258, *post.*
[15] Charities Act 1960, s. 17 (1).
[16] *Wallis* v. *S.-G. for New Zealand*, [1903] A.C. 173, P.C.; *Re Royal Society's Charitable Trusts*, [1955] 3 All E.R. 14; [1956] Ch. 87; *Re Belling*, [1967] 1 All E.R. 105; [1967] Ch. 425. Cf. Charities Act 1960, s. 28 (7).
[17] *Hauxwell* v. *Barton-upon-Humber U.D.C.*, [1973] 2 All E.R. 1022. Contrast the position with regard to "charity proceedings" discussed p. 206, *infra.*
[18] *Ibid.*, s. 28 (6).
[19] *Ibid.*, s. 28 (7).
[20] *Re Snowden*, [1969] 3 All E.R. 208; [1970] Ch. 700; and see [1968] 32 Con. 384 (P. H. Pettit); Report of the Charity Commissioners for 1969, paras. 26–31.
[21] *Nathan Report* (Cmd. 8710), paras. 661, 662.

encouraged, and this has been carried into effect by ss. 10–12[1] of the Charities Act 1960, which are entirely new.

Section 10[2] authorises the council of a county or of a district or London borough to maintain an index[3] of local charities[4] or of any class of local charities in the council's area, and to publish information therein contained. The index ·is to be open to public inspection at all reasonable times.

Section 11 enables the same local authorities to initiate and carry out, in co-operation with the charity trustees, a review of the working of any group of local charities with the same or similar purposes in the council's area. After consultation with the trustees the council may make a report on the review and recommendations arising from it to the Commissioners who, in a proper case, may act upon it by the exercise of their ordinary scheme-making power.[5] Councils having the above-mentioned power to initiate reviews may also co-operate with other persons in any review by them of the working of local charities in the council's area, or may join with other persons in initiating and carrying out such a review.[6] No review initiated by a council, however, is to extend to any charity without the consent of the charity trustees, nor to any ecclesiastical charity.[7] The Nathan Report,[8] in recommending legislation to this effect, said the objects of a review would be threefold, namely,

(1) to ascertain which trusts have endowments so small as to be plainly uneconomic units involving administrative trouble and expense, both locally and centrally, out of proportion to the benefits they confer;

(2) to ascertain which trusts have objects so out of accord with present-day conditions that their endowments are not used to the greatest advantage to the community; and

(3) to ascertain which trusts are doing valuable work and have insufficient funds.

The Commissioners, in reviewing the first ten years' working of the Act,[9] have stated the objects of a local review somewhat differently. They have said:

---

[1] As amended by the Local Government Act 1972, s. 272 and Sched. 30.

[2] As amended by the London Government Act 1963, ss. 1 (6) and 81 (9), and the Local Government Act 1972, s. 210 (9).

[3] The Commissioners are required to provide, on request, copies of relevant entries in the register of charities (discussed, *post*, pp. 208 *et seq.*). In practice the index may also contain informal references to local branches of national charities which are ineligible to be placed on the register. Such references have no legal consequences but may be of considerable practical value.

[4] Defined by s. 45 (1) in relation to any area as "a charity established for purposes which are by nature or by the trusts of the charity directed wholly or mainly to the benefit of that area or of part of it".

[5] A scheme can normally be made only on the application of a charity—but see p. 200 *supra*, n. 8. For details of schemes made resulting from a local review, see, e.g. Report for 1964, para. 35 and App. G; Report for 1971, paras. 84–89.

[6] Charities Act 1960, s. 11 (2).

[7] *Ibid.*, s. 11 (3). For the definition of ecclesiastical charity see s. 45 (1), referring to s. 75 (2), of the Local Government Act 1894.

[8] Cmd. 8710, para. 595.

[9] Report for 1970, para. 31.

"The aim is to work out with the different bodies of trustees an agreed plan of the future activities of the charities included in the review so as to ensure—

(a) that there is no duplication between the work of two charities in one area;

(b) that charities complement and do not duplicate the work and benefits of the statutory welfare service . . .; and

(c) that charity income is used to give the most effective help to those in need whom—for whatever reason—the statutory services cannot help in the way required."

Section 12 (1) empowers any local council[10] to make, with any charity established for purposes similar or complementary to services provided by the council, arrangements for co-ordinating the activities of the council and those of the charity in the interests of persons who may benefit from those services or from the charity. Complementary to this, sub-s. (2) empowers charity trustees, notwithstanding anything in the trusts of the charity, to do all or any of the following things in order to promote or make more effective the work of the charity, namely, to co-operate in any review undertaken under s. 11 or otherwise of the working of charities or any class of charities, to make arrangements with any local council or with another charity for co-ordinating their activities and those of the council or of the other charity, and to publish information of other charities with a view to bringing them to the notice of those for whose benefit they are intended. This is carried a stage further by s. 142 of the Local Government Act 1972 which empowers a local authority to make or assist in the making of, arrangements under which the public may obtain information concerning the services provided by the authority, government departments, charities and voluntary bodies within the area of the local authority concerned.

It is convenient to mention here that s. 37 of the Charities Act 1960[11] contains special provisions relating to parochial charities.[12] These provisions relate in the main to the transfer of property by the trustees to the parish council or their appointees, and to the appointment of trustees by the parish council or parish meeting.

f The court

The court has an inherent general jurisdiction[13] over charitable trusts and may accordingly enforce them, take steps to redress a breach of trust, direct a scheme [14] in order to enforce the more complete attainment of the charitable

---

[10] This includes councils not included in ss. 10 and 11 and is defined for this purpose in s. 12 (1) as amended byt he Local Government Act 1972, ss. 210 (9) (c), 272, and Sched. 30.

[11] As amended by the Local Government Act 1972, ss. 210 (9) (c), 272 and Sched. 30.

[12] Defined by s. 45 (1) in relation to any parish, as meaning "a charity the benefits of which are, or the separate distribution of the benefits of which is, confined to inhabitants of the parish, or of a single ancient ecclesiastical parish which included that parish or part of it, or of an area consisting of that parish with not more than four neighbouring parishes". Voluntary schools within the meaning of the Education Act 1944 are excluded—s. 37 (7).

[13] A.-G. v. Sherborne Grammar School Governors (1854), 18 Beav. 256.

[14] Either by directing a reference to chambers to settle the scheme, or by reference to the Commissioners under s. 18 (2) discussed infra, p. 212. In a simple case, or where the fund is very small, the court may act directly without any reference.

objects and alter and amend the trusts under the *cy-près* doctrine. The Charities Act 1960 provides that charity proceedings, i.e. proceedings in a court of an administrative nature,[15] may be taken either by the charity, or by any of the charity trustees, or by any person interested in the charity, or by any two or more inhabitants of the area of the charity, if it is a local charity.[16] Except in the case of an exempt charity, however, no charity proceedings can be entertained or proceeded with in any court unless the taking of the proceedings is authorised by order of the Commissioners,[17] who should not, however, without special reasons, give such authorisation where in their opinion the case can be dealt with by them under the powers[18] of the Act.[19] If the Commissioners refuse their authorisation, an application for leave may nevertheless be sought from a Chancery judge.[20]

The jurisdiction is based primarily, if not exclusively, on the existence of a trust. The point has several times been raised where a testator has given property to a non-existent institution and where there is clearly a general charitable intention. In such case if the gift is by way of trust, the court has jurisdiction and will direct a scheme; but if it is by way of direct gift the court has no jurisdiction and the matter falls within the royal prerogative and will be disposed of by the Crown by sign-manual, acting as it is said as *parens patriae*.[21]

The inherent jurisdiction was limited in relation to charities established by royal charter,[22] or by statute,[1] though it always had jurisdiction to see that the provisions of the charter or the statute were observed. There is, moreover, a difficulty as to jurisdiction over corporate charities. Where a corporate body holds property on charitable trusts there is clearly jurisdiction, but in many cases a corporation with exclusively charitable purposes simply holds property as part of its corporate funds. If jurisdiction depends on the existence of a trust a problem arises. It may be possible in the case of a charity incorporated by charter to evade the difficulty by holding that the corporate charity holds its property on trust for its charitable purposes,[2] but this argument is not available in the case of a company incorporated under the Companies Acts with exclusively charitable objects, for a company does not hold its property on trust either for its members or the objects set out in its memorandum of association.

---

[15] Section 28 (8). It does not, therefore, cover proceedings by way of construction of a testamentary document to determine whether a provision was effective to create a charitable trust, where only the Attorney-General, or the trustees, can start an action. *Re Belling*, [1967] 1 All E.R. 105; [1967] Ch. 425; *Hauxwell* v. *Barton-upon-Humber U.D.C.*, [1973] 2 All E.R. 1022, and see p. 203, *supra*.

[16] Section 28 (1). Cf. s. 18 and Section 1b of this chapter, p. 199, *ante*.

[17] Charities Act 1960, s. 28 (2).

[18] Especially s. 18, and see p. 200, *ante.*

[19] Charities Act 1960, s. 28 (3).   [20] *Ibid.*, s. 28 (5).

[21] See *Re Bennett*, [1959] 3 All E.R. 295; [1960] Ch. 18, where the somewhat conflicting cases from *Moggridge* v. *Thackwell* (1803), 7 Ves. 36, affirmed (1807), 13 Ves. 416, H.L., onwards are discussed; *Re Conroy* (1973), 35 D.L.R. (3d) 752.

[22] See now p. 212, *post*.

[1] See now p. 212, *post*.

[2] Even, it seems, although the charity came into existence before the creation of trusts— *A.-G.* v *St. Cross Hospital* (1853), 17 Beav. 435 (hospital founded in twelfth century).

Dicta[3] have, nevertheless, suggested that such a company is within the juris-diction, and such a company is clearly a charity for the purposes of the Charities Act 1960, provision being made for its being wound up on a petition presented by the Attorney-General.[4] Further, the statutory definition of charity[5] includes a corporate "institution" established for charitable purposes; "institu-tion" is defined[6] to include a trust, and trust is defined[6] in relation to a charity as meaning the provisions establishing it as a charity and regulating its purposes and administration, whether those provisions take effect by way of trust or not. It may be added that although there is no provision in the Charities Act 1960 to prevent a corporate charity from altering its objects so that it ceases to be exclusively charitable, s. 30 (2) ensures that such alteration will not affect the application of property held by the company at the time of the alteration.

g Visitors

Ecclesiastical and eleemosynary corporations[7] are subject to the jurisdiction of visitors in relation to their internal management. Ecclesiastical corporations are those which exist for the furtherance of religion and perpetuating the rights of the Church. For present purposes eleemosynary corporations[8] are such as are constituted for the perpetual distribution of the free alms or bounty of the founder of them to such persons as he has directed, mainly hospitals[9] and colleges.[10]

Ecclesiastical corporations are generally visitable by the Ordinary. So far as eleemosynary corporations are concerned the founder is said to be a legislator,[11] and may accordingly appoint visitors, and if no visitor is appointed by him, he and his heirs[12] are visitors by operation of law.[13] If the founder's heirs die out, or cannot be found,[14] or cannot act by reason of insanity[15] the visitorial power becomes vested in the Crown.[16] And, as it would be contrary to natural justice

---

[3] Per Cozens-Hardy L.J. in Re Church Army (1906), 94 L.T. 559, C.A., at 564, 565; Re Society for Training Teachers of the Deaf and Whittle's Contract, [1907] 2 Ch. 486.

[4] Charities Act 1960, s. 30 (1).

[5] Ibid., s. 45 (1).   [6] Ibid., s. 46.

[7] 1 Blackstone's Commentaries 470. As to civil corporations see pp. 481, 482, where it is pointed out that the Court of King's Bench (now presumably the Queen's Bench Division) has a supervisory jurisdiction, but it is doubtful whether the court acts in the capacity of visitor.

[8] This phrase is not a term of art with a judicially established definition. The narrowest possible meaning has been said to be charities for the relief of poverty, and in Re Armitage's Will Trusts, [1972] 1 All E.R. 708; [1972] Ch. 438, it was said to cover all charities directed to the relief of individual distress whether due to poverty, age, sickness or other similar individual afflictions. Modern universities, it had been contended, are for the purposes of visitation at least, treated as eleemosynary corporations, and, being created by royal charter, as founded by the Crown—(1970), 86 L.Q.R. 531 (J. W. Bridge).

[9] In the old sense of institutions for the maintenance of the needy, infirm or aged.

[10] See Phillips v. Bury (1694), Skinn. 447; Holt 715.

[11] Spencer v. All Souls' College (1767), Wilm. 163; Phillips v. Bury, supra.

[12] The effect of the abolition of inheritance by the Administration of Estates Act 1925, s. 45 is not clear.

[13] Phillips v. Bury, supra; Eden v. Foster (1726), 2 P.Wms. 325.

[14] R. v. St. Catherine's Hall, Cambridge (1791), 4 Term. Rep. 233; Ex parte Wrangham (1795), 2 Ves. 609; A.-G. v. Clarendon (Earl) (1810), 17 Ves. 491.

[15] A.-G. v. Dixie (1805), 13 Ves. 519.   [16] Exercised by the Lord Chancellor.

that a man should be judge in his own cause, the Court of Queen's Bench[17] has assumed jurisdiction where otherwise the same person would be both visitor and visited.[18] No technical words are required for the appointment of a visitor by the founder,[19] who may either appoint a general visitor, or divide up the visitorial power among two or more persons,[20] or appoint special visitors for a particular purpose. If a visitorial power is *prima facie* general, it requires particular words to abridge it in any respect.[1]

The nature of the visitorial power has been said to be *forum domesticum*, the private jurisdiction of the founder.[2] Subject to any special provisions in the statutes of the foundation, his ordinary duties and powers concern the election and removal of members of the corporation and its officers, the internal management of the corporation, construction of the statutes of the foundation, and judging claims and complaints by members. This jurisdiction covers claims by persons to become members of the foundation, such as rejected candidates for fellowships,[3] but does not extend to any questions between the foundation and people outside it.[4]

In any matter within his jurisdiction the power of the visitor is absolute and not subject to the control of court.[5] Outside his jurisdiction, the act of a visitor is a nullity. Thus if by the statutes of the foundation he is to conduct a general visitation not more than once in five years, he has no power to visit more often, but a general visitor has a standing constant authority at all times to hear complaints and redress grievances of particular members of the foundation.[6] A visitor can, however, be compelled to exercise his jurisdiction,[7] and the exercise of the visitorial power is a judicial act so that the dictates of natural justice, which require, for example, that both sides should be heard, must be observed.[8]

It should be added that if a corporation holds property as a trustee on a special trust, the court has jurisdiction in the ordinary way and the matter is outside the jurisdiction of the visitor.[9]

2 REGISTRATION OF CHARITIES

The provisions for registration contained in the Charities Act 1960 are not, in fact, the first in time. The statutory obligation to register imposed by the

---

[17] And presumably the High Court would now act in the same way.

[18] R. v. Chester (Bishop) (1728), 2 Stra. 797; R. v. Ely (Bishop) (1788), 2 Term. Rep. 290.

[19] A.-G. v. Middleton (1751), 2 Ves. Sen. 327; St. John's College, Cambridge v. Todington (1757), 1 Burr. 158.

[20] A.-G. v. Middleton, supra.

[1] R. v. Worcester (Bishop) (1815), 4 M. & S. 415.

[2] Per Hardwicke L.J. in Green v. Rutherford (1790), 1 Ves. Sen. 462, at p. 472.

[3] R. v. Hertford College (1878), 3 Q.B.D. 693, C.A.

[4] Davidson's Case cited in R. v. Grundon (1775), 1 Cowp. 315; R. v. Windham (1776), 1 Cowp. 377.

[5] R. v. Dunsheath, [1950] 2 All E.R. 741; [1951] 1 K.B. 127, D.C.; Thorne v. University of London, [1966] 2 All E.R. 338; [1966] 2 Q.B. 237, C.A. (the court has no jurisdiction to hear a complaint that failure in degree examinations in, inter alia, the law of trusts, was a result of negligence of the examiners); Herring v. Templeman, [1973] 2 All E.R. 581.

[6] Phillips v. Bury (1694), Skinn. 447; Holt 715.

[7] Whiston v. Rochester (Dean and Chapter) (1849), 7 Hare 532.

[8] R. v. Ely (Bishop) (1788), 2 Term. Rep. 290.

[9] Green v. Rutherford (1790), 1 Ves. Sen. 462, at p. 472; Whiston v. Rochester (Dean and Chapter), supra.

Charitable Donations Registration Act 1812[10] seems, however, to have been a dead letter almost from the time when it was passed and the provisions for the registration of certain kinds of charity under the War Charities Act 1940 and the National Assistance Act 1948[11] are quite independent, and for a quite different purpose, namely, the protection of the public by prohibiting public appeals by unregistered charities. The 1960 Act, accordingly, in practice covers new ground in making for the first time effective provision for the general registration of charities of all kinds in order to provide a central pool of information for the benefit of all persons interested.

The main section is section 4 which provides for the establishment and maintenance of a register by the Commissioners, containing particulars of the trusts of the charity and open to public inspection at all reasonable times. The register is kept on a card index system, comprising a name index, an objects index and a geographical index. In addition copies of the index of national charities are held at ten regional centres, and two copies of an index of all charities in Wales and Monmouthshire are available for inspection, one in the north and the other in the south of the principality.[12] All charities within the meaning of the Act[13] not excepted from the requirement of registration must be entered on the register; and an excepted charity may be entered on the register at the request of the charity, for instance, to publicise its work or to establish its charitable status, but may at any time, and must at the request of the charity, be removed from the register. The excepted charities fall into four categories[14]:

i Exempt charities.[15]

ii Any charity which is excepted by order or regulations. Regulations have been made excepting all universities which are not exempt charities;[16] all voluntary schools, within the meaning of the Education Acts 1944–1973, being charities and having no permanent endowment other than the premises of, or connected with, the school;[17] charities for the promotion of the efficiency of the armed forces;[18] certain religious charities,[19] and charities comprising funds, not being permanent endowments, belonging to units of the Boy Scouts Association or the Girl Guides Association, which are being accumulated for the purposes of the unit and which produce an income of more than £15 a year.[20]

iii Any charity having neither any permanent endowment, nor any income from property amounting to more than £15 a year, nor the use and occupation of any land.[1] The conditions are cumulative and must all be fulfilled if

---

[10] Repealed by Charities Act 1960, s. 39 and Fifth Schedule.   [11] Section 41.
[12] For the addresses see Appendix B to the Report of the Charity Commissioners for 1965.
[13] See Chapter 6, Section 2i, p. 194, ante.
[14] Charities Act 1960, s. 4 (4).
[15] See Chapter 6, Section 2i, p. 195, ante.
[16] S.I. 1966 No. 965.
[17] S.I. 1960 No. 2366.
[18] S.I. 1965 No. 1056. The regulation has certain exceptions.
[19] S.I. 1963 No. 2074; 1964 No. 1825.
[20] S.I. 1961 No. 1044. If not more than £15 p.a., see category (iii) immediately following.
[1] Charities Act 1960, s. 4 (4) (c). This is intended to link up with rating provisions, so that reference to the Central Register will establish readily whether an institution occupying land is eligible to claim the mandatory rating relief provided by the General Rate Act 1967.

the charity is to be excepted. The phrase "permanent endowment" is somewhat misleading for, as defined by sections 46 and 45 (3) it does not necessarily mean that the endowment must be retained as capital in perpetuity. A charity is deemed to have a permanent endowment for the purposes of the Act unless all the property held for the purposes of the charity may be expended for those purposes without distinction between capital and income. If capital is subject to restrictions not attached to income, the charity has a permanent endowment even though the capital may be entirely expended in appropriate circumstances. "Income from property" refers to the gross revenues of the charity, without bringing into account, however, anything for the yearly value of land occupied by the charity.[2]

iv No charity is required to be registered in respect of any registered place of worship.[3] This means in effect the meeting-places, recorded by the Registrar-General of Births, Deaths and Marriages, for the religious worship of Protestant Dissenters or other Protestants, Roman Catholics, Jews and any other body or denomination of persons other than the Church of England,[4] so long as it continues to be used *bona fide* as a place of religious worship. The exception extends to ancillary premises held on the same trusts as the meeting-place so recorded such as a forecourt, yard, garden, burial-ground, vestry or caretaker's house and, on a certificate of the Commissioners, a Sunday-school house or building.

It is the duty of the charity trustees of any charity which is neither registered nor excepted from registration to apply for it to be registered, and to supply all the documents and information required for this purpose.[5] Though no time limit is specified before which the duty must be carried out, any person who makes default may be required by order of the Commissioners to make it good, and failure to obey their order is punishable as a contempt of court.[6] The same sanction applies to the further duty of the charity trustees of any institution which is for the time being registered to notify the Commissioners if it ceases to exist, or if there is any change in its trusts, or in the particulars of it entered in the register.[7] The Commissioners are themselves under a duty[8] to remove from the register any institution which no longer appears to them to be a charity,[9] and also any charity which ceases to exist or does not operate.[10]

The most important effect of registration is that an institution is for all purposes other than rectification of the register conclusively presumed to be or have been a charity at any time when it is or was on the register of charities.[11]

---

[2] Charities Act 1960, s. 45 (4).
[3] For a definition, by reference to the Places of Worship Registration Act 1855 and the Charitable Trusts Act 1853, see Charities Act 1960, ss. 4 (9), 48 (1) and Sched. 6.
[4] It will be remembered that a corporation in the Church of England is not a charity for the purposes of the Act—s. 45 (2) discussed in Chapter 6, Section 2i, p. 195, *ante*.
[5] Charities Act 1960, s. 4 (6) (a).
[6] *Ibid.*, ss. 4 (6) and 41.   [7] *Ibid.*, s. 4 (6) (b).
[8] *Ibid.*, s. 4 (3).
[9] See the Report of the Charity Commissioners for 1967, Appendix D, Part II.
[10] It is not clear when a charity can be said not to operate. Presumably it does not cover the case where the trustees fail to act, where the proper course is merely to compel them to do so, or have new trustees appointed who will.
[11] Charities Act 1960, s. 5 (1).

To some extent the presumption operates retrospectively. Thus in *Re Muraw-ski's Will Trusts*[12] the question was whether at the date of the testatrix's death in 1964 the Bleakholt Animal Sanctuary was a charity. The Sanctuary was not registered as a charity until 1968. On evidence that at all material times before and after registration its objects were identical, the court felt bound to hold that the Sanctuary was a charity at the date of death. Provision is of course made for claims and objections to registration being adjudicated upon. This is done by the Commissioners with an appeal to the High Court.[13]

3 SCHEMES

a General

As we have seen,[14] a charitable trust does not fail for uncertainty, and an order for the direction of a scheme is the device available to the Court under its inherent jurisdiction to remedy uncertainty either in the substance of the trust[15] or the mode of administration, to get over some administrative difficulty or to amend the rules of the charity.[16] A scheme is not necessarily, or even generally, a scheme for the application of property *cy-près*.[17] It may be directed where the exact ambit of the charitable purpose is not clear,[18] where the trustees are dead,[19] or disclaim or refuse to act,[20] or have misapplied the trust property,[1] where the income of the charity has substantially increased,[2] and in other cases where it is an appropriate remedy.[3] But sometimes even a charitable trust cannot be saved by a scheme. Thus "if it is of the essence of a trust that the trustees selected by the settlor and no-one else shall act as the trustees of it and those trustees cannot or will not undertake the office, the trust must fail".[4] The terms of particular schemes vary considerably, and may be more or less complex depending on the circumstances of the particular case. The court has, of course, a discretion whether to order a scheme or not, and in *Re Hanbey's Will*

---

[12] [1971] 2 All E.R. 328.
[13] *Ibid.*, s. 5. On 1 Feb. 1974 there were 83,640 charities registered by the Commissioners, by which date they had rejected 1,616 applications and removed 847 charities from the register. On that date they took over from the Secretary of State for Education and Science 11,140 recreational charities and an estimated 17,150 educational charities. There have been two appeals to the High Court, one from the Commissioners and one from the Secretary of State.
[14] Chapter 6, Section 1a, p. 157, *ante*.
[15] There must be a trust—*Re Bennett*, [1959] 3 All E.R. 295; [1960] Ch. 18, and *ante*, p. 206.
[16] *Re Gott*, [1944] 1 All E.R. 293; [1944] Ch. 193. The details of the scheme will be settled by the Master in Chambers.
[17] *Re Robinson*, [1931] 2 Ch. 122. As to *cy-près* see section 4, p. 215, *post*.
[18] *Re White*, [1893] 2 Ch. 41, C.A.; *Re Gott*, *supra*.
[19] *Moggridge* v. *Thackwell* (1803), 7 Ves. 36 affd. (1807), 13 Ves. 416, H.L.; *Re Willis*, [1921] 1 Ch. 44, C.A. Cf. *Marsh* v. *A.-G.* (1860), 2 John & H. 61.
[20] *Reeve* v. *A.-G.* (1843), 3 Hare 191; *Re Lawton*, [1936] 3 All E.R. 378; *Re Lysaght*, [1965] 2 All E.R. 888; [1966] Ch. 191.
[1] *A.-G.* v. *Coopers' Co.* (1812), 19 Ves. 187.
[2] *Re Campden Charities* (1881), 18 Ch.D. 310, C.A.
[3] E.g. *Re Forbes* (1910), 27 T.L.R. 27; *Re Robinson*, [1923] 2 Ch. 332 (removing "abiding" condition that a black gown should be worn in the pulpit); *Re Dominion Students' Hall Trust*, [1947] Ch. 183 (removing colour bar from trust for Dominion students); *Re Lysaght*, *supra* (removing provision for religious discrimination).
[4] *Per* Buckley J. in *Re Lysaght*, [1965] 2 All E.R. 888, 896; [1966] Ch. 191, 207.

Trusts[5] refused to do so, where the effect would have been to defeat a gift over.

As we have seen, the Commissioners have the same power as the court for establishing a scheme, though generally only on the application of the charity.[6] Where the court directs a scheme for the administration of a charity to be established, the court may refer the matter to the Commissioners for them to prepare or settle a scheme and the court order may direct such scheme to come into effect without further reference to the court.[7] Further, where in the case of a charity, other than an exempt charity, the Commissioners are satisfied that the charity trustees ought to apply for a scheme, but have unreasonably refused or neglected to do so, the Commissioners may apply to the Home Secretary for him to refer the case to them with a view to a scheme, and if, after giving the charity trustees an opportunity to make representations to him, the Home Secretary does so, the Commissioners may proceed accordingly.[8] Their power under this last provision does not, however, enable them to alter the purposes of a charity, unless forty years have elapsed from the date of its foundation.

In addition to the inherent jurisdiction of the court, given concurrently in many cases, as we have seen, by the Act to the Commissioners, the Act provides for an extension of the jurisdiction in four respects:—

i   The inherent jurisdiction of the Court over charities founded by royal charter was limited, though the limits were not altogether clear.[9] Now it is provided[10] that a scheme relating to such a charity or the administration of its property may be made by the court[11] notwithstanding that it cannot take effect without the alteration of the charter. In such case the scheme must be so framed as not to come into effect unless or until Her Majesty thinks fit to make an appropriate amendment to the charter.[12]

ii   The inherent jurisdiction of the court over a charity regulated by statute is also limited in a somewhat similar way to that over charities founded by royal charter.[13] The court[14] has now been given statutory jurisdiction with respect to certain charities relating to allotments, seamen's and regimental funds, and some educational and local charities, by section 15 (3) and the Fourth Schedule.

iii   In the case of other charities regulated by statute, the Commissioners, but not the court, are now empowered,[15] if they consider that a scheme should

---

[5] [1955] 3 All E.R. 874; [1956] Ch. 264.   [6] See pp. 199, 200 *ante*.
[7] Section 18 (2).   [8] Section 18 (6) as yet unused.
[9] *Re Whitworth Art Gallery Trusts*, [1958] 1 All E.R. 176; [1958] Ch. 461; Cf. *Re Royal Society's Charitable Trusts*, [1955] 3 All E.R. 14; [1956] Ch. 87.   [10] Section 15 (1).
[11] Or, in a proper case, by the Commissioners acting under s. 18 (1). The first scheme made by the Commissioners under s. 15 concerned the British Red Cross Society—see Report of the Charity Commissioners for 1965, paras. 22–24. See also their Reports for 1967, paras. 50–56, 1971, paras. 46–51, and 1972, paras. 62–67.
[12] By Order in Council—s. 15 (2).
[13] *London Parochial Charities' Trustees* v. *A.-G.*, [1955] 1 All E.R. 1; *Re Shipwrecked Fishermen and Mariners' Royal Benevolent Society Charity*, [1958] 3 All E.R. 465; [1959] Ch. 220.
[14] And, in a proper case, the Commissioners—s. 18 (1).
[15] By s. 19. The procedure set out in this section also applies where the Commissioners wish to insert some provision in a scheme which otherwise would be beyond their powers, or where in any case it is proper for the scheme to be subject to Parliamentary review. See Reports of the Charity Commissioners for 1967, paras. 57–62, and 1972, paras. 68–74.

be established, to settle a scheme to which effect may be given by order of the Home Secretary made by statutory instrument.[16] The Commissioners can only proceed under these provisions on the like application or like reference from the Home Secretary as would be required if they were proceeding (without an order of the court) under section 18.[17]

iv Temporary *cy-près* scheme. Under section 19 (8) where the Commissioners are satisfied—

"(a) that the whole of the income of a charity cannot in existing circumstances be effectively applied for the purposes of the charity; and

(b) that, if those circumstances continue, a scheme might be made for applying the surplus *cy-près*; and

(c) that it is for any reason not yet desirable to make such a scheme"

they may authorise the trustees to apply a limited[18] amount of income for any purposes for which it might be made applicable by a *cy-près* scheme.

b Common investment funds

It is a frequent occurrence for a single body of trustees, particularly of a large charity, to hold and administer a number of separate funds associated with the main charity, each fund being held on separate (though possibly similar or even identical) trusts, and legally constituting a separate charity. Before the Charities Act 1960 the funds of such separate trusts had in general to be kept separate, even though held by the same trustees and held on similar trusts.   Exceptionally particular statutes[19] authorised particular bodies to amalgamate various trust funds held by them and to administer the amalgam as a single fund, and the court and the Commissioners sometimes made schemes, known as pooling schemes, to the like effect, but this was only possible where the separate trusts were administered by a single body of trustees.[1] Section 22 of the Act now authorises the court or the Commissioners, where two or more bodies of trustees wish to unite in pooling the endowments of the charities which they administer, to make and bring into effect schemes for the establishment of common investment funds under trusts which provide—

"(a) for property transferred to the fund by or on behalf of a charity participating in the scheme to be invested under the control of trustees appointed to manage the fund; and

(b) for the participating charities to be entitled . . . to the capital and income of the fund in shares determined by reference to the amount or value of the property transferred to it by or on behalf of each of them and to the value of the fund at the time of the transfers."

---

[16] The most recent are S.I. 1968 Nos. 1692 and 1694, S.I. 1971 Nos. 805 and 1982, S.I. 1972 No. 163 and S.I. 1973 Nos. 169 and 196.

[17] See pp. 199, 200, 212, *ante*.

[18] Up to £300 income accrued before the date of the order and up to £100 out of income accruing in each of the next three years.

[19] E.g. Liverpool University Act 1931; Universities and Colleges (Trusts) Act 1943 (Oxford and Cambridge universities and colleges therein, and Winchester College); Birmingham University Act 1948. Cf. Administration of Justice Act 1965 and S.I. 1965 No. 1467 as regards money in court.

[1] *Re Royal Society's Charitable Trusts*, [1955] 3 All E.R. 14; [1956] Ch. 87.

Such a scheme may involve the appointment of an entirely distinct body of trustees to manage the pooled endowments. A common investment scheme may be made on the application of any two or more charities[2]—it will be remembered that for the purposes of the Act each separate trust fund is a separate charity,[3] even where the trustees are the same persons[4]—and the scheme may make provision for, and for all matters connected with, the establishment, investment, management and winding up of the common investment fund. It may provide for a charity to deposit sums on such terms as to repayment and interest as may be set out in the scheme. The assets of the common invest- ment fund may, under the scheme, be vested in the Official Custodian who, if the scheme is made by the Commissioners or if they consent, may also be appointed as managing trustee with the same powers, duties and liabilities as other managing trustees. Where the scheme provides for the Official Custodian to exercise any discretion with respect to the investment of the fund, it must also provide for him to have competent advice. The common investment fund is itself deemed for all purposes to be a charity, and the assets of the fund are normally treated for the purposes of the Act as a permanent endowment. However, if the scheme establishing the fund admits to participation only charities not having a permanent endowment, the fund is treated as a charity not having a permanent endowment; and if the scheme admits only exempt charities, the fund is an exempt charity for the purposes of the Act.[5]

Since the decision in *Re University of London Charitable Trusts*[6] it has become the practice for the ordinary pooling scheme, as used before the Act, where a single body of trustees is administering a number of trusts, to be drafted as a common investment fund scheme under s. 22, and this will readily be done whenever it is shown to be useful.[7] As regards common investment fund schemes involving two or more bodies of trustees, up to the end of 1963 only three schemes had been made, and the Commissioners have indicated that they will not be willing to make such schemes unless there is some nexus, either geographical or functional, between the participating charities.[8] One of these three schemes is of more general interest. It set up what is known as the Charities Official Investment Fund,[9] and any charity[10] may participate in this fund, but only in respect of property held by the Official Custodian for Charities. Property may, however, be vested in the Official Custodian or with his consent transferred to him specifically for the purpose of enabling the charity to participate.

---

[2] All charities have power to participate in common investment schemes, unless expressly excluded by the trust instrument—s. 22 (8).
[3] See Chapter 6, Section 2i, pp. 194, 195, *ante*.
[4] *Re University of London Charitable Trusts*, [1963] 3 All E.R. 859; [1964] Ch. 282.
[5] Section 22 (9).
[6] *Supra*.
[7] See the Report of the Charity Commissioners for 1963, para. 47.
[8] Reports of the Charity Commissioners for 1962 and 1963, paras. 48 and 46 respectively.
[9] The scheme is set out in Appendix B to the Report of the Charity Commissioners for 1962.
[10] Subject to the qualification set out in n. 2 *supra*.

4 THE CY-PRÈS DOCTRINE

a General position[11]

In the case of a private trust, if the trust fails the beneficial interest results to the settlor or testator.[12] This may be the position also in the case of a charitable trust, though in practice the trust property is commonly saved for charity by the *cy-près* doctrine. Where this doctrine applies, even though the particular charitable trust fails, the trust property is applied for other charitable purposes *cy-près*, that is as near as possible,[13] to the original purposes which cannot be carried out. The procedure is for the establishment of a scheme by the court or the Commissioners.[14] There are one, and often two, conditions that have to be satisfied in order for the doctrine to apply, and these, as affected by the relevant provisions of the Charities Act 1960, are considered below. The Act now imposes a statutory duty on the trustee of a charitable trust to take steps, in an appropriate case, for trust property to be applied *cy-près*.[15]

Before considering the *cy-près* doctrine in detail, one particular situation should be mentioned. Where before the Perpetuities and Accumulations Act 1964, there was a gift to charity for a limited period only, the period at the end of the undisposed interest resulted to the grantor, notwithstanding the grantor had in fact purported to make some disposition over, if this was void for perpetuity. There was no case for *cy-près* application.[16] There is still no case for *cy-près* application, and there will still be a resulting trust, unless the case falls within s. 12 of the Perpetuities and Accumulations Act 1964, which provides that if and when it appears that the event which might cause the interest to determine must occur, if at all, outside the perpetuity period ascertained in accordance with the Act, the resulting trust becomes void and the determinable interest becomes absolute,[17] whether or not it is followed by a gift over.

b Impossibility or impracticability

Before the Act the rule was that *cy-près* application was only possible where it was impossible or impracticable to carry out the declared trust. The rule

---

[11] For a review of recent cases in other common law jurisdictions see (1972), 1 A.-A.L.R. 101 (L. A. Sheridan).

[12] See Chapter 4, Section 3, p. 115, *ante*.

[13] *Re Prison Charities* (1873), L.R. 61 Eq. 129; but the *cy-près* application may still be made even though there is no possible object closely resembling the one that has failed—*A.-G.* v. *Ironmongers Co.* (1841), Cr. & Ph. 208 affd. (1844), 10 Cl. & Fin. 908, H.L.

[14] Generally the Commissioners—s. 28 (2) and (3) discussed at p. 206, *ante*.

[15] Section 13 (5). The existence of the duty was previously proclaimed by Lord Simonds in *National Anti-Vivisection Society* v. *I.R.Comrs.*, [1947] 2 All E.R. 217, at p. 238; [1948] A.C. 31, at p. 74, H.L.

[16] *Re Randell* (1888), 38 Ch.D. 213; *Re Blunt's Trusts*, [1904] 2 Ch. 767; *Re Cooper's Conveyance Trusts*, [1956] 3 All E.R. 28; Contrast *Re Bowen*, [1893] 2 Ch. 491; *Re Peel's Release*, [1921] 2 Ch. 218, and see (1961), 25 Con. 56 (J. D. Davies).

[17] See (1964), 80 L.Q.R. 486, 527 (Morris and Wade). The resulting trust or possibility of reverter will still be valid if the determining event in fact happens within the perpetuity period and the same would be true of an express gift over.

covered both the case where the declared trust was initially impossible,[18] and the case of supervening impossibility,[19] and also cases where there was a surplus of funds after the particular charitable purpose had been fulfilled.[20] Although impossibility and impracticability were generously construed,[1] the court had no jurisdiction to apply *cy-près* so long as any lawful object of the testator's bounty was available, however inexpedient such object might appear to the court as compared with other objects, and Romilly M.R. has pointed out[2] that in several cases the court had considered itself bound to carry into effect "charities of the most useless description".

The old rule[3] has been considerably modified by section 13 (1) of the Charities Act 1960, which provides that, subject to any other necessary conditions being fulfilled, *cy-près* application may be directed in any of five sets of circumstances, namely:—

"(*a*) where the original purposes,[4] in whole or in part—
  (i) have been as far as may be fulfilled; or
  (ii) cannot be carried out, or not according to the directions given and to the spirit of the gift;

(*b*) where the original purposes provide a use for part only of the property available by virtue of the gift; or

(*c*) where the property available by virtue of the gift and other property applicable for similar purposes can be more effectively used in conjunction, and to that end can suitably, regard being had to the spirit of the gift, be made applicable to common purposes; or

(*d*) where the original purposes were laid down by reference to an area which then was but has since ceased to be a unit for some other purpose, or by reference to a class of persons or to an area which has for any reason since ceased to be suitable, regard being had to the spirit of the gift, or to be practical in administering the gift; or

(*e*) where the original purposes, in whole or in part, have, since they were laid down—
  (i) been adequately provided for by other means[5]; or

---

[18] E.g. *Biscoe* v. *Jackson* (1887), 35 Ch.D. 460, C.A.—trust to establish a soup kitchen and cottage hospital in Shoreditch, but no land available for the purpose. An unusual case of initial impracticability was *Re Lysaght*, [1965] 2 All E.R. 888; [1966] Ch. 191, where insistence on the provision for religious discrimination would have resulted in the trustee disclaiming the trusteeship. This would have occasioned complete failure of the trust as it was the exceptional case where the trust was conditional on acceptance of the office by the named trustee.

[19] E.g. *A.-G.,* v. *Ironmongers' Co.* (1841), Cr. & Ph. 208 affd. (1844), 10 Cl. & Fin. 908, H.L.—trust for redemption of Barbary slaves.

[20] *Re Monk,* [1927] 2 Ch. 197, C.A.; *Re North Devon and West Somerset Relief Fund Trusts,* [1953] 2 All E.R. 1032; *Re Raine,* [1956] 1 All E.R. 355; [1956] Ch. 417.

[1] E.g. *Re Dominion Students' Hall Trust,* [1947] Ch. 183 (removing colour bar from trust for Dominion students).

[2] In *Philpott* v. *St. George's Hospital* (1859), 27 Beav. 107, at p. 111; *Re Weir Hospital,* [1910] 2 Ch. 124, C.A.

[3] There were limited relaxations of this rule even before the 1960 Act under various statutes, in particular as to educational charities under the Endowed Schools Act 1869. These limited provisions have now been repealed.

[4] Where the application of the trust property has been altered or regulated by a scheme or otherwise, "original purposes" means the purposes for which the property is for the time being applicable—s. 13 (3).

[5] E.g. where the object of the charity has become the statutory responsibility of the central or local government authorities.

(ii) ceased, as being useless or harmful to the community or for other reasons, to be in law charitable; or

(iii) ceased <u>in any other way</u> to provide a suitable and effective method of using the property available by virtue of the gift, regard being had to the spirit of the gift."

The court is also given a limited power to enlarge the area of a charity's operations, without any need to show that any of the above conditions are fulfilled.[6] There has been little authority on this section, but it was held in *Re Lepton's Will Trusts*[7] that, in relation to a trust for payment of a fixed annual sum out of the income of a fund to charity A and payment of the residue of that income to charity B, the "original purposes" referred to in the section should be construed as referring to the trust as a whole.

As we shall see, it might have been important under the old law to know whether the case was one of initial or supervening impossibility, and cases of initial impossibility must now, it seems, for the same reason be distinguished from other *cy-près* occasions.[8] Suppose a testator gave a fund to trustees on trust for an individual for life, and then to found a defined institution of a charitable nature, and that at the date of the testator's death the fund would have been adequate to carry out the charitable purpose, but was inadequate when the life tenant died say thirty years later. Would this be a case of initial impossibility? The cases on the old law, which are presumably still applicable, decide that the question of initial impossibility or impracticability must be determined as at the time when the gift was made, not when it falls into possession so far as charity is concerned, i.e., in the case of a gift by will, on the death of the testator. The proper inquiry, in the case of a gift by will, is, therefore, whether at the date of the death of the testator it was practicable to carry the intentions of the testator into effect or whether at that date there was any reasonable prospect that it would be practicable to do so at some future time. If there is a negative answer to both parts of this inquiry, it is a case of initial impossibility or impracticability.[9] If there is a vested gift to charity which is not only to take effect at some future time but is also liable to be defeated on the happening of some event such as the birth of issue to the person holding a life interest, an inquiry as to its practicability should be approached on the footing that the gift will not be defeated, but will take effect at some future time in possession.[10]

c General charitable intention

We must now turn to consider the distinction which used to be drawn between initial and supervening impossibility, and which now seems to exist between initial impossibility and other *cy-près* occasions.[11] In the case of initial impossibility or impracticability the general rule was and is that *cy-près* applica-

---

[6] Section 13 (4) and Sched. 3, as amended by Local Government Act 1972, s. 210 (9) (*f*).
[7] [1971] 1 All E.R. 799; [1972] Ch. 276.
[8] Section 13 (2).
[9] *Re Moon's Will Trusts*, [1948] 1 All E.R. 300; *Re Wright*, [1954] 2 All E.R. 98; [1954] Ch. 347, C.A.; *Re White's Will Trusts*, [1954] 2 All E.R. 620; [1955] Ch. 188.
[10] *Re Tacon*, [1958] 1 All E.R. 163; [1958] Ch. 447, C.A.—but different considerations may be applicable to the case of a strictly contingent gift, *per* Evershed M.R. at 166, 454.
[11] Charities Act 1960, s. 13 (2).

tion is only permitted if a paramount intention of charity on the part of the donor is established. The classic statement of the law is contained in the judgment of Parker J. in *Re Wilson*,[12] where he said the authorities were to be divided into two classes. "First of all," he said, "we have a class of cases where, in form, the gift is given for a particular charitable purpose, but it is possible, taking the will as a whole, to say that, notwithstanding the form of the gift, the paramount intention, according to the true construction of the will, is to give the property in the first instance for a general charitable purpose rather than a particular charitable purpose, and to graft on to the general gift a direction as to the desires or intentions of the testator as to the manner in which the general gift is to be carried into effect." If this is the proper construction and the particular purpose is initially impossible, the gift will be applied *cy-près*.[13] "Then," he continued, "there is the second class of cases, where, on the true construction of the will, no such paramount general intention can be inferred, and where the gift, being in form a particular gift—a gift for a particular purpose— and it being impossible to carry out that particular purpose, the whole gift is held to fail."[14] It may be observed that there is some authority for thinking that where the whole of residue is given for a particular charitable purpose or purposes which fail in whole or in part, the court will need very little, if any, further indication to draw the inference of a general charitable intention.[15]

The position of the anonymous donor, such as the man who puts his contribution into a collecting box on a flag day, was discussed in several cases shortly before the passing of the Charities Act 1960.[16] Now, however, s. 14 (1) of the Act provides, with retrospective effect,[17] that

"Property given for specific charitable purposes which fail shall be applicable *cy-près* as if given for charitable purposes generally, where it belongs—
(a) to a donor who, after such advertisements and inquiries as are reasonable,[18] cannot be identified or cannot be found; or
(b) to a donor who has executed a written disclaimer of his right to have the property returned."

Further subsection (2) provides that—

"For the purposes of this section property shall be conclusively presumed (without any advertisement or inquiry) to belong to donors who cannot be identified, in so far as it consists—
(a) of the proceeds of cash collections made by means of collecting boxes or by other means not adapted for distinguishing one gift from another; or

---

[12] [1913] 1 Ch. 314, at 320, 321. See [1957] C.L.J. 87 (J. C. Hall) who observes that the meaning of the phrase "general charitable intention" is obscure and its application extremely difficult.

[13] *Biscoe* v. *Jackson* (1887), 35 Ch.D. 460, C.A.; *Re Hillier*, [1954] 2 All E.R. 59, C.A.; *Re Lysaght*, [1965] 2 All E.R. 888; [1966] Ch. 191.

[14] *Re Good's Will Trusts*, [1950] 2 All E.R. 653; *Re Ulverston and District New Hospital Building Fund*, [1956] 3 All E.R. 164; [1956] Ch. 622, C.A.

[15] *Re Raine*, [1956] 1 All E.R. 355; [1956] Ch. 417; *Re Griffiths* (1958), unreported, but cited in *Re Roberts*, [1963] 1 All E.R. at p. 680. See (1956), 72 L.Q.R. 170 (R. E. Megarry).

[16] See e.g. *Re Hillier*, *supra*; *Re Ulverston and District New Hospital Building Fund*, *supra*; *Re Gillingham Bus Disaster Fund*, [1958] 1 All E.R. 37; [1958] Ch. 300, affd., [1958] 2 All E.R. 749; [1959] Ch. 62, C.A., but no appeal on this point. See (1957), 20 M.L.R. 61 (G. H. Jones). Cf. *Re West Sussex Constabulary's Widows, Children and Benevolent (1930) Fund Trusts*, [1970] 1 All E.R. 544; [1971] Ch. 1.

[17] Charities Act 1960, s. 14 (7).

[18] *Re Henry Wood National Memorial Trusts*, [1967] 1 All E.R. 238.

(b) of the proceeds of any lottery, competition, entertainment, sale or similar money-raising activity, after allowing for property given to provide prizes or articles for sale or otherwise to enable the activity to be undertaken."

and under subsection (3)—

"The court may by order direct that property not falling within subsection (2) above shall for the purposes of this section be treated (without any advertisement or inquiry) as belonging to donors who cannot be identified, where it appears to the court either—

(a) that it would be unreasonable, having regard to the amounts likely to be returned to the donors, to incur expense with a view to returning the property; or

(b) that it would be unreasonable, having regard to the nature, circumstances and amount of the gifts, and to the lapse of time since the gifts were made, for the donors to expect the property to be returned."

Provision is made for a donor who cannot be identified or found to recover any part of his gift applied cy-près under these provisions, within twelve months after the date of the scheme, except in a case to which subsection (2) or (3) applies.

The first case in which the Commissioners used their powers under s. 14 concerned the Mile End Memorial Hall Fund.[19] It is a useful illustration of how these provisions work in practice. The facts were that a fund had been opened in 1945 to provide a memorial hall at Mile End but it was clear in 1964 that the trusts had failed for the fund then amounted to only £372. Of this £346 had been raised by whist drives, dances and concerts and the balance of £26 represented the subscription of 63 subscribers. A public meeting was held to discuss the fund, at which it was agreed to apply it to the extension of a war memorial and a church hall, objects which the Commissioners considered satisfactory under the cy-près doctrine. By virtue of s. 14 (2) (b) there was no difficulty as regarded the £346, but 62 of the 63 subscribers could be traced and so could not come under s. 14 (1) (a). These persons were invited to execute a written disclaimer so as to bring their subscriptions within s. 14 (1) (b). Only one of these persons desired the return of his subscription (which was, of course, returned) and the remainder could also be applied cy-près. The final result was a cy-près scheme allowing the trustees to use the money as proposed, subject to a provision for the retention of a small sum for twelve months to cover a possible claim by the one subscriber who could not be identified or found.

On cy-près occasions other than initial impossibility, it is not necessary to show a paramount intention of charity. Once money is effectually dedicated to charity in perpetuity, whether in pursuance of a general or a particular charitable intent, the testator's next of kin or residuary legatees are for ever excluded and no question of subsequent failure can affect the matter so far as they are concerned. It is a case for cy-près application.[20] There are, however, some cases dealing with surpluses after the particular charitable purpose has been fulfilled which apparently decide that in such cases a general charitable intention must be established in order to authorise cy-près application.[21]

---

[19] Reported in the Report of the Charity Commissioners for 1965, paras. 19, 20, 21.

[20] *Re Peel's Release*, [1921] 2 Ch. 218; *Re Wokingham Fire Brigade Trusts*, [1951] 1 All E.R. 454; [1951] Ch. 873; *Re British School of Egyptian Archaeology*, [1954] 1 All E.R. 887; *Re Wright*, [1954] 2 All E.R. 98; [1954] Ch. 347, C.A.; *Re Tacon*, [1958] 1 All E.R. 163; [1958] Ch. 447, C.A.

[21] *Re Welsh Hospital (Netley) Fund*, [1921] 1 Ch. 655; *Re North Devon & West Somerset Relief Fund Trusts*, [1953] 2 All E.R. 1032.

d Gifts to specified charitable institutions which cease to exist or have never existed

There are three different situations which must be considered in turn—

(i) *Gift to a specified charitable institution which once existed, but ceased to exist before the death of the testator.*[22] *Prima facie* the gift lapses in the same way as if it had been a gift to an individual. Thus in *Re Rymer*[1] there was a legacy "to the rector for the time being of St. Thomas's Seminary for the education of priests in the diocese of Westminster for the purposes of such seminary". Shortly before the testator's death the Seminary had been closed, the buildings sold, and the students transferred to another seminary near Birmingham. It was held that the legacy lapsed and fell into residue. However, as Wilberforce J. observed in *Re Roberts*,[2] "the position is that the courts have gone very far in the decided cases to resist the conclusion that a legacy to a charitable institution lapses, and a number of very refined arguments have been found acceptable with a view to avoiding that conclusion". In practice much depends on difficult and debatable questions of construction, and the courts may not infrequently be thought to have adopted a somewhat strained construction of the testator's words in order to reach the desired result.

(a) First, there may be no lapse because although the specified institution may apparently have disappeared the charity may be held not to have ceased to exist. *Re Faraker*[3] is the leading case in a series of decisions[4] which have established that so long as there are funds held in trust for the purposes of a charity the charity continues in existence and is not destroyed by any alteration in its constitution, name or objects made in accordance with law, or even by amalgamation with another charity. The vital point seems to be that there is a fund in existence for ever dedicated to charity. The *Re Faraker*[5] principle is readily applied where the gift is construed as a gift to augment the funds of the named charity and there is no difficulty where, as is common, the charity was founded as a perpetual charity which no-one has power to terminate. Where, however, a charitable organisation was founded, not as a perpetual charity, but as one liable to termination, and its constitution provided for the disposal of its funds in that event, then if the organisation has determined and its funds have been disposed of, the charity has ceased to exist and there is nothing to prevent the operation of the doctrine of lapse.[6] There is, however, some doubts as to whether the principle was properly applied in *Re Vernon's Will Trusts*,[7] a case of an incorporated charity which had been dissolved, where its work was being

---

[22] See generally (1969), 32 M.L.R. 283 (J. B. E. Hutton); (1972), 36 Con. 198 (R. B. M. Cotterrell).

[1] [1895] 1 Ch. 19, C.A. (a decision which has not received much favour in the courts *per* Wilberforce J. in *Re Roberts*, [1963] 1 All E.R. 674, at p. 681); *Re Tacon*, [1958] 1 All E.R. 163; [1958] Ch. 447, C.A.; *Re Slatter's Will Trusts*, [1964] 2 All E.R. 469.

[2] *Supra*, at p. 678.

[3] [1912] 2 Ch. 488, C.A.

[4] Including *Re Lucas* [1948] 2 All E.R. 22; [1948] Ch. 424, C.A.; *Re Bagshaw*, [1954] 1 All E.R. 227; *Re Roberts*, *supra*: *Re Slatter's Will Trusts*, *supra*, noted (1964), 28 Con. 313 (J. T. Farrard); see also *Re Hutchinson's Will Trusts*, [1953] 1 All E.R. 996; [1953] Ch. 387.

[5] *Supra*, C.A.

[6] *Re Stemson's Will Trusts*, [1969] 2 All E.R. 517; [1970] 1 Ch. 16; *Re Finger's Will Trusts*, [1971] 3 All E.R. 1050; [1972] Ch. 286.

[7] Decided in 1962 but not reported until [1971] 3 All E.R. 1061 n; [1972] Ch. 300, see *Re Finger's Will Trusts*, *supra* at pp. 1057; 295.

carried on by another body in unbroken continuance of the work originally conducted by the dissolved charity. The funds of the incorporated charity had, however, vested in the Ministry of Health under the National Health Service Act 1946 free from any trusts, and accordingly the funds had ceased to be dedicated to charity.

(b) Secondly, the gift may be construed as a gift for the purposes of the specified institution. It is well established that a gift for a particular purpose will lapse if the particular purpose has ceased to exist before the death of the testator[8] on a similar principle to that applied in *Re Rymer*.[9] *Re Lucas*[10] is an interesting illustration. There the main object of "The Huddersfield Home for Crippled Children" was to provide a holiday home for poor crippled children in leasehold premises at Lindley Moor given by the benefactor. On the expiry of the lease the home was closed. No other premises were acquired, and ultimately a *cy-près* scheme was made under which the modest funds held by the trustees were to be applied in sending poor crippled children to holiday or convalescent homes. At first instance it was held that a legacy given to the Home after it had in fact been closed was to be construed as a gift for the upkeep of the particular holiday home at Lindley Moor. After the closure of the home it was impossible to carry out this purpose, and it was accordingly held that the legacy lapsed. On appeal the decision was reversed but, as the Court of Appeal made clear, only because it took a different view on the question of construction. The Court of Appeal was only able to hold the legacy good because it construed the gift as one in augmentation of the funds of the Home. On this construction it was held that the principle of *Re Faraker*[11] applied to save the gift.

In practice, charitable purposes are not easily destroyed and may continue, thus giving no occasion for lapse, notwithstanding the fact that the original organisation or machinery for carrying out those purposes no longer exists.[12] This approach was used in several cases[13] in relation to gifts to hospitals taken over by the Minister of Health under the National Health Service Act 1946 between the date of the will and the date of death. The courts commonly held that the gift was to be construed as being for the work previously carried on by the hospital, and where the work was now being carried on by the appropriate Hospital Management Committee, directed payment to the Committee on trust to apply the money for the purposes of the particular hospital which was the object of the testator's bounty.

(c) Next, the two approaches in (a) and (b) above must be looked at in the light of the general statement made by Buckley J. in *Re Vernon's Will Trusts*[14] as to the principles to be applied to gifts to unincorporated charities on the one hand and corporate charities on the other. He expressed the logical view that every gift to an unincorporated charity must take effect as a gift for the purpose which the charity exists to serve. Such a gift will not fail for want of a trustee, and effect will be given to it by way of scheme notwith-

---

8 *Re Wilson*, [1913] 1 Ch. 314; *Re Tacon, supra*; *Re Slatter's Will Trusts*, [1964] 2 All E.R. 469; [1964] Ch. 512 noted (1964), 28 Con. 313 (J. T. Farrand).
9 *Supra*, C.A.
10 *Supra*, C.A.
11 *Supra*, C.A.
12 *Re Watt*, [1932] 2 Ch. 243 n; *Re Morrison* (1967), 111 Sol. Jo. 758.
13 E.g. *Re Morgan's Will Trusts*, [1950] 1 All E.R. 1097; [1950] Ch. 637; *Re Meyers*, [1951] 1 All E.R. 538; [1951] Ch. 534. The courts seem to have construed the purposes of the hospitals in these cases as that of carrying on their work on the particular premises, and this construction accordingly could not have saved a gift where the premises had ceased to be used for hospital work—*Re Hutchinson's Will Trusts*, [1953] 1 All E.R. 996; [1953] Ch. 387. See also *Re Little*, [1953] 2 All E.R. 852 where the same approach prevailed in a gift to a hospital for particular purposes.
14 [1971] 3 All E.R. 1061, n.; [1972] Ch. 300.

standing the disappearance of the charity in the lifetime of the testator,[15] unless there is something positive to show that the continued existence of the donee was essential to the gift. In the case of a gift to a corporate charity, however, Buckley J. said that there is simply a gift to the corporate body beneficially, which will lapse if that body ceases to exist before the death of the testator, unless there is positive evidence that that body took on trust for charitable purposes.

Re Vernon's Will Trusts[16] was adopted by Goff J. in Re Finger's Will Trusts.[17] In that case questions arose over two shares of residue, one given to the National Radium Commission, an unincorporated charity, and the other to the National Council for Maternity and Child Welfare, a corporate charity. Both charities had been dissolved between the date of the will and the date of death. Applying the above principles it was held that the gift to the unincorporated charity, the National Radium Commission did not fail. It was a purpose trust for the work of the commission, which was not dependent on the continued existence of the named charitable organisation. The charitable purposes of the commission could still be carried out and the appropriate share of residue was accordingly applicable under a scheme. The gift of the share to the corporate charity however failed, for the will did not show an intention that the gift should be held on trust for the purposes of the charity. It was an absolute gift to a corporate body which had ceased to exist before the death of the testatrix. This gift could not be claimed by the National Association for Maternity and Child Welfare, to which the Council had transferred its funds on its dissolution and which to all intents and purposes carried on the work of the Council. As will be seen later, the failure of the gift to the Council gave rise to the further question whether the share should pass on intestacy or was applicable cy-près.

The law as stated in Re Vernon's Will Trusts[16] and Re Finger's Will Trusts[17] is not without its difficulties—Goff J. in the latter case himself pointed out that the distinction between corporate and unincorporate charities produces anomalies. One such anomaly had appeared in Re Meyers,[18] and an absurd result had only been avoided by reliance on the special context in the will. In that case there were legacies to both unincorporate and corporate hospitals, all of which had been taken over by the Ministry of Health under the 1946 Act. There was no difficulty in construing the legacies to the unincorporate hospitals as gifts for the purposes of the work they carried on, and on that construction, as we have seen under (b) above they were valid. Prima facie, however, the gifts to the corporate hospitals were gifts to them beneficially (and not for the purposes of the work they carried on) and should accordingly lapse. Such a result, the judge observed, would be contrary to common sense and would produce an unacceptable difference between the gifts to corporate and unincorporate hospitals. On the true construction of that particular will he felt able to decide that the legacies were given to the corporate hospitals for the purposes of the work they carried on, and should go to the appropriate hospital management committees on trust to apply it for those purposes.

The main difficulty, however, it is submitted, lies in the proposition, as stated by Buckley J.,[19] that "if the gift [to an unincorporated charity] is to be permitted to take effect at all, it must be a bequest for a purpose, i.e. that charitable purpose which the named charity exists to serve." A gift to an unincorporate charity, it would seem to follow, must always be a gift for its purposes as under (b) above. Both the Re Rymer[20]

---

[15] In restating this proposition in Re Finger's Will Trusts, [1971] 3 All E.R. 1050; [1972] Ch. 286. Goff J. added the proviso that the work was still being carried on. In principle it would seem sufficient for the purpose to be capable of being carried out.

[16] [1971] 3 All E.R. 1061 n.; [1972] Ch. 300.

[17] Supra. The facts as stated below have been slightly simplified.

[18] [1951] 1 All E.R. 538; [1951] Ch. 534.

[19] In Re Vernon's Will Trusts, supra, at p. 1064; 303.

[20] [1895] 1 Ch. 19, C.A.

and *Re Faraker*[21] lines of cases, however, appear to assume the possibility of a gift to a charity (including an unincorporated charity) as distinct from a gift to a charitable purpose. A case which appears to raise the difficulty squarely, but which was not apparently referred to in either *Re Vernon's Will Trusts*,[22] or *Re Finger's Will Trusts*[1] is *Re Bagshaw*.[2] Here there was a legacy to the Bakewell and District War Memorial Cottage Hospital, the correct name of an unincorporated charity. Between the date of the will and the date of death the hospital run by the charity had been taken over under the National Health Service Act 1946 and was now carried on by the defendant Hospital Management Committee. The charity had changed its name to the Bakewell and District 1914–18 War Memorial Charity and also changed its purposes. On the basis of the principles laid down in *Re Vernon's Will Trusts*[22] and *Re Finger's Will Trusts*[1] one should, it seems, construe the legacy as a gift for the purposes of the work being carried on in the hospital buildings at the date of the will. The work was in fact being continued on the same premises by the appropriate hospital management committee. On the posited basis one would expect the legacy to be payable to the hospital management committee as explained in (b) above. Such an argument was put forward but failed. It was held that this was a gift to the charity correctly described by the testatrix as the Bakewell and District War Memorial Cottage Hospital. It was further held that the principle of *Re Faraker*[3] applied and that the legacy was accordingly payable to the Bakewell and District 1914–18 War Memorial Charity for its general purposes.

(d) Lastly, if the gift would otherwise fail, it may be possible to apply the *cy-près* doctrine. The non-existence of the specified charity at the date of death is treated as a case of initial impossibility, and the gift will be applied *cy-près*, provided a general charitable intention can be established. In *Re Harwood*[4] it was said to be very difficult to find such an intention where a testator had selected a particular charity and taken some care to identify it. Though difficult, it depends on the circumstances and is not impossible, as is shown by *Re Finger's Will Trusts*.[5] In that case, as we have seen,[6] the bequest of a share of residue to the National Council for Maternity and Child Welfare failed. Taking account of the facts that virtually the whole estate was dedicated to charitable purposes, that the Council had been mainly, if not exclusively, a co-ordinating body, and that the testatrix regarded herself as having no relatives, the judge found a general charitable intention and directed *cy-près* application.

(ii) *Specified institution in existence at the death of the testator but ceasing to exist before the gift becomes payable or is in fact paid over.* In this case there is no lapse and the testator's next of kin or residuary legatees are for ever excluded.[7] The property will be applied to charity, though it is not clear whether the correct view is that it falls to be administered by the Crown, who in practice applies it to analogous charitable purposes,[8] or that it is a case of *cy-près* application by the court.[9]

(iii) *Gift to what appears to be a specified charitable institution, but which it turns out has never existed.* This is, in effect, a case of initial impossibility and a class of

---

[21] [1912] 2 Ch. 488, C.A.   [22] [1971] 3 All E.R. 1061 n.; [1972] Ch. 300.
[1] [1971] 3 All E.R. 1050; [1972] Ch. 286.
[2] [1954] 1 All E.R. 227.
[3] *Supra*, C.A.
[4] [1936] Ch. 285; [1935] All E.R. Rep. 918 (Gift to the Wisbech Peace Society, Cambridge).
[5] *Supra*.
[6] *Supra*, p. 222.
[7] *Re Slevin*, [1891] 2 Ch. 236, C.A.; *Re Soley* (1900), 17 T.L.R. 118; *Re Tacon*, *supra*.
[8] *Re Slevin*, *supra*.
[9] *Re Soley*, *supra*; *Re Tacon*, *supra*.

case, moreover, in which the court will lean in favour of a general charitable purpose, and will accept even a small indication of the testator's intention as sufficient to show that a gift for a charitable purpose and not a particular charitable body was intended.[10] Harman L.J. once declared[11] that the court has leaned so far over in this sort of case that it has become almost prone, and, expressing his preference for an upright posture, he held that there was no general charitable intention in a case of this kind, where residue was also given to charity, for this would be to favour one charity against another. There may be other circumstances in the will which may negative the existence of a general charitable intention and thus prevent a *cy-près* application.[12]

It is respectfully submitted that Harman L.J.'s preference for an upright posture showed some weakening in *Re Satterthwaite's Will Trusts*,[13] where, simplifying the facts slightly, residue was to be divided equally between an anti-vivisection society (not in law charitable), seven animal charities and the "London Animal Hospital". None of the claimants was able to establish a claim to this last share,[14] which it was held must be applied *cy-près*, the Court finding a general charitable intention in the dispositions of residue notwithstanding that "one-ninth of residue was given to an anti-vivisection society which in law—unknown to the average testator—is not charitable".[15] In *Re Jenkins' Will Trusts*,[16] heard after *Re Satterthwaite's Will Trusts*[17] had been decided but before it had been reported, a one-seventh share of residue was given to an anti-vivisection society expressly to be used for non-charitable purposes, and the other six one-seventh shares to animal charities. The gift of the one-seventh share to the anti-vivisection society was held to fail as being impressed with a non-charitable purpose, and Buckley J. held that he could not find a general charitable intention in the residuary gift so as to enable him to apply this one-seventh share *cy-près*. As he put it[18]:

> "If you meet seven men with black hair and one with red hair, you are not entitled to say that there are eight men with black hair. In finding one gift for a non-charitable purpose among a number of gifts for charitable purposes, the court cannot infer that the testator or testatrix meant the non-charitable gift to take effect as a charitable gift when in its terms it is not charitable, even though the non-charitable gift may have a close relation to the purposes for which the charitable gifts are made."

It is not easy to distinguish this decision convincingly from *Re Satterthwaite's Will Trusts*.[19]

---

[10] *Re Davis*, [1902] 1 Ch. 876; *Re Harwood*, [1936] Ch. 285; [1935] All E.R. Rep. 918. Similarly if there are two or more possible claimants, but the one intended by the testator cannot be identified—*Re Songest*, [1956] 2 All E.R. 765, C.A.; *Re Conroy* (1973), 35 D.L.R. (3d) 752.

[11] *Re Goldschmidt*, [1957] 1 All E.R. 513, 514; (1957) 73 L.Q.R. 166.

[12] *Re Tharp*, [1942] 2 All E.R. 358.

[13] [1966] 1 All E.R. 919, C.A.

[14] It is submitted that there is much to be said for the claim of the third defendant as being *persona designata*.

[15] *Re Satterthwaite's Will Trusts*, *supra*, per Russell L.J. at p. 925.

[16] [1966] 1 All E.R. 926; [1966] Ch. 249.

[17] *Supra*. It is strange that this case was apparently not referred to in *Re Jenkins' Will Trusts* as the same person was counsel for the Attorney-General in both cases.

[18] *Re Jenkins' Will Trusts*, *supra*, at pp. 929; 256.   [19] *Supra*.

5 DEALINGS WITH CHARITY PROPERTY

Certain dealings with charity property are to a greater or lesser extent invalidated, unless an order of the court or of the Commissioners is first obtained, by section 29 of the Charities Act, 1960. Subsection (1) provides that no property forming part of the permanent endowment[20] of a charity shall, without such order,[21] be mortgaged or charged by way of security for the repayment of money borrowed, nor, in the case of land in England or Wales, be sold, leased, or otherwise disposed of. Decisions on previous legislation[22] suggest that a purported transaction made without the necessary order is void, not merely voidable,[1] and that the order must be obtained before the contract for the dealing is entered into and not merely before it is completed.[2]

The provisions of subsection (1) are extended by subsection (2) to any land which is held by or in trust for a charity and is or has at any time been occupied for the purposes of the charity, which is sometimes called "functional land". A dealing in functional land which is not part of the permanent endowment of a charity is, however, notwithstanding the absence of an order, valid in favour of a person who then or afterwards in good faith acquires an interest in or charge on the land for money or money's worth.

Section 29 provides for two classes of exceptions where no order is necessary —first certain types of dealings by any charity, and secondly, any type of dealings by certain charities. The first class of exceptions is set out in subsection (3), namely—

"(a) . . . any transaction for which general or special authority is expressly given (without the authority being made subject to the sanction of an order) by any statutory provision contained in or having effect under an Act of Parliament[3] or by any scheme legally established;[4] or

(b) . . . the granting of a lease for a term ending not more than twenty-two years after it is granted, not being a lease granted wholly or partly in consideration of a fine; or

(c) . . . any disposition of an advowson."

The second class of exceptions comprises exempt charities and charities excepted by order or regulations.[5] Various regulations have been made in relation to religious premises,[6] and the Commissioners have also made orders of more restricted scope.

---

[20] As to the meaning of this term see ss. 46, 45 (3) and 22 (9) discussed at pp. 210, 214, *ante*.

[21] A formal order is required: in the case of the Commissioners this means the order must be authenticated under their seal—*B.I.U. Estates Ltd.* v. *Chichester Diocesan Fund and Board of Finance (Incorporated)* (1963), 186 Estates Gazette 261; see also the Report of the Charity Commissioners for 1963, para. 67.

[22] Charitable Trusts Amendment Act 1855, s. 29.

[1] *Bishop of Bangor* v. *Parry*, [1891] 2 Q.B. 277.

[2] *Milner* v. *Staffordshire Congregational Union (Incorporated)*, [1956] 1 All E.R. 494; [1956] Ch. 275. Cf. *Manchester Diocesan Council for Education* v. *General Investments Ltd.*, [1970] 1 W.L.R. 241.

[3] E.g. Lands Clauses Consolidation Act 1845, s. 7.

[4] I.e. a scheme sanctioned by the court or the Commissioners—*Re Mason's Orphanage & London & North Western Railway Co.*, [1896] 1 Ch. 596, C.A.; *A.-G.* v. *National Hospital for Relief and Cure of the Paralysed and Epileptic*, [1904] 2 Ch. 252.

[5] Section 29 (4).

[6] S.I. 1961, Nos. 225 and 1282; S.I. 1962, Nos. 1421 and 1815; S.I. 1963, No. 1062.

CHAPTER 8

Trustees. *Appointment and Determination of Appointment*

I APPOINTMENT OF TRUSTEES

a Appointment by the settlor

The first trustees are normally appointed by the settlor or testator who creates the trust. In the case of a trust created by will the fact that the trustees appointed all predecease the testator,[1] or otherwise cease to exist,[2] or even that no trustees were originally appointed by the testator at all,[3] or that they all disclaim the trust, or that the trustee appointed is legally incapable of taking,[4] will not cause the trust to fail, even though the will may contain no provisions for the appointment of trustees. In such case the court will be able to appoint trustees under the powers hereafter discussed. In the meantime the personal representatives will be deemed to be constructive trustees, and accordingly it could not be successfully contended that the trust was not completely constituted. In the case of a trust created or purported to be created *inter vivos*, it seems clear that there can be no valid trust if the document relied upon as constituting the trust is a purported conveyance or transfer to trustees who are not named or otherwise identified, or who are already dead, or have otherwise ceased to exist or are not capable grantees. Such a document would be a nullity and completely ineffective to constitute a trust. If, however, a trust is once completely constituted, it is another matter. Accordingly where there is a conveyance or transfer to named persons, as trustees, a trust is validly created notwithstanding an effective disclaimer[5] by the trustees, and even though the settlor has died without having communicated the trust to the trustees. The reasoning in such case is that the

---

[1] *Re Smirthwaite's Trusts* (1871), L.R. 11 Eq. 251.
[2] *A.-G.* v. *Stephens* (1834), 3 My. & K. 347, *semble.*
[3] *Dodkin* v. *Brunt* (1868), L.R. 6 Eq. 580; *Pollock* v. *Ennis*, [1921] 1 I.R. 181.
[4] *Sonley* v. *Clock Makers' Company* (1780), 1 Bro.C.C. 81.
[5] As to disclaimer generally see Section 3a of this Chapter, p. 246, *post.*

conveyance or transfer is valid until disclaimer,[6] and accordingly the property passes to the trustees and the trust is completely constituted. On disclaimer the trust property is by operation of law revested in the settlor, or his personal representatives, if he is dead, subject to the trusts, notwithstanding the fact that a disclaimer is often said to make the conveyance void *ab initio*.[7] Again in such case the court has power to appoint new trustees.[8] To the above propositions, which are sometimes compendiously comprehended in the maxim that a trust will not fail for want of a trustee, there is one qualification which we have already met in connection with charities.[9] "If it is of the essence of a trust that the trustees selected by the settlor and no-one else shall act as the trustees of it and those trustees cannot or will not undertake the office, the trust must fail."[10]

Apart from his power to appoint the first trustees when creating the trust, the settlor has, as such, no power to appoint new or additional trustees, unless such a power is expressly reserved to him by the trust instrument.[11] It should be mentioned that in the case of an *inter vivos* trust there is no reason[12] why the settlor should not himself be one of the original trustees, and he will inevitably be the sole original trustee if the trust is created by the settlor simply declaring himself a trustee of property already vested in him alone.

b Appointment under an express power

It is not usual to insert an express power of appointing new trustees, as the statutory power hereafter discussed is usually regarded as adequate. The operation and effect of an express power is, of course, a question of construction of the particular words used, and it seems that such a power will be strictly construed.[13] It is doubtful whether under an express power the donee of the power can appoint himself to be a new trustee, either alone or jointly with other persons, even assuming that such an appointment is *prima facie*, as a matter of construction, within the power.[14] Kay J. has stated the equitable objection:

---

[6] It is settled that a transfer of property to a person without his knowledge, if made in proper form, vests the property in him at once, subject to his right to repudiate it when he learns of it: in other words assent is presumed until dissent is signified. *Siggers* v. *Evans* (1855), 5 E. & B. 367, *Standing* v. *Bowring* (1885), 31 Ch.D. 282, C.A.; *London and County Banking Co.* v. *London and River Plate Bank* (1888), 21 Q.B.D. 535, C.A. Cf. *Re Gulbenkian's Settlement Trusts* (No. 2), [1969] 2 All E.R. 1173; [1970] Ch. 408.

[7] Such a statement, it seems, signifies that as regards the person to whom the grant is made, he is in respect of his liabilities, his burdens and his rights, in exactly the same position as though no conveyance has been made to him. *Mallott* v. *Wilson*, [1903] 2 Ch. 494; but see *Re Parsons*, [1942] 2 All E.R. 496; [1943] Ch. 12, C.A.; *Re Stratton's Deed of Disclaimer*, [1957] 2 All E.R. 594; [1958] 1 Ch. 42, C.A.

[8] *Jones* v. *Jones* (1874), 31 L.T. 535; *Mallott* v. *Wilson*, [1903] 2 Ch. 494.

[9] Chapter 7, Section 3a, *ante*, p. 211.

[10] *Per* Buckley J. in *Re Lysaght*, [1965] 2 All E.R. 888, 896; [1966] Ch. 191, 207, citing *Reeve* v. *A.-G.* (1843), 3 Hare 191; *Re Lawton*, [1936] 3 All E.R. 378.

[11] As was done, for example, in *Noble* v. *Meymott* (1851), 14 Beav. 471.

[12] Note however the danger in respect of estate duty—*Oakes* v. *New South Wales Commissioner of Stamp Duties*, [1953] 2 All E.R. 1563; [1954] A.C. 57, P.C.

[13] See e.g. *Stones* v. *Rowton* (1853), 17 Beav. 308; *Re Norris* (1884), 27 Ch.D. 333.

[14] *Re Skeats' Settlement* (1889), 42 Ch.D. 522; *Re Newen*, [1894] 2 Ch.D. 297; see, however, the explanation of these cases in *Montefiore* v. *Guedalla*, [1903] 2 Ch. 723; doubted in *Re Sampson*, [1906] 1 Ch. 435.

"A man should not be judge in his own case; . . . he should not decide that he is the best possible person, and say that he ought to be the trustee. Naturally no human being can be imagined who would not have some bias one way or the other as to his own personal fitness, and to appoint himself among other people, or excluding them to appoint himself, would certainly be an improper exercise of any power of selection of a fiduciary character such as this is."[15]

In order to avoid duplication, cases on the construction in express powers of common form phrases which appear in the statutory power in identical or similar terms are discussed in relation to the latter, with an identifying note. They are not, of course, direct decisions on the statute, but, are likely to be applied by analogy, and, contrariwise, decisions on statutory phrases would almost certainly be followed in a case on an express power in similar terms.

c   Appointment under the provisions of section 36 of the Trustee Act 1925[16]

The statutory power contained in this section applies to all trusts, unless a contrary intention appears.[17]   Such a contrary intention is not, it seems, to be inferred from the mere fact that there is an express power in certain circumstances, and accordingly this would not prevent the appointment of new trustees under the statutory power in other circumstances to which the express power did not apply.[18]

Subsection (1) of section 36 provides as follows:—

"Where a trustee, either original or substituted, and whether appointed by a court or otherwise, is dead, or remains out of the United Kingdom for more than twelve months, or desires to be discharged from all or any of the trusts or powers reposed in or conferred on him, or refuses or is unfit to act therein, or is incapable of acting therein, or is an infant, then, subject to the restrictions imposed by this Act on the number of trustees,—

(a) the person or persons nominated for the purpose of appointing new trustees by the instrument, if any, creating the trust; or

(b) if there is no such person, or no such person able and willing to act, then the surviving or continuing trustees or trustee for the time being, or the personal representatives of the last surviving or continuing trustee;

may, by writing, appoint one or more other persons (whether or not being the persons exercising the power) to be a trustee or trustees in the place of the trustee so deceased, remaining out of the United Kingdom, desiring to be discharged, refusing, or being unfit or being incapable, or being an infant, as aforesaid."

The unanimous view of textbook writers, the assumption of practitioners, and the only inference to be drawn from the cases, is that a trustee in this section does not include a personal representative, notwithstanding that the definition section[19] specifically provides that "trustee, where the context admits, includes

---

[15] *Re Skeats' Settlement, supra*, per Kay J. at p. 527.
[16] Replacing Trustee Act 1893, s. 10. Similar provisions were first enacted in Lord Cranworth's Act, 23 & 24 Vict. c. 145, 1860.
[17] Trustee Act, 1925, s. 69 (2).
[18] *Cecil* v. *Langdon* (1884), 28 Ch.D. 1 C.A.;   *Re Wheeler and De Rochow*, [1896] 1 Ch.D. 315; *Re Sichel's Settlements*, [1916] 1 Ch. 358.
[19] Trustee Act 1925, s. 68 (17).

a personal representative". In the face of such unanimity of opinion, it is not surprising that no litigant' has yet been brave, or perhaps one should say rash, enough even to argue the contrary. It is, however, not easy to find in section 36 a context which clearly supplies the necessary contrary intention and it is noteworthy that in section 41 of the Trustee Act 1925,[20] which gives power to the court to appoint new trustees in certain circumstances, it was thought necessary to provide expressly that nothing therein contained gives power to appoint a personal representative. Of course if a personal representative has become a trustee, the statutory, or any other, power to appoint a new trustee will apply: the circumstances in which this transformation takes place were discussed in Chapter 2, Section 1f, p. 30, *ante*.

We must now consider the provisions of the subsection set out above in more detail.

(i) *The circumstances in which the statutory power may be exercised.*

These can be put under eight heads:

a "*where a trustee . . . is dead.*" It is specifically provided by subsection (8)[21] that this includes the case of a person nominated trustee in a will but dying before the testator, thus resolving the doubts previously caused by the differing views of the judges.[22] The statutory provision does not cover the case, which is seldom likely to occur in practice, where under an *inter vivos* trust a trustee appointed is already dead. In the absence of direct authority the cases cited in the previous note provide a close analogy, but, as stated, leave the point doubtful. Perhaps the better view is that of Parker V.C. in *Re Hadley*,[1] from which it would follow that in the case of such prior death the power of appointment would be exercisable. It will be remembered, however, that if all the trustees appointed under an *inter vivos* trust are already dead at the date of the deed there will be no valid trust at all.[2]

b "*where a trustee . . . remains out of the United Kingdom*[3] *for more than twelve months.*"[4] This means an uninterrupted period of twelve months, and it was accordingly held in *Re Walker*[5] that the event upon which the power arose had not happened when the period had been broken by a week's visit to London. If, however, the event has happened and the power has become

---

[20] Discussed at p. 235, *post.*
[21] Replacing earlier legislation tracing its ancestry to Lord Cranworth's Act.
[22] *Walsh* v. *Gladstone* (1844), 14 Sim. 2; *Winter* v. *Rudge* (1847), 15 Sim. 596; *Re Hadley* (1851), 5 De. G. & Sm. 67 (all cases on express powers, where doubts still remain).
[1] *Supra.*
[2] See p. 226, *ante.*
[3] This means Great Britain and Northern Ireland—Trustee Act 1925, s. 68 (20).
[4] For the protection of purchasers, s. 38 of the Trustee Act 1925 provides "(1) A statement, contained in any instrument coming into operation after the commencement of this Act by which a new trustee is appointed for any purpose connected with land, to the effect that a trustee has remained out of the United Kingdom for more than twelve months or refuses or is unfit to act, or is incapable of acting . . . shall, in favour of a purchaser of a legal estate, be conclusive evidence of the matter stated. (2) In favour of such purchaser any appointment of a new trustee depending on that statement, and any vesting declaration, express or implied, consequent on the appointment, shall be valid."
[5] [1901] 1 Ch. 259. Cf. *Re Moravian Society* (1858), 26 Beav. 101; *Re Arbib and Class's Contract*, [1891] 1 Ch. 601, C.A. (both decisions on express provisions).

exercisable, the trustee who has remained out of the United Kingdom can be removed against his will.[6]

c *"where a trustee . . . desires to be discharged from all or any of the trusts or powers reposed in or conferred on him."* It will be observed that this provision specifically authorises a trustee to retire from a part only of the trusts or powers reposed in or conferred on him, thus getting over the difficulty caused by cases which held that this could only be done with the aid of the court.[7]

d *"where a trustee . . . refuses . . . to act therein."*[8] This seems to cover the case of a trustee who disclaims the trust.[9]

c *"where a trustee . . . is unfit to act therein."*[10] It seems that a trustee who is bankrupt is unfit to act,[11] though in *Re Wheeler & De Rochow*[12] the court did not rely on this saying that, whether or not a trustee who became bankrupt was for that reason alone unfit to act, one who became bankrupt and absconded certainly was.

f *"where a trustee . . . is incapable of acting therein."*[13] The better view[14] seems to be that the incapacity to act must be personal incapacity, such as old age, with consequent bodily and mental infirmity,[15] or mental disorder,[16] but not bankruptcy.[17] Where a trustee who is incapable by reason of mental disorder is also entitled in possession to some beneficial interest in the trust property, it is specially provided[18] that no appointment of a new trustee in his place shall be made,[19] unless leave to make the appointment has been given by the authority having jurisdiction under Part VIII of the Mental Health Act 1959.

It was held during the First World War that an alien enemy was incapable of acting, on the ground that he could not bring an action to protect the trust property.[20] This decision does not appear to have been cited to the court

---

[6] *Re Stoneham's Settlement Trusts*, [1952] 2 All E.R. 694; [1953] Ch. 59.

[7] *Savile* v. *Couper* (1887), 36 Ch.D. 520; *Re Moss's Trusts* (1888), 37 Ch. D. 513. Cf. s. 39 Trustee Act 1925, discussed at p. 250, *post* (retirement without appointment of new trustees).

[8] Trustee Act 1925, s. 38, applies—see note 4, p. 229, *ante*.

[9] *Viscountess D'Adhemar* v. *Bertrand* (1865), 35 Beav. 19.

[10] Trustee Act 1925, s. 38, applies—see note 4, p. 229, *ante*.

[11] See *Re Roche* (1842), 2 Dr. & War. 287; *Re Hopkins* (1881), 19 Ch.D. 61, C.A., *per* Jessel M.R. at p. 63.

[12] [1896] 1 Ch. 315 Cf. *Re Barker's Trusts* (1875), 1 Ch.D. 43 and *Re Adams' Trust* (1879), 12 Ch.D. 634 where the question concerned the power of the court to appoint in place of a bankrupt trustee.

[13] Trustee Act 1925, s. 38, applies—see note 4, p. 229, *ante*.

[14] See e.g. *Re Bignold's Settlement Trusts* (1872), 7 Ch. App. 223; *Turner* v. *Maule* (1850), 15 Jur. 761; *Re. Watts' Settlement* (1851), 9 Hare 106, all decisions on express powers.

[15] *Re Lemann's Trusts* (1883), 22 Ch.D. 633; *Re Weston's Trusts*, [1898] W.N. 151 (cases on appointment by the court).

[16] *Re East* (1873), 8 Ch. App. 735 (express power) ; *Re Blake*, [1887] W.N. 173, C.A. Cf. *Kirby* v. *Leather*, [1965] 2 All E.R. 441; [1965] 2 Q.B. 367, C.A., *per* Winn L.J. at pp. 446; 387; compromised [1965] 3 All E.R. 927, H.L.

[17] *Turner* v. *Maule* (1850), 15 Jur. 761; *Re Watts' Settlement* (1851), 9 Hare 106 (both cases on express powers).

[18] In place of Trustee Act 1925, s. 36 (9) a new subsection to the above effect was substituted by the Mental Health Act 1959, s. 149 (1) and Sched. 7.

[19] Except by the person or persons nominated to appoint new trustees by the trust instrument.

[20] *Re Sichel's Settlements*, [1916] 1 Ch. 358.

during the Second World War in a case where the court refused to lay down a rule, but said that on the facts before it there was no evidence that the trustee, resident in enemy occupied territory, was really incapable of acting.[21] The court in fact rather avoided the issue by itself appointing a new trustee under section 41 of the Trustee Act 1925.[1]

The question whether a trustee becomes incapable of acting by going abroad is now less likely to arise in the case of the statutory power by reason of the provision already discussed that a new trustee may be appointed in place of a trustee who remains out of the United Kingdom for more than twelve months. In cases on express powers, it was held in two early cases that a trustee did not become incapable of acting by going abroad, even to such places as Australia[2] and China,[3] at that time very remote. In *Mennard* v. *Welford*,[4] however, it was held that a trustee who had been absent for 20 years and established a business in New York, was incapable of acting as a trustee of leasehold property in London, and in *Re Lemann's Trusts*[5] residence abroad was given as an obvious illustration of incapacity.

One case is specially provided for by the section itself.[6] Where a trustee is a corporation, and the corporation is or has been dissolved, it is deemed to be and to have been from the date of the dissolution incapable of acting in the trusts or powers reposed in or conferred on the corporation.

g "*where a trustee . . . is an infant.*" Although the appointment of an infant to be a trustee in relation to any settlement or trust is void,[7] an infant may be a trustee under a resulting, implied or constructive trust.[8]

h "*where a trustee has been removed under a power contained in the instrument creating the trust.*"[9] In such case the statutory power arises and operates in the case of an individual[10] who is removed, as if he were dead, and in the case of a corporation, as if the corporation desired to be discharged from the trust. It should be observed that this provision applies only in the case where a trustee has been removed under a power contained in the trust instrument. It does not confer any power to remove a trustee.

(ii) *The persons who can exercise the statutory power.*

The section, it will be observed, has a primary and a secondary category.

a "*The person or persons nominated for the purpose of appointing new trustees*"—There is no need for the nomination to refer to the statutory

---

[21] *Re May's Will Trusts*, [1941] Ch. 109.
[1] Discussed in the following sub-section, pp. 235 *et seq.*
[2] *Re Harrison's Trusts* (1852), 22 L.J. Ch. 69.
[3] *Withington* v. *Withington* (1848), 16 Sim. 104.
[4] (1853), 1 Sm. & Giff. 426 (express power). See *Re Bignold's Settlement Trusts* (1872), 7 Ch. App. 223 (appointment by court).
[5] (1883), 22 Ch.D. 633 (appointment by court).
[6] Trustee Act 1925, s. 36 (3).
[7] Law of Property Act 1925, s. 20. Note Law of Property Act, s. 15 which provides that the parties to a conveyance are presumed to be of full age until the contrary is proved.
[8] See e.g. *Re Vinogradoff*, [1935] W.N. 68.
[9] Trustee Act 1925, s. 36 (2).
[10] Presumably the subsection would be construed as contrasting an individual with a corporation, though it actually uses the words "trustee" and "corporation", thus, it seems, requiring the word "trustee" to be given two different meanings in one sentence.

power[11] and it is usual for the trust deed simply to provide that X shall have power to appoint new trustees. If someone is nominated to appoint new trustees in certain cases only, it should be noted that he is not regarded as nominated to exercise the statutory power in other cases not specifically mentioned.[12] As there is no need for the person nominated to appoint new trustees to have any beneficial interest under the trust, it is not surprising that it has been held that if a beneficiary is nominated to appoint new trustees, he may continue to exercise the power of appointment after alienating his interest, and without obtaining the consent of the alienees.[13] A curious point arises where two or more persons are jointly nominated to appoint new trustees. Here, unless a contrary intention can be found as a matter of construction, the old rule still applies that a bare power, given to two or more persons by name and not annexed to an estate or office, does not survive, but determines on the death of the first of the named persons to die.[14]

b "*The surviving or continuing trustees or trustee for the time being, or the personal representatives of the last surviving or continuing trustee*"—Power to appoint new trustees is given to persons in this second category where there is no one nominated to appoint, or where there is "no such person able and willing to act". It was held that there was no person able and willing to act where the persons jointly nominated were a husband and wife, who were at the relevant time living apart and unable to agree on the selection of new trustees,[15] and likewise where the donee of the power of appointment could not be found.[16]

A continuing trustee normally means a trustee who is to continue to act after the appointment of the new trustee has taken effect.[17] It is, however, specifically provided that the provisions of section 36 "relative to a continuing trustee include a refusing or retiring trustee, if willing to act in the execution of the provisions" of that section.[18] It is accordingly possible for all the surviving trustees together, or a sole trustee, to retire and at the same time to appoint new trustees or a new trustee to act in their or his place, which could not be done if this power was given to the continuing trustees or trustee in the *prima facie* sense. In thus obviating one difficulty, another has

---

[11] See *Re Walker & Hughes Contract* (1883), 24 Ch.D. 698.

[12] *Cecil* v. *Langdon* (1884), 28 Ch.D. 1, C.A.; *Re Wheeler and De Rochow*, [1896] 1 Ch. 315; *Re Sichel's Settlements*, [1916] 1 Ch. 358.

[13] *Hardaker* v. *Moorhouse* (1884), 26 Ch.D. 417 (express power). But see *Re Bedingfield & Herring's Contract*, [1893] 2 Ch. 332, at p. 337.

[14] *Re Harding*, [1923] 1 Ch. 182; [1922] All E.R. Rep. 557. The rule was held not to be abrogated by the Trustee Act 1892, s. 22, now replaced by the Trustee Act 1925, s. 18. Cf. *Bersel Manufacturing Co., Ltd.* v. *Berry*, [1968] 2 All E.R. 552, H.L.

[15] *Re Sheppard's Settlement Trusts*, [1888] W.N. 234.

[16] *Cradock* v. *Witham*, [1895] W.N. 75.

[17] *Travis* v. *Illingworth* (1865), 2 Drew. & Sm. 344; *Re Norris* (1884), 27 Ch.D. 333 (both cases on express powers); *Re Coates to Parsons* (1886), 34 Ch.D. 370. The last two cases disapprove contrary dicta in *Re Glenny and Hartley* (1884), 25 Ch.D. 611. These cases would still apply to the construction of the word 'continuing' in the case of an express power.

[18] Trustee Act 1925, s. 36 (8). A trustee who is compulsorily removed because he has remained out of the United Kingdom for more than twelve months is not a refusing or retiring trustee within the subsection and accordingly his concurrence is not required to an appointment of new trustees—*Re Stoneham's Settlement Trusts*, [1952] 2 All E.R. 694; [1953] Ch. 59.

arisen; namely, whether the continuing trustees or trustee *stricto sensu* can validly make an appointment without the concurrence of a refusing or retiring trustee. The answer seems to be that such an appointment is valid, unless it is shown that the refusing or retiring trustee was competent and willing to act, the onus being upon those who allege that this is so to establish it.[19] In practice it is desirable that a refusing or retiring trustee should join in the deed of appointment of new trustees, if this is possible.

The phrase "the last surviving or continuing trustee" has been held to include a sole trustee,[20] but where all the trustees of a will predecease the testator, the last of them to die does not come within the meaning of the phrase and consequently his personal representatives are not entitled to appoint.[21] Where the section does apply, it seems that the personal representatives of a last surviving or continuing trustee are not bound to exercise the statutory power of appointment.[1]

Subsection (4) provides that

"the power of appointment given . . . to the personal representatives of a last surviving or continuing trustee shall be . . . exercisable by the executors for the time being (whether original or by representation) of such surviving or continuing trustee who have proved the will of their testator or by the administrators for the time being of such trustee without the concurrence of any executor who has renounced or has not proved."

But, by subsection (5),

"a sole or last surviving executor intending to renounce, or all the executors where they all intend to renounce, shall have . . . power, at any time before renouncing probate, to exercise the power of appointment given by this section, . . . if willing to act for that purpose and without thereby accepting the office of executor."

Although a non-proving executor can exercise the power of appointment, his title to do so can only be proved by a proper grant of representation.[2]

(iii) *Mode of appointment*

An appointment under section 36 is merely required to be in writing, though it is normally made by deed in order to get the benefit of the vesting provisions contained in section 40.[3] It need not be contained in an instrument expressly executed for that purpose, if it can properly be construed as having that effect.[4] If the trust deed in terms requires an appointment to be made with some unusual form of execution or attestation or solemnity, such provisions are ineffective by reason of s. 159 of the Law of Property Act 1925, though the section expressly provides that it does not operate to defeat any direction making the consent of some person necessary to a valid appointment.[5] The appointment cannot, however, be made by will, that is to say a last surviving trustee cannot appoint a new trustee to take office at his own death in place of himself.[6]

---

[19] *Re Coates to Parsons* (1886), 34 Ch.D. 370.
[20] *Re Shafto's Trusts* (1885), 29 Ch.D. 247.
[21] *Nicholson* v. *Field*, [1893] 2 Ch. 511.
[1] *Re Knight's Will* (1884), 26 Ch.D. 82 *per* Pearson J. at p. 89 (not discussed on appeal).
[2] *Re Crowhurst Park, Sims-Hilditch* v. *Simmons*, [1974] 1 All E.R. 991.
[3] Discussed in Section 2 of this Chapter, p. 244, *post*.
[4] *Re Farnell's Settled Estates* (1886), 33 Ch.D. 599 (express power).
[5] Cf. *Lancashire* v. *Lancashire* (1848), 2 Ph. 657 (express power).
[6] *Re Parker's Trusts*, [1894] 1 Ch. 707.

(iv) *Appointment of additional trustees*

Even under subsection (1) the number of trustees may be increased, for this section authorises the appointment of "one or more other persons ... to be a trustee or trustees in the place of the trustee" who has already ceased or upon the appointment ceases to hold office. Subsection (6), however, authorises the appointment of an additional trustee or trustees in some circumstances, even where there is no vacancy in the trusteeship. Before 1926, unless of course there was an express power given, this was impossible except by means of an application to the court.[7] Subsection (6) provides as follows:—

> "Where a sole trustee, other than a trust corporation, is or has been originally appointed to act in a trust, or where, in the case of any trust, there are not more than three trustees (none of them being a trust corporation) either original or sub-stituted and whether appointed by the court or otherwise, then and in any such case—
>
> (a) the person or persons nominated for the purpose of appointing new trustees by the instrument, if any, creating the trust; or
>
> (b) if there is no such person, or no such person able and willing to act, then the trustee or trustees for the time being;
>
> may, by writing, appoint another person or other persons to be an additional trustee or additional trustees, but it shall not be obligatory to appoint any additional trustee, unless the instrument, if any, creating the trust, or any statutory enactment provides to the contrary, nor shall the number of trustees be increased beyond four by virtue of any such appointment."

One curious distinction, probably unintentional, should be observed between the provisions of this subsection and those of subsection (1). Here the appointor is given power to appoint "another person or other persons" to be an additional trustee or additional trustees, which has been construed as meaning that he cannot appoint himself.[8] In subsection (1), however, which, as we have seen, deals with the appointment of a new trustee or new trustees in place of a trustee who has already ceased or upon the appointment ceases to hold office, it is specifically provided that the appointor may appoint one or more other persons, whether or not being the persons exercising the power.[9]

(v) *Effect of appointment*

The Trustee Act 1925, section 36 (7), provides:

> "Every new trustee appointed under this section as well before as after all the trust property becomes by law, or by assurance, or otherwise, vested in him, shall have the same powers, authorities, and discretions, and may in all respects act as if he had been originally appointed a trustee by the instrument, if any, creating the trust."

---

[7] *Re Gregson's Trusts* (1886), 34 Ch.D. 209.

[8] *Re Power's Settlement Trusts*, [1951] 2 All E.R. 513; [1951] Ch. 1074, C.A., following the principle of *Re Sampson*, [1906] 1 Ch. 435. Cf. *Re Skeats' Settlement* (1889), 42 Ch.D. 522; *Re Newen*, [1894] 2 Ch. 297 (express powers).

[9] This express provision prevails over both the objections to the exercise by the appointor of the power of appointment in favour of himself, *viz.*, the objection of construction, which as we have just seen, prevails on the different wording of subsection (6), and the equitable objection that it is improper for a person having a fiduciary power to exercise it in his own favour—see pp. 227, 228 *ante*.

d Appointment by the court

i *Under the statutory power contained in the Trustee Act 1925.* Section 41 (1)[10] of the Act provides as follows:

"The court[11] may,[12] whenever it is expedient to appoint a new trustee or new trustees, and it is found inexpedient difficult or impracticable so to do without the assistance of the court, make an order appointing a new trustee or new trustees either in substitution for or in addition to any existing trustee or trustees, or although there is no existing trustee.

In particular and without prejudice to the generality of the foregoing provision, the court may make an order appointing a new trustee in substitution for a trustee who is incapable, by reason of mental disorder within the meaning of the Mental Health Act 1959, of exercising his functions as trustee, or is a bankrupt, or is a corporation which is in liquidation or has been dissolved."

Cases in which the court has made an appointment under the statutory power, apart from those specifically referred to in the section, include the following: where all the named trustees predeceased the testator[13]; where no trustees were named[14]; where a trustee had gone abroad with the intention of residing there permanently[15]; where a trustee was incapable of acting by reason of old age and consequent bodily and mental infirmity[16]; where a trustee was, so far as was known, in enemy occupied territory[17]; where there was a doubt as to whether the statutory, or an express, power of appointment was exercisable[18]; where the persons who should have exercised a power of appointment,[19] or one of them in the case of a joint power,[20] were resident abroad; where an infant had been nominated to appoint new trustees, for though an appointment by an infant may not be void, it is at least liable to be set aside and accordingly it would not be safe to act upon it[21]; and where there was friction between trustees, there being no dispute as to the facts, and even though this involved removing a trustee against her will.[22]

---

[10] As amended by the Mental Health Act 1959, s. 149 (1) and Sched. 7, Part 1, and the Criminal Law Act 1967, s. 10 and Sched. 3, Part III. This section replaces the Trustee Act 1893, s. 25 (1), which in turn replaced similar provisions first enacted in the Trustee Act 1850, s. 32.

[11] The court is defined in s. 67 (1) and normally means the High Court, or, where the estate or fund subject to the trust does not exceed £5,000, the County Court (County Courts Act 1959, s. 52 (1) (b) as amended by the Administration of Justice Act 1969, s. 5, and S.I. 1970 No. 672).

[12] The court delayed making an appointment in *Re Pauling's Settlement* (No. 2), [1963] 1 All E.R. 857 in order to protect the old trustees against possible liability for costs and estate duty.

[13] *Re Smirthwaite's Trusts* (1871), L.R. 11 Eq. 251.

[14] *Re Gillett's Trusts* (1876), 25 W.R. 23.

[15] *Re Bignold's Settlement Trusts* (1872), 7 Ch. App. 223.

[16] *Re Lemann's Trusts* (1883), 22 Ch.D. 633; *Re Phelps' Settlement Trusts* (1885), 31 Ch.D. 351, C.A.; *Re Weston's Trusts*, [1898] W.N. 151.

[17] *Re May's Will Trusts*, [1941] Ch. 109.

[18] *Re Woodgate's Settlement* (1857), 5 W.R. 448; *Re Bignold's Settlement Trusts*, supra.

[19] *Re Humphry's Estate* (1855), 1 Jur. (N.S.) 921.

[20] *Re Somerset*, [1887] W.N. 122.

[21] *Re Parsons*, [1940] 4 All E.R. 65; [1940] Ch. 973 and see (1941), 57 L.Q.R. 25 (R. E. Megarry).

[22] *Re Henderson*, [1940] 3 All E.R. 295; [1940] Ch. 764; Cf. *Letterstedt* v. *Broers* (1884), 9 App. Cas. 371, P.C.

The court, however, will not under section 41 interfere with an appointment of new trustees by a person having the statutory or an express power to do so,[1] even on an application by all the beneficiaries,[2] and even though the person with the power of appointment may have intended to exercise it corruptly.[3] The great respect shown by the court to such a power of appointment of new trustees is further established by the rule that even a decree for administration of the trusts by the court does not take away a power of appointing new trustees, though after decree the exercise of the power is subject to the supervision of the court.[4] In such case, if the person with the power of appointment nominates a fit and proper person, he must be appointed and the court will not appoint another person whom it might think more suitable. If, however, the court does not approve of the person nominated it will call for a fresh nomination. Persistent nomination of unsuitable persons would, however, amount to a refusal to appoint and the court would then make its own choice.[5]

The exercise by the court of its power to appoint trustees under section 41 frequently involves the removal of an existing trustee, possibly against his will. This section, however, as a matter of construction does not empower the court simply to discharge a trustee, unless at the same time it reappoints the continuing trustees in place of themselves and the retiring trustee. This, however, the court will not do in practice, either from want of jurisdiction or from a refusal to exercise it.[6]

It should be observed that section 41 (1) clearly empowers the court to appoint additional trustees,[7] and that subsection (4) provides in express terms that "nothing in this section gives power to appoint an executor or administrator".[8] The power will, of course, apply if the personal representative has become a trustee: the circumstances in which this may happen were discussed in Chapter 2, Section 1f, p. 30, *ante*.

ii *Under its inherent jurisdiction.* Prior to the Trustee Act 1850 the court had no statutory power to appoint new trustees, but appointments were commonly made by the Court of Chancery under its inherent jurisdiction to

---

[1] *Re Hodson's Settlement* (1851), 9 Hare 118; *Re Higginbottom*, [1892] 3 Ch. 132; *Re Brockbank*, [1948] 1 All E.R. 287; [1948] Ch. 206. Aliter, where the donee of the power is an infant—*Re Parsons, supra*. See also *Re Kensit*, [1908] W.N. 235.

[2] All the beneficiaries acting together could, however, direct the trustees to transfer the trust property to any other person or persons, or corporation, on identical trusts, see *Re Brockbank, supra*.

[3] *Re Hodson's Settlement, supra*. The abuse could, however, be dealt with by the court under its inherent jurisdiction in an action to restrain the corrupt exercise of the power and for the execution of the trusts by the court.

[4] The last proposition only applies when there has been a general administration order; it does not apply to an order for partial administration, unless an enquiry is ordered as to the appointment of new trustees, or proceedings are taken for this purpose—*Re Cotter*, [1915] 1 Ch. 307.

[5] *Re Gadd* (1883), 23 Ch.D. 134, C.A.; *Tempest* v. *Lord Camoys* (1882), 21 Ch.D. 571, C.A.; *Re Norris* (1884), 27 Ch.D. 333.

[6] *Re Chetwynd's Settlement*, [1902] 1 Ch. 692. See also *Re Dewhirst's Trusts* (1886), 33 Ch.D. 416, C.A.; *Re Gardiner's Trusts* (1886), 33 Ch.D. 590.

[7] Cf. *Re Gregson's Trusts* (1886), 34 Ch.D. 209.

[8] The court has such power in some circumstances under the Judicature Act 1925, s. 160 (2), and the Administration of Estates Act 1925, s. 23 (2).

supervise trusts and trustees.[9] There was nothing in the Act of 1850 or in the subsequent legislation replacing it to take away this jurisdiction. The statutory power should, however, be invoked if it is available, and in view of the wide wording of section 41, it is seldom necessary to rely on the inherent jurisdiction,[10] unless it is desired to remove a trustee against his will and there is a dispute as to the facts.[11]

iii *Under the Mental Health Act 1959.*[12] This Act, which substituted a new section in place of section 54 of the Trustee Act 1925, gives the authority having jurisdiction under Part VIII of that Act[13] concurrent jurisdiction with the High Court where a mental patient is a trustee and a receiver is acting for him,[14] except where the trust is being administered by the High Court, in relation to matters consequent on the making of provision by the said authority for the exercise of a power of appointing trustees or retiring from a trust. The object of this provision is to prevent the necessity of cases being transferred from one department to another.

iv *Under the Judicial Trustees Act 1896 and the Public Trustee Act 1906.* These statutes are considered in Sections 4 and 5 below.

v *Effect of appointment by the court.* The Trustee Act 1925, s. 43, provides:

> "Every trustee appointed by a court of competent jurisdiction shall, as well before as after the trust property becomes by law, or by assurance, or otherwise, vested in him, have the same powers, authorities, and discretions, and may in all respects act as if he had been originally appointed a trustee by the instrument, if any, creating the trust."

e The persons who may be appointed trustee

So far as legal capacity is concerned, any person who has capacity to hold property has capacity to be a trustee. The former restrictions on aliens,[15] corporations,[16] and married women have now been removed. The Crown, it seems, can be a trustee,[17] at any rate if it deliberately chooses to act as such,[18]

---

[9] See e.g. *Buchanan* v. *Hamilton* (1800), 5 Ves. 722; *Ockleston* v. *Heap* (1847), 1 De. G. & Sm. 640.

[10] *Dodkin* v. *Brunt* (1868), L.R. 6 Eq. 580. Here the court relied on the inherent jurisdiction.

[11] See p. 252, *post.*

[12] Section 149 (1) and Sched. 7.

[13] I.e. the Lord Chancellor, any judge of the Supreme Court nominated by the Lord Chancellor, the Master or Deputy Master of the Court of Protection or any officer of that court nominated by the Lord Chancellor—Mental Health Act 1959, ss. 118 (2), 100 (1) and (3).

[14] Also where an application for the appointment of a receiver has been made but not yet determined.

[15] See the Status of Aliens Act 1914, s. 17, as amended by the British Nationality Act 1948. There are, however, limitations as to ships and aircraft. An alien cannot be the owner of a British ship—Merchant Shipping Act 1894, s. 1, Status of Aliens Act 1914, s. 17, proviso (3), British Nationality Act 1948, s. 34 (3), Sched. 4, Pt. II; nor can an aircraft be registered in the United Kingdom in the name of an alien—Air Navigation Order 1966, S.I. 1966 No. 1184, art. 2(3).

[16] See Charities Act 1960, s. 38; *Re Thompson's Settlement Trusts,* [1905] 1 Ch. 229; *Bankes* v. *Salisbury Diocesan Council of Education Incorporated,* [1960] 2 All E.R. 372; [1960] Ch. 631.

[17] *Penn* v. *Lord Baltimore* (1750), 1 Ves Sen. 444 *per* Hardwicke L.C. at p. 453; *Burgess* v. *Wheate* (1757–9), 1 Eden. 177.

[18] *Civilian War Claimants Association, Ltd.* v. *R.,* [1932] A.C. 14, H.L., *per* Lord Atkin at p. 27.

but in practice should never be appointed a trustee if only by reason of the doubts and difficulties in enforcing the trust.[19] An infant cannot be validly appointed a trustee either of real or personal property,[1] though it seems that he can hold property, other than a legal estate in land,[2] upon a resulting, implied or constructive trust.[3]

Where an appointment of a new trustee is made by the court, it will be guided by certain rules in deciding who should be appointed. The Court of Appeal in *Re Tempest*[4] set out three principles. First, that in selecting a person for the office of trustee the court will have regard to the wishes of the author of the trust, expressed in, or plainly deduced from, the instrument containing it. Secondly, that the court will not appoint a person with a view to the interest of some of the *cestuis que trust*, in opposition to the interest of others. Thirdly, that the court will have regard to the question whether the appointment will promote or impede the execution of the trust. It appears from the same case, however, that the mere fact that a continuing trustee refuses to act with a proposed new trustee would not be sufficient to induce the court to refrain from appointing him. A more recent case[5] suggests a fourth principle, namely, that the court should not appoint a person who would be in a position where there would be a conflict between his duty and his interest.

In applying these principles the courts have held that certain categories of persons will not normally be appointed trustees, though in every case "the rule is not imperative, and when there are special circumstances, the court will exercise its discretion in judging whether the case is one in which the rule may be departed from".[6] Thus neither the tenant for life, nor any other *cestui que trust*, will normally be appointed.[7] If, perhaps because it is impossible to obtain the services of an independent trustee,[8] beneficiaries are appointed, an undertaking may be required in some such form as in *Re Lightbody's Trusts*,[9] where two beneficiaries were appointed trustees, and they were required to undertake that if either of them became a sole trustee he would use every endeavour to obtain the appointment of a co-trustee. Further, the court will not normally appoint the husband of a tenant for life[10]; indeed, it has been said that no near relative of parties interested should be appointed except in cases of absolute necessity,[11] though it is thought that the court would not take such a strict view

---

[19] See *Dyson v. A.-G.*, [1911] 1 K.B. 410, C.A.; *Esquimalt and Nanaimo Rail. Co. v. Wilson*, [1920] A.C. 358, P.C.; Hanbury, *Essays in Equity*, pp. 87–89; Holdsworth, *History of English Law*, Vol. IX, pp. 30–32.

[1] Law of Property Act 1925, s. 20.

[2] Cf. Law of Property Act 1925, s. 1 (6).

[3] *Re Vinogradoff*, [1935] W.N. 68.

[4] (1866), 1 Ch. App. 485.

[5] *Re Parsons*, [1940] 4 All E.R. 65; [1940] Ch. 973.

[6] *Ex parte Conybeare's Settlement* (1853), 1 W.R. 458, *per* Turner L.J. at p. 458.

[7] *Ex parte Conybeare's Settlement, supra*; *Re Clissold's Settlement* (1864), 10 L.T. 642; *Forster v. Abraham* (1874), L.R. 17 Eq. 351.

[8] Since the Public Trustee Act 1906, it will often be possible to appoint the Public Trustee; or a trust corporation or other professional trustee may be appointed if the trust instrument contains a charging clause—see p. 261, *post*.

[9] (1884), 52 L.T. 40. Similarly in *Re Parrott* (1881), 30 W.R. 97 (husband of tenant for life).

[10] *Re Parrott* (1881), 30 W.R. 97; *Re Coode* (1913), 108 L.T. 94.

[11] *Wilding v. Bolder* (1855), 21 Beav. 222 and see *Re Parsons, supra*.

today. The same rule applies to the solicitor of the tenant for life, or, presumably of any other of the *cestuis que trust*,[12] to a solicitor of an existing trustee,[13] and to the partner of an existing solicitor-trustee. It may be noticed that there is no principle that would prevent a bank from being appointed a trustee merely because one or all of the beneficiaries happen to be customers of the bank,[14] but the special facts may justify the court in refusing to appoint a particular bank, where, for example, the trustee has a discretionary power to advance to the life tenant out of capital, and the life tenant has a large overdraft with the bank proposed as trustee.[14]

A somewhat different category of persons who will not normally be appointed are persons outside the jurisdiction of the court. It is well established that there is no absolute bar to the appointment of persons resident abroad as trustees of an English trust, but equally well established that, apart from exceptional circumstances, it is not proper to make such an appointment. The most obvious exceptional circumstances in which such an appointment will normally be proper are where the beneficiaries have settled permanently in some country outside the United Kingdom and what is proposed to be done is to appoint new trustees in that country.[15] The court, however, refused to appoint trustees resident in Jersey in *Re Weston's Settlements*,[16] where the appointment was sought as part of a tax avoidance scheme which would have involved removing the trusts from England to Jersey.

It is generally said that the donee of a power of appointment should in making his appointment be guided by the same principles as would guide the court. In practice, however, persons whom the court would not normally appoint are frequently appointed, and such appointment will not normally be upset by the court.[17] Again it has been said that it is the duty of a trustee to consult beneficiaries before appointing a new trustee,[18] but although it is a desirable and usual practice to do so, the duty seems to be unenforceable for, as has been seen,[19] the court will not normally interfere with an appointment made by a person having power to do so, even at the instance of all the beneficiaries.[20]

---

[12] *Re Earl of Stamford*, [1896] 1 Ch. 288; *Re Spencer's Settled Estates*, [1903] 1 Ch. 75; *Re Cotter*, [1915] 1 Ch. 307.

[13] *Re Norris* (1884), 27 Ch.D. 333, where a solicitor trustee appointed his son and partner as co-trustee. The trusts were being administered by the court, and the court refused to sanction the appointment.

[14] *Re Northcliffe's Settlements*, [1937] 3 All E.R. 804, C.A. Cf. *Re Pauling's Settlement Trusts*, [1963] 3 All E.R. 1; [1964] Ch. 303, C.A.

[15] *Re Whitehead's Will Trust*, [1971] 2 All E.R. 1334.

[16] [1968] 3 All E.R. 338; [1969] 1 Ch. 223, C.A.

[17] *Re Earl of Stamford*, [1896] 1 Ch. 288 (solicitor of tenant for life); *Re Coode* (1913), 108 L.T. 94 (husband of tenant for life); *Re Norris* (1884), 27 Ch.D. 333 (as to the appointment of a father and son, solicitors in partnership). As to the case where the donee of the power of appointment is an infant see *Re Parsons*, [1940] 4 All E.R. 65; [1940] Ch. 973; (1941), 57 L.Q.R. 25 (R. E. Megarry).

[18] *O'Reilly* v. *Alderson* (1849), 8 Hare, 101.

[19] See p. 236, *ante*.

[20] Note however that where the court has directed a settlement to be made under the Infant Settlements Act 1855 (now repealed) it has allowed an objection to the proposed trustees on the ground that they were personally distasteful to a beneficiary—*Re Sampson & Wall* (1884), 25 Ch.D. 482, C.A.

In conclusion, it may be observed that the settlor himself is, of course, legally quite uninhibited in the choice of the original trustees; in practice, however, this is a vital matter and the choice of the trustees will affect the smooth running of the trusts and the safety of the interests of the beneficiaries.[1]

f The number of trustees

Apart from statute, on the one hand a sole trustee can act effectively, while on the other hand there is no limit to the number of trustees who may be appointed. Statutory provisions, however, impose limitations in many cases on both the maximum and minimum number of trustees.

As regards the maximum number of trustees who may be appointed section 34 (2) of the Trustee Act 1925 provides as follows:—

> "In the case of settlements[2] and dispositions on trust for sale[3] of land[4] made or coming into operation after the commencement[5] of this Act—
>
> (a) the number of trustees thereof shall not in any case exceed four, and where more than four persons are named as such trustees, the four first named (who are able and willing to act) shall alone be the trustees, and the other persons named shall not be trustees unless appointed on the occurrence of a vacancy;
>
> (b) the number of the trustees shall not be increased beyond four."[6]

Section 34 (2) is in terms restricted to settlements and dispositions on trust for sale of land,[7] and accordingly does not apply to trusts of pure personalty[8]; further, subsection (3) provides that the restrictions on the number of trustees do not apply:—

> "(a) in the case of land vested in trustees for charitable, ecclesiastical, or public[9] purposes[10]; or

---

[1] See Keeton, *Social Change in the Law of Trusts*, Chapter 1.

[2] Defined in Trustee Act 1925, s. 68 (15), and Settled Land Act 1925, s. 1. There are special provisions for the appointment of trustees of a settlement for the purposes of the Settled Land Act 1925. See especially ss. 30 and 34 of the Settled Land Act 1925.

[3] Defined in s. 68 (19) of the Trustee Act 1925.

[4] Defined in *ibid.*, s. 68 (6).

[5] I.e., 1st January, 1926–Trustee Act 1925, s. 71 (2).

[6] Where, in the case of a pre-1926 settlement or trust for sale of land there were more than four trustees on 1st January, 1926, s. 34 (1) of the Trustee Act 1925 provides that "no new trustees shall (except where as a result of the appointment the number is reduced to four or less) be capable of being appointed until the number is reduced to less than four, and thereafter the number shall not be increased beyond four".

[7] See also the express provision in s. 34 (3), where, however, the words "on trust for sale" would appear to have been omitted after the word "disposition".

[8] Nor does it seem to apply to every case where land is held on trust, for instance where land is conveyed to A,B,C,D and E on a bare trust for X absolutely. There seems to be no trust for sale here—s. 36 of the Law of Property Act 1925 does not appear to apply, since on the one hand the grantees do not take beneficially, and on the other hand the beneficial interest is not vested in joint tenants.

[9] Trusts of land belonging to an unincorporated society coming within the provisions of the Literary & Scientific Institutions Act 1854 are public trusts—*Re Cleveland Literary and Philosophical Society's Land*, [1931] 2 Ch. 247.

[10] Settled Land Act 1925, s. 29 (1), provides: "Any conveyance of land held [i.e., presumably, to be held after conveyance] on charitable, ecclesiastical or public trusts shall state that the land is held on such trusts". The same section also provided that such land is deemed to be settled land.

(b) where the net proceeds of the sale of the land are held for like purposes; or

(c) to the trustees of a term of years absolute limited by a settlement on trusts for raising money, or of a like term created under the statutory remedies[11] relating to annual sums charged on land."

On the appointment of a trustee the number of trustees may, subject to the above restrictions, be increased,[12] and, as we have seen,[13] an additional trustee or additional trustees may, subject to the same restrictions, be appointed under the provisions of section 36 (6) of the Trustee Act 1925.

As regards the minimum number of trustees, obviously as a result of deaths of trustees the number may be reduced to one, or, indeed, to none at all,[14] and legislation cannot prevent this happening. There are, however, two sets of relevant provisions.

First, in some cases it is provided that for some purposes a sole trustee (not being a trust corporation[15]) cannot act effectively. Thus a sole trustee for sale of land (not being a trust corporation) cannot give a valid receipt for the proceeds of sale or other capital money,[16] and similar provisions apply to the trustees of a settlement under the Settled Land Act 1925.[17] These provisions apply notwithstanding anything to the contrary contained in the relevant instruments.

Secondly, the better view, it is submitted, is that, provided no contrary intention was expressed in the power of appointment, equity did not insist upon the original number of trustees being maintained. Accordingly, on the appointment of new trustees the number of trustees might be increased[18] or reduced.[19] It followed that there was in general no obligation to keep up the number of trustees, and where, as was commonly the case, the power of appointment was vested in the continuing trustees, failure to replace the trustees who ceased for any reason to hold office was not normally a breach of trust. This was carried to the limit by the Court of Appeal, which held in Peacock v. Colling,[20] that, at any rate where the will contemplated a sole trustee acting, a sole continuing trustee was justified in refusing to appoint a second trustee, and consequently his failure to do so was not a breach of trust.

---

[11] See Law of Property Act 1925, s. 121.

[12] Trustee Act 1925, s. 37 (1) (a), which appears to apply to appointments under both an express and the statutory power. As to the latter, s. 36 (1) by itself would seem to have the same result.

[13] See p. 234, ante.

[14] But note Trustee Act 1925, s. 18 (2), discussed at p. 249, post.

[15] See Section 7, p. 261, infra.

[16] Law of Property Act 1925, s. 27 (2), as substituted by the Law of Property (Amendment) Act 1926, s. 7 and Schedule; Trustee Act 1925, s. 14 (2) as slightly amended by the Law of Property (Amendment) Act 1926, s. 7 and Schedule. See (1969) 33 Con. 240 (J. F. Garner) and Re Myhill, [1928] Ch. 100 and Re Wight and Best's Brewery Co. Ltd.'s Contract, [1929] W.N. 11.

[17] Settled Land Act 1925, ss. 18 (1), 94 (1), 95; Trustee Act 1925, s. 14 (2).

[18] Sands v. Nugee (1836), Donnelly 106; Meinertzhagen v. Davis (1844), 1 Coll. 335; but see Re Clark (1843), 2 Y. & C. Ch. Cas. 468. See now Trustee Act 1925, s. 37 (1) (a).

[19] Emmet v. Clark (1861), 3 Giff. 32; Re Cunningham & Bradley's Contract for Sale to Wilson, [1877] W.N. 258 (the statement in this case that there is a different rule in relation to charity trustees seems to be ill-founded—see Re Worcester Charities (1847), 2 Ph. 284; Re Shrewsbury Charities (1849), 1 Mac. & G. 84). Cf. Lonsdale (Earl) v. Beckett (1850), 4 De. G. & Sm. 73.

[20] (1885), 53 L.T. 620, C.A. Cf. Re Rendell's Trusts (1915), 139 L.T. Jo. 249.

There are now statutory provisions[1] to the effect that on the appointment of a trustee[2] it shall not be obligatory,

(a) subject to the provisions discussed above[3] to appoint more than one trustee where only one trustee was originally appointed, or

(b) to fill up the original number of trustees where more than two trustees were originally appointed.

The same section[4] further provides, however, that except where only one trustee was originally appointed, and a sole trustee when appointed will be able to give valid receipts for all capital money,[5] a trustee shall not be discharged from his trust unless there will be either a trust corporation or at least two individuals to act as trustees to perform the trust. A sole surviving trustee even of pure personalty accordingly cannot retire from the trust and appoint a sole trustee (not being a trust corporation) to act in his stead where more than one trustee was originally appointed, and in many cases a sole trustee, even though he be the first and only trustee originally appointed, is in the same position.[6]

The court has always had power and now has statutory jurisdiction under section 41 of the Trustee Act 1925 to increase the number of trustees on an appointment of new trustees,[7] or by appointing an additional trustee or trustees where there is no vacancy.[8] An appointment by the court is commonly made at the request of one or more of the beneficiaries, but although it has been held in some cases that a beneficiary was entitled to have a second,[9] or even a third,[10] trustee appointed, it is doubtful whether in strictness even all the beneficiaries acting together have an absolute right to require the appointment of even a second trustee.[11] Again, the court has always had power to reduce the number of trustees, and on the appointment of new trustees may do so under the statutory jurisdiction,[12] even in disregard of directions contained in the trust deed,[13] though it is not likely to take this course without any special circumstances being estab-

---

[1] Trustee Act 1925, s. 37 (1) (c).

[2] Presumably under either an express or the statutory power.

[3] See also Trustee Act 1925, s. 37 (2), which provides "Nothing in this Act shall authorise the appointment of a sole trustee, not being a trust corporation, where the trustee, when appointed, would not be able to give valid receipts for all capital money arising under the trust."

[4] Ibid., s. 37 (1) (c).

[5] Primarily where there is a trust of pure personalty, but also, semble, where X holds land on a bare trust for Y, i.e. where there is no trust for sale.

[6] I.e. where a sole trustee when appointed will be unable to give valid receipts for all capital money.

[7] See e.g. Birch v. Cropper (1848), 2 De. G. & Sm. 255; Plenty v. West (1853), 16 Beav. 356.

[8] See e.g. Grant v. Grant (1865), 34 L.J. Ch. 641; Re Gregson's Trusts (1886), 34 Ch.D. 209.

[9] Grant v. Grant, supra.

[10] Viscountess D'Adhemar v. Bertrand (1865), 35 Beav. 19.

[11] Re Badger's Settlement (1915), 113 L.T. 150. But the position may be different since 1925 where there is a sole trustee who cannot give a valid receipt for capital moneys.

[12] Re Fowler's Trusts (1886), 55 L.T. 546; Re Leslie's Hassop Estates, [1911] 1 Ch. 611.

[13] Re Leslie's Hassop Estates, supra.

lished.[14] As we have seen,[15] the court either cannot, or will not, under the statutory jurisdiction, reduce the number of trustees save on the appointment of new trustees, though it has inherent jurisdiction to do so in an action to administer the trust.

In deciding how many trustees should be appointed the court will, of course, comply with the restriction limiting the number of trustees to four, in those cases where section 34 of the Trustee Act 1925 applies, and in practice will never appoint a sole trustee where such trustee would not be able to give a valid receipt for capital moneys. Quite apart from statutory provisions, there are obvious dangers in the trust property being under the control of a sole trustee, and consequently it has been said[16] that "the court never commits a trust to the care of a single trustee, even in cases where no more than one was originally appointed" and one judge even affirmed[17] "I do not think it right to leave it to two". It seems, however, that although the court is reluctant to appoint a single trustee,[18] it will do so if special circumstances would make it more beneficial to the parties interested,[19] for instance where the trust fund is small and shortly to be distributed and the appointment of a second trustee would incur disproportionate expense.

g   Separate sets of trustees for distinct trusts

On an appointment[1] out of court of a trustee for the whole or any part of trust property, section 37 (1) (b)[2] of the Trustee Act 1925 provides—

"a separate set of trustees, not exceeding four, may be appointed for any part of the trust property held on trusts distinct from those relating to any other part or parts of the trust property, notwithstanding that no new trustees or trustee are or is to be appointed for other parts of the trust property, and any existing trustee may be appointed or remain one of such separate set of trustees, or, if only one trustee was originally appointed, then, save as hereinafter provided,[3] one separate trustee may be so appointed ".

The section apparently applies in a case where different parts of the trust property are for the time being held on distinct trusts, even though upon a certain event the trusts may ultimately coalesce.[4]

On an appointment of new trustees by the court,[5] it has always been possible

---

[14] Re Fowler's Trusts (1886), 55 L.T. 546.
[15] See p. 236, ante.
[16] Per Romilly M.R. in Viscountess D'Adhemar v. Bertrand (1865), 35 Beav. 19, 20.
[17] Bulkeley v. Earl of Eglinton, supra, per Page Wood V.C. at 994. This statement goes too far.
[18] I.e. an individual as opposed to a trust corporation.
[19] Sitwell v. Heron (1850), 14 Jur. 848; Re Reynault (1852), 16 Jur. 233.
[1] Presumably under either an express or the statutory power.
[2] Replacing s. 10 (2) (b) of the Trustee Act 1893 which in turn replaced the original provision in s. 5 of the Conveyancing Act 1882, which altered the then existing law.
[3] By sub-s. (2) set out supra, p. 242, in n. 3.
[4] Re Hetherington's Trusts (1886), 34 Ch.D. 211.
[5] It is not clear whether the Trustee Act 1925, s. 37, applies to an appointment by the court, though it seems to have been assumed that the original provision in s. 5 of the Conveyancing Act 1882 did so apply in Re Paine's Trusts (1885), 28 Ch.D. 725; Re Hetherington's Trusts (1886), 34 Ch.D. 211. But see Re Moss's Trusts (1888), 37 Ch.D. 513.

for separate sets of trustees to be appointed for different parts of the trust property held on distinct trusts,[6] though applications to the court are now much less common by reason of the existence of the statutory power just mentioned.

h   Liability[7] of the original trustees and the purported new trustees under an invalid appointment

If a purported appointment of new trustees in place of existing trustees is invalid, the existing trustees remain trustees and will be liable as such in case there is any loss to the trust estate, even though they act upon the assumption that the appointment was valid and take no further part in the administration of the trust. A purported new trustee under the invalid appointment may also be liable as a trustee *de son tort* if he on the like assumption has acted in the trust. These propositions are neatly illustrated by *Pearce* v. *Pearce*,[8] where A and B were trustees. A deed was prepared appointing C a new trustee in the place of B. It was executed by C, but not by the other parties, so that the appointment was invalid. At the same time the trust fund was transferred by A and B to A and C. Afterwards A and C authorised the husband of the tenant for life to receive the fund, and it was lost. It was held that both B and C were liable for the loss, in addition, of course, to A.

2   VESTING OF THE TRUST PROPERTY

a   New trustees

When new trustees are appointed it is clearly vital that the trust property shall be vested in them jointly with the continuing trustees, if any. Dealing first with an appointment out of court, the vesting of the trust property in the new trustees (including any continuing trustees) can be done by means of an ordinary conveyance or transfer by the old trustee or trustees in whom the property is vested, in the form appropriate to the particular kind of trust property. There will not always, however, be a need for this to be done, as by statute the trust property is in many cases automatically vested in the new and any continuing trustees, provided that the new trustees are appointed by deed.

The relevant provisions are contained in section 40 of the Trustee Act 1925, subsection (1) of which is in the following terms—

"Where by a deed[9] a new trustee is appointed to perform any trust, then—

(a) if the deed contains a declaration[10] by the appointor to the effect that any estate or interest in any land subject to the trust, or in any chattel so subject, or the right to recover or receive any debt or other thing in action so subject, shall vest in the persons who by virtue of the deed become or are the trustees

---

[6] See e.g. *Re Moss's Trusts, supra*; *Re Paine's Trusts, supra*; *Re Hetherington's Trusts, supra*.

[7] See, generally, Chapter 12, *post*, and in particular s. 61 of the Trustee Act 1925, discussed Section 3 d, p. 379, *post*.

[8] (1856), 22 Beav. 248.

[9] By sub-s. (6) the section applies to deeds of appointment executed on or after 1st January, 1882, in relation to trusts created at any time.

[10] See also sub-s. (3), which deals with the possibility that there may be defects in the form of an express vesting declaration.

for performing the trust, the deed shall operate,[11] without any conveyance or assignment, to ·vest in those persons as joint tenants and for the purposes of the trust the estate interest or right to which the declaration relates; and

(b) if the deed is made after the commencement of this Act and does not contain such a declaration, the deed shall, subject to any express provision to the contrary therein contained, operate as if it had contained such a declaration by the appointor extending to all the estates interests and rights with respect to which a declaration could have been made."

Certain cases are, however, expressly excluded from the operation of the section by subsection (4), and unfortunately they include some of the most usual kinds of trust property. They comprise the following :—

"(a) land conveyed by way of mortgage for securing money subject to the trust except land conveyed on trust for securing debentures or debenture stock;

(b) land held under a lease[12] which contains any covenant, condition or agreement against assignment or disposing of the land without licence or consent, unless, prior to the execution of the deed containing expressly or impliedly the vesting declaration, the requisite licence or consent has been obtained, or unless, by virtue of any statute or rule of law, the vesting declaration, express or implied, would not operate as a breach of covenant or give rise to a forfeiture;

(c) any share, stock, annuity or property which is only transferable in books kept by a company or other body, or in manner directed by or under an Act of Parliament."

There are special reasons why it is necessary to exclude the implied vesting provisions in each of these cases. In the first case, concerning mortgages, the object is to keep the trusts off the face of the mortgagor's title: trustees who lend money on a mortgage of land do not disclose the fact in the mortgage deed, nor is it disclosed in the transfer of mortgage which must be executed on the appointment of new trustees.[13] The second case, concerning leases, is to avoid the possibility of an inadvertent breach of covenant which would render the lease liable to be forfeited. The last case is necessary because the legal title to such property as stocks and shares depends upon the appropriate entry having been made in a register consequent upon the completion of a proper instrument of transfer and the whole system would break down if the legal title could pass in any other manner. A company deals with the registered shareholder as the legal owner of the shares, and does not recognize the existence of any trust which may affect them.

It should be mentioned that as regards registered land, the registrar is required

---

[11] Even where the estate, interest or right is not vested in the person making the appointment. Cf. s. 9, Law of Property Act 1925. This provision conveniently covers the case where, for instance, the person who appoints the new trustees is not himself a trustee. The section presumably does not enable a legal estate outstanding in some third party holding adversely to the trust to be vested in the new trustees, or even, it seems, according to Re King's Will Trusts, [1964] 1 All E.R. 833; [1964] Ch. 542, where the trustee holds the legal estate in some other capacity, such as personal representative.

[12] Defined by the subsection to include an under-lease and an agreement for a lease or under-lease.

[13] The Law of Property Act 1925, s. 112, provides that a purchaser shall not be deemed to have notice of any trust by reason of the fact that the transfer bears only a ten-shilling stamp and not any higher ad valorem duty which would normally be exigible. See also the Law of Property Act 1925, s. 113.

to give effect on the register to any vesting declaration, express or implied, made on the appointment or discharge of a trustee or otherwise, and to dispositions made in the name and on behalf of a proprietor by a person authorised to make the disposition. It is also declared that the provisions of the Trustee Act 1925, relating to the appointment and discharge of trustees and the vesting of trust property, shall apply to registered land subject to the proper entry being made on the register.[14]

b Vesting orders

Wide powers to make vesting orders are given to the court under sections 44–56[15] of the Trustee Act 1925. In particular, it is provided that where the court appoints or has appointed a trustee, or where a trustee has been appointed out of court under any statutory or express power, the court may make a vesting order vesting land or any interest therein in the persons who on the appointment are the trustees in any such manner and for any such estate or interest as the court may direct,[16] and may likewise make an order vesting in such persons the right to transfer or call for a transfer of stock, or to receive the dividends or income thereof, or to sue for or recover a thing in action.[17]

It should be mentioned that by rule 6 of the Judicial Trustee Rules 1972, on the appointment of a judicial trustee the court is required to make such vesting or other orders as may be required for vesting the trust property in the judicial trustee either as sole trustee or jointly with other trustees as the case requires.

3 TERMINATION OF TRUSTEESHIP

a Disclaimer[18]

A person who is appointed a trustee cannot be compelled to accept the office. He may disclaim[19] the office, which will also amount to a disclaimer of the estate,[20] at any time before acceptance, but once he has accepted it, it cannot thereafter be disclaimed.[1] Acceptance may be either express, or implied from the acts or conduct of the alleged trustee. Execution by the trustee of the trust deed will normally be regarded as an express acceptance of the trust,[2] and where a person is appointed by will to be executor and trustee, it seems that if he takes out probate of the will, he will be treated as having thereby also accepted the trust.[3] It is sometimes said that in the absence of evidence to the contrary,

---

[14] Land Registration Act 1925, s. 47.
[15] A new section was substituted for s. 54 by the Mental Health Act 1959, s. 149 (1) and Sched. 7, Part 1, which also amended s. 55. Cf. *Re Harrison's Settlement Trusts*, [1965] 3 All E.R. 795.
[16] Trustee Act 1925, s. 44. Alternatively, by s. 50, if it is more convenient the court may appoint a person to convey the land or any interest therein.
[17] Trustee Act 1925, s. 51.
[18] The effect of a valid disclaimer is discussed in Section 1a of this Chapter, p. 226, *ante*.
[19] At the cost of the trust estate—*Re Tryon* (1844), 7 Beav. 496.
[20] *Re Birchall* (1889), 40 Ch.D. 436, C.A.
[1] *Re Sharman's Will Trusts*, [1942] 2 All E.R. 74; [1942] Ch. 311, and see *Re Lister*, [1926] Ch. 149, C.A.
[2] *Jones* v. *Higgins* (1866), L.R. 2 Eq. 538.
[3] *Mucklow* v. *Fuller* (1821), Jac. 198; *Re Sharman's Will Trusts*, *supra*.

acceptance will be presumed,[4] but it is submitted that this statement is somewhat misleading unless coupled with the statement that mere inaction over a long period may itself be sufficient evidence of disclaimer.[5]

Whether by his conduct a person is deemed to have accepted the trust depends upon the view which the court takes of the facts of the case. In one case,[6] a testatrix had appointed a certain person as one of three executors and two trustees of her will. In discussing his position Romilly M.R. observed,[7] "He is one of the executors, he has never proved, but he has never renounced, and he says he has never acted in the trusts; but the court must look at his actions, and see to what character they are attributable. I think he has acted in the character which the testatrix had given him." In general, any interference with the subject matter of the trust by a person appointed trustee will be regarded as an acceptance of the trust, unless it can clearly be explained on some other ground. Thus where a man has permitted an action to be brought in the name of himself and the other trustees,[8] or given directions as to the sale of part of the trust property and made enquiries as to the accounts,[9] he has been held to have accepted the trust. In another case[10] there was a bequest of £1,100 and certain leasehold property to trustees. The only relevant act of the trustees was an assignment of the leasehold property to a beneficiary who had become absolutely entitled. It was held that the execution of the assignment amounted to an acceptance of the trusts not only of the leasehold property but also of the sum of £1,100, for there cannot be part acceptance and part disclaimer. Acceptance of part is regarded as acceptance of the whole, and accordingly prevents a disclaimer of any other parts.[11] Conversely partial disclaimer is impossible: to be effective disclaimer must be "of the totality of the office and estate and *ab initio*".[12]

On the other hand, a person appointed a trustee has been held not to have accepted the trust merely by holding the deed for about six months for safe custody,[13] and similarly in another, perhaps rather doubtful case, where the alleged trustee had actually signed a legacy duty receipt which he need not have done if he were not a trustee.[14] Again, the court has sometimes allowed that the dealing with the subject matter of the trust which is alleged to constitute acceptance of the trust was merely carried out in the capacity of agent to a trustee who had accepted,[15] though the court would doubtless be suspicious of such an explanation of his conduct by an alleged trustee.[16]

If the trust has not been accepted it may be disclaimed, the proper form being

---

[4] See e.g. Underhill's *Law of Trusts and Trustees*, 12th Ed., p. 250—the corresponding statement in an earlier edition was cited with approval in *Re Sharman's Will Trusts*, [1942] 2 All E.R. 74; [1942] Ch. 311; *Re Arbib and Class's Contract*, [1891] 1 Ch. 601, C.A.
[5] This last proposition is, however, itself a matter of dispute. See p. 248, *post.*
[6] *White v. Barton* (1854), 18 Beav. 192.
[7] *White v. Barton, supra* at p. 195.
[8] *Montfort v. Cadogan* (1810), 17 Ves. 485.
[9] *James v. Frearson* (1842), 1 Y. & C.Ch.Cas. 370.
[10] *Urch v. Walker* (1838), 3 My. & Cr. 702.
[11] *Re Lord and Fullerton's Contract*, [1896] 1 Ch. 228, C.A.
[12] Per Sargant L.J. in *Re Lister*, [1926] Ch. 149, 166, C.A.
[13] *Evans v. John* (1841), 4 Beav. 35.
[14] *Jago v. Jago* (1893), 68 L.T. 654.
[15] *Dove v. Everard* (1830), 1 Russ. & My. 231, *Lowry v. Fulton* (1839), 9 Sim. 104.
[16] *Conyngham v. Conyngham* (1750), 1 Ves. Sen. 522.

by a deed poll.[17]   As has been said,[18] "It is most prudent that a deed of dis-claimer[19] should be executed by a person named trustee, who refuses to accept the trust, because such deed is clear evidence of the disclaimer, and admits of no ambiguity; but there may be conduct which amounts to a clear disclaimer, and such appears to be the case here".   The conduct referred to was that of the alleged trustee who purchased real property and took a conveyance from one who could only have a title thereto on the basis of a disclaimer having been effected.[20]   An effective disclaimer may be made by an alleged trustee in the pleadings in an action brought against him for enforcement of the trust,[1] or even by his counsel at the bar.[2]

Although it has been said[3] that "a disclaimer, to be worth anything, must be an act whereby one entitled to an estate immediately and before dealing with it renounces it", the better view, it is submitted, is that although a disclaimer ought to be made without delay, there is no rule that it must be executed within any particular time,[4] and in several reported cases a disclaimer after twenty years or so has been held to be valid.[5]   Further it is submitted that the better view is that mere inaction by the alleged trustee over a long period may by itself be sufficient evidence of disclaimer, and the longer the period of inaction, the stronger the presumption of disclaimer.   This was the view taken by Lord Buckmaster[6] in *Re Clout & Frewer's Contract*,[7] applying the decisions in *Re Gordon*[8] and *Re Birchall*[9] and casting doubt on the contrary view expressed in *Re Uniacke*[10] and *Re Needham*,[11] that the longer the period of inaction the stronger the presumption of acceptance.

It has been said that one of several trustees cannot disclaim,[12] but it is submitted, with respect, that this *obiter dictum* cannot stand in the light of numerous cases where such a disclaimer has been held to be effective,[13] thus making the title of those trustees who do accept valid *ab initio*.   Finally it should perhaps be mentioned that just as acceptance of a trust makes a subsequent disclaimer impossible, so a valid disclaimer precludes the possibility of a subsequent acceptance.

---

[17] *Re Schar*, [1950] 2 All E.R. 1069; [1951] Ch. 280.
[18] *Per* Leach M.R. in *Stacey* v. *Elph* (1833), 1 My. & K. 195, at p. 199.
[19] It has been held that what is in form a deed of release which logically involves a prior acceptance, may operate as a disclaimer if this was the intention (*Nicloson* v. *Wordsworth* (1818), 2 Swans. 365).
[20] See also *Re Gordon* (1877), 6 Ch.D. 531; *Re Birchall* (1889), 40 Ch.D. 436, C.A.
[1] *Norway* v. *Norway* (1834), 2 My. & K. 278; *Bray* v. *West* (1838), 9 Sim. 429.
[2] *Foster* v. *Dawber* (1860), 1 Drew & Sm. 172.
[3] *Per* Kelly C.B. in *Bence* v. *Gilpin* (1868), L.R. 3 Exch. 76, 81.
[4] *Jago* v. *Jago* (1893), 68 L.T. 654.
[5] *Doe d. Chidgey* v. *Harris* (1847), 16 M. & W. 517 (16 years); *Peppercorn* v. *Wayman* (1852), 5 De G. & Sm. 230 (20 or 21 years).
[6] Sitting as a judge of first instance.
[7] [1924] 2 Ch. 230.
[8] (1877), 6 Ch.D. 531.
[9] (1889), 40 Ch.D. 436, C.A.
[10] (1844), 1 Jo. & Lat. 1.
[11] (1844), 1 Jo. & Lat. 34.
[12] *Per* Vaisey J. in *Re Schar*, [1950] 2 All E.R. 1069, at p. 1072; [1951] Ch. 280, at p. 285.
[13] See e.g. *Peppercorn* v. *Wayman* (1852), 5 De.G. & Sm. 230; *Re Birchall* (1889), 40 Ch.D. 436, C.A.

b Death

Trustees are invariably joint tenants and accordingly on the death of one of two or more trustees the trust estate, by reason of the *ius accrescendi*, devolves on the surviving trustees or trustee. It is now provided by statute, affirming the equitable rule,[14] that the office likewise devolves on the surviving trustees or trustee. The terms of s. 18 (1) of the Trustee Act 1925 are as follows—

> "Where a power or trust is given to or imposed on two or more trustees jointly, the same may be exercised or performed by the survivors or survivor of them for the time being."

It should be remembered that this provision does not abrogate the old rule that a bare power, given to two or more persons by name and not annexed to an estate or office, does not survive.[15] However it has been said[16] that

> "Every power given to trustees which enables them to deal with or affect the trust property is *prima facie* given them *ex officio* as an incident of their office, and passes with the office to the holders or holder thereof for the time being; whether a power is so given *ex officio* or not depends in each case on the construction of the document giving it, but the mere fact that the power is one requiring the exercise of a very wide personal discretion is not enough to exclude the *prima facie* presumption . . .: the testator's reliance on the individuals to the exclusion of the holders of the office for the time being must be expressed in clear and apt language."

Upon the death of a sole or last surviving trustee, the trust estate, since 1925, devolves on his personal representatives,[17] and it is provided by section 18 (2) of the Trustee Act 1925, that such personal representatives (excluding an executor who has renounced or has not proved),[18] "shall be capable of exercising or performing any power or trust which was given to, or capable of being exercised by, the sole or last surviving or continuing trustee, or other the trustees or trustee for the time being of the trust". It will be observed that this provision does not impose any obligation on the personal representatives to act, and it would seem therefore that the old law still applies, that "such a personal representative of a deceased trustee has an absolute right to decline to accept the position and duties of trustee if he chooses so to do".[19] Presumably, however, if such a personal representative chose to accept[20] the trust, he would thereafter be liable as a trustee in the ordinary way. Even if personal representatives do accept the trust, they can only act until the appointment of new trustees. In practice, they are themselves likely to be the appropriate persons to appoint new trustees, but if

---

14 See e.g. *Warburton* v. *Sandys* (1845), 14 Sim. 622.
15 *Re Harding*, [1923] 1 Ch. 182; [1922] All E.R. Rep. 557, see p. 232, *ante*.
16 *Per* Farwell J. in *Re Smith*, [1904] 1 Ch. 139, 144; *Re De Sommery*, [1912] 2 Ch. 622; *Crawford* v. *Forshaw*, [1891] 2 Ch. 261, C.A.
17 Administration of Estates Act 1925, ss. 1–3.
18 Trustee Act 1925, s. 18 (4).
19 *Per* Vaughan Williams L.J. in *Re Benett*, [1906] 1 Ch. 216, 225, C.A.; *Legg* v. *Mackrell* (1860), 2 De G.F. & J. 551; *Re Ridley*, [1904] 2 Ch. 774.
20 Taking out probate is not, of course, any evidence of an intention to accept a trust of which the deceased was trustee. Cf. the case where the will creates the trust and appoints a person executor and trustee—p. 246, *ante*.

some other person has such a power which is validly exercised, it will operate forthwith to oust the personal representatives for all purposes from the trust.[1]

Finally it should be mentioned that all the above provisions are subject to the restrictions imposed in regard to receipts by a sole trustee, not being a trust corporation.[2]

c   Retirement

A trustee may voluntarily retire from the trust under any of the following circumstances:

i   *Under an express power in the trust instrument.* There is no reason why an express power should not be inserted, but it is not now usual to do so as the statutory power next referred to is normally regarded as adequate.

ii   *Under the provisions of the Trustee Act 1925.* As we have seen, a trustee who desires to be discharged from all or any of the trusts may retire on the appointment of a new trustee in his place under the provisions of section 36 of the Trustee Act 1925.[3] In addition he may be able to retire without a new appointment under the provisions of section 39 of the Trustee Act 1925. This provides as follows—

> "Where a trustee is desirous of being discharged from the trust, and after his discharge there will be either a trust corporation or at least two individuals to act as trustees to perform the trust, then, if such trustee as aforesaid by deed declares that he is desirous of being discharged from the trust, and if his co-trustees and such other person, if any, as is empowered to appoint trustees, by deed consent[4] to the discharge of the trustee, and to the vesting in the co-trustees alone of the trust property, the trustee desirous of being discharged shall be deemed to have retired from the trust, and shall, by the deed, be discharged therefrom under this Act, without any new trustee being appointed in his place."

It appears that under this provision, as contrasted with the provisions of section 36, a trustee cannot retire from part of the trusts, as there is no phrase equivalent to "all or any of the trusts or powers". However, if separate sets of trustees have been appointed under section 37, it is submitted that a trustee will be able to retire therefrom under section 39, on the ground that the distinct trust is to be regarded as a trust and not merely part of a trust.

iii   *Under an order of the court.* As we have seen[5] the court either cannot or will not discharge a trustee under its statutory jurisdiction[6] except on the appointment of a new trustee. It has, however, inherent jurisdiction to do so in

---

[1] *Re Routledge's Trusts*, [1909] 1 Ch. 280.
[2] Trustee Act 1925, s. 18 (3).
[3] See Section I c, p. 228, *ante*. He may retire similarly under an appropriate express power of appointment.
[4] By the Public Trustee Act 1906, s. 5 (2) where the Public Trustee has been appointed a trustee, a co-trustee may retire under these provisions notwithstanding that there are not more than two trustees, and without any consents being obtained.
[5] See Section I d, p. 236, *ante*.
[6] Trustee Act 1925, s. 41.

an action to administer the trust.[7] The existence of the statutory power under section 39 means, however, that it is only rarely that it will be necessary to invoke the jurisdiction of the court. A case might, however, arise where, for instance, the trustee was physically incapable of executing the necessary deed,[8] or where a person with a power of appointment could not be found, or refused to give his consent.

It was said in one case[9] that "no person can be compelled to remain a trustee and act in the execution of the trust" but retirement without good cause was discouraged by the rule that if a trustee retired from mere caprice, he would have to pay the costs,[10] though he might be justified in wishing to retire and accordingly be allowed his costs when circumstances arising in the administration of the trust had altered the nature of his duties and involved him in difficulties and responsibilities which he had never contemplated.[11] However, since the Trustee Act 1925 appears to recognize that a trustee has a right to retire if he desires to do so, it would seem that a trustee should now normally be allowed the costs of an application to the court, if for any reason he is unable to take advantage of the statutory provisions.

Where a sole trustee wishes to retire, and it is impossible to find anyone who is willing to become the new trustee,[12] the court will not discharge him, so as to leave the trust without a trustee. An order may, however, be made in such case for the administration of the trust by the court, and although the trustee retains his office, the court will take care in working out the order that the trustee does not suffer.[13] Similar considerations will presumably apply,[14] where one of two trustees wishes to retire, and the sole continuing trustee would not be able to give valid receipts for capital moneys.[15]

iv *By consent of the beneficiaries.* If all the *cestuis que trust*, being *sui iuris*, consent to the retirement of a trustee, none of them will thereafter be able to call that trustee to account for anything that happens after the date of such retirement. It is by no means clear, however, that a trustee could rely upon such a retirement vis-à-vis his co-trustees, unless of course they also consent. In truth this is merely a special application of the rule[16] that a beneficiary who has concurred in or assented to a breach of trust cannot have any right of action in respect thereof. It is of course essential that each of the *cestuis que trust* who gives his consent shall be of full age and *sui iuris*, and that between them they comprise the entirety of the equitable interests under the trust.

v *By payment into court.* Under the Trustee Act 1925, s. 63,[17] trustees may

---

[7] *Re Chetwynd's Settlement*, [1902] 1 Ch. 692.
[8] *Re Stretton*, [1942] W.N. 95.
[9] *Forshaw* v. *Higginson* (1855), 20 Beav. 485 *per* Romilly M.R. at p. 487.
[10] *Forshaw* v. *Higginson, supra; Howard* v. *Rhodes* (1837), 1 Keen 581.
[11] *Forshaw* v. *Higginson, supra; Gardiner* v. *Downes* (1856), 22 Beav. 395.
[12] Since the Public Trustee Act 1906, it will usually be possible to appoint the Public Trustee, or a trust corporation may be appointed.
[13] *Courtenay* v. *Courtenay* (1846), 3 Jo. & Lat. 519; *Re Chetwynd's Settlement,*[1902] 1 Ch. 692.
[14] Cf. *Re Chetwynd's Settlement, supra.*
[15] See Section 1 f, p. 241, *ante.*
[16] Discussed in Chapter 12, Section 3 a, p. 370, *post.*
[17] Discussed in Chapter 11, Section 10, p. 358, *post.*

pay into court money or securities belonging to a trust. It has been said[18] "that payment of a trust fund into court is a retiring from the trust", and it is settled that having done so the trustees cannot prevent a *cestui que trust* from having the fund paid out to him,[19] nor can the trustees any longer exercise any of their discretionary powers.[20] It seems, however, that he does not in fact altogether cease to be a trustee, neither is the court nor the Accountant-General constituted a co-trustee.[1] He remains a trustee for the purpose of receiving notices,[2] and would be a necessary party to an action in relation to the fund.[3]

d Removal

i *Under an express power.* An express power of removal is not usually inserted under most kinds of trust. It is, however, commonly found in an equitable mortage to a bank by a deposit of title deeds, when the mortgagor often declares himself a trustee of the legal estate for the bank, which is given an express power to remove the mortgagor as trustee and appoint itself or some other person in his place.[4]

ii *Under the provisions of section 36 of the Trustee Act 1925.* As we have seen, on the appointment of a new trustee an existing trustee may be removed against his will if he remains out of the United Kingdom for more than twelve months, or refuses or is unfit to act therein, or is incapable of acting.

iii *Under the provisions of section 41 of the Trustee Act 1925.* As we have seen the court may, under this section, on the appointment of a new trustee, remove an existing trustee. It will not, however, simply discharge a trustee without appointing a new trustee,[5] nor will it exercise its statutory jurisdiction to remove a trustee where there is a dispute as to the facts.[6]

iv *By the court under its inherent jurisdiction.* The court has an inherent jurisdiction to remove a trustee in an action[7] for the administration or execution of a trust, without necessarily appointing a new trustee, and notwithstanding that the facts may be in dispute.[8] The Privy Council observed in *Letterstedt* v. *Broers*,[9] that there was little authority to guide them in deciding in what circumstances the jurisdiction should be exercised and they were not prepared to lay down any general rule beyond the very broad principle that their main

---

[18] *Per* Page Wood V.C. in *Re Williams' Settlement* (1858), 4 K. & J. 87, at p. 88.

[19] *Re Wright's Trusts* (1857), 3 K. & J. 419.

[20] *Re Tegg* (1866), 15 L.T. 236; *Re Coe's Trust* (1858), 4 K. & J. 199; *Re Nettlefold's Trusts* (1888), 59 L.T. 315.

[1] *Thompson* v. *Tomkins* (1862), 6 L.T. 305; *Barker* v. *Peile* (1865), 2 Drew & Sm. 340.

[2] *Thompson* v. *Tomkins, supra.*

[3] *Barker* v. *Peile, supra.*

[4] *London and County Banking Co.* v. *Goddard,* [1897] 1 Ch. 642; and see Key and Elphinstone's *Precedents in Conveyancing,* 15th Ed., Vol. 2, p. 237.

[5] See p. 236 *supra.* Also *Re Harrison's Settlement Trusts,* [1965] 3 All E.R. 795.

[6] *Re Combs* (1884), 51 L.T. 45 C.A. Cf. *Re Dove's Will Trust,* [1939] W.N. 230.

[7] Generally, this should be an action began by writ: see Chapter 12, Section 1g, *post,* p. 368.

[8] *Re Chetwynd's Settlement,* [1902] 1 Ch. 692; *Re Wrightson,* [1908] 1 Ch. 789; *Re Henderson,* [1940] 3 All E.R. 295; [1940] Ch. 764.

[9] (1884), 9 App. Cas. 371, at p. 385, P.C.

guide must be the welfare of the beneficiaries. It seems that although friction and hostility between a trustee and the beneficiaries is not necessarily or even normally a sufficient ground for the removal of a trustee,[10] the court may think it proper to take this into account and accordingly in some circumstances to remove a trustee, even though he has not been guilty of any breach of trust.[11]

4 JUDICIAL TRUSTEES

By the Judicial Trustees Act 1896[12] the High Court[13] is empowered, on application made by or on behalf of the person creating or intending to create a trust, or of a trustee of beneficiary, to appoint a person, known as a judicial trustee, to be a trustee of that trust. The object of the Act has been said[14] to have been "to provide a middle course in cases where the administration of the estate by the ordinary trustees had broken down and it was not desired to put the estate to the expense of a full administration. In those circumstances, a solution was found in the appointment of a judicial trustee, who acts in close concert with the court and under conditions enabling the court to supervise his transactions." The provisions of the Act do not seem, however, to have found much favour with practitioners: it is often possible, and thought more convenient, to deal with cases where a judicial trustee could be applied for, by appointing the Public Trustee, or some other corporate trustee.

A judicial trustee may be appointed either jointly with any other person[15] or as sole trustee, and if sufficient cause is shown, in place of all or any existing trustees.[16] It is expressly provided[16] that the appointment is to be made at the discretion of the court, and it follows that no one can claim to be entitled as of right to have an appointment made.[17] Thus the court in one case refused to make an appointment on the application of the mortgagees of one fifth of the reversion where one of two trustees wished to be discharged, and the tenant for life was prepared to appoint in his place a person to whom no objection was made.[18]

The Act does not contain any definition of "trust", and it was held in *Re Marshall's Will Trusts*[19] that that word must be given its ordinary meaning, the judge for the purpose of the case before him adopting the definition given by

---

[10] *Forster* v. *Davies* (1861), 4 De. G.F. & J. 133; *Re Wrightson, supra.*
[11] *Letterstedt* v. *Broers, supra*; *Re Consiglio Trust* (No. 1) (1973), 36 D.L.R. (3d) 658 (Ont. C.A.).
[12] Section 1 (1).
[13] Proceedings under the Act are assigned to the Chancery Division. The previous County Court jurisdiction determined on 31 August 1972 (except in relation to subsisting proceedings)—Judicial Trustee Rules 1972 (S.I. 1972 No. 1096).
[14] *Per* Jenkins J. in *Re Ridsdel*, [1947] 2 All E.R. 312, at pp. 316–7; [1947] Ch. 597, at p. 605.
[15] In *Re Martin*, [1900] W.N. 129, Kekewich J. expressed the opinion that the union of a judicial trustee and a private trustee was undesirable.
[16] Judicial Trustees Act 1896, s. 1 (1).
[17] *Re Ratcliff*, [1898] 2 Ch. 352.
[18] *Re Chisholm* (1898), 43 Sol. Jo. 43.
[19] [1945] 1 All E.R. 550; [1945] Ch. 217.

Underhill,[20] and holding that Settled Land Act trustees were trustees within that definition. In one respect, however, the meaning of trust is considerably extended for the purpose of the Judicial Trustees Act, which by section 1 (2) expressly provides that "the administration of the property of a deceased person, whether a testator or intestate, shall be a trust, and the executor or administrator a trustee, within the meaning of this Act". Accordingly the court, by appointing a judicial trustee, can in effect appoint a new personal representative,[1] which, as we have seen,[2] it has no power to do either under the provisions of the Trustee Act, 1925,[3] or the inherent jurisdiction.[4] Unless, however, the will appointed separate executors for different parts of the estate, the court has no powers to appoint a judicial trustee of the trusts affecting a part only of the estate. Unless this were done, the executorship would be indivisible, and there would not be created separate trusts within the meaning of the Act of 1896 with regard to particular assets.[5]

By section 1 (3) of the Act "any fit and proper person nominated for the purpose in the application may be appointed a judicial trustee, and, in the absence of such nomination, or if the court is not satisfied of the fitness of a person so nominated, an official of the court[6] may be appointed." An official of the court cannot, however, be appointed or act as judicial trustee for any persons in their capacity as members or debenture holders of, or being in any other relation to, any corporation or unincorporate body, or any club, or of a trust which involves the carrying on of any trade or business unless the Court, with or without special conditions to ensure the proper supervision of the trade or business, specifically directs. Apart from an official of the Court, the Rules[7] expressly provide that "any fit and proper person" includes—

(i)   an existing trustee of the trust;[8]
(ii) an executor or administrator of the estate of a deceased person the administration of whose property constitutes the trust;
(iii) a beneficiary;
(iv) a solicitor of the trust, or to a trustee or to a beneficiary;
(v)   a qualified accountant;[9] and
(vi) a person standing in any special position with regard to the trust.

---

[20] *Law of Trusts and Trustees*, 8th Ed., p. 3, *viz.*: "A trust is an equitable obligation, binding a person (who is called a trustee) to deal with property over which he has control (which is called the trust property) for the benefit of persons (who are called the beneficiaries or *cestuis que trust*), of whom he may himself be one and any one of whom may enforce the obligation." The definition is unchanged in the current (12th) edition.

[1] *Re Ratcliff*, [1898] 2 Ch. 352.

[2] See p. 236, *ante*.   [3] Section 41 (1).

[4] Note, however, the Judicature Act 1925, s. 160 (2), and the Administration of Estates Act 1925, s. 23 (2).   [5] *Re Wells*, [1967] 3 All E.R. 908.

[6] "Official of the Court" means the holder of any paid office in or connected with the court, and in practice, unless there are special reasons, should be the official solicitor of the court—Judicial Trustees Act 1896, s. 5, and Judicial Trustee Rules 1972, rr. 3 (1) and 6 (1) (b).   [7] Judicial Trustee Rules 1972, r. 6 (1).

[8] The corresponding provision (r. 5 (2)) in the 1897 Rules appears to have been overlooked in *Re Marshall's Will Trusts*, [1945] 1 All E.R. 350; [1945] Ch. 217. It is accordingly submitted that the difficulties felt as to the form of the order in that case are illusory.

[9] I.e. a person who is a member, or a firm, all the partners of which are members, of the Institute of Chartered Accountants in England and Wales or of the Association of Certified and Corporate Accountants—*Ibid.*, r. 3 (1).

The Public Trustee Act 1906[10] provides that the Public Trustee may, if he thinks fit, be appointed to be a judicial trustee.

Except where the judicial trustee is an official of the court, the court may require a judicial trustee to give security for the due application of the trust property under or to be under his control. It will not, however, normally require security to be given when the application is made by a person creating or intending to create a trust. Even where security is required the judicial trustee may be allowed to act before the security is completed.[11]

Once appointed a judicial trustee is, in general, "in the position of any other trustee and exercises all the powers of any other trustee".[12] There are various regulations as to the mode in which the trust must be administered, the more important of which are mentioned in their appropriate contexts. At this point it is sufficient to mention that "the court may, either on request or without request, give to a judicial trustee any general or special directions in regard to the trust or the administration thereof".[13] It is further provided[14] that the court may dispense with formal proof when it is satisfied that there is no reasonable doubt of any fact which affects the administration of a trust by a judicial trustee; that a judicial trustee may communicate with or be given directions by the court by letter without any further formality; and that any other thing required to be done in relation to the administration of the trust may be done in a simple and informal manner.

The court may at any time, if it considers that it is expedient to do so in the interests of the trust, either suspend, or remove[15] a judicial trustee. If a judicial trustee wishes to be discharged from his trust he must give notice to the court of the arrangements proposed for the appointment of a successor.[16] In practice, although a retiring judicial trustee has no overriding right under section 36 of the Trustee Act 1925 or otherwise to appoint his successor,[17] his nominee is likely to be appointed. The court, however, may appoint another person, or where the court considers it convenient or expedient in the interests of the trust so to do, the court may appoint an official of the court to be the new judicial trustee. Further, it is possible for any person interested in the trust to apply to the court for an order that there shall cease to be a judicial trustee of the trust, whether the person who is judicial trustee continues as an ordinary trustee or not. The court may make the order after ascertaining the wishes of all persons appearing to be interested, and must do so if all the persons so appearing concur.[18]

---

[10] Section 2 (1) (d). See also Re Johnston (1911), 105 L.T. 701 which seems to be authority for the proposition that where there is an existing judicial trustee, and it is desired to appoint the Public Trustee as an ordinary trustee, there must first be an order under the Judicial Trustee Rules 1972, r. 21, that there shall cease to be a judicial trustee of the trust.

[11] Judicial Trustee Rules 1972, r. 8.

[12] Per Jenkins J. in Re Ridsdel, [1947] 2 All E.R. 312, at p. 314; [1947] Ch. 597, 601.

[13] Judicial Trustees Act 1896, s. 1 (4).

[14] Judicial Trustee Rules 1972, rr. 12 and 26.

[15] Ibid., r. 18.

[16] Ibid., r. 20.

[17] Re Johnston (1911), 105 L.T. 701.

[18] Judicial Trustee Rules 1972, r. 21.

5 THE PUBLIC TRUSTEE

a General powers and duties

The Public Trustee, a corporation sole with perpetual succession and an official seal, is an office created by the Public Trustee Act 1906. He may act, either alone or jointly with any person or body of persons,[19] as an ordinary trustee,[1] a judicial trustee, or as custodian trustee,[2] but he may decline to accept any trust, though he cannot do so on the ground only of the small value of the trust property.[3] He is not permitted to accept any trust exclusively for religious or charitable purposes,[4] nor any trust under a deed of arrangement for the benefit of creditors,[5] nor the trust of any instrument made solely by way of security for money.[6] He must not, as a general rule, accept any trust which involves the management or carrying on of any business, but may, if he thinks fit, as regards such a trust

  i act as custodian trustee, but upon the conditions that

   (a) he shall not act in the management or carrying on of such business, and
   (b) he shall not hold any property of such a nature as will expose the holder thereof to any liability except under exceptional circumstances and when he is satisfied that he is fully indemnified or secured against loss; and

  ii accept as ordinary trustee under exceptional circumstances, but upon the conditions that except with the consent of the Treasury, he shall only carry on the same

   (a) for a short time not exceeding eighteen months, and
   (b) with a view to sale, disposition or winding-up, and
   (c) if satisfied that the same can be carried on without risk of loss.[7]

In practice, the tendency seems to be to appoint some other corporate trustee, such as a bank, rather than the Public Trustee.

b Mode of appointment

The Public Trustee may be appointed as ordinary trustee of any will or settlement or other instrument creating a trust, either as an original or a new trustee, or as an additional trustee, in the same cases and in the same manner and by the

---

[19] Public Trustee Act 1906, s. 2 (2).
[1] He can accept trusteeship only of an English trust—*Re Hewitt's Settlement*, [1915] 1 Ch. 228.
[2] Public Trustee Act 1906, s. 2 (1). This section read together with s. 15 and Public Trustee Rules 1912, r. 6, enables the Public Trustee to act as executor and administrator, and in effect by s. 6 (2) to be appointed as a new executor or administrator, either solely or jointly with the continuing executors or administrators; he is, by s. 3, also authorised to administer an estate, in lieu of administration by the court, where the gross capital is less than £1,000.
[3] Public Trustee Act 1906, s. 2 (3).
[4] *Ibid.*, s. 2 (5). E.g. a trust where the sole object involved the selection of charitable objects for the testator's bounty—*Re Hampton* (1918), 88 L.J. Ch. 103.
[5] Public Trustee Act 1906, s. 2 (4).
[6] Public Trustee Rules 1912, r. 6.
[7] Public Trustee Act 1906, s. 2 (4) and Public Trustee Rules 1912, r. 7.

same persons or by the court, as if he were a private trustee.[8] He can always be appointed as sole trustee, even though two or more trustees were originally appointed,[9] and notwithstanding a direction in the trust instrument that the number of trustees shall not be less than some specified number.[10] Indeed, the court may order that the Public Trustee be appointed as a new or additional trustee, notwithstanding an express direction to the contrary in the trust instrument.[11] Provision is, however, made for giving notice to the beneficiaries of any proposed appointment of the Public Trustee either as a new or additional trustee, and within 21 days of such notice any beneficiary can apply to the court for an order prohibiting the appointment being made.[12] In deciding whether it is expedient to make such an order, the court will not in ordinary circumstances take into account the fact of the expense that will be incurred by the appointment.[13]

The Public Trustee may be appointed to be custodian trustee of any trust:

(a) by order of the court made on the application of any person on whose application the court may order the appointment of a new trustee; or

(b) by the testator, settlor, or other creator of any trust; or

(c) by the person having power to appoint new trustees.[14]

There is no provision in the case of appointment as custodian trustee for giving notice to the beneficiaries.

An appointment of the Public Trustee as a judicial trustee is made by the court under the provisions of the Judicial Trustees Act 1896.[15]

No appointment of the Public Trustee as an ordinary trustee or as custodian trustee should be made (except by a testator[16]) unless and until the Public Trustee has given his formal consent to act.[17] This is usually incorporated in the deed of appointment. It seems, however, that if formal consent is given at some time after the appointment, the appointment will thereupon become effective and incapable of being withdrawn.[18] In any case, even under a will, the appointment will only become effective if and when the formal consent is given.[1]

---

[8] Public Trustee Act 1906, s. 5 (1).

[9] Ibid., s. 5 (1).

[10] Re Leslie's Hassop Estates, [1911] 1 Ch. 611 (appointment by the court); Re Moxon [1916] 2 Ch. 595; [1916–17] All E.R. Rep. 438 (appointment by persons having statutory power of appointment).

[11] Public Trustee Act 1906, s. 5 (3); Re Leslie's Hassop Estates, supra.

[12] Public Trustee Act 1906, s. 5 (4). It was said in Re Hope Johnstone's Settlement Trusts (1909), 25 T.L.R. 369 that the Public Trustee should only be appointed if there was no other way out of the difficulty, but in Re Drake's Settlement (1926), 42 T.L.R. 467, Romer J. stated that these observations were only intended to refer to settlements of the kind with which the judge was dealing (spendthrift settling his own property, after payment of debts, mainly for his own benefit) and were not of general application.

[13] Re Firth, [1912] 1 Ch. 806.

[14] Public Trustee Act 1906, s. 4 (1).

[15] Discussed in Section 4, p. 253, ante.

[16] Public Trustee Rules 1912, r. 8 (1). R. 8 (3) provides that a person appointed by will to be co-trustee with the Public Trustee should give the Public Trustee notice of his appointment.

[17] Ibid., r. 8 (1) and (2).

[18] Re Shaw, [1914] W.N. 141.

[1] Public Trustee Rules 1912, r. 8 (2); Re Shaw, supra.

c Position of Public Trustee after appointment

The general position is set out in section 2 (2) of the Act, which provides that the Public Trustee

> "shall have all the same powers, duties, and liabilities, and be entitled to the same rights and immunities and be subject to the control and orders of the court, as a private trustee acting in the same capacity".

He has no more power than a private trustee, where he is in the position of having conflicting interests, to make a bargain with himself, and he must accordingly in such circumstances come to the court for sanction to such a bargain.[2] The more important regulations and provisions affecting the Public Trustee are referred to in their respective contexts.

d Future of the Public Trustee

In March 1972 the Hutton Committee of Enquiry[3] reported on the Public Trustee Office. It stated that there was a falling demand for the services of the Public Trustee, and saw no reason to expect a change in the pattern. Consequently it recommended that the Public Trustee Office should be merged with the Official Solicitor's Department, that legislation should be introduced at the earliest possible moment to relieve the Public Trustee from the duty of accepting new business, and that settlors or beneficiaries of existing trusts should be approached and offered the opportunity to accept transfer to another trustee, free of all expenses to the trust and themselves.

The Government has stated that it is in general agreement with the committee's recommendations. No action has, however, been taken to bring these recommendations into effect.

6 CUSTODIAN TRUSTEES

The office of custodian trustee[4] was created by the Public Trustee Act 1906. The idea is quite simply that the trust property shall for greater security[5] be vested in a custodian trustee, while the management of the trust remains in the hands of the other trustees who are known as the managing trustees. It is accordingly provided, on the one hand,[6] that the trust property shall be transferred to the custodian trustee as if he were a sole trustee, and for that purpose vesting orders may, where necessary, be made under the Trustee Act 1925, and, on the other hand,[7] that the management of the trust property and the exercise of any power or discretion exercisable by the trustees under the trust shall remain vested in the trustees other than the custodian trustee. The custodian trustee is not to be reckoned as a trustee in determining the number of trustees for the purposes of the Trustee Act 1925.[8]

---

[2] *Re New Haw Estates Trust* (1912), 107 L.T. 191.   [3] Cmnd. 4913.

[4] Discussed generally in (1960), 24 Con. 196 (Spencer G. Maurice).

[5] The Public Trustee Act 1906, s. 7, provides that the Consolidated Fund shall be liable to make good all sums required to discharge any liability which the Public Trustee, if he were a private trustee, would be personally liable to discharge.

[6] *Ibid.*, s. 4 (2) (*a*).

[7] *Ibid.*, s. 4 (2) (*b*). The differences between a custodian trustee and managing trustees are discussed in *Forster* v. *Williams Deacon's Bank Ltd.*, [1935] Ch. 359; [1935] All E.R. Rep. 374, C.A.

[8] Public Trustee Act 1906, s. 4 (2) (*g*). The relevant provision is discussed in Section 1 f, p. 240, *ante.*

The Public Trustee Act 1906[9] which, as we have seen, provided that the Public Trustee could act as a custodian trustee, also declared that the provisions relating to a custodian trustee should apply in like manner (including a power to charge) to any banking or insurance company or other body corporate entitled by the rules[10] made thereunder to act as custodian trustee. This means:

(*a*) The Solicitor for the affairs of Her Majesty's Treasury;

(*b*) Any corporation which is constituted under the law of the United Kingdom or of any part thereof and having a place of business there and which is empowered by its constitution to undertake trust business (which for the purpose of this rule means the business of acting as trustee under wills and settlements and as executor and administrator), and which is—

(i) a company incorporated by special Act or Royal Charter, or

(ii) a company registered (whether with or without limited liability) under the Companies Act 1948 and having a capital (in stock or shares) for the time being issued of not less than £250,000, of which not less than £100,000 has been paid up in cash, or

(iii) a company registered without limited liability under the Companies Act 1948 of which one of the members is a company within any of the classes hereinbefore defined;

(*c*) Any corporation which is incorporated by special Act or Royal Charter or under the Charitable Trustees Incorporation Act 1872 which is empowered by its constitution to act as a trustee for any charitable purposes, but only in relation to trusts in which its constitution empowers it to act;

(*d*) Any corporation which is constituted under the law of the United Kingdom or of any part thereof and having its place of business there, and which is either—

(i) established for the purpose of undertaking trust business for the benefit of Her Majesty's Navy, Army, Air Force or Civil Service or of any unit, department, member or association of members thereof, and having among its directors or members any persons appointed or nominated by the Defence Council or any Department of State or any one or more of those Departments, or

(ii) authorised by the Lord Chancellor to act in relation to any charitable ecclesiastical or public trusts as a trust corporation, but only in connection with any such trust as is so authorised.

(*e*) Any Regional Hospital Board, Board of Governors of a teaching hospital or Hospital Management Committee constituted under the National Health Service Acts 1946 to 1968, but only in relation to any trust which such a Board or Committee is authorised to accept by virtue of section 59 of the said Act of 1946;[11]

---

[9] Public Trustee Act 1906, s. 4 (3).

[10] The Public Trustee Rules 1912, r. 30, as substituted by S.I. 1971 No. 1894 and amended by Gas Act 1972, s. 49 (1) and Sched. 6, Part II.

[11] This paragraph would appear to require amendment in the light of the National Health Service Reorganisation Act 1973, which abolished most of the authorities referred to in (e) and created new health authorities.

(f) The British Gas Corporation established under the Gas Act 1972 but only in relation to a pension scheme or pension fund established or maintained by the Corporation, by virtue of the powers conferred on them by that Act;

(g) Any of the following, namely—

(i) the Greater London Council,

(ii) [under the reorganisation of local authorities the references to councils and originally contained in (ii) and (iii) are to be construed as references to

(iii) the council of a county, a borough, a district or a parish (in Wales, a community)—Local Government Act 1972, s. 179. S. 120 provides for the vesting in the new local authorities of property held by the old authorities on charitable trusts].

(iv) the Council of the Isles of Scilly,

but only in relation to charitable or public trusts (and not ecclesiastical or eleemosynary trusts) for the benefit of the inhabitants of the area of the local authority concerned and its neighbourhood, or any part of that area".

The more important provisions regulating the relationship between the custodian trustee and the managing trustees are set out in section 4 (2) of the Act as follows:

"(c) As between the custodian trustee and the managing trustees, and subject and without prejudice to the rights of any other persons, the custodian trustee shall have the custody of all securities and documents of title relating to the trust property, but the managing trustee shall have free access thereto and be entitled to take copies thereof or extracts therefrom.

(d) The custodian trustee shall concur in and perform all acts necessary to enable the managing trustees to exercise their powers of management or any other power or discretion vested in them (including the power to pay money or securities into court), unless the matter in which he is requested to concur is a breach of trust, or involves a personal liability upon him in respect of calls or otherwise, but, unless he so concurs, the custodian trustee shall not be liable for any act or default on the part of the managing trustees or any of them.[12]

(e) All sums payable to or out of the income or capital of the trust property shall be paid to or by the custodian trustee: Provided that the custodian trustee may allow the dividends and other income derived from the trust property to be paid to the managing trustees or to such person as they direct, or into such bank to the credit of such person as they may direct, and in such case shall be exonerated from seeing to the application thereof and shall not be answerable for any loss or misapplication thereof.

(f) The power of appointing new trustees, when exercisable by the trustees, shall be exercisable by the managing trustees alone, but the custodian trustee shall have the same power of applying to the court for the appointment of a new trustee as any other trustee."

The Public Trustee cannot be appointed to act in the dual capacity of custodian trustee and managing trustee;[13] and accordingly where, the Public Trustee being custodian trustee, the managing trustee died, and it was desired that the Public Trustee should manage the trust, it was admitted that his

---

[12] See *I.R.Comrs.* v. *Silverts Ltd.*, [1951] 1 All E.R. 703; [1951] Ch. 521, C.A.

[13] A corporation capable of being appointed custodian trustee under the Rules is in the same position. *Forster* v. *Williams Deacon's Bank Ltd.*, [1935] Ch. 359; [1935] All E.R. Rep. 374 C.A.; *Arning* v. *James*, [1936] Ch. 158.

custodian trusteeship had to be terminated, before he could be appointed an ordinary trustee.[14]

The custodian trusteeship can be brought to an end by an order of the court, on an application for this purpose brought by the custodian trustee, or any of the managing trustees, or any beneficiary. Before making the order, the court requires to be satisfied that it is the general wish of the beneficiaries, or that on other grounds it is expedient, to terminate the custodian trusteeship.[15]

7 TRUST CORPORATIONS

In various circumstances it may be advantageous to have a corporate trustee, and when this is the case it will commonly be desirable that the corporate trustee shall be a trust corporation. While almost any corporate trustee could provide continuity of administration, a trust corporation[16] can in addition be expected to provide financial stability and professional expertise in managing the trust,[17] and can act alone in cases where at least two individual trustees would otherwise be required by statute.[18] The most familiar trust corporations are large banks and insurance companies having trustee departments, often separately incorporated, which offer their services as professional trustees. Clearly they will not be prepared to act unless they are remunerated, but they have no greater right to remuneration than any other trustee, though there are special provisions where they are appointed by the court.[19]

Technically, "trust corporation", for the purposes of the relevant 1925 Property Acts[20] is defined therein as meaning the Public Trustee or a corporation either appointed by the court in any particular case to be a trustee or entitled by rules made under the Public Trustee Act 1906, s. 4 (3), to act as custodian trustee;[1] it also, as a result of the Law of Property (Amendment) Act 1926, s. 3, includes the Treasury Solicitor, the Official Solicitor, and other officials prescribed by the Lord Chancellor, a trustee in bankruptcy and a trustee under a deed of arrangement, and in relation to charitable, ecclesiastical and public trusts, local or public authorities and other corporations prescribed by the Lord Chancellor.[2]

---

[14] *Re Squires Settlement* (1946), 115 L.J., Ch. 90.

[15] Public Trustee Act 1906, s. 4 (2) (*i*).

[16] But not only a trust corporation; where, for instance, a reputable firm of accountants has formed its own trust company, with unlimited liability, such a company may be able to offer sufficient *de facto* protection to the beneficiaries, as well as professional skills.

[17] See p. 263, *infra*, especially cases cited in n. 10.

[18] See p. 242, *supra*.

[19] See Chap. 10, sect. 2a(iii) and 2a(v), pp. 309, 310, *infra*.

[20] Law of Property Act 1925, Settled Land Act 1925, Trustee Act 1925, Administration of Estates Act 1925, and the Supreme Court of Judicature (Consolidation) Act 1925.

[1] See pp. 259, 260, *supra*.

[2] In addition some other bodies are created trust corporations for special limited purposes, e.g. the Church of England Pensions Board by the Church of England Pension Board (Powers) Measure 1952, s. 6.

CHAPTER 9

Duties of Trustees–I

Jessel M.R. has pointed out[1] that "it is a fallacy to suppose that every trustee has the same duties and liabilities". For instance, the duties of a trustee in bankruptcy to the bankrupt are not the same as those of an ordinary trustee to his beneficiary,[2] and, as has been mentioned,[3] the vendor under a contract for the sale of land is in a special position. Unless a special case is made out, however, a trustee is bound to perform the duties about to be discussed, in so far as they are appropriate to his trust.

Before considering these duties in detail a general picture should perhaps be drawn. On accepting a trust, new trustees "are bound to inquire of what the property consists that is proposed to be handed over to them and what are the trusts",[4] and they should examine all the relevant documents in order to ascertain that everything is in order. Thereafter "the duty of a trustee is properly to preserve the trust fund, to pay the income and the *corpus* to those who are entitled to them respectively, and to give all his *cestuis que trust*, on demand, information with respect to the mode in which the trust fund has been dealt with, and where it is".[5] "A trustee cannot assert a title of his own to trust property",[6] neither can he divest himself of the trust property, nor of a power given to him as incident to the execution of his trust.[7] If he "ventures to deviate from the letter of his trust, he does so under the obligation and at the peril of afterwards satisfying the court that the deviation was necessary or beneficial".[8] *Prima facie*, a trustee must act personally, and "as a general rule a trustee sufficiently discharges his duty if he takes in managing trust affairs all those precautions which an ordinary prudent man of business would take in

---

[1] *Earl of Egmont* v. *Smith* (1877), 6 Ch.D. 469, at p. 475; *Knox* v. *Gye* (1872), L.R. 5 H.L. 656 *per* Lord Westbury.

[2] *Re A Debtor* (No. 400 of 1940), [1949] 1 All E.R. 510; [1949] Ch. 236. As to the director of a company, see *Selangor United Rubber Estates, Ltd.* v. *Cradock* (No. 3), [1968] 2 All E.R. 1073.

[3] Chapter 4, Section 4, p. 120, *ante*.

[4] *Hallows* v. *Lloyd* (1888), 39 Ch.D. 686, at p. 691 *per* Kekewich J.

[5] *Low* v. *Bouverie*, [1891] 3 Ch. 82, C.A., *per* Lindley L.J. at p. 99.

[6] *Per* Page-Wood V.C. in *Frith* v. *Cartland* (1865), 2 Hem. & M. 417, at p. 420; [1861–73] All E.R. Rep, 608, at p. 610. Nor can he set up, as against his *cestuis que trust*, the adverse title of a third party—*Newsome* v. *Flowers* (1861), 30 Beav. 461.

[7] *Re Mills*, [1930] 1 Ch. 654; [1930] All E.R. Rep. 355, C.A.; cf. *Re Wills's Trust Deeds*, [1963] 1 All E.R. 390; [1964] Ch. 219; *Muir* v. *I.R. Comrs.* [1966] 3 All E.R. 38, C.A.

[8] *Harrison* v. *Randall* (1852), 9 Hare 397, 407 *per* Turner V.C.

managing similar affairs of his own".[9] It has been said[10] that "a paid trustee is expected to exercise a higher standard of diligence and knowledge than an unpaid trustee, and . . . a bank which advertises itself largely in the public Press as taking charge of administrations is under a special duty". As between beneficiaries with conflicting interests, a trustee must act impartially and it is "an inflexible rule of a Court of Equity that a person in a fiduciary position . . . is not, unless otherwise expressly provided, entitled to make a profit; he is not allowed to put himself in a position where his interest and duty conflict".[11]

The more important of the trustee's duties will be considered in some detail in this and the following chapter.

I DUTIES ON THE ACCEPTANCE OF THE TRUST

As we have seen,[12] a trustee cannot be compelled to accept the office of trustee, "but having once accepted it . . . he must discharge its duties, so long as his character of trustee subsists".[13] The law does not recognise any distinction between active and passive trustees, and a trustee will be fully liable to the *cestuis que trust* for any loss that occurs, where he has left the management of the trust to a co-trustee, even though the co-trustee may be the solicitor to the trust.[14] A trustee who has accepted the trust has been ordered by the court to concur with the other trustees in all proper and necessary acts of administration,[15] though in practice it would normally in such case be possible and more convenient to appoint a new trustee in his place. Before he accepts a trusteeship to which any discretionary power is annexed, a trustee must disclose any circumstances in his situation which might tend to induce him to exercise any such power unfairly. If he fails to do so and nevertheless accepts the trust, he cannot afterwards exercise the discretionary power for his own benefit.[16]

On their appointment it is the right and duty of trustees to see that their appointment has been properly made,[17] and to ascertain of what the trust property consists and the trusts upon which they are to hold it.[18] "They ought also to look into the trust documents and papers to ascertain what notices appear among them of incumbrances and other matters affecting the trust."[19] To

---

[9] *Speight* v. *Gaunt* (1883), 9 App. Cas. 1, H.L., *per* Lord Blackburn at p. 19; *Learoyd* v. *Whiteley* (1887), 12 App. Cas. 727, H.L.; *Eaton* v. *Buchanan*, [1911] A.C. 253, H.L. See (1973), 37 Con. 48 (D. R. Paling).

[10] *Per* Harman J. in *Re Waterman's Will Trusts*, [1952] 2 All E.R. 1054, at p. 1055; *National Trustees Coy. of Australasia, Ltd.* v. *General Finance Coy. of Australasia, Ltd.*, [1905] A.C. 373, P.C.; *Contra, Jobson* v. *Palmer*, [1893] 1 Ch. 71 *per* Romer J.

[11] *Bray* v. *Ford*, [1896] A.C. 44, H.L., *per* Lord Herschell at p. 51.

[12] See Chapter 8, Section 3 a, p. 246, *ante*.

[13] *Moyle* v. *Moyle* (1831), 2 Russ. & M. 710, at p. 715 *per* Brougham L.C. He will not be liable for failing to act in a trust which has never been brought to his notice—*Youde* v. *Cloud* (1874), L.R. 18 Eq. 634.

[14] *Bahin* v. *Hughes* (1886), 31 Ch.D. 390, C.A.; *Robinson* v. *Harkin*, [1896] 2 Ch. 415; *Re Turner*, [1897] 1 Ch. 536.

[15] *Ouchterlony* v. *Lynedoch* (1830), 7 Bli. N.S. 448, H.L.

[16] *Peyton* v. *Robinson* (1823), 1 L.J. O.S. Ch. 191. Cf. *Molyneux* v. *Fletcher*, [1898] 1 Q.B. 648; *Butler* v. *Butler* (1877), Ch.D. 116, C.A.

[17] *Harvey* v. *Olliver* (1887), 57 L.T. 239.

[18] *Harvey* v. *Olliver, supra*; *Hallows* v. *Lloyd* (1888), 39 Ch.D. 686.

[19] *Hallows* v. *Lloyd, supra, per* Kekewich J. at p. 691.

enable this to be done effectively, a trustee, being an individual, can be required to produce to his successors in office entries relating to the administration of the trust recorded by him in a diary or other document, and where there are two or more trustees they can be required to produce the minutes of their meetings. Similarly in the case of a corporate trustee, new trustees may even be able to demand production of the internal correspondence and memoranda of such a trustee: each individual document has to be considered on its merits.[20]

The trustees should ensure that the legal title to the trust property is duly transferred to them, and, if this is not possible, that their equitable rights are appropriately protected by notice to the legal owners, or otherwise.[21] If any part of the trust property is outstanding it is their duty to press for the payment or transfer of such trust property to them.[1] If the payment or transfer is not completed within a reasonable time the best course generally is to ask for the directions of the court as to whether they should bring appropriate legal proceedings for the purpose,[2] for while it has always been true that if they do not ask for the directions of the court, they will not be liable where their failure to sue was based on a well-founded belief that an action would be fruitless, the burden of proving that such belief was well-founded would rest on the trustees who asserted it.[3] However it now seems that under section 15 of the Trustee Act 1925[4] trustees who have acted in good faith[5] will not be liable in any case where failure to sue is the result of the positive exercise of their discretion and not the result of a mere passive attitude of leaving matters alone.[6] Again, where a settlement contains a covenant to settle after-acquired property, a new trustee is entitled, unless there are circumstances which should put him on enquiry, to assume that everything has been duly attended to up to the time of his becoming trustee.[7]

New trustees are bound to see that the trust funds are properly invested,[8] and the investment should be in the names of all the trustees,[9] or in the case of bearer securities held by a trustee not being a trust corporation they must be deposited for safe custody and collection of income with a banker or banking company.[10] Title deeds and non-negotiable securities may, however, be kept in the custody of one of the trustees, and in such case a co-trustee cannot, in the absence of special circumstances, require that they be removed from such custody and placed at a bank in a box accessible only to the trustees jointly.[11] They may,

---

[20] *Tiger* v. *Barclays Bank, Ltd.*, [1952] 1 All E.R. 85, C.A.
[21] But see Trustee Act 1925, s. 22 (1) and (2).
[1] See e.g. *McGacher* v. *Dew* (1851), 15 Beav. 84; *Westmoreland* v. *Holland* (1871), 23 L.T. 797.
[2] *Re Beddoe*, [1893] 1 Ch. 547, at p. 557; C.A.; *Bennett* v. *Burgis* (1846), 5 Hare 295. See R.S.C., O.85, r. 2 (3) (*c*).
[3] *Re Brogden* (1888), 38 Ch.D. 546 C.A.; *Re Hurst* (1890), 63 L.T. 665.
[4] Discussed generally in Chapter 11, Section 4, p. 341, *post*.
[5] See *Re Owens* (1882), 47 L.T. 61, C.A., *per* Jessel M.R. at p. 63.
[6] *Re Greenwood* (1911), 105 L.T. 509.
[7] *Re Strahan* (1856), 8 De G.M. & G. 291, C.A.
[8] *Re Strahan*, *supra*, and see Section 2 of this Chapter, p. 265, *post*.
[9] *Lewis* v. *Nobbs* (1878), 8 Ch.D. 591.
[10] Trustee Act 1925, s. 7, in effect making statutory the decision in *Re De Pothonier*, [1900] 2 Ch. 529.
[11] *Re Sisson's Settlement*, [1903] 1 Ch. 262; *Cottam* v. *Eastern Counties Rail. Co.* (1860), 1 John. & H. 243.

however, be deposited with a banker or banking company or any other company whose business includes the undertaking of the safe custody of documents.[12]

In the case of a trust of chattels, the trustees should ensure that there is a proper inventory,[13] which should be signed by a tenant for life who is let into possession.[14] If the trust property includes a lease containing a covenant that the tenant will at all times personally inhabit the demised premises, it seems that this covenant will bind the trustees.[15] In conclusion it should be observed that no trustee can be bound by a release of a power made by a previous holder of the office, even where the power is capable of release, which is commonly not the case.[16]

2 DUTIES IN RELATION TO INVESTMENT

Until the passing of the Law of Property Amendment Act 1859, trustees only had such power of investment as was expressly conferred upon them by the trust instrument. If there was no express power given it was at one time thought that they could invest in "well secured real estates or upon Government securities",[17] but before the 1859 Act was passed it seems to have been accepted that in such case they were bound to invest in Consols.[18] The 1859 Act, which has long since been repealed, conferred a limited statutory power of investment. Subsequent statutes extended the statutory power, and the position now is that trustees have wide powers of investment under the Trustee Investments Act 1961, which apply in so far as a contrary intention is not expressed. Securities in which trustees are authorised to invest under general statutory provisions are commonly referred to as trustee investments or trustee securities. In addition to or in lieu of the statutory power, express powers of investment may be conferred by the trust instrument.

a Express power of investment

The effect of any particular express provision is, of course, a question of construction of the particular words used. Some general observations may, however, be made. First, it seems that express investment clauses are now construed more generously than was once the case. The older view was[19] "that investment clauses purporting to add to the wide range of investments now authorised by law should be construed strictly for the protection of trustees and remaindermen; if a greater latitude is to be allowed testators and settlors should express its extent in clear terms". Accordingly directions to trustees to invest in such securities as they should think fit,[20] or, "at the discretion of my trustees",[1] have

---

[12] Trustee Act 1925, s. 21—the charges in relation to any such deposit are chargeable against income.

[13] *England* v. *Downs* (1842), 6 Beav. 269.

[14] *Temple* v. *Thring* (1887), 56 L.T. 283 following *Foley* v. *Burnell* (1783), 1 Bro. C. C. 274.

[15] *Lloyds Bank Ltd.* v. *Jones*, [1955] 2 Q.B. 298, C.A.

[16] *Re Wills's Trust Deeds*, [1963] 1 All E.R. 390; [1964] Ch. 219; *Muir* v. *I.R.Comrs.*, [1966] 3 All E.R. 38, C.A. and see (1968) 84 L.Q.R. 64 (A. J. Hawkins).

[17] *Pocock* v. *Reddington* (1801), 5 Ves. 794, at p. 800.

[18] *Prendergast* v. *Prendergast* (1850), 3 H.L.Cas. 195; *Thornton* v. *Ellis* (1852), 15 Beav. 193; *Raby* v. *Ridehalgh* (1855), 7 De G.M. & G. 104.

[19] *Re Maryon-Wilson's Estate*, [1912] 1 Ch. 55, C.A. *per* Farwell L.J. at pp. 66–67.

[20] *Re Braithwaite* (1882), 21 Ch.D. 121.

[1] *Bethell* v. *Abraham* (1873), L.R. 17 Eq. 24 where Jessel M.R. was inclined to limit the discretion to the time of investment, on the question whether the investment should be changed or not. See also *Re Hazeldine*, [1918] 1 Ch. 433.

been held only to entitle the trustees to invest in trustee securities. The modern view seems to be that although the onus remains on those who seek to say that a particular investment is within the meaning of an investment clause to establish it, the words of such a clause will be given a natural and not a restrictive interpretation. Accordingly it was held in *Re Harari's Settlement Trusts*,[2] where the earlier authorities are discussed, that there was no justification for implying any restriction on the meaning of an investment clause authorising trustees to invest "in or upon such investments as to them may seem fit". "I think," Jenkins J. said,[3] "the trustees have power, under the plain meaning of those words, to invest in any investments which, to adopt Kekewich J.'s observation,[4] they 'honestly think' are desirable investments for the investment of moneys subject to the trusts of the settlement".

Secondly, questions have arisen as to the meaning of the word "invest" as used in an investment clause. The judicial definition most commonly referred to is that of P.O. Lawrence J. in *Re Wragg*,[5] that "to invest" includes "as one of its meanings 'to apply money in the purchase of some property from which interest or profit is expected and which property is purchased in order to be held for the sake of the income which it will yield'". Probably it is safe to regard this as *the* meaning of the word in this context. In *Re Wragg*[5] itself the investment clause was held to authorise the purchase of real property for the sake of the income it would produce, but this case was distinguished in *Re Power*[6] where it was held that a power to invest in the purchase of freehold property did not authorise the purchase of a freehold house with vacant possession for the occupation of the beneficiaries. Of course an express power to purchase land other than as an investment, for instance as a residence for a beneficiary, may be given by the trust instrument; further by statute such a power is given to the trustees of a settlement under the Settled Land Act 1925,[7] though it must normally be exercised according to the direction of the tenant for life,[8] and is also given to trustees for sale of land by virtue of section 28 (1) of the Law of Property Act 1925.[9]

Thirdly, mention may be made of the construction placed on particular provisions contained in express investment clauses in various cases. A power to invest in "stocks" has been held to authorise an investment in fully-paid shares,[10] and, conversely, a power to invest in shares an investment in stock,[11] while a power to invest in "securities" has been held to include any stocks or shares or bonds by way of investment.[12] Where trustees were authorised to lend money to a particular firm, it was held that it was a breach of trust to continue the

---

[2] [1949] 1 All E.R. 430; *Re Peczenik's Settlement*, [1964] 2 All E.R. 339. See also *Re McEacharn's Settlement Trusts*, [1939] Ch. 858.
[3] *Re Harari's Settlement Trusts*, [1949] 1 All E.R. 430, at p. 434.
[4] In *Re Smith*, [1896] 1 Ch. 71, 76.
[5] [1919] 2 Ch. 58 at 64, 65; [1918–19] All E.R. Rep. 233, 237; *Re Peczenik's Settlement, supra*.
[6] [1947] 2 All E.R. 282; [1947] Ch. 572.   [7] Section 73 (1) (xi).
[8] Settled Land Act 1925, s. 75 (2).
[9] See p. 278, *post*.
[10] *Re McEacharn's Settlement Trusts*, [1939] Ch. 858. Cf. *Re Willis*, [1911] 2 Ch. 563.
[11] *Re Boys' Will Trusts*, [1950] 1 All E.R. 624.
[12] *Re Douglas's Will Trusts*, [1959] 2 All E.R. 620, affd. C.A., [1959] 3 All E.R. 785, but no appeal on this point. As to the meaning of "ordinary preferred stock or shares" see *Re Powell-Cotton's Re-settlement*, [1957] 1 All E.R. 404; [1957] Ch. 159.

loan after a change in the firm had occurred.[13] Only a very clear provision will be treated as authorising an investment on personal security, in the sense that there is no security beyond the liability of the borrower to repay, as opposed to a loan on the security of personal property. In *Khoo Tek Keong* v. *Ching Joo Tuan Neoh*[14] there was a very wide investment clause empowering the trustees "to invest all moneys liable to be invested in such investments as they in their absolute discretion think fit", but it was held that this did not authorise them to invest in personal security in the above sense, though it did authorise a loan on the security of personal property. One may contrast with this case *Re Laing's Settlement*[15] where the trustees were expressly authorised to invest "upon such personal credit without security as the trustees or trustee shall in their or his absolute and uncontrolled discretion think fit". On these clear words the trustees were held to be authorised to advance by way of loan, even to the tenant for life, on his personal security which, it was pointed out, was not really an advance on security at all.

Fourthly, it should be observed that if the trust instrument directs and requires trustees to make some specified investment they are under a duty to do so, even if it is one of which they disapprove, and accordingly they will not be under any liability in doing so even though this may result in a loss to the trust estate.[16]

Fifthly, an investment clause usually confers an express power to vary investments. In the absence of such a provision it has been held in a series of cases[17] that a power to vary is implied in a power of investment, the court observing in one case[18] that it would be most unfortunate if it were not so.[19]

Sixthly, there is a conflict of authority as to whether a power of investment "with the consent of X" gives X a beneficial power which he can use for his own benefit, or effectively release, or whether it gives X a fiduciary power which he should use in the interests of all the beneficiaries, and which he is unable to release. In the absence of a controlling context, the former view is perhaps to be preferred.[20]

Lastly, a settlor or testator can, it seems, validly confer on a trustee or someone else a power to enlarge the original investment clause.[21]

b The statutory power under the Trustee Investments Act 1961[1]

Until this Act came into force on 3rd August, 1961, the range of investments permitted to trustees under the general provisions contained in the Trustee Act

[13] *Re Tucker*, [1894] 1 Ch. 724—an appeal on this point was stood over until it was seen if any loss occurred—[1894] 3 Ch. 429, C.A.; *Smith* v. *Patrick*, [1901] A.C. 282, H.L.
[14] [1934] A.C. 529, P.C. See also *Pickard* v. *Anderson* (1872), L.R. 13 Eq. 608.
[15] [1899] 1 Ch. 593; *Re Godwin's Settlement* (1918), 119 L.T. 643.
[16] *Beauclerk* v. *Ashburnham* (1845), 8 Beav. 322; *Cadogan* v. *Essex (Earl)* (1854), 2 Drew. 227; *Re Hurst* (1890), 63 L.T. 665. See (1972), 36 Con. 260 (Penelope Pearce).
[17] Including *Hume* v. *Lopes*, [1892] A.C. 112, H.L.; *Re Pope's Contract*, [1911] 2 Ch. 442; *Re Pratt's Will Trusts*, [1943] 2 All E.R. 375; [1943] Ch. 326.
[18] *Re Pope's Contract, supra*, per Neville J.
[19] As to the statutory power to vary investments see the Trustee Investments Act 1961, s. 1 (1).
[20] See *Re Wise*, unreported, but discussed in (1954) 218 L.T. News. 116, in which Wynn-Parry J. followed *Dicconson* v. *Talbot* (1870), 6 Ch. App. 32 in preference to *Re Massingberd's Settlement* (1890) 63 L.T. 296.
[21] *Re Jewish Orphanage Endowments Trusts*, [1960] 1 All E.R. 764, not following dictum in *Re Tobacco Trade Benevolent Association*, [1958] 3 All E.R. 353. Cf. *Soldiers', Sailors' and Airmen's Families Association* v. *A.-G.*, [1968] 1 All E.R. 448 n.
[1] See generally (1962), 26 Con. 351 (A. Samuels) where references are given to much periodical literature.

1925, section 1,[2] as extended by later enactments,[3] was restricted in the main to fixed interest investments which would ultimately be repayable at par,[4] in particular excluding investment in "equities"[5] The earlier legislation, giving only a restricted power of investment, was intended as a safeguard. On the one hand it was intended to protect the trustees from liability to the beneficiaries for losses arising from their investment of the trust fund, and on the other hand it was intended to protect the trust fund as far as possible from loss as a result of imprudent investment. The legislation, however, failed to make allowance for the far-reaching changes in the economy and the investment situation which have since taken place, and which have greatly affected the relative security of different classes of investment. There is no real safety in the capital of a trust retaining a paper value of £10,000 if in the meantime the real value of the pound has, as a result of inflation, been reduced to fifty pence. And to a somewhat lesser extent the same is true in relation to income beneficiaries. Long before the 1961 Act, the individual investor was often able to provide a hedge against inflation by investing in investments which themselves appreciated in value so as to keep pace with the progress of inflation. In particular he could invest in equity stock and shares which represent the right, not to a fixed money income and a fixed capital sum, but to a share in the companies' profits and assets and are thus ultimately associated with real values and not with money values: moreover, they contain the possibility of growth owing to the practice adopted by most companies of retaining in the business a considerable part of the profits and so adding to the value of the equity. The 1961 Act was passed, somewhat belatedly, to enable trustees to invest more widely. In general terms it empowers trustees to invest up to half the trust funds, subject to certain safeguards, in the debentures and stock and shares (including equity stock and shares) of financial, industrial and commercial companies quoted on a recognized stock exchange. Trustee investments are now classified into narrower-range investments and wider-range investments, and the details of the investments, which were set out in the First Schedule to the 1961 Act, are reproduced, with subsequent amendments, in the Appendix at the end of this book. It is perhaps worth noting here that there is no power conferred by the Act on trustees to invest in the purchase of land.

Before explaining the scheme of the Act, a few preliminary points may be

---

[2] Repealed by the Trustee Investments Act 1961, s. 16 (2) and Sched. 5.

[3] E.g. Agricultural Credits Act 1928, s. 3; Local Government Act 1958, s. 54; House Purchase and Housing Act 1959, s. 1 (1) (a) and 1 (5), all likewise repealed by the Trustee Investments Act 1961, s. 16 (2) and Sched. 5.

[4] Note that many of these investments are highly sensitive to interest rates, and have been badly affected by the rise in these rates in recent years. They include Government stock ("gilt-edged securities", which is really money borrowed by the Government) which may be "dated", when it is redeemable at a fixed date (or a date to be fixed by the Government within strict limits, e.g. 1986–89); or "undated", or redeemable on or after a fixed date, when it is, or is virtually, irredeemable. In the latter category is the Treasury 2½ per cent Stock issued by the first Labour Government after the last war in pursuance of its "cheap money" policy. Mainly as a consequence of a rise in interest rates it now stands at only a little above a sixth of its face value, and clearly, particularly bearing in mind the effects of inflation, has in many cases proved a disastrous investment.

[5] I.e. the ordinary shares in a company as opposed to preference shares and debentures. See Companies Act 1948, s. 154 (5).

made. The powers of investment given to a trustee by the 1961 Act are not limited by any provision contained in a settlement or trust made before the Act was passed, but are exercisable only in so far as a contrary intention is not expressed[6] in a settlement or trust made thereafter. The power is to be exercised according to the discretion of the trustees with which the court will not normally interfere[7], but subject to any consent or direction required by the trust instrument or by statute.[8] A power to vary investments is expressly given.[9]

The scheme of the Act, as already mentioned, is first to classify the range of trustee investments into narrower-range investments and wider-range investments. The narrower-range investments are set out in Parts I and II of the First Schedule. Part I investments comprise such things as Defence Bonds, National Savings Certificates, and deposits in the National Savings Bank, while Part II investments consist, in general terms, of the old trustee securities with some additions. The wider-range investments which, as already stated, include equities, and also units in an authorized unit trust scheme, and shares (as opposed to deposits) in designated building societies, are set out in Part III of the First Schedule. The restrictions in Part IV of the First Schedule in relation to many of the Part II and Part III investments should be carefully observed. These are that any securities where the holder can be required to accept repayment of the principal, or the payment of any interest, otherwise than in sterling, are disqualified; and the equity investment is limited to stocks and shares in large public companies with a recent consistently satisfactory dividend record, which are fully paid up and quoted on a recognized stock exchange.

It may be added that the powers of investment may be increased by Order in Council by adding to any of the three parts of the First Schedule, and up to the present seven orders adding investments have been made.

A trustee can always invest any property in his hands, whether at the time in a state of investment or not, in narrower-range investments: it is always possible for the whole of the trust property to be invested in narrower-range investments. Turning to the wider-range investments, it is never possible for more than a half of the trust fund to be initially so invested, and even this can only be done if the trust fund has first been divided into two parts, equal in value at the time of the division. A trustee is empowered, but not required,[10] to make such a division which, once made, is final and irrevocable. The division of the trust fund into the narrower-range part and the wider-range part can only be made into equal parts, and not any other proportion, and no other division can thereafter be made.[11] Once made no property can be transferred from one part of the

---

[6] Similar words in the Trustee Act 1925, s. 69 (2), have been held to have the same meaning as "unless expressly forbidden" in the Trustee Act 1893, s. 1—*Re Warren*, [1939] 2 All E.R. 599; [1939] Ch. 684. Cf. *Re Rider's Will Trusts*, [1958] 3 All E.R. 135.

[7] *Lee* v. *Young* (1843), 2 Y. & C.Ch.Cas. 532. See generally, as to control of trustees' discretions, pp. 360 *et seq.*, *post*.

[8] Trustee Act 1925, s. 3.

[9] Trustee Investments Act 1961, s. 1 (1).

[10] *Ibid.*, s. 2. As to whether the provision for diversification in s. 6 (1), discussed at p. 272, *post*, might impose a duty to divide, *quære*.

[11] By the Trustee Investments Act 1961, s. 13, the Treasury may by order increase, but not reduce, the proportion of the wider-range part to the narrower-range part, either in one step or by several, to a maximum of three to one. Each time the proportion is increased one further division of the trust is permitted. No order has yet been made.

fund to another unless a compensating transfer is made in the other direction. In determining whether the division has been properly made a valuation in writing of any property obtained by a trustee from a person reasonably believed by him to be qualified to make it, such as a stockbroker, is conclusive.[12] Funds belonging to the narrower-range part must be invested in narrower-range investments, and any property invested in any other manner which is or becomes comprised in that part of the trust fund shall either be transferred to the wider-range part of the fund, with a compensating transfer, or be invested in narrower-range investments as soon as may be.[13] Funds belonging to the wider-range part may be invested either in wider-range or in narrower-range investments, or partly in some and partly in others. Where property accrues[14] to a trust fund after it has been divided in the above manner, then if it accrues to the trustee as owner or former owner of property comprised in either part of the fund, it is to be treated as belonging to that part of the fund, and in other cases must be dealt with in such a way[15] that the value of each part of the fund is increased by the same amount. It is expressly provided,[16] however, that where in the exercise of any power[17] or duty property falls to be taken out of the trust fund, there is no statutory restriction on the trustee's discretion as to the choice of property to be taken out. He may, accordingly, take the whole out of the narrower-range part with the result that the wider-range investments may thereafter exceed one half of the total trust funds.

c Relationship between the statutory power and other powers of investment[18]

The power conferred by the Trustee Investments Act 1961 is in addition to and not in derogation from any other powers of investment or postponing conversion, called in the Act "special powers", which a trustee may have been given expressly by the trust instrument, or which he may have obtained as a result of an order of the court,[19] or under a special statute, such as those private Acts which various local authorities had promoted for this purpose in the years before the Act was passed. Further, any special power conferred on a trustee before the passing of the Act to invest property in any investment for the time being authorised by law for the investment of that property is to be treated as referring to the power of investment under the 1961 Act.[20]

Property, including wider-range but excluding narrower-range investments, which a trustee has power to hold under a special power, apart from the special power last mentioned, and the provisions of section 1 of the Act and Part I of the Trustee Act 1925, is called "special-range property".

---

[12] *Ibid.*, s. 5.
[13] *Ibid.*, s. 2 (2).
[14] *Ibid.*, s. 2 (3).
[15] *Prima facie* by an apportionment, but if, for instance, it constitutes a wider-range investment, it might be appropriated to the wider-range part and a compensating transfer made.
[16] Trustee Investments Act 1961, s. 2 (4). See (1970) 120 N.L.J. 240 (R. T. Oerton).
[17] E.g. the statutory power of advancement under Trustee Act 1925, s. 32.
[18] Trustee Investments Act 1961, s. 3 and Sched. 2 and 3.
[19] E.g. under the Variation of Trusts Act 1958—see Chapter 10, Section 1 b, p. 301, *post.*
[20] Trustee Investments Act 1961, s. 3 (2).

The rules relating to special-range property are contained in the Second Schedule. Where a trust fund includes special-range property, it must be carried to a separate part of the fund, and the provisions as to division of the trust fund contained in section 2 (1) of the Act only apply to the residue of the trust fund. In such case, if the division is made, the fund will consist of three parts: a special-range part (which may include either or both wider-range investments and "unauthorised investments"[1]), a wider-range part and a narrower-range part. In order to maintain the principle behind this tripartite division, it is provided on the one hand that any property belonging to the narrower-range or wider-range part of the trust fund which is converted into special-range property, and any special-range property which accrues to a trust fund after division of the fund under section 2 (1), must be carried to the separate special-range part of the fund. There does not appear to be any provision to require special-range property to be bought equally out of the wider-range and narrower-range parts of the fund and consequently it seems that the whole of the narrower-range part of the fund may be sold and reinvested in special-range property, so that the whole fund is divided into a special-range part and a wider-range part. On the other hand, where special-range property is converted into property other than special-range property, it must be transferred to the narrower-range part or the wider-range part or apportioned between them, and if necessary a compensating transfer made, so as to ensure that the values of the narrower-range part and the wider-range part are each increased by the same amount.

By virtue of section 3 (4) the above provisions contained in section 3 (3) and the Second Schedule do not apply where the special power has been conferred or varied by the court or by an Act of Parliament relating specifically to the trusts in question made, in either case, within the period of ten years ending with the passing of the Act,[2] or by a local Act passed in the same Session as the 1961 Act. The position in such case is governed by the provisions set out in the Third Schedule, the effect of which seems to be that there is no special-range part of the fund but the trustees can make the ordinary division into a narrower-range part and a wider-range part. If they choose to do so the special power remains valid, but section 1 is not to be regarded as authorising the making or retention of any wider-range investment unless the whole of the narrower-range part is and will continue after such investment to be invested in narrower-range investments.[3]

d General principles to be applied

The mere fact that a certain type of investment is authorised by the trust instrument or by statute does not mean that it is necessarily proper to invest in it in any particular case: it is possible for investment in an authorised investment

---

[1] By unauthorised investments in this context are meant investments not included in any part of the First Schedule, e.g. shares in companies which do not satisfy the statutory conditions, and land. The trustee must, of course, be authorised to retain or purchase the property by the special power.

[2] 3rd August, 1961.

[3] Trustee Investments Act 1961, s. 3 (4) and Sched. 3.

to constitute a breach of trust. However wide the provisions of an express investment clause may be, it is submitted that they do not absolve trustees from their duty to consider whether a proposed investment is such as in its nature it is prudent and right for them as trustees to make. Even if they are given power to invest at their absolute discretion and as if they were absolute owners the better view, it is submitted, is that they must act as trustees in exercising the power in accordance with the following principles.[4] The general principles were restated in the leading case of *Re Whiteley*.[5] In the Court of Appeal Lopes L.J. said,[6] "The duty of a trustee in investing the money of his *cestuis que trust* may be thus defined. He must choose those investments only which are within the terms of his trust. In the selection of investments within the terms of his trust he must use the care and caution which an ordinary man of business, regardful of the pecuniary interests in the future of those having claims upon him, would exercise in the management of his own property. So much I think should be required of a trustee—it would be unreasonable to require more". In the House of Lords, Lord Watson expressed it this way:[7]

> "As a general rule the law requires of a trustee no higher degree of diligence in the execution of his office than a man of ordinary prudence would exercise in the management of his own private affairs. Yet he is not allowed the same discretion in investing the moneys of the trust as if he were a person *sui juris* dealing with his own estate. Business men of ordinary prudence may, and frequently do, select investments which are more or less of a speculative character; but it is the duty of a trustee to confine himself to the class of investments which are permitted by the trust, and likewise to avoid all investments of that class which are attended with hazard. So, so long as he acts in the honest observance of these limitations, the general rule already stated will apply".

Accordingly in *Re Whiteley*[8] itself, although the power of investment was wide enough to cover a mortgage on a freehold brickfield, it was held to be a breach of trust since the property was of a hazardous and wasting character.

The Trustee Investments Act 1961, section 6 (1), has, in effect, made statutory the above duty of trustees by providing that in the exercise of his powers of investment[9] a trustee shall have regard "to the suitability to the trust of investments of the description of investment proposed and of the investment proposed as an investment of that description". The same sub-section has, moreover, perhaps extended a trustee's duty as to investment by providing that he shall also have regard to "the need for diversification of investments of the trust, in so far as is appropriate to the circumstances of the trust". In many cases this need would, it is submitted, be satisfied by investing in one unit trust.

---

[4] *Khoo Tek Keong* v. *Ching Joo Tuan Neoh*, [1934] A.C. 529 P.C.; *Chapman* v. *Browne*, [1902] 1 Ch. 785 C.A.

[5] (1886), 33 Ch.D. 347, C.A.; affd. *sub. nom. Learoyd* v. *Whiteley* (1887), 12 App. Cas. 727, H.L.

[6] At 33 Ch.D. 358.

[7] At 12 App. Cas. 733.

[8] (1886), 33 Ch.D. 347, C.A.; affd. *sub. nom. Learoyd* v. *Whiteley* (1887), 12 App. Cas. 727, H.L.

[9] The section seems to apply equally to powers conferred by the Act and powers granted outside it.

e Obtaining advice

Section 6 (2) of the Trustee Investments Act 1961 provides that before exercising the statutory power of investment in any of the investments specified in Parts II or III of the First Schedule[10] a trustee must obtain and consider proper advice on the question whether the investment is satisfactory having regard to the matters mentioned in sub-section 1, set out above. The trustee is not, on the one hand, required to act on such advice, nor, on the other hand, is he necessarily protected if he does so: but, clearly, it would be difficult to establish a breach of trust if a trustee had *bona fide* relied on such advice, and such reliance would also normally enable him to obtain relief under section 61 of the Trustee Act 1925.[11] Proper advice, for the purpose of these provisions, means[12] the written[13] advice of a person who is reasonably believed by the trustee to be qualified by his ability in and practical experience of financial matters; and such advice may be given by a person notwithstanding that he gives it in the course of his employment as an officer or servant. The provisions as to obtaining advice do not, however, apply to one of two or more trustees where he is the person giving the advice to his co-trustees,[14] nor do they apply where powers of a trustee are lawfully exercised by an officer or servant competent under section 6 (4) just mentioned to give proper advice, as will frequently be the case where the trustee is a trust corporation.

The statutory provisions as to obtaining advice apply to loans on the security of land, notwithstanding that in such case a report has been obtained under section 8 of the Trustee Act 1925, though the advice in such case should not include advice on the suitability of the particular loan,[15] which will appear in the report.

No advice is required in respect of the investments specified in Part I of the First Schedule,[16] but otherwise the duties of trustees in connection with those investments are the same.

From a different angle it must be remembered that in choosing an investment trustees are under a duty to hold a balance between the interests of the beneficiaries and must not unduly favour the tenant for life as against the remainderman or *vice versa*.[17]

In the present investment situation the position of trustees is not easy. The sort of investment which will produce a high rate of interest which will suit the life tenant, is likely to be a fixed interest investment whose real value may well be eroded by inflation by the time the remaindermen come into possession,

---

[10] See Appendix. This provision also applies to investments in exercise of a special power under s. 3 (2), to which reference is made at p. 270, *ante*. See (1970), 120 N.L.J. 240 (R. T. Oerton).

[11] Discussed in Chapter 12, Section 3 d, p. 379, *post*.

[12] Trustee Investments Act 1961, s. 6 (4).

[13] *Ibid.*, s. 6 (5)—it is sufficient if the advice is originally given orally provided it is subsequently confirmed in writing.   [14] *Ibid.*, s. 6 (6).

[15] *Ibid.*, s. 6 (7).

[16] See Appendix.

[17] *Raby* v. *Ridehalgh* (1855), 7 De G.M. & G. 104; *Re Dick*, [1891] 1 Ch. 423, 431 C.A. affd. H.L. *sub. nom. Hume* v. *Lopes*, [1892] A.C. 112. See *Re Smith* (1971), 16 D.L.R. (3d) 130 (Ont. H.C.) affd. (1971), 18 D.L.R. (3d) 405 (Ont. C.A.) where the trustee was removed from office for breach of this duty.

while equities which it is hoped will show a capital appreciation and thus safeguard the position of remaindermen, will not produce a high enough rate of interest to satisfy the tenant for life.

f Investments on a mortgage of land

There are difficulties in ascertaining to what kinds of mortgage the power applies, though it always seems to have authorised an investment on a sub-mortgage.[18] On the one hand, the pre-1926 cases took the view that, unless expressly given, a power to invest on mortgage did not authorise investment on either a second, an equitable or a contributory mortgage. On the other hand, the power was by the Trustee Act 1925[19] extended to a charge by way of legal mortgage,[20] and it has been suggested[1] that the old restrictions have been swept away by the Trustee Investments Act 1961, which provides that mortgages of freehold property and leasehold property with at least sixty years to run are narrower-range investments requiring advice, the point being that, unless the context otherwise requires, mortgage is defined[2] by reference to the definition in the Trustee Act 1925[3] where it is declared to relate to every estate and interest regarded in equity as merely a security for money. The courts, however, have not yet considered whether the position has been affected either by the alterations made in the law of mortgages by the 1925 Property Acts, or by the Trustee Investments Act 1961, and a prudent trustee should accordingly refuse to advance money on a mortgage of any of the above kinds.

As to second mortgages, the main objection seems to have been that the trustees would not get the protection of a legal estate[4]: the Court of Appeal, however, in *Chapman* v. *Browne*,[5] in distinguishing certain Irish decisions,[6] pointed out that there were other objections,[7] so that they probably remain improper investments, notwithstanding the fact that since 1925 they may be legal, and their priority adequately protected by registration under the Land Charges Act 1972.[8] As to equitable mortgages, it always seems to have been assumed before 1926[9] that they were not proper investments on the ground that

---

[18] *Smethurst* v. *Hastings* (1885), 30 Ch.D. 490.

[19] Section 5 (2).

[20] Law of Property Act 1925, s. 87.

[1] Lewin on *Trusts*, 16th Ed., p. 370.

[2] Trustee Investments Act 1961, s. 17 (4).

[3] Trustee Act 1925, s. 68 (7).

[4] *Norris* v. *Wright* (1851), 14 Beav. 291; *Lockhart* v. *Reilly* (1857), 1 De G. & J. 464.

[5] [1902] 1 Ch. 785, C.A.

[6] *Smithwick* v. *Smithwick* (1861), 12 Ir. Ch. Rep. 181; *Crampton* v. *Walker* (1893), 31 L.R. Ir. 437. The position in Ireland was affected by the possibility of registration and other differences from English law.

[7] E.g. if the first mortgagee were to foreclose, the security might be lost if funds are not available to redeem him; if he were to go into possession, the whole of the income might stop.

[8] As a land charge class C (i) under s. 2 (4), previously the Land Charges Act 1925 s. 10; and see Law of Property Act 1925, s. 198.

[9] In *Swaffield* v. *Nelson*, [1876] W.N. 255 Jessel M.R. said that "it had never been decided that an investment upon equitable mortgage was unauthorised when there was power to invest on real securities, because it has always been assumed to be the law of the Court without calling for decision".

a subsequent legal mortgagee without notice, might obtain priority. The position is probably the same since 1925 where the equitable mortgage is protected by a deposit of deeds. In theory an equitable mortgagee who does not obtain the deeds and thus is able to and does register his mortgage[10] cannot be prejudiced by subsequent transactions entered into by the mortgagor,[11] and in such case it might be arguable that if it is a first mortgage it is a proper security for trustees. In practice, however, trustees should not lend on an equitable mortgage, whether protected by a deposit of deeds or not. As to contributory mortgages, i.e. where the trustees join with other persons, whether trustees or not, in a joint loan, the cases in which they have been held to be improper have been on the ground that they were outside the scope of an investment clause requiring investments to be made in the names or under the control of the trustees.[12] Apart from this point of construction, it would seem that a contributory mortgage is an improper investment as, to some extent, it puts the trust property out of the control of the trustees.

Assuming that the mortgage is one upon which trust money can properly be lent, the question arises as to how much can be lent. A trustee can protect himself in this respect by complying with the conditions of section 8 of the Trustee Act 1925[13] which provides that a trustee lending money on the security of any property on which he can properly lend will not be chargeable with breach of trust by reason only of the proportion borne by the amount of the loan to the value of the property at the time when the loan was made: in other words the trustee is not liable merely because the security becomes insufficient. These provisions are, it has been said,[14] intended to relieve trustees from a burden previously cast upon them by the court, and accordingly ought to be construed liberally in favour of the persons whom it is sought to relieve. In order to gain this protection the court must be satisfied[15]

> "(a) that in making the loan the trustee was acting upon a report as to the value of the property made by a person whom he reasonably believed to be[16] an able practical surveyor or valuer instructed and employed independently of any owner of the property, whether such surveyor or valuer carried on business in the locality where the property is situate or elsewhere; and
>
> (b) that the amount of the loan does not exceed two third parts of the value of the property as stated in the report; and
>
> (c) that the loan was made under the advice of the surveyor or valuer expressed in the report."

---

[10] As a land charge class C (iii) under the Land Charges Act 1972, s. 2 (4).

[11] In theory, therefore, it is safer for an equitable mortgagee not to obtain the title deeds, but to register. In practice, however, it seems to be more usual to obtain the deeds if possible.

[12] *Webb* v. *Jonas* (1888), 39 Ch.D. 660; *Re Massingberd's Settlement* (1890), 63 L.T. 296, C.A.; *Re Dive*, [1909] 1 Ch. 328.

[13] Re-enacting Trustee Act, 1893, s. 8, which re-enacted Trustee Act 1888, s. 4.

[14] *Re Solomon*, [1912] 1 Ch. 261, 271, which was concerned with the corresponding provision in the Trustee Act 1893.

[15] Trustee Act 1925, s. 8 (1) (*a*) (*b*) and (*c*).

[16] According to Kekewich J. the words "reasonably believed to be" do not govern the words "instructed and employed", which has to be proved as a fact—*Re Walker* (1890), 62 L.T. 449; *Re Somerset*, [1894] 1 Ch. 231, C.A., but this seems doubtful, see *Re Stuart*, [1897] 2 Ch. 583; *Shaw* v. *Cates*, [1909] 1 Ch. 389, 403; *Re Solomon*, [1912] 1 Ch. 261, 281.

The trustee must use his own discretion in selecting a surveyor or valuer[17] who must be independently employed by the trustee to make a report for him. The requirement of independence has been held not to be satisfied where the surveyor or valuer knew that his fees were ultimately to be met by the mortgagor,[18] nor where it was agreed that he would only be entitled to a fee if the mortgage was duly granted.[19] It does not matter, however, that the fee is to be a percentage of the amount of the loan advised,[20] and the trustee is not under a duty to inquire into the previous transactions of the surveyor to ascertain whether he has acted for the mortgagor on previous occasions.[1] The report must not only state the value of the property, but must advise that the property is a sufficient security for the proposed loan. This is not automatically two-thirds of the value: the surveyor or valuer should take all the relevant factors into account in advising for what amount it is a sufficient security,[2] but the trustee is entitled to assume that this has been done[3] even though the maximum loan of two-thirds is advised.[4]

The better view, it is submitted, is that section 8 affords no protection to a trustee if the property, by reason for instance of its hazardous or speculative character, is not a proper security for trustees to invest in at all,[5] though another view is that in every case it is simply a question of what amount a trustee may safely lend.[6]

There is no statutory duty imposed on a trustee to obtain a valuation under section 8,[7] though a trustee who fails to do so is unlikely to obtain relief under section 61 of the Trustee Act 1925.[8] In ascertaining the liability of a trustee where for any reason he is unable to rely on the protection of section 8, the rules which applied to any investment on mortgage before the Trustee Act 1888 will still be applicable. It was settled that trustees were "entitled to rely on expert advice as to the value of the property, but if they did so, it was their duty to see that the expert[9] was properly instructed—that he knew for whom and with what object he was advising, and that he was acting independently of the mortgagor. . . . Having thus been advised as to value, they had themselves to determine, and could not delegate it to a third party (even an expert) to determine, what amount they could prudently advance on the security in question".[10] It is by altering the law on this last point that section 8 has made the greatest change in the law. Certain general rules were laid down for the guidance of trustees in deciding this question, namely that not more than two-thirds of the value should

---

17 *Fry* v. *Tapson* (1884), 28 Ch.D. 268.
18 *Shaw* v. *Cates*, [1909] 1 Ch. 389; *Re Stuart*, [1897] 2 Ch. 583.
19 *Re Dive*, [1909] 1 Ch. 328; *Salisbury (Marquis)* v. *Keymer* (1909), 25 T.L.R. 278.
20 *Re Solomon*, [1912] 1 Ch. 261.
1 *Re Solomon, supra,* at p. 281.
2 *Re Dive, supra; Shaw* v. *Cates, supra.*
3 *Shaw* v. *Cates, supra; Re Solomon,* [1912] 1 Ch. 261.
4 *Re Solomon, supra.*
5 *Blyth* v. *Fladgate,* [1891] 1 Ch. 337; *Re Turner,* [1897] 1 Ch. 536; *Shaw* v. *Cates, supra.*
6 *Re Solomon,* [1912] 1 Ch. 261, 279.
7 *Palmer* v. *Emerson,* [1911] 1 Ch. 758.
8 Discussed in Chapter 12, Section 3d, *post,* p. 379.
9 He had to have local knowledge—*Budge* v. *Gummow* (1872), 7 Ch. App. 719; *Fry* v. *Tapson* (1884), 28 Ch.D. 268.
10 *Shaw* v. *Cates, supra, per* Parker J. at p. 396. See also *Fry* v. *Tapson, supra; Learoyd* v. *Whiteley, supra.*

be lent in the case of agricultural property, and not more than a half in the case of houses or buildings used in trade. These rules concerned the normal minimum margins, but the circumstances might require a larger margin to be adopted, and in exceptional cases, particularly in connection with houses, the trustee might be able to show that a smaller margin was adequate.

Where too much money is advanced on mortgage on what would otherwise be a proper investment, it is deemed to be an authorised investment for the smaller sum, and the trustee is only liable for the balance improperly advanced.[11] Trustees may validly agree not to call in the mortgage for up to seven years,[12] and they will be given similar protection to that given by section 8, even without obtaining a report, where on a sale of land they permit not more than two-thirds of the purchase price to remain outstanding on a legal mortgage.[13]

g Trustees holding a controlling interest in a company

As already mentioned,[14] the duty of a trustee is to conduct the business of the trust in such a way as an ordinary prudent man would conduct a business of his own. In *Re Lucking's Will Trusts*[15] Cross J. had to consider how this general principle should be applied to trustees holding a controlling interest in a private company. First he asked himself "What steps, if any, does a reasonably prudent man who finds himself a majority shareholder in a private company take with regard to the management of the company's affairs?" To this question he gave answer: "He does not, I think, content himself with such information as to the management of the company's affairs as he is entitled to as shareholder, but ensures that he is represented on the board. He may be prepared to run the business himself as managing director or, at least, to become a non-executive director while having the business managed by someone else. Alternatively, he may find someone who will act as his nominee on the board and report to him from time to time as to the company's affairs." Trustees holding a controlling interest, he concluded, ought in the same way, to ensure so far as they can that they have such information as to the progress of the company's affairs as directors would have, and act on that information appropriately. In *Re Lucking's Will Trusts*[16] itself trustees held a majority shareholding. One of the trustees was indeed on the board of the company, but he had failed to supervise adequately the drawings of the managing director in effect appointed by him, as a consequence of which the company lost some £15,000 on the managing director's bankruptcy. The failure of supervision was clearly a failure of the trustee-director's duty to the company *qua* director; the judge held that, being partly a representative of the trust, it was also a failure of his duty *qua* trustee, for which he was liable to the beneficiaries.

h Settled land and land held upon trust for sale

Capital money arising under a settlement within the Settled Land Act 1925 may be invested or otherwise applied in trustee investments or in various other

---

[11] Trustee Act 1925, s. 9.
[12] *Ibid.*, s. 10 (1).
[13] *Ibid.*, s. 10 (2).
[14] *Supra*, pp. 262, 263.
[15] [1967] 3 All E.R. 726.   [16] *Supra*.

modes set out in section 73 (1) of the Act. Most of the modes are closely connected with the management of the settled land, but there is included[17] the purchase of land in fee simple, or of leasehold land held for sixty years or more unexpired at the time of purchase. If a division into a narrower-range part and a wider-range part is made under section 2 (1) of the Trustee Investments Act 1961, it is not clear whether the land in the settlement is to be taken into account. The better view is, perhaps, that it is not, at any rate where the settled land, as is usually the case, is vested, not in the trustees of the settlement as statutory owners, but in the tenant for life. The investment or other application of capital money by the trustees must normally be made according to the direction of the tenant for life,[18] and in giving directions the tenant for life is in exactly the same position as an ordinary trustee exercising a discretionary power of investment,[19] though it is not clear whether he is, or the trustees of the settlement are, the person or persons to obtain advice under section 6 (2) of the Trustee Investments Act 1961.

The same powers of investment are given to trustees for sale of land by virtue of section 28 (1) of the Law of Property Act 1925, which gives them all the powers of a tenant for life and the trustees of a settlement under the Settled Land Act 1925.[20] It has been held, however, that if trustees for sale of land sell all the land subject to the trusts they cease to be trustees for sale of land and accordingly section 28 (1) ceases to apply.[21] Some doubt has, however, been cast on this decision by dicta in Re Wellsted's Will Trusts.[22]

i Retaining investments

Where the initial investment is authorised, it has been held,[23] in connection with an investment on mortgage, that the trustees are not bound to make periodical or further investigations as to either the title of the security or the solvency or sufficiency of the mortgagor, though such a duty may arise if there are circumstances which suggest that the security may be in jeopardy. Presumably similar principles apply to other kinds of investment. Where loss occurs due to retention of an authorised investment, the trustees will not be liable if they have retained it "honestly and prudently, in the belief that it was the best course to take in the interest of all parties. Trustees acting honestly, with ordinary prudence and within the limits of their trust, are not liable for mere errors of judgment".[24] Different considerations apply in deciding whether to invest upon a particular security, or whether to get rid of an existing security which was originally a proper investment.[25]

---

[17] Settled Land Act 1925, s. 73 (1) (xi).
[18] Ibid., s. 75 (2).
[19] Re Hunt's Settled Estates, [1905] 2 Ch. 418; affd. C.A. [1906] 2 Ch. 11.
[20] Re Wellsted's Will Trusts, [1949] 1 All E.R. 577; [1949] Ch. 296, C.A. And see s. 36 of the Law of Property Act 1925.
[21] Re Wakeman, [1945] 1 All E.R. 421; [1945] Ch. 177.
[22] Supra, per Cohen L.J. at 588, 319.
[23] Rawsthorne v. Rowley (1907), [1909] 1 Ch. 409 n., C.A.; cf. Re Brookes, [1914] 1 Ch. 558.
[24] Re Chapman, [1896] 2 Ch. 763, C.A. per Lindley L.J. at p. 776.
[25] Re Chapman, supra.

The Trustee Act 1925, section 4[26], provides that—

"A trustee shall not be liable for breach of trust by reason only of his continuing to hold an investment which has ceased to be an investment authorised by the trust instrument or by the general law."

Clearly this section does not afford protection to a trustee where on some other ground he was under a duty to realise an investment.

It does not seem that the liability of trustees in respect of retaining investments has been greatly increased by the Trustee Investments Act 1961, section 6 (3). This subsection provides, as regards investments in respect whereof advice had to be obtained by reason of section 6 (1) and (2) of the Act before they were made,[1] that a trustee must determine at what intervals the circumstances, and in particular the nature of the investment, make it desirable to obtain advice on the question whether the investment continues to be satisfactory, and must obtain and consider such advice accordingly.

j Miscellaneous statutory provisions incidental to powers of investment

Section 2 of the Trustee Act 1925 as amended[2] provides that trustees may invest in redeemable securities, even though the price exceeds the redemption value, and may retain until redemption any redeemable stock, shares, fund or security properly purchased.

Section 7 of the Trustee Act 1925 permits investment in bearer securities being otherwise authorised investments, unless expressly prohibited by the trust instrument. Except where the trustee is a trust corporation, bearer securities must be deposited for safe custody and collection of income with a bank or banking company. No bearer securities are authorised investments under the Trustee Investments Act 1961.

Section 10 (3) of the Trustee Act 1925 as amended[3] gives trustees holding securities of a company very wide powers to concur in any scheme or arrangement for the reconstruction of the company, the sale of the property and undertaking of the company to another company, the acquisition of the securities of the company or of control thereof, by another company, the amalgamation of the company with another company, and the release, modification or variation of any rights, privileges or liabilities attached to the securities. Subsection (4)[4] of the same section authorises the trustees, if any conditional or preferential right to subscribe for any securities in any company is offered to them in respect of their holding, to exercise the right, renounce it, or assign it for value, as they in their discretion shall think fit, and, if they choose to exercise the right, to retain the securities for any period for which the trustees had power to retain the holding in respect of which the right to subscribe for the securities was offered.

Lastly, mention may be made of section 41[5] of the Administration of Estates

---

[26] This section does not apply in cases where an investment ceased to be authorised by the Trustee Investments Act 1961, s. 3 (4) and Sched. 3, para. 1.

[1] But curiously not, *semble*, as regards any investments comprised in the original settlement—(1970), 120 N.L.J. 240 (R. T. Oerton).

[2] By the Trustee Investments Act 1961, s. 16 and Sched. 5.

[3] By Trustee Investments Act 1961, s. 9, altering the law laid down in *Re Walker's Settlement*, [1935] Ch. 567; [1935] All E.R. Rep. 790, C.A.

[4] As explained by the Trustee Investments Act 1961, s. 9 (2).

[5] As amended by the Intestates' Estates Act 1952, s. 5 and Sched. 2, and the Mental Health Act 1959, s. 149 (1) and Sched. 7.

Act 1925, which gives a power of appropriation to personal representatives, though it is important to remember that it does not apply to trustees. Sub-section 2 of this section provides that any property duly appropriated under the statutory power shall thereafter be treated as an authorised investment, and may be retained or dealt with accordingly.

k   Alteration of power of investment

The court has no jurisdiction, under its inherent jurisdiction, to authorise an unauthorised investment, save in emergency.[6] With regard to charities, the power of investment may be altered by way of scheme,[7] or it seems,[8] under the provisions of section 57 of the Trustee Act 1925.[9] Apart from charities, on general principles a trustee cannot be charged with a breach of trust if an "unauthorised" investment is made with the concurrence of the beneficiaries, provided that they are all *sui iuris* and between them entitled to the whole of the equitable interest.[10]

Where all the beneficiaries do not concur, it seems that the court may have jurisdiction to enlarge the power of investment under section 57 of the Trustee Act 1925,[11] though the position is not settled and the jurisdiction may be limited to sanctioning the sale of existing securities and authorising investment in specified new ones.[12] The apparent reluctance of the courts to enlarge powers of investment under section 57, did not at first extend to the jurisdiction given to them under the Variation of Trusts Act 1958.[13] Although in this respect the 1958 Act does not seem to be more widely worded than section 57, the courts at first under the 1958 Act, were very willing to authorise the enlargement of investment powers, either by adding a few words to the investment clause, or by substituting a new clause altogether.[14] It is not clear why there should have been this difference of approach to the two provisions.[15]

---

[6] *Chapman* v. *Chapman*, [1954] 1 All E.R. 798; [1954] A.C. 429 H.L. Cf. *Ovey* v. *Ovey*, [1900] 2 Ch. 524; *Re Powell-Cotton's Resettlement*, [1956] 1 All E.R. 60, C.A.

[7] *Re Royal Society's Charitable Trusts*, [1955] 3 All E.R. 14; [1956] Ch. 87; *Re Tobacco Trade Benevolent Association*, [1958] 3 All E.R. 353; *Re University of London Charitable Trusts*, [1963] 3 All E.R. 859; [1964] Ch. 282; and see Chapter 7, Section 3, p. 211, *ante*.

[8] *The Shipwrecked Fishermen & Mariners' Royal Benevolent Society Charity*, [1958] 3 All E.R. 465; [1959] Ch. 220; *Re Kolb's Will Trusts*, [1961] 3 All E.R. 811; [1962] Ch. 531, not following the view expressed by Vaisey J. in *Re Royal Society's Charitable Trusts*, *supra*.

[9] See Chapter 10, Section 1 b, p. 298, *post*.

[10] See Chapter 12, Section 3 a, p. 370, *post*.

[11] See the cases cited in note 8, *supra*.   There seems to be no justification for restricting the operation of s. 57 to charities. It should be observed that Vaisey J. in *Re Byng's Will Trusts*, [1959] 2 All E.R. 54, seems to have resiled from the view expressed by him in *Re Royal Society's Charitable Trusts*, *supra*.

[12] *Re Brassey's Settlement*, [1955] 1 All E.R. 577; *Re Coates' Will Trusts*, [1959] 2 All E.R. 51.

[13] Considered generally, *post*, pp. 301 *et seq.*

[14] *Re Coates' Will Trusts*, *supra*; *Re Byng's Will Trusts*, *supra*.

[15] There are some differences in the jurisdictions under these provisions. Under s. 57 the court must be satisfied that it is expedient, but there is no requirement that all or any of the beneficiaries must give their consent. Under the 1958 Act all the beneficiaries who are capable of doing so must assent to the proposed variation, and the court is merely empowered to assent on behalf of persons who are themselves unable to do so; further the court can, in general, only approve the variation if it is for the benefit of the beneficiaries on whose behalf it is assenting.

Neither of the above provisions, however, is of great practical importance so far as extending the powers of investment is concerned since the passing of the Trustee Investments Act 1961. The courts have made it clear that, notwithstanding the express provision that the 1961 Act does not affect the jurisdiction under the Variation of Trusts Act 1958,[16] the powers of investment given by the 1961 Act must now be taken to be *prima facie* sufficient. Since the 1961 Act, therefore, a very special case has to be made out in order to persuade the court to exercise its discretionary power of extending them under the Act of 1958,[17] and the practical effect of the 1961 Act has accordingly been to abridge the operation of the Act of 1958. Similar considerations would presumably also apply to an application under section 57 of the Trustee Act 1925.

3 DUTY TO ACT IMPARTIALLY AS BETWEEN THE BENEFICIARIES

One aspect of this duty that we have already come across[18] is the obligation to maintain an even hand as between the life tenant and remaindermen in considering the choice of investments. The most elaborate development, however, is in connection with the conflicting interests of tenant for life and remainderman.[19]

a The duty to convert

Where the will or settlement contains a direction, express or implied,[20] to convert, then the precise duty of the trustees will depend upon the terms of the direction, as affected by statutory provisions.[21] In the absence of any such direction, there is no duty to convert in the case of an *inter vivos* settlement, which must necessarily deal with specific property,[22] nor does any such duty arise in the case of a devise of real estate, whether specific or residuary,[1] or in the case of a specific legacy of personal estate.[2] A duty to convert may, however, be

---

[16] The Trustee Investments Act 1961, s. 15, provides "The enlargement of the investment powers of trustees by this Act shall not lessen any power of a court to confer wider powers of investment on trustees, or affect the extent to which any such power is to be exercised".

[17] *Re Cooper's Settlement*, [1961] 3 All E.R. 636; [1962] Ch. 826; *Re Kolb's Will Trusts*, [1961] 3 All E.R. 811; *Re Clarke's Will Trusts*, [1961] 3 All E.R. 1133. Similarly as regards charitable trusts by way of a scheme: *Re University of London Charitable Trusts*, [1963] 3 All E.R. 859, where a special case was made out. See also (1963), 27 Con. 127 (D. M. E. Evans).

[18] See p. 273, *supra*.

[19] The different position of personal representatives in the course of administration of the deceased's estate is discussed in *Re Hayes's Will Trusts*, [1971] 2 All E.R. 341.

[20] See e.g. *Flux* v. *Best* (1875), 31 L.T. 645 and cp. *Re Holloway* (1888), 60 L.T. 46.

[21] Section 25 (1) of the Law of Property Act 1925 provides that, in the absence of a contrary intention, a power to postpone sale is implied in every trust for sale of land, whenever created: further under s. 25 (4) in the case of dispositions or settlements coming into effect after 31st December, 1925, a trust either to retain or sell land is to be construed as a trust to sell the land with power to postpone the sale.

[22] *Re Van Straubenzee*, [1901] 2 Ch. 779.

[1] *Re Woodhouse*, [1941] 2 All E.R. 265; [1941] Ch. 332.

[2] See e.g. *Bethune* v. *Kennedy* (1835), 1 My. & Gr. 114; *Re Van Straubenzee*, *supra*, and the cases cited *infra* in connection with enjoyment *in specie*.

implied in the case of a residuary bequest contained in a will under what is known as the rule in *Howe* v. *Earl Dartmouth*.[3] This rule, and the reason for it, were thus explained by Wigram V.C. in *Hinves* v. *Hinves*,[4] ". . . where personal estate is given in terms amounting to a general residuary bequest to be enjoyed by persons in succession, the interpretation the Court puts upon the bequest is that the persons indicated are to enjoy the same thing in succession; and, in order to effectuate that intention, the Court as a general rule converts[5] into permanent investments so much of the personalty as is of a wasting or perishable nature[6] at the death of the testator, and also reversionary interests. The rule did not originally ascribe to testators the intention to effect such conversions, except in so far as a testator may be supposed to intend that which the law will do[7]; but the Court, finding the intention of the testator to be that the objects of his bounty shall take successive interests in one and the same thing, converts the property, as the only means of giving effect to that intention." Wasting property,[8] such as royalties in respect of copyright[9] and leaseholds,[10] and hazardous investments, are directed to be converted in order to do justice to the remainderman, who might otherwise get nothing at all, or property much depreciated in value: reversionary interests and other property not producing income are directed to be converted in order to do justice to the tenant for life, who might otherwise obtain nothing from these parts of the trust property. The traditional reasoning behind the rule is not altogether appropriate to contemporary conditions in which the remainderman may well prefer the hazard of an investment which stands a chance of maintaining its real value, as against one which, while maintaining its value on paper, is certain to depreciate in real terms in an inflationary situation. Conversely the tenant for life may well prefer a "safe" investment such as consols bringing in, at the date of writing, over 14 per cent interest. The difficulty has been mitigated by the fact that many

---

[3] (1802), 7 Ves. 137—a decision of Lord Eldon. See, generally, (1943), 7 Con. 128 (S. J. Bailey); (1952), 16 Con. 349 (L. A. Sheridan).

[4] (1844), 3 Hare 609, 611; see also *Alcock* v. *Sloper* (1833), 2 My. & K. 699; *Tickner* v. *Old* (1874), L.R. 18 Eq. 422; *Re Fawcett*, [1940] Ch. 402.

[5] Baggallay L.J. put this more accurately in *Macdonald* v. *Irvine* (1878), 8 Ch.D. 101, 112, C.A., where he said that the court will direct the conversion.

[6] Also unauthorised investments, which are always deemed to be more or less hazardous— *Macdonald* v. *Irvine* (1878), 8 Ch.D. 101, C.A.

[7] In *Simpson* v. *Lester* (1858), 4 Jur. N.S. 1269. Kindersley V.C. said the rule was "purely an artificial rule . . . often calculated to defeat what the testator would have wished in order to give effect to his intentions".

[8] Terminable annuities are commonly referred to as wasting assets, and there is no doubt that there is a duty to convert them. It seems to have been assumed in early cases dealing with government long annuities that, apart from *Howe* v. *Earl Dartmouth*, terminable annuities would be income to which the tenant for life would be entitled. Such annuities were capable of exact valuation and were apportioned, under the rule in *Howe* v. *Earl Dartmouth*, in order to be fair to the remainderman, in accordance with rules iii and iv in sub-section (*b*), *post*, pp. 286, 287 (*Tickner* v. *Old* (1874), L.R. 18 Eq. 422). Under the modern law annuities not capable of exact valuation and, indeed, it would seem, all annuities, are regarded as instalments of capital and not income, it being said that there is no tree of which they can be said to be the fruit. Each payment must accordingly be apportioned in compliance with rules v and vi of sub-section (*b*), *post*, pp. 287, 288.

[9] *Re Sullivan*, [1930] 1 Ch. 84.

[10] Many of the older cases concern leaseholds, but it is doubtful whether the rule applies to leaseholds since 1925—see the discussion at pp. 289-290, *post*.

"equities" are no longer regarded as hazardous investments, under the Trustee Investment Act 1961.

The rule in *Howe* v. *Earl Dartmouth*, it has been observed,[11] "has been since affirmed, as often as it has been referred to, and is unquestionably the law. But the testator may take the case of any particular bequest out of this rule ...". There are a large number of reported cases where the question has been whether on the true construction of the will an intention is to be found that the rule in *Howe* v. *Earl Dartmouth* shall not apply. The above citation[12] from the judgment of Wigram V.C. in *Hinves* v. *Hinves*[13] in fact continues: "But if the will expresses an intention that the property as it existed at the death of the testator shall be enjoyed *in specie*, although the property be not in a technical sense specifically bequeathed, to such a case the rule does not apply." Dicta are to be found in *Hinves* v. *Hinves*[13] and other cases[14] to the effect that small indications of intention will prevent the application of the rule, but the true view, it is submitted, is that expressed by Cozens-Hardy M.R. in *Re Wareham*,[15] "that the rule in *Howe* v. *Earl Dartmouth* must be applied, unless it appears on the construction of the particular will that the testator has shown an intention that the rule shall not apply. The burden of proving this rests on the tenant for life who claims to enjoy the property *in specie*".

Whether the rule in *Howe* v. *Earl Dartmouth* is held to be excluded is thus in each case a question of the true construction of the particular will. The intention that the rule shall not apply may be express, or may be implied from directions in the will which are inconsistent with the application of the rule. Typically the rule will be excluded if the court finds an intention that the tenant for life should enjoy the property *in specie*,[16] or that the remainderman should take the identical property comprised in the residuary gift,[17] or, which indeed follows from either of the preceding intentions, that all the beneficiaries in turn shall enjoy the estate as existing at the time of the death.[18] The intention to exclude the rule may alternatively be found not in directions as to the beneficial enjoyment, but in directions in relation to conversion. Thus the rule will of course be excluded if there is an immediate express trust for sale and will be excluded by implication if the court finds an intention that the property should be converted at some time fixed by the will by reference to a given number of years after the testator's death, or to the falling in of a life;[19] or that the residuary estate should be divided on the death of the tenant for life.[20] The same result follows from finding an intention that whether the property should be sold, and, if so, when it should be sold, should be left to the discretion of the trustees or of some other person, for instance by giving trustees power to retain existing investments, or to sell and

---

[11] *Per* Romilly M.R. in *Morgan* v. *Morgan* (1851), 14 Beav. 72, 82.
[12] *Supra*, p. 282.
[13] (1844), 3 Hare 609, 611.
[14] E.g. *Morgan* v. *Morgan, supra*; *Simpson* v. *Lester, supra*.
[15] [1912] 2 Ch. 312, 315, C.A.; *Macdonald* v. *Irvine* (1878), 8 Ch.D. 101, C.A.; see also *Re Eaton* (1894), 70 L.T. 761.
[16] See e.g. *Marshall* v. *Bremner* (1854), 2 Sm. & G. 237; *Boys* v. *Boys* (1860), 28 Beav. 436.
[17] *Harris* v. *Poyner* (1852), 1 Drew. 174; *Holgate* v. *Jennings* (1857), 24 Beav. 623.
[18] *Re Gough*, [1957] 2 All E.R. 193; [1957] Ch. 323.
[19] *Alcock* v. *Sloper* (1833), 2 My. & K. 699; *Rowe* v. *Rowe* (1861), 29 Beav. 276.
[20] *Re Barratt*, [1925] Ch. 550. Cf. *Re Evans' Will Trusts*, [1921] 2 Ch. 309.

convert the same as they should in their absolute discretion think fit,[1] or by giving them a mere power to sell if and when they should consider it expedient.[2] But a power to vary securities supports the application of the rule by showing the testator intended a conversion.[3] Contrary to what was at one time thought to be the law, in considering whether the rule in *Howe* v. *Earl Dartmouth* is excluded, there is no distinction between hazardous and wasting investments,[4] and reversionary interests are in the same position.[5]

Special mention should be made of the application of the rule in *Howe* v. *Earl Dartmouth* to leaseholds. There is some doubt as to whether the rule originally applied to long leaseholds[6] to which the reason for the rule is hardly appropriate, but in any case it is now clear that the rule cannot apply to leaseholds held for a term exceeding 60 years, since these are now authorised investments under the Settled Land Act 1925.[7] Indeed, it is now doubtful whether since 1925 there is ever an implied duty to convert even short leaseholds under the rule in *Howe* v. *Lord Dartmouth*[8]: dicta which suggest that the rule no longer applies have, however, met with adverse criticism, but it will be convenient to discuss this in connection with another point in the following subsection.

b The duty to apportion

If there is no duty to convert, express[9] or implied, whether as a matter of construction or as a rule of law under the rule in *Howe* v. *Earl Dartmouth*, the tenant for life is of course entitled to the income *in specie*, if any,[10] and the remainderman will in turn become entitled to the capital *in specie*. Suppose, however, there is a duty to convert, no matter how it arises, and suppose, moreover, there is some lapse of time before the conversion actually takes place. In such circumstances if the tenant for life during such period were to take the income *in specie*, this would be liable to result in unfairness—in the case of a wasting asset, for instance, it might be unfair to the remainderman, for the tenant for life might get a large income for a number of years and the remainderman get nothing at all, while in the case of a reversionary interest producing no income, it might, conversely, be unfair to the tenant for life. Equity will not allow failure to carry out a duty to affect the rights of the beneficiaries, and, basing itself on the maxim that equity looks upon that as done which ought to be done, has laid down somewhat elaborate rules as to the

---

[1] *Re Bates*, [1907] 1 Ch. 22; *Re Wilson*, [1907] 1 Ch. 394. In *Re Bates, supra*, Kekewich J. put it another way, namely, that the power to retain the shares added them to the list of authorised investments. Cf. s. 25 (4) of the Law of Property Act 1925, p. 281, note 21, *ante*.

[2] *Re Pitcairn* (1896), 2 Ch. 199; and see *Re Bentham* (1906), 94 L.T. 307; *Re Rogers*, [1915] 2 Ch. 437.

[3] *Morgan* v. *Morgan* (1851), 14 Beav. 72; *Re Llewellyn's Trust* (1861), 29 Beav. 171.

[4] *Re Nicholson*, [1909] 2 Ch. 111.

[5] *Re Pitcairn*, [1896] 2 Ch. 199.

[6] Though not relevant to the decision, it was assumed it did so apply before 1926 in *Berton*, [1939] Ch. 200.

[7] Section 73 (1) (xi); *Re Gough*, [1957] 2 All E.R. 193.

[8] *Re Brooker*, [1926] W.N. 93; *Re Trollope's Will Trusts*, [1927] 1 Ch. 596.

[9] There is no duty to convert where trustees are merely given a discretionary power to convert if and when they think fit—*Re Leonard* (1880), 43 L.T. 664.

[10] *Re Pitcairn*, [1896] 2 Ch. 199; *Rowlls* v. *Bebb*, [1900] 2 Ch. 107, C.A.

apportionment that is to take place in such circumstances. There is, of course, no reason why the testator should not make what provision he likes with regard to the intermediate income, and if expressly or by implication he gives the income *in specie* pending sale to the tenant for life, his wish will prevail.[11] Similarly he may make what provisions he chooses where the property in question is a reversionary interest producing no income.[12] In practice it is very common for a professionally drawn will to contain appropriate express provisions.[13]

Subject to any such expression of a contrary intention, the rules about to be discussed apply whether the duty to convert is express, statutory, or implied under the rule in *Howe* v. *Lord Dartmouth* or otherwise. It should be observed that the rule in *Howe* v. *Lord Dartmouth* is often taken to refer not only to the duty to convert already discussed, for which the case is an authority, but also to the duty to apportion when conversion is delayed, which at most is a corollary of the main rule.[14] Indeed, it is commonly taken[15] to refer to the corresponding duty to apportion in the case of an express or statutory trust for conversion, which would be more properly called the rule in *Gibson* v. *Bott*.[16] The rules as to apportionment are the same however the duty to convert arises.

Assuming that there is a duty to convert, the income to which the tenant for life is entitled depends to a large extent upon the type of property, in accordance with the following rules.

i *Authorised investments.* The tenant for life is of course entitled to the whole income of authorised investments as from the date of death.[17] It will be convenient to mention at this point the position where there is an authorised investment upon some security such as a mortgage, the interest upon which falls into arrears, if when the security is realised it is not sufficient to pay the capital debt and arrears of interest in full. The loss in such case has to be shared between the tenant for life and the remainderman, the sum actually realised being apportioned upon the principles laid down in *Re Atkinson*,[18] namely, in the proportion which the amount due for arrears of interest bears to the amount due in respect of the capital debt. The tenant for life, in making this calculation, is only allowed simple interest.[19]

ii *Realty.* No apportionment has to be made. As Kekewich J. said in *Re Searle*[20]: "where there is a trust for sale with a power to postpone[1] which has been exercised, or where the sale without any impropriety has been postponed,

---

[11] *Re Crowther*, [1895] 2 Ch. 56; *Re Elford*, [1910] 1 Ch. 814.
[12] *Re Pitcairn*, *supra*; *Rowlls* v. *Bebb*, *supra*.
[13] For precedents see Prideaux, *Precedents in Conveyancing*, 25th ed., Vol. 3, pp. 750–752: Key and Elphinstone's *Precedents in Conveyancing*, 15th ed., Vol. 2, pp. 926–928.
[14] See (1952), 16 Con. 349 (L. A. Sheridan); (1943), 7 Con. 128 and 191 (S. J. Bailey).
[15] *Re Brooker*, [1926] W.N. 93; *Re Trollope's Will Trusts*, [1927] 1 Ch. 596; *Re Berton*, [1938] 4 All E.R. 286; [1939] Ch. 200.
[16] (1802), 7 Ves. 89. The distinction was taken by Romer J. in *Re Parry*, [1946] 2 All E.R. 412; [1947] Ch. 23.
[17] *Meyer* v. *Simonsen* (1852), 5 De G. & Sm. 723; *Brown* v. *Gellatly* (1867), 2 Ch. App. 751.
[18] [1904] 2 Ch. 160, C.A.; *Re Walker's Settlement Trusts*, [1936] Ch. 280.
[19] *Re Moore*, (1885), 54 L.J.Ch. 432.
[20] [1900] 2 Ch. 829, 824; *Re Oliver*, [1908] 2 Ch. 74; *Re Woodhouse*, [1941] 2 All E.R. 265; [1941] Ch. 322.
[1] A power to postpone is implied in every trust for sale of land, whenever created, unless a contrary intention appears—Law of Property Act 1925, s. 25 (1) and (3).

the rents and profits of the real estate until sale are payable to the person who would be entitled to the income of the proceeds of sale".

iii   *Unauthorised pure personalty.* The following rules as to how this apportionment is to be carried out where there is no express power to postpone conversion are mainly taken from the decision of Farwell J. in *Re Fawcett.*[2] The tenant for life is not in this case entitled to the actual income, but there has to be an apportionment. In most cases the tenant for life is likely, as a result of such apportionment, to receive less than the actual income, though in some cases it may operate in his favour. There is no longer any distinction made between unauthorised investments which could only be realised at a serious loss to the estate, and those which could easily be realised without such loss.

(a) where unauthorised investments are retained unsold at the end of one year from the death of the testator, the tenant for life is entitled to receive, not the actual income, but interest at the rate of 4 per cent per annum from the date of death until realisation, on the value taken one year after the date of death, i.e. at the end of the executors' year, by which time the conversion ought to have taken place.

(b) where unauthorised investments are sold during the year following the death of the testator, the tenant for life is entitled to receive from the date of death until realisation the like interest on the net proceeds of sale.[3]

(c) subject to head (f) below, upon realisation, whether during or after the end of the executors' year, the net proceeds of sale must be re-invested in authorised investments and thereafter rule i above will apply.

(d) the unauthorised investments for the time being unsold must be treated *en bloc* as one aggregate.[4]

(e) any excess of income from unauthorised investments beyond the interest payable to the life tenant under heads (a) or (b) above, must be invested in authorised investments, to the income of which thereafter rule i above will apply.

(f) interest in respect of unauthorised investments is payable out of the interest arising from them or, in so far as that is insufficient, out of the proceeds of their realisation; any interest for the time being in arrear is payable (but calculated as simple interest only) out of subsequent income from unauthorised investments, which are for the time being retained, and out of the proceeds of their sale when realised.

(g) neither excess income from unauthorised investments which at the end of any accounting period is available under head (e) above for investment in authorised investments, nor proceeds of realisation of unauthorised investments not required at the date of realisation to pay interest under head (f) above which are accordingly available to be invested in authorised investments, are applicable towards payment of subsequently accruing interest in respect of unauthorised investments still retained.

---

[2] [1940] Ch. 402. See also *Dimes* v. *Scott* (1828), 4 Russ. 195; *Meyer* v. *Simonsen* (1852), 5 De G. & Sm. 723; *Brown* v. *Gellatly* (1867), 2 Ch. App. 751.
[3] *Re Berry,* [1961] 1 All E.R. 529; [1962] Ch. 97.
[4] *Re Owen,* [1912] 1 Ch. 519.

iv *Unauthorised pure personalty—the effect of a power to postpone conversion.* The preliminary point is whether the inclusion of such a power shows an intention that the tenant for life should enjoy the income *in specie* until a conversion takes place. This depends upon whether the power is inserted for benefit of the tenant for life, or merely for the more convenient realisation of the] estate.[5] In order to entitle the tenant for life *in specie* there must be something more than a bare power to postpone. As Eve J. explained in *Re Slater*,[6] "A mere trust for conversion, with an ancillary power to postpone the conversion, does not of itself give the income of the property before conversion *in specie* to the tenant for life. One must find further indications of the testator's intention, and must consider the will carefully". Where the necessary indications are found, and even though there is an express provision excluding the rules as to apportionment, the tenant for life will *prima facie* only be entitled to the income *in specie* so long as the trustees postpone the sale in proper exercise of their discretion.[7]

In the absence of any indication that the tenant for life is to take the income *in specie*, there must be an apportionment notwithstanding the power to postpone conversion.[8] The difference made by the insertion of a power to postpone was fully discussed by Romer J. in *Re Parry*.[9] It means, he pointed out, that there is no duty upon the executor to sell at once, or within a year, or at any other time, and accordingly there is no reason for assuming a notional conversion at once, or within a year, or at any other time.

> "The essential equity, however—the balance between the successive interests—remains equally compelling even where there is no immediate obligation to convert and property is retained for the benefit of the estate as a whole. It is accordingly rational, and indeed obvious, to substitute a valuation of the testator's assets in the place of a hypothetical sale; and, if so, it is difficult to think of a better date for the valuation than the day when the testator died and the assets passed to his executors".[10]

Accordingly the tenant for life is entitled to receive interest at the rate of 4 per cent per annum from the date of the death until realisation, on the value taken at the date of death. Subject to the consequential variations due to the different date of valuation, the directions set out in rule iii above, heads (c)–(g) will, however, presumably apply.

v *Reversionary interests the Rule in Re Earl of Chesterfield's Trusts.*[11] Here the property is producing no income, and accordingly until it falls in there is

---

[5] *Re Inman*, [1915] 1 Ch. 187.
[6] (1915), 113 L.T. 691, 693; and see *Re Chance*, [1962] 1 All E.R. 942; [1962] Ch. 593.
[7] This seems right on principle, and may be inferred from *Rowlls* v. *Bebb*, [1900] 2 Ch. 107, C.A. (dealing however with a reversionary interest); *Re Godfree*, [1914] 2 Ch. 110. In *Re Fisher*, [1943] Ch. 377, this was held to be so in the case of the statutory trust for sale on intestacy under s. 33 of the Administration of Estates Act 1925, though on the wording of sub-ss. (1) (4) and (5) it would seem arguable that the tenant for life takes the income *in specie* in any event. Cf. *Re Sullivan*, [1930] 1 Ch. 84.
[8] *Re Chaytor*, [1905] 1 Ch. 233; *Re Parry*, [1946] 2 All E.R. 412; [1947] Ch. 23; *Re Berry*, [1961] 1 All E.R. 529; [1962] Ch. 97. In *Re Parry* counsel reserved the right to contend before a higher tribunal that the power to postpone excluded the duty to apportion.
[9] *Supra*, where the relevant cases are carefully considered.
[10] *Per* Romer J. in *Re Parry*, [1946] 2 All E.R. at p. 422; [1947] Ch. at p. 45.
[11] (1883), 24 Ch.D. 643 following with some variation *Wilkinson* v. *Duncan* (1857), 23 Beav. 469; *Beavan* v. *Beavan* (1869), 24 Ch.D. 649 n.

nothing to apportion. When it eventually does fall in, or is realised, an apportionment has to be made in order to be fair to the tenant for life. The apportionment is made by ascertaining the sum which, put out at interest at 4 per cent per annum on the day of the testator's death, and accumulating at compound interest calculated at that rate with yearly rests and deducting income tax, would, with the accumulations of interest, have produced, at the day of receipt, the amount actually received. The sum so ascertained must be treated as capital, and the residue as income payable to the tenant for life. The rule applies not only to a reversionary interest in its strict sense,[12] but to other sums which have to be treated as postponed capital payments even though they may have some appearance of income. Thus the rule has been applied to a policy of assurance on the life of another which fell in some years after the death of the testator,[13] to sums payable to the estate after the testator's death in consideration of past service[14], to the instalments of the purchase price of a business sold by the testator and payable after his death,[15] to a determinable annuity, and payments analogous thereto,[16] and to payment of a sum due from an insolvent estate which was grossly insufficient to satisfy a bond debt.[17] It was also applied to sums paid in respect of claims under Part I of the Town and Country Planning Act 1954[18] in Re Chance[19], which also decides that it makes no difference that when the asset ultimately comes in, it brings with it or contains within it interest. It is the fact that the asset is not producing anything in the meantime that gives rise to the claim by the tenant for life for recoupment. But the court has refused to apply the rule where the interest of the testator at the date of death was not a reversionary interest, but an absolute interest, the income of which was temporarily charged in favour of a third person.[20]

vi *Reversionary interests—the effect of a power to postpone conversion.* On similar principles to those discussed under rule iv above, a mere power to

---

[12] *Re Hobson* (1886), 53 L.T. 627; *Re Flower* (1890), 62 L.T. 216 reversed on other grounds (1890), 63 L.T. 201 C.A.; *Rowlls* v. *Bebb*, [1900] 2 Ch. 107, C.A. Cp. *Re Holliday's Will Trusts*, [1947] 1 All E.R. 695, [1947] Ch. 402.

[13] *Re Morley*, [1895] 2 Ch. 738.

[14] *Re Payne*, [1943] 2 All E.R. 675. Cf. *Re Fisher*, [1943] Ch. 377.

[15] *Re Hollebone*, [1919] 2 Ch. 93; [1918–19] All E.R. Rep. 323.

[16] *Re Hey's Settlement Trusts*, [1945] Ch. 294; *Re Guinness's Settlement*, [1966] 2 All E.R. 497. Contrast, however, *Crawley* v. *Crawley* (1835), 7 Sim. 427, followed in *Re Whitehead*, [1894] 1 Ch. 678 where the court simply ordered each payment to be treated as capital and invested accordingly, the tenant for life thereafter to receive the income on the investments. The distinction was noted in *Re Hollebone, supra*, Eve J. merely observing that the facts were quite different. The cases were apparently approved in *Re Payne, supra*, and *Re Hey's Settlement Trusts, supra*, but in each of these the court went on to order apportionment on the principle of *Re Earl of Chesterfield's Trust, supra*. It is to be noted that *Crawley* v. *Crawley, supra*, was decided before the rule in *Re Earl of Chesterfield's Trust* was settled, and it is submitted that on such facts an apportionment under the rule should be made.

[17] *Cox* v. *Cox* (1869), L.R. 8 Eq. 343; and see *Re Duke of Cleveland's Estate*, [1895] 2 Ch. 542. For unusual applications of the rule see *Re Godden*, [1893] 1 Ch. 292; *Re Hengler*, [1893] 1 Ch. 586—this doubtful case is difficult to reconcile with *Re Owen*, [1912] 1 Ch. 519 and seems to depend on a wrong admission by counsel that the rule in *Re Earl of Chesterfield's Trusts* applied.

[18] *Re Chance*, [1962] 1 All E.R. 942; [1962] Ch. 593.

[19] *Supra.*

[20] *Re Holliday's Will Trusts*, [1947] 1 All E.R. 695; [1947] Ch. 402.

postpone does not affect the duty to apportion when the reversion eventually
falls in or a sale eventually takes place. The apportionment must be carried out
according to the principles set out in rule v above. If, however, there is a
power to postpone which is properly[1] exercised then there may be other
indications in the will that it is the testator's intention that no apportionment
is to take place, and if so this will be effective. In practice, it is usual to exclude
the operation of the rule in *Re Earl of Chesterfield's Trust.*

vii *Leaseholds.* Before 1926, both the duty to convert under the rule in
Howe v. *Earl Dartmouth* and the duty to apportion during such period as the
property was retained unconverted, applied equally to leaseholds as to other
forms of personal property.[2] The better view, it is submitted, is that the length
of the lease was immaterial.[3]

The effect of the Law of Property Act 1925[4] is somewhat uncertain. So far as
apportionment is concerned, it seems clear that, in the absence of a direction to
the contrary, a tenant for life is now entitled to the whole of the rents and profits
arising from leaseholds, where the leasehold is held on a trust for sale whether
express,[5] or implied either by statute,[6] or even, probably, by the rule in
Howe v. *Earl Dartmouth* itself,[7] though it has been suggested[8] that section 28 (2)
does not apply in the last case on the ground that there is no "disposition" on
trust for sale as required by the Act. What is more difficult, however, is to
discover whether, in the absence of any express or statutory trust for sale, the
rule in *Howe* v. *Earl Dartmouth* continues to operate so as to impose a duty to
convert in the case of leaseholds. It has been held that the rule can no longer
apply to leaseholds held for a term exceeding 60 years, since these are now
authorised investments under section 73 (1) (xi) of the Settled Land Act 1925.[9]
So far as shorter leaseholds are concerned there still seems to be a duty to
convert, though it can be argued that the rule must be deemed to have ceased
to be applicable in view of provisions which, if it applied, would operate to
defeat its purpose, namely, section 25 (1) of the Law of Property Act 1925,
which gives an indefinite power to postpone sale and section 28 (2) which, as
we have just seen, probably gives the whole income to the tenant for life.
It is submitted, nevertheless, that the duty to convert under the rule in *Howe* v.
Earl Dartmouth still applies[10] and that dicta in *Re Brooker,*[11] *Re Trollope's Will
Trusts*[12] and *Re Berton*[13] which appear to contradict this are really concerned

---

[1] *Rowlls* v. *Bebb,* [1900] 2 Ch. 107, C.A.; *Re Hey's Settlement Trusts,* [1945] Ch. 294; *Re
   Guinness's Settlement,* [1966] 2 All E.R. 497.
[2] See e.g. *Re Game,* [1897] 1 Ch. 881; *Re Wareham,* [1912] 2 Ch. 312, C.A.
[3] See (1932), 4 C.L.J. 357, 364 (S. J. Bailey); *Re Berton,* [1938] 4 All E.R. 286; [1939] Ch.
   200. But see Jarman on *Wills,* 8th Ed., Vol. II, p. 1223.
[4] Section 28 (2).
[5] *Re Brooker,* [1926] W.N. 93; *Re Trollope's Will Trusts,* [1927] 1 Ch. 596.
[6] *Re Berton, supra.* This was a case of undivided shares where a trust for sale was implied
   under s. 34 (3) of the Law of Property Act 1925, and see (1942), 6 Con. 155 (S. J. Bailey).
[7] Assuming the rule continues to operate—see the immediately following discussion.
[8] Nathan and Marshall, *A Casebook on Trusts,* 5th Ed., pp. 417, 418. *Contra,* Lewin on
   Trusts, 16th Ed., p. 236; Snell's *Equity,* 27th Ed., p. 219.
[9] *Re Gough,* [1957] 2 All E.R. 193; [1957] Ch. 323.
[10] See (1939), 3 Con. 236 (S. J. Bailey). *Contra* Jarman on *Wills,* 8th Ed., Vol. II, p. 1225.
[11] *Supra.*
[12] *Supra.*
[13] *Supra.*

only with the rules as to apportionment. The practical importance lies chiefly in whether the leasehold will be settled land governed by the Settled Land Act 1925, or land held on trust for sale, which is excluded from the Settled Land Act 1925[14] and governed by the Law of Property Act 1925.

viii *Rate of interest.* It will have been observed that in making an apportionment, both in the case of wasting or hazardous investments, and in the case of reversionary interests, the rate of interest is stated to be 4 per cent. There was, however, a period in the early part of this century when the rate was reduced to 3 per cent. In both types of case the reduction was introduced by Kekewich J., first in *Re Goodenough*[15] in the case of reversionary interests, and then in *Re Woods*[16] in the case of wasting or hazardous investments. The rate was restored to 4 per cent in *Re Baker*[17] and *Re Beech*[18] and has ever since continued to be applied.[19] Perhaps the time has come for a reappraisal, as has happened in other contexts. For example the rate of interest on judgment debts, which was fixed at 4 per cent by the Judgments Act 1838, was increased to $7\frac{1}{2}$ per cent by an order[20] made under the Administration of Justice Act 1970, and the rate of interest payable on legacies has been raised from 4 per cent to 5 per cent.[21]

ix For the avoidance of doubt, it may be observed that the above rules as to apportionment only apply to property found in a particular state of investment at the date of the death. They have no application where trustees commit a breach of trust by making an unauthorised investment. Trustees in such case "have discharged their liability in favour of the *cestuis que trust* who are entitled to the capital in remainder, when they have made good the capital and any increase which that capital has received."[22] Increase here "does not mean increase by way of interest, but increase by way of profit—some accumulations, something by way of accretion to the capital."[1] Accordingly if the tenant for life has received more than 4 per cent, he cannot be called upon to account for the balance over that amount to the remainderman, even though it be the trustee himself who is the tenant for life.[2] If the unauthorised investment proves to be insufficient, the loss[3] has to be thrown rateably on the tenant for life and remainderman. The sum available has to be divided in the proportion which the dividends which the tenant for life would have received had the wrongful

---

[14] Section 1 (7) added by the Law of Property (Amendment) Act 1926, s. 7 and Sched.
[15] [1895] 2 Ch. 537 followed in *Re Duke of Cleveland's Estate,* [1895] 2 Ch. 542; *Rowlls* v. *Bebb,* [1900] 2 Ch. 107, C.A.
[16] [1904] 2 Ch. 4.
[17] [1924] 2 Ch. 271.
[18] [1920] 1 Ch. 40 followed in *Re Fawcett,* [1940] Ch. 402; *Re Parry,* [1946] 2 All E.R. 412; [1947] Ch. 23; *Re Berry,* [1961] 1 All E.R. 529; [1962] Ch. 97.
[19] In *Re Ellis,* [1935] Ch. 193; [1934] All E.R. Rep. 58. Farwell J. refused to take judicial notice of the fact that a trustee could not then get 4 per cent on trustee securities, saying this was a matter for evidence.
[20] S.I. 1971, No. 491. And see *The Funabashi,* [1972] 2 All E.R. 181; *Cremer* v. *General Carriers S.A.,* [1974] 1 All E.R. 1.
[21] S.I. 1972, No. 1898 amending R.S.C., O. 44 s. 19.
[22] *Stroud* v. *Gwyer* (1860), 28 Beav. 130, 141 *per* Romilly M.R.; *Slade* v. *Chaine,* [1908] 1 Ch. 522, C.A.
[1] *Slade* v. *Chaine, supra, per* Kekewich J. at p. 526.
[2] *Re Hoyles,* [1912] 1 Ch. 67.
[3] For present purposes it is assumed that any personal remedy against the trustee who has committed the breach of trust is worthless.

investment not been made bear to the value of the sum wrongly invested. The tenant for life must, of course, give credit for monies actually received, though he is not liable to refund any over payment.[4]

c Where stock or shares are sold or purchased by trustees cum dividend

In such cases the general rule is that there is no apportionment between capital and income.[5] This is purely a rule of convenience as a result of which the beneficiaries have to take the rough with the smooth in order to ease the burden falling on trustees. The court, however, may depart from the general rule where its application would cause a glaring injustice, though it seems that this jurisdiction will only be exercised in extreme circumstances.[6] If at the date of the purchase of stock or shares, however, dividends have been earned and declared, though not paid, they must go to capital when they are ultimately paid and not to the tenant for life.[7]

d The "windfall" principle

Questions sometimes arise as to whether the tenant for life or remainderman is entitled to extraordinary payments made by a company, which may be given some name such as "cash bonus" or "capital profits dividend". On the one hand it is a basic principle that a limited company not in liquidation can make no payment by way of return of capital to its shareholders except as a step in an authorised reduction of capital. Any other payment made by it by means of which it parts with moneys or other property to its shareholders must and can only be made by way of dividing profits. Accordingly, whatever the payment may be called, if it is paid to a trustee shareholder it will *prima facie* belong to the person beneficially entitled to the income of the trust estate, *i.e.*, the tenant for life as opposed to the remainderman.[8] As Vaisey J. put it,[9] "These accretions to the normal income of the trust fund are sometimes metaphorically described as "windfalls", and when they have left the parent tree, I can see no principle for notionally replacing them on the boughs from which they have fallen".

Thus in *Re Bates*[10] a company sold some of its assets at a price well above the value as appearing in the company's balance sheet. The profit on the sale was distributed as a cash bonus, and it was held that the tenant for life was entitled

---

[4] *Re Bird*, [1901] 1 Ch. 916.
[5] *Bulkeley* v. *Stephens*, [1896] 2 Ch. 241. Cf. *Re Henderson*, [1940] 1 All E.R. 623; [1940] Ch. 368.
[6] *Bulkeley* v. *Stephens, supra*; *Re Firth*, [1938] 2 All E.R. 217; [1938] Ch. 517; *Re Maclaren's Settlement Trusts*, [1951] 2 All E.R. 414. Clauson J.'s decision in *Re Winterstoke's Will Trusts*, [1937] 4 All E.R. 63; [1938] Ch. 158, seems out of line with the other cases.
[7] *Re Peel's Settled Estates*, [1910] 1 Ch. 389.
[8] *Hill* v. *Permanent Trustee Company of New South Wales Ltd.*, [1930] A.C. 720, P.C. (where the guiding principles are clearly laid down); *Re Doughty*, [1947] 1 All E.R. 207; [1947] Ch. 263, C.A.; *Re Harrison's Will Trusts*, [1949] Ch. 678, see generally (1951), 67 L.Q.R. 195 (S.J. Bailey).
[9] *Re Kleinwort's Settlement Trusts*, [1951] 2 All E.R. 328, at p. 330; [1951] Ch. 860, at p. 863.
[10] [1928] Ch. 682.

to the whole payment. Similarly in *Re Tedlie*[11] a company sold a considerable part of its assets to another company, receiving in payment shares and a sum of cash. Following this transaction the company had a large surplus of assets over debts, capital and what was required for carrying on the business retained. Shares[12] and cash were paid to the shareholders, and it was held that a trustee shareholder must pay the whole to the tenant for life. By an application of the same principle it was held in *Thomson's Trustees* v. *Thomson*[13] that if trustees sell stock at an increased price by reason of some anticipated right to receive an income payment, the price received must be proportionately appropriated to the claims of the tenant for life. Again in *Re Whitehead's Will Trusts*[14] the question arose where trustees, as holders under a unit trust, received what were called capital distributions. The court held that in case of doubt the trustees must enquire into the source of any such distribution and treat it as income or capital just as if they were the direct shareholders of the shares included in the portfolio. On the other hand, where the company is being wound up, the situation is entirely different, and distributions made to shareholders, including trustees, are capital.[15] And as a result of statute,[16] the same rule applies to a distribution out of moneys in a company's share premium account.[17]

Even though the above rules may appear to operate harshly in a particular case, it seems that the courts have power to make an apportionment only where the trustees have been guilty of some breach of trust.[18] These rules, however, cease to be applicable where a company has taken the necessary steps to capitalise its profits. All limited companies having a share capital now have power,[19] if authorised by their articles,[20] to increase their capital. If, instead of paying out its profits as dividend, a company uses the profits to pay for a new issue of shares which are issued as bonus shares to the shareholders, trustee-shareholders must hold the bonus shares as part of the capital of the trust and must not hand them over to the tenant for life as income. The point is that if the company does this it is not in fact parting with its money at all, and the money ceases for all time to be divisible as profits and can only be paid to the shareholders on a reduction of capital or in a winding-up. The same principle has been applied even though no new paid-up capital in the strict sense of the word has been created, as where the profits are used to pay for an issue of unsecured loan stock.[1] "The real application of the principle is to assets, from which

---

[11] (1922), 126 L.T. 644. See also the Thomas Tilling cases—*Re Sechiari*, [1950] 1 All E.R. 417; *Re Kleinwort's Settlement Trusts*, [1951] 2 All E.R. 328; [1951] Ch. 860; *Re Rudd's Will Trusts*, [1952] 1 All E.R. 254 discussed (1953), 17 Con. 22 (A. J. Bland).

[12] I.e., the shares in the other company.

[13] [1955] S.C. 476. Cp. *Manclark* v. *Thomson's Trustees*, [1958] S.C. 147.

[14] [1959] 2 All E.R. 497; [1959] Ch. 579.

[15] *Re Armitage*, [1893] 3 Ch. 337, C.A.; *Re Palmer* (1912), 28 T.L.R. 301; *I.R.Comrs.* v. *Burrell*, [1924] 2 K.B. 52, C.A.

[16] Companies Act 1948, s. 56.

[17] *Re Duff's Settlement*, [1951] 2 All E.R. 534; [1951] Ch. 923, C.A.

[18] *Re Kleinwort's Settlement Trusts*, *supra*; *Re Maclaren's Settlement Trusts*, [1951] 2 All E.R. 414; *Re Rudd's Will Trusts*, [1952] 1 All E.R. 254; *Re Morris's Will Trusts*, [1960] 3 All E.R. 548.

[19] Companies Act 1948, s. 61 (1).

[20] If not so authorised, the articles can be altered for the purpose.

[1] *Re Outen's Will Trusts*, [1962] 3 All E.R. 478; [1963] Ch. 291.

any further character of divisible profits has been taken away, whatever may be the substituted character thereafter impressed upon them."[2]

Thus in the leading case of *Bouch* v. *Sproule*[3] the directors of a company proposed to distribute certain accumulated profits as a bonus dividend, to allot new shares to each shareholder, and to apply the bonus dividend in payment of the new shares. This proposal was carried out and it was held that the real nature of the transaction was that the undivided profits should be appropriated as an increase of the capital stock, and the tenant for life accordingly had no claim either to the bonus dividend or to the new shares. Lord Herschell in this case approved the statement of Fry L.J. in the court below[4] that the company alone decides whether to capitalise its profits or not, and provided its decision is properly carried out, its decision will bind beneficiaries claiming under a shareholder. Whether there has been capitalisation of profits or not is therefore a question of fact in each case. In considering this question from one point of view Atkin L.J. observed,[5] "the intention of the company is dominant for all purposes. Did the company intend to distribute as profits or as capital?". From another point of view, however, Lord Sumner has said,[6] "the only intention, that the company has, is such as is expressed in or necessarily follows from its proceedings. It is hardly a paradox to say that the form of a company's resolutions and instruments is their substance".[7] Accordingly although the question is as to the intention of the company the court will not be bound by a company's statement as to what it intended to do or as to the effect of what it has done, if it has failed to take the necessary steps for effective capitalisation.[8] If the intention of the company to capitalise is clear, however, the fact that an option is given to the shareholders to take cash instead of the new shares makes no difference and since, in practice, the cash offer is always less favourable than the offer of bonus shares, the trustees will be under a duty to accept the offer in its most favourable, that is to say its capitalised, form.[9] If, however, there is such an option given but no intention to capitalise, then if the cash option is properly exercised, the cash will go to the tenant for life,[10] but if the trustees, as they normally should, accept the offer of new shares as being more advantageous, the tenant for life will only be entitled to so much of the value of the new shares as represented the dividend applied by the trustees in taking them up, the balance of such value forming part of the capital of the trust.[11] The point is that the issue of new shares in such circumstances necessarily depreciates the value of the old ones.

---

[2] *Per* Lord Sumner in *I.R. Comrs.* v. *Fisher's Executors*, [1926] A.C. 395, at p. 410, H.L. Cf. *I. R. Comrs.* v. *Parker*, [1966] 1 All E.R. 399, [1966] A.C. 141, H.L.

[3] (1887), 12 App. Cas. 385, H.L.   [4] (1885), 29 Ch.D. 635, 653, C.A.

[5] *I.R. Comrs.* v. *Burrell*, [1924] 2 K.B. 52, at p. 68, C.A.

[6] *I.R. Comrs.* v. *Fisher's Executors*, [1926] A.C. 395, at p. 411, H.L.

[7] See also *I.R. Comrs.* v. *Blott*, [1921] 2 A.C. 171, H.L.; *Re Taylor*, [1926] Ch. 923; *I.R. Comrs.* v. *Wright*, [1927] 1 K.B. 333, C.A.

[8] *Re Piercy*, [1907] 1 Ch. 289; *Re Bates*, [1928] Ch. 682; *Re Thomas*, [1916] 2 Ch. 331, 343, C.A. *per* Cozens Hardy M.R.

[9] *Re Evans*, [1913] 1 Ch. 23; *Re Malam*, [1894] 3 Ch. 578.

[10] *Re Despard* (1901), 17 T.L.R. 478. The question whether it was proper for the trustees to exercise the cash option does not seem to have been raised, though it would seem that the inevitable effect of the whole transaction must have been to reduce the value of the trust shares.

[11] *Re Northage* (1891), 64 L.T. 625; *Re Malam*, [1894] 3 Ch. 578.

CHAPTER 10

Duties of Trustees—II

---

1 DUTY NOT TO DEVIATE
FROM THE TERMS OF THE TRUST[1]

The fundamental principle is that a trustee must faithfully observe the directions contained in the trust instrument and, "as a rule, the court has no jurisdiction to give, and will not give, its sanction to the performance by trustees of acts with reference to the trust estate which are not, on the face of the instrument creating the trust, authorised by its terms".[2] The House of Lords has made it clear in *Chapman* v. *Chapman*[3] that under the inherent jurisdiction the exceptions to this rule are very limited. These exceptions must now be discussed, together with various important statutory provisions which are relevant.[4] Two other exceptions are more conveniently considered elsewhere, namely the rule that if all the beneficiaries being of full age and capacity act together they can consent to what would otherwise be a breach of trust so as to free the trustees from any liability,[5] and, indeed, even bring the trust to an end,[6] and the *cy-près* doctrine in relation to charities.[7] Mention should also be made of the statutory exceptions under the Matrimonial Causes Act 1973, which gives a wide jurisdiction to the court to vary trusts in cases of divorce, nullity and judicial separation,[8] and under the Mental Health Act 1959, which gives the Court of Protection power to settle the property of a patient, and in certain circumstances to vary such a settlement.[9]

---

[1] See, generally (1965), 43 C.B.R. 181 (A. J. McClean).
[2] *Re New*, [1901] 2 Ch. 534, 544, C.A., *per* Romer L.J.
[3] [1954] 1 All E.R. 798; [1954] A.C. 429 affirming the judgment of the majority in C.A., [1953] 1 All E.R. 103; [1953] Ch. 218.
[4] See (1954), 17 M.L.R. 420 (O. R. Marshall).
[5] See Chapter 12, Section 3a, *post*, pp. 370 *et seq*. If the proposed act can affect only some of the beneficiaries, only those who may be affected need consent in order to protect the trustees—but those beneficiaries must all be of full age and capacity.
[6] See Section 7, p. 333, *post*.
[7] See Chapter, 7, Section 4, p. 215 *ante*.
[8] See *Jones* v. *Jones*, [1972] 3 All E.R. 289.
[9] Mental Health Act 1959, s. 103 (1) (*d*) and 103 (4). The power to vary is given where any material fact was not disclosed when the settlement was made, or where there has been any substantial change in circumstances. Cf. *Re R.H.C.*, [1963] 1 All E.R. 524 (*Ct. of Protection*).

a   The inherent jurisdiction

Adopting the classification used by Lord Morton in *Chapman* v. *Chapman*,[10] the cases can be grouped under four heads—

i   "*Cases in which the court has effected changes in the nature of an infant's property, e.g., by directing investment of his personalty in the purchase of freeholds.*"   In looking at these cases it must be remembered that under the old law, there were important differences between the law relating to realty and that relating to personalty.   Before the Wills Act 1837, which provided that no will made by any person under the age of 21 should be valid,[11] a male infant on attaining the age of 14, and a female infant on attaining the age of 12, could dispose by will of personalty,[12] but not of realty.   Until 1926 therefore the position was that on the death of an infant his realty passed to his heir-at-law,[13] while his personalty passed to his next-of-kin, or before the Wills Act 1837 to the legatees if he had made a valid will.   It followed that a conversion of property to which an infant was absolutely entitled would not change the infant's beneficial interest, though it would affect rights of succession and before 1838 might affect his power of testamentary disposition.   Accordingly trustees were not permitted to change the nature of an infant's property,[14] but where it was shown to be for the benefit of the infant the court might be prepared to make an appropriate order,[15] though it became the practice in such case to insert a provision in the order that in equity the property should notionally retain its unconverted form until the infant attained his majority.[16]   A similar jurisdiction was exercised in the case of persons of unsound mind.[17]

ii   "*Cases in which the court has allowed the trustees of settled property to enter into some business transaction which was not authorised by the settlement.*"   The principle of this exception is stated in perhaps its widest form in the leading case of *Re New*.[18]   In delivering the judgment of the Court of Appeal, Romer L.J. said,[1]

> "In the management of a trust estate . . . it not infrequently happens that some peculiar state of circumstances arises for which provision is not expressly made by the trust instrument, and which renders it most desirable, and it may be even essential, for the benefit of the estate and in the interest of all the *cestuis que trust*, that certain acts should be done by the trustees which in ordinary circumstances

---

[10] [1954] 1 All E.R. 798, at pp. 807, 808; [1954] A.C. 429, at p. 451, H.L.
[11] Subject to an exception under s. 11, extended by the Wills (Soldiers and Sailors) Act 1918. 18 was substituted for 21 by the Family Law Reform Act 1969, in respect of wills made after 31 December, 1969.
[12] It is respectfully submitted that Lord Denning's reference to the age of 17 is an error, perhaps a confusion with the age at which an infant could at one time become an executor —*Chapman* v. *Chapman*, *supra*, in C.A. at pp. 132, 270.
[13] If there was no heir-at-law, realty would escheat to the lord of the fee; in no case would it pass under an infant's will or to his next-of-kin.
[14] *Witter* v. *Witter* (1730), 3 P.Wms. 99.
[15] *Inwood* v. *Twyne* (1762), Amb. 417.
[16] *Lord Ashburton* v. *Lady Ashburton* (1801), 6 Ves. 6; and see *A.-G.* v. *Marquis of Ailesbury* (1887), 12 App. Cas. 672, H.L.
[17] *A.-G.* v. *Marquis of Ailesbury*, *supra*.
[18] [1901] 2 Ch. 534, C.A.   [1] At p. 544.

they would have no power to do. In a case of this kind, which may reasonably be supposed to be one not foreseen or anticipated by the author of the trust, where the trustees are embarrassed by the emergency that has arisen and the duty cast upon them to do what is best for the estate, and the consent of all the beneficiaries cannot be obtained by reason of some of them not being *sui juris* or in existence, then it may be right for the court, and the court in a proper case would have jurisdiction, to sanction on behalf of all concerned such acts on behalf of the trustees as we have above referred to. . . . Of course, the jurisdiction is one to be exercised with great caution, and the court will take care not to strain its powers . . . it need scarcely be said that the court will not be justified in sanctioning every act desired by trustees and beneficiaries merely because it may appear beneficial to the estate; and certainly the court will not be disposed to sanction transactions of a speculative or risky character."

This exception includes, and can perhaps be regarded as,[2] an extension of the principle of what are referred to as the salvage cases, where, in the case of absolute necessity, such as repairs vital to prevent further damage to settled land, the court has sanctioned a transaction such as the mortgage or sale of part of an infant's beneficial interest.[3] The Court of Appeal in *Re Montagu*,[4] following earlier cases,[5] made it quite clear that the fact that the proposed scheme would benefit the infant, or indeed all the beneficiaries, was not enough. The application failed in *Re Montagu*[6] itself, Lopes L.J. observing,[7] "If the buildings were falling down it would be a case of actual salvage and would stand differently".

The proposal put forward in *Re New*,[8] was that the trustees, as holders of certain shares, should be empowered to concur in a proposed reconstruction of a mercantile company, as a result of which they would receive shares and debentures in the proposed new or reconstructed company. In sanctioning the scheme the court put the trustees on an undertaking to apply for leave to retain such shares and debentures if they desired to retain them for more than a year. This decision, it was said two years later in *Re Tollemache*[9] "constitutes the high-water mark of the exercise by the court of its extraordinary jurisdiction in relation to trusts". In the later case what was sought, and refused, was authority for the trustees to acquire—as the relevant trusts did not permit them to do—a mortgage of the tenant for life's interest, a transaction which it was claimed could not prejudice the remaindermen and would enable the tenant for life to enjoy a large addition to her income by reason of the fact that a higher rate of interest was payable under the mortgage than was being received on the authorised trust investments.

---

[2] See (1954), 17 M.L.R. 420 (O. R. Marshall).
[3] *Re Jackson* (1882), 21 Ch.D. 786; *Conway* v. *Fenton* (1888), 40 Ch.D. 512; *Re De Teissier's Settled Estates*, [1893] 1 Ch. 153.
[4] [1897] 2 Ch. 8, C.A.
[5] E.g. *Calvert* v. *Godfrey* (1843), 6 Beav. 97; *Re Jackson, supra*.
[6] *Supra.*
[7] At p. 11.
[8] *Supra.*
[9] [1903] 1 Ch. 955, C.A. *per* Cozens-Hardy L.J. at p. 956; Romer L.J., who had delivered the judgment of the court in *Re New*, *supra*, in effect said the same thing. See also the judgment of Kekewich J. in the court below, [1903] 1 Ch. 457.

iii *"Cases in which the court has allowed maintenance out of income which the settlor or testator directed to be accumulated."* Unlike the previous two exceptions, this exception involves modification or re-moulding of the beneficial trusts. The classic explanation of this exception was given by Pearson J. in *Re Collins*,[10] namely,

> "that where a testator has made a provision for a family, using that word in the ordinary sense in which we take the word, that is the children of a particular *stirps* in succession or otherwise, but has postponed the enjoyment, either for a particular purpose or generally for the increase of the estate, it is assumed that he did not intend that these children should be left unprovided for or in a state of such moderate means that they should not be educated properly for the position and fortune which he designs them to have, and the Court has accordingly found from the earliest time that where an heir-at-law is unprovided for, maintenance ought to be provided for him. Lord Hardwicke has extended that to the case of a tenant for life. . . ."[11]

The jurisdiction here does not depend on the infancy of the life tenant,[12] nor is it confined to cases of emergency or necessity.[13]

iv *"Cases in which the court has approved a compromise on behalf of infants and possible after-born beneficiaries."* There is no doubt that the court has jurisdiction where rights are in dispute: but if the court approves a compromise in such case it is not really altering the trusts, which are, *ex hypothesi*, still in doubt and un-ascertained. The House of Lords, however, in *Chapman* v. *Chapman*[14] decided that there was no jurisdiction to sanction an alteration or re-arrangement of beneficial interests where there was no compromise of disputed rights, and the Court of Appeal has since decided that there cannot be said to be any disputed rights where there is merely an ambiguity in, for instance, an investment clause and it would be to the common advantage of all the beneficiaries to have a new clause substituted therefor.[15]

b Statutory exceptions

i *Section 53 of the Trustee Act 1925.*[16] The section provides as follows—

> "Where an infant is beneficially entitled to any property the court may, with a view to the application of the capital or income thereof for the maintenance, education, or benefit[17] of the infant, make an order—
>
> (a) appointing a person to convey such property; or

---

[10] (1886), 32 Ch.D. 229, 232; *Havelock* v. *Havelock* (1881), 17 Ch.D. 807.

[11] Instead of presumed intent, Farwell J. in *Re Walker*, [1901] 1 Ch. 879 based the jurisdiction on the construction of the will, and Denning L.J., dissenting in *Re Downshire's Settled Estates*, [1953] 1 All E.R. at p. 134; [1953] Ch. at p. 273, C.A., simply on the benefit to the children.

[12] *Revel* v. *Watkinson* (1748), 1 Ves. Sen. 93.

[13] *Haley* v. *Bannister* (1820), 4 Madd. 275, where maintenance was allowed to a father although the mother had ample means of her own to bring up the children.

[14] [1954] 1 All E.R. 798; [1954] A.C. 429, H.L. See (1954), 17 M.L.R. pp. 427–431 (O. R. Marshall); *Re Barbour's Settlement, National Westminster Bank, Ltd.* v. *Barbour*, [1974] 1 All E.R. 1188.

[15] *Re Powell-Cotton's Re-Settlement*, [1956] 1 All E.R. 60, C.A. Contrast *Re Lord Hylton's Settlement*, [1954] 2 All E.R. 647, C.A.

[16] See (1957), 21 Con. 448 (O. R. Marshall).

[17] These are words of the widest import—*Re Heyworth's Settlement*, [1956] 2 All E.R. 21, at p. 23; [1956] Ch. 364, at p. 370.

(b) in the case of stock, or a thing in action, vesting in any person the right to transfer or call for a transfer of such stock, or to receive the dividends or income thereof, or to sue for and recover such thing in action, upon such terms as the court may think fit."

Under this section it was held in *Re Gower's Settlement*[18] that where there was an infant tenant in tail in remainder of Blackacre with divers remainders over, the court could effectually authorise a mortgage of Blackacre (subject to the interests having priority over the infant's tenancy in tail) framed so as to vest in the mortgagee a security which would be as effective a bar against the infant's issue taking under the entail and the subsequent remaindermen as if the infant were of full age and had executed the conveyance in accordance with the Fines and Recoveries Act 1833.

It was expressly assumed in *Re Gower's Settlement*[19] that the requirement of the section that the mortgage should be made "with a view to the application of the capital or income thereof for the maintenance, education or benefit of the infant" was satisfied. It was held that there was no such "application" in *Re Heyworth's Settlements*[20] where it was proposed to put an end to the trusts created by the settlement by selling the infant's contingent reversionary interest to the life tenant for an outright cash payment. This decision was distinguished in *Re Meux's Will Trusts*[1] where the proceeds of sale were to be settled. It was held that the sale and settlement of the proceeds of sale were to be regarded as a single transaction, which did constitute an "application" for the purposes of the section.[2] And in *Re Bristol's Settled Estates*[3] a person was appointed to execute a disentailing assurance to bar the infant's entail with a view to a settlement to b made with the assistance of the court under the Variation of Trusts Act 1958 [e]

ii *Section 57 (1) of the Trustee Act 1925.* This section, which does not apply to trustees of a settlement for the purposes of the Settled Land Act 1925,[5] provides as follows:

"Where in the management or administration of any property vested in trustees any sale, lease, mortgage, surrender, release, or other disposition, or any purchase investment, acquisition, expenditure, or other transaction, is in the opinion of the court expedient, but the same cannot be effected by reason of the absence of any power for that purpose vested in the trustees by the trust instrument, if any, or by law, the court may by order confer upon the trustees, either generally or in any particular instance, the necessary power for the purpose, on such terms, and subject to such provisions and conditions, if any, as the court may think fit and may direct in what manner any money authorised to be expended, and the costs of any transaction, are to be paid or borne as between capital and income."

Although it was conceded by counsel before the House of Lords in *Chapman* v. *Chapman*[6] that this section could not apply, Lord Morton stated his agreement with the comments on the section contained in the majority judgment in

---

[13] [1934] Ch. 365; [1934] All E.R. Rep 796; *Re Lansdowne's Will Trusts*, [1967] 1 All E.R. 888; [1967] Ch. 603.
[19] *Supra.*
[20] [1956] 2 All E.R. 21; [1956] Ch. 364.
[1] [1957] 2 All E.R. 630; [1958] Ch. 154; *Re Lansdowne's Will Trusts, supra.*
[2] Cf. *Re Ropner's Settlements Trusts*, [1956] 3 All E.R. 332.—a decision on similar words in s. 32 of the Trustee Act 1925.
[3] [1964] 3 All E.R. 939.   [4] Discussed, *post*, p. 301.
[5] Trustee Act, 1925 s. 57 (4).
[6] [1954] 1 All E.R. 798; [1954] A.C. 429, H.L.

the Court of Appeal,[7] which is authority for the following propositions. It was presumably the intention of Parliament, in enacting this section, to confer new powers on the court rather than to codify or define the existing powers under the inherent jurisdiction, though it may well be that the new extended jurisdiction does in some degree overlap the old. The section envisages

    a   an act unauthorised by a trust instrument,[8]

    b   to be effected by the trustees thereof

    c   in the management or administration of the trust property,

    d   which the court will empower them to perform,

    e   if in its opinion the act is expedient, i.e. expedient for the trust as a whole.[9]

Of primary importance is the interpretation of the words "management" and "administration", which are largely, though very possibly not entirely, synonymous. The subject-matter of both words in section 57 is trust property which is vested in trustees, and "trust property" cannot by any legitimate stretch of the language include the equitable interests which a settlor has created in that property. The application of both words is confined to the managerial supervision and control of trust property on behalf of beneficiaries, and the section accordingly does not permit the remoulding of the beneficial interests. The object of section 57, it was said,[10] is

> "to secure that trust property should be managed as advantageously as possible in the interests of the beneficiaries, and, with that object in view, to authorise specific dealings with the property which the court might have felt itself unable to sanction under the inherent jurisdiction, either because no actual 'emergency' had arisen or because of inability to show that the position which called for intervention was one which the creator of the trust could not reasonably have foreseen, but it was no part of the legislative aim to disturb the rule that the court will not re-write a trust or to add to such exceptions to that rule as had already found their way into the inherent jurisdiction".

Later in the judgment the majority adopted the statement of Farwell J. in *Re Mair*,[11] that "if and when the court sanctions an arrangement or transaction under section 57, it must be taken to have done it as though the power which is being put into operation had been inserted in the trust instrument as an overriding power". Perhaps Farwell J. put it even more clearly later in his judgment where he said[12] "the effect of the court permitting the exercise by trustees of some power which is not in the trust document itself, and, therefore, something which the trustees could not do except by the direction of the court, is the same as though that power had been inserted as an overriding power in the trust document".

Applications under section 57 are almost invariably heard and disposed of in chambers and accordingly not reported. There are, however, a few reported cases which show that in the exercise of its jurisdiction under this section the

---

[7] [1953] 1 All E.R. 103; [1953] Ch. 218, C.A.
[8] *Re Pratt*, [1943] 2 All E.R. 375; [1943] Ch. 326.
[9] *Re Craven's Estate*, [1937] 3 All E.R. 33; [1937] Ch. 423.
[10] *Per* Evershed M.R. and Romer L.J. in *Re Downshire's Settled Estates*, [1953] 1 All E.R. 103, 119 and see also pp. 129 and 132; [1953] Ch. 218, 248, 264 and 265. And see *Municipal and General Securities Co. Ltd.* v. *Lloyds Bank, Ltd.*, [1949] 2 All E.R. 937; [1950] Ch. 212.
[11] [1935] Ch. 562, at p. 565; [1935] All E.R. Rep. 736, at pp. 737-8.
[12] *Supra* at 566, 738.

court has authorised the sale of settled chattels,[13] a partition of land[14] and a sale of land where the necessary consent could not be obtained.[15] It has authorised two residuary estates left on identical charitable trusts to be blended into one fund.[16] It has, apparently commonly, authorised capital money to be expended on paying off the tenant for life's debts, on having its replacement secured by a policy of insurance so that the beneficial interests remain unaltered,[17] but although it has in exceptional circumstances sanctioned a similar expenditure of capital to purchase the life tenant's interest,[18] it is doubtful whether it would do so in an ordinary case, as it would come "at least very near to altering the beneficial interests of the tenant for life".[19] The court has also authorised the sale of a reversionary interest which under the trust instrument was not to be sold until it should fall into possession.[20]

iii *Section 64 of the Settled Land Act 1925*. This section, which applies also to land held upon trust for sale,[1] provides as follows—

> "(1) Any transaction[2] affecting or concerning the settled land, or any part thereof, or any other land (not being a transaction otherwise authorised by this Act, or by the settlement) which in the opinion of the court would be for the benefit of the settled land, or any part thereof, or the persons interested under the settlement, may, under an order of the court, be effected by a tenant for life, if it is one which could have been validly effected by an absolute owner."

According to the majority judgment of the Court of Appeal in *Re Downshire's Settled Estates*[3] the jurisdiction under this section is more ample in regarp to the subject-matter to which it relates than is section 57 of the Trustee Act 1925. The jurisdiction here is not limited to managerial and administrative acts, but may be exercised provided that the court is satisfied that the transaction proposed is for the benefit of either the settled land or some part thereof, or of the persons interested under the settlement—but not necessarily of both; also that the transaction should affect or concern the settled land or any other land.[4]

---

[13] *Re Hope's Will Trust*, [1929] 2 Ch. 136.
[14] *Re Thomas*, [1930] 1 Ch. 194; [1929] All E.R. Rep. 129.
[15] *Re Beale's Settlement Trusts*, [1932] 2 Ch. 15; [1931] All E.R. Rep. 637.
[16] *Re Harvey*, [1941] 3 All E.R. 284. The contrary decision in *Re Royal Society's Charitable Trusts*, [1955] 3 All E.R. 14; [1956] Ch. 87, where *Re Harvey* does not appear to have been cited, would seem to be wrong in the light of *Re Shipwrecked Fishermen and Mariners' Royal Benevolent Society Charity*, [1958] 3 All E.R. 465; [1959] Ch. 220.
[17] *Re Salting*, [1932] 2 Ch. 57; [1932] All E.R. Rep. 857; *Re Mair*, [1935] Ch. 562; [1935] All E.R. Rep. 736. These cases must be read in the light of the observations of the majority of the Court of Appeal in *Re Downshire's Settled Estates*, [1953] 1 All E.R. 103, at pp. 119–121; [1953] Ch. 218, at pp. 249–251 and see *Re Forster's Settlement*, [1954] 3 All E.R. 714.
[18] *Re Forster's Settlement, supra*.
[19] *Re Forster's Settlement, supra*, per Harman J. at p. 720.
[20] *Re Cockerell's Settlement Trusts*, [1956] 2 All E.R. 172; [1956] Ch. 372.
[1] Law of Property Act, 1925, s. 28 (1); *Re Simmons' Trusts*, [1955] 3 All E.R. 818; [1956] Ch. 125.
[2] Defined by sub-s. 2, as amended by the Settled Land and Trustee Acts (Courts General Powers) Act 1943 and the Statute Law (Repeals) Act 1969, to include "any sale, exchange, assurance, grant, lease, surrender, reconveyance, release, reservation, or other disposition, and any purchase or other acquisition, and any covenant, contract, or option, and any application of capital money, and any compromise or other dealing, or arrangement".
[3] [1953] 1 All E.R. 103; [1953] Ch. 218, C.A.
[4] Whether settled or not and whether within or without England.

The last qualification is satisfied by transactions indirectly, as well as directly, operating upon the settled land (or other land), provided that in the former case the effect is real and substantial by ordinary common-sense standards, as distinct from that which is oblique or remote and merely incidental.

iv *The Settled Land and Trustee Acts (Court's General Powers) Act 1943.* This Act, as amended by the Emergency Laws (Miscellaneous Provisions) Act 1953,[5] permanently extends[6] the jurisdiction of the court under section 57 of the Trustee Act 1925 and section 64 of the Settled Land Act 1925, giving it power, in certain circumstances, taking all relevant matters into account,[7] to authorise any expense of action taken or proposed in or for the management of settled land, or of land held on trust for sale, to be treated as a capital outgoing, notwithstanding that in other circumstances that expense could not properly have been so treated.

The circumstances referred to are that the court is satisfied that the action taken or proposed was or would be for the benefit of the persons entitled under the settlement, or under the trust for sale; and either

(a) that the available income from all sources of a person who, as being beneficially entitled to possession or receipt of rents and profits of the land or to reside in a house comprised therein, might otherwise have been expected to bear the expense has been so reduced as to render him unable to bear that expense, or unable to bear it without undue hardship; or

(b) where there is no such person, that the income available for meeting that expense has become insufficient.

v *The Variation of Trusts Act 1958.*[8] This Act was passed as a result of the recommendations of the Law Reform Committee following the House of Lords decision in *Chapman* v. *Chapman.*[9] It gives the court a discretionary power[10] to approve on behalf of any of four classes of persons, any arrangement varying or revoking all[11] or any of the trusts upon which property is held, or enlarging the powers of the trustees of managing or administering any of the property subject to the trusts.

The word "arrangement" used in the Act has been said[12] to be "deliberately used in the widest possible sense so as to cover any proposal which any person may put forward for varying or revoking the trusts", and there is some authority as to the extent of the jurisdiction of the court in these matters. In looking at the cases it seems that the maxim "equity looks to the intent rather than the form" has, in effect, been applied. On the one hand, Wilberforce J. has pointed out[13] that if the arrangement, though presented as a "variation", is in truth a complete new re-settlement, the court has no jurisdiction to approve it. If an arrangement changes the whole substratum of the trust, then it may well be that it

---

[5] Section 9.
[6] *Re Scarisbrick Resettlement Estates*, [1944] 1 All E.R. 404; [1944] Ch. 229.
[7] Section 1 (3) of the Settled Land and Trustee Acts (Court's General Powers) Act 1943.
[8] Discussed generally in (1963), 27 Con. 6 (D. M. E. Evans); (1969), 33 Con. 113 and 183 (J. W. Harris).
[9] [1954] 1 All E.R. 798; [1954] A.C. 429, H.L.
[10] *Re Oakes' Settlement Trusts*, [1959] 2 All E.R. 58; *Re Van Gruisen's Will Trusts*, [1964] 1 All E.R. 843 n.
[11] *Re Seale's Marriage Settlement*, [1961] 3 All E.R. 136; [1961] Ch. 574.
[12] *Re Steed's Will Trusts*, [1960] 1 All E.R. 487, at p. 492; [1960] Ch. 407, at p. 419, C.A. *per* Evershed M.R.
[13] In *Re Towler's Settlement Trusts*, [1963] 3 All E.R. 759; [1964] Ch. 158, at pp. 762; 162.

cannot be regarded as a variation. On the other hand, Megarry J. has said[14] that "if an arrangement, while leaving the substratum, effectuates the purpose of the original trust by other means, it may still be possible to regard that arrangement as merely varying the original trusts, even though the means employed are wholly different, and even though the form is completely changed".

The four classes of persons referred to in the Act are therein defined[15] as follows:

"(a) any person having, directly or indirectly, an interest, whether vested or contingent, under the trusts who by reason of infancy or other incapacity is incapable of assenting, or

(b) any person (whether ascertained or not) who may become entitled, directly or indirectly, to an interest under the trusts as being at a future date or on the happening of a future event a person of any specified description or a member of any specified class of persons, so however that this paragraph shall not include any person who would be of that description, or a member of that class, as the case may be, if the said date had fallen or the said event had happened at the date of the application to the court, or

(c) any person unborn, or

(d) any person[16] in respect of any discretionary interest of his under protective[17] trusts where the interest of the principal beneficiary[17] has not failed or determined."

Except as regards the last class under paragraph (d), the court must not approve an arrangement on behalf of any person unless the carrying out thereof would be for the benefit of "that person".[18] One aspect of this is that a proposed arrangement may well involve some sort of risk to the beneficiary upon whose behalf the court is asked to give its approval, but this will not prevent the court giving its sanction if it is a risk that an adult would be prepared to take.[19] Another aspect, emphasizing the words "that person", appeared in *Re Cohen's Settlement Trusts*,[20] where the court was concerned with a class of persons unborn. It was held that the court was not concerned with the interests of the class as a whole, but with the individual members of it. Accordingly it followed that the court could not approve a variation where, among persons yet unborn who might become entitled to beneficial interests under the settlement in its original form, there might be a person or persons who by the effect of the proposed variation would be deprived of the beneficial interest he or they might otherwise have taken

---

[14] In *Re Ball's Settlement*, [1968] 2 All E.R. 438; [1968] 1 W.L.R. 899 at pp. 442, 905.

[15] Variation of Trusts Act 1958, s. 1 (1).

[16] Including an unascertained or unborn person—*Re Turner's Will Trusts*, [1959] 2 All E.R. 689; [1960] Ch. 122.

[17] Defined by s. 1 (2) by reference to s. 33 of the Trustee Act 1925. See *Re Wallace's Settlements*, [1968] 2 All E.R. 209.

[18] Proviso to s. 1 (1) of the Variation of Trusts Act 1958; *Re Clitheroe's Settlement Trusts*, [1959] 3 All E.R. 789. It was held that the peculiar discretionary trust in *Re Bristol's Settled Estates*, [1964] 3 All E.R. 939, did not fall within para. (d), and a benefit had accordingly to be found. In that case a discretionary trust arose for six months after the death of the principal beneficiary, even if he had never suffered any forfeiture of his life interest.

[19] *Re Cohen's Will Trusts*, [1959] 3 All E.R. 523. Note that in some cases the court may require the risk to be covered by insurance. See *Re Brook's Settlement*, [1968] 3 All E.R. 416 for a discussion of the risk that may be involved in the possibility of the judge taking what turns out later to have been a wrong view of the law.

[20] [1965] 3 All E.R. 139.

without obtaining any counter-balancing advantage. But it is no bar to the court giving approval that in some circumstances an unborn person would obtain no benefit, where probably in fact the arrangement would be to his advantage. This is simply the risk that, as mentioned above, the court is entitled to take, if it thinks fit, on behalf of the unborn person.[1] It may be added that the fact that as between the adult beneficiaries the arrangement does not represent a fair bargain does not prevent the court from approving the arrangement in a proper case.[2]

According to *obiter dicta* of Megarry J. in *Re Holt's Settlement*,[3] the benefit referred to is "plainly not confined to financial benefit, but may extend to moral or social benefit". It was, he said, "speaking in general terms, . . . most important that young children 'should be reasonably advanced in a career and settled in life before they are in receipt of an income sufficient to make them independent of the need to work'". Thus it might, under the Act, be a "benefit" to an infant to suffer the financial detriment of a postponement in the date of the absolute vesting of his interest. On the facts in *Re Holt's Settlement*[4] it was held that the financial advantages of the proposed arrangement were overwhelming, and accordingly there was no need for any "balance sheet" of advantages and disadvantages. The principle that an element of financial benefit is unnecessary actually formed part of the *ratio decidendi* in *Re C.L.*[5] where the court approved an arrangement on behalf of an elderly, wealthy widow who was a patient under the Mental Health Act, 1959. Under the arrangement she gave up life interests in trust funds for no consideration at all, for the benefit of adopted daughters. The object was to save estate duty and the actual cost to the patient would be trifling, taking account of income tax and sur-tax, the patient's spending income being substantially in excess of her requirements.

Neither of these cases appears to have been cited in *Re Weston's Settlements*[6] where Lord Denning M.R. expressed a similar view:[7] "The court should not consider merely the financial benefit to the infants or unborn children, but also their educational and social benefit. There are many things in life more worthwhile than money." In this case the proposed scheme involved the appointment by the court[8] of new trustees resident outside the jurisdiction and variation of the trusts to enable the trust property to be discharged from the trusts of the existing English settlement and made subject to similar trusts under a Jersey settlement. The object was admittedly tax avoidance. Applying the principle mentioned above Lord Denning said: "One of these things [more worthwhile than money] is to be brought up in this our England, which if still 'the envy of less happier lands'. I do not believe it is for the benefit os

---

[1] *Re Holt's Settlement*, [1968] 1 All E.R. 470; [1969] 1 Ch. 100.

[2] *Re Berry's Settlement*, [1966] 3 All E.R. 431 n.

[3] [1968] 1 All E.R. 470; [1969] 1 Ch. 100.

[4] *Supra.*

[5] [1968] 1 All E.R. 1104; [1969] 1 Ch. 587 (Ct. of Protection). Cf. the meaning of "benefit" in connection with advancement, discussed *infra* p. 349.

[6] [1968] 3 All E.R. 338; [1969] 1 Ch. 223, C.A. See also *Re Remnant's Settlement Trusts*, [1970] 2 All E.R. 554; [1970] Ch. 560 (forfeiture clause on practising Roman Catholicism a deterrent in the selection of a husband and a source of possible family dissension: deletion accordingly a benefit).

[7] At p. 342; 245.

[8] Under s. 41 of the Trustee Act 1925, discussed *supra*, pp. 235 *et seq.*

children to be uprooted from England and transported to another country simply to avoid tax. . . . The Court of Chancery should not encourage or support [the avoidance of tax]—it should not give its approval to it—if by so doing it would imperil the true welfare of the children, already born or yet to be born.". Accordingly he dismissed the appeal from the judge's refusal to approve the scheme.[9] The decision was criticised in *The Times*[10] on the grounds that these were matters of judgment for parents, and that the court was trespassing on the preserves of family life. Professor Crane,[11] however, is not wholly convinced by this criticism and thinks that the mathematics should carry less weight when the application involves removing the trust from the jurisdiction of the court. Harman L.J. in *Re Weston's Settlements*[12] preferred to dismiss the appeal on the ground that the linchpin[13] of the scheme was the exercise by the court of its power to appoint new trustees, and that the judge was entitled in the exercise of his discretion to refuse to exercise it so as to remove the trusts to Jersey. The settlements, he said, were English settlements and should remain so unless some good reason connected with the trusts themselves could be put forward.[14]

The jurisdiction given to the court by the Act is not confined to settlements governed by English law.[15] As to the principles which are to be applied, it has been said[16] that, in exercising the "very wide, and, indeed, revolutionary discretion" conferred upon it by the Act, "the court must regard the proposal as a whole, and, so regarding it, then ask itself whether in the exercise of its jurisdiction it should approve that proposal on behalf of the person who cannot give a consent, because he is not in a position to do so". "It is the arrangement which has to be approved, not just the limited interest of the person on whose behalf the court's duty is to consider it."[16] The court must be satisfied that the arrangement is a fair and proper one in the light of the purpose of the trust as appears from the trust instrument and any other relevant evidence available. Accordingly the Court of Appeal in *Re Steed's Will Trusts*[17] refused to approve a scheme which "cut at the root of the testator's wishes and intentions". This case was not, apparently, cited to Pennycuick J. in *Re Remnant's Settlement Trusts*,[18] where an arrangement was approved which clearly defeated the

---

[9] *Re Seale's Marriage Settlement*, [1961] 3 All E.R. 136; [1961] Ch. 574 was distinguished. There the whole family had emigrated to Canada and become Canadian citizens. The children were being educated there. Irrespective of tax advantages there were manifest administrative advantages in having the trusts administered locally. This decision has been followed since *Re Weston's Settlement* in *Re Windeatt's Will Trusts*, [1969] 2 All E.R. 324.

[10] 1 August, 1968.

[11] (1968), 32 Con. 431. See also (1969) 85 L.Q.R. 15 (P. V. Baker).

[12] *Supra.*

[13] Though commonly new trustees outside the jurisdiction could be appointed otherwise than by the court under an express, or the statutory, power.

[14] The third judge in the Court of Appeal, Danckwerts L.J., agreed with both Lord Denning M.R. and Harman L.J.

[15] *Re Ker's Settlement Trusts*, [1963] 1 All E.R. 801; [1963] Ch. 553; *Re Paget's Settlement*, [1965] 1 All E.R. 58.

[16] *Re Steed's Will Trusts*, [1960] 1 All E.R. 487, at p. 493; [1960] Ch. 407, at p. 421, C.A.; and see *Re Lister's Will Trusts*, [1962] 3 All E.R. 737; *Re Munro's Settlement Trusts*, [1963] 1 All E.R. 209; *Re Michelham's Will Trusts*, [1963] 2 All E.R. 188.

[17] *Supra.*

[18] [1970] 2 All E.R. 554; [1970] Ch. 560 (facts in n. 6 on p. 303).

testator's intentions, the judge saying this was "a serious but by no means conclusive consideration".

It does not matter that the object of the proposed variation is to improve the position of the beneficiaries from the point of view of taxation or death duties, and this is in fact the most frequent motive behind applications under the Act.[19] The court will not, however, sanction an arrangement involving approval of an appointment which was a fraud on a power.[20] Where evidence of fraud is not clear Megarry J. has explained[21] what the attitude of the court should be: "If to a fair, cautious and enquiring mind the circumstances of the appointment, so far as known, raise a real and not a merely tenuous suspicion of a fraud on the power, the approval of the court ought to be withheld until that suspicion is dispelled". He added that although the court should act as an alert and persistent watch dog, it ought not to be required to discharge the functions of a bloodhound or a ferret. The Act almost certainly does not empower the court to direct a settlement of an infant's property, though in special circumstances it may defer an infant's right to capital.[22] Nor is an application under the Act appropriate to cover the contingency of the birth of a child to a woman believed in fact to be past the age of child-bearing. Funds may properly be administered on the footing that at a certain age, normally in the middle or late fifties, a woman has become incapable of childbearing. In a clear case no application to the court is necessary, but if an application is made to the court it will be to the ordinary administrative jurisdiction.[1] There is no reason why, in an appropriate case, such an application to the administrative jurisdiction should not be combined with an application for an order under the Act in relation to other persons.[2]

The exact effect of an order under the Act has given rise to some difficulty. So far as it goes the statement of Lord Reid in the House of Lords in Re Holmden's Settlement Trusts[3] seems both clear and conclusive: "Under the Variation of Trusts Act 1958, the court does not itself amend or vary the trusts of the original settlement. The beneficiaries are not bound by variations because the court has made the variation. Each beneficiary is bound because he has consented to the variation. If he was not of full age[4] when the arrangement was made, he is bound because the court was authorised by the Act of 1958 to approve of it on his behalf and did so by making an order. If he was of full age and did not in fact consent he is not affected by the order of the court and he is

---

[19] See Re Holmden's Settlement Trusts, [1966] 2 All E.R. 661; [1966] Ch. 511, C.A. per Denning M.R. at 665; 527; affd. [1968] 1 A.E.R. 148; [1968] A.C. 685, H.L.; Re Sainsbury's Settlement, [1967] 1 All E.R. 878; (1968), 32 Con. 194 (G. R. Bretten). Note, however, that in Re Weston's Settlements, [1968] 1 All E.R. 720 (affd. on different grounds by C.A. [1968] 3 All E.R. 338; [1969] 1 Ch. 223). Stamp J. refused to sanction what he called "a cheap exercise in tax avoidance" as distinct from "a legitimate avoidance of liability to taxation".

[20] Re Robertson's Will Trusts, [1960] 3 All E.R. 146.

[21] Re Wallace's Settlement, [1968] 2 All E.R. 209. See also Re Brook's Settlement, [1968] 3 All E.R. 416; (1969), 32 M.L.R. 317 (S. Cretney).

[22] Re Towler's Settlement Trusts, [1963] 3 All E.R. 759; [1964] Ch. 158.

[1] Re Pettifor's Will Trusts, [1966] 1 All E.R. 913; [1966] Ch. 257.

[2] Re Westminster Bank, Ltd.'s Declaration of Trust, [1963] 2 All E.R. 400n.

[3] [1968] 1 All E.R. 148; [1968] A.C. 685 H.L.

[4] The principle here stated to apply to an infant must apply equally to any other class of person under s. 1 (1).

not bound.[5] So the arrangement must be regarded as an arrangement made by the beneficiaries themselves. The court merely acted on behalf of or as representing those beneficiaries who were not in a position to give their own consent and approval."

Unfortunately in *Re Holmden's Settlement Trust*[6] no mention seems to have been made of the difficulty raised by s. 53 (1) (c) of the Law of Property Act 1925[7] which would seem to require that the beneficiaries, other than those on whose behalf the court was giving its approval, should sign[8] some document in writing. *Prima facie* it would not be enough for counsel to give his assent to the arrangement in court.

The difficulty was, however, carefully considered by Megarry J. in *Re Holt's Settlement*,[9] who thought there was much to be said for the view that "the Act of 1958 does no more than empower the court to supply on behalf of the infants, unborn persons and others mentioned in s. 1 (1) that binding approval which they cannot give, leaving the other beneficiaries to provide their own approval in some other document which will bind them." If this view were right, he went on, though it would be possible to get over the difficulty of s. 53 (1) (c) for the future by obtaining signatures from adult beneficiaries it would mean that in many past cases the order would have affected no variation of the trusts.

The contrary view, that there is no need for the adult beneficiaries to sign any document, depended on the decision in *Re Viscount Hambleden's Will Trusts*[10] where it was held that an order of the court under the Act *ipso facto* varied the terms of the trust without the execution of the arrangement or any other document by or on behalf of any beneficiary, apart from those on whose behalf s. 1 (1) of the Act empowers the court to approve the arrangement. This decision, it was pointed out, must have been acted on in thousands of cases, and in order to accord with the practice and with considerations of convenience, the judge followed it in *Re Holt's Settlement*,[9] admittedly by "straining a little at the wording in the interests of legislative efficacy".[11] Megarry J. accepted with some hesitation two grounds which were put forward by counsel to defeat the argument based on s. 53 (1) (c). First, that by conferring an express power on the court to do something by order, Parliament in the Act of 1958 had provided by necessary implication an exception to s. 53 (1) (c). Secondly that where, as on the facts before him, the arrangement consisted of a specifically enforceable agreement made for valuable consideration, the beneficial interest would have passed to the respective purchasers on the making of the agreement. This would be a case of constructive trust excluded from the operation of s. 53 (1) (c) by sub-section (2).[12] Neither of these grounds seems altogether convincing, but the result is undeniably convenient.

---

[5] Though not apparently cited to the court, there was an earlier decision to this effect in *Re Suffert's Settlement*, [1960] 3 All E.R. 561; [1961] Ch. 1.
[6] [1968] 1 All E.R. 148; [1968] A.C. 685, H.L.
[7] Discussed *supra* pp. 56, 57.
[8] The section permits signature by a lawfully authorised agent.
[9] [1968] 1 All E.R. 470; [1969] 1 Ch. 100.
[10] [1960] 1 All E.R. 353.
[11] *Per* Megarry J. in *Re Holt's Settlement, supra*, at p. 476; 115.
[12] See pp. 57, 820, *supra*.

It is expressly provided[13] that the jurisdiction given by the Act is additional to that given by section 57 of the Trustee Act 1925 and section 64 of the Settled Land Act 1925. Although in most ways the jurisdiction under the 1958 Act is wider, there are differences between these provisions which mean that it may sometimes be necessary to bring proceedings under one of the other Acts. Thus under section 57 of the Trustee Act 1925 the court must be satisfied that the proposed transaction is expedient, but there is no requirement that all or any of the beneficiaries must give their consent for an order to be effective. Under the 1958 Act, as we have seen, approval of an arrangement will only be fully effective if all the beneficiaries who are *sui iuris* give their consent; moreover in giving its approval on behalf of beneficiaries who are unable to give their consent, the court can in general only do so if the proposed arrangement is for their benefit.

2 DUTY NOT TO PROFIT FROM HIS TRUST

In *Bray* v. *Ford*,[14] Lord Herschell said:[15] "It is an inflexible rule of a Court of Equity that a person in a fiduciary position . . . is not, unless otherwise expressly provided, entitled to make a profit; he is not allowed to put himself in a position where his interest and duty conflict." The liability arises from the mere fact of a profit having been made by the fiduciary. "The profiteer, however honest and well-intentioned, cannot escape the risk of being called upon to account."[16] Various aspects of this general principle must be considered.

a Duty to act without remuneration[17]

As early as 1734,[18] it was said to be "an established rule that a trustee . . . shall have no allowance for his care and trouble: the reason of which seems to be, for that on these pretences, if allowed, the trust estate might be loaded, and rendered of little value". The rule is strictly applied, for instance to a trustee who spends much time and trouble in managing a business to the great advantage of the beneficiaries,[19] and a solicitor-trustee is in no different position.[20] A solicitor-trustee cannot evade the rule by employing a firm of which he is a member to transact legal business in connection with the trust,[1] and it makes no difference that there is an agreement that the solicitor-trustee will have no share in the profit costs,[2] or that the solicitor-trustee is merely entitled to a fixed salary.[3] However where a solicitor-trustee could properly employ an outside solicitor,[4] he "may employ his partner to act as solicitor for himself and his co-

---

[13] Variation of Trusts Act 1958, s. 1 (6).

[14] [1896] A.C. 44, H.L.; *Regal (Hastings) Ltd.* v. *Gulliver*, [1942] 1 All E.R. 378, H.L.

[15] At p. 51; *Brown* v. *I.R.Comrs.*, [1964] 3 All E.R. 119, H.L., per Lord Upjohn at p. 127.

[16] Per Lord Russell of Killowen in *Regal (Hastings) Ltd.* v. *Gulliver*, *supra*, at p. 386.

[17] He can, of course, claim out-of-pocket expenses.

[18] *Robinson* v. *Pett* (1734), 3 P. Wms. 249, 251.

[19] *Brocksopp* v. *Barnes* (1820), 5 Madd. 90; *Barrett* v. *Hartley* (1866), L.R. 2 Eq. 789.

[20] *Moore* v. *Frowd* (1837), 3 My. & Cr. 45; *Todd* v. *Wilson* (1846), 9 Beav. 486. But a solicitor-trustee who lends trust money on mortgage is not required to account for profit costs received in acting for the mortgagor—*Whitney* v. *Smith* (1869), 4 Ch. App. 513.

[1] *Re Corsellis* (1887), 34 Ch.D. 675, C.A.; *Re Doody*, [1893] 1 Ch. 129, C.A.

[2] *Re Gates*, [1933] Ch. 913; [1933] All E.R. Rep. 546.

[3] *Re Hill*, [1934] Ch. 623; [1934] All E.R. Rep. 617, C.A.

[4] See now s. 23 of the Trustee Act 1925 and Section 3, p. 320, *post*.

trustees with reference to the trust affairs, and may pay him the usual charges, provided that it has been expressly agreed between himself and his partner that he himself shall not participate in the profits or derive any benefit from the charges. Nothing short of this will be sufficient."[5]

The rule does not, however, mean that there is necessarily anything illegal or improper in a trustee receiving remuneration, but the onus is on the trustee to point to some provision in the trust instrument or some rule of law which establishes his right thereto. As Lord Normand said more recently,[6] the rule "is not that reward for services is repugnant to the fiduciary duty, but that he who has the duty shall not take any secret remuneration or any financial benefit not authorised by the law, or by his contract, or by the trust deed under which he acts, as the case may be". A trustee may establish his right to remuneration upon any of the following grounds.

i   *The provisions of the trust instrument.* There has never been any doubt but that the trust instrument may authorise the payment of remuneration to a trustee,[7] though a provision to this effect always receives a strict interpretation from the courts.[8] Thus if a solicitor-trustee is given the right to charge for his professional services, he can only charge for services strictly professional, and not for business "not strictly professional which might have been performed, or would necessarily have been performed in person by a trustee not being a solicitor".[9] The precise scope of a charging clause is, of course, a question of construction of the particular words used, and the words of a particular clause may, for instance, entitle a solicitor-trustee to charge for services not strictly professional.[10] Even if not needed at first, a charging clause[11] should be inserted, so that a professional trustee can be appointed later, if desired.[12]

ii   *Contract with the cestuis que trust.* Such a contract by a trustee for remuneration may be valid, though it would be viewed with great jealousy by the courts.[13] If, however, the trustee, having accepted the trust, merely contracted to carry out his duties as trustee, it would seem that there might well be no valid contract at all,

---

[5] *Re Doody, supra, per* Stirling J. at p. 134 stating this to be the effect of *Clack* v. *Carlon* (1861), 30 L.J. Ch. 639. For a precedent see Key and Elphinstone's *Precedents in Conveyancing* 15th Ed., Vol. 2, p. 441.

[6] In *Dale* v. *I.R.Comrs.,* [1953] 2 All E.R. 671, at p. 674; [1954] A.C. 11, 27, H.L.

[7] *Webb* v. *Earl of Shaftesbury* (1802), 7 Ves. 480; *Willis* v. *Kibble* (1839), 1 Beav. 559. See, generally (1952), 16 Con. 13 (G. Boughen Graham).

[8] *Re Gee,* [1948] 1 All E.R. 498; [1948] Ch. 284.

[9] *Per* Warrington J. in *Re Chalinder & Herington,* [1907] 1 Ch. 58, at p. 61, and see *Re Chapple* (1884), 27 Ch.D. 584; *Clarkson* v. *Robinson,* [1900] 2 Ch. 722.

[10] *Re Ames* (1883), 25 Ch.D. 72; *Re Fish,* [1893] 2 Ch. 413, C.A. See also *Re Pedley,* [1927] 2 Ch. 168.

[11] For precedents see e.g. Prideaux, *Precedents in Conveyancing,* 25th Ed., Vol. 3, p. 829; Key and Elphinstone's *Precedents in Conveyancing* 15th Ed. Vol. 2, pp. 977–978.

[12] It may be mentioned that where a will appoints a solicitor-trustee, and there is a charging clause, the solicitor-trustee's charges are for most purposes treated as a legacy—*Re Pooley* (1888), 40 Ch.D. 1, C.A.; *Re White,* [1898] 2 Ch. 217, C.A.; *Re Brown,* [1918] W.N. 118. Since it ranks as a legacy, if the assets are insufficient it will abate proportionally with the other legacies unless there is some provision giving it priority, and it will be avoided by s. 15 of the Wills Act 1837 if the trustee is an attesting witness (but see *Re Royce's Will Trusts,* [1959] 3 All E.R. 278; [1959] Ch. 626, C.A. and the Wills Act 1968). However, it is earned income for the purposes of tax—*Dale* v. *I.R. Comrs.,* [1953] 2 All E.R. 671; [1954] A.C. 11, H.L.

[13] *Ayliffe* v. *Murray* (1740), 2 Atk. 58.

on the ground of absence of consideration, unless the contract were under seal.[14]

iii *Order of the court.* The court, under the inherent jurisdiction, can authorise the payment of remuneration, either prospectively or retrospectively,[15] to a trustee, whether appointed by the court or not.[16] It is clear, however, that the "jurisdiction should be exercised only sparingly and in exceptional cases",[17] and there are few reported cases where it has been done.

iv *The rule in Cradock* v. *Piper.*[18] This rule, though well established, is also "exceptional and anomalous and not to be extended".[19] It permits a solicitor-trustee or his firm to receive the usual profit costs, for work done in a suit not on behalf of the solicitor-trustee alone, but on behalf of himself and a co-trustee, provided that the costs of appearing for and acting for the two have not added to the expense which would have been incurred if he or his firm had appeared only for his co-trustee. The rule is limited to the costs incurred in respect of business done in an action, or other legal proceedings.[20]

v *Statutory provisions.* By section 42 of the Trustee Act 1925 it is provided that—

> "where the court appoints a corporation, other than the Public Trustee, to be a trustee[1] either solely or jointly with another person, the court may authorise the corporation to charge such remuneration for its services as trustee as the court may think fit."

The Judicial Trustees Act 1896 provides[2] that the court may assign remuneration to a person whom it appoints as a judicial trustee.

The Public Trustee is authorised[3] to charge fees fixed by the Treasury with the sanction of the Lord Chancellor, irrespective of any provision in the trust instrument, and fees not exceeding those chargeable by the Public Trustee may likewise be charged by any body properly appointed to be a custodian trustee.[4] It is not, however, possible to take advantage of this latter provision by appointing a bank, for instance, separately as custodian trustee and managing trustee.[5]

---

[14] Cf. Cheshire and Fifoot, *The Law of Contract*, 8th Ed., pp. 77 *et seq.*; (1956), 72 L.Q.R. 490 (A. L. Goodhart).

[15] The dictum in *Brocksopp* v. *Barnes* (1820), 5 Madd. 90, to the effect that the trustee must apply to the court before accepting the trust has not been applied in later cases, e.g. *Re Macadam*, [1945] 2 All E.R. 664; [1946] Ch. 73; *Re Masters*, [1953] 1 All E.R. 19; *Boardman* v. *Phipps* [1966] 3 All E.R. 721; [1967] 2 A.C. 46, H.L.

[16] *Re Freemen's Settlement Trusts* (1887), 37 Ch.D. 148; *Re Masters, supra*; *Re Worthington*, [1954] 1 All E.R. 677.

[17] Per Upjohn J. in *Re Worthington*, [1954] 1 All E.R. 677, where the court could not find sufficient exceptional circumstances; *Re Barbour's Settlement, National Westminster Bank, Ltd.* v. *Barbour*, [1974] 1 All E.R. 1188.

[18] (1850), 1 Mac. & G. 664; *Broughton* v. *Broughton* (1855), 5 De G.M. & G. 160.

[19] Per Upjohn J. in *Re Worthington, supra*, at 679; *Re Corsellis* (1887), 34 Ch.D. 675, C.A.; *Re Doody, supra*, C.A.

[20] *Re Barber* (1886), 34 Ch.D. 77; *Re Corsellis, supra*, C.A.

[1] By s. 68 (17) "trustee" is defined so as to include a personal representative—*In the Estate of Young* (1934), 151 L.T. 221; *Re Masters*, [1953] 1 All E.R. 19.

[2] Section 1 (5).

[3] Public Trustee Act 1906, s. 9, as amended by the Administration of Justice Act 1965, s. 2; Public Trustee (Fees) Act 1957 and orders made thereunder.

[4] *Ibid.*, s. 4 (3).

[5] *Forster* v. *Williams Deacon's Bank Ltd.*, [1935] Ch. 359; [1935] All E.R. Rep. 374, C.A.; *Arning* v. *James*, [1936] Ch. 158.

The Hutton Committee of Enquiry into the Public Trustee Office[6] proposed new legislation in relation to the Public Trustee and recommended that it should include a provision enabling all professional or corporate trustees to charge for their services whether or not the trust instrument or will includes a charging clause. As yet no action has been taken to carry these recommendations into effect.

vi   *Custom.* The existence of any valid custom is very doubtful. In *Brown* v. *I.R. Comrs.*[7] a Scottish solicitor had received money from a number of his clients, too small in individual amounts or held for too short a time to make individual investment worth while in the interest of the client, but which, in the aggregate, amounted to a large floating sum. This money was put on deposit so as to earn interest for the solicitor which he claimed to be entitled to retain. There was no question of professional malpractice, for the practice had been recognised as proper by the Council of the Law Society of Scotland, whose opinion, however, was held to be ill-founded. The solicitor had based his claim on the grounds of implied agreement and custom. Both grounds proved to be inadequately supported by evidence, and dicta of their Lordships[8] leave it very doubtful whether such a custom would be recognised by the law of either Scotland or England.

vii   *Foreign remuneration.* It appears from *Re Northcote's Will Trusts*[9] that if in the course of administering assets abroad, trustees receive remuneration without their volition, they will not be called to account. In that case executors took out an English grant, and on doing so were required by the Inland Revenue to undertake to obtain a grant in New York State in respect of American assets. They duly obtained such a grant, and got in the American assets, for doing which the law of that State allowed them agency commission. It was held that in those circumstances there was no equity against the trustees requiring them to disgorge what they had put in their pockets from an outside source.

b   Obligation to account as a constructive trustee for profits received by virtue of his position as trustee

Various cases may be mentioned to illustrate the wide principle, continually re-stated, that "whenever a trustee, being the ostensible owner of property, acquires any benefit as the owner of that property, that benefit cannot be retained by himself, but must be surrendered for the advantage of those who are beneficially interested".[10] The principle applies equally to a custodian trustee,[11] and to other persons in a fiduciary position including agents,[12] solicitors,[13]

---

[6] Cmnd. 4913.

[7] [1964] 3 All E.R. 119, H.L.

[8] *Brown* v. *I.R. Comrs.*, *supra*, *per* Lord Evershed at 125, Lord Guest at 126 and Lord Upjohn at 128. As to solicitors, the law has been altered by the Solicitors Act 1965, s. 8

[9] [1949] 1 All E.R. 442.

[10] *Per* Lord Cairns L.C. in *Aberdeen Town Council* v. *Aberdeen University* (1877), 2 App. Cas. 544, 549, H.L.

[11] *Re Brooke Bond & Co., Ltd.'s Trust Deed*, [1963] 1 All E.R. 454; [1963] Ch. 357, where, however, the court authorised the custodian trustee to retain the profits.

[12] See e.g. *Parker* v. *McKenna* (1874), 10 Ch. App. 96 *per* Lord Cairns at p. 118.

[13] *Brown* v. *I.R.Comrs.*, [1964] 3 All E.R. 119, H.L.

company directors,[14] company promoters[15] and partners[1] though its application and precise scope must be moulded according to the nature of the relationship.[2] In *Reading* v. *A.-G.*[3] there was held to be a fiduciary relationship between the Crown and an army sergeant stationed in Cairo who, on several occasions, while in uniform, boarded a private lorry and escorted it through Cairo, thus enabling it to pass the civilian police without being inspected. The Crown was held to be entitled to the money he received for the misuse of his uniform and position. In the Court of Appeal in that case it was said[4] that in this context "a fiduciary relation exists (a) whenever the plaintiff entrusts to the defendant property tangible or intangible (as, for instance, confidential information) and relies on the defendant to deal with such property for the benefit of the plaintiff or for purposes authorised by him and not otherwise; and (b) whenever the plaintiff entrusts to the defendant a job to be performed, for instance, the negotiation of a contract on his behalf or for his benefit, and relies on the defendant to procure for the plaintiff the best terms available."

The cases can be loosely grouped as follows—

i *Fees paid to trustee directors.* On one side of the line are *Re Francis*,[5] where trustees were required to account for remuneration which they voted to themselves as directors by virtue of their holding of the trust shares; and *Re Macadam*[6] where trustees had power as such, and by virtue of the articles of the company, to appoint two directors of it. By the exercise of this power they appointed themselves, and were held liable to account for the remuneration they received for their services as directors,[7] because they had acquired it by the direct use of their trust powers. Cohen J. observed[8] ". . . the root of the matter . . . is: Did the trustee acquire the position in respect of which he drew the remuneration by virtue of his position as trustee?"

On the other side of the line is *Re Dover Coalfield Extension Ltd.*,[9] where it was held that the directors were not liable to account for their remuneration. They had become directors before they held any trust shares, and although the trust shares were subsequently registered in their names in order to qualify them to continue as directors, it was not by virtue of the use of those shares that they either became entitled or continued to earn their fees. Again in *Re Lewis*,[10] the point was that the trustee did not receive the remuneration by virtue of the use of his position as a trustee, but by an independent bargain with the firm

---

[14] *Regal (Hastings), Ltd.* v. *Gulliver*, [1942] 1 All E.R. 378, H.L.; *Selangor United Rubber Estates, Ltd.* v. *Cradock (No. 3)*, [1968] 2 All E.R. 1073.

[15] *Jubilee Cotton Mills, Ltd.* v. *Lewis*, [1924] A.C. 958, H.L.

[1] *Aas* v. *Benham*, [1891] 2 Ch. 244, C.A.; *Thompson's Trustee* v. *Heaton*, [1974] 1 All E.R. 1239.

[2] *New Zealand Netherlands Society Oranje Inc.* v. *Kuys*, [1973] 2 All E.R. 1222 P.C. (officer of an unincorporated non-profit making society).

[3] [1951] 1 All E.R. 617; [1951] A.C. 507, H.L. See (1968), 84 L.Q.R. 472 (Gareth Jones).

[4] [1949] 2 All E.R. 68, at p. 70; [1949] 2 K.B. 232, at p. 236. See Goff & Jones, The Law of Restitution, p. 458.

[5] (1905), 92 L.T 77.

[6] [1945] 2 All E.R. 664; [1946] Ch. 73.

[7] The court however allowed remuneration under the inherent jurisdiction—see *Re Masters*, [1953] 1 All E.R. 19.

[8] [1945] 2 All E.R. at 672; [1946] Ch. at 82.

[9] [1908] 1 Ch 65, C.A.

[10] (1910), 103 L.T. 495; [1908–10] All E.R. Rep. 281.

employing him. And from *Re Gee*,[11] where the earlier cases were reviewed, it appears that if the use of, or failure to use, the trust votes could not prevent the appointment of the trustee to a remunerative position in the company, he will not be called upon to account; further, there is no reason why a trustee should not use the votes attached to his own shares, as opposed to those attached to the trust shares, in favour of his own appointment. It may be added that there is, of course, no reason why, as in *Re Llewellin's Will Trusts*,[12] a testator holding a majority of shares should not effectively empower his trustees to appoint themselves as directors and arrange for their remuneration without being liable to account therefor.

ii *Other cases in which trustees accountable for payments received.* In *Williams* v. *Barton*,[13] the defendant, one of two trustees of a will, was clerk to stockbrokers on the terms that he should get a half commission on business introduced by him. He persuaded his co-trustee to employ his firm, and was held accountable for the half commission received by him. On principle any payment made to a trustee to induce him to act in any particular way in connection with the trust business must be held by him as a part of the trust funds. Thus in *Sugden* v. *Crossland*,[14] a payment of £75 made to a trustee in consideration of his retiring from the trust and appointing the person making the payment as a new trustee and in *Re Smith*,[15] a payment of £300 commission on investing the trust funds in the debentures of a particular company, were 'directed to be held as a part of the trust funds. A very curious case was *Re Payne's Settlement*,[16] where an eccentric mortgagor devised the equity of redemption to the mortgagee, with whom he had no other relationship. The mortgagee happened to be a trustee, and it was held he took the equity of redemption as a part of the trust estate.

iii *Court acting to prevent trustee profiting.* The same fundamental principle may call for somewhat different action in different circumstances. Thus in *Wright* v. *Morgan*[1] it was held that an option to purchase trust property could not be validly assigned to a trustee as it would involve him in a conflict of duty and interest,[2] and for the same reason the court granted an injunction in *Re Thomson*,[3] to restrain an executor carrying on the testator's business as yacht agent from setting up in competition.

iv *Cases involving other fiduciary relationships.* A leading case is *Boardman* v. *Phipps*,[4] where the facts, somewhat simplified, were that B at all material times

---

[11] [1948] 1 All E.R. 498; [1948] Ch. 284; *Re Northcote's Will Trusts*, [1949] 1 All E.R. 442.
[12] [1949] 1 All E.R. 487; [1949] Ch. 225. Similarly in *Re Sykes*, [1909] 2 Ch. 241, C.A., a trustee was held entitled to retain profits made in supplying goods to the estate in connection with a business by virtue of a clause in the will. And see *Re Waterman's Will Trusts*, [1952] 2 All E.R. 1054.
[13] [1927] 2 Ch. 9.
[14] (1856), 3 Sm. & Giff. 192.
[15] [1896] 1 Ch. 71.
[16] (1886), 54 L.T. 840.
[1] [1926] All E.R. Rep. 201; [1926] A.C. 788, P.C.
[2] Even though the price was to be fixed by valuation there would be a conflict in relation to the time of sale; the trustee, *qua* trustee, would want to sell when prices were high, but *qua* individual would want the sale to take place when they were low.
[3] [1930] 1 Ch. 203. Whether or not an injunction is granted may depend on the nature of the business. Cf. *Moore* v. *M'Glynn*, [1894] 1 Ir. R. 74.
[4] [1966] 3 All E.R. 721; [1967] 2 A.C. 46, H.L. See (1968), 84 L.Q.R. 472 (Gareth Jones).

acted as solicitor to the trustees, and for the co-appellant P, one of the beneficiaries. The trust property included shares in a private company. In 1956
B and F, the active trustee, a chartered accountant, considered that the position
of the company was unsatisfactory and that something must be done to
improve it. Following the 1956 annual general meeting of the company, B
and P decided, with the knowledge of two of the three trustees, including F,
that they should try to obtain control of the company by purchasing shares.
The trustees had no power to invest trust moneys in shares of the company.
B, purporting to act on behalf of the trustees as shareholders, obtained much
information from the company, and after long and difficult negotiations B
and P, in July 1959, purchased more than two-thirds of the shares, virtually
all the remainder being still held by the trustees. A considerable profit subsequently arose from capital distributions on the shares. It was accepted that
B had acted with complete honesty throughout. At the time of the purchase
of the shares, the beneficiaries were absolutely entitled in possession to their
respective shares (following the death of an annuitant in November 1958),
which were in fact distributed in 1960. The action was brought by one of the
beneficiaries, having an interest in five eighteenths of the trust fund, claiming
that B and P were constructive trustees of a corresponding five eighteenths
of the shares purchased, and were liable to account to him for the profit
thereon. The claim succeeded, and was affirmed by the Court of Appeal and
ultimately by the House of Lords (though here only by a bare majority),
on the ground that both the information which satisfied B and P that the
purchase of the shares would be a good investment and the opportunity to bid
for them came to them as a result of B's acting or purporting to act on behalf
of the trustees for certain purposes. In so holding the majority took the view
that the claimant beneficiary was "a fortunate man in that the rigour of equity
enabled him to participate in the profits" and directed that payment should be
allowed on a liberal scale to B and P in respect of their work and skill in
obtaining the shares and the profits in respect thereof[5]. Lord Upjohn, dissenting,
in the House of Lords fully accepted "the fundamental rule of equity that a
person in a fiduciary capacity must not make a profit out of his trust, which is
part of the wider rule that a trustee must not place himself in a position where
his duty and his interest may conflict". There seems, however, something to
be said for his opinion that it was an over-rigid application of the rule to apply
it to the facts of *Boardman* v. *Phipps*,[6] and that the dictum of Lord Selborne L.J.
in *Barnes* v. *Addy*[7] should have been applied: "It is equally important to maintain the doctrine of trusts which is established in this court, and not to strain it by
unreasonable construction beyond its due and proper limits. There would be
no better mode of undermining the sound doctrines of equity than to make
unreasonable and inequitable applications of them."

Another case is *Industrial Development Consultants* v. *Cooley*[8] where the
defendant was managing director of the plaintiff company. The defendant was

---

[5] Account would, of course, also be taken of their expenditure.
[6] *Supra.*
[7] (1874), 9 Ch. App. 244, at p. 251.
[8] [1972] 2 All E.R. 162.

privately offered a contract by a third party, who made it clear that he was not willing to contract with the plaintiffs. The defendant concealed the offer from the plaintiffs and obtained his release from his employment with them. About a week later he entered into a contract with the third party. He was held liable to account to the plaintiffs for all the benefit he had received or would receive under the contract with the third party. He had been in a fiduciary relationship with the plaintiffs, and in breach of his fiduciary duty had failed to disclose information of concern to the plaintiffs, and had indeed embarked on a deliberate course of conduct which had put his personal interest as a potential contracting party in direct conflict with his fiduciary duty as managing director of the plaintiffs. Whether the benefit of the contract would have been obtained for the plaintiffs but for the defendant's breach of fiduciary duty was held to be irrelevant.

c The rule in Keech v. Sandford[9]

This rule can be regarded as a particular application of the wide principle discussed in Section 2b, *supra*. The particular application is concerned primarily with the renewal of leases. Where a trustee who held a lease for the benefit of a *cestui que trust*, has made use of the influence which his situation has enabled him to exercise to get a new lease, he will be compelled in equity to hold the new lease thus acquired as a constructive trustee for the benefit of the *cestui que trust*. The length to which the doctrine has been carried is exemplified by *Keech* v. *Sandford*[10] itself. There despite express proof of the lessor's refusal[11] to renew the lease for the benefit of the *cestui que trust*, the rule was still adhered to that the trustee, who had subsequently had a lease granted to himself, must hold it for the *cestui que trust*. In his judgment Lord Chancellor King observed[12] that it might seem hard "that the trustee is the only person of all mankind who might not have the lease; but it is very proper that rule should be strictly pursued, and not in the least relaxed; for it is very obvious what would be the consequence of letting trustees have the lease on refusal to renew to *cestui que use*".[13] The renewed lease is regarded in equity as an accretion to or graft upon the original term and subject accordingly to the same trusts. The doctrine is not restricted to cases where the old lease was renewable by custom or agreement, or where the new lease was obtained by surrender or before the expiration of the old lease: it applies also where there is no obligation to grant a new lease, and notwithstanding the fact that the old lease has expired.[14]

The principle that a trustee who renews a lease will be treated as a constructive trustee of the renewed lease or, to put it another way, the presumption of

---

[9] (1726), Sel. Cas. Ch. 61. See (1972), 36 Con. 159 (D. R. Paling) where the pleadings are transcribed. Many of the relevant cases are reviewed in *Re Biss*, [1903] 2 Ch. 40, C.A. See also (1969), 33 Con. 161 (S. Cretney).

[10] *Supra*.

[11] Cf. *Blewett* v. *Millett* (1774), 7 Bro. Parl. Cas. 367, where co-trustees refused to concur in a renewal, yet the trustee who renewed was held liable; *Killick* v. *Flexney* (1792), 4 Bro. C.C. 161.

[12] *Keech* v. *Sandford, supra*, at p. 62.

[13] I.e., there would be too great an opportunity for the trustee to defraud the beneficiaries of their interests.

[14] *Pickering* v. *Vowles* (1783), 1 Bro. C.C. 197.

personal incapacity to retain the benefit, has been extended to other cases where there is a fiduciary relationship. Apart from the case of the trustee, there are other persons in connection with whom the presumption cannot be rebutted,[15] namely, personal representatives,[16] agents, tenants for life[17] and presumably in most cases as a result of the Law of Property Act 1925[18] joint tenants and tenants in common. In some other cases, namely, mortgagors,[19] mortgagees,[20] and partners,[1] the presumption of personal incapacity has been said to be "at most a rebuttable presumption of fact".[2] These seem to be the only cases in which any such presumption arises, and the Court of Appeal in Re Biss[3] expressly disapproved of dicta[4] suggesting that if any person, only partly interested in an old lease, obtained from the lessor a renewal, he must be held a constructive trustee of the new lease, whatever might be the nature of his interest or the circumstances under which he obtained the new lease. In Re Biss[5] itself it was held that the principle in Keech v. Sandford[6] did not apply. There a lessor granted a lease for seven years of a house in which the lessee carried on a profitable business. On the expiration of the term the lessor refused to renew, but allowed the lessee to remain as tenant from year to year at an increased rent. During that tenancy the lessee died intestate, leaving a widow and three children, one being an infant. The widow alone took out administration to her husband's estate, and she and the two adult children, one of whom was a son, continued to carry on the business under the existing yearly tenancy. The widow and son each applied to the lessor for a new lease for the benefit of the estate, which he refused to grant but, having determined the yearly tenancy by notice, he granted to the son, who had never become an administrator of his father's estate, "personally" a new lease for three years at a still further increased rent. The widow, as sole administratrix, applied to have the new lease treated as taken by the son for the benefit of the estate. The court, however, in the absence of a fiduciary relationship, held the son entitled to keep the lease for his own benefit.

Another way in which the rule in Keech v. Sandford[7] has been extended is by its application to the acquisition by a trustee[8] of the reversion expectant on a

---

[15] Re Biss, [1903] 2 Ch. 40, C.A.; Re Knowles' Will Trusts, [1948] 1 All E.R. 866, C.A.
[16] Including an executor de son tort—Mulvany v. Dillon (1810), 1 Ball & B. 409.
[17] James v. Dean, (1805), 15 Ves. 236; Lloyd-Jones v. Clark-Lloyd, [1919] 1 Ch. 424, C. A. and now see ss. 16 (1) and 107, Settled Land Act 1925.
[18] Sections 34–36. But not if the legal estate is vested in outside trustees. In such case there is no fiduciary relationship, either in the case of tenants in common—Kennedy v. de Trafford, [1897] A.C. 180, H.L., or of joint tenants—Re Biss, supra.
[19] Leigh v. Burnett (1885), 29 Ch.D. 231.
[20] Nelson v. Hannam and Smith, [1942] 2 All E.R. 680; [1943] Ch. 59, C.A.
[1] Clegg v. Fishwick (1849), 1 Mac. & G. 294; Clegg v. Edmondson (1857), 8 De G.M. & G. 787.
[2] Re Biss, supra, per Collins M.R. at p. 56.
[3] Supra.
[4] Per Lord Bathurst L.C. in Rawe v. Chichester (1773), Amb. 715; and see Palmer v. Young[1] (1684), 1 Vern. 276; [1903] 2 Ch. 65 n.
[5] Supra.
[6] Supra.
[7] Supra.
[8] Or other person in the appropriate fiduciary relationship.

lease.[9] The earlier cases, however, laid down a distinction for which no really satisfactory justification can be put forward.[10] This was that the rule applied to purchases of reversions on leases when the leases were renewable by custom or agreement,[11] on the ground that it deprived the beneficiaries of the chance of a renewal for their benefit, but not where there was no right or custom of renewal.[12] This distinction does not appear to have been mentioned to the Court of Appeal in *Protheroe* v. *Protheroe*,[13] where it was held that the purchased reversion was held on trust although there was presumably no right or custom of renewal. It was a case where the husband held the lease of what had been the matrimonial home as trustee for himself and his wife in equal shares, and after the parties had separated and the wife had filed a petition for divorce, he purchased the freehold reversion. It was held that the freehold reversion must be regarded in equity as acquired on the same trusts as the lease.

It should be observed that where a man is held to be a constructive trustee under the rule in *Keech* v. *Sandford*,[14] he is entitled to a lien on the property for the expenses of renewal,[15] and the costs of permanent improvements,[16] and he is entitled to be indemnified against the covenants in the new lease.[17] Further, although if the lease comprises business premises upon which the trustee carries on a business he will be accountable for the whole of the profits, the form of enquiry will vary according to the circumstances, and allowances may be made to the trustee for his time, energy and skill.[18]

Finally, it may be mentioned that a claim based on the rule in *Keech* v. *Sandford*[19] may fail by reason of some general defence such as laches, which is particularly important if the alleged constructive trust extends to a business being carried on by the trustee on the subject matter of the renewed lease.[20]

d   Purchase by a trustee of the trust property[1]

"Any trustee purchasing[2] the trust property is liable to have the purchase set

---

[9] See also *Owen* v. *Williams* (1773), Amb. 734 where a sum of money paid in consideration of giving up a claim to renewal, was ordered to be held upon the same constructive trusts as the renewed lease would have been; *Giddings* v. *Giddings* (1827), 3 Russ. 241 where the rule was applied to an underlessee who obtained not a renewal of the underlease (which the underlessor in any case had not power to grant) but a new lease from the head lessor; and cf. *Yem* v. *Edwards* (1857), 1 De G. & J. 598.

[10] See (1969), 33 Con. 161 (S. Cretney) for an historical explanation coupled with the opinion that the distinction is now irrelevant.

[11] *Re Lord Ranelagh's Will* (1884), 26 Ch.D. 590; *Phillips* v. *Phillips* (1885), 29 Ch.D. 673, C.A. Cf. *Griffith* v. *Owen*, [1907] 1 Ch. 195.

[12] *Longton* v. *Wilsby* (1897), 76 L.T. 770; *Bevan* v. *Webb*, [1905] 1 Ch. 620. And see *per* Wilberforce J. at first instance in *Phipps* v. *Boardman*, [1964] 2 All E.R. 187, at p. 202.

[13] [1968] 1 All E.R. 1111, C.A. See (1968), 32 Con. 220 (F. R. Crane) and (1968), 31 M.L.R. 707 (P. Jackson). See also *Thompson's Trustee* v. *Heaton*, [1974] 1 All E.R. 1239.

[14] *Supra.*

[15] *Bradford* v. *Brownjohn* (1868), 3 Ch. App. 711; *Isaac* v. *Wall* (1877), 6 Ch.D. 706; *Re Lord Ranelagh's Will* (1884), 26 Ch.D. 590.

[16] *Mill* v. *Hill* (1852), 3 H.L. Cas. 828; *Rowley* v. *Ginnever*, [1897] 2 Ch. 503.

[17] *Mill* v. *Hill* (1852), 3 H.L. Cas. 828.

[18] *Re Jarvis*, [1958] 2 All E.R. 336.   [19] *Supra.*

[20] *Clegg* v. *Edmondson* (1857), 8 De G.M. & G. 787; *Re Jarvis*, [1958] 2 All E.R. 336.

[1] See (1936), 49 H.L.R. 521 (A. W. Scott); (1955), 8 C.L.P. (O. R. Marshall).

[2] The rule applies equally to the grant of a lease—*Ex parte Hughes* (1802), 6 Ves. 617; *A.-G.* v. *Earl of Clarendon* (1810), 17 Ves. 491.

aside, if in any reasonable time the *cestui que trust* chooses to say, he is not satisfied with it."[3] The transaction is voidable at the instance of the beneficiaries,[4] even though the particular dealing may in fact be perfectly fair,[5] and even beneficial to the trust estate.[6] "The purchase is not permitted in any case, however honest the circumstances; the general interests of justice requiring it to be destroyed[7] in every instance; as no court is equal to the examination and ascertainment of the truth in much the greater number of cases."[8] The rule cannot be evaded by carrying out the transaction by means of a nominee,[9] and it applies to a sale to someone such as a partner, where the trustee may directly or indirectly benefit from the transaction[10]: It seems strictly not to apply to a sale by a trustee to his wife, but such a transaction would be viewed by the courts with great suspicion[11]: it does not apply to a sale to a company of which the trustee is a member, though the circumstances may throw upon the company the onus of showing that the sale was fair and honest,[12] and the rule will apply if the company is a mere nominee for the trustee.[13] In one case, which seems to have evaded criticism, although it appears doubtful on principle, a sale by a trustee, at his request, to the trustees of his marriage settlement was held to be valid notwithstanding that the trustee himself helped out with the purchase price.[14] There is no objection to a trustee completing a purchase where the contract came into existence before the fiduciary relationship.[15]

If a trustee sells to a stranger to the trust, and subsequently re-purchases the trust property for himself, the sale cannot always be set aside. If the sale to the stranger has not been completed the vendor-trustee is never allowed to purchase the benefit of the contract for himself. "So long as the contract remains executory, and the trustee . . . has power either to enforce it or to rescind or alter it, as long as it remains in that state he cannot re-purchase the property from his own purchaser, except for the benefit of his principal."[16] After the sale to a stranger has been completed, however, a subsequent re-purchase by the trustee may be

---

[3] *Campbell* v. *Walker* (1800), 5 Ves. 678 *per* Arden M.R. at 680.

[4] Note that one of several beneficiaries cannot insist on the property being reconveyed to the trust without the consent of the other beneficiaries. His remedy is to demand a resale as discussed *infra* p. 318—*Holder* v. *Holder*, [1966] 2 All E.R. 116, at p. 128 (this point did not arise on appeal [1968] 1 All E.R. 665; [1968] Ch. 353, C.A.).

[5] See e.g. *Campbell* v. *Walker*, *supra*—sale by public auction, trustee taking no unfair advantage; *Dyson* v. *Lum* (1866), 14 L.T. 588.

[6] It was early settled, after some doubts, that the right of the *cestui que trust* does not depend on the trustee making a profit. *Ex parte Lacey* (1802), 6 Ves. 625; *Ex parte Bennett* (1805), 10 Ves. 381.

[7] The effect is, as stated above, to make the transaction voidable, not void *ab initio*.

[8] *Ex parte James* (1803), 8 Ves. 337, *per* Eldon L.C. at 345; *Ex parte Lacey* (1802), 6 Ves. 625; *Randall* v. *Errington* (1805), 10 Ves. 423.

[9] *Silkstone and Haigh Moor Coal Co.* v. *Edey*, [1900] 1 Ch. 167; *Re Sherman*, [1954] 1 All E.R. 893; [1954] Ch. 653.

[10] *Ex parte Moore* (1882), 45 L.T. 558; *Ex parte Forder*, [1881] W.N. 117, C.A.

[11] *Burrell* v. *Burrell's Trustees*, [1915] S.C. 333; *Ferraby* v. *Hobson* (1847), 2 Ph. 255; (1949), 13 Con. 248 (J. G. Fleming).

[12] *Farrar* v. *Farrar's Ltd.* (1888), 40 Ch.D. 395, C.A.

[13] *Silkstone & Haigh Moor Coal Co.* v. *Edey*, *supra*.

[14] *Hickley* v. *Hickley* (1876), 2 Ch.D. 190.

[15] *Vyse* v. *Foster* (1874), L.R. 7 H.L. 318; *Re Mulholland's Will Trusts*, [1949] 1 All E.R. 460.

[16] *Parker* v. *McKenna* (1874), 10 Ch. App. 96, *per* Mellish L.J. at 125; *Williams* v. *Scott*. [1900] A.C. 499, P.C.; *Delves* v. *Gray*, [1902] 2 Ch. 606.

good provided that the court is satisfied that there was no agreement or under-standing for re-purchase at the time of the sale to the stranger, that the original sale price was adequate and the sale *bona fide*; in order to set aside a re-purchase by a trustee it is not enough merely to show that the trustee had a hope that he would be able to purchase at some time in the future, or that, having in fact repurchased, he ultimately made a profit on a re-sale many years later.[17]

The right to avoid the purchase is valid not only as against the trustee, but also against any subsequent purchaser with notice.[18] Alternatively if the trustee has re-sold at a profit, the *cestuis que trust* can adopt the sale and require the trustee to account for the profit.[19] If the trustee has not re-sold, the court may require him to offer the property for re-sale: if a greater price is offered than that paid by the trustee, the sale to the trustee will be set aside; otherwise he will be held to his bargain.[1] On general principles the *cestuis que trust*, having full knowledge of the facts,[2] may waive their rights and affirm the purchase by the trustee, and after a long period of acquiescence will be deemed to have done so under the equitable doctrine of laches[3]: mere lapse of time will not be enough, though it may be some evidence of laches.

The rule applies in all its stringency to a trustee who has recently retired, whether or not with a view to the sale[4], but ceases to apply after a long period of retirement, such as twelve years,[5] unless there are circumstances of doubt or suspicion. It does not apply to a trustee who disclaims the trust,[6] nor, it seems, to trustees who have no active duties to perform.[7] Normally, of course, the rule applies equally to an executor, but it was held, on appeal, not to do so on the special facts of *Holder* v. *Holder*.[8] The defendant in that case was, as it was assumed, technically an executor by reason of the fact that he had intermeddled with the estate. His interference had, however, been of a minimal character, and ceased before he executed a deed of renunciation, which at all relevant times had been wrongly assumed to have been effective. He had taken no part in the arrangements for the sale, which had been by public auction, and the beneficiaries had not looked to him to protect their interests.

Finally, mention should be made of exceptions to the general rule. In the

---

[17] *Baker* v. *Peck* (1861), 4 L.T. 3; *Re Postlethwaite* (1888), 60 L.T. 514, C.A.
[18] *Cookson* v. *Lee* (1853), 23 L.J. Ch. 473; *Aberdeen Town County Council* v. *Aberdeen University* (1877), 2 App. Cas. 544, H.L. It follows that, at any rate in the case of land, the trustee will find it almost impossible to find a purchaser. On setting aside a sale to a trustee, he is liable to account for the rents and profits, but without interest—*Silkstone & Haigh Moor Coal Co.* v. *Edey*, [1900] 1 Ch. 167.
[19] *Baker* v. *Carter* (1835), 1 Y. & Coll. Ex. 250.
[1] *Ex parte Hughes* (1802), 6 Ves. 617; *Ex parte Lacey* (1802), 6 Ves. 625; *Dyson* v. *Lum* (1866), 14 L.T. 588; *Holder* v. *Holder*, [1966] 2 All E.R. 116, at first instance.
[2] *Randall* v. *Errington* (1805), 10 Ves. 423; *Holder* v. *Holder*, *supra*, C.A. and see pp. 372, 373, *post*.
[3] Right not lost in *A.G.* v. *Dudley (Lord)* (1815), Coop. G. 146 (22 years); *Chalmer* v. *Bradley* (1819), 1 Jac. & W. 51 (45 years); *Watson* v. *Toone* (1820), 6 Madd. 153 (20 years); *Aberdeen Town Council* v. *Aberdeen University* (1877), 2 App. Cas. 544, H.L. (80 years); *Re Sherman*, [1954] 1 All E.R. 893; [1954] Ch. 653 (19 years).
[4] *Wright* v. *Morgan*, [1926] A.C. 788; [1926] All E.R. Rep. 201, P.C.
[5] *Re Boles & British Land Company's Contract*, [1902] 1 Ch. 244.
[6] *Stacey* v. *Elph* (1833), 1 My. & K. 195; *Clark* v. *Clark* (1884), 9 App. Cas. 733, P.C.
[7] *Parkes* v. *White* (1805), 11 Ves. 209—trustees to preserve contingent remainders.
[8] [1968] 1 All E.R. 665; [1968] Ch. 353, C.A.

first place, the court can give the trustee leave to purchase the trust property, but it will not do so, if the *cestuis que trust* object, until all other ways of selling the property at an adequate price have failed.[9] Dicta in *Holder* v. *Holder*,[10] however, suggest that the court might now be prepared to exercise its discretion more readily than indicated by some of the earlier cases. Secondly, a provision in the trust instrument authorising a purchase by a trustee will be effective according to its terms. Thirdly, there are statutory provisions[11] to enable the tenant for life under a strict settlement, who holds the legal estate on trust for all the beneficiaries, to purchase the settled land.

e Purchase by the trustee from the *cestui que trust* of his equitable interest

A distinction has to be drawn between this case and the last. Lord Eldon put it succinctly in *Ex parte Lacey*[12]: "The rule I take to be this; not, that a trustee cannot buy from his *cestui que trust*, but, that he shall not buy from himself." Elsewhere[13] he stated the position as to purchase by a trustee from his *cestui que trust* ". . . a trustee may buy from the *cestui que trust*, provided there is a distinct and clear contract, ascertained to be such after a jealous and scrupulous examination of all the circumstances, proving, that the *cestui que trust* intended, the trustee should buy; and there is no fraud, no concealment, no advantage taken, by the trustee of information, acquired by him in the character of trustee". A later Lord Chancellor[14] restated the matter in these words: "there is no rule of law which says that a trustee shall not buy property from a *cestui que trust*, but it is a well-known doctrine of equity that if a transaction of that kind is challenged in proper time, a Court of Equity will examine into it, will ascertain the value that was paid by the trustee, and will throw upon the trustee the onus of proving that he gave full value, and that all information was laid before the *cestui que trust* when it was sold". Facts which would assist a trustee in upholding a purchase by him include the fact that the purchase was arranged by the *cestui que trust*,[15] or that he pressed the trustee to purchase,[16] or the fact that no other purchaser could be found.[17] These principles, and not those discussed in subsection (d) above, also apply where a trustee purchases the trust property with the consent of the *cestuis que trust*, for this is in effect a purchase from the *cestuis que trust*.[18]

The principles laid down in the judgments cited above apply in general to any person in a fiduciary position.[19] Thus, for instance, on a purchase by a solicitor from his client "the solicitor must establish that the sale was as advantageous to the client as it could have been if the solicitor had used his utmost endeavours to sell

---

[9] *Farmer* v. *Dean* (1863), 32 Beav. 327; *Tennant* v. *Trenchard* (1869), 4 Ch. App. 537.
[10] *Supra*, C.A., at pp. 677, 680; 398, 402, 403.
[11] Section 68 of the Settled Land Act 1925; see *Dicconson* v. *Talbot* (1870), 6 Ch. App. 32.
[12] *Supra*, at p. 626.
[13] *Coles* v. *Trecothick* (1804), 9 Ves, 233, at p. 247.
[14] Lord Cairns in *Thomson* v. *Eastwood* (1877), 2 App. Cas. 215, at p. 236, H.L., approved in *Dougan* v. *Macpherson*, [1902] A.C. 197, H.L., where the trustee failed to disclose a valuation to the *cestui que trust*.
[15] *Coles* v. *Trecothick, supra.*
[16] *Morse* v. *Royal*, (1800), 12 Ves. 355; *Luff* v. *Lord* (1864), 34 Beav. 220.
[17] *Clarke* v. *Swaile* (1762), 2 Eden 134 (actually a case of solicitor and client).
[18] See *Williams* v. *Scott*, [1900] A.C. 499, P.C.; *Coles* v. *Trecothick, supra.*
[19] *Tate* v. *Williamson* (1866), 2 Ch. App. 55.

the property to a stranger, and that the burthen of proving this lies on the solicitor, or any persons claiming through him".[20] In practice, a solicitor who wishes to buy from his client should see to it that the client is independently advised.[1]

3 DUTY NOT TO DELEGATE THE TRUST

a The equitable rules, apart from statute

The original principle was that "trustees who take on themselves the management of property for the benefit of others have no right to shift their duty on other persons".[2] It was early recognised, however, that administration of a trust would often be impracticable unless exceptions were permitted, and thus it can now be said that "the law is not that trustees cannot delegate: it is that trustees cannot delegate unless they have authority to do so".[3] Lord Hardwicke[4] said that trustees could "act by other hands" on the ground of legal necessity,[5] or what he called moral necessity, from the usage of mankind. The ground of moral necessity, which was much the more important of these exceptions, was fully discussed, particularly by the Court of Appeal, in *Speight* v. *Gaunt*[6] which, as Kay J. pointed out in *Fry* v. *Tapson*,[7] "did not lay down any new rule, but only illustrated a very old one, *viz.*, that trustees acting according to the ordinary course of business, and employing agents as a prudent man of business would do on his own behalf, are not liable for the default of an agent so employed". In deciding whether the employment of an agent by a trustee was proper, the standard adopted was the conduct of the ordinary prudent man of business in managing his own affairs.

In appointing an agent the trustees must exercise their personal discretion in making their choice of agent[8]; they cannot delegate the choice to someone, such as their solicitor, though they may of course ask him, or another person, for advice or even for the names of suitably qualified persons.[9] An important,

---

[20] *Spencer* v. *Topham* (1858), 22 Beav. 573 *per* Romilly M.R. at 577. Here the sale was upheld, although the solicitor re-sold two years later at a fancy price making a profit of £970; *Luddy's Trustee* v. *Peard* (1886), 33 Ch.D. 500 and cf. *Johnson* v. *Fesemeyer* (1858), 2 De G. & J. 13.

[1] *Cockburn* v. *Edwards* (1881), 18 Ch.D. 449, C.A.; *Barron* v. *Willis*, [1900] 2 Ch. 121, C.A., affd. H.L., [1902] A.C. 271.

[2] *Per* Langdale M.R. in *Turner* v. *Corney* (1841), 5 Beav. 515, at p. 517.

[3] *Pilkington* v. *I.R.Comrs.*, [1962] 3 All E.R. 622; [1964] A.C. 612, H.L., *per* Lord Radcliffe at p. 630, 639.

[4] In *Ex parte Belchier* (1754), Amb. 218.

[5] The illustration given by Lord Hardwicke in *Ex parte Belchier*, *supra*, was the rule that "if trustees join in giving a discharge, and one only receives, the other is not answerable, because his joining in the discharge was necessary"—a discharge by one of two or more trustees would be ineffective. Another illustration would be where a broker is employed to purchase investments, it being impossible to purchase them in any other way.

[6] (1883), 22 Ch.D. 727, C.A.; (1883), 9 App. Cas. 1, H.L.; *Learoyd* v. *Whiteley* (1887), 12 App. Cas. 727, H.L.

[7] (1884), 28 Ch.D. 268, at p. 280.

[8] *Re Weall* (1889), 42 Ch.D. 674. A direction in a will that a particular person is to be solicitor to the trust imposes no trust or duty on the trustees to employ him—*Foster* v. *Elsley* (1881), 19 Ch.D. 518; and see *Re Duke of Cleveland's Settled Estates*, [1902] 2 Ch. 350.

[9] *Robinson* v. *Harkin*, [1896] 2 Ch. 415.

if obvious, limitation is that they must only employ an agent to do work within the scope of the usual business of the agent.[10] Thus trustees may employ a broker for investment, or a solicitor for legal work, or a rent collector to collect rents,[11] but they have been held liable for delegating the investment of trust funds to a solicitor, when those funds were misapplied,[12] and it has been held that as it is no part of the ordinary business of a solicitor to receive trust moneys, if a trustee "allows the trust money to go into the hands of the solicitor, unless there is some extraordinary reason for doing so, he is just as much liable as if he put it into his own pocket".[13] It followed from this that, until altered by statute,[14] trustees could not, under ordinary circumstances, properly authorise solicitors or other agents to receive the purchase monies on a sale of the trust property and accordingly a purchaser could insist that vendor-trustees should attend personally to receive the purchase monies, or alternatively direct that the monies should be paid into a joint account at a bank.[15]

b   Section 23 of the Trustee Act 1925

The position as to the employment of an agent has, according to Maugham J. in *Re Vickery*,[16] been revolutionised by this section. Subsection (1) provides as follows:

> "Trustees or personal representatives may, instead of acting personally, employ and pay an agent, whether a solicitor, banker, stockbroker, or other person, to transact any business or do any act required to be transacted or done in the execution of the trust, or the administration of the testator's or intestate's estate, including the receipt and payment of money, and shall be entitled to be allowed and paid all charges and expenses so incurred . . ."[17]

The effect of this provision is that a trustee "is no longer required to do any actual work himself, but he may employ a solicitor or other agent to do it, whether there is any real necessity for the employment or not".[18] It is submitted, however, that there is nothing in section 23 (1) to modify the duty of a trustee, if he does appoint an agent, to use his discretion in selecting him, nor to authorise the employment of an agent otherwise than within the scope of the usual business of the agent.

In addition to the general power to employ agents in subsection (1), section 23 of the Trustee Act 1925 also provides as follows:

---

[10] *Fry* v. *Tapson* (1884), 28 Ch.D. 268.
[11] *Wilkinson* v. *Wilkinson* (1825), 2 Sim. & St. 237. It was held here that the trustees of the will did not by reason of such proper employment lose legacies of £5 per annum expressly given to them for their trouble in administering the trust.
[12] *Rowland* v. *Witherden* (1851), 3 Mac. & G. 568.
[13] Per Kay J. in *Dewar* v. *Brooke* (1885), 52 L.T. 489, at pp. 492, 493.
[14] Trustee Act 1888, s. 2, replaced by Trustee Act 1893, s. 17, now reproduced, with amendments, in Trustee Act 1925, s. 23 (3), discussed at p. 322, *post*.
[15] *Ghost* v. *Waller* (1846), 9 Beav. 497; *Re Bellamy and Metropolitan Board of Works* (1883), 24 Ch.D. 387, C.A.; *Re Flower & Metropolitan Board of Works* (1884), 27 Ch.D. 592.
[16] [1931] 1 Ch. 572; [1931] All E.R. Rep. 562.
[17] Such payment has always been allowed in the case of a proper appointment—*Bonithon* v. *Hockmore* (1685), 1 Vern. 316; *Re Weall* (1889), 42 Ch.D. 674.
[18] Per Maugham J. in *Re Vickery, supra*, at pp. 581; 565.

"(2) Trustees or personal representatives may appoint any person to act as their agent or attorney for the purpose of selling, converting, collecting, getting in, and executing and perfecting insurances[19] of, or managing or cultivating, or otherwise administering any property, real or personal, moveable or immoveable, subject to the trust or forming part of the testator's or intestate's estate, in any place outside the United Kingdom or executing or exercising any discretion or trust or power vested in them in relation to any such property, with such ancillary powers, and with and subject to such provisions and restrictions as they may think fit, including a power to appoint substitutes . . ."

This provision is wider than subsection (1) in that it authorises a trustee to appoint an agent not only to perform ministerial acts, but also to exercise the discretions which, it is submitted, cannot be delegated under subsection (1). Subsection (2), however, only applies as regards property outside the United Kingdom.[20] Though this is a new subsection, it in effect merely makes statutory the pre-existing law.[1]

Subsection (3)[2] provides:

"Without prejudice to such general power of appointing agents as aforesaid—

(a) A trustee may appoint a solicitor to be his agent to receive and give a discharge for any money or valuable consideration or property receivable by the trustee under the trust, by permitting the solicitor to have the custody of, and to produce, a deed having in the body thereof or endorsed thereon a receipt for such money or valuable consideration or property, the deed being executed, or the endorsed receipt being signed, by the person entitled to give a receipt for that consideration;

(b) . . . and the production of any such deed by the solicitor shall have the same statutory validity and effect as if the person appointing the solicitor had not been a trustee[3];

(c) A trustee may appoint a banker or solicitor to be his agent to receive and give a discharge for any money payable to the trustee under or by virtue of a policy of insurance, by permitting the banker or solicitor to have the custody of and to produce the policy of insurance with a receipt signed by the trustee . . ."

The interpretation put upon section 23 (1) in *Re Vickery*[4] has been said to render subsection (3) "meaningless and unnecessary".[5] The general provision under subsection (1) certainly seems wide enough to cover the matters dealt with in subsection (3), which is expressly stated to be without prejudice to the general power in subsection (1), and, as we shall see, the protection given to a trustee in respect of the acts of the agent may well be much wider under subsection (1). A purchaser from the trustees may, however, be entitled to require the trustees to act under subsection (3) in order to ensure that he gains the protection afforded by section 69 of the Law of Property Act 1925.

---

[19] "Obviously a misprint for 'assurances' " *per* Eve J. at first instance in *Green* v. *Whitehead*, [1930] 1 Ch. 38, at p. 45, C.A.

[20] *Green* v. *Whitehead, supra.*

[1] *Stuart* v. *Norton* (1860), 14 Moo. P.C.C. 17.

[2] Re-enacting with amendments. s. 17 of the Trustee Act 1893, which in turn replaced s. 2 of the Trustee Act 1888.

[3] This refers to s. 69 of the Law of Property Act 1925 (replacing s. 86 of the Conveyancing Act 1881) which protects a purchaser by providing that a receipt in a deed or endorsed thereon is sufficient authority for payment to the solicitor producing it.

[4] [1931] 1 Ch. 572; [1931] All E.R. Rep. 562.

[5] (1931), 47 L.Q.R. 331 (H. Potter).

c Liability of a trustee for the defaults of an agent[6]

At times some of the judges have taken the view that a trustee is inevitably liable for the default of an agent, even though properly appointed and supervised.[7] The view which has prevailed, however, is that if, assuming the employment is proper, "and without any other misconduct or default on the part of the trustees, a loss takes place through any fraud or neglect of the agents employed, the trustees are not liable to make good such loss".[8] As Lindley L.J. observed in the same case in the Court of Appeal[9]: "I wish most emphatically to say that if trustees are justified by the ordinary course of business in employing agents, and they do employ agents in good repute and whose fitness they have no reason to doubt, and employ those agents to do that which is in the ordinary course of their business, I protest against the notion that the trustees guarantee the solvency or honesty of the agents employed."

Apart from statute, a trustee was, however, liable for loss caused to the trust estate by the default of an agent, if the employment of the agent could not be justified according to the principles set out above, or if the trustee failed to supervise the agent properly, in particular, by leaving the trust funds in the agent's hands for longer than was reasonably necessary.

This position has at least been maintained, and the protection offered to trustees perhaps extended, by statute. The earliest provision, now represented by section 30 (1) of the Trustee Act 1925,[10] "incorporated, generally, into instruments creating trusts the common indemnity clause which was usually inserted in such instruments".[11] The section provides as follows:

> "(1) A trustee shall be chargeable only for money and securities actually received by him notwithstanding his signing any receipt for the sake of conformity, and shall be answerable and accountable only for his own acts, receipts, neglects, or defaults, and not for those of any other trustee, nor for any banker, broker, or other person with whom any trust money or securities may be deposited,[12] nor for the insufficiency or deficiency of any securities nor for any other loss,[13] unless the same happens through his own wilful default."

The section was considered by the court in *Re Vickery*[14], where a sole executor in May, 1927, employed a solicitor, under section 23 (1), not merely to obtain

---

[6] See the valuable discussion in (1959), 22 M.L.R. 381 (G. H. Jones).
[7] E.g. Romilly M.R. in *Bostock* v. *Floyer* (1865), 35 Beav. 603; *Hopgood* v. *Parkin* (1870), L.R. 11 Eq. 74; *Sutton* v. *Wilders* (1871), L.R. 12 Eq. 373.
[8] *Speight* v. *Gaunt* (1883), 9 App. Cas. 1, H.L., *per* Selborne L.C., at p. 4; *Benett* v. *Wyndham* (1862), 4 De G.F. & J. 259; *Fry* v. *Tapson* (1884), 28 Ch.D. 268.
[9] (1883), 22 Ch.D. 727, at p. 762, C.A.
[10] Replacing s. 24 of the Trustee Act 1893 which replaced s. 31 of the Law of Property Amendment Act 1859 (Lord St. Leonards' Act). This last Act is erroneously referred to as Lord Cranworth's Act by Maugham J. in *Re Vickery*, [1931] 1 Ch. 572; [1931] All E.R. Rep. 562—Lord Cranworth's Act is the Powers of Trustees and Mortgagees, etc. Act 1860 (23 & 24 Vict. c. 145).
[11] *Re Brier* (1884), 26 Ch.D. 238, C.A. *per* Selborne L.C. at 243.
[12] I.e. properly deposited—*Re Brier, supra*, C.A.
[13] I.e. "some other analogous loss" *per* Maugham J. in *Re Vickery*, [1931] 1 Ch. 572; [1931] All E.R. Rep. 562. Cf. *Re Lucking's Will Trusts*, [1967] 3 All E.R. 726, *per* Cross J. at p. 732.
[14] *Supra*.

probate and wind-up the estate, but also to collect sums in the Post Office Savings Bank and in Savings Certificates. On the facts as found by the judge the defendant executor was first given reason for suspecting that the solicitor was unworthy of confidence in September 1927. Before then the executor had already pressed for an immediate settlement, and after that date he kept on pressing, and kept on being assured that a settlement would take place. Receiving no satisfaction the defendant put the matter into the hands of another solicitor in early December, but ultimately the first solicitor absconded without accounting for the sums he had collected which were accordingly wholly lost. In considering the application of section 30 (1), the main problem was as to the meaning of "wilful default". Before 1926, it seems that wilful default was held to include want of ordinary prudence on the part of trustees.[15] In this case, however, Maugham J. adopted the definition, in a different context, in *Re City Equitable Fire Insurance Co.*,[16] namely "either a consciousness of negligence or breach of duty, or a recklessness in the performance of a duty", and held on the facts that wilful default had not been established.

Whether or not the right result was reached, there is much to be said for the view that Maugham J. was wrong in adopting this definition of wilful default and that the definition in the earlier trustee cases should have been the one applied.[17] However, it is submitted that Maugham J.'s definition is easier to reconcile with the relevant provisions of section 23.

Subsection (1) of section 23, part of which was set out above,[18] continues and concludes:

". . . and shall not be responsible for the default of any such agent if employed in good faith".

A preliminary point is that employed means, it is submitted, properly employed[19] thus preserving the obligation of the trustee to make a personal choice, and to employ an agent only within the scope of his usual business. The main difficulty is to reconcile section 30 (1) which retains the trustee's liability for his agent's acts if due to the trustee's own wilful default, with this provision which apparently relieves him from liability in the case of an honest, though imprudent employment. It is submitted with some diffidence that what Maugham J. in effect did in *Re Vickery*,[20] rightly or wrongly, was to equate lack of good faith with wilful default in the narrower sense. If the word "employed" is not restrictively construed as referring only to the original act of employment, but to employment at the relevant time, it seems to follow that where an agent causes loss but the loss is also due to the wilful default of the trustee in the *Re Vickery* sense, the agent cannot be said to be employed in good faith. Accordingly if he cannot gain protection under section 30 (1) by reason of his own wilful default, he cannot be in any better position under section 23 (1) which

---

15 See *Re Chapman*, [1896] 2 Ch. 763, C.A. *per* Lindley L.J. at 776.
16 [1925] Ch. 407, C.A., accepted by Astbury J. in *Re Munton*,[1927] 1 Ch .262, C.A. (the point was not discussed in the Court of Appeal).
17 See (1959), 22 M.L.R. 381 (G. H. Jones).
18 See p. 321, *ante*.
19 Cf. *Re Brier*, *supra*, in connection with "deposited" in s. 30
20 *Supra*.

requires good faith.[21] An alternative view which has been put forward[1] to reconcile these two provisions, is to give "wilful default" the wider construction, including want of ordinary prudence on the part of the trustees, and to say that "in good faith" in this context means in good faith and without negligence.

There is not the same difficulty with subsection (2), which concludes—

> "and shall not, by reason *only*[2] of their having made such appointment, be responsible for any loss arising thereby".

In other respects a trustee must rely for his protection on section 30. If the true view is that the protection afforded by section 23 (1) is wider than that afforded by section 30, it seems that a trustee would be well advised to act under section 23 (1) rather than section 23 (2) whenever possible.

With regard to appointments under subsection (3), both (a) and (c), it is provided that

> "a trustee shall not be chargeable with a breach of trust by reason *only*[3] of his having made or concurred in making any such appointment".

There is, moreover, an important proviso, that

> "nothing in this subsection shall exempt a trustee from any liability which he would have incurred if this Act and any enactment replaced by this Act had not been passed, in case he permits any such money, valuable consideration, or property to remain in the hands or under the control of the banker or solicitor for a period longer than is reasonably necessary to enable the banker or solicitor, as the case may be, to pay or transfer the same to the trustee".

Beyond this a trustee must rely for his protection on section 30. For the reason given in connection with section 23 (2) a trustee may be well advised to act under the general power in section 23 (1) rather than under the more limited power under section 23 (3).

d Liability of trustee for his own breach of trust

There is nothing in the statutory provisions just discussed to affect a trustee's liability for his own breach of trust, and it is irrelevant that the breach of trust complained of is in some way connected with an agent. Accordingly it is submitted that a trustee is still personally liable for his own breach of trust if he does not take due care in the choice of an agent,[4] or if he fails to take proper care and custody of the trust funds, as by putting or leaving them in the hands of an agent for longer than is reasonably necessary. Of course, if he properly leaves the trust funds in the hands of an agent, such as a bank, whose normal work it is to undertake the safe custody of money, he will not be liable.[5]

---

[21] Thus Maugham J. said "where an executor employs a solicitor or other agent to receive money belonging to the estate, in reliance on s. 23 (1) of the Trustee Act 1925, he will not be liable for a loss of the money occasioned by the misconduct of the agent unless the loss happens through 'wilful default' of the executor, using those words as implying, as the Court of Appeal have decided, either a consciousness of negligence or breach of duty or a recklessness in the performance of a duty" (*Re Vickery, supra*, at pp. 583–584, 567).

[1] (1959), 22 M.L.R. 381 (G. H. Jones).

[2] The author's italics.

[3] The author's italics.

[4] See cases cited in notes 8–13, pp. 320 and 15, p. 321, *ante*.

[5] Section 11 of the Trustee Act 1925, a new provision which permits temporary deposit pending investment, was declaratory of the existing law. But see *Cann* v. *Cann* (1884), 51 L.T. 770, the principle of which—that the deposit must only be for a reasonable period —still applies.

This view is supported by *Speight* v. *Gaunt*[6] where there is no suggestion that the trustee should be vicariously liable for the default of the broker employed by him: the question was whether the trustee was guilty of a breach of trust in paying the £15,000 to the broker for investment. In *Speight* v. *Gaunt*[7] the trustees in fact escaped liability by showing that in paying over the money they acted without negligence, in accordance with the usage of an ordinary prudent man of business, but in *Wyman* v. *Paterson*[8] the trustees were held liable for their gross breach of trust in leaving the trust funds in the hands of the law agents for longer than was reasonably necessary. "The first duty of the trustees was to preserve the trust fund under their own control."[9]

The view that a trustee cannot rely on the statutory provisions to absolve him from liability for his own breach of trust is supported by the construction taken of express immunity clauses purporting to relieve trustees from liability for the default of their agents. The House of Lords has repeatedly said[10] that clauses of this kind do not protect against positive breach of duty. Thus Lord Davey observed, in *Wyman* v. *Paterson*,[11] "If trustees think fit to delegate their duties to their law agent in a matter in which they cannot properly authorise him to act for them, or to treat him as their banker, they are not, in my opinion, protected by a clause of immunity from liability for the intromissions of factors or agents". And with reference to section 31 of Lord St. Leonards' Act,[12] the Earl of Selborne L.C. observed[13] that the immunity was only given when the trust moneys were *properly* deposited with the banker, broker or other person.

It should be made clear, however, that the distinction between the primary liability of a trustee for his own default, and his vicarious liability for the defaults of his agents, is not discussed in the cases.

e   Delegation by power of attorney under section 25 of the Trustee Act 1925 as amended by section 9 of the Powers of Attorney Act 1971

It is convenient to consider this provision separately, as delegation under it leaves the trustee liable for the acts or defaults of the donee of the power of attorney in the same manner as if they were the acts or defaults of the donor.[14] In so far as the provisions overlap this would be a reason for a trustee preferring to act under section 23 (1). Section 25 (1) provides as follows—

> "Notwithstanding any rule of law or equity to the contrary, a trustee may by power of attorney, delegate for a period not exceeding twelve months the execution or exercise of all or any of the trusts, powers and discretions vested in him as trustee, either alone or jointly with any other person or persons."

---

[6] (1883), 22 Ch.D. 727, C.A.; (1883), 9 App. Cas. 1, H.L., and see *Wyman* v. *Paterson*, [1900] A.C. 271, H.L.
[7] *Supra.*
[8] *Supra.*
[9] *Wyman* v. *Paterson*, *supra*, per Lord Davey at 288.
[10] *Knox* v. *Mackinnon* (1888), 13 App. Cas. 753, H.L.; *Rae* v. *Meek* (1889), 14 App. Cas. 558, H.L.; *Wyman* v. *Paterson*, [1900] A.C. 271, H.L.
[11] *Supra*, at p. 289,
[12] Now replaced by s. 30 of the Trustee Act 1925.
[13] *Re Brier* (1884), 23 Ch.D. 238, C.A.
[14] Trustee Act 1925, as amended, s. 25 (5).

It will be observed that this provision authorises the delegation of powers[15] and discretions as well as merely ministerial acts. The persons who may be donees of a power of attorney under this section include a trust corporation, but not (unless a trust corporation) the only other co-trustee of the donor of the power.[16] An instrument creating a power of attorney must be attested by at least one witness[17] and written notice containing details of the power must be given by the trustee within seven days to each of the other trustees and any person who has power to appoint a new trustee, whether alone or jointly. The notice must contain the reason why the power is given, though this need not appear in the power itself. Failure to give notice does not, however, prejudice a person dealing with the donee of the power.[18] The Powers of Attorney Act 1971 gives protection to the donee of a power of attorney and third persons where the power of attorney has been revoked without their knowledge. The donee will not incur any liability, and in favour of the third party the transaction will be valid.[19]

f Miscellaneous provisions

The Trustee Act 1925 authorises the employment of agents such as surveyors, valuers, accountants and bankers for special work in connection with a trust. These special powers are referred to in their appropriate contexts.

4 DUTY OF TRUSTEES TO ACT UNANIMOUSLY

"There is no law that I am acquainted with which enables the majority of trustees to bind the minority. The only power to bind is the act of [them all]."[20] Subject to any contrary provision in the trust instrument, only the joint exercise by trustees of their powers and discretions will be valid,[21] and only a receipt by all the trustees will give a good discharge to a purchaser:[22] the trust fund should be under the joint control of all the trustees,[1] and if one trustee obtains control of some or all of the fund, and misapplies it, his co-trustees will be fully liable,[2] though they may escape liability if they can show that the trustee properly obtained control of the fund and that the co-trustees acted promptly to get the money invested in their joint names.[3] Nor, it seems, will trustees be liable for

---

[15] Apparently including the power of delegation under s. 23 but not including the power under s. 25 itself—s. 25 (6).

[16] Trustee Act 1925, as amended, s. 25 (2).

[17] Ibid., s. 25 (3).

[18] Ibid., s. 25 (4).

[19] Powers of Attorney Act 1971, s. 5.

[20] Luke v. South Kensington Hotel Co. (1879), 11 Ch.D. 121, C.A. per Jessel M.R. at 125; Re Mayo, [1943] 2 All E.R. 440; [1943] Ch. 302; Phipps v. Boardman, [1965] 1 All E.R. 849, C.A. affd. sub-nom. Boardman v. Phipps, [1966] 3 All E.R. 721; [1967] 2 A.C. 46, H.L.

[21] But a trustee will not be liable and the joint act of the trustees will be valid if a dissenting trustee, acting bona fide, modifies his original view in deference to the views of his co-trustees and agrees to the proposed act—Re Schneider (1906), 22 T.L.R. 223.

[22] Lee v. Sankey (1873), L.R. 15 Eq. 204; Re Flower & Metropolitan Board of Works (1884), 27 Ch.D. 592.

[1] Consterdine v. Consterdine (1862), 31 Beav. 330.

[2] Rodbard v. Cooke (1877), 36 L.T. 504; Lewis v. Nobbs (1878), 8 Ch.D. 591 (but on the facts see now s. 7 of the Trustee Act 1925, discussed supra, Chapter 9, Section 2j).

[3] Thompson v. Finch (1856), 8 De G.M. & G. 560; Carruthers v. Carruthers, [1896] A.C. 659, H.L.

moneys belonging to the trust which their co-trustee gets into his possession without their knowledge or consent and by a fraud upon them.[4]

Exceptionally, one of several trustees may be authorised, on the grounds of practical convenience, to receive income,[5] though no trustee should be authorised to do this whose co-trustees have any reason to believe that he is liable to misapply the income,[6] and on general principles his co-trustees must see to the money being brought under their joint control with all due despatch. Where the trust property includes an investment in a limited company, the Articles of Association in practice invariably provide that trusts shall not be recognised,[7] and that in the case of joint holders, dividends will be payable to the first named, who can give an effectual receipt therefor.[8]

The different rule in relation to charity trustees has already been discussed.[9]

5 DUTY OF TRUSTEES TO HAND OVER THE TRUST FUNDS TO THE RIGHT PERSONS

a The extent of the duty

Obviously trustees are under an obligation to distribute the trust property only to the beneficiaries who are properly entitled thereto. Accordingly trustees have been held liable to the persons rightly entitled where they have paid the wrong persons through acting on the faith of a marriage certificate which turned out to be a forgery,[10] or through acting on the wrong construction of the trust instrument.[11] Strictly, it remains a breach of trust notwithstanding the fact that the payment is made upon legal advice,[12] though, as is explained elsewhere,[13] this may be a factor which would induce the court to relieve the trustees under section 61 of the Trustee Act 1925. Exceptionally, where illegitimate persons or their relatives are entitled to property by reason of the provisions contained in sections 14–16 of the Family Law Reform Act 1969, statutory protection is given to trustees and personal representatives who, without notice of a claim, distribute the estate without having ascertained that there is no person entitled to any interest therein by reason of these provisions. The section[14] does not, however, prejudice the right of any person entitled under the Act to follow the property, or any property representing it, into the hands of any person, other than a purchaser, who may have received it.

---

[4] *Barnard* v. *Bagshaw* (1862), 3 De G. J. & Sm. 355—crossed cheque entrusted to co-trustee for delivery to beneficiary. Cf. *Re Bennison* (1889), 60 L.T. 859, where trustee was held liable on similar facts with the essential difference that the beneficiary should not have been paid by cheque, the strict duty of the trustees being to purchase stock to satisfy a specific legacy.

[5] *Townley* v. *Sherborne* (1633), Bridg. 35.   [6] *Gough* v. *Smith*, [1872] W.N. 18.

[7] See Companies Act 1948, s. 117 and Sched. 1, Table A, Art. 7; Gower, *Modern Company Law*. 3rd Ed., p. 388.

[8] *Ibid.*, Art. 121.

[9] In Chapter 7, Section 1a, *ante*, p. 197.

[10] *Eaves* v. *Hickson* (1861), 30 Beav. 136; *Sporle* v. *Barnaby* (1864), 11 L.T. 412.

[11] *Re Hulkes* (1886), 33 Ch.D. 552; *Ministry of Health* v. *Simpson*, [1950] 2 All E.R. 1137; [1951] A.C. 251, H.L.

[12] *National Trustees Company of Australasia Ltd.* v. *General Finance Company of Australasia, Ltd.*, [1905] A.C. 373, P.C.

[13] See Chapter 12, Section 3d, p. 379, *post*.

[14] Section 17, Family Law Reform Act 1969.

Trustees will not be liable if they have accounted to an apparent beneficiary on the face of the trust documents, without notice of any facts or documents which might indicate that some other person is in fact entitled. Thus if a power of appointment has been exercised, apparently properly, in favour of X and the trustees having made all reasonable inquiries pay the trust funds to him, they will not be liable to pay again if it turns out that there was a prior appointment to Y of which the trustees had no notice.[15] Again, a payment to the apparent beneficiary will be a good discharge to the trustees, if they have no notice of the fact that the beneficiary has assigned or charged his interest,[16] and it seems they can safely pay to a person entitled in default of appointment on apparently satisfactory evidence that no appointment has ever been made.[17]

Conversely, trustees will be liable to pay again if they ignore a derivative title of which they have notice, whether actual or constructive.[18] Trustees have a right to call upon anyone who claims to be a *cestui que trust* to prove his title,[19] but they cannot raise questions where the validity or invalidity of the doubt is not essential to their safety;[20] nor, on distribution of the fund, can they require delivery of the assignment or other documents whereby the *cestui que trust* establishes his derivative title.[1]

Where the trustees have a reasonable doubt as to title of a claimant, as, for instance, where he claims under an appointment which may be a fraud on a power,[2] they should apply to the court and act under its directions.[3]

b   Section 27 of the Trustee Act 1925

This section,[4] which applies notwithstanding a provision to the contrary in the trust instrument,[5] gives considerable protection to trustees on the distribution of the trust property. Sub-section 1 provides that trustees may give notice[6] by advertisement in the *London Gazette* and, where land is involved, in a news-

---

15 *Cothay* v. *Sydenham* (1788), 2 Bro. C.C. 391.
16 *Leslie* v. *Baillie* (1843), 2 Y. & C. Ch. 91; *Re Lord Southampton's Estate* (1880), 16 Ch.D. 178.
17 *Re Cull's Trusts* (1875), L.R. 20 Eq. 561; *Williams* v. *Williams* (1881), 17 Ch.D. 437.
18 *Hallows* v. *Lloyd* (1888), 39 Ch.D. 686; *Re Neil* (1890), 62 L.T. 649; *Davis* v. *Hutchings*, [1907] 1 Ch. 356.
19 *Hurst* v. *Hurst* (1874), 9 Ch. App. 762.
20 *Devey* v. *Thornton* (1851), 9 Hare 222—where beneficiary is dead cannot raise doubts as to the title of apparently properly constituted executors or administrators.
1 *Re Palmer*, [1907] 1 Ch. 486.
2 It is submitted that cases such as *Campbell* v. *Home* (1842), 1 Y. & C. Ch. 664; *Firmin* v. *Pulham* (1848), 2 De G. & Sm. 99, charging trustees with costs where the appointment was held to be valid would not be followed. The courts are now more ready to allow costs, partly by reason of the simpler and less expensive procedure available.
3 *Talbot* v. *Earl of Radnor* (1834), 3 My. & K. 252; *Merlin* v. *Blagrave* (1858), 25 Beav. 125.
4 As amended by the Law of Property Amendment Act 1926, s. 7 and Schedule. It replaces, with amendments, s. 29 of the Law of Property (Amendment) Act 1859 (Lord St. Leonards' Act).
5 Trustee Act 1925, s. 27 (3).
6 At any rate in the case of a trust arising under a will, as soon as possible—*Re Kay*, [1897] 2 Ch. 518.

paper circulating in the district in which the land is situated,[7] and "such other like notices, including notices elsewhere than in England and Wales, as would, in any special case, have been directed by a court of competent jurisdiction in an action for administration"[8] of their intention to distribute. The notice must require any person interested to send particulars of his claim to the trustees within the time, not being less than two months, fixed in the notice.[9] The notices should follow the wording of section 27 so as to indicate that it is not merely the claims of creditors which are required to be sent in, but also those of beneficiaries.[10]

At the expiration of the time fixed by the notice, the trustees, provided they make all appropriate searches, can safely distribute having regard only to those claims, whether formal or not, of which they have notice, whether as a result of the advertisement or otherwise.[11] The trustees will be as fully protected as if they had administered under an order of the court.[12] So far as claimants are concerned, however, it is expressly provided that nothing in the section prejudices the right of any person to follow the property, or any property representing the same, into the hands of any person, other than a purchaser, who may have received it.[13]

6 DUTIES IN RELATION TO INFORMATION, ACCOUNTS AND AUDIT

a Duty to account

"It is the first duty of an accounting party [including a trustee] . . . to be constantly ready with his accounts."[14] He must not only keep proper accounts, and allow a *cestui que trust* to inspect them, but must also, on demand, give a *cestui que trust* information and explanations as to the investment of and dealings with the trust property.[15] Some cases apparently lay down that the trustees must, *prima facie*, actually render an account to each *cestui que trust*, and that it is not enough merely to make an offer to him, or his accountant, or some other person, to inspect and take copies.[16] Other cases suggest a *cestui que trust* can only demand a copy of the accounts if he is prepared to pay the expense himself,[17]

---

[7] On similar language in other statutes it has been held that *The Sporting Life* circulates in Westminster (*R.* v. *Westminster Betting Licensing Committee*, [1963] 2 All E.R. 544; [1963] 2 Q.B. 750, D.C.), and that *The Times* is a local paper circulating in Rickmansworth (*Re Southern Builders and Contractors (London) Ltd.* (1961), *Times*, 10th October).

[8] See *Re Bracken* (1889), 43 Ch.D. 1, C.A.; *Re Letherbrow*, [1935] W.N. 34; *Re Holden*, [1935] W.N. 52.

[9] Or the last of the notices, if more than one is given.

[10] *Re Aldhous*, [1955] 2 All E.R. 80.

[11] Trustee Act 1925, s. 27 (2).

[12] *Re Frewen* (1889), 60 L.T. 953.

[13] Trustee Act 1925, s. 27 (2) (a).

[14] *Per* Plumer M.R. in *Pearse* v. *Green* (1819), 1 Jac. & W. 135, at p. 140; *Kemp* v. *Burn* (1863), 4 Giff. 348. As to judicial trustees, see Judicial Trustee Rules, S.I. 1972 No. 1096, rr. 13–15.

[15] *Springett* v. *Dashwood* (1860), 2 Giff. 521; *Re Tillott*, [1892] 1 Ch. 86.

[16] *Kemp* v. *Burn* (1863), 4 Giff. 348; *Re Watson* (1904), 49 Sol. Jo. 54.

[17] *Ottley* v. *Gilby* (1845), 8 Beav. 602.

though this may be so only when the accounts are long and complex so that the preparation of a copy would be expensive.[18] *A fortiori*, a person merely claiming to be a *cestui que trust* cannot demand information at the cost of the trust estate, at any rate where the trustee could only give it after obtaining professional advice.[19]

In *Low* v. *Bouverie*[20] it was held that it was "no part of the duty of a trustee to tell his *cestui que trust* what incumbrances the latter has created, nor which of his incumbrancers have given notice of their respective charges" on the ground that "it is no part of the duty of a trustee to assist his *cestui que trust* in selling or mortgaging his beneficial interest and in squandering or anticipating his fortune". Now, however, it is provided by section 137 (8) of the Law of Property Act 1925 that a *cestui que trust*[1] may require, subject to the payment of costs, production of all notices in writing of dealings with the equitable interest which have been served on the trustees.

A *cestui que trust* is *prima facie*, in the absence of special circumstances, entitled to production and inspection of all trust documents in the possession of the trustees, which clearly include title deeds and other documents relating to the title to the trust property and the nature and content of his own beneficial interest,[2] and he is also entitled to be given any necessary authority to verify the information given and to ascertain that the trust property is free from any incumbrances.[3] This right to inspect the trust documents is a proprietary right. "The beneficiary is entitled to see all the trust documents because they are trust documents and because he is a beneficiary. They are in a sense his own."[4] This right came into conflict, in *Re Londonderry's Settlement*[5] with the principle that trustees exercising a discretionary power are not bound to disclose to their beneficiaries the reasons actuating them in coming to a decision. The facts of this case were that under the settlement the defendant was, in default of appointment, an income beneficiary, and also a member of the class among whom the trustees of the settlement had power, exercisable with the consent of the appointors therein defined, to appoint shares of capital. Being dissatisfied with the share appointed to her, she demanded the disclosure of various classes of documents including the agenda of meetings of the trustees, correspondence between individual trustees and appointors, correspondence between the trustees and appointors or any of them on the one hand and beneficiaries on the other hand, and minutes of meetings of the trustees so far as they related to the exercise by the trustees of the power of appointment. The Court of Appeal

---

[18] *Re Watson, supra.*
[19] *Re Bosworth* (1889), 58 L.J. Ch. 432.
[20] [1891] 3 Ch. 82, C.A., *per* Lindley L.J. at p. 99.
[1] In fact, any person interested in the equitable interest.
[2] *Simpson* v. *Bathurst* (1869), 5 Ch. App. 193; *Re Cowin* (1886), 33 Ch.D. 179; *Re Londonderry's Settlement*, [1964] 3 All E.R. 855; [1965] Ch. 918, C.A.; (1965), 81 L.Q.R. 192 (R. E. Megarry).
[3] *Re Tillott*, [1892] 1 Ch. 86.
[4] *Per* Lord Wrenbury in *O'Rourke* v. *Darbishire*, [1920] A.C. 581; [1920] All E.R. Rep. 1, H.L. at pp. 626; 17.
[5] [1964] 3 All E.R. 855; [1965] Ch. 918, C.A.

held[6] that the trustees were not bound to disclose these documents, but the grounds are not altogether clear. So far as at any rate some of the documents are concerned, it seems to have been held that they were not strictly "trust documents", so that the defendant beneficiary did not have even a *prima facie* right of inspection. There was no attempt at a comprehensive definition of the term "trust documents", but Salmon L.J. suggested that they have three characteristics in common "(i) they are documents in the possession of the trustees as trustees; (ii) they contain information about the trust which the beneficiaries are entitled to know; (iii) the beneficiaries have a proprietary interest in the documents and, accordingly, are entitled to see them". If, however, any of the documents in question were properly to be described as trust documents, then it was held that they were protected for the special reason which protects the trustees' deliberations on a discretionary matter from disclosure. Where necessary this over-rides the *prima facie* right of the beneficiary to inspection. The reasons[7] given for this prevailing principle are that the discretionary power having been given to the trustees, it is for them to exercise it, and the exercise cannot be challenged so long as it is *bona fide*: that disclosure would be likely to embitter family feelings and the relationship between the trustees and the beneficiaries and consequently would not be for the good of the beneficiaries as a whole, and might make the lives of the trustees intolerable: and that it might be difficult to persuade persons to act as trustees if the rule were otherwise. It should be added that if the trustees choose to give reasons, their soundness can be considered by the court.[8]

Trustees under an express trust are not merely required to give information on demand, but, when there is an infant beneficiary, are under a positive duty to inform him of his interest on his coming of age.[9] It seems, however, that executors are under no such duty,[10] the distinction being said to be due to the fact that a will is open to public inspection.

It may be mentioned that trustees may well be held personally liable for the costs of any proceedings made necessary by their failure to carry out the above duties.[11]

b Audit

There are three statutory provisions. First, Section 22 (4) of the Trustee Act 1925 provides—

---

[6] The order was rather carefully made "without prejudice to any right of the defendant to discovery in separate proceedings against the plaintiffs and subject to any order the court may think fit to make in particular circumstances", and subject to a proviso excluding written professional legal advice as to how trustees are in law entitled to exercise such powers.

[7] None of their reasons convinces Alec Samuels writing in (1965), 28 M.L.R. 220, who contends that in modern society trustees should be required to give their reasons on request.

[8] See (1965), 81 L.Q.R. 192 (R. E. Megarry).

[9] *Burrows* v. *Walls* (1855), 5 De G.M. & G. 233; *Brittlebank* v. *Goodwin* (1868), L.R. 5 Eq. 545; *Hawksley* v. *May*, [1955] 3 All E.R. 353; [1956] 1 Q.B. 304. As to whether this involves an obligation to inform the beneficiary of the rule in *Saunders* v. *Vautier* (1841), Cr. & Ph. 240, discussed *infra* in Section 7, see (1970), 34 Con. 29 (Alec Samuels).

[10] *Re Lewis*, [1904] 2 Ch. 656, C.A.; *Re Mackay*, [1906] 1 Ch. 25; *Hawksley* v. *May*, *supra*.

[11] See e.g. *Re Skinner*, [1904] 1 Ch. 289; *Re Holton's Settlement Trusts* (1918), 119 L.T. 304. Illiteracy and consequent inability to keep accounts is no defence—an agent could be employed (*Wroe* v. *Seed* (1863), 4 Giff. 425).

"Trustees may, in their absolute discretion, from time to time, but not more than once in every three years unless the nature of the trust or any special dealings with the trust property make a more frequent exercise of the right reasonable, cause the accounts of the trust property to be examined or audited by an independent accountant, and shall, for that purpose, produce such vouchers and give such information to him as he may require; and the costs of such examination or audit, including the fee of the auditor, shall be paid out of the capital or income of the trust property, or partly in one way and partly in the other, as the trustees, in their absolute discretion, think fit, but, in default of any direction by the trustees to the contrary in any special case, costs attributable to capital shall be borne by capital and those attributable to income by income."

Secondly, section 13 of the Public Trustee Act 1906, "an exceedingly drastic enactment",[12] enables any trustee or beneficiary to apply to the Public Trustee for an audit of the whole accounts of a trust at any time whatever, subject to the proviso that the application cannot be made within one year after there has been a prior audit. There is no limit backwards beyond which the audit is not to be extended, and the audit can only be prevented by an application to the court to stay the exercise of the *prima facie* right conferred by the Act. The sanction against insisting improperly on an investigation of the trust accounts is the liability of the applicant to be ordered to pay the costs of the audit.[13]

Lastly there is provision for annual audit by the court in the case of a judicial trustee.[14]

7 DUTIES WHERE *CESTUI QUE TRUST* IS SOLELY AND BENEFICIALLY ENTITLED

Where the entire equitable interest is presently vested in a *cestui que trust* who is of full age and capacity, he can require the trustee to convey the trust property to him and thus bring the trusts to an end, notwithstanding that the trust instrument may contain contrary provisions. It would, of course, be quite a different matter if the *cestui que trust* merely had a contingent interest, contingent, for instance, upon his attaining a specified age. Page Wood V.C. explained the position in *Gosling* v. *Gosling*[15] as follows: "The principle of this court has always been to recognise the right of all persons who attain the age of [18][16] to enter upon the absolute use and enjoyment of the property given to them by a will,[17] notwithstanding any directions by the testator to the effect that they are not to enjoy it until a later age—unless, during the interval, the property is given for the benefit of another.[18] If the property is once theirs, it is useless for the testator to attempt to impose any fetter upon their enjoyment of it in full so soon as they attain [18]."[16,19] It may be mentioned that trustees may be validly empowered by the trust instrument to pay a beneficiary at an earlier age than 18, but even so

---

[12] *Per* Parker J. in *Re Oddy*, [1911] 1 Ch. 532, at p. 537; [1911–13] All E.R. Rep. 744, at p. 745.
[13] *Re Oddy, supra; Re Utley* (1912), 106 L.T. 858.
[14] Judicial Trustee Rules, S.I. 1972 No. 1096, rr. 13–15.
[15] (1859), Johns, 265, 272; *Re Johnston* (1894), 3 Ch. 204.
[16] 18 substituted for 21 to take account of the Family Law Reform Act 1969, s. 1.
[17] Or trust instrument *inter vivos*.
[18] See e.g. *Re Coleman* (1888), 39 Ch.D. 443, C.A.
[19] See *Re Bowden*, [1936] Ch. 71.

an infant beneficiary cannot compel payment before coming of age.[20] A leading case is *Saunders* v. *Vautier*,[21] which is commonly cited to support the general principle, though the ratio has been more narrowly stated by Lord Davey[1] to be "that where there is an absolute vested gift made payable at a future event, with direction to accumulate the income in the meantime, and pay it with the principal, the court will not enforce the trust for accumulation in which no person has any interest but the legatee, or (in other words) the court holds that a legatee[2] may put an end to an accumulation which is exclusively for his benefit". Conversely, if the beneficiary refused to accept a transfer of the trust funds in such a case, the trustees would be entitled, if they wished, to pay them into court.[3] Again, where there is a gift of an annuity, the annuitant is entitled to demand in lieu thereof payment of the cash which would be needed to purchase it.[4] The general principle applies in the same way where the *cestui que trust* is a charity, whether corporate or incorporate,[5] but not where the alleged beneficiary is "charity" in the abstract, there being provisions for the future ascertainment of particular charitable institutions.[6] It may also be observed that although an indefinite gift of income to an individual carries the right to *corpus*,[7] this is not so in the case of a similar gift to charity, for such a gift could be enjoyed by the charity to its fullest extent in perpetuity.[8]

The same principle applies where there are two or more *cestuis que trust*, each *sui iuris*, who are between them entitled to the whole equitable interest. Provided they are both or all agreed, they can bring the trust to an end by requiring the trust funds to be paid over to them or as they may direct. This principle has been held applicable not only to joint tenants and tenants in common, but also to the objects of a discretionary trust,[9] the certificate holders under a unit trust[10] and cases where the beneficiaries are entitled in succession.[11] It is important to remember, however, as Lord Maugham has pointed out,[12] that "the rule has no operation unless all the persons who have any present or contingent interest in the property, are *sui iuris* and consent". Accordingly it seems that the principle will not apply where the

---

[20] *Re Somech*, [1956] 3 All E.R. 523; [1957] Ch. 165, and see s. 21 of the Law of Property Act 1925, whereby a married infant can give a valid receipt for income.

[21] (1841), Cr. & Ph. 240; *I.R. Comrs.* v. *Executors of Hamilton-Russell*, [1943] 1 All E.R. 474, C.A.

[1] In *Wharton* v. *Masterman*, [1895] A.C. 186, at p. 198, H.L.

[2] Assuming, of course, he is of full age and capacity—*Re Jump*, [1903] 1 Ch. 129.

[3] *I.R. Comrs.* v. *Executors of Hamilton-Russell, supra.*

[4] *Re Robbins*, [1907] 2 Ch. 8, C.A., and cf. *Parkes* v. *Royal Botanic Society of London*(1908), 24 T.L.R. 508. As to the valuation of the annuity see *Re Castle*, [1916] W.N. 195; *Westminster Bank* v. *I.R. Comrs.*, [1954] 1 All E.R. 240.

[5] *Wharton* v. *Masterman*, [1895] A.C. 186, H.L.

[6] *Re Jefferies*, [1936] 2 All E.R. 626.

[7] *Re Levy*, [1960] 1 All E.R. 42; [1960] Ch. 346, C.A.

[8] *Re Levy, supra; Re Beesty's Will Trusts*, [1964] 3 All E.R. 82; [1966] Ch. 223.

[9] *Re Nelson* (1918), [1928] Ch. 920 n. C.A.; *Re Smith*, [1928] Ch. 915; *Re Beckett's Settlement*, [1940] Ch. 279.

[10] *Re A.E.G. Unit Trust (Managers) Ltd's Deed*, [1957] 2 All E.R. 506; [1957] Ch. 415.

[11] *Anson* v. *Potter* (1879), 13 Ch.D. 141; *Re White*, [1901] 1 Ch. 570.

[12] In *Re Blake, Berry* v. *Geen*, [1938] 2 All E.R. 362, at p. 366; [1938] A.C. 575, at p. 582, H.L.; *Biggs* v. *Peacock* (1882), 22 Ch.D. 284, C.A.

only beneficiaries who do not consent are the unborn issue of a woman in fact past the age of child-bearing, for there remains the theoretical possibility of further beneficiaries coming into existence.[13] It is irrelevant for this purpose that the trustees, in an appropriate case, may properly distribute the trust funds on the basis that a particular woman is past the age of child-bearing.[14]

It remains to consider whether one of several beneficiaries, being *sui iuris* and absolutely entitled in possession to a share in the trust property, can require a transfer of that share to him. In general, according to Cozens-Hardy M.R. in *Re Marshall*,[15] "the right of a person, who is entitled indefeasibly in possession to an aliquot share of property, to have that share transferred to him is one which is plainly established by law". So far as personalty is concerned, the rule will normally be applied, though it is said that in very special circumstances, where it would unduly prejudice the other beneficiaries, such a beneficiary may be unable to insist on a transfer.[16] Cozens-Hardy M.R., however, went on to explain[17] an important exception in relation to land. "There is also another case which is equally plain and established by law, that where real estate is devised in trust for sale and to divide the proceeds between A, B, C and D—some of the shares being settled and some of them not—A has no right to say 'Transfer to me my undivided fourth of the real estate, because I would rather have it as real estate than personal estate'. The court has long ago said that that is not right, because it is a matter of notoriety, of which the court will take judicial notice, that an undivided share of real estate never fetches quite its proper proportion of the proceeds of sale of the entire estate; therefore, to allow an undivided share to be elected to be taken as real estate by one of the beneficiaries would be detrimental to the other beneficiaries."[18] A beneficiary may now, it is true, apply to the court for an order for sale under section 30 of the Law of Property Act 1925, which would convert the realty into personalty but the court will not interfere[19] if the trustees properly exercise the power to postpone sale which they will usually have either expressly or by implication.[20] It is perhaps arguable that in the case of a statutory trust, or where there is an appropriate express provision, a beneficiary of full age with a majority interest vested in possession may require the trustees to give effect to his desire for a sale by reason of section 26 (3)[1] of the Law of Property Act 1925, which directs trustees for sale so far as practicable to consult such a beneficiary and to give effect to his wishes. The section, however, only directs the trustees

---

13 *Re Whichelow*, [1953] 2 All E.R. 1558.
14 See, e.g., *Re Westminster Bank Ltd's Declaration of Trust*, [1963] 2 All E.R. 400 n.; *Re Pettifor's Will Trusts*, [1966] 1 All E.R. 913; [1966] Ch. 257 and contrast *Re Cazenove* (1919), 122 L.T. 181.
15 [1914] 1 Ch. 192, 199, C.A.
16 *Re Sandeman's Will Trusts*, [1937] 1 All E.R. 368; *Re Weiner's Will Trusts*, [1956] 2 All E.R. 482.
17 *Ubi supra.*
18 *Re Horsnaill*, [1909] 1 Ch. 631; *Re Kipping*, [1914] 1 Ch. 62, C.A. As to whether in a suitable case an appropriation could be required, *quære*— per Harman J. in *Re Weiner's Will Trusts*, *supra*.
19 *Gisborne* v. *Gisborne* (1877), 2 App. Cas. 300, H.L.; *Tempest* v. *Lord Camoys* (1882), 21 Ch.D. 571, C.A.; *Re Whichelow*, [1953] 2 All E.R. 1558.
20 Under s. 25 (1) of the Law of Property Act 1925.
As substituted by the Law of Property (Amendment) Act 1926, s. 7 and Sched.

to give effect to his wish in so far as is consistent with the general interest
of the trust, and where trustees *bona fide* exercise a power to postpone sale
they may well be able to argue that to do otherwise would be inconsistent
with the general interest of the trust. Once all the shares are vested in possession, however, it is submitted that the court would normally order a sale
under section 30, unless for some special reason it would be inequitable to do
so,[2] or a partition might be made under section 28 (3) of the Law of Property
Act 1925[3].

---

[2] See e.g. *Jones* v. *Challenger*, [1960] 1 All E.R. 785; [1961] 1 Q.B. 177, C.A.; *Re A Debtor,
    Trustee* v. *Solomon*, [1966] 3 All E.R. 255; *sub. nom. Re Solomon, A Bankrupt*, [1967]
    Ch. 573; *Jackson* v. *Jackson*, [1971] 3 All E.R. 774, C.A. Cf. *Waller* v. *Waller*, [1967]
    1 All E.R. 305; *Irani Finance, Ltd.* v. *Singh*, [1970] 3 All E.R. 199; [1971] Ch. 59, C.A.,
    and see (1973), 37 Con. 270 (J. A. Saunders and A. McGregor).
[3] This section is discussed in (1970), 34 Con. 123 (E. H. Bodkin).

CHAPTER 11

Powers of Trustees

1 POWER OF SALE

a Existence of a power of sale

Although a trustee does not necessarily have a power of sale over the trust property, in most cases he will have such a power, either granted expressly or by implication by the trust instrument, or under some statutory provision, or exceptionally by virtue of an order of the court.[1]

So far as land is concerned, if it is settled land as defined by section 1 of the Settled Land Act 1925 the power of sale given by that Act is not conferred upon the trustees of the settlement (though they may, exceptionally, have it if they happen to be also the statutory owners), but on the tenant for life, and even if expressly purported to be conferred on the trustees of the settlement by the settlement itself, it is exercisable by the tenant for life.[2] If the land is not settled land, it will in most cases necessarily be held by trustees on an express or implied trust for sale, though usually with a power to postpone sale.[3] Thus, for example, under statutory provisions, a trust for sale is implied "where any property, vested in trustees by way of security, becomes, by virtue of the statutes of limitation, or of an order for foreclosure or otherwise, discharged from the right of redemption"[4]; or, in the absence of a contrary provision, where land is purchased by the trustees of a personalty settlement[5]; or where "land is expressed to be conveyed to any persons in undivided shares and those persons are of full age"[6]; or "where a legal estate (not being settled land) is beneficially limited to or held in trust for any persons as joint tenants"[7]; and in any case where trustees are authorised to pay or apply capital money subject to the trust for any purpose or in any manner, they have power to raise the money required by sale of all or any

---

[1] E.g. under s. 57 of the Trustee Act 1925.
[2] Settled Land Act 1925, ss. 108, 109. Cf. Trustee Act 1925, s. 12 (3).
[3] Either express, or implied under Law of Property Act 1925, s. 25.
[4] Law of Property Act 1925, s. 31 (1).
[5] Ibid., s. 32.
[6] Ibid., s. 34 (2) and s. 35.
[7] Ibid., s. 36 (1).

part of the trust property for the time being in possession.[8] Further, apart from statute, trustees who purchase land in breach of trust can sell and make a good title even to a purchaser with notice, provided only that all the beneficiaries are not at once competent and desirous to take the land *in specie*.[9] Even in the comparatively rare case of a trust of land where the land is neither settled land nor held upon trust for sale, as may, for instance, be the case where the trustee holds upon a bare trust for a sole *cestui que trust* of full age absolutely entitled, the trustee will have a power of sale by virtue of section 1 (1) of the Trustee Investments Act 1961,[10] unless a contrary intention is expressed.[11]

With regard to property other than land there may be an express trust for or power of sale, or one may be implied, for instance, under the rule in *Howe* v. *Lord Dartmouth*.[12] In other cases a power of sale will be implied under statutory provisions, such as section 16 of the Trustee Act 1925, or section 31 of the Law of Property Act 1925, or the Trustee Investments Act 1961, above mentioned. Special provisions in the Settled Land Act 1925 apply to heirlooms, in the widest sense, i.e., personal chattels settled so as to devolve with settled land, or to devolve therewith as nearly as may be in accordance with the law or practice in force at the date of the settlement, or settled together with land, or upon trusts declared by reference to the trusts affecting land. These can be sold by the tenant for life,[13] but only on obtaining an order of the court.[14] Further, where personal chattels are settled without reference to settled land on trusts creating entailed interests therein, the trustees are given a power of sale, with the consent of the usufructuary for the time being of full age, by section 130 (5) of the Law of Property Act 1925. Where this section did not apply and the trustees had no power of sale,[15] it was held in *Re Hope's Will Trust*[16] that the court could order a sale under section 57 of the Trustee Act 1925.

b   Statutory provisions relating to sales

The Trustee Act 1925 contains various provisions, which are chiefly of interest to the conveyancer, and for present purposes need not be considered in detail. By section 12 (1) a trustee having a trust for or power of sale

---

[8] Trustee Act 1925, s. 16. This section applies notwithstanding any contrary provision in the trust instrument, but does not apply to charity trustees, nor to the trustees of a settlement, not being also the statutory owners.

[9] *Patten to Edmonton Guardians* (1883), 48 L.T. 870; *Re Jenkins and Randall's Contract*, [1903] 2 Ch. 362.

[10] "A trustee may invest any property in his hands, whether at the time in a state of investment or not . . ." This implies a power to sell in order to make the investment—cf. *Hume* v. *Lopes*, [1892] A.C. 112, H.L.; *Re Pratt's Will Trusts*, [1943] 2 All E.R. 375; [1943] Ch. 326.

[11] Trustee Investments Act 1961, s. 1 (3). This has been held to mean "unless expressly forbidden"; cf. *Re Warren*, [1939] 2 All E.R. 599; [1939] Ch. 684; *Re Rider's Will Trusts*, [1958] 3 All E.R. 135.

[12] Discussed in Chapter 9, Section 3, pp. 281 *et seq.*, *ante*.

[13] Exceptionally the statutory owners, who may be the trustees of the settlement.

[14] Settled Land Act 1925, s. 67.

[15] It was not argued that they had a power of sale under s. 1 (1) of the Trustee Act 1925, now repealed and replaced by s. 1 (1) of the Trustee Investments Act 1961.

[16] [1929] 2 Ch. 136; [1929] All E.R. Rep. 561.

"may sell or concur with any other person in selling[17] all or any part of the property, either subject to prior charges or not, and either together or in lots,[18] by public auction or by private contract, subject to any such conditions respecting title or evidence of title or other matter as the trustee thinks fit, with power to vary any contract for sale, and to buy in at any auction, or to rescind any contract for sale and to re-sell, without being answerable for any loss".

A trust or power to sell or dispose of land, moreover, "includes a trust or power to sell or dispose of part thereof, whether the division is horizontal, vertical, or made in any other way".[19] Further, no beneficiary can impeach a sale made by a trustee on "the ground that any of the conditions subject to which the sale was made may have been unnecessarily depreciatory, unless it also appears that the consideration for the sale was thereby rendered inadequate",[20] and it cannot after the execution of the conveyance be impeached as against the purchaser on such ground "unless it appears that the purchaser was acting in collusion with the trustee at the time when the contract for sale was made".[1]

In general it must be remembered that trustees "have an overriding duty to obtain the best price which they can for their beneficiaries",[2] even though accepting a higher offer may mean resiling from an existing offer at a late stage in the negotiations contrary to the dictates of commercial morality. Trustees must, however, act with proper prudence, and may accept an existing lower offer if to probe a higher one would involve a serious risk that both offers would fall through.

It must also be remembered that trustees for sale "in relation to land or to manorial incidents and to the proceeds of sale, have all the powers of a tenant for life and the trustees of a settlement under the Settled Land Act 1925, including in relation to the land the powers of management conferred by that Act during a minority".[3]

2 POWER TO GIVE RECEIPTS

Notwithstanding anything to the contrary in the instrument, if any, creating the trust,[4] section 14 (1) of the Trustee Act 1925 now provides:

---

[17] Apart from statute trustees could, and indeed should, concur with other persons, if they can thereby get a higher price: *Re Cooper and Allen's Contract for Sale to Harlech* (1876), 4 Ch.D. 802. There must be a proper apportionment and the apportioned part due to the trustees paid to them, unless there is some special provision in the trust instrument—*Re Parker and Beech's Contract* (1887), 56 L.T. 95, C.A.

[18] See *Re Judd and Poland and Skeleher's Contract*, [1906] 1 Ch. 684, C.A.

[19] Trustee Act 1925, s. 12 (2).

[20] *Ibid.*, s. 13 (1). Cf. *Dance* v. *Goldingham* (1873), 8 Ch. App. 902; *Dunn* v. *Flood* (1885), 28 Ch.D. 586, C.A. Both decided prior to any statutory provisions.

[1] Trustee Act 1925, s. 13 (2). This does not prevent an action against the trustees for breach of trust. See also *ibid.*, s. 17.

[2] *Buttle* v. *Saunders*, [1950] 2 All E.R. 193 *per* Wynn Parry J. at 195; *Re Cooper and Allen's Contract for Sale to Harlech, supra*; (1950), 14 Con. 228 (E. H. Bodkin).

[3] Law of Property Act 1925, s. 28 (1) (amended by the Law of Property (Amendment) Act 1926, s. 7 and Sched.) and see s. 26 (3) of the Law of Property Act 1925 (as likewise amended) as to the obligation of trustees under a statutory trust for sale to consult their beneficiaries.

[4] Trustee Act 1925, s. 14 (3).

"The receipt in writing of a trustee for any money, securities, or other personal property or effects payable, transferable, or deliverable to him under any trust or power shall be a sufficient discharge to the person paying, transferring, or delivering the same and shall effectually exonerate him from seeing to the application or being answerable for any loss or misapplication thereof."

By subsection (2),[5] however, this section does not affect the statutory provisions[6] which require capital money arising under the Settled Land Act 1925 and the proceeds of sale or other capital money arising under a trust for sale of land, to be paid to at least two trustees of a settlement or trustees for sale as the case may be, except where the trustee is a trust corporation. Nor, it seems clear, does the section alter the rule[7] that where there are two or more trustees, a valid receipt can only be given by all of them acting jointly.

3 POWER TO INSURE

Unless there is some express provision in the trust instrument, trustees are under no duty to insure the trust property, and accordingly will not be liable for failure to insure if the trust property should be destroyed or damaged.[8] Nor, originally, did they have any power to insure, unless conferred by the trust instrument expressly or by implication.[9] Now, however, they have a statutory power[10] to "insure against loss or damage by fire[11] any building or other insurable property[12] to any amount, including the amount of any insurance already on foot, not exceeding three fourth parts of the full value of the building or property". The premiums are payable out of income.[13] The section does not impose any duty on the trustees to insure, and does not apply to a bare or simple trust, where the trustee is bound forthwith to convey any building or property to a beneficiary absolutely, upon being requested to do so.[14]

The following section[15] deals with the application of insurance moneys in four cases, namely, where the policy has been kept up under any trust in that behalf, or under any power statutory or otherwise,[16] or in performance of any covenant or of any obligation statutory or otherwise,[17] or by a tenant for life

---

[5] As slightly amended by the Law of Property (Amendment) Act 1926.

[6] Settled Land Act 1925, s. 94 (1); Law of Property Act 1925, s. 27 (2) as re-enacted with amendments by the Law of Property (Amendment) Act 1926.

[7] Discussed in Chapter 10, Section 4, p. 327, *ante*.

[8] *Re McEacharn* (1911), 103 L.T. 900.

[9] *Re Bennett*, [1896] 1 Ch. 778, C.A.

[10] Trustee Act 1925, s. 19 (1), replacing Trustee Act 1893, s. 18, which replaced Trustee Act 1888, s. 7.

[11] But not other risks, such as burglary—*Re Earl of Egmont's Trusts*, [1908] 1 Ch. 821. It is submitted that the statutory power is inadequate.

[12] Including chattels settled so as to devolve as heirlooms with settled land—*Re Earl of Egmont's Trusts*, [1908] 1 Ch. 821.

[13] Trustee Act 1925, s. 19 (1).

[14] *Ibid.*, s. 19 (2).

[15] *Ibid.*, s. 20 (1). For the old law, see *Re Quicke's Trusts*, [1908] 1 Ch. 887 and cases there cited; *Re Bladon*, [1911] 2 Ch. 350.

[16] E.g. Settled Land Act 1925, s. 102 (2) (e).

[17] E.g. Settled Land Act 1925, s. 88.

impeachable for waste.[18] In any of these cases money receivable by trustees or any beneficiary[19] under a policy of insurance against the loss or damage, whether by fire or otherwise,[20] of any property subject to a trust or to a settlement within the meaning of the Settled Land Act 1925, is capital money for the purposes of the trust or settlement as the case may be. Detailed provisions for the carrying through the application in different circumstances are set out in subsection (3), and, subject to obtaining the specified consents, the trustees are empowered, by subsection (4), to apply the money in rebuilding, reinstating, repairing or replacing the property lost or damaged. Subsection (5), moreover, expressly saves the other rights, whether statutory or otherwise, of any person to require the insurance money to be applied in rebuilding, reinstating, or repairing the property lost or damaged—for instance, under the Fires Prevention (Metropolis) Act 1774, section 83, which despite its title, is of general application.[1] This latter act provides that on the request of any person interested the insurers must cause the insurance money to be laid out and expended towards rebuilding, reinstating or repairing the house or building burnt down, demolished or damaged by fire, unless all the persons interested agree as to its disposition, to the satisfaction of the insurers.

4 POWER TO COMPOUND LIABILITIES

Section 15 of the Trustee Act 1925,[2] provides as follows:

"A personal representative, or two or more trustees[3] acting together,[4] or, subject to the restrictions imposed in regard to receipts by a sole trustee not being a trust corporation, a sole acting trustee where by the instrument, if any, creating the trust, or by statute, a sole trustee is authorised to execute the trusts and powers reposed in him, may, if and as he or they think fit—

(a) accept any property, real or personal, before the time at which it is made transferable or payable; or

(b) sever and apportion any blended trust funds or property; or

(c) pay or allow any debt or claim on any evidence that he or they think sufficient; or

(d) accept any composition or any security, real or personal, for any debt or for any property, real or personal, claimed; or

(e) allow any time of payment of any debt; or

---

[18] He is impeachable for waste unless, as is commonly the case, there is a contrary provision in the trust instrument—*Pardoe* v. *Pardoe* (1900), 82 L.T. 547.

[19] By s. 20 (2) of the Trustee Act 1925, if receivable by a beneficiary it must be paid by him to the trustees, or into court.

[20] Cf. Trustee Act 1925, s. 19 (1) and n. 11, *supra*.

[1] *Sinnott* v. *Bowden*, [1912] 2 Ch. 414; [1911–13] All E.R. Rep. 752.

[2] Replacing with amendments the Trustee Act 1893, s. 21. The first statutory provision was in the Powers of Trustees and Mortgagees, etc. Act 1860 (Lord Cranworth's Act), s. 30. Apart from statute see *Blue* v. *Marshall* (1735), 3 P. Wms. 381.

[3] Including a judicial trustee. *Re Ridsdel*, [1947] 2 All E.R. 312; [1947] Ch. 597; see also *Re Shenton*, [1935] Ch. 651; [1935] All E.R. Rep. 920, D.C.

[4] Presumably the general principle that all the trustees must act unanimously applies. It is submitted that under this section trustees have no power to compromise a claim by one of themselves. According to *Re Houghton*, [1904] 1 Ch. 622, however, one executor can, on other grounds, compromise a claim by a co-executor. Cf. *De Cordova* v. *De Cordova* (1879), 4 App. Cas. 692, P.C.

(*f*) compromise,[5] compound, abandon, submit to arbitration, or otherwise settle any debt, account, claim, or thing whatever relating to the testator's or intestate's estate or to the trust;

and for any of those purposes may enter into, give, execute, and do such agreements, instruments of composition or arrangement, releases, and other things as to him or them seem expedient, without being responsible for any loss occasioned by any act or thing so done by him or them in good faith."

There is not a great deal of authority on this section, which is drafted in wide terms. It appears to extend to the claims of beneficiaries, as well as to claims against the trust by strangers to it.[6] *Re Ridsdel*[7] decides the fairly obvious point that although a payment under section 15 (f) must be made in compromise of a claim, it does not follow that, to justify a compromise payment, it must be established that the claim, if there had not been a compromise, would have succeeded. As the judge observed, if this were so the power of compromise would be reduced in effect to a nullity. Further, it seems that the section only protects a trustee where he has done some act or at least exercised some active discretion and will not avail him where he has adopted a mere passive attitude of leaving matters alone.[8]

5 POWERS IN RELATION TO REVERSIONARY INTERESTS

New provisions in section 22 of the Trustee Act 1925 give considerable protection to trustees where trust property includes any share or interest in property not vested in the trustees, or the proceeds of the sale of any such property, or any other thing in action. Subsection (1) provides that on the same falling into possession, or becoming payable or transferable the trustees may—

"(*a*) agree or ascertain the amount or value thereof or any part thereof in such manner as they may think fit;

(*b*) accept in or towards satisfaction thereof, at the market or current value, or upon any valuation or estimate of value which they may think fit, any authorised investments;

(*c*) allow any deductions for duties, costs, charges and expenses which they may think proper or reasonable;

(*d*) execute any release in respect of the premises so as effectually to discharge all accountable parties from all liability in respect of any matters coming within the scope of such release;

without being responsible in any such case for any loss occasioned by any act or thing so done by them in good faith."

Subsection (2) restricts the obligations of trustees during the period before such

---

[5] "Compromise" in other contexts, has been held to require either some dispute as to the claimant's rights, or some difficulty in enforcing them—*Mercantile Investment & General Trust Co.* v. *River Plate Trust, Loans & Agency Co.,* [1894] 1 Ch. 578; *Chapman* v. *Chapman,* [1954] 1 All E.R. 798; [1954] A.C. 429 H.L.

[6] *Re Warren* (1884), 51 L.T. 561; *Eaton* v. *Buchanan,* [1911] A.C. 253, H.L.; cf. *Abdallah* v. *Rickards* (1888), 4 T.L.R. 622.

[7] *Supra.*

[8] *Re Greenwood* (1911), 105 L.T. 509.

property falls into possession, but it is expressly provided that nothing therein contained "shall relieve the trustees of the obligation to get in and obtain payment or transfer of such share or interest or other thing in action on the same falling into possession".

6 POWER OF MAINTENANCE OF INFANTS

a Express powers

In view of the wide statutory power hereafter discussed, it is no longer so usual or vital to insert express powers of maintenance, and it is not proposed to deal with them in great detail, particularly as much turns in such case on the construction of the particular words used. A primary question may be whether the alleged power is not in fact an imperative trust to apply the income, or so much of it as may be required, for or towards the maintenance of the infant. Thus there was held to be an imperative trust in *Re Peel*,[9] and a line of cases[10] which the Court of Appeal has accepted as binding, though agreeing that criticism is well founded, has decided that "a trust to apply the whole or part as the trustees may think fit of the income for the maintenance of the children is an obligatory trust and compels the trustees to maintain the children where that trust occurs in the marriage settlement to which the father is a party".[11] Accordingly the father in such case, notwithstanding his own ability to maintain his children, can compel the trustees to apply an adequate portion of the income for this purpose. It was made clear, however, by the Court of Appeal at the same time,[12] that this line of cases is not to be extended.

Where the trustees have, on the construction of the instrument, a true discretionary power of maintenance, they must, in exercising it, consider what is most for the benefit of the infant, and must not be deterred from doing what is for his benefit because it is also a benefit to the father, though they must not act with a view to the father's benefit apart from the infant's.[13] Nor, it is thought, should they be forgetful of the principles which the court would apply in granting maintenance.[14] In general the court will not interfere with or overrule the *bona fide* exercise by trustees of their discretion.[15] Where, however, trustees fail to exercise their discretion one way or the other, the court may make an appropriate order. Thus, on the one hand, past maintenance has been allowed where the trustees were apparently unaware of their discretionary power,[16] and, on the other hand, a father has been compelled to repay the whole of the income paid to him by the trustees without their exercising any discretion at all[17]; and where trustees had failed to exercise any discretion as to which of two

---

[9] [1936] Ch. 161; [1935] All E.R. Rep. 179.
[10] Including *Meacher* v. *Young* (1834), 2 My. & K. 490; *Thompson* v. *Griffin* (1841), Cr. & Ph. 317.
[11] Per Jessel M.R. in *Wilson* v. *Turner* (1883), 22 Ch.D. 521, at p. 525, C.A.
[12] *Wilson* v. *Turner, supra.*
[13] *Re Lofthouse* (1885), 29 Ch.D. 921, C.A. Applied to a statutory trust—*Re Sayers and Philip* (1974), 38 D.L.R. (3d) 602 (Saskatchewan C.A.).
[14] See p. 348, *post.*
[15] See p. 361, *post.*
[16] *Stopford* v. *Lord Canterbury* (1840), 11 Sim. 82.
[17] *Wilson* v. *Turner, supra.*

funds the allowance for maintenance should be paid out of, the court exercised it by directing that it should be paid primarily out of that fund from which it was most for the infant's benefit that it should be taken.[18]

It may be added that it has been held that a provision in an express maintenance clause that no income is to be applied while the infant is in the custody or control of the father, or while the father has anything to do with the education or bringing up of the child, is valid.[19]

b Statutory power

i *History.* The first statutory power was contained in Lord Cranworth's Act in 1860,[20] which was repealed and replaced by section 43 of the Conveyancing Act 1881. This latter provision still applies to instruments coming into force before 1st January, 1926, but has otherwise been repealed,[21] and is now replaced by section 31 of the Trustee Act 1925, which correspondingly does not apply where the instrument under which the infant's interest arises[1] came into operation before 1926.[2] This section has itself been amended by the Family Law Reform Act 1969, which has reduced the age of majority to 18. Terms in the section such as "infant", "infancy" and "minority" are to be construed accordingly.

ii *The present law.* As amended, section 31 (1), the language of which, it has been said, "is by no means easy to follow",[3] now provides as follows:

"Where any property is held by trustees in trust[4] for any person for any interest whatsoever, whether vested or contingent, then, subject to any prior interests or charges affecting that property—

  (i) during the infancy of any such person,[5] if his interest so long continues, the trustees may, at their sole discretion, pay to his parent or guardian, if any, or otherwise apply for or towards his maintenance, education, or benefit,[6] the whole or such part, if any, of the income of that property as may, in all the circumstances, be reasonable, whether or not there is—

  (a) any other fund applicable to the same purpose; or

  (b) any person bound by law to provide for his maintenance or education; and

---

[18] *Re Wells* (1889), 43 Ch.D. 281.
[19] *Re Borwick's Settlement*, [1916] 2 Ch. 304.
[20] 23 & 24 Vict. c. 145, s. 26.
[21] Law of Property Act 1925, Sched. 7.
[1] Where a power of appointment is exercised, this means the document exercising the power and not the document creating the power—*Re Dickinson's Settlements*, [1939] Ch. 27 (a convenient, if not wholly convincing, decision).
[2] Trustee Act 1925, s. 31 (5).
[3] Per Evershed M.R. in *Re Vestey's Settlement*, [1950] 2 All E.R. 891, at p. 897; [1951] Ch. 209, at p. 216, C.A.
[4] This does not include a sum of income allocated to an infant as being the object of a discretionary trust—*Re Vestey's Settlement, supra.*
[5] In a class gift to persons contingently on attaining the age of 21, it does not matter that one or more members of the class have attained that age—*Re Holford*, [1894] 3 Ch. 30, C.A. The different rule that used to apply to realty before 1926—*Re Averill*, [1898] 1 Ch. 523—seems to be abrogated by s. 175 of the Law of Property Act 1925.
[6] The same words in s. 53 of the Trustee Act 1925 were said to be of the widest import in *Re Heyworth's Settlements*, [1956] 2 All E.R. 21, at p. 23; [1956] Ch. 364, at p. 370.

(ii) if such person on attaining the age of eighteen has not a vested[7] interest in such income, the trustees shall thenceforth pay the income of that property and of any accretion thereto under subsection (2) of this section to him, until he either attains a vested interest therein or dies, or until failure of his interest . . ."

A settlor may adopt the section with variations,[8] or exclude it by a contrary intention,[9] express or implied, which may be shown even by a direction for accumulation,[10] notwithstanding that the direction itself is void.[11] Obviously, as the subsection makes clear, the power of maintenance cannot affect prior interests and charges, and by subsection 3 it only applies in the case of a contingent interest if the limitation or trust carries the intermediate income of the property, expressly including a future or contingent legacy by the parent of, or a person standing *in loco parentis* to, the legatee, if and for such period as, under the general law, the legacy carries interest[12] for the maintenance of the legatee. In many cases, quite irrespective of the relationship between the testator and the devisee or legatee, a testamentary disposition will carry the intermediate income (unless otherwise disposed of[13]) under section 175 of the Law of Property Act 1925, which provides that this shall be so[14] in the case of a contingent or future specific devise or bequest of property, whether real or personal; a contingent residuary devise of freehold land; and a specific or residuary devise of freehold land to trustees upon trust for persons whose interests are contingent or executory. Further, apart from the section, a contingent gift of residuary personalty carries the intermediate income,[15] but probably not a residuary bequest, whether vested or contingent, expressly deferred to a future date which must come sooner or later.[16]

A future or contingent pecuniary legacy is not within section 175, and *prima facie* does not carry the intermediate income. Exceptionally, however, the court presumes an intention that it does carry the intermediate income in three cases,[17] namely,

(a) where the legacy is given by a testator to his infant child, or to an infant to whom he stands *in loco parentis*,[18] no other fund being provided for his

---

[7] This provision does not apply if such person has a vested interest, even if it is liable to be divested—*Re McGeorge*, [1963] 1 All E.R. 519; [1963] Ch. 544.

[8] E.g. by substituting "they may think fit" for "may, in all the circumstances, be reasonable".

[9] Trustee Act 1925, s. 69 (2) as explained in *I.R.Comrs* v. *Bernstein*, [1961] 1 All E.R. 320; [1961] Ch. 399, C.A.; *Re Evans' Settlement*, [1967] 3 All E.R. 343 (both actually decisions on s. 32 Trustee Act 1925); *Re McGeorge, supra.*

[10] *Re Turner's Will Trusts*, [1936] 2 All E.R. 1435; [1937] Ch. 15, C.A.; *Re Ransome's Will Trusts*, [1957] 1 All E.R. 690; [1957] Ch. 348; *I.R.Comrs.* v. *Bernstein, supra.*

[11] *Re Ransome's Will Trusts, supra.*

[12] At 5 per cent, provided the income available is sufficient—Trustee Act 1925, s. 31 (3).

[13] See *Re Reade-Revell*, [1930] 1 Ch. 52; *Re Stapleton*, [1946] 1 All E.R. 323.

[14] Subject to the provisions relating to accumulations in ss. 164–166 of the Law of Property Act 1925 and s. 13 of the Perpetuities & Accumulations Act 1964.

[15] *Countess of Bective* v. *Hodgson* (1864), 10 H.L.Cas. 656; *Re Taylor*, [1901] 2 Ch. 134.

[16] *Re Geering*, [1962] 3 All E.R. 1043; [1964] Ch. 136; *Re McGeorge*, [1963] 1 All E.R. 519; [1963] Ch. 544; *Re Nash*, [1965] 1 All E.R. 51; and see (1963), 79 L.Q.R. 184 (P. V. B.).

[17] *Re Raine*, [1929] 1 Ch. 716.

[18] Only the father comes within the exception *qua* parent; if the mother is to come within it, it must be shown she was *in loco parentis*—*Re Eyre*, [1917] 1 Ch. 351.

maintenance.[19] This exception applies to a contingent legacy,[20] but only where the contingency is the attainment of full age by the infant legatee, or previous marriage.[21]

(b) where the will indicates, expressly or by implication, an intention that the income should be used for the maintenance of an infant legatee, not necessarily standing in any special relationship to the testator. It does not matter in this case that the legacy is contingent on some event other than the attainment of majority, or previous marriage.[1] The exception has been held to apply where trustees have been given a discretionary power to apply the whole or any part of the share to which the legatee might be entitled in or towards his advancement in life or otherwise for his benefit,[2] or, in another case, for the purpose of his education.[3]

(c) where a legacy is, expressly or by implication, directed to be set aside so as to be available for the legatee so soon as the contingency happens.[4]

The trustees, in deciding whether to exercise their statutory power, and, if so, to what extent, are directed[5] to have regard to the age of the infant and his requirements and generally to the circumstances of the case, and in particular to what other income, if any, is applicable for the same purposes; and where they have notice that the income of more than one fund is applicable, then, so far as practicable, unless the entire income of the funds is used or the court otherwise directs, a proportionate part only of the income of each fund should be applied. It has been held[6] that section 31 does not exclude the operation of the Apportionment Act 1870. This may produce a somewhat anomalous result where income is received after a beneficiary has attained the age of eighteen. In so far as such income is apportioned in respect of the period before he was eighteen, the income cannot be applied for maintenance, because the trustees cannot exercise their discretion in advance so as to affect the income when it is received, and they cannot apply it in arrear, because the infancy will have ceased.

Subsection (2) provides that any balance of the income not applied for the maintenance, education or benefit of the infant under subsection (1), shall be accumulated during the infancy (or until his interest previously determines), though during this period the accumulations, or any part thereof, may be applied as if they were income arising in the current year. Subsection (2) further provides for the destination of the accumulations[6] as follows:

"(i) If any such person—
   (a) attains the age of eighteen years, or marries under that age, and his interest
   in such income during his infancy or until his marriage is a vested interest;
   or

---

[19] Re Moody, [1895] 1 Ch. 101; Re George (1877), 5 Ch.D. 837, C.A.
[20] Re Bowlby, [1904] 2 Ch. 685, C.A.
[21] Re Abrahams, [1911] 1 Ch. 108.
[1] Re Jones, [1932] 1 Ch. 642.
[2] Re Churchill, [1909] 2 Ch. 431. Cf. Re Stokes, [1928] Ch. 716.
[3] Re Selby-Walker, [1949] 2 All E.R. 178.
[4] Re Medlock (1886), 54 L.T. 828; Re Clements, [1894] 1 Ch. 665; Re Woodin, [1895] 2 Ch. 309, C.A.
[5] Trustee Act 1925, s. 31 (1) proviso.
[6] Re Joel's Will Trusts, [1966] 2 All E.R. 482; [1967] Ch. 14.

(b) on attaining the age of eighteen years or on marriage under that age becomes entitled to the property from which such income arose in fee simple, absolute or determinable, or absolutely, or for an entailed interest;

the trustees shall hold the accumulations in trust for such person absolutely, but without prejudice to any provision with respect thereto contained in any settlement by him made under any statutory powers during his infancy, and so that the receipt of such person after marriage, and though still an infant, shall be a good discharge; and

(ii) In any other case the trustees shall, notwithstanding that such person had a vested interest in such income, hold the accumulations as an accretion to the capital of the property from which such accumulations arose, and as one fund with such capital for all purposes, and so that, if such property is settled land, such accumulations shall be held upon the same trusts as if the same were capital money arising therefrom."

In (i) (b) it appears[7] that the words "in fee simple, absolute or determinable" apply exclusively to realty; that the word "absolutely" applies exclusively to personalty; and that the words "for an entailed interest" apply alike to realty and personalty, and it has been held[7] that a person cannot be said to be entitled "absolutely" if his interest is liable to be divested, for instance by the exercise of a power of appointment. Under (ii) the "capital of the property from which such accumulations arose" is the share which the infant ultimately obtains. Accordingly, in a gift to a class of or including infants the accumulations of income allocated to an infant but not used for his maintenance under sub-s. (1) continue to be held on trust for him, even though his share in the capital may subsequently be reduced by an increase in the size of the class. If the infant dies before attaining a vested interest, his share accrues to the other shares and carries the accumulations with it, becoming a part of the common fund of capital.[8] It should be added[9] that although the section applies to a vested annuity as if the annuity were the income of property held by trustees in trust to pay the income thereof to the annuitant for the same period for which the annuity is payable, accumulations made during the infancy of the annuitant must be held in trust for the annuitant or his personal representatives absolutely.

iii *Interests arising under instruments made before 1 January, 1970.*[10] Such interests are unaffected by the Family Law Reform Act 1969, which has to be read in its original form, i.e. 21 instead of 18 in sub-sections 1 (ii) and 2 (i) (a) and (b), and references to "infant", "infancy" and "minority" being construed in relation to an age of majority of twenty-one. The only qualification is that where as a result trustees have power, under s. 31 (1), to pay the income to the parent or guardian of a person who has attained the age of eighteen, or to apply it for or towards his maintenance, education or benefit, they are also given power to pay it to that person himself.[11]

It should be stressed that in deciding whether or not an interest falls under this head one is concerned to know when the instrument was made, not when it came into effect. In particular, a will made before 1 January, 1970, is not to

---

[7] *Re Sharp's Settlement Trusts*, [1972] 3 All E.R. 151; [1973] Ch. 331.
[8] *Re Joel's Will Trusts, supra; Re Sharp's Settlement Trusts, supra.*
[9] As provided by Trustee Act 1925, s. 31 (4).
[10] And coming into force after 31 December, 1925: Trustee Act 1925, s. 31 (5).
[11] Family Law Reform Act 1969, s. 1 (4) and Sched. 3, para. 5.

be treated as made on or after that date by reason only that the will is confirmed by a codicil executed on or after that date.[12]

c Power of the court

Although it will now seldom be necessary to invoke it, the court has an inherent jurisdiction to allow maintenance out of an infant's property. As Lord Redesdale explained in *Wellesley* v. *Wellesley*[13] the court has an unquestionable jurisdiction "with respect to the income of the property, to take care of it for the benefit of the children, to apply it for the benefit of the children, as far as it may be beneficial for them that it should be so applied, and to accumulate any surplus, if any surplus there should be". Although income will primarily be used, in exceptional circumstances the court will even resort to capital for maintenance:[14] according to Romilly M.R.[15] "it has frequently happened that this court has considered it necessary that the capital of infants should be applied for their maintenance, where there has been no other means for their support".

The court has normally applied the rule "that however large a child's fortune may be, whilst the father is of ability to maintain the child, he must perform his duty, and no part of the child's fortune is to be applied for that purpose".[16] The rule, however, is not strictly applied, and the surrounding circumstances, such as the means of the father, the size of the infant's fortune, and even the effect on other members of the family, have been taken into account. Thus maintenance was allowed in 1813[17] to a father with an income of £6,000 p.a., the court thinking that the father should not be expected to put down his establishment in any part to educate his children, when they had large incomes of their own. Again, where there was a gift to a class of children, some of whom were excluded under the rule in *Andrews* v. *Partington*,[18] the court allowed maintenance without regard to the father's ability, on the ground that otherwise his estate would be diminished which would be liable to operate unfairly to the excluded children.[19] It may be added that even where the father is not of ability, or dead, the means of the mother are disregarded and the court does not apply the rule stated in *Douglas* v. *Andrews*[20] to the mother.[1]

As has been mentioned, where trustees have been given a power of maintenance, the court will not normally interfere with its exercise, and even where

---

[12] Family Law Reform Act 1969, s. 1 (4) and (7) and Sched. 3, para. 1.
[13] (1828), 2 Bli. N.S. 124, at p.133, 134, H.L.
[14] *Ex parte Green* (1820), 1 Jac. & W. 253; *Ex parte Chambers* (1829), 1 Russ. & My. 577.
[15] In *Robison* v. *Killey* (1862), 30 Beav. 520, at p. 521.
[16] *Per* Langdale M.R. in *Douglas* v. *Andrews* (1849), 12 Beav. 310, at p. 311.
[17] *Jervoise* v. *Silk* (1813), Coop. G. 52.
[18] (1791), 3 Bro. C.C. 401. Under this rule membership of a class of possible beneficiaries may be closed earlier than it would normally close, with the result that afterborn persons answering the description of the class will be excluded from membership. The rule is a rule of convenience in order to expedite the distribution of estates. See Megarry and Wade, *The Law of Real Property*, 3rd Ed., pp. 237 *et seq.*, 508 *et seq.*; Morris and Leach, *The Rule against Perpetuities*, 2nd Ed., pp. 110 *et seq.* The rule was recently described in *Re Henderson's Trusts*, [1969] 3 All E.R. 769, C.A., by Harman L.J. as "a sacrifice . . . on the altar of early vesting" and by Karminski L.J. as "a veteran long-lived but not universally admired".
[19] *Hoste* v. *Pratt* (1798), 3 Ves. 730.
[20] *Supra.*
[1] *Haley* v. *Bannister* (1820), 4 Madd. 275; *Douglas* v. *Andrews, supra.*

they have not been given any such power, if they in fact use income[2]—or even capital[3]—for maintenance, the court will, in a proper case, allow the payment in the accounts.

Further powers of the court have already been dealt with in Chapter 10, Section 1, especially p. 297, *ante*.

7 POWER OF ADVANCEMENT[4]

a Express powers

Before 1926 an express power of advancement was frequently conferred on trustees under settlements of personalty, though since 1925 reliance is commonly placed on the statutory power hereafter discussed. In *Pilkington* v. *I.R. Comrs.*,[5] Viscount Radcliffe explained that the general purpose and effect of such a power was to enable trustees

> "in a proper case to anticipate the vesting in possession of an intended beneficiary's contingent or reversionary interest by raising money on account of his interest and paying or applying it immediately for his benefit. By so doing they released it from the trusts of the settlement and accelerated the enjoyment of his interest (though normally only with the consent of a prior tenant for life); and where the contingency upon which the vesting of the beneficiary's title depended failed to mature or there was a later defeasance or, in some cases, a great shrinkage in the value of the remaining trust funds, the trusts as declared by the settlement were materially varied through the operation of the power of advancement".

The exact scope of a power of advancement, of course, depends upon the words of the particular clause under consideration. "Advancement" is itself "a word appropriate to an early period of life"[6] and means the establishment in life of the beneficiary who was the object of the power or at any rate some step that would contribute to the furtherance of his establishment. To avoid uncertainties, other words were commonly inserted, such a phrase as "or otherwise for his benefit" being of the widest import.[7] Viscount Radcliffe has explained[8] the combined phrases "advancement and benefit" as meaning "any use of the money which will improve the material situation of the beneficiary", and it has been held to authorise, for instance, a payment for the purpose of discharging the beneficiary's debts,[9] a payment made to the beneficiary's husband, on his personal security, for the purpose of setting him up in trade,[6] payments for the maintenance and education of a beneficiary,[10] and, of particular importance in modern conditions, an advancement made in order to avoid estate duty, although the beneficiary may not require it at the time it is made for any special

---

[2] *Brown* v. *Smith* (1878), 10 Ch.D. 377, C.A. As to charging past maintenance on *corpus* see *Re Hambrough's Estate*, [1909] 2 Ch. 620; *Re Badger*, [1913] 1 Ch. 385, C.A.
[3] *Prince* v. *Hine* (1859), 26 Beav. 634; *Worthington* v. *M'Craer* (1856), 23 Beav. 81.
[4] See, generally, (1958), 22 Con. 413 (D. W. M. Waters).
[5] [1962] 3 All E.R. 622, at p. 627; [1964] A.C. 612, at p. 633, H.L.
[6] *Re Kershaw's Trusts* (1868), L.R. 6 Eq. 322.
[7] *Lowther* v. *Bentinck* (1874), L.R. 19 Eq. 166; *Pilkington* v. *I.R. Comrs.*, [1962] 3 All E.R. 622; [1964] A.C. 612, H.L. at pp. 627; 633, H.L.
[8] In *Pilkington* v. *I.R. Comrs.*, *supra*, at pp. 628; 635, H.L.
[9] *Lowther* v. *Bentinck*, *supra*.
[10] *Re Breeds' Will* (1875), 1 Ch.D. 226; *Re Garrett*, [1934] Ch. 477; [1934] All E.R. Rep. 128.

purpose.[11] However wide the power, the trustees must, of course, be satisfied that the proposed exercise will benefit the beneficiary.[12] The courts, however, do not take too narrow a view of what represents a benefit. At any rate in the case of a wealthy beneficiary who regards himself as being under a moral obligation to make charitable donations, it may be for his benefit for the trustees to raise capital and pay it over to a charity in order to relieve him of his moral obligation. The trustees cannot, however, do this against the beneficiary's will, for it is of the essence of the matter that the beneficiary himself should recognise the moral obligation.[13]

Three final points may be added. First, if the power is given only during infancy, and the beneficiary has attained 18,[14] or for a limited purpose which can no longer be effected,[15] the power ceases to be exercisable, and the trustees will, of course, be personally liable to refund if they exercise the power improperly.[16] Secondly, where a beneficiary has an interest which will determine if he does any act whereby if the income were payable to him he would be deprived of the right to receive the same, it will not normally be forfeited if that beneficiary consents to the exercise of a power of advancement—whether express or statutory.[17] This is expressly provided for in the statutory protective trusts under section 33 of the Trustee Act 1925. Thirdly, on basic equitable principles the exercise of the power must be *bona fide*, and, accordingly, it was held to be a breach of trust in *Molyneux* v. *Fletcher*[18] where trustees advanced money to a beneficiary on the understanding that the money advanced would be used to repay a debt owed to one of the trustees by the beneficiary's husband.

b   The statutory power contained in section 32 of the Trustee Act 1925

This is a new provision, subsection (1) of which provides as follows—

"Trustees may at any time or times pay or apply any capital money subject to a trust, for the advancement or benefit, in such manner as they may, in their absolute discretion, think fit, of any person entitled to the capital of the trust property or of any share thereof, whether absolutely or contingently on his attaining any specified age or on the occurrence of any other event, or subject to a gift over on his death under any specified age or on the occurrence of any other event, and whether in possession or in remainder or reversion, and such payment or application may be made notwithstanding that the interest of such person is liable to be defeated by the exercise of a power of appointment or revocation, or to be diminished by the increase of the class to which he belongs."

It adopts without qualification the accustomed wording "for the advancement or benefit, in such manner as they may, in their absolute discretion, think fit" which, as we have seen in connection with express powers, is of the widest import.

---

[11] *Re Collard's Will Trusts*, [1961] 1 All E.R. 821; [1961] Ch. 293; *Pilkington* v. *I.R. Comrs.*, *supra* (both decisions on the statutory power).

[12] *Re Moxon's Will Trusts*, *supra* (on the statutory power); *Re Pauling's Settlement Trusts* [1963] 3 All E.R. 1; [1964] Ch. 303, C.A. Cf. *Molyneux* v. *Fletcher*, [1898] 1 Q.B. 648.

[13] *Re Clore's Settlement Trusts*, [1966] 2 All E.R. 272.

[14] *Clarke* v. *Hogg* (1871), 19 W.R. 617; Family Law Reform Act 1969, s. 1.

[15] *Re Ward's Trusts* (1872), 7 Ch. App. 727.   [16] *Simpson* v. *Brown* (1864), 11 L.T. 593.

[17] *Re Shaw's Settlement Trusts*, [1951] 1 All E.R. 656; [1951] Ch. 833; *Re Rees' Will Trusts*, [1954] 1 All E.R. 7; [1954] Ch. 202.

[18] [1898] 1 Q.B. 648.

It applies to contingent interests even where there is a double contingency such as surviving the life interest and attaining a specified age.[19] The section does not apply to trusts constituted or created before 1926,[20] and for this purpose trusts contained in a will executed before 1926 where the testator died after 1925,[1] and trusts declared by an appointment made after 1925 executing a general power of appointment created before 1926[2] have been treated as being constituted or created after 1925. However, where a special power was created before 1926, trusts created by an appointment made after 1925 were regarded as constituted by the original instrument and section 32 accordingly was held not to apply.[3] Like section 31, a settlor may incorporate this section with variations,[4] or exclude it altogether by a contrary intention, express or implied.[5]

Until recently it was arguable that an advancement of money for a beneficiary could not be made by trustees by way of a settlement of capital when the powers and discretions in the new trust were not contemplated in the original trust instrument. The situation arose in several cases where the beneficiary had no immediate need of the money, and the creation of a sub-trust was designed to avoid estate duty. The House of Lords has now decided[6] that such a scheme is within the scope of section 32, pointing out that the propriety of requiring a settlement of moneys found for advancement was recognised as long ago as 1871 in *Roper-Curzon* v. *Roper-Curzon*[7] and that it can make no difference whether trustees require resettlement as a condition of advancement, or themselves appoint new trusts, appropriating certain investments to the new trusts, of which they may also be the trustees.[8] Care must be taken however to bear in mind the operation of the rule against perpetuities, particularly where the trustees have to appoint new trusts themselves because the beneficiary being advanced is an infant and therefore incapable of making a settlement. In such case as regards the rule against perpetuities there is an effective analogy between powers of advancement and special powers of appointment, and failure to realise this meant, in *Re Abrahams' Will Trusts*,[9] that many of the declared trusts were void for perpetuity, so that the character of the settlement was wholly altered. It followed that the trustees had never addressed their minds to the question whether the settlement, as modified by the rule against perpetuities, was "for the advancement or benefit" of the beneficiary, as required by section 32. There had accordingly never been a valid exercise by the trustees of the power of advancement and the purported

---

[19] *Re Garrett*, [1934] Ch. 477; [1934] All E.R. Rep. 128.
[20] Trustee Act 1925, s. 32 (3). Cf. the different wording under Trustee Act 1925, s. 31 (5).
[1] *Re Darby* (1943), 59 T.L.R. 418; *Re Taylor's Will Trusts* (1950), 66 T.L.R. (Pt. 2) 507.
[2] *Re Bransbury's Will Trusts*, [1954] 1 All E.R. 605.
[3] *Re Batty*, [1952] 1 All E.R. 425; [1952] Ch. 280; *Re Leigh's Marriage Settlement*, [1952] 2 All E.R. 57.
[4] E.g. by altering or omitting proviso (a), *infra*.
[5] Trustee Act 1925, s. 69 (2); *Re Rees' Will Trusts*, [1954] 1 All E.R. 7; [1954] Ch. 202; I.R. Comrs. v. *Bernstein*, [1961] 1 All E.R. 320; [1961] Ch. 399, C.A.; *Re Evans' Settlement*, [1967] 3 All E.R. 343.
[6] *Pilkington* v. *I.R. Comrs.*, *supra*, cf. *Re Wills' Will Trusts*, [1958] 2 All E.R. 472; [1959] Ch. 1.
[7] *Supra*.
[8] Cf. *Re Collard's Will Trusts*, *supra*. As regards the rule against perpetuities there is an effective analogy between powers of advancement and special powers of appointment.
[9] [1967] 2 All E.R. 1175; [1969] 1 Ch. 463. See also *Pilkington* v. *I.R. Comrs.* per Upjohn L.J. in C.A. at [1961] 2 All E.R. at pp. 340, 341; [1961] Ch. at pp. 488, 489 and per Lord Radcliffe in H.L. at [1962] 3 All E.R. at pp. 631, 632; [1964] A.C. at pp. 641, 642.

settlement by the trustees was ineffective. It was observed in *Re Abrahams'*
Will Trusts,[10] however, that this drastic result would not necessarily follow where
the rule against perpetuities operated to invalidate only a comparatively small
part of the settlement.

By the proviso to subsection (1) the statutory power is subject to certain
important restrictions, namely,

"(a) the money so paid or applied for the advancement or benefit of any person
shall not exceed altogether in amount one-half of the presumptive or vested
share or interest of that person in the trust property; and

(b) if that person is or becomes absolutely and indefeasibly entitled to a share in the
trust property the money so paid or applied shall be brought into account as
part of such share; and

(c) no such payment or application shall be made so as to prejudice any person
entitled to any prior life or other interest, whether vested or contingent, in the
money paid or applied unless such person is in existence and of full age and
consents in writing to such payment or application."

Under proviso (c) it has been held that the objects of a discretionary trust are
not persons whose consent to the exercise of the power is required, even where
these discretionary trusts have come into operation.[11]   But if there is a person
whose consent is required, the court has not got power to dispense with it.[12]

Finally, it is important to observe that the operation of the statutory power
is restricted by subsection (2), which provides:

"This section applies only where the trust property consists of money or securities
or of property held upon trust for sale calling in and conversion, and such money or
securities, or the proceeds of such sale calling in and conversion are not by statute[13] or
in equity[14] considered as land, or applicable as capital money for the purposes of the
Settled Land Act, 1925."

It has been held[15] that the final phrase of this subsection does not prevent the
section from applying to the proceeds of sale of land held upon trust for sale,
although by virtue of section 28 of the Law of Property Act, 1925, such proceeds
may be applied as capital money under the Settled Land Act 1925.

c   Power of the court

The court may, in exceptional circumstances, apply capital for the maintenance or advancement of an infant,[16] or allow such payment made by the trustee
without any express power to do so,[17] and may also exercise its statutory
jurisdiction for this purpose under section 53 of the Trustee Act 1925.[18]

---

[10] *Supra.*
[11] *Re Harris' Settlement* (1940), 162 L.T. 358; *Re Beckett's Settlement*, [1940] Ch. 279.
[12] *Re Forster's Settlement*, [1942] 1 All E.R. 180; [1942] Ch. 199. *Quære*, if an application
were made under Trustee Act 1925, s. 57.
[13] E.g. Settled Land Act 1925, s. 75 (5).
[14] *Semble*, under the equitable doctrine of conversion, discussed in Chapter 16, *post.*
[15] *Re Stimpson's Trusts*, [1931] 2 Ch. 77; [1931] All E.R. Rep. 809.
[16] E.g. to pay the expenses of emigration—*Re Mary England* (1830), 1 Russ. & My. 499;
Clay v. *Pennington* (1837), 8 Sim. 359.
[17] *Worthington* v. *M'Craer* (1856), 23 Beav. 81.
[18] Discussed in Chapter 10, Section 1b, p. 297, *ante.*

8. RIGHT TO REIMBURSEMENT FOR COSTS AND EXPENSES

a Reimbursement out of the trust estate

The right of each trustee to be indemnified out of the trust property has always been recognised. Lord Eldon explained, in *Worrall* v. *Harford*,[19] "It is in the nature of the office of a trustee, whether expressed in the instrument, or not, that the trust property[20] shall reimburse him all the charges and expenses incurred in the execution of the trust. That is implied in every such deed". The position has now been made statutory, by section 30(2) of the Trustee Act 1925,[1] which provides—

"A trustee may reimburse himself or pay or discharge out of the trust premises all expenses incurred in or about the execution of the trusts or powers."

The right to reimbursement naturally only applies to expenses which are properly incurred,[2] which have included, for instance, calls on shares which the trustee has been obliged to pay,[3] damages and costs awarded to a third party in an action against the trustee as legal owner of the trust property,[4] and liabilities incurred in carrying on a business, where authorised to do so by the trust instrument.[5] Where trustees are authorised to carry on a business by will,[6] the right of trustees to an indemnity, though good as against the beneficiaries, will not prevail against the testator's creditors at the date of death, unless they have assented to the business being carried on, and such assent will not be inferred from their merely standing by with knowledge that the business was being carried on and abstaining from interfering.[7] If the trustees are only authorised to use certain assets in the business, their indemnity will be against these assets only.[8] Trustees may, if they wish, pay claims which are statute-barred, and will be entitled to the usual indemnity in respect thereof, notwithstanding that the beneficiaries do not wish the claim to be paid.[9]

---

[19] (1802), 8 Ves. 4, 8; *Walters* v. *Woodbridge* (1878), 7 Ch.D. 504, C.A.; *Re Whitley*, [1962] 3 All E.R. 45.

[20] *Re Earl of Winchilsea's Policy Trusts* (1888), 39 Ch.D. 168.

[1] Replacing Trustee Act 1893, s. 24, which in turn replaced the Law of Property Amendment Act 1859, s. 31 (Lord St. Leonards' Act).

[2] *Leedham* v. *Chawner* (1858), 4 K. & J. 458; *Ecclesiastical Commissioners* v. *Pinney*, [1900] 2 Ch. 736, C.A.; *Re Grimthorpe's Will Trusts*, [1958] 1 All E.R. 765; [1958] Ch. 615.

[3] *Re National Financial Company* (1868), 3 Ch. App. 791; *James* v. *May* (1873), L.R. 6 H.L. 328.

[4] *Benett* v. *Wyndham* (1862), 4 De G.F. & J. 259; *Re Raybould*, [1900] 1 Ch. 199.

[5] *Re Evans* (1887), 34 Ch.D. 597, C.A.; *Dowse* v. *Gorton*, [1891] A.C. 190, H.L.; *Re Oxley*, [1914] 1 Ch. 604, C.A. Under a will, the personal representatives are in any event impliedly authorised to carry on the business for the purpose of winding it up so soon as reasonably possible.

[6] In general, the rules apply equally whether the trust is created *inter vivos* or by will, though most of the cases are on wills—*Re Johnson* (1880), 15 Ch.D. 548.

[7] *Dowse* v. *Gorton, supra; Re Oxley, supra.*

[8] *Re Johnson, supra. Cf. Re Webb* (1890), 63 L.T. 545; *Strickland* v. *Symons* (1884), 26 Ch.D. 245, C.A.

[9] *Budgett* v. *Budgett*, [1895] 1 Ch. 202; contrast the position of executors—*Re Wenham*, [1892] 3 Ch. 59.

As between the beneficiaries, the trustees' costs and expenses are normally payable out of capital,[10] but so far as the trustees are concerned their right to "indemnity against all costs and expenses properly incurred by them in the execution of the trust is a first charge on all the trust property, both income and corpus".[11] This indemnity, which thus gives the trustees a lien on the trust property, takes priority to the claims both of beneficiaries and third parties,[12] and is unaffected by the fact that a beneficiary has assigned his equitable interest to a stranger.[13] Trustees who have such a lien may at any time apply to the court to enforce it; they are not bound to wait until the trust property happens to be turned into money.[14] Exceptionally, however, the court may refuse to enforce the lien, where to do so would destroy the trusts altogether, though in such case the court has held the trustees entitled to the possession of the title deeds, and prohibited any disposition of the trust property without discharging the trustees' lien.[15] According to *Gordon* v. *Trail*,[16] it would seem that the claim of trustees does not extend to interest, even where they have advanced moneys to meet some liability when trust moneys were not available. It is submitted, however, that the courts do not follow this rule strictly, particularly where the advance benefits the trust estate, or where it is used to pay a debt carrying interest.[17] In any case where the trustees have committed a breach of trust, they can only claim their indemnity after they have first made good to the trust estate the loss caused by the breach of trust.[18] As we shall see,[19] where the trustee mixes his own moneys and trust moneys, the trust has a first and paramount charge over the mixed fund, and, similarly, where a trustee expends his own money in the purchase or improvement of trust property, the claim of the trustee for indemnity is subject to the prior claim of the beneficiaries under the trust.[20]

In some cases the above principles have been extended so as to give the trustee an indemnity and a lien on the trust property where the trustee has expended his own money in the preservation of the trust property, as by paying the premiums on an insurance policy.[1] The court in one case even allowed a partial indemnity where the trustee, under the impression that he would be repaid out of the estate, had *bona fide* used his own moneys together with trust moneys in rebuilding the mansion house, although this was a breach of trust which the court considered it would have had no jurisdiction to authorise had it been asked to do so.[2] The indemnity was, however, limited to the amount

---

[10] *Carter* v. *Sebright* (1859), 26 Beav. 374.
[11] *Per* Selbourne L.C. in *Stott* v. *Milne* (1884), 25 Ch.D. 710, at p. 715, C.A.; *Re Exhall Coal Co.* (1866), 35 Beav. 449.
[12] *Re Knapman* (1881), 18 Ch.D. 300, C.A.; *Dodds* v. *Tuke* (1884), 25 Ch.D. 617; *Re Turner*, [1907] 2 Ch. 126, C.A.
[13] *Re Knapman, supra.*
[14] *Re Pumfrey* (1882), 22 Ch.D. 255.
[15] *Darke* v. *Williamson* (1858), 25 Beav. 622.
[16] (1820), 8 Price 416.
[17] *Re Beulah Park Estate* (1872), L.R. 15 Eq. 43; *Finch* v. *Pescott* (1874), L.R. 17 Eq. 554.
[18] *McEwan* v. *Crombie* (1883), 25 Ch.D. 175; cf. *Re Knott* (1887), 56 L.J. Ch. 318.
[19] See Chapter 15, Section 2b, p. 462, *post.*
[20] *Re Pumfrey* (1882), 22 Ch.D. 255.
[1] *Re Leslie* (1883), 23 Ch.D. 552; *Re Smith's Estate*, [1937] Ch. 636.
[2] *Jesse* v. *Lloyd* (1883), 48 L.T. 656.

which happened to be in court,[3] this being about half the sum advanced and clearly less than the amount by which the estate had benefited. Again, in *Rowley* v. *Ginnever*,[4] a constructive trustee of property, who expended money in improving what he *bona fide* believed to be his own property, was held to be entitled to be recouped his expenditure to the extent of the improved value.

Agents, such as solicitors, employed by the trustees, even though described as solicitors to the trust, are in law retained by the trustees and therefore have no direct claim against the trust estate. Nevertheless they may be entitled to be subrogated to the rights of the trustees against the estate,[5] though they cannot be in a better position than the trustees, and if, for instance, the trustees have committed a breach of trust, this must first be made good. Where trustees have properly carried on a business, it is clear that creditors of the business are similarly subrogated to the trustees' rights, subject to the qualification mentioned. Another instance is that if the trustees' indemnity is limited to certain assets, the creditors' right will be limited in a similar way.[6] Each trustee has a separate right of indemnity, which will not necessarily be affected by the fact that another trustee has committed a breach of trust. Since a creditor may sue the trustee with a subsisting indemnity, it follows that he does not lose his right of subrogation by reason of the fact that one of two or more trustees is a defaulter.[7]

b Personal liability of *cestui que trust* to indemnify trustees

It is not every *cestui que trust* who is liable to indemnify his trustee.[8] There seem to be only two cases: first, where there is a simple trust in favour of a beneficiary, *sui iuris*, solely and absolutely entitled in equity. As explained in *Hardoon* v. *Belilios*,[9] "where the only *cestui que trust* is a person *sui iuris*, the right of the trustee to indemnity by him against liabilities incurred by the trustee by his retention of the trust property has never been limited to the trust property; it extends further, and imposes upon the *cestui que trust* a personal obligation enforceable in equity to indemnify his trustee". Secondly, where the settlor is also a beneficiary, Jessel M.R. stated in *Jervis* v. *Wolferstan*,[10] "I take it to be a general rule that where persons accept a trust at the request of another, and that other is a *cestui que trust*, he is personally liable to indemnify the trustees for any loss accruing in the due execution of the trust". In any case where a *cestui que trust* is personally liable to indemnify his trustee, his liability is not terminated by an assignment of his beneficial interest.[11]

It may be added that, unless the rules provide to the contrary, members of a

---

[3] A somewhat haphazard solution on no clear principle.
[4] [1897] 2 Ch. 503.
[5] *Staniar* v. *Evans* (1886), 34 Ch.D. 470; cf. *Re Blundell* (1888), 40 Ch.D. 370; *Re Raybould*, [1900] 1 Ch. 199.
[6] *Re Johnson* (1880), 15 Ch.D. 548; *Re Evans* (1887), 34 Ch.D. 597, C.A.; *Re Blundell*, supra.
[7] *Re Frith*, [1902] 1 Ch. 342.
[8] See, however, the views of Wigram V.C. in *Phene* v. *Gillan* (1845), 5 Hare 1; *Parsons* v. *Spooner* (1846), 5 Hare 102.
[9] [1901] A.C. 118, at p. 124, P.C.
[10] (1874), L.R. 18 Eq. 18, at p. 24; *Fraser* v. *Murdoch* (1881), 6 App. Cas. 855, H.L.; *Hobbs* v. *Wayet* (1887), 36 Ch.D. 256.
[11] *Matthews* v. *Ruggles-Brise*, [1911] 1 Ch. 194.

club are assumed not to be under any liability beyond their subscriptions, and are under no obligation to indemnify trustees of club property.[12]

c Costs of legal proceedings

It is convenient to make separate mention of costs, although the above rules apply equally to them, it being expressly provided[13] that on a taxation of trustee's costs, no costs are to be disallowed except in so far as they should not, in accordance with the duty of the trustee as such, have been incurred or paid, and should for that reason be borne by him personally. In accordance with the above principles a trustee is entitled to an indemnity for his costs where he properly brings or defends an action on behalf of the trust whether successfully or unsuccessfully, and it does not matter that in the action he is incidentally defending himself against charges made against him personally in relation to his administration of the trust provided it is for the benefit of the trust.[14] In practice, the prudent course is for the trustees to ask for the directions of the court before taking part in any legal proceedings:[15] if they are given leave to sue or defend, they will then be entitled to their costs in any event. If, however, they go ahead without obtaining such leave, and the proceedings are unsuccessful, it will be for the trustees to establish that the costs so incurred were properly incurred.[16] The advice of counsel, though an important factor, is not conclusive on this point.[17] Of course, even if it is proper to bring or defend the proceedings, excessive or unnecessary costs therein will be disallowed.[18] And where the costs are due to breach of trust or misconduct by the trustees, the court has a discretion which it will usually exercise against the trustees.[19] It was said in *Carroll* v. *Graham*[20] that trustees holding a merely neutral position, and not intending to argue, ought not to appear by separate counsel on appeal. In practice, however, this view has seldom been followed,[1] and the contrary view seems to have prevailed, that trustees ought to appear in the Court of Appeal, because it is necessary for them to see that the order which relates to the administration of the estate is properly carried out.[2] It may be added that the right of a trustee to costs extends to the costs of successfully defending proceedings brought against him for breach of trust. This right is only lost by misconduct. As Ungoed-Thomas J. explained in *Re Spurling's Will Trusts*,[3] "if costs of successfully defending claims to make good to a trust fund for alleged breach of trust were excluded, it would drive a coach and four through the very

---

[12] *Wise* v. *Perpetual Trustee Company Ltd.*, [1903] A.C. 139, P.C.
[13] R.S.C., O. 62, r. 31.
[14] *Walters* v. *Woodbridge* (1878), 7 Ch.D. 504, C.A.; *Re Dunn*, [1904] 1 Ch. 648.
[15] *Re Beddoe*, [1893] 1 Ch. 547, C.A.; *Chettiar* v. *Chettiar*, [1962] 2 All E.R. 238, P.C.
[16] *Re Beddoe, supra; Re Yorke*, [1911] 1 Ch. 370.
[17] *Stott* v. *Milne* (1884), 23 Ch.D. 710, C.A.; *Re Beddoe, supra*.
[18] *Re England's Settlement Trusts*, [1918] 1 Ch. 24; *Re Robertson*, [1949] 1 All E.R. 1042; *Re Whitley*, [1962] 3 All E.R. 45.
[19] *Easton* v. *Landor* (1892), 62 L.J. Ch. 164, C.A.; *Re Knox's Trusts*, [1895] 2 Ch. 483, C.A.; *Re Chapman* (1894), 72 L.T. 66, C.A.
[20] [1905] 1 Ch. 478, C.A.
[1] *Catterson* v. *Clark* (1906), 95 L.T. 42, C.A.; contrast *Re Barry's Trusts*, [1906] 2 Ch. 358, C.A.
[2] *Re Stuart*, [1940] 4 All E.R. 80, C.A.; *Chettiar* v. *Chettiar, supra*, P.C.
[3] [1966] 1 All E.R. 745, 758.

raison d'être which Sir George Jessel M.R. invoked[4] for the principle which he lays down; namely, the safety of trustees, and the need to encourage persons to act as such by protecting them 'if they have done their duty or even if they have committed an innocent breach of trust'". To this last proposition *Re Dargie*,[5] which unfortunately does not appear to have been cited to the court in *Re Spurling's Will Trusts*,[6] suggests one qualification, namely that trustees are not necessarily entitled to costs on an indemnity basis in hostile litigation designed to define and secure the personal rights of the trustees as individuals.

Difficulty has been felt in some cases[7] in allowing trustees their costs where the court has declared the settlement void as against a trustee in bankruptcy, or void generally on the ground of undue influence or otherwise. In the more recent cases, however, the court seems to have regarded the costs as being within its discretion, and has allowed costs to trustees who have acted *bona fide*.[8]

9 RIGHT TO A DISCHARGE ON TERMINATION OF TRUSTS

In general, a trustee cannot demand a release by deed from the *cestuis que trust* on handing over the trust property in accordance with the terms of the trust.[9] As Kindersley V.C. explained in *King* v. *Mullins*,[10] "in the case of a declared trust; where the trust is apparent on the face of a deed; the fund clear; the trust clearly defined; and the trustee is paying either the income or the capital of the fund; if he is paying it in strict accordance with the trusts, he has no right to require a release under seal". He has, however, a right to a receipt for the funds paid over, and an acknowledgment that the accounts are settled.[11] But if he is a trustee of two separate trusts, he cannot refuse to pay over funds to which a *cestui que trust* is clearly entitled under one trust by reason of some dispute in connection with the other.[12]

In some cases, however, a release may be demanded. In *King* v. *Mullins*[13] Kindersley V.C. continued, on the facts of the case before him, that where "there was no writing to indicate either what the trusts were or the amount of the trust fund; and . . . what the trustee has been asked to do is not in accordance with the tenor of the trusts" , . . . it is "not illegal in the trustee to demand a release by deed". Again, where the beneficial interest has been resettled, although the trustees of the original settlement are not entitled to a release from the trustees of the resettlement, but only an acknowledgment of

---

[4] In *Turner* v. *Hancock* (1882), 20 Ch.D. 303, at p. 305.
[5] [1953] 2 All E.R. 577; [1954] Ch. 16.
[6] *Supra.*
[7] See e.g. *Re Butterworth, Ex parte Russell* (1882), 19 Ch.D. 588, C.A.; *Dutton* v. *Thompson* (1883), 23 Ch.D. 278, C.A.
[8] *Re Holden* (1887), 20 Q.B.D. 43, D.C.; *Ideal Bedding Co. Ltd.* v. *Holland*, [1907] 2 Ch. 157; *Bullock* v. *Lloyds Bank, Ltd.*, [1954] 3 All E.R. 726; [1955] Ch. 317.
[9] *Chadwick* v. *Heatley* (1845), 2 Coll. 137; *Re Roberts' Trusts* (1869), 38 L.J. Ch. 708.
[10] (1852), 1 Drew. 308, 311, where the different position of an executor is contrasted.
[11] *Chadwick* v. *Heatley, supra; Re Heming's Trust* (1856), 3 K. & J. 40.
[12] *Price* v. *Loaden* (1856), 21 Beav. 508.
[13] *Re Cater's Trusts (No. 2)* (1858), 25 Beav. 366; *Tiger* v. *Barclays Bank, Ltd.*, [1951] 2 All E.R. 262; [1951] 2 K.B. 556 affirmed, but not on this point; [1952] 1 All E.R. 85, C.A. Cf. *Re Hoskins' Trusts* (1877), 5 Ch.D. 229; on appeal 6 Ch.D. 281, C.A.

the receipt of the money paid,[14] it has been said[15] that in such case they are entitled to a release from the *cestui que trust* to whom the money was due.

10 PAYMENT INTO COURT

The statutory power[16] for trustees, or the majority of them, to pay trust funds into court is one which it is now seldom advisable for them to adopt, as they are likely to be made liable for at least the costs of payment out if they neglect some less expensive or more convenient procedure, such as advertising for claimants under section 27,[17] or raising a question for the decision of the court by means of an originating summons.[18] Moreover, "a trustee cannot pay into court merely to get rid of a trust he has undertaken to perform",[19] and the fact that he has been so advised by counsel will not assist him.[19]

Subject to what has been said, trustees may be justified in paying into court where there is a *bona fide* doubt as to whom they should pay,[20] or where they cannot get a valid discharge from the *cestuis que trust*, by reason of their incapacity, or otherwise.[1] But trustees have been held liable to pay costs where payment in was made when the trustees knew that the person claiming the fund was on his way from Australia to establish his claim,[2] and would be held liable if they paid in instead of paying a beneficiary entitled in default of appointment, satisfactory evidence having been produced that no appointment had been made.[3]

11 APPLICATIONS TO THE COURT

Trustees, and any person claiming to be interested in the relief sought as *cestui que trust*, may apply to the court by means of an originating summons for directions and for the determination, without an administration of the trust, of any question arising in the administration of the trust.[4] This "is exactly equivalent to the old practice of commencing an administration suit, raising the

---

[14] *Supra.*
[15] *Re Cater's Trusts (No. 2), supra.*
[16] Trustee Act 1925, s. 63 (as amended by the Administration of Justice Act 1965, s. 36 and Sched. 3), replacing Trustee Act 1893, s. 42, which replaced Trustees Relief Act 1847, s. 1. See generally, (1968), 84 L.Q.R. 64 (A. J. Hawkins).
[17] Discussed in Chapter 10, Section 5 b, p. 329, *ante.*
[18] *Re Giles* (1886), 55 L.J. Ch. 695.
[19] *Per* Romilly M.R. in *Re Knight's Trusts* (1859), 27 Beav. 45, 49.
[20] *Re Maclean's Trusts* (1874), L.R. 19 Eq. 274; *Hockey* v. *Western*, [1898] 1 Ch. 350, C.A.; *Re Davies* (1914), 59 Sol. Jo. 234.
[1] *Re Parker's Will* (1888), 39 Ch.D. 303 (more fully reported in 58 L.J. Ch. 23), C.A.; *Re Salomons* [1920] 1 Ch. 290. Cf. Administration of Estates Act 1925, s. 42.
[2] *Re Elliott's Trusts* (1873), L.R. 15 Eq. 194.
[3] *Re Cull's Trusts* (1875), L.R. 20 Eq. 561 (though trustees were here allowed costs as it was the first case of its kind and the trustees had been advised by counsel); see also *Re Foligno's Mortgage* (1863), 32 Beav. 131; *Re Leake's Trusts* (1863), 32 Beav. 135.
[4] R.S.C., O. 85, r. 2 and O. 5, rr. 1 and 4. A summons may be brought, e.g. for the construction of the trust instrument; as to whether the trustees should bring or defend an action (*Re Moritz*, [1959] 3 All E.R. 767; [1960] Ch. 251; *Re Eaton*, [1964] 3 All E.R. 229 n.); as to whether a fund may be distributed on the basis that a person is dead (*Re Newson-Smith's Settlement*, [1962] 3 All E.R. 963 n.) or a woman past child-bearing (*Re Westminster Bank Ltd.'s Declaration of Trust*, [1963] 2 All E.R. 400 n.).

particular point by the pleadings, getting an inquiry or direction upon that point, and then staying further proceedings in the suit".[5] The procedure is simpler but the jurisdiction of the court has not been enlarged.[6] It is also possible to apply by originating summons for the administration of the trust.[7] The court, however, is not bound to make an administration order if the questions between the parties can be properly determined without it,[8] and in fact will only undertake the administration of a trust as a last resort. A trustee may have to pay the costs of the summons personally if he does not make out his case for administration by the court, and the court holds the view that some other process would have dealt with the difficulty more satisfactorily.[9]

It should be observed that a settlor[10] or testator cannot deprive a beneficiary of his right to go to the court, at any rate on questions of law. The reasons for this rule were explained by Danckwerts J. in *Re Wynn's Will Trusts*[11] where he said,[12] "a provision which refers the determination of all questions and matters of doubt arising in the execution of the trusts of a will to the trustees, and which attempts to make such determination conclusive and binding upon all persons interested under the will, is void and of no effect; because it is both repugnant to the benefits which are conferred by the will upon the beneficiaries; and also because it is contrary to public policy as being an attempt to oust the jurisdiction of the court to construe the will and control the construction and administration of a testator's will and estate". It is submitted that the rule applies to invalidate not only wide general clauses such as that mentioned by the judge, but any clause which purports to give trustees power to decide on a question of law, as opposed to one which gives trustees power to decide on a question of fact, provided in this last case that the state of affairs on which the trustees have to form their opinion is sufficiently defined. Thus, on the one hand, in *Re Raven*[13] a provision that in case of doubt the trustees should decide the identity of the institution intended to benefit was held to be void, while, on the other hand, in *Re Coxen*[14] a gift over "if, in the opinion of my trustees, she shall have ceased permanently to reside therein" was held to be validly made dependent on the decision of the trustees, who were described as "judges of fact for this purpose". A similar distinction is drawn where contracting parties seek to oust the jurisdiction of the court.[15] The converse of this is that a private person cannot impose on a judge a jurisdiction or duty to adjudicate by providing for instance, for a power of revocation "with the consent of a judge of the Chancery Division."[16]

---

[5] *Per* Fry L.J. in *Re Medland* (1889), 41 Ch.D. 476, 492, C.A.

[6] *Re King*, [1907] 1 Ch. 72.

[7] R.S.C., O. 5, r. 1 and assumed in O. 85. As to the effect of an order on a trustee's powers, see (1968), 84 L.Q.R. 64 (A. J. Hawkins).

[8] R.S.C., O. 85, r. 5.

[9] See *Re Wilson* (1885), 28 Ch.D. 457; *Re Blake* (1885), 29 Ch.D. 913, C.A.

[10] The cases concern wills but the same principles would seem applicable in *inter vivos* trusts.

[11] [1952] 1 All E.R. 341; [1952] Ch. 271.

[12] At p. 346; 278, 279.

[13] [1915] 1 Ch. 673; [1914–15] All E.R. Rep. 353; *Re Wynn's Will Trusts, supra*.

[14] [1948] 2 All E.R. 492; [1948] Ch. 747; *Re Jones*, [1953] 1 All E.R. 357; [1953] Ch. 125 and see *Dundee General Hospitals Board of Management* v. *Walker*, [1952] 1 All E.R. 896, H.L.

[15] See *Re Davstone Estates, Ltd.'s Leases*, [1969] 2 All E.R. 849, and cases there cited.

[16] *Re Hooker's Settlement*, [1954] 3 All E.R. 321; [1955] Ch. 55.

Some further points should be observed in relation to trustees. On the one hand wherever trustees have a discretionary power and are in doubt how, in the relevant circumstances, they ought to exercise it, they can go to the court and obtain directions as to what is the proper thing for them to do.[17] The court will not, however, accept from trustees the surrender for the future of a discretion which involves considering from time to time changing circumstances. It will not relieve the trustees of their obligation to apply their minds to the problem and, if they cannot themselves arrive at a satisfactory answer, to inform the court of the relevant circumstances, and seek the court's direction from time to time.[18]

A quite different point is whether trustees should initiate an appeal from a decision of the court. Contrasting views were expressed in *Re Londonderry's Settlement*[19] where Harman L.J. said[20] "Trustees seeking the protection of the court are protected by the court's order and it is not for them to appeal." In the same case, however, Salmon L.J. stated[21]: "In my view the trustees were fully justified in bringing this appeal. Indeed it was their duty to bring it since they believed rightly that an appeal was essential for the protection of the general body of beneficiaries." It is submitted that trustees should not normally appeal, but that they have a discretionary power to do so which they may exercise in exceptional circumstances. It will only be very rarely, however, that they will be justified in bringing an appeal.

12 CONTROL OF TRUSTEES' POWERS

So far as a trustee's duties are concerned, he is under an obligation to carry them out, and if he fails to do so will be liable for breach of trust. In relation to the exercise of a discretionary power, however, his obligation is limited to a duty to consider from time to time whether he should exercise it, and in particular he must consider a request by a person within the ambit of a power for it to be exercised in his favour.[1] A trustee who considers whether or not to exercise a power and acts *bona fide* is not likely to have his decision upset.

a Control by beneficiaries

As we have seen,[2] all the beneficiaries, being *sui iuris*, can together terminate the trusts. They cannot however, so long as the trust continues, control the trustees in the *bona fide* exercise of their powers and discretions under the trust. The point has arisen, *inter alia*, in connection with the appointment of new trustees, and in one such case, *Re Brockbank*,[3] Vaisey J. observed, "If the court, as a matter of practice and principle, refuses to interfere with the legal power to

---

[17] *Talbot* v. *Talbot*, [1967] 2 All E.R. 920; [1968] Ch. 1, C.A.
[18] *Re Allen-Meyrick's Will Trusts*, [1966] 1 All E.R. 740.
[19] [1964] 3 All E.R. 855; [1965] Ch. 918, C.A.
[20] At pp. 858; 930.
[21] At pp. 862; 936.
[1] *Re Manisty's Settlement*, [1973] 2 All E.R. 1203, at p. 1210.
[2] Chap. 10, Sect. 7, *supra*, p. 333.
[3] [1948] 1 All E.R. 287, at p. 289; [1948] Ch. 206, at p. 210.

appoint new trustees,[4] it is, in my judgment, *a fortiori* true that the beneficiaries cannot do so". There has been no judicial attempt to reconcile with this proposition section 26 (3)[5] of the Law of Property Act 1925, which states that, in the trusts to which it applies, trustees for sale "shall so far as practicable consult" and "shall, so far as consistent with the general interest of the trust, give effect to the wishes" of all, or a majority in value, of the persons of full age for the time being beneficially interested in possession in the rents and profits of the land until sale.

Apart from this section Romer L.J., in a case[6] where the trust fund comprised shares in a private company, stated "the beneficiaries are entitled to be treated as though they were the registered shareholders in respect of trust shares with the advantages and disadvantages (e.g., restrictions imposed by the articles) which would be involved in that position and that they could compel the trustee directors, if necessary, to use their votes as the beneficiaries—or as the court, if the beneficiaries themselves are not in agreement—should think proper, even to the extent of altering the articles of association if the trust shares carry votes sufficient for that purpose". As Upjohn J. has pointed out in *Re Whichelow*,[7] however, it is difficult to reconcile this statement with the principle upon which *Re Brockbank*[8] and the cases cited in note 4, *supra*, were decided.

b Control by the court

The jurisdiction of the court to interfere with discretionary powers of trustees against their will is limited.[9] The discretion, after all, has been given to the trustees and not to the court. It seems to be settled that where the trustees are expressly given an uncontrollable discretion by the trust instrument, the court will not interfere in the absence of *mala fides*, even though the court may be clearly of opinion that the trustees are not acting judiciously.[10] Where there is a simple or unenlarged discretion, the position is less certain. One view is that the same principle applies and accordingly the court will not interfere if the power is exercised *bona fide*, and the terms of the power are duly observed. The court could even on this view interfere on the ground of fraud, *mala fides* or improper exercise of the power, or where the trustees had failed or refused to consider whether or not to exercise a discretionary power.[11] It would be an improper exercise of a power for trustees to act "capriciously", which was explained in *Re Manisty's Settlement*[12] as meaning where they act "for reasons which . . . could be said to be irrational, perverse, or irrelevant to any sensible expectation of

---

[4] As is clearly the case—*Tempest* v. *Lord Camoys*, *supra*, C.A.; *Re Higginbottom*, [1892] ? Ch. 132.
[5] As substituted by the Law of Property (Amendment) Act 1926, s. 7 and Sched.
[6] *Re Butt*, [1952] 1 All E.R. 167, at p. 172; *sub. nom. Butt* v. *Kelson*, [1952] Ch. 197, at p. 207, C.A.—the other members of the Court of Appeal concurred in the judgment.
[7] [1953] 2 All E.R. 1558.
[8] *Supra*.
[9] See, generally, (1957), 21 Con. 55 (L. A. Sheridan); (1967) 31 Con. 117 (A. J. Hawkins).
[10] *Gisborne* v. *Gisborne* (1877), 2 App. Cas. 300, H.L.; *Tabor* v. *Brooks* (1878), 10 Ch.D. 273.
[11] *Brophy* v. *Bellamy* (1873), 8 Ch. App. 798, C.A.; *Tempest* v. *Lord Camoys* (1882), 21 Ch.D. 571; [1881–5] All E.R. Rep. 836, C.A.; *Re Burrage* (1890), 62 L.T. 752; *Re Bryant*, [1894] 1 Ch. 324.
[12] [1973] 2 All E.R. 1203, 1210; *McPhail* v. *Doulton*, [1970] 2 All E.R. 228; [1971] A.C. 424, H.L., *per* Lord Wilberforce at pp. 247; 456.

the settlor; for example, if they chose a beneficiary by height or complexion or by the irrelevant fact that he was a resident of Greater London". Some judges, however, have asserted the jurisdiction of the court to control the exercise by trustees of discretionary powers given to them, and have interfered where the trustees have "not exercised a sound discretion", as it was put by Fry J. in *Re Roper's Trusts*,[13] It is unfortunate that the Court of Appeal avoided giving judgment on this point in *Re Lofthouse*,[14] though in the course of argument Cotton L.J. observed[15]: "You have, in my mind, to show that the trustees are not exercising their discretion honestly." It is submitted that the better view is that the court has no power to override the proper exercise by trustees of their discretion, even though the court may think it injudicious, and relevant dicta in the more recent cases seem to support this proposition.[16] It should be added that trustees exercising a discretionary power are not bound to disclose to their beneficiaries the reasons actuating them in coming to a decision,[17] though if they do give reasons, their soundness can be considered by the court.[18] It follows that in practice beneficiaries will usually find it very difficult to find evidence to persuade the court to act.

---

[13] (1879), 11 Ch.D. 272; *Re Hodges*, (1878), 7 Ch.D. 754; *Klug v. Klug*, [1918] 2 Ch. 67, often cited in this context, is explicable on either view on the facts as found by the judge. These are that one trustee wished to exercise a power of advancement while the other trustee refused to do so for extraneous reasons without having exercised her discretion at all. Admittedly, however, the court referred to the court's control over trustees' discretion. See also *Re D'Epinoix's Settlement*, [1914] 1 Ch. 890.

[14] (1885) 29 Ch.D. 921, C.A.

[15] At p. 929.

[16] *Re Whichelow*, [1953] 2 All E.R. 1558; *Re Steed's Will Trusts*, [1959] 1 All E.R. 609; [1959] Ch. 354; on appeal, [1960] 1 All E.R. 487; [1960] Ch. 407, C.A.; *Re Gulbenkian's Settlement Trusts*, [1968] 3 All E.R. 785; [1970] A.C. 508, H.L. *per* Lord Reid at pp. 518; 787; *Barker v. Addiscott*, [1969] 3 All E.R. 685; *sub. nom. Re 90 Thornhill Road, Tolworth, Surrey*, [1970] Ch. 261.

[17] See p. 331, *ante.*

[18] *Re Beloved Wilkes' Charity* (1851), 3 Mac. & G. 440; *Re Londonderry's Settlement*, [1964] 3 All E.R. 855; [1965] Ch. 918, C.A.

CHAPTER 12

Breach of Trust

1 LIABILITY OF TRUSTEES TO BENEFICIARIES

a General position

Failure to comply with any of the duties of a trustee, whether by a positive act, for instance, investing the trust funds in unauthorised investments, or by a failure to act,[1] for instance, neglecting to get the trust funds transferred into his name, constitutes a breach of trust, for which the trustee will be liable. The liability extends to all loss[2] thereby caused directly or indirectly[3] to the trust estate, and, even where no loss can be shown, to any profit which has accrued to the trustee.[4] It is equally a breach of trust whether committed fraudulently by a trustee for his own purposes, or innocently, for the benefit of the trust estate and ignorant of the fact it was a breach of trust. Exceptionally, it has been said that a trustee will not be held liable for a technical breach of trust which was actually for the benefit of the *cestuis que trust*, at any rate where it is one which the court would have authorised,[5] though in practice this seems to be restricted to the use of trust funds for unauthorised maintenance or advancement. Even in such case, however, the trustee acts "under the obligation and at the peril of afterwards satisfying the Court that the deviation was necessary or beneficial",[6] and accordingly he will usually be well advised to ask the court to authorise the transaction[7] before he acts. There are innumerable cases in the reports where the court has made it clear that it believes the trustee has *bona fide*

---

[1] *Grayburn* v. *Clarkson* (1868), 3 Ch.App. 605.

[2] But see Trustee Act 1925, s. 9.

[3] *Bateman* v. *Davis* (1818), 3 Madd. 98; *Lander* v. *Weston* (1855), 3 Drew. 389.

[4] Where the breach of trust results in a profit for which the trustees have to account, this is the limit of their liability—*Vyse* v. *Foster* (1872), 8 Ch.App. 309 affd. (1874), L.R. 7 H.L. 318.

[5] *Lee* v. *Brown* (1798), 4 Ves. 362; *Brown* v. *Smith* (1878), 10 Ch.D. 377, C.A. It has been judicially observed that the great use of a trustee is to commit judicious breaches of trust—*Perrins* v. *Bellamy*, [1899] 1 Ch. 797, at p. 798, C.A., as modified in *National Trustees Company of Australasia Ltd.* v. *General Finance Company of Australasia*, [1905] A.C. 373, at pp. 375, 376, P.C.

[6] *Harrison* v. *Randall* (1852), 9 Hare 397, at p. 407, *per* Turner V.C.

[7] See Chapter 10, Section 1, *supra* pp. 275 *et seq*.

done what he thought best for the *cestuis que trust*, but nevertheless has held him liable for all the consequences of even a technical breach of trust.

It may be noted that in considering the liability of trustees it is immaterial how the trust was created, and whether it was for valuable consideration, or by the voluntary gift of the very trustees who are now being sued.[8]

b   Measure of damage in particular circumstances

Where trustees were under a duty to sell unauthorised investments, and neglected or delayed doing so, they will be liable for the difference between the price for which they could have been sold at the proper time, and the price eventually obtained on the actual sale.[9] Conversely where trustees improperly realised a proper investment, whether or not followed by an improper investment, they will be liable either to replace the investment sold, or to pay the difference in the price between the amount actually obtained and the value of such an investment at the date of the commencement of the proceedings.[10]

Where trustees have made an unauthorised investment, they are liable for all loss which is incurred when it is realised.[11] If trustees were directed to make a specific investment, and either made no investment at all or invested in something else, they will be required to provide the amount of that specified investment which could have been purchased with the trust funds at the time when the investment should have been made.[12] In such case account will be taken of any payments, such as calls on shares, that they would necessarily have made if they had properly carried out the directions as to investment.[13] Where, however, trustees were not directed to invest in one specified investment, but were given a choice, and yet made no investment at all, they are only liable to replace the trust fund, for it would be impossible to say which investment they would have chosen and for what other sum they could be held liable.[14]

In what has been said it has been assumed that there has been a loss to the trust estate: it need hardly be said that if the breach of trust has resulted in some profit accruing, this must be held by the trustees as a part of the trust property. Moreover, if trustees have committed more than one breach of trust, a gain in one cannot be set off against a loss in another: the gain on the one transaction becomes subject to the trusts, and the trustees are liable to replace the loss on the other.[15] The general rule is even clearer where there are in fact two separate funds, even though the trustees and the trusts may be the same.[16]

---

[8] *Smith* v. *French* (1741), 2 Atk. 243; *Drosier* v. *Brereton* (1851), 15 Beav. 221.
[9] *Grayburn* v. *Clarkson* (1868), 3 Ch.App. 605; *Dunning* v. *Gainsborough (Earl)* (1885), 54 L.J. Ch. 991.
[10] *Phillipson* v. *Gatty* (1850), 7 Hare 516, affd. 2 H. & Tw. 459; *Re Massingberd's Settlement* (1890), 63 L.T. 296, C.A.
[11] *Knott* v. *Cottee* (1852), 16 Beav. 77.
[12] *Brychall* v. *Bradford* (1822), 6 Madd. 235; *Pride* v. *Fooks* (1840), 2 Beav. 430.
[13] *Briggs* v. *Massey* (1882), 51 L.J. Ch. 447, C.A.
[14] *Shepherd* v. *Mouls* (1845), 4 Hare 500; *Robinson* v. *Robinson* (1851), 1 De G.M. & G. 247.
[15] *Dimes* v. *Scott* (1828), 4 Russ. 195; *Wiles* v. *Gresham* (1854), 2 Drew. 258; affd. 5 De. G.M. & G. 770; *Re Barker* (1898), 77 L.T. 712. *Fletcher* v. *Green* (1864), 33 Beav. 426, if rightly decided, must be explained on the ground that the gains and losses could be set against each other because they all arose out of the same transaction.
[16] *Wiles* v. *Gresham, supra.*

In the case of an unauthorised investment, the *cestuis que trust*, if they are all *sui iuris* and together comprehend the entire equitable interest, can, if they so agree, adopt the unauthorised investment as part of the trust property.[17] As was explained in *Wright* v. *Morgan*,[18] "If a trustee has made an improper investment . . . the *cestuis que trustent* (*sic*) as a whole have a right, if they choose, to adopt the investment and to hold it as trust property". It may well be that if they do this, they can nevertheless call on the trustee to make good any loss to the trust estate, but the law is not clear.[19] The advice of the Privy Council in *Wright* v. *Morgan*[1] continued: "But if there is not unanimity, then it is not trust property, but the trustee who has made it must keep the investment himself. He is debtor to the trust for the money which has been applied in its purchase".[2] More accurately, perhaps, the duty of the trustee to sell the unauthorised investment if the *cestuis que trust* do not choose to adopt it is subject to the right of the trustee to take it over on replacing the trust funds.[3] Until this is done the *cestuis que trust* retain a lien on the unauthorised investment.

It should be mentioned that if trustees made an unauthorised investment, which brought in a greater income than an authorised investment would have done, and this income has been paid to the tenant for life, the trustees cannot call upon the tenant for life to pay the excess income to capital, nor can it be set off against future income.[4] It makes no difference that the tenant for life and the trustee are the same person.[5] The point seems to be that the capital is intact, and there is no question of a profit to the trustee. This rule may be contrasted with the position where trustees fail to convert under the rule in *Howe* v. *Lord Dartmouth*,[6] or an express trust for sale.[7]

c Interest

Where a trustee is required to replace a loss caused to the trust estate, he is normally liable, in addition, to pay interest at 4 per cent.[8] However in various circumstances a trustee may be liable for a higher rate.[9] Thus if he has actually received more he will be liable for what he has actually received. If he ought to have received more, he will be liable for what he ought to have received, as,

---

[17] *Re Patten and Guardians of the Poor of Edmonton Union* (1883), 52 L.J. Ch. 787; *Re Jenkins and Randall's Contract*, [1903] 2 Ch. 362.
[18] [1926] A.C. 788, at p.799; [1926] All E.R. Rep. 201, at p. 206, P.C.
[19] *Re Lake*, [1903] 1 K.B. 439; *contra, semble, Thornton* v. *Stokill* (1855), 1 Jur. N.S. 751.
[1] *Supra.*
[2] *Sharp* v. *Jackson*, [1899] A.C. 419, H.L.
[3] *Re Salmon* (1889), 42 Ch.D. 351, C.A.; *Re Lake, supra; Head* v. *Gould*, [1898] 2 Ch. 250.
[4] *Stroud* v. *Gwyer* (1860), 28 Beav. 130; *Slade* v. *Chaine*, [1908] 1 Ch. 522, C.A.; *Learoyd* v. *Whiteley*, [1887] 12 App. Cas. 727, H.L.
[5] *Re Hoyles* (No. 2), [1912] 1 Ch. 67.
[6] (1802), 7 Ves. 137.
[7] *Dimes* v. *Scott* (1827), 4 Russ. 195, and see Chapter 9, Section 3, p. 281, *ante*.
[8] *A.-G.* v. *Alford* (1855), 4 De G.M. & G. 843; *Imperial Mercantile Credit Association* v. *Coleman* (1873), L.R. 6 H.L. 189; *Re Hulkes* (1886), 33 Ch.D. 552. It is submitted that *Re Barclay*, [1899] 1 Ch. 674 and *Re Whiteford*, [1903] 1 Ch. 889 which required 3 per cent would not now be followed—cf. the cases in connection with the rule in *Howe* v. *Lord Dartmouth, supra*, discussed in Chapter 9, Section 3b, p. 290, *ante*.
[9] *Jones* v. *Foxall* (1852), 15 Beav. 388; *A.-G.* v. *Alford, supra*, explained in *Mayor etc. of Berwick upon Tweed* v. *Murray* (1857), 7 De G.M. & G. 497.

for instance, where he calls in a mortgage carrying a high rate of interest.[10] If he is fairly presumed to have received more, as where he has used the trust money for his own purposes, he will normally be charged 5 per cent: in particular where he has employed the trust money in trade, the *cestuis que trust* have the option of claiming 5 per cent, or alternatively the actual profits,[11] or, if the trustee has mixed his own moneys and the trust moneys, a proportionate share of the profits.[12] They cannot, however, claim profits for part of the time and interest for the remainder.[13] It is not altogether clear in what cases interest is simple and in what compound: according to dicta in some cases, which perhaps represent the better view, where the trustee is made liable for compound interest, it is not by way of a punishment for his conduct, but because this fairly represents what he is presumed to have received,[14] but other cases in which compound interest has been charged stress fraud or great misconduct on the part of the trustee.[15] It seems that compound interest will be charged as a matter of course where there was a duty to accumulate.[16]

d Joint and several liability to beneficiaries

It is settled that where two or more trustees are liable for a breach of trust, their liability is joint and several: this means that the *cestuis que trust* can claim the whole loss from any one trustee,[17] or two or more jointly, or all of them, and even where a judgment is obtained against all of them, may execute the whole judgment against any one.[18] The *cestuis que trust* are not concerned with the liability of the trustees *inter se*. So far as the *cestuis que trust* are concerned "all parties to a breach of trust are equally liable; there is between them no primary liability".[19] The above rules apply equally where the trustees comprise or include constructive trustees,[20] such as persons who have knowingly received trust property in breach of trust, or who, having received it innocently have dealt with it in a manner inconsistent with the performance of trusts of which

---

[10] See *Jones* v. *Foxall*, (1852), 15 Beav. 388.

[11] *Vyse* v. *Foster* (1872), 8 Ch. App. 309; affd. (1874), L.R. 7 H.L. 318; *Re Davis*, [1902] 2 Ch. 314; *Gordon* v. *Gonda*, [1955] 2 All E.R. 762, C.A.

[12] *Docker* v. *Somes* (1834), 2 My. & K. 655; *Lord Provost of Edinburgh* v. *Lord Advocate* (1879), 4 App. Cas. 823, H.L.

[13] *Heathcote* v. *Hulme* (1819), 1 Jac. & W. 122; *Vyse* v. *Foster* (1872), 8 Ch. App. 309, at p. 334.

[14] *Vyse* v. *Foster, supra*, at p. 333; *A.-G.* v. *Alford* (1855), 4 De G.M. & G. 843; *Burdick* v. *Garrick* (1870), 5 Ch. App. 233. Only simple where trustee has allowed money already there to remain in trustees' trade—*Brown* v. *Sansome* (1825), M'Clel. & Yo. 427; *Smith* v. *Nelson* (1905), 92 L.T. 313.

[15] *Jones* v. *Foxall* (1852), 15 Beav. 388; *Gordon* v. *Gonda*, [1955] 2 All E.R. 762, C.A.

[16] *Re Emmet's Estate* (1881), 17 Ch.D. 142; *Gilroy* v. *Stephens* (1882), 51 L.J. Ch. 834; *Re Barclay*, [1899] 1 Ch. 674.

[17] *Walker* v. *Symonds* (1818), 3 Swan. 1, 75; *Re Harrison*, [1891] 2 Ch. 349; *McCheane* v. *Gyles* (No. 2), [1902] 1 Ch. 911. But if all the trustees are dead, an action cannot normally be brought against the personal representatives of one trustee, not being the survivor of the trustees, without joining the personal representatives of the survivor, or having new trustees appointed and joining them as defendants—*Re Jordan*, [1904] 1 Ch. 260.

[18] *A.-G.* v. *Wilson* (1840), Cr. & Ph. 1, 28; *Fletcher* v. *Green* (1864), 33 Beav. 426.

[19] *Per* Leach M.R. in *Wilson* v. *Moore* (1833), 1 My. & K. 126, at p. 146; affd. (1834), 1 My. & K. 337; *Edwards* v. *Hood-Barnes*, [1905] 1 Ch. 20.

[20] See Chapter 4, Section 5, p. 122, *ante*.

they have become aware.[1] The liability continues against the estate of a deceased or bankrupt trustee,[2] but the estate of a deceased trustee is not liable for what he left in a proper state of investment at his death.[3] Since the liability is joint and several, *cestuis que trust* who have recovered in part from one trustee, may prove in the bankruptcy of another trustee for the whole amount of the loss, and not merely for the balance, though they cannot, of course, in the aggregate recover more than their loss.[4]

Retired trustees remain liable for their own breaches of trust but are not normally liable for breaches of trust committed by their successors. If, however, a trustee is asked to commit a breach of trust, and refuses, he should take care before appointing, or resigning in order to enable the appointment of, a new trustee who he has reason to believe may be more accommodating. The position, according to Kekewich J. in *Head* v. *Gould*,[5] is

> "that in order to make a retiring trustee liable for a breach of trust committed by his successor you must show, and show clearly, that the very breach of trust which was in fact committed was not merely the outcome of the retirement and new appointment, but was contemplated by the former trustee when such retirement and appointment took place. . . . It will not suffice to prove that the former trustees rendered easy or even intended, a breach of trust, if it was not in fact committed. They must be proved to have been guilty as accessories before the fact of the impropriety actually perpetrated".

Again, a new trustee is not liable for breaches of trust committed by his predecessors, and "is entitled to assume that everything has been duly attended to up to the time of his becoming trustee".[6] However, if he discovers a breach of trust, he should take appropriate steps to remedy it, if necessary by proceedings against the old trustees, as part of his duty to get in the trust property and to see that it is in a proper state of investment.[7]

e Trustee-beneficiary

It is settled that if a trustee, who is also a beneficiary, is in default and liable to the trust estate, he will not be allowed to claim, as against his *cestuis que trust*, any beneficial interest in the trust estate, until he has made good his default.[8] It makes no difference that he acquired his beneficial interest derivatively, for instance, under the will or on the intestacy of an original beneficiary.[9] And if the trustee has assigned his beneficial interest, his assignee is in no better position, even though the default takes place after the assignment.[10] But if the same persons happen to be the trustees of two separate trusts, even though created by

---

1 *Blyth* v. *Fladgate*, [1891] 1 Ch. 337; *Cowper* v. *Stoneham* (1893), 68 L.T. 18.
2 See e.g., *Dixon* v. *Dixon* (1878), 9 Ch.D. 587; *Edwards* v. *Hood-Barnes, supra*.
3 *Re Palk* (1892), 41 W.R. 28.
4 *Edwards* v. *Hood-Barnes, supra*.
5 [1898] 2 Ch. 250, 273–274.
6 *Re Strahan* (1856), 8 De G.M. & G. 291, at p. 309 *per* Turner L.J.
7 See Chapter 9, Section 1, p. 263, *ante*.
8 *Re Rhodesia Goldfields Ltd.*, [1910] 1 Ch. 239. See *Selangor United Rubber Estates, Ltd.* v. *Cradock (No.* 4), [1969] 3 All E.R. 965.
9 *Jacubs* v. *Rylance* (1874), L.R. 17 Eq. 341; *Doering* v. *Doering* (1889), 42 Ch.D. 203; *Re Dacre*, [1916] 1 Ch. 344, C.A.
10 *Doering* v. *Doering, supra; Re Towndrow*, [1911] 1 Ch. 662.

the same will, then their beneficial interest under one cannot be impounded to make good their default in connection with the other.[11]

f Injunction

An injunction may be obtained in appropriate circumstances to restrain an apprehended breach of trust. This is discussed in Chapter 13, Section 6h, p. 424, post.

g Procedure

At one time[12] it was not possible for a beneficiary in proceedings commenced by summons, to ask for or obtain, otherwise than by consent, an order founded on breach of trust or inquiries pointing to wilful default[13]—in such case the inherent jurisdiction had to be invoked in an action commenced by writ. Under the present rules, an action must still be begun by writ where there is a claim based on an allegation of fraud,[14] but in other cases it appears to be left to the discretion of the plaintiff,[15] and it is expressly provided that the court may grant any relief to which the plaintiff may be entitled by reason of any breach of trust, wilful default or other misconduct of the defendant notwithstanding that the action was begun by originating summons.[16] Nevertheless it has been stated[17] that "proceedings by beneficiaries against trustees of a contentious nature, charging the trustees with breach of trust or with default in the proper performance of their duties, whether the matters with which the trustees are charged are matters of commission or omission, ought normally to be commenced by writ and not by originating summons", on the ground that in such proceedings the trustees ought to know before the trial precisely what is alleged against them.

2 LIABILITY OF TRUSTEES *INTER SE*

a Townley v. Sherborne

It has been recognised since *Townley* v. *Sherborne*[18] in 1634 that a trustee is not liable for the acts and defaults of his co-trustee, and the Trustee Act 1925, section 30 (1),[19] now provides—

---

[11] *Re Towndrow*, [1911] 1 Ch. 662.
[12] I.e. before the 1962 Revision of the Rules of the Supreme Court (S.I. 1962 No. 2145). The current rules are the 1965 rules (S.I. 1965 No. 1776).
[13] *Dowse* v. *Gorton*, [1891] A.C. 190, H.L., per Lord Macnaghten at p. 202; *Re Hengler*, [1893] W.N. 37; cf. *Re Newland*, [1904] W.N. 181.
[14] R.S.C., O. 5, r. 2 (b).   [15] R.S.C., O. 5, rr. 1 and 4.
[16] R.S.C., O. 85, r. 4. This provision is without prejudice to the power of the court to make an order under O. 28, r. 8, that the proceedings be continued as if begun by writ.
[17] Per Buckley J. in *Re Sir Lindsay Parkinson & Co. Ltd.'s Trusts Deed*, [1965] 1 All E.R. 609, at p. 610.
[18] (1634), Bridg. J. 35. For a recent illustration see *Re Lucking's Will Trusts*, [1967] 3 All E.R. 726.
[19] See Chapter 10, Section 3, p. 320, *ante*.

"A trustee shall be chargeable only for money and securities actually received by him notwithstanding his signing any receipt for the sake of conformity, and shall be answerable and accountable only for his own acts, receipts, neglects, or defaults, and not for those of any other trustee . . . unless the same happens through his own wilful default."

Apart from statute, a trustee was, however, said to be liable in three cases;[20] first, where, being recipient, he handed over money without securing its due application; secondly, where he permitted a co-trustee to receive money without making due inquiry as to his dealing with it; and thirdly, where he became aware of a breach of trust, either committed or meditated, and abstained from taking the needful steps to obtain restitution or redress.[21] It followed that it was by no means easy for a trustee to escape liability even where the active breach of trust was committed by a co-trustee, and the trustee's position was, apparently, not mitigated by the common indemnity clause.[22] According to *Re Brier*,[23] the statutory indemnity, now contained in section 30 (1) merely incorporates generally into instruments creating trusts the common indemnity clause, but it may perhaps be that this view requires modification in the light of the construction put on "wilful default" in *Re Vickery*.[24]

It is submitted that should section 30 (1) be held to give a wider protection to trustees, a way for beneficiaries to get round it, as with delegation to agents which rests on similar principles, might be to charge the trustee for his own act or default, for instance, failing to carry out his own duty to get the trust funds under his control and to take proper care and custody of them, which would be broken by leaving them in the hands of a co-trustee for longer than was reasonably necessary,[25] or in failing to carry out his duty to keep a watch over the conduct of his co-trustees.[26]

b Contribution between trustees

It seems that where all the trustees concerned have been guilty of fraud, one trustee who is compelled to pay the whole cannot claim any contribution from the others.[1] The general rule, however, is that as between themselves the trustees are equally liable, and one who is compelled to pay more than his fair share can enforce contribution from the others.[2] The right extends to the personal representatives of a deceased trustee, where the breach of trust took place before, even though the loss only occurred after, his death.[3] The general

---

[20] *Per* Westbury L.C. in *Wilkins* v. *Hogg* (1861), 5 L.T. 467, at p. 470.

[21] See *Boardman* v. *Mosman* (1779), 1 Bro.C.C. 68; *Shipbrook* v. *Hinchingbrook* (1810), 16 Ves. 477; *Booth* v. *Booth* (1838), 1 Beav. 125.

[22] See e.g. *Dix* v. *Burford* (1854), 19 Beav. 409; *Brumridge* v. *Brumridge* (1858), 27 Beav. 5.

[23] (1884), 26 Ch.D. 238, C.A.

[24] [1931] 1 Ch. 572, discussed in Chapter 10, Section 3, p. 320, *ante*.

[25] See e.g., *Wyman* v. *Paterson*, [1900] A.C. 271, H.L.

[26] *Styles* v. *Guy* (1849), 1 Mac. & G. 422.

[1] *Lingard* v. *Bromley* (1812), 1 Ves. & B. 114; *Tarleton* v. *Hornby* (1835), 1 Y. & C. Ex. 333; *A.-G.* v. *Wilson* (1840), Cr. & Ph. 1, at p. 28. Snell's *Equity*, 27th Ed. p. 284 suggests that this rule has not survived the Law Reform (Married Women and Tortfeasors) Act 1935, s. 6. *Contra* (1948), 64 L.Q.R. 47 (P. H. Winfield).

[2] *Chillingworth* v. *Chambers*, [1896] 1 Ch. 685, C.A.; *Robinson* v. *Harkin*, [1896] 2 Ch. 415.

[3] *Jackson* v. *Dickinson*, [1903] 1 Ch. 947.

rule applies as between so-called active and passive trustees for, as pointed out in *Bahin* v. *Hughes*;[4] a passive trustee by doing nothing may neglect his duty more than a trustee who acts honestly, though erroneously.

Exceptionally, however, a trustee may not be entitled to contribution, but indeed will be liable to indemnify his co-trustees. This will be the case where a trustee has got the money into his hands and made use of it,[5] or where the active trustee was a solicitor, who was relied on by the other trustees.[6] A solicitor-trustee is not, however, necessarily bound to indemnify a co-trustee merely because he is a solicitor: he will be under no such obligation if it appears that the co-trustee was an active participator in the breach of trust, and is not proved to have participated merely in consequence of the advice and control of the solicitor.[7] Further a trustee who is also, or subsequently becomes, a *cestui que trust*, is bound, at any rate where he has received some benefit by the breach of trust,[8] to indemnify his co-trustee to the extent of his interest in the trust fund, and not merely to the extent of any benefit he may have received by the breach of trust.[9] A new trustee who is also a *cestui que trust*, however, although he may be liable to the other *cestuis que trust* for failure to have an existing breach of trust put right on his appointment, is not liable to indemnify the original trustees under this head, but is himself entitled to be indemnified by the original trustees who were also responsible for the breach the primary cause of the loss.[10]

3 DEFENCES OF A TRUSTEE TO PROCEEDINGS FOR BREACH OF TRUST

a Consent or concurrence of the *cestui que trust*

A beneficiary who consents to or concurs in a breach of trust,[11] or subsequently confirms it or grants a release to the trustees,[12] or even merely acquiesces in it,[13] will not, in general, be able to succeed in a claim against the trustees[14] whether or not he has derived any benefit thereby.[15] In order to have this result, as will be elaborated later, the beneficiary must, at the relevant time, have been fully cognizant of the circumstances affecting his rights. Although a beneficiary whose interest is reversionary is not bound to assert his title until his interest

---

[4] (1886), 31 Ch.D. 390, C.A.; *Bacon* v. *Camphausen* (1888), 58 L.T. 851.
[5] *Bahin* v. *Hughes, supra,* at 395, C.A.
[6] *Chillingworth* v. *Chambers,* [1896] 1 Ch. 685, C.A.; *Re Turner,* [1897] 1 Ch. 536; *Re Linsley,* [1904] 2 Ch. 785.
[7] *Head* v. *Gould,* [1898] 2 Ch. 250.
[8] *Chillingworth* v. *Chambers, supra, per* Kay L.J. at p. 707: contrast Lindley L.J. at p. 700.
[9] *Chillingworth* v. *Chambers, supra,* C.A.
[10] *Re Fountaine,* not reported on this point in [1909] 2 Ch. 382, C.A., but referred to in Underhill's *Law of Trusts and Trustees,* 12th Ed., pp. 670, 671.
[11] *Brice* v. *Stokes* (1805), 11 Ves. 319; *Nail* v. *Punter* (1832), 5 Sim. 555; *Evans* v. *Benyon* (1887), 37 Ch.D. 329, C.A.
[12] *Farrant* v. *Blanchford* (1863), 1 De G.J. & S. 107.
[13] *Walker* v. *Symonds* (1818), 3 Swan. 1; *Stafford* v. *Stafford* (1857), 1 De G. & J. 193.
[14] *A fortiori,* a *cestui que trust* who is also a trustee cannot claim from a co-trustee in respect of a breach of trust in which they have both joined—*Butler* v. *Carter* (1868), L.R. 5 Eq. 276.
[15] *Fletcher* v. *Collis,* [1905] 2 Ch. 24, C.A.

falls into possession, he may in the meantime assent to a breach of trust so as to bar his claims in respect thereof, though the mere fact that he knows of the breach of trust and does nothing about it will not by itself be enough.[16] It need hardly be said that the fact that one beneficiary has consented to a breach of trust will not affect the rights of other beneficiaries who have not done so, and if necessary, the court will order an inquiry as to which beneficiaries have given their consent.[17] Further, the concurrence, release or acquiescence of a person not *sui iuris* is generally ineffective;[18] but although, accordingly, as Wigram V.C. said,[19] "the release of infants is worth nothing in law", the court will not permit an infant who, by fraudulently misrepresenting his age, persuades trustees to pay him money in breach of trust, to claim the money over again on attaining his majority.[20] Again, on general principles, a consent or release obtained by undue influence will not avail a trustee.[1] "A consent which is not a free one is no consent at all".[2]

Whether a beneficiary has consented to or concurred in a breach of trust is a question of fact. No particular formalities are required, but it has been said[3] that a trustee would not be justified in committing a breach of trust "if, in a casual conversation, the *cestui que trust* happened to say to the trustee 'I wish you would invest the trust money so as to get a higher rate of interest'". Similarly, a release does not need to be a formal release under seal in order to be effective; any expression of an intention to waive the breach of trust, if supported by some consideration, however slight, will be regarded as equivalent to a release.[4] A release may even be inferred from conduct,[5] but a beneficiary does not waive his rights in respect of a breach of trust merely by accepting a part of what is due to him with knowledge that the trustee has committed a breach of trust.[6] Where a trustee relies on acquiescence by the beneficiary he must, it seems, show more than the mere passing of time and failure to act. If a long time has passed, however, very slight acts may suffice to establish acquiescence, and Campbell L.C. has even said[7] that "although the rule be that the onus lies on the party relying on acquiescence to prove the facts from which the consent of the *cestui que trust* is to be inferred, it is easy to conceive cases in which, from great lapse of time, such facts might and ought to be presumed".[8]

[16] *Life Association of Scotland* v. *Siddal* (1861), 3 De G.F. & J. 58.
[17] *Brice* v. *Stokes* (1805), 11 Ves. 319; *Wilkinson* v. *Parry* (1828), 4 Russ. 272; *Ghost* v. *Waller* (1846), 9 Beav. 497.
[18] *Montford (Lord)* v. *Lord Cadogan* (1816), 19 Ves. 635.
[19] *Overton* v. *Banister* (1844), 3 Hare 503, at p. 506.
[20] *Overton* v. *Banister, supra; Wright* v. *Snowe* (1848), 2 De G. & Sm. 321.
[1] *Farrant* v. *Blanchford* (1863), 1 De G.J. & Sm. 107; *Lloyd* v. *Attwood* (1859), 3 De G. & J. 614.
[2] Per Stuart V.C. in *Stevens* v. *Robertson* (1868), 18 L.T. 427, at p. 428.
[3] *Rehden* v. *Wesley* (1861), 29 Beav. 213, at p. 215 per Romilly M.R.
[4] *Stackhouse* v. *Barnston* (1805), 10 Ves. 453.
[5] *Egg* v. *Devey* (1847), 10 Beav. 444.
[6] *Re Cross* (1882), 20 Ch.D. 109, C.A.
[7] *Life Association of Scotland* v. *Siddal* (1861), 3 De G.F. & J. 58, at p. 77. Cf. *Knight* v. *Bowyer* (1858), 2 De G. & J. 421, at p. 443 per Turner L.J.
[8] In the following cases, acquiescence was established—*Jones* v. *Higgins* (1866), L.R. 2 Eq. 538; *Sleeman* v. *Wilson* (1871), L.R. 13 Eq. 36; in the following cases it was not—*Griffiths* v. *Porter* (1858), 25 Beav. 236; *Re Jackson* (1881), 44 L.T. 467.

There are many cases which stress that, whether relying on concurrence,[9] release, or acquiescence, a trustee must establish full knowledge on the part of the *cestui que trust*. In connection with a release Westbury L.C. explained in *Farrant* v. *Blanchford*:[10] "where a breach of trust has been committed from which a trustee alleges that he has been released, it is incumbent on him to shew that such release was given by the *cestui que trust* deliberately and advisedly, with full knowledge of all the circumstances, and of his own rights and claims against the trustee; for it is impossible to allow a trustee who has incurred personal liability to deal with his *cestui que trust* for his own discharge upon any other ground than the obligation of giving the fullest information, and of shewing that the *cestui que trust* was well acquainted with his own legal rights and claims, and gave the release freely and without pressure or undue influence of any description". Accordingly releases have been set aside where executed under a mistake of fact,[11] where a solicitor-trustee was allowed costs to which he was not entitled, the *cestui que trust* not being professionally advised,[12] where the *cestui que trust* was in a humble condition of life and had no professional assistance, the facts not being accurately represented to him nor the effect of the release fully explained,[13] and where the release was executed shortly after the *cestui que trust* attained his majority and purported to involve the examination of complicated accounts.[14] Moreover, a release in general terms will not extend to matters of which the parties were ignorant,[15] and may be restricted in its operation by the recitals and the context.[16]

Similarly, where a trustee relies on acquiescence, it has been said[17] to be "essential that the person who acquiesces must know exactly the nature of the thing to which his acquiescence is supposed to be given. He must know that, and he must know also the effect of his acquiescence," and, more recently, Danckwerts J., in *Re Howlett*,[18] referred to *Cockerell* v. *Cholmeley*[19] "as authority for the proposition that in order to found a defence of acquiescence the party against whom the plea is raised must know not only the facts but also the consequences. That seems to me to be substantially correct". The House of Lords in *Bullock* v. *Downes*[20] held on the same principles that there can be no acquiescence where there is a common misapprehension as to the rights of the *cestui que trust*. Cross J. has, however, pointed out[1] that a conflicting statement in *Stafford* v. *Stafford*[2] was not referred to in *Re Howlett*,[3] and has himself

---

[9] *Buckeridge* v. *Glass* (1841), Cr. & Ph. 126.

[10] (1863), 1 De G.J. & Sm. 107, at p. 119; *Thomson* v. *Eastwood* (1877), 2 App. Cas. 215, H.L.

[11] *Hore* v. *Becher* (1842), 12 Sim. 465.

[12] *Todd* v. *Wilson* (1846), 9 Beav. 486 distinguishing *Stanes* v. *Parker* (1846), 9 Beav. 385 where the *cestui que trust* was professionally advised.

[13] *Aspland* v. *Watte* (1855), 20 Beav. 474.

[14] *Wedderburn* v. *Wedderburn* (1838), 4 My. & G. 41; *Parker* v. *Bloxam* (1855), 20 Beav. 295.

[15] *Ramsden* v. *Hylton* (1751), 2 Ves. Sen. 304; *Pritt* v. *Clay* (1843), 6 Beav. 503.

[16] *Lindo* v. *Lindo* (1839), 1 Beav. 496.

[17] Per Stuart V.C. in *Strange* v. *Fooks* (1863), 4 Giff. 408, at p. 413; *Marker* v. *Marker* (1851), 9 Hare 1; *Stretton* v. *Ashmall* (1854), 3 Drew. 9.

[18] [1949] 2 All E.R. 490, at p. 492; [1949] Ch. 767, at p. 775.

[19] (1830), 1 Russ. & My. 418. affd. on appeal (1832), 6 Bli. N.S. 120.

[20] (1860), 9 H.L.Cas. 1.

[1] At first instance in *Holder* v. *Holder*, [1966] 2 All E.R. 116, at p. 127.

[2] (1857), 1 De G. & J. 193 per Knight Bruce L.J. at p. 202: "Generally, when the facts are known from which a right arises, the right is presumed to be known: and I am not satisfied that in the present case, upon the materials before us, it would be right to ascribe to the lady any degree of ignorance of her rights".   [3] *Supra*.

expressed the view[4] that "in cases of alleged acquiescence one cannot lay down a hard and fast rule to this effect that knowledge of the legal consequences of known facts is or is not essential to the success of the plea." According to another recent decision a nice distinction has to be drawn between knowledge by the beneficiary of what he is doing and its legal effect, and knowledge of the fact that what he is concurring in is a breach of trust. At any rate where a trustee relies on the concurrence of a beneficiary—and on principle there seems no reason why the rule in relation to release or acquiescence should be any different—Wilberforce J. in *Re Pauling's Settlement*,[5] accepted the view of the Court of Appeal in *Evans v. Benyon*[6] as correctly representing the law. There it was said that a person who, knowing that a trustee was distributing a settled fund, consented to and was active in the distribution, could not afterwards claim against the trustee even though he did not know at the time that he was beneficially interested and although he did not know that the division was a breach of trust.[7] All the members of the Court of Appeal in *Holder* v. *Holder*[8] expressly approved the general statement of the law made by Wilberforce J. in *Re Pauling's Settlement*,[9] where he said,[10] after reviewing the authorities: "The result of these authorities appears to me to be that the court has to consider all the circumstances in which the concurrence of the *cestui que trust* was given with a view to seeing whether it is fair and equitable that, having given his concurrence, he should afterwards turn round and sue the trustees: that, subject to this, it is not necessary that he should know that what he is concurring in is a breach of trust, provided that he fully understands what he is concurring in, and that it is not necessary that he should himself have directly benefited by the breach of trust."

b Impounding the beneficial interest of the *cestui que trust*

Quite apart from statute, a *cestui que trust* who instigated or requested a trustee to commit a breach of trust could be called upon to indemnify the trustee, in respect of his liability to make good the loss to the trust estate, out of his beneficial interest;[11] where the *cestui que trust* had merely consented to the breach of trust, and obtained no personal benefit thereby, the trustee had no right to impound his beneficial interest by way of indemnity,[12] but if the *cestui que trust* had consented to and obtained a personal benefit from the breach of trust, the trustee was apparently entitled to an indemnity out of the beneficial interest, though only to the extent of the benefit.[13] The right does not depend on

---

[4] In *Holder* v. *Holder, supra*, at p. 128.
[5] [1961] 3 All E.R. 713, at p. 730. The Court of Appeal expressed no opinion on this point in the same case on appeal in [1963] 3 All E.R. 1; [1964] Ch. 303.
[6] (1887), 37 Ch.D. 329, C.A.; *Re Hulkes* (1886), 33 Ch.D. 552.
[7] Note, however, that the Court was in fact of opinion that he knew both of his beneficial interest and of the breach of trust.
[8] [1968] 1 All E.R. 665; [1968] Ch. 353, C.A.
[9] *Supra*.
[10] *Supra*, at p. 730.
[11] *Raby* v. *Ridehalgh* (1855), 7 De G.M. & G. 104; *Sawyer* v. *Sawyer* (1885), 28 Ch.D. 595, C.A.; *Chillingworth* v. *Chambers*, [1896] 1 Ch. 685, C.A.
[12] *Sawyer* v. *Sawyer, supra; Fletcher* v. *Collis*, [1905] 2 Ch. 24, C.A.
[13] *Booth* v. *Booth* (1838), 1 Beav. 125; *Chillingworth* v. *Chambers, supra*.

possession of the trust fund, and so will continue in favour of a former trustee where a new trustee is appointed.[14]

The equitable right has been extended by statute, now represented by section 62 of the Trustee Act 1925,[15] which applies whether the breach of trust was committed before or after the passing of the Act.[16] Section 62 (1)[17] provides as follows—

> "Where a trustee commits a breach of trust at the instigation or request or with the consent in writing[18] of a beneficiary, the court may, if it thinks fit, make such order as to the court seems just, for impounding all or any part of the interest of the beneficiary in the trust estate by way of indemnity to the trustee or persons claiming through him."

The statement with regard to the corresponding provision of the 1888 Act applies here,[19] namely, that it "was intended to enlarge the power of the court as to indemnifying trustees, and to give greater relief to trustees, and was not intended and did not operate to curtail the previously existing rights and remedies of trustees, or to alter the law except by giving greater power to the court".[20] Although the section gives the court a discretion, it is a judicial discretion, and in any case where it would have impounded the interest of a beneficiary before the statutory provisions, it will be bound to make a similar order under the Act.[1] Accordingly, the power to impound is not lost on the one hand by an assignment, even for value, of the beneficial interest,[2] nor, on the other hand, by the appointment of new trustees.[3]

In order to rely successfully on section 62, the trustee must establish that the *cestui que trust* at least knew the facts which rendered what he was instigating, or requesting, or consenting to, a breach of trust. It is not enough, therefore, to show that the *cestui que trust* pressed for a particular investment if it also appears that he left it to the trustees to determine whether it was a proper one for the moneys proposed to be advanced.[4]

It should also be observed that, again apart from statute, it has always been the practice of the court when administering the estate of a deceased person or a trust, "in cases where trustees have under an honest mistake overpaid one beneficiary, in the adjustment of the accounts between the trustees and the *cestui que trust*, to make allowance for the mistake in order that the trustee may so far as possible be recouped the money which he has inadvisedly paid".[5] The overpaid beneficiary will not however be compelled to refund the over-

---

[14] *Re Pauling's Settlement (No. 2)*, [1963] 1 All E.R. 857; [1963] Ch. 576.
[15] Replacing Trustee Act 1893, s. 45, which in turn replaced Trustee Act 1888, s. 6.
[16] Trustee Act 1925, s. 62 (2).
[17] As amended by the Married Women (Restraint upon Anticipation) Act 1949, s. 1 (4) and Sched. 2.
[18] The words "in writing" apply only to consent and not to instigation or request— *Griffith* v. *Hughes*, [1892] 3 Ch. 105; *Re Somerset*, [1894] 1 Ch. 231, C.A.
[19] *Re Pauling's Settlement (No. 2)*, supra.
[20] *Bolton* v. *Curre*, [1895] 1 Ch. 544, 549 per Romer J.; *Fletcher* v. *Collis*, [1905] 2 Ch. 24, C.A.
[1] *Re Somerset*, [1894] 1 Ch. 231, C.A.; *Bolton* v. *Curre, supra.*
[2] *Bolton* v. *Curre, supra.*   [3] *Re Pauling's Settlement (No. 2), supra.*
[4] *Re Somerset*, [1894] 1 Ch. 231, C.A.; *Mara* v. *Browne*, [1895] 2 Ch. 69, reversed, but not on this point, [1896] 1 Ch. 199, C.A.
[5] *Per* Neville J. in *Re Musgrave*, [1916] 2 Ch. 417, at p. 423; *Re Robinson*, [1911] 1 Ch. 502; [1911–13] All E.R. Rep. 296; *Re Ainsworth*, [1915] 2 Ch. 96.

payment, but further payments will be withheld until the accounts have been put straight.[6] Exceptionally it has been held that a trustee-beneficiary who has overpaid the other beneficiaries and underpaid himself is not allowed to correct his mistake,[7] though it is obviously different where he has overpaid himself.[8] Further, this principle only applies to trusts and estates, and not, for instance, to overpayments made under a covenant.[9]

c Limitation and laches

The rules as to the limitation of actions against trustees are set out in the Limitation Act 1939. The Act applies to trustees as defined by the Trustee Act 1925 and accordingly includes trustees holding on implied and constructive trusts and personal representatives.[10] There may be applied to the relevant provisions of the Act, the remarks of Kekewich J. in *Re Timmis*[11] on section 8 of the Trustee Act 1888, which they replace:

"The intention of the statute was to give a trustee the benefit of the lapse of time when, although he had done something legally or technically wrong, he had done nothing morally wrong or dishonest, but it was not intended to protect him where, if he pleaded the statute, he would come off with something he ought not to have, i.e., money of the trust received by him and converted to his own use".

The main section of the Limitation Act 1939 dealing with trustees is section 19, subsection (1) of which provides as follows—

"No period of limitation prescribed by this Act shall apply to an action by a beneficiary under a trust, being an action—

(a) in respect of any fraud or fraudulent breach of trust to which the trustee was a party or privy; or

(b) to recover from the trustee trust property or the proceeds thereof in the possession of the trustee, or previously received by the trustee and converted to his use".

As regards fraud, Lord Davey said,[12] on similar words in the 1888 Act, that "if fraud, or a non-discovery of fraud, is to be relied on to take a case out of the Statute of Limitations, it must be the fraud of or in some way imputable to the person who invokes the aid of the Statute of Limitations". It was said in an Irish case[13] that the fraud must amount to dishonesty, but Wright J., in *Re Sale Hotel and Botanical Gardens Ltd.*,[14] thought it impossible to hold that moral fraud was required for the purposes of this provision.

---

[6] *Downes* v. *Bullock* (1854), 25 Beav. 54; affd. (1860), 9 H.L.Cas. 1; *Bate* v. *Hooper* (1855), 5 De G.M. & G. 338; but contrast *Hood* v. *Clapham* (1854), 19 Beav. 90.
[7] *Re Horne*, [1905] 1 Ch. 76, but see *Re Reading*, [1916] W.N. 262.
[8] *Re Reading*, *supra*.
[9] *Re Hatch*, [1919] 1 Ch. 351; [1918–19] All E.R. Rep. 357.
[10] Limitation Act 1939, s. 31 (1); Trustee Act 1925, s. 68 (17).
[11] [1902] 1 Ch. 176, 186.
[12] *Thorne* v. *Heard*, [1895] A.C. 495, at p. 506, H.L.; and see *G. L. Baker Ltd.* v. *Medway Building and Supplies, Ltd.*, [1958] 2 All E.R. 532, order discharged on another ground, [1958] 3 All E.R. 540, C.A.
[13] *Collings* v. *Wade*, [1896] 1 I.R. 340, C.A.
[14] (1897), 77 L.T. 681, reversed on another point (1898), 78 L.T. 368, C.A.

As regards possession, or receipt and conversion to the trustee's use, the slight change in the wording from the 1888 Act probably does not alter the substance.[15] Accordingly, on the one hand, trustees who paid themselves annuities, by mistake without deduction of tax, were held to be within the subsection as regarded the amount attributable to tax, and thus unable to rely on the defence of limitation.[16] And in *Re Howlett*[17] a trustee who remained in occupation of trust property for his own purposes was held to be chargeable with an occupation rent and to be considered as still having it in his own pocket so as to be unable to escape under the provisions of the Limitation Act 1939. On the other hand, the subsection was held not to apply, and the trustees thus able to rely on the Act, where, for instance, the trustee had used the trust funds in the maintenance of an infant beneficiary,[18] where the trust funds had been lost,[19] and where the trust funds had been lent on mortgage, and the mortgagor used the monies to pay off a debt to a bank in which one of the trustees was a partner.[20]

Subject to these exceptions, and to any other provisions of the Act—which do not include claims for pure breach of trust—section 19 (2) provides that no action by a beneficiary to recover trust property or in respect of any breach of trust shall be brought after the expiration of six years from the date on which the right of action accrued. Time runs from the date of the breach of trust, not from the time the loss accrued,[1] for instance, where trustees pay annuities to other persons, by mistake not deducting tax,[2] where they fail to convert in accordance with the directions in the trust instrument,[3] or where they invest on insufficient security.[4] By a proviso to this subsection, however, the right of action is not to be deemed to have accrued to any beneficiary entitled to a future interest in the trust property, until the interest falls into possession. It has accordingly been held that where a person has two separate interests in property, one in possession and one reversionary, he will not be barred as to the latter merely because he is barred as to the former.[5] Section 19 (3) however provides that no beneficiary whose own claim has been barred can derive any benefit from a judgment or order obtained by any other beneficiary. Thus if a trust fund is lost, and the claim of the tenant for life is barred, the trustees, if compelled to replace the trust fund by the remainderman, will be personally entitled to the income so long as the life interest subsists.[6] It may be added that the six year period of limitation in an action for an account prescribed by section 2 (2)

---

15 *Re Howlett*, [1949] 2 All E.R. 490; [1949] Ch. 767.
16 *Re Sharp*, [1906] 1 Ch. 793.
17 *Supra; Wassell* v. *Leggatt*, [1896] 1 Ch. 554; *Re Eyre-Williams*, [1923] 2 Ch. 533.
18 *Re Page*, [1893] 1 Ch. 304; *Re Timmis*, [1902] 1 Ch. 176.
19 *Re Tufnell* (1902), 18 T.L.R. 705; *Re Fountaine*, [1909] 2 Ch. 382; [1908–10] All E.R. Rep. 969, C.A.
20 *Re Gurney*, [1893] 1 Ch. 590.
1 *Re Somerset*, [1894] 1 Ch. 231, C.A.; *Want* v. *Campain* (1893), 9 T.L.R. 254.
2 *Re Sharp*, [1906] 1 Ch. 793.
3 *Re Swain*, [1891] 3 Ch. 233.
4 *Re Bowden* (1890), 45 Ch.D. 444; *Re Somerset, supra;* and see *How* v. *Winterton*, [1896] 2 Ch. 626, C.A. (failure to accumulate); *Re Tufnell* (1902), 18 T.L.R. 705 and *Re Fountaine*, [1909] 2 Ch. 382; [1908–10] All E.R. Rep. 969, C.A. (allowing co-trustee, a solicitor to receive trust monies).
5 *Mara* v. *Browne*, [1895] 2 Ch. 69 reversed, but not on this point, [1896] 1 Ch. 199, C.A.
6 *Re Somerset, supra.*

seems not to apply to a claim against a trustee by virtue of subsection (7).[7] An account, however, is usually sought as ancillary to another claim, and presumably the period of limitation, if any, appropriate to the main claim would also be applied to the ancillary one,[8] and if the only claim was for an account, the period prescribed by subsection (2) would probably be applied by analogy.

Reference should also be made to section 20 of the Act which provides for a twelve year period of limitation in an action in respect of any claim to the personal estate of a deceased person. Time in this case runs from the date when the right to receive the share or interest accrued, which may be an earlier date than the date on which he can first bring an action to recover it.[9] In the case of an immediate legacy, it is submitted that it means the date of death,[10] but a later date may be specified expressly or by implication in the will,[11] and there can be no right to receive the interest until there are sufficient assets to cover the claim in the hands of the personal representatives.[12]

The relationship between section 19 (2) and 20 is not altogether clear. Under the law in operation before the Act of 1939 it was vital to ascertain whether a personal representative had become a trustee. If the personal representative had not become a trustee the action was one to recover a legacy under section 8 of the Real Property Limitation Act 1874 and the period was twelve years, whereas if the personal representative had become an express trustee section 8 of the Trustee Act 1888 applied and the period of the limitation was only six years. An illustration of the first situation was *Re Richardson*[13] where the widow of a testator who died in 1909 was entitled to the whole residue absolutely. After the widow's death in 1917, the beneficiaries under her will claimed an account of the testator's estate. It was held that as the only duty of the personal representative was to administer the estate as such, the appropriate period of limitation was twelve years, and accordingly the claim must succeed. The second type of situation is illustrated by *Re Oliver*,[14] where a testatrix who died in 1890 gave the residue of her real and personal estate to her executors on trust for sale and conversion, and directed them to set aside £2,000 out of the proceeds to be held by them upon trust for L during her widowhood, and on her death or remarriage to fall into residue. Subject to this life interest the residue was given to her six children in equal shares. L died in 1916 and in an action brought in 1925 it was held that there was a trust for the residuary legatees and their claim was accordingly statute barred. After 1925, the Trustee Act 1888 would *prima facie* have applied wherever a man died

---

[7] *Moody* v. *Poole Corporation*, [1945] 1 All E.R. 536; [1945] K.B. 350, C.A.; cf. *Re Howlett supra*.

[8] *How* v. *Winterton*, [1896] 2 Ch. 626, C.A.

[9] *Hornsey Local Board* v. *Monarch Investment Building Society* (1889), 24 Q.B.D. 1, C.A.; contra, Kekewich J. in *Re Pardoe*, [1906] 1 Ch. 265 (overruled on another point, [1906] 2 Ch. 340, C.A.), but previous decision of Court of Appeal not cited.

[10] *Hornsey Local Board* v. *Monarch Investment Building Society, supra; contra, Re Johnson* (1885), 29 Ch.D. 964 (end of executor's year).

[11] *Prior* v. *Horniblow* (1836), 2 Y. & C. Ex. 200; *Rudd* v. *Rudd*, [1895] 1 Ir. 15, C.A.

[12] *Re Johnson, supra; Re Ludlam* (1890), 63 L.T. 330; cf. *Re Owen*, [1894] 3 Ch. 220.

[13] [1920] 1 Ch. 423, C.A. Cf. *Re Davis*, [1891] 3 Ch. 119, C.A.; *Re Barker*, [1892] 2 Ch. 491; *Re Lacy*, [1899] 2 Ch. 149.

[14] [1927] 2 Ch. 323; *Re Bowden* (1890), 45 Ch.D. 444; *Re Swain*, [1891] 3 Ch. 233; *Re Timmis*, [1902] 1 Ch. 177.

intestate, by reason of the express trusts set up by the Administration of Estates Act 1925.[15]

Some writers[16] take the view that the same distinction has to be drawn under the Act of 1939, but it is submitted that the better view is that this distinction is no longer relevant.[17] Section 20 of the Act of 1939 is more widely worded than the corresponding provision of the Real Property Limitation Act 1874 and it is submitted that an "action in respect of [a] claim to the personal estate of a deceased person"[18] remains such notwithstanding that the personal representative may for some purposes have become a trustee. This view is supported by Re Diplock[19] in two ways. In a general way it is supported by the indication of the proper approach to section 20 given by Lord Simonds in the House of Lords, in a speech concurred in by all the other Law Lords present, when he said[20] "there is nothing in the ancestry of the section which justifies, much less requires, a narrower meaning being given to its words than they ordinarily bear". More specifically, it is supported by the observations of the Court of Appeal[1] as to the position of an administrator on intestacy. The Court affirmed the proposition that after 1925 and before the 1939 Act such an administrator would be a trustee for the next-of-kin and that the relevant period of limitation would apparently be six years under the Trustee Act 1888. However, under the 1939 Act, such a case would, it was said, be governed by section 20 and the limitation period would accordingly be twelve years, thus increasing the statutory period applicable.

Finally, in relation to the Limitation Act 1939, two points may be noted. First, that the general provisions as to the extension of the period of limitation by reason of disability,[2] concealed fraud and mistake[3] apply to actions against trustees. Secondly, that the periods of limitation may be extended, in appropriate cases, under the provisions of the Limitation (Enemies and War Prisoners) Act 1945. It does not seem necessary now to discuss those provisions.

Where the Limitation Act 1939 does not apply[4] the question arises whether it can be barred by the plaintiff's delay in bringing the action, i.e., by laches. In practice, lapse of time is commonly pleaded together with acquiescence and it has been said that lapse of time is simply evidence of assent or acquiescence.[5] Further in a number of cases it has been stated that mere delay by itself can

---

15 Sections 33 and 46.
16 Preston and Newsom, *Limitation of Actions*, 3rd Ed., p. 188; Halsbury's *Laws of England*, 3rd Ed., Vol. 24, p. 282; Williams, *Law of Wills*, 4th Ed., pp. 184, 185.
17 Franks, *Limitations of Actions*, pp. 49, 50.
18 Limitation Act 1939, s. 20.
19 [1948] 2 All E.R. 318; [1948] Ch. 465, C.A.; *affirmed sub nom. Ministry of Health* v. *Simpson*, [1950] 2 All E.R. 1137; [1951] A.C. 251, H.L.
20 At pp. 1148; 276, 277, respectively.
1 *Supra*, at 342, 343; 511–513, *semble*; approved by the House of Lords *supra*, at 1147; 276.
2 Section 22.
3 Section 26. *Eddis* v. *Chichester Constable*, [1969] 2 All E.R. 912; [1962] 2 Ch. 345, C.A. *Archer* v. *Moss*, [1971] 1 All E.R. 747; *sub nom. Applegate* v. *Moss*, [1971] 1 Q.B. 406, C.A.; *King* v. *Victor Parsons & Co.*, [1973] 1 All E.R. 206, C.A.
4 *Re Pauling's Settlement Trust*, [1961] 3 All E.R. 713, 735, affirmed on this point, [1963] 3 All E.R. 1; [1964] Ch. 300, C.A.
5 *Morse* v. *Royal* (1806), 12 Ves. 355; *Life Association of Scotland* v. *Siddal* (1861), 3 De G.F. & J. 58.

never bar the plaintiff,[6] but that there must either be acquiescence or a change in the situation of the defendant or innocent third parties in the meantime who would be unfairly prejudiced if the claim were to be admitted. On the other hand in *Re Sharpe*,[7] Lindley L.J. said[8] "that staleness of demand as distinguished from the Statute of Limitations and analogy to it may furnish a defence in Equity to an equitable claim was settled at least as early as *Smith* v. *Clay*".[9] It is submitted that mere delay may be sufficient to bar a claim, where the balance of justice or injustice in affording or refusing relief so requires, as seems bound to be the case sooner or later.[10] In practice, however, wherever possible, the court prefers to rely on acquiescence.

d Section 61 of the Trustee Act 1925[11]

This section provides—

"If it appears to the court that a trustee . . . is or may be personally liable for any breach of trust . . . but has acted honestly and reasonably, and ought fairly to be excused for the breach of trust and for omitting to obtain the directions of the court in the matter in which he committed such breach, then the court may relieve him either wholly or partly from personal liability for the same."

"The provisions of the section", it has been said,[12] "were intended to enable the Court to excuse breaches of trust where the circumstances of the particular case showed reasonable conduct, but it was never meant to be used as a sort of general indemnity clause for honest men who neglect their duty". The onus of showing that he acted not only honestly but also reasonably rests on the trustee,[13] and unless both these matters are established "the court cannot help the trustees; but if both are made out, there is then a case for the Court to consider whether the trustee ought fairly to be excused for the breach, looking at all the circumstances".[14] By "fairly" is meant in fairness to the trustee and to other people who may be affected.[15] Although the court has refused to fetter its discretion and insists that each case must be dealt with according to its own circumstances,[16] it is helpful to look at some of the decisions, particularly on the question of reasonableness. Before doing so it may be observed that the courts have said that the section should not be narrowly construed.[17] It can even be

---

[6] *Blake* v. *Gale* (1886), 32 Ch.D. 571, C.A.; *Rochefoucauld* v. *Boustead*, [1897] 1 Ch. 196, C.A.; *Re Lacey*, [1907] 1 Ch. 330, C.A.

[7] [1892] 1 Ch. 154, C.A.

[8] At p. 168.   [9] (1767), 3 Bro.C.C. 639 n.

[10] *Lindsay Petroleum Oil Co.* v. *Hurd* (1874), L.R. 5 P.C. 221 (where there is an important statement of the doctrine); *Erlanger* v. *New Sombrero Phosphate Co.* (1878), 3 App. Cas. 1218, H.L.; *Brooks* v. *Muckleston*, [1909] 2 Ch. 519.

[11] Re-enacting, with slight alterations Judicial Trustees Act 1896, s. 3, decisions on which are usually applicable to s. 61. The section need not be specially pleaded—*Singlehurst* v. *Tapscott Steam Ship Company*, [1899] W.N. 133, C.A., though it is better that it should be. See generally (1955), 19 Con. 420 (L. A. Sheridan).

[12] *Evans Williams* v. *Byron* (1901), 18 T.L.R. 172 *per* Byrne J. at 176.

[13] *Re Stuart*, [1897] 2 Ch. 583.

[14] *Per* Sir Ford North, giving the advice of P.C. in *National Trustees Company of Australasia* v. *General Finance Company of Australasia*, [1905] A.C. 373, at p. 381 on the corresponding provision of the Victorian Trusts Act 1901; *Re Turner*, [1897] 1 Ch. 536.

[15] *Marsden* v. *Regan*, [1954] 1 All E.R. 475, C.A.

[16] *Re Turner, supra; Re Kay*, [1897] 2 Ch. 518.

[17] *Re Allsop*, [1914] 1 Ch. 1, C.A.

applied to cases where a trustee has paid the wrong person,[18] and the maxim *ignorantia iuris non excusat* does not in the least prevent the court from granting relief.[19] There must, however, have been a breach of trust—the section cannot be used to excuse trustees from a breach of trust they wish to commit in the future.[20] On another point it seems clear that the court will be much less ready to grant relief to a professional trustee who is being paid for his services in performing his duties.[1]

Turning to the cases in *Re Stuart*,[2] the court said it was fair to consider whether the trustee would have acted in the same way if he had been dealing with his own property. If he would, it is a point in his favour, though not enough by itself to show that he acted reasonably.[3] The taking and acceptance of advice by someone reasonably believed to be qualified to give it has a similar effect.[4] It was also held in *Re Stuart*[5] that the statutory regulations[6] as to investment on mortgage set up a standard of reasonable conduct and that failure to comply with them makes it difficult for the court to grant relief, though it is not an absolute bar to doing so. In *Chapman* v. *Browne*[7] the trustees were held not to have acted reasonably, where they never really considered whether the security was one which it was right and proper for a trustee to take, and in *Wynne* v. *Tempest*[8] the court refused relief where a trustee had left the trust money in the hands of his co-trustee, a solicitor, without sufficient reason. Indeed Kekewich J. regarded it not merely as a failure to act reasonably, but as dishonest in this context, where a trustee "does nothing, swallows wholesale what is said by his co-trustee, never asks for explanation, and accepts flimsy explanations".[9] A final illustration of refusal of relief by the court is *Ward-Smith* v. *Jebb*[10] where the court would assist neither a solicitor trustee nor his lay co-trustee, who had made payments out of a trust fund on the erroneous assumption that a certain person was entitled by reason of the Adoption of Children Act, 1949, having failed to observe the provisions of the Act, which made it quite clear that it did not apply on the facts of the case. Accepting the general rule that a trustee must exercise that degree of care which a prudent man would exercise in respect of his own affairs, Buckley J. applied it to the facts before him by saying[11]: "A prudent man, whose affairs were affected by a statute would either satisfy himself that he fully understood its effect or would seek legal advice.

---

[18] *Re Allsop, supra; Re Wightwick's Will Trusts*, [1950] 1 All E.R. 689; [1950] Ch. 260. But see *Ward-Smith* v. *Jebb* (1964), 108 Sol.Jo. 919, discussed *infra*, p. 380.
[19] *Holland* v. *Administrator of German Property*, [1937] 2 All E.R. 807.
[20] *Re Rosenthal*, [1972] 3 All E.R. 553.
[1] *National Trustees Company of Australasia* v. *General Finance Company of Australasia*, [1905] A.C. 373, P.C.; *Re Windsor Steam Coal Co.* (1901) *Ltd.*, [1929] 1 Ch. 151, C.A.; *Re Pauling's Settlement Trusts*, [1963] 3 All E.R. 1; [1964] Ch. 303, C.A.
[2] [1897] 2 Ch. 583; *Re Barker* (1898), 77 L.T. 712.
[3] Per Farwell J. in *Re Lord De Clifford's Estate*, [1900] 2 Ch. 707, at p. 716, "The fact that he has acted with equal foolishness in both cases will not justify relief under this statute".
[4] *Marsden* v. *Regan*, [1954] 1 All E.R. 475, C.A.
[5] *Supra.*
[6] Trustee Act 1925, s. 8.
[7] [1902] 1 Ch. 785, C.A.
[8] (1897), 13 T.L.R. 360; *Re Second East Dulwich etc. Building Society* (1899), 68 L.J. Ch. 196.
[9] *Re Second East Dulwich etc. Building Society, supra*, at 198.
[10] (1964), 108 Sol.Jo. 919.
[11] *Ibid.*

A solicitor trustee could not be heard to say that it was reasonable to apply a lower standard to him." The lay trustee was in no better position, in the absence of any evidence that he had relied on the advice of the solicitor or any other legal adviser. The question of any indemnity between the two trustees was not before the court.

On the other hand, in *Re Lord De Clifford's Estate*[12] executors were relieved where, during five years administration of the estate, and knowing that large sums were required for administration purposes, they paid various sums to their solicitors in reliance on their statements that they were required for those purposes. Over ninety per cent of the sums were in fact so applied, but the balance was lost on the solicitors' bankruptcy. Similarly where executors failed to call in a small debt, where the terms of the will might fairly bring a business man to the conclusion there was no duty to do so.[13] According to the circumstances it may[14] or may not be reasonable to act without seeking the directions of the court.

e Discharge in bankruptcy

A claim in respect of a breach of trust is provable in bankruptcy,[15] and in general, an order of discharge releases a bankrupt from all debts provable in bankruptcy.[16] This provision applies to all claims in respect of a breach of trust, except where the debt or liability was incurred by means of any fraud or fraudulent breach of trust to which the bankrupt trustee was a party.[17] Although, as stated, in the case of a non-fraudulent breach of trust the discharge bars the right to the original debt due from the trustee, his duties, character and functions as debtor are perfectly distinct from those which belong to him as trustee, and those of the trustee are not affected by the bankruptcy. Accordingly it is the duty of a defaulting trustee to prove in his own bankruptcy just as much as if he were a perfect stranger to it, and it is a clear breach of trust for him to fail to do so. This further breach of trust subsequently attaching to the trustee in that character is unaffected by the discharge, and the trustee accordingly remains liable for it, to the amount of the dividends he would have received under the bankruptcy.[18]

4 CRIMINAL LIABILITY OF TRUSTEES

Under the Larceny Act 1916[19] fraudulent conversion by a trustee was a special offence, and there were restrictions on the institution of a prosecution thereunder. This Act was repealed by the Theft Act 1968 under which a trustee is liable for ordinary theft, without any special restrictions on prosecution, "if he dishonestly appropriates property belonging to another with the intention of permanently depriving the other of it".[20] For the purposes of the Act, in the case of trust property, the persons to whom it belongs are to be regarded as

---

[12] [1900] 2 Ch. 707; *Perrins v. Bellamy*, [1899] 1 Ch. 797, C.A.
[13] *Re Grindey*, [1898] 2 Ch. 593, C.A.; *Re Mackay*, [1911] 1 Ch. 300.
[14] *Re Gee*, [1948] 1 All E.R. 498; [1948] Ch. 284.
[15] Bankruptcy Act 1914, s. 30 (1) and (3).
[16] *Ibid.*, s. 28 (2).
[17] *Ibid.*, s. 28 (1) (b).
[18] *Orrett v. Corser* (1855), 21 Beav. 52.
[19] Section 21.
[20] Theft Act 1968, s. 1 (1).

including "any person having a right to enforce the trust",[21] i.e. the beneficiaries or, in the case of a charitable trust, the Attorney-General. In the case of
unenforceable trusts, it would presumably include the person entitled to the
residue, from which it would follow that it would not be theft if the trustee was
himself solely entitled to the residue.[1] Though in general a person cannot steal
land, a trustee can and will do so if "he appropriates the land or anything
forming part of it by dealing with it in breach of the confidence reposed in
him."[2] This does not, however, represent any extension of the law, since it
was a possible subject of fraudulent conversion under the provisions of the
Larceny Act 1916 mentioned above.

Finally, it may be mentioned that under the Debtors Act 1869, section 4, a
trustee who has been ordered by the court to pay any sum in his possession or
under his control is, on default, liable to imprisonment for a period of up to a year.

---

[21] Theft Act 1968, s. 5 (2).
[1] Nor, of course, would the trustee in such case be liable for breach of trust.
[2] Theft Act 1968, s. 4 (2) (a).

CHAPTER 13

Injunctions

1 MEANING AND NATURE OF AN INJUNCTION

a Meaning and jurisdiction

An injunction is an order[1] of the court directing a person or persons to refrain from doing some particular act or thing or, less often, to do some particular act or thing. It is an equitable remedy which originally could only be obtained in the Court of Chancery or the Court of Exchequer in equity.[2] A limited power to grant injunctions was first given to the common law courts by the Patent Law Amendment Act 1852 and then, by the Common Law Procedure Act 1854,[3] the common law courts were given so wide a jurisdiction to grant injunctions in all cases of breach of contract or other injury that, as Baggalay L.J. observed,[4] they had a more extensive jurisdiction as regarded the granting of injunctions than the Court of Chancery itself.

These statutes have been repealed and the Judicature Acts[5] have transferred to the High Court all the jurisdiction, including the jurisdiction to grant injunctions, previously exercised both by the Court of Chancery and the common law courts. The jurisdiction may, of course, be exercised by every division of the High Court, though in practice most applications for an injunction are made to the Chancery Division.[6]

In addition to the above provisions the Judicature Acts[7] also declare that "the

---

1 Formerly a writ of injunction issuing under an order of the court was required, but now there is simply a judgment or order.
2 The equity jurisdiction of the Court of Exchequer was abolished by the Court of Chancery Act 1841.
3 Common Law Procedure Act 1854, ss. 79 and 82.
4 In *Quartz Hill Consolidated Gold Mining Co.* v. *Beall* (1882), 20 Ch.D. 501, 509, C.A.
5 Judicature Act 1873, s. 16, now replaced by Judicature Act 1925, s. 18 (2).
6 The County Court has jurisdiction to grant an injunction but only as ancillary to a claim for money or, presumably, other relief within the substantive jurisdiction of the court—County Courts Act 1959, s. 74 as amended by the Administration of Justice Act 1969, s. 6. *R.* v. *Cheshire County Court Judge,* [1921] 2 K.B. 694; [1921] All E.R. Rep. 344, C.A.; *De Vries* v. *Smallridge,* [1928] 1 K.B. 482; [1927] All E.R. Rep. 613, C.A.; *Thompson* v. *White,* [1970] 3 All E.R. 678. An injunction may, however, be granted independently of any other claim on a counter-claim—County Courts Act 1959, s. 65.
7 Judicature Act 1925, s. 45, replacing Judicature Act 1873, s. 25 (8).

High Court may grant . . . an injunction . . . by an interlocutory order[8] in all cases in which it appears to the court to be just or convenient so to do . . . either unconditionally or on such terms and conditions as the court thinks just".

The exact effect of these statutory provisions is a matter of some doubt, for contradictory dicta are to be found in the spate of decisions on this matter at the end of the last century. It seems fairly safe, however, to say that, in general, the old equitable principles still apply, and it may well be that the intention of the Judicature Act 1873 was merely to obviate certain technical difficulties in regard to the grant of injunctions.[9] In discussing this matter cases on the jurisdiction of the court to appoint a receiver may be cited as authorities as this jurisdiction depends on the same statutory provision.

An attractive view is "that, where there is a legal right which was, independently of the [Judicature Act], capable of being enforced either at law or in equity, then whatever may have been the previous practice, the High Court may interfere by injunction in protection of that right".[10] In other words where, before the Judicature Acts, some court would have had power to grant some remedy, there is now jurisdiction

> "to superadd to what would have been previously the remedy, a remedy by way of injunction, altering therefore not in any way the rights of the parties so as to give a right to those who had no legal right before, but enabling the court to modify the principle on which it had previously proceeded in granting injunctions, so that where there is a legal right the court may, without being hampered by its old rules, grant an injunction where it is just or convenient to do so for the purpose of protecting or asserting the legal rights of the parties".[11]

An illustration of this view is the case of *Aslatt* v. *Southampton Corporation*.[12] There a meeting of the defendant corporation had been summoned to declare the office of alderman held by the plaintiff void on the ground of an alleged disqualification, and to elect a successor. Having decided the issue of disqualification in favour of the plaintiff, the judge had to consider whether he would issue an injunction to restrain the defendant corporation from declaring void the office of alderman held by the plaintiff. There was no precedent for

---

[8] This means an order other than a final judgment or decree in an action, and may accordingly be made after judgment—*Smith* v. *Cowell* (1880), 6 Q.B.D. 75, C.A. And what can be done by interlocutory application can *a fortiori* be done at the trial of the action—*Beddow* v. *Beddow* (1878), 9 Ch.D. 89; *North London Rail. Co.* v. *Great Northern Rail. Co.* (1883), 11 Q.B.D. 30, C.A., *per* Cotton L.J. at p. 39.

[9] *Fletcher* v. *Rodgers* (1878), 27 W.R. 97, C.A.; *Day* v. *Brownrigg* (1878), 10 Ch.D. 294, C.A.; *Gaskin* v. *Balls* (1879), 13 Ch.D. 324, C.A.

[10] *Per* Cotton L.J. in *North London Rail. Co.* v. *Great Northern Rail. Co.*, *supra*, at p. 40; *Steamship Den of Airlie Ltd.* v. *Mitsui & Co. Ltd.* (1912), 106 L.T. 451, C.A.; *Duchess of Argyll* v. *Duke of Argyll*, [1965] 1 All E.R. 611, 634; [1967] Ch. 302, 344. Cf. *Montgomery* v. *Montgomery*, [1964] 2 All E.R. 22; [1965] P. 46.

[11] *Per* Cotton L.J., *ubi supra*, at p. 39. Dicta to some extent supporting this view may be found in *Anglo-Italian Bank* v. *Davies* (1878), 9 Ch.D. 275, C.A. (Jessel M.R. and Cotton L.J.); *Smith* v. *Cowell* (1880), 6 Q.B.D. 75, C.A. (Lord Esher); *Thomas* v. *Williams* (1880), 14 Ch.D. 864 (Fry J.); *Quartz Hill Consolidated Gold Mining Co.* v. *Beall* (1882), 20 Ch.D. 501, C.A. (Jessel M.R.); *Manchester and Liverpool District Banking Company* v. *Parkinson* (1888), 2 Q.B.D. 173, C.A.; *Monson* v. *Tussauds Ltd.*, [1894] 1 Q.B. 671, C.A. (Lopes L.J.).

[12] (1880), 16 Ch.D. 143; *Hedley* v. *Bates* (1880), 13 Ch.D. 498; *Richardson* v. *Methley School Board*, [1893] 3 Ch. 510.

such an injunction, for a very good reason as the judge explained,[13] namely "that the Courts of Common Law which exercised jurisdiction over cases of this kind had no power to grant an injunction, because the Act[14] enabling them to do so was not passed until a very recent date, and therefore you could not have an injunction so far as the Common Law was concerned; nor was it the habit of the Court of Chancery to grant an injunction in aid of a legal right where the man was in possession of an office". The judge, however, held that as a result of the Judicature Act 1873[15] he had jurisdiction to protect the plaintiff and prevent a serious injury by granting an appropriate injunction.

Although section 25 (8)[16] was passed to amend and declare the law to be thereafter administered, it is doubtful whether the above view can be sustained in the light of decisions and strong dicta to the effect that the statutory provisions have not in any respect enlarged the jurisdiction, and that an injunction can only be granted in a case where it could have been granted in like case by some court before 1875. One may start with *North London Rail. Co.* v. *Great Northern Rail. Co.*[17] where Lord Esher expressed the view, *obiter*, that the Judicature Act 1873 had not dealt with jurisdiction at all, but only with procedure; and was inclined to hold that if no court would have had the power of issuing an injunction before the Judicature Act, no part of the High Court had power to issue such an injunction after it. Notwithstanding that Lord Esher expressly declared it was not necessary to decide this latter point, and that the only other judge, Cotton L.J., took, as we have seen, a different view, the Court of Appeal has subsequently, on at least three occasions,[18] expressly declared that this case decides that the Act gave no power to the court to grant an injunction in a case in which no court would have granted one before the Act. In the light of these clear decisions it would seem that the restrictive interpretation of the Act must prevail, except possibly in the House of Lords. Even on this restrictive view, however, it seems that the court may now be more ready to grant injunctions in cases where, though there was jurisdiction to do so, they were not previously granted in practice.[19]

It is quite clear in any case that no injunction can be granted where there has been no violation of any right in the plaintiff. For instance, in *Day* v. *Brownrigg*[20] the plaintiff lived in a house that for some sixty years had been called "Ashford Lodge". The defendant's adjoining house had been known for some forty years as "Ashford Villa". The plaintiff was held to have no claim to an injunction

---

[13] *Aslatt* v. *Southampton Corporation* (1880), 16 Ch.D. 143, 147, *per* Jessel M.R. But note the comment of Chitty J. on Jessel M.R.'s views in *Hayward* v. *East London Waterworks Coy.* (1884), 28 Ch.D. 138, 146.

[14] I.e. the Common Law Procedure Act 1854.

[15] Section 25 (8), now replaced by s. 45 of the Judicature Act, 1925.

[16] Judicature Act 1873.

[17] (1883), 11 Q.B.D. 30, C.A. Cf. the same judge's dicta in *Smith* v. *Cowell* (1880), 6 Q.B.D. 75, C.A. and *Manchester and Liverpool District Banking Co.* v. *Parkinson* (1888), 2 Q.B.D. 173, C.A.

[18] *Holmes* v. *Millage*, [1893] 1 Q.B. 551, C.A.; *Kitts* v. *Moore*, [1895] 1 Q.B. 253, C.A.; *Morgan* v. *Hart*, [1914] 2 K.B. 183, C.A.

[19] *Bonnard* v. *Perryman*, [1891] 2 Ch. 269, C.A.; *Cummins* v. *Perkins*, [1899] 1 Ch. 16, C.A.

[20] (1878), 10 Ch.D. 294, C.A.; *Street* v. *Union Bank of Spain & England* (1885), 30 Ch.D. 156; *White* v. *Mellin*, [1895] A.C. 154, H.L.; *Webster* v. *Webster*, [1916] 1 K.B. 714; *Sports and General Press Agency Ltd.* v. *"Our Dogs" Publicity Co. Ltd.*, [1917] 2 K.B. 125, C.A.

when the defendant altered the name of his house to "Ashford Lodge", not-withstanding the resulting inconvenience. Since there is no right of property in the name of a house, the plaintiff had suffered no legal injury.

Where the statute uses the phrase "just or convenient"[21] it must be read "just, as well as convenient".[22] It is undisputed that these "well-known words do not confer an arbitrary or unregulated discretion on the court":[1] "what is right or just must be decided, not by the caprice of the judge, but according to sufficient legal reasons or on settled legal principles".[2] When it is said that equitable remedies are discretionary, what is meant is that the court is entitled to take into account certain collateral matters, such as the conduct of the parties, in addition to considering their bare legal rights, in deciding whether to grant an equitable remedy. It may be added that it follows that an appeal court will be slow to interfere with an order made by the trial judge in his discretion, unless it appears that he has acted on wrong principles.

b   Remedy *in personam*

In granting an injunction "the court acts *in personam*, and will not suffer anyone within its reach to do what is contrary to its notions of equity, merely because the act to be done may be, in point of locality, beyond its jurisdiction".[3] A person who is residing abroad, and physically outside the jurisdiction, is nevertheless within the reach of the court if service out of the jurisdiction can properly be made upon him under rules of court,[4] and the same is true of a company incorporated abroad.[5] The court, however, will consider carefully before it grants an injunction in these cases, and, as a general rule, will not adjudicate on questions relating to the title to or the right to the possession of immovable property out of the jurisdiction,[6] nor will it give effect to a contractual or equitable right *in personam* which the *lex situs* would treat as incapable of creation.[7]

c   Where a particular remedy is provided by statute

If a right of property which is created or confirmed by statute is infringed, it is settled that the fact that a particular remedy is provided for an infringement of that right by statute does not oust the jurisdiction of the court to grant an injunction. Even though the statutory remedy may be the only remedy available for the past infringement, the court may grant an injunction to

---

[21] See p. 384, *ante*.
[22] *Day* v. *Brownrigg*, *supra*, *per* Jessel M.R. at p. 307; *Beddow* v. *Beddow* (1878), 9 Ch.D. 89.
[1] *Per* Davey L.J. in *Harris* v. *Beauchamp Bros.*, [1894] 1 Q.B. 801, 809, C.A.
[2] *Per* Jessel M.R. in *Beddow* v. *Beddow*, *supra*, at p. 93.
[3] *Per* Cranworth L.C. in *Carron Iron Co.* v. *Maclaran* (1855), 5 H.L.Cas. 416, at 436, 437; *Hope* v. *Carnegie* (1868), L.R. 7 Eq. 254. See, however, *"Morocco Bound" Syndicate, Ltd.* v. *Harris*, [1895] 1 Ch. 534.
[4] *Re Liddell's Settlement Trusts*, [1936] 1 All E.R. 239; [1936] Ch. 365, C.A. The relevant rules are to be found in R.S.C., O. 11.
[5] *Hospital for Sick Children* v. *Walt Disney Productions Inc.*, [1967] 1 All E.R. 1005; [1968] Ch. 52, C.A.
[6] *Deschamps* v. *Miller*, [1908] 1 Ch. 856.
[7] *Bank of Africa, Ltd.* v. *Cohen*, [1909] 2 Ch. 129, C.A.

prevent further infringements in the future,[8] unless the statute expressly or by implication provides to the contrary.[9] Where, however, a statute creates an offence and provides a summary remedy, the generally accepted view has been that a person who is aggrieved by the commission of the offence but who has no property right which is infringed thereby, can do no more than use the statutory remedy; he is not entitled to an injunction.[10] In *Duchess of Argyll* v. *Duke of Argyll*,[11] however, Ungoed-Thomas J. repudiated this view in a case where a threatened breach of the Judicial Proceedings (Regulation of Reports) Act 1926[12] would involve an injury to the plaintiff's reputation. Even though his decision may represent a "rational and sensible development to correspond with the different needs and values in a different age",[13] it is submitted that it cannot be confidently relied upon as all the contrary authorities do not appear to have been considered. In any case, however, as we shall see,[14] the Attorney-General may be able to claim an injunction if the public interest is affected.

2 CLASSIFICATION OF INJUNCTIONS

a Prohibitory and mandatory

The prohibitory or restrictive injunction, by which a person is directed to refrain from doing some particular act or thing, is the original basic form, the mandatory injunction, by which a person is directed to perform some positive act, being a later development. This is demonstrated by the fact that until the turn of the century an order, even though mandatory in substance, had to be drafted in a prohibitory form. Thus the court would not, for instance, make an order directing a building to be pulled down, but would order the defendant not to allow it to remain on the land. Since the decision in *Jackson* v. *Normanby Brick Co.*,[15] however, it has been the rule that if an injunction is mandatory in substance, it should be made in direct mandatory form.

At one time it was thought that particular caution had to be exercised by the court in granting a mandatory injunction,[16] but it is now settled that there is no distinction in principle between granting a prohibitory and a mandatory injunction: every injunction requires to be granted with care and caution, but it is not more needed in one case than the other.[17] The court will not hesitate to

---

[8] *Stevens* v. *Chown*, [1901] 1 Ch. 894; *Devonport Corporation* v. *Tozer*, [1903] 1 Ch. 759, C.A.; *Carlton Illustrators* v. *Coleman & Co., Ltd.*, [1911] 1 K.B. 771.

[9] *Evans* v. *Manchester, Sheffield and Lincolnshire Rail. Co.* (1887), 36 Ch.D. 626; *Stevens* v. *Chown, supra*.

[10] *Patent Agents Institute* v. *Lockwood*, [1894] A.C. 347, H.L.; *Devonport Corporation* v. *Tozer, supra*; *Thorne* v. *British Broadcasting Corporation*, [1967] 2 All E.R. 1225, C.A.

[11] [1965] 1 All E.R. 611; [1967] Ch. 302.

[12] This Act made it an offence to publish details, with certain exceptions, of matrimonial proceedings.

[13] *Per* Ungoed-Thomas J. in *Duchess of Argyll* v. *Duke of Argyll, supra*, at p. 634; 344.

[14] See Section 7 g, p. 422, *post*.

[15] [1899] 1 Ch. 438, C.A. Occasionally orders were made in the positive form even before this date—*Bidwell* v. *Holden* (1890), 63 L.T. 105.

[16] *Great North of England, Clarence and Hartlepool Junction Rail. Co.* v. *Clarence Rail. Co.* (1845), 1 Coll. 507; *Isenberg* v. *East India House Estate Co., Ltd.* (1863), 3 De G.J. & Sm. 263.

[17] *Smith* v. *Smith* (1875), L.R. 20 Eq. 500; *Lawrence* v. *Horton* (1890), 59 L.J. Ch. 440.

grant a mandatory injunction in any appropriate case,[18] but whenever it does so, it must be careful to see that the defendant knows exactly what he has to do, and this means not as a matter of law but as a matter of fact.[19]

There is obviously an analogy between a mandatory injunction and a decree of specific performance. As we shall see there are certain contracts of which specific performance cannot be obtained,[20] and one cannot get round this by making a claim for a mandatory injunction. Thus the court will not grant an injunction ordering the defendant to do something which is impossible,[21] or which cannot be enforced or which is unlawful,[22] and as a general rule[23] it will not grant an injunction which would involve the court in constant super-intendence of works of building or repair,[1] nor one ordering the performance of a continuous act which requires the continuous employment of people,[2] or the carrying on of a business.[3] Again the court will not normally make an order requiring a defendant to perform personal services,[4] nor one to enforce an obligation entered into by a person that he will not apply to Parliament, or that he will not oppose an application to Parliament by another person,[5] or to compel the sale and delivery of chattels not specific or ascertained.[6]

b Perpetual and interlocutory

A perpetual injunction is one which has been granted after the right thereto has been established in an ordinary action in which both sides have been fully heard, and it is intended to settle finally the relations between the parties in connection with the matter in dispute, so as to relieve the plaintiff from the need for bringing a series of actions as his rights are from time to time infringed by the defendant. The word "perpetual" does not necessarily signify that the order is to remain permanently effective: in some cases the defendant may be entitled to require that the operation of the injunction be expressly limited to a specified period as, for instance, where a man has entered into a valid contract not to enter into competition with his former employer in a defined area for, say, three years after leaving the employment.

An interlocutory injunction, on the other hand, is only a temporary measure

---

[18] *Hermann Loog* v. *Bean* (1884), 26 Ch.D. 306, C.A.; *Puddephatt* v. *Leith*, [1916] 1 Ch. 200. See *Charrington* v. *Simons & Co., Ltd.*, [1971] 2 All E. R. 588, C.A. and see p. 414 *infra*.
[19] *Redland Bricks, Ltd.* v. *Morris*, [1969] 2 All E.R. 576; [1970] A.C. 652, H.L.
[20] See Chapter 14, Section 2, p. 429, *post*.
[21] *A.-G.* v. *Colney Hatch Lunatic Asylum* (1868), 4 Ch. App. 146.
[22] *Pride of Derby and Derbyshire Angling Association, Ltd.* v. *British Celanese, Ltd.*, [1953] 1 All E.R. 179; [1953] Ch. 149, C.A. *per* Evershed M.R. at 198; 181.
[23] *Semble*, it may do so in exceptional circumstances, as in the case of specific performance. See *Wolverhampton Corporation* v. *Emmons*, [1901] 1 K.B. 515, C.A.; *A.-G.* v. *Colchester Corporation*, [1955] 2 All E.R. 124; [1955] 2 Q.B. 207 at pp. 128; 216.
[1] *A.-G.* v. *Staffordshire County Council*, [1905] 1 Ch. 336; cf. *Ryan* v. *Mutual Tontine Westminster Chambers Association*, [1893] 1 Ch. 116, C.A.; *Kennard* v. *Cory Bros.*, [1922] 2 Ch. 1, C.A.
[2] *Powell Duffryn Steam Co.* v. *Taff Vale Rail. Co.* (1874), 9 Ch. App. 331; *Ryan* v. *Mutual Tontine Westminster Chambers Association, supra*.
[3] *A.-G.* v. *Colchester Corporation*, [1955] 2 All E.R. 124; [1955] 2 Q.B. 207.
[4] *Lumley* v. *Wagner* (1852), 1 De G.M. & G. 604. Cf. *Hill* v. *C. A. Parsons & Co., Ltd.*, [1971] 3 All E.R. 1345; [1972] Ch. 305, C.A.; and see pp. 433, 434, *infra*.
[5] *Bilston Corporation* v. *Wolverhampton Corporation*, [1942] Ch. 391; [1942] 2 All E.R. 447.
[6] *Sky Petroleum, Ltd.* v. *VIP Petroleum, Ltd.*, [1974] 1 All E.R. 954—an exceptional case where order made. See p. 430, *infra*.

framed so as to continue in force until the trial of the action, or until further order,[7] with the object of preserving matters *in statu quo* in the meantime. In an appropriate case, however, the court may grant an interlocutory injunction even though from a practical point of view it disposes of the matter. This has been done, for instance, where it has been applied for in order to remove a trespasser, who had plainly no defence to the action and merely sought to delay his eviction as long as possible;[8] and, again, to prevent a member of a private association from being deprived of his right to vote at the annual general meeting.[9]

Generally an interlocutory injunction will only be granted on notice, so as to give the defendant a full opportunity to resist the claim. In a case of urgency, however, it may be granted *ex parte*.[10] Generally on an *ex parte* application,[11] and sometimes in applications on notice where, for instance, the defendant has not had time properly to answer the plaintiff's affidavits, the court will grant only an interim injunction. The form and procedure differ slightly in the different divisions, but in the Chancery Division, an interim injunction is usually granted until the next motion day[12] for which proper notice of motion[13] can be given, or further order.[14] The court may hear an *ex parte* application for an injunction at any time after the writ has been issued, even before it has been served on the defendant[15]: indeed in a case of extreme urgency, where delay might be fatal, the court has jurisdiction to grant an injunction before the issue of the writ or originating summons, even on a Sunday.[16]

The purpose of an interlocutory injunction, i.e. the preservation of the *status quo*, means that it is generally of a prohibitory nature. In exceptional circumstances, however, a mandatory injunction may be granted on an interlocutory application.[17] A phrase commonly used to describe the kind of situation in which the court might properly be expected to grant a mandatory

---

[7] For instance, it may be dissolved if the defendant can show it was granted on the suppression or misrepresentation of material facts.

[8] *Manchester Corporation* v. *Connolly*, [1970] 1 All E.R. 961; [1970] Ch. 420, C.A.

[9] *Woodford* v. *Smith*, [1970] 1 All E.R. 1091n.

[10] Likewise an injunction will normally only be varied or discharged on notice, but exceptionally act *ex parte*—*London City Agency(JCD), Ltd.* v. *Lee*, [1969] 3 All E.R. 1376; [1970] Ch. 597. An *ex parte* application may be opposed. As to the procedures see *Pickwick International Inc. (G.B.), Ltd.* v. *Multiple Sound Distributors, Ltd.*, [1972] 3 All E.R. 384.

[11] But an application to restrain the marriage of a ward of court will usually be granted generally until further order—*Norris* v. *Ormond*, [1883] W.N. 58.

[12] Technically, every day in term is, in the Chancery Division, a motion day (*Chaffers* v. *Baker* (1854), 5 De G.M. & G. 482), but in practice motions are heard during term on two days in each week. Special arrangements are made during the law vacations.

[13] At least two clear days (R.S.C., O. 8, r. 2 (2)), excluding Saturdays, Sundays, bank holidays, Christmas Day and Good Friday (R.S.C., O. 3, r. 2 (5)).

[14] I.e. order made before the day named—*Bolton* v. *London School Board* (1878), 7 Ch.D. 766.

[15] *Re H's Estate* (1875), 1 Ch.D. 276 (application for a receiver); *Colebourne* v. *Colebourne* (1876), 1 Ch.D. 690. And see *Beese* v. *Woodhouse*, [1970] 1 All E.R. 769, C.A.

[16] *Carr* v. *Morice* (1873), L.R. 16 Eq. 125; *Thorneloe* v. *Skoines* (1873), L.R. 16 Eq. 126; *Chanoch* v. *Hertz* (1888), 4 T.L.R. 331; *Re N.*, [1967] 1 All E.R. 161; [1967] Ch. 512; *L.* v. *L.*, [1969] 1 All E.R. 852; [1969] P. 25, and see R.S.C., O. 29, r. 1.

[17] *Daniel* v. *Ferguson*, [1891] 2 Ch. 27, C.A.; *Allport* v. *Securities Company, Ltd.* (1895), 72 L.T. 533.

E.T.   17

injunction or an interlocutory application is "stealing a march". One example is *Von Joel* v. *Hornsey*,[18] where the defendant, knowing that the plaintiff wished to serve a writ upon him, deliberately evaded service of the writ for some days and in the meantime hurried on with the building of which the plaintiff, as he well knew, was complaining. A more recent case is *Esso Petroleum Co., Ltd.* v. *Kingswood Motors (Addlestone), Ltd.*[19] where there was a five year solus tie agreement between Esso and Kingswood. As part of a scheme to defeat the tie, Kingswood's garage was conveyed to a third party, Impact. The facts were somewhat complex, but the judge had no doubt that Impact had unlawfully procured a direct breach of Kingswood's contract with Esso. Accordingly a mandatory injunction was granted ordering a reconveyance of the garage to Kingswood.

c *Quia timet* injunction

Although an injunction is directed to the future, it is, in general, based on some infringement or, in the case of an interlocutory injunction, alleged infringement of the plaintiff's rights. It is, however, possible to obtain injunctions, both interlocutory and perpetual, based on an injury which is merely threatened or apprehended, although no infringement of the plaintiff's rights has yet occurred. The House of Lords, in *Redland Bricks, Ltd.* v. *Morris*,[20] said that there are two types of cases. First, where the defendant has as yet done no hurt to the plaintiff but is threatening and intending (so the plaintiff alleges) to do works which will render irreparable harm to him or his property if carried to completion: such cases are normally concerned with negative injunctions. Secondly, the type of case where the plaintiff has been fully recompensed both at law and in equity for the damage he has suffered but where he alleges that the earlier actions of the defendant may lead to future causes of action. The typical case is where the defendant has withdrawn support from the plaintiff's land. Such withdrawal of support only constitutes a cause of action when damage is suffered, and any further damage arising from the original withdrawal will constitute a fresh cause of action. In such cases a mandatory injunction may well be the appropriate remedy.

The jurisdiction to grant a *quia timet* injunction has been said to be "as old as the hills",[21] but "no one can obtain a *quia timet* order by merely saying '*Timeo*' ".[1] Chitty J. said[2] "that the plaintiff must show a strong case of probability that the apprehended mischief will, in fact, arise"; in other words the plaintiff must prove that the threatened or intended act would be an inevitable violation of his right. Inevitable has been explained as meaning, in this context, a "very

---

[18] [1895] 2 Ch. 774, C.A. But refused in *Shepherd Homes, Ltd.* v. *Sandham*, [1970] 3 All E.R. 402; [1971] Ch. 340 (breach of negative covenant).
[19] [1973] 3 All E.R. 1057; [1974] Q.B. 142. See p. 420, *infra.*
[20] [1969] 2 All E.R. 576; [1970] A.C. 652, H.L.
[21] A.-G. v. *Long Eaton Urban Council*, [1915] 1 Ch. 124, C.A. *per* Cozens-Hardy at p. 127.
[1] *Per* Lord Dunedin in *A.-G. for Dominion of Canada* v. *Ritchie Contracting and Supply Co., Ltd.*, [1919] A.C. 999, P.C., at p. 1005.
[2] In *A.-G.* v. *Manchester Corporation*, [1893] 2 Ch. 87, at p. 92; *Litchfield–Speer* v. *Queen Anne's Gate Syndicate (No. 2), Ltd.*, [1919] 1 Ch. 407; [1918–19] All E.R. Rep. 1075; *Redland Bricks, Ltd.* v. *Morris*, [1969] 2 All E.R. 576; [1970] A.C. 652, H.L.

great probability",[3] or that "the result is one which all reasonable men skilled in the matter would expect would happen".[4]

On a given set of facts, different minds may come to different conclusions as to whether a strong case of probability can be made out and the cases accordingly do not show a clear dividing line. Thus the court thought that there was a sufficient degree of probability in *Dicker* v. *Popham, Radford & Co.*,[5] where the defendant was erecting a building which, if completed, would infringe the plaintiff's alleged right to light; in *Hepburn* v. *Lordan*,[6] where the defendant was storing and drying damp hemp, and the plaintiff brought evidence to show that there was an inherent risk of combustion which, if it occurred, would spread to his adjoining building; in *Goodhart* v. *Hyatt*,[7] where the plaintiff had a right to have pipes to convey water through the defendant's land, and the defendant was building a house over part of the line of pipes, which would render their repair more difficult and expensive; and in *Adair* v. *Young*,[8] where the only pumps on board a certain ship were pumps which were an infringement of the plaintiff's patent. On the other hand, the court will not grant an injunction where there is nothing more than a mere possibility of future injury, or mere speculation of possible mischief which may never happen at all.[9] Thus the plaintiff failed to make out a case of sufficient probability, and an injunction was refused, in *Earl of Ripon* v. *Hobart*,[10] to restrain a defendant from erecting and using a steam engine which it was alleged would constitute a nuisance, on the ground that it could be used in such a way that it would not infringe the plaintiff's rights; in *Fletcher* v. *Bealey*,[11] to restrain a defendant from polluting a river by depositing chemicals, from which in time a noxious liquid would flow, on certain land close to the river, on the ground that the liquid could be prevented from reaching the river, and that by the time the flow began some method of rendering it innocuous might have been discovered; in *A.-G.* v. *Manchester Corporation*,[12] to restrain the erection of a small-pox hospital, on the ground that the danger to the health of the neighbourhood was not sufficiently established; in *Coates* v. *Coates*,[13] to restrain the breach of a covenant against competition after the dissolution of a partnership, when the notice to dissolve the partnership had not expired; and in *Draper* v. *British Optical Association*,[14] to restrain the holding of a meeting to consider the removal of the plaintiff from the defendant association, for it was to be assumed that they would not remove him unless entitled to do so.

In particular, a *quia timet* injunction will readily be granted where the plaintiff establishes his right, and that the defendant has claimed and insisted on his right

---

[3] Per Jessel M.R. in *Pattisson* v. *Gilford* (1874), L.R. 18 Eq. 259, at p. 264.
[4] Per Chitty J. in *Phillips* v. *Thomas* (1890), 62 L.T. 793, at p. 795.
[5] (1890), 63 L.T. 379; *Potts* v. *Levy* (1854), 2 Drew. 272.
[6] (1865), 2 Hem. & M. 345; *M'Murray* v. *Cadwell* (1889), 6 T.L.R. 76.
[7] (1883) 25 Ch.D. 182.
[8] (1879) 12 Ch.D. 13, C.A.
[9] *Coates* v. *Coates* (1821), 6 Madd. 287; *Worsley* v. *Swann* (1882), 51 L.J. Ch. 576, C.A.
[10] (1834), 3 My. & K. 169; *Haines* v. *Taylor* (1847), 2 Ph. 209.
[11] (1885), 28 Ch.D. 688 (the plaintiff's right to bring another action later in case of actual injury or imminent danger, was expressly reserved).
[12] [1893] 2 Ch. 87; *A.-G.* v. *Nottingham Corporation*, [1904] 1 Ch. 673.
[13] (1821), 6 Madd. 287.
[14] [1938] 1 All E.R. 115.

to do an act which would be an infringement of the plaintiff's right,[15] or has threatened or given notice of his intention to do such act.[16] In any such case it is not as a rule a sufficient defence to a claim for an injunction for the defendant to say that he has no present intention of doing the act in question.[17] Conversely in *Cowley (Lord)* v. *Byas*,[18] an injunction was refused where the defendant not only stated that he had no present intention of using the land as a cemetery, but said also that if he should at any time thereafter wish to do so, he would give the plaintiff two months' notice of his intention in order to give him an opportunity to bring proceedings to try and prevent his doing so. Another example is *Jenkins* v. *Hope*,[19] an action to restrain the infringement of a patent, where the defendant on service of the writ, at once offered to undertake not to infringe and to pay the plaintiff's costs. The plaintiff nevertheless went on with the action and at the hearing, the offer of an undertaking being renewed, the court refused an injunction, giving the plaintiff costs only up to the date of the original offer, and of the day's appearance in court.[20] The general principle seems to be that "it would be wrong for [the] court in *quia timet* proceedings to grant relief by way of injunction to compel the defendants to do something which they appear to be willing to do without the imposition of an order of the court".[21]

Where a mandatory injunction is sought in *quia timet* proceedings the question of the cost to the defendant of doing works to prevent or lessen the likelihood of a future apprehended wrong must be an element to be taken into account. On the one hand, where the defendant has acted wantonly and quite unreasonably in relation to his neighbour he may be ordered to repair his wanton and unreasonable acts by doing positive work to restore the *status quo* even if the expense to him is out of all proportion to the advantage thereby accruing to the plaintiff. On the other hand, where the defendant has acted reasonably, although in the event wrongly, the cost of remedying by positive action his earlier activities is more important for two reasons. First, because *ex hypothesi* no legal wrong has occurred (for which he has not been recompensed) and may never occur or only on a small scale. Secondly, because if ultimately heavy damage does occur the plaintiff is in no way prejudiced for he has his action at law and all his consequential remedies in equity. With these considerations the cost to the defendant of carrying out a mandatory order must be balanced against the anticipated possible damage to the plaintiff, and if, on such balance, it seems unreasonable to inflict such expenditure on one who for this purpose is no more than a potential wrongdoer then the court must exercise its jurisdiction accordingly.[1]

---

[15] *Shafto* v. *Bolckow, Vaughan & Co.* (1887), 34 Ch.D. 725; *Phillips* v. *Thomas* (1890), 62 L.T. 793.

[16] *Potts* v. *Levy* (1854), 2 Drew. 272; *McEacharn* v. *Colton*, [1902] A.C. 104, P.C.; *Thornhill* v. *Weeks*, [1913] 1 Ch. 438.

[17] *Hext* v. *Gill* (1872), 7 Ch. App. 699; *Leckhampton Quarries Co. Ltd.* v. *Ballinger* (1904), 20 T.L.R. 559.

[18] (1877), 5 Ch.D. 944, C.A.

[19] [1896] 1 Ch. 278.

[20] *Semble*, the plaintiff was entitled to have the undertaking given in court.

[21] *Bridlington Relay, Ltd.* v. *Yorkshire Electricity Board*, [1965] 1 All E.R. 264, 269; [1965] Ch. 436, 445, *per* Buckley J.

[1] *Redland Bricks, Ltd.* v. *Morris*, [1969] 2 All E.R. 576; [1970] A.C. 652, H.L.

3 INTERLOCUTORY INJUNCTIONS

a Principle

"In all cases of applications for interlocutory injunctions the governing principle is that pending the settlement of the dispute between the parties the court will as far as possible keep matters *in statu quo*"[2] and it is a jurisdiction which has been said[3] to be one of the most valuable functions of the Court of Chancery. However, in some kinds of case the court will be slow to restrain the defendant, but will leave him to go ahead at his own risk if it turns out at the trial that his actions are wrongful. Thus the court will not normally restrain a defendant in a libel action who says he is going to justify; or a defendant in a copyright action who has a reasonable defence of fair dealing; or a defendant in an action for breach of confidence who has a reasonable defence of public interest. The reason in all those cases is that the defendant, if he is right, is entitled to publish, and the law is reluctant to intervene to suppress freedom of speech.[4]

An interlocutory injunction is never granted as a matter of course:[5] it is always a matter of discretion. From one point of view it has accordingly been said[6] that whether an interlocutory injunction should be granted depends upon a great variety of circumstances, and it is utterly impossible to lay down any general rule upon the subject, by which the discretion of the court ought in all cases to be regulated, but from another point of view, the discretion being, of course, a judicial discretion, it has been observed[7] that in appropriate circumstances it is a "matter of right that upon proper terms the property shall be maintained *in statu quo* pending the trial". The current tendency in the Court of Appeal[8] seems to be to stress the discretionary element. Thus in *Hubbard* v. *Vosper*[9] Lord Denning M.R. said: "In considering whether to grant an interlocutory injunction, the right course for a judge is to look at the whole case. He must have regard not only to the strength of the claim, but also to the strength of the defence, and then decide what is best to be done. Sometimes it is best to grant an injunction so as to maintain the *status quo* until the trial. At other times it is best not to impose a restrain on the defendant but leave him to go ahead . . . The remedy by interlocutory injunction is so useful that it should be kept flexible and discretionary. It must not be made the subject of strict rules." In the following subsections we shall consider circumstances that have com-

---

[2] *Per* Buckley L.J. in *Jones* v. *Pacaya Rubber and Produce Co., Ltd.*, [1911] 1 K.B. 455, at p. 457, C.A.; *Hilton* v. *Lord Granville* (1841), Cr. & Ph. 283; *Eastern Trust Co.* v. *McKenzie Mann & Co., Ltd.*, [1915] A.C. 750, P.C.

[3] *Greenslade* v. *Dare* (1853), 17 Beav. 502, at p. 504 *per* Romilly M.R.

[4] *Hubbard* v. *Vosper*, [1972] 1 All E.R. 1023; [1972] 2 Q.B. 84, C.A.

[5] *Potter* v. *Chapman* (1750), Amb. 98.

[6] *Saunders* v. *Smith* (1838), 3 My & Cr. 711, at p. 728 *per* Cottenham L.C. (where an injunction was refused to restrain the sale of the first edition of Smith's Leading Cases, as being an infringement of copyright in various law reports).

[7] *Jones* v. *Pacaya Rubber and Produce Co., Ltd.*, *supra*, C.A. *per* Buckley L.J. at p. 458; *Harman Pictures, N.V.* v. *Osborne*, [1967] 2 All E.R. 324.

[8] Particularly among the Common Law members.

[9] [1972] 1 All E.R. 1023, at p. 1029; [1972] 2 Q.B. 84, at p. 96, C.A. cited with approval by Sachs L.J. in *Evans Marshall & Co. Ltd.* v. *Bertola SA.*, [1973] 1 All E.R. 992, 1004, C.A.

monly to be taken into account.   As one would expect, the plaintiff has a harder task on an *ex parte* application.[10]

b *Prima facie* case

Where the plaintiff asks the court to protect by interlocutory injunction some right which he asserts, he must show at least a *prima facie* case in support of his title thereto though it is not necessary to establish a case which will entitle him to relief at all events at the trial.[11] In a doubtful case an injunction will normally,[12] but not necessarily,[13] be refused.   Until recently the cases appeared to decide that what is necessary is that the court shall be satisfied that there is a serious question to be tried at the hearing, and that on the facts before it there is a probability that the plaintiff is entitled to relief.[14] Accordingly Brightman J. in *Gallagher* v. *Post Office*[15] said, "I am only entitled to grant interlocutory relief if the plaintiffs establish a probability of succeeding at the trial or make out a strong *prima facia* case."[16] Kerr J. took the same view at first instance in *Evans Marshall & Co. Ltd.* v. *Bertola SA.*[17] but was reversed on appeal.   There was little citation of relevant authority, but the Court of Appeal stated unanimously and clearly that there is no rule of law which precludes the grant of an interlocutory injunction unless there is sufficient prospect of a permanent injunction being obtained at the trial.   It was accepted, however, that the likelihood of success at the trial will normally be an important factor for the court to consider in the exercise of its discretion.   Similarly if the plaintiff seeks an injunction to prevent the exercise by the defendant of some alleged legal right, upon the ground that the right either does not exist or is doubtful, it is the duty of the plaintiff to satisfy the court that there are substantial grounds for doubting the existence of the legal right.[18] No injunction will, however, be granted in respect of an injury of a temporary nature which has already come to an end.[19]

c Irreparable damage

It is a general rule that a plaintiff will not be granted an interlocutory injunction unless he is able to show that if it is not granted, he will suffer irreparable damage,[20] i.e. "the damage must be substantial and one which could not be

---

[10] *Eothen Films, Ltd.* v. *Industrial and Commercial Education—Macmillan, Ltd.*, (1966), *Times*, 26 October, C.A.

[11] *Glascott* v. *Lang* (1838), 3 My. & Cr. 45.

[12] *Spotteswoode* v. *Clark* (1846), 1 Coop. *temp.* Cott. 254.

[13] *Ollendorff* v. *Black* (1850), 4 De G. & Sm. 209; *Electric Telegraph Co.* v. *Nott* (1847), 2 Coop. *temp.* Cott. 41.

[14] *Preston* v. *Luck* (1884), 27 Ch.D. 497, C.A.

[15] [1970] 3 All E.R. 712, at p. 717.

[16] The phrase "strong *prima facie* case" was used by Cottenham L.C. in *Hilton* v. *Lord Granville* (1841), Cr. & Ph. 283; Lord Denning used the phrase "good *prima facie* case" in *Chaplin* v. *Leslie Frewin (Publishers), Ltd.*, [1965] 3 All E.R. 764, 769; [1966] Ch. 71, 88, C.A. See also *Esso Petroleum Co., Ltd.* v. *Kingswood Motors (Addlestone) Ltd.*, [1973] 3 All E.R. 1057; [1974] Q.B. 142.

[17] [1973] 1 All E.R. 992, C.A. (not reported at first instance).

[18] *Sparrow* v. *Oxford, Worcester and Wolverhampton Rail. Co.* (1851), 9 Hare 436; *on appeal* (1852), 2 De G.M. & G. 94.

[19] *Shersby* v. *South-Eastern Rail. Co.* (1849), 13 L.T.O.S. 252.

[20] *Johnson* v. *Shrewsbury and Birmingham Rail. Co.* (1853), 3 De G.M. & G. 914.

adequately remedied by a pecuniary payment".[21] Thus where a railway
company blocked up a mode of access to a rival's station, the court took the
view that the inevitable diversion of traffic could not be measured or estimated
and it was accordingly a case of irreparable damage,[22] and in another case[23]
the court granted an injunction against a declaration of dividend by a company,
holding the damage to be irreparable since if it were ultimately held to be
improperly declared, it would never be recovered (even if measurable) from the
persons to whom it was paid. Again, in a writ to impeach the conveyance of an
advowson, an injunction was granted to restrain the institution of a clerk. If the
injunction had been refused and a clerk appointed, he would be irremovable,
and the court would be unable to give any effective remedy.[24]

d Balance of convenience

If both the right of the plaintiff and the infringement of it by the defendant
seem clear, and irreparable damage is likely to arise from the infringement, it is
prima facie the duty of the court to grant an interlocutory injunction to restrain
any further infringement pending the trial of the action.[25] In particular this will
be so where there is a plain and uncontested breach of a clear covenant not to do
a particular thing,[1] or where there is an admitted trespass even though it may
do no harm to the plaintiff.[2] Generally, however, there is some doubt either as
to the plaintiff's alleged right, or its alleged infringement by the defendant, and
in such case the court normally puts great importance on what is called the
balance of convenience. What this means is that in order to persuade the court
to grant the injunction sought the plaintiff must normally be able to show that
the inconvenience that he will suffer if the injunction is refused is greater than
the inconvenience that the defendant will suffer if the injunction is granted,[3]
and in considering this question the nature of the respective injuries which the
plaintiff and defendant would suffer will be taken into account. The onus is on
the plaintiff to show that the inconvenience that he would suffer exceeds that

---

[21] *Litchfield–Speer* v. *Queen Anne's Gate Syndicate (No. 2), Ltd.*, [1919] 1 Ch. 407, at p. 411 *per*
P.O. Lawrence J.; *Pinchin* v. *London and Blackwall Rail. Co.* (1854), 5 De G.M. & G.
851.

[22] *London and North Western Rail. Co.* v. *Lancashire and Yorkshire Rail. Co.* (1867), L.R.
4 Eq. 174.

[23] *Bloxam* v. *Metropolitan Rail. Co.* (1868), 3 Ch. App. 337; *Mogul S.S. Co.* v. *McGregor
Gow* (1885), 15 Q.B.D. 476, D.C.

[24] *Greenslade* v. *Dare* (1853), 17 Beav. 502; *Armstrong* v. *Armstrong* (1854), 21 Beav. 71;
Garrett v. *Salisbury and Dorset Junction Rail. Co.* (1866), L.R. 2 Eq. 358.

[25] *Wilkinson* v. *Rogers* (1864), 2 De G.J. & Sm. 62 esp. *per* Turner L.J. at p. 69; *Cory* v.
Yarmouth and Norwich Rail. Co. (1844), 3 Hare. 593.

[1] *Hampstead and Suburban Properties, Ltd.* v. *Diomedous*, [1968] 3 All E.R. 545; [1969]
1 Ch. 248. Cf. *Texaco, Ltd.* v. *Mulberry Filling Station, Ltd.*, [1972] 1 All E.R. 513.

[2] *Woollerton & Wilson, Ltd.* v. *Richard Costain, Ltd.*, [1970] 1 All E.R. 483. The suspension
of the operation of the injunction in this case, so as virtually to nullify its effect, was
criticised in (1970), 33 M.L.R. 552 (G. Dworkin), and opinion on the correctness of the
decision reserved by C.A. in *Charrington* v. *Simons Co., Ltd.*, [1971] 2 All E.R. 588, at
p. 592.

[3] In addition to the cases cited in note 25, *supra*, see e.g. *Hilton* v. *Granville (Earl)* (1841),
Cr. & Ph. 283; *Grafton* v. *Watson* (1884), 51 L.T. 141, C.A.; *Hivac Ltd.* v. *Park Royal
Scientific Instruments Ltd.*, [1946] 1 All E.R. 350; [1946] Ch. 169, C.A.; *Emerald Construction
Co., Ltd.* v. *Lowthian*, [1966] 1 All E.R. 1013, C.A.

of the defendant,[4] and it is, of course, only where the plaintiff has first made out
a *prima facie* case that the court has to go on to consider the balance of convenience.[5]   It may be added that the court never grants injunctions on the
principle that they will do no harm to the defendant, if he does not intend to
commit the act in question.[6]

e Delay and acquiescence

Delay or laches, and, *a fortiori*, acquiescence by the plaintiff in the infringement of his rights may disentitle him to an interlocutory injunction,[7] particularly
if the defendant has incurred expenditure in the meantime.   The meaning of
acquiescence has been discussed in a number of cases: it involves a knowledge by
the plaintiff of his rights infringed by the defendant,[8] and an encouragement or
even merely passive inaction by the plaintiff on the strength of which the defendant has expended money or altered his position in violation of the plaintiff's
rights.   Thus Lord Cottenham[9] said, "If a party, having a right, stands by and
sees another dealing with the property in a manner inconsistent with that right,
and makes no objection while the act is in progress, he cannot afterwards complain", and in slightly different words Romilly M.R. explained,[10] "if one man
stand by and encourage another, though but passively, to lay out money, under
an erroneous opinion of title, or under the obvious expectation that no obstacle
will afterwards be interposed in the way of his enjoyment, the court will not
permit any subsequent interference with it, by him who formally[11] promoted
and encouraged those acts of which he now either complains or seeks to take
advantage".   The fact that the plaintiff has indicated that he is willing to accept
the payment of a sum of money as the price of giving up his rights may well
persuade the court not to grant an injunction, though it does not take away its
jurisdiction to do so in a proper case,[12] though a demand for payment will not
constitute acquiescence if it is shown that the plaintiff assumed at the relevant
time that the defendant had statutory power to do the thing complained of.[13]

---

[4] *Child* v. *Douglas* (1854), 5 De G.M. & G. 739.
[5] *Challender* v. *Royle* (1887), 36 Ch.D. 425, C.A.; *Republic of Peru* v. *Dreyfus Bros. & Co.*
    (1888), 38 Ch.D. 348.
[6] *Coffin* v. *Coffin* (1821), Jac. 70; *H.V.E. (Electric), Ltd.* v. *Cufflin Holdings, Ltd.*, [1964] 1 All
    E.R. 674, C.A.
[7] *Great Western Rail. Co.* v. *Oxford, Worcester and Wolverhampton Rail. Co.* (1853), 3 De
    G.M. & G. 341; *Bovill* v. *Crate* (1865), L.R. 1 Eq. 388; *Isaacson* v. *Thompson* (1871),
    41 L.J. Ch. 101.
[8] *Ramsden* v. *Dyson* (1866), L.R. 1 H.L. 129; *Weldon* v. *Dicks* (1878), 10 Ch.D. 247 (*Per*
    Malins V.C. at p. 262, "There can only be acquiescence where there is knowledge");
    Willmott v. *Barber* (1880), 15 Ch.D. 96; *Armstrong* v. *Sheppard and Short, Ltd.*, [1959]
    2 All E.R. 651; [1959] 2 Q.B. 384, C.A.
[9] In *Leeds (Duke)* v. *Earl Amherst* (1846), 2 Ph. 117, 123; *Russell* v. *Watts* (1883), 25 Ch.D.
    559, C.A. esp. *per* Cotton L.J. at p. 576; affd. (1885) 10 App. Cas. 590 H.L.; *Northumber-
    land (Duke)* v. *Bowman* (1887), 56 L.T. 773.
[10] *Rochdale Canal Co.* v. *King* (1853), 16 Beav. 630, 633, 634; *Williams* v. *Earl Jersey* (1841),
    Cr. & M. 91.
[11] *Semble,* a misprint for "formerly".
[12] *Gort (Viscountess)* v. *Clark* (1868), 18 L.T. 343. Cf. *Ainsworth* v. *Bentley* (1866), 14 W.R.
    630; *McKinnon Industries Ltd.* v. *Walker* (1951), 95 Sol. Jo. 559 P.C.
[13] *Pentney* v. *Lynn Paving Commissioners* (1865), 12 L.T. 818.

Questions have often arisen in connection with the enforcement of covenants restrictive of the user of land. If it is shown that the plaintiff took no steps to enforce a covenant on prior breaches, this may show acquiescence and an intent to abandon any building scheme there may be, in which case no injunction will be granted.[14] In general, however, the mere fact that the plaintiff has waived his right to sue for breaches in the past, does not constitute acquiescence as to the future so as to prevent him from suing for some subsequent infraction, particularly if the earlier infractions were trivial in character.[15] Even acquiescence, however, may be explained away, for instance, where the plaintiff had been led to believe that the violation of his right would only be temporary,[16] or where he had not at the earlier time the necessary documents to establish his right,[17] or where he had been assured by the defendant that steps were being taken to prevent continued violation of his rights[18]; and if he has acquiesced in some infringement of his rights causing him only slight injury, this does not prevent him from obtaining an interlocutory injunction if the injury is subsequently considerably increased.[19] Moreover no equity arises if the defendant expended money with knowledge of the true legal position.[20]

f Clean hands[1]

"The jurisdiction to interfere is purely equitable, and it must be governed by equitable principles".[2] One of the principles is that the court will not grant equitable relief to a litigant unless he comes, as it is said, with clean hands. On this principle, as Lord Eldon observed,[3] "many cases have occurred in which injunctions are applied for, and are granted or refused, not upon the ground of the right possessed by the parties, but upon the ground of their conduct and dealings before they applied to the court for the injunction to preserve and protect that right".

g Conditions and undertakings

At the hearing of an interlocutory injunction the court is not called upon to decide finally on the rights of the parties: the court will confine itself

---

[14] *Roper* v. *Williams* (1822), Turn. & R. 18.
[15] *Peek* v. *Matthews* (1867), L.R. 3 Eq. 515; *Kilbey* v. *Haviland* (1871), 24 L.T. 353; *German* v. *Chapman* (1877), 7 Ch.D. 271, C.A.
[16] *Gordon* v. *Cheltenham and Great Western Union Rail. Co.* (1842), 5 Beav. 229. Cf. *Innocent* v. *North Midland Railway Co.* (1839), 1 Ry. & Can. Cas. 242.
[17] *Coles* v. *Sims* (1854), 5 De G.M. & G. 1.
[18] *A.-G.* v. *Birmingham Borough Council* (1858), 4 K. & J. 528; *Innocent* v. *North Midland Rail. Co.* (1839), 1 Ry. & Can. Cas. 242.
[19] *Bankart* v. *Houghton* (1860), 27 Beav. 425.
[20] *Rennie* v. *Young* (1858), 2 De G. & J. 136.
[1] The principle is more fully discussed in connection with perpetual injunctions, *post*, p. 402.
[2] Per Turner L.J. in *Great Western Rail. Co.* v. *Oxford, Worcester and Wolverhampton Rail. Co.* (1853), 3 De G. M. & G. 341, 359.
[3] *Blakemore* v. *Glamorganshire Canal Navigation* (1832), 1 My. & K. 154, 168; *Sheard* v. *Webb* (1854), 23 L.T.O.S. 48; *Jarvis* v. *Islington Corporation* (1909), 73 J.P. Jo. 323.

to the immediate object of the proceedings and so far as possible it will not prejudge the case.[4] It will impose only such a restraint as may be required to stop the mischief complained of and to keep things as they are until the hearing.[5]

The price that the plaintiff has since the middle of the nineteenth century been almost[6] invariably called upon to pay[7] for the grant of an interlocutory injunction, is entry into what is called the "usual undertaking" as to damages. By this the plaintiff undertakes that he will abide by any order as to damages which the court may make if it should eventually turn out that he was not entitled to the interlocutory injunction and the defendant has suffered damage thereby.[8] Fairly soon after the introduction of this undertaking it was argued that if the action was dismissed the court no longer had any jurisdiction over the parties and the undertaking could not be enforced. The argument, which, if successful, would have made the undertaking nugatory, was conclusively rejected in *Newby* v. *Harrison*,[9] and an undertaking is equally enforceable if the plaintiff discontinues his action.[10] Contrary to the view expressed by Jessel M.R.,[11] an undertaking is perfectly valid and enforceable even though the injunction was obtained by the plaintiff *bona fide*, without any misrepresentation, suppression of the facts, or other default on his part.[12] It makes no difference whether in granting the injunction the judge made an error of law or of fact.[13] The court has technically no power to compel the plaintiff to enter into an undertaking, but it has power in practice since it can indicate that an injunction will be refused unless the undertaking is given.[14]

It is not unusual, on a motion for an injunction, for no injunction to be granted but for the defendant to offer and the plaintiff to accept an undertaking by the defendant in terms similar to those claimed in the injunction. In such case a cross-undertaking in damages, similar to the usual undertaking above mentioned, will automatically be inserted in the order, unless the contrary is

---

[4] *Skinners' Co.* v. *Irish Co.* (1835), 1 My. & Cr. 162; *Preston* v. *Luck* (1884), 27 Ch.D. 497 C.A.

[5] *Blakemore* v. *Glamorganshire Canal Navigation, supra.*

[6] For an exceptional case see *Fenner* v. *Wilson*, [1893] 2 Ch. 656, where the injunction, though in one sense interlocutory, in another sense was final and not subject to review.

[7] *Graham* v. *Campbell* (1878), 7 Ch.D. 490, C.A.; *Tucker* v. *New Brunswick Trading Co. of London* (1890), 44 Ch.D. 249, C.A. Possibly not in a clear case of fraud—*Ingram* v. *Stiff* (1859), cited in John. 220, though on appeal an undertaking was required—33 L.T.O.S. 195.

[8] Note that the court will not make an order as to damages until either the plaintiff has failed on the merits at the trial, or it is established before trial that the injunction ought not to have been granted in the first instance—*Ushers Brewery, Ltd.* v. *P. S. King & Co. (Finance), Ltd.*, [1971] 2 All E.R. 468; [1972] Ch. 148.

[9] (1861), 3 De G.F. & J. 287; *Ross* v. *Buxton*, [1888] W.N. 55.

[10] *Newcomen* v. *Coulson* (1878), 7 Ch.D. 764.

[11] In *Smith* v. *Day* (1882), 21 Ch.D. 421, C.A., where the history of undertakings is discussed.

[12] *Griffith* v. *Blake* (1884), 27 Ch.D. 474, C.A.

[13] *Hunt* v. *Hunt* (1884), 54 L.J. Ch. 289.

[14] *Tucker* v. *New Brunswick Trading Co. of London* (1890), 44 Ch.D. 249, C.A.; *A.-G.* v. *Albany Hotel Co.*, [1896] 2 Ch. 696, C.A., *per* North J. at first instance at 700; *Howard* v. *Press Printers Ltd.* (1904), 91 L.T. 718, C.A.

expressly agreed at the time.[15] It follows from what has been said above that the court cannot compel the defendant to offer an undertaking, though it may exert pressure by indicating that an injunction is likely to be granted if no offer of an undertaking is made.

Where an injunction is granted on the usual undertaking, the court may, if it doubts the plaintiff's ability to pay any damages that may be ordered under the undertaking, make the injunction conditional on the plaintiff's depositing a specified sum of money with the parties' solicitors,[16] or giving security to the satisfaction of the court.[17] The court has also as a condition of granting an injunction, where an action concerned the payment of a sum of money, required the plaintiff to pay the amount in dispute into court,[18] and in other cases to undertake to prosecute the action with due diligence.[19]

It may be added that the court may require the defendant to enter into an undertaking as a condition of refusing an injunction: thus the defendant, in appropriate circumstances, may be required to undertake to keep an account to assist the court, should the plaintiff succeed at the trial, in ascertaining what damage he has suffered in the meantime.[20] Other undertakings required include an undertaking not to attempt to induce certain persons to break their contracts,[21] and, where an injunction was sought to restrain building, an undertaking to pull down the building complained of if the plaintiff should succeed in the action.[1]

Finally, special mention should be made of the position where an injunction is sought by the Attorney-General on behalf of the Crown. It used to be the established practice that, when the Crown sought an interlocutory injunction, the court would not require it to give an undertaking in damages. Both members of the Court of Appeal who discussed the point in *Secretary of State for Trade and Industry* v. *F. Hoffman-La Roche and Co. AG.*[2] observed that this should no longer be the practice since the Crown Proceedings Act 1947, which has in large measure assimilated the position of the Crown in litigation to that of a subject. Where a government department appears as an ordinary litigant it may in many cases be proper for it to give an undertaking in damages. Where, however, the Attorney-General appears on behalf of the Crown, even though nominally on behalf of a government department, for the purpose of enforcing the law, it is a different matter. In such a case the Crown cannot and should not be required to give an undertaking.

---

[15] *Practice Note*, [1904] W.N. 203; *G.M.B.H. Oberrheinische Metallwerke* v. *Cocks*, [1906] W.N. 127. Cf. *Howard* v. *Press Printers Ltd.*, *supra*; *Hanning* v. *Gable-Jeffreys Properties, Ltd.*, [1965] 1 All E.R. 924.

[16] *Baxter* v. *Claydon*, [1952] W.N. 376.

[17] *Harman Pictures, N.V.* v. *Osborne*, [1967] 2 All E.R. 324.

[18] *Hill* v. *Kirkwood* (1880), 42 L.T. 105, C.A. (to restrain sale by mortgagee); *Jones* v. *Pacaya Rubber and Produce Co. Ltd.*, [1911] 1 K.B. 455 C.A.; *Cavenagh* v. *Cohen* (1919), 147 L.T. Jo. 252.

[19] *Newson* v. *Pender* (1884), 27 Ch.D. 43, C.A.

[20] *Mitchell* v. *Henry* (1880), 15 Ch.D. 181, C.A.; *Holophone Ltd.* v. *Berend & Co. Ltd.* (1897), 15 R.P.C. 18. See also *Wall* v. *London and Northern Assets Corporation*, [1898] 2 Ch. 469, C.A.

[21] *Wright* v. *Hennessey* (1894), 11 T.L.R. 14, D.C.

[1] *Ford* v. *Gye* (1858), 6 W.R. 235; *Wilson* v. *Townend* (1860), 1 Dr. & Sm. 324.

[2] [1973] 3 All E.R. 945, C.A.

h Motion as trial of action

An application for an interlocutory injunction may, by the consent of the parties, be treated as the trial of the action. If this is done the plaintiff, if he succeeds, will be granted a perpetual, not merely an interlocutory injunction, while if he fails his claim is finally dismissed. The parties may be induced to give their consent to this procedure by the fact that their dispute will thus be decided more cheaply and more expeditiously than by allowing the matter to go on to trial in the normal way. It is, however, only a possible procedure where the dispute between the parties is a matter of law. Evidence on the hearing of an interlocutory injunction is on affidavit, and accordingly this is not a suitable procedure where there is a dispute as to the facts.

4 PERPETUAL INJUNCTIONS

a General principles

There are two important principles that have to be kept in mind. What has been called "the very first principle of injunction law is that *prima facie* you do not obtain injunctions to restrain actionable wrongs, for which damages are the proper remedy".[3] A perpetual injunction, as we have seen, is intended to relieve the plaintiff from the necessity of bringing a series of actions to protect his right each time it is infringed, and is, therefore, particularly appropriate where the injury is continuous, or in any case where the repetition, or in the case of a *quia timet* application the commission, of an injury is reasonably apprehended and the remedy of damages would be inadequate,[4] as is typically the case in nuisance or infringement of rights such as patents or copyrights. The second principle is that, being an equitable remedy, the award of an injunction is discretionary. This proposition, though generally[5] true, tends to be misleading, and, even if it is recognised that the discretion is a judicial discretion to be exercised in accordance with precedent, it is easy to over-estimate the discretion which the court has. From a practical point of view Lord Evershed M.R.'s statement[6] is more helpful: "It is, I think, well settled that, if A proves that his proprietary rights are being wrongfully interfered with by B, and that B intends to continue his wrong, then A is *prima facie* entitled to an injunction, and he will be deprived of that remedy only if special circumstances exist, including the circumstance that damages are an adequate remedy for the

---

[3] *Per* Lindley L.J. in *London and Blackwall Rail. Co.* v. *Cross* (1886), 31 Ch.D. 354, at p. 369, C.A.; *Dollfus* v. *Pickford* (1854), 2 W.R. 220; *Staight* v. *Burn* (1869), 5 Ch. App. 163.

[4] See *Hodgson* v. *Duce* (1856), 28 L.T.O.S. 155, where the court took into account that the defendant was a pauper, and a mere award of damages would accordingly be a mockery of justice. In *Pride of Derby and Derbyshire Angling Association, Ltd.* v. *British Celanese, Ltd.*, [1953] 1 All E.R. 179; [1953] Ch. 149, C.A., the angling association complained of the pollution of a river. As reported in [1953] Ch. at 181, Evershed M.R. pointed out that damages would be a wholly inadequate remedy for the association which had "not been incorporated in order to fish for monthly sums".

[5] See, however, for an exception, Section 7a, p. 413, *post*.

[6] In *Pride of Derby and Derbyshire Angling Association, Ltd.* v. *British Celanese, Ltd.*, *supra*, at 197; 181; *Shelfer* v. *City of London Electric Lighting Co.*, [1895] 1 Ch. 287, C.A.; *Cowper* v. *Laidler*, [1903] 2 Ch. 337.

wrong that he has suffered".[7] The existence of the discretion merely means that, to a limited extent largely dictated by precedent, the court may, indeed must, "have regard not only to the dry strict rights of the plaintiff and defendant, but also to the surrounding circumstances, to the rights or interests of other persons which may be more or less involved".[8] The main illustrations of special circumstances which have to be taken into account are discussed in the following subsections.[9]

b Small damage

When it was necessary to bring separate actions in different courts for damages and an injunction, it was held that the fact that at law only a very small or nominal sum was recovered by way of damages was not *per se* a sufficient ground for refusing an injunction,[10] particularly where there was the possibility of a series of actions to recover damages from time to time. In general the fact that the plaintiff has not suffered substantial damage does not prevent him from obtaining an injunction if he can establish an infringement of a legal right.[11] Sometimes, however, the court may regard the matter as too trivial[12] to entitle the plaintiff to "the formidable weapon of an injunction",[13] and an injunction will not necessarily be granted to restrain a trespass or a nuisance where the infringement is only temporary or occasional.[14] Thus the court refused an injunction in *Behrens* v. *Richards*[15] where it was sought to restrain members of the public from using tracks on the plaintiff's land situate on an unfrequented part of the coast, which use caused no damage; and in *Society of Architects* v. *Kendrick*,[16] where members of the plaintiff society were accustomed to use the letters M.S.A. after their names. The plaintiff society sought to restrain the defendant, a non-member, from doing likewise, but the court refused an injunction on the ground that the matter was too trivial. Further, in exceptional circumstances,

---

[7] Or as the same judge said more recently, in *Armstrong* v. *Sheppard and Short, Ltd.*, [1959] 2 All E.R. 651, at p. 655; [1959] 2 Q.B. 384, at p. 394, C.A. "A proprietor who establishes a proprietary right is *ex debito justitiae* entitled to an injunction, unless it can be said against him that he has raised such an equity that it is no longer open to him to assert his legal or proprietary title".

[8] Per Kindersley V.C. in *Wood* v. *Sutcliffe* (1851), 2 Sim.N.S. 163, at p. 165.

[9] See also Section 6, p. 408, *post*, as to the award of damages in lieu of an injunction.

[10] *Rochdale Canal Co.* v. *King* (1851), 2 Sim.N.S. 78; *Wood* v. *Sutcliffe* (1851), 2 Sim.N.S. 163, where sums of one shilling and one farthing were referred to.

[11] *Goodson* v. *Richardson* (1874), 9 Ch. App. 221; *Marriott* v. *East Grinstead Gas and Water Co.*, [1909] 1 Ch. 70 (both cases of pipes being laid in soil under a highway, which was of no value to the owner). Cf. *Armstrong* v. *Sheppard and Short, Ltd.*, *supra*.

[12] Cf. *Harrison* v. *Good* (1871), L.R. 11 Eq. 338 per Bacon V.C. at 352, "if the violation is so slight, formal and unsubstantial that the plaintiff can have no ground in conscience to complain of it, the court will not grant an injunction."

[13] Per Buckley J. in *Behrens* v. *Richards*, [1905] 2 Ch. 614, at p. 621.   [14] *Supra*.

[15] *Supra*; *Ward* v. *Kirkland*, [1966] 1 All E.R. 609; [1967] Ch. 194 (right to use drain to convey bath water—court refused injunction to restrain additional user of same drains for effluent from water closets).

[16] (1910), 26 T.L.R. 433. Contrast *Society of Accountants and Auditors* v. *Goodway*, [1907] 1 Ch. 489 (Incorporated Accountant) and *Society of Accountants in Edinburgh* v. *Corporation of Accountants, Ltd.* (1893), 20 R. 750 (Ct. of Sess.), where injunctions were granted. It seems to depend on the status of the plaintiff body. The Society of Architects was described by the judge as "a private joint stock company, which for payment purported to give people the right to use a certain combination of mystic letters the meaning of which ... nobody in the court, except counsel for the plaintiffs, knew".

particularly where a mandatory injunction is sought, the court may take into account the fact that an injunction would inflict serious damage on the defendant with no compensatory advantage to the plaintiff, as in *Doherty* v. *Allman*,[17] where the court refused an injunction to restrain ameliorating waste by a tenant under a lease with over nine hundred years left to run.

c Delay and acquiescence[18]

Mere lapse of time or laches does not affect the plaintiff's right to a perpetual injunction, unless the claim itself is barred.[19] This is, of course, in complete contrast to an application for an interlocutory injunction.[20] Lapse of time is, however, commonly an important factor to be taken into account in deciding whether there has been acquiescence, which may bar a claim even to a perpetual injunction. But "to justify the court in refusing to interfere at the hearing of a cause there must be a much stronger case of acquiescence than is required upon an interlocutory application, for at the hearing of a cause it is the duty of the court to decide upon the rights of the parties, and the dismissal of the bill upon the ground of acquiescence amounts to a decision that a right which has once existed is absolutely and for ever lost".[1]

d Clean hands

Being an equitable remedy the principle expressed in the maxim that "he who comes into equity must come with clean hands" applies. Thus an injunction has been refused to a plaintiff who had wrongfully taken away partnership books,[2] and in *Telegraph Despatch and Intelligence Co.* v. *McLean*[3] a plaintiff in breach of an implied undertaking in a contract was held not entitled to an injunction to enforce an express undertaking therein entered into by the defendant. Again in *Litvinoff* v. *Kent*[4] a landlord had reserved a right of re-entry for breach only of the covenant in the lease to pay rent. This covenant had not been broken, but the landlord nevertheless re-entered and excluded the tenant from the demised premises. The tenant, the plaintiff in the proceedings, sought an injunction, but this was refused on the grounds that he had been guilty of breaches of other covenants in the lease and was using the premises for an illegal purpose. The point has often arisen in connection with a building scheme where numerous purchasers have entered into restrictive covenants with their common vendor for each other's benefit. In such case a plaintiff who has not complied with the covenants himself may be unable to enforce them against another,[5] but there is no rigid rule and an injunction may yet be obtained where the plaintiff's breach was only trifling, or where he has broken a much

---

[17] (1878), 3 App. Cas. 709, H.L.; *Meux* v. *Cobley*, [1892] 2 Ch. 253; *Sharp* v. *Harrison*, [1922] 1 Ch. 502.
[18] As to the meaning of acquiescence, see p. 397, *ante*.
[19] *Rochdale Canal Co.* v. *King* (1851), 2 Sim.N.S. 78; *Savile* v. *Kilnor* (1872), 26 L.T. 277; *Fullwood* v. *Fullwood* (1878), 9 Ch.D. 176.
[20] *Turner* v. *Mirfield* (1865), 34 Beav. 390; *Proctor* v. *Bennis* (1897), 36 Ch.D. 740, C.A.
[1] *Johnson* v. *Wyatt* (1863), 2 De G.J. & Sm. 18 *per* Turner L.J. at 25; *Illingworth* v. *Manchester and Leeds Rail. Co.* (1840), 2 Ry. & Can. Cas. 187; *Patching* v. *Dubbins* (1853), Kay. 1.
[2] *Littlewood* v. *Caldwell* (1822), 11 Price, 97; *Williams* v. *Roberts* (1850), 5 Hare 315.
[3] (1873), 8 Ch. App. 658; *Stiff* v. *Carsell* (1850), 2 Jur. N.S. 248.
[4] (1918), 34 T.L.R. 298.
[5] *Goddard* v. *Midland Rail. Co.* (1891), 8 T.L.R. 126.

less important covenant than the one he seeks to enforce.[6] This same qualification applies to other types of case; thus in *Besant* v. *Wood*[7] a husband was not debarred from enforcing provisions in a separation deed by reason of trifling breaches of covenant on his part. Further "the cleanliness required is to be judged in relation to the relief that is sought".[8] Thus in *Duchess of Argyll* v. *Duke of Argyll*[9] the plaintiff was held not to be disentitled to an injunction to restrain the publication by her ex-husband of intimate confidences between husband and wife by reason of the fact that it was her subsequent immorality that was the basis for the divorce and the termination of the marriage.

The same basic idea is behind the maxim that "he who seeks equity must do equity", though here one is looking to the future rather than the past. The equitable remedy of an injunction will not be granted to a plaintiff, even though his past conduct is impeccable, if he is not both able and willing to carry out any obligation he has undertaken towards the defendant.[10]

It should be added that according to *Holmes* v. *Eastern Counties Railway Co.*[11] where it would be unduly hard to refuse the plaintiff an injunction on the ground of his conduct, because this would leave him with no adequate remedy, the court may grant the injunction and register its disapproval of his conduct by depriving him of costs. It does not seem from the reports, however, that the courts are very ready to adopt this course.

Finally some cases which are at first sight apparently decided on the ground that the plaintiff has forfeited his right to an injunction by his conduct, are in fact decided on the ground that the alleged contractual right has ceased to exist either because the plaintiff has himself repudiated the contract or acted in such a way as to entitle the defendant to treat it as being at an end.[12]

e **Third parties**

Again owing to the fact that it is an equitable remedy, the court in deciding whether or not an injunction should be granted may take into consideration the effect that the grant of an injunction would have on third parties.[13] Thus in *Maythorn* v. *Palmer*[14] the defendant employee had entered into a limited and valid covenant not to enter into the employment of anyone other than the plaintiff. He entered into the employment of a third party who knew nothing about his undertaking to the plaintiff. The plaintiff's claim to an injunction was refused, partly on the ground of the injury this would do to the third party, who was not a party to the action.

---

[6] *Chitty* v. *Bray* (1883), 48 L.T. 860; *Meredith* v.*Wilson* (1893), 69 L.T. 336; *Hooper* v. *Bromet* (1903), 89 L.T. 37 affd. (1904), 90 L.T. 234, C.A.

[7] (1879), 12 Ch.D. 605.

[8] *Duchess of Argyll* v. *Duke of Argyll*, [1965] 1 All E.R. 611; [1967] Ch. 302, *per* Ungoed-Thomas J. at 626; 332.

[9] *Supra.* This was a motion for an interlocutory injunction, but the principle seems equally applicable to a claim for a perpetual injunction.

[10] *Measures Bros., Ltd.* v. *Measures*, [1910] 2 Ch. 248, C.A.

[11] (1857), 3 K. & J. 675.

[12] *Fechter* v. *Montgomery* (1863), 33 Beav. 22—cf. *Grimston* v. *Cuningham*, [1894] 1 Q.B. 125, D.C.; *General Billposting Co., Ltd.* v. *Atkinson*, [1909] A.C. 118, H.L.; *Measures Bros., Ltd.* v. *Measures, supra.*

[13] *Maythorn* v. *Palmer* (1864), 11 L.T. 261; *Hartlepool Gas and Water Co.* v. *West Hartlepool Harbour and Rail. Co.* (1865), 12 L.T. 366; cf. *Tubbs* v. *Esser* (1909), 26 T.L.R. 145.

[14] *Supra.*

f Declarations and suspension of injunction

In some circumstances, where *prima facie* the plaintiff is entitled to an immediate injunction, the court may merely make a declaration as to the plaintiff's right, with liberty to apply for an injunction should this become necessary: this may be done, for instance, where there seems to be no probability that the violation of the plaintiff's rights will be repeated.[15] The court also took this course in *Stollmeyer* v. *Trinidad Lake Petroleum Co., Ltd.*[16] where there was a clear infringement of the plaintiff's right, but the damage caused to the plaintiff was insignificant, though the grant of an injunction would seriously affect local industry. In this case the right to apply for an injunction was suspended for two years.

In other cases, for example, where it would be impossible, difficult or unduly hard on the defendant to comply with an injunction forthwith, the court may adopt the device of granting an immediate injunction, but suspending its operation for a specified time, and the defendant may even be given liberty to apply for an extension of the suspension.[17] This has frequently been done in cases against a local authority for the pollution of a stream by sewage and similar cases where immediate cessation of the nuisance would in fact be impossible,[18] or on the ground of considerations of public welfare.[19] And it has also been done where the defendant body is in the course of promoting a bill in Parliament authorising it to do the thing complained of,[20] or even to enable it to promote such a bill.[1] This course may also be followed where the grant of an immediate injunction coming into effect forthwith would cause difficulties with third parties.[2]

In any case where either of the above devices is adopted, the court may require the defendant, if he wishes to avoid an immediately operative injunction, to undertake to pay damages from time to time as any damage is in fact suffered by the plaintiff.[3]

5 ENFORCEMENT OF AN INJUNCTION[4]

Failure to comply with an injunction is a contempt of court[5] and it now seems established that this is so even though the infringements of the injunction were

---

[15] *A.-G.* v. *Birmingham, Tame and Rea District Drainage Board*, [1910] 1 Ch. 48, C.A. affd., [1912] A.C. 788, H.L.; *Race Relations Board* v. *Applin*, [1973] 2 All E.R. 1190; [1973] Q.B. 815, C.A. (no repetition of acts complained of for 20 months).

[16] [1918] A.C. 485, P.C.

[17] *Reinhardt* v. *Mentasti* (1889), 42 Ch.D. 685; *Frost* v. *King Edward VII Welsh etc., Association*, [1918] 2 Ch. 180 compromised on appeal (1918) 35 T.L.R. 138; *Stollmeyer* v. *Petroleum Development Co., Ltd.*, [1918] A.C. 498 n. P.C.

[18] *A.-G.* v. *Lewes Corporation*, [1911] 2 Ch. 495; *Phillimore* v. *Watford Rural District Council*, [1913] 2 Ch. 434.

[19] *Prices' Patent Candle Co., Ltd.* v. *London County Council*, [1908] 2 Ch. 526, C.A. per Cozens-Hardy M.R. at p. 544.

[20] *A.-G.* v. *South Staffordshire Waterworks Co.* (1909), 25 T.L.R. 408.

[1] *Roberts* v. *Gwyrfai District Council*, [1899] 2 Ch. 608, C.A.

[2] *Tubbs* v. *Esser* (1909), 26 T.L.R. 145.

[3] *Stollmeyer* v. *Trinidad Lake Petroleum Co., Ltd.*, [1918] A.C. 485, P.C.; *Stollmeyer* v. *Petroleum Development Co. Ltd.*, [1918] A.C. 498 n., P.C.

[4] An undertaking given to the court is enforceable in the same way—*Biba, Ltd.* v. *Stratford Investments, Ltd.*, [1972] 3 All E.R. 1041; [1973] Ch. 281.

[5] It is equally a contempt of court for a third party knowingly to aid and abet the breach of an injunction. See *Acrow (Automation), Ltd.* v. *Rex Chainbelt Inc.*, [1971] 3 All E.R. 1175, C.A. and contrast *Thorne R.D.C.* v. *Bunting (No. 2)*, [1972] 3 All E.R. 1084, C.A.

things done, reasonably and despite all due care and attention, in the belief, based on legal advice, that they were not infringements. In other words, when an injunction prohibits an act, that prohibition is absolute and is not to be related to intent unless otherwise stated on the face of the order.[6] Disobedience is regarded as wilful unless it is shown that it was merely casual, or accidental and unintentional. Nor is it sufficient by way of answer to an allegation that a court order has not been complied with, for the person concerned to say that he "did his best". The quality of non-compliance, which varies over an enormous range, is, however, of the utmost importance to the court in deciding what penalty should be imposed. The penalty in fact reflects faithfully the court's view of the conduct of the person to whom the order was addressed.[7]

Prior to the coming into force of the revised rules of court,[8] the primary remedy for contempt of court in the case of an individual was imprisonment[9] by means[10] of attachment or committal.[11] Attachment or committal being impracticable in the case of a corporation, it was provided[12] that where a corporation wilfully disobeyed an injunction it could be enforced by sequestration against the corporate property, or by attachment against the directors or other officers thereof, or by a writ of sequestration against their property.[13] Sequestration was also a method of enforcing a mandatory injunction against an individual,[14] and possibly also a breach of a prohibitory injunction where the defendant had rendered committal or attachment impossible by keeping out of the way or fleeing the country. In the case both of an individual and a corporation it seems the court could always impose the lesser penalty of a fine,[15]

---

[6] *Fairclough* v. *Manchester Ship Canal*, (1897), 41 Sol. Jo. 225, less fully reported; [1897] W.N. 7 C.A.; *Steiner Products, Ltd.* v. *Willy Steiner, Ltd.*, [1966] 2 All E.R. 387; *Re Agreement of Mileage Conference Group of the Tyre Manufacturers' Conference, Ltd.*, [1966] 2 All E.R. 849 (R.P.C.). *Knight* v. *Clifton*, [1971] 2 All E.R. 378; [1971] Ch. 700, C.A. *Heatons Transport (St. Helens), Ltd.* v. *Transport and General Workers Union*, [1972] 3 All E.R. 101; [1973] A.C., at p. 78, H.L.

[7] *Howitt Transport, Ltd.* v. *Transport and General Workers Union*, [1973] I.C.R. 1 *per* Donaldson J. esp. at pp. 10 and 11.

[8] The Rules of the Supreme Court 1965 came into force on 1 October, 1966. The old Rules referred to in this section were those made in 1883.

[9] In the case of a mandatory order a person committed will be released where the length of imprisonment served is regarded as adequate punishment for disobedience to the court's order, and where the court thinks that continued imprisonment will not secure compliance with the order—6 months in *Re Barrell Enterprises, Ltd.*, [1972] 3 All E.R. 631, C.A.

[10] The two methods were alternative. See the old R.S.C., O. 44, r. 2 (1) the note to which in the Annual Practice 1965, discusses briefly the history of attachment and committal.

[11] In an extreme case, on an *ex parte* application—*Warwick Corporation* v. *Russell*, [1964] 2 All E.R. 337.

[12] See the old R.S.C., O. 42, r. 31.

[13] There would be no remedy against directors or other officers under this provision unless the corporation had itself been guilty of a punishable contempt.

[14] Old R.S.C., O. 43, r. 6.

[15] *Phonographic Performance, Ltd.* v. *Amusement Caterers (Peckham), Ltd.*, [1963] 3 All E.R. 493; [1964] Ch. 195; *Ronson Products, Ltd.* v. *Ronson Furniture, Ltd.*, [1966] 2 All E.R. 381; [1966] Ch. 603; *Steiner Products, Ltd.* v. *Willy Steiner, Ltd., supra*; *The "Jarlinn"*, [1965] 3 All E.R. 36; [1965] 2 Lloyd's Rep. 191; *The "Calyx"*, [1966] 1 Lloyd's Rep. 701 (Mayor's and City of London Court). The fine may be large, e.g. £50,000 in *Goad* v. *Amalgamated Union of Engineering Workers* (No. 3), [1973] I.C.R. 108.

or merely order the offending party to pay costs and, if it thought fit, damages.[16] It should be observed that a distinction was made between mandatory and prohibitory injunctions as regards service of the injunction.[17]   A mandatory injunction would only be enforced by a committal order or a writ of sequestration if the judgment or order had actually been served on the defendant,[18] while in the case of a prohibitory injunction it was sufficient to show that he had notice in fact, by reason of his presence in court when the order was made or some informal notice by telegram or otherwise.[19] A defendant who had merely had informal notice might, however, escape liability if he could establish that he had a *bona fide* and reasonable belief that no injunction had in fact been granted.[20]

Under the new rules some changes have been made. The existing power to imprison an individual for contempt of court, or to impose a fine,[21] seems to be unaltered save that in the case of imprisonment proceedings must in every case be by committal, attachment having been abolished. Probably in the exercise of the general power to commit for contempt of court under the new O. 52, the old distinction between mandatory and prohibitory injunctions as regards service of the order remains.[1] Further, the old O. 42, r. 31 which, as already mentioned, provided means for enforcing an injunction against a corporation, has been replaced by the new and wider O. 45, r. 5 which provides means for enforcing an injunction against both an individual and a body corporate. One or more of the following means are made available, viz:—

" (i) with the leave of the court, a writ of sequestration against the property of that person;
 (ii) where that person is a body corporate, with the leave of the court, a writ of sequestration against the property of any director or other officer of the body;
(iii) subject to the provisions of the Debtors Acts 1869 and 1878, an order of committal against that person or, where that person is a body corporate, against any such officer."

The following observations may be made on the new order.

(a) although under (i) sequestration appears to be generally available in order to enforce an injunction against both an individual and a body corporate, it may be that the court would only give leave for a writ of sequestration to issue

---

[16] *Fairclough* v. *Manchester Ship Canal, supra; Re Agreement of Mileage Conference Group of the Tyre Manufacturers' Conference, Ltd., supra.*
[17] See *Hyde* v. *Hyde* (1888), 13 P.D. 166, C.A.; *Kistler* v. *Tettmar*, [1905] 1 K.B. 39, C.A.; *Re Tuck*, [1906] 1 Ch. 692, C.A.; *Husson* v. *Husson*, [1962] 3 All E.R. 1056; *Ronson Products, Ltd.* v. *Ronson Furniture, Ltd., supra*, and old R.S.C., O. 41, r. 5.
[18] An exception was where the defendant, knowing of the order, had wilfully evaded service—*Hyde* v. *Hyde, supra; Kistler* v. *Tettmar, supra; R.* v. *Wigand*, [1913] 2 K.B. 419, D.C.; *Re Suarez*, [1918] 1 Ch. 176, C.A.
[19] *Husson* v. *Husson, supra; Re Suarez, supra; Ronson Products, Ltd.* v. *Ronson Furniture, Ltd., supra.*
[20] *Re Bishop, ex parte Langley* (1879), 13 Ch.D. 110, C.A.
[21] See O. 52, r. 9.
[1] In *Ronson Products, Ltd.* v. *Ronson Furniture, Ltd., supra*, Stamp J. said that this was not a merely historical or technical distinction.

against an individual in the sort of case where it would have been available under the old rules.

(b) the order expressly provides for an order of committal against a person who has disobeyed an injunction. This is additional to the general power to commit for contempt of court under O. 52.

(c) the order, unlike its predecessor, appears at first sight to make the means of enforcement available in the case of simple disobedience to an injunction, not only in the case of wilful disobedience. If this were so, then so far as (i) and (ii) are concerned, the court might well refuse to grant leave in the absence of wilful disobedience, but leave is not required under (iii) and it would seem to be arguable that a committal order should be made under O. 45 r. 5[2] though the injunction had not been wilfully disobeyed or contumaciously disregarded. The view stated in the Supreme Court Practice,[3] however, that the change in the rule has not altered the practice, produces a more reasonable result and will probably be followed, though the grounds for it are not completely convincing. It would be more consistent, too, with the recent observation[4] of O'Connor J. that "where parties seek to invoke the power of the court to commit people to prison and deprive them of their liberty, there has got to be quite clear certainty about it". It is clear, however, as was recently pointed out by Lord Wilberforce[5] that the omission of the word "wilfully" in the new Order cannot improve the position of a party who has disobeyed an order.

(d) unless the court dispenses with the requirement, a mandatory injunction cannot be enforced under O. 45, r. 5 unless a copy of the order has been served personally on the person required to do the act in question.[6] The old rules,[7] however, as to service in the case of prohibitory injunctions, have now been expressly written into the order.[8]

Two final points may be added. First, under O. 45, r. 8[9] the court without prejudice to its powers in relation to contempt may direct that an act to be done be carried out by some person appointed by the court at the cost of the disobedient party. Secondly, the court has jurisdiction to commit for contempt for breach of an injunction even though the injunction has ceased to have effect.[10]

---

[2] It would seem to be otherwise if committal is sought under O. 52.
[3] 1970 Ed., Vol. I, p. 637.
[4] P. A. Thomas & Co. v. Mould, [1968] 1 All E.R. 963, 967; [1968] 2 Q.B. 913, 923.
[5] In Heaton's Transport (St. Helens), Ltd. v. Transport and General Workers Union, [1972] 3 All E.R. 101; [1973] A.C. 15, H.L. at pp. 117, 109.
[6] O. 45, r. 7 (2) and (7) as amended by S.I. 1967, No. 829. In the case of a body corporate, if enforcement is sought against an officer, there must normally have been personal service on that officer—O. 45, r. 7 (3).
[7] See supra, p. 406.
[8] S.I. 1967, No. 829 adding a new O. 45, r. 6.
[9] Replacing the old O. 42, r. 30.
[10] Jennison v. Baker, [1972] 1 All E.R. 997; [1972] 2 Q.B. 52, C.A., where it was held on this point that the county court has the same power as the High Court.

6 DAMAGES IN LIEU OF AN INJUNCTION

a Jurisdiction

Before Lord Cairns' Act[11] the Court of Chancery had no power to award damages,[12] but by section 2 the court was empowered to award damages in addition to or in substitution for an injunction.[13] This enabled the court to give damages in some cases where damages could not have been obtained in a court of common law, where, for instance, the injury was merely threatened or apprehended,[14] or where the right was purely equitable,[15] and it applied even though the damage was only nominal.[16] Although Lord Cairns' Act has been repealed,[17] the jurisdiction has been preserved, as explained by the House of Lords in *Leeds Industrial Co-operative Society Ltd.* v. *Slack*,[18] and the present position is that all divisions of the High Court now have both this jurisdiction and also, under the Judicature Acts,[19] the jurisdiction which the common law courts had to award damages before 1875. In view of the latter jurisdiction it will now only be necessary to rely on Lord Cairns' Act in exceptional cases, such as a *quia timet* application, where the common law courts had no jurisdiction before 1875, or in a case where the measure of damage under Lord Cairns' Act would be higher than at common law.[20] There is no provision giving any division of the High Court power to award damages in a case where no court had power to do so before 1875.

The object of Lord Cairns' Act was said, in *Ferguson* v. *Wilson*,[21] to be to prevent a litigant being bandied about from one court to another and to enable the Court of Chancery to do complete justice by awarding damages where, before the Act, it would have refused an injunction and left the plaintiff to bring his action for damages at law. Since Lord Cairns was himself a member of the court in which this explanation was given it is presumably accurate, but, if so, it seems that the Act was not effective for its purpose, since it has been held in a number of cases,[22] including *Ferguson* v. *Wilson*[23] itself, that the court could only

---

[11] Chancery Amendment Act 1858.

[12] But an account might be ordered in certain cases where the defendant had made a profit.

[13] Or specific performance. Since the same principles apply the cases cited below include cases on specific performance.

[14] *Leeds Industrial Co-operative Society Ltd.* v. *Slack*, [1924] A.C. 851, H.L.

[15] E.g. a restrictive covenant, in respect of a subsequent purchaser to whom the burden did not pass at common law—*Eastwood* v. *Lever* (1863), 4 De G.J. & S. 114. Damages could likewise be obtained in addition to or in substitution for specific performance where damages could not be obtained at common law by reason of the absence of writing to satisfy the Statute of Frauds, but where there was a sufficient act of part performance—*Lavery* v. *Pursell* (1888), 39 Ch.D. 508.

[16] *Sayers* v. *Collyer* (1884), 28 Ch.D 103, C.A.

[17] By the Statute Law Revision Act 1883, s. 3.

[18] *Supra*.

[19] Judicature Act 1925, ss. 36–43, re-enacting the Judicature Act 1873, s. 24.

[20] See p. 412, *infra*.

[21] (1866), 2 Ch. App. 77 *per* Turner L.J. (a case on specific performance).

[22] E.g. *Holland* v. *Worley* (1884), 26 Ch.D. 578, (where Pearson J. observed that the authorities added to rather than removed the difficulties); *Proctor* v. *Bayley* (1889), 42 Ch.D. 390, C.A.; *Lavery* v. *Pursell* (1888), 39 Ch.D. 508.

[23] *Supra*.

exercise the jurisdiction to award damages where it would have granted an injunction before the Act, or in cases where the injunction was refused by reason of a change in circumstances between the filing of the bill and the trial, but would have been granted on the facts as at the time of the filing of the bill. Fry L.J. expressed it succinctly in *Proctor* v. *Bayley*[24] on appeal from the Chancery Court of the County Palatine of Lancaster[1] which had only the jurisdiction of the old Court of Chancery, "Under Lord Cairns' Act there is no jurisdiction to give damages except in substitution for or in addition to an injunction. Unless, therefore, the plaintiff can establish his right to an injunction, his case wholly fails". The Act does not in fact appear to have given the court power to award damages where before it the injunction would have been refused and the matter left to the common law courts. But in most cases, as we have seen, the High Court can now award damages under the old common law jurisdiction irrespective of whether the plaintiff has a claim to an injunction or not. It is interesting to observe that the original reason for passing the Act seems to have been forgotten, and Jessel M.R. thought[2] that the Act was designed to prevent a man obtaining an extortionate sum as the price of giving up his legal right to an injunction, for instance, against some comparatively trifling infringement of a right to light by a property developer.

b Principles to be applied

Whatever doubts there may have been about the jurisdiction, the Act clearly gave the court power to award damages in lieu of an injunction where it had jurisdiction to grant an injunction if it thought fit, with the result in such case that the court found itself with a discretion whether to award damages or grant an injunction. The court has assumed a similar discretion where, as a result of the Judicature Acts, it has both the equitable jurisdiction to grant an injunction and the common law jurisdiction to award damages. The courts do not seem to distinguish between these two discretions in considering whether to award an injunction or damages, although if they exercise it in favour of damages there may be, as we shall see,[3] a difference in the measure of damage. In exercising their discretion, the courts have made it clear that if, according to ordinary principles, a plaintiff has made out his case for an injunction, the court will not award damages in substitution therefor, except under very exceptional circumstances.[4] The mere fact that an injunction would almost certainly do no good

---

[24] (1889), 42 Ch.D. 390, 401, C.A.

[1] The Chancery Court of Lancaster (but not of Durham) was given the jurisdiction of the Chancery Division of the High Court by s. 3 of the Chancery of Lancaster Act, 1890. Both courts were abolished by the Courts Act 1971.

[2] In *Aynsley* v. *Glover* (1874), L.R. 18 Eq. 544, at p. 555, only eight years after *Ferguson* v. *Wilson* (1866), 2 Ch. App. 77. Cf. Buckley J. in *Cowper* v. *Laidler*, [1903] 2 Ch. 337 who did not think it extortion to ask a price which a property for exceptional reasons in fact commands.

[3] See p. 412, *infra*.

[4] "The cases do, however, show that Lord Cairns' Act did not revolutionise the principles on which the equitable jurisdiction had been administered up to that time and that some special case must be shown before the court should exercise the jurisdiction under that Act"—*per* Stamp J. in *Sefton* v. *Topham's Ltd.*, [1964] 3 All E.R. 876, at p. 894. No point was taken on Lord Cairns' Act on appeal—[1965] 3 All E.R. 1; [1966] Ch. 1140, C.A.; [1966] 1 All E.R. 1039; [1967] 1 A.C. 50, H.L.

to the plaintiff does not seem to be sufficient.[5] In particular, as Lindley L.J. said in *Shelfer* v. *City of London Electric Lighting Co.*,[6] "ever since Lord Cairns' Act was passed the Court of Chancery has repudiated the notion that the legislature intended to turn that Court into a tribunal for legalizing wrongful acts; or in other words, the Court has always protested against the notion that it ought to allow a wrong to continue simply because the wrongdoer is able and willing to pay for the injury he may inflict". Lord Sumner expressed the same idea in colourful language in *Leeds Industrial Co-operative Society* v. *Slack*,[7] which involved the infringement of a right to light. "For my part", he said, "I doubt, as Sir George Jessel doubted,[8] whether it is complete justice to allow the big man, with his big building and his enhanced rateable value and his improvement of the neighbourhood, to have his way, and to solace the little man for his darkened and stuffy little house by giving him a cheque that he does not ask for".

In *Shelfer* v. *City of London Electric Lighting Co.*[9] A. L. Smith L.J. gave it as his opinion that "as a good working rule" damages in substitution for an injunction may be given if—

(i) the injury to the plaintiff's legal rights is small, and

(ii) is one which is capable of being estimated in money, and

(iii) is one which can be adequately compensated by a small money payment, and

(iv) the case is one in which it would be oppressive to the defendant to grant an injunction.

Though this rule has been followed and applied in a number of cases,[10] it was pointed out in *Slack* v. *Leeds Industrial Co-operative Society Ltd.*,[11] where the rule was accepted as valid, that it must be read in its context, including in particular the judge's preceding observation that if the plaintiff's legal right has been invaded, he is *prima facie* entitled to an injunction. It came in for more severe criticism in *Fishenden* v. *Higgs & Hill Ltd.*[12] where it was said[13] to be the "high water mark of what might be called definite rules". It was further said[13] that the rule was not intended to be exhaustive or to be rigidly applied, and that the tests were, as A. L. Smith L.J. himself recognised, of imperfect application— what, for instance, is meant by a "small"[14] injury, or "adequate" compensation. Another member of the court,[15] after observing that the rule was contained in an *obiter dictum*, observed[15] that, though it might have been valid in the sort of

---

[5] *Per* Stamp J. at first instance in *Sefton* v. *Topham's Ltd.*, *supra*, at p. 894.

[6] [1895] 1 Ch. 287, C.A., at pp. 315, 316.

[7] [1924] A.C. 851, H.L., at p. 872.

[8] In *Krehl* v. *Burrell* (1878), 7 Ch.D. 551, at p. 554 affd. C.A., (1879), 11 Ch.D. 146.

[9] [1895] 1 Ch. 287, C.A., at pp. 322, 323; cf. *Aynsley* v. *Glover* (1874), L.R. 18 Eq. 544.

[10] E.g. *Price* v. *Hilditch*, [1930] 1 Ch. 500; *Kelsen* v. *Imperial Tobacco Co. (of Great Britain & Ireland), Ltd.*, [1957] 2 All E.R. 343; [1957] 2 Q.B. 334.

[11] [1924] 2 Ch. 475, C.A.

[12] (1935), 153 L.T. 128, C.A.

[13] *Per* Hanworth M.R. at p. 138.

[14] Some assistance is obtained from *Slack* v. *Leeds Industrial Co-operative Society Ltd.*, *supra*, which says that this is meant comparatively and not absolutely, and *Fishenden* v. *Higgs & Hill Ltd.*, *supra*, which decides that it does not matter if "comparatively small damages" constitute absolutely a "not inconsiderable sum".

[15] Maugham L.J. at p. 144.

case then before the court, i.e. nuisance by noise and vibration, it was "not a universal or even a sound rule in all cases of injury to light". However, in the most recent case, *Morris* v. *Redland Bricks, Ltd.*[16] no reference was made to any criticism or qualification of the rule, which all the members of the Court of Appeal accepted as good law, though there was disagreement as to its application to the facts. These concerned a market garden cultivated by the plaintiffs on eight acres of land adjoining land belonging to the defendant brick company. The defendant company excavated earth and clay from their land thereby withdrawing support from the plaintiff's land, as a result of which a small part of the plaintiff's land slipped, and further slipping of up to perhaps an acre of the plaintiff's land was likely to occur in the future. An acre of the land was worth about £1,500. The only sure way of restoring support and preventing further slipping might cost £30,000 to £35,000. The majority of the Court of Appeal thought that only part (iv) of the rule was satisfied, and accordingly the grant of an injunction was affirmed, though Sellers L.J. dissenting, considered that all four parts of the rule were satisfied and that it was a case for damages.

The exercise of the court's discretion has been discussed in several cases. On the one hand Lord Macnaghten has stated[17] that while the amount of damages that it is supposed could be recovered does not furnish a satisfactory test, an injunction and not damages should be awarded if the injury cannot fairly be compensated by money; or if the defendant has acted in a high-handed manner,[18] or if he has endeavoured to steal a march upon the plaintiff or to evade the jurisdiction of the court. And it has been held[19] that in general damages will not be granted *in lieu* of an injunction against the pollution of a stream, or nuisance by noise or smell,[20] as it is impossible to measure what the future damage would be. On the other hand Lord Macnaghten, in the same case,[1] observed that where there is a real question as to whether the plaintiff's rights have been infringed, and the defendant has acted fairly and not in an unneighbourly spirit, the court should incline to damages rather than an injunction, and Lindley L.J. has suggested,[2] as examples of circumstances where the court would exercise its discretion by awarding damages, trivial and occasional nuisances; cases in which a plaintiff has shown that he only wants money; vexatious and oppressive cases; cases where the plaintiff has so conducted himself as to render it unjust to give him more than pecuniary relief, and cases where damages is really an adequate remedy. And in several cases[3] it has been held that a fairly weak case of

---

[16] [1967] 3 All E.R. 1, C.A. Note, however, that this decision was reversed on appeal to the House of Lords, *sub nom. Redland Bricks, Ltd.* v. *Morris*, [1969] 2 All E.R. 576; [1970] A.C. 652, where this point was not discussed. All their Lordships agreed with Lord Upjohn that the Court of Appeal should not have considered Lord Cairns' Act at all. The question at issue was simply whether or not a mandatory *quia timet* injunction should be granted. Neither side had sought to rely on Lord Cairns' Act, and indeed it would have been impractical to do so, the action having been started in the county court with its limited jurisdiction as to damages.

[17] In *Colls* v. *Home and Colonial Stores, Ltd.* [1904] A.C. 179, H.L., at p. 193.

[18] Cf. *Price* v. *Hilditch*, [1930] 1 Ch. 500.

[19] *Pennington* v. *Brinsop Hall Coal Co.* (1877), 5 Ch.D. 769.

[20] *Wood* v. *Conway Corporation*, [1914] 2 Ch. 47, C.A.

[1] *Colls* v. *Home and Colonial Stores, Ltd.*, supra, H.L.; *Kine* v. *Jolly*, [1905] 1 Ch. 480, C.A.

[2] In *Shelfer* v. *City of London Electric Lighting Co.*, [1895] 1 Ch. 287, C.A., at p. 317.

[3] *Lockwood* v. *London & North Western Rail. Co.* (1868), 19 L.T. 68; *Sayers* v. *Collyer* (1884), 28 Ch.D. 103, C.A., esp. *per* Fry L.J. at p. 110.

quiescence by the plaintiff may be a ground for awarding damages *in lieu* of an injunction. While it is not doubted that in the circumstances suggested damages might well be awarded rather than an injunction, it would seem that on principle, in some cases at any rate, this should not be under any discretionary power given to the court by Lord Cairns' Act, but by an application of the ordinary principles which, apart from that Act, would prevent the grant of an injunction in such cases,[4] leaving the court only with the old common law jurisdiction to give damages. An illustration of the sort of case in which the court will exercise its discretion by giving damages is an unreported case[5] decided by Jessel M.R. where the injury was very trifling compared with the injury that the defendant would suffer if the injunction were granted.[6] The same judge has also suggested[7] that as a general rule an injunction should be awarded if the defendant knew he was doing wrong and took his chance about being disturbed in doing it. Again in *Bowes* v. *Law*,[8] James V.C. applied Lord Cairns' Act and awarded damages saying,[9]

> "I am of opinion, having regard to all the circumstances, and considering that no substantial annoyance has been occasioned to the plaintiff, and no substantial injury done to any right of property of his, that a declaration will be sufficient for the purpose of protecting the title, and I do not think it necessary to give the plaintiff the power of doing such an unreasonable and unneighbourly act as that of taking down this vinery, which is a great convenience to the defendant, and the taking down of which would not confer on the plaintiff himself any benefit."

And in *Sharp* v. *Harrison*[10] Astbury J. stated the general proposition that damages and not an injunction should be granted where the plaintiff had not really suffered any damage and an injunction would inflict damage upon the defendant out of all proportion to the relief which the plaintiff ought to obtain.

c Measure of damage

If damages are awarded in substitution for an injunction under Lord Cairns' Act, the measure of damage is not necessarily the same as if a claim was made for damages at common law. In *Wroth* v. *Tyler*[11] the point arose in a specific performance action which, as has been mentioned, is also governed in this respect by Lord Cairns' Act. Specific performance of a contract for the sale of land was refused and the question was whether the damages should be £1,500, the difference between the contract price and the market price of the property as at the date of the breach, i.e. the date fixed for completion, or £5,500 being the same difference as at the date of the trial. Even assuming that the first figure would represent the measure of damage at common law, as *prima facie*

---

[4] See Section 4, p. 400, *ante*.
[5] Identified as *Batt* v. *Earl Derby* (1874), by Kekewich J. in *Dicker* v. *Popham Radford & Co.* (1890), 63 L.T. 379 and mentioned at (1874) L.R. 18 Eq. 555.
[6] See also *Holland* v. *Worley* (1884), 26 Ch.D. 578; *Greenwood* v. *Hornsey* (1886), 33 Ch.D. 471.
[7] *Smith* v. *Smith* (1875), L.R. 20 Eq. 500. Cf. *Ough* v. *King*, [1967] 3 All E.R. 859, C.A., where there appears to have been no appeal against the refusal of an injunction though the defendant knew his acts might, and as the court held did, infringe the plaintiff's rights.
[8] (1870), L.R. 9 Eq. 636.
[9] At p. 642.
[10] [1922] 1 Ch. 502.
[11] [1973] 1 All E.R. 897.

it would, it was held that under Lord Cairns' Act the damages awarded must in fact constitute a true substitute for specific performance, namely £5,500. Only damages on this basis could put the plaintiff into as good a position as if the contract had been performed.

Another difficulty that sometimes arises is, as has been pointed out,[12] "that damages cannot be an adequate substitute for an injunction unless they cover the whole area which would have been covered by the injunction". The sum awarded has to cover not only past damage, whether accruing before or after the issue of the writ,[13] but also damage merely threatened or apprehended. Of course, in the case of a purely *quia timet* application, it will comprise only damage which has not yet occurred.[14] Moreover in a proper case the court may grant damages as to the past and an injunction as to the future.[15]

7 INJUNCTIONS IN PARTICULAR TYPES OF CASES

It is impossible to consider exhaustively the various circumstances which may give rise to a claim for an injunction. An injunction is commonly claimed in aid of a legal right, in which case a mere equitable owner, though he may obtain an interlocutory injunction, can only obtain a perpetual injunction by joining the legal owner in the action,[16] but it may also be granted to give effect to a purely equitable right, for instance to restrain a breach of trust,[17] equitable waste, or the breach of a restrictive covenant enforceable only in equity under the doctrine of *Tulk* v. *Moxhay*.[18] Some of the types of case in which an injunction is commonly claimed will now be briefly considered.

a To restrain a breach of contract

There is a close relationship between an injunction to restrain a breach of contract and a decree of specific performance. The terms of a contract may be affirmative or negative, or partly one and partly the other. Subject to the restrictions dealt with in the following chapter, specific performance is the natural remedy to enforce an affirmative term, while the injunction is appropriate to enforce a negative one. So far as jurisdiction to grant an interlocutory injunction is concerned, the general principles discussed above apply, but there are special considerations in regard to a claim for a perpetual injunction.

i *Purely negative terms.* Where it is sought to restrain by perpetual injunction the threatened breach of a purely negative contract or covenant, the court, in general, has no discretion to exercise. The classic statement on this point, though strictly only an *obiter dictum*, is that of Lord Cairns in *Doherty* v.

---

[12] Per Fry J. in *Fritz* v. *Hobson* (1880), 14 Ch.D. 542, 557.

[13] *Fritz* v. *Hobson, supra*; *Wroth* v. *Tyler, supra* (specific performance).

[14] *Leeds Industrial Co-operative Society Ltd.* v. *Slack*, [1924] A.C. 851, H.L.

[15] *Martin* v. *Price*, [1894] 1 Ch. 276, C.A.; *Gilling* v. *Gray* (1910), 27 T.L.R. 39. Cf. *Lipman* v. *Pulman & Sons, Ltd.* (1904), 91 L.T. 132.

[16] *Performing Right Society Ltd.* v. *London Theatre of Varieties Ltd.*, [1924] A.C. 1, H.L. Cf. *E. M. Bowden's Patents Syndicate Ltd.* v. *H. Smith & Co.*, [1904] 2 Ch. 86.

[17] See Section 7h, p. 424, *post*.

[18] (1848), 2 Ph. 774. See, e.g. Megarry and Wade, *The Law of Real Property*, 3rd Ed., pp. 753 *et seq.*; Cheshire, *Modern Law of Real Property*, 11th Ed., pp. 578 *et seq.*

Allman[19]: "If parties, for valuable consideration, with their eyes open, contract that a particular thing shall not be done, all that a Court of Equity has to do is to say, by way of injunction, that which the parties have already said by way of covenant, that the thing shall not be done; and in such case the injunction does nothing more than give the sanction of the process of the Court to that which already is the contract between the parties. It is not then a question of the balance of convenience or inconvenience, or of the amount of damage or of injury—it is the specific performance, by the Court, of that negative bargain which the parties have made, with their eyes open, between themselves." Thus, in the old case of *Martin* v. *Nutkin*,[20] the plaintiffs, objecting to being disturbed by the ringing of the bell on Hammersmith parish church at 5 a.m. daily, agreed to erect a cupola, clock and new bell in consideration of the defendants refraining from ringing the bell at such a time. The plaintiffs duly carried out their part of the bargain, but after some two years abstinence the defendants recommenced the ringing of the 5 a.m. bell. The plaintiffs were granted an appropriate injunction.

In these cases there is no need for the plaintiff to prove damage, except, it seems, in an action by a reversioner.[21] The general rule is that "if the construction of the instrument be clear and the breach clear, then it is not a question of damage, but the mere circumstance of the breach of covenant affords sufficient ground for the court to interfere by injunction".[22] It is no defence, therefore, to show that the plaintiff has not suffered any loss by reason of the breach, or even that the breach is more beneficial to him than strict performance of the contract would have been,[1] and accordingly in *Marco Productions, Ltd.* v. *Pagola*,[2] where theatrical performers expressly agreed not to perform for any other person during the period of the contract, the plaintiffs were entitled to an injunction though they could not show that they would suffer greater damage by the defendants performing elsewhere than by their remaining idle. Nor can the court take into account that the matter is one of public importance, and that the granting of an injunction would cause inconvenience to the public.[3] The principles as to the granting of injunctions are the same whether the injunction is sought in aid of the legal right where there is privity of contract or privity of estate,[4] or in aid of an equitable claim only, as in the case of restrictive covenants enforceable under the rule in *Tulk* v. *Moxhay*.[5]

Where a mandatory injunction is sought for breach of a negative term, Lord Cairns' statement of the law is subject to some qualification, for it seems that in such case the court retains a residual discretion and may refuse an injunction

---

[19] (1878), 3 App. Cas. 709, at p. 720, H.L.
[20] (1724), 2 P.Wms. 266.
[21] *Johnstone* v. *Hall* (1856), 2 K. & J. 414.
[22] *Per* Page Wood V.C. in *Tipping* v. *Eckersley* (1855), 2 K. & J. 264, at p. 270; *Wells* v. *Attenborough* (1871), 24 L.T. 312; *Cooke* v. *Gilbert* (1892), 8 T.L.R. 382, C.A.
[1] *Mexborough (Earl)* v. *Bower* (1843), 7 Beav. 127; *Dickenson* v. *Grand Junction Canal Co.* (1852), 15 Beav. 260.
[2] [1945] 1 All E.R. 155; [1945] K.B. 111.
[3] *Lloyd* v. *London, Chatham and Dover Rail. Co.* (1865), 2 De G.J. & Sm. 568; *Price* v. *Bala and Festiniog Rail. Co.* (1884), 50 L.T. 787.
[4] *Spencer's Case* (1583), 5 Co. Rep. 16a; Law of Property Act 1925, ss. 140–142.
[5] (1848) 2 Ph. 744; *Manners (Lord)* v. *Johnson* (1875), 1 Ch.D. 673; *Richards* v. *Revitt* (1877), 7 Ch.D. 224.

if the circumstances are wholly exceptional. Thus in *Sharp* v. *Harrison*[6] a mandatory injunction was refused, where the plaintiff had suffered no damage, an injunction would inflict damage upon the defendant out of all proportion to the relief which the plaintiff ought to obtain, and the defendant was willing to give certain undertakings.

The extent of this residual discretion must not be overrated, however, and dicta at first instance in *Charrington* v. *Simons & Co., Ltd.*,[7] and in *Shepherd Homes, Ltd.* v. *Sandham*[8] to the effect that the criterion is whether a mandatory order, and if so what kind of mandatory order, will produce a fair result, must be viewed with considerable suspicion in the light of the comment of the Court of Appeal in the former case.[9] It may be added that it seems clear that the court cannot refuse an injunction or award damages *in lieu* even of a mandatory injunction where the defendant's breach has caused substantial damage.[10]

ii *Contract containing both affirmative and negative stipulations.* In many cases a party's obligation under a contract will expressly involve both affirmative and negative stipulations. It seems that as a general rule, the negative stipulations will be enforced by means of an injunction,[11] notwithstanding the fact that the affirmative stipulations may not be enforceable by means of a decree of specific performance. The negative stipulation to be enforceable must, however, be negative in substance as well as in form. In *Davis* v. *Foreman*[12] there was, in a contract of personal service, a stipulation in negative form by an employer not to give notice except for misconduct or breach of agreement. It was held that this was affirmative in substance, to retain the employee in his employment, and an injunction was consequently refused. An injunction will not, moreover, be granted if it would really amount to an indirect way of compelling specific performance of an agreement, where that remedy could not be obtained directly.

These matters may be illustrated[13] by reference to contracts of personal service, which cannot be enforced by a decree of specific performance. The foundation of this branch of the law is *Lumley* v. *Wagner*[14] where the defendant had agreed to sing at the plaintiff's theatre during a certain period of time, and had also expressly agreed not to sing elsewhere without the plaintiff's written authority. The court would not grant specific performance of the affirmative stipulation, but granted an injunction to restrain the defendant from singing elsewhere than in the plaintiff's theatre. This decision has been consistently followed, though it is regarded as anomalous and will not be extended.[15] Further an injunction will not be granted where its effect would be to leave the defendant with the two alternatives only of remaining idle or performing his contract, i.e. where the grant of the remedy would amount to enforcing specific

---

[6] [1922] 1 Ch. 502. The maxim *de minimis non curat lex* may apply—*Cooke* v. *Gilbert* (1892), 8 T.L.R. 382, C.A. *per* Lindley L.J. at 383; *Harrison* v. *Good* (1871), L.R. 11 Eq. 338.

[7] [1970] 2 All E.R. 257, 261 *per* Buckley J. (order varied, [1971] 2 All E.R. 588, C.A.)

[8] [1970] 3 All E.R. 402, at p. 412; [1971] Ch. 340, at p. 351 *per* Megarry J.

[9] *Charrington* v. *Simons & Co., Ltd.*, [1971] 2 All E.R. 588, at p. 592.

[10] *Achilli* v. *Tovell*, [1927] 2 Ch. 243.   [11] *Donnell* v. *Bennett* (1883), 22 Ch.D. 835.

[12] [1894] 3 Ch. 654; *Kirchner & Co.* v. *Gruban*, [1909] 1 Ch. 413; *Warner Bros. Pictures Inc.* v. *Nelson*, [1936] 3 All E.R. 160; [1937] 1 K.B. 209.

[13] See also, as to contracts requiring constant supervision, *Phipps* v. *Jackson* (1887), 56 L.J. Ch. 550; *Ryan* v. *Mutual Tontine Westminster Chambers Association*, [1893] 1 Ch. 116, C.A.

[14] (1852), 1 De G.M. & G. 604.

[15] *Whitwood Chemical Co.* v. *Hardman*, [1891] 2 Ch. 416, C.A.

performance of an agreement to which that latter remedy would not be directly applied. So in *Rely-A-Bell Burglar and Fire Alarm Co., Ltd.* v. *Eisler*,[16] the court, while granting a declaration as to the plaintiff's legal right and awarding damages, refused to grant an injunction to enforce a stipulation by an employee not to enter into *any* other employment during the term of the contract. The niceness of the distinctions that have to be drawn in this context appears by comparing this decision with that in *Warner Bros. Pictures Inc.* v. *Nelson*,[17] where the defendant film actress agreed not to render any services *in that capacity* for any other person during the term of the contract,[18] and the court granted an injunction. The defendant here was not confronted with the dilemma faced by the defendant in the *Rely-A-Bell Case*[19]: there were other ways in which she might earn a living, and it was irrelevant that the alternative ways might well be less remunerative. She might be tempted to perform her contract though she must not be compelled to do so, The above principles were considered in *Page One Records, Ltd.* v. *Britton*[20] where a group of musicians known as "The Troggs" had appointed the plaintiff company as their manager for five years, and had agreed not to engage any other person to act as manager or agent for them. An argument based on *Warner Bros. Pictures Inc.* v. *Nelson*,[21] to the effect that The Troggs could, without employing any other manager or agent, continue as a group on their own, or seek other employment of a different nature, failed, however. The judge held that, as a practical matter on the evidence before him, to grant an injunction would compel The Troggs to continue to employ the plaintiff company as their manager and agent. "It would", he added, "be a bad thing to put pressure on The Troggs to continue to employ as a manager and agent in a fiduciary capacity one, who, unlike the plaintiff in those cases[22] who had merely to pay the defendant money, has duties of a personal and fiduciary nature to perform and in whom The Troggs, for reasons good, bad or indifferent, have lost confidence and who may, for all I know, fail in its duty to them." The way in which cases such as *Warner Bros. Pictures Inc.* v. *Nelson*[21] were distinguished is not altogether convincing. The members of "The Troggs" were presumably as capable of earning their living by some other means as the defendant film actress in the former case.

iii *No express negative stipulation.* Further problems arise where there is no express negative stipulation and the question is whether one should be implied from an affirmative stipulation which is incapable of being directly enforced by specific performance, or, which often comes to the same thing, whether what on the face of it is an affirmative stipulation is in substance a negative one and should be treated as such. It does not seem possible to frame an adequate test to decide when the courts will imply a negative stipulation, but it is possible to get considerable guidance from decided cases.

In general, "when a plaintiff comes into this court upon an agreement which does not contain any such direct negative clause, and where you must infer the

---

[16] [1926] Ch. 609; *Whitwood Chemical Co.* v. *Hardman, supra.*
[17] [1936] 3 All E.R. 160; [1937] 1 K.B. 209.
[18] The court was prepared to sever the covenants as drafted.
[19] *Supra.*
[20] [1967] 3 All E.R. 822.
[21] *Supra.*
[22] *Lumley* v. *Wagner, supra: Warner Bros. Pictures Inc.* v. *Nelson, supra.*

negative from the necessity of the case, the instances in which the court has found it possible to act are very few and special".[23] Mere inconsistency of the proposed course of conduct with the positive obligation under the contract is not enough. It is necessary to point to something specific which the defendant has by implication agreed not to do.[1] Accordingly on the one hand the court will not import a negative quality into an agreement if this would in effect result in specific performance of a contract for which that remedy is not directly available. Thus so far as contracts for personal service are concerned, although the Court of Appeal has indicated[2] that it is not impossible for a negative stipulation to be implied, it is extremely difficult and no negative stipulation will be implied simply from an employee's covenant to devote all his time to his employer's business[3] or to act exclusively for his employer.[4] Again it has been held[5] that where specific performance of an agreement of a lease could not be obtained by reason of the infancy of one of the two defendants, no injunction against the granting of a lease to any other person should be decreed, and in another case concerning a contract for the sale and delivery of chattels which was not specifically enforceable, that no injunction should be granted to restrain the vendor from selling elsewhere.[6] Further no injunction will be granted where it would really be ancillary to a decree of specific performance which cannot be obtained.[7]

On the other hand, in *Metropolitan Electric Supply Co., Ltd.* v. *Ginder*[8] a covenant by the defendant "to take the whole of the electric energy required" for certain premises from the plaintiff was held to be in substance a covenant not to take it from anyone else; in *Manchester Ship Canal Co.* v. *Manchester Racecourse Co.*[9] a contract to give "first refusal" was held to involve a negative covenant not to part with the property without giving that first refusal, which could be enforced by injunction; in *Jones* v. *Tankerville*,[10] where there was a contract for the purchase of timber to be cut and removed by the purchaser, and the vendor forcibly ousted the purchaser's workmen, the court granted an injunction to restrain the vendor from preventing due execution of the contract; and in *Smith* v. *Peters*,[11] where there was a contract for a sale at a valuation, an injunction was granted to restrain the vendor from refusing to allow the valuer to enter and inspect the premises.

---

[23] *Per* Page Wood V.C. in *Peto* v. *Brighton, Uckfield and Tunbridge Wells Rail. Co.* (1863), 1 H. & M. 468, 486.

[1] *Bower* v. *Bantam Investments, Ltd.*, [1972] 3 All E.R. 349.

[2] *Mutual Reserve Fund Life Assurance* v. *New York Life Insurance Co.* (1896), 75 L.T. 528, C.A. *per* Lindley L.J. at 530.

[3] *Whitwood Chemical Co.* v. *Hardman*, [1891] 2 Ch. 416, C.A.; *Mortimer* v. *Beckett*, [1920] 1 Ch. 571. Cf. *Frith* v. *Frith*, [1906] A.C. 254, P.C.

[4] *Mutual Reserve Fund Life Assurance* v. *New York Life Insurance Co. supra.* Cf. *Clarke* v. *Price* (1819), 2 Wils. Ch. 157.

[5] *Lumley* v. *Ravenscroft*, [1895] 1 Q.B. 683, C.A.

[6] *Fothergill* v. *Rowland* (1873), L.R. 17 Eq. 132.

[7] *Baldwin* v. *Society for Diffusion of Useful Knowledge* (1838), 9 Sim. 393; *Phipps* v. *Jackson* (1887), 3 T.L.R. 387.

[8] [1901] 2 Ch. 799; *Catt* v. *Tourle* (1869), 4 Ch. App. 654; *Esso Petroleum Co., Ltd.* v. *Harper's Garage (Stourport), Ltd.*, [1967] 1 All E.R. 699; [1968] A.C. 269, H.L. Cf. *Clegg* v. *Hands* (1890), 44 Ch.D. 503, C.A.

[9] [1901] 2 Ch. 37, C.A. Cf. *Gardner* v. *Coutts & Co.*, [1967] 3 All E.R. 1064 (an action for damages only).

[10] [1909] 2 Ch. 440.

[11] (1875), L.R. 20 Eq. 511. Cf. *Hart* v. *Herwig* (1873), 8 Ch. App. 860.

iv   *De Mattos* v. *Gibson*[12]. Mention should be made of the principle laid down by Knight Bruce L.J. in *De Mattos* v. *Gibson*[12] namely that "reason and justice seem to prescribe that, at least as a general rule, where a man, by gift or purchase, acquires property from another, with knowledge of a previous contract, lawfully and for valuable consideration made by him with a third person, to use and employ the property for a particular purpose in a specified manner, the acquirer shall not, to the material damage of the third person, in opposition to the contract and inconsistently with it, use and employ the property in a manner not allowable to the giver or seller". The principle, discredited in *London County Council* v. *Allen*[13] and *Barker* v. *Stickney*,[14] but resuscitated by the Privy Council in *Lord Strathcona S.S. Co., Ltd.* v. *Dominion Coal Co., Ltd.*[15] was held to be invalid by Diplock J. in *Port Line, Ltd.* v. *Ben Line Steamers, Ltd.*,[16] who held that he was not bound by the Privy Council decision in the *Strathcona* case,[17] and that *De Mattos* v. *Gibson*[18] is to be explained on the ground taken by Lord Chelmsford L.C. at the trial of the action, who treated the right to an injunction as depending on the same principle as the right to damages in *Lumley* v. *Gye*,[19] namely, that it is a tort knowingly to procure a breach of contract by another person.

v   *Defences*. Finally it may be added that the clean hands doctrine[20] applies, and a plaintiff may also become disentitled to an injunction by reason of his laches or acquiescence,[1] or by reason of the effect that the grant of an injunction would have on third parties.[2]

b   To restrain legal proceedings

Before the coming into operation of the Judicature Act 1873 the Court of Chancery would restrain by injunction the prosecution of proceedings in a common law court where their continuance was inequitable, such an injunction being known as a "common injunction" as opposed to other injunctions which were "special". On the fusion of the courts by the Judicature Acts, the common injunction ceased to exist, it being expressly provided[3] that no cause or proceeding at any time pending in the High Court of Justice or before the Court of Appeal should be restrained by prohibition or injunction, though every matter of equity on which an injunction against the prosecution of any such cause or proceeding might formerly have been obtained, either unconditionally or on any terms or conditions, might be relied on by way of defence thereto.

The Judicature Acts do not, however, prohibit the High Court from granting an injunction to restrain a person from instituting proceedings,[4] or continuing

---

[12] (1858) 4 De G. & J. 276, at p. 282.
[13] [1914] 3 K.B. 642, C.A.
[14] [1919] 1 K.B. 121, C.A.
[15] [1926] A.C. 108, P.C.
[16] [1958] 1 All E.R. 787; [1958] 2 Q.B. 146. See (1958), 21 M.L.R. 433 (G. H. Treitel).
[17] *Supra.*
[18] *Supra.*
[19] (1853) 2 E. & B. 216.   [20] See Section 4d, p. 402, *ante.*
[1] See Section 4c, p. 402, *ante.*   [2] See Section 4e, p. 403, *ante.*
[3] Judicature Act 1873, s. 4 (5), repealed and replaced by the Judicature Act 1925, s. 41. See *Llewellyn* v. *Carrickford*, [1970] 2 All E.R. 24 (garnishee proceedings within section).
[4] *Besant* v. *Wood* (1879), 12 Ch.D. 605.

pending proceedings, in other courts, such as a County Court,[5] a magistrates' court,[6] and the courts of a foreign country.[7] In *Johns* v. *Chatalos*,[8] however, the court expressly left open the question whether or not the Chancery Division has jurisdiction to grant an injunction to restrain a party from enforcing an order of a county court which is said to be a nullity.

c To protect membership of clubs, trade unions and other unincorporated bodies

Members of unincorporated bodies can only be expelled from membership if the rules so provide and the procedure there set out is strictly complied with. The court, accordingly, can only intervene if it can be shown that the purported expulsion was not authorised by the rules,[9] or that the proceedings were irregular,[10] or not consonant with the principles of natural justice,[11] or that there was *mala fides* or malice in arriving at the decision.[12] If, however, a member is wrongfully expelled, he may seek a declaration that the purported expulsion is null and void, and an injunction to restrain the club, trade union, or other body from acting on the basis that he is not a member. At one time the jurisdiction of the court to grant an injunction was thought to be based purely on the member's right of property,[13] but recent decisions indicate that the jurisdiction is founded on the contractual rights of the expelled member.[14] An injunction will, however, only be granted to prevent a member's expulsion if it is necessary to protect a proprietary right of his, or to protect him in his right to earn his livelihood.[15] It will not be granted to give a member the right to enter a social club, unless there are proprietary rights attached to it, because purely as a matter of contract it is too personal to be specifically enforced.[16]

d To restrain the commission or repetition of a tort

Injunctions have frequently been granted to prevent a threatened or appre-

---

[5] *Murcutt* v. *Murcutt*, [1952] 2 All E.R. 427; [1952] P. 266.
[6] *Thames Launches, Ltd.* v. *Corporation of the Trinity House of Deptford Strond*, [1961] 1 All E.R. 26; [1961] Ch. 197; *Hedley* v. *Bates* (1880), 13 Ch.D. 498; *Stannard* v. *St. Giles, Camberwell, Vestry* (1882), 20 Ch.D. 190, C.A.
[7] *Settlement Corporation* v. *Hochschild*, [1965] 3 All E.R. 486; [1966] Ch. 10.
[8] [1973] 3 All E.R. 410.
[9] *Lee* v. *Showmen's Guild of Great Britain*, [1952] 1 All E.R. 1175; [1952] 2 Q.B. 329, C.A. *Bonsor* v. *Musicians' Union*, [1955] 3 All E.R. 518; [1956] A.C. 105, H.L.
[10] *Young* v. *Ladies' Imperial Club*, [1920] 2 K.B. 523, C.A.
[11] *Lawlor* v. *Union of Post Office Workers*, [1965] 1 All E.R. 353; [1965] Ch. 712.
[12] *Burn* v. *National Amalgamated Labourers' Union of Great Britain and Ireland*, [1920] 2 Ch. 364; *Byrne* v. *Kinematograph Renters Society, Ltd.*, [1958] 2 All E.R. 579; *Annamunthodo* v. *Oilfields Workers' Trade Union*, [1961] 3 All E.R. 621; [1961] A.C. 945, P.C.
[13] *Rigby* v. *Connol* (1880), 14 Ch.D. 482.
[14] *Lee* v. *Showmen's Guild of Great Britain*, [1952] 1 All E.R. 1175; [1952] 2 Q.B. 329, C.A. per Denning L.J. at 1180, 341, 342; *Bonsor* v. *Musicians' Union, supra*, per Lord Morton at 524, 127; *Byrne* v. *Kinematograph Renters Society, Ltd.*, [1958] 2 All E.R. 579. Cf. *Nagle* v. *Feilden*, [1966] 1 All E.R. 689, [1966] 2 Q.B. 633, C.A.
[15] As to a right to membership when this is necessary to enable him to earn his living, see *Faramus* v. *Film Artistes' Association*, [1964] 1 All E.R. 25; [1964] A.C. 925, H.L.; *Nagle* v. *Feilden*, [1966] 1 All E.R. 689; [1966] 2 Q.B. 633, C.A., noted (1966), 82 L.Q.R. 319 (A. L. Goodhart); (1966), 29 M.L.R. 424 (R. W. Rideout).
[16] *Baird* v. *Wells* (1890), 44 Ch.D. 661; *Lee* v. *Showmen's Guild of Great Britain, supra*. It follows that no injunction will lie at the suit of a member of a proprietary club.

hended trespass, nuisance[17] and waste, whether legal or equitable. Recently it has been held that if a person, without just cause or excuse, deliberately interferes with the trade or business of another, and does so by unlawful means, then he is acting unlawfully and, in a proper case, an injunction can be granted against him.[18]

So far as an injunction to restrain the publication of a libel is concerned, this was wholly impossible prior to the Common Law Procedure Act 1854. Courts of Equity had no jurisdiction in matters of libel,[19] and courts of law had no power to issue injunctions. Such a power was conferred on the common law courts by the Common Law Procedure Act 1854, though there is no reported instance of its exercise, prior to *Saxby* v. *Easterbrook*.[20] By the Judicature Act 1873 the High Court acquired the powers previously possessed by both common law and equity courts, and after that Act, the Chancery Division began to grant injunctions to restrain the publication of libels.[1] Where, however, an interlocutory injunction is sought the jurisdiction is "of a delicate nature. It ought only to be exercised in the clearest cases, where any jury would say that the matter complained of was libellous, and where if the jury did not so find the court would set aside the verdict as unreasonable."[2] It will not normally be exercised when the defendant says that he intends to justify the libel or to claim that it is fair comment on a matter of public interest.[3] The orthodox reason why it was and is regarded as such a delicate jurisdiction to exercise is that ever since Fox's Act[4] the question of libel or no libel, even in civil actions, has been a question for the jury, and if the court is to be justified in granting an interlocutory injunction it must come to a decision upon the question of libel or no libel before the jury has decided whether it was a libel or not.[5] The alternative, and according to Lord Denning M.R. the better, reason is the importance in the public interest that the truth should out. In his view[6]: "There is no wrong done if it is true, or if it is fair comment on a matter of public interest. The court will not prejudice the issue by granting an injunction in advance of publication."

It may be added that the jurisdiction to restrain the publication of a libel does not distinguish between a libel affecting trade or property and one affecting character only, and extends to an action of slander as well as to an action of libel.[7]

---

[17] E.g. *Halsey* v. *Esso Petroleum Co., Ltd.*, [1961] 2 All E.R. 145, and see *Rugby Joint Water Board* v. *Walters*, [1966] 3 All E.R. 497; [1967] Ch. 397 (to restrain riparian owner from abstracting water for extraordinary purposes).

[18] *Acrow (Automation), Ltd.*, v. *Rex Chainbelt Inc.*, [1971] 3 All E.R. 1175, C.A.; *Esso Petroleum Co., Ltd.* v. *Kingswood Motors (Addlestone), Ltd.*, [1973] 3 All E.R. 1057. See (1972), 88 L.Q.R. 177 (P. Rayner).

[19] *Prudential Assurance Co.* v. *Knott* (1875), 10 Ch. App. 142.

[20] (1878), 3 C.P.D. 339, D.C.

[1] *Quartz Hill Consolidated Gold Mining Co.* v. *Beall* (1882), 20 Ch.D. 501, C.A.; *Bonnard* v. *Perryman*, [1891] 2 Ch. 269, C.A.; *White* v. *Mellin*, [1895] A.C. 154, H.L.

[2] *Per* Lord Esher M.R. in *Coulson* v. *Coulson* (1887), 3 T.L.R. 846, C.A.; *Bonnard* v. *Perryman, supra; Monson* v. *Tussauds Ltd.*, [1894] 1 Q.B. 671, C.A.

[3] *Fraser* v. *Evans*, [1969] 1 All E.R. 8; [1969] 1 Q.B. 349, C.A.

[4] The Libel Act, 1792.

[5] *Monson* v. *Tussauds Ltd., supra.*

[6] In *Fraser* v. *Evans, supra*, at pp. 10; 361.

[7] *Hermann Loog* v. *Bean* (1884), 26 Ch.D. 306, C.A.

e To protect copyright, patent rights and trade marks

An injunction is the appropriate remedy to restrain the infringement of any of these rights, the substantive law now being largely statutory.[8]

f To restrain the improper use of confidential information

Under this head the court can, for instance, grant an injunction to restrain an employee or ex-employee from divulging trade secrets, whether they are in the nature of secret processes,[9] or a list of customers.[10] An injunction has been granted to restrain the improper use or disclosure of trade secrets, even though the details of the secrets were not disclosed to the court at the trial,[11] but the usual procedure is for this difficulty to be dealt with by having the matter heard in private.[12] In particular, as between traders where the question most often arises, the broad principle is "that if information be given by one trader to another in circumstances which make that information confidential then the second trader is disentitled to make use of the confidential information for purposes of trade by way of competition with the first trader".[13] The principle is not, however, restricted to traders, and thus, for instance, a printer is not entitled to make additional copies for his own purposes of a drawing he has undertaken to reproduce,[14] a person who attends oral lectures can be restrained from publishing them for profit,[15] and a spouse can be prevented from publishing confidences communicated during marriage.[16]

Though the jurisdiction is undoubted it is not altogether clear, as Turner V.C. observed in *Morison* v. *Moat*,[17] whether it is based on a right of property,[18] breach of an implied contract,[19] or breach of trust or confidence.[20] Most of the cases refer to breach of contract or trust, and it has been suggested[1] that "confidence postulates an implied contract; that where the court is satisfied of the existence of the confidential relation, then it at once infers or implies the contract arising from that confidential relation," "though the obligation to respect confidence is not limited to where the parties are in contractual relation-

---

[8] Copyright Act 1956; Patents Acts 1949 and 1957; Trade Marks Act 1938.
[9] *Morison* v. *Moat* (1851), 9 Hare 241; *Alperton Rubber Co.* v. *Manning* (1917), 116 L.T. 499; *Cranleigh Precision Engineering, Ltd.* v. *Bryant*, [1964] 3 All E.R. 289.
[10] *Robb* v. *Green*, [1895] 2 Q.B. 315, C.A.
[11] *Amber Size & Chemical Co., Ltd.* v. *Menzel*, [1913] 2 Ch. 239.
[12] *Mellor* v. *Thompson* (1885), 31 Ch.D. 55, C.A.
[13] Per Evershed M.R. in *Terrapin, Ltd.* v. *Builders' Supply Co. (Hayes), Ltd.*, [1960] R.P.C. 128, 131 C.A. based on *Saltman Engineering Co., Ltd.* v. *Campbell Engineering Co., Ltd.* (1948), 65 R.P.C. 203, C.A. Followed in *Peter Pan Manufacturing Corporation* v. *Corsets Silhouette, Ltd.*, [1963] 3 All E.R. 402. And see *Seager* v. *Copydex, Ltd.*, [1967] 2 All E.R. 415, C.A.
[14] *Prince Albert* v. *Strange* (1849), 1 Mac. & G. 25; *Tuck & Sons* v. *Priester* (1887), 19 Q.B.D. 629, C.A.
[15] *Abernethy* v. *Hutchinson* (1825), 1 H. & Tw. 28.
[16] *Duchess of Argyll* v. *Duke of Argyll*, [1965] 1 All E.R. 611; [1967] Ch. 302.
[17] *Supra.*
[18] *Abernethy* v. *Hutchinson*, supra.
[19] *Tuck & Sons* v. *Priester*, supra, *Robb* v. *Green*, supra.
[20] *Yovatt* v. *Winyard*, (1820), 1 Jac. & W. 394. *Fraser* v. *Evans*, [1969] 1 All E.R. 8; [1969] 1 Q.B. 349, C.A.
[1] By Kekewich J. in *Merryweather* v. *Moore*, [1892] 2 Ch. 518, 522. See, generally, Turner, *The Law of Trade Secrets*, pp. 175 et seq.; *Nichrotherm Electrical Co. Ltd.* v. *Percy*, [1957] R.P.C. 207, C.A.

18

ship".[2] More recently the view has been clearly expressed[3] that a breach of confidence or trust or faith can arise independently of any right of property or contract, other, of course, than any contract which the imparting of the confidence in the relevant circumstances may itself create.

In any case it is clear that an injunction can be obtained not only against the original guilty party, but against any third party who knowingly obtained the confidential information in breach of confidence or in any other fraudulent manner.[4] Indeed, even if a man obtains the confidential information innocently, once he gets to know that it was originally given in confidence, he can be restrained from breaking that confidence.[5]

g To protect public rights

Even if the "court has no jurisdiction to prevent the commission of acts which are merely criminal or merely illegal, and do not affect any rights of property",[6] it may intervene by injunction at the suit of the Attorney-General to prevent the commission of some apprehended or threatened act which is illegal and affects the public generally. Thus although, as we have seen,[7] where a statute creates an offence, without creating a right of property, and provides a summary remedy, an individual may be unable to claim an injunction, the Attorney-General can bring proceedings if the public interest is affected,[8] unless, it would seem, the statute expressly provides that the statutory remedy is to be the only one.[9] It is not essential for the defendant to have been convicted of the offence before the court is asked by the Attorney-General to exercise its discretion.[10]

The Attorney-General, who is the guardian of the public interest, may sue *ex officio*, or under the relator procedure. Under this procedure a member of the public, known as the relator, may seek the Attorney-General's consent to the institution of proceedings in which the Attorney-General is the nominal plaintiff. If the Attorney-General gives his consent, the relator becomes responsible for the conduct of the proceedings and is liable for the costs. The traditional

---

[2] *Per* Greene M.R. in *Saltman Engineering Co. Ltd.*, v. *Campbell Engineering Co., Ltd.* (1948), 65 R.P.C. 203, 211, C.A.

[3] *Per* Ungoed-Thomas J. in *Duchess of Argyll* v. *Duke of Argyll, supra,* at 619; 322.

[4] *Morison* v. *Moat* (1851) 9 Hare 241; *Lord Ashburton* v. *Pape*, [1913] 2 Ch. 469, C.A.; *Duchess of Argyll* v. *Duke of Argyll*, [1965] 1 All E.R. 611; [1967] Ch. 302.

[5] *Fraser* v. *Evans*, [1969] 1 All E.R. 8; [1969] 1 Q.B. 349, C.A.; *Butler* v. *Board of Trade*, [1970] 3 All E.R. 593; [1971] Ch. 680.

[6] *Per* Turner L.J. in *Emperor of Austria* v. *Day* (1861), 3 De G.F. & J. 217, 253; *Macaulay* v. *Shackell* (1827), 1 Bli. N.S. 96, 127; *Springhead Spinning Co.* v. *Riley* (1868), L.R. 8 Eq. 551. This is denied, however, in the most recent decision, *Duchess of Argyll* v. *Duke of Argyll, supra.*

[7] See Section 1c, p. 386, ante. But note that an individual may sue to enforce legal rights vested in the inhabitants of a parish—*Wyld* v. *Silver*, [1962] 3 All E.R. 309; [1963] 1 Q.B. 169, C.A.

[8] *A.-G.* v. *Bastow*, [1957] 1 All E.R. 497; [1957] 1 Q.B. 514; *A.-G.* v. *Smith*, [1958] 2 All E.R. 557; [1958] 2 Q.B. 173; *A.-G.* v. *Harris*, [1960] 3 All E.R. 207; [1961] 1 Q.B. 74, C.A.

[9] *Evans* v. *Manchester, Sheffield & Lincolnshire Railway* (1887), 36 Ch.D. 626; *Stevens* v. *Chown*, [1901] 1 Ch. 894.

[10] *A.-G.* v. *Chaudry*, [1971] 3 All E.R. 938, C.A.

view is that it is entirely a matter for the Attorney-General to decide whether he should commence litigation or not, and that the court has no jurisdiction to control the exercise of his discretion.[11] The only control is parliamentary. In connection with the relator procedure this view has recently been challenged by Lord Denning M.R. who said,[12] *obiter*, that "in the last resort, if the Attorney-General refuses leave in a proper case, or improperly or unreasonably delays in giving leave, or his machinery works too slowly, then a member of the public, who has a sufficient interest, can himself apply to the court itself".

Once the matter is before the court it is for the court to decide what the result of the litigation shall be,[13] though in a case in which the Attorney-General is acting *ex officio*, the very fact that the Attorney-General has initiated proceedings, thereby showing that in his opinion the acts of the defendant warrant an injunction, will carry weight with the court. In particular, where the Attorney-General establishes deliberate and still continuing breaches of the law, the court will in the exercise of its discretion normally grant an injunction, unless after hearing both sides it comes to the conclusion that the matter is too trivial to warrant it, or that an injustice would be caused by it, or that there is some other good reason for refusing to enforce the general right of the public to have its laws obeyed. The mere fact that there is no immediate injury in a narrow sense to the public is not a ground for refusing an injunction at the instance of the Attorney-General who, representing the community, has a larger and wider interest in seeing that the laws are obeyed and order maintained. Thus in a narrow sense there was no public injury, possibly even a public benefit, in, for instance, *A.-G.* v. *Sharp*[14] where the defendant persistently ran omnibuses without the proper licence, and *A.-G.* v. *Harris*,[15] where the defendants sold flowers from stalls erected on the pavement near a cemetery in breach of the Manchester Police Regulation Act 1844. Indeed in the latter case Pearce L.J. admitted that in one sense and from one point of view the defendants' acts were trivial in themselves and insufficient to justify an injunction. An injunction was nevertheless granted on the wider view of the matter, that the public ought not to be denied their general and not unimportant right to put an end to continuing and deliberate breaches of statute. The narrow view, in the words of Sellers L.J. in the same case,[16] disregards "the effect on the administration of and respect for the law if the defendants can continue in the future on the same lines as in the past, to laugh at the law, and say they are immune from its restraints so long as they pay recurringly a small price for their immunity". Further in an action by the Attorney-General the court, although retaining its discretion, ought to be slow to say that the Attorney-General should first have exhausted other remedies.[17]

---

[11] *A.-G.* v. *Birmingham, Tame and Rea District Drainage Board*, [1910] I Ch. 48, C.A. (affd. [1912] A.C. 788, H.L.); *A.-G.* v. *Harris*, *supra*, C.A.

[12] *A.-G.* v. *Independent Broadcasting Authority*, [1973] I All E.R. 689; [1973] I Q.B. 629, C.A. at p. 698; 649.

[13] *A.-G.* v. *Birmingham, Tame and Rea District Drainage Board*, *supra*, *A.-G.* v. *Harris*, *supra*.

[14] [1931] I Ch. 121; [1930] All E.R. Rep. 741, C.A.

[15] [1960] 3 All E.R. 207; [1961] I Q.B. 74, C.A.; *A.-G.* v. *Chaudry*, [1971] 3 All E.R. 938, C.A.

[16] *Ibid.*, at p. 214, 91.

[17] *A.-G.* v. *Bastow*, [1957] I All E.R. 497; [1957] I Q.B. 514.

h To restrain a breach of trust

In this case an injunction is granted not in aid of a legal right, but to protect some purely equitable claim. Thus, for instance, in *Dance* v. *Goldingham*[18] trustees for sale of land inserted depreciatory conditions of sale without reasonable cause. An injunction to restrain completion of sale was issued against both the trustees and the purchaser,[19] the court holding it irrelevant that the plaintiff had only a small interest under the trust, and that she was an infant and that the action may have been started from some other motive. More recently, in *Waller* v. *Waller*,[20] a wife sought an injunction to restrain her husband from making or completing any sale of the matrimonial home without her consent. She and her husband were tenants in common in equity, but the legal estate was vested in the husband alone. Notwithstanding the imposition of the statutory trust for sale,[21] the husband alone entered into a contract of sale with a third party, without having appointed another trustee and without consulting his wife. The injunction was granted.[22] Other cases show that an injunction may be granted to restrain trustees from distributing the estate otherwise than in accordance with the terms of the trust instrument,[1] from introducing ministers into the pulpit who were not ministers of the Church of Scotland, in breach of the provisions of the trust,[2] or otherwise disturbing the management of a chapel by the majority of trustees,[3] from demolishing a building,[4] from mortgaging the trust property unnecessarily,[5] or from selling it to anyone at a less price than that offered by the reversioner and without first communicating with him.[6]

i In matrimonial and other family matters

In divorce or other matrimonial proceedings injunctions may be granted even after decree absolute,[7] to restrain one spouse from forcing his or her society on the other or otherwise molesting the other,[8] though recently in *Freedman* v. *Freedman*,[9] Ormrod J. observed "there is an obvious tendency these days to ask

---

[18] (1873), 8 Ch. App. 902. See, generally, *Balls* v. *Strutt* (1841), 1 Hare 146.
[19] The question whether the purchaser might have a personal right of action against the trustees was left open.
[20] [1967] 1 All E.R. 305.
[21] *Bull* v. *Bull*, [1955] 1 All E.R. 253; [1955] 1 Q.B. 234, C.A., and see Megarry and Wade, *Law of Real Property*, 3rd Ed., pp. 423, 424.
[22] The third party was not a party to the proceedings, and the injunction was granted on an undertaking by the wife to join him as a defendant, and he was given liberty to apply to discharge the injunction.
[1] *Fox* v. *Fox* (1870), L.R. 11 Eq. 142.
[2] *Milligan* v. *Mitchell* (1837), 3 My. & Cr. 72.
[3] *Perry* v. *Shipway* (1859), 4 De G. & J. 353.
[4] *Ludlow Corporation* v. *Greenhouse* (1827), 1 Bli. N.S. 17.
[5] *Rigall* v. *Foster* (1853), 18 Jur. 39.
[6] *Wheelwright* v. *Walker* (1883), 23 Ch.D. 752.
[7] *Devas* v. *Devas*, [1969] 3 All E.R. 1543. *Beasley* v. *Beasley* [1969] 1 W.L.R. 226 (not cited in *Devas* v. *Devas*) suggests, perhaps, that an injunction against molestation will only be granted after decree absolute where young children are involved.
[8] *McGibbon* v. *McGibbon*, [1973] 2 All E.R. 836; [1973] Fam. 170; *Stewart* v. *Stewart*, [1973] 1 All E.R. 31; [1973] Fam. 21.
[9] [1967] 2 All E.R. 680n.

the court to invoke this power very much too light-heartedly". In refusing
the application the judge said that if the husband did not want "to endure the
insults of his wife" he should leave the matrimonial home, as he was in a position
to do. Injunctions may also be granted for other purposes, for instance, to
restrain a wife from allowing a letter written by her to be handed to a child of
the marriage,[10] or to prevent a child being taken out of the jurisdiction.[11] In
other proceedings an injunction may be granted to restrain the marriage of an
infant ward of court.[12] And the court has power, either in divorce proceedings,
or at common law, or under the Matrimonial Homes Act 1967, to exclude a
spouse from the matrimonial home, even where it belongs to that spouse,
though it is recognised that this is a drastic step which the court will be slow to
take.[13]

j In company matters

The legal capacity of a company regulated by the Companies Act 1948 is
defined by the memorandum of association, and if a company attempts to do an
ultra vires act, i.e. one beyond its legal powers, even a single shareholder has a
right to resist it, notwithstanding that it may have been sanctioned by all the
directors and a large majority of the shareholders, and the court will interpose
on his behalf by injunction.[14] A mere creditor, as opposed to a shareholder,
however, has no such right, and, as Lord Hatherley L.C. observed,[15] he cannot
claim "the interference of this court on the ground that he, having no interest
in the company, except the mere fact of being a creditor, is about to be
defrauded by reason of their making away with their assets".

---

[10] *R.* v. *R. & I.*, [1961] 3 All E.R. 461.
[11] *Harris* v. *Harris* (1890), 63 L.T. 262.
[12] *Smith* v. *Smith* (1745), 3 Atk. 304; *Pearce* v. *Crutchfield* (1807), 14 Ves. 206.
[13] *Hall* v. *Hall*, [1971] 1 All E.R. 762, C.A.; *Phillips* v. *Phillips*, [1973] 2 All E.R. 423, C.A.
(injunction granted excluding divorced husband from home of which he was joint
tenant with his ex-wife); *McCleod* v. *McCleod* (1973), 117 Sol. Jo. 679 (injunction
excluding husband from matrimonial home of which wife was tenant).
[14] *Simpson* v. *Westminster Palace Hotel Co.* (1860), 8 H.L.Cas., 712; *Mosely* v. *Koffyfontein
Mines Ltd.*, [1911] 1 Ch. 73, C.A. affd. *sub nom. Koffyfontein Mines Ltd.* v. *Mosley,* [1911]
A.C. 409, H.L.; *Parke* v. *Daily News, Ltd.*, [1962] 2 All E.R. 929; [1962] Ch. 927.
[15] *Mills* v. *Northern Railway of Buenos Ayres Co.* (1870), 5 Ch. App. 621, 628. As to
debenture holders see Gower, *Company Law*, 3rd Ed., pp. 86, 123.

CHAPTER 14

Specific Performance

1 NATURE OF REMEDY

a Meaning

This equitable remedy consists of an order of the court directing a party to a contract to perform his obligations thereunder according to its terms. It has been said[1] that it "presupposes an executory as distinct from an executed agreement, something remaining to be done, such as the execution of a deed or a conveyance, in order to put the parties in the position relative to each other in which by the preliminary agreement they were intended to be placed". In this passage Lord Selborne was drawing a broad distinction between the class of executory agreements, such as agreements for the sale of land and marriage articles, and the principles applicable to specific performance of them on the one hand, and on the other a very different class of agreements which he described[2] as "ordinary agreements for work and labour to be performed, hiring, and service, and things of that sort", for which specific performance is not available. The strict or proper sense of the term "specific performance" apparently designates the first type of case where an executory agreement is to be followed by the execution of a more formal instrument. However the term is commonly used, and will henceforward be used in this work, as including the equitable right to specific relief in respect of an intermediate class of agreements which do not call for the execution of a further instrument. The principles applicable seem to be exactly the same.[3]

The basis of the jurisdiction to grant specific performance has always been the inadequacy of the common law remedy of damages for breach of contract. "The Court gives specific performance instead of damages, only when it can by that means do more perfect and complete justice."[4] Thus the common law remedy may be regarded as inadequate, and specific performance may be available in an appropriate case, where only nominal damages could be recovered by

---

[1] Per Lord Selborne L.C. in Wolverhampton and Walsall Rail. Co. v. London and North Western Rail. Co. (1873), L.R. 16 Eq. 433, at p. 439; approved by Lord Macnaghten in Tailby v. Official Receiver (1888), 13 App. Cas. 523, at p. 547, H.L.
[2] Ubi supra.
[3] Australian Hardwoods Pty. Ltd. v. Commissioner for Railways, [1961] 1 All E.R. 737, P.C.
[4] Per Lord Selborne L.C. in Wilson v. Northampton and Banbury Junction Rail. Co. (1874), 9 Ch. App. 279, 284; Flint v. Brandon (1803), 18 Ves. 159.

an action at law,[5] or where there is a continuing obligation which would necessitate a series of actions at law for damages.[6] Further there are, on the one hand, as we shall see, many cases where specific performance is not available although damages may be obtained, and on the other hand, although originally specific performance was not granted unless the plaintiff had first recovered damages at law,[7] it has long since been recognized that in some cases specific performance may be granted though there is no right to recover damages at law at all. Thus damages at law can only be awarded for a *breach* of contract, but a breach of contract is not absolutely essential to a claim for specific performance. Accordingly the plaintiff in *Marks* v. *Lilley*[8] was held to be justified in issuing a writ for specific performance of a contract for the sale of land after the date fixed for completion had passed, although no notice had been served making time the essence of the contract, and in *Hasham* v. *Zenab*[9] even before the date for completion had been reached. Further specific performance may be granted of a contract for which an action at law will not lie by reason of failure to comply with s. 40 of the Law of Property Act 1925, where there is a sufficient act of part performance.[10] Indeed it seems that the fact that an action at law will not lie,[11] or even that it is doubtful if it will,[12] may itself be a ground for granting specific performance. And specific performance may be granted where equity takes a less rigid view than the common law; thus in *Mortlock* v. *Buller*[13] Lord Eldon pointed out that specific performance with compensation[14] might be granted when some unessential misdescription would defeat an action at law, and similarly where the plaintiff, though he has substantially performed some condition, has not done it with such exactitude as to be able to claim performance at common law.[15] As Lord Redesdale explained,[16] "a Court of Equity frequently decrees specific performance where the action at law has been lost by the default of the very party seeking the specific performance, if it be, notwithstanding, conscientious that the agreement should be performed, as in cases where the terms of the agreement have not been strictly performed on the part of the person seeking specific performance; and to sustain an action at law, performance must be averred according to the very terms of the contract. Nothing but specific execution of the contract, so far as it can be executed, will do justice in such a case."

The question has not infrequently arisen as to the effect of a clause in the contract that if the primary obligation is not performed, a specified sum of

---

[5] *Sed quaere.* Nominal damages are awarded because the plaintiff is regarded as having suffered no loss, and it is arguable that they should accordingly be regarded as adequate.
[6] See *Beswick* v. *Beswick*, [1967] 2 All E.R. 1197; [1968] A.C. 58, H.L.
[7] *Dodsley* v. *Kinnersley* (1761), Amb. 403.
[8] [1959] 2 All E.R. 647.
[9] [1960] A.C. 316, P.C.; *Manchester Diocesan Council for Education* v. *Commercial & General Investments, Ltd.*, [1969] 3 All E.R. 1593; [1970] 1 W.L.R. 241. Of course the decree would not order performance to take place before the date for completion. See also (1960), 76 L.Q.R. 200 (R. E. Megarry).
[10] Part performance will not ground an action for damages at law in a case to which s. 40 applies, though in some cases it may, under Lord Cairns' Act, enable the court to award damages in lieu of specific performance—*Lavery* v. *Pursell* (1888), 39 Ch.D. 508, 518.
[11] *Wright* v. *Bell* (1818), 5 Price 325.
[12] *Buxton* v. *Lister* (1746), 3 Atk. 383; *Doloret* v. *Rothschild* (1824), 1 Sim. & St. 590.
[13] (1804), 10 Ves. 292.   [14] See p. 437, *post*.
[15] *Davis* v. *Hone* (1805), 2 Sch. & Lef. 341.   [16] In *Davis* v. *Hone*, *supra*, at 347.

money is to be paid either by way of penalty or as liquidated damages. The answer depends upon whether on the true construction of the contract, the defendant is intended to be able to choose either to do the thing specified in the contract or, alternatively, to pay the specified sum, or whether the intention is that he is bound to do the specified thing, the money clause being added by way of security. If the first construction is the correct one, specific performance cannot be obtained for the parties have in effect agreed that damages will be an adequate remedy and thus taken away the basis of a claim for specific perform-ance.[17] If however the second construction is the true one, the court will decide the claim for specific performance disregarding the presence of the money clause. It makes no difference for this purpose whether the sum is intended as a penalty[18] or as liquidated damages, such as the common case of forfeiture of a deposit on a sale of land.[19] In deciding the question of construction, the court leans in favour of the second construction, i.e. in favour of the availability of specific performance.[20]

b Remedy *in personam*

In relation to specific performance equity, as always, acts *in personam*. The leading case is *Penn* v. *Lord Baltimore*[21] where Lord Hardwicke L.C. decreed specific performance of an English agreement relating to the boundaries between Pennsylvania and Maryland, despite the inability of the court to enforce its remedy *in rem*. In the latest case[1] specific performance was decreed of a contract for the sale of land outside the jurisdiction[2] against a defendant within it.

c Discretionary character

"From the very first, when specific performance was introduced it has been treated as a question of discretion whether it is better to interfere and give a remedy which the common law knows nothing at all about, or to leave the parties to their rights in a Court of Law."[3] It is undoubted however that this discretion is not arbitrary or capricious, but is governed so far as possible by fixed rules and principles.[4] As Romilly M.R. explained,[5] the discretion "must be exercised according to fixed and settled rules; you cannot exercise a discretion by merely considering what, as between the parties, would be fair to be done; what one person may consider fair, another person may consider very unfair; you must have some settled rule and principle upon which to determine how that discretion is to be exercised". These rules and principles will be considered in the following section. The result is that in many cases, where the parties are under no disability and there is nothing objectionable in the nature or circum-

---

[17] *Magrane* v. *Archbold* (1813), 1 Dow. 107; *Legh* v. *Lillie* (1860), 6 H. & N. 165.

[18] *Howard* v. *Hopkyns* (1742), 2 Atk. 371; *Logan* v. *Weinholt* (1833), 7 Bli. N.S. 1.

[19] *Crutchley* v. *Jerningham* (1817), 2 Mer. 502 *per* Lord Eldon at 506. Cf. cases of negative contracts specifically enforced by an injunction such as *Coles* v. *Sims* (1854), 5 De G.M. & G.1; *Bird* v. *Lake* (1863), 1 Hem. & M. 111.

[20] *Ranger* v. *Great Western Rail. Co.* (1854), 5 H.L.Cas. 72.

[21] (1750), 1 Ves. Sen. 444; [1558–1774] All E.R. Rep. 99.

[1] *Richard West and Partners (Inverness), Ltd.* v. *Dick*, [1969], 1 All E.R. 289 *affd.* [1969], 1 All E.R. 943; [1969] 2 Ch. 424, C.A.

[2] It was actually in Scotland.

[3] *Per* Rigby L.J. in *Re Scott* and *Alvarez's Contract*, [1895] 2 Ch. 603, at p. 615, C.A.

[4] *White* v. *Damon* (1802), 7 Ves. 30; *Lamare* v. *Dixon* (1873), L.R. 6 H.L. 414.

[5] In *Haywood* v. *Cope* (1858), 25 Beav. 140, at p. 151.

stances of the contract, a decree of specific performance is as much a matter of course in equity as damages at common law,[6] and will be ordered even though the judge may think it to be a hard case for the defendant.[7] But, as will be seen, matters which would be irrelevant at common law, such as the conduct of the plaintiff, may be material in a claim for specific performance.[8] Further the court may have to take into account other equitable doctrines. Thus in *Langen and Wind, Ltd.* v. *Bell*[9] the purchaser brought a specific performance action for the sale of shares, under a contract whereby the purchase price could not be ascertained for about two years after the agreed date for the transfer of the shares. The court had regard to the equitable principle that an unpaid vendor is entitled to a lien on the subject matter of the sale, and refused to grant an order for specific performance except in a form which would effectively safeguard the equitable lien.

d Damages in addition to or in substitution for specific performance

The same statutory provisions apply as apply in the case of a claim for an injunction, which were discussed together with the relevant cases in Chapter 13, Section 6, p. 408, *ante.*

e Specific performance with compensation

This is discussed in Section 2e, p. 437, *post.*

2 GROUNDS ON WHICH SPECIFIC PERFORMANCE MAY BE REFUSED

Specific performance will not, of course, be granted unless there is, in accordance with the law of contract, a concluded contract, complete and certain,[10] and even such a contract will not be enforced by specific performance if it is illegal or against the policy of the law,[11] even though valid according to the law of the country where it was made.[12] Assuming, however, that these matters are satisfied, we must consider certain classes of contract of which specific performance will nevertheless not be granted and certain defences, which may be available. The matters more commonly arising will now be discussed but the list does not purport to be exhaustive.

a Contracts relating to personal property

In general, specific performance of a contract relating to real property is granted as a matter of course, but it was settled at an early date that specific performance would not as a general rule be granted of a contract relating to

---

[6] *Hall* v. *Warren* (1804), 9 Ves. 605.
[7] *Haywood* v. *Cope* (1858), 25 Beav. 140.
[8] *Cox* v. *Middleton* (1854), 2 Drew. 209; *Lamare* v. *Dixon* (1873), L.R. 6 H.L. 414.
[9] [1972] 1 All E.R. 296; [1972] Ch. 685.
[10] See *Waring & Gillow Ltd.* v. *Thompson* (1913), 29 T.L.R. 154, C.A.; *Pallant* v. *Morgan*, [1952] 2 All E.R. 951; [1953] Ch. 43. Cf. *Bigg* v. *Boyd Gibbins, Ltd.*, [1971] 2 All E.R. 183, C.A.
[11] *Rees* v. *Bute (Marquis)*, [1916] 2 Ch. 64. It is not clear how heavy is the burden of proof— see *Aubin* v. *Holt* (1855), 2 K. and J. 66; *De Hoghton* v. *Money* (1866), 2 Ch. App. 164.
[12] *Hope* v. *Hope* (1857), 8 De G.M. & G. 731, at p. 743.

personal property, primarily on the ground that damages is an adequate remedy. Thus, for instance, specific performance will not be granted of a contract to transfer government or other stock or shares freely available on the market,[13] or coal[14] or other merchandise.

Where, however, for some reason damages would not be an adequate remedy, specific performance may be granted. This principle does not always seem to have been correctly applied. It is submitted that it does not cover the grant of a decree of specific performance by Lord Hardwicke in *Taylor* v. *Neville*,[15] where there was a contract for the sale of 800 tons of iron to be paid for and delivered over a certain number of years and by instalments; nor, probably, at any rate in modern conditions, the illustrations given by the same judge,[16] of a ship-carpenter purchasing timber, convenient to him by reason of its vicinity, and the owner of land with timber on it selling the timber in order to clear the land. Specific performance may, however, properly be granted on this principle where there is a contract for the purchase of articles of unusual beauty, rarity and distinction, or of a chattel of peculiar value to the plaintiff.[17] Thus, though refused on other grounds, it would have been granted in *Falcke* v. *Gray*[18] of a contract to purchase two china jars apparently worth at least £200, and no objection seems to have been taken to the jurisdiction in *Thorn* v. *Public Works Commissioners*[19] which involved a contract for the purchase of the arch-stone, the spandrill stone, and the Bramley Fall stone contained in the old Westminster Bridge which had been pulled down. Again specific performance may be granted of a contract for the transfer of shares,[20] or other property[21] not freely available on the market. An analogous remedy sometimes available is an order for delivery of a specific chattel wrongfully detained by the defendant where the claim does not arise under contract,[1] and where damages would not be an adequate remedy.[2]

Finally statute[3] has intervened to empower the court to grant the buyer[4] a

---

[13] *Cuddee* v. *Rutter* (1720), 5 Vin. Abr. 538 pl. 21; *sub nom. Cud* v. *Rutter* 1. P. Wms. 570; *Adderley* v. *Dixon* (1824), 1 Sim. & St. 607; *Pooley* v. *Budd* (1851), 14 Beav. 34.

[14] *Dominion Coal Co. Ltd.* v. *Dominion Iron & Steel Co. Ltd.*, [1909] A.C. 293 P.C.

[15] Cited in *Buxton* v. *Lister* (1746), 3 Atk. 383, at p. 384; but doubted in *Pollard* v. *Clayton* (1855), 1 K. & J. 462.

[16] In *Buxton* v. *Lister, supra.*

[17] Ships seem to be readily so regarded—*De Mattos* v. *Gibson* (1859), 4 De. G. & J. 276, at p. 299; *Hart* v. *Herwig* (1873), 8 Ch. App. 860, at p. 866; *Behnke* v. *Bede Shipping Co., Ltd.*, [1927] 1 K.B. 649; [1927] All E.R. Rep. 689—but it must depend on the facts.

[18] (1859), 4 Drew. 651. See also *Phillips* v. *Lamdin*, [1949] 1 All E.R. 770; [1949] 2 K.B. 33.

[19] (1863), 32 Beav. 490.

[20] *Duncuft* v. *Albrecht* (1841), 12 Sim. 189; *Cheale* v. *Kenward* (1858), 3 De G. & J. 27; cf. *Sri Lanka Omnibus Co. Ltd.* v. *Perera*, [1952] A.C. 76, P.C. As to choses in action see *Adderley* v. *Dixon* (1824), 1 Sim. & St. 607; *Cogent* v. *Gibson* (1864), 33 Beav. 557.

[21] *Sky Petroleum, Ltd.* v. *VIP Petroleum, Ltd.*, [1974] 1 All E.R. 954 (petroleum where no alternative source of supply).

[1] *Pusey* v. *Pusey* (1684), 1 Vern. 273; *Duke of Somerset* v. *Cookson* (1735), 3 P. Wms. 390; *Fells* v. *Read* (1796), 3 Ves. 70. Since the Common Law Procedure Act 1854, s. 78, the defendant may in detinue be deprived of the right to retain the chattel on payment of its value—the form of the appropriate order is set out in Appendix A to the R.S.C., Form No. 64. See *Whiteley, Ltd.* v. *Hilt*, [1918] 2 K.B. 808, at p. 819, C.A.

[2] This last point could not be established in *Dowling* v. *Betjamann* (1862), 2 J. & H. 544, where the plaintiff had in effect put a price on the chattel.

[3] Sale of Goods Act 1893, s. 52, replacing s. 2 of the Mercantile Law Amendment Act 1856.

[4] But not the seller.

decree of specific performance in any action for breach of contract to deliver specific or ascertained goods. "Specific goods" means, under the definition section of the Act,[5] "goods identified and agreed upon at the time a contract of sale is made", and "ascertained" probably means identified in accordance with the agreement after the time a contract of sale is made.[6] Under the Act the court has a discretion whether or not to grant specific performance, which it will exercise on the established equitable principles.[7] In no case does it matter whether the property has passed to the buyer or not,[8] though if the property has passed the same principles will apply to the alternative remedy of a claim in detinue for delivery of the specific chattel.[9]

b Voluntary contracts

Lord Hardwicke's dictum[10] that "the court never decrees specifically without a consideration" has been consistently followed, and it makes no difference that the contract is under seal. The rule, which can be regarded as an application of the maxim that equity will not assist a volunteer,[11] applies equally to a contract to create a trust or settlement.[12]

A curious point arose recently in *Mountford* v. *Scott*.[13] In that case an option to purchase was granted for what was admitted to be a token consideration. Before the option had expired the grantor purported to withdraw his offer. The grantee subsequently exercised the option, and was held entitled to specific performance. The point is that if an option is validly granted, it creates an equitable interest in the land over which it is exercisable, even though the option may have been granted gratuitously or for a token payment. Such equitable interest will be protected in equity whether or not it was created for valuable consideration.

c Contracts requiring constant superintendence

The Court of Appeal has regarded it as an established rule that the court will not grant specific performance of a contract involving continuous acts on the part of the defendant which would require watching over and constant supervision by the court,[14] and the principle has recently been said to be established

---

[5] Sale of Goods Act 1893, s. 62.
[6] *Per* Atkin L.J. in *Re Wait*, [1927] 1 Ch. 606, 630, C.A.
[7] *Behnke* v. *Bede Shipping Co., Ltd.*, [1927] 1 K.B. 649; [1927] All E.R. Rep. 689.
[8] *Re Wait, supra, per* Hanworth M.R. at 617; *Cohen* v. *Roche*, [1927] 1 K.B. 169, at p. 180.
[9] See note 1, p. 430, *ante*, and *Cohen* v. *Roche, supra*, at pp. 180, 181.
[10] In *Penn* v. *Lord Baltimore* (1750), 1 Ves. Sen. 444, at p. 450; *Colman* v. *Sarrel* (1789), 3 Bro. C. C. 12; *Groves* v. *Groves* (1829), 3 Y. & J. 163.
[11] *Ford* v. *Stuart* (1852), 15 Beav. 493, at p. 501.
[12] *Jefferys* v. *Jefferys* (1841), Cr. & Ph. 138; *Listor* v. *Hodgson* (1867), L.R. 4 Eq. 30.
[13] [1974] 1 All E.R. 248.
[14] *Ryan* v. *Mutual Tontine Westminster Chambers Association*, [1893] 1 Ch. 116, C.A.; *Joseph* v. *National Magazine Co., Ltd.*, [1958] 3 All E.R. 52; [1959] Ch. 14. But in *Wolverhampton Corporation* v. *Emmons*, [1901] 1 K.B. 515, C.A., A. L. Smith M.R. said, at 523, that he had never seen the force of the rule.

beyond argument.[15] On this principle specific performance has been refused of
contracts to appoint a porter to carry out certain specified duties,[16] of a house-
keeper to be in attendance during certain fixed hours,[17] of stipulations in a
farming lease,[18] and of contracts to construct railways.[19]

The general rule is subject to exceptions, and there are numerous cases in
relation to contracts to build and repair. These are at first sight difficult to
reconcile, but a general explanation was given by Collins L.J. in *Wolverhampton
Corporation* v. *Emmons*.[20] In early times, he said, courts of equity

> "seem to have granted decrees for specific performance in such cases. Then came a
> period in which they would not grant such decrees on the ground that the Court
> could not undertake to supervise the performance of the contract. Later on again they
> seem to have attached less importance to this consideration, and returned to some
> extent to the more ancient practice, holding that they could order specific perfor-
> mance in certain cases in which the works were specified by the contract in a suffi-
> ciently definite manner."[21]

The conditions which have to be fulfilled if the exception is to apply and
specific performance is to be granted were set out by Romer L.J. in the same
case.[1] "The first," he said, "is that the building work, of which he seeks to enforce
the performance, is defined by the contract; that is to say, that the particulars
of the work are so far definitely ascertained that the court can sufficiently see
what is the exact nature of the work of which it is asked to order the performance.[2] The second is that the plaintiff has a substantial interest in having the
contract performed, which is of such a nature that he cannot adequately be
compensated for breach of the contract by damages.[3] The third is that the
defendant has by the contract obtained possession of land on which the work is
contracted to be done." This last condition was criticised in *Carpenters Estates,
Ltd.* v. *Davies*[4] and it is submitted that the formulation in that case is to be
preferred, namely, that the plaintiff must establish that the defendant is in
possession of the land on which the work is contracted to be done. The point is
that the plaintiff cannot go on the land in order to do the work himself or
through other agents. In the two cases last mentioned in the text the conditions
were fulfilled and specific performance was granted. Their facts, slightly

---

[15] *Dowty Boulton Paul, Ltd.* v. *Wolverhampton Corporation*, [1971] 2 All E.R. 277 *per*
Pennycuick V.C. at p. 284.
[16] *Ryan* v. *Mutual Tontine Westminster Chambers Association, supra*, C.A.
[17] *Barnes* v. *City of London Real Property Co.*, [1918] 2 Ch. 18.
[18] *Phipps* v. *Jackson* (1887), 3 T.L.R. 387.
[19] *Peto* v. *Brighton, Uckfield and Tunbridge Wells Rail. Co.* (1863), 1 Hem. & M. 468; *Wheatley*
v. *Westminster Brymbo Coal Co.* (1869), L.R. 9 Eq. 538, at p. 552 where Malins V.C. said
"this court will not undertake either the construction of a railway, the management of a
brewery, or the management of a colliery, or anything of the kind".
[20] [1901] 1 K.B. 514, 524, C.A.; *Molyneux* v. *Richard*, [1906] 1 Ch. 34.
[21] See *Greenhill* v. *Isle of Wight Rail. Co.* (1871), 23 L.T. 885, where several of the cases are
discussed; *Fortescue* v. *Lostwithiel and Fowey Rail. Co.*, [1894] 3 Ch. 621.
[1] *Wolverhampton Corporation* v. *Emmons*, [1901] 1 K.B. 515, C.A. at p. 525.
[2] *South Wales Rail. Co.* v. *Wythes* (1854), 5 De G.M. & G. 880.
[3] If the building is to take place on the plaintiff's land, damages will normally be adequate
because some other contractor can be paid to do the job and any increased price be
recovered as damages.
[4] [1940] 1 All E.R. 13; [1940] Ch. 160.

simplified, were in *Wolverhampton Corporation* v. *Emmons*[5] that the plaintiff corporation, in pursuance of a scheme of street improvement, sold and conveyed to the defendant a plot of land abutting on a street, the defendant covenanting with the corporation that he would erect buildings thereon in accordance with certain plans and specifications within a certain time. The defendant failed to erect the buildings. In the other case, *Carpenters Estates, Ltd.* v. *Davies*,[6] a vendor who sold certain land to purchasers for building development, retaining other land adjoining it, failed to perform his covenant to make certain roads and lay certain mains, sewers and drains on the land retained.

In relation to a covenant to repair contained in a lease, Lord Eldon laid down[7] that a landlord cannot obtain an order for specific performance in the case of a tenant's covenant to repair. However, in the case of a landlord's covenant to repair it was held in *Jeune* v. *Queen's Cross Properties, Ltd.*[8] that an order could be made where there has been a plain breach of a covenant to repair and there is no doubt at all what is required to be done to remedy the breach. In that case, where the order was made, it was observed that obviously it was a jurisdiction which must be exercised with care.

d Contracts for personal work or service

"The courts, as such, have never dreamt of enforcing agreements strictly personal in their nature."[9] The commonly put forward reasons are partly the difficulty of supervision and partly the undesirability on grounds of public policy of compelling persons to continue personal relations with each other against their will. Fry L.J. put the latter reason rather dramatically in *De Francesco* v. *Barnum*,[10] saying "the courts are bound to be jealous, lest they should turn contracts of service into contracts of slavery". Other factors are that damages is normally an adequate remedy, and in many cases, where an employee has been replaced, the difficulty of reinstatement.

Megarry J. has recently suggested,[11] however, that the reasons are "more complex and more firmly bottomed on human nature". He speculated on the effect of a decree of specific performance of a contract to sing. "If a singer contracts to sing, there could no doubt be proceedings for committal if, ordered to sing, the singer remained obstinately dumb. But if instead the singer sang flat, or sharp, or too fast or too slowly, or too loudly, or too quietly, . . . the threat of committal would reveal itself as a most unsatisfactory weapon; for who could say whether the imperfections of the performance were natural or self-induced? To make an order with such possibilities of evasion would be vain; and so the order will not be made." Nevertheless, in Megarry J.'s view

---

[5] *Supra.*
[6] *Supra.*
[7] In *Hill* v. *Barclay* (1810), 16 Ves. 402. The decision was put on the ground of want of mutuality—see *infra*, p. 435.
[8] [1973] 3 All E.R. 97.
[9] *Per* Jessel M.R. in *Rigby* v. *Connol* (1880), 14 Ch.D. 482, at p. 487. Some early cases to the contrary have not been followed, *viz. Ball* v. *Coggs* (1710), 1 Bro. Parl. Cas. 140; *East India Co.* v. *Vincent* (1740), 2 Atk. 83.
[10] (1890), 45 Ch.D. 430, 438. See (1969), 32 M.L.R. 532 (G. de N. Clark).
[11] *C. H. Giles & Co., Ltd.* v. *Morris*, [1972] 1 All E.R. 960, at p. 969.

it depends on the circumstances of the particular case, and though there is always a strong reluctance on the part of the court to decree specific performance of a contract for personal services, there is no rigid rule to this effect. *Hill* v. *C. A. Parsons & Co., Ltd.*[12] is another case which suggests a growing unwillingness on the part of the courts to regard themselves as bound by an inflexible rule. The case was actually concerned with a motion for an interlocutory injunction, but is directly relevant as this could only be granted with a view to specific performance of the contract at the hearing. The majority[13] of the Court of Appeal granted the injunction on the ground of special circumstances in particular that damages would not be an adequate remedy, and that a combination of the injunction and the coming into operation of the Industrial Relations Act 1971 would safeguard the plaintiff's position. There are also earlier decisions in which it has been held that in exceptional circumstances specific performance may be decreed of some personal obligation, where it forms only a small part of a larger contract which is otherwise suitable for such an order.[14]

In relation to the general rule, in addition to the ordinary contract of service, such as the employment of a valet, coachman or cook referred to in *Johnson* v. *Shrewsbury and Birmingham Rail. Co.*,[15] specific performance has been refused on this ground of a contract between a company and its managing director,[16] of an agreement to compose and write reports of cases in the Court of Exchequer,[17] of an agreement to supply drawings of maps,[18] of a claim to fill the office of receiver to the Bishop of Ely,[19] of an agreement to sing at a theatre,[20] and of articles of apprenticeship.[21] The same principle applies to any contract of agency.[22]

It should be added that there is a vital distinction between an order to perform a contract for services and an order to procure the execution of such a contract. The mere fact that the contract to be made is one of which the court would not order specific performance—such as the service agreement as managing director of a company in *C. H. Giles & Co., Ltd.* v. *Morris*[23] is no ground for refusing to decree that the contract be entered into. In the last cited case the defendants were properly ordered to procure the execution of the service agreement.

---

[12] [1971] 3 All E.R. 1345; [1972] Ch. 305, C.A.
[13] The two common law members, reversing the Chancery judge at first instance. *Per* Lord Denning M.R. at p. 1359. "It is the common lawyers who now do equity!"
[14] *Fortescue* v. *Lostwithiel & Fowey Rail. Co.*, [1894] 3 Ch. 621; *Kennard* v. *Cory* [1922] 2 Ch. 1, C.A.; *Beswick* v. *Beswick*, [1967] 2 All E.R. 1197; [1968] A.C. 58, H.L., *per* Lord Upjohn at pp. 1218; 97. *C. H. Giles & Co., Ltd.* v. *Morris*, [1972] 1 All E.R. 960, at p. 969.
[15] (1853), 3 De. G.M. & G. 914, at p. 926.
[16] *Bainbridge* v. *Smith* (1889), 41 Ch.D. 462, C.A.
[17] *Clarke* v. *Price* (1819), 2 Wils. Ch. 157.
[18] *Baldwin* v. *Society for the Diffusion of Useful Knowledge* (1838), 9 Sim. 393.
[19] *Pickering* v. *Bishop of Ely* (1843), 2 Y. & C. Ch. 249.
[20] *Lumley* v. *Wagner* (1852), 1 De. G.M. & G. 604.
[21] *Webb* v. *England* (1860), 29 Beav. 44; *De Francesco* v. *Barnum* (1890), 45 Ch.D. 430.
[22] *Chinnock* v. *Sainsbury* (1860), 3 L.T. 258; *Brett* v. *East India and London Shipping Co.* (1864), 2 Hem. & M. 404; *Morris* v. *Delobbel-Flipo*, [1892] 2 Ch. 352.
[23] *Supra.*

e Contracts wanting in mutuality

English judges and writers[24] commonly state and apply the general rule that specific performance will not be granted unless the remedy is mutual, i.e. if by reason of personal incapacity, the nature of the contract or any other matter A cannot obtain specific performance against B, then B will not be granted specific performance against A even though, taking A's obligation by itself, this would be an appropriate remedy. According to Kekewich J.[25] it "is a technical doctrine, but like many other technical doctrines, founded on common sense. It comes simply to this, that one party to a bargain shall not be held bound to that bargain when he cannot enforce it against the other."

In accordance with this general rule an infant cannot obtain a decree of specific performance,[26] for specific performance cannot be decreed against him[1] and a plaintiff against whom specific performance could not be decreed because his obligation is to do something of a personal or continuous nature[2] cannot obtain specific performance even though this is *prima facie* appropriate to the defendant's obligation.[3] It should be observed, however, that it has long been settled that in the case of the ordinary contract for the sale and purchase of land, the vendor is as much entitled to a decree of specific performance as the purchaser, notwithstanding that the purchaser's obligation is merely to pay the purchase price. This has been explained by Lord St. Leonards[4] on the ground that damages would not be an adequate remedy—"a seller wants the exact sum agreed to be paid to him, and he wants to divest himself legally of the estate, which after the contract was no longer vested in him beneficially. This is accomplished by specific performance, whereas, at law, he would be left with the estate on his hands, and would recover damages...." In the same case Lord Campbell observed[5] that the remedy must necessarily be afforded to the vendor as well as the purchaser, from the application of the doctrine of conversion on the signing of the contract.

The point of time at which mutuality has to be shown causes some difficulty. Judicial approval[6] has been given to the statement in the leading textbook on specific performance[7] that the mutuality of a contract is to be judged of at the time it is entered into. And certainly if there is mutuality at that moment, a party who has by his own neglect or default lost his right to the remedy since

---

[24] Ames in *Lectures On Legal History*, pp. 370 *et seq.* criticises the usual statement of the rule owing to its being at variance with a number of generally accepted propositions. He would substitute the principle "Equity will not compel specific performance by a defendant if, after performance, the common-law remedy of damages would be his sole security for the performance of the plaintiff's side of the contract".

[25] *Wylson* v. *Dunn* (1887), 34 Ch.D. 569, at p. 576.

[26] *Flight* v. *Bolland* (1828), 4 Russ. 298.

[1] *Lumley* v. *Ravenscroft*, [1893] 1 Q.B. 683, C.A.

[2] See Sections 2c and d, pp. 431, 433, *ante.*

[3] *Pickering* v. *Bishop of Ely* (1843), 2 Y. & C. Ch. 249; *Johnson* v. *Shrewsbury and Birmingham Rail. Co.* (1853), 3 De. G.M. & G. 914; *Page One Records, Ltd.* v. *Britton*, [1967] 3 All E.R. 822.

[4] In *Eastern Counties Rail. Co.* v. *Hawkes* (1855), 5 H.L.C. 331, at p. 376.

[5] In *Eastern Counties Rail. Co.* v. *Hawkes, supra*, at p. 360.

[6] *Per* Sargant J. in *Bayley & Shoesmith's Contract* (1918), 87 L.J. Ch. 626, at p. 628.

[7] Fry, 4th Ed., p. 201 (now 6th Ed., p. 222).

the date of the contract cannot successfully plead want of mutuality as a defence to an action against him.[8]

Without derogating from the last point, certain cases, however, seem to indicate that it may be sufficient that there is mutuality at the time the specific performance action is commenced, or even at the date of the hearing. These cases have been of the kind where a vendor of land has at the date of the contract neither been in a position to convey the land himself nor had power to compel a conveyance of it by some other person, but where subsequently he has acquired this position or power. It is clear in such circumstances that if the purchaser had acted promptly on discovering the defect of title, he could have repudiated the contract so as to disable the vendor from successfully bringing a specific performance action against him.[9] But if after ascertaining the defect the purchaser still treated the contract as subsisting, he does not retain the right to repudiate at any subsequent moment he may choose. The vendor can in such case be granted a decree of specific performance provided he can show a good title at the relevant time. Lord Campbell in *Eastern Counties Rail. Co.* v. *Hawkes*[10] is sometimes cited[11] as authority for the proposition that the relevant time is the commencement of the action for specific performance and that want of mutuality at that time will be fatal. It is submitted, however, that this case is rather authority for the proposition that mutuality at this point of time suffices, even though the defendant subsequently loses his right to specific performance by his neglect or default. A vendor can, it seems, obtain specific performance if he can show a good title at the time of the hearing of the action, even though for default of title the remedy was mutual neither at the date of the contract nor at the date of the commencement of the action.[12] A further related point concerns the position where at the time of the action the plaintiff has already performed all his obligations under the contract, though there may not have been mutuality when the contract was entered into. It is submitted that want of mutuality is not a defence in such a case, and that any other rule would be most inequitable.[13]

Three exceptions to the requirement of mutuality may be noted. First, if, as is commonly the case, the contract is the one which requires writing under section 40 of the Law of Property Act 1925 a plaintiff may obtain specific performance even though, not having signed any document, it would be impossible for specific performance to be ordered against him.[14] This has been explained[15] on the ground that the statute only requires the writing to be signed by the party to be charged, and that the bringing of the action necessarily means that the remedy becomes mutual, because the plaintiff's pleadings in the action,

---

[8] *South Eastern Rail. Co.* v. *Knott* (1852), 10 Hare 122. Cf. *Hope* v. *Hope* (1857), 8 De G.M. & G. 731; *O'Regan* v. *White*, [1919] 2 I.R. 339.

[9] *Halkett* v. *Dudley (Earl)*, [1907] 1 Ch. 590; *Procter* v. *Pugh*, [1921] 2 Ch. 256; *Elliott* v. *Pierson*, [1948] 1 All E.R. 939; [1948] Ch. 452.

[10] (1855), 5 H.L.C. 331, at p. 365.

[11] Williams on *Vendor and Purchaser*, 4th Ed., Vol. 2, pp. 1053-1054.

[12] *Hoggart* v. *Scott* (1830), Taml. 500; *Chamberlain* v. *Lee* (1840), 10 Sim. 444; *Salisbury* v. *Hatcher* (1842), 2 Y. & C. Ch. 54.

[13] See *O'Regan* v. *White*, [1919] 2 I.R. 339 and (1968), 32 Con. 384 (P. H. Pettit).

[14] *Seton* v. *Slade* (1802), 7 Ves. 265; *Morgan* v. *Holford* (1852), 1 Sm. & G. 101.

[15] E.g. by Leach M.R. in *Flight* v. *Bolland* (1828), 4 Russ. 298, at p. 301.

which will need to contain the necessary particulars of the contract, must be signed by the plaintiff or his authorised agent.

Secondly, it has been said that the holder of an option to purchase may be able to obtain specific performance even though the other party may have no such right against him.[16] This may be explained, however, on the ground that specific performance could not be obtained prior to the exercise of the option, after which there would be mutuality.

Thirdly, an exception arises in connection with the grant of specific performance with compensation,[17] a special variant of the remedy limited to cases of misdescription in a contract for the sale of land, whether the misdescription relates to the title, or the quantity or quality of the land. In other words it is only available where the vendor is unable to convey to the purchaser property exactly corresponding to that which he has contracted to convey, and not even in the case where there has been a mis-statement not incorporated in the contract but in the form of a misrepresentation inducing it.[18] When specific performance with compensation is granted the court, exceptionally, does more than simply enforce the agreement between the parties. It enforces an agreement somewhat different than that agreed upon, and compels the acceptance of compensation which the parties never agreed to give or receive. Compensation in every case means compensation to the purchaser and not to the vendor. The general position is, on the one hand, that where the vendor cannot fulfil the exact terms of the contract, but can convey to the purchaser substantially what he had contracted to get,[19] either the vendor or the purchaser may obtain a decree of specific performance with compensation. If, however, it is impossible to estimate the amount of compensation, specific performance will be refused.[20] Where, on the other hand, the vendor cannot even convey to the purchaser substantially what he contracted to get the remedies are not mutual. In such case the vendor is not entitled to specific performance at all, but the purchaser can, as a general rule,[21] elect to take all that the vendor is able to convey to him, and to have a proportionate abatement from the purchase money, provided that this is capable of computation.[20] The purchaser may, of course, alternatively rescind the contract.[1]

---

[16] McCarthy and Stone, Ltd. v. Julian S. Hodge & Co., Ltd., [1971] 2 All E.R. 973, at p. 980, per Foster J.

[17] For a fuller general discussion see Fry, op. cit., pp. 566 et seq. A succinct general statement is to be found in Rutherford v. Acton-Adams, [1915] A.C. 866, at pp. 869, 870, P.C. The contract in practice commonly contains special provisions. As to the extent of a claim for damages where even extinguishment of the purchase price would not be adequate compensation, see Grant v. Dawkins, [1973] 3 All E.R. 897.

[18] A purchaser may have other remedies in such cases, e.g. rescission, or damages for deceit if the vendor has been fraudulent, or possibly damages for breach of a collateral contract. See Rutherford v. Acton-Adams, supra.

[19] As to what is meant by substantial in this context, reference should be made to Fry, op. cit., and works on Conveyancing such as Williams on Vendor and Purchaser, 4th Ed., Vol. I, pp. 723 et seq.

[20] Westmacott v. Robins (1862), 4 De G.F. & J. 390; Cato v. Thompson (1882), 9 Q.B.D. 616, C.A.

[21] Not, however, if innocent third parties would be prejudiced—Thomas v. Dering (1837), 1 Keen 729. And some general defence such as those discussed below may be available.

[1] See Chapter 15, Section 4, p. 473, post.

f   Contracts capable of partial performance only[2]

Suppose that a contract contains two terms, under one of which X is obliged to do an act for which, taken by itself, specific performance would be an appropriate remedy, and under the other he is obliged to do an act, say of a personal nature,[3] for which it is not. Will it be possible to get a decree ordering X specifically to perform the first act alone? The general answer was given by Romilly M.R. in *Ford* v. *Stuart*:[4] "No matter is more fully settled in this court than that a contract cannot be specifically performed in part; it must be wholly performed, or not at all, and a part of a contract may be of such a nature as to vitiate the whole". Thus in *Ogden* v. *Fossick*[5] an agreement was entered into between Fossick and Ogden that Fossick should grant Ogden a lease of a coal wharf at a certain rent, and should be employed throughout the tenancy at a salary of £200 p.a. plus a commission on the coal sold at the wharf. Although the first part of the agreement was typical of the kind of matter of which specific performance is decreed, this remedy was refused on the ground that it was inseparably connected with the second part of the agreement which was clearly of the kind of which specific performance is not granted. It is an *a fortiori* case where the term sought to be enforced by specific performance is merely an ancillary or subsidiary term of a contract, the principal terms of which are unenforceable by specific performance. Thus in *South Wales Rail. Co.* v. *Wythes*[6] specific performance was refused of an agreement to give a bond to the amount of £50,000 to secure the performance of a contract to execute works for which specific performance was clearly not appropriate, and again in *Brett* v. *East India and London Shipping Co., Ltd.*[7] of an undertaking to advertise the plaintiff as the defendant's broker when the contract of employment as such could obviously not be enforced.

There is an exception or apparent exception to the above rule where the contract is divisible, i.e., where on its true construction there is not one contract containing two or more parts, but two or more separate agreements. In such case specific performance will lie in appropriate circumstances for breach of one separate agreement.[8] This is what happened in *Wilkinson* v. *Clements*,[9] from which it seems that the burden of proof that the contract is divisible lies upon the person who alleges that this is so, Mellish L.J. observing[10] that as a general rule all agreements must be considered as entire and indivisible. Where property is sold in one lot the contract will generally be so considered, as in

---

[2] See also Chapter 13 Section 7a, p. 415, *ante*, as to the enforcement by injunction of a contract of which specific performance will not be granted.
[3] See section 4d of this Chapter, p. 433, *ante*.
[4] (1852), 15 Beav. 493, at p. 501; *Merchant's Trading Co.* v. *Banner* (1871), L.R. 12 Eq. 18, at p. 23.
[5] (1862), 4 De. G.F. & J. 426; *Frith* v. *Frith*, [1906] A.C. 254, P.C.; *Barnes* v. *City of London Real Property Co.*, [1918] 2 Ch. 18.
[6] (1854), 5 De G.M. & G. 880.
[7] (1864), 2 Hem. & M. 404.
[8] *Wilkinson* v. *Clements* (1872), 8 Ch. App. 96; *Odessa Tramways Co.* v. *Mendel* (1878), 8 Ch.D. 235, C.A.
[9] *Supra*.
[10] *Wilkinson* v. *Clements*, *supra*, at 110.

Roffey v. *Shallcross*[11] where two undivided one-seventh shares of land were sold in one lot. A good title could be made to one share only, and specific performance was refused. Where, however, property is sold in separate lots specific performance can normally be obtained in relation to one lot, even though it may be unobtainable in relation to the others.[12]

g   Where a decree of specific performance would be useless

In such cases a decree will not be granted. Thus it has been refused of an agreement to enter into a partnership at will, which could be dissolved immediately afterwards,[13] of an agreement to grant a deputation of an office which was clearly revocable,[14] and of an agreement to grant a lease for a term expired before the action was heard.[15] Similarly specific performance will not be granted of an agreement for a lease for a very short term. Chitty J. took it as settled[16] that it would not be granted of an agreement for a year, one ground being the practical one that you could not in the ordinary course get the action heard and the decree made within the year. On the other hand it has been granted of a tenancy from year to year.[17]

h   Contracts to lend or advance money

Such contracts are not enforceable by specific performance, whether or not the loan is to be secured by mortgage. The reason is that the remedy at law is adequate—the borrower can borrow the money elsewhere, and claim at law if he is compelled to pay a higher rate of interest, and likewise the lender has a simple money demand if his money has lain idle or been invested less advantageously.[18] Exceptionally, by statute,[19] a contract with a company to take up and pay for any debentures of a company may be enforced by an order for specific performance.

Specific performance can, however, be obtained of a contract to execute a mortgage, i.e., of an agreement to give security, when the money has been actually advanced.[20]

It should be observed that it is quite possible for a decree of specific performance to be obtained in appropriate circumstances of a contract to make a money payment. For instance a purchaser of land is commonly compelled to pay the purchase price in a specific performance action at the instance of a vendor,

---

[11] (1819), 4 Madd. 227.
[12] *Lewin* v. *Guest* (1826), 1 Russ. 325; *Casamajor* v. *Strode* (1834), 2 My & K. 706.
[13] *Hercy* v. *Birch* (1804), 9 Ves. 357.
[14] *Wheeler* v. *Trotter* (1737), 3 Swan. 174.
[15] *De Brassac* v. *Martyn* (1863), 9 L.T. 287; *Turner* v. *Clowes* (1869), 20 L.T. 214. The cases contemplate the possibility of a decree being made in very special circumstances.
[16] In *Lavery* v. *Pursell* (1888), 39 Ch.D. 508, at p. 519; *Glasse* v. *Woolgar* (No. 3) (1897), 41 Sol. Jo. 573, C.A.; *Deverell* v. *Milne* (1918), 34 T.L.R. 576. Cf. *De Brassac* v. *Martyn, supra.*
[17] *Manchester Brewery Co.* v. *Coombs*, [1901] 2 Ch. 608; *Lever* v. *Koffler*, [1901] 1 Ch. 543; *Zimbler* v. *Abrahams*, [1903] 1 K.B. 577, C.A.
[18] *Larios* v. *Bonany y Gurety* (1873), L.R. 5 P.C. 346; *Western Wagon and Property Co.* v. *West*, [1892] 1 Ch. 271. *Loan Investment Corporation of Australasia* v. *Bonner*, [1970] N.Z.L.R. 724, P.C.
[19] Companies Act 1948, s. 92.
[20] *Ashton* v. *Corrigan* (1871), L.R. 13 Eq. 76; *Hermann* v. *Hodges* (1873), L.R. 16 Eq. 18.

where as has been seen[1] damages is not regarded as an adequate remedy, and it
has been held that it makes no difference that the price is payable by instalments,
or that the price is not payable to the plaintiff but to some third party.[2] Similarly
the Minister of Transport can sue for specific performance of the agreement
between himself and the Motor Insurers' Bureau,[3] under which the Bureau
agreed that if a judgment for an injured person against a motorist was not
satisfied in full within seven days, the Bureau would pay the amount of the
judgment to the injured person.[4] Hitherto it has generally been thought that
the courts would be unwilling to extend the limited type of case in which specific
performance of a contract to make a money payment would be granted, but
Beswick v. *Beswick*[5] perhaps heralds a more liberal approach.

i A contract to refer to arbitration

Such a contract is not specifically enforceable.[6] It may, however, be indirectly
enforced under the provisions of the Arbitration Act 1950,[7] which gives the
court a discretionary power to stay an action in respect of any dispute which the
parties have by writing agreed to refer to arbitration. If the court exercises this
power the plaintiff must either give up his claim or proceed by arbitration.

Specific performance may, however, be granted of the award of the arbitrator
"because the award supposes an agreement between the parties, and contains
no more than the terms of that agreement ascertained by a third person".[8]
It follows that it is enforceable on the same principles and subject to the same
limitations as an ordinary contract.

j Partnership agreements

As a general rule the court will not decree specific performance of an agreement to perform and carry on a partnership,[9] for this would involve the court
in constant superintendence of the partnership affairs. *A fortiori* the rule applies
in the case of a partnership at will where, as we have seen, specific performance
would be useless as either party could forthwith dissolve the partnership.[10]

Exceptionally it seems that, where there has been part performance of the
partnership agreement, the parties may be compelled specifically to perform a
term to execute a partnership deed, incorporating any subsequent variations
to the original agreement which may have been made between the partners.[11]

---

[1] See p. 435, *supra.*
[2] *Beswick* v. *Beswick*, [1967] 2 All E.R. 1197; [1968] A.C. 58, H.L. And see (1967) 30 M.L.R.
690–693 (G. H. Treitel).
[3] The agreement is set out in a note to *Hardy* v. *Motor Insurers' Bureau*, [1964] 2 Q.B. 745
at pp. 770–775.
[4] *Gurtner* v. *Circuit*, [1968] 1 All E.R. 328; [1968] 2 Q.B. 587, C.A.
[5] *Supra.*
[6] *South Wales Rail. Co.* v. *Wythes* (1854), 5 De G.M. & G. 880, C.A.; *Doleman & Sons* v.
Ossett Corporation, [1912] 3 K.B. 257, C.A.
[7] Section 4(1) replacing earlier legislation, first contained in the Common Law Procedure
Act, 1854, s. 11.
[8] Per Lord Eldon in *Wood* v. *Griffith* (1818), 1 Swans. 43, 54.
[9] *Scott* v. *Rayment* (1868), L.R. 7 Eq. 112.
[10] *Hercy* v. *Birch* (1804), 9 Ves. 357.
[11] *England* v. *Curling* (1844), 8 Beav. 129; *Sichel* v. *Mosenthal* (1862), 30 Beav. 371. See
Lindley on *Partnership*, 13th ed., p. 503.

k Contracts to leave property by will

In these cases, an action for damages will clearly lie against the covenantor's estate if the contract is not carried out, and the Court of Appeal had no doubt in *Synge* v. *Synge*[12] of the power of the court, where the contract related to a defined piece of real property, to decree a conveyance of that property after the death of the covenantor against all persons claiming under him as volunteers.[13] Specific performance will not, however, be decreed where the covenantor is merely donee of a testamentary power of appointment.[14]

l Misrepresentation and mistake

As we shall see,[15] both misrepresentation and mistake[16] may be grounds for rescission, and in such case will *a fortiori* be a defence to an action for specific performance. Both pleas have, however, a wider scope for the latter purpose. Misrepresentation, even though not sufficient to induce a court to rescind a contract, may be sufficient to defeat a claim for specific performance,[17] the point being that rescission has the drastic effect of avoiding the contract for all purposes, while refusing specific performance leaves it open to the plaintiff to seek other remedies, such as damages. It is commonly the wiser course to seek rescission, if this is possible, rather than to wait to raise the defence of misrepresentation if a specific performance action is brought,[18] particularly as in the latter case the burden of proof rests on the defendant to show that he repudiated the contract upon, or at least within a reasonable time after, discovery of the truth.[19]

Mistake may be a defence to a specific performance action even where there has been a mistake in a popular rather than the technical sense. This does not mean that a man can be careless in entering into a contract, and then avoid liability simply by alleging or even proving that he did so under a mistake,[1] for to allow this would open the door to perjury and fraud. If, however, he can establish that he made a *bona fide* mistake, and that he had a reasonable ground for the mistake, it may well be thought inequitable to grant specific performance. This is likely to be the case where the plaintiff has contributed to the

---

[12] [1894] 1 Q.B. 466, C.A. *Schaefer* v. *Schuhmann*, [1972] 1 All E.R. 621; [1972] A.C. 572, P.C.

[13] There seems no reason to doubt that other persons may be bound by the equitable interest and liable to specific performance according to the ordinary rules, including the registration provisions of the Land Charges Act 1972 and the Law of Property Act 1925.

[14] *Re Parkin*, [1892] 3 Ch. 510; *Re Evered*, [1910] 2 Ch. 147, C.A.; *Re Cooke*, [1922] 1 Ch. 292.

[15] Chapter 15, Section 4b, pp. 475, 476, *post.*

[16] Mistake may also give the court jurisdiction to rectify the contract. See Chapter 15, Section 5, p. 478, *post.*

[17] *Cadman* v. *Horner* (1810), 18 Ves. 10, at p. 12; *Re Banister* (1879), 12 Ch.D. 131, at p. 142, C.A.; *Re Terry and White's Contract* (1886), 32 Ch.D. 14, 29 C.A.

[18] *Fenn* v. *Craig* (1838), 3 Y. & C. Ex. 216, 222; Cf. *Aaron's Reefs* v. *Twiss*, [1896] A.C. 273, at p. 293, H.L.

[19] *Dawes* v. *Harness* (1875), L.R. 10 C.P. 166; *United Shoe Machinery Co. of Canada* v. *Brunet*, [1909] A.C. 330, at p. 338, P.C.; *First National Reinsurance Co.* v. *Greenfield*, [1921] 2 K.B. 260, 266, D.C.

[1] *Swaisland* v. *Dearsley* (1861), 29 Beav. 430; *Goddard* v. *Jeffreys* (1881), 51 L.J. Ch. 57; *Tamplin* v. *James* (1880), 15 Ch.D. 215, C.A.

defendant's mistake,[2] even though unintentionally.[3] Thus in *Denny* v. *Hancock*[4] on a sale by auction the plan annexed to the particulars showed on the western boundary ground covered by small trees or shrubs. On inspection of the property before the sale with the plan in his hand the defendant found on the western side a shrubbery with an iron fence outside it, and within the fence three very large and fine elm trees. He successfully bid for the property in the belief that he was buying everything up to the fence, but the real boundary was denoted by stumps largely concealed by shrubs, and the elm trees were outside it. It was held, on appeal, that the defendant's mistake was induced by the plan for which the vendors were responsible, and the vendors' specific performance action was accordingly dismissed. Further, Lord Macnaghten has said[5] that it cannot be disputed that a unilateral mistake by the defendant may be a good defence to a specific performance action even when the mistake has not been induced or contributed to by any act or omission on the part of the plaintiff, though most of such cases have been cases where a hardship amounting to injustice would have been inflicted upon the defendant by holding him to his bargain, and it was unreasonable to hold him to it. It has indeed been judicially suggested[6] that some of the cases have gone too far. *Malins* v. *Freeman*[7] may perhaps be one of these cases, where specific performance was refused against a purchaser, whose agent had mistakenly bid for the wrong property, the mistake being an unreasonable one not in any way contributed to by the vendor.

The mistake has, in effect, been held to be a reasonable one and specific performance refused, where it was caused by some ambiguity, even though the defendant was the author of the ambiguity.[8] One case is *Webster* v. *Cecil*[9] where the defendant, due to an arithmetical error, offered his property to the plaintiff for £1,250, instead of £2,250. The plaintiff, though his previous offer of £2,200 had been refused and he must have known of the mistake, accepted the offer and brought his action for specific performance. The action was dismissed. A case may also arise for refusing specific performance where through the ignorance, neglect or error of the vendor's agent, property not intended to be sold is included in the sale.[10]

m   Hardship and want of fairness

Even though there may not be fraud or other vitiating element which would support a claim for rescission, unfairness, inequality, hardship, oppression or sharp practice by the plaintiff may be a sufficient reason for the court to refuse a

---

[2] *Mason* v. *Armitage* (1806), 13 Ves. 25; *Higginson* v. *Clawes* (1808), 15 Ves. 516; *Moxey* v. *Bigwood* (1862), 4 De G.F. & J. 351.

[3] *Baskcomb* v. *Beekwith* (1869), L.R. 8 Eq. 100; *Bray* v. *Briggs* (1872), 26 L.T. 817.

[4] (1870), 6 Ch. App. 1.

[5] In *Stewart* v. *Kennedy* (No. 1) (1890), 15 App. Cas. 75, 105, H.L.; *Jones* v. *Rimmer* (1880), 14 Ch.D. 588, C.A.

[6] *Tamplin* v. *James, supra, per* James L.J. at 221.

[7] (1837), 2 Keen, 25 doubted by Kekewich J. in *Van Praagh* v. *Everidge,* [1902] 2 Ch. 266 reversed on another ground [1903] 1 Ch. 434, C.A.

[8] *Butterworth* v. *Walker* (1864), 11 L.T. 436; *Wycombe Rail. Co.* v. *Donnington Hospital* (1866), 1 Ch. App. 268; *Douglas* v. *Baynes,* [1908] A.C. 477, P.C.

[9] (1861), 30 Beav. 62. See the comment of James L.J. in *Tamplin* v. *James, supra,* at 221.

[10] *Alvanley* v. *Kinnaird* (1849), 2 Mac. & G. 1; *Leslie* v. *Thompson* (1851), 9 Hare 268; *Re Hare and O'More's Contract,* [1901] 1 Ch. 93.

decree of specific performance, while leaving open the possibility of a claim for damages.[11] Mere inadequacy of consideration is not however by itself a ground for refusing a decree, even though it may in fact cause considerable hardship to the defendant,[12] and this principle applies to a sale at a valuation. Thus specific performance was granted[13] where it was admitted that the valuation appeared very high and perhaps exorbitant, in the absence of any other factor such as fraud, mistake or misconduct by the valuer, but the additional presence of any of these other factors may be a defence to such a claim.[14] On the same principle it is no defence that the purpose for which the defendant entered into the contract cannot be carried out, as where he had purchased a lease and it turned out that the activities intended to be carried on there were prohibited by the lease.[15] Inadequacy of consideration may however be an important factor where combined with other circumstances,[16] and may be evidence, and in an extreme case conclusive evidence, of fraud.[17]

Questions of fairness, hardship and the like have to be judged as at the time when the contract was entered into,[18] and subsequent events are in general irrelevant. Thus, for instance, "if, in a compromise or a family arrangement, a person professes to give up something to which he fairly supposes he is entitled, and it afterwards turns out that he had nothing whatever to give up, this fact will not prevent the court carrying that family arrangement or agreement into effect."[19] Again, although the court may refuse specific performance of an award by an arbitrator based on a submission which is unfair, unreasonable and improvident,[20] it will not refuse to enforce an award merely on the ground that the award itself is unreasonable,[1] for this is a matter subsequent to the contract, i.e., the agreement to submit the case to an arbitrator, and the parties in choosing a judge for themselves are deemed to have taken this risk.[2] Exceptionally specific performance may be refused where by reason of the plaintiff's acts subsequent to the contract it would be inequitable and unreasonable to enforce it,[3]

---

[11] *Twining* v. *Morrice* (1788), 2 Bro. C. C. 326; *Willan* v. *Willan* (1810), 16 Ves. 72; *Martin* v. *Mitchell* (1820), 2 Jac. & W. 413.

[12] *Kimberley* v. *Jennings* (1836), 6 Sim. 340. It is submitted that the early cases to the contrary, followed in *Falcke* v. *Gray* (1859), 4 Drew. 651, are no longer good law.

[13] *Collier* v. *Mason* (1858), 25 Beav. 200; *Weekes* v. *Gallard* (1869), 21 L.T. 655.

[14] *Emery* v. *Wase* (1803), 8 Ves. 505; *Chichester* v. *M'Intire* (1830), 4 Bli. N.S. 78; *Eads* v. *Williams* (1854), 4 De G.M. & G. 674.

[15] *Morley* v. *Clavering* (1860), 29 Beav. 84; *Haywood* v. *Cope* (1858), 25 Beav. 140.

[16] *Cockrell* v. *Taylor* (1852), 15 Beav. 103; and see *James* v. *Morgan* (1663), 1 Lev. 111, the geometric progression trick where a horse was sold at a barleycorn a nail, doubling it for each nail on the horse's feet.

[17] *Griffith* v. *Spratley* (1787), 1 Cox. Eq. Cas. 383; *Stilwell* v. *Wilkins* (1821), Jac. 281.

[18] *Revell* v. *Hussey* (1813), 2 Ball & B. 280; *Lawder* v. *Blachford* (1815), Beat. 522; *Eastern Counties Rail. Co.* v. *Hawkes* (1855), 5 H.L.C. 331.

[19] Per Romilly M.R. in *Lawton* v. *Campion* (1854), 18 Beav. 87, at p. 93; *Pickering* v. *Pickering* (1839), 2 Beav. 31; *Heap* v. *Tonge* (1851), 9 Hare 90.

[20] *Nickels* v. *Hancock* (1855), 7 De G.M. & G. 300.

[1] It would be different if the award were fraudulent, or excessive i.e., beyond the arbitrator's powers.

[2] *Wood* v. *Griffith* (1818), 1 Swan. 43.

[3] *Duke of Bedford* v. *British Museum Trustees* (1822), 2 My. & K. 552.

particularly where his conduct has acted as a trap for the defendant, even though unintentionally.[4] But clearly hardship which the defendant has brought upon himself is no defence.[5]

In deciding questions as to the fairness of a contract the court considers the surrounding circumstances—if the consideration is inadequate and there are suspicious circumstances the court may refuse a decree, though there may not be enough to enable it to set the contract aside. Relevant factors may include weakness of mind, not amounting to insanity, age, illiteracy, poverty, want of advice, and financial distress.[6] The fact that an agreement was obtained from the defendant while he was intoxicated may also be a defence.[7] The question is whether in all the circumstances it would be unfair and inequitable to grant specific performance, and it is not enough for the defendant simply to show that he had, for instance, had several drinks before he signed the contract and had not taken legal advice.[8] It is not on the other hand necessary to show any intentional unfairness or misconduct on the part of the plaintiff.[9]

In general the court will not grant specific performance of an agreement if the consequence would be a forfeiture,[10] though it is, of course, otherwise if the state of affairs is due to the defendant's own acts.[11] The facts of the cases are individual, and by way of illustration mention may be made of three cases where specific performance was refused, viz., *Wedgwood* v. *Adams*,[12] where trustees personally undertook with the purchaser of trust property to see it freed from incumbrances, and it appeared that the purchase money would be inadequate to an uncertain extent; *Denne* v. *Light*[13] where the purchaser might have found himself with no means of access to his land: and *Hope* v. *Walters*[14] where the court refused to "thrust down the throat of an innocent buyer the obligation of becoming the landlord of a brothel".

The hardship or unfairness which may cause the court to refuse a decree may be suffered by a third party[15] rather than the defendant.[16] In particular the court will not normally grant specific performance if this would necessarily involve

---

[4] *Dowson* v. *Solomon* (1859), 1 Dr. & Sm. 1.

[5] *Pembroke* v. *Thorpe* (1740), 3 Swan. 482; *Storer* v. *Great Western Rail. Co.* (1842), 2 Y. & C. Ch. 48.

[6] *Kemeys* v. *Hansard* (1815), Coop. G. 125; *Martin* v. *Mitchell* (1820), 2 Jac. & W. 413; *Stanley* v. *Robinson* (1830), 1 Russ. & My. 527.

[7] *Cooke* v. *Clayworth* (1811), 18 Ves. 12; *Cox* v. *Smith* (1868), 19 L.T. 517. Cf. *Matthews* v. *Baxter* (1873), L.R. 8 Exch. 132.

[8] *Lightfoot* v. *Heron* (1839), 3 Y. & C. Ex. 586.

[9] *Twining* v. *Morrice* (1788), 2 Bro. C. C. 326; *Mortlock* v. *Buller* (1804), 10 Ves. 292.

[10] *Helling* v. *Lumley* (1858), 3 De G. & J. 493; *Warmington* v. *Miller*, [1973] 2 All E.R. 372; [1973] Q.B. 877, C.A.

[11] *Helling* v. *Lumley, supra.*

[12] (1843), 6 Beav. 600; *Watson* v. *Marston* (1853), 4 De G.M. & G. 230.

[13] (1857), 8 De G.M. & G. 774 (the judgment of Knight Bruce L.J. is worth reading for its entertainment value alone).

[14] [1900] 1 Ch. 257, C.A., per Lindley M.R. at 258; *Talbot* v. *Ford* (1842), 13 Sim. 173; *Hamilton* v. *Grant* (1815), 3 Dow. 33.

[15] But not, *semble*, by the public—*Raphael* v. *Thames Valley Railway Co.* (1866), L.R. 2 Eq. 37 reversed (1867) 2 Ch. App. 147. Aliter if it would be a fraud on the public—*Post* v. *Marsh* (1880), 16 Ch.D. 395.

[16] *Thomas* v. *Dering* (1837), 1 Keen. 729; *McKewan* v. *Sanderson* (1875), L.R. 20 Eq. 65.

breach of a prior contract with a third party,[17] or would require a person to do an act which he is not lawfully competent to do.[18] Again there are many cases where the court has refused a decree against trustees on the ground that performance by them would constitute a breach of trust,[19] or even that it is reasonably and seriously doubtful whether it is a breach of trust.[20] If, however, an innocent breach of trust has already been committed as a result of a contract, the court may grant specific performance and compel the other party to carry out his part of the bargain.[21]

n Rights of third parties

In contracts for the sale of land problems have sometimes arisen where a purchaser has sought specific performance against a vendor who is unable to give a good title without the consent of some third person, or where he has contracted to give vacant possession and some third person is in possession. Megarry J. recently summarized the position in *Wroth* v. *Tyler*[22] as follows: "A vendor must do his best to obtain any necessary consent to the sale; if he has sold with vacant possession he must, if necessary, take proceedings to obtain possession from any person in possession who has no right to be there or whose right is determinable by the vendor, at all events if the vendor's right to possession is reasonably clear; but I do not think that the vendor will usually be required to embark on difficult or uncertain litigation in order to secure any requisite consent or obtain vacant possession. Where the outcome of any litigation depends on disputed facts, difficult questions of law or the exercise of a discretionary jurisdiction, then I think the court would be slow to make a decree of specific performance against the vendor which would require him to undertake such litigation." In *Wroth* v. *Tyler*[1] itself the judge refused to decree specific performance which would compel the defendant to take legal proceedings against his wife, who had, after the contract and without his knowledge, registered rights of occupation under the Matrimonial Homes Act 1967, and with whom he was still living.

o Conduct of the plaintiff

In general, a plaintiff who seeks specific performance must come with clean hands, i.e., he must have fulfilled all conditions precedent and performed, or at least have tendered performance, of all the terms of the contract which he has

---

[17] *Willmott* v. *Barber* (1880), 15 Ch.D. 96; *Manchester Ship Canal Co.* v. *Manchester Racecourse Co.*, [1901] 2 Ch. 37, C.A.; *Sefton (Earl)* v. *Tophams, Ltd.*, [1965] 3 All E.R. 1; [1966] Ch. 1140, C.A. This point was not discussed on appeal *sub nom. Tophams, Ltd.* v. *Sefton (Earl)*, [1966] 1 All E.R. 1039; [1967] 1 A.C. 50, H.L.
[18] *Tolson* v. *Sheard* (1877), 5 Ch.D. 19, C.A.; *Oceanic Steam Navigation Co.* v. *Sutherberry* (1880), 16 Ch.D. 236, C.A.; *Warmington* v. Miller, *supra*, C.A.
[19] *Maw* v. *Topham* (1854), 19 Beav. 576; *Sneesby* v. *Thorn* (1855), 7 De. G.M. & G. 399; *Naylor* v. *Goodall* (1877), 37 L.T. 422.
[20] *Rede* v. *Oakes* (1864), 4 De G.J. & S. 505.
[21] *Briggs* v. *Parsloe*, [1937] 3 All E.R. 831.
[22] [1973] 1 All E.R. 897, at p. 913.
[1] *Supra*.

been under a duty to perform, and he must, seeking equity, be prepared to do equity, i.e., to perform all his future obligations under the contract.[2]

Though not necessarily dependent upon any default by the plaintiff, it is convenient to mention first the obvious principle that where a contract is subject to the performance of some condition precedent there can be no decree of specific performance unless and until the condition has been performed.[3] Thus specific performance has been refused of a covenant to renew a lease conditional on compliance with repairing covenants,[4] and of an agreement to take a lease of a public house conditional on the grant of a licence,[5] where the respective conditions had not been fulfilled. The condition remains capable of fulfilment, in a case between vendor and purchaser, at any time until the time fixed for completion of the contract.[6] Conditions may be express or implied, as a matter of construction of the contract,[7] and the performance of a condition precedent may be waived by the person or persons who alone benefit therefrom.

Turning to the terms of the contract, the plaintiff must be able to show he has performed all the essential terms of the contract, express or implied, which he was under a duty to have performed by the time the writ was issued.[8] The breach of a non-essential or trivial term is not, however, necessarily fatal to a specific performance action,[9] nor is it absolutely vital to show the exact performance which would be required at law.[10] Non-performance of a term by the plaintiff cannot be used as a defence where the defendant has waived performance,[11] or where non-performance has been caused by the defendant's acts or defaults.[12] Moreover if the term which has not been performed is independent and collateral to the contract sought to be enforced, even though contained in the same document, the non-performance will not prevent specific performance being obtained.[13] If there is a stipulation in the contract intended to benefit the plaintiff, he may waive it and obtain specific performance, provided the stipulation is in terms for the exclusive benefit of the plaintiff.[14]

Somewhat similar to what has just been discussed are the cases which show that a plaintiff who has repudiated his obligations under a contract, or who has done acts at variance with it, may be refused specific performance. Thus an

---

[2] *Australia Hardwoods Pty, Ltd.* v. *Commissioner for Railways*, [1961] 1 All E.R. 737, at p. 742, P.C.

[3] *Regent's Canal Co.* v. *Ware* (1857), 23 Beav. 575; *Scott* v. *Liverpool Corporation* (1858), 3 De G. & J. 334.

[4] *Bastin* v. *Bidwell* (1881), 18 Ch. 238; *Greville* v. *Parker*, [1910] A.C. 335, P.C.

[5] *Modlen* v. *Snowball* (1861), 4 De. G.F. & J. 143.

[6] *Smith* v. *Butler*, [1900] 1 Q.B. 694, C.A.; *Re Sandwell Park Colliery Co.*, [1929] 1 Ch. 277; *Aberfoyle Plantations, Ltd.*, v. *Cheng*, [1959] 3 All E.R. 910; [1960] A.C. 115, P.C.

[7] *Williams* v. *Brisco* (1882), 22 Ch.D. 441, C.A.

[8] *Modlen* v. *Snowball* (1861), 4 De. G.F. & J. 143; *Tildesley* v. *Clarkson* (1862), 30 Beav. 419.

[9] *Dyster* v. *Randall*, [1926] Ch. 932; cf. *Oxford* v. *Provand* (1868), L.R. 2 P.C. 135.

[10] *Davis* v. *Hone* (1805), 2 Sch. & Lef. 341.

[11] *Lamare* v. *Dixon* (1873), L.R. 6 H.L. 414.

[12] *Hotham* v. *East India Co.* (1787), 1 Term. Rep. 638; *Murrell* v. *Goodyear*(1860), 1 De G.F. & J. 432.

[13] *Green* v. *Low* (1856), 22 Beav. 625; *Phipps* v. *Child* (1857), 3 Drew 709.

[14] *Heron Garage Properties, Ltd.* v. *Moss*, [1974] 1 All E.R. 421. Cf. *Scott* v. *Bradley*, [1971] 1 All E.R. 583; [1971] Ch. 850.

employer who has wrongfully dismissed a servant cannot specifically enforce a term in restraint of trade contained in the service contract,[15] and a vendor who, having given possession under the contract, repossesses the property cannot obtain specific performance.[16] There is also a line of cases which show that a tenant under an agreement for a lease who is in breach of his obligations thereunder cannot compel a lease to be granted.[17] Again the act must not be merely trivial and unsubstantial,[18] and the doctrine of waiver applies.[19]

Failure to perform representations which induced the defendant to enter into the contract may also be a defence to a claim for specific performance, even though the representations were not such as would ground an action at law.[20] Further the plaintiff must be ready and willing to perform all the terms of the contract which have yet to be performed by him. Thus a purchaser who has committed an available act of bankruptcy of which the vendor has notice cannot enforce the contract, because he is incapable of so paying the purchase money to the vendor as that the latter shall be certain of being able to retain it against the trustee, should bankruptcy supervene.[1] And in one case the fact that the vendor could not produce the title deeds, which had been destroyed by fire, prevented him from getting specific performance.[2]

p Laches

In equity, in general, the rule has always been that time is not of the essence of the contract and accordingly a plaintiff may obtain specific performance even though he has not performed the terms of the contract to be carried out by him at the time specified.[3] There is no reason, however, why the parties should not agree that time should be of the essence of the contract, in which case specific performance will not be granted if the time limit has not been observed by the plaintiff as to his part,[4] and even though not originally of the essence, time may be made of the essence by serving an appropriate notice at the proper time.[5]

Even though time is not of the essence of the contract, long delay by the plaintiff[6] in performing his part, or in bringing proceedings, may defeat his claim to specific performance. The plaintiff must come to the court promptly,

---

[15] *Measures* v. *Measures*, [1910] 2 Ch. 248, C.A.

[16] *Knatchbull* v. *Grueber* (1815), 1 Madd. 153 affd. (1817), 3 Mer. 124.

[17] *Coatsworth* v. *Johnson* (1886), 55 L.J. Q.B. 220, C.A.; *Swain* v. *Ayres* (1888), 21 Q.B.D. 289, C.A.

[18] *Parker* v. *Taswell* (1838), 2 De G. & J. 559; *Besant* v. *Wood* (1879), 12 Ch.D. 605.

[19] *Gregory* v. *Wilson*, (1852), 9 Hare 683.

[20] *Myers* v. *Watson* (1851), 1 Sim. N.S. 523; *Lamare* v. *Dixon, supra.*

[1] *Dyster* v. *Randall*, [1926] Ch. 932. Similarly as to the vendor's bankruptcy—*Lowes* v. *Lush* (1808), 14 Ves. 547. As to insolvency without bankruptcy see *Crosbie* v. *Tooke* (1833), 1 My. & K. 431; *Neale* v. *Mackenzie* (1837), 1 Keen 474.

[2] *Bryant* v. *Busk* (1827), 4 Russ. 1. But secondary evidence may suffice—*Moulton* v. *Edmonds* (1859), 1 De G.F. & J. 246.

[3] Cf. 41 of the Law of Property Act 1925, replacing s. 25(7) of the Judicature Act 1873.

[4] *Steedman* v. *Drinkle*, [1916] 1 A.C. 275, P.C.

[5] *Green* v. *Sevin* (1879), 13 Ch.D. 589; *Howe* v. *Smith* (1884), 27 Ch.D. 89, C.A.; *Stickney* v. *Keeble*, [1915] A.C. 386, H.L.; *Smith* v. *Hamilton*, [1950] 2 All E.R. 928; [1951] Ch. 174.

[6] It makes no difference whether he is vendor or purchaser—*Rich* v. *Gale* (1871), 24 L.T. 745.

and as soon as the nature of the case will permit.[7] It is impossible to lay down definite times, but to give an idea three and a half years' delay was a good defence in *Eads* v. *Williams*,[8] and less than two years in *Southcomb* v. *Exeter (Bishop)*[9] and *Lord James Stuart* v. *London & North Western Railway Co.*[10] As little as three and a half months was held to be enough in *Glasbrook* v. *Richardson*,[11] a case concerning the sale of a colliery, said however to be "a property of an extremely speculative character, approaching a trade" to which special considerations applied. If the writ has been issued promptly, it seems that delay in bringing the action to trial will not normally defeat the plaintiff's claim to specific performance. This result will only follow if the plaintiff by his conduct has lulled the defendant into a belief that he is going to ask for damages only and not specific performance.[12]

Laches will not, however, defeat a claim nearly so soon, if at all, where the plaintiff is in possession and is the equitable owner, and the action is brought merely to clothe the plaintiff with the legal estate. Thus in such circumstances specific performance was decreed of an agreement for a lease after eighteen years delay in *Sharp* v. *Milligan*,[13] and of a contract for the sale of land after ten years in *Williams* v. *Greatrex*.[14] To have this effect the possession of the plaintiff must be possession under the contract.[15]

It need hardly be said that the defendant may waive, or by his conduct be deemed to have waived, the defence on the ground of laches.[16]

q   Absence of writing

Section 40 of the Law of Property Act 1925,[17] which provides that "no action may be brought upon any contract for the sale or other disposition of land or any interest in land, unless the agreement upon which such action is brought, or some memorandum or note thereof, is in writing, and signed by the party to be charged or by some other person thereunto by him lawfully authorised", applies just as much to a claim for specific performance as to a claim for damages. Notwithstanding the statute, however, the Court of Chancery would grant specific performance in the absence of writing where there was a sufficient act of part performance, and this exceptional rule is expressly preserved by section 40(2) of the Law of Property Act 1925. The doctrine of part performance is adequately discussed in the standard text books on real property and contract.[18]

---

[7]   *Eads* v. *Williams* (1854), 4 De G.M. & G. 674.
[8]   *Supra.*
[9]   (1847), 6 Hare 213.
[10] (1852), 1 De G.M. & G. 721.
[11] (1874), 23 W.R. 51. Cf. *Wroth* v. *Tyler*, [1973] 1 All E.R. 897.
[12] *Du Sautoy* v. *Symes*, [1967] 1 All E.R. 25; [1967] Ch. 1146.
[13] (1856), 22 Beav. 606; *Shepheard* v. *Walker* (1875) L.R. 20 Eq. 659.
[14] [1956] 3 All E.R. 705, C.A. applying a dictum of Lord Redesdale in *Crofton* v. *Ormsby* (1806), 2 Sch. & Lef. 583, who contemplated forty or fifty years delay.
[15] *Mills* v. *Haywood* (1877), 6 Ch.D. 196, C.A.
[16] *Seton* v. *Slade* (1802), 7 Ves. 265; *King* v. *Wilson* (1843), 6 Beav. 124.
[17] Replacing a part of s. 4 of the Statute of Frauds 1677.
[18] E.g. Megarry & Wade, *The Law of Real Property*, 3rd Ed., pp. 569 *et seq.* (the fullest account); Cheshire, *Modern Real Property*, 11th Ed., pp. 379 *et seq.*; Cheshire & Fifoot, *Law of Contract*, 8th Ed., pp. 191 *et seq.*

CHAPTER 15

Other Equitable Remedies

1 THE APPOINTMENT OF A RECEIVER, OR RECEIVER AND MANAGER

a Receivers

The jurisdiction of the Court of Chancery to appoint a receiver has been said to be one of the oldest equitable remedies.[1] A receiver may be appointed on the one hand in order to preserve property which is in danger, or on the other hand to enable a person to obtain the benefit of his rights over property, or to obtain payment of his debt, where the legal remedies are inadequate. Generally, the appointment may extend over any form of property, provided it is capable of assignment, but there are important restrictions, which are discussed later,[2] on the kinds of property over which a receiver by way of equitable execution may be appointed. A receiver has been described[3] as "a person who receives rents or other income paying ascertained outgoings, but who does not . . . manage the property in the sense of buying or selling or anything of that kind". This description is not comprehensive, for the purpose of the appointment may be simply to preserve property pending the settlement of legal proceedings, the property in the meantime bringing in no income. In any case the duty of the receiver is to take possession of the relevant property: thus if a receiver is appointed over real or leasehold property, the order will usually direct any parties to the action who may be in possession to deliver it up to the receiver, and if the land is in the possession of tenants they will be directed to attorn to the receiver; while if the receiver is appointed over personal estate the order should direct parties in possession to deliver such estate to the receiver, together with all the securities therefor in their hands, and all other books and papers relating thereto.

Originally the remedy was a purely equitable one exercised by the Court of Chancery, but it has now been made statutory,[4] and is capable of being granted

---

[1] *Hopkins* v. *Worcester & Birmingham Canal Co.* (1868), L.R. 6 Eq. 437, *per* Giffard V.C. at 447; *Rowley* v. *Ridley* (1784), 2 Dick. 622.

[2] See pp. 457 *et seq., post.*

[3] *Per* Jessel M. R. in *Re Manchester and Milford Railway Co.* (1880), 14 Ch.D. 645, at p. 653, C.A.; *Evans* v. *Coventry* (1854), 3 Drew. 75; *Wright* v. *Vernon* (1855), 3 Drew. 112.

[4] Judicature Act 1925, s. 45, replacing s. 25 (8) of the Judicature Act 1873. See also R.S.C., O. 30.

by any division of the High Court,[5] the Court of Appeal,[6] the House of Lords,[7] and inferior courts having equity jurisdiction,[8] "in all cases in which it appears to the court to be just or convenient so to do".[9] The "order may be made either unconditionally or on such terms and conditions as the court thinks just".[10] The result of these statutory provisions is that the court will now grant a remedy in many cases where it would not in practice have done so before the Judicature Acts,[11] though the principles on which the court acts have not been changed and it seems that it will still not appoint a receiver where before those Acts the Court of Chancery would have had no jurisdiction to do so.[12]

A person appointed receiver is required to give security[13] for what he shall receive as such receiver; the appointment may be conditional upon security being given, or the receiver may be ordered to give security by a given date, with liberty to act at once, on an undertaking by the applicant to be answerable for what he shall receive or become liable to pay.

b Managers

Where it is desired to continue a trade or business, it is not sufficient to appoint a receiver for, as we have seen, he has no authority for this purpose. Though not so old a remedy as appointing a receiver,[14] the court has, however, for many years had jurisdiction for this purpose to appoint a manager, and normally the same person is appointed and known as the receiver and manager.[15] The effect is that the management of the business is carried on by the court, through its officer, but the court will only do this for a limited period of time, for the purpose of preserving the assets.[16] "Nothing is better settled than that this Court does not assume the management of a business or undertaking except with a view to the winding up and sale of the business or undertaking."[17] Accordingly in the first instance a manager will not normally be appointed for longer than three months, though this may be extended from time to time if a proper case is made out.

---

[5] Most commonly, in practice, in the Chancery Division, except that receivers by way of equitable execution are frequently appointed in the Queen's Bench Division. A receiver may be appointed by a court of bankruptcy—*Re Goudie*, [1896] 2 Q.B. 481.

[6] *Hyde* v. *Warden* (1876), 1 Ex. D. 309, C.A.

[7] *Houlditch* v. *Donegall (Marquess)* (1834), 2 Cl. & Fin. 470.

[8] Judicature Act 1925, s. 202; as to County Courts, County Courts Act 1959, s. 75.

[9] Judicature Act 1925, s. 45(1).

[10] *Ibid.*, s. 45(2).

[11] *Re Whiteley* (1887), 56 L.T. 846; *Cummins* v. *Perkins*, [1899] 1 Ch. 16, C.A.

[12] *Holmes* v. *Millage*, [1893] 1 Q.B. 551, C.A.; *Harris* v. *Beauchamp*, [1894] 1 Q.B. 801, C.A.; *Morgan* v. *Hart*, [1914] 2 K.B. 183, C.A. Cf. *Kitts* v. *Moore*, [1895] 1 Q.B. 253, C.A. and see the discussion of the same provisions in relation to injunctions, Chapter 13, Section 1a, pp. 384 et seq., ante.

[13] R.S.C., O. 30, r. 2.

[14] *Re Newdigate Colliery Ltd.*, [1912] 1 Ch. 468, C.A.

[15] *Re Manchester and Milford Rail. Co.* (1880), 14 Ch.D. 645, at p. 653, C.A.

[16] *Waters* v. *Taylor* (1808), 15 Ves. 10; *Taylor* v. *Neate* (1888), 39 Ch.D. 538.

[17] *Gardner* v. *London Chatham and Dover Railway* (1867), 2 Ch. App. 201, *per* Cairns L.J. at 212.

c **Who may be appointed as receiver, or receiver and manager**

Any party to the action, but not a stranger thereto,[18] may nominate a person to be appointed as receiver. In making the appointment the general principle is that the person appointed should be independent and impartial. *Prima facie*, therefore, the court will not appoint a party to the action,[19] or anyone who has shown a partiality for one of the parties,[20] or whose interest may conflict with his duties.[21] Again the court will not normally appoint a person who should act as a check on the receiver. Thus a trustee will not normally be appointed receiver of the trust property, for the *cestuis que trust* should be able to rely on him to control the receiver,[1] nor will the court appoint the next friend of an infant plaintiff,[2] and in one case Lord Eldon even refused to appoint the son of the next friend.[3] Similarly the court will not normally appoint the solicitor having the conduct of the cause,[4] nor any member of the firm of solicitors acting for the plaintiff.[5]

The court may, however, and frequently does, depart from this general principle if the parties consent, and even without their consent if a proper case is made out. Thus if a receiver is appointed on the dissolution of a partnership, a solvent partner will usually be appointed as receiver, if he has not behaved improperly,[6] in order that the partnership business may be wound up to the best advantage of all concerned.[7] Again where a company is in liquidation and the duties to be performed by the liquidator and the receiver are identical, the court will in general appoint the liquidator as receiver to avoid additional expense and to prevent conflict between them.[8] However in *Boyle* v. *Bettws Llantwit Colliery Co.*[9] the plaintiffs successfully applied to be appointed receivers. They were the unpaid vendors of the property of a company in voluntary liquidation. The liquidator had no funds to re-open the colliery or carry on the workings, while the plaintiffs, who were said to be "really the owners of the colliery",[10] were willing to provide funds for this purpose.

It may be added that an infant cannot be appointed as receiver,[11] and there are other personal qualities which are likely to be regarded as valid objections to appointment. Thus it seems that the court will be reluctant to appoint a person who may be protected against the ordinary remedies against a receiver,

---

18 *A.-G.* v. *Day* (1817), 2 Madd. 246.
19 *Re Lloyd* (1879), 12 Ch.D. 447, C.A.
20 *Blakeway* v. *Blakeway* (1833), 2 L.J. Ch. 75; *Wright* v. *Vernon* (1855), 3 Drew. 112.
21 *Fripp* v. *Chard Railway Co.* (1853), 11 Hare 241.
1 *Sykes* v. *Hastings* (1805), 11 Ves. 363; *Sutton* v. *Jones* (1809), 15 Ves. 584.
2 *Stone* v. *Wishart* (1817), 2 Madd. 64.
3 *Taylor* v. *Oldham* (1822), Jac. 527.
4 *Garland* v. *Garland* (1793), 2 Ves. 137.
5 *Re Lloyd*, *supra*.
6 *Young* v. *Buckett* (1882), 51 L.J. Ch. 504.
7 *Collins* v. *Barker*, [1893] 1 Ch. 578; *Harrison-Broadley* v. *Smith*, [1964] 1 All E.R. 867, C.A., at 872.
8 *Re Joshua Stubbs Ltd.*, [1891] 1 Ch.D. 475, C.A.; *British Linen Co.* v. *South American and Mexican Co.*, [1894] 1 Ch. 108, C.A.
9 (1876), 2 Ch.D. 726.
10 At p. 728.
11 Co. Litt. 171b, 172a.

such as a peer,[12] or a member of the House of Commons.[13] And where a receiver and manager is to be appointed, which will involve trading, it seems that a beneficed clergyman of the Church of England[14] is ineligible. Moreover by statute[15] a body corporate is not qualified for appointment as receiver[16] of the property of a company.

Two or more persons may be appointed as joint receivers,[17] or exceptionally as separate receivers of different parts of the assets.[18]

d   Salary and allowance

Unless otherwise ordered, a receiver or manager appointed by the court will be allowed a proper salary or allowance.[19]   Any remuneration allowed is payable out of the assets in the receiver's hands, but the receiver has no personal claim for his remuneration from the parties to the action, even though they all consent to his appointment.[1]   A trustee who is appointed receiver will not usually be allowed remuneration,[2] though he may be in exceptional circumstances.[3]   Similarly a party to an action who is appointed receiver will normally be required to act without remuneration,[4] but it seems that remuneration may be allowed in partnership cases,[5] and in any case he may be paid for any extraordinary trouble and expense beyond what his duties as receiver required, provided it was for the benefit of the estate.[6]   In practice the receiver should apply to the court for directions before undertaking the exceptional work or expense, otherwise he runs the risk that additional remuneration will not be allowed.

There is no settled scale for calculating the remuneration,[7] which is usually fixed by the master in chambers.   It depends on the circumstances of each case—the difficulty of collection and the amount of work involved—and seems usually to vary, in the case of a receiver of annual rents and profits, from about two to five per cent, and in the case of gross sums from about one and a quarter to one and a half.   A fixed salary, however, may be allowed in lieu of a commission,[8] or a lump sum where the work of the receiver is to get in capital sums.

---

[12] *A.-G.* v. *Gee* (1813), 2 Ves. & B. 208.
[13] *Wellesley* v. *Duke of Beaufort* (1831), 2 Russ. & My. 639; *Lechmere Charlton's Case, Re Ludlow Charities* (1837), 2 My. & Cr. 316; *Re Armstrong*, [1892] 1 Q.B. 327.
[14] Pluralities Act 1838, s. 29.
[15] Companies Act 1948, s. 366; *Portman Building Society* v. *Gallwey*, [1955] 1 All E.R. 227.
[16] The disqualification apparently does not apply to appointment as manager. Cf. s. 367 of the Companies Act 1948.
[17] *Duder* v. *Amsterdamsch Trustees Kantoor*, [1902] 2 Ch. 132.
[18] *British Linen Co.* v. *South American and Mexican Co.*, [1894] 1 Ch. 108, C.A.
[19] R.S.C., O. 30, r. 3.
[1] *Boehm* v. *Goodall*, [1911] 1 Ch. 155.
[2] *Pilkington* v. *Baker* (1876), 24 W.R. 234.
[3] *Newport* v. *Bury* (1857), 23 Beav. 30; *Re Bignell*, [1892] 1 Ch. 59, C.A.
[4] *Sargant* v. *Read* (1876), 1 Ch.D. 600; *Taylor* v. *Neate* (1888), 39 Ch. D. 538.
[5] *Davy* v. *Scarth*, [1906] 1 Ch. 55.
[6] *Potts* v. *Leighton* (1808), 15 Ves. 273; *Harris* v. *Sleep*, [1897] 2 Ch. 80, C.A.
[7] At one time the standard rate was 5%—*Day* v. *Croft* (1840), 2 Beav. 488, but this had ceased to be the rule by *Prior* v. *Bagster* (1887), 57 L.T. 760.
[8] *Re Bignell*, [1892] 1 Ch. 59, C.A.

e Position of receiver

A receiver is an officer of the court. It is his duty to take possession of the property over which he is appointed and his possession and acts are the possession and acts of the court.[9] As Chitty J. expressed it,[10] "A receiver is not an agent for any other person, and a receiver is not a trustee. The receiver is appointed by the order of the court and is responsible to the court, and cannot obey the directions of the parties in the action." By reason of the fact that the receiver is an officer of the court, any interference by anyone with his possession of the property he has been directed to receive is a contempt of court, even though the order appointing him is perfectly erroneous.[11] Interference may be punished by committal,[12] and restrained by the issue of an injunction.[13] Thus in *Dixon* v. *Dixon*[14] an injunction was granted to the receiver and manager of a partnership business to restrain one of the old partners from inducing employees of the receiver to leave his employment and enter the employment of a rival business set up by the old partner, even though due notice was given to the receiver and breach of contract was neither instigated nor committed. Apart from physical interference it would be a contempt of court to institute legal proceedings to assert a right over property of which the receiver has either taken or been directed to take possession[15] without first obtaining the leave of the court, which will, however, readily be given unless it is perfectly clear that there is no foundation for the claim.[16] There will, however, be no actionable interference if the order for a receiver does not make it clear on the face of it that he is to be receiver over the property in dispute,[17] nor where the order is made conditional on the giving of security, and security has not yet been given.[18]

A receiver is appointed by the court for the benefit of all parties,[19] to preserve the property pending the settlement of their rights without in any way affecting the rights themselves.[1] Not being an agent for anyone, a receiver is personally liable for his acts, for instance contracts entered into in carrying on a business,[2] or existing contracts adopted as his own.[3] He is, however, entitled to an indemnity out of the assets for all costs and expenses not improperly incurred,[4]

---

[9] *Aston* v. *Heron* (1834), 2 My. & K. 390; *Re Flowers & Co.*, [1897] 1 Q.B. 14, C.A.
[10] In *Bacup Corporation* v. *Smith* (1890), 44 Ch.D. 395, 398.
[11] *Ames* v. *Birkenhead Docks Trustees* (1855), 20 Beav. 332.
[12] *Helmore* v. *Smith* (No. 2) (1886), 35 Ch.D. 449, C.A.
[13] *Dixon* v. *Dixon*, [1904] 1 Ch. 161.
[14] *Supra.*
[15] *Ames* v. *Birkenhead Docks Trustees*, *supra*; *Defries* v. *Creed* (1865), 12 L.T. 262.
[16] *Hawkins* v. *Gathercole* (1852), 1 Drew 12; *Lane* v. *Capsey*, [1891] 3 Ch. 411; *Brenner* v. *Rose*, [1973] 2 All E.R. 535. Provided such leave is obtained an action may be brought against a receiver even by the person at whose instance he was appointed—*L.P. Arthur (Insurance), Ltd.* v. *Sisson*, [1966] 2 All E.R. 1003.
[17] *Crow* v. *Wood* (1856), 13 Beav. 271.
[18] *Edwards* v. *Edwards* (1876), 2 Ch.D. 291, C.A.
[19] *Bertrand* v. *Davis* (1862), 31 Beav. 429; *Davy* v. *Scarth*, [1906] 1 Ch. 55.
[1] *Ward* v. *Royal Exchange Shipping Co.* (1887), 58 L.T. 174, 178; *Durran* v. *Durran* (1904), 91 L.T. 187.
[2] *Burn, Boulton and Hayward* v. *Bull*, [1895] 1 Q.B. 276, C.A.; *Moss S.S. Co.* v. *Whinney*, [1912] A.C. 254, H.L.
[3] *Re Botibol*, [1947] 1 All E.R. 26.
[4] *Burt, Boulton and Hayward* v. *Bull*, *supra*, C.A.; *Strapp* v. *Bull*, [1895] 2 Ch. 1, C.A.

including the costs of an action brought against him as receiver where the defence was for the benefit of the trust estate,[5] but, as with a claim for remuneration, he is not entitled to any personal indemnity,[6] even though he has been appointed with the consent of all parties.[7] Further by the doctrine of subrogation, the receiver's creditors will be entitled to the same rights against the property as the receiver himself.[8]

f Cases in which a receiver may be appointed by the court

Except where the appointment is to enforce an equitable mortgage or charge, or by way of equitable execution, the general ground on which a receiver is appointed is for the protection and preservation of property for the benefit of the persons who are, or, as a result of litigation are ultimately held to be, beneficially interested. It was said in *Owen* v. *Homan*[9] that where "the property is as it were *in medio*, in the enjoyment of no one, the court can hardly do wrong in taking possession. It is the common interest of all parties that the court should prevent a scramble". Until the Judicature Acts, however, it was the rule that a receiver would not be appointed against a person in possession of real estate claiming under a legal title,[10] except where the plaintiff could set up a case of fraud or other exceptional circumstance.[11] Though it has been held that the rule no longer applies on the ground[12] that the court has power to appoint a receiver whenever it is just and convenient to do so, in practice in such case the court is slow to exercise its discretionary power.[13] It is unlikely to do so where the defendant is in actual possession,[14] but will be more ready where there are tenants who might otherwise be under the risk of being required to pay their rents a second time.[15] Other matters will also be taken into account, such as the length of the defendant's possession, the relative apparent strength of his and the plaintiff's titles and their respective financial positions.[16]

The main types of case in which a receiver may be appointed are as follows:—

i *Pending the grant of probate or letters of administration.* In these circumstance a receiver may be appointed to protect the assets of the estate,[1] and similarly if a sole executor dies a receiver may be appointed pending a fresh grant being obtained.[2] Until the Administration of Justice Act 1970 there was a conflict

---

[5] *Re Dunn*, [1904] 1 Ch. 648; contrast *Walters* v. *Woodbridge* (1878), 7 Ch.D. 504, C.A. where the defence was merely to vindicate the receiver's character against charges of personal fraud and misconduct in his office and not to benefit the estate.

[6] *Ex parte Izard* (1883), 23 Ch.D. 75, C.A.; *Batten* v. *Wedgwood Coal and Iron Co.* (1884), 28 Ch.D. 317.

[7] *Boehm* v. *Goodall*, [1911] 1 Ch. 155.

[8] *Re London United Breweries, Ltd.*, [1907] 2 Ch. 511.

[9] (1853), 4 H.L.Cas. 997, at p. 1032.

[10] *Earl Talbot* v. *Hope Scott* (1858), 4 K. & J. 96; *Carrow* v. *Ferrior* (1868), 3 Ch. App. 719.

[11] *Hugonin* v. *Baseley* (1806), 13 Ves. 105; *Lloyd* v. *Passingham* (1809), 16 Ves. 59.

[12] See p. 450, *ante*; *Berry* v. *Keen* (1882), 51 L.J. Ch. 912, C.A.; *Foxwell* v. *Van Grutten*, [1897] 1 Ch. 64, C.A.

[13] *Foxwell* v. *Van Grutten*, *supra.*

[14] *Marshall* v. *Charteris*, [1920] 1 Ch. 520.

[15] *John* v. *John*, [1898] 2 Ch. 573, C.A.

[16] *John* v. *John*, *supra.*

[1] *Re Oakes*, [1917] 1 Ch. 230; *Jackman* v. *Sutcliffe*, [1942] 2 All E.R. 296; [1942] Ch. 453.

[2] *Re Parker* (1879), 12 Ch.D. 293; *Re Clark*, [1910] W.N. 234.

between the jurisdiction of the Chancery Division to appoint a receiver, and that of the Probate Division to appoint an administrator *pendente lite*. It is no longer necessary to know how this conflict was resolved, because the Act, which re-named the Probate, Divorce and Admiralty Division the Family Division, also transferred contentious probate proceedings to the Chancery Division. Further, O. 76, r. 15 (2) of the Rules of the Supreme Court has assimilated the accounts of an administrator *pendente lite* and a receiver. The proper procedure now is to apply for an administrator *pendente lite* if probate proceedings have been started, but if this is not the case then an administration action should be commenced asking for the appointment of a receiver.

ii   *As against executors and trustees.* The court may dispossess an executor or trustee of the trust estate by appointing a receiver if a strong case is made out.[3] Gross misconduct or personal disability on the part of the executor or trustee, such as wasting or misapplication of the assets, may justify the appointment of a receiver,[4] or even mere mismanagement without any corrupt intention.[5] Mere poverty is not a sufficient ground,[6] but insolvency is a different matter, unless it can be clearly shown that, knowing of the insolvency, the testator or settlor nevertheless appointed him as executor or trustee, or, in the case of an executor, deliberately refrained from altering his will, with the intention that the insolvent executor should act.[7] A receiver has also been appointed where a sole executor remained outside the jurisdiction,[8] but this will not normally be done where one of several trustees has gone abroad, or is inactive or disclaims.[9]

iii   *In partnership cases.* The court will readily appoint a receiver if it can be shown, when the application is made, that the partnership is at an end.[10] The court, however, finds itself in a difficulty if the defendant claims that the partnership is continuing. On the one hand, if a receiver is appointed, the effect is to bring to an end the partnership which one party claims to have a right to be continued; while, on the other hand, if a receiver is not appointed, it leaves the defendant at liberty to go on with the business with risk of loss and prejudice to the plaintiff.[11] The court tries to weigh the various factors, but will not in general appoint a receiver unless it appears reasonably clear either that the partnership is already at an end or that the court will order a dissolution at the trial.[12] For similar reasons the court will be slow to appoint a receiver if the defendant denies the existence of the alleged partnership, though there is no rigid rule preventing it.[13]

---

[3] *Middleton* v. *Dodswell* (1806), 13 Ves. 266; *Bainbridge* v. *Blair* (1835), 4 L.J. Ch. 207.
[4] *Evans* v. *Coventry* (1854), 5 De G.M. & G. 911; *Swale* v. *Swale* (1836), 22 Beav. 584; *Brooker* v. *Brooker* (1857), 3 Sm. & G. 475.
[5] *Whitehead* v. *Bennett* (1845), 6 L.T.O.S. 185.
[6] *Anon.* (1806), *supra*; *Howard* v. *Papera* (1815), 1 Madd. 142.
[7] *Re H's Estate* (1875), 1 Ch.D. 276; *Langley* v. *Hawk* (1820), 5 Madd. 46.
[8] *Collas* v. *Hesse* (1864), 10 L.T. 221; *Dickins* v. *Harris* (1866), 14 L.T. 98.
[9] *Browell* v. *Reed* (1842), 1 Hare 434.
[10] *Pini* v. *Roncoroni*, [1892] 1 Ch. 633; *Taylor* v. *Neate* (1888), 39 Ch.D. 538.
[11] *Madgwick* v. *Wimble* (1843), 6 Beav. 495.
[12] *Goodman* v. *Whitcomb* (1820), 1 Jac. & W. 589; *Smith* v. *Jeyes* (1841), 4 Beav. 503.
[13] *Floydd* v. *Cheney*, [1970] 1 All E.R. 446; [1970] Ch. 602.

iv *Companies.* Receivers are usually appointed under express powers in debentures or debenture trust deeds,[14] though any such appointment may be superseded by an appointment by the Court.[15] An appointment may be made by the court at the instance of shareholders or the company itself where, for instance, there is no governing body, or such disputes between the directors that the management is not being carried on.[16] Debenture holders may ask the court to appoint a receiver if their security is in jeopardy,[17] even though they have reserved a power under the debentures which has not yet become exercisable.[18] The mere fact that the security is insufficient is not enough:[19] there must also be evidence that the security is in jeopardy, as, for instance, where the company is threatening to distribute all its assets among the shareholders,[20] or where it has ceased to be a going concern.[1]

v *Mortgages.* Before the Judicature Acts a receiver would not be appointed at the instance of a legal mortgagee. The view taken was that he must take possession himself if he wanted it, and he was not entitled to have another person put in to act for him, when he could take possession for himself.[2] Since the Acts, however, the court may appoint a receiver at the instance of a legal mortgagee when it thinks it just and convenient to do so,[3] and it may do so, if a special case is made out, even though the mortgagee has gone into possession or himself appointed a receiver under an express power so to do.[4] A legal mortgagee almost invariably has power to appoint a receiver himself.[5]

An equitable mortgagee or chargee has, however, always had a right to have a receiver appointed by the court,[6] where there has been no prior incumbrancer in possession,[7] on the ground that he was unable to take possession for himself.[8] He has this right whenever there has been a breach of any of the mortgagor's obligations, or even without this, where the security is in jeopardy.[9] Where

---

[14] See p. 459, *post.*
[15] *Re Maskelyne British Typewriter Ltd.,* [1898] 1 Ch. 133, C.A.; *Re Slogger Automatic Feeder Co., Ltd.,* [1915] 1 Ch. 478.
[16] *Trade Auxiliary Co.* v. *Vickers* (1873), L.R. 16 Eq. 298, C.A.; *Stanfield* v. *Gibbon,* [1925] W.N. 11.
[17] *McMahon* v. *North Kent Ironworks,* [1891] 2 Ch. 148; *Edwards* v. *Standard Rolling Stock Syndicate,* [1893] 1 Ch. 574.
[18] *McMahon* v. *North Kent Ironworks, supra.*
[19] *Re New York Taxicab Co.,* [1913] 1 Ch. 1, distinguishing *Re Victoria Steamboats, Ltd.,* [1897] 1 Ch. 158.
[20] *Re Tilt Cove Copper Co., Ltd.,* [1913] 2 Ch. 588.
[1] *Hubbuck* v. *Helms* (1887), 56 L.T. 232. See also *Re London Pressed Hinge Co.,* [1905] 1 Ch. 576; *Re Braunstein & Marjolaine,* [1914] W.N. 335.
[2] *Re Prytherch,* [1889] 42 Ch. D. 590.
[3] *Pease* v. *Fletcher* (1875), 1 Ch. D. 273; *Tillett* v. *Nixon* (1883), 25 Ch.D. 238; *Re Prytherch, supra.*
[4] *County of Gloucester Bank* v. *Rudry Merthyr Coal Co.,* [1895] 1 Ch. 629, C.A.
[5] See p. 459, *post.*
[6] *Tanfield* v. *Irvine* (1826), 2 Russ. 149; *Sollory* v. *Leaver* (1869), L.R. 9 Eq. 22; *Re Crompton & Co. Ltd.,* [1914] 1 Ch. 954, 967.
[7] *Berney* v. *Sewell* (1820), 1 Jac. & W. 647.
[8] The ground, however, seems doubtful as regards an equitable mortgagee. See, *Barclays Bank, Ltd.* v. *Bird,* [1954] 1 All E.R. 449; [1954] Ch. 274; Megarry & Wade, *Law of Real Property,* 3rd Ed., pp. 917, 918.
[9] See cases cited in notes 17 to 20 and 1, *supra.*

the application is made by a subsequent incumbrancer, and the appointment is made in the usual form, expressly without prejudice to the rights of prior incumbrancers, a prior incumbrancer can take possession without leave of the court.[10] Where no reservation is made of the rights of prior incumbrancers, they are not in fact destroyed, but can only be exercised if the leave of the court is first obtained, which will not in practice be refused.[11]

(vi) *Creditors*. In *Cummins v. Perkins*[12] Lindley M.R. observed that the authorities clearly showed "that, quite independently of the Judicature Act 1873, if a plaintiff had a right to be paid out of a particular fund he could in equity obtain protection to prevent that fund from being dissipated so as to defeat his rights". It was, he said, "settled that a person who had a right to be paid out of a particular fund could obtain an injunction (and if an injunction, it followed on principle that he could obtain a receiver) in a proper case to protect the fund from being misapplied".[13]

(vii) *Between vendor and purchaser*. In appropriate cases a receiver may be appointed both in actions for specific performance and for rescission. Thus it has been done where proceedings had been brought to set aside a sale for fraud where the court thought it hardly possible that the transaction could stand, though it was also said that this was not the usual practice.[14] More commonly it has been done in order to preserve the property, for instance where the property is a mine and it is clearly desirable to keep it working,[15] or a farm which should clearly be kept in a state of cultivation.[16] And an unpaid vendor may be granted a receiver for the protection of his lien.[17]

(viii) *Other instances* have included cases where the owner of a chattel was suing for its return from a bailee, who claimed a lien over it;[18] pending a reference to arbitration;[19] and pending litigation in a foreign court.[20]

(ix) *A receiver for a mental patient* may be appointed under the provisions of the Mental Health Act 1959.[1] He has wider power and duties than an ordinary receiver and his special position, dependent on statute, is outside the scope of this book.[2]

(x) Lastly, there is the rather special case of the receiver by way of equitable execution. Before the Judicature Acts the Court of Chancery would come to the aid of a judgment creditor who was unable to enforce his judgment by a common law writ of execution, by appointing a receiver over certain assets of

---

[10] *Underhay v. Read* (1887), 20 Q.B.D. 209, C.A.
[11] *Re Metropolitan Amalgamated Estates Ltd.*, [1912] 2 Ch. 497.
[12] [1899] 1 Ch. 16, 19, 20, C.A.
[13] See also *Kearns v. Leaf* (1864), 1 H. & M. 681; *Owen v. Homan* (1853), 4 H.L.Cas. 997.
[14] *Stilwell v. Wilkins* (1821), Jac. 281.
[15] *Boehm v. Wood* (1820), 2 Jac. & W. 236; *Gibbs v. David* (1875), L.R. 20 Eq. 373.
[16] *Hyde v. Warden* (1876), 1 Ex. D. 309, C.A.
[17] *Munns v. Isle of Wight Railway Co.* (1870), 5 Ch. App. 414. Cf. *Cook v. Andrews*, [1897] 1 Ch. 266.
[18] *Hatton v. Car Maintenance Co. Ltd.*, [1915] 1 Ch. 621; [1911–13] All E.R. Rep. 890, where the receiver was authorised to allow the owner to use the chattel.
[19] *Law v. Garrett* (1878), 8 Ch. D. 26, C.A.; *Compagnie du Sénégal v. Smith* (1883), 49 L.T. 527.
[20] *Transatlantic Co. v. Pietroni* (1860), John. 604.
[1] Section 105.
[2] See e.g. *Re Oppenheim's Will Trusts*, [1950] 2 All E.R. 86; [1950] Ch. 633.

the debtor. Despite its title, equitable execution is not really execution at all, but equitable relief which the court gives because execution at law cannot be had. "It is not execution, but a substitute for execution".[3]

Before the Judicature Acts, the Court of Chancery would only appoint a receiver where the plaintiff could show first, that he had exhausted his legal remedies and, secondly, that the judgment debtor had an equitable interest in property which could have been reached at law, if he had had the legal interest in it, instead of an equitable interest in it. On the first point, since the Judicature Acts, which, as we have seen, give the court jurisdiction to appoint a receiver whenever it appears just or convenient to do so,[4] it has been unnecessary to go through the "useless and absurd form"[5] of issuing a barren writ of execution,[6] though apart from cases within the Administration of Justice Act 1956[7] it is still in general necessary to show that there is no remedy available at law.[8] Again, apart from the provisions of the 1956 Act, the second point remains valid, and accordingly a receiver will not be appointed of property which could never be taken in execution at law. The Court in fact will not grant equitable execution by the appointment of a receiver in a case where prior to the Judicature Acts no court had jurisdiction to grant such relief.[9] Thus a receiver has been refused over future earnings,[10] a patent which was not producing any profits,[11] and a sum the payment of which to the debtor was wholly contingent and dependent on the will of another person.[12] Obvious cases for the appointment of a receiver are over an interest in a settlement of personalty,[13] even when reversionary,[14] or a legacy or share of residue under a will.[15] Other property over which a receiver by way of equitable execution has been appointed includes a tenancy in common[16] of the proceeds of sale of land,[17] debts and sums of money payable to a judgment debtor to which garnishee proceedings are not

---

[3] Per Bowen L.J. in Re Shephard (1889), 43 Ch.D. 131, at p. 137, C.A.; Levasseur v. Mason and Barry Ltd., [1891] 2 Q.B. 73, C.A.; Holmes v. Millage, [1893] 1 Q.B. 551, C.A.

[4] See p. 450, ante.

[5] Per Jessel M.R. in Anglo-Italian Bank v. Davies (1878), 9 Ch.D. 275, C.A., at p. 285; Re Watkins, Ex parte Evans (1879), 13 Ch.D. 252, at p. 260, C.A.

[6] Re Whiteley (1887), 56 L.T. 846; Hills v. Webber (1901), 17 T.L.R. 513, C.A.

[7] Section 36, discussed infra.

[8] Harris v. Beauchamp Bros., [1894] 1 Q.B. 801, C.A.; Holmes v. Millage, supra, C.A.; Morgan v. Hart, [1914] 2 K.B. 183, C.A.

[9] Holmes v. Millage, supra, C.A.; Edwards & Co. v. Picard, [1909] 2 K.B. 903, C.A. and see supra, p. 450.

[10] Holmes v. Millage, supra; Cadogan v. Lyric Theatre, [1894] 3 Ch. 338, C.A.

[11] Edwards & Co. v. Picard, supra.

[12] R. v. Lincolnshire County Court Judge (1887), 20 Q.B.D. 167, D.C.

[13] Oliver v. Lowther (1880), 42 L.T. 47; Webb v. Stenton (1883), 11 Q.B.D. 518, C.A.; Ideal Bedding Co. v. Holland, [1907] 2 Ch. 157.

[14] Fuggle v. Bland (1883), 11 Q.B.D. 711, D.C.; Tyrrell v. Painton, [1895] 1 Q.B. 202, C.A.

[15] Re Anglesey (Marquis), [1903] 2 Ch. 727.

[16] Or, semble, a joint tenancy—Hills v. Webber, supra, C.A.

[17] Stevens v. Hutchinson, [1953] 1 All E.R. 699; [1953] Ch. 299. According to this decision a person who has been appointed a receiver of the proceeds of sale of land is not a "person interested" for the purposes of s. 30 of the Law of Property Act 1925. Cf. Cooper v. Critchley, [1955] 1 All E.R. 520; [1955] Ch. 431, C.A.; Irani Finance, Ltd. v. Singh, [1970] 3 All E.R. 199; [1971] Ch. 59, C.A.; National Westminster Bank, Ltd. v. Allen, [1971] 3 All E.R. 201; [1971] 2 Q.B. 718.

applicable,[18] rents of land outside the jurisdiction,[19] and goods in the possession of a third party, subject to that third party's lien.[20] Generally, in determining whether it is just or convenient to appoint a receiver by way of equitable execution, the court must have regard to the amount of the debt claimed, the amount likely to be obtained by the receiver, and the probable costs of his appointment.[1]

It remains to say that by section 36 of the Administration of Justice Act 1956,[2] which has really "made a revolutionary change in the enforcement of judgments",[3] the power of the court to appoint a receiver by way of equitable execution was extended[4] so as to operate in relation to all legal estates and interests in land, whether or not a charge has been imposed on that land[5] under section 35 for the purpose of enforcing the judgment; and the power is in addition to and not in derogation of any power of any court to appoint a receiver in proceedings for enforcing such a charge. Since the writ of elegit was abolished by the same Act,[6] the remedy of a judgment creditor against land is either the imposition of a charge,[7] or the appointment of a receiver, or both.

g Appointment out of court

It is possible for a receiver to be appointed out of court, and indeed this is commonly done under mortgages and debentures, and may be done in other cases, for instance where partners by agreement appoint a receiver and manager to wind up the partnership business.[8] An express power to appoint a receiver was at one time commonly inserted in mortgage deeds, but reliance is now usually placed on the statutory power contained in the Law of Property Act 1925.[9] On the other hand, although in most cases debentures and debenture trust deeds are mortgages to which the statutory power would apply,[10] they still commonly include an express power in order to confer extended powers on the receiver. Strictly speaking, any discussion of a receiver appointed out of court is out of place in a chapter on equitable remedies, but it seems desirable to consider briefly the position of such a receiver by way of contrast and comparison.

---

[18] *Westhead* v. *Riley* (1883), 25 Ch.D. 413.
[19] *Mercantile Investment and General Trust Co.* v. *River Plate Trust Loan and Agency Co.*, [1892] 2 Ch. 303 (though in the circumstances the court refused to make the appointment.)
[20] *Levasseur* v. *Mason and Barry Ltd.*, [1891] 2 Q.D. 73, C.A.
[1] R.S.C., O. 51, r. 1.
[2] As to the County Court jurisdiction see ss. 141 and 142 of the County Courts Act 1959.
[3] *Per* Danckwerts L.J. in *Barclays Bank, Ltd.* v. *Moore*, [1967] 3 All E.R. 34, C.A. at p. 37.
[4] But see *Re Pope* (1886), 17 Q.B.D. 743, C.A.
[5] In s. 35 "land or interest in land" does not include the beneficial interest of a joint tenant or tenant in common under a trust for sale of land—*Irani Finance, Ltd.* v. *Singh*, [1970] 3 All E.R. 199; [1971] Ch. 59, C.A., criticised (1971), 34 M.L.R. 441 (Stephen Cretney)— but where joint tenants of land at law and in equity are jointly liable on a judgment debt, a changing order can be made on their legal interest in the land—*National Westminster Bank, Ltd.* v. *Allen*, [1971] 3 All E.R. 201; [1971] 2 Q.B. 718.
[6] Section 34.   [7] Under s. 35.
[8] *Turner* v. *Major* (1862), 3 Giff. 442. For different examples see *Knight* v. *Bowyer* (1858), 2 De G. & J. 421; *Cradock* v. *Scottish Provident Institutions*, [1893] W. N. 146; affd, [1894] W.N. 88, C.A.
[9] Section 101 (1) (iii) and 109 replacing Conveyancing Act 1881, ss. 19 (1) (iii) and 24. The first statutory power was in Lord Cranworth's Act 1860.
[10] Cf. *Knightsbridge Estates Trust Ltd.* v. *Byrne*, [1940] 2 All E.R. 401; [1940] A.C. 613, H.L. *Contra, Blaker* v. *Herts & Essex Waterworks Co.* (1889), 41 Ch.D. 399, at 405, 406.

Unlike a receiver appointed by the court, a receiver or manager appointed out of court is *prima facie* an agent for the person appointing him.[11] However, the statutory provisions in the case of mortgages and the usual express provisions in debentures make the receiver the agent of the mortgagor or company, as the case may be, with the object of making the mortgagor or company liable for the receiver's acts or defaults. Notwithstanding any such provision the receiver is primarily concerned to look after the interests of the person who appointed him.[12] A receiver appointed out of court ceases to be an agent for any person if he is superseded by a receiver appointed by the court,[13] and, on general principles of agency, his authority will be terminated by the death of the principal.[14] And if, under a debenture, a receiver is appointed as agent for the company, the appointment will terminate on the commencement of liquidation of the company, whether voluntary or compulsory.[15] Since a receiver appointed out of court is a mere agent, he incurs no personal liability for acts properly done by him as receiver,[16] though he may make himself personally liable for some transaction by giving his personal promise to carry it out,[17] and may always make himself liable for breach of warranty of authority.

In general, there are no restrictions as to who may be appointed receiver out of court. The statutory disability[18] of a body corporate to act as receiver of property of a company, however, applies, and it is an offence for an undischarged bankrupt to act as receiver or manager of the property of a company unless appointed by the court.[19]

Where a receiver is appointed out of court under the statutory power, he is entitled to such remuneration, not exceeding five per cent on the gross amount of all money received, as is specified in the appointment, and if no rate is specified then at the rate of five per cent or at such other rate as the court thinks fit to allow.[20] If a receiver of a company is appointed for debenture holders, he will be entitled to remuneration at the rate specified in the debenture or debenture trust deed, though if the company goes into liquidation the court may fix the remuneration. In this latter case the rate may be lower than that specified in the debenture or debenture trust deed, and the court may make its order with retrospective effect and require any excess remuneration retained by the receiver to be repaid.[1] If there is no provision for remuneration, a receiver may be entitled to claim on a *quantum meruit.*[2]

2 FOLLOWING THE TRUST PROPERTY—TRACING ORDERS

The question here is how far a legal or equitable owner can follow or trace property which has come into the hands of another. This involves a claim *in rem*

---

[11] *Knight* v. *Boywer* (1858), 2 De G. & J. 421; *Ford* v. *Rackham* (1853), 17 Beav. 485.
[12] *Re B. Johnson & Co. (Builders), Ltd.*, [1955] 2 All E.R. 775; [1955] Ch. 634, C.A.
[13] *Hand* v. *Blow*, [1901] 2 Ch. 721, C.A.
[14] *Semble*, this is not the case when the appointment is made under the statutory power by reason of the definition in the Law of Property Act 1925, s. 205 (1) (xvi).
[15] *Gosling* v. *Gaskell*, [1897] A.C. 575, H.L.; *Thomas* v. *Todd*, [1926] 2 K.B. 511.
[16] *Owen & Co.* v. *Cronk*, [1895] 1 Q.B. 265, C.A.
[17] *Robinson Printing Co.* v. *Chic, Ltd.*, [1905] 2 Ch. 123.
[18] Companies Act 1948, s. 366.
[19] *Ibid.*, s. 367.   [20] Law of Property Act 1925, s. 109 (6).
[1] Companies Act 1948, s. 371.   [2] *Prior* v. *Bagster* (1887), 57 L.T. 760.

as opposed to a claim *in personam*, which will be particularly valuable if for any reason a claim *in personam* will not lie, or if the defendant is bankrupt, when it may enable the claimant to obtain priority over the general creditors. In order to acquire a proper understanding of the position in equity it is desirable to consider first the position at common law.[3] It should, however, be observed that following or tracing is not strictly a remedy at all, but a preliminary step necessary in some circumstances to obtain an appropriate remedy. If it is possible to follow property at common law the remedy sought used to be an order for the return of the chattel or payment of its full value—though since the Common Law Procedure Act 1854[4] it has been possible to ask for an order for specific delivery, at the discretion of the court. In equity the appropriate relief includes an order to restore an unmixed fund and a declaration of charge.

a Following property at common law

At common law the legal owner of an asset who is deprived of the possession thereof has a right to follow it no matter into whose hands it may come, and notwithstanding that it may change its form, so long as he retains the property[5] in the asset in its original or converted form, and so long as the means of identifying the asset in its original or converted form continue to exist.[6] The right is not restricted to tangible assets, such as the sovereigns in a bag or a strong box referred to in the older cases, but applies equally to a chose in action, such as a banker's debt to his customer.[7] Moreover it has long been settled that the right to follow at common law is not determined by a change in the form of the asset, provided it can still be identified, as by the purchase of other property, or paying money into a separate account at a bank, and, perhaps, making payments out of the account for the purchase of other assets which can be shown to have been purchased wholly with it.[8] The difficulty which may arise is as to the continued identification of the asset, particularly if at some stage of the chain of events it has been converted into money, bearing in mind that the common law right is based on the notion that the unauthorised conversion of the asset from one form into another was an act capable of ratification by the owner of the original asset.[9] Accordingly one important limitation on the common law

---

[3] It is submitted that the remedies at law and in equity should be kept distinct, but see *Nelson* v. *Larholt*, [1947] 2 All E.R. 751; [1948] 1 K.B. 339; *G. L. Baker, Ltd.* v. *Medway Building and Supplies Ltd.*, [1958] 2 All E.R. 532 (reversed on other grounds, [1958] 3 All E.R. 540, C.A.) and my comment in (1959) 22 M.L.R. 87. Cf. (1971), 34 M.L.R. 12 and (1973), 2 A.A.L.R. 198 (F.O.B. Babafemi).

[4] Section 78.

[5] As in the typical case of principal and agent; contrast the case where there is merely the relationship of debtor and creditor, where there is no right to follow.

[6] *Miller* v. *Race* (1785), 1 Burr. 452; *Banque Belge* v. *Hambrouck*, [1921] 1 K.B. 321, C.A.; *Re Diplock's Estate*, [1947] 1 All E.R. 522; [1947] Ch. 716, per Wynn-Parry at pp. 534, 535, 744–747; affd on this point but reversed on others, [1948] 2 All E.R. 318; [1948] Ch. 465, C.A.; C.A. decision affirmed *sub nom. Ministry of Health* v. *Simpson*, [1950] 2 All E.R. 1137; [1951] A.C. 251, H.L., where, however, the claim *in rem* was not considered.

[7] *Banque Belge* v. *Hambrouck*, *supra*; *Re Diplock's Estate*, *supra*, C.A.

[8] *Taylor* v. *Plumer* (1815), 3 M. & S. 562; *Banque Belge* v. *Hambrouck*, *supra*; *Re Diplock's Estate*, *supra*.

[9] Per Lord Parker of Waddington in *Sinclair* v. *Brougham*, [1914] A.C. 398, at p. 441; [1914–15] All E.R. Rep. 622, at p. 643, H.L.; *Re Diplock's Estate*, [1948] 2 All E.R. 318, at p. 345; [1948] Ch. 465, at p. 518, C.A. But see Lord Denning's extra-judicial comment in (1949), 65 L.Q.R. 37, 41.

remedy was that the common law found itself unable to identify money in a mixed fund. This has been explained as being due to the materialistic approach of the common law coupled with and encouraged by the limited range of remedies available to it, particularly the absence of the equitable device of a declaration of charge.[10] Once the money of A became mixed with the money of B, identification in a physical sense became impossible and the common law was helpless. It made no difference whether the mixing was of sovereigns in a bag, funds in a banking account, or by the purchase of property partly with A's money and partly with B's. The difficulty was purely one of fact.[11]

Another limitation on the common law remedy was inevitable as the common law did not recognise equitable interests in property. A beneficiary under a trust could not at law follow the property in the hands of the trustee, though he could take steps in equity to compel the trustee to follow the trust property into the hands of a stranger to the trust.

It should be added that the right at law is not restricted to cases where there is a fiduciary relationship.[12]

b Tracing in equity

(i) *General position.* The law was exhaustively considered by the Court of Appeal in *Re Diplock's Estate*,[13] explaining the earlier important House of Lords decision in *Sinclair* v. *Brougham*,[14] from which it appears that the remedy in equity is much wider than the remedy at common law. The facts of *Re Diplock's Estate*[13] were refreshingly simple. Caleb Diplock, who died in 1936, by his will directed his executors to apply his residuary estate of over a quarter of a million pounds "for such charitable institution or institutions or other charitable or benevolent object or objects in England as my acting executors or executor may in their or his absolute discretion select". The executors had distributed over £200,000 among 139 charitable institutions before the validity of this disposition was successfully challenged by the next-of-kin.[15] Having exhausted their primary remedy against the personal representatives for their misapplication of the residuary estate,[16] the next-of-kin sought to recover the balance from the wrongly paid charities, claiming alternatively *in personam* and *in rem*. The claim *in personam* was allowed by the House of Lords, affirming the Court of Appeal. The claim *in rem*, i.e. the right of the next-of-kin to trace their claims into the hands of the charities, did not come before the House of Lords but was considered at length by the Court of Appeal. It is, of course, the claim *in rem* with which we are now concerned. The general principle laid down is that whenever there is an initial fiduciary relationship, the beneficial owner of an equitable

---

10   *Re Diplock's Estate*, [1948] 2 All E.R. 318; [1948] Ch. 465, C.A., at pp. 346; 520 respectively.
11   *Taylor* v. *Plumer* (1815), 3 M. & S. 562; *Re Diplock's Estate, supra*, C.A.
12   *Sinclair* v. *Brougham*, [1914] A.C. 398; [1914–15] All E.R. Rep. 622, H.L., *per* Haldane L.C. at pp. 420; 631.
13   *Supra.*
14   [1914] A.C. 398; [1914–15] All E.R. Rep. 622.
15   *Chichester Diocesan Fund* v. *Simpson*, [1944] 2 All E.R. 60; [1944] A.C. 341, H.L., and see Chapter 2, Section 3c, p. 38, *ante*.
16   Not surprisingly, the executors could not satisfy the claims of the next-of-kin and terms of compromise were approved by the court. It is believed that at least one of the executors committed suicide as a consequence of taking on the executorship.

proprietary[17] interest in property can trace it into the hands of anyone holding the property, except a *bona fide* purchaser for value without notice whose title, is, as usual, inviolable.[18] It is settled, at least as far as the Court of Appeal,[19] and probably in the House of Lords,[20] that there is no right to trace unless there was at some stage a fiduciary relationship of some kind sufficient to give rise to an equitable right of property. It is not restricted to the relationship of trustee and *cestui que trust* under a trust, actual or constructive, but includes other relationships, not precisely laid down, such as that of principal and agent. But if there has never been any fiduciary relationship at all, there is no right to trace: it is not enough merely to show a case of unjust enrichment, i.e. that the property of A has, without justification, got into the hands of B. It has been pointed out[1] that the requirement of an initial fiduciary relationship produces the paradoxical result that a person having merely an equitable interest may be in a better position to follow or trace than one who is both the legal and equitable owner, since the equitable remedy is more persistent than the legal one.

The equitable remedy, by contrast with the common law remedy, recognised and protected equitable interests, and the metaphysical approach of equity, coupled with and encouraged by the far reaching remedy of a declaration of charge, enabled equity to identify money in a mixed fund. "Equity, so to speak, is able to draw up a balance sheet, on the right hand side of which appears the composite fund, and on its left hand side the two or more funds of which it is deemed to be made up".[2] The appropriate equitable form of relief may accordingly be either in the form of an order to restore an unmixed sum of money (or property acquired by means of such a sum), or a declaration of charge on a mixed fund (or property acquired by means of such a fund).

The remedy is somewhat restricted where it is sought to trace into the hands of an innocent volunteer, as he is called, that is someone who takes without notice but does not give value. Even here there is no difficulty in tracing into the hands of an innocent volunteer if there is no question of mixing.[3] But if the volunteer mixes the money with money of his own, or receives it mixed from the fiduciary agent, there is an important limitation. Although the volunteer must admit the claim of the equitable owner, "he is not precluded from setting up his own claim in respect of the moneys of his own which have been contri-

---

[17] See *Lister* v. *Stubbs* (1890), 45 Ch.D. 1, C.A.; (1959), 75 L.Q.R. 234 (R. H. Maudsley) at 243 *et seq.* But note that in the administration of a deceased's estate a mere unsatisfied creditor has a similar equitable right to follow assets of the estate into the hands of devisees and legatees and those claiming through them for the purpose of obtaining payment—see *Salih* v. *Atchi*, [1961] A.C. 778, P.C.

[18] *Thomson* v. *Clydesdale Bank*, [1893] A.C. 282, H.L.; *Coleman* v. *Bucks & Oxon Union Bank*, [1897] 2 Ch. 243; *Sinclair* v. *Brougham*, [1914] A.C. 398; [1914–15] All E.R. Rep. 622, H.L. *Re Diplock's Estate*, [1948] 2 All E.R. 318; [1948] Ch. 465, C.A., at pp. 356, 539. Cf. *Nelson* v. *Larholt*, [1947] 2 All E.R. 751; [1948] 1 K.B. 339; *G. L. Baker, Ltd.* v. *Medway Building and Supplies, Ltd.*, [1958] 2 All E.R. 532 (this point was not discussed on appeal—[1958] 3 All E.R. 540).

[19] *Re Diplock's Estate, supra*, C.A.

[20] *Sinclair* v. *Brougham, supra*, H.L., *per* Lords Haldane, Parker and Atkinson. *Contra, semble*, Lord Dunedin.

[1] (1959), 75 L.Q.R. 234 (R. H. Maudsley), a valuable article on this topic. The requirement of fiduciary relationship is criticised by Goff and Jones, *The Law of Restitution*, pp. 40–43.

[2] *Re Diplock's Estate*, [1948] 2 All E.R. 318, at p. 346; [1948] Ch. 465, at p. 520, C.A.

[3] *Banque Belge* v. *Hambrouck*, [1921] 1 K.B. 321, C.A.; *Re Diplock's Estate*, [1948] 2 All E.R. 318, at p. 359; [1948] Ch. 465, at p. 539, C.A.

buted to the mixed fund. The result is that they share *pari passu*. It would be inequitable for the volunteer to claim priority for the reason that he is a volunteer: it would be equally inequitable for the true owner of the money to claim priority over the volunteer, for the volunteer is innocent and cannot be said to act unconscionably if he claims equal treatment for himself".[4] It may be added that "money" is used in a wide sense to include not only cash in hand but cash at the bank and cheques.[5] Further consideration must be given to tracing into a mixed fund.

(ii) *Mixing of trust property with the trustee's*[6] *own property.* In the rare case where the amalgam of mixed assets is such that they cannot be sufficiently distinguished and treated separately, the whole amalgam is regarded as trust property. In the leading case of *Lupton* v. *White*[7] the defendant, an accounting party, had mixed the plaintiff's lead ore of unascertainable amount with his own lead ore, and Lord Eldon referred to

> "the great principle, familiar both at law and in equity, that, if a man, having undertaken to keep the property of another distinct, mixes it with his own, the whole must both at law and in equity be taken to be the property of the other, until the former puts the subject under such circumstances, that it may be distinguished as satisfactorily, as it might have been before that unauthorised mixture upon his part".

The point is that the onus is on the trustee to distinguish th e separate assets, and to the extent that he fails to do so, they belong to the trust.

Generally, however, it is possible to distinguish the separate contributions of the trust property and the trustee's own property to the mixed fund, and here the basic principle is that the *cestui que trust* is entitled to a first charge on the mixed fund or any property which is purchased thereout.[8] Commonly the mixing takes place in an active banking account when, under the rule in *Re Hallett's Estate*,[9] the trustee is presumed to draw out his own moneys first, and is deemed not to draw on the trust moneys until his own moneys have been exhausted, no matter in what order the moneys were paid in. This is said to be based on a presumption against a breach of trust—or rather a further breach of trust, for any mixing of trust moneys and other moneys is of course improper. Thus if a trustee has £1,000 of his own money in his account, pays in first £2,000 of trust moneys and then a further £1,000 of his own money, and subsequently withdraws £2,000 for his own purposes, the *cestuis que trust* are entitled to say that the £2,000 remaining in the account is trust property. The presumption is not, however, extended to enable a *cestui que trust* to claim, once the trust funds have been drawn upon, that any subsequent payment in of private moneys is to be treated as being made in replacement of such withdrawals in breach of trust.[10]

---

[4] *Re Diplock's Estate*, [1948] 2 All E.R. 318, at p. 357; [1948] Ch. 465, at p. 539, C.A.; *Sinclair* v. *Brougham*, [1914] A.C. 398; [1914–15] All E.R. Rep. 622, H.L.; cf. Maudsley, *op. cit.*, pp. 249 *et seq.*

[5] *Re Diplock's Estate*, [1948] 2 All E.R. 318, at pp. 347, 348; [1948] Ch. 465, at pp. 521, 522, C.A.

[6] Trustee in this section is used, where the context admits, to include other fiduciary agents.

[7] (1805), 15 Ves. 432; *Re Tilley's Will Trusts*, [1967] 2 All E.R. 303; [1967] Ch. 1179.

[8] *Re Hallett's Estate* (1880), 13 Ch.D. 696, C.A.; *Re Pumfrey* (1882), 22 Ch.D. 255; *Re Oatway*, [1903] 2 Ch. 356; *Re Diplock's Estate*, [1948] 2 All E.R. 318, 356; [1948] Ch. 465, 539, C.A.

[9] (1880), 13 Ch. D. 696, C.A.

[10] *Roscoe (James)(Bolton), Ltd.* v. *Winder*, [1915] 1 Ch. 62.

Thus if in the illustration given above the £2,000 had been withdrawn before the £1,000 private moneys had been paid in, the *cestuis que trust* would only have been able to claim £1,000 of the balance in the account as trust property.

The rule in *Re Hallett's Estate*[11] does not, however, operate so as to derogate from the basic principle that the *cestui que trust* is entitled to a first charge on the mixed fund or any property which is purchased thereout. In *Re Oatway*[12] the trustee had mixed his own and trust moneys in a banking account. He drew on this account to purchase shares, leaving a balance exceeding the amount of the trust moneys paid in. He subsequently made further drawings which exhausted the account, so that it was useless to proceed against the account: these later drawings were dissipated and did not result in any traceable assets. On these facts it was held that the *cestuis que trust* had a charge on the shares for the trust money paid into the account. The original charge on the mixed fund would, it was said, continue on each and every part thereof, notwithstanding changes of form, unless and until the trust money paid into the mixed account was restored and the trust fund reinstated by the due investment of the money in the joint names of the proper trustees.

Re Oatway[13] did not raise the question whether a *cestui que trust* is entitled to any profit made out of the purchase of property by a trustee out of a fund consisting of his personal moneys which he mixed with the trust moneys, and the discussion of this problem in *Re Tilley's Will Trusts*[14] was *obiter*, for reasons that are explained below. The question may arise in perhaps three main ways: suppose a mixed banking account of £1,000 trust moneys and £2,000 of the trustee's own moneys. First, the trustee may use the whole £3,000 to purchase an asset; secondly, he may withdraw £2,000 for this purpose, leaving enough in the account to restore the £1,000 trust moneys; or, thirdly, he may withdraw £2,500 for the same purpose, leaving only £500 in the account. Suppose further that the purchased asset doubles in value—what claim could the *cestuis que trust* make in each case?

In the first situation, where the whole of a mixed fund is used to purchase an asset one view is that the *cestui que trust* does not get any benefit from the increase in value, but is merely in the words of Jessel M.R. in *Re Hallett's Estate*,[15] "entitled to a charge on the property purchased for the amount of the trust money laid out in the purchase". Maudsley,[16] though he considered the other view would be a more satisfactory solution, thought that the limited right of the *cestuis que trust* recognised by this dictum represented the existing state of the law, and Lewin[17] thought the contrary would only be arguable in the House of Lords. Ungoed-Thomas J., however, in *Re Tilley's Will Trusts*[18] has expressed the view that the charge of the *cestuis que trust* on the purchased property

---

[11] *Supra.*
[12] [1903] 2 Ch. 356.
[13] *Supra.*
[14] [1967] 2 All E.R. 303; [1967] Ch. 1179. This case is discussed in (1968), 26 C.L.J. 28 (Gareth Jones).
[15] (1880), 13 Ch.D. 696, at p. 709.
[16] (1959), 75 L.Q.R. 234, at p. 246.
[17] *Law of Trusts*, 16th Ed., p. 654.
[18] *Supra.* The High Court of Australia has also adopted this view—*Scott* v. *Scott* (1963), 109 C.L.R. 649.

will be not merely for the amount of the trust moneys but for a proportionate part of the increased value. The dictum of Jessel M.R. cited above, and a similar dictum by Lord Parker in *Sinclair* v. *Brougham*[19] were distinguished and explained on the ground that in those cases the judges were not addressing their minds to the question whether the beneficiary could claim a proportion of the property corresponding to his own contribution to its purchase. Ungoed-Thomas J.'s view can be supported by contending that the trustee would otherwise be profiting from his breach of trust, and is consistent with the undoubted rule[20] that if a trustee wrongly uses trust money alone to pay the whole of the purchase price in respect of the purchase of an asset, the beneficiaries can elect either to treat the purchased asset as trust property or to treat the purchased asset as security for the recouping of the trust money. The effect of applying the opinion of Ungoed-Thomas J. is to give the *cestuis que trust* the same right of election where the asset is purchased out of a mixed fund with regard to the proportionate part thereof.

In the second situation it seems that the inference to be drawn even from *Re Tilley's Will Trusts*[1] is that the *cestuis que trust* would have no claim to any part of the profits, but would be restricted to their claim to the £1,000 remaining in the account on the basis of *Re Hallett's Estate*.[2] Suppose, however, that before the matter comes before the court the trustee has withdrawn and dissipated the remaining £1,000. As we have seen the *cestuis que trust* will have a charge on the purchased property, but will it be for the amount of the trust moneys or for a proportionate part of the increased value. The language of *Re Oatway*[3] suggests the former, but Ungoed-Thomas J. in *Re Tilley's Will Trusts*[4] has pointed out that the question of a profit was not raised and the judgment was therefore not directed towards that point. It would seem a strange result, however, if the position of the beneficiaries were to be improved by the trustee dissipating the balance of the account.

The third situation would, as to the £500 trust money necessarily used in the purchase, seem to be governed by the same principles as the first, and as to the other £500 by the same principles as the second.

Even on the basis of the principles set out in *Re Tilley's Will Trusts*[5] the mere fact that a mixed fund has been used to purchase an asset is not necessarily enough to enable a beneficiary to claim that he is entitled to adopt the purchase to the extent to which the trust moneys have contributed thereto, and that he is accordingly entitled to a due proportion of the profits. Such a claim actually failed in *Re Tilley's Will Trusts*[6] itself where a sole trustee, who was also life tenant of the trust, had mixed the trust moneys with her own moneys in her bank account, which became overdrawn on the purchase of an asset, though subsequent payments in of her own moneys left the account in credit to an amount exceeding the amount of the trust fund. The trustee carried out many

---

[19] [1914] A.C. 398; [1914–15] All E.R. Rep. 622, at pp. 442; 643.
[20] See *ante*, p. 365.
[1] *Supra*.
[2] *Supra*.
[3] *Supra*.
[4] [1967] 2 All E.R. 303, at p. 308; [1967] Ch. 1179, at p. 1185.
[5] *Supra*.
[6] *Re Tilley's Will Trusts, supra*, at p. 313; 1193.

property dealings, had ample overdraft facilities and had no need, nor, as the judge found, any intention of relying on the trust moneys for the purchase. Ungoed-Thomas J.'s view[7] was "that if, having regard to all the circumstances of the case objectively considered, it appears that the trustee has in fact, whatever his intention, laid out trust moneys in or towards a purchase, then the beneficiaries are entitled to the property purchased and any profits which it produces to the extent to which it has been paid for out of the trust moneys". Applying this test he held that the trust moneys were not so laid out: they were not invested in properties at all but merely went in reduction of the trustee's overdraft which was in reality the source of the purchase moneys.

(iii) *Mixing of two trust funds, or of trust moneys with moneys of an innocent volunteer.* Where the contest is between two claimants to a mixed fund made up of moneys held on behalf of the two of them respectively and mixed together by the trustee, they share *pari passu*, and if property is acquired by means of the mixed fund, each is entitled to a charge *pari passu* and neither is entitled to priority over the other.[8] Further, as against the trustee, they can agree to take the property itself, so as to become tenants in common in shares proportional to the amounts for which either could claim a charge.[9] The same rules apply where moneys of a *cestui que trust* and an innocent volunteer are mixed, whether the mixing is done by the innocent volunteer or the trustee,[10] though it has been argued[11] that this puts the innocent volunteer in too favourable a position. The suggestion is that it is unreasonable that, as is the law, an innocent volunteer who purchases, say, £2,000 stock, half with his own and half with trust moneys, and then withdraws half and spends it on living expenses is regarded as withdrawing it rateably from the trust funds and his own funds and is accordingly entitled to share the remaining half equally with the *cestui que trust*. The position, as will be seen, might be even more extreme if the funds were in an active banking account to which the rule in *Clayton's Case*[12] applied, when the innocent volunteer might be entitled to the whole remaining funds.

The above rules as to mixing are modified where the mixing takes place in an active banking account. Where a trustee mixes the funds of two separate trusts,[13] or a volunteer mixes trust moneys with his own moneys,[14] the rule in *Clayton's Case*[15] applies. This rule of convenience, based on so-called presumed intention, is to the effect that withdrawals out of the account are presumed to be made in the same order as payments in, that is to say, first in, first out. The rule will not be extended beyond banking accounts and only applies where there is one unbroken account. Moreover, the rule will not apply if the fund is "unmixed", and a specific withdrawal is earmarked as trust money. Accordingly in

---

[7] In *Re Tilley's Will Trusts*, [1967] 2 All E.R. 303; [1967] Ch. 1179, at p. 313; 1193.

[8] *Re Diplock's Estate*, [1948] 2 All E.R. 318, at pp. 353, 354, 356; [1948] Ch. 475, at pp. 533, 534, 539, C.A.; *Sinclair v. Brougham*, [1914] A.C. 398; [1914–15] All E.R. Rep. 622, H.L. See Maudsley, *op cit.*, pp. 246 et seq.

[9] *Sinclair v. Brougham*, *supra*, per Lord Parker at p. 442; 643; *Re Tilley's Will Trusts*, *supra*.

[10] *Re Diplock's Estate*, *supra*, C.A., at pp. 349, 354, 357; 524, 534, 539; *Sinclair v. Brougham*, *supra*.   [11] Maudsley, *op. cit.*

[12] *Devaynes v. Noble, Clayton's Case* (1816), 1 Mer. 529, 572.

[13] *Re Hallett's Estate*, (1880), 13 Ch.D. 696; *Re Stenning*, [1895] 2 Ch. 433.

[14] *Re Diplock's Estate*, *supra*, C.A., at pp. 364, 554.

[15] *Supra*. For recent applications in other contexts see: *Re Yeovil Glove Co., Ltd.*, [1964] 2 All E.R. 849; [1965] Ch. 148, C.A.; *Re James R. Rutherford & Sons, Ltd.*, [1964] 3 All E.R. 137. For an unorthodox view, see (1963), 79 L.Q.R. 388 (D. A. McConville).

Re Diplock's Estate[16] a charity which paid £1,500 trust moneys into its current account, and later drew out the same sum which it placed in a Post Office Savings Bank account and treated as "Diplock" money was held bound by its own appropriation. The whole sum could accordingly be traced by the next of kin, the rule in *Clayton's Case*[17] not being applicable.

(iv) *Identification.* Tracing is only possible so long as the fund can be followed in a true sense, i.e. so long as, whether mixed or unmixed, it can be located and identified. It presupposes the continued existence of the money either as a separate fund or as part of a mixed fund or as latent in property acquired by means of such a fund. If, on the facts of any individual case, such continued existence is not established, equity is as helpless as the common law itself. Thus tracing is impossible where an innocent volunteer spends the trust money on a dinner,[18] or on education or general living expenses. Again, where an innocent volunteer uses trust money in the alteration and improvement of assets which he already owns, it by no means necessarily follows that the money can be said to be present in the adapted property. In every true sense the money may have disappeared. An example was given in *Re Diplock's Estate*:[19]

> "The owner of a house who, as an innocent volunteer, has trust money in his hands given to him by a trustee uses that money in making an alteration to his house so as to fit it better to his own personal needs. The result may add not one penny to the value of the house. Indeed, the alteration may well lower its value, for the alteration, though convenient to the owner, may be highly inconvenient in the eyes of a purchaser. Can it be said in such cases that the trust money can be traced and extracted from the altered asset? Clearly not, for the money will have disappeared leaving no monetary trace behind.[20]"

Yet again the right to trace comes to an end if an innocent volunteer uses the trust money to pay off a debt, even though secured, and even though the money was given to him for this purpose. The effect of such payment is that the debt is extinguished and any security ceases to exist, and the *cestui que trust* cannot claim to be subrogated to the rights of the creditor.[21] It might, perhaps, be otherwise if the debt paid off constituted a loan which has been used to purchase some identifiable asset.

(v) *Claim inequitable.* The general principle that tracing, an equitable remedy, will not be granted in a case where it would lead to an inequitable result, was an additional reason why trust moneys used by an innocent volunteer in alterations to his house could not be traced.[22] The equitable remedy is a declaration of charge, enforceable by sale. This would be equitable where the land was purchased with moneys of the innocent volunteer mixed with trust moneys, but it would be different where the innocent volunteer has contributed not money but the land itself. Where this is his contribution it would be inequitable to

---

[16] [1948] 2 All E.R. 318, at pp. 363, 364; [1948] Ch. 465, at pp. 551, 552, C.A. (reversed on the facts at pp. 429–432; 559).
[17] (1816), 1 Mer. 529.
[18] *Re Diplock's Estate, supra*, C.A., at 347; 521.
[19] *Supra*, C.A., at pp. 361, 547.
[20] Another difficulty in such case would be as to whether the charge should be on the whole of the land or only on that part which was altered or reconstructed.
[21] *Re Diplock's Estate, supra*, C.A., at 362; 549.
[22] *Re Diplock's Estate, supra*, C.A., at pp. 361; 547–548.

compel the innocent volunteer to take a charge merely for the value[1] of the land, and a declaration of charge is the only possible remedy available.

(vi) *Interest.* Where a tracing claim succeeds, it appears that the claimant is entitled to interest, i.e. the interest in fact earned by the trust moneys or the property into which they have been traced.[2]

c The claims *in personam*

It is convenient to mention here the alternative claim by the next of kin in *Re Diplock's Estate*[3] against the innocent recipients by means of a direct action *in personam* in equity. The House of Lords expressly affirmed the Court of Appeal judgment on this point, which had asserted the right of an unpaid or underpaid creditor, legatee or next of kin to bring a direct action in equity against the persons to whom the estate had been wrongfully distributed. Contrary to what had previously been commonly thought, it makes no difference whether the wrongful distribution was due to a mistake of law or fact;[4] it does not matter that the wrongful recipient has no title at all and was a stranger to the estate, and there is no requirement that the estate must be administered by the court. The Court of Appeal observed[5] "as regards the conscience of the defendant on which in this, as in other jurisdictions, equity is said to act, it is *prima facie*, at least, a sufficient circumstance that the defendant, as events have proved, has received some share of the estate to which he was not entitled". Nevertheless it seems somewhat inequitable that an innocent volunteer can be called upon to refund—admittedly without interest—until the claim is barred by the Limitation Act, for he may well alter his position on the assumption that the payment was valid.[6] The claim, however, is subject to the qualification that the primary remedy is against the wrongdoing executor or administrator, and the direct claim in equity against those overpaid or wrongly paid is limited to the amount which the *cestui que trust* cannot recover in the primary action.

Finally it must be made clear that it is at least doubtful whether a direct action in equity lies in similar circumstances in the execution of a trust as opposed to the administration of the estate of a deceased person. In the House of Lords, Lord Simonds, whose speech was concurred in by all the other Law Lords, said[7]

"it is important in the discussion of this question to remember that the particular branch of the jurisdiction of the Court of Chancery with which we are concerned relates to the administration of assets of a deceased person. While in the development of this jurisdiction certain principles were established which were

---

[1] You cannot have a charge for land, and a charge for the value of land is an entirely different thing.
[2] *Re Diplock's Estate*, [1948] 2 All E.R. 318, at pp. 345, 346; [1948] Ch. 465, at pp. 517, 557, C.A.
[3] *Supra.*
[4] Contrast the common law action for money had and received which will only lie where there is a mistake of fact.
[5] In *Re Diplock's Estate, supra*, C.A. at 337; 503.
[6] (1957), 73 L.Q.R. 48 (G. H. Jones), cf. (1961), 24 M.L.R. 85 (R. Goff).
[7] *Re Diplock*, [1950] 2 All E.R. 1137, at p. 1140; [1951] A.C. 251, at pp. 265–266, H.L. But see *G. L. Baker, Ltd.* v. *Medway Building and Supplies, Ltd.*, [1958] 3 All E.R. 540, C.A.; *Eddis* v. *Chichester Constable*, [1969] 1 All E.R. 546 affd. without reference to this point [1969] 2 All E.R. 912; [1969] 2 Ch. 345, C.A.

common to it and to the comparable jurisdiction in the execution of trusts, I do not find in history or in logic any justification for an argument which denies the possibility of an equitable right in the administration of assets because, as it is alleged, no comparable right existed in the execution of trusts".

3 ACCOUNT

a Actions of account

At common law an action of account could be brought in certain special cases, namely, against a guardian in socage, a bailiff and a receiver,[8] and by statute,[9] by one joint tenant or tenant in common against another, to compel him to account where he had received more than his fair share.[10] The common law action, however, which might be alternative to some other action such as an action in debt, *assumpsit*, or for money had and received was said by Alderson B.[11] to be "so inconvenient, that it has been long discontinued, and parties have gone into a court of equity in preference."[12] Lord Redesdale has explained this more fully. "The writ of account at common law," he said,[13] "did not exclude, but rather was superseded by, the jurisdiction of the courts of equity on this subject; because the proceeding in equity was found to be the more convenient mode of calling parties to account—partly on account of the difficulty attending the process under the old writ of account, but chiefly from the advantage of compelling the party to account upon oath, according to the practice of courts of equity."

It did not follow from this that a person with a legal claim had a right to an account in equity, as he would normally have in an equitable matter, such as where a *cestui que trust* sought an account from his trustee, or a mortgagor from a mortgagee in possession. The Court of Chancery refused to lay down definite rules as to when it would allow a bill for an account, and when it would leave the plaintiff to his action at law. Thus Cottenham L.C. said[14] it was "impossible with precision to lay down rules or establish definitions as to the cases in which it may be proper for this court to exercise this jurisdiction". The principle on which the court acted was, however, reasonably clear: jurisdiction would not be exercised where the matter could be as fully and conveniently dealt with by a court of common law.[15]

---

[8] See *The Earl of Devonshire's Case* (1607), 11 Co. Rep. 89a.

[9] Administration of Justice Act 1705, s. 27, now repealed by the Law of Property (Amendment) Act 1924, s. 10 and Sched. 10.

[10] *Sturton* v. *Richardson* (1844), 13 M. & W. 17; *Ex parte Bax* (1751), 2 Ves. Sen. 388.

[11] In *Sturton* v. *Richardson, supra*, at p. 20; Blackstone's *Commentaries,* Vol. III, 164.

[12] It was resuscitated, however, by the plaintiff in *Godfrey* v. *Saunders* (1770), 3 Wils. K.B. 73, because his action in Chancery had been "fruitlessly depending there for more than twelve years".

[13] *A.-G.* v. *Dublin Corporation* (1827), 1 Bli. N.S. 312, 337; *Carlisle Corporation* v. *Wilson* (1807), 13 Ves. 276.

[14] *North-Eastern Rail. Co.* v. *Martin* (1848), 2 Ph. 758, 762 in some reports *sub nom. South-Eastern Rail. Co.* v. *Martin*.

[15] *Shepard* v. *Brown* (1862), 4 Giff. 203; *Southampton Dock Co.* v. *Southampton Harbour & Pier Board* (1870), L.R. 11 Eq. 254; (1964), 80 L.Q.R. 203 (S. J. Stoljar).

In practice, equity would normally exercise its jurisdiction in the following cases. First, where there were mutual accounts, unless these were extremely simple.[16] Secondly where there was some confidential relationship between the parties, as between principal and agent, or between partners.[17] A principal could normally maintain an action of account against the agent by reason of the confidence reposed and the fact that the only way of ascertaining the state of the account was by the equitable procedure of discovery,[18] but the agent had no corresponding right for the facts were within his knowledge and he placed no special confidence in his principal.[19] Thirdly where the account was so complicated that a court of law would be incompetent to examine it, a question of degree left somewhat indefinite.[20] Fourthly, Lindley L.J. has said[1] that an account would be ordered where the plaintiff would have had a legal right to have money ascertained and paid to him by the defendant, if the defendant had not wrongfully prevented it from accruing. Fifthly, as regards waste, although this was normally a tort for which a remedy lay at law, an account would be ordered where an injunction was also sought, and waste had already been committed, in order to prevent the need for two actions,[2] and in any case of equitable waste, which was not recognised at common law.[3] Sixthly, an account was also ordered as incident to an injunction, but not otherwise, in cases of infringement of patent rights.[4]

The Judicature Acts[5] have now assigned actions for an account to the Chancery Division. However in a simple case an account may be taken in the Queen's Bench Division,[6] but normally it will be transferred to the Chancery Division[7] or referred to an official referee.[8]

b Wilful default

In addition to the ordinary order for an account, an order may be made for an account on the footing of wilful default, under which the accounting party will be charged not merely with what he has actually received, but also with what,

---

[16] *Foley* v. *Hill* (1844) 1 Ph. 399; *Phillips* v. *Phillips* (1852), 9 Hare 471; *Fluker* v. *Taylor* (1855), 3 Drew. 183.

[17] But there is no such relationship between a banker and his customers—*Foley* v. *Hill, supra*.

[18] *Beaumont* v. *Boultbee* (1802), 7 Ves. 599; *Mackenzie* v. *Johnson* (1819), 4 Madd. 373.

[19] *Padwick* v. *Stanley* (1852), 9 Hare 627.

[20] *Taff Vale Rail. Co.* v. *Nixon* (1847), 1 H.L.Cas. 111; *North Eastern Rail. Co.* v. *Martin* (1848), 2 Ph. 758; *Phillips* v. *Phillips, supra*.

[1] In *London, Chatham & Dover Rail. Co.* v. *South Eastern Rail. Co.*, [1892] 1 Ch. 120, 140, C.A.; affd., [1893] A.C. 429, H.L.; *M'Intosh* v. *Great Western Railway* (1850), 2 Mac. & G. 74.

[2] *Jesus College* v. *Bloom* (1745), 3 Atk. 262; *Parrott* v. *Palmer* (1834), 3 My. & K. 632.

[3] *Duke of Leeds* v. *Earl of Amherst* (1846), 2 Ph. 117.

[4] *Smith* v. *London & South Western Rail. Co.* (1854), 1 Kay. 408; *Price's Patent Candle Co.* v. *Bauwen's Patent Candle Co.* (1858), 4 K. & J. 727; *De Vitre* v. *Betts* (1873), L.R. 6. H.L. 319; see now Patents Act 1949, s. 60.

[5] Judicature Act 1873, s. 34, repealed and replaced by Judicature Act 1925, s. 56 (1) (b).

[6] *York* v. *Stowers*, [1883] W.N. 174.

[7] *Leslie* v. *Clifford* (1884), 50 L.T. 590, D.C.

[8] *Newbould* v. *Steade* (1882), 49 L.T. 649, C A

but for his wilful default, he ought to have received. In general, in order to obtain an account on this footing, the plaintiff must allege in his pleadings, and prove, at least one act of wilful default,[9] though this is not necessary in the case of a mortgagee in possession where an account is always ordered on this footing as a matter of course.[10] If in the course of an ordinary account facts come out which, if proved at the hearing, would have entitled the plaintiff to a decree on the footing of wilful default, an account on this footing may be added,[11] though it seems to be necessary in such case for an appropriate amendment to be made to the pleadings.[12] This does not in any way relax the rule that at least one instance of wilful default must be established before an account on this footing can be ordered.[13] An account on the footing of wilful default can now be made in proceedings on an originating summons.[14]

c Settled accounts

The plea of settled accounts, sometimes less happily referred to as account stated, is a defence to an action of account. It is a plea that the account between the parties has been agreed for valuable consideration, and consequently cannot be gone into again. It is an available plea where there have been mutual debits and credits. Romer J. explained the principle in *Anglo-American Asphalt Co.* v. *Crowley Russell & Co.*:[15]

> "Where A owes, or may owe, B money, and B owes, or may owe, A money, and in their accounts they strike a balance and agree that balance, that truly represents the financial result of their transactions. There is mutuality in it, and whereas A may be giving up something or B may be giving up something, for the purpose of settling the matter between them, they expressly or by implication agree to a conventional position which is established by striking a balance, and that results in what is called a settled account. But that has no application to a case . . . where the whole accounting is to be rendered by one party to the other."

In order to constitute a settled account, it is not necessary that it be signed by the parties, nor that vouchers should be delivered up.[16] It seems, indeed, that settled accounts could be orally agreed and proved, though this may be difficult to establish in practice.[17]

---

[9] *Sleight* v. *Lawson* (1857), 3 K. & J. 292; R.S.C., O. 18, r. 12. Cf. *Re Wells*, [1962] 2 All E.R. 826, C.A.

[10] *Mayer* v. *Murray* (1878), 8 Ch.D. 424; *White* v. *City of London Brewery* (1889), 42 Ch.D. 237, C.A.

[11] *Re Youngs* (1885), 30 Ch.D. 421, C.A. Note that in an action for active breaches of trust, relief can only be granted in respect of breaches alleged in the pleadings and established at the trial—*Re Wrightson*, [1908] 1 Ch. 789.

[12] *Job* v. *Job* (1877), 6 Ch.D. 562; *Mayer* v. *Murray, supra; Re Symons* (1882), 21 Ch.D. 757.

[13] *Re Youngs, supra.*

[14] R.S.C., O. 85, r. 4. As to the old rule see *Re Hengler*, [1893] W.N. 37. Cf. Chapter 12, Section 1g, p. 368, *ante*.

[15] [1945] 2 All E.R. 324, at p. 331; *Hunter* v. *Belcher* (1864), 2 De G.J. & Sm. 194. Cf. *Siquiera* v. *Noronha*, [1934] A.C. 332, P.C.

[16] *Willis* v. *Jernegan* (1741), 2 Atk. 251; *Yourell* v. *Hibernian Bank*, [1918] A.C. 372, H.L.

[17] *Phillips-Higgins* v. *Harper*, [1954] 1 All E.R. 116; affd., [1954] 2 All E.R. 51; [1954] 1 Q.B. 411, C.A.

As has been said above, the normal effect of a plea of settled accounts is to prevent the accounts being reconsidered.[18] Exceptionally settled accounts may be re-opened on the ground of fraud or mistake, the effect of which is that the whole accounts may be reconsidered or new accounts taken. Alternatively the court may merely grant the plaintiff liberty to surcharge and falsify.[19] The main factors which are taken into account by the court in deciding whether the plaintiff is to be allowed to re-open the account, or merely to surcharge and falsify, are whether the claim is based on fraud or only mistake, and whether there is any fiduciary relationship between the parties. The number and amount of the errors is also material and the time that has elapsed since the accounts were settled.

According to Cottenham L.C. in *Allfrey* v. *Allfrey*,[20] the original rule was that in the case of mistakes and omissions an order to surcharge and falsify was appropriate, but that in a case of fraud the accounts should be re-opened.[1] Later, he said, it was held[2] that even in a case of fraud an order to surcharge and falsify might be the appropriate remedy. Either order, he pointed out, might cause injustice and in deciding which order should be made care should be taken that the innocent and injured party should not suffer. It is submitted, however, that Jessel M.R. was right[3] in continuing to regard the re-opening of the accounts as *prima facie* the proper remedy in a case of fraud. But after a long time it may well be that even for fraud the proper remedy would be to surcharge and falsify.[4]

Where there is no fraud, the relationship between the parties is of particular importance. Though an account may be re-opened for mistake alone,[5] the *prima facie* remedy here is an order to surcharge and falsify. If, however, there is a fiduciary relationship between the parties, the court will generally be prepared to re-open the accounts, even for mistake.[6]

It may be added that the court has statutory jurisdiction to re-open a settled account with a moneylender under the Moneylenders Act 1900.[7]

4 RESCISSION

a General

The right to rescind a contract is a right which a party to a contract may have in certain circumstances to declare that he no longer accepts the contract but entirely rejects and repudiates it. In such case, unless and until the party entitled

---

[18] *Darthez* v. *Lee* (1836), 2 Y. & C.Ex. 5; *Newen* v. *Wetten* (1862), 31 Beav. 315.

[19] *Per* Hardwicke L.C. in *Pit* v. *Cholmondeley* (1754), 2 Ves.Sen. 565, at p. 566: "If any of the parties can show an omission for which credit ought to be, that is a surcharge; or if any thing is inserted, that is a wrong charge, he is at liberty to show it, and that is falsification; but that must be by proof on his side." But this does not entitle the defendant to insert items in his own favour, *Mozeley* v. *Cowie* (1877), 47 L.J. Ch. 271.

[20] (1849), 1 Mac. & G. 87.

[1] See *Vernon* v. *Vawdrey* (1740), 2 Atk. 119; *Oldaker* v. *Lavender* (1833), 6 Sim. 239.

[2] *Brownell* v. *Brownell* (1786), 2 Bro.C.C. 62; *Millar* v. *Craig* (1843), 6 Beav. 433.

[3] See *Gething* v. *Keighly* (1878), 9 Ch.D. 547.

[4] *Millar* v. *Craig* (1843), 6 Beav. 433. But accounts have been ordered to be re-opened for fraud after many years—*Vernon* v. *Vawdry, supra* (23 years); *Allfrey* v. *Allfrey, supra* (17 years).

[5] *Pritt* v. *Clay* (1843), 6 Beav. 503.

[6] *Williamson* v. *Barbour* (1877), 9 Ch.D. 529; *Gething* v. *Keighly, supra; Re Webb,* [1894] 1 Ch. 73, C.A.

[7] Section 1.

to do so repudiates the contract, which repudiation must normally be communicated to the other party,[8] it remains fully valid and binding, but an effective repudiation terminates the contract, puts the parties *in statu quo ante* and restores things, as between them, to the position in which they stood before the contract was entered into. Strictly speaking rescission is the act of a party and not the act of a court: if the court makes an appropriate order this is little more than a judicial recognition of the fact that the expression by the party of his determination to repudiate the contract was an effective rescission of the contract.[9] It may be asked, therefore, why the matter should come before the court at all. This may happen for a variety of reasons: for instance, the other party may refuse to accept the repudiation and bring an action on the contract, to which the defence may be that the contract has been rescinded; or, the party who claims the right to rescind, perhaps knowing that his claim is not accepted by the other party, may prefer to bring an action to have the contract set aside; or, commonly, there may be some consequential question on which the decision of the court is required, as to the steps that have to be taken to arrive at the *restitutio in integrum*, the restoring of the parties to their original positions, which is an essential concomitant of rescission. It was because of the ancillary relief commonly sought that, originally, questions of rescission generally arose in the Court of Chancery. The accounts and inquiries that might be necessary to enable *restitutio in integrum* to be implemented could not usually be carried out in a court of common law.[10] Also a court of equity might be prepared to set aside a contract in circumstances which would not render it voidable at common law. But if *restitutio in integrum* merely required the repayment of money paid, or the recovery of property transferred, and the contract was voidable at common law, the matter could be completely remedied by a common law action for money had or received,[11] or trover.[12] Actions for setting aside deeds or other written instruments are now assigned to the Chancery Division.[13]

It may be, of course, that the act relied upon as a ground for rescission will also be a ground for an independent action in tort. Thus a fraudulent misrepresentation which induces a man to enter into a contract may give him a right of action for damages at common law for the tort of deceit. If this is so it may be either alternative or additional to rescission:[14] the party defrauded may either affirm the contract and be compensated for his loss by damages for the tort, or rescind and yet bring his action for deceit to cover any loss beyond

---

[8] Exceptionally communication is not required where election to rescind is shown by retaking goods transferred under the contract, or, at any rate in a case of fraud, where the other party has made communication impossible—*Car and Universal Finance Co.,Ltd.* v. *Caldwell*, [1964] 1 All E.R. 290; [1965] 1 Q.B. 525, C.A.; *Newtons of Wembley, Ltd.* v. *Williams*, [1964] 3 All E.R. 532; [1965] 1 Q.B. 560, C.A.

[9] *Aaron's Reefs, Ltd.* v. *Twiss*, [1896] A.C. 273, H.L.; *United Shoe Machinery Co. of Canada* v. *Brunet*, [1909] A.C. 330, P.C.; *Abram Steamship Co.* v. *Westville Shipping Co.*, [1923] A.C. 773, H.L.

[10] *Erlanger* v. *New Sombrero Phosphate Co.* (1878), 3 App. Cas. 1218, *per* Lord Blackburn at p. 1278.

[11] *Stone* v. *City and County Bank* (1877), 3 C.P.D. 282, C.A.; *Kettlewell* v. *Refuge Assurance Co.*, [1908] 1 K.B. 545, C.A.; affd., [1909] A.C. 243, H.L.

[12] *Jones* v. *Keene* (1841), 2 Mood. & R. 348.

[13] Judicature Act 1925 s. 56 (1) (b).

[14] *Newbigging* v. *Adam* (1886), 34 Ch.D. 582, C.A., *per* Bowen L.J. at 592, affd. *sub nom.* *Adam* v. *Newbigging* (1888), 13 App. Cas. 308, H.L.

restitutio in integrum, which, however, in many cases will be merely nominal.

It may be added that the contract may expressly give a party to it the right to rescind in certain circumstances. Such a right of rescission should however be kept distinct from the right which one party to a contract may have, where the other party has broken a term thereof going directly to the substance of the contract, to repudiate the contract *in toto* and so be relieved from performing his part of it, while retaining the right to sue for damages for breach of contract.[15] In general it will be remembered that breach of contract by one party does not absolve the other party from carrying out his obligation thereunder: the only remedy is damages.

b Grounds upon which rescission may be granted

The main grounds on which a contract may be rescinded are mentioned briefly below, but for a fuller discussion the reader is referred to books on the law of contract,[16] and other works mentioned in the footnotes.

i *Fraudulent misrepresentation.* This rendered a contract voidable both at law and in equity. For this purpose what is relevant is fraud in the common law sense, sometimes called actual fraud, which will sustain an action of deceit. A fraud is proved when it is shown that a false representation has been made knowingly, or without belief in its truth, or recklessly, careless whether it be true or false.[17] The fraudulent party need not have acted with a corrupt motive,[18] but the false statement must have been made with the intent that it should be acted on,[19] and it must actually have been acted on by the other party.[20]

ii *Innocent misrepresentation.* As such, this had no effect at common law, unless incorporated into the contract.[1] In equity, although it might be a good defence to a specific performance action, it was, somewhat illogically, not for a long time regarded as sufficient to enable a court of equity to set the contract aside.[2] From the middle of the nineteenth century, however, the courts of equity have asserted this jurisdiction,[3] which Jessel M.R. explained, in *Redgrave* v. *Hurd*,[4] either on the ground that equity would not permit a man to get a benefit from a statement made by him which has in fact been proved false, or that it would be fraudulent to allow a man to insist upon a contract obtained by the aid of his own false statement. Since the Misrepresentation Act 1967,[5] rescission has been equally available where the misrepresentation has become a term of the contract.

iii *Mere silence.* This does not usually amount to a representation, but it may do so if the concealment gives to the truth which is told the character of

---

[15] *Heilbutt* v. *Hickson* (1872), L.R. 7 C.P. 438; *Wallis* v. *Pratt*, [1910] 2 K.B. 1003, C.A.
[16] E.g. Cheshire and Fifoot, *The Law of Contract*, 8th Ed., Part IV, Chap. II.
[17] *Derry* v. *Peek* (1889), 14 App. Cas. 337, H.L.
[18] *Polhill* v. *Walter* (1832), 3 B. & Ad. 114.
[19] *Peek* v. *Gurney* (1873), L.R. 6 H.L. 377.
[20] *Smith* v. *Chadwick* (1884), 9 App. Cas. 187, H.L.
[1] See, generally, L. A. Sheridan, *Fraud in Equity*, pp. 10 *et seq.*
[2] *Attwood* v. *Small* (1838), 6 Cl. & Fin. 232; *Bartlett* v. *Salmon* (1855), 6 De G.M. & G. 33.
[3] *Reese River Silver Mining Co.* v. *Smith* (1869), L.R. 4 H.L. 64; *Torrance* v. *Bolton* (1872), 8 Ch.App. 118.
[4] (1881), 20 Ch.D. 1 at 12, 13, C.A.
[5] Section 1. The Act came into force on 22 April, 1967. It is criticized in (1967), 30 M.L.R. 369 (P. S. Atiyah and G. H. Treitel); (1967), 31 Con. 234 (J. R. Murdock).

falsehood,[6] or if there is a duty to make disclosure, as is the case where the contract is one *uberrimae fidei*.[7]

iv *Executed contracts entered into as a result of misrepresentation.* If the misrepresentation was fraudulent the fact that the contract has been completed does not destroy the right of rescission. Before the Misrepresentation Act 1967 it was the law that there could be no rescission for innocent misrepresentation after completion of a contract for the sale of land,[8] or, probably, the execution of a formal lease.[9] This rule was less firmly established in other cases.[10] The Act now provides[11] that rescission may be allowed for innocent misrepresentation where the contract has been performed in the same way as where the representation is fraudulent.

v *Mistake.* On principle it is submitted that mistake, if it operates at all, operates equally at law and in equity to make the purported contract void *ab initio*. If the alleged mistake is not operative at common law, the court has no jurisdiction to set aside a contract for that mistake in equity. *Solle* v. *Butcher*,[12] a much criticized decision,[13] but yet a decision of the Court of Appeal, apparently decides, however, that where the contract is not void at law, the court may order rescission where both parties have contracted under a mutual mistake and misapprehension as to their relative and respective rights and rescission would not prejudice third parties.

vi *Constructive fraud.* A contract may be rescinded in equity on the ground of constructive fraud. This term includes in particular undue influence, which will be presumed in the case of certain fiduciary relationships[14] and may be established in other cases by evidence,[15] taking advantage of weakness or necessity, including catching bargains with expectant heirs, breach of fiduciary duty, such as a purchase by a trustee of the trust property, and frauds on a power.[16]

c Loss of the right to rescission

This may occur in various ways.

i *Affirmation of the contract.* Where a man has a right of rescission, he has a choice either to rescind the contract or to affirm it, and if, having full knowledge of the relevant facts, he, either by express words or by unequivocal acts, affirms

---

[6] *Oakes* v. *Turquand* (1867), L.R. 2 H.L. 325.

[7] Principally, contracts of insurance of all kinds.

[8] *Early* v. *Garrett* (1829), 9 B. & C. 928; *Wilde* v. *Gibson* (1848), 1 H.L.Cas. 605.

[9] *Angel* v. *Jay*, [1911] 1 K.B. 666, D.C.; *Edler* v. *Auerbach*, [1949] 2 All E.R. 692; [1950] 1 K.B. 359.

[10] *Seddon* v. *North Eastern Salt Co., Ltd.*, [1905] 1 Ch. 326; [1904–7] All E.R.Rep. 817; cf. *Leaf* v. *International Galleries*, [1950] 1 All E.R. 693; [1950] 2 K.B. 86, C.A.; *Long* v. *Lloyd*, [1958] 2 All E.R. 402, C.A.

[11] Section 1.

[12] [1949] 2 All E.R. 1007; [1950] 1 K.B. 671, C.A., applied *Grist* v. *Bailey*, [1966] 2 All E.R. 875; [1967] Ch. 532; *Magee* v. *Pennine Insurance Co., Ltd.*, [1969] 2 All E.R. 891, C.A.

[13] (1950), 66 L.Q.R. 169 (A. L. Goodhart); (1952), 15 M.L.R. 297 (C. Grunfeld); (1954), 70 L.Q.R. 385 (C. J. Slade); (1961), 24 M.L.R. 421 (P. S. Atiyah and F. A. R. Bennion) Contrast Cheshire, *op. cit.*, p. 199.

[14] Trustee and *cestui que trust*, solicitor and client, parent and child, guardian and ward, fiancé and fiancée, medical, religious and other advisers and their patients, etc.

[15] E.g. *Williams* v. *Bayley* (1866), L.R. 1 H.L. 200.

[16] See, generally, L. A. Sheridan, *Fraud in Equity*, pp. 71 *et seq.*

the contract, his election has been determined for ever.[17] Although the question remains open until he elects one way or the other, lapse of time and acquiescence will furnish evidence of an election to affirm the contract, and when the lapse of time is great it would probably in practice be treated as conclusive evidence to show that he had so determined. The court will, of course, on equitable principles, take all the circumstances into account,[18] including the nature of the contract,[1] and the presence or absence of fraud.[2]

ii *Restitutio in integrum*. Rescission is not permitted unless it is possible for the contract to be rescinded *in toto*,[3] and the parties replaced *in statu quo ante*. On the one hand, this means that rescission necessarily involves the restoration of money paid or property transferred under the contract which has been avoided; where there is no independent right of action for damages, as may still be the case even after the Misrepresentation Act 1967 where rescission is decreed for innocent misrepresentation,[4] this includes a right to an indemnity against liabilities necessarily incurred or created under the contract which has been avoided, but this may well be something less than what would be recoverable in an action for damages.[5] On the other hand, it follows that if it is not possible to restore the parties to their pre-contract position then the remedy of rescission will not lie.[5] In applying this rule the courts are primarily concerned with the restoration of the defendant to his pre-contract position and do not lay stress on the restoration of the plaintiff.[6] Further the rule is not applied too literally, the court fixing its eyes on the goal of doing what is practically just, and being more drastic in exercising its discretionary remedy of rescission in a case of fraud than in a case of innocent misrepresentation.[7] The equitable course may not be rescission at all but may be to enforce specific performance with compensation.

iii *Rights of third parties*. If an innocent third party has acquired for value an interest in property affected by the contract which would be prejudiced by

---

[17] *Clough* v. *London and North Western Rail. Co.* (1871), L.R. 7 Ex. Ch. 26.
[18] See, generally, *Lindsay Petroleum Co.* v. *Hurd* (1874), L.R. 5 P.C. 221; *Erlanger* v. *New Sombrero Phosphate Co.* (1878), 3 App. Cas. 1218, H.L.; *Senanayake* v. *Cheng*, [1965] 3 All E.R. 296; [1966] A.C. 63, P.C.
[1] *Leaf* v. *International Galleries*, [1950] 1 All E.R. 693, C.A. (where a claim to rescind an executed contract for the sale of goods for innocent misrepresentation was barred by five years delay, although the plaintiff brought his action as soon as he knew the true facts); *Re Scottish Petroleum Co.* (1883), 23 Ch.D. 413, at p. 434, C.A. (where shares are allotted in a going concern it is doubtful if repudiation in a fortnight would be soon enough).
[2] *Charter* v. *Trevelyan* (1844), 11 Cl. & Fin. 714; *Spackman* v. *Evans* (1868), L.R. 3 H.L. 171.
[3] *Thorpe* v. *Fasey*, [1949] 2 All E.R. 393; [1949] Ch. 649.
[4] Section 2 (1) of the Misrepresentation Act 1967 did not altogether abolish the common law rule laid down in *Gilchester Properties, Ltd.* v. *Gomm*, [1948] 1 All E.R. 493. A misrepresentor may defend an action for damages by proving that "he had reasonable ground to believe and did believe up to the time the contract was made that the facts represented were true". *Quaere*, whether non-disclosure can even constitute misrepresentation for the purposes of this section.
[5] *Clarke* v. *Dickson* (1858), E.B. & E. 148; *Urquhart* v. *Macpherson* (1878), 3 App.Cas. 831, P.C.; and cases cited in the following two footnotes.
[6] *Western Bank of Scotland* v. *Addie* (1867), L.R. 1 Sc. & Div. 145; *Spence* v. *Crawford*, [1939] 3 All E.R. 271, H.L.
[7] *Newbigging* v. *Adam* (1886), 34 Ch.D. 582, C.A.; *Lagunas Nitrate Co.* v. *Lagunas Syndicate*, [1899] 2 Ch. 392, C.A.; *Spence* v. *Crawford*, *supra*.

rescission, the person who would otherwise have a right to rescind will be precluded from exercising it.[8]   The right of rescission being, it is submitted, a mere equity, this is a correct application of the basic principle that such a right is ineffective against a subsequent purchaser for value without notice of either a legal estate or an equitable interest.[9]

iv   *Misrepresentation Act* 1967.   In any case of innocent misrepresentation giving rise to a right of rescission, the court may declare the contract subsisting and award damages in lieu of rescission, if of opinion that it would be equitable to do so, having regard to the nature of the misrepresentation and the loss that would be caused by it if the contract were upheld, as well as to the loss that rescission would cause the other party.

5   RECTIFICATION OF DOCUMENTS

a   General

Where a transaction is embodied in a written instrument which, by mistake, does not express the true agreement of the parties the remedy of rectification may be available.   Where it is ordered, such alterations or amendments will be made in the written instrument as may be necessary to express the true agreement, and after such rectification "the written agreement does not continue to exist with a parol variation; it is to be read as if it had been originally drawn in its rectified form".[10]   This may have the result of validating with retrospective effect some act which was invalidly done under the instrument in its original form.[11]   It is vital to realize that it is only the written expression of the parties' agreement which is rectified, never the agreement itself.   "Courts of Equity do not rectify contracts; they may and do rectify instruments purporting to have been made in pursuance of the terms of contracts."[12]   "In order to get rectification, it is necessary to show that the parties were in complete agreement on the terms of their contract, but by an error wrote them down wrongly. . . . If you can predicate with certainty what their contract was, and that it is, by a common mistake, wrongly expressed in the document, then you rectify the document".[13]   The remedy is available in respect of nearly all kinds of documents, such as a conveyance of land,[14] a lease,[15] a settlement,[16] a bill of exchange,[17] a policy of life[18]

---

[8]   *Clough* v. *London and North Western Rail. Co.* (1871), L.R. 7 Exch. 26, 35; *Scholefield* v. *Templer* (1859), Johns. 155; affd., 4 De G. & J. 429; *Oakes* v. *Turquand* (1867), L.R. 2, H.L. 325.

[9]   It is doubtful if it even binds a purchaser with notice, unless the equity is ancillary to, or dependent on, an equitable estate or interest in the land—*National Provincial Bank, Ltd.* v. *Ainsworth,* [1965] 2 All E.R. 472; [1965] A.C. 1175, H.L., esp. *per* Lord Upjohn at 488; 1238.

[10]   *Per* Sterndale M.R. in *Craddock Bros., Ltd.* v. *Hunt,* [1923] 2 Ch. 136, at p. 151; [1923] All E.R. Rep. 394, at p. 402, C.A.; *Johnson* v. *Bragge,* [1901] 1 Ch. 28.

[11]   *Malmesbury* v. *Malmesbury* (1862), 31 Beav. 407, at p. 418.

[12]   *Per* James V.C. in *Mackenzie* v. *Coulson* (1869), L.R. 8 Eq. 368, at p. 375.

[13]   *Per* Denning L.J. in *Frederick E. Rose (London), Ltd.* v. *Wm. H. Pim, Junr. & Co., Ltd.,* [1953] 2 All E.R. 739, at p. 747; [1953] 2 Q.B. 450, at p. 461, C.A.

[14]   *White* v. *White* (1872), L.R. 15 Eq. 247.

[15]   *Murray* v. *Parker* (1854), 19 Beav. 305.

[16]   *Welman* v. *Welman* (1880), 15 Ch.D. 570.

[17]   *Druiff* v. *Parker* (1868), L.R. 5 Eq. 131.

[18]   *Collett* v. *Morrison* (1851), 9 Hare, 162.

or marine[19] insurance, a building contract[20] and a disentailing deed[1] but not a will,[2] except in a case of fraud, nor the articles of association of a company.[3]

Rectification must be kept distinct from the power of the court to correct an obvious mistake or error on the face of the instrument *as a matter of construction*, where this can be done without recourse to extrinsic evidence. As Amphlett L.J. said in *Burchell* v. *Clark*,[4] "the courts of law and equity—for the rule was the same in both—where there is a manifest error in a document will put a sensible meaning on it by correcting or reading ·the error as corrected". There are innumerable instances in the reports of this being done, a recent instance being *Re Doland*.[5] In this case a testator disposed of his residuary estate in percentages and gave two per cent to W.F.L. The testator further provided that if the gift of any share should fail his trustees should hold "my residuary estate" upon trust for H.C. and P.R.C. absolutely. The gift to W.F.L. having failed it was argued that the whole of the residuary estate passed to H.C. and P.R.C. The court, however, held that the words "such share of" must be inserted before "my residuary estate". The mistake may be corrected on this principle whether it involves inserting words omitted, as in the case cited, deleting words,[6] altering words, as for instance in *Wilson* v. *Wilson*,[7] by reading Mary for John, where in a separation deed the trustees had apparently covenanted to indemnify the husband against liability for *his* debts, or re-arranging them.[8] This constructional escape from what would otherwise be an intolerable result was thus explained by Knight-Bruce L.J. in *Key* v. *Key*:[9]

> "There are many cases upon the construction of documents in which the spirit is strong enough to overcome the letter; cases in which it is impossible for a reasonable being, upon a careful perusal of an instrument, not to be satisfied from its contents that a literal, a strict, or an ordinary interpretation given to particular passages, would disappoint and defeat the intention with which the instrument, read as a whole, persuades and convinces him that it was framed. A man so convinced is authorised and bound to construe the writing accordingly."

It must be emphasized that this constructional escape is only available where, without the aid of extrinsic evidence, both the error on the face of the document, and the intention of the parties, are manifest from the document itself.

---

[19] *Motteux* v. *London Assurance Co.* (1739), 1 Atk. 545.

[20] *Simpson* v. *Metcalf* (1854), 24 L.T. O.S. 139; *A. Roberts & Co., Ltd.* v. *Leicestershire County Council*, [1961] 2 All E.R. 545; [1961] Ch. 555.

[1] Notwithstanding s. 47 of the Fines and Recoveries Act 1833—*Hall-Dare* v. *Hall-Dare* (1885), 31 Ch.D. 251, C.A.; *Meeking* v. *Meeking*, [1917] 1 Ch. 77.

[2] *Harter* v. *Harter* (1873), L.R. 3 P. & D. 11; *Collins* v. *Elstone*, [1893] P. 1. Cf. *Re Morris*, [1970] 1 All E.R. 1057; [1971] P. 62.

[3] *Evans* v. *Chapman* (1902), 86 L.T. 381; *Scott* v. *Frank F. Scott (London), Ltd.*, [1940] 3 All E.R. 508; [1940] Ch. 794, C.A.

[4] (1876), 2 C.P.D. 88, 97, C.A.

[5] [1969] 3 All E.R. 713; [1970] Ch. 267; *Coles* v. *Hulme* (1828), 8 B. & C. 568 (the accidental omission of the word 'pounds' said to be a 'moral certainty'); *Re Bird's Trusts* (1876), 3 Ch.D. 214.

[6] E.g. deleting "not"—*Wilson* v. *Wilson* (1854), 5 H.L.Cas. 40, at p. 67 *per* Lord St. Leonards.

[7] *Supra; Fitch* v. *Jones* (1855), 5 E. & B. 238 (date 1854 read as 1855); *Scholefield* v. *Lockwood* (No. 2) (1863), 32 Beav. 436 (in a series of deeds £1,400 in one place written as £1,200).

[8] *Re Bacharach's Will Trusts*, [1958] 3 All E.R. 618; [1959] Ch. 245; *Re Whitrick* [1957] 2 All E.R. 467, C.A.

[9] (1853), 4 De G.M. & G. 73, at p. 84.

b Evidence

The rule which applies in the construction of documents, that parol evidence is not admissible to add to, vary or subtract from a written instrument, clearly cannot apply in an action for rectification which is, of course, based on the proposition that the written instrument fails to carry out the true agreement of the parties. Evidence must necessarily be admitted of the true agreement which is allegedly not expressed in the written instrument.[10] There are many dicta to the effect that "the burden of proof lies upon the plaintiff,[11] and that this court, upon an application to reform an executed deed, looks at the evidence in a very jealous manner".[12] There has often been cited Lord Thurlow's dictum[13] that there must be "strong, irrefragable evidence"[14] which Lord Chelmsford L.C. later explained as requiring "something more than the highest degree of probability" saying it must "leave no fair and reasonable doubt upon the mind that the deed does not embody the final intention of the parties". More recently, however, Russell L.J., giving the judgment of the Court of Appeal,[15] adopted the phrase "convincing proof", and said he preferred neither to use the old-fashioned word "irrefragable", nor to import from the criminal law the phrase "beyond all reasonable doubt". He expressly approved the judgment of Simonds J. in *Crane* v. *Hegeman-Harris Co. Inc.*,[16] who said that the jurisdiction is one "which is to be exercised only upon convincing proof that the concluded instrument does not represent the common intention of the parties . . . and is further satisfied as to what their common intention was."

The court has jurisdiction on the one hand to rectify a document solely on the evidence afforded by a perusal of it,[17] and, on the other hand, may act purely on oral evidence,[18] and on the uncontradicted evidence of the person seeking relief.[19] It is too late to seek rectification after an agreement has been construed by the court and money paid under a judgment founded on that construction,[1] or if the contract is no longer capable of performance,[2] and rectification will not be decreed to the prejudice of a *bone fide* purchaser for value who has acquired an interest in the property dealt with by the instrument.[3] In accordance with familiar equitable principles a claim may be barred by laches and acquiesence.[4] It

---

[10] See e.g. *per* Cozens-Hardy M.R. in *Lovell and Christmas Ltd.* v. *Wall* (1911), 104 L.T. 85, 88, C.A.

[11] I.e. the person claiming rectification.

[12] *Per* Romilly M.R. in *Wright* v. *Goff* (1856), 22 Beav. 207, at p. 214; *Tucker* v. *Bennett* (1887), 38 Ch.D. 1, C.A.

[13] In *Dowager Countess Shelburne* v. *Earl of Inchiquin* (1784), 1 Bro.C.C. 338, at p. 341.

[14] In *Fowler* v. *Fowler* (1859), 4 De G. & J. 250, at p. 264.

[15] *Joscelyne* v. *Nissen*, [1970] 1 All E.R. 1213; [1970] 2 Q.B. 86, C.A.

[16] [1939] 1 All E.R. 662 (see n. 9, p. 481, *infra*).

[17] *Banks* v. *Ripley*, [1940] 3 All E.R. 49; [1940] Ch. 719; *Fitzgerald* v. *Fitzgerald*, [1902] 1 Ir. Rep. 477, C.A.

[18] *Lackersteen* v. *Lackersteen* (1860), 30 L.J. Ch. 5; *M'Cormack* v. *M'Cormack* (1877), 1 L.R. Ir. 119.

[19] *Edwards* v. *Bingham* (1879), 28 W.R. 89; *Hanley* v. *Pearson* (1879), 13 Ch.D. 545.

[1] *Card* v. *Moss* (1886), 33 Ch.D 22, C.A.

[2] *Borrowman* v. *Rossell* (1864), 16 C.B. N.S. 58.

[3] *Garrard* v. *Frankel* (1862), 30 Beav. 445; *Smith* v. *Jones*, [1954] 2 All E.R. 823.

[4] *Beaumont* v. *Bramley* (1822), Turn. & R. 41 (20 years); *Fredensen* v. *Rothschild*, [1941] 1 All E.R. 430 (30 years); *Burroughes* v. *Abbott*, [1922] 1 Ch. 86; [1921] All E.R. Rep. 709 (12 years—rectification granted).

may be added that it may be more difficult to persuade the court that there has been a common mistake where the matter has been dealt with through professional advisers.[5]

c Common mistake

The general rule is that in order "to justify the Court in reforming an executed deed, it must appear that there has been a mistake common to both the contracting parties, and that the agreement has been carried into effect by the deed in a manner contrary to the intention of both".[6] In *Mackenzie* v. *Coulson*,[7] indeed, James V.C. said "it is always necessary for a plaintiff to show that there was an actual concluded contract antecedent to the instrument which is sought to be rectified: and that such contract is inaccurately represented in the instrument". This laid down the rule rather too rigidly, and was at one time held to lead to the result that the contract of an urban authority, which was only capable of contracting under seal, could never be rectified for it was impossible that there could be any prior enforceable contract.[8] The rule is now settled that while it is necessary to show that the parties were in complete agreement on the terms of their contract, it is not necessary to find a concluded and binding contract between the parties antecedent to the instrument which it is sought to rectify.[9] There must, however, be some outward expression of their continuing common intention in relation to the provision in dispute.[10]

Where the necessary antecedent agreement is established, rectification can be granted of a written agreement, even though that agreement is complete in itself and has been carried out by a more formal document based upon it.[11] Nor is it a valid objection to a claim for rectification that the contract in question is one that is required by law to be in writing, and that the evidence of the antecedent agreement is merely oral,[12] for the jurisdiction to order rectification is outside the scope of such provisions, and the contract when rectified will satisfy them. If a contract is rectified, the court may order specific performance of the contract as rectified in the same action.

It is not enough to establish the existence of an antecedent agreement whose terms differ from those of the instrument which is sought to be rectified, unless it is also established that the instrument was intended to carry out the terms of the agreement and not to vary them. If the evidence shows that the parties have changed their intentions and the instrument represents their altered intentions there is no case for rectification.[13] As Simonds J. said in *Gilhespie* v. *Burdis*,[14] "in order to establish [rectification], it must be shown beyond all

---

[5] *Hazell, Watson and Viney, Ltd.* v. *Malvermi*, [1953] 2 All E.R. 58.
[6] Per Romilly M.R. in *Murray* v. *Parker* (1854), 19 Beav. 305, 308, 309.
[7] (1869), L.R. 8 Eq. 368, 375; *Ewing and Lawson* v. *Hanbury & Co.* (1900), 16 T.L.R. 140.
[8] *Higgins Ltd.*, v. *Northampton Corporation*, [1927] 1 Ch. 128.
[9] *Joscelyne* v. *Nissen*, [1970] 1 All E.R. 1213; [1970] 2 Q.B. 86, C.A., expressly approving the judgment of Simonds J. in *Crane* v. *Hegeman Harris Co. Inc.*, [1939] 1 All E.R. 662 (affd. [1939] 4 All E.R. 68, C.A. but not on this point). Omitted passage at first instance printed as note to *Prenn* v. *Simmonds*, [1971] 3 All E.R. 237, H.L. at p. 245.
[10] Per Denning L.J. in *Frederick E. Rose (London), Ltd.* v. *Wm. H. Pim, Junr. & Co., Ltd.*, [1953] 2 All E.R. 739; [1953] 2 Q.B. 450, C.A.; *Joscelyne* v. *Nissen, supra*, C.A. The necessity for an outward expression is attacked in (1971), 87 L.Q.R. 532 (Leonard Bromley).
[11] *Craddock Bros., Ltd.* v. *Hunt*, [1923] 2 Ch. 136; [1923] All E.R. Rep. 394, C.A.
[12] *Craddock Bros., Ltd.* v. *Hunt, supra*; *United States* v. *Motor Trucks*, [1924] A.C., 196, P.C.
[13] *Breadalbane* v. *Chandos* (1837), 2 My. & Cr. 711.   [14] (1943), 169 L.T. 91, 92.

reasonable doubt that up till the moment of execution of the agreement, it was the common intention of the parties that something should find a place in the agreement which is not there as expressed by the agreement". At one time this was carried further in connection with marriage settlements than it is today. The courts have always been ready to rectify a post-nuptial settlement in order to bring it into conformity with ante-nuptial articles,[15] but used to refuse to interfere in the case of an ante-nuptial settlement, unless expressly made in performance of articles, on the ground that the parties must be taken to have changed their intention. Since *Bold* v. *Hutchinson*,[16] however, the courts have held that in the case of an ante-nuptial settlement rectification will be granted of the settlement both where there is a reference to the articles and a variance between them, and also where there is no reference, but satisfactory evidence to show that the variance was due to a mistake. The same point has arisen where a written agreement for a lease has been followed by a regular lease with, however, some differences in the terms. It has been held that in such case the *prima facie* conclusion must be that there was a new agreement with which the lease is in conformity.[17]

Since the principle behind rectification is to make the written instrument correspond with the parties' intentions, there can be no rectification where some term is deliberately omitted or put in a particular form,[18] even though this may have been done because of a mistaken belief by the parties that the inclusion of the term would be supererogatory,[19] or (in a sub-lease) a breach of covenant contained in the head lease,[20] or illegal.[1] The document in any such case expresses the parties' intentions, and it is irrelevant that they might have had different intentions if all the material facts had been present to their minds.[2] On similar grounds, rectification will not be granted where a person has deliberately executed a document, though under protest and threatening in due course to bring proceedings for rectification.[3] Rectification can, however, be granted notwithstanding that the clause in question is a perfectly proper one usually contained in documents of that kind,[4] and the fact that the instrument may have been drawn up by the person claiming rectification is not an absolute bar to relief.[5] Again there was held to be no case for rectification of a contract for horse beans, though it was established that both parties were under the mistaken belief that horse beans were the same things as feveroles.[6]

Another question is whether rectification is possible where there is a mistake of law as opposed to a mistake of fact, i.e. where the mistake is as to the legal

---

15 *Bold* v. *Hutchinson* (1855), 5 De G.M. & G. 558; *Cogan* v. *Duffield* (1876), 2 Ch.D. 44, C.A.
16 *Supra; Viditz* v. *O'Hagan*, [1899] 2 Ch. 569; *King* v. *King-Harman* (1873), I.R. 7 Eq. 446.
17 *Hills* v. *Rowland* (1853), 4 De G.M. & G. 430.
18 *Rake* v. *Hooper* (1900), 83 L.T. 669.
19 *Worrall* v. *Jacob* (1817), 3 Mer. 256.
20 *City and Westminster Properties* (1934), *Ltd.* v. *Mudd*, [1958] 2 All E.R. 733; [1959] Ch. 129.
1 *Irnham* (*Lord*) v. *Child* (1781), 1 Bro.C.C. 92.
2 *Barrow* v. *Barrow* (1854), 18 Beav. 529; *Tucker* v. *Bennett* (1887), 38 Ch.D. 1, C.A.; cf. *Carpmael* v. *Powis* (1846), 10 Beav. 36.
3 *Eaton* v. *Bennett* (1865), 34 Beav. 196.
4 *Torre* v. *Torre* (1853), 1 Sm. & G. 518.
5 *Ball* v. *Storie* (1823), 1 Sim. & St. 210; *Fowler* v. *Scottish Equitable Ins. Co.* (1858), 28 L.J. Ch. 225.
6 *Frederick E. Rose (London), Ltd.* v. *Wm. H. Pim, Junr. & Co., Ltd.*, [1953] 2 All E.R. 739; [1953] 2 Q.B. 450, C.A.

effect and consequences of the words used. Dicta can be found in general terms denying altogether,[7] or admitting[8] the possibility of rectification on this ground. The better view, it is submitted, is that if the parties addressed their minds to, and were under a common mistake as to the legal effect of a provision in a deed, rectification may be an appropriate remedy. The question has arisen in connection with covenants to pay an annual sum "free of tax". The Income Tax Acts[9] were until recently[10] thought to make such a provision contained in an agreement void, though the effect presumably intended could be achieved by adopting the formula "such a sum as, after the deduction of tax at the standard rate, will amount to" the net sum intended to be received by the covenantee. In two cases[11] the courts altered a free of tax provision into the above mentioned formula on proof that this would carry out the agreed intention of the parties. These decisions were approved by the Court of Appeal in *Whiteside* v. *Whiteside*,[12] though in that case the court actually refused to grant rectification of a similar provision. The main reason for the refusal was on the ground that the parties had themselves executed a supplemental deed rectifying the position, so that there was no dispute or issue between the parties—the object of the action was to put the husband in a position to claim deductions from sur-tax as against the revenue authorities. It was clearly intimated, however, that if the husband had refused to execute the supplemental deed and a rectification action had been brought by the wife, it would have succeeded.[13] It may be added that "if there is a written contract which accurately gives effect to the agreement or common intention of the parties, the fact that a statute, passed later, in effect provides that that intention shall be frustrated and that the instrument shall not operate according to its tenor, seems to afford no ground for rectification."[14]

d Unilateral mistake

The general rule is that there cannot be rectification if the mistake is merely unilateral.[15] Thus there could be no rectification of a separation deed although the husband and the husband's and wife's respective solicitors were under a common mistake, where the wife thought she was getting under the deed

---

[7] *Midland Great Western Railway of Ireland* v. *Johnson* (1858), 6 H.L.C. 798, *Napier* v. *Williams*, [1911] 1 Ch. 361; *Jackson* v. *Stopford*, [1923] 2 I.R. 1, C.A.

[8] *Stone* v. *Godfrey* (1854), 5 De G.M. & G. 76, 90; *Rogers* v. *Ingham* (1876), 3 Ch.D. 351, C.A.; *Whiteside* v. *Whiteside*, [1949] 2 All E.R. 913; [1950] Ch. 65, C.A.

[9] Now s. 106 of the Taxes Management Act 1970 replacing similar provisions in earlier Acts.

[10] *Ferguson* v. *I.R. Comrs.*, [1969] 1 All E.R. 1025; [1970] A.C. 442, H.L. This case decides that an agreement to pay an annual sum "free of tax" means an agreement to pay a net sum after deducting tax, and that the gross sum is to be calculated by the formula set out in the text above.

[11] *Burroughes* v. *Abbott*, [1922] 1 Ch. 86; [1921] All E.R. Rep. 709; *Jervis* v. *Howle and Talke Colliery Co. Ltd.*, [1936] 3 All E.R. 193; [1937] Ch. 67.

[12] *Supra.*

[13] Kerr on *Fraud and Mistake*, 7th Ed., p. 565, points out that this intimation should have been sufficient to enable the husband to get the deduction he claimed from the Revenue. The mere fact that rectification may incidentally give the plaintiff some tax advantage is not a bar to relief—*Re Colebrook's Conveyances*, [1973] 1 All E.R. 132.

[14] *Per* Asquith J. in *Pyke* v. *Peters*, [1943] K.B. 242, 250.

[15] *Fowler* v. *Fowler* (1859), 4 De G. & J. 250; *Sells* v. *Sells* (1860), 1 Drew & Sm. 42; *Earl Bradford* v. *Earl of Romney* (1862), 30 Beav. 431.

what in fact the deed, according to its terms, gave her.[16] To this general rule there are exceptions, the scope of which, however, is not clearly settled. In the first place it seems that the court can rectify an instrument where one party only is mistaken, but the other party is guilty of fraud, whether actual, or constructive or equitable. Thus in several cases[17] a marriage settlement has been rectified where the intended husband acted as the intended wife's fiduciary agent in the preparation of the settlement, and failed to inform or explain to her the inclusion therein of unusual provisions advantageous to him. The principle is not restricted to marriage settlements.[18]

Secondly, recent cases[19] lay down the principle that "a party is entitled to rectification of a contract on proof that he believed a particular term to be included in the contract and that the other party concluded the contract with the omission or a variation of that term in the knowledge that the first party believed the term to be included".[20]   Pennycuick J. has said[1] "the exact basis of the principle appears to be in some doubt. If the principle is correctly based upon estoppel[2] it seems to me that it is not an essential ingredient of the right of action to establish any particular degree of obliquity to be attributed to the defendant in such circumstances. If, on the other hand, the principle is rested on fraud, obviously dishonesty must be established". It has been pointed out,[3] however, that this dilemma is perhaps illusory, since the concept of equitable estoppel involves conduct which, in equity at least, would be regarded as fraudulent. The facts of *A. Roberts & Co., Ltd.* v. *Leicestershire County Council*[4] were that the plaintiff company and the defendant council agreed the terms of a building contract to be completed within eighteen months. Officers of the council decided to substitute thirty months for eighteen, and submitted a contract to the plaintiff company specifying the longer period without taking any steps to draw the plaintiff's attention to the alteration. The directors and the secretary of the plaintiff company executed the contract, not having observed the altered date and believing the period for completion specified therein was eighteen months. It was held, on the above principle, that the company was entitled to rectification.

Thirdly, there is a small group of cases[5] which suggest that there may be an exception to the rule that mistake must be common in cases between vendor and purchaser. In these cases of unilateral mistake the court has given the defendant the option of accepting rectification of the instrument against him

---

[16] *Gilhespie* v. *Burdis* (1943), 169 L.T. 91; *Fowler* v. *Scottish Equitable Insurance Co.* (1858), 28 L.J. Ch. 225.

[17] *Clark* v. *Girdwood* (1877), 7 Ch.D. 9, C.A.; *Lovesy* v. *Smith* (1880), 15 Ch.D. 655.

[18] *Hoblyn* v. *Hoblyn* (1889), 41 Ch.D. 200; *McCausland* v. *Young*, [1949] N.I. 49.

[19] *Cohen* v. *Docks and Inland Waterways Executive* (1950), 84 Ll.L.R. 97, C.A.; *A. Roberts & Co., Ltd.* v. *Leicestershire County Council*, [1961] 2 All E.R. 545; [1961] Ch. 555.

[20] *Per* Pennycuick J. in *A. Roberts & Co., Ltd.* v. *Leicestershire County Council*, supra, at 551; 570.

[1] *A. Roberts & Co., Ltd.* v. *Leicestershire County Council*, supra, at 552; 570.

[2] As suggested by Snell's *Principles of Equity*, 27th Ed., p. 614.

[3] (1961), 77 L.Q.R. 313 (R. E. Megarry).

[4] *Supra.*

[5] *Garrard* v. *Frankel* (1862), 30 Beav. 445; *Harris* v. *Pepperell* (1867), L.R. 5, Eq. 1; *Bloomer* v. *Spittle* (1872), L.R. 13 Eq. 427 said to be wholly unintelligible by Neville J. in *Beale* v. *Kyte*, [1907] 1 Ch. 564; [1904–7] All E.R. Rep. 931; *Paget* v. *Marshall* (1884), 28 Ch.D. 255.

or having the contract rescinded. This option seems to involve an illogicality, for rectification assumes a binding contract incorrectly expressed in the instrument, while rescission for mistake assumes that the contract was void *ab initio*. It has been suggested[6] that this can be supported as putting the parties back into the position which they would have been in if the mistake had not occurred—in effect the defendant is given the choice of accepting or rejecting the real offer intended by the plaintiff. Elsewhere, however, it has been declared that these cases are only supportable on the ground of fraud,[7] and there seems much to be said for the view that unilateral mistake is not a ground for rectification unless there is fraud, or the principle of *A. Roberts & Co., Ltd.* v. *Leicestershire County Council*[8] applies.

Fourthly, a quasi-exception appeared in *Wilson* v. *Wilson*.[9] In that case the defendant wished to purchase a house and, his own income being insufficient to qualify him for a loan, he requested the plaintiff to join him in an application to a building society for this purpose. The plaintiff agreed to do so, and in due course the house was conveyed into their joint names and the conveyance expressly declared that they were beneficially interested as joint tenants. It was held on the facts that the plaintiff never made any contribution to the purchase price, and that the common intention of the plaintiff and the defendant was that the beneficial ownership should be solely vested in the defendant. It was held that the conveyance should be rectified by striking out that part of it which declared the beneficial interests, notwithstanding the fact that the vendor was not a party to the action.[10] It was pointed out by the court that the vendor would not be concerned with or affected by the part of the deed that was being rectified, and that the declaration of beneficial trusts could perfectly well have been contained in a separate document. Though superficially a unilateral mistake by the purchasers, in substance there was a common mistake by the plaintiff and defendant in that the expressed declaration of beneficial interests did not represent the terms of their agreement.

e Voluntary settlements

The court has jurisdiction to rectify a voluntary settlement, not only at the instance of the settlor, but even at the instance of a beneficiary who is a volunteer.[11] Rectification will not, however, be decreed against the wishes of the settlor,[12] even though it is clear that the document does not represent his intentions at the time of the execution thereof. "No amount of evidence, however conclusive, proving that he did so intend, will at all justify the court in compelling him to introduce a clause into the deed which he does not choose to introduce now, although he might at the time have wished to have done so."[13] However, if

---

[6] See *per* Bacon V.C. in *Paget* v. *Marshall* (1884), 28 Ch.D. 255, at p. 267; *Solle* v. *Butcher*, [1949] 2 All E.R. 1107; [1950] 1 K.B. 671, C.A., *per* Denning L.J. at pp. 696; 1122.

[7] *May* v. *Platt*, [1900] 1 Ch. 616; *Blay* v. *Pollard*, [1930] 1 K.B. 628, C.A., at pp. 633, 634, *per* Scrutton L.J.

[8] [1961] 2 All E.R. 545; [1961] Ch. 555.   [9] [1969] 3 All E.R. 945.

[10] The consequence was that the property was held on trust for the defendant who had put up the purchase price.

[11] *Thompson* v. *Whitmore* (1860), 1 John. & H. 268.

[12] *Brown* v. *Kennedy* (1863), 33 Beav. 133, at p. 147, affd. 4 De G.J. & S. 217; *Lister* v. *Hodgson* (1867), L.R. 4 Eq. 30; *Weir* v. *Van Tromp* (1900), 16 T.L.R. 531.

[13] *Per* Romilly M.R. in *Lister* v. *Hodgson, supra,* at p. 34.

the settlor is dead "and it is afterwards proved, from the instructions or otherwise, that beyond all doubt the deed was not prepared in the exact manner which he intended, then the deed may be reformed, and those particular provisions necessary to carry his intention into effect may be introduced".[14] In the case of a voluntary settlement the burden of proof is perhaps even heavier and in particular the court is slow to act on the evidence of the settlor alone, unsupported by other evidence such as written instructions, even though the rectification sought would make the settlement more in accord with recognised precedents and may have reasonably been intended.[15] Further in *Weir* v. *Van Tromp*[16] Byrne J. observed that he had not been referred to any case where judgment had in fact been given in favour of reforming a voluntary settlement at the instance of a volunteer.

It may be added that in the case of a deed poll the need for a common mistake is necessarily modified and it may well be sufficient to prove a mistake on the part of the settlor.[17]

6 DELIVERY UP AND CANCELLATION OF DOCUMENTS

In some circumstances a court of equity was prepared to order a void document to be delivered up for cancellation. The idea behind this remedy is that it is inequitable that the defendant should be allowed to remain in possession of an apparently valid document, with the risk to the plaintiff that an action may possibly be brought against him on the document many years later, when evidence to support his defence may have become difficult or impossible to obtain. Thus if a document is voidable, and avoided, for fraud, whether actual or constructive, delivery up can be ordered.[18] Where, however, the document is void at law, and the invalidity appears on its face so that there is no risk of a successful action being brought on it, delivery up will not be ordered.[19] Where the invalidity does not so appear, however, it has long been held that the court has jurisdiction to order delivery up,[20] though there was at one time doubt as to the position.[1]

All kinds of documents may be ordered to be delivered up, for instance negotiable instruments,[2] forged instruments,[3] policies of insurance,[4] and documents which, as it has been said, form a cloud upon title to land.[5] The

---

[14] *Ibid.*; *Weir* v. *Van Tromp, supra.*

[15] *Rake* v. *Hooper* (1900), 83 L.T. 669; *Constandinidi* v. *Ralli*, [1935] Ch. 427; *Van der Linde* v. *Van der Linde*, [1947] Ch. 306.

[16] (1900), 16 T.L.R. 531.

[17] *Wright* v. *Goff* (1856), 22 Beav. 207; *Killick* v. *Gray* (1882), 46 L.T. 583.

[18] *Duncan* v. *Worrall* (1822), 10 Price 31; *Hoare* v. *Bremridge* (1872), 8 Ch. App. 22; *Brooking* v. *Maudslay, Son and Field* (1888), 38 Ch.D. 636.

[19] *Gray* v. *Mathias* (1800), 5 Ves. 286; *Simpson* v. *Lord Howden* (1837), 3 My. & Cr. 97.

[20] *Davis* v. *Duke of Marlborough* (1819), 2 Swan. 108, at p. 157; *Underhill* v. *Horwood* (1804), 10 Ves. 209.

[1] *Ryan* v. *Mackmath* (1789), 3 Bro. C.C. 15.

[2] *Wynne* v. *Callander* (1826), 1 Russ. 293.

[3] *Peake* v. *Highfield* (1826), 1 Russ. 559.

[4] *Bromley* v. *Holland* (1802), 7 Ves. 3; *Kemp* v. *Pryor* (1802), 7 Ves. 237.

[5] *Bromley* v. *Holland, supra; Hayward* v. *Dimsdale* (1810), 17 Ves. 111.

document must, however, be altogether void, and not merely void as against creditors.[6]   Nor will a document be ordered to be delivered up where it is alleged that there would be a good defence to an action at law, but the document is neither void nor voidable.[7] The proper remedy in such case has been said to be an action to perpetuate the testimony,[8] but it is conceived that some other remedy, such as an action for a declaration, might be more appropriate.

Delivery up and cancellation being an equitable remedy, it has been said that it will only be granted on terms which will do justice to both parties, an illustration of the maxim that he who seeks equity must do equity. Thus in *Lodge* v. *National Union Investment Co., Ltd.*[9] where a borrower gave certain securities to the lender under a moneylending contract which was illegal and void under the Money-lenders Act 1900,[10] the court was only prepared to order delivery up of the securities on the terms that the borrower should repay such of the money borrowed as was still outstanding. The Privy Council, however, has declared[11] that this case "cannot be treated as having established any wide general principle that governs the action of courts in granting relief in moneylending cases". It seems that where the moneylending contract is merely unenforceable[12] as opposed to illegal and void, the lender is, paradoxically, in a worse position, for in such case the borrower can recover his securities without any terms being imposed. To impose terms would be an indirect way of enforcing a contract declared unenforceable by statute.[13]

It should be added that the Court of Appeal has held[14] on similar facts to those in *Lodge* v. *National Union Investment Co., Ltd.*[15] that a declaration that the transaction is illegal and void may be made without any terms being imposed, on the ground that a declaration is not "equitable relief" or "true equitable relief". This ground is not altogether convincing for a declaration has long been recognised in equity, though under the inherent jurisdiction there was only power to make a declaration as ancillary to some other remedy.[16] Statutes[17] gave the Court of Chancery jurisdiction to make a declaratory order without granting consequential relief, but this was strictly construed so as to apply only where some other relief was in fact available, though not sought or granted.[18] It is not clear why this remedy should have ceased to be equitable

---

[6] *Ideal Bedding Co. Ltd.* v. *Holland*, [1907] 2 Ch. 157.

[7] *Brooking* v. *Maudsley, Son and Field* (1888), 38 Ch.D 638. Cf. *Onions* v. *Cohen* (1865), 2 Hem. & M. 354.

[8] *Brooking* v. *Maudsley Son and Field, supra.*

[9] [1907] 1 Ch. 300; [1904–7] All E.R. Rep. 333.

[10] Section 2.

[11] *Kasumu* v. *Baba-Egbe*, [1956] 3 All E.R. 266, at p. 270; [1956] A.C. 539, at p. 549, P.C.

[12] This is the effect of the Moneylenders Act 1927, s. 6, which Act repealed s. 2 of the Act of 1900.

[13] *Cohen* v. *J. Lester Ltd.*, [1938] 4 All E.R. 188; [1939] 1 K.B. 504; *Kasumu* v. *Baba-Egbe, supra.*

[14] *Chapman* v. *Michaelson*, [1909] 1 Ch. 238, C.A.

[15] [1907], Ch. 300; [1904–7] All E.R. Rep. 333.

[16] *Ferrand* v. *Wilson* (1845), 4 Hare 344, at p. 385; *Clough* v. *Ratcliffe* (1847), 1 De G. & Sm. 164, 178. The only case to the contrary seems to be *Taylor* v. *A.-G.* (1837), 8 Sim. 413. See generally, Zamir, *The Declaratory Judgment.*

[17] Court of Chancery Act 1850; Court of Chancery Procedure Act 1852.

[18] *Jackson* v. *Turnley* (1853), 1 Drew. 617, 628; *Lady Langdale* v. *Briggs* (1856), 8 De G.M. & G. 391, at p. 428; *Rooke* v. *Lord Kensington* (1856), 2 K. J. & 753, at p. 761.

when the Judicature Acts and the Rules made thereunder extended the remedy to all divisions of the High Court "whether or not any consequential relief is or could be claimed.[19]

Finally, it seems that whether or not a declaration is sought, it may be possible to recover securities without repayment by means of an action in trover or detinue.[20]

7 PERPETUATION OF TESTIMONY

A court of equity would entertain a suit for the perpetuation of testimony where, for instance, a man was in possession of land, and had reason to suppose that another was intending to impeach his title thereto on the ground that his title deeds were fraudulent—but intended to postpone bringing his action until all those who could give evidence as to the genuineness of the deeds were dead. Being in undisturbed possession he could not bring any action against that other, and this proceeding enabled him to take steps to prevent the invalid claim subsequently succeeding for want of rebutting evidence.[1]   The jurisdiction is now set out in the Rules of the Supreme Court[2] as follows, but the original equitable principles still apply.

> "Any person who would under the circumstances alleged by him to exist become entitled, upon the happening of any future event, to any honour, title, dignity, or office, or to any estate or interest in any real or personal property, the right or claim to which cannot be brought to trial by him before the happening of such event, may begin an action to perpetuate any testimony which may be material for establishing such right or claim."

It is settled that an action for this purpose will not succeed if the matter in question could be brought before a court in some other form of proceedings.[3] Thus, for instance, the court will refuse to deal with the matter if it could be dealt with by obtaining a declaration of legitimacy.[4] Nor will it succeed if the matter is already the subject of an existing action against the plaintiff.[5]

If the order to perpetuate testimony is made, evidence may be taken down from all possible witnesses—it is not restricted to the evidence of old and infirm witnesses, or to a single witness who alone can speak to the matter, as is the case where evidence in taken *de bene esse* for use in contemporary proceedings. The evidence will be sealed up and kept in the custody of the court, and will only be brought out if and when occasion requires. If the matter is ultimately litigated, the evidence thus taken can only be used if the witnesses have died in the meantime, though this strict rule has been somewhat relaxed to cover cases where the witness is too ill or otherwise incapable of travelling, or is prevented from attending the court by accident.[6]

---

[19] R.S.C., O. 15, r. 16. See *Mellstrom* v. *Garner*, [1970] 2 All E.R. 9, C.A.
[20] See *Lodge* v. *National Union Investment Co., Ltd.*, [1907] 1 Ch. 300; [1904–7] All E.R. Rep. 333.
[1] See *Ellice* v. *Roupell* (No. 1) (1863), 32 Beav. 299.
[2] O. 39, r. 15.
[3] *Angell* v. *Angell* (1822), 1 Sim. & St. 83; *West* v. *Lord Sackville*, [1902] 2 Ch. 378, C.A.
[4] Now under the Matrimonial Causes Act 1973, s. 45. See the cases cited in note 3, *supra*.
[5] *Earl Spencer* v. *Peek* (1867), L.R. 3 Eq. 415.
[6] *Biddulph* v. *Lord Camoys* (1855), 20 Beav. 402; *Beresford* v. *A.-G.*, [1918] P. 33, C.A.; affd. (1918), *Times*, 24th July, H.L.

8 NE EXEAT REGNO

The issue of the writ *ne exeat regno* is a process whereby an equitable creditor can have the debtor arrested and made to give security if, but only if, the debtor is about to leave the realm. It is essential that the debt shall be an equitable and not a legal one. In connection with this writ the provisions of s. 6 of the Debtors Act 1869 are applied by analogy. This means that four conditions have to be satisfied before the writ can be issued, namely (i) The action is one in which the defendant would formerly have been liable to arrest at law (ii) A good cause of action for at least £50 is established (iii) There is "probable cause" for believing that the defendant is "about to quit England" unless he is arrested, and (iv) The absence of the defendant from England will materially prejudice the plaintiff in the prosecution of his action, as opposed to the execution of any judgment he may obtain. Even if these four conditions are satisfied—and the standard of proof is high—the issue of an order is discretionary.

There is no record of the writ being issued since 1893,[7] and the law was recently fully reviewed by Megarry J. in an unsuccessful application for this now rarely-sought remedy in *Felton* v. *Callis*.[8]

---

[7] *Lewis* v. *Lewis* (1893), 68 L.T. 198.
[8] [1968] 3 All E.R. 673; [1969] 1 Q.B. 200. See (1972), 88 L.Q.R. 83 (J. W. Bridge).

CHAPTER 16

Conversion and Reconversion

1 CONVERSION

a Meaning of conversion

English law has divided property into two categories, realty and personalty, which in many respects were, before the 1925 Property Legislation, governed by different rules, perhaps the most important difference being that on a man's death intestate, his realty passed to his heir-at-law,[1] while his personalty passed to his next-of-kin.[2] This difference has now disappeared and the law of real and personal property has been assimilated in many respects by the 1925 Property Legislation,[3] but the distinction between realty and personalty may still be material in some circumstances, for instance in relation to death duties,[4] or if, in his will, a testator has made separate dispositions of his real and personal property. Under the doctrine of conversion property in one category will, in certain circumstances, be treated in equity as if it were in the other. Suppose, for instance, that a settlor conveyed realty to trustees on trust to sell it forthwith and hold the proceeds of sale on trust for X and Y in equal shares. If, after the trustees had carried out their duty and actually converted the realty to personalty X died having by his will left all his realty to R and all his personalty to P, clearly X's half share in the trust property would pass to P; and if these events had happened before 1926 and X had died intestate, X's interest would have passed to his next-of-kin and not his heir-at-law. Under the doctrine of conversion the result would be exactly the same even though X died before the trustees had carried out their duty. In general there is a notional conversion as soon as there is a duty to convert and, in equity, the rights of the parties will be worked out accordingly on the basis of the maxim that what ought to be done

---

[1] Ascertained in accordance with common law rules as amended by the Inheritance Act 1833 and the Law of Property Amendment Act 1859. For details see Megarry and Wade, *Law of Real Property*, 3rd ed., pp. 515 *et seq.*

[2] Ascertained in accordance with the Statutes of Distribution 1670 and Administration of Indestates' Estates 1685 and the Statute of Frauds 1677. See Megarry and Wade, *op. cit.,* pp. 528 *et seq.*

[3] On the particular difference referred to see Administration of Estates Act 1925, **ss.** 33 and 45-52, and Intestates' Estates Act 1952.

[4] See e.g. Beattie, *Elements of Estate Duty*, 8th Ed., pp. 10, 11, 12.

must be considered as done.[5] Equity will not allow the rights of persons to be affected by the delay or failure of trustees to carry out their duty. The classic statement of the general principle is to be found in the judgment of Sewell M.R. in *Fletcher* v. *Ashburner*,[6] who observed that "nothing was better established than this principle, that money directed to be employed in the purchase of land, and land directed to be sold and turned into money, are to be considered as that species of property into which they are directed to be converted; and this in whatever manner the direction is given; whether by will, by way of contract, marriage articles, settlement, or otherwise, and whether the money is actually deposited or only covenanted to be paid, whether the land is actually conveyed or only agreed to be conveyed. The owner of the fund or the contracting parties may make land money, or money land". It should be pointed out, however, that in this quotation land must be construed as meaning realty. Land is now normally construed, and is defined in the Law of Property Act 1925,[7] as including leaseholds, which are personalty, and the doctrine of conversion is primarily[8] concerned with the conversion of realty into personalty, and *vice versa*. If money is given to trustees to be laid out in the purchase of land, including both freehold and leasehold land, there is no conversion unless and until there is conversion in fact.[9] Not uncommonly in this context, however, it will be found that the word "land" is used in the sense of realty, and care must be taken to ascertain whether the word is being used in the wider or the narrower sense.

The doctrine of conversion, where it applied, applied not only in relation to the devolution of the estates of deceased persons, but for all purposes. It was applied as against the Crown, for instance in relation to death duties[10], and a good illustration in another context is *Sweetapple* v. *Bindon*,[11] a case under the pre-1926 law. There a testatrix bequeathed £300 to be laid out in the purchase of real property, and settled to the use of her daughter and her daughter's children, with limitations over if the daughter died without issue. The daughter married and had a child, but both were dead at the date of the action, no purchase of real property having been made with the £300. In the action the widower of the daughter claimed to be tenant by the curtesy of the fund of £300, tenancy by the curtesy being an interest to which a widower was, in certain circumstances, entitled in relation to his deceased's wife's realty, though never as to her personalty. It was held that the money was to be considered as realty and that the claim must succeed.

We must now consider the different types of circumstances in which the doctrine of conversion applies.

---

[5] *Trafford* v. *Boehm* (1746), 3 Atk. 440; *Hutcheon* v. *Mannington* (1791), 1 Ves. 366.
[6] (1799), 1 Bro. C. C. 497, at p. 499.
[7] S. 205 (1) (ix).
[8] See *post*, p. 498.
[9] *Davies* v. *Goodhew* (1834), 6 Sim. 585.
[10] *A.-G.* v. *Dodd* [1894] 2 Q.B. 150, D.C.; *A.-G.* v. *Johnson*, [1907] 2 K.B. 885.
[11] (1705), 2 Vern. 536.

b Under a direction contained in a will or settlement

Where a settlor or testator has directed[12] his trustees to purchase or to sell realty, the property, subject to what follows, is treated as if it had actually been converted from the time when the instrument came into effect. For a direction to have this effect it is essential that it shall be imperative: if it is left merely optional whether the trustees purchase or sell the realty, as the case may be, the rights of the parties will depend on the actual state of the property. The general principle of conversion in this context was clearly stated by Pollock M.R. in Re Twopeny's Settlement:[13] "where the quality of real estate is 'imperatively and definitively'[14] fixed upon personalty (or vice versa) equity will treat the personalty (or realty as the case may be) as having acquired the quality indicated, even though it is not found to have been actually turned into realty or personalty; because equity treats what ought to be done as done, and will not allow the rights of beneficiaries to be altered by a failure on the part of trustees to carry out their trust".

It is a question of construction, which may well give rise to difficulty, as to whether a particular will or settlement imposes an imperative direction, or merely confers on trustees a discretionary power.[15] A mere declaration that personalty is to devolve or pass to persons successively as realty or vice versa does not, however, operate as a conversion, and is ineffective to achieve its intended purpose, though it might possibly in some contexts add a little weight to an argument that the instrument as a whole imposes an imperative trust for conversion.[16] Again the mere fact that personalty was given to trustees on limitations appropriate to realty, a great part of which must have failed if applied to personalty, was not by itself held to justify the court in finding an implied trust for conversion,[17] though it was important evidence which, added to the rest of the will or settlement, might enable the court to do so.[18]

Two points were treated as well settled by Morton L.J. giving the judgment of the Court of Appeal in Duke of Marlborough v. A.-G. [19] first, "that, if real property is vested in trustees upon trust for sale with the consent[20] of A B., the consent is treated as intended to regulate the exercise of the trust for sale but not to prevent the trust for sale from being an immediate trust; and if there is an immediate trust for sale, whether subject to consent or not, the trust operates

---

[12] Expressly or by implication—Mower v. Orr (1849), 7 Hare 473. But the court must have some material from which to draw the necessary inference—there was none in Cornick v. Pearce (1848), 7 Hare 477.

[13] [1924] 1 Ch. 522, at p. 529, C.A.

[14] This phrase is taken from the judgment of Loughborough L.C. in Walker v. Denne (1793), 2 Ves. 170, at p. 184; Wheldale v. Partridge (1800), 5 Ves. 388.

[15] Re Hotchkys (1886), 32 Ch.D. 408, C.A.; Re Bird, [1892] 1 Ch. 279; Re Newbould (1914), 110 L.T. 6, C.A.

[16] Hyett v. Mekin (1884), 25 Ch.D. 735; Re Walker, [1908] 2 Ch. 705; Re Aspinall's Settled Estates, [1916] 1 Ch. 15.

[17] Evans v. Ball (1882), 47 L.T. 165, H.L.

[18] Cowley v. Hartstonge (1813), 1 Dow. 361; Evans v. Ball, supra. These cases have been shorn of most of their importance by the 1925 Property Legislation, as a result of which personalty may be subjected to the same limitations as realty, though some limitations may, perhaps, still be regarded as more appropriate to realty.

[19] [1945] 1 All E.R. 165, 175; [1945] Ch. 145, at p. 154, C.A.

[20] Or "at the request"—Re Ffennell's Settlement, [1918] 1 Ch. 91.

at once to effect a conversion",[21] and secondly, "that the existence of a power to postpone sale does not prevent conversion taking place".[22] A trust for sale with power to postpone the sale, which gives rise to a conversion, must, of course, be distinguished from a trust to retain with a power of sale, which does not, though as a matter of construction it may not be easy to decide into which category a particular trust falls. There may also be found a trust to retain or sell land, but the difficulties to which such a trust gave rise[23] have now been removed, as regards dispositions and settlements coming into operation after 31st December, 1925, by a statutory provision[1] that a trust either to retain or sell land is to be construed as a trust to sell with power to postpone the sale. Accordingly under such a trust realty is converted into personalty.

The direction must be effectual if it is to cause a conversion—"nothing short of an absolute and effective trust for sale can in equity create a conversion of realty into personalty".[2] Thus there is no conversion if the trust for sale is void for perpetuity, even though there may have been an actual conversion.[3] In such case if the beneficial trusts do not themselves offend against the perpetuity rule, they will be good, but the beneficiaries will take interests in realty.[3] It should be noted, however, that since the Perpetuities and Accumulations Act 1964, it is uncertain whether or not the rule against perpetuities still applies to a trust for sale. Section 8 of the Act provides that the rule shall no longer operate to invalidate "a power conferred on trustees . . . to sell . . . property for full consideration". There is as yet no authority as to whether this covers an imperative trust for sale as well as a mere power of sale. A similar point on section 32 of the Law of Property Act 1925 was left open in Re Hanson.[4]

Where the doctrine of conversion applies, it takes place in the case of a will as from the date of the death of the testator, and in the case of a deed as from the date of its execution, even though the direction is only to convert at some future time.[5]

It may be added that occasionally one may come across a case of double conversion, where the effect is that the property retains its original form throughout. This would be the case where realty was given to trustees upon trust to sell it and lay out the proceeds in the purchase of other real estate.[6] In such case,

---

[21] A.-G. v. Dodd, [1894] 2 Q.B. 150, D.C.; O'Grady v. Wilmot, [1916] 2 A.C. 231, H.L.; Re Ffennell's Settlement, [1918] 1 Ch. 91.

[22] Re Raw (1884), 26 Ch.D. 601; Gresham Life Assurance Society v. Crowther, [1915] 1 Ch. 214; [1914–15] All E.R. Rep. 991, C.A. A power to postpone sale is now implied in all trusts for sale of land unless a contrary intention appears—Law of Property Act 1925, s. 25(1).

[23] It seems that such a direction did not cause a conversion in the absence of a controlling context—Re Johnson, [1915] 1 Ch. 435; Re White's Settlement, [1930] 1 Ch. 179.

[1] Law of Property Act 1925, s. 25(4).

[2] Per Stirling J. in Goodier v. Edmunds, [1893] 3 Ch. 455, at p. 462.

[3] Re Daveron, [1893] 3 Ch. 421; Goodier v. Edmunds, supra; Re Appleby, [1903] 1 Ch. 565, C.A.

[4] [1928] Ch. 96.

[5] Griffith v. Ricketts (1849), 7 Hare 299; Clarke v. Franklin (1858), 4 K. & J. 257. But note Section 2b, post, p. 499.

[6] Sperling v. Toll (1747), 1 Ves. Sen. 70; Cf. Re Bird, [1892] 1 Ch. 279; Re Duke of Cleveland's Settled Estates, [1893] 3 Ch. 244, C.A. Unless the purchased real estate is to be held on trust for sale.

whatever the actual state of the trust property, the beneficiaries would be treated as having interests in realty.

c Under statutory provisions

If a statute imposes a trust for sale on land, the usual consequences of conversion will follow, unless the statute provides to the contrary.[7] There are several examples of a statutory trust for sale under the 1925 Property Legislation,[8] and there is a series of illustrative cases in relation to the transitional provisions of the Law of Property Act 1925,[9] which imposed a trust for sale on land which, immediately before 1st January, 1926, was held in undivided shares vested in possession. In all of these cases a testator dying after 1925 had made a pre-1926 will devising an undivided share in realty. As a result of the imposition of a statutory trust for sale and the doctrine of conversion he had, at the date of his death, only an interest in the proceeds of sale, i.e. personalty.[10] The question was whether the devise had been adeemed. The Court of Appeal held on such facts in Re Kempthorne[11] that the gift failed, the principle being that "if the testator uses language that can only be construed as a devise of real estate, and, notwithstanding the imposition of the statutory trusts, he dies without altering or confirming his will, the conversion effected by the statutory trusts adeems the devise, because there is nothing left for that devise to operate on".[12] This logical conclusion was in practice likely to defeat the intentions of testators, and was particularly unfortunate as the imposition of the statutory trust for sale was merely a conveyancing device and was not intended to alter or affect substantive rights.[13] The courts were accordingly ready to listen to arguments circumventing this logic, and held the conversion immaterial and the gift valid if the testator used language wide enough to carry any interest in the property whether it was in law real or personal property.[14] Again, if the will was republished by a codicil executed after 1925,[15] even though it merely placed on record the cancellation and destruction of a previous codicil with intent to revoke it,[16] the gift would be good.

---

[7] Conversion under the Fines and Recoveries Act 1833 was for certain purposes only—Re Dickson's Settled Estates, [1921] 2 Ch. 108, C.A.

[8] See e.g. Law of Property Act 1925, ss. 34–36; Settled Land Act 1925, s. 36; Administration of Estates Act 1925, s. 33. Note, however, that s. 16 (4) of the Law of Property Act 1925 and s. 53 (3) of the Administration of Estates Act 1925 provide that nothing in those Acts is to affect liability in relation to estate duty—A.-G. v. Public Trustee and Tuck, [1929] 2 K.B. 77; Re Wheeler, [1929] 2 K.B. 81 n.

[9] Sched. 1, Part IV as amended by the Law of Property (Amendment) Act 1926, s. 7 and Sched. and s. 35.

[10] Note, however, that this is an "interest in land" for the purposes of s. 40 of the Law of Property Act 1925—Cooper v. Critchley, [1955] 1 All E.R. 520; [1955] Ch. 431, C.A. —and s. 54 of the Land Registration Act 1925 (right to lodge a caution)—Elias v. Mitchell, [1972] 2 All E.R. 153; [1972] Ch. 652. Cf. Irani Finance, Ltd. v. Singh, [1970] 3 All E.R. 199; [1971] Ch. 59, C.A.

[11] [1930] 1 Ch. 268; [1929] All E.R. Rep. 495, C.A., following Re Price, [1928] Ch. 579.

[12] Per Farwell J. in Re Newman, [1930] 2 Ch. 409, at p. 417; [1930] All E.R. Rep. 617, at p. 619.

[13] Re Galway's Will Trusts, [1949] 2 All E.R. 419, at p. 421; [1950] Ch. 1, 9, per Harman J.

[14] Re Mellish, [1929] 2 K.B. 82 n ("all my share or interest"); Re Newman, supra.

[15] Re Wheeler, [1929] 2 K.B. 81 n; Re Warren, [1932] 1 Ch. 42; [1931] All E.R. Rep. 702.

[16] Re Harvey, [1947] 1 All E.R. 349; [1947] Ch. 285.

It seems that the imposition of the statutory trusts may cause a case of double conversion. One case of a statutory trust for sale is where a legal estate is held on trust for any persons as joint tenants.[17] Suppose then that a testator gave a fund of money to trustees and directed them to use it in the purchase of real estate for A and B as joint tenants. The will would operate to convert the fund into realty and the statutory trusts to convert it back into personalty, so that as the result A and B would be treated as having interests in personalty whatever the actual state of the property might be. The same result, might perhaps, be reached on these facts under section 32 of the Law of Property Act 1925, which provides that "where a settlement of personal property or of land held upon trust for sale contains a power to invest money in the purchase of land, such land shall, unless the settlement otherwise provides, be held by the trustees on trust for sale". It is not clear, however, whether this section applies where there is a trust for the purchase of land as opposed to a mere power.[18]

It may be added that statutes sometimes provide that for some, or all, purposes an actual conversion should have no effect on the nature of the property which is to retain its unconverted form. Thus under the Settled Land Act 1925[19] capital money is "for all purposes of disposition, transmission, and devolution," but not in relation to death duties,[20] to be treated as land.[1]

d Under an order of the court

It is clearly established as a general principle that if the court by an order directs the sale or purchase of realty, this operates as a conversion as from the date of the order.[2] The general principle may, however, be affected by statutory provisions. Thus under the Mental Health Act 1959,[3] where the court orders the disposal of real property belonging to a patient,[4] any property representing it is to be treated as if it were real property so long as it remains part of the patient's estate,[5] and the judge, in ordering any disposal of property which apart from section 107 would result in the conversion of personal property into real property, may direct that the property representing the property disposed of shall, so long as it remains the property of the patient or forms part of his estate, be treated as if it were personal property.[6]

---

[17] Law of Property Act 1925, s. 36(1).
[18] See *Re Hanson*, [1928] Ch. 96. The section, which replaces s. 10(1) of the Conveyancing Act 1911, only applies to settlements coming into operation after 31st December, 1911.
[19] Section 75(5).
[20] *Midleton (Earl)* v. *Baron Cottesloe*, [1949] 1 All E.R. 841; [1949] A.C. 418, H.L.
[1] "Land" includes leaseholds which are personalty, but the Court of Appeal has explained that if settled freeholds are sold, the capital money would be treated as freehold, if settled leaseholds, as leasehold; *Re Cartwright*, [1938] 4 All E.R. 209; [1939] Ch. 90, C.A. See also *Re Cutcliffe's Will Trusts*, [1940] 2 All E.R. 297; [1940] Ch. 565.
[2] *Steed* v. *Preece* (1874), L.R. 18 Eq. 192; *Fauntleroy* v. *Beebe*, [1911] 2 Ch. 257, C.A.; *Re Silva*, [1929] 2 Ch. 198; [1929] All E.R. Rep. 546.
[3] Section 107 replacing s. 123 of the Lunacy Act 1890.
[4] I.e., a person incapable, by reason of mental disorder, of managing and administering his property—s. 101 of the Mental Health Act 1959.
[5] *Ibid.*, s. 107(1).
[6] *Ibid.*, s. 107(2). *A.-G.* v. *Marquis of Ailesbury* (1887), 12 App. Cas. 672, H.L.; *Re Silva*, *supra.* Cf. *Re Searle*, [1912] 2 Ch. 365.

e Under a contract for the sale of land

It is familiar law, going back at least to *Lady Foliamb's* case[7] that a contract for the sale of land causes a conversion. Vaisey J. restated the law in *Hillington Estates Co.* v. *Stonefield Estates, Ltd.*[8]—

"when there is a contract by A to sell land to B at a certain price, B becomes the owner in equity of the land, subject, of course, to his obligation to perform his part of the contract by paying the purchase money; but subject to that, the land is the land of B, the purchaser. What is the position of A, the vendor? He has, it is true, the legal estate in the land, but, for many purposes, from the moment the contract is entered into he holds it as trustee for B, the purchaser. True, he has certain rights in the land remaining, but all those rights are conditioned and limited by the circumstance that they are all referable to his right to recover and receive the purchase-money. His interest in the land when he has entered into a contract for sale is not an interest in land; it is an interest in personal estate, in a sum of money . . .".

It follows, as a result of the application of the doctrine of conversion, that if the vendor has died between contract and completion, any specific devise of the property contained in a will preceding[9] the contract is revoked or adeemed,[10] and the right to receive the purchase money goes to the person entitled to the personal property. On the death of the purchaser between contract and completion, the property correspondingly passes to the person entitled to his real property, though since Locke King's Acts[11] he takes it subject to the liability to pay the whole or the balance of the purchase price as the case may be.

In order for the doctrine of conversion to apply there must be a valid contract of sale, and, as Jessel M.R. pointed out in *Lysaght* v. *Edwards*,[12] as regards real estate there is no valid contract unless the vendor is in a position to make title according to the contract, or the purchaser has accepted the title notwithstanding the fact that it is not a good one. Though it is commonly said[13] that there is conversion under a contract only where the contract is enforceable by specific performance, the availability of this remedy does not seem to be an altogether satisfactory criterion.[14]

The doctrine of conversion applies in the ordinary way to a contract imposed by statute,[15] and the point has arisen in connection with land taken by compulsory purchase. In such case the notice to treat does not operate as a conversion,[16] even though the owner has stated the price which he is willing to

---

[7] (1651), cited in *Daire* v. *Beversham* (1661), Nels. 76. Cf. Chapter 4, Section 4, p. 120, *ante*.

[8] [1952] 1 All E.R. 853; [1952] Ch. 627, at pp. 856; 631. See (1960) 24 Con. 47 (P. H. Pettit).

[9] If subsequent to the contract, it is a question of construction of the will whether the disposition therein contained extends to the purchase money. See *Re Calow*, [1928] Ch. 710; [1928] All E.R. Rep. 518.

[10] Strictly, it seems to be revocation by alteration of estate, see (1957), 21 Con. 152; *Andrew* v. *Andrew* (1856), 4 W.R. 520.

[11] The Real Estate Charges Acts 1854, 1867 and 1877 now repealed and replaced by the Administration of Estates Act 1925, s. 35.

[12] (1876), 2 Ch.D. 499.

[13] E.g. *Per* Lord Westbury L.C. in *Holroyd* v. *Marshall* (1862), 10 H.L.C. 191 at 209–210; *Per* Lord Parker in *Howard* v. *Miller*, [1915] A.C. 318, at p. 326, P.C.

[14] See *Rose* v. *Watson* (1864), 10 H.L.C. 672; *Gordon Hill Trust* v. *Segall*, [1941] 2 All E.R. 379, C.A. Some of the latent difficulties in this field are discussed in (1960), 24 Con. 47.

[15] E.g. Coal Act 1938—*Re Galway's Will Trusts*, [1949] 2 All E.R. 419; [1950] Ch. 1.

[16] *Haynes* v. *Haynes* (1861), 1 Dr. & Sm. 426.

take, if he dies before it has been accepted.[17] Again if there is agreement on the price per acre to be paid, but the quantity of land to be taken has not yet been ascertained, there is no conversion.[18] Where, however, the notice to treat has been followed by ascertainment of the price, whether by agreement or arbitration or some other procedure, there is a complete valid contract and conversion takes place in the ordinary way.[19] "A somewhat analogous case is enfranchisement under the Leasehold Reform Act 1967, under which a leaseholder who satisfies certain conditions may convert his interest from leasehold, i.e., personalty into freehold, i.e. realty. There is as yet no authority on the application of the doctrine of conversion to this situation, but it would seem on principle clearly to apply, perhaps at the point of time when the tenant as well as the landlord becomes irrevocably bound to the enfranchisement process.[20]

f Under an option to purchase

If T, having made his will devising all his realty to R and bequeathing all his personalty to P, and having granted X an option to purchase Blackacre, died before X had exercised the option, one would expect, on principle, that Blackacre would pass to R, who would become entitled to the proceeds of sale if X subsequently exercised the option thereby creating a valid contract of sale. Under the rule in *Lawes* v. *Bennett*,[1] however, the proceeds of sale would, in such case, be payable to P,[2] Blackacre being treated for the purpose of devolution on death as devolving from the date of the exercise of the option as proceeds of sale and not as real estate. It would make no difference that the option was not even exercisable until after T's death.[3] Though generally castigated as an illogical anomaly in many of the subsequent cases, it is now acknowledged to be settled law, certainly as far as the Court of Appeal[4] and probably, having stood so long, in the House of Lords.

It has been made clear in a series of cases[5] that conversion does not take place at the date when the option is granted, but only at the time when it is exercised. Thus in the illustration given, R would get an estate or interest defeasible by the exercise of the option, upon which event and not before conversion would take place. It follows from this that any rents and profits which accrue between the date of death and the exercise of the option would go to R and not to P.[6] If there is conversion, it seems to make no difference that the contract is not carried through to completion.[7]

Prima facie, the rule in *Lawes* v. *Bennett*[8] applies whether the option precedes the will, as in *Lawes* v. *Bennett*[8] itself or whether the will precedes the option,

---

[17] *Re Battersea Park Acts* (1863), 32 Beav. 591.
[18] *Ex parte Walker* (1853), 1 Drew. 508.
[19] *Harding* v. *Metropolitan Railway Co.* (1872), 7 Ch. App. 154; *Watts* v. *Watts* (1873), L.R. 17 Eq. 217.
[20] For a full discussion see (1969), 33 Con. 43 & 141 (J. Tiley).
[1] (1785), 1 Cox. Eq. Cas. 167; *Weeding* v. *Weeding* (1861), 1 John & H. 424.
[2] Unless, perhaps, the sale was a collusive transaction between X and P to oust R.
[3] *Re Isaacs*, [1894] 3 Ch. 506, where the rule was applied on intestacy before 1926, as between the heir-at-law and next-of-kin.
[4] *Re Marlay*, [1915] 2 Ch. 264, C.A.; *Re Carrington*, [1932] 1 Ch. 1; [1931] All E.R. Rep. 658, C.A.; and see [1950] C.L.P. 30 (O. R. Marshall).
[5] *Re Isaacs*, [1894] 3 Ch. 506; *Re Marlay*, *supra*; *Re Carrington*, *supra*.
[6] *Townley* v. *Bedwell* (1808), 14 Ves. 591; *Collingwood* v. *Row* (1857), 26 L.J. Ch. 649.
[7] *Re Blake*, [1917] 1 Ch. 18.
[8] (1785) 1 Cox. Eq. Cas. 167.

as in *Weeding* v. *Weeding.*[9] It may, however, be possible to argue successfully that a case falls outside the rule, where the option comes first and the will contains a specific devise of the property. The principle, as stated by Page Wood V.C.,[10] is that "when you find that, in a will made after a contract giving an option of purchase, the testator, knowing of the existence of the contract, devises the specific property which is the subject of the contract without referring in any way to the contract he has entered into, there it is considered that there is sufficient indication of an intention to pass that property to give to the devisee all the interest, whatever it may be, that the testator had in it". This excepting principle has been applied not only where the will follows the option,[11] but also where the will was merely republished after the option by the execution of a codicil,[12] and even where the will and the option were executed on the same day, thought it was uncertain which in fact came first.[13]

Owing to its anomalous character the courts will only apply the doctrine of conversion under *Lawes* v. *Bennett*[14] in deciding claims between persons entitled respectively to the real and personal property of a deceased grantor of an option. Thus it was not applied in *Edwards* v. *West*[15] where under the terms of a lease the landlord covenanted to insure, and the tenant had the option to purchase for a fixed sum. Before the time for exercising the option, the buildings demised were burnt, and the landlord received the insurance money. The tenant then exercised his option to purchase, but his claim to receive the insurance money as part of his purchase failed.

Notwithstanding the general reluctance to extend the doctrine of *Lawes* v. *Bennett*,[16] the Court of Appeal felt itself bound to apply the doctrine in *Re Carrington*,[17] where there was a specific legacy given of certain shares over which an option to purchase was granted, which was exercised after the testator's death. On the basis that the doctrine of conversion applied, it was held that the specific legacy of the shares was adeemed. It has been forcibly contended[18] that this decision is an unwarrantable extension of the *Lawes* v. *Bennett*[19] doctrine, by reason of the fact that the doctrine of conversion proper is concerned with conversion from real into personal property and *vice versa*, and not with a mere change from one kind of personalty to another. It is, however, a clear decision of the Court of Appeal, and has necessarily been followed since in a court of first instance.[20]

g   Partnership property

Real property belonging to partners has always been regarded in equity as personalty,[1] and this has now been made the statutory rule, subject to the

---

9 (1861), 1 John. & H. 424.
10 In *Weeding* v. *Weeding* (1861), 1 John. & H. 424, at p. 431.
11 *Drant* v. *Vause* (1842), 1 Y. & C. Ch. 580.
12 *Emuss* v. *Smith* (1845), 2 De G. & Sm. 722.
13 *Re Pyle*, [1895] 1 Ch. 724.
14 (1785), 1 Cox Eq. Cas. 167.
15 (1878), 7 Ch.D. 858. Cf. *Reynard* v. *Arnold* (1875), 10 Ch. App. 386.
16 *Supra.*
17 [1932] 1 Ch. 1; [1931] All E.R. Rep. 658, C.A.
18 By Professor Hanbury in (1933), 49 L.Q.R. 173.
19 *Supra.*
20 *Re Rose*, [1948] 2 All E.R. 971; [1949] Ch. 78.
1 *A.-G.* v. *Hubbuck* (1884), 13 Q.B.D. 275, C.A.

expression of a contrary intention, not only as between the partners, including the personal representatives of a deceased partner, but as between the persons entitled to the real and personal property of a deceased partner.[2]

2 FAILURE OF CONVERSION

a Reasons for failure

The objects for which a conversion is directed by a settlor or testator may fail, in whole or in part, for various reasons, for instance, some or all of the beneficiaries under a will may predecease the testator,[3] or some of the trusts may be void as directing accumulations beyond the permitted period.[4] In such cases the question may arise as to who is entitled to the lapsed or void interest, and the same question may arise where the entire equitable interest is not disposed of,[5] or where there is a surplus after carrying out the object of the conversion.[6]

b Total failure

If the objects of the conversion fail entirely at or before the time when the duty to convert arises,[7] the better view[8] is that there is no conversion at all, for there has never been a point of time when anyone could claim that the conversion should take place. The rule is the same whether the question arises under a deed[9] or a will,[10] and it makes no difference that there has been conversion in fact.[11] In the case of a future trust to convert it may well be that there is a period of time when it is uncertain whether or not the beneficial trusts will entirely fail, in which case it will be uncertain whether there is conversion or not until the prior uncertainty is resolved.

c Partial failure

If, for instance, realty is given to trustees on trust for sale, and to hold the proceeds of sale in trust for X and Y in equal shares, there is a partial failure of the objects of conversion if for any reason the gift to X cannot take effect, though the gift to Y is good. In such case if the conversion was directed by a deed, the rule is that the conversion is fully effective for all purposes, and the trustees hold X's half share on a resulting trust for the settlor who accordingly is regarded as having an interest in personalty.[12] It followed, before 1926, that if

---

[2] Partnership Act 1890, s. 22.
[3] *Bedford* v. *Bedford* (1865), 35 Beav. 584; *Hereford* v. *Ravenhill* (1839), 1 Beav. 481.
[4] Law of Property Act 1925, s. 164, as amended by the Perpetuities and Accumulations Act 1964, s. 13, replacing Accumulations Act 1800. *Re Perkins* (1909), 101 L.T. 345; *Re Walpole*, [1933] Ch. 431.
[5] *Watson* v. *Hayes* (1839), 5 My. & Cr. 125; *Flint* v. *Warren* (1848), 16 Sim. 124.
[6] *Wright* v. *Wright* (1809), 16 Ves. 188; *Maugham* v. *Mason* (1813), 1 Ves. & B. 410.
[7] Normally the date of the execution of a deed, and the death of the testator in the case of a will, though it may be later in the case of a future trust to convert.
[8] It has been said alternatively that there is a resulting trust for the settlor or testator of the property in its unconverted form.
[9] *Clarke* v. *Franklin* (1858), 4 K. & J. 257; *Re Lord Grimthorpe*, [1908] 2 Ch. 675, C.A.
[10] *Smith* v. *Claxton* (1820), 4 Madd. 484; *Bagster* v. *Fackerell* (1859), 26 Beav. 469; *Re Hopkinson*, [1922] 1 Ch. 65; *Re Walpole*, [1933] Ch. 431; [1933] All E.R. Rep. 988.
[11] *Davenport* v. *Coltman* (1842), 12 Sim. 588; *Re Hopkinson, supra*.
[12] *Hewitt* v. *Wright* (1780), 1 Bro. C. C. 86; *Clarke* v. *Franklin* (1858), 4 K. & J. 257.

the settlor was dead his next-of-kin and not his heir-at-law would be entitled, and though the question cannot now arise on intestacy, under a will a residuary legatee and not a residuary devisee would be entitled. The converse is equally true in the case of a direction to invest personalty in the purchase of realty.[13]

The position is rather more complicated where the direction to convert is contained in a will, where there may be differences between the rules as to conversion from realty to personalty and as to conversion from personalty to realty. First, let us consider partial failure of objects under a will directing the sale of realty. Here the undisposed-of interest results to the person entitled to the testator's realty,[14] either *in toto*, or *pro rata* if the will involved a disposition of realty and personalty comprising a mixed fund.[15] Before 1926, this rule had two bases, namely,

(i) that conversion was, *prima facie*, directed for the purposes of the will only and was irrelevant in deciding who was entitled if the interest was, in the events which happened, undisposed of, and the person entitled was accordingly the person entitled to the property in its unconverted form; and

(ii) that the person who satisfied this description, i.e., the heir-at-law, could only be disinherited by express words or a necessary implication.[16]

Thus even an express declaration that the proceeds of sale should not in any event lapse or result for the benefit of the heir-at-law would not affect the position in the absence of an express gift to the next-of-kin.[17] The first of these bases still holds good though the second has been removed by the 1925 Property Legislation.

Most of the reported cases in fact arose before 1926 and involved a conflict between the claims of the next-of-kin and the heir-at-law. There was, of course, no reason why a testator should not have expressly provided that in case of partial failure the interest that failed should go not to the heir-at-law but to another, and although, as mentioned in the preceding paragraph, a mere declaration was ineffective, it was successfully argued in a few cases that on the true construction of a will the share undisposed of was included in a residuary legacy.[18] The same problem may arise after 1925 where the testator has disposed separately of his residuary realty and his residuary personalty.

A further question is as to the form in which the property is taken. The rule is that although the interest goes to the person entitled to the property in its unconverted form, he takes it in its converted form, for the trustees are under a duty to convert in order to carry out the objects which have not failed.[19] Thus before 1926, if before the interest had been handed over to the heir-at-law of the testator he had died intestate, the interest would have passed to his next-of-kin, and similarly, both before and after 1926, under the will of the person entitled, it would pass to a residuary legatee and not a residuary devisee.

---

[13] *Wheldale* v. *Partridge* (1803), 8 Ves. 227; *Clarke* v. *Franklin* (1858), 4 K. & J. 257.
[14] *Ackroyd* v. *Smithson* (1780), 1 Bro. C. C. 503; *Re Richerson*, [1892] 1 Ch. 379.
[15] *Ackroyd* v. *Smithson, supra; Salt* v. *Chattaway* (1841), 3 Beav. 576; *Spencer* v. *Wilson* (1873), L.R. 16 Eq. 501.
[16] *City of London* v. *Garway* (1706), 2 Vern. 571.
[17] *Fitch* v. *Weber* (1848), 6 Hare 145; *Edwards* v. *Tuck* (1856), 23 Beav. 268.
[18] *Kennell* v. *Abbott* (1799), 4 Ves. 802; *Green* v. *Jackson* (1835), 2 Russ. & My. 238.
[19] *Smith* v. *Claxton* (1820), 4 Madd. 484; *Wilson* v. *Coles* (1860), 28 Beav. 215; *Re Richerson, supra.*

Turning to the conversion of personalty into realty, the corresponding rule applies as to who is entitled to the interest which has failed, i.e. the person entitled to the property in its unconverted form.[20] It is not altogether clear, however, whether the corresponding rule also applies that he takes the property in its converted form. Chitty J. thought that he would in *Re Richerson*,[1] which seems more consistent with principle, but in *Curteis* v. *Wormald*,[2] Jessel M.R. and James L.J. in the Court of Appeal, said that the next-of-kin would take it as they found it, though this may perhaps be explained on the ground that all the money had actually been converted into land.[3] This explanation is not, however, available in the case of *Hereford* v. *Ravenhill*[4] where it was held the residuary legatee took the property in the unconverted form in which it in fact was.

Finally it should be added that, except perhaps as regards the last point dealt with, the actual state of the property is irrelevant in ascertaining the rights of the parties, whether it is partial failure on conversion of realty to personalty or *vice versa*.[5]

3 RECONVERSION

In some circumstances where a conversion has been directed a beneficiary is entitled to elect to call for the property in its unconverted form, in which case equity treats the notionally converted property as restored to its original state. This process is known as reconversion. We shall consider in the following subsections, first, who can reconvert, and secondly, how election may be made.

a Entire equitable interest in property absolutely vested

If the entire equitable interest in property is vested absolutely and indefeasibly in a person *sui iuris*, that person can elect to take the property in its actual state. Any other rule would, indeed, be absurd, for otherwise, after conversion, the beneficiary could call for the property to be transferred to him under the rule in *Saunders* v. *Vautier*,[6] and then proceed by a further sale or purchase, to restore the property to its original form. The common-sense of the matter was pithily expressed by Trevor M.R.'s observation[7] that "a court of equity will not decree a vain thing". The general position was stated by Lord Cranworth as follows:[8] "where, by a settlement, land has been agreed to be converted into money, or money to be converted into land, a character is imposed upon it until somebody entitled to take it in either form chooses to elect that, instead of its being converted into money, or instead of its being converted into land, it shall remain in

---

[20] *Cogan* v. *Stephens* (1835), 1 Beav. 482 n.; *Hereford* v. *Ravenhill* (1839), 1 Beav. 481 and (1842), 5 Beav. 51; *Simmons* v. *Pitt* (1873), 8 Ch. App. 978; *Curteis* v. *Wormald* (1878), 10 Ch.D. 172, C.A.

[1] [1892] 1 Ch. 379.

[2] *Supra*.

[3] The judgment apparently did not deal with the small sum not actually converted—See *Re Richerson*, [1892] 1 Ch. 379, at p. 384.

[4] (1842), 5 Beav. 51.

[5] *Johnson* v. *Woods* (1840), 2 Beav. 409; *Bective* v. *Hodgson* (1864), 10 H.L.Cas. 656.

[6] (1841), Cr. & Ph. 240 discussed in Chapter 10, Section 7, p. 333, *ante*.

[7] In *Benson* v. *Benson* (1710), 1 P. Wms. 130, at p. 131.

[8] In *Harcourt* v. *Seymour* (1851), 2 Sim. N.S. 12, at pp. 45, 46.

the form in which it is actually found. There can be no doubt that that is the law; and the only question in each particular case is whether there have been acts sufficient to enable the court to say that the party has so determined". Thus if trustees held Blackacre in fee simple on trust for sale for X absolutely, and X elected to take Blackacre as land, on X's death the trustees would *prima facie* hold Blackacre on trust for X's residuary devisee and not for his residuary legatee. After X had made his election the trustees would no longer be under a duty to sell Blackacre, indeed it would be a breach of trust for them to do so, though a purchaser would be protected under statutory provisions.[9]

In one case, indeed, reconversion takes place automatically without any declaration or act on the part of the person entitled. This happens where, as the expression is, the property is "at home", that is to say where not only the equitable interest, but the whole property, both legal and equitable, is vested in one person.[10] Thus if H had covenanted to lay out £5,000 in the purchase of real property to be settled in the form usual in the classic realty settlement, including an ultimate remainder in fee simple to H, there would have been an immediate conversion, and, notwithstanding that the covenant had never been carried out, on H's death leaving wife or issue surviving him, the fee simple remainder would have passed to the persons entitled to H's realty. If, however, all the other persons entitled under the limitations of the settlement had pre-deceased H, who was at his death indefeasibly entitled to the entire legal and equitable interest, the property would have been treated as reconverted and the fund would have passed to the persons entitled to H's personalty. The point is that there would no longer be anyone in existence who could enforce the trust for conversion. The same principle was applied in *Re Cook*[11] where as a result of section 36 of the Law of Property Act 1925 the legal estate in Blackacre became vested in a husband and wife on a statutory trust for sale for themselves as joint tenants. At this stage each joint tenant clearly had an equitable interest in personalty. On the death of the husband the entire interest in the property, both legal and equitable, became vested in the wife. The question was whether the bequest by the wife of "all my personal estate" would carry the equitable interest in Blackacre to the residuary legatee. It was held in effect that there was a reconversion on the death of the husband, and that the wife could not be a trustee for herself alone, there being no separation of the legal and equitable interests. Blackacre, accordingly, was realty in the hands of the wife and did not pass under the gift of "all my personal estate".

b Undivided shares

Before 1926, two or more tenants in common, between them absolutely entitled in equity, could, provided they acted unanimously, reconvert in the same way as a single equitable owner. Where, however, the tenants in common were not agreed a distinction was drawn between a trust to convert land into money and money into land, on the ground that land is liable to lose its value if not sold as one parcel, and that one co-owner must not be allowed to act to

---

[9] *Re Cotton's Trustees and the School Board for London* (1882), 19 Ch.D. 624; Law of Property Act 1925, s. 23. Cf. *Re Jenkins & Randall's Contract*, [1903] 2 Ch. 362.

[10] *Chichester* v. *Bickerstaff* (1693), 2 Vern. 295; *Pulteney* v. *Darlington* (1783), 1 Bro. C.C 223; affd. (1796), 7 Bro. C.C. 530, H.L.; *Wheldale* v. *Partridge* (1803), 8 Ves. 227.

[11] [1948] 1 All E.R. 231; [1948] Ch. 212.

the prejudice of the others. Accordingly where money was directed to be laid out in the purchase of realty to be held on trust for tenants in common, any tenant could reconvert and was entitled to his share in money irrespective of the wishes of the others.[12] Where, however, there was a trust for sale of real property it was said to be "repugnant to the principles on which the doctrine of conversion and reconversion rest, to hold that one of the legatees of an undivided share in the produce of real estate directed by the testator to be converted into personalty could, without the assent of the others, elect to take his share as unconverted, and in the shape of real estate".[13] Nothing short of unanimity would suffice.[14] Since 1925, as we have seen,[15] the practical result is substantially the same, though it seems that it is no longer possible for tenants in common to reconvert so as to give themselves interests in realty.[16]

c Remaindermen

Though the cases[17] are not wholly consistent, it seems that, in some circumstances at any rate, a remainderman can elect to take property in its unconverted form. It is, of course, clear on the one hand that no election can prejudice persons with prior interests, and, on the other hand, that any election made is liable to be affected by an actual conversion that takes place before the interest falls into possession. It was said in Re Sturt,[18] after a careful consideration of the cases, that no case had gone further than Meek v. Devenish[19] which decided that a man entitled absolutely in a contingent event might, before it happened, effectually elect to reconvert if it happened before his death. It was held in Re Sturt[20] itself that a person with a contingent or defeasible interest could not by his will effect a reconversion which would become operative if the contingent interest became absolute at some time after his death.

d Persons under disability

An infant[21] cannot elect, though in an appropriate case the court may sanction his election or elect for him.[22] Similarly a patient under the Mental Health Act 1959[1] cannot elect,[2] but the Court of Protection may act on his behalf.

e Evidence

To establish reconversion "it is necessary to have sufficient evidence of the election to be derived from declarations or acts and conduct of the parties, and

---

[12] Seeley v. Jago (1717), 1 P. Wms. 389.
[13] Per Romilly M.R. in Holloway v. Radcliffe (1857), 23 Beav. 163, at p. 172; Re Jenkins and Randall's Contract, [1903] 2 Ch. 362; Re Heathcote (1887), 58 L.T. 43. Cf. s. 28 (3) of the Law of Property Act 1925, as slightly amended by the Mental Health Act 1959, s. 149 (1) and Sched. 7, Part I.
[14] Spencer v. Harrison (1879), 5 C.P.D. 97.
[15] Chapter 10, Section 7, p. 333, ante.
[16] This seems to be the effect of ss. 34 and 35 of the Law of Property Act 1925 and s. 36 of the Settled Land Act 1925.
[17] Crabtree v. Bramble (1747), 3 Atk. 680; Sisson v. Giles (1863), 3 De G. J. & S, 614.
[18] [1922] 1 Ch. 416.   [19] (1877), 6 Ch.D. 566.   [20] Supra.
[21] Seeley v. Jago (1717), 1 P. Wms. 389; Van v. Barnett (1812), 19 Ves. 102.
[22] Robinson v. Robinson (1854), 19 Beav. 494.
[1] Section 101; Wilder v. Pigott (1882), 22 Ch.D. 263; Re Douglas & Powell's Contract, [1902] 2 Ch. 296.
[2] Re Wharton (1854), 5 De G.M. & G. 33; Re Douglas and Powell's Contract, supra.

where it is sought to establish such an election by a person or persons only entitled so to elect subject to the rights of third persons to insist upon a sale, it must be shewn in like manner that such persons have assented".[3] Very slight evidence will suffice,[4] though it is not certain whether a mere parol declaration would be adequate.[5]

In the case of a trust for sale of land, the mere retention of the land unsold for a long time may be enough,[6] unless this is to be explained for instance by reason of the existence of an unexpired option to purchase over the land.[7] Other matters which have been held to show election including getting possession of the trust deeds,[8] taking steps to transfer the land to another,[9] paying off a charge that would normally have been paid out of the proceeds of sale[10] and making a statement, in relation to a claim for legacy duty, that the land had been retained to his own use.[11] There may even be election by infection, as it were. If two properties are clearly being dealt with by a testator in the same way, and it is shown that there was reconversion as to one by the testator, it may be assumed that reconversion was also intended as to the other.[12]

In the case of money to be converted into land, reconversion will not be presumed merely from long enjoyment of the income from the unconverted personalty.[13]

---

[3] Per Byrne J. in Re Douglas and Powell's Contract, [1902] 2 Ch. 296, 312.

[4] Pulteney v. Darlington (1783), 1 Bro. C.C. 223; Wheldale v. Partridge (1803), 8 Ves. 227.

[5] Edwards v. Warwick (Countess) (1723), 2 P.Wms. 171; Pulteney v. Darlington (1783) 1 Bro. C.C. 223, 236; Wheldale v. Partridge, (1803), 8 Ves. 227, at p. 236, suggest it would, but this is doubted in Bradish v. Gee (1754), Amb. 229.

[6] Dixon v. Gayfere (No. 2) (1853), 17 Beav. 433 (2 years not enough); Brown v. Brown (1864) 33 Beav. 399 (3½ years not enough); Re Gordon (1877), 6 Ch.D. 531 (9 years); Griesbach v. Fremantle (1853), 17 Beav. 314 (16 years).

[7] Re Lewis (1885), 30 Ch.D. 654.

[8] Davies v. Ashford (1845), 15 Sim. 42; Potter v. Dudeney (1887), 56 L.T. 395.

[9] Potter v. Dudeney, supra.

[10] Re Davidson (1879), 11 Ch.D. 341, C.A.

[11] Griesbach v. Freemantle (1853), 17 Beav. 314; cf. Sharp v. St. Sauveur (1871), 7 Ch. App. 343.

[12] Potter v. Dudeney (1887), 56 L.T. 395; contrast Meredith v. Vick (1857), 23 Beav. 559.

[13] Gillies v. Longlands (1851), 4 De G. & Sm. 372; Re Pedder's Settlement (1854), 5 De G. M. & G. 890.

CHAPTER 17

Satisfaction, Ademption and Performance

Satisfaction was defined by Lord Romilly[1] as "the donation of a thing with the intention that it is to be taken either wholly or in part in extinguishment of some prior claim of the donee". This can perhaps best be made clear by giving illustrations of the types of circumstances in which questions of satisfaction may arise

(i) A owes B £500. Subsequently A makes a will giving B a legacy of £X00. Can B claim both his debt and the legacy in full?
  This type of case is discussed in Section 1, *post*, p. 506.

(ii) A owes B £500. Subsequently A pays B £X00, without reference to the debt. Can B still claim the debt in full?
  This type of case is discussed in Section 2, *post*, p. 511.

(iii) A father covenants in his daughter's marriage settlement to pay £5,000 to the trustees thereof. He subsequently makes a will leaving the daughter a settled legacy of £X,000, and then dies without having paid any money to the trustees. Is the father's estate liable to pay both the £5,000 under the marriage settlement and also the legacy settled by the will?
  This, and the following two types of case, are discussed in Section 3, *post*, p. 512.

(iv) By his marriage settlement a father has covenanted to provide portions of £1,000 for each of the children of the marriage. His wife dies, leaving two children of the marriage, and by a settlement made on his remarriage the father, *inter alia*, conveys Blackacre to trustees upon trust to raise £X,000 to be settled on the children of his first marriage in equal shares. Can the children claim under both settlements?

(v) By will a father gives £5,000 to his daughter Susie. Subsequently, on Susie's marriage, he pays, or covenants to pay, £X,000 to the trustees of her marriage settlement. Can Susie claim under both the will and the settlement?

---

[1] In *Lord Chichester* v. *Coventry* (1867), L.R. 2 H.L. 71, at p. 95, adopting White and Tudor's *Leading Cases in Equity*, now 9th Ed., Vol. II, pp. 326–327.

(vi) By will A gives B £2,000 for a particular purpose. Subsequently A hands over £X,000 to B for the same purpose. On A's death can B claim the legacy in full?

This type of case is discussed in Section 4, *post*, p. 527.

(vii) A by will gives B a legacy of £700. Elsewhere in the will, or in a codicil, he gives B a legacy of £X00. Can B claim both legacies in full?

The term "satisfaction" has been used to include all the above types of case. More strictly satisfaction is restricted to the first four types of case, as presupposing an existing legal obligation, which does not arise, of course, under the will of a living person. The next two types of case are properly described as cases of ademption, or sometimes equitable ademption to distinguish another and perhaps stricter sense of the term where a testamentary disposition fails by reason of the fact that the subject of the disposition has ceased to exist as a part of the testator's estate at the time of his death. The last type of case is purely a question of construction of the testamentary instrument or instruments as to whether the provisions are intended to be cumulative or substitutional. As such it is outside the scope of this book.[2]

In every case it is a question of the intention of the settlor or testator whether the prior claim is satisfied. Of course the intention that there is or is not to be satisfaction may appear expressly or by implication on the true construction of the instrument itself,[3] in which case the usual rule applies that parol evidence will not be admitted to contradict, add to or vary a written instrument. Where there is no such provision there is in many cases a presumption of satisfaction: if there is neither a provision contained in the instrument nor a presumption applicable, both benefits can be claimed. We must now turn to discuss the variant presumptions of satisfaction and ademption which may arise in the types of circumstances set out above.

1 SATISFACTION OF ORDINARY DEBTS BY LEGACIES

a The general rule

The presumption of satisfaction is to the effect that if a testator gives a legacy to his creditor the legacy being at least equal in amount to the debt, there is a presumption that the testator does not intend the creditor to have both his debt and the legacy, but intends the legacy to be in extinguishment of the claim of the creditor. Where the presumption applies the effect is that if the creditor-legatee wishes to have the legacy, he must give up his claim to his debt. The

---

[2] Reference may be made to Jarman on *Wills*, 8th Ed., Vol. 2, pp. 1101 *et seq.* The leading case is *Hooley* v. *Hatton* (1773), 1 Bro. C.C. 390 n. where *prima facie* rules of construction to be applied are laid down.

[3] Questions of construction may arise on such a declaration. See *Cooper* v. *Cooper* (1873), 8 Ch. App. 813 for a discussion of a line of authority "in which the use of precedents has, sometimes, caused the courts of this country, first to slide into manifest error, and afterwards to follow that error under the notion that they are bound to do so" (*per* Lord Selborne L.C. at 825).

presumption is commonly regarded as being founded on *Talbott* v. *Duke of Shrewsbury*[4] where "it was said by Mr. Vernon and agreed to by the Master of the Rolls[5] that if one, being indebted to another in a sum of money, does by his will give him as great, or greater sum of money than the debt amounts to, without taking any notice at all of the debt, that this shall nevertheless be in satisfaction of the debt, so as that he should not have both the debt and the legacy". *Talbott* v. *Shrewsbury*[6] is not in fact the earliest case where the presumption was applied,[7] and it appears that the statement of the general rule therein contained was a mere dictum, as the will actually directed that legacies should be taken in discharge of debts.[8] Nevertheless the existence of the rule has been consistently accepted ever since this decision, and it will prevail in the absence of other relevant circumstances.[9] Though consistently accepted, the rule has also been consistently criticized—"no sooner was it established than learned judges of great eminence expressed their disapproval of it, and invented ways to get out of it".[10] Thus Lord Hardwicke said he would not have adopted such a rule in a case of first impression and observed[11] that the courts "have said indeed they would not break the rule, but at the same time have said, they would not go one jot further, and have been fond of distinguishing cases since, if possible", and more than a century later Kindersley V.C. said[12] the "principle being established, successive judges have said they cannot alter it. But what they have done is to rely on the minutest shade of difference to escape from that false principle".

b Differences between the legacy and the debt

The differences which will prevent the presumption of satisfaction from arising may be differences either of amount or in kind. It was settled at an early date that there is no presumption of satisfaction where the legacy is less in amount than the debt, not even satisfaction *pro tanto*.[13] Similarly if the legacy is given on a condition or a contingency,[14] or is of an uncertain amount, such as a share of residue, it is or may be less beneficial than the debt and is therefore no satisfaction, even though it in fact turns out to be more beneficial.[15]

---

[4] (1741), Prec. Ch. 394.

[5] Sir J. Trevor.

[6] *Supra.*

[7] See e.g. *Atkinson* v. *Webb* (1704), 2 Vern. 478; *Brown* v. *Dawson* (1705), 2 Vern. 498.

[8] See the argument of counsel in *Re Rattenberry*, [1906] 1 Ch. 667, at p. 668.

[9] E.g. *Re Rattenberry*, [1906] 1 Ch. 667; *Re Haves*, [1951] 2 All E.R. 928.

[10] Per Stirling J. in *Re Horlock*, [1895] 1 Ch. 516, at p. 518.

[11] *Richardson* v. *Greese* (1743), 3 Atk. 65, at p. 68; *Mathews* v. *Mathews* (1755), 2 Ves. Sen. 635.

[12] *Hassell* v. *Hawkins* (1859), 4 Drew. 468, at p. 470.

[13] *Gee* v. *Liddell* (No. 1) (1866), 35 Beav. 621; *Coates* v. *Coates*, [1898] 1 I.R. 258. Aliter in *Hammond* v. *Smith* (1864), 33 Beav. 452, where, however, the intention that the legacy should be in part payment of the debt was communicated to the debtor and not objected to by him.

[14] *Mathews* v. *Mathews* (1755), 2 Ves. Sen. 635; *Tolson* v. *Collins* (1799), 4 Ves. 483; *Sanford* v. *Irby* (1825), 4 L.J. O.S. Ch. 23.

[15] *Devese* v. *Pontet* (1785), 1 Cox. Eq. Cas. 188; *Lady Thynne* v. *Earl of Glengall* (1848), 2 H.L.Cas. 131.

Again there is no satisfaction if there is some other difference between the debt and the legacy which makes the legacy less advantageous to the creditor. Thus if the legacy is by the will expressly made payable at a later date than the debt, there is no satisfaction.[16] Where there is no special provision as to the date of payment of the legacy, so that it is payable at the end of the executor's year, the cases are in conflict. According to Re Horlock,[17] where there was a debt of £300 payable within three months of death, and a legacy of £400, as to which no time of payment was fixed, there is no satisfaction in such a case, since there is a difference in the times of payment. If this is right, the effect would be virtually to abolish the rule, for the payment of legacies can never be enforced for a year after the death,[18] while debts are normally payable at once. The contrary and, it is submitted, the better view was taken in Re Rattenberry[19] where Swinfen Eady J. pointed out that Lord Hardwicke had decided in Clark v. Sewell[20] that a legacy in satisfaction of a debt where no time is fixed for payment carries interest from the date of death, contrary to the normal rule. This can be regarded as preventing the legacy, by reason of the delay in payment, from being less beneficial than the debt. The same reasoning is not applicable where the "debt" consists of an annuity, and it has been held accordingly that there was no satisfaction where the annuity under the deed was payable quarterly[1] or half-yearly,[2] while under the will the first payment would not become due until a year after the testator's death, and similarly where under the deed it was payable quarterly in advance, under the will, quarterly in arrear.[3] But there can be satisfaction of an annuity, as in Atkinson v. Littlewood,[4] where both under the deed and under the will, the payments were to be made on the same special quarter days.

Another question which has arisen is whether a debt carrying interest, some of which is due at the date of death, is satisfied by a legacy of the capital sum. Thus in Fitzgerald v. National Bank, Ltd.[5] there was a debt of £100 carrying interest at the rate of 5 per cent and a legacy of £100. At the date of death £3 was due on account of interest. It was argued that the legacy was accordingly less than the debt and the presumption of satisfaction did not arise. The judge, however, held that it was a case of satisfaction since the "debt" did not include the interest due thereon and consequently was equal to the legacy. This doubtful decision was

---

[16] Adams v. Lavender (1824), M'Cle. & Yo. 41; Re Roberts (1902), 50 W.R. 469.
[17] [1895] 1 Ch. 516 purporting to follow Re Dowse (1881), 50 L.J. Ch. 285, which, however, was a case of an annuity.
[18] Even if directed to be paid before, according to the generally accepted opinion. The cases do not make the point very clearly—Benson v. Maude (1821), 6 Madd. 15; Brooke v. Lewis (1822), 6 Madd. 358. There are dicta to the contrary in Re Riddell, [1936] 2 All E.R. 1600 (not reported on this point in [1936] Ch. 747); Re Pollock, [1943] 2 All E.R. 443; [1943] Ch. 338.
[19] [1906] 1 Ch. 667.
[20] (1744), 3 Atk. 96.
[1] Re Stibbe (1946), 175 L.T. 198.
[2] Re Dowse (1881), 50 L.J. Ch. 285.
[3] Re Van den Bergh's Will Trusts, [1948] 1 All E.R. 935 (but this was said by the judge to be. in this case, a subsidiary question).
[4] (1874), L.R. 18 Eq. 595; Re Haves, [1951] 2 All E.R. 928.
[5] [1929] 1 K.B. 394; [1928] All E.R. Rep. 596.

based on the ground that at the time when *Talbott* v. *Duke of Shrewsbury*[6] was decided a debt had to be sued for in an action of debt, while interest thereon had to be sued for separately in an action of assumpsit, and that "debt" in the rule accordingly excluded interest thereon. If rightly decided, an action would presumably lie for any arrears of interest due.[7]

Other differences which may rebut the presumption of satisfaction are that the debt is secured, while the legacy is not,[8] that the debt—an annuity—is free of taxes, while the legacy is not,[9] that the legacy is of an annuity liable to forfeiture, while the covenanted annuity is not,[10] and, possibly, that the debt is payable to one set of trustees, while the legacy is payable to a different set of trustees,[11] even though on the same trusts, or to the *cestui que trust*.[12] It is sometimes said[13] that a legacy cannot be a satisfaction of a debt owed by the testator in a fiduciary capacity, for instance as a trustee. It is submitted, however, that the better view is that the presumption of satisfaction may apply in such case, though perhaps here it is even more easy to rebut it than usual. The presumption was applied in *Tennant* v. *Tennant*,[14] and in many cases where the presumption has not been applied, it has been on other grounds, and the fact that the debt has been due from the testator as a trustee or executor has not been mentioned.[15] The mere fact that the creditor-legatee is also appointed executor is irrelevant.[16] It should also be observed that "it is a general rule of satisfactions that the thing to be considered as a satisfaction should be exactly of the same nature".[17] Thus a debt cannot be satisfied by a devise of land, and an annuity cannot be satisfied by a life interest in a house and furniture.[18]

c Debts to which the presumption applies

Since the rule is based on the presumed intention of the testator, it follows that no debt can be satisfied unless it was in existence when the will was made.[19] Again there is no satisfaction in the case of an open and running account for in as much as the testator could not be supposed to know what the balance of a

---

[6] (1714), Prec. Ch. 394.
[7] In *Fitzgerald* v. *National Bank*, *supra*, the arrears had been paid before the action was heard.
[8] *Re Stibbe* (1946), 175 L.T. 198; *Hales* v *Darell* (1840), 3 Beav. 324; Cf. *Re Haves*, [1951] 2 All E.R. 928.
[9] *Atkinson* v. *Webb* (1704), 2 Vern. 478.
[10] *Re Van den Bergh's Will Trusts*, [1948] 1 All E.R. 935.
[11] *Pinchin* v. *Simms* (1861), 30 Beav. 119; *contra, semble, Atkinson* v. *Littlewood* (1874), L.R. 18 Eq. 595.
[12] *Smith* v. *Smith* (1861), 3 Giff. 263; *Re Hall*, [1918] 1 Ch. 562. See also *Fairer* v. *Park* (1876), 3 Ch.D. 309.
[13] E.g. Halsbury's Laws of England, 3rd Ed., Vol. 14, p. 606.
[14] (1847), 9 L.T.O.S. 217; *Barkham* v. *Dorwine* (1712), 2 Eq. Cas. Abr. 352. Note that in *Bensusan* v. *Nehemias* (1851), 4 De G. & Sm. 381 both the debt and the legacy were payable to settlement trustees.
[15] E.g. *Drewe* v. *Bidgood* (1825), 2 Sim. & St. 424; *Rowe* v. *Rowe* (1848), 2 De G. & Sm. 294; *Fairer* v. *Park* (1876), 3 Ch.D. 309; *contra, Taylor* v. *Taylor* (1858), 33 L.T.O.S. 88.
[16] *Re Rattenberry*, [1906] 1 Ch. 667.
[17] Per Lord Hardwicke in *Barret* v. *Beckford* (1750), 1 Ves. Sen. 519, at p. 521; *Alleyn* v. *Alleyn* (1750), 2 Ves. Sen. 37.
[18] *Coates* v. *Coates*, [1898] 1 I.R. 258.
[19] *Thomas* v. *Bennet* (1725), 2 P. Wms. 341; *Fowler* v. *Fowler* (1735), 3 P. Wms. 353.

running account would be, or whether he owed any money or not, he could not intend the legacy to be in satisfaction of a debt which he did not know that he owed.[20] It is not a running account, where the creditor has merely deposited moneys with the testator, who from time to time makes repayments, and there is no possibility of the testator becoming the creditor.[1] Nor will a negotiable instrument be satisfied by a legacy.[2]

It should be observed that if the debt was in existence when the will was made, the presumption of satisfaction will apply notwithstanding that the debt was subsequently paid during the testator's lifetime, at any rate where the amount of the legacy exactly equals the debt. The legacy in such case will accordingly fail to take effect.[3]

If the debt is entered into by a document contemporaneous with the will, so that both must have been present to the mind of the testator when he executed each of them, it is a strong reason against applying the presumption of satisfaction.[4]

d Direction to pay debts, or to pay debts and legacies

"It seems tolerably clear that a direction for payment either of debts and legacies,[5] or of debts simpliciter,[6] is treated as being, whether or not artificially— and I do not think it is particularly artificial—something which *prima facie* takes the case altogether out of the rule".[7] It is something from which the court will readily infer an intention by the testator that the creditor shall have both his debt and the legacy. It was held in *Wathen* v. *Smith*,[8] however, that "debt" in this context did not include liability on a bond or covenant to pay a sum of money after the testator's death. This unsatisfactory view, however, can hardly stand in the light of subsequent authorities.[9]

e Debt due to a child of the testator

It seems that where the debt is an ordinary debt,[10] the fact that the creditor-legatee is a child of the testator makes no difference to the application of the rule.[11] The same is true where the creditor-legatee is the wife of the testator.[12]

---

[20] *Rawlins* v. *Powel* (1715), 1 P. Wms. 297; *Buckley* v. *Buckley* (1887), 19 L.R. Ir. 544.
[1] *Edmunds* v. *Low* (1857), 3 K. & J. 318.
[2] *Carr* v. *Easterbrooke* (1797), 3 Ves. 561; *Re Roberts* (1902), 50 W.R. 469.
[3] *Re Fletcher* (1888), 38 Ch.D. 373.
[4] *Horlock* v. *Wiggins* (1888), 39 Ch.D. 142, C.A.
[5] *Chancey's Case* (1725), 1 P. Wms. 408; *Field* v. *Mostin* (1778), 2 Dick. 543; *Hassell* v. *Hawkins* (1859), 4 Drew. 468.
[6] *Cole* v. *Willard* (1858), 25 Beav. 568; *Re Huish* (1889), 43 Ch.D. 260; *Re Manners*, [1949] 2 All E.R. 201; [1949] Ch. 613, C.A. *Edmunds* v. *Low* (1857), 3 K. & J. 318 is not good law on this point.
[7] *Re Manners* [1949] 2 All E.R. 201, at p. 204; [1949] Ch. 613, at p. 618, C.A. *per* Evershed M.R.
[8] (1819), 4 Madd. 325.
[9] *Cole* v. *Willard* (1858), 25 Beav. 568; *Re Huish* (1889) 43 Ch.D. 260; *Re Stibbe* (1946), 175 L.T. 198; *Re Manners, supra,* C.A.
[10] See Section 3, p. 512, *post*, for the rule in the case of a portions debt.
[11] *Tolson* v. *Collins* (1799), 4 Ves. 483; *Edmunds* v. *Low* (1857), 3 K. & J. 318.
[12] *Cole* v. *Willard*, (1858), 25 Beav. 568; *Atkinson* v. *Littlewood* (1874), L.R. 18 Eq. 595.

f Admissibility of extrinsic evidence

As has already been seen, the presumption of satisfaction is deemed to represent the intention of the settlor, and accordingly the presumption may be rebutted, or, indeed, reinforced, by some express provision in the will or by implied expressions of intention therein contained.[13] For instance the court may infer an intention that the legacy shall be in addition to the debt from the motive expressed in the bequest of the legacy. Moreover, as has been explained, differences, even slight ones, between the debt and the legacy are construed as indicating an intention that the creditor shall have his legacy as well as his debt.[14]

As to how far extrinsic evidence is admitted, the rules are the same as in relation to other cases of satisfaction, and are discussed in Section 3j, p. 526, *post*.

2 SATISFACTION OF A DEBT BY AN *INTER VIVOS* PAYMENT

a Debt due to a child from its parent

In *Wood* v. *Briant*[15] Lord Hardwicke observed[16] "There are very few cases where a father will not be presumed to have paid the debt he owes to a daughter, when, in his lifetime, he gives her in marriage a greater sum than he owed her; for it is very unnatural to suppose that he would choose to leave himself a debtor to her and subject to an account." This decision was followed in *Plunkett* v. *Lewis*,[17] which in turn was treated by the Court of Appeal, in *Crichton* v. *Crichton*,[18] as showing that a debt[19] owing by a parent to a child is presumed to be satisfied by the subsequent payment to him, on marriage or some other occasion, of a sum equal to or greater than the debt. There is not much authority, but the rules seem to correspond so far as possible with those applying to the type of satisfaction dealt with in the previous section. It was made clear in *Crichton* v. *Crichton*[20] that in this sort of case there could be no satisfaction *pro tanto*, and that the debt must have been in existence at the time of the *inter vivos* advance.

b Other cases

Although the above cases refer to payments by a parent to a child, it is doubtful in principle whether this relationship is essential: there is at least one case[1] where it was assumed there could be satisfaction between a brother and

---

13 *Davie* v. *Messiter* (1861), 3 L.T. 874; *Douce* v. *Torrington* (1833), 2 My. & K. 600; *Glover* v. *Hartcup* (1864), 34 Beav. 74.

14 *Charlton* v. *West* (1861), 30 Beav. 124.

15 (1742), 2 Atk. 521; *Seed* v. *Bradford* (1750), 1 Ves. Sen. 501; *Chave* v. *Farrant* (1810), 18 Ves. 8.

16 At p. 522.

17 (1844), 3 Hare 316.

18 [1896] 1 Ch. 870, C.A.

19 There seems no reason to restrict it to liability for a breach of trust, which was in question in *Crichton* v. *Crichton*, *supra*, itself.

20 *Supra*.

1 *Drewe* v. *Bidgood* (1825), 2 Sim. & St. 424.

sister, though held in the circumstances that there was not. It will be remembered, as Plumer M.R. expressed it in *Goldsmid* v. *Goldsmid*,[2] that "where there is a question of satisfaction, there must be a reference to the intention. Satisfaction is a substitution of one thing for another: and the question in cases of that kind is whether the substituted thing was given for the thing proposed". Though less likely to arise in practice, it would seem that the presumption of satisfaction should be stronger in the absence of the parent-child relationship.

3 SATISFACTION OF A PORTIONS DEBT BY A LEGACY OR BY A SUBSEQUENT PORTION: ADEMPTION OF A LEGACY BY A PORTION

a Double portions

It will be observed that this one section deals with three different types of circumstances. This is by reason of the fact that the presumption which arises is in each case based on the leaning of the courts against double portions and consequently the rules are, in general, the same, and authorities on one type of case are authorities also on another. There are, however, some differences, which will be explained in due course, between ademption of a legacy on the one hand and the two cases of satisfaction on the other hand. Cottenham L.C. explained the matter thus in *Pym* v. *Lockyer*[3]:

"All the decisions upon questions of double portions depend upon the declared or presumed intention of the donor. The presumption of equity is against double portions, because it is not thought probable, when the object appears to be to make a provision, and that object has been effected by one instrument, that a repetition of it in a second should be intended as an addition to the first. The second provision, therefore, is presumed to be intended as a substitution for, and not as an addition to, that first given."

As applied to the ademption of a legacy by a subsequent portion Greene M.R. put it the following way in *Re Vaux*[4]:

"The rule against double portions rests upon two hypotheses: first of all, that under the will the testator has provided a portion and, secondly, that by the gift *inter vivos* which is said to operate in ademption of that portion either wholly or *pro tanto*, he has again conferred a portion. The conception is that the testator having in his will given to his children that portion of the estate which he decides to give to them, when after making his will he confers upon a child a gift of such a nature as to amount to a portion, then he is not to be presumed to have intended that that child should have both, the gift *inter vivos* being taken as being on account of the portion given by the will."

This presumption of ademption has been held to apply to an appointment under a special power of appointment.[5] Again, as applied to the satisfaction of a portions debt by a legacy, Cotton L.J. said in *Montagu* v. *Earl of Sandwich*,[6]

---

[2] (1818), 1 Wils. Ch. 140, 149.
[3] (1841), 5 My. & Cr. 29 at 34–5.
[4] [1938] 4 All E.R. 703, at p. 708–9, [1939] Ch. 465, at p. 481, C.A.; *Ex parte Pye* (1811), 18 Ves. 140, *per* Lord Eldon.
[5] *Re Peel's Settlement*, [1911] 2 Ch. 165.
[6] (1886), 32 Ch. D. 525, at p. 534, C.A.; *Weall* v. *Rice* (1831), 2 Russ. & My. 251, *per* Leach M.R.

"as between father and son the presumption arises that a father does not intend to give double portions to his children; that is to say, if a father has made a provision by way of covenant in favour of his child before the date of his will; then unless it appears upon the will or by parol testimony . . . that he intends to give the benefit conferred by will in addition to that which is already secured to the child by covenant, then the child will not take both".

On the one hand, as regards the satisfaction of portions debts by legacies,[7] it should perhaps be made clear that if the portion has actually been paid, no question of satisfaction can arise.[8] A legacy cannot be intended as a substitution for something that has already been given. Thus if, for instance, on his son's marriage a father paid £5,000 to the trustees of his marriage settlement, a subsequent legacy to the settlement trustees would be payable in full. But if he merely covenanted to pay £5,000 to the trustees and did not pay it in his lifetime, and by a subsequent will gave them a legacy, the presumption of satisfaction would *prima facie* apply. On the other hand, where the will comes first, there is no reason why a legacy therein contained should not be adeemed by a covenant contained in a subsequent settlement just as much as by actual payment.[9] It should be observed, however, that a will may contain a provision, known as hotchpot,[10] requiring a child to bring into account advancements actually made during the father's lifetime. The exact effect of such a provision depends upon the construction of the particular words used and is outside the scope of this book.[11] Again, on an intestacy children who wish to share in the distribution of the estate will normally have to bring into hotchpot any money or property received from their parent during his lifetime by way of advancement or upon marriage.[12]

Though the presumptions of satisfaction and ademption have their supporters,[13] there has been considerable criticism from early times. The more common attitude of the courts is perhaps typified by the forthright statement of Bowen L.J. in *Montagu* v. *Earl of Sandwich*[14]: "whatever may be the view to be taken of the rule against double portions, it is a rule that exists; and there is nothing worse than frittering away an existing rule. . . . Feeling no confidence that in applying this doctrine of double portions in this particular case we are giving effect to the real intention of the testator . . . I record my judgment accordingly in favour of the appeal as a sacrifice made upon the altar of authority."

---

[7] Or subsequent portions, i.e. where the father subsequently makes an actual payment *inter vivos* to or for the benefit of his child, such payment being regarded as a portion.
[8] *Taylor* v. *Cartwright* (1872), L.R. 14 Eq. 167.
[9] *Hopwood* v. *Hopwood* (1859), 7 H.L.Cas. 728; *Stevenson* v. *Masson* (1873), L.R. 17 Eq. 78. In *Clarke* v. *Burgoine* (1767), 1 Dick. 353, legacies were adeemed in part by a payment on marriage and in part by a covenant to make a further payment on death.
[10] As to the derivation of this word Littleton explained . . . "this word is in English a pudding; for in this pudding is not commonly put one thing alone but one thing with other things together"—Coke upon Littleton 176a Sect. 267. And see (1962), 78 L.Q.R. at p. 262 (J. E. S. Simon).
[11] See e.g. Jarman on *Wills*, 8th Ed., Vol. 2, pp. 1156 *et seq.*
[12] Section 47(1)(iii) of the Administration of Estates Act 1925. For a useful general discussion of this subsection see (1961), 25 Con. 468 (J. T. Farrand).
[13] E.g. Lord Cottenham in *Lady Thynne* v. *Earl of Glengall* (1848), 2 H.L.Cas. 131, at p. 153.
[14] (1886), 32 Ch.D. 525, at p. 544, C.A.; *Re Lacon*, [1891] 2 Ch. 482, C.A.

b Meaning of a portion

As appears from the above citations it is essential, in order for a presumption of satisfaction or ademption to arise, for both the relevant provisions to be gifts or advancements in the nature of portions.[15] In considering what is meant by the term "portion", it seems permissible to refer to decisions on the hotchpot provisions on intestacy, mentioned above, to be found in section 47(1)(iii) of the Administration of Estates Act 1925. This subsection replaces the Statute of Distribution 1670, which referred to advances "by portion". Jenkins L.J. in *Re Hayward*,[16] in a judgment concurred in by the other members of the court, after referring to the different language, stated his view that section 47(1)(iii) was, if anything, narrower than the provisions of the Statute of Distribution 1670, but that decisions on the old Act were, generally speaking, applicable to the new.

Lord Jenkins has pointed out, in two different cases, two factors which tend to confuse the matter. One is[17] "that the word 'advancement' seems to be used in two ways. First, there is the typical gift by way of advancement for establishing a child in life; the child is there spoken of as being advanced because he is forwarded in life and made to stand better with the world." This is the meaning with which we are concerned. Secondly, where for instance a legacy is adeemed by a subsequent portion "the word 'advancement' is sometimes used . . . as being an advancement or anticipation of the interest under the will". It may be added that in the same case, in the court of first instance,[18] Upjohn J. referred to yet another sense of the word, namely "whether a sum of money paid by a parent to a child is by way of advancement or whether the child held the money from the parent on a resulting trust. When any payment is made by a parent to a child, there may be a presumption of advancement in that sense,[19] but that type of advancement is not the advancement with which we are now concerned, which is an advancement by way of portion." Further "portion" is not restricted to provision for younger children, in the sense in which it is commonly used in connection with a strict settlement.[20] The other factor was pointed out by Lord Jenkins, when a judge of first instance, in *Re George's Will Trusts*,[1] a case of ademption. Here it was contended "that, having regard to its character and the circumstances in which it was made, the testator's gift *inter vivos* . . . was not in the nature of a portion at all, and, alternatively, that, if this gift was in itself in the nature of a portion, its character and the circumstances in which it was made were sufficient to rebut the presumption. The question of portion or no portion being necessarily to a great extent a question of the testator's intention, it is hardly possible to distinguish circumstances relied on as tending to show that the gift *inter vivos* was not in the nature of a portion at all from circumstances relied on as tending to rebut the presumption on the footing that it was in itself in the nature of a portion."

---

15 *Re Lacon*, [1891] 2 Ch. 482, at p. 497; [1891–4] All E.R. Rep. 286, at p. 292, C.A.; *Re George's Will Trusts*, [1948] 2 All E.R. 1004, at p. 1008; [1949] Ch. 154, at p. 159.
16 [1957] 2 All E.R. 474, at p. 477; [1957] Ch. 528, at p. 535, C.A.
17 *Re Hayward*, [1957] 2 All E.R. 474, at p. 480; [1957] Ch. 528, at p. 540, C.A.
18 [1956] 3 All E.R. 608, at p. 611.
19 See Chapter 4, Section 2d, p. 104, *ante*.
20 *Re Stephens*, [1904] 1 Ch. 322.
 1 [1948] 2 All E.R. 1004, at p. 1009; [1949] Ch. 154, at p. 159.

According to Kay L.J.,[2] "a 'portion' means such a share of the father's personal property as he intends to be a provision for that son, or . . . a substantial part of the provision for that son". This, however, is hardly adequate, and according to Jenkins L.J.,[3] "the nearest approach to a definition of what is an advancement that our case law has achieved" is contained in two short judgments[4] of Jessel M.R. in *Taylor* v. *Taylor*.[5] In the first he said[6] "I have always understood that an advancement by way of portion is something given by the parent to establish the child in life, or to make what is called a provision for him. . . . You may make the provision by way of marriage portion on the marriage of the child. You may make it on putting him into a profession or business in a variety of ways . . . [or by] a father giving a large sum to a child in one payment." However "it is not every payment made to a child which is to be regarded as an advancement, or advancement by way of portion. In every case to which I have been referred there has either been a settlement itself, or the purpose for which the payment was made has been shewn to be that which every one would recognize as being for establishing the child or making a provision for the child." And in the second judgment, according to his view, "nothing was an advancement unless it were given on marriage, or to establish the child in life. *Prima facie*, an advancement must be made in early life; but any sum given by way of making a permanent provision for the child would come within the term establishing in life."

A legacy, including a gift of residue,[7] from a father to a child "is presumed to be intended to be a portion; because providing for the child is a duty which the relative situation of the parties imposes upon the parent",[8] though the principle would not apply universally, for instance to a bequest of personal chattels.[9] And, as appears from *Taylor* v. *Taylor*,[10] a provision made on the marriage of a child is always regarded as being a portion. There is however no reason why a gift, although not made on marriage or any other special occasion with reference to the donee, should not constitute a portion.[11]

In *Taylor* v. *Taylor*[12] it was held on the one hand, that sums given for the following purposes constituted advancements by way of by portion for the purpose of the Statute of Distribution 1670, namely, the payment of the admission fee to one of the Inns of Court in the case of a child intended for the Bar,[13] the price, following a change of career,[14] of a commission and outfit of a child

---

[2] In *Re Lacon*, [1891] 2 Ch. 482, at p. 501; [1891–4] All E.R. Rep. 286, at p. 293, C.A.

[3] In *Re Hayward*, [1957] 2 All E.R. 474, at p. 478; [1957] Ch. 528, at p. 537, C.A.

[4] Alleged "advancements by portion" under the Statute of Distribution 1670, were made by a father to two sons: the first judgment deals with payments made to one son, the second with payments to the other.

[5] (1875), L.R. 20 Eq. 155.

[6] At pp. 157–158.

[7] *Lady Thynne* v. *Earl of Glengall* (1848), 2 H.L. Cas. 131; *Montefiore* v. *Guedalla* (1859), 1 De G. F. & J. 93; *Stevenson* v. *Masson* (1873), L. R. 17 Eq. 78.

[8] *Pym* v. *Lockyer* (1841), 5 My. & Cr. 29, at p. 35 *per* Lord Cottenham; *Ex parte Pye* (1811), 18 Ves. 140, 151 *per* Lord Eldon. So held or assumed in all cases of ademption.

[9] *Re Tussaud's Estate* (1878), 9 Ch.D. 363, C.A., *per* Jessel M.R. at 367.

[10] (1875), L.R. 20 Eq. 155; *Re Tussaud's Estate, supra*.

[11] *Leighton* v. *Leighton* (1874), L.R. 18 Eq. 458.

[12] *Supra*.

[13] Similarly in *Boyd* v. *Boyd* (1867), L.R. 4 Eq. 305 in relation to a premium to a solicitor.

[14] *Hoskins* v. *Hoskins* (1706), Prec. Ch. 263; *Andrew* v. *Andrew* (1878), 30 L.T. 457.

entering the army, and following yet another change of career the price of plant and machinery and other payments for the purpose of starting a child in business. On the other hand, the following were held not to be advancements by way of portion, namely, the payment of a fee to a special pleader for the same child, on the ground that this was in the nature of a payment for preliminary education,[15] the price, after becoming an officer in the army, of an outfit and passage money for him and his wife on going out to India with his regiment, and the payment of debts incurred by him in India, this being in the nature of temporary assistance. The decision on this last point was preferred by the Court of Appeal in Re Scott[16] to the contrary decisions in Boyd v. Boyd[17] and Re Blockley.[18]

The size of the gift is a matter of importance. Referring again to Jessel M.R.'s first judgment in Taylor v. Taylor[19] the rule is that "if in the absence of evidence you find a father giving a large sum to a child in one payment, there is a presumption that that is intended to start him in life or make a provision for him; but if a small sum is so given you may require evidence to show the purpose". On the one hand, the presumption that the gift of a large sum constitutes a portion was affirmed by the Court of Appeal in Re Scott[20] and Re Hayward,[1] the decision in Re Livesey's Settlement Trusts,[2] which at first sight seems to be to the contrary, being explained in Re Hayward,[3] as turning upon the language of the particular document. Although the relative size of the amount of the gift compared with the size of the testator's estate is a factor to be taken into account, in order to raise a presumption of satisfaction or ademption "it must be shown that the fund in question was sufficiently substantial in itself to be in the nature of a permanent provision without pressing too far the question of proportion."[4] Thus in Re Hayward,[5] admittedly a border line case, it was held that the gifts did not constitute advancements under section 47(1)(iii) of the Administration of Estates Act 1925, although they amounted to over £500 and the value of the net estate, exclusive of the gifts, was less than £1,800. The decision in this case might have been different had the donee been younger; he was forty-three years old at the date of the gift and it will be remembered that Jessel M.R. in Taylor v. Taylor[6] stated that prima facie, an advancement must be made in early life. On the other hand, not only is a single small gift, such as £100 to a daughter to buy a wedding outfit,[7] not a portion, but "the court has never added up small sums in order to show that if the child claims those sums as well as the larger provision made for him by the parent, he would be taking a

---

[15] Contrast Boyd v. Boyd [1867], L.R. 4 Eq. 305.

[16] [1903] 1 Ch. 1, C.A.

[17] Supra.

[18] (1885), 29 Ch.D. 250. Supported by Ansley v. Bainbridge (1830), 1 Russ. & My. 657; Auster v. Powell (1863), 1 De G.J. & S. 99 not referred to in Re Scott, [1903] 1 Ch. 1, C.A.

[19] (1875), L.R. 20 Eq. 155, at p. 158.

[20] Supra.

[1] [1957] 2 All E.R. 474; [1957] Ch. 528, C.A

[2] [1953] 2 All E.R. 723.

[3] Supra.

[4] Per Jenkins L.J. in Re Hayward, [1957] 2 All E.R. 474, at p. 482; [1957] Ch. 528, at p. 542, C.A.

[5] Supra.

[6] (1875), L.R. 20 Eq. 155.   [7] Ravenscroft v. Jones (1864), 4 De G J. & S. 224.

double portion".[8] As regards annuities, Lord Eldon had no doubt, in *Lord Kircudbright* v. *Lady Kircudbright*,[9] that an annuity was an advance by way of portion under the Statute of Distribution. In *Hatfield* v. *Minet*,[10] however, where by a separation deed a father covenanted to pay annuities to his children, it was held that so much of the annuities as were paid in the father's lifetime were not in the nature of advancements, but that the value of the annuities must be estimated as at the date of death and brought into hotchpot. And in *Watson* v. *Watson*[11] an annual allowance of £60 was held not to be a portion.

A portion is commonly money, but may, of course, comprise securities such as stock or shares in a limited company. Setting a child up in business may involve buying the goodwill of a business for a child and giving him stock in trade, which was given as a typical instance of a portion by Jessel M.R. in *Taylor* v. *Taylor*,[12] and in *Re George's Will Trusts*[13] Jenkins J. had "no doubt that a gift by a farmer to his son of live and dead stock with which to set up in business as a farmer may be in the nature of a portion, and, in the absence of circumstances tending to show the contrary, would generally be regarded as such". It was further held in this case that the fact that the gift was in a sense a forced one, did not prevent the gift from being a portion: the facts were that in 1940 the county war agricultural committee had threatened the father with eviction for inefficient farming and in the following year had actually served notice on him to vacate the farm. The committee was persuaded to withdraw the notice on being satisfied that control of the farm was being transferred to the son under a scheme which involved the gift of the live and dead stock in question.

c Donor must be father or *in loco parentis*

The presumptions of satisfaction and ademption only arise where both provisions in question are made by the child's father or by some other person who stands *in loco parentis* to him.[14] *Prima facie*, there is no presumption, and the child is entitled to both provisions, not only where the donor is completely unrelated, but equally where he or she, as the case may be, is the mother,[15] grandfather,[16] grandmother,[17] uncle,[18] or other collateral relative.[19] Further no presumption arises as between a father and an illegitimate child.[20]

---

8 *Per* Wigram V.C. in *Suisse* v. *Lowther* (1843), 2 Hare 424; *Watson* v. *Watson* (1864), 33 Beav. 574; *Re Peacock's Estate* (1872), L.R. 14 Eq. 236.

9 (1802), 8 Ves. 51.

10 (1878), 8 Ch.D. 136, C.A.

11 *Supra.*

12 (1875), L.R. 20 Eq. 155.

13 [1948] 2 All E.R. 1004, at p. 1009; [1949] Ch. 154, at p. 160.

14 *Ex parte Pye* (1811), 18 Ves. 140; *Powys* v. *Mansfield* (1837), 3 My. & Cr. 359; *Suisse* v. *Lowther* (1843), 2 Hare 424; *Fowkes* v. *Pascoe* (1875), 10 Ch. App. 343.

15 *Bennet* v. *Bennet* (1879), 10 Ch.D. 474; *Re Ashton* (1897), 2 Ch.D. 574, reversed on other grounds, [1898] 1 Ch. 142, C.A. *Contra, Mayd* v. *Field* (1876), 3 Ch.D. 587, where, however, the point was not taken.

16 *Roome* v. *Roome* (1744), 3 Atk. 181; *Re Dawson,* [1919] 1 Ch. 102; [1918–19] All E.R. Rep. 866; Cf. *Pym* v. *Lockyer* (1841), 5 My. & Cr. 29; *Campbell* v. *Campbell* (1866), L.R. 1 Eq. 383.

17 *Lyddon* v. *Ellison* (1854), 19 Beav. 565.

18 *Brown* v. *Peck* (1758), 1 Eden. 139; *Powys* v. *Mansfield, supra.*

19 *Shudal* v. *Jekyll* (1743), 2 Atk. 516; *Williams* v. *Duke of Bolton* (1768), 1 Bick. 405.

20 *Ex parte Pye, supra; Wetherby* v. *Dixon* (1815), 19 Ves. 407.

If the gifts have not been made by the father of the child, the question arises whether the donor was, at the relevant time,[1] *in loco parentis* to him. Whether in any case a person has put himself *in loco parentis* to a child has been said[2] to be "probably one of the most difficult of legal problems to solve". Lord Cottenham considered the question in *Powys v. Mansfield*[3] saying that he readily adopted Lord Eldon's definition in *Ex parte Pye*[4] and continuing "Lord Eldon says [one *in loco parentis*] is a person 'meaning to put himself in *loco parentis*; in the situation of the person described as the lawful father of the child'; but this definition must, I conceive, be considered as applicable to those parental offices and duties to which the subject in question has reference, namely, to the office and duty of the parent to make provision for the child." He went on to stress the importance of the intention of the person alleged to be *in loco parentis*, and the fact that one is concerned with the duty to make financial provision. Recently it has been emphasised that the matter is dependent on the circumstances of the individual case.[5]

Applying the above principles, it was held in *Powys v. Mansfield*,[6] that a rich unmarried uncle, whose brother had not got the means of adequately providing for his children, and who had furnished, through the father, the means of their maintenance and education, and negotiated the marriage settlement of a niece, to which the father was not a party, putting in the necessary money, was *in loco parentis* to the niece, notwithstanding the fact that she had continued to live with her father until her marriage.[7] Similarly in *Booker v. Allen*[8] where the donor, a near relative, had not only contributed to the maintenance and education of the child from the time she lost her father in early infancy, but was consulted as to the place of her education, was regarded by her as the person whose consent was necessary to her marriage and had expressly taken upon himself the obligation to make a provision for her in that event. The court was, perhaps, too easily persuaded that the grandfather was *in loco parentis* in *Campbell v. Campbell*,[9] but refused to extend this status in *Fowkes v. Pascoe*[10] to a woman who had made gifts to the son of her daughter-in-law, though he had lived with her for some years before his marriage, stayed with her on his visits to London, and had been given a handsome present on his marriage. It would seem to be easier, as would be expected, to establish that one is *in loco parentis* to another where there is a close blood relationship, whether legitimate or not.

---

[1] In *Watson v. Watson* (1864), 33 Beav. 574, a case of ademption, this was said to be the date of the will; on principle it would seem that the relationship must exist at the date of both gifts—in practice, once established it is unlikely to determine.

[2] *Per* James L.J. in *Fowkes v. Pascoe* (1875), 10 Ch. App. 343, at p. 350.

[3] (1837), 3 My. & Cr. 359, at p. 367.

[4] (1811), 18 Ves. 140.

[5] *Per* Danckwerts L.J. giving the judgment of the Court of Appeal in *Re Paradise Motor Co., Ltd.*, [1968] 2 All E.R. 625.

[6] (1837), 3 My. & Cr. 359; *Monck v. Monck* (1810), 1 Ball. & B. 298 (elder to younger brother.)

[7] Similarly in *Pym v. Lockyer* (1841), 5 My. & Cr. 29, where a grandfather was held to be *in loco parentis* to grandchildren although their father was living and had maintained them during childhood.

[8] (1831), 2 Russ. & My. 270.

[9] (1866), L.R. 1 Eq. 383; cf. *Lyddon v. Ellison* (1854), 19 Beav. 565.

[10] (1875), 10 Ch. App. 343.

A qualification to what has been said above arises where both portions are settled by a father or someone *in loco parentis* on a child, his or her spouse, and their children. If the limitations in the settlement and the will are identical, then the presumption of satisfaction or ademption will apply not only to the interest of the child, but equally to the interests of the other beneficiaries: the effect of differences in the limitations is considered below.[11]

It may be added, in conclusion, that parol evidence is, of course, admissible to establish that the donor was *in loco parentis* to the child at the relevant times.[12]

d Satisfaction and ademption *pro tanto*

It was at one time thought[13] that where, for instance, a father bequeathed a legacy of £10,000 to a child, and subsequently advanced him £5,000 on marriage, the legacy was wholly adeemed, the idea apparently being that the father was fully entitled to change his mind about the amount which would be an appropriate provision for the child. The matter was carefully considered by Lord Cottenham in *Pym* v. *Lockyer*,[14] and his decision has always been regarded as establishing that ademption or satisfaction is only *pro tanto*, so that in the illustration given, the legacy would only be adeemed to the extent of the subsequent advance of £5,000, and the balance of £5,000 would remain payable.

It may happen that a will contains two provisions bestowing portions on a child, and the question may arise as to which of these is adeemed by a subsequent advancement. The answer is, that which the latter portion most closely resembles. Thus in *Montefiore* v. *Guedalla*,[15] a father by his will gave an absolute pecuniary legacy to a son and also settled on him and his family a share of residue. On the son's marriage, the father transferred property to the trustees of his marriage settlement. It was held this was an ademption *pro tanto* of the gift of residue and not of the absolute legacy.

The value of an advancement has to be ascertained as at the time when it was made,[16] less any estate duty which may be payable thereon by reason of the death of the donor within the statutory period.[17] Similarly in ascertaining the value of shares of residue, estate duty on free personalty has first to be deducted.[18]

e Both portions must be provided by, and for, the same persons

On the first point, that both portions must be provided by the same person, the rule stated by Romilly M.R.[19] applies to both satisfaction and ademption, namely, that "satisfaction can only arise where the person who makes the payment is himself the party bound to pay, or is the owner of the estate charged with the payment". On the other point, that both portions must be provided for the same persons, equity looks to the substance of the matter, and there are

---

[11] See Section 3h, p. 523, *post*.
[12] *Booker* v. *Allen* (1831), 2 Russ. & My. 270; *Powys* v. *Mansfield* (1837), 3 My. & Cr. 359.
[13] See e.g. *Ex parte Pye* (1811), 18 Ves. 140.
[14] (1841), 5 My. & Cr. 29; *Lady Thynne* v. *Earl of Glengall* (1848), 2 H.L.Cas. 131; *Montefiore* v. *Guedalla* (1859), 1 De G.F. & J. 93; *Re Pollock* (1885), 28 Ch.D. 552, C.A.
[15] (1859), 1 De G.F. & J. 93.
[16] *Watson* v. *Watson* (1864), 33 Beav. 574.
[17] *Re Beddington*, [1900] 1 Ch. 771; cf. *Re Crocker*, [1916] 1 Ch. 25.
[18] See *Re Turner's Will Trusts*, [1968] 1 All E.R. 321.
[19] *Samuel* v. *Ward* (1856), 22 Beav. 347, 350; *Douglas* v. *Willes* (1849), 7 Hare, 318.

innumerable cases where there has been held to be ademption or satisfaction where the portions have been payable to different trustees, but the respective beneficial limitations have been substantially the same.[20] There have also been a number of cases where the question has been whether a legacy to a daughter has been adeemed by a subsequent advancement to her husband. The cases are somewhat confused but it is submitted that on principle the better view is that expressed by Romilly M.R. in a case[21] actually concerned with an express provision. He said,[21] "Nothing turns on the fact that it was given to her husband rather than to the wife: if, in truth, the money was paid by way of marriage portion, or by way of advancement, it falls within the provision, whoever received it." The crux of the matter is whether the money, although paid to the husband, was paid by way of the wife's portion. Thus the same judge observed in a later case,[22] "I do not know of any case in which it has yet been determined that the gift of a sum of money to the husband of a daughter, by her father, *simpliciter*, after the marriage, and not in consequence of any promise previous to the marriage taking place (which might have a very different effect), has been held to be an ademption of a legacy given to the daughter". In this latter case[1] it was held there was no ademption of a legacy to the daughter, where some three weeks after her marriage the father gave £400 to the husband and when thanked said "that he hoped it would do him good". On the other hand, there was ademption in *Nevin* v. *Drysdale*[2] where there was a legacy of £500 to the wife, and a subsequent payment of £400 to the husband in pursuance of an ante-nuptial understanding that the wife's father would contribute towards the furnishing of the matrimonial home. The presumption was not rebutted by evidence of a promise by the father to contribute a further £600.

It is difficult to reconcile *Cooper* v. *Macdonald*[3] with the above principles: this case seems to be decided on the view that there can never be ademption where or in so far as the persons taking under the several instruments are different. Accordingly it was held that there was no ademption of a share of residue settled on the wife and her children by the payment under the terms of her marriage settlement of £1,000 absolutely to the husband, notwithstanding that it was expressed to be given as a marriage portion.[4]

f Application of the doctrines to benefit strangers

It is not altogether clear how far, if at all, someone not a child can claim the benefit of these presumptions. The question does not seem to have been raised prior to *Meinertzagen* v. *Walters*,[5] where Mellish L.J. stated that "in the ordinary

---

[20] E.g. *Lady Thynne* v. *Earl of Glengall* (1848), 2 H.L.Cas. 131; *Russell* v. *St. Aubyn* (1876), 2 Ch.D. 398; *Romaine* v. *Onslow* (1876), 24 W.R. 899 and see section 3h, p. 523, *post*.
[21] *M'Clure* v. *Evans* (1861), 29 Beav. 422, at p. 425.
[22] *Ravenscroft* v. *Jones* (1863), 32 Beav. 669, at pp. 670–671, affd. (1864), 1 De G.J. & S. 224; where one judge refused to express an opinion on this point and the other seems to have disagreed with Romilly M.R.
[1] *Ravenscroft* v. *Jones, supra.*
[2] (1867), L.R. 4 Eq. 517; the same result in *Kirk* v. *Eddowes* (1844), 3 Hare, 509, depended on extrinsic evidence of intention.
[3] (1873), L.R. 16 Eq. 258.
[4] There was, however, ademption of the share of residue as to £4,000 by the same settlement covenanted to be paid to trustees as a provision for the daughter.
[5] (1872), 7 Ch. App. 670, at p. 674.

case of a legacy, where a legacy has been left to a child, and then a gift has been made which amounts to an ademption of that legacy, there certainly appears to be no possible way of holding it to be an ademption so as to carry out the general rule against double portions, except by holding that whoever has the residue benefits by it; because by the necessity of the case the persons who have the residue must benefit by the fact of the previous legacy not being paid from any cause whatever". Though not discussed therein, this view is supported by cases[6] where the presumption of ademption has been applied although the residuary legatee was a stranger, and to some extent by the existence of cases where it has not been considered necessary in the reports to state to whom residue has been given.[7]

In *Meinertzagen* v. *Walters*,[8] however, the court refused to allow a stranger to benefit where residue was given to children and a stranger, and an advancement was made to a child, the principle, according to *obiter dicta* in *Re Heather*,[9] and the decision at first instance in *Re Vaux*[10] being that a rule designed to produce equality[11] among children ought not to be applied so as to reduce their shares for the benefit of a stranger. Thus if a father gave his residue worth £9,000 equally between A and B, his children, and X, a stranger, and subsequently advanced £2,000 to A, X would receive £3,000 only, but as between A and B, A's share of residue has been adeemed *pro tanto* and accordingly B would get £4,000, and A £2,000, which together with the advance he had already received would, of course, make him equal to B. Again, suppose a father having two children A and B, by his will gave a legacy of £3,000 to A and his residue equally between A and B and X, a stranger, and subsequently made an advancement of £3,000 to A, and died leaving a net estate of £15,000. In distributing the estate, the presumption of ademption would not be applied for the benefit of X, who accordingly would get one-third of the residue of £12,000 (net estate less the legacy of £3,000), namely, £4,000. The net assets available for distribution would now be £11,000. As between A and B the presumption of ademption would apply, the legacy of £3,000 would be treated as adeemed by the *inter vivos* advancement and accordingly A and B would each get £5,500. Consequently A would have had, in the result, £3,000 more than B, which was presumably the testator's intention.

It remains doubtful, however, whether the general statement in *Re Vaux*,[12] that in the case of ademption of a legacy the rule is not to be used to benefit a stranger, applies where the sole residuary legatee is a stranger.

g The operation of the presumptions

Where the presumption of ademption applies, the legatee has no option, the legacy having gone his only choice is to take the subsequent portion. Where, however, it is the presumption of satisfaction that applies, he cannot be com-

---

[6] *Trimmer* v. *Bayne* (1802), 7 Ves. 508; *Booker* v. *Allen* (1831), 2 Russ. & M. 270.
[7] *Debeze* v. *Mann* (1789), 2 Bro. C.C. 519; *Robinson* v. *Whitley* (1804), 9 Ves. 577.
[8] (1872), 7 Ch. App. 670, at p. 674.
[9] [1906] 2 Ch. 230.
[10] [1938] Ch. 581, reversed C.A., [1939] Ch. 465, where it was not necessary to discuss this point.
[11] Or proportionate division as intended by the testator.
[12] *Supra*, at first instance, at pp. 589, 591.

pelled to take the second provision offered *in lieu* of that to which he is legally entitled under the settlement or covenant: all he can be compelled to do is to elect or choose between them. The distinction is that in cases of ademption the first benefit is given by a will, which is a revocable instrument which the testator can alter as he pleases, and consequently when he subsequently gives benefits in circumstances which give rise to the presumption of ademption, he is assumed to have intended to substitute the second gift for the first, which he had the power of altering at his pleasure. The law uses the word *ademption*, because the bequest contained in the will is thereby *adeemed*, that is, taken out of the will. In cases of satisfaction, however,[13] where, for instance, a father, on the marriage of a child, enters into a covenant to pay money to the trustees of the marriage settlement, he cannot unilaterally avoid or alter that covenant, and if he gives benefits by his will to the same objects, in circumstances which give rise to the presumption of satisfaction, he necessarily gives the objects of the covenant the right to elect whether they will take under the covenant, or whether they will take under the will.

It may be added that if, for example, a father covenants with the trustees of his daughter's marriage settlement to pay them a sum of money to be settled on the daughter and her children, and by his will bequeaths a legacy to the daughter absolutely, the daughter may be called upon to elect, but this cannot affect the rights of the children under the covenant.[14]

h Rebutting the presumptions

It need hardly be said that if the donor has, in his second provision, expressed an intention that it is to be in addition to, and not in satisfaction or ademption of, the first, his intention must be carried out. In other cases, since the presumptions are based on the presumed intention of the donor, it is always open to the donee to rebut a presumption by intrinsic or extrinsic evidence. In this context it is important to remember that it is much easier to rebut the presumption in a case of satisfaction than in a case of ademption. The reason for this was emphasised in *Chichester* v. *Coventry*:[15] in a case of ademption the will, a revocable instrument, comes first, and if the father subsequently gives a portion to a child on marriage or otherwise, it may very reasonably be supposed that he has anticipated the benefit provided by the will and has intended to substitute for it the new provision, either wholly or *pro tanto*. But if the father first makes an irrevocable settlement, and subsequently makes his will, it is easy to suppose that an additional benefit was intended, bearing in mind that, without the consent of the donee, he cannot substitute the benefits he has chosen to confer by his will for those that have already been secured by the settlement. It follows from this that, on the one hand, circumstances which will rebut the presumption of ademption will, *a fortiori*, rebut the presumption of satisfaction; but, on the other hand, cases which decide that certain circumstances rebut the presumption of satisfaction cannot be relied on in connection with ademption. It is now proposed to consider

---

[13] *Chichester* v. *Coventry* (1867), L.R. 2 H.L. 71, at pp. 90–91; *Lady Thynne* v. *Earl of Glengall* (1848), 2 H.L.Cas. 131; *McCarogher* v. *Whieldon* (1867), L.R. 3 Eq. 236.
[14] *Chichester* v. *Coventry, supra.*
[15] *Supra; Re Tussaud's Estate* (1878), 9 Ch.D. 363, C.A.; *Montagu* v. *Earl of Sandwich* (1886), 32 Ch.D. 525, C.A.

the effect of intrinsic evidence derived from the nature of the two provisions.

(i) *Differences in the limitations.* Dealing first with the presumption of satisfaction, the rule is that differences between the limitations contained in the two provisions will rebut the presumption of satisfaction, unless the differences are merely slight.[16] Unfortunately the courts have accepted the view[17] that "it is not possible to define what are to be considered as slight differences between two provisions. Slight differences are such as, in the opinion of the judge, leave the two provisions substantially of the same nature; and every judge must decide that question for himself". It is submitted, nevertheless, that some guidance can be obtained from previous decisions. On the one hand, the differences were held to be slight, and the presumption of satisfaction not rebutted, in *Weall* v. *Rice*,[18] where under both provisions the wife (the daughter of the settlor) took a life interest to her separate use, but only in the will was she restrained from anticipation and alienation; under both provisions the husband was given a life estate, but in the will only it was provided "he nevertheless maintaining and educating" the children; under the settlement the children took as tenants in common in tail with cross remainders, while under the will they took as tenants in common in fee, with a provision, in law void, for cross remainders on the death of any child under 25; in *Lady Thynne* v. *Earl of Glengall*,[19] where by a marriage settlement one-third of the sum of £100,000 was paid and the remaining two-thirds covenanted to be paid to four trustees on trust for the wife (the settlor's daughter) for life, to her separate use, with remainder to the children *of the marriage* as the husband and wife should *jointly* appoint; and by the will half of the residue was given to two of the settlement trustees on trust for the wife's separate use for life with remainder for *her* children generally as *she* should by deed or will appoint; and in *Russell* v. *St. Aubyn*,[20] where by the settlement the husband, by the will the wife (the settlor's daughter) had the first life interest, the will only making the husband's interest determinable upon his bankruptcy or alienation; by the settlement there was a *joint* power of appointment by the husband and wife, or the survivor of them, among the *children of the marriage*, while by the will a power of appointment was given to the *wife alone* among *her* children generally or more remote issue. The ultimate limitations on failure of issue were also different.

On the other hand, the differences were held to be great enough to rebut the presumption of satisfaction in *Chichester* v. *Coventry*,[1] where the settlor covenanted to pay £10,000 to the trustees of his daughter's marriage settlement, on trust for the husband for life (subject to the wife's pin money of £200 p.a.), with remainder to the wife for life, with remainder to the children of the marriage as the wife should appoint; and by the will half the residue was given to the wife for her separate use for life, with remainder to such persons, excluding the husband,

---

[16] *Weall* v. *Rice* (1831), 2 Russ. & M. 251; *Lady Thynne* v. *Earl of Glengall* (1848), 2 H.L. Cas, 131; *Chichester* v. *Coventry* (1867), L.R. 2 H.L. 71; *Russell* v. *St. Aubyn* (1876), 2 Ch.D. 398; *Re Tussaud's Estate* (1878), 9 Ch.D. 363, C.A.

[17] *Per* Leach M.R. in *Weall* v. *Rice* (1831), 2 Russ. & M. 251, at p. 268; *Chichester* v. *Coventry supra*; *Re Tussaud's Estate, supra.*

[18] *Supra.*

[19] (1848), 2 H.L. Cas. 131.

[20] (1876), 2 Ch.D. 398.

[1] *Supra.* Much stress was laid in this case on the direction in the will to pay debts and legacies.

as she should appoint: in *Re Tussaud's Estate*[2] where by the daughter's marriage settlement she was first given a general power of appointment with the consent of trustees, and in default of appointment there were successive life interests to the wife and husband, followed by a remainder to the children of the marriage and on failure of these trusts an ultimate limitation to the husband absolutely; and by the will the wife alone had a life interest, with remainder to *her* children, and on failure of these trusts the property would fall into residue and go to the testator's sons; and in *Re Vernon*,[3] where under the daughter's marriage settlement there were successive life interests to wife and husband, with remainder to such of their issue as they jointly or the survivor of them should appoint and in default of appointment a trust for the children of the marriage; and by the will the limitations were to the wife for life, remainder to her children, but if she should die without leaving any child surviving her, to any husband she should leave surviving her for life, and then the fund to fall into residue.

Sometimes the difference alleged is that the will makes provision for one only, or some only of the beneficiaries under the prior settlement. In such case, as Lord Romilly explained in *Chichester* v. *Coventry*,[4] "a provision by will may satisfy one part of the covenant without satisfying the other parts of it; for instance, that if a father, on the marriage of his daughter, should settle £10,000 on her for life, remainder to the children of the marriage, a bequest of £10,000 to that daughter would satisfy her life interest in the £10,000, but would not satisfy or touch the interests of her children". Similarly a bequest to the children of the marriage, omitting the parent, could be a satisfaction of so much of the covenant as related to them, without affecting the right of the parent to claim under the covenant. This principle was applied, for instance, in *Re Blundell*,[5] where by the marriage settlement of his daughter a father covenanted to pay some £5,500 to trustees to be settled on certain trusts for the wife, husband and children, the wife taking the first life interest. Subsequently, by his will, the father gave the wife a share of residue worth much more than £5,500 for her separate use absolutely. It was held that there was satisfaction of the wife's life interest, but not of the interests of the other beneficiaries under the settlement.[6]

Turning to the ademption of legacies by subsequent portions, there are numerous cases where it was held that differences in the limitations did not prevent ademption, but there does not seem to be any reported case in which the presumption has been rebutted solely on this ground. Thus there was ademption in *Durham* v. *Wharton*,[7] where by the will £10,000 was settled on a daughter for life, with remainder to such of her children as she should appoint, and in default of appointment equally, and if there should be no children, the fund was to fall into residue; and by the marriage settlement, the father agreed to give £15,000 to the intended husband expressly as the marriage portion, who agreed to secure to his wife pin money of £500 a year, a jointure of £1,200 and portions for the

---

[2] (1878), 9 Ch.D. 363, C.A.
[3] (1906), 95 L.T. 48.
[4] (1867), L.R. 2 H.L. 71, 95.
[5] [1906] 2 Ch. 222; *McCarogher* v. *Whieldon* (1867), L.R. 3 Eq. 236; *Mayd* v. *Field* (1876), 3 Ch.D. 587.
[6] Notwithstanding the fact that they acquired an interest derivatively by reason of an after-acquired property clause in the settlement.
[7] (1836), 10 Bli. N.S. 526.

daughters and younger sons of the marriage; in *Powys* v. *Mansfield*,[8] where by the will there were limited successive life interests to the wife and husband, and remainder to the wife's children; by the settlement successive life interests to husband and wife and remainder to the *younger* children of the *marriage*; and in *Stevenson* v. *Masson*,[9] where the will gave the daughter an absolute legacy, and the settlement provided for the covenanted sum to be settled.

(ii) *Gifts must be eiusdem generis.* Here the cases do not draw any distinction between the presumptions of ademption and satisfaction. Both apply not only to gifts of money, but also to gifts of other forms of personal property, such as shares in a partnership business,[10] though not, it seems, to devises of land.[11] In *Bellasis* v. *Uthwatt*,[12] however, Lord Hardwicke laid down that "the thing given in satisfaction must be of the same nature, and attended with the same certainty, as the thing in lieu of which it is given, and land is not to be taken in satisfaction for money,[13] nor money for land". This was applied in *Holmes* v. *Holmes*,[14] where the presumption of ademption was rebutted by the difference in nature between a legacy of money and an advance of a share in a partnership. The Court of Appeal in *Re Jaques*[15] affirmed that the law laid down in these cases had not been changed, disapproving the interpretation placed by North J.[16] on the earlier Court of Appeal decision in *Re Lawes*.[17] The court made clear, however, that if a thing is given by reference to its pecuniary value, then it is treated as equivalent to a gift of money. As Jessel M.R. observed,[18] "where a testator gives to a child a beneficial lease or share of works, or any other thing, and says nothing about the value, he is not to be taken to be giving it in satisfaction of a pecuniary bequest; but where he does refer to the value the presumption of satisfaction may arise".

The difference between a gift of money and a gift of consols,[19] or bearer bonds,[20] is disregarded for this purpose, but if one gift is absolute, the other contingent, this difference rebuts the presumption,[1] unless the contingency is so remote that the settlor did not think it should be taken into consideration.[2]

At one time it was thought that there could neither be an ademption of residue by a subsequent advancement, nor a satisfaction of a portions debt by a gift of

---

[8] (1837), 3 My. & Cr. 359.
[9] (1873), L.R. 17 Eq. 78. See also *Phillips* v. *Phillips* (1864), 34 Beav. 19; *Re Furness*, [1901] 2 Ch. 346.
[10] *Re Lacon*, [1891] 2 Ch. 482, C.A. (satisfaction); *Re George's Will Trusts*, [1948] 2 All E.R. 1004; [1949] Ch. 154 (ademption).
[11] *Davys* v. *Boucher* (1839), 3 Y. & C. Ex. 397.
[12] (1737), 1 Atk. 426, at p. 428.
[13] *Chaplin* v. *Chaplin* (1734), 3 P. Wms. 245; cf. *Re Aynsley*, [1915] 1 Ch. 172, C.A.
[14] (1783), 1 Bro. C.C. 555; *Davys* v. *Boucher*, supra.
[15] [1903] 1 Ch. 267, C.A.
[16] In *Re Vickers* (1888), 37 Ch.D. 525.
[17] (1881), 20 Ch.D. 81, C.A.; *Bengough* v. *Walker* (1808), 15 Ves. 507.
[18] In *Re Lawes* (1881), 20 Ch.D. 81, at p. 88 C.A.; *Re George's Will Trusts*, supra.
[19] *Pym* v. *Lockyer* (1841), 5 My. & Cr. 29; *Twining* v. *Powell* (1845), 2 Coll. 262; *Watson* v. *Watson* (1864), 33 Beav. 574.
[20] *Re Jupp*, [1922] 2 Ch. 359.
[1] *Bellasis* v. *Uthwatt* (1737), 1 Atk. 426 (satisfaction); *Spinks* v. *Robins* (1742), 2 Atk. 491 (ademption).
[2] *Powys* v. *Mansfield*, supra, per Lord Cottenham at pp. 374, 375.

residue. Since *Lady Thynne* v. *Earl of Glengall*,[3] however, it has been consistently held that there can be both ademption of and satisfaction by a gift of residue.

(iii) *Differences between the times of payment* do not rebut the presumption of ademption or satisfaction, at any rate where the difference is only a matter of months.[4]

(iv) *Direction for the payment of debts prior to ascertainment of residue contained in the will.* So far as the presumption of ademption is concerned, any such direction is irrelevant, for a previous will can throw no light on the intention with which a subsequent advance was made.[5] In connection with the satisfaction of a portions debt by a subsequent will, however, a provision giving to a beneficiary under the covenant a share of residue, after payment of debts, shows an intention that the beneficiary shall first be paid what is due under the covenant, and then take in addition his share of what is left.[6] The obligation under the covenant, however, may not be a "debt" within the provision in the will, in which case the presumption of satisfaction will not be rebutted on this ground.[7]

i   Ademption—subsequent advancement followed by a codicil

If the presumption of ademption applies, a subsequent codicil has no effect. "It is very true that a codicil republishing a will makes the will speak as from its own date for the purpose of passing after-purchased lands, but not for the purpose of reviving a legacy revoked, adeemed, or satisfied. The codicil can only act upon the will as it existed at the time; and, at the time, the legacy revoked, adeemed, or satisfied formed no part of it".[8] Contrary, however, to the further opinion of Lord Cottenham in the same case, it has been held that the codicil can be taken into account in deciding the intention with which the advancement was made.[9]

j   The admission of extrinsic evidence

The Court of Appeal stated clear rules in *Re Tussaud's Estate*,[10] though without a full discussion of the somewhat conflicting dicta to be found in earlier cases. First, the rules are the same whether it is a case of satisfaction or ademption. Secondly, if the second instrument contains an expression of intention as to whether there is or is not to be satisfaction, parol evidence will not be admitted to contradict it.[11] Thirdly, if there is no such expression of intention, and no presumption of satisfaction or ademption, extrinsic evidence will not be admitted

---

[3] (1848), 2 H.L. Cas. 131; *Montefiore* v. *Guedalla* (1859), 1 De G.F. & J. 93; *Dawson* v. *Dawson* (1867), L.R. 4 Eq. 504; *Cooper* v. *Macdonald* (1873), L.R. 16 Eq. 258

[4] *Davys* v. *Boucher* (1839), 3 Y. & C. Ex. 397; *Stevenson* v. *Masson* (1873 , L.R. 17 Eq. 78.

[5] *Dawson* v. *Dawson*, *supra*; *Cooper* v. *Macdonald*, *supra*.

[6] *Chichester* v. *Coventry* (1867), L.R. 2 H.L. 71; *Smyth* v. *Johnston* (1875), 31 L.T. 876.

[7] *Re Vernon* (1906), 95 L.T. 48.

[8] Per Lord Cottenham in *Powys* v. *Mansfield* (1837), 3 My. & Cr. 359, at p. 376; *Montagu* v. *Montagu* (1852), 15 Beav. 565; *Hopwood* v. *Hopwood* (1859), 7 H.L. Cas. 728; cf. *Re Warren*, [1932] 1 Ch. 42.

[9] *Ravenscroft* v. *Jones* (1864), 4 De G. J. & S. 224; *Re Scott*, [1903] 1 Ch. 1, C.A.

[10] (1878), 9 Ch.D. 363, C.A.

[11] *Kirk* v. *Eddowes* (1844), 3 Hare, 509.

to raise a plea of satisfaction or ademption.[12] Fourthly, however, if in the circumstances equity raises a presumption of satisfaction or ademption, parol evidence is admissible to rebut that presumption, and also, in such case, counter-evidence is admissible to fortify it.[13] It seems doubtful whether, as stated in *Kirk* v. *Eddowes*,[14] the parol evidence is restricted to declarations made con-temporaneously with the second provision: it seems that they are also admissible whether made before or afterwards.[15]

In any case the onus of rebutting a presumption raised by equity rests upon those who allege that in the circumstances it does not apply.[16]

4 ADEMPTION OF LEGACIES GIVEN FOR A PARTICULAR PURPOSE

The same principles as have been discussed in the preceding section apply, even though the testator is neither the father nor stands *in loco parentis* to the legatee, where he "gives a legacy for one particular purpose only, and after that applies a sum of money to the same purpose".[17] The crux of the matter is what constitutes a particular purpose: on the one hand, it was held that there was no particular purpose and accordingly no presumption of ademption where a testator bequeathed a legacy of £200 to his wife to be paid within ten days of his death, and subsequently, during his last illness, gave her a cheque for £200;[18] and where he gave a legacy to a trustee for the benefit of an infant, and sub-sequently a gift of the same sum to the same trustee for the same purpose[19]— in substance they were merely gifts to the infant and no particular purpose was declared.[20] On the other hand, there was held to be a particular purpose and accordingly a presumption of ademption in *Re Corbett*,[1] where there was a legacy to the trustees of the endowment fund of a hospital followed by an *inter vivos* gift of the same amount to the same trustees; and in *Re Jupp*,[2] where both legacy and *inter vivos* gift were to the trustees of a fund the income of which was to be expended in making up the aggregate income of three sisters, strangers to the testator, to a certain sum, and in meeting their extraordinary expenses incurred through illness or other causes, the balance after the death or marriage of all the sisters to be divided among the subscribers in proportion to their contributions.

---

[2] *Hall* v. *Hill* (1841), 1 Dr. & War. 94. Contra, *Monck* v. *Monck* (1810), 1 Ball & B.298; *Kirk* v. *Eddowes* (1844), 3 Hare, 509, in cases where the second transaction is not made by an instrument in writing; and see *Re Shields*, [1912] 1 Ch. 591 perhaps restricting this to cases of agreement between donor and donee.
[13] *Powys* v. *Mansfield* (1837), 3 My. & Cr. 359; *Kirk* v. *Eddows, supra.*
[14] *Supra.*
[15] *Weall* v. *Rice* (1831), 2 Russ. & M. 251; *Robinson* v. *Whiteley* (1804), 9 Ves. 577.
[16] *Papillon* v. *Papillon* (1841), 11 Sim. 642; *Hopwood* v. *Hopwood* (1859), 7 H.L. Cas. 728.
[17] *Roome* v. *Roome* (1744), 3 Atk. 181, at p. 183 *per* Fortescue M.R.; *Debeze* v. *Mann* (1789), 2 Bro. C.C. 519; *Re Pollock* (1885), 28 Ch.D. 552, C.A.
[18] *Pankhurst* v. *Howell* (1870), 6 Ch. App. 136.
[19] *Re Smythies*, [1903] 1 Ch. 259.
[20] *Re Corbett*, [1903] 2 Ch. 326; *Re Jupp*, [1922] 2 Ch. 359.
[1] *Supra.*
[2] *Supra.*

This head of satisfaction or ademption was, perhaps, slightly extended by the Court of Appeal in *Re Pollock*[3] to cases where the bequest and subsequent gift are "expressed to be made in fulfilment of some moral obligation recognised by the testator, and originating in a definite external cause, though not of a kind which (unless expressed) the law would have recognised, or would have presumed to exist".[4] The idea behind this is said to be the same as that which lies behind the presumption against double portions, namely that as the purpose of both gifts was to fulfil one and the same antecedent obligation or duty, a double fulfilment was presumably not intended. The need for the intention to fulfil a moral obligation to be expressed in the bequest was stressed in *Re Jupp*.[5] *Re Pollock*[3] itself is the leading case in this field, where it was held that there was a presumption of ademption *pro tanto*: the facts were that a legacy of £500 was given by the testatrix to a niece of her deceased husband, with the words "according to the wish of my late beloved husband", and a subsequent gift was described in contemporaneous entries in her diary as "a legacy from" the niece's "uncle John", i.e. the testatrix's husband.

5 PERFORMANCE

a Generally

Performance is closely related to satisfaction, and in the older cases one finds that what would now be classified as performance is commonly referred to as satisfaction by implication. The doctrine has been much reduced in importance by the changes made in the law of intestate succession by the Property Legislation of 1925. The principle behind the cases has been said[6] to be that "where a man covenants to do an act, and he does an act which may be converted to a completion of this covenant, it shall be supposed that he meant to complete it", or, in other words,[7] "that a person is to be presumed to do that which he is bound to do; and if he has done anything, that he has done it in pursuance of his obligation". The cases fall naturally into two groups.

b Covenant to purchase and settle land

Where a man has covenanted to purchase and settle land,[8] or to convey and settle land,[9] or to pay money to trustees to be laid out by them in the purchase of land,[10] and has failed to carry out his obligation; but has nevertheless subsequently to the covenant purchased lands, the court will, under this doctrine, presume that the purchase was made in performance or part performance of the covenant.

---

[3] (1885), 28 Ch.D. 552, C.A.
[4] *Re Pollock*, (1885), 28 Ch.D. 552, at p. 556, C.A., per Selborne L.C.
[5] [1922] 2 Ch. 359.
[6] *Per* Kenyon M.R. in *Sowden* v. *Sowden* (1785), 1 Cox. Eq. Cas. 165, at p. 166; *Weyland* v. *Weyland* (1742), 2 Atk. 632.
[7] *Per* Brougham L.C. in *Tubbs* v. *Broadwood* (1831), 2 Russ. & M. 487, at p. 493.
[8] *Lechmere* v. *Lady Lechmere* (1735), Cas. temp. Tal. 80.
[9] *Deacon* v. *Smith* (1746), 3 Atk. 323.
[10] *Sowden* v. *Sowden* (1785), 1 Cox. Eq. Cas. 165.

The effect of the doctrine, and indeed many of the rules, can be seen from the leading case of *Lechmere* v. *Lady Lechmere*:[11] it will be remembered that when this case was decided, on intestacy realty descended to the heir-at-law but personalty passed to the next of kin. In *Lechmere* v. *Lady Lechmere*,[11] Lord Lechmere, by marriage articles in 1719, covenanted to lay out £30,000 within one year of the marriage in the purchase, with the consent of trustees, of freehold lands in fee simple in possession, to be settled on Lord Lechmere for life and after his death a jointure to his widow, with remainder to the sons of the marriage in tail male, and an ultimate remainder to Lord Lechmere in fee simple. At the date of the marriage Lord Lechmere was already seised of some lands in fee simple. After the marriage he purchased and contracted to purchase several estates in fee simple, but not within the year nor with the consent of the trustees: he also purchased some estates for lives, and some reversionary estates in fee, expectant upon lives. None of these estates was settled in accordance with the covenant. Lord Lechmere died in 1727 intestate and without issue, but leaving his widow surviving him. Under the doctrine of conversion it was held that the £30,000 ought to be treated as land and go to the heir-at-law, who was, of course, entitled to all the realty of which Lord Lechmere died seised. The heir-at-law accordingly claimed, first, all the deceased's realty, and, secondly, that £30,000 should be raised out of personalty and laid out in accordance with the articles with the result that it would pass to him under the ultimate remainder. The next of kin, while admitting the *prima facie* validity of the claim, argued that the estates purchased by Lord Lechmere must be taken to have been made in part performance of the covenant, and their value deducted from the £30,000 claimed by the heir-at-law. The next-of-kin's plea had a limited success. It was held that the estates of which Lord Lechmere was already in possession could not be regarded as performance of the covenant in the articles, since they were acquired before there was any obligation capable of being performed. Again the estates for lives and the reversionary estates expectant upon lives, being of a different nature from those covenanted to be settled, could not be taken in part performance. The estates in fee purchased or contracted to be purchased were, however, to be taken in part performance of the covenant, notwithstanding that they were not purchased within a year of the marriage, for time is not of the essence of the matter, nor with the consent of the trustees, for this was merely to prevent unreasonable purchases and does not matter if the purchases made are in fact reasonable.

The same presumption of performance was held to apply in *Tubbs* v. *Broadwood*,[12] where the obligation to purchase was imposed, not by covenant or contract, but by statute.

c   Covenant to leave money

Where a man has covenanted that he will leave, or that his executors will pay, a sum of money or a share of his personalty to another, and has then died intestate, but that other has taken a share of the personalty under the law of

---

[11] *Supra.* See also *Hucks* v. *Hucks* (1754), 2 Ves. Sen. 568; *Davys* v. *Howard* (1762), 6 Bro. Parl. Cas. 370.
[12] (1831), 2 Russ. & M. 487.

intestate succession, such share is presumed to be taken in performance, or part performance, of the covenant. The leading case is *Blandy* v. *Widmore*,[13] where by marriage'articles a man covenanted to leave his wife £620 on his death: he died intestate, but the wife's share on intestacy was worth more than £620. It was held that this must be taken in performance of the covenant. This was followed in *Lee* v. *Cox and D'Aranda*,[14] and in *Garthshore* v. *Chalie*,[15] where the cases were fully discussed by Lord Eldon. The doctrine has been held to apply to a case where a father covenanted to exercise a special power of appointment by will in favour of a daughter, and failed to do so, the daughter also being one of the persons entitled in default of appointment.[16]

The fact that the direction is to pay, say, three or six months after death, while, in the administration of the estate, payment could not be claimed until a year after the death, does not matter,[17] but it is different if there is a covenant by a man to pay during his lifetime which is broken before his death. Thus in *Oliver* v. *Brickland*,[18] a man covenanted to pay a sum of money within two years of his marriage, and if he died that his executors should pay it. He lived more than two years and died intestate. It was held that the widow's share on intestacy was not to be taken in performance of the covenant.

Further it was held before 1926, when the next-of-kin on intestacy invariably took a capital sum, that this was not performance of a covenant to leave an annuity.[19] It is not decided whether this rule will apply after 1925 to cases where a surviving spouse takes a life interest in half the residuary estate.[20]

Finally, it should be observed that the doctrine only applies where a man dies intestate,[1] though it was extended in *Goldsmid* v. *Goldsmid*[2] to a case where by reason of the death or renunciation of the executor the estate had to be distributed according to the rules applicable to an intestacy.

---

[13] (1715), 1 P. Wms. 324.
[14] (1747), 3 Atk. 419, *sub nom. Lee* v. *D'Aranda and Cox*, 1 Ves. Sen. 1.
[15] (1804), 10 Ves. 1; cf. *Re Hall*, [1918] 1 Ch. 562.
[16] *Thacker* v. *Key* (1869), L.R. 8 Eq. 408.
[17] *Garthshore* v. *Chalie, supra.*
[18] Cited in *Lee* v. *Cox and D'Aranda* (1747), 3 Atk. 419; 1 Ves. Sen. 1, but *sub nom. Oliver* v. *Brighouse* in the report in Ves. Sen.
[19] *Couch* v. *Stratton* (1799), 4 Ves. 391; *Salisbury* v. *Salisbury* (1848), 6 Hare, 526.
[20] See Intestates' Estates Act 1952 amending s. 46 of the Administration of Estates Act 1925.
[1] *Haynes* v. *Mico* (1781), 1 Bro. C.C. 129; *Devese* v. *Pontet* (1785), 1 Cox. Eq. Cas. 188; *Goldsmid* v. *Goldsmid* (1818), 1 Swans 211.
[2] *Supra.*

CHAPTER 18

The Equitable Doctrine of Election

Election "is a principle which the courts apply in the exercise of an equitable jurisdiction enabling them to secure a just distribution in substantial accordance with the general scheme of the instrument".[1] More particularly, as Lord Cairns observed,[2] by this doctrine "where a deed or will professes to make a general disposition of property for the benefit of a person named in it, such person cannot accept a benefit under the instrument without at the same time conforming to all its provisions, and renouncing every right inconsistent with them". In other words, as Lord Redesdale said,[3] "the general rule is, that a person cannot accept and reject the same instrument, and this is the foundation of the law of election". The very name of the corresponding doctrine in Scottish law, approbate and reprobate, brings out the same point. Though, in general, the rules elaborating this general principle apply equally to deeds and wills, it is convenient to treat its application to each of them separately.

1 ELECTION UNDER A WILL

a Application of the doctrine to wills

"The ordinary principle is clear that if a testator gives property by design or by mistake which is not his to give, and gives at the same time[4] to the real owner of it other property, such real owner cannot take both".[5] Thus if a testator by his will devises Blackacre, which in fact belongs to George, to Mary, and elsewhere in the will bequeaths George a legacy of £5,000, George will have to elect. George cannot, of course, be compelled to give up his own property,

---

[1] *Per* Lord Haldane in *Brown* v. *Gregson*, [1920] A.C. 860, at p. 868; [1920] All E.R. Rep. 730, at p. 734, H.L.

[2] In *Codrington* v. *Codrington* (1875), L.R. 7 H.L. 854, at pp. 861, 862. Cf. *Re Edwards*. [1957] 2 All E.R. 495; [1958] Ch. 168, C.A.

[3] In *Birmingham* v. *Kirwan* (1805), 2 Sch. & Lef. 444, at p. 450.

[4] *Prima facie* the two gifts must be contained in the same instrument, but two wills— *Douglas-Menzies* v. *Umphelby* [1908] A.C. 224 P.C.—or two contemporaneous documents—*Bacon* v. *Cosby* (1851), 4 De G. & Sm. 261—may be treated as one for this purpose.

[5] *Per* James V.C. in *Wollaston* v. *King* (1869), L.R. 8 Eq. 165.

Blackacre, over which the testator had no disposing power. What he can be compelled to do, however, if necessary by proceedings in the courts[6], is to elect, as it is said, to take either under the will or against it. If he elects to take under the will, he will be entitled to receive all the benefits given to him by the will, but will have to allow his own property, of which the testator wrongfully purported to dispose, to be treated as if it belonged to the testator,[7] i.e., in the case put he will be entitled to his legacy of £5,000, but will have to convey Blackacre to Mary. Alternatively he may elect to take against the will, which means that he insists, as he is fully entitled to, on keeping his own property. If he does this, however, the benefits which he would otherwise be able to claim under the will must be used so far as may be necessary to compensate the person who is disappointed by this insistence on keeping his own property. Thus, in the case put, if George insists on keeping Blackacre, Mary will be disappointed of her testamentary expectations. George, however, will not get his legacy of £5,000 in full. Mary will be paid out of it the value of Blackacre, and George will be able to claim only the balance. If Blackacre should be worth more than £5,000, Mary cannot get more than that sum: in such case George will clearly get nothing under the will, but will, of course, continue to hold Blackacre.

b   Legal basis of the doctrine

In the early cases[8] the doctrine is often said to be based upon a tacit or implied condition that the person to whom the testator has given his own property is only to take if he allows his property to go over to the person to whom the testator has purported to give it. This theory has rather fallen into disfavour, for, as has been pointed out, while failure to comply with an express condition would cause forfeiture of the interest granted, under the doctrine of election a person who insists on keeping his own property only has his interest under the will taken away so far as necessary to compensate the person disappointed for his disappointment.

Again it is only in a limited sense that the doctrine can be said to depend on the intent of the testator. In *Cooper* v. *Cooper*[9] Lord Cairns said in so many words that the rule did not proceed either upon an expressed intention, or upon a conjecture of a presumed intention. In the same case Lord Hatherly said that the only relevant intent, apart from an intention to dispose of property not belonging to the testator, was the ordinary intent implied in the case of any man who makes a will that he intends that every part of it shall be effective. Effect is given to this latter intent, erroneously based though it usually is on a wrong belief that property belonging to another belonged to the testator, by the doctrine of election. This theory has been applied in cases such as *Re Vardon's Trusts*[10] where the beneficial interest given to the person called upon to elect had been given on terms rendering it inalienable. This restriction was held to show a particular intention inconsistent with and capable of rebutting the general intention that every part of the will should take effect and accordingly there was no case for election.

---

[6]   *Douglas* v. *Douglas* (1871), L.R. 12 Eq. 617.
[7]   It becomes subject to all the incidents to which it would have been subject if it had been the testator's property, such as his debts—*Re Williams*, [1915] 1 Ch. 450.
[8]   See e.g. *Noys* v. *Mordaunt* (1706), 2 Vern. 581; *Streatfield* v. *Streatfield* (1735), Cas. temp. Talbot 176; *Bor* v. *Bor* (1756), 3 Bro. Parl. Cas. 167; *Ker* v. *Wauchope* (1819), 1 Bli. 1.
[9]   (1874), L.R. 7 H.L. 53.
[10]   (1885), 31 Ch.D. 275 C.A. (a case upon election under a deed).

Probably, however, it is best to adopt the view of Lord Cairns[11] that the doctrine of equity "proceeds on a rule of equity founded upon the highest principles of equity, and as to which the court does not occupy itself in finding out whether the rule was present or not present to the mind of the party making the will". As was said more recently[12] "it is a doctrine by which equity fastens on the conscience of the person who is put to his election and refuses to allow him to take the benefit of a disposition contained in the will, the validity of which is not in question, except on certain conditions".

ι Compensation not forfeiture

Although there was doubt expressed in some of the earliest cases on election, it was fairly soon settled that if a person elected to take against the will, he did not lose his legacy altogether, but only to the extent necessary to compensate the persons disappointed thereby for their disappointment.[13] Of course, depending on the relative values, it might be that the entire legacy would be needed for the purposes of compensation. It is, however, clear that no more compensation can be required than the value of the testator's own property given to the person called upon to elect, even though this be inadequate to compensate for the disappointment. "The obligation [to compensate] is only to the extent of the benefit he derives: it cannot go beyond that".[14] Jessel M.R.[15] has pointed out that what really happens when a person elects to take against the will is that he claims both to keep his own property and also to take the benefits under the will: equity then steps in and declares that he can only take the latter benefits subject to the obligation to make compensation. As it was expressed in an early case[16] "The equity of this court is to sequester the devised estate *quousque* till satisfaction is made to the disappointed devisee".

The same principles have been applied in more complex cases. Clearly if more than one person is disappointed, the compensation, if election is made against the will, must be made to the beneficiaries in proportion to their disappointment.[17] Where, in addition, more than one person was called upon to elect, it was held in *Re Booth*[18] that persons electing to take against the will were respectively bound to make compensation to other persons so electing, as well as to persons who took under the will only, for any disappointment caused by such election, the compensation being limited to the extent of the benefits received under the will by the several persons electing to take against it. It was further held that all compensation so paid to any person electing to take against the will must be included in the benefits received by him under the will.

In any case where election is made against the will, the amount of compensation which has to be paid must be ascertained as at the date of the death of the testator.[19]

---

[11] In *Cooper* v. *Cooper* (1874), L.R. 7 H.L. 53, at p. 67; *Brown* v. *Gregson*, [1920] A.C. 860; [1920] All E.R. Rep. 730, H.L.

[12] *Re Mengel's Will Trusts*, [1962] 2 All E.R. 490; [1962] Ch. 791; *per* Buckley J. at pp. 492; 797.

[13] See e.g. *Rich* v. *Cockell* (1804), 9 Ves. 369; *Ker* v. *Wauchope* (1819), 1 Bli. 1.

[14] *Per* Jessel M.R. in *Pickersgill* v. *Rodger* (1876), 5 Ch. D. 163, at p. 174.

[15] In *Pickersgill* v. *Rodger*, *supra*.

[16] *Per* de Grey L.C.J. cited by Loughborough L.C. in *Lady Cavan* v. *Pulteney* (1795), 2 Ves. Jnr. 544, at p. 560.

[17] *A.G.* v. *Fletcher* (1835), 5 L.J. Ch. 75.

[18] [1906] 2 Ch. 321. [19] *Re Hancock*, [1905] 1 Ch. 16.

d   Election under a power of appointment

Before going further it will be convenient to mention special powers of appointment in relation to election. Where a testator has a special power of appointment by will he can only appoint to or among a limited number or class of persons—the objects of the power—and if he fails to make a valid appointment other persons, who may or may not also be the objects of the power, will be entitled. Such other persons taking in default of appointment do not claim under the will, but under the instrument creating the power. They are in effect the owners of the property, though their interests are liable to be defeated by an exercise of the power of appointment. Accordingly if the testator purports to appoint to persons not objects of the power, which appointment is, of course, ineffective, he can be and is regarded as wrongfully purporting to dispose of property belonging to the persons entitled in default of appointment, who will be called upon to elect if they are also given other property of the testator's own. This means that they can either elect to take under the will, by allowing the non-objects to take the property wrongfully appointed to them; or against the will, by insisting on their claims as persons entitled in default, in which case the non-objects will have to be compensated out of the gift of the testator's own property.

There will, however, be no case for election where the appointor, having made an appointment in favour of an object of the power, seeks to impose a trust or condition in favour of a non-object. As Page Wood V.C. explained in *Woolridge* v. *Woolridge*,[20] "where there is an absolute[1] appointment by will in favour of a proper object of the power, and that appointment is followed by attempts to modify the interest so appointed in a manner which the law will not allow, the court reads the will as if all the passages in which such attempts are made were swept out of it, for all intents and purposes, i.e., not only so far as they attempt to regulate the quantum of interest to be enjoyed by the appointee in the settled property, but also so far as they might otherwise have been relied upon as raising a case of election". *A fortiori* mere precatory words attached to an appointment do not raise a case of election.[2]

e   The essentials of election

"The essentials of election are that there should be an intention on the part of the testator or testatrix to dispose of certain property; secondly that the property should not in fact be the testator's or testatrix's own property; and thirdly, that a benefit should be given by the will to the true owner of the property".[3] It is clear that it is wholly immaterial whether the testator thought he had power to dispose of the property over which he had in fact no such power, or whether he knowingly purported to dispose of property not his own. In nearly every case the testator in fact has made a mistake as to his power of disposition, very often by exercising a power of appointment in favour of someone not an object of the power, but the rule in regard to election applies in precisely the same way whether

---

[20] (1859), Johns 63, 69; *Churchill* v. *Churchill* (1867), L.R. 5 Eq. 44; *Re Neave*, [1938] 3 All E.R. 220; [1938] Ch. 793. Cf. *White* v. *White* (1882), 22 Ch.D. 555.
[1] Cf. the rule in *Lassence* v. *Tierney* (1849), 1 Mac. & G. 551; *Hancock* v. *Watson*, [1902] A.C. 14, H.L.
[2] *Blacket* v. *Lamb* (1851), 14 Beav. 482; *Langslow* v. *Langslow* (1856), 21 Beav. 552.
[3] *Re Edwards*, [1957] 2 All E.R. 495, at p. 499; [1958] Ch. 168, at p. 175, C.A. *per* Jenkins L.J.

or not the testator knows he is purporting to dispose of the property of another.[4]

An apparent intention on the face of the will to dispose of property which in fact at the date of the death does not belong to the testator will not give rise to a case for election, if the true view of the matter is that there is no real intention to make the apparent testamentary disposition. This may happen as a result of ademption. If, for example, a testator by his will devised Blackacre of which he was the owner at the date of the will to X, and subsequently in his lifetime sold and conveyed Blackacre to Y, the devise in the will to X must obviously fail. The devise is said to have been adeemed, which means that the will has to be read as if there were no gift of that property in the will at all. "The true position in such a case is", it has been said, "that the testamentary disposition has clean gone".[5] Accordingly the testator would not be regarded as manifesting any intention to devise Blackacre and no case for election could arise, even though a legacy were given to Y. The Court of Appeal, in *Re Edwards*,[6] held that the same principle applied where the testatrix had entered into a specifically enforceable contract relating to the property between the date of the will and the date of her death, thus bringing into play the doctrine of conversion.

In order to raise a case of election it is vital that the intention to dispose shall relate to property which does not belong to the testator. The courts are naturally slow to hold that a person has purported to dispose of property over which he has no power of disposition, and if general words are used by a testator they will *prima facie* be taken to refer only to property over which he has such power and thus not raise a case of election.[7] "A man must be presumed to have intended to have devised what he actually possessed. The *onus probandi* lay on the parties who alleged the contrary".[8] Questions have often been raised in cases where a testator has used words which would be wide enough to carry an absolute interest but where he has in fact only a limited interest: in general in such cases, the provision will be construed as referring only to the limited interest. "It is difficult in any case to apply the doctrine of election where the testator has some present interest in the estate disposed of, though it may not be entirely his own".[9] In such case, "the court will lean as far as possible to a construction which would make him deal only with that to which he was entitled".[10] Where, however, on its true construction, the will must be taken to refer not only to the limited interest of the testator, but also to the interest of another, there may be a case for election: there is no rule that only a positive declaration to that effect can show the wider intention.[11] Thus in *Padbury* v.

---

[4] *Cooper* v. *Cooper* (1874), L.R. 7 H.L. 53; *Pitman* v. *Crum Ewing*, [1911] A.C. 217, H.L.; *Re Harris*, [1909] 2 Ch. 206 and see *Re Brooksbank* (1886), 34 Ch.D. 160.

[5] *Re Edwards*, [1957] 2 All E.R. 495, at pp. 500, 501; [1958] Ch. 168, at p. 177, C.A., per Jenkins, L.J.

[6] *Supra*, and see (1957), 21 Con. 152. Cf. *Plowden* v. *Hyde* (1852), 2 Sim. N.S. 171.

[7] See e.g. *Blomart* v. *Player* (1826), 2 Sim. & St. 597; *Re Harris*, [1909] 2 Ch. 206; *Re Booker* (1886), 54 L.T. 239.

[8] *Per* Turner L.J. in *Evans* v. *Evans* (1863), 2 New. Rep. at p. 408, 410.

[9] *Per* Lord Eldon in *Lord Rancliffe* v. *Lady Parkyns* (1818), 6 Dow. 149, at p. 185; *Miller* v. *Thurgood* (1864), 33 Beav. 496.

[10] *Howells* v. *Jenkins* (1863), 2 J. & H. 706 per Page Wood V.C. at 713; affd. 1 De G.J. & Sm. 617; *Re Mengel's Will Trusts*, [1962] 2 All E.R. 490; [1962] Ch. 791; *Galvin* v. *Devereux*, [1903] 1 Ir. Rep. 185.

[11] *Winton* v. *Cliftour* (1856), 8 De G.M. & G. 641; *Usticke* v. *Peters* (1858), 4 K. & J. 437.

Clark,[12] for instance, the testator, who was entitled only to a moiety of a freehold house, devised "all that my freehold messuage or tenement, with the garden . . . now on lease to X and in his occupation" to one and gave property of his own to the owner of the other moiety. Elsewhere in his will he devised a moiety of another property to which he was entitled in proper words. It was held that the intention to dispose of the entirety of the freehold house was clear, and accordingly the other owner of a moiety thereof was put to his election. And in *Re Mengel's Will Trusts*,[13] where the property of the testator and his wife was subject to the Danish law of community of assets, it was held that the testator, by his bequest of "all my personal and household goods and effects" purported to dispose of the whole property in those goods, i.e., both his own share and the share of his wife,[14] though in the same will the disposition of residue was held to extend only to the testator's own property, in accordance with the principle that a mere general devise or bequest will not raise a case of election. Exceptionally even a gift of residue has been held to raise a case of election where in the context, on the true construction of the will, the testator intended to refer thereby to the property of a beneficiary.[15]

It can now be regarded as settled[16] that the intention of the testator to dispose of property not his own must appear from the will itself: if on the face of it the will does not appear to attempt to dispose of another's property, extrinsic evidence will not be admitted directed to show that the testator regarded himself as the owner of some other's property and must have intended to dispose of it by some general or residuary disposition. The early case of *Pulteney* v. *Lord Darlington*[17] held to the contrary, but has been disapproved in numerous cases and it is submitted that the rule set out above, as stated in subsequent cases,[18] now represents the law.

f Gift of the testator's own property

There can be no case for election unless the testator has given some of his own property to the person called upon to elect, out of which compensation can be made in case he elects to take against the instrument. Thus in *Bristow* v. *Warde*[19] a father had a power of appointment over certain stock in favour of his

---

[12] (1850), 2 Mac. & G. 298; *Miller* v. *Thurgood* (1864), 33 Beav. 496; *Wilkinson* v. *Dent* (1871) 6 Ch. App. 339.

[13] [1962] 2 All E.R. 490; [1962] Ch. 791.

[14] It is difficult to understand, however, how the court came to the conclusion that there was a case for election, since the wife's interest under community of assets was not given to a stranger, but to the wife herself.

[15] *Re Allen's Estate*, [1945] 2 All E.R. 264, criticised on another point Cheshire, *Private International Law*, 8th Ed., p. (1945), 494; 10 Con. 102 (J. H. C. Morris); Dicey and Morris, *Conflict of Laws*, 9th Ed., p. 611. And see *Orrell* v. *Orrell* (1871), 6 Ch. App. 302.

[16] But see Jessel M.R. in *Pickersgill* v. *Rodger* (1876), 5 Ch.D. 163, 171 where cases subsequent to *Pulteney* v. *Lord Darlington*, a decision of Thurlow L.C. cited in *Pole* v. *Lord Somers* (1801), 6 Ves. 309, at p. 314, and *Hinchcliffe* v. *Hinchcliffe* (1797), 3 Ves. 516, at p. 521, do not appear to have been cited.

[17] *Supra*, followed with reluctance in *Druce* v. *Denison* (1801), 6 Ves. 385; *Guillebaud* v. *Meares* (1829), 7 L.J.O.S. Ch. 136.

[18] *Doe d. Oxenden* v. *Chichester* (1816), 4 Dow. 65; *Clementson* v. *Gandy* (1836), 1 Keen, 309; *Re Harris*, [1909] 2 Ch. 206.

[19] (1794), 2 Ves. 336; *Re Fowler's Trust* (1859), 27 Beav. 362; *Re Aplin's Trusts* (1865), 13 W.R. 1062.

children, who were also entitled in default of appointment. He appointed part of the stock to his children, and a part to persons not objects of the power, but gave no property of his own to his children. It was held that there was no case for election, the children being fully entitled to keep both what was appointed to them, and also what came to them in default of appointment by reason of the invalid appointment to non-objects. But in *Whistler* v. *Webster*,[1] on similar facts, save that the children were also given legacies out of the testator's own property, the children had to elect. "In all cases there must be some free disposable property given to the person, which can be made a compensation for what the testator takes away".[2] Provided, however, that the testator's own property which is given is bounty, it makes no difference that it is expressly given in payment of a statute barred obligation.[3]

g Alienability of the property wrongfully purported to be disposed of

Where the property of the person whom it is alleged should elect is not freely alienable, so that it would be impossible for him to elect effectively to take under the will, no case for election arises. Thus in *Re Chesham*[4] the testator purported to dispose in favour of younger brothers of heirlooms over which his eldest son had no power of disposition, and gave that son other benefits. It was held that there was no case for election and that the eldest son was accordingly entitled to enjoy the heirlooms and take the other benefits in full.

It was contended, indeed, in *Re Dicey*[5] that election only arises when the person on whom the obligation falls can, if he elects in favour of the will, secure that the relevant provisions of the will take effect precisely according to their terms. There, subject to the testatrix's life interest, the proceeds of sale of Blackacre belonged as to one half to the defendant and as to a quarter each to the plaintiff and the plaintiff's brother. The testatrix purported to devise the whole of Blackacre to the plaintiff and gave other property of her own to the defendant. Accordingly the most that the defendant could do, by electing to take under the will, was to secure for the plaintiff an absolute beneficial interest in three quarters of the proceeds of sale of Blackacre. The court, however, refused to hold that the obligation to elect should depend on the chance of the existence of some outstanding interest in the property, however small it might be, in a third party, which was unaffected by the question of election. The defendant, therefore, had to elect. In so deciding the court affirmed the decision in *Fytche* v. *Fytche*[6] that if two or more persons are called on to elect each of them has not only an individual obligation but an individual right to elect and can exercise it independently of the way in which the right may be exercised by the other or others. The following illustration was given in *Re Dicey*.[7]

---

[1] (1794), 2 Ves. 367.
[2] *Bristow* v. *Warde* (1794), 2 Ves. 336, at p. 350, *per* Loughborough L.C.
[3] *Re Fletcher's Settlement Trusts*, [1936] 2 All E.R. 236.
[4] (1886), 31 Ch.D. 466.
[5] [1956] 3 All E.R. 696; [1957] Ch. 145, C.A.
[6] (1868), 19 L.T. 343; less well reported in (1868), L.R. 7 Eq. 494; *Cooper* v. *Cooper* (1874), L.R. 7 H.L. 53.
[7] [1956] 3 All E.R. 696, at p. 702; [1957] Ch. 145, at p. 158, *per* Romer L.J., reading the judgment of C.A.

"A testator gives Blackacre or the proceeds of its sale to A. Blackacre in fact belongs to B, C and D as joint tenants and the testator gives legacies to each of these persons. Each of them has a separate and individual right and obligation to elect for or against the will notwithstanding that the gift to A can only take full effect according to the terms if B, C and D all elect in favour of the will. In other words, a class is not exempted from the principle of election merely because each can contribute only a part of the total subject-matter of the gift which the testator has purported to effect".

The principle is exactly the same if persons are entitled successively instead of concurrently.[8]

h   The rule against perpetuities

Although there has been powerful adverse criticism,[9] it can now, for practical purposes, be regarded as settled that where a testator exercises a special power of appointment in such a way that the appointment is void by reason of its offending against a rule of law such as the rule against perpetuities, there is no case for election. The persons entitled in default of appointment will be entitled to claim the property as invalidly appointed, and also to claim in full any benefits given to them by the testator out of his own property, even though they might be able to carry out the testator's wishes without any infringement of the rule. This might be possible because the perpetuity period in the case of a special power of appointment runs from the date when the power was created not from the date when it is exercised, but the limitations in a void appointment might well be good if contained in a settlement or trust set up on the testator's death by the persons who it would be claimed should elect.[10]   The reason behind this rule is said to be that the court will not assist a testator to evade a rule of law founded on public policy,[11] and it has been said[12] that the will must be read as if the clause which is void for perpetuity were not there. The matter has not been before the courts since the passing of the Perpetuities and Accumulations Act 1964, which does not, however, affect the position directly though it perhaps makes the reasons given sound less convincing.

i   Claim dehors the will

In *Wollaston* v. *King*[13] it was clearly stated that "the rule as to election is to be applied as between a gift under a will and a claim dehors the will, and adverse to it, and is not to be applied as between one clause in a will and another clause in the same will". There a testatrix had a special power of appointment. By her will she made an appointment of a part of the fund which was void for perpetuity and then made a general residuary appointment to three objects of the

---

8 *Ward* v. *Baugh* (1799), 4 Ves. 623.
9 See Gray on *Perpetuities*, 4th Ed., § 541 *et seq.*; Morris and Leach, *The Rule against Perpetuities*, 2nd Ed., p. 158.   The argument is that there is no difference in principle between an appointment void for remoteness, and one which is void as being an excessive exercise of the power.
10 *Wollaston* v. *King* (1869), L.R. 8 Eq. 165; *Re Oliver's Settlement*, [1905] 1 Ch. 191; *Re Nash*, [1910] 1 Ch. 1 C.A. overruling *Re Bradshaw*, [1902] 1 Ch. 436.
11 See e.g., *Re Oliver's Settlement*, [1905] 1 Ch. 191, but see Gray, *op. cit.*
12 *Re Warren's Trusts* (1884), 26 Ch.D. 208, at p. 219, *per* Pearson J.
13 (1869), L.R. 8 Eq. 165, at p. 174.

power, who were also given other benefits by the will out of the testatrix's own property. This was not a case of default of appointment, for in so far as the appointment failed, it was swept up in the general residuary appointment which accordingly applied to the whole fund. It was held, therefore, that there was no case for election: the residuary appointees took the whole fund under the residuary appointment in the will, and the other benefits also under the will.

Although the above rule was accepted in *Bate* v. *Willats*,[14] and repeated, *obiter*, by Viscount Maugham in *Lissenden* v. *C.A.V. Bosch Ltd.*,[1] it has met with academic criticism[2] and was not applied by Neville J. in the curious case of *Re Macartney*.[3] There the testator by his will gave a sum of colonial stock to his daughter Maggie and all his shares in Company X to his seven children including Maggie, in varying proportions. The testator held substantially all the issued share capital of the company, and that company had promoted company Y and held 90 per cent of its issued share capital. The colonial stock was in fact held by the testator in trust for company Y, so that the gift to Maggie failed. The court held that the legatees of the shares of company X could not take the benefit of their legacies without compensating Maggie in respect of her legacy of the stock, and that such compensation was a charge on their legacies in an amount equal to the value of the stock on the death of the testator. It is clear that this decision cannot stand with the above stated rule in *Wollaston* v. *King*,[4] and it is accordingly submitted that it is wrongly decided. It is further submitted that in all cases, not only in most cases as stated in *Re Macartney*,[5] where there are two claims made under the will, the only question is one of finding the intention of the testator on the true construction of the will itself. There are other grounds on which the decision in *Re Macartney*[6] seems to be unsatisfactory. As decided, it did not give the legatees of the shares any right of election at all: they had no choice to take either under or against the will, for the court decreed that they were to take the shares charged with the payment of a sum to compensate Maggie. There was no alternative—save to refuse the legacy altogether—and it was made clear that the other benefits received from the testator were not in any way liable. Even assuming that there was a *prima facie* case for election, it is submitted that *Re Chesham*[7] was not and cannot be validly distinguished, for on the facts of *Re Macartney*[8] it does not seem that the legatees of the shares had the power, even if they wished, to transfer the colonial stock to Maggie. The stock belonged to company Y and a gift of the company's property to a stranger would be *ultra vires* the company.[9] Indeed, Neville J. seems to have failed to recognise the significance of the interposition of companies X and Y between the legatees of the shares and the colonial stock. He apparently took it for granted that the legatees of the shares in company X were the beneficial owners

---

[14] (1877), 37 L.T. 221.
[1] [1940] 1 All E.R. 425, at p. 429; [1940] A.C. 412, at p. 419, H.L.
[2] See Gray on *Perpetuities*, 4th Ed. § 541 *et seq.* The main point made is that the appointees do not really claim under the will, but under the instrument creating the power.
[3] [1918] 1 Ch. 300.
[4] (1869), L.R. 8 Eq. 165.
[5] [1918] 1 Ch. 300.
[6] *Supra.*
[7] (1886), 31 Ch.D. 466 and see *supra* p. 537.
[8] *Supra.*
[9] See Gower, *Modern Company Law*, 3rd Ed., pp. 91, 92.

of the stock in fact beneficially owned by company Y, but, even disregarding the further remove, shareholders in a company have long since ceased to be regarded as having any equitable interest in the assets of the company: they "are not, in the eye of the law, part owners of the undertaking".[10] This being so it would seem to follow that no case for election arose.

j Election by the heir

It is settled that a case for election arises in English law where a testator has purported or attempted to dispose of foreign land in a way not effective by the foreign law[11] and has given either English land[12] or, being domiciled in England, any moveables[13] to the foreign heir who takes that land. Such heir, claiming adversely to the will, will, *prima facie*, be called upon to elect, not only where or in so far as the foreign law deprives the testator of any power of disposition over the property,[14] but also where the testator had a power of disposition, but his purported exercise of it is ineffective because of failure to comply with the necessary formalities.[15]

The *prima facie* rule that there is a case for election where a testator has disposed of foreign land in a way not effective by the foreign law, has, in accordance with the principle previously discussed,[16] no application where it would be impossible for the foreign heir, who it is alleged should elect, to deal with the property which devolves on him as heir in accordance with the terms of the will. Thus it was held that there was no case for election where a testator declared trusts of his Argentine land, which were invalid by Argentine law, because his children, who took as foreign heirs and who were given other benefits by the will, could not by any act of their own render the lands subject to the trusts of the will, such trusts being invalid by the law of the Argentine whether created *inter vivos* or by will.[17]

Before 1926 the position of the heir-at-law of English real estate caused some difficulty. Problems arose where there had been an ineffective disposition by will of realty, which consequently passed to the heir-at-law, and where the heir-at-law had been given other benefits by the will.[18] The heir-at-law was abolished by the Administration of Estates Act 1925,[1] in respect of deaths after

---

[10] Per Evershed M.R. in *Short* v. *Treasury Commissioners*, [1947] 2 All E.R. 298, at p. 301; [1948] 1 K.B. 116, at p. 122, C.A.; affd., [1948] 2 All E.R. 509; [1948] A.C. 534, H.L.; and see Gower, *op. cit.*, p. 319.

[11] It will be remembered that Scottish law is foreign law for this purpose. The Scottish law of approbate and reprobate has often been said to be the same as the English doctrine of election, and Scottish cases where the testator has made a disposition of English realty ineffective by English law may accordingly be cited as authorities also on the English doctrine—*Ker* v. *Wauchope* (1819). 1 Bli. 1; *Pitman* v. *Crum Ewing*, [1911] A.C. 217, H.L.; *Lissenden* v. *C.A.V. Bosch Ltd.*, [1940] 1 All E.R. 425; [1940] A.C. 412, H.L.

[12] Governed by the *lex situs*.

[13] Governed by the *lex domicilii*.

[14] *Haynes* v. *Foster*, [1901] 1 Ch. 361; *Re Ogilvie*, [1918] 1 Ch. 492.

[15] *Dundas* v. *Dundas* (1830), 2 Dow. & Cl. 349; *Orrell* v. *Orrell* (1871), 6 Ch. App. 302; *Brown* v. *Gregson*, [1920] A.C. 860; [1920] All E.R. Rep. 730, H.L.

[16] See p. 537, *ante*.

[17] *Brown* v. *Gregson*, *supra*; *Hewit's Trustees* v. *Lawson* (1891), 18 R. (Ct. of Sess.) 793.

[18] This is now mainly of historical interest, and is discussed in the First Ed., pp. 471, 472.

[1] Section 45—except as regards entailed interests.

1925, and there do not seem to be any circumstances in which the persons entitled on intestacy can be called on to elect.[2] The primary reason is that in relation to property passing to persons on intestacy, the testator cannot, by an ineffective disposition thereof, be said to be purporting to dispose of property not his own but belonging to the intestate successors, for the intestate successors have no beneficial interest in any of the assets, unless or until an assent or conveyance is made in their favour.[3] Secondly, where a gift in a will is for any reason ineffective, in practice a similar disposition by the intestate successors by way of compensation would likewise be ineffective for the same reason

This subsection should not be concluded without mentioning by way of contrast the rule that if a legacy is given upon the express condition that the heir should give up the realty, he will forfeit the legacy if he refuses to do so.[4] The distinction between the doctrine of election and the case of an express condition was completely settled at an early date, though often criticised as anomalous.[5] The anomaly was clear enough at a time when the doctrine of election was regarded as based on an implied condition[6] but is less apparent on the view taken in more modern cases that the doctrine of election is based directly on principles of equity, and is settled as giving rise to compensation, not forfeiture.[7]

k Derivative interests

Where X, the person who should have elected, dies without having done so[8] there may be two alternative sets of circumstances. On the one hand, the same person may be entitled, under X's will or on his intestacy, so far as it passes thereunder, both to the property of X of which the original testator wrongfully purported to dispose, and also to the original testator's property given beneficially to X. In such case, that person will have the same right and duty of electing as X had during his lifetime.[9] On the other hand X's own property may go to A, and the property of the original testator given to him to B. In such case it is sometimes said that there is a presumed election against the instrument. It is clear that X's own property passes to A unfettered, while B only takes the original testator's property after compensation has been made out of it to the persons disappointed. In fact, as Jessel M.R. observed in *Pickersgill v. Rodger*,[10] there is in such case no power of election in the ordinary sense. "You must treat the case as if each of those two persons took his property separately, and then, as I said before, you must discover upon whose property the obligation lies to make good what is required to satisfy the disappointed legatees".

---

[2] *Contra, semble,* Snell, *Principles of Equity,* 27th Ed., p. 490.
[3] See. p. 31, *supra*: Hanbury's *Modern Equity,* 9th Ed., p. 483.
[4] *Boughton* v. *Boughton* (1750), 2 Ves. Sen. 12.
[5] *Carey* v. *Askew* (1786), 1 Cox. Eq. Cas. 241; *Sheddon* v. *Goodrich* (1803), 8 Ves. 481; *Brodie* v. *Barry* (1813), 2 Ves. & B. 127.
[6] See Section 1 b, p. 532, *ante.*
[7] See Section 1 c, *supra.*
[8] It is submitted that the decision in *Re Carpenter* (1884), 51 L.T. 773 that in such case the personal representatives have the same right and duty of electing was made *per incuriam.*
[9] *Cooper* v. *Cooper* (1874), L.R. 7 H.L. 53.
[10] (1876), 5 Ch.D. 163, at p. 174.

There will, however, be no case for election where a person claims derivatively through a person who has himself elected. Thus where a married woman elected to take against a will and retain her interest in Blackacre it was held, after her death, that her husband, as tenant by the curtesy therein, could not be called upon to elect, notwithstanding that he had himself also received benefits under the will.[11] Clearly to have decided otherwise would have meant that the persons disappointed would have been claiming compensation a second time. Further, there will be no case for compensation where the derivative claim is made through someone who could not be called upon to elect, because, for instance, he was given no benefits by the will.[12]

1 Mode and time of election

It is clear that a person is fully entitled to ascertain the respective values of the properties involved and any other relevant information before he makes his election,[13] and it seems that the court will in general entertain an action for this purpose if necessary.[14] "Two things," it has been stated,[15] "are essential to constitute a settled and concluded election by any person who takes an interest under a will, which disposes of property belonging to that person. There must be, in the first place, clear proof that the person put to his election was aware of the nature and extent of his rights; and, in the second place, it must be shewn that, having that knowledge, he intended to elect". An election made in ignorance of the relevant circumstances will not be binding.[16]

Election may either be express, or may be inferred from the circumstances, and from the acts of the person under an obligation to elect, where the two essentials set out above are satisfied. Moreover it seems that an express election must be communicated to, or the fact of an unequivocal act have come to the knowledge of, the persons who will be affected by the election.[17] Receiving the income of or dealing with property *prima facie* implies an election to take it,[18] but even doing so for a long period will not necessarily raise an inference of election where it was done without full knowledge of the rights involved,[19] and "if a party being bound to elect between two properties, not being called upon so to elect, continues in the receipt of the rents and profits of both, such

---

[11] *Cavan* v. *Pulteney* (1795–7), 2 Ves. Jnr. 544; 3 Ves. 384.
[12] *Grissell* v. *Swinhoe* (1869), L.R. 7 Eq. 291.
[13] *Chalmers* v. *Storil* (1813), 2 Ves. & B. 222; *Pigott* v. *Bagley* (1825), M'Cle. & Yo. 569.
[14] *Douglas* v. *Douglas* (1871), L.R. 12 Eq. 617 *per* Wickens V.C.
[15] *Per* Romilly M.R. in *Worthington* v. *Wiginton* (1855), 20 Beav. 67, at p. 74; *Spread* v. *Morgan* (1865), 11 H.L. Cas. 588 (election under a deed); *Wilson* v. *Thornbury* (1875), 10 Ch. App. 239.
[16] *Pusey* v. *Desbouverie* (1734), 3 P. Wms. 315; *Kidney* v. *Coussmaker* (1806), 12 Ves. 136.
[17] In *Re Shepherd*, [1942] 2 All E.R. 584; [1943] Ch. 8, where there was an express condition of election, it was held that there was no election, where the interest under the will was reversionary, by writing letters, announcing an intention of electing in a certain way, to trustees who were not persons interested in the election.
[18] *Giddings* v. *Giddings* (1827), 3 Russ. 241; *Dewar* v. *Maitland* (1866), L.R. 2 Eq. 834.
[19] *Reynard* v. *Spence* (1841), 4 Beav. 103; *Fytche* v. *Fytche* (1868), 19 L.T. 343 less well reported in L.R. 7 Eq. 494; *Re Turner* (1892), 66 L.T. 758. Cf. *Sopwith* v. *Maugham* (1861), 30 Beav. 235 (a case on an express condition).

receipt, affording no proof of preference, cannot be an election to take the one and reject the other".[20]

The only disabilities which may now prevent a person from electing are infancy and mental disorder. In cases of infancy the court has sometimes directed that election is to be deferred until the infant attains full age,[1] but the usual practice today is for an election to be made on his behalf after any necessary inquiry as to what would be most for his benefit.[2] As regards a person incapable by reason of mental disorder of managing and administering his property and affairs, the court has similar powers and an appropriate election will normally be made for him, after due enquiry as to what is for his benefit, by the Court by Protection.[3]

2 ELECTION UNDER A DEED

In general it is thought that the rules relating to election under a deed are the same as those relating to election under a will, being based on the same basic principle that a person cannot accept and reject the same instrument. One difference, as Lord Selbourne pointed out in *Codrington* v. *Lindsay*,[4] is that the rule in the case of wills that there must be a clear intention on the part of the testator to give that which is not his property is not applicable or appropriate in the case of deeds. A case for election may arise where X has agreed, as consideration for benefits he is to receive thereunder, to bring property into a settlement. If it turns out that for some reason the agreement to bring property into the settlement cannot be enforced, X will have to elect. He can either put his property into the settlement as agreed, when he will be entitled to the agreed benefits; or he can refuse to settle his property, in which case his interest under the settlement will be used, so far as may be required, to compensate other persons entitled under the settlement for their disappointment. Thus in *Anderson* v. *Abbott*[5] there was a post-nuptial, i.e. a voluntary, settlement under which the husband and wife covenanted to settle the after-acquired property of the wife. Some after-acquired property was in fact duly transferred to the trustees, and as to this the trust was completely constituted. After the death of the husband, the wife claimed successfully that she could not be compelled to settle her after-acquired property, although it was within the terms of the covenant. The court held, however, that if she stood on her rights and refused to do so, the

---

[20] *Per* Lord Cottenham in *Padbury* v. *Clark* (1850), 2 Mac. & G. 298, at p. 306; *Spread* v. *Morgan* (1865), 11 H.L. Cas. 588.

[1] *Boughton* v. *Boughton* (1750), 2 Ves. Sen. 12.

[2] *Blunt* v. *Lack* (1856), 26 L.J. Ch. 148; *Prole* v. *Soady* (1859), 2 Giff. 1; *Re Montagu*, [1896] 1 Ch. 549.

[3] See Mental Health Act 1959, Part VIII, and cf. *Wilder* v. *Pigott* (1882), 22 Ch.D. 263; *Re Earl of Sefton*, [1898] 2 Ch. 378, C.A.

[4] (1873), 8 Ch. App. 578, at pp. 587, 588 affd. H.L. *sub nom. Codrington* v. *Codrington* (1875), L.R. 7 H.L. 854.

[5] (1857), 23 Beav. 457; *Brown* v. *Brown* (1866), L.R. 2 Eq. 481; *Codrington* v. *Codrington* (1875), L.R. 7 H.L. 854. But note *Campbell* v. *Ingilby* (1856), 21 Beav. 567 affirmed on different grounds 1 De G. & J. 393, as explained by the judge who decided it in *Brown* v. *Brown*, *supra*, and doubted by James L.J. in *Codrington* v. *Lindsay* (1873), 8 Ch. App. 578, at p. 593.

other persons entitled under the settlement would be able to claim compensation out of her interest therein. Lord Selborne in *Codrington* v. *Lindsay*,[6] after referring to numerous cases, said

> "in all of them the party who, claiming by a title not bound by the deeds, thereby withdrew part of the consideration for which the deeds were intended to be made, was held obliged to give up, by way of compensation, what he or she was entitled to under the deeds, or *ex converso* . . . was held bound, if taking the benefit of the deeds, to adopt and make good the contract forming the consideration for those benefits, as to matters by which, without such election, he would not have been bound".[7]

Finally it may be mentioned that the suggestion made in some early cases[8] that the rule as to deeds was different from that as to wills, involving forfeiture and not compensation, did not find favour with the courts, and later cases take it for granted that the doctrine here is also one of compensation.[9]

---

[6] (1873), 8 Ch. App. 578, at p. 587. Cf. *Aspden* v. *Seddon* (1876), 1 Ex.D. 496, C.A.; *Halsall* v. *Brizell*, [1957] 1 All E.R. 371.

[7] E.g. *Mosley* v. *Ward* (1861), 29 Beav. 407.

[8] See e.g. *Green* v. *Green* (1816), 2 Mer. 86.

[9] See e.g. *Codrington* v. *Codrington*, *supra*; *Spread* v. *Morgan* (1865), 1 H.L. Cas. 588; *Hamilton* v. *Hamilton*, [1892] 1 Ch. 396.

Appendix

Trustee Investments Act 1961, First Schedule, as amended by the London Government Act 1963, the National Loans Act 1968, the Post Office Act 1969 and the Local Government Act 1972. Investments which have been added to the Schedule subsequently by Statutory Instrument are printed in italics.

PART I

NARROWER-RANGE INVESTMENTS NOT REQUIRING ADVICE

1. In Defence Bonds, National Savings Certificates and Ulster Savings Certificates, *Ulster Development Bonds,*[1] *National Development Bonds,*[2] and *British Savings Bonds.*[3]

2. In deposits in the National Savings Bank, ordinary deposits in a trustee savings bank and deposits in a bank or department thereof certified under subsection (3) of section nine of the Finance Act 1956.[4]

PART II

NARROWER-RANGE INVESTMENTS REQUIRING ADVICE

1. In securities issued by Her Majesty's Government in the United Kingdom, the Government of Northern Ireland or the Government of the Isle of Man, not being securities falling within Part I of this Schedule and being fixed-interest securities registered in the United Kingdom or the Isle of Man, Treasury Bills or Tax Reserve Certificates.

2. In any securities the payment of interest on which is guaranteed by Her Majesty's Government in the United Kingdom or the Government of Northern Ireland.

---

[1] S.I. 1962, No. 2611.
[2] S.I. 1964, No. 703.
[3] S.I. 1968, No. 470.
[4] At present, only the Birmingham Municipal Bank (S.I. 1958, No. 923, as amended by S.I. 1959, No. 300).

3. In fixed-interest securities issued in the United Kingdom by any public authority or nationalised industry or undertaking in the United Kingdom.

4. In fixed-interest securities issued in the United Kingdom by the government of any overseas territory within the Commonwealth[5] or by any public or local authority within such a territory, being securities registered in the United Kingdom.

References in this paragraph to an overseas territory or to the government of such a territory shall be construed as if they occurred in the Overseas Service Act, 1958.

5. In fixed-interest securities issued in the United Kingdom by the International Bank for Reconstruction and Development, being securities registered in the United Kingdom.

In fixed-interest securities issued in the United Kingdom by the Inter-American Development Bank.[6]

In fixed-interest securities issued in the United Kingdom by the European Investment Bank or by the European Coal and Steel Community, being securities registered in the United Kingdom[7].

6. In debentures issued in the United Kingdom by a company incorporated in the United Kingdom, being debentures registered in the United Kingdom.

7. In stock of the Bank of Ireland *and in Bank of Ireland 7 per cent Loan Stock* 1986/91.[8]

8. In debentures issued by the Agricultural Mortgage Corporation Limited or the Scottish Agricultural Securities Corporation Limited.

9. In loans to any authority to which this paragraph applies charged on all or any of the revenues of the authority or on a fund into which all or any of those revenues are payable, in any fixed-interest securities issued in the United Kingdom by any such authority for the purpose of borrowing money so charged, and in deposits with any such authority by way of temporary loan made on the giving of a receipt for the loan by the treasurer or other similar officer of the authority and on the giving of an undertaking by the authority that, if requested to charge the loan as aforesaid, it will either comply with the request or repay the loan.

This paragraph applies to the following authorities, that is to say—

(a) any local authority in the United Kingdom;

(b) any authority all the members of which are appointed or elected by one or more local authorities in the United Kingdom;

---

[5] It is not clear at what point of time the territory must be within the Commonwealth: the choice would seem to lie between the date of the issue of the securities, and the date at which it is proposed to acquire them for the trust. The point is of particular importance in connection with South African securities issued before 31st May, 1961 when the Union of South Africa became a republic and ceased to be a member of the Commonwealth.

[6] S.I. 1964, No. 1404.
[7] S.I. 1972, No. 1818.
[8] S.I. 1966, No. 401.

(c) any authority the majority of the members of which are appointed or elected by one or more local authorities in the United Kingdom, being an authority which by virtue of any enactment has power to issue a precept to a local authority in England and Wales, or a requisition to a local authority in Scotland, or to the expense of which, by virtue of any enactment, a local authority in the United Kingdom is or can be required to contribute;

(d) the Receiver for the Metropolitan Police District or a combined police authority (within the meaning of the Police Act, 1946);

(e) the Belfast City and District Water Commissioners.

(f) the Great Ouse Water Authority.[9]

(g) any district council in Northern Ireland.[10]

10. In debentures or in the guaranteed or preference stock of any incorporated company, being statutory water undertakers within the meaning of the Water Act 1948[11], or any corresponding enactment in force in Northern Ireland and having during each of the ten years immediately preceding the calendar year in which the investment was made paid a dividend of not less than $3\frac{1}{2}$ per cent[12] on its ordinary shares.

11. In deposits by way of special investment in a trustee savings bank or in a department (not being a department certified under subsection (3) of section nine of the Finance Act, 1956) of a bank any other department of which is so certified.

12. In deposits in a building society designated under section one of the House Purchase and Housing Act, 1959.

13. In mortgages of freehold property in England and Wales or Northern Ireland and of leasehold property in those countries of which the unexpired term at the time of investment is not less than sixty years, and in loans on heritable security in Scotland.

14. In perpetual rent-charges charged on land in England and Wales or Northern Ireland and fee-farm rents (not being rent-charges) issuing out of such land, and in feu-duties or ground annuals in Scotland.

PART III

WIDER-RANGE INVESTMENTS

1. In any securities issued in the United Kingdom by a company incorporated in the United Kingdom, being securities registered in the United Kingdom and not being securities falling within Part II of this Schedule.

---

9 S.I. 1962, No. 658.

10 S.I. 1973 No. 1332. This order gets over the difficulty that the Local Government Act (Northern Ireland) 1972 which reorganised local authorities in Northern Ireland, did not amend paragraph 4 (c) of Part IV. The power under s. 12 of the Act to add to the First Schedule by Order does not apply to Part IV.

11 See Water Act 1948, s. 1, which substituted a new definition

12 Before 1973, 5 per cent—see S.I. 1973 No. 1393.

2. In shares in any building society designated under section one of the House Purchase and Housing Act, 1959.

3. In any units, or other shares of the investments subject to the trusts, of a unit trust scheme in the case of which there is in force at the time of investment an order of the Board of Trade under section seventeen of the Prevention of Fraud (Investments) Act, 1958, or of the Ministry of Commerce for Northern Ireland under section sixteen of the Prevention of Fraud (Investments) Act (Northern Ireland), 1940.

PART IV
Supplemental

1. The securities mentioned in Parts I to III of this Schedule do not include any securities where the holder can be required to accept repayment of the principal, or the payment of any interest, otherwise than in sterling.

2. The securities mentioned in paragraphs 1 to 8 of Part II, other than Treasury Bills or Tax Reserve Certificates, securities issued before the passing of this Act by the Government of the Isle of Man, securities falling within paragraph 4 of the said Part II issued before the passing of this Act or securities falling within paragraph 9 of that Part, and the securities mentioned in paragraph 1 of Part III of this Schedule, do not include—

(a) securities the price of which is not quoted on a recognised stock exchange within the meaning of the Prevention of Fraud (Investments) Act, 1958, or the Belfast stock exchange;

(b) shares or debenture stock not fully paid up (except shares or debenture stock which by the terms of issue are required to be fully paid up within nine months of the date of issue).

3. The securities mentioned in paragraph 6 of Part II and paragraph 1 of Part III of this Schedule do not include—

(a) shares or debentures of an incorporated company of which the total issued and paid up share capital is less than one million pounds;

(b) shares or debentures of an incorporated company which has not in each of the five years immediately preceding the calendar year in which the investment is made paid a dividend on all the shares issued by the company, excluding any shares issued after the dividend was declared and any shares which by their terms of issue did not rank for the dividend for that year.

For the purposes of sub-paragraph (b) of this paragraph a company formed—

(i) to take over the business of another company or other companies, or

(ii) to acquire the securities of, or control of, another company or other companies,

or for either of those purposes and for other purposes shall be deemed to have paid a dividend as mentioned in that sub-paragraph in any year in which such a dividend has been paid by the other company or all the other companies, as the case may be.

4. In this Schedule, unless the context otherwise requires, the following expressions have the meanings hereby respectively assigned to them, that is to say—

"debenture" includes debenture stock and bonds, whether constituting a charge on assets or not, and loan stock or notes;

"enactment" includes an enactment of the Parliament of Northern Ireland;

"fixed-interest securities" means securities which under their terms of issue bear a fixed rate of interest;

"local authority" in relation to the United Kingdom, means any of the following authorities—

(a) in England and Wales, the council of a county, a borough, an urban or rural district or a parish, the Common Council of the City of London, the Greater London Council, and the Council of the Isles of Scilly;

(b) in Scotland, a local authority within the meaning of the Local Government (Scotland) Act, 1947[13];

(c) in Northern Ireland, the council of a county, a county or other borough, or an urban or rural district[14];

"ordinary deposits" and "special investment" have the same meanings respectively as in the Trustee Savings Banks Act, 1954;

"securities" includes shares, debentures, Treasury Bills and Tax Reserve Certificates;

"share" includes stock;

"Treasury Bills" includes bills issued by Her Majesty's Government in the United Kingdom and Northern Ireland Treasury Bills.

5. It is hereby declared that in this Schedule "mortgage", in relation to free-hold or leasehold property in Northern Ireland, includes a registered charge which, by virtue of subsection (4) of section forty of the Local Registration of Title (Ireland) Act, 1891, or any other enactment, operates as a mortgage by deed.

6. References in this Schedule to an incorporated company are references to a company incorporated by or under any enactment and include references to a body of persons established for the purpose of trading for profit and incorpor-ated by Royal Charter.

7. The references in paragraph 12 of Part II and paragraph 2 of Part III of this Schedule to a building society designated under section one of the House Purchase and Housing Act, 1959, include references to a permanent society incorporated under the Building Societies Acts (Northern Ireland), 1874 to 1940 for the time being designated by the Registrar for Northern Ireland under subsection (2) of that section (which enables such a society to be so designated for the purpose of trustees' powers of investment specified in paragraph (a) of subsection (1) of that section).

---

[13] As from 16 May 1975 substitute the Local Government (Scotland) Act 1973, by virtue of s. 211 (1) and Sched. 27, Part 1, para. 1 of that Act.

[14] See n. 10, p. 547, *supra*.

Index